THE
New Humanities
READER

THE
New Humanities
READER

Richard E. Miller

RUTGERS UNIVERSITY

Kurt Spellmeyer

RUTGERS UNIVERSITY

HOUGHTON MIFFLIN COMPANY   Boston   New York

Acknowledgments

This project has been a long time in the making. It has been helped along by the hard work and dedication of the assistant directors of the Rutgers Writing Program, the writing program's teaching faculty and staff, and the undergraduates at our university. We are fortunate to work in an environment where so many people are willing to innovate and to give curricular change a try. We are grateful, as well, for Houghton Mifflin's commitment to this project: the folks in custom publishing, our editors for the national edition of this volume, and the sales reps have all helped us fine tune our vision for the new humanities. Now, all that remains to do is what always remains: to think connectively, to read creatively, and to write one's way to new ways of seeing.

Editor-in-Chief: Pat Coryell
Sponsoring Editor: Suzanne Phelps Weir
Senior Project Editor: Florence Kilgo
Production Editorial Assistant: Marlowe Shaeffer
Production/Design Coordinator: Lisa Jelly
Senior Manufacturing Coordinator: Jane Spelman
Senior Marketing Manager: Cindy Graff Cohen

Cover: Veiled woman: © Chris Lisle/Corbis; Traffic, New York City: © Edmond Van Hoorick/PhotoDisc; Native American Drawings: © Albert J. Copley/PhotoDisc; Field of Wheat: © Eyewire Collection.

Library of Congress Control Number: 2001133314

ISBN: 0-618-21605-7

123456789-DOC-06 05 04 03 02

CONTENTS

PREFACE

This book probably differs from most you have encountered, at least those that you have encountered in school. Initially, the readings collected here might appear to have nothing more in common than their concern with contemporary issues—the jobless future, the degradation of the environment, the conflict between scientific expertise and spiritual conviction, the spread of terrorist networks. Rather than arrange the readings under helpful rubrics such as "Civilization and Nature" or "Society and the Individual," we have organized them alphabetically by author, with the result being thought-provoking juxtapositions. An essay on the information society, for example, is followed by one that concerns a young woman's experience after entering a military academy. Generally, the books taught in school tell students how to think, but ours has a different purpose. We wanted to put in your hands a book that would compel you to make connections for yourself as you think, read, and write about the events that are likely to shape your future life.

Although the articles and essays in this book deal with subjects as diverse as the anthropology of art and the transformation of the workplace, the book is not really "about" art or work or any of the other subjects explored by the readings we have selected. Instead, this book is about the need for new ways of thinking, and it does not pretend that those ways of thinking are widely practiced today. Our world has seen more change in the last hundred years than it had seen in the previous thousand. From the media we get daily reports on subjects that our great-grandparents might have found incomprehensible: breakthroughs in cloning; mergers of U.S. firms with Japanese or German partners; a global treaty on biological weapons; a new account of the universe in the first seconds after the Big Bang; the melting of the polar icecaps; legislation to extend health-care benefits to same-sex couples. Such events are truly without precedent.

Never before have people faced uncertainty in so many different areas. Will the Internet be a negative influence, contributing to the forces that have pulled apart our family unit, or will it strengthen our neighborhoods and communities? Will the global economy create widespread unemployment and environmental decline, or will it usher in an era of undreamed-of prosperity and peace? Will encounters between different cultures, long separated by geography, lead to a new renaissance, or must such meetings always end in balkanization and violence? Unlike the questions posed by the standard textbook, the answers to these questions aren't waiting for any of us in the teacher's edition. Not even the best educated and the most experienced among us can foresee with certainty how the life of our times will turn out. If our problems today are much more sweeping than those before encountered by humankind, they are also more complex. Globalization is not just an issue for economists, or political scientists, or historians, or anthropologists: it is an issue for all of them—and us—together. The degradation of the biosphere is not just an ecological matter, but a political, social, and cultural matter as well.

The uniqueness of our time requires that we devise new understandings of ourselves and of the world. One purpose of this book is to provide a forum for these understandings to emerge. It may seem strange, perhaps, that we would have such lofty goals in a course for undergraduates. Surely the experts are better equipped to respond to issues of the sort our world now confronts than are beginning students in our colleges and universities. But this assumption may be unjustified. While the forms of expertise available today clearly have great value, most of the current academic disciplines were created more than a century ago, and the divisions of knowledge on which they are based reflect the needs of a very different society. It is worth remembering, for example, that in 1900 cars were a new technology, and airplanes and radios had yet to be invented. Scientists still debated the structure of the atom. The British Empire dominated three-fourths of the globe, and "culture" meant the traditions of Western Europe's elite, never more than one-tenth of one percent of the population of that region. In a certain sense, the current generation of college students, teachers, and administrators needs to reinvent the university itself, not by replacing one department or methodology with another, but by forging broad connections across areas of knowledge that still remain in relative isolation.

New Humanities for New Times: The Search for Coherence

Some readers of this book will be surprised by the absence of material from the traditional humanities: poems and plays, photographs of paintings and statues, excerpts from great works of philosophy such as Plato's *Republic* and Descartes's *Discourse on Method*. Clearly, no one should leave Aristotle or Shakespeare or Toni Morrison unread. And anyone unfamiliar with Leonardo da Vinci, Frida Kahlo, Thelonious Monk, and Georgia O'Keeffe has missed a priceless opportunity. Yet this book has grown out of the belief that the humanities today must reach farther than in centuries past. Without intending to do so, traditional humanists may have contributed to the decline of their own enterprise. One could even argue that the humanities have seen their principal task as the preservation of the past rather than the creation of the future. Humanists have often left real-world activities and concerns to other fields, while devoting themselves to passive contemplation, aesthetic pleasure, and partisan critique. Consequently, most people outside the university have come to consider the humanities as something closer to entertainment, wish fulfillment, or a covert form of politics, while regarding the sciences as the only real truth.

The humanities today must be understood in a new way: not as a particular area of knowledge but as the human dimension of *all* knowledge. Engineering may lie outside the traditional humanities, but it enters the domain of the New Humanities when we begin to consider the impact of engineering on everyday life, as Henry Petroski does in his essay on the role that structural failures play in the design process. When we define the humanities in this way, it may come as a surprise that some of our society's foremost humanists work in fields quite far removed from the traditional humanities. Stephen Jay Gould, one of the writers in this collection, is a distinguished paleontologist who has played a leading role in American cultural life. Well-versed in Western arts and letters, he also brings to his writing the knowledge and insight of a highly accomplished scientist. Marcia Angell, a pathologist and the former editor-in-chief of the *New England Journal of Medicine,* has helped to safeguard our society as a whole by changing the way the legal system understands scientific evidence.

The New Humanities, as represented by this book, brings change in another way as well: they invite us to take knowledge obtained at the university beyond the confines of the university itself. In a certain sense, this means that we all must become our own best teachers: we must find in our own lives—our problems, values, dreams, and commitments—an organizing principle we will not find in a curriculum which is bound to seem disorganized. The great, unspoken secret of the university is that the curriculum has no center: specialization makes sure of that. Historians write primarily for historians; literary critics for other critics. As we shuttle back and forth between these specialized disciplines, the only coherence we gain is the coherence we have constructed for ourselves. Under these conditions, what the New Humanities can teach us is a different way of using knowledge, a way of thinking that synthesizes many different fields of study.

Specialized learning in the disciplines typically deals with the "how," but it often leaves unanswered the "why." There has never been a course called "Life 101," and given the complexity of our world, such a course seems unlikely. But something important will be missing if we leave the "why" questions unexplored. Should we continue to pursue technological-utopia? Does modern science mean the end of religion? Is social inequality an acceptable price to pay for economic growth? Any attempt to answer these questions requires specialized knowledge, yet knowledge alone is not enough. Because a cogent, well-informed case can be made on either side of almost every issue, the source of our ultimate commitments must reach deeper. We might say that the "why" questions shape these commitments because they address our most basic and most personal relations to other people and to the world. In different ways, these questions ask us how we choose to live. No expert can choose on our behalf, because no expert can live our lives for us or define what our experiences should mean to us.

The coherence missing from the curriculum is not a quality of knowledge but of our own lives. In itself, no amount of learning can produce a sense of coherence. That sense arises, instead, from a creative and synthetic activity on our part as we interact with the world. Again and again, we need to make connections between discrete areas of knowledge and between knowledge and our personal experience. This coherence is never complete because there is always something more to learn that remains unconnected, but we might think of coherence, not as a goal reached once and for all but as an ideal worth pursuing continuously. Of course, cynicism and fragmentation are always options, too, and they require no special effort. One could easily live as though nothing and no one mattered, but in such a case, learning and living become exercises in futility. The New Humanities offers a better path.

Knowledge in Depth and Knowledge of the World

As everyone understands, formal education has been carefully designed to keep disciplines separate. In economics classes, we typically read economics; in history classes, we typically read history. This approach allows information to be imparted in small, efficiently managed packages. We can divide, say, biology from chemistry, and then we can divide biology into vertebrate and inverterbrate, and chemistry into organic and inorganic. We start with the general and move to the particular: ideally, we learn in depth, with increasing mastery of details that become more and more refined. At the end of the semester, if everything goes well, we can distinguish between an ecosystem and a niche, a polymer and a plastic, a neo-Kantian and a neo-Hegelian. We can contrast Hawthorne's treatment of the outsider with Salinger's, or we can explain the debate about whether slavery or states' rights actually caused the Civil War.

Knowledge in depth is indispensable. But it can also create a sense of disconnection, the impression that education is an empty ritual without real-world consequences beyond the receipt of a grade and the fulfillment of a requirement. In the classroom, we learn to calculate sine and cosine without ever discovering how these calculations might be used and why they were invented. Searching for symbols in a poem or a short story becomes a mental exercise on par with doing a crossword puzzle. Instead of reflecting on why events have happened and how they get remembered and recorded, we refine our ability to recapitulate strings of dates and names. At its worst, learning in depth can produce a strange disconnect: the purpose of learning becomes learning itself, while activity in the real world becomes incidental, even difficult to imagine. As students reach the final years of high school, they may understand vaguely that they ought to know *Hamlet,* and should be able to identify *The Declaration of Independence,* and explain how photosynthesis has influenced the shape of leaves, but in response to an actual tragedy, an environmental disaster, or a real-life legal crisis, they might feel unqualified to speak and unprepared to act.

College-level learning can offer an escape from this predicament by giving students greater freedom to choose what they will study, and in many cases the subjects they choose are closely related to their real-world objectives. But even with this new-found freedom, the problem of disconnection crops up in other ways. After years of hard work, a student who has mastered electrical engineering may still leave college poorly informed about the globalized, commercial environment in which most engineers now do their work. Students well-versed in Renaissance drama or the history of World War I may find their own lives after graduation much more difficult to explain. For some people, this problem of disconnection may arise long before graduation. One who sets out to memorize facts from, say, a social psychology textbook may find that these facts grow increasingly stale. Easily memorized one day, they are quickly forgotten the next. The risk of knowledge in depth is that we lose our sense of the larger world and we forget that a field like psychology, for all its current sophistication, began with tentative and somewhat clumsy questions about the mind. Ironically, the more we treat an area of knowledge as a reality in itself, the less we may be able to understand and use what we have supposedly learned.

There is another kind of knowledge that we begin to create when we ask ourselves how our learning pertains to the world outside the classroom. This line of questioning is more complex than it might initially seem because the larger world is never simply out there waiting for us. All knowledge begins as a knowledge of parts and fragments. Even our knowledge of the private lives we know in most detail. Each of our private lives may seem complete, in itself, just as a field like psychology can seem to explain everything once we are immersed in its methods and its facts. But this sense of completeness is an illusion produced by the limits of our perspective. Beyond the reach of what we know here and now, nothing seems to matter. We begin to get a glimpse of the larger world, however, when we shift our focus from one reality to another; then do we discover the deficiencies in our previous ways of thinking, and then are we able to think in new and different ways. This movement from the known to the unknown is the essence of all learning; indeed, the most successful learners are generally those who have developed the highest tolerance for not knowing—those who continue to question and explore issues beyond their own areas of specialization, entertaining alternatives that others might find unimaginable.

Knowledge itself can be defined in many ways: as a quantity of information, as technical expertise, as cultivated taste, as a special kind of self-awareness. And as varied as these definitions may appear, they share an underlying principle. Whatever the form knowledge may take, it always emerges from a process we might call *connecting*. The eighteenth-century English scientist Sir Isaac Newton, who first understood the complex relations between force, mass, and acceleration, may have been inspired by connecting his scientific work with his deeply held religious convictions about the rational perfection of God and His Creation. Many other notable thinkers likewise found inspiration through connection. Roughly two hundred years after Newton's discoveries had sparked a technological revolution, a young lawyer born in India, Mohandas K. Gandhi, drew on Henry David Thoreau's *Civil Disobedience,* written in support of abolitionists just before the Civil War, to launch a campaign of passive resistance against the racist government of South Africa. Two years before Gandhi spent his first term in jail as a political prisoner, a French artist and intellectual, Marcel Duchamps, shocked the art world with a painting—*Nude Descending a Staircase*—inspired by scientific photographs of athletes in motion. Whether we are talking about physics or political systems, epidemiology or aesthetics, knowledge by its very nature brings together disparate worlds of thought and action.

Creative Reading: From Explicit to Implicit

The selections in this book are intended for creative reading. The humanities should do more than convey information or give professors a chance to demonstrate their brilliance. After all, studies have consistently demonstrated that we retain little of what we have been taught unless we put that knowledge to use. At its best, education should offer beginners the chance to practice the same activities that more accomplished thinkers engage in: beyond receiving knowledge, beginners should participate in the making of knowledge. The articles and chapter collected in this book offer many opportunities for such participation. All of the selections are challenging, some because they are long and complex, some because they draw on specialized disciplines, and some because they open up unusual perspectives. These are not readings that lend themselves to simple summaries and multiple-choice answers. Instead, they require discussion—they were written to elicit activity and response.

It is important not to think of essays such as these as truths to be committed to memory or arguments to be weighed and then accepted or rejected. It might be more useful to see them in much the same way we now see Internet sites. Every site on the Internet is linked to countless others by the connections that Web authors and programmers have forged. As a result of their cumulative efforts, one site links us to another and then to the next, on and on for as long as we care to go. In some ways, even the most useful and informative written texts are less sophisticated than the simplest Web sites, and the Internet can transform the labor of many days—sifting through periodicals and rummaging through the library stacks—into the work of a few hours. Yet the Web also has limitations that the printed word does not. The Web, after all, can show us only those pathways that someone has already made semipermanent. By contrast, *all* connections to the printed text are *virtual* connections: any text can be linked to any other text in a web of inquiry and analysis potentially much vaster than the Internet itself.

When we surf the Internet, we find only what others want us to find, but the connections we personally forge between one text and the next may truly be uncharted terrain.

Texts can be connected to other texts in any way a reader finds helpful and credible. But the ideas set forth in a text also offer a potential network of connections waiting to be made. Of course, every text has an explicit dimension: the words on the page in their most literal form and the order in which ideas are presented. Because of this explicit content, it is possible to memorize and repeat, more or less verbatim, the information that a text provides. We might try to remember, for example, all the major authors Karen Armstrong reviews in "Does God Have a Future?" Yet the meaning of a text is something more than what the words on the page explicitly state. A text becomes meaningful only through the implicit connections it motivates. To understand a text, as opposed to simply repeating it, is to move back and forth from the explicit to the implicit until an interpretation takes shape. In Armstrong's case what matters more than the particular figures she mentions is the overall direction of religious thought in the twentieth-century—a direction Armstrong traces out but leaves for us to understand and assess.

Remember that these implicit dimensions are always virtual. An essay on the politics of AIDS, for example, may not be explicitly related to an article on bicycles in West Africa. But between them a connection could still be made, an important and original one. While some connections might seem potentially more fruitful and easily forged than others, improbable connections have sometimes revealed enormous vistas of knowledge. In practice this means that the most creative readers are also those most willing to take constructive risks, exploring connections that others have overlooked. At the same time, a connection must be credible, and the more sustained that connection becomes—the more deeply and widely it extends across the details of the texts at hand—the more persuasive the interpretation that arises from it.

The most basic form of interpretation starts when we connect one part of a text with other parts. Consider, for example, the first sentence of Jonathan Boyarin's "Waiting for a Jew." "My story begins in a community," he writes, "with an illusion of wholeness." Needless to say, this statement can stand alone, but it also serves as a point of departure. Practically every detail that follows in Boyarin's account can be connected in some way to this key phrase "the illusion of wholeness." Sometimes the experiences he recalls may appear to underscore the word *illusion,* confirming the irreparable loss of the community in which he had grown up. But other moments in his narrative might speak directly to *wholeness*—to the persistence of communities of shared belief in the midst of a larger, unbelieving world. Explicitly, of course, Boyarin's text makes no such point, but implicitly the point is waiting to be made, and by making it we become interpreters of the text.

When we read for content, we are reading to preserve the knowledge made by others. But when we read for implicit connections, we become cocreators with the authors themselves. To recapitulate some portion of

Boyarin's narrative might help us pass a quiz or defend a point of view in the context of a debate, but when we use Boyarin's narrative as an opportunity to make connections of our own, we join in the same questioning that started him on his path. The purpose of such reading is not to get the "right answer" but to understand more fully the world in which we live, a process literally without end. In this sense, the best interpretations leave the texts behind as they move forward, toward other questions and other texts.

Connective Thinking: The Search for a Shared Horizon

Much of formal education promotes mimetic, or imitative, thinking: we learn to reproduce information already collected and organized by someone else. Mimetic thinking presupposes the adequacy of knowledge in its present state. But what happens when we discover that our knowledge leaves something out? Perhaps the lecture in English class this afternoon contradicted a point made yesterday in anthropology class. Or perhaps an assigned article has described an aspect of the social world in a manner that we find inaccurate or disconcerting. On occasions like these, when we encounter the limits or defects of knowledge, mimetic thinking cannot help us; instead, we are obliged to think connectively—to think *across* domains of knowledge rather than thinking from within them.

Sometimes connective thinking happens in response to crisis. The complex of knowledge we call immunology, for example, has advanced rapidly in an effort to counter the spread of HIV and AIDS. So, too, a growing crisis in farming, caused by the overuse of pesticides, has spurred extensive research in plant genetics. But whether or not real-world crises bear down on us, the construction of knowledge of any kind necessarily produces contradictions. In his essay "Playing God in the Garden," Michael Pollan describes the reactions of Idaho farmers to the biotech industry. Even if we do not share Pollan's ambivalence about genetic engineering, few readers would doubt the truthfulness of the evidence he presents. And fewer still would question Pollan's abilities: his account is well written, carefully researched, and coherently organized. It is precisely the coherence of Pollan's case, however, that limits its value for readers. At best, because he is just one person, he can offer us only one perspective.

As soon as we have read more than a single text, we encounter discontinuous images and perspectives of the world that we must somehow reconcile. Precisely because most accounts are more or less true to the perspectives they adopt, the way out of this discontinuity seldom lies with a blanket rejection of one perspective or another, a simple "right" or "wrong." Instead, the most constructive and creative response is to search for a larger shared horizon, a new way of thinking that is broad enough in scope to do justice to both accounts. This search is not quite the same as "compare and contrast." After all, we can endlessly compare and contrast details that are relatively trivial and that do not bridge the gaps between texts. A shared horizon, on the other hand, is more inclusive than either text alone and often connects them on the level of implications, not explicit claims. And once a shared horizon presents itself, the connections we make gradually prompt to questions we pose—and answer—for ourselves.

When a theorist of management like Peter Drucker considers the emerging "knowledge society," he foresees an era of unprecedented personal freedom and upward mobility. On the other hand, Benjamin Barber, a political scientist and contemporary of Drucker, describes an America that he regards as socially fragmented and politically paralyzed. Confronting these two images of the same society, we are bound to question their relation to one another. Are the two views in contradiction? Perhaps you will find Barber's view more persuasive, or perhaps you will prefer Drucker's. No two essays, however, are simply in contradiction. To a greater or lesser extent, they also will confirm and complicate one another. We might assume that democracy and the free market go together, as Drucker thinks, but the values of the free market may in some ways undermine democratic attitudes, as Barber fears. We might believe, as Barber does, that people ought to get more involved with their government, but perhaps, as Drucker argues, the apparatus of government is no longer in control of our society. The point is not to say "yes" to one writer and "no" to the other. Nor is it to declare that everybody has "a right to his or her own opinion." Instead, we can explore the different ways each discussion might fit together and then evaluate the real-world consequences of these combinations.

Connective thinking is creative and independent in a way that mimetic thinking can never be. No matter how well we summarize the views of Drucker and Barber, this is not the same as connecting them within the context of a larger question or debate. Yet these connections are never waiting for us fully formed: there is always the need for a leap of imagination. Drucker's principal concern is the organization of work; Barber's is the collapse of American political life. At first, when we consider these differences, no shared horizon may present itself, but we must not stop there. Our advice is not to stop at what the authors have said but to ask about the implications for each of us—to ask how the issues they have raised might impact us personally. Barber and Drucker might appear worlds apart at first, but a shared horizon may begin to open up when we think about the forms of political life that might be possible in a society where knowledge is power, or when we start to imagine the economic changes that might give Americans more time to be active in their communities or, instead, that might throw them out of work.

Writing to Tell, Writing to See

Mimetic thinking goes hand in hand with writing to tell—writing for the purpose of demonstrating mastery over an existing body of information.

In American schools, the classic example of writing to tell is the venerable book report. Like mimetic thinking, writing to tell has its appropriate place. Connective thinking calls, however, for writing of a different kind, which might be described as writing to see. In this case, the writer has to do something more than recount the knowledge of others; like connective thinking, it is an active pursuit in which the writer takes that knowledge somewhere new. In the act of writing to tell, people give answers. In the process of writing to see, we start with a question inspired by others and go on to explore what they have left unexplored; we engage in the kind of writing that higher education at its best can foster: exploratory writing, writing to see. A good example of writing to see is Ellen Dissanayake's "The Core of Art: Making Special." Although Dissanayake draws extensively from previous thinkers on aesthetics, evolutionary biology, and ethology, she connects each thinker to the next in a way that reveals her own position. While she could not have reached her final position without her sources' help, her thinking goes beyond theirs.

It may be the case that Dissanayake's research began with a key question—"What is art?"—already firmly in mind. But she may have formulated that question only after the broad, diverse reading we see evidenced in her copious notes. What seems certain, no matter how her project began, is that Dissanayake discovered at some stage in her research a fundamental discontinuity between the West's tradition of elite arts and the accounts offered by anthropologists of grassroots creativity in non-Western societies. On the one hand, Western tradition tends to view the arts as the restricted domain of the talented and brilliant; on the other, ordinary people across the globe engage in art-making as a part of their everyday lives.

Discontinuity is where the most valuable and valued writing starts. From time immemorial, teachers of English have told their students to begin the task of writing only after they know clearly what they want to say. These instructions have always expressed more fantasy than truth. Typically, a position—a thesis or argument—will remain fairly vague until we have done a great deal of preliminary writing. Discontinuities lead us to the search for a shared horizon, and from this shared horizon our own questions come. Then, provided we are willing to push far enough, a coherent position begins to emerge, not all at once in a grand vision but cumulatively, with one insight building on the next. At some point, as these insights begin to cohere, we discern the direction of our thoughts, a direction that writing itself has revealed. We write and then we see where our writing has taken us. Only then are we in a position to convey our discoveries to others in a well-crafted presentation.

In order for Dissanayake to become a source for our own writing, we need to start with a question that her work leaves unresolved. If art is, as she believes, a universal human behavior, then what are we to make of museums, galleries, and professional artists? Why is it that we call certain paintings "art" but not cartoons or popular movies? If we ourselves see cartoons and movies as trivial, we may find Dissanayake's ideas less than entirely persuasive. But her ideas may also force us to rethink some of our basic assumptions: Where is it written, after all, that art has to be exclusive and difficult? As we set out to answer questions like these, we might also draw on David Abram's observations about the Balinese way of life. Or we might make fruitful connections to Drucker's thoughts on the increasingly specialized character of work. Our assessment of the place of the aesthetic in contemporary culture might emerge from the synthesis of the work of these three writers. We might decide that "entertainment" is actually art, or we might consider the disappearance of art from everyday life a development closely related to our growing distance from nature.

Developing a Position

A position is not exactly an argument in the ordinary sense of the word. In everyday speech, the term *argument* suggests an adversarial stance: we might argue for, or against, Drucker's positive assessment of corporate culture. "Making an argument" tends to mean deciding ahead of time what you think about an issue and then finding "support" to back up your points. There is, however, another way. Instead of simply ratifying an existing belief, each of us can use the readings to formulate a position of our own. To do so is to imagine ourselves in a different way, not as combatants but as participants in an ongoing conversation. Even if we read a writer with distaste, what matters most are the questions raised, not the answers given. Precisely because the search for a position begins with some degree of uncertainty, it requires a willingness on our part to suspend judgment and to pursue ideas wherever they might lead. It is important to remember that this pursuit does not require complete assent or unwavering commitment. We can always explore ideas that we eventually reject. The proper spirit for writing to see might be described as exploratory and experimental.

An experiment involves a "dialogue" between projection and revision. First, we imagine or "project" an outcome based on our prior knowledge and experience. We make an educated guess about the conclusion we will probably draw from our reading of an author or authors. Perhaps we start with the claim that Chris McCandless, the young man whose travels and death Jon Krakauer retraces, was spoiled and self-deceiving. Yet when we turn to Alexander Stille's account of alternative attitudes toward the natural world, our opinion of McCandless may grow less clear. As we write, our thinking may appear to lose its way and we may realize, after three or four pages, that we have contradicted ourselves. Perhaps McCandless's actions now seem justified, even commendable. Instead of treating this change in our position as a failure or a lapse, we should appreciate its value as a discovery, which we could make only after a great deal of hard work. And rather than return to our original stance, we should revise what we have written in order to present a revised position. But revision, too, involves experiment and discovery. The point of a new draft is never simply to change a position: the point is also to explain how and why the position has changed.

The Spirit of the New Humanities

Because we can learn from everything, no one should fear making mistakes. We should never forget that the greatest thinkers of every age have often been refuted later, whereas ordinary people have sometimes lived more wisely than they were given credit for. Not so long ago, the best-educated Europeans believed that all celestial bodies beyond the moon hung immobilized in space. The learned taught that matter in every form could be reduced to the basic elements of earth, air, fire, and water. Medical experts sternly warned against the perils of regular bathing and eating whole grains. In sexual reproduction, men were supposed to contribute the blueprint, while women provided the raw material. One could spend a lifetime enumerating the follies that have passed for knowledge. And when we pause to consider such a checkered history, we might decide that education is itself a folly.

But maybe not. Instead of expecting knowledge to be true once and for all, we might try to see it as pragmatic and provisional, always subject to revision given further evidence or new circumstances. In our society today, the sciences may offer the best example of this experimentalist attitude, but some philosophers and artists of every generation have also refused the twin consolations of dogmatism and disillusionment. In the years ahead, our society will face many challenges—environmental, social, cultural, economic, and political—that are sure to seem overwhelming. Given the high level of uncertainty that has become a constant feature of our lives, people may be drawn to ideologies that promise truths exempt from all revision and insulated from the challenges of diversity. If this book does nothing else, we hope that it will offer an alternative more compatible with the values espoused by the readings we have chosen: trust in the world, and trust in ourselves.

R.E.M.
K.S.

DAVID ABRAM

DAVID ABRAM IS an ecologist, anthropologist, and philosopher, but it is work with magic that has most shaped his research on the connections between the environment, human experience, and modes of perception. After the magic trick has been performed, Abram believes, we are left "without any framework of explanation. We are suddenly floating in that open space of direct sensory experience, actually encountering the world without preconceptions, even if just for a moment." How would our thinking about the earth and our place on it change if we could suspend our preconceptions about our own central importance? This is the question that Abram brings to the fields of ecopsychology and environmental philosophy.

"The Ecology of Magic" is drawn from Abram's book, *The Spell of the Sensuous: Perception and Language in a More-Than-Human World*, which explores our perception of the natural world and the way we use language and symbols to process our experience. In "The Ecology of Magic," Abram describes his travels through Sri Lanka, Indonesia, and Nepal to study the lifeways of magicians and healers. During the course of his research, Abram came to see the role of traditional magicians and healers as bridging the gap between humankind and nature; "the shaman or sorcerer," he tells us, "is the exemplary voyager in the intermediate realm between the human and the more-than-human worlds."

Abram could be characterized as just such a voyager. After receiving his doctorate in philosophy from the State University of New York at Stony Brook, he and his wife founded the Alliance for Wild Ethics, an organization that focuses on raising ecological awareness. When asked to explain why he draws so heavily on academic discourse and continues to write for an academic audience when his thinking has taken him in such unconventional directions, Abram answered that his goal in writing *The Spell of the Sensuous* was "to bridge the gap between the world of the imagination—the kind of magical world of these

Abram, David. "The Ecology of Magic." *The Spell of the Sensuous: Perception and Language in a More-Than-Human World*. New York: First Vintage Books, 1997. 3–29.

Quotations come from Scott London's interview with David Abram for the National Public Radio series, *Insight & Outlook* <http://www.scottlondon.com/insight/scripts/abram.html>.

indigenous, traditional societies—and the world of academia, the intelligentsia, and the scientific elite. But I didn't want to do that just by writing a scholarly or scientific analysis of indigenous, animistic ways of thinking. I wanted to do the opposite. I wanted to do an animistic analysis of rationality and the Western intellect, and to show that our Western, civilized ways of thinking are themselves a form of magic."

To learn more about David Abram and the practice of shamanism, visit the Link-O-Mat at <www.newhum.com>.

■ ■

The Ecology of Magic

A Personal Introduction to the Inquiry

Late one evening I stepped out of my little hut in the rice paddies of eastern Bali and found myself falling through space. Over my head the black sky was rippling with stars, densely clustered in some regions, almost blocking out the darkness between them, and more loosely scattered in other areas, pulsing and beckoning to each other. Behind them all streamed the great river of light with its several tributaries. Yet the Milky Way churned beneath me as well, for my hut was set in the middle of a large patchwork of rice paddies, separated from each other by narrow two-foot-high dikes, and these paddies were all filled with water. The surface of these pools, by day, reflected perfectly the blue sky, a reflection broken only by the thin, bright green tips of new rice. But by night the stars themselves glimmered from the surface of the paddies, and the river of light whirled through the darkness underfoot as well as above; there seemed no ground in front of my feet, only the abyss of star-studded space falling away forever.

I was no longer simply beneath the night sky, but also *above* it—the immediate impression was of weightlessness. I might have been able to reorient myself, to regain some sense of ground and gravity, were it not for a fact that confounded my senses entirely: between the constellations below and the constellations above drifted countless fireflies, their lights flickering like the stars, some drifting up to join the clusters of stars overhead, others, like graceful meteors, slipping down from above to join the constellations underfoot, and all these paths of light upward and downward were mirrored, as well, in the still surface of the paddies. I felt myself at times falling through space, at other moments floating and drifting. I simply could not dispel the profound vertigo and giddiness; the paths of the fireflies, and their reflections in the water's surface, held me in a sustained trance. Even after I crawled back to my hut and shut the door on this whirling world, I felt that now the little room in which I lay was itself floating free of the earth.

Fireflies! It was in Indonesia, you see, that I was first introduced to the world of insects, and there that I first learned of the great influence that insects—such diminutive entities—could have upon the human senses. I had traveled to Indonesia on a research grant to study magic—more precisely, to study the relation between magic and medicine, first among the traditional sorcerers, or *dukuns,* of the Indonesian archipelago, and later among the *dzankris,* the traditional shamans of Nepal. One aspect of the grant was somewhat unique: I was to journey into rural Asia not outwardly as an anthropologist or academic researcher, but as a magician in my own right, in hopes of gaining a more direct access to the local sorcerers. I had been a professional sleight-of-hand magician for five years back in the United States, helping to put myself through college by performing in clubs and restaurants throughout New England. I had, as well, taken a year off from my studies in the psychology of perception to travel as a street magician through Europe and, toward the end of that journey, had spent some months in London, England, exploring the use of sleight-of-hand magic in psychotherapy, as a means of engendering communication with distressed individuals largely unapproachable by clinical healers.[1] The success of this work suggested to me that sleight-of-hand might lend itself well to the curative arts, and I became, for the first time, interested in the relation, largely forgotten in the West, between folk medicine and magic.

It was this interest that led to the aforementioned grant, and to my sojourn as a magician in rural Asia. There, my sleight-of-hand skills proved invaluable as a means of stirring the curiosity of the local shamans. For magicians—whether modern entertainers or indigenous, tribal sorcerers—have in common the fact that they work with the malleable texture of perception. When the local sorcerers gleaned that I had at least some rudimentary skill in altering the common field of perception, I was invited into their homes, asked to share secrets with them, and eventually encouraged, even urged, to participate in various rituals and ceremonies.

But the focus of my research gradually shifted from questions regarding the application of magical techniques in medicine and ritual curing toward a deeper pondering of the relation between traditional magic and the animate natural world. This broader concern seemed to hold the keys to the earlier questions. For none of the several island sorcerers that I came to know in Indonesia, nor any of the *dzankris* with whom I lived in Nepal, considered their work as ritual healers to be their major role or function within their communities. Most of them, to be sure, *were* the primary healers or "doctors" for the villages in their vicinity, and they were often spoken of as such by the inhabitants of those villages. But the villagers also sometimes spoke of them, in low voices and in very private conversations, as witches (or "lejaks" in Bali), as dark magicians who at night might well be practicing their healing spells backward (or while turning to the left instead of to the right) in order to afflict people with the very diseases that they would later work to cure by day. Such suspicions seemed fairly common in Indonesia, and often were harbored with regard to the most effective and powerful healers, those who were most renowned for their skill in driving out illness. For it was assumed that a magician, in order to expel malevolent influences, must have a strong understanding of those influences and demons—even, in some areas, a close rapport with such powers. I myself never consciously saw any of those magicians or shamans with whom I became acquainted engage in magic for harmful purposes, nor any convincing evidence that they had ever done so. (Few of the magicians that I came to know even accepted money in return for their services, although they did accept gifts in the way of food, blankets, and the like.) Yet I was struck by the fact that none of them ever did or said anything to counter such disturbing rumors and speculations, which circulated quietly through the regions where they lived. Slowly, I came to recognize that it was through the agency of such rumors, and the ambiguous fears that such rumors engendered in the village people, that the sorcerers were able to maintain a basic level of privacy. If the villagers did not entertain certain fears about the local sorcerer, then they would likely come to obtain his or her magical help for every little malady and disturbance; and since a more potent practitioner must provide services for several large villages, the sorcerer would be swamped from morning to night with requests for ritual aid. By allowing the inevitable suspicions and fears to circulate unhindered in the region (and sometimes even encouraging and contributing to such rumors), the sorcerer ensured that *only* those who were in real and profound need of his skills would dare to approach him for help.

This privacy, in turn, left the magician free to attend to what he acknowledged to be his primary craft and function. A clue to this function may be found in the circumstance that such magicians rarely dwell at the heart of their village; rather, their dwellings are commonly at the spatial periphery of the community or, more often, out beyond the edges of the village—amid the rice fields, or in a forest, or a wild cluster of boulders. I could easily attribute this to the just-mentioned need for privacy, yet for the magician in a traditional culture it seems to serve another purpose as well, providing a spatial expression of his or her symbolic position with regard to the community. For the magician's intelligence is not encompassed *within* the society; its place is at the edge of the community, mediating *between* the human community and the larger community of beings upon which the village depends for its nourishment and sustenance. This larger community includes, along with the humans, the multiple nonhuman entities that constitute the local landscape, from the diverse plants and the myriad animals—birds, mammals, fish, reptiles, insects—that inhabit or migrate through the region, to the particular winds and weather patterns that inform the local geography, as well as the various landforms—forests, rivers, caves, mountains—that lend their specific character to the surrounding earth.

The traditional or tribal shaman, I came to discern, acts as an intermediary between the human community and the larger ecological field, ensuring that there is an appropriate flow of nourishment, not just from the landscape to the human inhabitants, but from the human community back to the local earth. By his constant rituals, trances, ecstasies, and "journeys," he ensures that the relation between human society and the larger society of beings is balanced and reciprocal, and that the village never takes more from the living land than it returns to it—not just materially but with prayers, propitiations, and praise. The scale of a harvest or the size of a hunt are always negotiated between the tribal community and the natural world that it inhabits. To some extent every adult in the community is engaged in this process of listening and attuning to the other presences that surround and influence daily life. But the shaman or sorcerer is the exemplary voyager in the intermediate realm between the human and the more-than-human worlds, the primary strategist and negotiator in any dealings with the Others.

And it is only as a result of her continual engagement with the animate powers that dwell beyond the human community that the traditional magician is able to alleviate many individual illnesses that arise *within* that community. The sorcerer derives her ability to cure ailments from her more continuous practice of "healing" or balancing the community's relation to the surrounding land. Disease, in such cultures, is often conceptualized as a kind of systemic imbalance within the sick person, or more vividly as the intrusion of a demonic or malevolent presence into his body. There are, at times, malevolent influences within the village or tribe itself that disrupt the health and emotional well-being of susceptible individuals within the community. Yet such destructive influences within the human community are commonly traceable to a disequilibrium between that community and the larger field of forces in which it is embedded. Only those persons who, by their everyday practice, are involved in monitoring and maintaining the relations *between* the human village and the animate landscape are able to appropriately diagnose, treat, and ultimately relieve personal ailments and illnesses arising *within* the village. Any healer who was not simultaneously attending to the intertwined relation between the human community and the larger, more-than-human field, would likely dispel an illness from one person only to have the same problem arise (perhaps in a new guise) somewhere else in the community. Hence, the traditional magician or medicine person functions primarily as an intermediary between human and nonhuman worlds, and only secondarily as a healer.[2] Without a continually adjusted awareness of the relative balance or imbalance between the human group and its nonhuman environ, along with the skills necessary to modulate that primary relation, any "healer" is worthless—indeed, not a healer at all. The medicine person's primary allegiance, then, is not to the human community, but to the earthly web of relations in which that community is embedded—it is from this that his or her power to alleviate human illness derives—and this sets the local magician apart from other persons.

The primacy for the magician of nonhuman nature—the centrality of his relation to other species and to the earth—is not always evident to Western researchers. Countless anthropologists have managed to overlook the ecological dimension of the shaman's craft, while writing at great length of the shaman's rapport with "supernatural" entities. We can attribute much of this oversight to the modern, civilized assumption that the natural world is largely determinate and mechanical, and that which is regarded as mysterious, powerful, and beyond human ken must therefore be of some other, nonphysical realm *above* nature, "supernatural."

The oversight becomes still more comprehensible when we realize that many of the earliest European interpreters of indigenous lifeways were Christian missionaries. For the Church had long assumed that only human beings have intelligent souls, and that the other animals, to say nothing of trees and rivers, were "created" for no other reason than to serve humankind. We can easily understand why European missionaries, steeped in the dogma of institutionalized Christianity, assumed a belief in supernatural, otherworldly powers among those tribal persons whom they saw awestruck and entranced by nonhuman (but nevertheless natural) forces. What is remarkable is the extent to which contemporary anthropology still preserves the ethnocentric bias of these early interpreters. We no longer describe the shamans' enigmatic spirit-helpers as the "superstitious claptrap of heathen primitives"—we have cleansed ourselves of at least *that* much ethnocentrism; yet we still refer to such enigmatic forces, respectfully now, as "supernaturals"—for we are unable to shed the sense, so endemic to scientific civilization, of nature as a rather prosaic and predictable realm, unsuited to such mysteries. Nevertheless, that which is regarded with the greatest awe and wonder by indigenous, oral cultures is, I suggest, none other than what we view as nature itself. The deeply mysterious powers and entities with whom the shaman enters into a rapport are ultimately the same forces—the same plants, animals, forests, and winds—that to literate, "civilized" Europeans are just so much scenery, the pleasant backdrop of our more pressing human concerns.

The most sophisticated definition of "magic" that now circulates through the American counterculture is "the ability or power to alter one's consciousness at will." No mention is made of any *reason* for altering one's consciousness. Yet in tribal cultures that which we call "magic" takes its meaning from the fact that humans, in an indigenous and oral context, experience their own consciousness as simply one form of awareness among many others. The traditional magician cultivates an ability to shift out of his or her common state of consciousness precisely in order to make contact with the other organic forms of sensitivity and awareness with which human existence is entwined. Only by temporarily shedding the accepted perceptual logic of his culture can the sorcerer hope to enter into relation with other species on their own terms; only by altering the common organization of his senses will he be able to enter into a rapport with the multiple nonhuman sensibilities that animate the local landscape. It is this, we might say, that defines a shaman: the ability to readily slip out of the perceptual boundaries that demarcate his or her particular culture—boundaries reinforced by social customs, taboos, and most importantly, the common speech or language—in order to make contact with, and learn from, the other powers in the land. His magic is precisely this heightened receptivity to the meaningful solicitations—songs, cries, gestures—of the larger, more-than-human field.

Magic, then, in its perhaps most primordial sense, is the experience of existing in a world made up of multiple intelligences, the intuition that every form one perceives—from the swallow swooping overhead to the fly on a blade of grass, and indeed the blade of grass itself—is an *experiencing* form, an entity with its own predilections and sensations, albeit sensations that are very different from our own.

To be sure, the shaman's ecological function, his or her role as intermediary between human society and the land, is not always obvious at first blush, even to a sensitive observer. We see the sorcerer being called upon to cure an ailing tribesman of his sleeplessness, or perhaps simply to locate some missing goods; we witness him entering into trance and sending his awareness into other dimensions in search of insight and aid. Yet we should not be so ready to interpret these dimensions as "supernatural," nor to view them as realms entirely "internal" to the personal psyche of the practitioner. For it is likely that the "inner world" of our Western psychological experience, like the supernatural heaven of Christian belief, originates in the loss of our ancestral reciprocity with the animate earth. When the animate powers that surround us are suddenly construed as having less significance than ourselves, when the generative earth is abruptly defined as a determinate object devoid of its own sensations and feelings, then the sense of a wild and multiplicitous otherness (in relation to which human existence has always oriented itself) must migrate, either into a supersensory heaven beyond the natural world, or else into the human skull itself—the only allowable refuge, in this world, for what is ineffable and unfathomable.

But in genuinely oral, indigenous cultures, the sensuous world itself remains the dwelling place of the gods, of the numinous powers that can either sustain or extinguish human life. It is not by sending his awareness out beyond the natural world that the shaman makes contact with the purveyors of life and health, nor by journeying into his personal psyche; rather, it is by propelling his awareness laterally, outward into the depths of a landscape at once both sensuous and psychological, the living dream that we share with the soaring hawk, the spider, and the stone silently sprouting lichens on its coarse surface.

The magician's intimate relationship with nonhuman nature becomes most evident when we attend to the easily overlooked background of his or her practice—not just to the more visible tasks of curing and ritual aid to which she is called by individual clients, or to the larger ceremonies at which she presides and dances, but to the content of the prayers by which she prepares for such ceremonies, and to the countless ritual gestures that she enacts when alone, the daily propitiations and praise that flow from her toward the land and *its* many voices.

All this attention to nonhuman nature was, as I have mentioned, very far from my intended focus when I embarked on my research into the uses of magic and medicine in Indonesia, and it was only gradually that I became aware of this more subtle dimension of the native magician's craft. The first shift in my preconceptions came rather quietly, when I was staying for some days in the home of a young "balian," or magic practitioner, in the interior of Bali. I had been provided with a simple bed in a separate, one-room building in the balian's family compound (most compound homes, in Bali, are comprised of several separate small buildings, for sleeping and for cooking, set on a single enclosed plot of land), and early each morning the balian's wife came to bring me a small but delicious bowl of fruit, which I ate by myself, sitting on the ground outside, leaning against the wall of my hut and watching the sun slowly climb through the rustling palm leaves. I noticed, when she delivered the fruit, that my hostess was also balancing a tray containing many little green plates: actually, they were little boat-shaped platters, each woven simply and neatly from a freshly cut section of palm frond. The platters were two or three inches long, and within each was a little mound of white rice. After handing me my breakfast, the woman and the tray disappeared from view behind the other buildings, and when she came by some minutes later to pick up my empty bowl, the tray in her hands was empty as well.

The second time that I saw the array of tiny rice platters, I asked my hostess what they were for. Patiently, she explained to me that they were offerings for the household spirits. When I inquired about the Balinese term that she used for "spirit," she repeated the same explanation, now in Indonesian, that these were gifts for the spirits of the family compound, and I saw that I had understood her correctly. She handed me a bowl of sliced papaya and mango, and disappeared around the corner. I pondered for a minute, then set down the bowl, stepped to the side of my hut, and peered through the trees. At first unable to see her, I soon caught sight of her crouched low beside the corner of one of the other buildings, carefully setting what I presumed was one of the offerings on the ground at that spot. Then she stood up with the tray, walked to the other visible corner of the same building, and there slowly and carefully set another offering on the ground. I returned to my bowl of fruit and finished my breakfast. That afternoon, when the rest of the household was busy, I walked back behind the building where I had seen her set down the two offerings. There were the little green platters, resting neatly at the two rear corners of the building. But the mounds of rice that had been within them were gone.

The next morning I finished the sliced fruit, waited for my hostess to come by for the empty bowl, then quietly headed back behind the buildings. Two fresh palm-leaf offerings sat at the same spots where the others had been the day before. These were filled with rice. Yet as I gazed at one of these offerings, I abruptly realized, with a start, that one of the rice kernels was actually moving.

Only when I knelt down to look more closely did I notice a line of tiny black ants winding through the dirt to the offering. Peering still closer, I saw that two ants had already climbed onto the offering and were struggling with the uppermost kernel of rice; as I watched, one of them dragged the kernel down and off the leaf, then set off with it back along the line of ants advancing on the offering. The second ant took another kernel and climbed down with it, dragging and pushing, and fell over the edge of the leaf, then a third climbed onto the offering. The line of ants seemed to emerge from a thick clump of grass around a nearby palm tree. I walked over to the other offering and discovered another line of ants dragging away the white kernels. This line emerged from the top of a little mound of dirt, about fifteen feet away from the buildings. There was an offering on the ground by a corner of my building as well, and a nearly identical line of ants. I walked into my room chuckling to myself: the balian and his wife had gone to so much trouble to placate the household spirits with gifts, only to have their offerings stolen by little six-legged thieves. What a waste! But then a strange thought dawned on me: what if the ants were the very "household spirits" to whom the offerings were being made?

I soon began to discern the logic of this. The family compound, like most on this tropical island, had been constructed in the vicinity of several ant colonies. Since a great deal of cooking took place in the compound (which housed, along with the balian and his wife and children, various members of their extended family), and also much preparation of elaborate offerings of foodstuffs for various rituals and festivals in the surrounding villages, the grounds and the buildings at the compound were vulnerable to infestations by the sizable ant population. Such invasions could range from rare nuisances to a periodic or even constant siege. It became apparent that the daily palm-frond offerings served to preclude such an attack by the natural forces that surrounded (and underlay) the family's land. The daily gifts of rice kept the ant colonies occupied—and, presumably, satisfied. Placed in regular, repeated locations at the corners of various structures around the compound, the offerings seemed to establish certain boundaries between the human and ant communities; by honoring this boundary with gifts, the humans apparently hoped to persuade the insects to respect the boundary and not enter the buildings.

Yet I remained puzzled by my hostess's assertion that these were gifts "for the spirits." To be sure, there has always been some confusion between our Western notion of "spirit" (which so often is defined in contrast to matter or "flesh"), and the mysterious presences to which tribal and indigenous cultures pay so much respect. I have already alluded to the gross misunderstandings arising from the circumstance that many of the earliest Western students of these other customs were Christian missionaries all too ready to see occult ghosts and immaterial phantoms where the tribespeople were simply offering their respect to the local winds. While the notion of "spirit" has come to have, for us in the West, a primarily anthropomorphic or human association, my encounter with the ants was the first of many experiences suggesting to me that the "spirits" of an indigenous culture are primarily those modes of intelligence or awareness that do *not* possess a human form.

As humans, we are well acquainted with the needs and capacities of the human body—we *live* our own bodies and so know, from within, the possibilities of our form. We cannot know, with the same familiarity and intimacy, the lived experience of a grass snake or a snapping turtle; we cannot readily experience the precise sensations of a hummingbird sipping nectar from a flower or a rubber tree soaking up sunlight. And yet we do know how it feels to sip from a fresh pool of water or to bask and stretch in the sun. Our experience may indeed be a variant of these other modes of sensitivity; nevertheless, we cannot, as humans, precisely experience the living sensations of another form. We do not know, with full clarity, their desires or motivations; we cannot know, or can never be sure that we know, what they know. That the deer does experience sensations, that it carries knowledge of how to orient in the land, of where to find food and how to protect its young, that it knows well how to survive in the forest without the tools upon which we depend, is readily evident to our human senses. That the mango tree has the ability to create fruit, or the yarrow plant the power to reduce a child's fever, is also evident. To humankind, these Others are purveyors of secrets, carriers of intelligence that we ourselves often need: it is these Others who can inform us of unseasonable changes in the weather, or warn us of imminent eruptions and earthquakes, who show us, when foraging, where we may find the ripest berries or the best route to follow back home. By watching them build their nests and shelters, we glean clues regarding how to strengthen our own dwellings, and their deaths teach us of our own. We receive from them countless gifts of food, fuel, shelter, and clothing. Yet still they remain Other to us, inhabiting their own cultures and displaying their own rituals, never wholly fathomable.

Moreover, it is not only those entities acknowledged by Western civilization as "alive," not only the other animals and the plants that speak, as spirits, to the senses of an oral culture, but also the meandering river from which those animals drink, and the torrential monsoon rains, and the stone that fits neatly into the palm of the hand. The mountain, too, has its thoughts. The forest birds whirring and chattering as the sun slips below the horizon are vocal organs of the rain forest itself.[3]

Bali, of course, is hardly an aboriginal culture; the complexity of its temple architecture, the intricacy of its irrigation systems, the resplendence of its colorful festivals and crafts all bespeak the influence of various civilizations, most notably the Hindu complex of India. In Bali, nevertheless, these influences are thoroughly intertwined with the indigenous animism of the Indonesian archipelago; the Hindu gods and goddesses have been appropriated, as it were, by the more volcanic, eruptive spirits of the local terrain.

Yet the underlying animistic cultures of Indonesia, like those of many islands in the Pacific, are steeped as well in beliefs often referred to by ethnologists as "ancestor worship," and some may argue that the ritual reverence paid to one's long-dead human ancestors (and the assumption of their influence in present life), easily invalidates my assertion that the various "powers" or "spirits" that move through the discourse of indigenous, oral peoples are ultimately tied to nonhuman (but nonetheless sentient) forces in the enveloping landscape.

This objection rests upon certain assumptions implicit in Christian civilization, such as the assumption that the "spirits" of dead persons necessarily retain their human form, and that they reside in a domain outside of the physical world to which our senses give us access. However, most indigenous tribal peoples have no such ready recourse to an immaterial realm outside earthly nature. Our strictly human heavens and hells have only recently been abstracted from the sensuous world that surrounds us, from this more-than-human realm that abounds in its own winged intelligences and cloven-hoofed powers. For almost all oral cultures, the enveloping and sensuous earth remains the dwelling place of both the living *and* the dead. The "body"—whether human or otherwise—is not yet a mechanical object in such cultures, but is a magical entity, the mind's own sensuous aspect, and at death the body's decomposition into soil, worms, and dust can only signify the gradual reintegration of one's ancestors and elders into the living landscape, from which all, too, are born.

Each indigenous culture elaborates this recognition of metamorphosis in its own fashion, taking its clues from the particular terrain in which it is situated. Often the invisible atmosphere that animates the visible world—the subtle presence that circulates both within us and between all things—retains within itself the spirit or breath of the dead person until the time when that breath will enter and animate another visible body—a bird, or a deer, or a field of wild grain. Some cultures may burn, or "cremate," the body in order to more completely return the person, as smoke, to the swirling air, while that which departs as flame is offered to the sun and stars, and that which lingers as ash is fed to the dense earth. Still other cultures may dismember the body, leaving certain parts in precise locations where they will likely be found by condors, or where they will be consumed by mountain lions or by wolves, thus hastening the reincarnation of that person into a particular animal realm within the landscape. Such examples illustrate simply that death, in tribal cultures, initiates a metamorphosis wherein the person's presence does not "vanish" from the sensible world (where would it go?) but rather remains as an animating force within the vastness of the landscape, whether subtly, in the wind, or more visibly, in animal form, or even as the eruptive, ever to be appeased, wrath of the volcano. "Ancestor worship," in its myriad forms, then, is ultimately another mode of attentiveness to nonhuman nature; it signifies not so much an awe or reverence of human powers, but rather a reverence for those forms that awareness takes when it is *not* in human form, when the familiar human embodiment dies and decays to become part of the encompassing cosmos.

This cycling of the human back into the larger world ensures that the other forms of experience that we encounter—whether ants, or willow trees, or clouds—are never absolutely alien to ourselves. Despite the obvious differences in shape, and ability, and style of being, they remain at least distantly familiar, even familial. It is, paradoxically, this perceived kinship or consanguinity that renders the difference, or otherness, so eerily potent.[4]

Several months after my arrival in Bali, I left the village in which I was staying to visit one of the pre-Hindu sites on the island. I arrived on my bicycle early in the afternoon, after the bus carrying tourists from the coast had departed. A flight of steps took me down into a lush, emerald valley, lined by cliffs on either side, awash with the speech of the river and the sighing of the wind through high, unharvested grasses. On a small bridge crossing the river I met an old woman carrying a wide basket on her head and holding the hand of a little, shy child; the woman grinned at me with the red, toothless smile of a beetle nut chewer. On the far side of the river I stood in front of a great moss-covered complex of passageways, rooms, and courtyards carved by hand out of the black volcanic rock.

I noticed, at a bend in the canyon downstream, a further series of caves carved into the cliffs. These appeared more isolated and remote, unattended by any footpath I could discern. I set out through the grasses to explore them. This proved much more difficult than I anticipated, but after getting lost in the tall grasses, and fording the river three times, I at last found myself beneath the caves. A short scramble up the rock wall brought me to the mouth of one of them, and I entered on my hands and knees. It was a wide but low opening, perhaps only four feet high, and the interior receded only about five or six feet into the cliff. The floor and walls were covered with mosses, painting the cave with green patterns and softening the harshness of the rock; the place, despite its small size—or perhaps because of it—had an air of great friendliness. I climbed to two other caves, each about the same size, but then felt drawn back to the first one, to sit cross-legged on the cushioning moss and gaze out across the emerald canyon. It was quiet inside, a kind of intimate sanctuary hewn into the stone. I began to explore the rich resonance of the enclosure, first just humming, then intoning a simple chant taught to me by a balian some days before. I was delighted by the overtones that the cave added to my voice, and sat there singing for a long while. I did not notice the change in the wind outside, or the cloud shadows darkening the valley, until the rains broke—suddenly and with great force. The first storm of the monsoon!

I had experienced only slight rains on the island before then, and was startled by the torrential downpour now sending stones tumbling along the cliffs, building puddles and then ponds in the green landscape below, swelling the river. There was no question of returning home—I would be unable to make my way back through the flood to the valley's entrance. And so, thankful for the shelter, I recrossed my legs to wait out the storm. Before long the rivulets falling along the cliff above gathered themselves into streams, and two small waterfalls cascaded across the cave's mouth. Soon I was looking into a solid curtain of water, thin in some places, where the canyon's image flickered unsteadily, and thickly rushing in others. My senses were all but overcome by the wild beauty of the cascade and by the roar of sound, my body trembling inwardly at the weird sense of being sealed into my hiding place.

And then, in the midst of all this tumult, I noticed a small, delicate activity. Just in front of me, and only an inch or two to my side of the torrent, a spider was climbing a thin thread stretched across the mouth of the cave. As I watched, it anchored another thread to the top of the opening, then slipped back along the first thread and joined the two at a point about midway between the roof and the floor. I lost sight of the spider then, and for a while it seemed that it had vanished, thread and all, until my focus rediscovered it. Two more threads now radiated from the center to the floor, and then another; soon the spider began to swing between these as on a circular trellis, trailing an ever-lengthening thread which it affixed to each radiating rung as it moved from one to the next, spiraling outward. The spider seemed wholly undaunted by the tumult of waters spilling past it, although every now and then it broke off its spiral dance and climbed to the roof or the floor to tug on the radii there, assuring the tautness of the threads, then crawled back to where it left off. Whenever I lost the correct focus, I waited to catch sight of the spinning arachnid, and then let its dancing form gradually draw the lineaments of the web back into visibility, tying my focus into each new knot of silk as it moved, weaving my gaze into the ever-deepening pattern.

And then, abruptly, my vision snagged on a strange incongruity: another thread slanted across the web, neither radiating nor spiraling from the central juncture, violating the symmetry. As I followed it with my eyes, pondering its purpose in the overall pattern, I began to realize that it was on a different plane from the rest of the web, for the web slipped out of focus whenever this new line became clearer. I soon saw that it led to its own center, about twelve inches to the right of the first, another nexus of forces from which several threads stretched to the floor and the ceiling. And then I saw that there was a *different* spider spinning this web, testing its tautness by dancing around it like the first, now setting the silken cross weaves around the nodal point and winding outward. The two spiders spun independently of each other, but to my eyes they wove a single intersecting pattern. This widening of my gaze soon disclosed yet another spider spiraling in the cave's mouth, and suddenly I realized that there were *many* overlapping webs coming into being, radiating out at different rhythms from myriad centers poised—some higher, some lower, some minutely closer to my eyes and some farther—between the stone above and the stone below.

I sat stunned and mesmerized before this ever-complexifying expanse of living patterns upon patterns, my gaze drawn like a breath into one converging group of lines, then breathed out into open space, then drawn down into another convergence. The curtain of water had become utterly silent— I tried at one point to hear it, but could not. My senses were entranced.

I had the distinct impression that I was watching the universe being born, galaxy upon galaxy. . . .

Night filled the cave with darkness. The rain had not stopped. Yet, strangely, I felt neither cold nor hungry—only remarkably peaceful and at home. Stretching out upon the moist, mossy floor near the back of the cave, I slept.

When I awoke, the sun was staring into the canyon, the grasses below rippling with bright blues and greens. I could see no trace of the webs, nor their weavers. Thinking that they were invisible to my eyes without the curtain of water behind them, I felt carefully with my hands around and through the mouth of the cave. But the webs were gone. I climbed down to the river and washed, then hiked across and out of the canyon to where my cycle was drying in the sun, and headed back to my own valley.

I have never, since that time, been able to encounter a spider without feeling a great strangeness and awe. To be sure, insects and spiders are not the only powers, or even central presences, in the Indonesian universe. But they were *my* introduction to the spirits, to the magic afoot in the land. It was from them that I first learned of the intelligence that lurks in nonhuman nature, the ability that an alien form of sentience has to echo one's own, to instill a reverberation in oneself that temporarily shatters habitual ways of seeing and feeling, leaving one open to a world all alive, awake, and aware. It was from such small beings that my senses first learned of the countless worlds within worlds that spin in the depths of this world that we commonly inhabit, and from them that I learned that my body could, with practice, enter sensorially into these dimensions. The precise and minuscule craft of the spiders had so honed and focused my awareness that the very web-work of the universe, of which my own flesh was a part, seemed to be being spun by their arcane art. I have already spoken of the ants, and of the fire-flies, whose sensory likeness to the lights in the night sky had taught me the fickleness of gravity. The long and cyclical trance that we call malaria was also brought to me by insects, in this case mosquitoes, and I lived for three weeks in a feverish state of shivers, sweat, and visions.

I had rarely before paid much attention to the natural world. But my exposure to traditional magicians and seers was shifting my senses; I became increasingly susceptible to the solicitations of nonhuman things. In the course of struggling to decipher the magicians' odd gestures or to fathom their constant spoken references to powers unseen and unheard, I began to *see* and to *hear* in a manner I never had before. When a magician spoke of a power or "presence" lingering in the corner of his house, I learned to notice the ray of sunlight that was then pouring through a chink in the roof, illuminating a column of drifting dust, and to realize that that column of light was indeed a power, influencing the air currents by its warmth, and indeed influencing the whole mood of the room; although I had not consciously seen it before, it had already been structuring my experience. My ears began to attend, in a new way, to the songs of birds—no longer just a melodic background to human speech, but meaningful speech in its own right, responding to and commenting on events in the surrounding earth. I became a student of subtle differences: the way a breeze may flutter a single leaf on a whole tree, leaving the other leaves silent and unmoved (had not that leaf, then, been brushed by a magic?); or the way the intensity of the sun's heat expresses itself in the precise rhythm of the crickets. Walking along the dirt paths, I learned to slow my pace in order to *feel* the difference between one nearby hill and the next, or to taste the presence of a particular field at a certain time of day when, as I had been told by a local *dukun,* the place had a special power and proffered unique gifts. It was a power communicated to my senses by the way the shadows of the trees fell at that hour, and by smells that only then lingered in the tops of the grasses without being wafted away by the wind, and other elements I could only isolate after many days of stopping and listening.

And gradually, then, other animals began to intercept me in my wanderings, as if some quality in my posture or the rhythm of my breathing had disarmed their wariness; I would find myself face-to-face with monkeys, and with large lizards that did not slither away when I spoke, but leaned forward in apparent curiosity. In rural Java, I often noticed monkeys accompanying me in the branches overhead, and ravens walked toward me on the road, croaking. While at Pangandaran, a nature preserve on a peninsula jutting out from the south coast of Java ("a place of many spirits," I was told by nearby fishermen), I stepped out from a clutch of trees and found myself looking into the face of one of the rare and beautiful bison that exist only on that island. Our eyes locked. When it snorted, I snorted back; when it shifted its shoulders, I shifted my stance; when I tossed my head, it tossed *its* head in reply. I found myself caught in a nonverbal conversation with this Other, a gestural duet with which my conscious awareness had very little to do. It was as if my body in its actions was suddenly being motivated by a wisdom older than my thinking mind, as though it was held and moved by a logos, deeper than words, spoken by the Other's body, the trees, and the stony ground on which we stood.

Anthropology's inability to discern the shaman's allegiance to nonhuman nature has led to a curious circumstance in the "developed world" today, where many persons in search of spiritual understanding are enrolling in workshops concerned with "shamanic" methods of personal discovery and revelation. Psychotherapists and some physicians have begun to specialize in "shamanic healing techniques." "Shamanism" has thus come to connote an alternative form of therapy; the emphasis, among these new practitioners of popular shamanism, is on personal insight and curing. These are noble aims, to be sure, yet they are secondary to, and derivative from, the primary role of the indigenous shaman, a role that cannot be fulfilled without long and sustained exposure to wild nature, to its patterns and vicissitudes. Mimicking the indigenous shaman's curative methods without his intimate knowledge of the wider natural community cannot, if I am correct, do anything more than trade certain symptoms for others, or shift the locus of disease from place to place within the human community. For the source of stress lies in the relation *between* the human community and the natural landscape.

Western industrial society, of course, with its massive scale and hugely centralized economy, can hardly be seen in relation to any particular landscape or ecosystem; the more-than-human ecology with which it is directly engaged is the biosphere itself. Sadly, our culture's relation to the earthly biosphere can in no way be considered a reciprocal or balanced one: with thousands of acres of nonregenerating forest disappearing every hour, and hundreds of our fellow species becoming extinct each month as a result of our civilization's excesses, we can hardly be surprised by the amount of epidemic illness in our culture, from increasingly severe immune dysfunctions and cancers, to widespread psychological distress, depression, and ever more frequent suicides, to the accelerating number of household killings and mass murders committed for no apparent reason by otherwise coherent individuals.

From an animistic perspective, the clearest source of all this distress, both physical and psychological, lies in the aforementioned violence needlessly perpetrated by our civilization on the ecology of the planet; only by alleviating the latter will we be able to heal the former. While this may sound at first like a simple statement of faith, it makes eminent and obvious sense as soon as we acknowledge our thorough dependence upon the countless other organisms with whom we have evolved. Caught up in a mass of abstractions, our attention hypnotized by a host of human-made technologies that only reflect us back to ourselves, it is all too easy for us to forget our carnal inherence in a more-than-human matrix of sensations and sensibilities. Our bodies have formed themselves in delicate reciprocity with the manifold textures, sounds, and shapes of an animate earth—our eyes have evolved in subtle interaction with *other* eyes, as our ears are at-tuned by their very structure to the howling of wolves and the honking of geese. To shut ourselves off from these other voices, to continue by our lifestyles to condemn these other sensibilities to the oblivion of extinction, is to rob our own senses of their integrity, and to rob our minds of their co-herence. We are human only in contact, and conviviality, with what is not human.

Although the Indonesian islands are home to an astonishing diversity of birds, it was only when I went to study among the Sherpa people of the high Himalayas that I was truly initiated into the avian world. The Himalayas are young mountains, their peaks not yet rounded by the endless action of wind and ice, and so the primary dimension of the visible landscape is over-whelmingly vertical. Even in the high ridges one seldom attains a view of a distant horizon; instead one's vision is deflected upward by the steep face of the next mountain. The whole land has surged skyward in a manner still evident in the lines and furrows of the mountain walls, and this ancient dynamism readily communicates itself to the sensing body.

In such a world those who dwell and soar in the sky are the primary powers. They alone move easily in such a zone, swooping downward to be-come a speck near the valley floor, or spiraling into the heights on invisible currents. The wingeds, alone, carry the immediate knowledge of what is un-folding on the far side of the next ridge, and hence it is only by watching them that one can be kept apprised of climatic changes in the offing, as well as of subtle shifts in the flow and density of air currents in one's own valley. Several of the shamans that I met in Nepal had birds as their close familiars. Ravens are constant commentators on village affairs. The smaller, flocking birds perform aerobatics in unison over the village rooftops, twisting and swerving in a perfect sympathy of motion, the whole flock appearing like a magic banner that floats and flaps on air currents over the village, then de-scends in a heap, only to be carried aloft by the wind a moment later, rip-pling and swelling.

For some time I visited a Sherpa *dzankri* whose rock home was built into one of the steep mountainsides of the Khumbu region in Nepal. On one of our walks along the narrow cliff trails that wind around the mountain, the *dzankri* pointed out to me a certain boulder, jutting out from the cliff, on which he had "danced" before attempting some especially difficult cures. I recognized the boulder several days later when hiking back down toward the *dzankri*'s home from the upper yak pastures, and I climbed onto the rock, not to dance but to ponder the pale white and red lichens that gave life to its surface, and to rest. Across the dry valley, two lammergeier condors floated between gleaming, snow-covered peaks. It was a ringing blue Himalayan day, clear as a bell. After a few moments I took a silver coin out of my pocket and aimlessly began a simple sleight-of-hand exercise, rolling the coin over the knuckles of my right hand. I had taken to practicing this somewhat monotonous exercise in response to the endless flicking of prayer-beads by the older Sherpas, a practice usually accompanied by a repetitively chanted prayer: "*Om Mani Padme Hum*" (O the Jewel in the Lotus). But there was no prayer accompanying my revolving coin, aside from my quiet breathing and the dazzling sunlight. I noticed that one of the two condors in the distance had swerved away from its partner and was now floating over the valley, wings outstretched. As I watched it grow larger, I realized, with some delight, that it was heading in my general direction; I stopped rolling the coin and stared. Yet just then the lammergeier halted in its flight, motionless for a moment against the peaks, then swerved around and headed back toward its partner in the distance. Disappointed, I took up the coin and began rolling it along my knuckles once again, its silver surface catching the sunlight as it turned, reflecting the rays back into the sky. Instantly, the condor swung out from its path and began soaring back in a wide arc. Once again, I watched its shape grow larger. As the great size of the bird became apparent, I felt my skin begin to crawl and come alive, like a swarm of bees all in motion, and a humming grew loud in my ears. The coin continued rolling along my fingers. The creature loomed larger, and larger still, until suddenly, it was there—an immense silhouette hovering just above my head, huge wing feathers rustling ever so slightly as they mastered the breeze. My fingers were frozen, unable to move; the coin dropped out of my hand. And then I felt myself stripped naked by an alien gaze infinitely more lucid and precise than my own. I do not know for how long I was transfixed, only that I felt the air streaming past naked knees and heard the wind whispering in my feathers long after the Visitor had departed.

I returned to a North America whose only indigenous species of condor was on the brink of extinction, mostly as a result of lead poisoning from bullets in the carrion it consumes. But I did not think about this. I was excited by the new sensibilities that had stirred in me—my newfound awareness of a more-than-human world, of the great potency of the land, and particularly of the keen intelligence of other animals, large and small, whose lives and cultures interpenetrate our own. I startled neighbors by chattering with squirrels, who swiftly climbed down the trunks of their trees and across lawns to banter with me, or by gazing for hours on end at a heron fishing in a nearby estuary, or at gulls opening clams by dropping them from a height onto the rocks along the beach.

Yet, very gradually, I began to lose my sense of the animals' own awareness. The gulls' technique for breaking open the clams began to appear as a largely automatic behavior, and I could not easily feel the attention that they must bring to each new shell. Perhaps each shell was entirely the same as the last, and *no* spontaneous attention was really necessary. . . .

I found myself now observing the heron from outside its world, noting with interest its careful high-stepping walk and the sudden dart of its beak into the water, but no longer feeling its tensed yet poised alertness with my own muscles. And, strangely, the suburban squirrels no longer responded to my chittering calls. Although I wished to, I could no longer focus my awareness on engaging in their world as I had so easily done a few weeks earlier, for my attention was quickly deflected by internal, verbal deliberations of one sort or another—by a conversation I now seemed to carry on entirely within myself. The squirrels had no part in this conversation.

It became increasingly apparent, from books and articles and discussions with various people, that other animals were not as awake and aware as I had assumed, that they lacked any real language and hence the possibility of thought, and that even their seemingly spontaneous responses to the world around them were largely "programmed" behaviors, "coded" in the genetic material now being mapped by biologists. Indeed, the more I spoke *about* other animals, the less possible it became to speak *to* them. I gradually came to discern that there was no common ground between the unlimited human intellect and the limited sentience of other animals, no medium through which we and they might communicate with and reciprocate one another.

As the expressive and sentient landscape slowly faded behind my more exclusively human concerns, threatening to become little more than an illusion or fantasy, I began to feel—particularly in my chest and abdomen—as though I were being cut off from vital sources of nourishment. I was indeed reacclimating to my own culture, becoming more attuned to its styles of discourse and interaction, yet my bodily senses seemed to be losing their acuteness, becoming less awake to subtle changes and patterns. The thrumming of crickets, and even the songs of the local blackbirds, readily faded from my awareness after a few moments, and it was only by an effort of will that I could bring them back into the perceptual field. The flight of sparrows and of dragonflies no longer sustained my focus very long, if indeed they gained my attention at all. My skin quit registering the various changes in the breeze, and smells seemed to have faded from the world almost entirely, my nose waking up only once or twice a day, perhaps while cooking, or when taking out the garbage.

In Nepal, the air had been filled with smells—whether in the towns, where burning incense combined with the aromas of roasting meats and honeyed pastries and fruits for trade in the open market, and the stench of organic refuse rotting in the ravines, and sometimes of corpses being cremated by the river; or in the high mountains, where the wind carried the whiffs of countless wildflowers, and of the newly turned earth outside the villages where the fragrant dung of yaks was drying in round patties on the outer walls of the houses, to be used, when dry, as fuel for the household fires, and where smoke from those many home fires always mingled in the outside air. And sounds as well: the chants of aspiring monks and adepts blended with the ringing of prayer bells on near and distant slopes, accompanied by the raucous croaks of ravens, and the sigh of the wind pouring over the passes, and the flapping of prayer flags, and the distant hush of the river cascading through the far-below gorge.

There the air was a thick and richly textured presence, filled with invisible but nonetheless tactile, olfactory, and audible influences. In the United States, however, the air seemed thin and void of substance or influence. It was not, here, a sensuous medium—the felt matrix of our breath and the breath of the other animals and plants and soils—but was merely an absence, and indeed was constantly referred to in everyday discourse as mere empty space. Hence, in America I found myself lingering near wood fires and even garbage dumps—much to the dismay of my friends—for only such an intensity of smells served to remind my body of its immersion in an enveloping medium, and with this experience of being immersed in a world of influences came a host of body memories from my year among the shamans and village people of rural Asia.

I began to find other ways, as well, of tapping the very different sensations and perceptions that I had grown accustomed to in the "undeveloped world," by living for extended periods on native Indian reservations in the southwestern desert and along the northwestern coast, or by hiking off for weeks at a time into the North American wilderness. Intermittently, I began to wonder if my culture's assumptions regarding the lack of awareness in other animals and in the land itself was less a product of careful and judicious reasoning than of a strange inability to clearly perceive other animals—a real inability to clearly see, or focus upon, anything outside the realm of human technology, or to hear as meaningful anything other than human speech. The sad results of our interactions with the rest of nature were being reported in every newspaper—from the depletion of topsoil due to industrial farming techniques to the fouling of groundwater by industrial wastes, from the rapid destruction of ancient forests to, worst of all, the ever-accelerating extinction of our fellow species—and these remarkable and disturbing occurrences, all readily traceable to the ongoing activity of "civilized" humankind, did indeed suggest the possibility that there was a perceptual problem in my culture, that modern, "civilized" humanity simply did not perceive surrounding nature in a clear manner, if we have even been perceiving it at all.

The experiences that shifted the focus of my research in rural Indonesia and Nepal had shown me that nonhuman nature can be perceived and experienced with far more intensity and nuance than is generally acknowledged in the West. What was it that made possible the heightened sensitivity to extrahuman reality, the profound attentiveness to other species and to the Earth that is evidenced in so many of these cultures, and that had so altered my awareness that my senses now felt stifled and starved by the patterns of my own culture? Or, reversing the question, what had made possible the absence of this attentiveness in the modern West? For Western culture, too, has its indigenous origins. If the relative attunement to environing nature exhibited by native cultures is linked to a more primordial, participatory mode of perception, how had Western civilization come to be so exempt from this sensory reciprocity? How, that is, have we become so deaf and so blind to the vital existence of other species, and to the animate landscapes they inhabit, that we now so casually bring about their destruction?

To be sure, our obliviousness to nonhuman nature is today held in place by ways of speaking that simply deny intelligence to other species and to nature in general, as well as by the very structures of our civilized existence—by the incessant drone of motors that shut out the voices of birds and of the winds; by electric lights that eclipse not only the stars but the night itself; by air "conditioners" that hide the seasons; by offices, automobiles, and shopping malls that finally obviate any need to step outside the purely human world at all. We consciously encounter nonhuman nature only as it has been circumscribed by our civilization and its technologies: through our domesticated pets, on the television, or at the zoo (or, at best, in carefully managed "nature preserves"). The plants and animals we consume are neither gathered nor hunted—they are bred and harvested in huge, mechanized farms. "Nature," it would seem, has become simply a stock of "resources" for human civilization, and so we can hardly be surprised that our civilized eyes and ears are somewhat oblivious to the existence of perspectives that are not human at all, or that a person either entering into or returning to the West from a nonindustrial culture would feel startled and confused by the felt absence of nonhuman powers.

Still, the current commodification of "nature" by civilization tells us little or nothing of the perceptual shift that made possible this reduction of the animal (and the earth) to an object, little of the process whereby our senses first relinquished the power of the Other, the vision that for so long had motivated our most sacred rituals, our dances, and our prayers.

But can we even hope to catch a glimpse of this process, which has given rise to so many of the habits and linguistic prejudices that now structure our very thinking? Certainly not if we gaze toward that origin from within the midst of the very civilization it engendered. But perhaps we may make our stand along the *edge* of that civilization, like a magician, or like a person who, having lived among another tribe, can no longer wholly return to his own. He lingers half within and half outside of his community, open as well, then, to the shifting voices and flapping forms that crawl and hover beyond the mirrored walls of the city. And even there, moving along those walls, he may hope to find the precise clues to the mystery of how those walls were erected, and how a simple boundary became a barrier, only if the moment is timely—only, that is, if the margin he frequents is a temporal as well as a spatial edge, and the temporal structure that it bounds is about to dissolve, or metamorphose, into something else.   ■

NOTES

1. This work was done at the Philadelphia Association, a therapeutic community directed by Dr. R. D. Laing and his associates.

2. A simple illustration of this may be found among many of the indigenous peoples of North America, for whom the English term "medicine" commonly translates a word meaning "power"—specifically, the sacred power received by a human person from a particular animal or other nonhuman entity. Thus, a particular *medicine person* may be renowned for her "badger medicine" or "bear medicine," for his "eagle medicine," "elk medicine," or even "thunder medicine." It is from their direct engagement with these nonhuman powers that medicine persons derive their own abilities, including their ability to cure human ailments.

3. To the Western mind such views are likely to sound like reckless "projections" of human consciousness into inanimate and dumb materials, suitable for poetry perhaps, but having nothing, in fact, to do with those actual birds or that forest. Such is our common view. This text will examine the possibility that it is civilization that has been confused, and not indigenous peoples. It will suggest, and provide evidence, that one perceives a world at all only by projecting oneself into that world, that one makes contact with things and others only by actively participating in them, lending one's sensory imagination to things in order to discover how they alter and transform that imagination, how they reflect us back changed, how they are different from us. It will suggest that perception is *always* participatory, and hence that modern humanity's denial of awareness in nonhuman nature is borne not by any conceptual or scientific rigor, but rather by an inability, or a refusal, to fully perceive other organisms.

4. The similarity between such animistic world views and the emerging perspective of contemporary ecology is not trivial. Atmospheric geochemist James Lovelock, elucidating the well-known Gaia hypothesis—a theory stressing the major role played by organic life in the ceaseless modulation of the earth's atmospheric and climatic conditions—insists that the geological environment is itself constituted by organic life, and by the products or organic metabolism. In his words, we inhabit "a world that is the breath and bones of our ancestors." See, for instance, "Gaia: The World as Living

Organism," in the *New Scientist*, December 18, 1986, as well as *Scientists on Gaia*, ed. Stephen Schneider and Penelope Boston (Cambridge: M.I.T. Press, 1991).

■ *QUESTIONS FOR MAKING CONNECTIONS WITHIN THE READING* ■

1. David Abram's essay begins with a description of his travels in eastern Bali and ends with his return to the United States. What happens to Abram during the course of his travels? When he says, "I began to *see* and to *hear* in a manner I never had before," what does he mean?

2. Abram tells us that one cannot become a shaman without "long and sustained exposure to wild nature, to its patterns and vicissitudes." What is "wild nature"? How does it differ from the kinds of nature one finds in a city, a suburb, or a state park? How does Abram's experience of "wild nature" differ from the experience one has in a city, a suburb, or a state park?

3. As Abram reflects on the differences between how he felt when he was in Indonesia and how he felt on his return to the United States, he considers the possibility that Westerners might have "a real inability to clearly see, or focus upon, anything outside the realm of human technology, or to hear as meaningful anything other than human speech." What is it that Abram would like for us to focus on instead?

■ *QUESTIONS FOR WRITING* ■

1. In "The Ecology of Magic," Abram describes how his travels made him "a student of subtle differences." What does it mean to become such a student? What does one notice? And why is it important to notice such things?

2. As Abram sees it, there is a qualitative difference between the ways Westerners experience nature and the ways shamans experience nature. And yet, somehow, Abram himself was able to transcend the difference and access these other ways of feeling. What made it possible for Abram to do this? Could anyone have the experiences Abram describes?

■ *QUESTIONS FOR MAKING CONNECTIONS BETWEEN READINGS* ■

1. In "The Ecology of Magic," Abram places a very high value on evidence drawn from personal experience. How does this kind of evidence differ from the evidence that Marcia Angell discusses in "Science in the Courtroom: Opinions Without Evidence"? What role does experiential

evidence play in the courtroom, the classroom, the dormitory room? What role should evidence of this kind play in these public places?

2. Abram defines humanity in the following way: "We are human only in contact, and conviviality, with what is not human." In "Playing God in the Garden," Michael Pollan discusses biogenetic engineering as one way that the food industry redefines the relationship between humans, plants, and animals. Is it possible to have a "convivial" relationship with "what is not human" in the age of technology? What relationship should humans have to the natural world?

For additional suggestions about making connections between readings, visit the Link-O-Mat and More Sample Assignments at <www.newhum.com>.

LILA ABU-LUGHOD

WHEN LILA ABU-LUGHOD was completing her graduate work in anthropology at Harvard University in the late 1970s, she designed a fieldwork project that took her to Egypt to study interpersonal relations between male and female members of a nomadic Bedouin community. Once there, Abu-Lughod noticed that the people she was living with frequently punctuated their talk, both in public and in private, by reciting short pieces of poetry. Although this wasn't what she had come to study, Abu-Lughod became fascinated by the fact that there was a "radical difference between the sentiments expressed in [the oral poetry] and those expressed about the same situations in ordinary social interactions and conversations." Abu-Lughod's first book, *Veiled Sentiments: Honor and Poetry in a Bedouin Society* (1986), grew out of her efforts to understand what produced these two very different ways of using language.

Currently a professor of Anthropology and Middle Eastern Studies at New York University, Abu-Lughod is internationally recognized for her contributions to feminist ethnography and the study of gender politics in the Muslim world. What makes Abu-Lughod's work so distinctive and so unsettling is her inclination to insist on the importance of carefully examining both the actions and the assumptions that make up our everyday lives. Thus, while Abu-Lughod works to understand how women can gain power in patriarchal societies, she also encourages all who pursue such research to consider what women lose when they adopt the lifeways and the values of modern society. "Feminists, leftists, progressives, and other intellectuals still haven't questioned the idea of development, progress, modernity, as wholly a good thing," she has said. "No one has challenged this concept . . . —that we have to follow a certain path, and as people get educated, they will get more enlightened."

Abu-Lughod, Lila. "Honor and Shame." *Writing Women's Worlds: Bedouin Stories.* Berkeley: University of California Press, 1993. 205–242.

Initial quotation from *Veiled Sentiments: Honor and Poetry in a Bedouin Society* (University of California Press, 1986); closing quotation from Sarwat Ahmad, "A Muddled Modernity," *Cairo Times*, Vol. 3, Issue 1, March 4–17, 1999. <http://www.cairotimes.com/content/issues/Women/lughod.html>.

In "Honor and Shame," which comes from Abu-Lughod's second book, *Writing Women's Worlds: Bedouin Stories* (1993), Abu-Lughod focuses our attention on this question quite directly. What does Kamla, the subject of "Honor and Shame," stand to gain by breaking with her tradition and completing her education? What does she stand to lose? Under the circumstances, what outcome should one hope for? By telling Kamla's story in just this way, Abu-Lughod incites the very sentiments she most wants her readers to explore.

To learn more about Lila Abu-Lughod and Bedouin culture, visit the Link-O-Mat at <www.newhum.com>.

Honor and Shame

Say to the believing men that they should lower their gaze and guard their modesty; that will make for greater purity for them. And God is well acquainted with all that they do.

And say to the believing women that they should lower their gaze and guard their modesty; that they should not display their beauty and ornaments except what (ordinarily) appear thereof; that they should draw their veils over their bosoms and not display their beauty except to their husbands, their fathers, their husbands' fathers, their sons, their husband's sons, their brothers or their brothers' sons, or their sisters' sons, or their women, or the slaves their right hands possess, or male attendants free of sexual desires, or small children who have no carnal knowledge of women.

Qur'an 24:30–31

In a letter dated July 30, 1989, Kamla, another daughter of Gateefa and Sagr, wrote to tell me her good news.

In the Name of God the All-Merciful and Compassionate. It gives me pleasure to send this letter to my dear sister, Dr. Lila, hoping from God on high, the All-Powerful, that it reaches you carrying love and greetings to you and your family while you are all in the best of health and in perfect happiness.

By name she mentioned my brother and sisters (none of whom she has met) and asked me to convey her greetings and those of her family to them and to my parents, as well as to the one American friend of mine they had met ten years ago—in short, to everyone they knew about in my life in

America. I had confided during my last visit that I would be getting married soon. She asked if I had; if so, she wrote, she sent a thousand congratulations and hoped, God willing, that he was a good man who would understand me. She hoped also that their new in-law was a noble man, the best in all of America, and that they would meet him soon. After wishing me many children (six boys and six girls) and more greetings, she squeezed her piece of news onto the bottom of the page.

> Your sister Kamla has become engaged to Engineer Ibrahim Saleem, Aisha's brother.

I could hardly believe it. We had teased Kamla about him ever since his name had been floated four years before as a prospect. This was the match she scarcely dared hope her father would arrange. Not that she had ever met the young man. What mattered was that he was educated, came from a family that believed in educating girls, and lived in a town. She would be able to escape the kind of life her family lived, a life that annoyed her—the only one in her family, male or female, to have made it through high school—more and more.

Because she complained so much, I had asked her in the summer after she graduated to write me an essay on how young Bedouin women's lives were changing and what of the past she hoped the Awlad 'Ali would retain and what she wished they would abandon. She had proudly told me that her teacher had sent off for publication an essay on Awlad 'Ali weddings she had written in school. You can trace, in the stilted words of her essay and the candid comments (in parentheses) she made as she read it aloud to me, the outlines of the new world she hoped to gain by marrying the likes of Engineer Ibrahim Saleem.

The Education of Girls

An Essay on the Young Bedouin Woman of Egypt and the Changes in Her Life over 40 Years

If we are to speak of the Bedouin girl in Egypt we find that her life differs from one era to another. The circumstances of the home and family relations change from one age to another. If we go back to discuss the way she was around forty years ago, we find that the Bedouin girl was living a life in which she was of no value. When she came of age, or maturity (as the Egyptians say—I mean the years when she is ready for marriage), *she had to do housework at her family's home—for example, cooking, washing clothes, and preparing firewood.* (Her only value was in the housework she did—the sweeping and washing—and if she didn't do it they'd laugh at her and gossip about her laziness. She was forced to do it, even if she weren't capable. No matter what her health was like. I'm talking about those who were my age, from around the age of twelve on.)

Also, she used to spin and weave, even though it is very difficult, painful, and strenuous. (When she was around fifteen, her mother or any woman in the household, an aunt for instance, would teach her. It's supposed to be the mother, though. Her goal was to teach her daughter to spin and to make something, anything. The important thing was for her to weave something, if only a border for the tent.) *She had to learn this skill.* (This is what is important for the Bedouins, housework, weaving, and such things. Forty years ago this was what a girl had to put up with.)

Kamla had been resenting housework. Now that she had finished school she rarely left the house. With two sisters, she was responsible for the cooking and cleaning one day out of three. On another of those days she was in charge of baking bread with them. She was on call much of the rest of the time, seeing to it that her little brothers and sisters were bathed, dressed, and staying out of mischief. Piles of laundry collected in the back room to be done when there was time.

Where before she had worn clean clothes for school, studied with her brothers in a quiet room of her own, and been given few household duties, now she had no privileges. Her clothes were as caked with dough and soot as her sisters'. Kamla's only escape was listening to the radio. She carried my transistor with her wherever in the house or courtyard she was working. She kept an eye on the time so as not to miss the radio soap operas. When she was free, she stared into space as she listened to Egyptian music, talk shows, and the news. So attached was she to the radio that I called it her sweetheart. Her mother, irritable from fatigue herself, scolded her and threatened to lock up the radio. When Gateefa complained, "My daughters are becoming lazy sluts," Kamla, like her sisters, simply ignored her.

Kamla had scored high enough on her final exams to secure a place in the agricultural college for which her high school had prepared her. She had no special interest in agriculture and had gone to this secondary school only because the regular high school was on the far side of town. Her uncles had given her a choice: quit school or go to the nearby agriculture school. School was still much on her mind. Her essay continued:

Education for the Bedouin girl used not to exist. It was impossible for her to study. (Forty years ago she lived a life, as I said earlier, that had no value at all.) *She was governed by the customs and traditions that the Bedouin families followed. These customs and traditions forbade a girl to leave the house under any circumstances. So going to school* (this is an example) *would be the greatest shame. She couldn't say that she wished to study, no matter what. Even if, as they say, she was the daughter of a tribal leader.* (So for example, a girl's father would be a tribal leader and she'd want to study, but her relatives would say no you can't. She'd say, but I'm the daughter of the head of a lineage. I must learn. They'd forbid her.)

This hypothetical example was, of course, from her own experience. She had been allowed to continue her schooling against the wishes of her uncles. They wanted to pull her out when she was no longer little. Because she was so determined, she and her parents had put up with the uncles' general suspicion and occasional accusations. She was a fierce child who had early on decided she wanted to go to school. She was not allowed to enroll in the public school, though, because, as is often the case, her father had never registered her birth. Yet still she went each day, as a visitor, borrowing her brothers' books. After three years of this her teacher finally required her to register officially. Haj Sagr went and had her papers drawn up. From then on she came in at the top of her class, while her brothers and male cousins flunked out. I had recorded in my notes from 1979 her bashful reaction when her brother told their father she had been appointed school monitor. Sagr had been hugging his youngest son, then in his first year of school, proudly predicting that his son would come out above the rest.

The primary school had been within sight of the camp, and its students were mostly relatives and neighbors. The secondary school, though, was about three kilometers away. Kamla's class had only four Bedouin girls; the rest of the girls were Egyptians from town. To get to this school she had to walk along the road past houses of people who did not know her. She said she walked with her head down, looking neither right nor left, but she still had to endure catcalls from men driving by.

Her relatives' suspicions were harder to cope with. One aunt had come twice to Gateefa to accuse Kamla of taking her son's schoolbook to give to a boy from a neighboring tribe. Kamla's mother had defended her. True, she had given the boy a schoolbook, but it was in exchange for a book that he had given her the previous year. And the book was one that her father had bought her, not one she had taken from her cousin. Fortunately, when they questioned the aunt's son, he backed Gateefa.

Kamla and her mother were angrier when Kamla's uncle told Haj Sagr that he had seen his niece Kamla walking home with a boy. Gateefa felt she'd been hit in the stomach with a rock. She argued, to me, "If it were true, why didn't he stop for her and put her in the car? Why didn't he get out and beat her right there, if he really saw her? If he's so afraid for her, why doesn't he ever offer to drive her to school?"

Kamla told the story as she knew it. She believed the problem began during her second year of high school. Her uncle had not wanted her to continue, but Sagr had defended his daughter's right to stay in school. Furious, her uncle did everything he could to prevent her from studying. If, for example, guests came to the house, he would knock on her door to ask her to make the tea. She'd try to escape, sneaking off to study outdoors under the trees. Two days before her final exams (when, as we all know, she added, nerves are on edge), she was walking home from school. Across the road a boy she had known since she was small was going the same direction.

Because she always walked with her head down, she noticed her uncle drive by only after he had passed. He went straight to her father and told him, "Your daughter was walking hand in hand with a boy." Her father had questioned him carefully, then called in Kamla's mother. Gateefa in turn had come to her ("And you know how upset she gets!" she said to me) to ask her about it. Kamla refused to say "yes, no, or maybe" unless her uncle came and accused her to her face.

Her father, she said lovingly, believed in her. He asked her why she didn't walk home from school with her cousin, and she explained that she was not about to go out of her way just to walk with him. If he wished to walk with her along her route before cutting off to his house, he was welcome to. Kamla's uncle had also told her father that this cousin had informed him that the boy waited for Kamla at the school gates to walk home with her every day. Fortunately for Kamla, her cousin happened to pass by the house that afternoon. Sagr called him over to question him—right in front of her uncle. The boy swore that he had never said such a thing. That ended it.

Arranged Marriage

The next paragraph of Kamla's essay took up the matter of marriage. Commenting on it, Kamla said, "This was a topic the Bedouin girl would hear nothing about and wasn't supposed to have anything to do with."

She had no right to an opinion in any matter, however much the matter might concern her personally. She had no say even in the choice of a husband. She had absolutely no say in this matter. (And to this day, no matter how educated she's become, very seldom does she have any opinion. The Bedouin girl has no say.) *In this matter what she had to do was carry out her family's orders even if she didn't want to. It was not right for her to refuse.* (Even if she didn't want him, she had to agree to it against her will. Even if he was older than she was, for example, or very different from her, she had to agree to what the family wanted. For example, if they said I had to marry someone and I didn't want him—I hated him—but if my kinsmen had agreed to the match and told me I had to marry him, what I would have to do, despite my wishes, was marry him.)

I was surprised that Kamla depicted women as powerless in decisions about marriage. She had heard the same stories I had—stories, like her grandmother Migdim's, of resistance to marriages arranged for them by their kinsmen. She knew plenty of young women like one who, in love with someone else, had married Kamla's cousin but then had gone home to her father's household at the slightest provocation, eventually forcing her husband to divorce her. The specter of forced marriage, especially to paternal cousins, may have loomed large for Kamla because she, like her sister Sabra, was waiting. As her mother joked with a friend, "Kamla's got her diploma. Now we're going to give her the other diploma!"

Her religious training at school had given Kamla moral ammunition against arranged marriage. The Prophet, she would explain, says that it is wrong to marry someone you have never seen. Moreover, the girl must give her consent: the bride's relatives are supposed to ask her opinion. Kamla is not sure her opinion will be sought. Already she has made it known throughout the women's community that she does not want to marry her cousin Salih, the young man closest to her in age who has been lined up with her, at least according to the calculations of his father and uncles about marriages between their children.

Kamla is fond of Salih, but he is "like a brother." She and her sisters boldly ask him to get them things they want from town; they reach into his pockets to grab the latest cassettes he has brought for himself. Kamla sometimes teases him, threatening to make him wash the dishes and sweep the floor if he marries her. Kamla even jokes with his mother. I had seen the woman grab Kamla and warn her to be good or else she'd exercise her prospective rights as a mother-in-law and make her quit school. Kamla broke free easily, laughing as she shouted defiantly, "Not until I come to live with you!"

Women in the camp mutter that Salih is not right for Kamla. Even her grandmother half supports her. Although Migdim tries to persuade her granddaughters of the virtues of marrying cousins, she is angry with her sons for wanting "what nothing good will come of"—this set of matches within the family between children who have grown up together and say they feel like siblings. She fumed, "Her father wants Kamla for Salih, and Kamla says she won't marry him. And Salih says he won't marry Kamla. She's older than he is!"

Her unmarried granddaughters enjoy provoking Migdim by maligning cousin marriage. They say they want out: they want to marry men who live far away so they can have new lives.

"They're good for nothing!" insisted one of Kamla's cousins once about her male cousins.

Migdim scolded her, "You slut! What is this outrage? You gypsy!"

She and her sister laughed wildly, "Damn them, our cousins! What do you see in them?"

A cousin agreed, "They're all ugly. Not a handsome one among them. No, we'll marry outsiders, Grandma, ugly or handsome."

Kamla shook her head. "I'm marrying an Egyptian! Someone educated."

Her grandmother retorted, "Your father won't agree to it!"

Kamla hugged her grandmother. "We're just talking with you to see what you'll say. Is there anything in our hands, Grandma? Or in my father's? Only God knows what will happen."

Generations

In the past, according to Kamla, a girl had no say in the matter of marriage because, as her essay continued,

> *They thought that girls shouldn't be concerned with anything but clothing and food and drink. In her kinsmen's eyes a girl had no value.* (Even now it's true. You might think conditions had changed and advanced a bit, but it's still true.) *They did not know that a girl had something she valued more than food and such things—and that was feelings.* (Feelings were forbidden to the girl.) *But she had feelings and sensitivity and affections just like any other person on this earth.* (This is true. There is no person God has created without feelings or sensitivity.) *Her kinsmen had feelings and sensitivities and affections.* (Take my father, for example. My father loved in the days of his youth; but then he thinks a girl doesn't have any such feelings.) *But they did not care if the girl had feelings. Her feelings and desires were not important.*

Kamla laughed conspiratorially as she read the next section.

> *So, for example, if she loved a person, she could not show this love, however precious and strong her love was. She would be very afraid that her relatives would hear about it, because they considered it a big scandal for a girl to love, even though they had. They say that only men have the right—a young woman does not have the right to know or speak with any man except her brothers and their relatives. All of this has governed the Bedouin girl for as long as she has lived on this earth.* (This is true. For example, if a boy meets a girl and talks with her, they say it doesn't matter—"He's a man." But you, the girl, if you do this? They don't say anything to him. If my father heard that my brother was in love with someone and talked with her, he wouldn't say anything. But if it was me? That would be dealt with very differently.)

This talk of love and vocabulary of feelings was new. Ever since I had known Kamla, from the age of twelve or so, she had been a tough little girl, the kind who would say to her uncle's new wife, "I don't even know what this 'love' is. I hear about it in songs and hear about this one giving her necklace and that one her ring, but I don't know what they are feeling." She used to amuse her great-aunts when they hugged her and teased her about which of her young cousins she would grow up to marry by proudly shouting, "I'm never going to marry."

Just a year before she wrote this essay she had demanded of her mother, "Does a woman have to marry? Does she have to have someone to tell her what to do, to boss her around?"

"Yes, a woman has to marry," Gateefa had answered. "If she doesn't, people will say, 'The poor thing!'"

But things had changed. Kamla now quoted from a book she had read at school: it was natural as one entered adolescence to begin thinking about members of the opposite sex. She admitted that such things had never even crossed her mind before. But then it had happened. It was at her cousin Selima's wedding that she had first revealed to me the new experiences she had begun to have at school. During a quiet period of the day before the wedding we had gone for a stroll on the hillside. Scattered on the ridge were groups of women in twos and threes, sisters who rarely saw each other, aunts and their nieces, old friends, also talking privately.

Looking into the distance—and, as it turned out, toward a certain house—Kamla had asked me, "What do you think, Lila? Is it wrong for two people to think about each other all the time?" I was puzzled. She told me about a young man at school—a well-behaved and good person, she added quickly—who had taken notice of her. He had asked her friends whether they could persuade her to agree to talk to him. She had refused at first. Finally she agreed to a brief meeting, with friends present. He wanted to know if she would be willing to marry him if he got his father to request her from Haj Sagr. She wondered if there was any hope that her father would accept. Knowing the family, I said I doubted it.

Usually she was more realistic. When I would ask whom she wanted to marry she would give various answers. She was adamant about her cousins: "If they think I'm going to take any of these, my cousins, or anyone from the camp, they're wrong." Then she would deny that she cared whether or not it was the boy she knew from school. The brother of their family friend Aisha would be just fine. As long as the man was educated. Backtracking she would say, "It's not even important that he's well educated. But he must be knowledgeable." The boys in her camp didn't know anything; they would not know how to get on in the world. Dependent on their fathers to feed, dress, and marry them off, they were incapable of taking care of themselves. "They're men in name only," she scoffed.

She blamed her elder kinsmen, especially her father, for her cousins' failures. Despite the double standard in matters of the heart, she acknowledged that her cousins and her brothers were having almost as hard a time dealing with their old-fashioned elders as she was. One time when I returned from a short trip to Cairo, Kamla greeted me with the news that her grandmother was distraught because her cousin Salih, the woman's favorite grandson, had run away from home after his father had hit him. No one knew where he had gone.

I would hear the story several times from Migdim, once as she told it to a visiting niece who began by asking, "Who hit Salih?"

"His father hit him."

"And why?"

"He went to a wedding at So-and so's and they say he drank liquor."

"Liquor? What kind of liquor?"

Migdim didn't know much about it. "The stuff you drink that makes them drunk. They said he drank. Each of the men came and asked him. They'd told his father on him."

"Beer, must have been beer." Migdim's niece knew things. Her husband, now dead, was rumored to have been a womanizer and an alcoholic.

Migdim did not want her story interrupted. "His father came here and hit him."

"Beer. Liquor?—why a bottle costs twenty-five pounds! There is beer and white water. The beer costs two pounds fifty a bottle."

Migdim went on. "I said, 'Son, listen, sometimes he hits his sisters just to get half a pound from them. Another time he'll need a pound. By God, he doesn't have a piaster.' I said, 'Son, your boy didn't drink. He doesn't have any money.' Salih told him, 'Father, I didn't buy any. Dad, I didn't taste it. Dad, I didn't drink.' Every time he said something, his father would give him a slap. And in the end he looked for something big to hit him with, but we grabbed it away."

Her niece was shocked.

"The women stopped him. The boy cried and cried—and I was crying too—until his eyes were red. And he said, 'Swear to God, I'll go to Libya. I'm leaving.' I thought maybe he'd go stay with his maternal uncle. That would have been fine. In the end, though, they said he headed east."

Migdim went on about her own feelings. The night Salih left, she says, her head never touched the pillow. She and his sisters sat up crying all night. "It was hard on me. He really was so generous, he was generous. I swear to God, that time he got a job with his uncle out west and had some money, he'd give me five pounds, his sister five pounds, his aunt five pounds, and his nephews one pound each. So generous. And in the morning, he never left without coming to say, 'Good morning, Grandmother. How are you, Grandma?' And he'd kiss me from this side and that. He was always there around me."

Although they thought Salih was wrong to run away, the other women in the community were angrier with his father. One of them had tried to calm the man, saying, "It's something that's already happened. If the boy went astray it has passed, and if it didn't really happen, then people lied. He's your son." The man had refused to be calmed.

Migdim was upset that her son was now threatening to pursue the boy. She says she cursed him, "You've gone crazy, my son, and you've made him go crazy. If you got him angry, may God bring you no success! May God not grant you success!"

Her niece commiserated.

Migdim continued, "I told him, 'If you hit him, may God not favor you! You should just talk to him. How can you say you're going to make him go out to herd the camels, living for three or four months on unleavened bread? You drove him crazy! Why didn't you scold him gently and say, 'Son, this is wrong, this is shameful?'"

Migdim's niece gave an alternative. The man should have said to his son, "Okay, it was the first time. Now say it will be the last time." She added, "After all, someone invited him, rottenest of invitations. The boys figured it would pass, but they caught it."

Had Salih really bought the liquor? Who was with him? The women of the family disagreed. Migdim cursed the family that held the wedding. "May God ruin their houses, those who had a wedding and brought—I don't know what dog it was who brought a box and sold bottles from it— who was it?" Others knew that beer was often sold at these kinds of weddings, where professional performers entertained. They suspected that the drinking had gone on. All the women agreed that the boys were just kids who didn't know better; his father should have reprimanded the boy, "My son, this is wrong. This is the Devil's work."

Kamla, too, criticized her father and her uncles, but not just for the way they had reacted to this rumor of alcohol. She thought they were mistaken to be so strict with the boys. They wanted the boys to be straight, but all they would get from applying this pressure was stubbornness. The pressure, she warned, would produce the opposite of what they wanted. She gave examples. The men wouldn't let the boys play soccer. "What's wrong with soccer? It's exercise." They wouldn't let them have a television, go to cafés, or visit the local cafeteria where videos are shown. Needless to say, they wouldn't permit them to grow their hair long. The men wouldn't even let the boys get jobs, making them stay on the land and tend the new fig trees. Noting that her brothers and cousins had no money, Kamla added, "They treat them like girls. If only they would give them a bit of freedom."

The freedom she wants for them, and perhaps for herself, is the subject of a popular song, an early recording by 'Awadh al-Maalky, that includes a comical tale of woe. The singer is moved, he begins, by the suffering that customs of the past have caused a young man. Hundreds of others have come to him to complain. Assuming the voice of the aggrieved young man, the poet describes what happened in the three marriages his kin arranged for him: when he reached out on the wedding night to touch his first bride, he discovered she was completely bald; the second bride, though beautiful with long thick braids, could not speak; the third tried to strangle him in his sleep—she was insane. The young man declares he won't marry again unless he is allowed to choose his own bride. Resuming his own voice the singer comments on the young man's predicament with some advice to the elders:

My warnings are to the old man
who imprisons the freedom of the young,
who has forgotten a thing called love,
affection, desire, burning flames,
forgotten the strength of lovers' fire,
the fire of lovers who long for one another.
What's exquisite is that they're afraid,
they say, any minute my prying guard will turn up:
my father's about to catch us.

The Dangers of Schooling

Kamla thinks her elders are wrong to fear an abuse of freedom. Her essay described what happened when her generation began to go to school.

> *Life began to change for the Bedouins, a change of conditions and location. Those Bedouins who began living in town started sending their sons and also their daughters to school to learn right from wrong, prayer, and writing.* (That was my father's single goal in educating us. He wanted us to know this. They don't put us in school to learn—who cared if I got educated? My own reason for being there was to learn right from wrong and the Qur'an. That's all.) *After that they would pull them out of school.* (Even if a girl was clever and came out first in her class, once she had learned right from wrong and had come to understand, they would say to her, "Come on, that's enough.") *Some might let her stay through secondary school.* (Like me. After I finished secondary school, that was it.) *The Bedouin girl could even gain such a mastery of learning and knowledge* (it would be great if every girl could go to high school) *that she could enter university.* (In Alexandria you'll find Bedouin girls who've gone to university.)

Kamla was grateful to have been allowed to continue so long in school. She had dreamt, when still in primary school, of going to college to study politics and economics. At the time, she says with amazement, she didn't understand the problem of being a girl. She had hope. Now they tease her younger sister for similar ambitions. Her father had proudly congratulated the younger girl for a good report card and said it was a pity her brothers had given her such a hard time when she announced that she wanted to be a doctor. Kamla was scornful. "They'll make her quit long before she becomes a doctor."

The problem with being a girl, as Kamla explained in her essay, was what other people would say and think about her family if they let her go to school.

> *What happened was that people began competing over the schooling of girls.* (For example, my father sees Aisha's father, who has educated all his daughters; so my father looks at him and says, "Why should he educate his daughters and not me? I have to educate my daughters." One looked at the next until all of them started educating their daughters. . . . But around here, they see that others' daughters aren't in school. No one here has daughters in university. In Marsa Matruh they all sent their girls to school, each imitating the other. My father looks over at Aisha's father and his daughters. If one of them did anything wrong—may God protect us!—*anything* wrong, my father and all of them would decide not to follow. But when I look, I see that the Bedouin girl does not give up her Bedouin values. The girls went to school and nothing bad happened.) *They put them in school, and the girls repaid their precious trust. The Bedouin girl made them see clearly that their daughter was as good as any girl from the biggest city—in intelligence and level of learn-*

ing. She would get the highest grades in all fields of learning. (This is true. If, for example, you compare someone from Marsa Matruh and someone from Cairo who've both graduated from the same school, you'll find them equally good. You'll even find that the Bedouin girl is better because she is also modest, pious, and respectful of her traditions and customs—better than the Egyptian girl who may have graduated from medical school but does not dress properly. Everything in her lifestyle is not right. Even if she gets educated, the Bedouin girl is better. You know, the Bedouins used to think that girls were a scandal. They used to think that if a Bedouin girl left the house she would have to do something wrong. They were sure of it. They'd say she can't go out—she's an idiot, she can't think. Like a beast of burden, she wouldn't know right from wrong. But when she got educated she showed them that what they had thought was wrong.)

Kamla still struggled against community opinion. Her relatives opposed sending her to college. An aunt put it bluntly: "What? Let her study in Alexandria? She's a kid. What does she know? Someone might take advantage of her. If it were here in our territory, it would be fine. But it's in Alexandria. She's gotten enough schooling."

Her father was more honest about their concerns. He had defied his brothers (with Aisha and perhaps even me in mind) to let her complete high school. The summer she graduated a school friend of Kamla's came to visit. She was dressed differently from the girls in our camp, having adopted the modern Islamic modest dress that included a severe headcovering. Haj Sagr knew her family; she spoke freely to Kamla's father, while his own daughter sat silent. The young woman told him how they wished they could go on to college. At first he tried to dismiss the idea by asking what use agricultural college (the only kind they were qualified to enter) would be for a girl. Then he got to the heart of the problem: "What would people say? 'His daughter's in college. I wonder if she's really studying or just going out a lot.'" Even if she were truly doing nothing wrong, he said, people would talk. The young woman argued with him, but he ended, as Kamla had predicted, by saying, "Listen, if your father agrees to it, tell him I'll agree too."

He inquired about her family situation, and she told him her father was refusing to marry any of his daughters to cousins. His excuse was that blindness ran in the family. Kamla was encouraged, momentarily, when her father agreed that a girl who is educated should be married to an educated man so there could be mutual understanding. But then Haj Sagr suddenly reversed his argument. He told Kamla's friend that he had been willing to send his daughters to school because he wanted them to know how to organize their lives, their home, and their children. An educated mother could help her children with their schoolwork. Therefore, he said, he would prefer to keep these girls in the family: even if their husbands were not educated, the next generation of the family would benefit. If you give women to outsiders, he noted, the benefits go to the other tribe.

His model was Aisha, the woman whose father had been an old friend, whose husband was Sagr's business partner, and whose brother he was eventually to accept as a son-in-law. Aisha was the only college-educated Bedouin woman they knew. Whenever she and her children accompanied her husband on a visit, Kamla assumed special charge. Although all the women were warm, it was Kamla who saw to it that Aisha got water for ablutions, a prayer mat when she wanted, and who kept the conversation going.

Aisha was tall, slender, and elegant. She wore nicely styled full-length, long-sleeved dresses. Instead of the usual black headcloth, she wore the fashionable modern headcovering that now marks Muslim modesty and piety. Unlike the Egyptian women who sometimes visited, she did not turn up her nose at the food that was offered her, and she was relaxed with the women of the household. She'd just laugh when old Migdim teased her about her husband. "After He created your husband's tribe, God created the donkey." Insults were expected between people from Aisha's tribe and that of her husband.

Aisha was and was not part of their world. A distant relative, she had people and interests in common with Migdim, Gateefa, and the others, but she was defensive about her family. Although they lived in the city, she was quick to tell stories that showed her brothers to be proper Bedouins. Describing her own wedding, she recalled how her husband—whose family were real desert Bedouins—came to her house the evening before the ceremony. He had brought along a Western-style suit, intending to have his photograph taken with her. Her brothers, she reported, had said, "If you're coming to have dinner with us, that's fine, you are very welcome. But if you're coming for anything else, don't bother."

Later she would try to cover for her sister, who made an unconventional marriage. We had met this young woman once, a student of pharmacology at Alexandria University who came to visit dressed in a long woolen suit, her hair covered with a turban and scarf, an alternative "Islamic" style. We heard later that her brothers had agreed to a marriage offer from an Egyptian doctor living in Marsa Matruh. Aisha insisted that even though the groom was Egyptian, her brothers had required a Bedouin engagement ceremony, where sheep are brought and eaten, first, before the Egyptian-style engagement party the groom's family wanted. She also claimed that they held a traditional henna party on the eve of the wedding—before the Egyptian-style wedding in a club. She denied that anyone except one brother had attended the wedding itself, but I didn't believe her: I knew she knew how scandalous it would be to admit that the bride's relatives had attended such a wedding.

Aisha switched easily between the Bedouin and Egyptian dialects. When she and her husband entertained Bedouins in their home, she served the men the customary lamb and rice but otherwise remained in a separate room from them. When they were with Egyptian friends, she served different foods and they all ate together. They even got different videos to entertain their guests. For Bedouins they always rented the same film about the Libyans' struggle against the Italian colonists. Their guests, Aisha explained, loved the early scenes showing a traditional Libyan Bedouin wedding and the scenes of men fighting on horseback. Egyptian films, she said, contained risqué scenes, so these were never shown to Bedouin guests. Aisha also owned two photo albums: one she showed to their more traditional Bedouin friends and family; the other one she kept hidden because it contained photographs, taken with a self-timer, of herself holding hands with her husband. Yet Aisha worried about trying to raise her two small children in an apartment on the outskirts of Alexandria. She did not want them to play with the neighbors. She feared they were learning bad language, and she apologized for their having picked up the Egyptian dialect. Her five-year-old daughter had just begun school and had started to deny that she was an Arab. "She says she's Egyptian," her mother reported. "You know," Aisha said earnestly to Kamla, "Egyptians aren't like us."

Egyptians

Could Bedouin identity be maintained after schooling? Kamla's essay took up this question.

> *The Bedouin girl preserves the traditions and customs she was raised by.* (People stay with what they have grown up with because they came of age with it. Me, for example, I grew up knowing this was shameful and that was not right, there are customs, there's respect and modesty. Even when I'm old and my hair is grey, I'll have to follow these.) *She has sense and preserves her family's reputation.* (Of course, she'd be afraid that if she did something wrong they'd pull her out of school.) *The Bedouin girl tries to overcome the special obstacles she must confront.* (For example, she doesn't let her customs and traditions, or people's talk—saying this is wrong and that is shameful— make her fall behind other girls. The Bedouin girl follows her customs but in a way that doesn't tie her up or block the path before her.) *She attempts to live a life enlightened by learning, happiness, and contributions to her country and family.* (She gives to her country. The Bedouin girl feels for her country and understands the meaning of Egypt as much as any girl from Cairo. The girl living in the Western Desert has feelings for Egypt that may be even stronger than the Egyptian girl's. The educated Bedouin girl knows the meaning of her country. . . . Boy, if my father heard this!)

Kamla's comment about her father gives a clue as to the obstacles she faces as she moves between home and her state school run by Egyptian teachers. While Haj Sagr bemoans the Awlad 'Ali's lack of foresight in failing to request an independent state from the British and chafes against every government restriction on his activities, Kamla patriotically defends Egypt and speaks proudly of President Mubarak. Once, when her father confronted her for being a few hours late from a school trip, she argued back. He then scolded her for raising her voice and waving her hands as she spoke. "This is the work of Egyptians!" he yelled. Anger fighting fear, she answered, "I *am* an Egyptian. And they are the best people, and this is the best country!"

Kamla listened closely to the detailed reports of city life that Safiyya, her father's second wife, gave each time she returned from visits to her brothers' homes. These were brothers whose sons were becoming lawyers. Kamla was also riveted to broadcasts of Egyptian radio melodramas, with plots like that of "Bride by Computer," about a young man whose life is nearly ruined by computer matchmaking. Kamla can envision this world better than her sisters can, although she was as puzzled as they were about what a computer might be, and just as disapproving of the female characters in this conservative moral tale.

The plot of this serial, as the girls explained, followed the usual formula: A man loves someone but cannot marry her; in the end, though, he succeeds in getting her. The main character was a young Egyptian who worked in a company. When his mother objected to him marrying a co-worker whom he loved, a friend suggested he "talk to the computer to find a bride." The results, predictably, were disastrous. The first bride was a doctor. "She worked day and night," Kamla recalled. "Even the night of the wedding she was busy."

"You know what she was doing?" Kamla's neighbor intervened. "She was doing experiments with mosquitoes and rats."

"So he divorced her," Kamla went on. "He got engaged to another girl but didn't marry her. After he got engaged to her, she wanted him to go swimming with her and to dance with her, to act like foreigners."

The neighbor was excited. "The day he wanted to marry her she told him she wanted him to come over. He went there and found it wild. There was loud music."

Sabra explained. "She was at a nightclub. When he got there she said, 'Play that music,' and people started dancing. She asked him if he knew how to dance. He said no. She said, 'Look, see that man who's moving wildly on the floor?' The girl moved wildly as well, asking them to play a foreign tape."

The young women laughed as they described her. "She said to him, 'Get up, get up.' But he wouldn't go with her. He wouldn't dance with her."

When they paused I asked, "What was the problem with the third bride?"

The girls were confused. Sabra ventured, "I don't know, she had put . . . she had made a workshop in the house. They had a guest room, and she put her workshop in that room."

"No, she turned the bedroom into a factory."

"And she started fighting with her in-laws. She experimented on the old woman. She gave her something to try that made her almost die. When the man came home from work he asked his wife, 'Where is my mother?' She told him, 'I took her to the hospital.' He asked, 'Why, what's the matter?' He couldn't bear that any harm would come to his mother. When he went to see her she talked to him. She said, 'She was doing an experiment and I'm the one who drank the medicine.'"

They giggled as Kamla repeated, "The old woman almost died. He said, 'No, if she wants to kill my mother, I don't want her.'"

"He loved his mother," Sabra noted.

"And the fourth one, he brought her and then couldn't get any peace. She gave him a headache. She'd bring the onions and potatoes to peel. The man would be resting on the bed and she'd climb up next to him at night to peel potatoes. She'd say, 'Put down that newspaper and let's talk, me and you.'"

The girls found it hilarious to think of the woman peeling potatoes in bed. One of them explained, "She was a real peasant."

Kamla argued, "It's just lies. A peasant woman wouldn't do that."

Her neighbor was emphatic. "She was a peasant from Upper Egypt. They are like that."

Kamla will only go so far in her defense of Egyptians. She often criticized their neighbors, a poor family who had lived among Egyptians and had picked up different ways. As evidence of their immorality she disclosed that the men and women ate together. Another nearby household fared little better. They knew no modesty, she said: the son listened to cassettes in front of his father, and the young daughter-in-law neither covered her hair with a black headcloth nor avoided her father-in-law.

In her essay, and even more clearly in her commentary, Kamla underlined this distinction between Bedouin morality and Egyptian immorality. Still writing about the young Bedouin woman who had become educated, she said:

> *She doesn't forget her origins or her customs and traditions. She raises her children as well as the people of the city do.* (Now we're talking about what the Bedouin woman does after she gets educated. Does she forget her duties as a mother? The difference between the Bedouins and the Egyptians is that when the Egyptian woman has a baby, she gives it to her mother to raise for her, and she takes it to day care. She doesn't do her duty to the child nor give it the required care. For example, she nurses only up to the fortieth day or at most for two months. And then she leaves it with her mother, her sister, or day care and goes out to work. But the Bedouin woman gives the child its due, even if she's educated and has an advanced degree. Not her mother, not anyone else—she herself does the work.
>
> And she raises her child according to her customs. Let's say she's a Bedouin who marries an Egyptian or an educated Bedouin. She doesn't raise her child by the customs or traditions of the Egyptians. She raises her

child with the customs and traditions of the Bedouin, except that she is slightly more informed. I mean, she tells her daughter, "This is shameful" and "That is right." Take an educated Bedouin girl like me, for example. If I were to marry an educated man and live the city life, I wouldn't let my daughter follow the ways of the Egyptians where a girl wears short dresses or goes out to clubs. No, of course that is wrong. We must be modest. It is wrong for us Bedouins, and we must respect our traditions. This is necessary. You wouldn't find an educated Bedouin woman allowing her daughter to do things that she could not do when she was with her family. Or maybe even if her parents permitted it, the girl herself would not do it. "No," she'd know, "that's wrong." Bedouin women are the ones who really know how to raise their daughters. They are better than Egyptians because the Egyptian woman won't hit her daughter. Very rarely do you find an Egyptian who can hit her daughter. But the Bedouin woman, if her daughter does something wrong, she must hit her. Even if she's not that young. She must hit her to teach her right and wrong. You don't learn right from wrong if you're not beaten. The Egyptians don't do it and their girls—well, you know . . .)

Poets have long reflected on the differences between Bedouins and their peasant neighbors. Only fragments are remembered, however, like the lines of a love story about a wealthy peasant and a beautiful Bedouin girl named Khawd. Drought had driven her family into his fields in search of pasture for their herds. He allowed them to stay and graze their animals when he saw Khawd. One day, though, his beloved announced that her family had decided to return to the desert; she asked him to migrate with them. In despair the young man answered:

O Khawd, I have no camels that I might travel your distances
I have nothing but buffalo and cows, who will find no pastures near you

Kamla's aunt Dhahab had once recited a short poem on a similar theme—it was her comment when I declined her polite suggestion that I marry her son so that I could come live with her. The song came, she said, from a story about a bull who fell in love with a camel and tried to follow her into the desert. She warned him that he would exhaust himself if he tried, since he had to eat and drink every day and she drank only every five days. He said that for her sake he'd drink only every other day, but she knew he couldn't keep up with her. She told him:

You'll kill yourself bellowing
O bull, if you try to follow . . .

Some women were tolerant of moral differences between themselves and Egyptians. I talked once about television with two poor women who had recently moved to the area from near the Libyan border. They said they found television entertaining to watch when they had no work to do. Their favorite shows, of course, were the Egyptian serialized dramas.

I was curious. "But the Egyptians on these programs are not like you, are they?"

One of them laughed. "The Egyptians are citified, not like the Bedouins, the poor things."

They explained that it didn't matter because they would never watch television with people they should respect and be modest in front of. Girls would never watch if their fathers were there; women would leave the room if their husbands had visitors.

"So you don't feel embarrassed by what you see on television?"

"No, if you're by yourself it doesn't matter," replied the older of the two.

"What if you see people in love?"

The younger of the two women laughed. "They're free to do that. We don't worry about them. The Egyptians have no modesty. They have no religion. They just do everything. It's their way."

The older one agreed. "Yes, let them do what they want. We just laugh at them."

Kamla and Sabra had a younger sister who loved television. She thought her father was wrong not to let them have a TV set. Although she conceded that foreign films were immoral, she argued that Egyptian films were different. Haj Sagr had taken away the television set when he heard that the girls were watching films in which people hugged and kissed each other. "He didn't want us watching. He said it was shameful." But these films and stories, she persisted, always showed the correct path in the end, even though they had people doing such things in early scenes. Egyptian films show how the girl who went off with a man later realized that he had tricked and used her. The importance of proper moral behavior always became clear ultimately.

Kamla's sister wondered anyway what her father could be thinking when he worried about his daughters' exposure to these things. Realistically she asked, "Where do we ever go? Nowhere but this house or the rest of the camp, where it's all family. Where does he think these things could happen?"

Kamla's father did fear the influence of Egyptians on the Bedouin community. In his opinion, the most serious problem the Bedouins faced was that of intermarriage between Bedouins and Egyptians. In the past, he maintained, no Arab, even the simplest shepherd, would give his daughter in marriage to "a peasant," as they used to call all Egyptians, even if the man were a company president. Things were more difficult now. Whereas before the area had been almost completely Bedouin, now, in regions like theirs that were close to large towns, Egyptians made up fifty percent of the population.

The trouble with the Egyptian presence, he went on, was that the Egyptian girls looked so pretty. They always dressed up, combed out their hair, and wore short dresses. A group of Bedouin elders had met recently to discuss what to do about these women who "walk around naked." Their concern was that the young men would find them attractive and want to marry them. And their fathers, wanting to make them happy, might agree. If the young men married Egyptian girls, there would no longer be any difference between Bedouin and Egyptian in the next generation. Sagr had warned the elders of this danger at the meeting. He admitted, though, that the process would be hard to stop now that the boys see these girls in school. Although he was afraid that Bedouin girls might pick up attitudes and habits from Egyptians—like having boyfriends, which the Egyptian girls don't think twice about—his real fear was intermarriage. That would bring about the end of tribal bonds.

Europeans

Sagr sensed the gradual shift in the boundaries of the moral community. Egyptians and Awlad 'Ali are being brought together by roads, newspapers, radio, television, schools, agricultural cooperatives, the army, and Parliament. With foreigners—Europeans—however, the divide remains absolute. Even Kamla, who sometimes pleaded with me, exasperated with her rambunctious little brothers and sisters, to take her away with me ("Put me in your suitcase and get me out of here!") and who proudly told me about several young Bedouin women with M.A.'s in veterinary medicine who had been sent, tattoos and all, to London for further training—even she did not approve of the Godless Europeans. Unlike Egyptian Christians, she argued, Europeans do not recognize God. "Every Muslim, even the most ignorant and uneducated, knows that there is a God and that He created all things." Worse, Europeans do not pray. When I contradicted her to say that many prayed in church, she challenged me. "What? What kind of person prays with his shoes on? May God protect us!"

The Westerner's lack of faith in God provides powerful imagery for inhumanity. Kamla's uncle's wife once lamented her lost brother with a poem that exploited this view:

The European, with all his lack of faith,
wept when I told him of my condition . . .

To show the magnitude of their compassion for girls, women sang a wedding rhyme that also mentioned Europeans:

God protect every girl
even the Christian woman's daughter

Kamla has not seen the new tourists who visit the Western Desert, but she has heard about them. In 1986 a favorite commercial cassette was the song called "The Japanese Woman" by the young Bedouin star Si'daawy al-Git'aany. The singer, identifying himself by tribe, says he lost his heart to a foreigner. (Although he calls her Japanese, the details of his song suggest a melding of many nationalities.)

Spanning many verses, the tale begins with his first sight of the woman. She had come to Egypt to relax, he sings, and in the gardens of a summer resort hotel in Marsa Matruh she was swinging on a swing. Her father, sitting on a chair ("like a boss") was grotesque and frightening: a European Christian with a long beard eating platefuls of pork and drinking quantities of beer. "We are Bedouins who like the desert," the singer goes on, "and they are Europeans. Fate brought us together." In her company he forgot his cares, and although they were accustomed to different ways, she made him lose interest in Bedouin women, who only cared about tying up goats and waiting for the sheep to come home in the evening.

She wore a cross and made him sit on chairs. Oh, he knew their ways were different, but he went astray, unable to stop himself from falling in love with a Christian. As she sat under an umbrella they talked. He had been to school and knew her language. She asked him to come home with her, but he first wanted to show her his home and the desert snail shells. Then she telephoned the governor and got permission for him to travel with her. So there he found himself, walking behind her, carrying her suitcases to board an airplane. Like a bird it took off, and he was scared. Everything is by God's will—that a man from the desert should end up with a Japanese woman.

Contrasting her country with his, he finds that the sea is to the south instead of the north. Her country is famous for its buses and trucks, he sings, whereas our women know only how to spin and to churn butter in goatskin bags. The moral contrasts are harsher. There, women's hair is uncovered and men wear straw baskets on their heads instead of skull caps. Women go wherever they wish and everyone says hello to them.

Accompanying his lover to a nightclub, he found people dancing like birds as someone howled while playing the piano. People got drunk and started fighting and throwing things around. His story would make a good soap opera, he sings. Things were different once they got to her country and she lost interest in him. The song ends with a refrain about the treachery of women, an ending that always got a rise out of Kamla and her sisters. "He got what he deserved," they insisted. "Who told him to go chasing after the foreigner, carrying her suitcases?"

Piety

Kamla reflected, in her essay, on what aspects of Bedouin life she would like to see preserved. Her father would have been proud of the list of positive features she drew up.

We all know that everything in life has its good qualities and its bad. (Weren't you asking what was good about the Bedouins and what wasn't?) *The virtues of the Bedouins are:*

1. *Their piety and their total adherence to the traditions of the Prophet, despite their lack of education.* (This is the thing I hope will continue until Judgment Day. This is the best thing—that they are religious. Even though ninety percent of them aren't educated, they are pious. Long clothing, respect, and modesty. The woman is as pious as the man. No woman can talk with a man she doesn't know or have him visit her at home. And she doesn't show her face or talk with any older man. This is what I hope Bedouin women and girls will never abandon.)
2. *Their total respectfulness. The old respect the young, and the young respect the old, whether they are strangers or kin.*
3. *Their generosity.* (It's true. You won't find anything on this earth like the generosity of the Bedouins. Even someone they don't know—they must invite him to the house and bring him food. Maybe no one else has this quality. I hope the Bedouins will hold on to this.)
4. *Hospitality and respect for the guest.*
5. *The ties of kinship that link various parts of the family and the cooperation of relatives in all situations.* (The other thing I want them to hold onto is this mutual assistance—they help each other in all circumstances. For example, even someone from a family that is related distantly to another must help a person from that family. Even among the women. When a Bedouin woman sets up a loom, for instance, her neighbors come to help her. Others always come to help. I wish the whole world—never mind just families—the whole world would help each other and that Muslims would cooperate the way our religion tells us to. Ninety-nine percent of Bedouin women haven't been educated. But they are pious. They're ignorant and illiterate, but they dress the right way, they fear God, and they pray. Sometimes they don't even know how to pray properly, but they pray anyhow. They are totally respectable, and they follow the traditions of the Prophet. They say the Prophet used to do this, the Prophet used to do that. They learn it from their husbands or their educated sons.)

Interestingly, Kamla had little to say about any of the traditional virtues except the first, piety. Although she was vehement in asserting their importance, perhaps she could not afford to think through their implications. She was proud of her father's generosity and hospitality, for instance, but it was also a source of tension, since the burden of feeding his many guests fell on the overworked women of the household. And if she were to think about how the extensive bonds between kin are to be maintained, she would have to admit the virtues of marriages to paternal cousins, the kind of marriage she wanted desperately to avoid.

Piety was a different matter. Like many, Kamla was becoming defensive in the face of new pressure from those sympathetic to Islamic activists in Egypt. She was correct to point out how tied up with their faith her kin were. They reckoned the months by the Islamic lunar calendar, the years by the annual religious feasts, age by the number of years a person has fasted the month of Ramadan, and the hours of the day by the five times for prayer. All the older women and many of the younger ones prayed regularly. Doing without the accouterments of city people, women simply prayed where they were, facing southeast and laying a small kerchief on the ground before them. The men like Kamla's father tended to know more. They would have learned as children to recite the Qur'an, and they continued to learn from the lectures at the mosque every Friday.

Their reactions to the sanctimonious Egyptians—and now to some Bedouins from the cities, who were becoming, as they put it, "followers of the model," meaning the life of the Prophet—have been mixed. The older women are not cowed. They argue, as Kamla did, that they have always worn modest clothing and covered their hair with a headcloth. They resent being told that some of the ways they have demonstrated their devoutness are wrong.

Kamla is more unsure. Sometimes she defends these Muslim Sisters and Brothers and sometimes she goes along with the old Bedouin women as they make fun of them. One evening, having recited some poetry and told some traditional tales for my benefit, Kamla's aunt Dhahab turned to her niece and asked, "Hey Kamla, have you given Lila any songs?"

Kamla was coy. "I'm not a song person. I'm just a simple person minding my own business. I'm with God. I'm pious and know my Lord."

Her sister hooted, perhaps thinking of Kamla's love of the radio and scandalous movie magazines. But Kamla went on, only half joking, "Auntie, I've become pious. I don't have anything to do with songs."

Her aunt mocked her. "What's this? You've become pious?" Everyone laughed as the old aunt continued, "God's blessings! God's blessings! So, you're joining the 'Beard Family'?"

There was a commotion, with everyone talking at once about the topic that was so often in the air these days: the Islamists. Kamla spoke on their behalf. "They say, 'We are religious people, . . . following God's path, the path to heaven.'"

Her aunt was hardly convinced. "I swear to God, they've never seen heaven. God is the only judge. God is present."

Sabra thought they should be more respectful. But she admitted, "May God protect them, they do some things that aren't necessary. Do you know what our aunt who lives out west says? She says they say that the sugar dolls are wrong, even the food we make to celebrate the Prophet's birthday. Rotten life! The special food for the birthday that the whole world celebrates—they say it is forbidden!"

Her aunt concurred. "Have you ever heard of such a thing!"

Some women were even more irreverent. Once when an old friend from the nearby town was visiting, the evening conversation turned to the topic of these new religious types. She complained that they had forbidden celebrations of saints' birthdays, including the candy and meat eaten at them. They had said it was wrong to call any holyman "Saint So-and-so." She said, "They have forbidden everything. Why, the next thing you know they'll forbid the clothes we wear and make us go around naked."

She then described to the group gathered around her how these people dressed. She told them about the wife of a Muslim Brother called Mr. Muhammad who had moved to her town. The woman was offering lessons on religion every Tuesday afternoon for any woman who wished to learn. She wore a veil that covered her head and her face, "except for her eyes"; she wore gloves, a dress down to the ground, and shoes. As the old woman put it, "She looks like a ghost."

Kamla showed off her knowledge of religion. "It is wrong for a woman to veil her face. What is required is that your head be covered; it is fine to expose your hands, your feet, and your face."

The old woman then commented on the men. "They all run around with those beards. Why, Doctor Ahmed's sticks out like this! It looks like pubic hair."

Kamla had to raise her voice to be heard over the wild laughter. "But Auntie, the beard is a tradition of the Prophet."

Kamla's cousin Salih had tried briefly to grow a beard, but the teasing had been merciless. No matter how many times Kamla told them it was the tradition of the Prophet, Gateefa and his other aunts accused him of looking like a Coptic priest. He finally shaved it off.

Kamla had confided to me that she would have liked to replace her kerchief with the new Islamic headcovering but she was afraid her family would object. A photograph of her with her school friends revealed that she was the only one among them not wearing the new modest dress. Yet Kamla criticized some of her classmates who wore this type of clothing but added flowers and multicolored headbands to their veils. She said their religion teacher had given them a real talking to and had confiscated their flowers and headbands saying, "If you want to take on the veil, do it seriously." Kamla said she would adopt this kind of headcovering "if God opens the way for me and I get to marry someone educated."

A New Order

The final part of Kamla's essay was to have been about what she hoped would change in her community. All she had written, though, was this:

As for the bad things, I will talk about them.

She read this final sentence and looked at me. "What are the wrongs I wish the Bedouins would finish with? I've already discussed these. First, their ideas about girls. They are totally meaningless and wrong. I wish they would give her the opportunity to get educated. They see her as a worthless being. You know this, Lila. . . . This is what I hope the Bedouins will leave behind. They should see that a girl is a person, a noble person created just as God created men. She has feelings, sensitivities, and desires.

"Another thing I wish is that they wouldn't let their customs and traditions rule them to such an extent that they believe that the customs of the city people are wrong and theirs right. Whenever they see that a person is educated, they say he's wrong, we're right. I wish they would respect the educated. I wish they would preserve their customs and traditions but be a bit more advanced. A girl who goes to school doesn't forget her customs and traditions, no matter how educated she becomes. Even if she goes to Europe or America, the Bedouin girl will preserve her customs and traditions. They should give her more freedom.

"Another thing I wish is that they would get more organized. I wish they would put a little order in their lives. Among Bedouins, order is completely lacking. In every area of their lives—in terms of food, in having too many children, in the way they raise the children—there's no order. And in the house—anything goes!"

I was curious about what Kamla meant by "order." She gave examples from close to home. "Say you've got two brothers living in one house. If they organized their lives, they'd put each one in his own house. And the business of marrying more than one wife—I wish they'd change their views on this. It is the biggest sin. The Prophet—it is not forbidden, but the Prophet said only if you can treat them fairly. But a man can't, it can't be done. Even if he has money, he can't. As a person, in his thoughts and his actions, he can't be fair. He'll like one more than another.

"The generation that's coming now, after my father's and mother's, they wouldn't think of it or do it. Why? So they won't have a house with thirty or forty people living in it. A household with two women in it will have thirty or forty people in it. Their lives will be lousy. They won't have good food, good clothes, or good childrearing. They won't be clean. A woman alone in her own house can handle her children. When there are two women, one will say, 'Why should I hit my children when that one doesn't hit hers?' They watch each other. When one does something, the other is looking. If one cleans and washes and the other doesn't, she says, 'Why should I do this when she doesn't?' If she is alone, a woman won't be able to say that. Who's going to do it for her? She'll do it herself and she'll know what's what. When she's alone she doesn't have to depend on anyone. And even her daughter will turn out well, like her mother. The other way they're always getting into fights over any little thing. Even without my saying this, you know it, Lila. This is what I wish would change.

"Bedouins think that as long as they have a house and can eat, drink, and be clothed, that's enough. That's life. And they marry and have kids and marry again. But a man should live a more ordered and relaxed life. Should a man come home at the end of his day tired from working and find it filthy and the kids and women fighting? He comes wanting to relax, and finds this? This is what makes someone say, 'No, there should be order.'"

For years I had heard Kamla's call for order. Living in a household of twenty or more, half of whom are under ten years old, can be chaotic. Fed up, Kamla would sometimes say, "This isn't a house, it's a breeding station!" She and Sabra often teased their mother, calling her Shalabiyya, the name of a character they had seen in a family planning advertisement on television. Shalabiyya was a woman with too many children: in her lap, on her shoulders, on her head. When she tried to draw water or milk the cow, they climbed all over her and trailed behind her. Gateefa would apologize, "We can't change the way we are."

When Kamla was young, she would come home from school announcing that she was going to marry an Egyptian doctor and have only one child. Other times she'd say she was going to have only two children, both daughters. She was going to live alone in a house with her husband, just them, no relatives. Bedouin men, she would say, make women work hard and don't pay attention to them. Even if the woman is ill, the man won't lift a finger to help, not even to pick up a crying baby. Egyptian men help their wives, respect them, and treat them well. When Kamla's younger sister, echoing their father, accused Egyptians of being stingy and not offering food to their guests, Kamla defended them to support her favorite theme. She argued that they just did things in an organized manner; they had special meal times, unlike the Bedouins who brought out food whenever anyone stopped by.

Perhaps because tensions between her father's wives had recently intensified, Kamla was impassioned in her final commentary. "Even without becoming educated, the Bedouins could organize their lives. It is enough to marry just one. Or if a man wants to marry more than one, he should put each wife in her own house. They won't fight then. But if the two are together, you'll always find this one saying, 'That one did and said' and that one saying, 'This one said this and did that.' Even if they are friends, the people outside the household won't let them be. Someone will come and say, 'That one said this' and 'This one said that.' Women are famous for this kind of talk.

"Yes, Bedouin women are famous for their talk. The Prophet said, 'Women—if not for their tongues, women would go to heaven.' They asked him, 'Why should a woman go to heaven?' He said, 'Because she gives milk.' Praise be to God, milk flows from her. And beyond that, she works harder than a man. She's weaker—that's right, she's weak compared to the man, whom nothing bothers—but she has to work more. She has children and cares for them. They asked the Prophet, 'So what is it that keeps her from entering heaven?' He said, 'It is because of her tongue.' In a second she'll turn things around. She'll gossip about everyone. Women talk about people more than men do."

Kamla is critical of the older women in her community. She confessed, too, that she belonged to two worlds. With her sisters and cousins she talked about the things they knew, not letting on that she was different. But there were so many things she could talk to her school friends about that she could not talk about with the girls in her family—things like politics. Sometimes she seemed to accept her double life with equanimity. When I saw her spinning with her aunt one day, I asked, "Hey Kamla, so you know how to spin too?" She had laughed. "Yes, I can go either way. If it turns out I'm to be citified, I'll do that. And if it turns out I'll be a Bedouin, I'll know how."

When I suggested that she might be lonely if she moved into a house of her own, she was adamant: "No, I won't miss them at all." Yet this is someone who is fiercely proud of her father for being an important man who is also generous and pious. Despite occasional confrontations, she spends, like her sisters, nearly every evening sitting close to her mother and talking. Even her brood of little siblings only sometimes drives her really crazy. The youngest she can rarely resist grabbing to hug. Delighted by this two-year-old's every new accomplishment, she whispers new words in her ear and kisses her when she repeats them.

Most of the time, though, she says she wants to get out. I worry about Kamla's blithe confidence that life in the city will be so much better. I disagree with her assessment of Bedouin women's lives. I argue with Kamla that she deliberately ignores the richness of their relationships and the way they have always struggled back (and were expected to). Her own life is evidence. There was not a single woman in the camp who had not admired her for being a willful little girl. Even her father had been amused by her opinions and determination. As she had grown up, her strength of purpose had enabled her to withstand the social pressure against her going to school. The independence she displayed reminded me of her grandmother Migdim, with her stories of resistance to marriage and her struggles to have her way with her sons. It even reminded me of her mother, Gateefa, who had earned the respect of her husband.

Yet when her letter arrived I was happy for her—happy that it was her fate not to have to marry her cousin after all and glad that her father had been willing to take her wishes into consideration. Armed with romantic visions inspired by Egyptian radio melodramas, cloying love songs, and her tattered collection of hokey postcards showing blonde brides and grooms looking deeply into each other's eyes, she will go off to live with her Egyptianized, educated husband in a small and ordered household. She will never work outside the home. She will rarely even leave her apartment. She expects to clean the house, cook meals, and serve her husband. If God brings children, she'll take care of them and raise them well.

Because she has none of his sister Aisha's feminine refinement, I was worried. What would her husband think when he first saw this sturdy young woman with her wide feet and callused hands? Because she is the daughter of a wealthy tribal leader, the fabric of her dresses would be expensive and she would bring many with her; but they would have been tailored by local seamstresses, whose renditions of city clothes are always awkward. And would she know how to dress for the wedding night, this girl who had to fight her mother's horrified accusations of immodesty when she wore a home-made bra? Would Engineer Ibrahim Saleem find charming her outspoken ways?

I wrote back to wish her all happiness and to apologize for not being able to attend the wedding. An older sister would sing at the henna party on the eve of the wedding, so I looked through my collection of Bedouin wedding songs to see if any seemed right. I ended my letter with three that I hoped would mean something to her. The first let her know how much I thought of her family:

> Her father has a good name
> and those who have come to marry will find happiness . . .

The second reminded her that I knew how much she wanted this:

> Her morning is blessed
> she got what she desired and was honored . . .

And the third expressed my best wishes for this young woman, vulnerable and beautiful as are all young brides heading off into the unknown:

> Neighbors, come say farewell
> a gazelle from our land is about to journey . . .   ■

■ QUESTIONS FOR MAKING CONNECTIONS WITHIN THE READING ■

1. One of the challenges that readers of Abu-Lughod's "Honor and Shame" must tackle is keeping track of the relationships between all of the people mentioned in the essay. Who is Kamla? What is her relationship to Abu-Lughod, Gateefa, Haj Sagr, Migdim, Salih, Aisha, Sabra, and Dhahab? Draw a chart that shows the relationships between all of the central figures in "Honor and Shame."

2. Who are the Bedouin? What is their relationship to Egypt? To Islam? What does it mean, within the context of Abu-Lughod's "Honor and Shame," to be "Egyptianized"?

3. "Honor and Shame" ends with a confession: Kamla acknowledges that she has "belonged to two worlds" and that she lives a "double life." What

are the two worlds that she inhabits? Which world does she wish to live in? Which world does Abu-Lughod want her to live in?

■ QUESTIONS FOR WRITING ■

1. At one point in her discussion of her essay on the education of Bedouin girls, Kamla stops midsentence and says, "Boy, if my father heard this!" This is one of many private moments that Abu-Lughod records and repeats for the readers of "Honor and Shame" to consider. What is gained by recording such moments? What is lost ? Does the study of another culture require such violations of privacy?

2. In a sense, "Honor and Shame" is an essay about student writing: Kamla reads aloud and comments on an essay that she has written for school; Abu-Lughod listens, responds to, and comments on what Kamla has written and then provides additional background to illustrate, extend, and complicate the assertions Kamla has made. Is Abu-Lughod studying Kamla? Is she teaching her? Who benefits from the work Abu-Lughod has done with Kamla's essay?

■ QUESTIONS FOR MAKING CONNECTIONS BETWEEN READINGS ■

1. *"As for the bad things, I will talk about them."* In Abu-Lughod's "Honor and Shame," Kamla records her thoughts about how life has changed for Bedouin girls over the past forty years. How would James C. Scott interpret the stories that Kamla has told? How many different transcripts are present in "Honor and Shame"? Who is best positioned to read and interpret these transcripts?

2. Abu-Lughod confides, "I worry about Kamla's blithe confidence that life in the city will be so much better." Would Peter F. Drucker share Abu-Lughod's concerns about what lies ahead for Kamla? Is Kamla a participant in "The Age of Social Transformation"? What role can those outside the "developed world" hope to play in the "knowledge society"?

For additional suggestions about making connections between readings, visit the Link-O-Mat and More Sample Assignments at <www.newhum.com>.

MARCIA ANGELL

AFTER GRADUATING FROM Boston University School of Medicine and becoming a board-certified pathologist, Marcia Angell joined the editorial staff of the *New England Journal of Medicine* in 1979 and was promoted to Executive Editor in 1988 and interim Editor-in-Chief in 1999. Currently Senior Lecturer in the Department of Social Medicine at Harvard Medical School, Angell writes and speaks publicly on medical ethics, health policy, and the nature of medical evidence. In 1997, *Time* magazine named Marcia Angell one of the twenty-five most influential Americans.

Angell is the author of the critically-acclaimed *Science on Trial: The Clash of Medical Evidence and the Law in the Breast Implant Case* (1996), which explores the influence that "junk science" has in the court system and in the public sphere more generally. Arguing that the value of science resides in its commitment to assessing evidence objectively, Angell details the ways this commitment is undermined in the courts, where scientists are tempted to sell their expert opinions to the highest bidder.

Angell's more recent work explores how conflicts of interest in the scientific community are further undermining the unfettered pursuit of truth. As Angell sees it, it is the responsibility of scientific journals like the *New England Journal of Medicine* and of academic medical centers to conduct objective research projects and to subject the results of such projects to rigorous and unbiased analysis. Fulfilling this responsibility has become increasingly difficult, Angell believes, precisely because the doctors, scientists, and technicians who carry out this research rely on medical and pharmaceutical corporations to fund their work. This is a problem because:

> the mission of investor-owned companies is quite different from the mission of academic medical centers. The primary purpose of the former is to

---

Angell, Marcia. "Science in the Courtroom: Opinions Without Evidence." *Science on Trial: The Clash of Medical Evidence and the Law in the Breast Implant Case*. New York: W. W. Norton, 1997. 111–132.

Quotation taken from Angell's remarks at the Health and Human Services Conference on Financial Conflicts of Interest, 8/16/2000, Bethesda, Md. <http://www.aspe.hhs.gov/sp/coi/angell.htm>.

increase the value of their shareholders' stock, which they do by securing patents and marketing their products. Their purpose is not to educate, nor even to carry out research, except secondarily or as a means to their primary end. I believe academics often forget this, and allow themselves to believe that marketing is really education.

In *Science in the Courtroom: Opinions Without Evidence,* we find Angell asking a similar set of questions: What ethical standards should scientists be held to? What role should science have in a civil society? And is it possible to preserve science's commitment to service and disinterestedness once scientists move out of the laboratory and into the courtroom and the marketplace?

To learn more about Marcia Angell and scientific objectivity, visit the Link-O-Mat at <www.newhum.com>.

■　■

Science in the Courtroom: Opinions Without Evidence

Dow's conduct in exposing thousands of women to a painful and debilitating disease, and the evidence that Dow gained financially from its conduct, may properly be considered in imposing an award of punitive damages.
—*Judge Procter Hug, August 26, 1994*

[. . .] Maria Stern and her lawyer, Nancy Hersh (with fellow attorney Dan Bolton's help), were the first to go for the legal brass ring by alleging that [breast] implants cause connective tissue disease. Stern's disease was never clearly defined in the media, although some press reports referred to it as "arthritis." Until this case, product liability suits against breast implant manufacturers, of which there was a small trickle, had been limited to settlements of no more than $15,000 to $20,000 for local complications.[1] With the 1984 Stern case, all that changed. It was inevitable that after Stern there would be more such cases. After all, many women had connective tissue disease (about 1 in 100) and many had breast implants (also about 1 in 100). Thus, one could expect—on the basis of chance alone—that about 10,000 of the roughly 100 million adult women in the United States would have both.

Once it got out that a link between the two conditions had been accepted in court, women who had both implants and connective tissue disease would be bound to consider whether they, too, should sue. Even those who only thought they might have connective-tissue-like disease also began to take notice. For any who lagged behind, there was plenty of encouragement from many plaintiffs' attorneys.

The issue in the Stern case, as would be true of any product liability suit, was whether the manufacturer of the implants (Dow Corning, in this case) had sold her a defective product that caused her harm. To make the case required that Stern demonstrate two conditions: first, that she was harmed, and second, that the harm was most likely caused by the implants. In addition to demonstrating these conditions, which would satisfy the standard known as "strict liability," there was the question of negligence. Was the manufacturer guilty of knowingly or heedlessly selling a dangerous product? To show negligence required that a third condition be demonstrated—that the manufacturer knew or should have known that the implants were harmful. Theoretically, the first two of these conditions must be met for any product liability suit to be successful. That is theory. In practice, as we shall see, a product liability suit can be spectacularly successful without any of the conditions being fulfilled.

Conditions two and three depend on the satisfaction of the one before it. The manufacturer cannot be held negligent if the implants didn't cause the harm, and the implants cannot be blamed if there is no harm. In most of the breast implant cases that have been brought to trial (but not necessarily in the far more numerous cases settled out of court), the plaintiff has been clearly ill. (In the Stern case, because the records were sealed as a part of an out-of-court settlement after the verdict, it is difficult to be certain about the nature of her medical problems.) The major job of the plaintiff's attorney, therefore, has not been to show that the plaintiff is ill, but to show that the illness was caused by the implants. To do so requires convincing the jury by a "preponderance of the evidence." This is a more relaxed standard than the requirement in a criminal case that the verdict be "beyond a reasonable doubt." But aside from its relative liberality, the phrase "preponderance of the evidence" tells us less than it might seem. It suggests confusingly that there are two kinds of medical evidence—evidence for and evidence against a causal relationship. In practice, this is highly unlikely: either there is evidence for a relationship or there isn't. In the absence of such evidence, the default position must be that there is no link. The burden of proof is on those who assert the relationship.

Sometimes the phrase "preponderance of the evidence" is translated to mean that the jury finds the disease more likely than not to be caused by the breast implants. Or sometimes the same concept is expressed by saying that the breast implants contributed more than 50 percent to the causation of the disease—that is, but for the implants, the disease would not have developed.[2] While neither of these alternative formulations is entirely satisfying, they are an improvement over the vague term "preponderance of the evidence." Furthermore, they can be translated into epidemiologic terms. If connective tissue disease in a typical woman with implants is more likely than not to be caused by implants, it follows that in a large population of women, the majority of cases of connective tissue disease would be due to breast implants. In other words, this cause would have to outweigh all other contributing causes put together. To outweigh all other causes means that women with implants would have to be at least twice as likely to develop the disease as women without implants. ([. . .] There is no evidence that they do.)

Notice that what is at issue here is not how certain we are of the effect of implants, but how big the effect is. The degree of certainty is an entirely different matter. I mention the distinction, because some legal scholars confuse the concepts of the size of the effect (as, for example, when it is said that implants contribute more than 50 percent to the disease) with the degree of confidence we can have that it is true. For a scientific finding to be accepted, it is customary to require a 95 percent probability that it is not due to chance alone (I am here giving a shorthand version of a much more complicated statistical concept). Comparing the size of an effect with the probability that a given finding isn't due to chance is comparing apples and oranges. It would be possible to find a huge effect with a low degree of certainty, or a tiny effect with a high degree of certainty. The distinction between the size of an effect and the probability that a particular finding is not due to chance is important in debates about science in the courtroom. It is sometimes said that the reason plaintiffs in court may be awarded damages without good scientific evidence is that the legal standard is more liberal than the scientific standard. According to this argument, all the plaintiff has to do is show preponderance of the evidence, whereas science requires 95 percent confidence about a finding. Not only does this argument confuse size with certainty, but it also confuses the whole with the part. The degree of certainty scientists require refers to the results of a given study, not to a limitless body of evidence. The fundamental issue in both science and the courtroom should be the same—that is, the quality of the evidence. Can we rely on it?

So far, I have been speaking mainly about populations. But courtroom trials are not about populations, they are about individuals. The question is whether breast implants caused disease in *this* woman. Is there any basis for such a judgment? I do not believe there is. Given the absence of any scientific information on individual differences in women's responses to breast implants, we can only look at the individual as an *average* woman with implants. We have no basis, at least in the current state of knowledge, for making a judgment about a particular woman. We therefore *must* appeal to epidemiologic data—that is, to studies of populations. We have to assume that whatever is true on average is true of the particular woman. As it happens, we think this way intuitively. When we wonder whether someone we know developed lung cancer because he smokes, we automatically consider what we know about the risks of smoking in a population. We can't be sure that cigarette smoking caused disease in this particular man, because there is no test to answer that question in his case, but we think it probably did because we know a lot about the risks of smoking in populations. Without considering what we know about populations, we have no basis for our opinion. Despite our intuitive realization that particular cases must be considered in the light of what we know about the general situation, that is not what juries are instructed to do. They are asked to judge the particular case on the basis of the evidence presented in court, and no matter how unsatisfactory that evidence is, they must reach a verdict. They cannot say, as scientists can, that they will not form an opinion until they get more or better evidence.

Science in the courtroom is paradoxical in that it always yields a firm conclusion, yet never does. Each plaintiff who claims that breast implants caused her connective tissue disease requires a verdict, and a verdict is always reached. But even though the issue is settled for the last plaintiff, it is not settled for the next one. The question must be revisited over and over, for every woman who comes to court claiming a connection. Even so, it is not argued completely from scratch. An earlier verdict for a plaintiff provides a powerful presumption in the next case (for technical reasons, a verdict for a defendant does not). Nevertheless, verdicts can differ, no matter how similar the women's cases. In contrast, scientists almost never claim to have settled a "case." Their findings are conditional. More work is nearly always required. But for any one scientific question, the weight of the accumulated evidence tends to converge toward an answer. Eventually the probability of the answer will be great enough to warrant general acceptance of the conclusion.

In product liability cases, expert testimony by scientists is usually central. The question of causation is, after all, a scientific one. But scientific questions are handled very differently in the courtroom than they are outside the courtroom. The difference turns on the relationship between evidence and opinion. In both science and law, of course, "expert" opinion is important. But what that means in the two professions is as far apart as day and night. [. . .] Scientists, no matter how expert, must provide the evidence on which their opinions are based. When they complete a research study, it is necessary to present their evidence before their conclusions will be accepted. Even when they are commenting on the general state of their field, it is customary for them to cite explicitly the basis of their opinions. For example, medical researchers sometimes publish summaries of what is already known about a subject. Called "review articles," these summaries are analogous to expert testimony in court, in that they are evaluations of the state of knowledge. But even review articles must refer to the published research being evaluated (unpublished work usually counts for very little in science). In addition, it is expected that authors of review articles will be as even-handed as possible—that is, reasonably comprehensive and unbiased in the selection of the work they discuss. Indeed, an important question for peer reviewers is whether a review article is objective and balanced.

Expert testimony in the courtroom is very different. In contrast to scientific procedures, an expert witness in court is *expected* to give an educated guess, not to produce evidence.[3] Whether expert testimony is admitted in court turns largely on the witness's "credibility"—which means his or her credentials. Does the expert have the appropriate training and experience? Even these rather minimalist standards are often only loosely applied. In the courtroom, one scientist can seem much like another. Some distinctly second-rate scientists testify in trial after trial and consult in case after case, sometimes even earning their living that way. In essence they become well-practiced, professional witnesses, whose major talent is convincing juries, not evaluating evidence. In fact, they may cite no evidence at all, or allude to evidence only vaguely, without giving its source. Sometimes, they refer to their own, unpublished work as evidence, but no one has the opportunity to evaluate its validity or even to know whether it exists. Many reputable scientists refuse to be expert witnesses in court, probably in part because they find the adversarial process an unsatisfactory way to arrive at scientific conclusions and therefore feel uncomfortable participating in it. Often experts are chosen whose field is not relevant to the scientific question that needs answering. In many of the breast implant cases, for example, plaintiffs' attorneys have relied on pathologists or toxicologists to speculate about how breast implants might cause connective tissue disease, rather than calling on epidemiologists who would get to the question of whether they actually do. In the Stern case, for example, her key witnesses consisted of a pathologist, a toxicologist, and an immunologist.[4] Even more troubling, expert witnesses are selected by the contesting lawyers, paid by them, and their testimony is rehearsed in advance—circumstances unlikely to ensure competence, let alone objectivity. In fact, the whole point is precisely to find a "qualified" witness who will be scientifically committed to your side. The irony here is that a lawyer may employ a scientist to offer eccentric views in a court proceeding that is supposed to hold manufacturers to generally accepted, mainstream standards.

After contributing so decisively to the handsome verdict in the Stern case, Dan Bolton was on a roll. He left Hersh and Hersh and went on to become a partner in another firm and a magnet for breast implant suits. The decision in Bolton's next big case—the case of Mariann Hopkins—was appealed all the way to the Supreme Court, which refused to review it. In its own way, this case was even more influential than the Stern case, because it was instrumental in the FDA ban.

Mariann Hopkins, of Sebastopol, California, a secretary at Sonoma State University in nearby Rohnert Park and the wife of a San Francisco firefighter, was in her early thirties when she underwent a double mastectomy in 1976 because of fibrocystic disease of the breast.[5] This is a very common condition that produces tender nodules in the breasts, particularly just before menstrual periods. Whether it is a precursor of breast cancer or not has been debated for decades. The consensus is that it usually isn't, although some forms of it may increase the risk. In any case, Hopkins evidently did not want to take the chance. After her mastectomy she had her breasts reconstructed with silicone-gel-filled implants, manufactured by Dow Corning. Within a few months, one of them ruptured, and to maintain symmetry she had them both replaced.

Three years later, in 1979, she was told she had an autoimmune disorder called mixed connective tissue disease. This is a devastating disease, with clinical features of systemic lupus, rheumatoid arthritis, polymyositis, and scleroderma, all rolled into one. Typically, the disease produces very high levels of antibodies against constituents of the patient's own cells. Mixed connective tissue disease is incurable, and Hopkins had to be treated indefinitely with corticosteroids, which can produce a variety of serious side effects. In 1986, seven years after the diagnosis, Hopkins gave up her job because of her disabling disease. The same year she again had her breast implants replaced because one had ruptured.

In 1987, Hopkins's mother told her that she had heard there was a link between ruptured breast implants and autoimmune disorders. Hopkins queried her doctors, who told her they knew of no such connection. She later said the rheumatologist who was treating her mixed connective tissue disease, Dr. Stephen Gospe, was "very patronizing. He said people always need something to blame and I might as well accept my illness." The next year, however, Hopkins happened to turn on the evening news as she came into her house from the grocery store and saw a clip of Bolton, along with Sybil Goldrich, talking about the effects of silicone leakage on the immune system. (Goldrich [. . .] is co-founder of the advocacy group Command Trust Network; Bolton was at the time testifying before the November 1988 FDA advisory panel.) To Hopkins, seeing Bolton on television was little short of a miracle. As she said later, "If I'd turned it on one minute later, I would have missed it." But she didn't miss it, and she straightaway phoned Bolton in San Francisco. Hopkins said of that conversation, "I learned there were other women besides myself who'd had problems with implants. I said 'Why haven't I heard of this?' He said, 'Because there have been suits filed against Dow Corning and they have settled out of court, and then all the documents are kept under lock and key.'" The next month, she and Bolton filed suit against Dow Corning in federal court in San Francisco.[6]

At the trial three years later, in 1991, Bolton called three expert witnesses to testify as to the cause of Hopkins's disease—Marc Lappé, Nir Kossovsky, and Frank Vasey. Because these three [. . .] have been so important in breast implant litigation, it is worth examining their credentials in some detail. Lappé, who [. . .] has a Ph.D. in experimental pathology, testified in the Stern case, as well as the Hopkins case, according to an article in *American Lawyer*.[7] In both cases, his testimony primarily concerned his interpretation of the Dow Corning laboratory studies. In his view Dow Corning's animal studies indicated that breast implants may have contributed to Stern's and Hopkins's illnesses. A 1995 computer search of Lappé's own publications, as compiled by the National Library of Medicine, is revealing. [. . .] He published his theory about the way in which implants might cause autoimmune disease in an article in the journal *Medical Hypotheses,* confidently titled, "Silicone-Reactive Disorder: A New Autoimmune Disease Caused by Immunostimulation and Superantigens." As a hypothesis, it contributed no new evidence. In its 1994 review of the scientific evidence in the breast implant controversy, the British Department of Health said Lappé's paper "has nothing to add to the issue of a causal relationship between silicones, immunological responsiveness and disease."[8] Of Lappé's 50-some scientific papers in the National Library of Medicine's database, only one other dealt with the subject of breast implants. (His other papers have dealt mainly with the ethics of genetic screening.) He also published a 1991 book, *Chemical Deception: The Toxic Threat to Health and the Environment.*[9]

Kossovsky is an M.D. certified in anatomic pathology, the study of diseased tissues.[10] An assistant professor at the UCLA Medical Center, he has been a very popular and effective plaintiffs' witness in breast implant cases. At the time of the Hopkins trial, Kossovsky was in his early thirties and looked younger. Pleasantly voluble, with an engaging, eager manner, Kossovsky gives the impression of wanting nothing more than to explain the immune system to the jury. He believes that silicone changes body tissues in such a way that the body no longer recognizes them as native. In its effort to reject what it interprets as "foreign" invaders, the body mounts an autoimmune reaction that leads to connective tissue disease. Despite Kossovsky's long-standing attachment to this theory, there is still no good evidence for it.

Bolton's third witness on causation was Frank Vasey, the chief of the Division of Rheumatology at the University of South Florida College of Medicine.[11] Rheumatology is the medical specialty concerned with connective tissue disease. Vasey, a physician, has reported a group of patients with breast implants who had connective tissue disease or symptoms suggestive of it, most of whom felt better after the implants were removed.[12] In medical practice, it is not unusual for a specialist who attracts patients with a certain type of problem to gain erroneous impressions about its frequency or its association with other conditions. Without controls and appropriate population sampling techniques, it is easy to draw conclusions that will not stand up to later, more careful epidemiologic analysis. Even a large clinical experience, while possibly suggestive, cannot substitute for a cohort or case-control study in getting at whether implants cause disease. The history of medicine is replete with examples of mistaken "clinical impressions" based on uncontrolled and often undocumented personal experience. One of the major advances in modern medicine is the realization that to be reliable, personal experience must be supported by rigorous research.

None of Bolton's witnesses was an epidemiologist. Yet this is the only kind of specialist who could authoritatively speak to the issue of a possible link between breast implants and connective tissue disease.

Perhaps the most startling testimony on the other side was that of Hopkins's own rheumatologist, Stephen Gospe. Gospe had definitively diagnosed Hopkins's mixed connective tissue disease in 1979, but he believed her symptoms began even before she received her first set of implants in 1976. Indeed, because of suggestive symptoms, her internist, Dr. Louis Pelfini, had in 1975 ordered a test for autoimmune disease, which at the time was inconclusive. Because her symptoms persisted, Pelfini sent her to Gospe in 1979. Gospe's testimony that her symptoms had begun before her first implants were placed in 1976 might have been expected to undermine the plaintiff's case. But evidently it didn't trouble the jurors. On December 13, 1991, the jury awarded Hopkins $7.34 million. Dow Corning was found guilty of fraud and malice in marketing the implants.[13] The evidence included the Dow Corning memo instructing salespeople to wash off demonstration implants so that plastic surgeons would not notice the oiliness of the envelope. The Hopkins case reached its climax just as David Kessler [commissioner of the FDA appointed by President Bush in 1990] was deciding whether to permit implants to stay on the market. This timing, nearly everyone agrees, greatly influenced the FDA's ultimate decision.

Dow Corning (which went out of the implant business a few months after the Hopkins decision)[14] appealed to the U.S. Court of Appeals for the Ninth Circuit. Signaling the significance of the case, two renowned lawyers joined the fray in the appeal. Harvard Law School professor Laurence Tribe headed the Hopkins-Bolton team. Shirley Hufstedler, Jimmy Carter's former secretary of education and a former judge of the Ninth Circuit, joined Frank Woodside III for Dow Corning's defense. The defense's appeal was based on two arguments. The first concerned the statute of limitations, a technical argument of interest to lawyers but probably no one else. The second argument was whether the testimony had established that it was more probable than not that there was a causal connection between Hopkins's breast implants and her mixed connective tissue disease—the second necessary condition for a product liability judgment. The first condition had clearly been met: no one doubted that Hopkins was sick. But the other two conditions were in contention, and the satisfaction of the third (that Dow Corning had been negligent or wanton) was contingent on proving the second (that the implants most likely caused the mixed connective tissue disease). The appellate court was asked to consider whether the lower court had adequate evidence for this finding. And in particular, was it correct in relying on the expert testimony Bolton had assembled?

Dow's Woodside (a physician as well as a lawyer) had argued in lower court that Lappé, Kossovsky, and Vasey were not qualified to testify as experts on causation, but the trial judge had disagreed. The appeal was largely based on the same argument, and again it was dismissed. Although the appeals court noted that scientific testimony must be "not only relevant, but reliable," it ruled that the testimony of Kossovsky, Lappé, and Vasey had met this standard. Kossovsky and Vasey, according to the court, had based their opinions in part on "preliminary results" of epidemiological studies they were conducting. Four years later, in a search of the medical literature, I was unable to find that either of them has published a rigorous epidemiologic study that could shed light on the question of causation. Lappé was said to be "a recognized expert on the immunological effects of silicone in the human body," although a search of the National Library of Medicine's comprehensive database shows that he has published very little on the subject.

Judge Procter Hug, writing for the Court of Appeals, not only accepted the testimony of the three witnesses, but his opinion indicated that he was utterly convinced about the substance of the matter—not just about the procedural questions.[15] He was certain, even if most scientists were not, that breast implants cause mixed connective tissue disease. Referring to the many thousands of women who have Dow Corning implants, the judge said, "Each of these women was at risk of encountering the same fate from which Hopkins suffered." As for Dow Corning, he said, "Dow's conduct in exposing thousands of women to a painful and debilitating disease, and the evidence that Dow gained financially from its conduct, may properly be considered in imposing an award of punitive damages." The harshness of Judge Hug's conclusion reflected the emphasis in the case on the Dow Corning documents. Dow Corning petitioned the U.S. Supreme Court for review. The petition was refused, thus letting stand the appellate court's decision.[16] Bolton's experts had done their job well.

With the astonishing explosion of scientific knowledge over the last century, and particularly in the last 50 years, expert testimony has become increasingly important in the courts. In particular, there are few product liability suits in which expert testimony is not central. In the *Hopkins* case, for example, the testimony of Lappé, Kossovsky, and Vasey was pivotal. But even as expert testimony became commonplace in the courtroom, legal scholars and judges began to fret about its role. Who was an expert? How should expert testimony be received and what weight should it have? As far back as 1858, the U.S. Supreme Court foresaw the problems in store. It observed then that "experience has shown that opposite opinions of persons professing to be experts may be obtained to any amount," and it went on to complain that cross-examination of all these experts was virtually useless, "wasting the time and wearying the patience of both court and jury, and perplexing, instead of elucidating, the questions involved."[17]

In 1897, possibly because it had heard enough, the Supreme Court decided to cut things short by limiting cross-examination of experts. In considering an insanity defense for a man accused of murder, an expert witness had been asked in lower court, "What does medical science teach as to that?" Incredibly, the witness was told by the trial judge that he didn't have to answer that question. On appeal, the Supreme Court agreed, saying that once an expert gives his opinion, the court should take it or leave it. It would be "opening the door to too wide an inquiry to interrogate him as to what other scientific men [*sic*] have said upon such matters, or in respect to the general teachings of science thereon, or to permit books of science to be offered in evidence." The message, then, was not to delve into something as arcane as scientific evidence. Whatever a qualified witness said was okay.

This decision pretty much settled the issue until a federal trials court in 1923 reached the polar opposite conclusion in *Frye v. United States*. In *Frye*, the issue in contention was whether a "lie detector test" (which in those days was simply a blood pressure reading) would be admitted as evidence. The court refused to admit it, on the grounds that there was not yet a scientific consensus about the validity of this new method. Far from agreeing with the Supreme Court that experts needn't take into account the work of other scientists, the *Frye* court said that testimony *must* speak to the work of others—that is, it was admissible only if it incorporated principles and methods generally accepted by the relevant scientific community. The Court of Appeals agreed. Thus was born the "general acceptance" standard for expert testimony, a subject of intense legal debate for the next 70 years. This standard had the effect of excluding a good deal of what has become known as "junk science"—patently absurd testimony by zealots, incompetents, or opportunists. But the *Frye* standard was by no means accepted in all courts. Its opponents claimed, somewhat improbably, that it would tend to exclude novel, farsighted testimony by modern-day Galileos.[18] There is no record of this happening once, let alone often. Furthermore, even if a modern-day Galileo did not make it into court at first, that fact would not stop him from prevailing in the scientific community. Courts do not determine scientific acceptance, as implied by the argument that we need to keep our courts open to the hidden Galileos in our midst.

What the don't-ask-don't-tell approach of the 1897 Supreme Court had in common with the *Frye* decision was that both avoided coming to grips with the substantive issue of how to define good scientific evidence that would qualify for admissibility in court. *Frye* evaded the issue by setting up a proxy, and a very good proxy it was: Good science was determined by other scientists through their usual methods—peer review and publication, criticism, replication—and, most important, by its reliability in predicting future results. (These were not the words of *Frye*, but they are its effect.) In 1975 new Federal Rules of Evidence were signed into law by President Ford. These detailed rules for admitting evidence into federal courts contain criteria for scientific testimony that include validity but omit the requirement for general acceptance in the scientific community. Whether the new, more liberal Rules superseded *Frye* or not was not clear. Some courts went with *Frye*, others with the Rules, and others simply followed their own instincts. The courts thus continued their chaotic approach to the problem, even while product liability suits were burgeoning and scientists themselves were having a difficult time keeping up with the rapid advances in their own fields.

In 1993 the U.S. Supreme Court finally grasped the nettle and attempted to deal substantively with the problem of expert testimony in the courts. The case that occasioned the Supreme Court's attention, *Daubert v. Merrell Dow Pharmaceuticals,* was in many respects similar to the breast implant cases. [19] The case was brought against Merrell Dow Pharmaceuticals in 1984 by the parents of two boys who had been born with only rudimentary arms, a well-known congenital mishap (these sorts of defects occur in about 1 in 1,000 births). The parents alleged that the defect had been caused by Merrell Dow's Bendectin, an antihistamine-like drug that the two mothers had taken during pregnancy to combat morning sickness. Bendectin was an extraordinarily popular drug, prescribed for pregnant women almost as routinely as vitamins. Some 17 million women took it (as did I) between 1958 and 1983. It is not surprising, then, that even if there were no connection, babies with upper-limb defects would sometimes be born to mothers who had taken Bendectin, just as connective tissue disease would sometimes develop in women who had breast implants even if there were no causal connection between the implants and the disease.

Merrell Dow's Frank Woodside (who would later be Dow Corning's attorney in the Hopkins case) had argued at first that the case should not be tried at all. He pointed out that there had been many epidemiologic studies published in the scientific literature, involving some 130,000 women, none of which had been able to show a connection between Bendectin and birth defects. The plaintiffs, however, produced eight expert witnesses who testified to Bendectin's ability to cause birth defects, although they could point to no epidemiologic evidence. One witness testified that she had reanalyzed the published studies that Woodside cited and had come to the opposite conclusion, although she had not published her work. The trial court, citing *Frye,* agreed that the plaintiffs had produced no admissible evidence. The appeals court agreed. The Supreme Court was then asked to speak to the narrow issue of whether Frye was the appropriate standard or whether it had been superseded by the 1975 Rules of Evidence. Merrell Dow favored *Frye,* since it had worked well for them, but the plaintiffs wanted the less stringent Federal Rules of Evidence to prevail.

The Supreme Court dispensed quickly with the narrow question. Yes, the Federal Rules did supersede *Frye,* and the case was passed back to the appeals court to hear again under those rules. The Supreme Court made no attempt to decide whether Bendectin caused birth defects, only what the standards for the admissibility of expert evidence should be. But the Court also devoted considerable attention to elucidating the meaning of those standards and how they were to be applied, thus finally dealing with the issue of what constitutes good science. A large number of interested individuals and organizations, including the *New England Journal of Medicine,* were aware of the enormous impact the *Daubert* decision might have. The Court was therefore flooded with amici briefs on both sides. These revealed interesting schisms within the scientific community. Many favored the *Frye* standard (as did we), because they felt it would reduce the amount of junk science finding its way to the courts. We argued that testimony should be based on research that had been duly published in peer-reviewed journals. But equally reputable scientists came down on the other side, because they felt the "general acceptance" criterion was too restrictive and elitist. And many lawyers also opposed the *Frye* standard because they believed it would preempt the responsibility of juries to decide the facts.

In the end both sides in the *Daubert* case claimed victory—or defeat, depending on whether one is inclined to see the glass as half full or half empty. The Supreme Court said that while the Federal Rules applied, this did not mean that all expert testimony would be admissible. Far from it. Federal judges are now required to undertake "a preliminary assessment of whether the reasoning or methodology underlying the testimony is scientifically valid and of whether that reasoning or methodology properly can be applied to the fact in issue." Thus, judges are to be the gatekeepers who decide whether to admit expert testimony. This was not what either side thought they wanted. The *Frye* proponents wanted the scientific community to be gatekeepers. The other side didn't want any gatekeepers; let the juries decide on the basis of the cross-examination. But in *Daubert,* the Supreme Court said that judges must decide, and they must do so by learning how to think like scientists. Expert testimony must be both "reliable" and "relevant," and judges should decide in advance whether it was. Writing for the majority, Justice Harry Blackmun emphasized the importance of relevance by pointing out that testimony about the effect of the phases of the moon on irrational behavior might be quite valid as to the astronomical data, but totally irrelevant in drawing any inference about behavior. What is relevant in one context may not be in another. This requirement that expert testimony be apposite to the matter at hand was at issue in the appeal of the *Hopkins* decision.

Many concerned about the increasingly contentious relations between law and science welcomed the *Daubert* decision. Bert Black, a lawyer and then-chair of the American Bar Association's Standing Committee on Scientific Evidence, and Francisco Ayala, a scientist and then-president of the American Association for the Advancement of Science, together with a colleague, Carol Saffran-Brinks, wrote a celebratory analysis in the *Texas Law Review.*[20] Despite the fact that both Black and Ayala had participated in an amicus brief on behalf of Merrell Dow—technically the losing side—they saw the actual written judgment as a cause for hope that the days of junk science in the courtroom were numbered. In particular, they approved of the sophisticated analysis of what good science is. The Supreme Court embraced the notion of Karl Popper, the philosopher of science, that good science requires formulating a question that can be answered. In other words, any hypothesis must be capable of being tested. It is useless to come up with a theory, no matter how plausible, that cannot be proved or disproved. Black and his colleagues, in a section on the "pathological science" that stems from ignoring the necessity for testing and corroboration, describe it as "characterized by a fixation on effects that are difficult to detect, a readiness to disregard prevailing ideas and theories, and an unwillingness to conduct meaningful experimental testing." This description is relevant in the breast implant controversy. The common contention that breast implants cause diseases that cannot be objectively described is a theory that cannot be tested. Doctors who believe in it simply assert that such diseases exist and that they know them when they see them.

For those who might have thought the Supreme Court's *Daubert* decision heralded a new, more rational era in the courts, let alone mere consistency, subsequent events are instructive. The Supreme Court decided the *Daubert* case in 1993, sending it back to the Ninth Circuit Appeals Court for reconsideration. By coincidence, this was the same court that considered the appeal in the Hopkins case in 1994. The *Daubert* decision was handed down after the Hopkins verdict but before the appeal. A major issue in the petition to the U.S. Supreme Court was the failure of the Ninth Circuit Appeals Court to adhere to the *Daubert* criteria. As we have seen, the appellate court found the expert testimony in Hopkins admissible even though its decision was handed down after the *Daubert* decision. Just a year later, however, the same court found that the testimony that Bendectin caused birth defects was *not* admissible. [21] I believe that in *neither* case had the testimony clearly met the Supreme Court's requirement for reliability and relevance. Even more difficult to comprehend is the fact that the Supreme Court itself, after its insightful analysis of good science in *Daubert* in 1993, let stand the Hopkins decision in 1995. (If you are having trouble following all this, it is not your fault, or even mine.) The inconsistency of the decisions surely underscores the continuing confusion about what kind of scientific evidence should be admitted in court. The *Daubert* decision doesn't seem to have helped much, at least not yet.

As I have noted, scientific testimony in the courtroom is often at most only marginally related to scientific evidence. To be sure, there are superficial matters of form that may suggest a resemblance between science in and out of the courtroom. Expert witnesses may wear white coats, be called "doctor," purport to do research, and talk scientific jargon. But too often they are merely adding a veneer to a foregone, self-interested conclusion. Sometimes they spin theories that they say are supported by their expertise or experience. Or they may refer vaguely to research. Very often, however, the "research" is their own and it is unpublished and unavailable. The point is that they are not required to produce their evidence, and they usually do not. The result is a growing gap between scientific reality and what passes for it in the courtroom. The *Daubert* decision was a brave step toward remedying the situation, but it was not enough.   ∎

NOTES

1. See A. Frankel, "From Pioneers to Profits," *American Lawyer,* June 1992:82.

2. For a fuller analysis, see B. Black, "Matching Evidence about Clustered Health Events with Tort Law Requirements," *American Journal of Epidemiology,* 132 (1990):579–86.

3. For more information on the role of expert testimony in the courtroom, see L. Loevinger, "Science as Evidence," *Jurimetrics Journal,* winter 1995:153–90. Also B. Black, "Evolving Legal Standards for the Admissibility of Scientific Evidence," Science, 239, no. 4847 (1988):1508–12.

4. See A. Frankel, "From Pioneers to Profits," *American Lawyer,* June 1992:82.

5. Biographical details about Mariann Hopkins, and the case chronology, primarily come from two sources: the decision of the United States Court of Appeals for the 9th Circuit, August 26, 1994 (*Mariann Hopkins v. Dow Corning Corp.* 33F.3d 1116 1994), and the Petition for a Writ of Certiorari to the U.S. Supreme Court (*Dow Corning v. Mariann Hopkins,* No. 94-861, 1994). See also J. M. Adams, "Victim of Silicone Breast Implants Wants Value Placed on Women's Lives," *Chicago Tribune,* February 9, 1992, p. 21.

6. Hopkins quotes are taken from J. M. Adams, "Victim of Silicone Breast Implants Wants Value Placed on Women's Lives," *Chicago Tribune,* February 9, 1992, p. 21, and A. Frankel, "From Pioneers to Profits," *American Lawyer,* June 1992:82.

7. See A. Frankel, "From Pioneers to Profits," *American Lawyer,* June 1992:82.

8. See D. M. Gott and J. J. B. Tinkler, "Evaluation of Evidence for an Association between the Implantation of Silicones and Connective Tissue Disease: Data Published from the End of 1991 to July 1994" (London: Medical Devices Directorate, December 1994).

9. See M. Lappé, *Chemical Deception: The Toxic Threat to Health and the Environment* (San Francisco: Sierra Club, 1991).

10. Kossovsky's credentials are documented in the *Official ABMS Directory of Board Certified Medical Specialists,* 27th ed. (Philadelphia: Reed Reference Publishing, 1995).

11. Vasey's credentials are documented in the *Official ABMS Directory of Board Certified Medical Specialists,* 27th ed. (Philadelphia: Reed Reference Publishing, 1995).

12. For Vasey's position, see his book, F. B. Vasey and J. Feldstein, *The Silicone Breast Implant Controversy: What Women Need to Know* (Freedom, Calif.: Crossing Press, 1993).

13. The verdict was widely publicized. See, for example, W. Carlsen, "Jury Awards $7.3 Million in Implant Case," *San Francisco Chronicle,* December 14, 1991, p. A13, and J. M. Adams, "Victim of Silicone Breast Implants Wants Value Placed on Women's Lives," *Chicago Tribune,* February 9, 1992, p. 21. See also the decision of the United States Court of Appeals for the 9th Circuit, August 26, 1994 (*Mariann Hopkins v. Dow Corning Corp.* 33F.3d 1116 1994).

14. Dow Corning announced it was pulling out of the breast implant market in March 1992. See E. Neuffer, "Maker Quits Implant Market," *Boston Globe,* March 20, 1992, p. 1.

15. See the decision of the United States Court of Appeals for the 9th Circuit, August 26, 1994 (*Mariann Hopkins v. Dow Corning Corp.* 33F.3d 1116 1994).

16. The U.S. Supreme Court's refusal to review the Hopkins case received widespread attention. See, for example, R. Carelli, "Justices Uphold Breast Implant Award," *Boston Globe,* January 10, 1995, p. 6.

17. For an account of the history of science in the courtroom, including *Frye* and the Federal Rules of Evidence, see L. Loevinger, "Science as Evidence," *Jurimetrics Journal,* winter 1995:153–90.

18. For more on the debate, see S. Begley, "The Meaning of Junk," *Newsweek,* March 22, 1993, and D. Freedman, "Who's to Judge? New Guidelines for Scientific Evidence," *Discover,* 15, no. 1 (1994):78.

19. Details of the *Daubert* case come primarily from the Supreme Court's decision (*Daubert v. Merrell Dow Pharmaceuticals,* No. 92-102, June 28, 1993, 113 S Ct 2768 1993) and "Brief of the New England Journal of Medicine, Journal of the American Medical Association, and Annals of Internal Medicine of Amicus Curiae in Support of Respondent" (*Daubert v. Merrell Dow Pharmaceuticals,* No. 92-102), Kaye, Scholer, Fierman, Hays & Handler (New York), January 19, 1993.

20. See B. Black, F. J. Ayala, and C. Saffran-Brinks, "Science and the Law in the Wake of *Daubert:* A New Search for Scientific Knowledge," *Texas Law Review,* 72, no. 4 (1994):715–802.

21. The 9th Circuit's decision in the Bendectin appeal was written by Judge Alex Kozinski. See *Daubert v. Merrell Dow Pharmaceuticals,* No. 90-55397, January 4, 1995. The decision received widespread attention in the popular and scientific press. See, for example, "Birth Defect Lawsuit that Set Science Standard Is Dismissed," *New York Times,* January 8, 1995, p. 19, and M. Barinaga, "Bendectin Case Dismissed," *Science,* 267 (January 13, 1995):167.

▪ QUESTIONS FOR MAKING CONNECTIONS WITHIN THE READING ▪

1. In order to get a handle on Angell's argument, it's important to understand what a product liability case is and how such cases are handled by the courts. What did the prosecutor have to show in the case against Dow Corning? What is the difference between a judgment based on a "preponderance of the evidence" and a judgment that is "beyond a reasonable doubt"?

2. Angell makes her argument about the role that scientific evidence should play in the courtroom by working through the litigation of the product liability cases against Dow Corning. What are the major events in the Stern case? In the Hopkins case? What is the connection between these cases? Who are the major figures in each case? And what conclusions does Angell want us to reach after having read about these cases?

3. Following the twists and turns in how the courts handle scientific evidence is no easy task. Indeed, Angell herself concedes this point at the end of "Science in the Courtroom," when she observes, "If you are having trouble following all this, it is not your fault, or even mine." And yet, being able to see the difference between the *Frye* decision and the *Daubert* decision is crucial if one is to understand Angell's conclusion that the "*Daubert* decision was a brave step toward remedying the situation, but it was not enough." What is the *Frye* decision? The *Daubert* decision? And what role did these decisions play in the litigation of the Stern case and the Hopkins case?

▪ QUESTIONS FOR WRITING ▪

1. As Angell sees it, both the 1897 Supreme Court decision on expert testimony and the *Frye* decision "avoided coming to grips with the substantive issue of how to define good scientific evidence that would qualify for admissibility in court." What is Angell's standard for "good scientific evidence"? What kind of evidence does she believe should count in product liability cases? Who should decide what counts as evidence in the courtroom?

2. "The question of causation is, after all, a scientific one." Angell makes this observation as if it were obvious and yet, on further inspection, it's clear that not everyone would agree with it. What does it mean to say that the question of causation is a scientific matter? And, if everyone could be made to agree with this statement, how would the court system have to change?

▪ QUESTIONS FOR MAKING CONNECTIONS BETWEEN READINGS ▪

1. In "False Science, False Promises," Jasper Becker details what happened when the political agenda in Mao's China was allowed to shape the scientific research carried out in that country. Marcia Angell is similarly concerned with the relationship between the scientific community and the government's legislative and judicial bodies. What should the relationship between science and politics be? Is it possible for scientists to be completely objective? Is this an ideal, a myth, a reality, or something else altogether?

2. In "Science in the Courtroom," Marcia Angell has few kind words to say about scientists who are paid to testify in court. Michael Pollan, in "Playing God in the Garden," subjects statements made by the scientists who work for Monsanto to a similar level of scrutiny. What happens when science moves into the boardroom? Are the problems that arise different from those that arise when science moves into the courtroom?

For additional suggestions about making connections between readings, visit the Link-O-Mat and More Sample Assignments at <www.newhum.com>.

KAREN ARMSTRONG

IN 1981, KAREN ARMSTRONG published *Through the Narrow Gate*, a controversial account of her experiences as a Sister of the Society of the Holy Child Jesus, a Roman Catholic order. Armstrong had left the convent and the Church in 1972, "wearied by religion" and "worn out by years of struggle" and had spent the intervening years pursuing a doctorate in literature and teaching at a girls' school. Although she was gratified by the success of her book, Armstrong has described the real turning point in her life as having occurred during a series of trips she made to Jerusalem beginning in 1982. Shocked both by the Israeli invasion of Lebanon and by the Palestinian intifada, Armstrong found herself questioning just how much Westerners—herself, included—knew or understood about the living conditions and the beliefs of Muslims living in the Middle East.

After realizing that Westerners "were posing as a tolerant and compassionate society and yet passing judgments from a position of extreme ignorance and irrationality," Armstrong committed herself to combating cross-cultural misperceptions and religious misunderstandings. She has written a number of books that explore relations between Judaism, Christianity, and Islam, including *Holy War: The Crusades and Their Impact on Today's World* (1991); *Mohammed: A Biography of the Prophet* (1992); and *Islam: A Short History* (2000). She has also written, most recently, a biography, *Buddha* (2001), and *The Battle for God* (2000), a study of the rise of fundamentalism.

The selection that follows comes from *A History of God: The 4,000-Year Quest of Judaism, Christianity and Islam*, where Armstrong sets out to catalog ways that Jews, Christians, and Muslims have named and understood the experience of the divine. While working on this book, Armstrong has said that she came to understand the difference between religion per se and neurological conditions that skeptics believe are at the root of mystical visions and insights: "the difference is

Armstrong, Karen. "Does God Have a Future?" *A History of God: The 4,000-Year Quest of Judaism, Christianity and Islam.* New York: Knopf, 1993. 377–399.

Biographical information and opening and closing quotations drawn from the Random House Web site <http://www.randomhouse.com/modernlibrary/karmstrong.html>. Middle quotation drawn from M. M. Ali's profile of Karen Armstrong in the *Washington Report on Middle East Affairs*, Feb. 1993, p. 38. <http://www.washington-report.org/backissues/0293/9302038.htm>.

compassion," Armstrong notes, "which in religion is ethically based." By asking, "Does God have a future?" Armstrong bids her readers to consider what roles organized religion and personal experiences of the divine will have in the years to come.

To learn more about Karen Armstrong and the role of religion in contemporary society, visit the Link-O-Mat at <www.newhum.com>.

■   ■

Does God Have a Future?

As we approach the end of the second millennium, it seems likely that the world we know is passing away. For decades we have lived with the knowledge that we have created weapons that could wipe out human life on the planet. The Cold War may have ended, but the new world order seems no less frightening than the old. We are facing the possibility of ecological disaster. The AIDS virus threatens to bring a plague of unmanageable proportions. Within two or three generations, the population will become too great for the planet to support. Thousands are dying of famine and drought. Generations before our own have felt that the end of the world is nigh, yet it does seem that we are facing a future that is unimaginable. How will the idea of God survive in the years to come? For 4000 years it has constantly adapted to meet the demands of the present, but in our own century, more and more people have found that it no longer works for them, and when religious ideas cease to be effective they fade away. Maybe God really is an idea of the past. The American scholar Peter Berger notes that we often have a double standard when we compare the past with our own time. Where the past is analyzed and made relative, the present is rendered immune to this process and our current position becomes an absolute: thus "the New Testament writers are seen as afflicted with a false consciousness rooted in *their* time, but the analyst takes the consciousness of *his* time as an unmixed intellectual blessing."[1] Secularists of the nineteenth and early twentieth centuries saw atheism as the irreversible condition of humanity in the scientific age.

There is much to support this view. In Europe, the churches are emptying; atheism is no longer the painfully acquired ideology of a few intellectual pioneers but a prevailing mood. In the past it was always produced by a particular idea of God, but now it seems to have lost its inbuilt relationship to theism and become an automatic response to the experience of living in a secularized society. Like the crowd of amused people surrounding Nietzsche's madman, many are unmoved by the prospect of life without God.

Others find his absence a positive relief. Those of us who have had a difficult time with religion in the past find it liberating to be rid of the God who terrorized our childhood. It is wonderful not to have to cower before a vengeful deity, who threatens us with eternal damnation if we do not abide by his rules. We have a new intellectual freedom and can boldly follow up our own ideas without pussyfooting around difficult articles of faith, feeling all the while a sinking loss of integrity. We imagine that the hideous deity we have experienced is the authentic God of Jews, Christians and Muslims and do not always realize that it is merely an unfortunate aberration.

There is also desolation. Jean-Paul Sartre (1905–80) spoke of the God-shaped hole in the human consciousness, where God had always been. Nevertheless, he insisted that even if God existed, it was still necessary to reject him, since the idea of God negates our freedom. Traditional religion tells us that we must conform to God's idea of humanity to become fully human. Instead, we must see human beings as liberty incarnate. Sartre's atheism was not a consoling creed, but other existentialists saw the absence of God as a positive liberation. Maurice Merleau-Ponty (1908–61) argued that instead of increasing our sense of wonder, God actually negates it. Because God represents absolute perfection, there is nothing left for us to do or achieve. Albert Camus (1913–60) preached a heroic atheism. People should reject God defiantly in order to pour out all their loving solicitude upon mankind. As always, the atheists have a point. God had indeed been used in the past to stunt creativity; if he is made a blanket answer to every possible problem and contingency, he can indeed stifle our sense of wonder or achievement. A passionate and committed atheism can be more religious than a weary or inadequate theism.

During the 1950s, Logical Positivists such as A. J. Ayer (1910–91) asked whether it made sense to believe in God. The natural sciences provided the only reliable source of knowledge because it could be tested empirically. Ayer was not asking whether or not God existed but whether the idea of God had any meaning. He argued that a statement is meaningless if we cannot see how it can be verified or shown to be false. To say "There is intelligent life on Mars" is not meaningless since we can see how we could verify this once we had the necessary technology. Similarly a simple believer in traditional Old Man in the Sky is not making a meaningless statement when he says: "I believe in God," since after death we should be able to find out whether or not this is true. It is the more sophisticated believer who has problems, when he says: "God does not exist in any sense that we can understand" or "God is not good in the human sense of the word." These statements are too vague; it is impossible to see how they can be tested; therefore, they are meaningless. As Ayer said: "Theism is so confused and the sentences in which 'God' appears so incoherent and incapable of verifiability or falsifiability that to speak of belief or unbelief, faith or unfaith, is logically impossible."[2] Atheism is as unintelligible and meaningless as theism. There is nothing in the concept of "God" to deny or be skeptical about.

Like Freud, the Positivists believed that religious belief represented an immaturity which science would overcome. Since the 1950s, linguistic philosophers have criticized Logical Positivism, pointing out that what Ayer called the Verification Principle could not itself be verified. Today we are less likely to be as optimistic about science, which can only explain the world of physical nature. Wilfred Cantwell Smith pointed out that the Logical Positivists set themselves up as scientists during a period when, for the first time in history, science saw the natural world in explicit disjunction from humanity.[3] The kind of statements to which Ayer referred work very well for the objective facts of science but are not suitable for less clear-cut human experiences. Like poetry or music, religion is not amenable to this kind of discourse and verification. More recently linguistic philosophers such as Antony Flew have argued that it is more rational to find a natural explanation than a religious one. The old "proofs" do not work: the argument from design falls down because we would need to get outside the system to see whether natural phenomena are motivated by their own laws or by Something outside. The argument that we are "contingent" or "defective" beings proves nothing, since there could always be an explanation that is ultimate but not supernatural. Flew is less of an optimist than Feuerbach, Marx or the Existentialists. There is no agonizing, no heroic defiance but simply a matter-of-fact commitment to reason and science as the only way forward.

[. . .] However, [. . .] not all religious people have looked to "God" to provide them with an explanation for the universe. Many have seen the proofs as a red herring. Science has been felt to be threatening only by those Western Christians who got into the habit of reading the scriptures literally and interpreting doctrines as though they were matters of objective fact. Scientists and philosophers who find no room for God in their systems are usually referring to the idea of God as First Cause, a notion eventually abandoned by Jews, Muslims and Greek Orthodox Christians during the Middle Ages. The more subjective "God" that they were looking for could not be proved as though it were an objective fact that was the same for everybody. It could not be located within a physical system of the universe, any more than the Buddhist nirvana.

More dramatic than the linguistic philosophers were the radical theologians of the 1960s who enthusiastically followed Nietzsche and proclaimed the death of God. In *The Gospel of Christian Atheism* (1966), Thomas J. Altizer claimed that the "good news" of God's death had freed us from slavery to a tyrannical transcendent deity: "Only by accepting and even willing the death of God in our experience can we be liberated from a transcendent beyond, an alien beyond which has been emptied and darkened by God's self-alienation in Christ."[4] Altizer spoke in mystical terms of the dark night of the soul and the pain of abandonment. The death of God represented the silence that was necessary before God could become meaningful again. All our old conceptions of divinity had to die before theology could be reborn. We were waiting for a language and a style in which God could once more become a possibility. Altizer's theology was a passionate dialectic which attacked the dark God-less world in the hope that it would give up its secret. Paul Van Buren was more precise and logical. In *The Secular Meaning of the Gospel* (1963), he claimed that it was no longer possible to speak of God acting in the world. Science and technology had made the old mythology invalid. Simple faith in the Old Man in the Sky was clearly impossible, but so was the more sophisticated belief of the theologians. We must do without God and hold on to Jesus of Nazareth. The Gospel was "the good news of a free man who has set other men free." Jesus of Nazareth was the liberator, "the man who defines what it means to be a man."[5]

In *Radical Theology and the Death of God* (1966), William Hamilton noted that this kind of theology had its roots in the United States, which had always had a utopian bent and had no great theological tradition of its own. The imagery of the death of God represented the anomie and barbarism of the technical age, which made it impossible to believe in the biblical God in the old way. Hamilton himself saw this theological mood as a way of being Protestant in the twentieth century. Luther had left his cloister and gone out into the world. In the same way, he and the other Christian radicals were avowedly secular men. They had walked away from the sacred place where God used to be to find the man Jesus in their neighbor out in the world of technology, power, sex, money and the city. Modern secular man did not need God. There was no God-shaped hole within Hamilton: he would find his own solution in the world.

There is something rather poignant about this buoyant sixties optimism. Certainly, the radicals were right that the old ways of speaking about God had become impossible for many people, but in the 1990s it is sadly difficult to feel that liberation and a new dawn are at hand. Even at the time, the Death of God theologians were criticized, since their perspective was that of the affluent, middle-class, white American. Black theologians such as James H. Cone asked how white people felt they had the right to affirm freedom through the death of God when they had actually enslaved people in God's name. The Jewish theologian Richard Rubenstein found it impossible to understand how they could feel so positive about Godless humanity so soon after the Nazi Holocaust. He himself was convinced that the deity conceived as a God of History had died forever in Auschwitz. Yet Rubenstein did not feel that Jews could jettison religion. After the near-extinction of European Jewry, they must not cut themselves off from their past. The nice, moral God of liberal Judaism was no good, however. It was too antiseptic; it ignored the tragedy of life and assumed that the world would improve. Rubenstein himself preferred the God of the Jewish mystics. He was moved by Isaac Luria's doctrine of *tsimtsum*, God's voluntary act of self-estrangement which brought the created world into being. All mystics had seen God as a Nothingness from which we came and to which we will return. Rubenstein agreed with Sartre that life is empty; he saw the God of the mystics as an imaginative way of entering this human experience of nothingness.[6]

Other Jewish theologians have also found comfort in Lurianic Kabbalah. Hans Jonas believes that after Auschwitz we can no longer believe in the omnipotence of God. When God created the world, he voluntarily limited himself and shared the weakness of human beings. He could do no more now, and human beings must restore wholeness to the Godhead and the world by prayer and Torah. The British theologian Louis Jacobs, however, dislikes this idea, finding the image of *tsimtsum* coarse and anthropomorphic: it encourages us to ask *how* God created the world in too literal a manner. God does not limit himself, holding his breath, as it were, before exhaling. An impotent God is useless and cannot be the meaning of human existence. It is better to return to the classic explanation that God is greater than human beings and his thought and ways are not ours. God may be incomprehensible, but people have the option of trusting this ineffable God and affirming *a* meaning, even in the midst of meaninglessness. The Roman Catholic theologian Hans Kung agrees with Jacobs, preferring a more reasonable explanation for tragedy than the fanciful myth of *tsimtsum*. He notes that human beings cannot have faith in a weak God but in the living God who made people strong enough to pray in Auschwitz.

Some people still find it possible to find meaning in the idea of God. The Swiss theologian Karl Barth (1886–1968) set his face against the Liberal Protestantism of Schleiermacher, with its emphasis on religious experience. But he was also a leading opponent of natural theology. It was, he thought, a radical error to seek to explain God in rational terms not simply because of the limitations of the human mind but also because humanity has been corrupted by the Fall. Any natural idea we form about God is bound to be flawed, therefore, and to worship such a God was idolatry. The only valid source of God-knowledge was the Bible. This seems to have the worst of all worlds: experience is out; natural reason is out; the human mind is corrupt and untrustworthy; and there is no possibility of learning from other faiths, since the Bible is the only valid revelation. It seems unhealthy to combine such radical skepticism in the powers of the intellect with such an uncritical acceptance of the truths of scripture.

Paul Tillich (1868–1965) was convinced that the personal God of traditional Western theism must go, but he also believed that religion was necessary for humankind. A deep-rooted anxiety is part of the human condition: this is not neurotic, because it is ineradicable and no therapy can take it away. We constantly fear loss and the terror of extinction, as we watch our bodies gradually but inexorably decay. Tillich agreed with Nietzsche that the personal God was a harmful idea and deserved to die:

> The concept of a "Personal God" interfering with natural events, or being "an independent cause of natural events," makes God a natural object beside others, an object among others, a being among beings, maybe the highest, but nevertheless *a* being. This indeed is not only the destruction of the physical system but even more the destruction of any meaningful idea of God.[7]

A God who kept tinkering with the universe was absurd; a God who interfered with human freedom and creativity was a tyrant. If God is seen as a self in a world of his own, an ego that relates to a thou, a cause separate from its effect, "he" becomes *a* being, not Being itself. An omnipotent, all-knowing tyrant is not so different from earthly dictators who made everything and everybody mere cogs in the machine which they controlled. An atheism that rejects such a God is amply justified.

Instead we should seek to find a "God" above this personal God. There is nothing new about this. Ever since biblical times, theists had been aware of the paradoxical nature of the God to which they prayed, aware that the personalized God was balanced by the essentially transpersonal divinity. Each prayer was a contradiction, since it attempted to speak to somebody to whom speech was impossible; it asked favors of somebody who had either bestowed them or not before he was asked; it said "thou" to a God who, as Being itself, was nearer to the "I" than our own ego. Tillich preferred the definition of God as the Ground of being. Participation in such a God above "God" does not alienate us from the world but immerses us in reality. It returns us to ourselves. Human beings have to use symbols when they talk about Being-itself: to speak literally or realistically about it is inaccurate and untrue. For centuries the symbols "God," "providence" and "immortality" have enabled people to bear the terror of life and the horror of death, but when these symbols lose their power there is fear and doubt. People who experience this dread and anxiety should seek the God above the discredited "God" of a theism which has lost its symbolic force.

When Tillich was speaking to laypeople, he preferred to replace the rather technical term "Ground of being" with "ultimate concern." He emphasized that the human experience of faith in this "God above God" was not a peculiar state distinguishable from others in our emotional or intellectual experience. You could not say: "I am now having a special 'religious' experience," since the God which is Being precedes and is fundamental to all our emotions of courage, hope and despair. It was not a distinct state with a name of its own but pervaded each one of our normal human experiences. A century earlier Feuerbach had made a similar claim when he had said that God was inseparable from normal human psychology. Now this atheism had been transformed into a new theism.

Liberal theologians were trying to discover whether it was possible to believe and to belong to the modern intellectual world. In forming their new conception of God, they turned to other disciplines: science, psychology, sociology and other religions. Again, there was nothing new in this attempt. Origen and Clement of Alexandria had been Liberal Christians in this sense in the third century when they had introduced Platonism into the Semitic religion of Yahweh. Now the Jesuit Pierre Teilhard de Chardin (1881–1955) combined his belief in God with modern science. He was a paleontologist with a special interest in prehistoric life and drew upon his understanding of evolution to write a new theology. He saw the whole evolutionary struggle as a divine force which propelled the universe from matter to spirit to personality and, finally, beyond personality to God. God was immanent and incarnate in the world, which had become a sacrament of his presence. De Chardin suggested that instead of concentrating on Jesus the man, Christians should cultivate the cosmic portrait of Christ in Paul's epistles to the Colossians and Ephesians: Christ in this view was the "omega point" of the universe, the climax of the evolutionary process when God becomes all in all. Scripture tells us that God is love, and science shows that the natural world progresses towards ever-greater complexity *and* to greater unity in this variety. This unity-in-differentiation was another way of regarding the love that animates the whole of creation. De Chardin has been criticized for identifying God so thoroughly with the world that all sense of his transcendence was lost, but his this-worldly theology was a welcome change from the *contemptus mundi* which had so often characterized Catholic spirituality.

In the United States during the 1960s, Daniel Day Williams (b. 1910) evolved what is known as Process theology, which also stressed God's unity with the world. He had been greatly influenced by the British philosopher A. N. Whitehead (1861–1947), who had seen God as inextricably bound up with the world process. Whitehead had been able to make no sense of God as an-other Being, self-contained and impassible, but had formulated a twentieth-century version of the prophetic idea of God's pathos:

> I affirm that God does suffer as he participates in the ongoing life of the society of being. His sharing in the world's suffering is the supreme instance of knowing, accepting, and transforming in love the suffering which arises in the world. I am affirming the divine sensitivity. Without it, I can make no sense of the being of God.[8]

He described God as "the great companion, the fellow-sufferer, who understands." Williams liked Whitehead's definition; he liked to speak of God as the "behavior" of the world or an "event."[9] It was wrong to set the supernatural order over against the natural world of our experience. There was only one order of being. This was not reductionist, however. In our concept of the natural we should include *all* the aspirations, capacities and potential that had once seemed miraculous. It would also include our "religious experiences," as Buddhists had always affirmed. When asked whether he thought God was separate from nature, Williams would reply that he was not sure. He hated the old Greek idea of *apatheia*, which he found almost blasphemous: it presented God as remote, uncaring and selfish. He denied that he was advocating pantheism. His theology was simply trying to correct an imbalance, which had resulted in an alienating God which was impossible to accept after Auschwitz and Hiroshima.

Others were less optimistic about the achievements of the modern world and wanted to retain the transcendence of God as a challenge to men and women. The Jesuit Karl Rahner has developed a more transcendental theology, which sees God as the supreme mystery and Jesus as the decisive manifestation of what humanity can become. Bernard Lonergan also emphasized the importance of transcendence and of thought as opposed to experience. The unaided intellect cannot reach the vision it seeks: it is continually coming up against barriers to understanding that demand that we change our attitudes. In all cultures, human beings have been driven by the same imperatives: to be intelligent, responsible, reasonable, loving and, if necessary, to change. The very nature of humanity, therefore, demands that we transcend ourselves and our current perceptions, and this principle indicates the presence of what has been called the divine in the very nature of serious human inquiry. Yet the Swiss theologian Hans Urs von Balthasar believes that instead of seeking God in logic and abstractions, we should look to art: Catholic revelation has been essentially Incarnational. In brilliant studies of Dante and Bonaventure, Balthasar shows that Catholics have "seen" God in human form. Their emphasis on beauty in the gestures of ritual, drama and in the great Catholic artists indicates that God is to be found by the senses and not simply by the more cerebral and abstracted parts of the human person.

Muslims and Jews have also attempted to look back to the past to find ideas of God that will suit the present. Abu al-Kalam Azad (d. 1959), a notable Pakistani theologian, turned to the Koran to find a way of seeing God that was not so transcendent that he became a nullity and not so personal that he became an idol. He pointed to the symbolic nature of the Koranic discourse, noting the balance between metaphorical, figurative and anthropomorphic descriptions, on the one hand, and the constant reminders that God is incomparable on the other. Others have looked back to the Sufis for insight into God's relationship with the world. The Swiss Sufi Frithjof Schuon revived the doctrine of the Oneness of Being *(Wahdat al-Wujud)* later attributed to Ibn al-Arabi, which asserted that since God is the *only* reality, nothing exists but him, and the world itself is properly divine. He qualifies this with the reminder that this is an esoteric truth and can only be understood in the context of the mystical disciplines of Sufism.

Others have made God more accessible to the people and relevant to the political challenge of the time. In the years leading up to the Iranian revolution, the young lay philosopher Dr. Ali Shariati drew enormous crowds from among the educated middle classes. He was largely responsible for recruiting them against the shah, even though the mullahs disapproved of a good deal of his religious message. During demonstrations, the crowds used to carry his portrait alongside those of the Ayatollah Khomeini, even though it is not clear how he would have fared in Khomeini's Iran. Shariati was convinced that Westernization had alienated Muslims from their cultural roots and that to heal this disorder they must reinterpret the old symbols of their faith. Muhammad had done the same when he had given the ancient pagan rites of the *hajj* a monotheistic relevance. In his own book *Hajj*, Shariati took his readers through the pilgrimage to Mecca, gradually articulating a dynamic conception of God which each pilgrim had to create imaginatively for him- or herself. Thus, on reaching the Kabah, pilgrims would realize how suitable it was that the shrine is empty: "This is not your final destination; the Kabah is a sign so that the way is not lost; it only shows you the direction."[10] The Kabah witnessed to the importance of transcending all human expressions of the divine, which must not become ends in themselves. Why is the Kabah a simple cube, without decoration or ornament? Because it represents "the secret of God in the universe: God is shapeless, colorless, without simularity, whatever form or condition mankind selects, sees or imagines, it is not God."[11] The *hajj* itself was the antithesis of the alienation experienced by so many Iranians in the postcolonial period. It represents the existential course of each human being who turns his or her life around and directs it toward the ineffable God. Shariati's activist faith was dangerous: the Shah's secret police tortured and deported him and may even have been responsible for his death in London in 1977.

Martin Buber (1878–1965) had an equally dynamic vision of Judaism as a spiritual process and a striving for elemental unity. Religion consisted entirely of an encounter with a personal God, which nearly always took place in our meetings with other human beings. There were two spheres: one the realm of space and time where we relate to other beings as subject and object, as I-It. In the second realm, we relate to others as they truly are, seeing them as ends in themselves. This is the I-Thou realm, which reveals the presence of God. Life was an endless dialogue with God, which does not endanger our freedom or creativity, since God never tells us *what* he is asking of us. We experience him simply as a presence and an imperative and have to work out the meaning for ourselves. This meant a break with much Jewish tradition, and Buber's exegesis of traditional texts is sometimes strained. As a Kantian, Buber had no time for Torah, which he found alienating: God was not a lawgiver! The I-Thou encounter meant freedom and spontaneity, not the weight of a past tradition. Yet the *mitzvot* are central to much Jewish spirituality, and this may explain why Buber has been more popular with Christians than with Jews.

Buber realized that the term "God" had been soiled and degraded, but he refused to relinquish it. "Where would I find a word to equal it, to describe the same reality?" It bears too great and a complex a meaning, has too many sacred associations. Those who do reject the word "God" must be respected, since so many appalling things have been done in its name.

> It is easy to understand why there are some who propose a period of silence about "the last things" so that the misused words may be redeemed. But this is not the way to redeem them. We cannot clean up the term "God" and we cannot make it whole; but, stained and mauled as it is, we can raise it from the ground and set it above an hour of great sorrow. [12]

Unlike the other rationalists, Buber was not opposed to myth: he found Lurianic myth of the divine sparks trapped in the world to be of crucial symbolic significance. The separation of the sparks from the Godhead represent the human experience of alienation. When we relate to others, we will restore the primal unity and reduce the alienation in the world.

Where Buber looked back to the Bible and Hasidism, Abraham Joshua Heschel (1907–72) returned to the spirit of the Rabbis and the Talmud. Unlike Buber, he believed that the *mitzvot* would help Jews to counter the dehumanizing aspects of modernity. They were actions that fulfilled God's need rather than our own. Modern life was characterized by depersonalization and exploitation: even God was reduced to a thing to be manipulated and made to serve our purposes. Consequently religion became dull and insipid; we needed a "depth theology" to delve below the structures and recover the original awe, mystery and wonder. It was no use trying to prove God's existence logically. Faith in God sprang from an immediate apprehension that had nothing to do with concepts and rationality. The Bible must be read metaphorically like poetry if it is to yield that sense of the sacred. The *mitzvot* should also be seen as symbolic gestures that train us to live in God's presence. Each *mitzvah* is a place of encounter in the tiny details of mundane life and, like a work of art, the world of the *mitzvot* has its own logic and rhythm. Above all, we should be aware that God needs human beings. He is not the remote God of the philosophers but the God of pathos described by the prophets.

Atheistic philosophers have also been attracted by the idea of God during the second half of the twentieth century. In *Being and Time* (1927) Martin Heidegger (1899–1976) saw Being in rather the same way as Tillich, though he would have denied that it was "God" in the Christian sense: it was distinct from particular beings and quite separate from the normal categories of thought. Some Christians have been inspired by Heidegger's work, even though its moral value is called into question by his association with the Nazi regime. In *What Is Metaphysics?*, his inaugural lecture at Freiburg, Heidegger developed a number of ideas that had already surfaced in the work of Plotinus, Denys and Erigena. Since Being is "Wholly Other," it is in fact Nothing—no thing, neither an object nor a particular being. Yet it is what makes all other existence possible. The ancients had believed that nothing came from nothing, but Heidegger reversed this maxim: *ex nihilo omne qua ens fit.* He ended his lecture by posing a question asked by Leibniz: "Why are there beings at all, rather than just nothing?" It is a question that evokes the shock of surprise and wonder that has been a constant in the human response to the world: why should anything exist at all? In his *Introduction to Metaphysics* (1953), Heidegger began by asking the same question. Theology believed that it had the answer and traced everything back to Something Else, to God. But this God was just another being rather than something that was wholly other. Heidegger had a somewhat reductive idea of the God of religion—though one shared by many religious people—but he often spoke in mystical terms about Being. He speaks of it as a great paradox; describes the thinking process as a waiting or listening to Being and seems to experience a return and withdrawal of Being, rather as mystics feel the absence of God. There is nothing that human beings can do to think Being into existence. Since the Greeks, people in the Western world have tended to forget Being and have concentrated on beings instead, a process that has resulted in its modern technological success. In the article written toward the end of his life titled "Only a God Can Save Us," Heidegger suggested that the experience of God's absence in our time could liberate us from preoccupation with beings. But there was nothing we could do to bring Being back into the present. We could only hope for a new advent in the future.

The Marxist philosopher Ernst Bloch (1885–1977) saw the idea of God as natural to humanity. The whole of human life was directed toward the future: we experience our lives as incomplete and unfinished. Unlike animals, we are never satisfied but always want more. It is this which has forced us to think and develop, since at each point of our lives we must transcend ourselves and go on to the next stage: the baby must become a toddler, the toddler must overcome its disabilities and become a child, and so forth. All our dreams and aspirations look ahead to what is to come. Even philosophy begins with wonder, which is the experience of the not-knowing, the not-yet. Socialism also looks forward to utopia, but, despite the Marxist rejection of faith, where there is hope there is also religion. Like Feuerbach, Bloch saw God as the human ideal that has not yet come to be, but instead of seeing this as alienating he found it essential to the human condition.

Max Horkheimer (1895–1973), the German social theorist of the Frankfurt school, also saw "God" as an important ideal in a way that was reminiscent of the prophets. Whether he existed or not or whether we "believe in him" is superfluous. Without the idea of God there is no absolute meaning, truth or morality: ethics becomes simply a question of taste, a mood or a whim. Unless politics and morality somehow include the idea of "God," they will remain pragmatic and shrewd rather than wise. If there is no absolute, there is no reason that we should not hate or that war is worse than peace. Religion is essentially an inner feeling that there *is* a God. One of our earliest dreams is a longing for justice (how frequently we hear children complain: "It's not fair!"). Religion records the aspirations and accusations of innumerable human beings in the face of suffering and wrong. It makes us aware of our finite nature; we all hope that the injustice of the world will not be the last word.

The fact that people who have no conventional religious beliefs should keep returning to central themes that we have discovered in the history of God indicates that the idea is not as alien as many of us assume. Yet during the second half of the twentieth century, there has been a move away from the idea of a personal God who behaves like a larger version of us. There is nothing new about this. As we have seen, the Jewish scriptures, which

Christians call their "Old" Testament, show a similar process; the Koran saw al-Lah in less personal terms than the Judeo-Christian tradition from the very beginning. Doctrines such as the Trinity and the mythology and symbolism of the mystical systems all strove to suggest that God was beyond personality. Yet this does not seem to have been made clear to many of the faithful. When John Robinson, Bishop of Woolwich, published *Honest to God* in 1963, stating that he could no longer subscribe to the old personal God "out there," there was uproar in Britain. A similar furor has greeted various remarks by David Jenkins, Bishop of Durham, even though these ideas are commonplace in academic circles. Don Cupitt, Dean of Emmanuel College, Cambridge, has also been dubbed "the atheist priest": he finds the traditional realistic God of theism unacceptable and proposes a form of Christian Buddhism, which puts religious experience before theology. Like Robinson, Cupitt has arrived intellectually at an insight that mystics in all three faiths have reached by a more intuitive route. Yet the idea that God does not really exist and that there is Nothing out there is far from new.

There is a growing intolerance of inadequate images of the Absolute. This is a healthy iconoclasm, since the idea of God has been used in the past to disastrous effect. One of the most characteristic new developments since the 1970s has been the rise of a type of religiosity that we usually call "fundamentalism" in most of the major world religions, including the three religions of God. A highly political spirituality, it is literal and intolerant in its vision. In the United States, which has always been prone to extremist and apocalyptic enthusiasm, Christian fundamentalism has attached itself to the New Right. Fundamentalists campaign for the abolition of legal abortion and for a hard line on moral and social decency. Jerry Falwell's Moral Majority achieved astonishing political power during the Reagan years. Other evangelists such as Maurice Cerullo, taking Jesus' remarks literally, believe that miracles are an essential hallmark of true faith. God will give the believer anything that he asks for in prayer. In Britain, fundamentalists such as Colin Urquhart have made the same claim. Christian fundamentalists seem to have little regard for the loving compassion of Christ. They are swift to condemn the people they see as the "enemies of God." Most would consider Jews and Muslims destined for hellfire, and Urquhart has argued that all oriental religions are inspired by the devil.

There have been similar developments in the Muslim world, which have been much publicized in the West. Muslim fundamentalists have toppled governments and either assassinated or threatened the enemies of Islam with the death penalty. Similarly, Jewish fundamentalists have settled in the Occupied Territories of the West Bank and the Gaza Strip with the avowed intention of driving out the Arab inhabitants, using force if necessary. Thus they believe that they are paving a way for the advent of the Messiah, which is at hand. In all its forms, fundamentalism is a fiercely reductive faith. Thus Rabbi Meir Kahane, the most extreme member of Israel's Far Right until his assassination in New York in 1990:

> There are not several messages in Judaism. There is only one. And this mes-
> sage is to do what God wants. Sometimes God wants us to go to war, some-
> times he wants us to live in peace. . . . But there is only one message: God
> wanted us to come to this country to create a Jewish state.[13]

This wipes out centuries of Jewish development, returning to the Deuteron-
omist perspective of the Book of Joshua. It is not surprising that people who
hear this kind of profanity, which makes "God" deny other people's human
rights, think that the sooner we relinquish him the better.

Yet [. . .], this type of religiosity is actually a retreat from God. To make
such human, historical phenomena as Christian "Family Values," "Islam" or
"the Holy Land" the focus of religious devotion is a new form of idolatry.
This type of belligerent righteousness has been a constant temptation to
monotheists throughout the long history of God. It must be rejected as inauthentic. The God of Jews, Christians and Muslims got off to an unfortunate
start, since the tribal deity Yahweh was murderously partial to his own people. Latter-day crusaders who return to this primitive ethos are elevating the
values of the tribe to an unacceptably high status and substituting man-
made ideals for the transcendent reality which should challenge our prejudices. They are also denying a crucial monotheistic theme. Ever since the
prophets of Israel reformed the old pagan cult of Yahweh, the God of
monotheists has promoted the ideal of compassion.

[. . .] Compassion was a characteristic of most of the ideologies that were
created during the Axial Age. The compassionate ideal even impelled Buddhists to make a major change in their religious orientation when they introduced devotion (bhakti) to the Buddha and bodhisattvas. The prophets
insisted that cult and worship were useless unless society as a whole
adopted a more just and compassionate ethos. These insights were developed by Jesus, Paul and the Rabbis, who all shared the same Jewish ideals
and suggested major changes in Judaism in order to implement them. The
Koran made the creation of a compassionate and just society the essence of
the reformed religion of al-Lah. Compassion is a particularly difficult virtue.
It demands that we go beyond the limitations of our egotism, insecurity and
inherited prejudice. Not surprisingly, there have been times when all three
of the God-religions have failed to achieve these high standards. During the
eighteenth century, deists rejected traditional Western Christianity largely
because it had become so conspicuously cruel and intolerant. The same will
hold good today. All too often, conventional believers, who are not fundamentalists, share their aggressive righteousness. They use "God" to prop up
their own loves and hates, which they attribute to God himself. But Jews,
Christians and Muslims who punctiliously attend divine services yet deni-
grate people who belong to different ethnic and ideological camps deny one
of the basic truths of their religion. It is equally inappropriate for people
who call themselves Jews, Christians and Muslims to condone an in-

equitable social system. The God of historical monotheism demands mercy not sacrifice, compassion rather than decorous liturgy.

There has often been a distinction between people who practice a cultic form of religion and those who have cultivated a sense of the God of compassion. The prophets fulminated against their contemporaries who thought that temple worship was sufficient. Jesus and St. Paul both made it clear that external observance was useless if it was not accompanied by charity: it was little better than sounding brass or a tinkling cymbal. Muhammad came into conflict with those Arabs who wanted to worship the pagan goddesses alongside al-Lah in the ancient rites, without implementing the compassionate ethos that God demanded as a condition of all true religion. There had been a similar divide in the pagan world of Rome: the old cultic religion celebrated the status quo, while the philosophers preached a message that they believed would change the world. It may be that the compassionate religion of the One God has only been observed by a minority; most have found it difficult to face the extremity of the God-experience with its uncompromising ethical demands. Ever since Moses brought the tablets of the Law from Mount Sinai, the majority have preferred the worship of a Golden Calf, a traditional, unthreatening image of a deity they have constructed for themselves, with its consoling, time-honored rituals. Aaron, the high priest, presided over the manufacture of the golden effigy. The religious establishment itself is often deaf to the inspiration of prophets and mystics who bring news of a much more demanding God.

God can also be used as an unworthy panacea, as an alternative to mundane life and as the object of indulgent fantasy. The idea of God has frequently been used as the opium of the people. This is a particular danger when he is conceived as an-other Being—just like us, only bigger and better—in his own heaven, which is itself conceived as a paradise of earthly delights. Yet originally, "God" was used to help people to concentrate on this world and to face up to unpleasant reality. Even the pagan cult of Yahweh, for all its manifest faults, stressed his involvement in current events in profane time, as opposed to the sacred time of rite and myth. The prophets of Israel forced their people to confront their own social culpability and impending political catastrophe in the name of the God who revealed himself in these historical occurrences. The Christian doctrine of Incarnation stressed the divine immanence in the world of flesh and blood. Concern for the here and now was especially marked in Islam: nobody could have been more of a realist than Muhammad, who was a political as well as a spiritual genius. As we have seen, later generations of Muslims have shared his concern to incarnate the divine will in human history by establishing a just and decent society. From the very beginning, God was experienced as an imperative to action. From the moment when—as either El or Yahweh—God called Abraham away from his family in Haran, the cult entailed concrete action in this world and often a painful abandonment of the old sanctities.

This dislocation also involved great strain. The Holy God, who was wholly other, was experienced as a profound shock by the prophets. He demanded a similar holiness and separation on the part of his people. When he spoke to Moses on Sinai, the Israelites were not allowed to approach the foot of the mountain. An entirely new gulf suddenly yawned between humanity and the divine, rupturing the holistic vision of paganism. There was, therefore, a potential for alienation from the world, which reflected a dawning consciousness of the inalienable autonomy of the individual. It is no accident that monotheism finally took root during the exile to Babylon, when the Israelites also developed the ideal of personal responsibility, which has been crucial in both Judaism and Islam.[14] [. . .] The Rabbis used the idea of an immanent God to help Jews to cultivate a sense of the sacred rights of the human personality. Yet alienation has continued to be a danger in all three faiths: in the West the experience of God was continually accompanied by guilt and by a pessimistic anthropology. In Judaism and Islam there is no doubt that the observance of Torah and Shariah has sometimes been seen as a heteronymous compliance with an external law, even though we have seen that nothing could have been further from the intention of the men who compiled these legal codes.

Those atheists who preached emancipation from a God who demands such servile obedience were protesting against an inadequate but unfortunately familiar image of God. Again, this was based on a conception of the divine that was too personalistic. It interpreted the scriptural image of God's judgment too literally and assumed that God was a sort of Big Brother in the sky. This image of the divine Tyrant imposing an alien law on his unwilling human servants has to go. Terrorizing the populace into civic obedience with threats is no longer acceptable or even practicable, as the downfall of communist regimes demonstrated so dramatically in the autumn of 1989. The anthropomorphic idea of God as Lawgiver and Ruler is not adequate to the temper of post-modernity. Yet the atheists who complained that the idea of God was unnatural were not entirely correct. [. . .] Jews, Christians and Muslims have developed remarkably similar ideas of God, which also resemble other conceptions of the Absolute. When people try to find an ultimate meaning and value in human life, their minds seem to go in a certain direction. They have not been coerced to do this; it is something that seems natural to humanity.

Yet if feelings are not to degenerate into indulgent, aggressive or unhealthy emotionalism, they need to be informed by the critical intelligence. The experience of God must keep abreast of other current enthusiasms, including those of the mind. The experiment of Falsafah was an attempt to relate faith in God with the new cult of rationalism among Muslims, Jews and, later, Western Christians. Eventually Muslims and Jews retreated from philosophy. Rationalism, they decided, had its uses, especially in such empirical studies as science, medicine and mathematics, but it was not entirely appropriate in the discussion of a God who lay beyond concepts. The Greeks had already sensed this and developed an early distrust of their native metaphysics. One of the drawbacks of the philosophic method of discussing God was that it could make it sound as though the Supreme Deity were simply an-other Being, the highest of all the things that exist, instead of a reality of an entirely different order. Yet the venture of Falsafah was important, since it showed an appreciation of the necessity of relating God to other experiences—if only to define the extent to which this was possible. To push God into intellectual isolation in a holy ghetto of his own is unhealthy and unnatural. It can encourage people to think that it is not necessary to apply normal standards of decency and rationality to behavior supposedly inspired by "God."

From the first, Falsafah had been associated with science. It was their initial enthusiasm for medicine, astronomy and mathematics which had led the first Muslim Faylasufs to discuss al-Lah in metaphysical terms. Science had effected a major change in their outlook, and they found that they could not think of God in the same way as their fellow Muslims. The philosophic conception of God was markedly different from the Koranic vision, but Faylasufs did recover some insights that were in danger of being lost in the *ummah* at that time. Thus the Koran had an extremely positive attitude to other religious traditions: Muhammad had not believed that he was founding a new, exclusive religion and considered that all rightly guided faith came from the One God. By the ninth century, however, the *ulema* were beginning to lose sight of this and were promoting the cult of Islam as the one true religion. The Faylasufs reverted to the older universalist approach, even though they reached it by a different route. We have a similar opportunity today. In our scientific age, we cannot think about God in the same way as our forebears, but the challenge of science could help us to appreciate some old truths.

[. . .] Albert Einstein had an appreciation of mystical religion. Despite his famous remarks about God not playing dice, he did not believe that his theory of relativity should affect the conception of God. During a visit to England in 1921, Einstein was asked by the Archbishop of Canterbury what were its implications for theology. He replied: "None. Relativity is a purely scientific matter and has nothing to do with religion."[15] When Christians are dismayed by such scientists as Stephen Hawking, who can find no room for God in his cosmology, they are perhaps still thinking of God in anthropomorphic terms as a Being who created the world in the same way as we would. Yet creation was not originally conceived in such a literal manner. Interest in Yahweh as Creator did not enter Judaism until the exile to Babylon. It was a conception that was alien to the Greek world: creation *ex nihilo* was not an official doctrine of Christianity until the Council of Nicaea in 341. Creation is a central teaching of the Koran, but, like all its utterances about God, this is said to be a "parable" or a "sign" (*aya*) of an ineffable truth. Jewish and Muslim rationalists found it a difficult and problematic doctrine, and many rejected it. Sufis and Kabbalists all preferred the Greek metaphor of emanation. In any case, cosmology was not a scientific description of the origins of the world but was originally a symbolic expression of a spiritual and psychological truth. There is consequently little agitation about the new science in the Muslim world: [. . .] the events of recent history have been more of a threat than has science to the traditional conception of God. In the West, however, a more literal understanding of scripture has long prevailed. When some Western Christians feel their faith in God undermined by the new science, they are probably imagining God as Newton's great Mechanick, a personalistic notion of God which should, perhaps, be rejected on religious as well as on scientific grounds. The challenge of science might shock the churches into a fresh appreciation of the symbolic nature of scriptural narrative.

The idea of a personal God seems increasingly unacceptable at the present time for all kinds of reasons: moral, intellectual, scientific and spiritual. Feminists are also repelled by a personal deity who, because of "his" gender, has been male since his tribal, pagan days. Yet to talk about "she"—other than in a dialectical way—can be just as limiting, since it confines the illimitable God to a purely human category. The old metaphysical notion of God as the Supreme Being, which has long been popular in the West, is also felt to be unsatisfactory. The God of the philosophers is the product of a now outdated rationalism, so the traditional "proofs" of his existence no longer work. The widespread acceptance of the God of the philosophers by the deists of the Enlightenment can be seen as the first step to the current atheism. Like the old Sky God, this deity is so remote from humanity and the mundane world that he easily becomes *Deus Otiosus* and fades from our consciousness.

The God of the mystics might seem to present a possible alternative. The mystics have long insisted that God is not an-Other Being; they have claimed that he does not really exist and that it is better to call him Nothing. This God is in tune with the atheistic mood of our secular society, with its distrust of inadequate images of the Absolute. Instead of seeing God as an objective Fact, which can be demonstrated by means of scientific proof, mystics have claimed that he is a subjective experience, mysteriously experienced in the ground of being. This God is to be approached through the imagination and can be seen as a kind of art form, akin to the other great artistic symbols that have expressed the ineffable mystery, beauty and value of life. Mystics have used music, dancing, poetry, fiction, stories, painting, sculpture and architecture to express this Reality that goes beyond concepts. Like all art, however, mysticism requires intelligence, discipline and self-criticism as a safeguard against indulgent emotionalism and projection. The God of the mystics could even satisfy the feminists, since both Sufis and Kabbalists have long tried to introduce a female element into the divine.

There are drawbacks, however. Mysticism has been regarded with some suspicion by many Jews and Muslims since the Shabbetai Zevi fiasco and the decline of latter-day Sufism. In the West, mysticism has never been a mainstream religious enthusiasm. The Protestant and Catholic Reformers either outlawed or marginalized it, and the scientific Age of Reason did not encourage this mode of perception. Since the 1960s, there has been a fresh interest in mysticism, expressed in the enthusiasm for Yoga, meditation and Buddhism, but it is not an approach that easily consorts with our objective, empirical mentality. The God of the mystics is not easy to apprehend. It requires long training with an expert and a considerable investment of time. The mystic has to work hard to acquire this sense of the reality known as God (which many have refused to name). Mystics often insist that human beings must deliberately create this sense of God for themselves, with the same degree of care and attention that others devote to artistic creation. It is not something that is likely to appeal to people in a society which has become used to speedy gratification, fast food and instant communication. The God of the mystics does not arrive readymade and prepackaged. He cannot be experienced as quickly as the instant ecstasy created by a revivalist preacher, who quickly has a whole congregation clapping its hands and speaking in tongues.

It is possible to acquire some of the mystical attitudes. Even if we are incapable of the higher states of consciousness achieved by a mystic, we can learn that God does not exist in any simplistic sense, for example, or that the very word "God" is only a symbol of a reality that ineffably transcends it. The mystical agnosticism could help us to acquire a restraint that stops us rushing into these complex matters with dogmatic assurance. But if these notions are not felt upon the pulse and personally appropriated, they are likely to seem meaningless abstractions. Secondhand mysticism could prove to be unsatisfactory as reading the explanation of a poem by a literary critic instead of the original. [. . .] Mysticism was often seen as an esoteric discipline, not because the mystics wanted to exclude the vulgar herd but because these truths could only be perceived by the intuitive part of the mind after special training. They mean something different when they are approached by this particular route, which is not accessible to the logical, rationalist faculty.

Ever since the prophets of Israel started to ascribe their own feelings and experiences to God, monotheists have in some sense created a God for themselves. God has rarely been seen as a self-evident fact that can be encountered like any other objective existent. Today many people seem to have lost the will to make this imaginative effort. This need not be a catastrophe. When religious ideas have lost their validity, they have usually faded away painlessly: if the human idea of God no longer works for us in the empirical age, it will be discarded. Yet in the past people have always created new symbols to act as a focus for spirituality. Human beings have always created a faith for themselves, to cultivate their sense of the wonder and ineffable significance of life. The aimlessness, alienation, anomie and violence that characterize so much of modern life seem to indicate that now that they are not deliberately creating a faith in "God" or anything else—it matters little what—many people are falling into despair.

In the United States, [. . .] ninety-nine percent of the population claim to believe in God, yet the prevalence of fundamentalism, apocalypticism and "instant" charismatic forms of religiosity in America is not reassuring. The escalating crime rate, drug addiction and the revival of the death penalty are not signs of a spiritually healthy society. In Europe there is a growing blankness where God once existed in the human consciousness. One of the first people to express this dry desolation—quite different from the heroic atheism of Nietzsche—was Thomas Hardy. In "The Darkling Thrush," written on December 30, 1900, at the turn of the twentieth century, he expressed the death of spirit that was no longer able to create a faith in life's meaning:

I leant upon a coppice gate
    When Frost was spectre-grey
And Winter's dregs made desolate
    The weakening eye of day.
The tangled bine-stems scored the sky
    Like strings of broken lyres,
And all mankind that haunted nigh
    Had sought their household fires.

The land's sharp features seemed to be
    The Century's corpse outleant,
His crypt the cloudy canopy,
    The wind his death-lament.
The ancient pulse of germ and birth
    Was shrunken hard and dry,
And every spirit upon earth
    Seemed fervourless as I.

At once a voice arose among
    The bleak twigs overhead
In a full-hearted evensong
    Of joy illimited;
An aged thrush, frail, gaunt, and small,
    In blast-beruffled plume,
Had chosen thus to fling his soul
    Upon the growing gloom.

So little cause for carolings
    Of such ecstatic sound
Was written on terrestrial things
    Afar or nigh around,
That I could think there trembled through
    His happy good-night air
Some blessed Hope, whereof he knew
    And I was unaware.

Human beings cannot endure emptiness and desolation; they will fill the vacuum by creating a new focus of meaning. The idols of fundamentalism are not good substitutes for God; if we are to create a vibrant new faith for the twenty-first century, we should, perhaps, ponder the history of God for some lessons and warnings. ■

NOTES

1. Peter Berger, *A Rumour of Angels* (London, 1970), p. 58.
2. A. J. Ayer, *Language, Truth and Logic* (Harmondsworth, 1974), p. 152.
3. Wilfred Cantwell Smith, *Belief and History* (Charlottesville, 1985), p. 10.
4. Thomas J. J. Altizer, *The Gospel of Christian Atheism* (London, 1966), p. 136.
5. Paul Van Buren, *The Secular Meaning of the Gospel* (London, 1963), p. 138.
6. Richard L. Rubenstein, *After Auschwitz, Radical Theology and Contemporary Judaism* (Indianapolis, 1966), passim.
7. Paul Tillich, *Theology and Culture* (New York and Oxford, 1964), p. 129.
8. Alfred North Whitehead, "Suffering and Being," in *Adventures of Ideas* (Harmondsworth, 1942), pp. 191–92.
9. *Process and Reality* (Cambridge, 1929), p. 497.
10. Ali Shariati, *Hajj,* trans. Laleh Bakhtiar (Teheran, 1988), p. 46.
11. Ibid., p. 48.
12. Martin Buber, "Gottesfinsternis, Betrachtungen zur Beziehung zwischen Religion und Philosophie," quoted in Hans Kung, *Does God Exist? An Answer for Today,* trans. Edward Quinn, (London, 1978), p. 508.
13. Quoted in Raphael Mergui and Philippa Simmonot, *Israel's Ayatollahs; Meir Kahane and the Far Right in Israel* (London, 1987), p. 43.
14. Personal responsibility is also important in Christianity, of course, but Judaism and Islam have stressed it by their lack of a mediating priesthood, a perspective that was recovered by the Protestant Reformers.
15. Philipp Frank, *Einstein: His Life and Times* (New York, 1947), pp. 189–90.

■ *QUESTIONS FOR MAKING CONNECTIONS WITHIN THE READING* ■

1. Armstrong's title poses a question: Does God have a future? A more conventional writer might answer that question with a "Yes" or a "No," supported by a series of arguments. But Armstrong does something else, demonstrating an approach some readers might find unexpected in the context of a "philosophical" issue. How would you characterize this approach? Is the absence of a final answer consistent with Armstrong's approach, or does it call that approach into doubt?

2. By means of direct quotation and paraphrase, many thinkers make their voices heard through Armstrong's own words. At times, this chorus of voices may become so closely fused that readers might have trouble

distinguishing Armstrong's own views from the views of the thinkers she draws on. At what moments in the argument does Armstrong speak for herself, and at what moments do other writers speak through her words? Would you say that her accounts of other writers' views are uniformly neutral, or are there places where Armstrong's descriptions become more openly evaluative?

3. How has Armstrong organized this chapter? Why does she start where she does? What is her criteria for choosing examples? Why does she end where she does? Is she making an argument or offering a neutral description of the way things are?

■ QUESTIONS FOR WRITING ■

1. Would you say Armstrong herself believes in God? What does "belief" mean to her? What does "God" mean? In what ways does her understanding of religion differ from those you have held or may now hold? Does the word God become nonsensical if people from different times and places have understood it in different ways?

2. Armstrong concludes her argument by citing Thomas Hardy's poem, "The Darkling Thrush," in its entirety. In what sense does Hardy's poem provide a conclusion to Armstrong's discussion? What does the poem have to say that Armstrong couldn't say for herself? Why has she given a poet the final word on the future of God?

■ QUESTIONS FOR MAKING CONNECTIONS BETWEEN READINGS ■

1. We might say that in "Waiting for a Jew: Marginal Redemption at the Eighth Street Shul," Jonathan Boyarin also takes on Armstrong's question, "Does God have a future?" But Boyarin poses the question in a rather different way, concerned less with the disappearance of God than with the disappearance of a community of believers. As he recalls, the religious community of his childhood is today "as obliterated as any *shtetl* in Eastern Europe." If the survival of God depends on the reinvention of such communities in the ways that Boyarin describes, then what are we to make of Armstrong's call for a turn away from a "personal God" and toward a more mystical religion? Will this turn renew waning communities of faith or will it only hasten their disappearance?

2. When Armstrong refers to the future of God, she has in mind primarily the notions of God embraced by theologians and philosophers in Western Europe and the United States. In "The Ganges' Next Life," however, Alexander Stille offers a portrait of religious life among Hindus in South

Asia. After reading both Armstrong and Stille, would you say that the "death of God" is a problem only for the West? What forces does Armstrong identify with the gradual decline of religious conviction? Given what Stille tells us about India, are those same forces at work in Veer Bhadra Mishra's world, or does his society face challenges very different from the ones that Armstrong describes?

For additional suggestions about making connections between readings, visit the Link-O-Mat and More Sample Assignments at <www. newhum.com>.

BENJAMIN R. BARBER

BENJAMIN R. BARBER, one of the most distinguished political theorists of our time, is the author of the international bestseller, *Jihad vs. McWorld: How Globalism and Tribalism Are Reshaping the World* (1995), the classic *Strong Democracy* (1984), and, most recently, *The Truth of Power: Intellectual Affairs in the Clinton White House* (2001), in which he draws on the six years he spent as an informal adviser to the president to show the limited influence intellectuals have on the shaping of public policy. The challenge for democratic leaders in the twenty-first century, Barber believes, will be to find ways for civil society to fulfill its responsibility to mediate between public and private, between community and individual, and between the power of public communities and the liberty of private individuals, a challenge made all the more difficult in a time when citizens and governments tend to confuse the freedom to shop with electoral democracy.

In the wake of the attacks of September 11, 2001, Barber's argument, first made in *Jihad vs. McWorld*, that the two greatest threats to democracy at the end of the twentieth century were religious fundamentalism and economic and cultural globalization now seems prophetic. If democracy is to survive into the twenty-first century and thrive as a form of mass political organization, Barber has argued recently, the United States, Britain, and their allies cannot simply defeat terrorism militarily; rather, these nations will all "have to open a second civic and democratic front aimed, not against terrorism 'per se,' but against the anarchism and social chaos—the economic reductionism and its commercializing homogeneity—that have created the climate of despair and hopelessness that terrorism has so effectively exploited."

Barber is currently Kekst Professor of Civil Society at the University of Maryland and one of the principal organizers of The Democracy Collaborative, an international consortium of the world's leading academic centers and citizen

---

Barber, Benjamin R. "Time, Work, and Leisure in a Civil Society." *A Place For Us: How to Make Society Civil and Democracy Strong.* New York: Hill and Wang, 1998. 124–147.

Biographical information drawn from materials available at the *Walt Whitman Center* <http://www.wwc.rutgers.edu>. Quotation taken from Benjamin R. Barber's "Ballots versus Bullets," *Financial Times*, Oct. 20, 2001 <http://www.christusrex.org/www1/icons/ barber.html>.

engagement organizations concerned with studying and promoting civil society. "Time, Work, and Leisure in a Civil Society," the concluding chapter in Barber's *A Place for Us: How to Make Society Civil and Democracy Strong* (1998), reflects on the crucial role that free time plays in nurturing a citizenry committed to avoiding the excesses of fundamentalism, on the one hand, and global capitalism, on the other.

To learn more about Benjamin R. Barber and the effort to sustain democratic societies, visit the Link-O-Mat at <www.newhum.com>.

Time, Work, and Leisure in a Civil Society

Work, leisure, and civil society compete for a single scarce resource: time. How often we complain that we simply do not have enough hours in the day for the myriad civic and volunteer activities of the third sector when we are through with the demands of the other two. Some people seem to run to work to find the social pleasures no longer available in high-pressured two- and three-job families, while even the socially responsible insist politics (defined as voting, jury service, and tax-paying) already requires of them more public work than their schedules can afford. Here we stumble on a series of paradoxes that seem at once to encumber and to amplify the promise of civil society.

The first is the economic reality of jobs vanishing at the very moment when we are reaffirming the ideology of work, calling the work ethic our core value in the politics of welfare reform. Unemployment may be down, but employability is replacing employment, serial job-holding has taken the place of a career, and outsourced and consultancy style work has been substituted for full-time in-house work. The net result of these stealth forms of downsizing and disemployment is a labor force that enjoys a "full employment" economy only because it struggles to stay afloat in an insecure new workplace defined by ever-changing part-time, unpensioned, sometime jobs, often two or three per worker or per family. Many universities, for example, have taken advantage of retiring tenured professors who, counting the generous health and retirement benefits package, were earning up to $150,000 a year to teach four courses, by replacing them with itinerant graduate students or Ph.D.s who earn $10,000 ($2,500 per course) per year. Such beneficiaries of the soaring economy must take two or three such positions just to make ends meet, and they face the prospect of a lifetime of such piecework and will have to teach in several different institutions, carrying course loads three or four times as onerous as those of their well-paid tenured "colleagues," but without health or retirement benefits. They will pursue academic "careers" with no tenure, no permanent home, no collegiality, no loyalty from or to their institutions, and no relationship to their students (who will also be getting short-changed). But they will be "employed," and their fragmented professional lives may even yield two or more "jobs" in the Labor Department's glowing annual statistical reports on the full-employment economy.

Employers will of course claim they are merely seeking new flexible arrangements, "but what this means in reality," says Sara Horowitz, the director of the advocacy group Working Today, "is people are working increasingly without benefits. They're working not only without health coverage but without the protections of the major labor legislation of this century: pensions, minimum wage, occupational safety, unemployment insurance, age discrimination. The list goes on."[1] Nearly half of the part-time work force say they want to work more, and involuntary part-timers make significantly less than those who work part-time out of choice.[2]

Among those who are employed, the gap between rich and poor grows. This huge divide between the extremely well paid minority and a hard-working but ever less secure majority defines the new economic reality. Hence, on the one hand, sociologists like William Julius Wilson demonstrate that poverty and urban breakdown are the consequence of the disappearance of inner-city jobs, and, on the other, economists like Jeremy Rifkin prophesy a far graver disappearance of work as we know it, and a painful transition to a "near-workerless information society."[3] Industrial and service firms continue to downsize, and the traditional responses to increased productivity—opening up new economic sectors, for example, as when farm disemployment was compensated by new industrial jobs, or continuing economic growth—have reached their limit. The new information technology, highly specialized and automated, needs nothing like the vast army of workers once employed in agriculture, industry, and the service sector. In this new "regime of production," where computers have "increased exponentially the 'multiplied productive powers' of labor," the "principal effect of technological change—labor displacement—is largely unmitigated by economic growth."[4]

Yet, at this very point, anti-government and anti-welfare ideologists are demanding that work be the focal point in our solution to problems of poverty and welfare; and even the most progressive reformers are responding to corporate downsizing and the export of jobs with a vigorous (often protectionist) call for the "creation of good jobs for Americans in the United States"[5]—this, despite the fact that, as the journalist Thomas Friedman has said, "the bulk of job loss today is produced by technological change and deregulation and only 29 percent can be attributed to freer trade."[6] Scarce jobs are even under pressure from America's growing prison population (1.1 million today, more than triple what it was in 1980); the costs of incarceration ($25 billion a year) are offset by putting inmates to work,[7] and it is as if criminals are being authorized to continue their careers in prison, "stealing" jobs from the civilian population. New workfare programs also skim jobs from the shallow pool at the bottom of the economic ladder.

The second paradox is that while many people are disemployed in our society, those who work seem to be working harder than ever, giving labor an even greater value, and making "unearned" leisure seem more odious than ever before. One-third of the working force work more than forty-five hours a week, up from one-quarter just a few years ago.[8] Those who do not work at all understandably respond to their enforced free time with anger, passivity, despondency, or despair, making them poor candidates (despite their "leisure time") for volunteer activities. The culture of work compels them to seek relief in employment rather than creative leisure. "Before I was working, I was depressed all the time. I couldn't sleep at night," says a typical welfare-to-work success. As society applauds her display of industry in her new job, she exults, "Nowadays, I sleep like a baby."[9] If the unemployed are sleepless in their idleness, those still employed are frantic in their industriousness, leaving themselves little time for family or relaxation, let alone the demanding activities of civil society. No wonder that while participation in annual sign-a-check style "membership" organizations is up, participation in organizations requiring time and effort is down.[10]

The third and final paradox turns on contradictions in the voluntary part of civil society itself. While volunteerism is still prevalent in the United States and growing impressively elsewhere, a deep prejudice argues against linking it to income or incentives of any kind. The ideology that rejects welfare without work also criticizes voluntarism for pay or for educational vouchers. (As we have seen, this was a leading criticism of President Clinton's Learn and Serve Program at the Corporation for National Service.) The ethical asymmetry here means that while you should not get something (pay) without giving something (working!), you also should not get anything for giving. At the very time when linking income to voluntary service, homemaking, or other types of public work could solve the problems of vanishing work in the traditional industrial and service sectors, ideology condemns the solution.

These paradoxes arise out of beliefs about the nature of work and of income, about labor and human dignity, that have persisted for more than a millennium. They set culture and mores against the very solutions that in fact lie at hand. They manifest a cultural lag in which our values are stalled in the nineteenth century as our economy enters the twenty-first. The rehabilitation of civil society is promised by economic changes but it is sorely challenged by this cultural lag.

It was not always thus. For most of our history, through a providential symmetry, work for pay simultaneously yielded the income needed for men and women to survive and the productivity needed for economies to flourish. In our civilization, work has thus endowed human life with meaning, dignity, and status. Since economic health has been a condition for, as well as a consequence of, the growth of democracy, work has also been seen as undergirding the virtues of a free society. This link is manifest in the classical connection between the Protestant lionization of industry, thrift, and work and the growth of capitalist democracy.

But what appears in our history as an ineluctable economic law is in fact little more than a coincidence. The symmetry between those two epic achievements—income for individual workers, productivity for society at large—may seem to express a powerful moral logic: if a person is to eat, then surely that person must labor. Yet the moral logic evolved to fit the economic necessity, and the economic necessity is largely circumstantial, the contingent result of inefficiency and the limited historical productivity of labor as simple animal effort. Consumption and production have been linked in the wage relationship, but the conditions of consuming and producing have not. People need wages to sustain the buying power upon which their consumption in a market society depends, but productivity does not necessarily need wage earners to sustain it. After all, the mythic Eden into which our species was imagined to have been born offered prosperity without labor and fecundity without pain. The promise of a future Eden in which productivity again is a gift of divine imagination has quickened the pulse of economic utopians ever since, all the way down to Marx and Engels and their heirs. Friedrich Engels imagined a lifting of the economic yoke in which

> anarchy in social production is replaced by systematic, definite organization. The struggle for individual existence disappears. Then for the first time man, in a certain sense, is finally marked off from the rest of the animal kingdom, and emerges from mere animal conditions of existence into really human ones. . . . It is the ascent of man from the kingdom of necessity to the kingdom of freedom.[11]

The utopians dream on, but the realists dream only of more work. The decoupling of consumption and production through increased labor productivity and the intervention of efficient machines, if it comes to pass as historical actuality, is likely to be disruptive rather than utopian, a prelude to global unemployment and the spread of poverty rather than to global freedom and the spread of a civic culture in which human beings loosen the bonds of nature and truly become its lords.[12] The journalist William Greider, like Stanley Aronowitz before him, gloomily awaits a convergence of "cheap people and expensive machines" which, he believes, will produce a persistent oversupply of goods and undersupply of consumption—a "bidding war for employment" that allows global corporations to descend to "the bottom of the global wage" supply where there is a "seemingly inexhaustible supply of new recruits."[13]

Greider's dilemma—too much efficiency, increasing "labor arbitrage," fewer and fewer jobs, less income for workers and thus less cash for consumption, and so an even greater oversupply—is not easily addressed. This seemingly natural symmetry of work and income, of labor and prosperity, has meant that political and moral systems have grown up around the normative centrality of labor. Work has anchored our value system and centered our civic culture from the earliest days of the modern era. Protestants associated work with virtue because they believed it was God's price for redemption in the face of human sinfulness; John Locke's liberalism made it the key to all value, which he understood to arise out of the mixing of our self-owned bodily labor with nature's bounty and which he therefore viewed as a projection of our essential selves into the inert materials of the common world. Marx took this Lockean "labor theory of value" and converted it into a rationale for revolution, arguing that if men had to labor to earn wages, they deserved full title to everything their labor had created, the "surplus value" or profit left over after all the costs of production were paid. In our democracy today, work serves as a vital key to status, dignity, income, republican virtue, and most of the other things our society values. As Judith Shklar observed in her last (and most original) book, *American Citizenship*, the classical notion of public virtue, which equated citizenship with politics (the sovereign and noblest form of human activity), was quickly superseded in America by a "vision of economic independence, of self-directed 'earning' as the ethical basis of citizenship." We are, she noted, "citizens only if we 'earn.'"[14]

To this day, then, our political and moral regime is predicated on the notion that to be a responsible human being is to work, to be engaged in the production of those goods necessary to our common flourishing—feeding our family and fueling prosperity. Hence the paradoxes of a threatened age after work, when what should appear as a promised liberation in fact looms as a calamity. Ideology is unable to catch up to economic progress, and both progressives and conservatives cling to work as the key to morality and citizenship. Even a progressive commoner like James Carville writes in his populist polemic *We're Right, They're Wrong!*, "work and training for work are core values. They are the values that built this country."[15] For William Julius Wilson, the source of the ghetto's poverty as well as its despair is neither racism nor the collapse of families but the disappearance of work. The remedy for economic nationalists, social progressives, and radical egalitarians is jobs, jobs, and more jobs: old jobs, new jobs, traditional jobs, reengineered jobs, full-time jobs, part-time jobs, essential jobs, make-work jobs.[16]

Nothing new here. Given the traditional value system, modern progressivism has always campaigned not just for political emancipation and electoral suffrage but for economic justice, for jobs, and for fair and equitable wages. In the same spirit, but with an inverted political spin, modern conservatism has campaigned to assure that women and men do a day's work in return for whatever benefits they receive from the government. If we are to be paid fairly for work, we must work fairly for our pay, especially if "pay" takes the form of welfare or other government benefits. Welfare's moral entailment is workfare.

The recent rebellion against government-sponsored welfare programs has been a rebellion against the notion that people, even (or especially!) if they are teens with illegitimate babies, should somehow receive the where-withal to live without "earning" it through work. "Earning" means doing paid labor, not homemaking or child-rearing or civic volunteering, not creating culture or enjoying freedom or filling leisure. Wages for labor in private-sector work has been the buckle linking work to income, labor to dignity, and employment to power and status. To work without adequate income is servitude of one kind, wage slavery, but to receive income without working is servitude of another: welfare dependency. These are the formulas by which the moral logic of work is played out in our democracy. This logic has turned our political parties into virtual twins, each devoted to one part of the formula linking income to "earning" and earning to work. Even when—other things being equal—we prefer that women stay at home with children ("family values"), we still believe that if the state pays the freight, mothers must carry the load and do something besides child care to "earn" their benefits. Work at private-sector jobs is obligatory. These moral calculations facilitated the economies of industrial-age societies in which labor power was still the key to productivity and growth, but they are disastrous for an information-age society where automation, robotics, and reengineering will offer productivity without labor and prosperity without jobs.

For all its seeming natural symmetry, the relationship between work and productivity has always been more contingent and variable than industrial-age ethics allowed. Not only have some labored while others did not (the reality of labor differentiation, the problem of distributive justice), but what counted as labor and what labor counted for have been contested. To the Greeks, labor by itself defined only mere animal existence, while leisure was the condition for freedom, politics, and truly "human" forms of being. Labor was relegated to animals, slaves, and (in the household) women, while citizens (men) enjoyed their freedom from private work by pursuing the public work of politics and culture, leaving private household economies to the drones. The gods, with whom they aspired to kinship, were divine creatures of leisure, not laborers in some Olympian vineyard. In his book *Leisure: The Basis of Culture*, Josef Pieper thus recalls that it was the gods "taking pity on mankind, born to work," who decreed festivals and leisure time so that in the company of the muses "they might nourish themselves in festive companionship" and so "again stand upright and erect."[17] Hannah Arendt and other German and American celebrants of classical republicanism have always distinguished man the laborer (*homo laborans*) from his nobler cousins man the actor, maker, and playful creator (*homo faber, homo ludens*), whose creative and productive activity established him as more than a mere instrument of bodily labor.[18] In Aristotle's view, man the contemplative philosopher manifested the highest form of virtue, seeking the ennobling leisure of contemplative gods.

With the passing of classical republicanism, bodily work was integrated into civic value systems, while leisure became associated with what in classical times was its very opposite—slothfulness. Enough of the classical world's utopian humanism remained, however, to keep alive the quest for liberation from the yoke of labor. The history of production has thus been a history of labor's growing productivity, augmented by machines, first mechanical and then electronic and digital. Increased efficiency inevitably meant decreased dependency on human labor. The ox did the work of many men, the wheel multiplied the efficiency of the ox, the steam and internal-combustion engines enhanced the efficacy of the wheel. Each increment in efficiency decreased the claims of industry on human labor and represented another step on the journey to liberation. Where classical democracy had allowed the few to enjoy leisure on the backs of slavery, had allowed the liberty of the few to depend on the servitude of the many, and freedom to be a product of inequality, now there appeared the promise of liberty for all, rooted in the emancipation of productivity from human labor altogether—Engels's "ascent to the kingdom of freedom," Nietzsche's heroic realm of self-invented men.

Hence today, when we can foresee an "end of work" and none of us can deny that the requirements of human labor have been radically transformed by automation, what once seemed a natural fact of human existence looks more and more like a coincidental outcome of inefficiency that can be and is being overcome. When just a little more than a century ago most Americans labored on farms to produce enough food for their own fellow citizens alone, today less than 2 percent of us feed all of America and much of the world besides. No one thinks she is morally compelled to cultivate her own garden in order to be entitled to eat, or to grow with her own hands the food she feeds her own children.

The industrial economy lags behind agriculture by a century or two, but the advent of automation permits a reengineering of industrial society where an ever diminishing proportion of us will be able to produce the goods and services needed by the growing world population.[19] For even service jobs are subject to automation, as anyone who once depended on secretaries, bank tellers and telephone operators knows. Surely the question is no longer *if* but only *when* the trends of our economy mandating what Jeremy Rifkin has called the end of work as we know it will dominate our economic and civic institutions.

Yet we still think, in the old way, that entitlement rests on labor contribution. Through the device of wage labor, the incomes of women and men as consumers are directly related to their participation in production,

whether or not production requires their presence. And the economic participation defined by work is not just crucial to income and consumption but
suffuses democracy's most visible values: status, power, and dignity. As
once in the nineteenth century the populist progressive Eugene Debs could
aver that "the man who by honest toil earns an honest living is a peer of the
realm," so the modern populist progressive James Carville affirms: "I believe with all my heart that outside of love and faith, the most sacred thing
you can render in this world is your labor."[20] Accordingly, the neo-liberal
Micky Kaus calls for a new "civic liberalism" in which

> liberals would, in effect, make work the prerequisite for full citizenship. The
> work ethic could assume its place as the basis of a unifying, egalitarian cul-
> ture in which the affluent as well as the poor judge themselves, not by how
> much money they make but by whether they are pulling their weight.[21]

But the trouble with Kaus's formula is that the weight of the modern economy is already being pulled by machines and computers and robots and
does not require that women and men stay in harness to draw "their"
weight—which is "theirs" no longer for some pertinent economic reason but
only for moral and psychological reasons that continue to sacralize work.

When work for pay has this sacred aspect, then decoupling work from
productivity, which the modern economy has done, becomes a sacrilege, a
rabid secular heresy, and it challenges our political, economic, and social
institutions. How should we deal with a flourishing economy in which an
increasing percentage of the work force is cast as mere spectators? What
once happened to a farm economy, which went in a century from employing nearly 80 percent of the population to employing but 2 percent, is happening in the industrial economy today, and it will happen in the service
sector in the years to come. As Jeremy Rifkin puts it: "The wholesale substitution of machines for workers is going to force the very nation to rethink
the role of human beings in the social process. Redefining opportunities and
responsibilities for millions of people in a society absent of mass formal employment is likely to be the single most pressing social issue of the coming
century."[22] Yet the new enforced leisure seems heretical in the face of work's
traditional sanctity, while "technical" solutions of the kind proffered by
Rifkin and other economists are unlikely to succeed if they smack of sloth,
or if they "privilege" those who do not "earn a living" yet are supported in
their living anyway.

We have to find new ways to distribute the fruits of nonlabor-based productivity to the general population, *whether or not they work for their living.*
Otherwise, more and more citizens will become poor in economic and social
terms (low income, low status), and the system itself, capable theoretically
of surviving without an extensive work force, will be undermined and destroyed by political instability, new forms of class war, and—most ironic of

all—by not enough income-earning consumers to buy all the goods in this labor-free world. The system will fail not because of economic inadequacy but because of hyper-adequacy: its capacity to function efficiently and productively without significant labor input. Once it has failed, the only means to break this kind of logjam will be Malthusian: catastrophes of starvation, inequality, civil strife, and war that reduce the population and break the economic machine in ways that eventually create new jobs. But ending civilization as we have known it over five thousand years does not seem a very efficient way to deal with downsizing. Do we have an alternative?

Imagine a world in which only one in two or perhaps one in five work to produce goods sufficient to the needs of the others. Unemployed and de-salaried, how will the others benefit from the remarkable productivity of the few who still work? (These latter will of course for the most part be knowledge workers—what Robert Reich calls symbolic-analyst workers.) Current assumptions tend to give credit to executives and shareholders for increased efficiencies, leaving workers to suffer the consequences of downsizing. But what are all those workers who are no longer needed to do to gain status in society? to "earn" a living that society will be able to afford to give them for free? to share in the efficiencies they helped to create but which now render them superfluous? to occupy their leisure time without feeling lazy or despondent? to feel independent and worthy of the goods that an efficient system of economic distribution will eventually have to make available to all, whether or not they work?

The dependency syndrome that stalks the lives of welfare recipients in our time demonstrates how bleak and demeaning it is to live without work in a world whose chief values are still defined by it. Indeed, the rush of middle-class women into paid work over the last several decades, as part of their search for status and dignity, suggests just how impoverished non-work occupations outside the private-market sector have become. And this has occurred just when private-market labor is becoming economically redundant, just when public forms of work—community service, child rearing, cultural or civic efforts, the work of play—are needed more than ever.

"From each according to ability, to each according to need" had a radical ring in the nineteenth century. But what if nothing at all is required "from" most of us, while all of us go on having more and more "needs" that can be filled without our contributing anything? How much more radical it is to proclaim: "From each, nothing at all, in return for the fulfillment of all your needs!" And how much more morally disruptive! Gain without pain? Bounty absent the sweat of bent brows? Eden regained? Yet the decoupling of work and productivity suggests the need for just such peculiar and ironic moral formulas.

To be sure, interim remedies can be found in technical economic adjustments that continue to value work. And were global population control ever to produce a significant population decline, it is conceivable that the global labor oversupply might be reduced (although at the price of fewer potential consumers, too). Interim adjustments are already being experimented with in Europe. As the growing productivity decreases the number of jobs, the remaining ones can be carved up and reparceled more equitably.

Lionel Jospin's socialist government in France has introduced a law mandating a thirty-five-hour work week for all French workers by the year 2000, with no diminution of wages, on the controversial theory that it will produce more jobs; as insurance, he is also proposing to create 700,000 new positions, half of them in the civil society sector (the government bearing 80 percent of the cost and the private sector 20 percent), an innovation that would give official status to the idea of "public work" as wage-worthy labor. Under the pressure of a strike, the government has also legislated early-retirement opportunities for truckers. Early retirement takes workers out of the marketplace, making room for the young, but it also taxes an already overburdened social security system. Indeed, the problem the Prime Minister will eventually face is how to pay for these conscientious innovations, especially if downsizing offsets whatever gains in jobs the thirty-five-hour week and a shorter working career may bring. Still, Jospin's economic plan is the first in the Western world to recognize that employment, public sector work, and leisure are responsibilities of government no less pressing than those of the productivity and profitability of business.

Elsewhere in Europe, both the state and the private sectors are pursuing technical solutions to the labor market crisis. Automobile companies in Germany (Volkswagen and BMW, for example) have agreed to shorten work schedules and reduce the work week to under thirty hours in return for union concessions.[23] At least some of the growing anti-foreigner sentiment in Austria, Germany, and Switzerland arises out of a fear of disemployment—even though many guest workers do unskilled labor natives have traditionally refused to do. More than twenty years ago, I urged that jobs be divided where feasible, so that women and men could continue to work half time for a single family wage, allowing them both to be involved in their families as well as their workplaces—an idea also championed by Betty Friedan and others.[24]

The Clinton Administration under the leadership of former Labor Secretary Robert Reich committed itself to job retraining and education for multiple careers. The wishful and wistful assumption here was that the problem was the export of jobs, not their diminishing number globally. It is certainly true that unemployment in the United States today is remarkably low, and some will argue that the "decline of work" is an illusion, a short-term effect of another shift in market and economic production of the kind that drove millions of agricultural workers from the fields in the late nineteenth century, only to see them resurface and achieve new success in industrial cities a few decades later. There are not, however, an infinite number of new economic sectors. And the "people" jobs in the service sector, where much of the employment slack is being taken up, are subject to automation. In any case, many of these new jobs are part-time and underpaid, without the traditional benefits of a full-time industrial job, and they have less significance in an economy where families share two or three jobs to scratch out a living that a single job might once have provided.

The smart talk about "life-time employability" rather than lifetime employment is a way of disguising the increasing marginality of labor in the information economy. Talk about the booming economy and endless jobs rings hollow to workers, more than two-thirds of whom reported in a recent survey that "despite the best economic conditions in a generation . . . their sense of job security is lower and their job stress higher than it used to be."[25] With corporations' share of national income up to a near record of 11 percent, and (with real wages falling) labor's share of corporate profits down to 8 percent, their perceptions are accurate.[26] Even Federal Reserve Chairman Alan Greenspan, as enthusiastic a booster of the current economy as we are likely to find, has said, "It is one thing to believe that the economy, indeed the job market, will do well overall, but quite another to feel secure about one's individual situation, given the accelerated pace of corporate restructuring and the heightened fear of skill obsolescence that has apparently characterized this expansion."[27]

Joblessness is a problem for producers as well as laborers, for the former understand that the latter are also consumers. At the very beginning of the age of mass production, Henry Ford observed that unless those who made his cars earned enough to buy them, their productivity would be wasted and the automobile industry would fail. Nothing has changed: even if a day comes when cars can be made without significant human labor power at all, they cannot be sold unless consumers can afford to buy them—whether with wages or with some other form of income by which the benefits of efficient productivity are distributed. Yet when producers need far fewer employees than consumers, their tactical maneuvering can only be halfhearted. They continue to downsize even as they wring their hands. They persist in talking about "growth" and new jobs even as they merge. Will Boeing and McDonnell-Douglas really keep all the jobs that two independent companies provided, now that they are a single company searching for efficiencies to make their merger profitable?[28] The United Parcel Service settled on a new contract with the Teamsters with terms favorable to the latter, but UPS had to downsize to pay for its concessions. The result? Better-paid but fewer jobs, and another installment in the story of economic polarization.

Indeed, nearly all the prudent tactical adjustments one can imagine share a common defect: they ignore the long-term implications for work of the automated knowledge-based economy, and consequently they compete for and try (in what can only be futile ways) to distribute and divide and retrain for an ever-diminishing number of jobs. Shorter work weeks, Roosevelt-era WPA-style government-sponsored jobs, restrictions on self-service such as New Jersey's ban on pumping your own gas, split and shared jobs, early retirement, and education and retraining programs may delay the onset of the value crisis, but they cannot restore work to its previous place of honor, or provide anything like the number of long-term, full-wage, pension- and insurance-carrying jobs that industrial capitalism generated at its labor-intensive pinnacle. In the long run, work itself must either be redefined or severed completely from income, so that human welfare does not depend on labor to get (not "earn") a "living."

The pernicious effect of the end of work on status and dignity can be only temporarily deferred by economic remedies. A permanent improvement requires society to decouple income from production, consumers from producers, work from entitlement. This would be a momentous and monumental transformation of our work-linked civic value system. And however feasible it may become in technical economic terms (Rifkin, Aronowitz, and others describe several prudent strategies for the transition), there are daunting political and moral hurdles. And it would require a revision of the moral logic which for centuries has made work the source of virtue and civic entitlement.

Can a civilization built around wage labor undergo such a conversion? Can our workaholic society dissociate leisure from pejorative linkages to the "leisure classes," to laziness, and to economic parasitism? Champions of leisure from Aristotle to Sebastian de Grazia who have seen in it the foundations of intellectual virtue and the very source of our civilization have tried to pry it apart from the association with sloth and inactivity.[29] But cultures like ours suffused with the work ethic find it difficult to appreciate the difference. They seem likely to continue to view women and men without jobs as economic parasites feeding off the labor of others, even when there are no jobs for them to fill and no good economic reason for them to earn through work the income the hyperproductive economy needs them to receive in order for them to be efficient consumers (and what they need to live).

The challenge is political as well as economic. We need moral grounds and civic reasons to reinforce the new economic logic in which work and productivity are severed. Here is where the dilemmas of civil society in the age of McWorld's global economy—too little time and space for third-sector activity—can give us hope. For if the linkage of work and wages has accounted for many of our civilization's virtues, it has also been the source of a paramount vice: in monopolizing time and defining status in terms of labor alone, work has crowded out our social and civic agenda. Democracy depends on leisure, on time to be educated into civil society, time to participate in deliberation, time to serve on juries, occupy municipal magistracies, volunteer for civic activities. Wilde was right: there weren't enough free evenings to accommodate his radical political principles; and advocates of civil society must worry about securing afternoons and weekends as well. Unable both to work and to participate in democracy, we were led to depend on representative institutions where others did the work of governance for us. The "iron law" dictating that representative government would inevitably become oligarchical is rooted largely in the inability of those represented to find time to oversee and get involved in self-governance. The early democratic republics of our civilization, understanding democracy to mean self-government in a strictly literal sense, demanded much of their citizens, and flourished only inasmuch as citizens were released from the burdens of labor. In Athens, our first "free society," it was ironically a system of slavery that permitted free Athenians to be full-time citizens. They were free to debate the peace and fight the wars because slaves did the work and produced the goods. In early Switzerland, where a communal version of direct democracy was established over seven hundred years ago, it was a pastoral economy that left long winters of leisure in which the free Swiss could cultivate their institutions and establish peasant armies capable of defending their mountain fortress as well as serving the mercenary needs of neighbors.

By contrast, the peasant agricultural societies of the rest of Europe, steeped in endless work, were producing what Edward Banfield later called a morally backward society weighed down by drudgery and defined by passivity. Karl Marx identified such features of the agricultural society with what he called the "idiocy of rural life": indenture to the soil as prelude to more human forms of bondage like wage slavery. Sunrise-to-sundown labor leaves little time in which to practice civic statecraft or indulge the apprenticeship of liberty, and it abandons the muses of art to commerce and to an inevitable commercialization of culture. Industrial societies have done little better in managing time: the proletariat has for the most part found precious little room in its endless days of hard labor and long decades of drudgery either for revolution or for reform, let alone for civility or for culture, content today to be placated with electronic circuses. Working, shopping, watching—the job place, the mall, and the television—leave neither time nor place for politics or art or civic culture, except in the lives of the disemployed and disempowered. But the disillusion and despondency of spreading unemployment have been felt more as spurs to despair than opportunities for civic engagement or edifying leisure. The women and men who have the most to gain from suffrage are those least likely to practice it, even if only once a year.[30] Nor, short of a cultural and moral transformation, are the unemployed and the welfare poor likely to respond to marginalization by spending their free time in civic voluntarism or cultural self-improvement.

How very cunning the cunning of reason is: at the very moment the human race finally stands on the threshold of the workless world for which it has labored these many millennia, it turns and flees in horror back into servitude. Give us back our chains! it cries. Take back the liberty the miraculous achievements of technology proffer and give us, instead, jobs! We would rather work than face the greater burden of freedom, than reembrace a democratic civil society or give up private labor in the name of economic survival and shoulder the weight of public work in the name of human improvement.

Democracy's logic is clear: if productivity has demanded work and work has become associated with status and power, democracy has demanded leisure but, in its modern absence, has had to settle for second-class representative institutions. In societies where the title "wage earner" brings more respect than the title "citizen," who can blame people for adopting a moral code in which voting is discretionary but work mandatory? By tying civic virtue to the labor of shopkeepers and yeoman farmers, by tying citizenship to property-holding and the A-type Calvinist habits that made it possible, America's early republicans knit together a leisureless work economy with the thinner civic virtues of a representative democracy. Their strategy has today become part of the problem. Judith Shklar has incisively demonstrated that work is more crucial to the core values of our democracy than anything else. But, under those conditions, labor's diminishing role in the face of the post-modern economy's efficiency becomes not merely an economic but a political issue. The end of work threatens the end of civic status and the end of dignity as well.

Here is where our two stories intersect to produce a quite miraculous prospect. The story of rising, ever more efficient productivity which renders human labor redundant converges with the tale of vanishing civic time in the face of government and market gargantuanism: here there is a unique opportunity for the restitution of civic life. Where the stories converge, the downsizing and unemployment associated with labor obsolescence in a post-modern hyper-efficient economy are transformed into the promise of a civil society, a leisure society in which civic culture is finally cut loose from commerce and made the focus of citizens liberated from work. The commercial malls that have encroached on our civic space can be rolled back by political will, as the commercialization of time that has filled our days with labor is rolled back by economic necessity.

The final victory of emancipation through work is emancipation from work. Forced for eons to earn its daily bread by the sweat of bent brows in a place East of Eden, humankind is abruptly offered an escape back into the garden in which human needs are largely met through the products not of human labor but of human imagination. For machines and robotics and computers are human imagination made manifest, a surrogate for Eden's bountiful God that frees us to enjoy imagination as an end in itself—education, play, politics, and art as forms of association and creativity. Private market work gives way to public and civic work, activity on behalf of art and family, neighborhood and polity, religion and school.[31] We are given the opportunity to use labor's material gifts to pursue not just material needs (shopping!) but civilization—if we can remember that work is the instrument and culture the object and can wean ourselves from the seductive tyrannies of production and consumption.

The strategies we require here are not economic and technical but political and cultural: making hobbies as rewarding as work, making civic volunteering as income-producing as commercial labor, making just distribution a function of need, making imagination a faculty worthy of remuneration, making art and culture objects of social support, making high-quality education—above all, civic education—accessible to all. The economic strategies follow: once the political will is in place to decouple work and reward, many feasible innovations are possible—for example, the law professor Bruce Ackerman's proposal for a once-in-a-lifetime capital grant to all people to create a stake-holders' society in which everyone is economically vested, or Tony Atkinson's idea of a "participation income" that would be pegged to civic engagement of every kind, and would separate the distribution of productivity's earnings from wage labor (a proposal in which Tony Blair's new Labour government in Britain has shown some interest).[32] But first a change in deep cultural perspective is needed.

At this moment, standing on the threshold of a new era, those with time on their hands should feel no shame in their hearts. Their unwanted leisure can be the occasion for more than envy, or depression, or lassitude, or simple rage, which they feel only because we have equated the active life exclusively with labor activity in the market sector. Even at play, we "labor" with an industry that robs us of leisure's succor and its promise. But public and civic work, as well as homemaking and family work, should not be discretionary, while wage-earning market labor is obligatory. Quite the other way around.

At present, the disemployed and underemployed and unemployed—whether mothers or homemaking fathers, downsized information society cast-offs or hard-core welfare cases—hardly can be considered a leisure class in potentia, ready to enter the "kingdom of freedom." "Our future," writes the economist Lester C. Thurow, "is the masterless American laborer, wandering from employer to employer, unable to build a career."[33] But Thurow's pessimism depends on a work-centered culture in which status and dignity usually disappear along with work, and the only "career" worth talking about is a wage-earning workplace career, in which leisure time is thought of as an evasion of rather than an opportunity to assume responsibility and civic obligations. Feminism has had a difficult time with homemaking because the home lacks both the pecuniary rewards and the public virtues of the economic workplace. Even cultural conservatives who celebrate family values are outraged by women without providers who stay home to raise children: thus the universal drive to compel welfare mothers to "work," even where there are neither appropriate jobs available nor an economic need for their labor, and even where their "work" at home might yield greater benefits for their children and for society at large.

To be fired, to be a housewife, to be a welfare mother, or to be a homemaker, to be unemployed or to be an unpaid civic volunteer, is in every case to be without power, without status, and without entitlement; and thus without dignity. The transformation of the role of work in our economic system will hence have to await the transvaluation of our civic and moral systems—something at which we will have to "work" exactly in this new public sense.[34] Those with time on their hands are potentially our most promising citizens. Homemakers and retired folks and those no longer "needed" by an efficient production system are more needed than ever by civil society. Freed from the onus of contributing to economic capital, women and men can become potential creators of social capital. In the age after work, democracy can rediscover the missing citizens stolen from it by the long epoch of value squeezed from labor. Civil society can finally have its own work force. Democracy can be our most magnanimous employer. Citizenship can again be the most human of all occupations.

If history has then conspired against civility in the manner portrayed here—squeezing civil society between the hammer of big government and the anvil of markets—it appears now to be conspiring with it. In a provocative realization of Marx's prophecy anticipating a new world of abundance no longer rooted in endless labor, our society is moving toward conditions that could nourish the resuscitation of civil society—not just public work but public play, cultural leisure as well as civic labor, fun no less than ferment, the joys of living in place of the burdens of earning a living. And the question we face, it becomes ever more apparent, is not whether history will permit the rehabilitation of civil society, but whether we habit-mired human beings will be able to make good on history's promise and, through acts of bold political imagination and moral transformation, convert the deficits of a world after work into the assets of a flourishing democracy—a civil society that is once again truly a place for us.   ■

NOTES

1. Cited by Steven Greenhouse, "Item in Tax Bill Poses Threat to Job Benefits," *The New York Times*, July 20, 1997, p. 18. The formula corporations have used to "restructure" the workplace has been to reclassify employees as "consultants" and "independent contractors"—which allows firms to stop paying pension, health, and other traditional benefits.

      When asked whether they preferred higher pay or sustained benefits, 62 percent of workers polled in one survey reported they would rather keep their benefits than have a pay raise.

2. Robert Kuttner, "Take the High Road on Labor," *The Berkshire Eagle*, Aug. 10, 1997, p. A9. Kuttner reports that Manpower, Inc., the temp agency, is today America's largest employer. See also Chris Tilly, *Half a Job*.

3. William Julius Wilson, *When Work Disappears: The World of the New Urban Poor* (1996); and Jeremy Rifkin, *The End of Work* (1995), p. 59.

4. Stanley Aronowitz and William DiFazio, *The Jobless Future: Sci-Tech and the Dogma of Work* (1994), p. 21. "In the wake of the shrinking social wage, joblessness, the supplanting of good full-time jobs by mediocre badly paid part-time jobs tends to thwart the ability of the economic system to avoid chronic overproduction and underconsumption." This is the theme explored in the setting of the global economy by William Greider in his *One World, Ready or Not* (1997).

5. Kenneth M. Dolbeare and Janette K. Hubble, *USA 2012: After the Middle Class Revolution* (1996), p. 89.

6. Thomas L. Friedman, "Down With Chips!" *The New York Times*, Oct. 6, 1997.

7. "Need Work? Go to Jail," *U.S. News and World Report,* Dec. 9, 1996, p. 66.

8. Figures from a Princeton Survey Research Associates Poll, *U.S.A. Today,* cover story, Aug. 29, 1997. The poll revealed that in 1997 33 percent of the work force worked more than forty-five hours a week, up from 27 percent six years earlier. In 1991, Juliet Schor found that Americans were working on average 163 more hours (nearly an extra month) per year in 1990 than they had in 1970 (Juliet Schor, *The Overworked American,* 1991). This increase in working hours is not due to a growing zest for work, but the result of families "trapped in an Alice in Wonderland world, running faster and faster just to stay in place." Barry Bluestone and Stephen Rose, "Overworked and Underemployed," in *The American Prospect,* March/April 1997, p. 64.

   Arlie Russell Hochschild suggests that, among those who do not have to work harder to make ends meet, many nonetheless actually prefer work to home—such is the power of the culture of work over the culture of home and civil society. When people go looking in the workplace for the civic and social values once imparted in the home and neighborhood, the inversion of work and leisure values is complete. See Hochschild, *The Time Bend: When Work Becomes Home and Home Becomes Work* (1997).

9. Don Terry, "Public Housing Program Opens Door to World of Work," *The New York Times,* Jan. 6, 1997.

10. This is the conclusion of Robert Putnam's work on membership in voluntary associations. See Putnam, "Bowling Alone," as well as his "The Strange Disappearance of Civic America," *The American Prospect,* Winter 1996. The many critics who have challenged Putnam for overstating the decline of voluntarism have not separated passive and active forms. Andrew Greeley claims that voluntary service in the United States is higher since 1980, but he also agrees that when the figures are corrected for religion (a primary venue for voluntary activity), the United States loses its lead over other nations. See Andrew Greeley, "The Other Civic America: Religion and Social Capital," *The American Prospect,* May–June 1997. Meanwhile, Sidney Verba and his colleagues note that voluntary activity is badly skewed economically, with the rich volunteering far more than the poor. See Sidney Verba, Kay L. Schlozman, and Henry E. Brady, "The Big Tilt: Participatory Inequality in America," *The American Prospect,* May–June 1997.

11. Frederick Engels, *Socialism: Scientific and Utopian,* in Karl Marx and Frederick Engels, *Selected Works* (Moscow, 1951), II, pp. 140–41.

12. The dream of work is no mere turn of phrase. A recently employed ex-welfare recipient enthused: "I can start dreaming again. It feels good to get up every morning and know you have a job to go to." Cited in Don Terry, "Public Housing Program Opens Door to World of Work," *The New York Times,* Jan. 6, 1997.

13. William Greider, *One World, Ready or Not: The Manic Logic of Global Capitalism* (1997), pp. 69–70ff.

14. Judith N. Shklar, *American Citizenship: The Quest for Inclusion* (1991), p. 67.

15. James Carville, *We're Right, They're Wrong!* (1995), p. xvii.

16. See William Julius Wilson, *When Work Disappears: The World of the New Urban Poor* (1996).

17. Joseph Pieper, *Leisure: The Basis of Culture* (1963), p. 19, paraphrasing Plato. This theme, long neglected in the current literature on work and the economy, is fruitfully examined in Sebastian de Grazia's classic work *Time, Work, and Leisure* (1962).

18. See Hannah Arendt, *The Human Condition* (1958). Arendt's complex discussion favors the active life over the merely contemplative but roots action in a context of

contemplation. In accord with what she recognizes as an "unusual" distinction between the labor of bodies and the work of hands, she also prefers man the maker and creator (*homo faber*) to man the mere laborer, man as animal (*homo laborans*). The modern victory of man the laborer is associated by her with many of the ills of modern life.

19. Rifkin shows persuasively that the service economy—particularly the white-collar service economy of accountants, bankers, lawyers, and brokers, where so many of the "new" jobs are found—is also subject to forces of automation that will give it the same fate as agriculture and the industrial economy. Layoffs and downsizing at information corporations like AT&T point the way.

20. Debs cited by Micky Kaus, *The End of Equality* (New York, 1992), p. 136. Carville, *Ibid.*

21. Kaus, p. 140.

22. Rifkin, p. xv.

23. Rifkin offers an illuminating review of such technical solutions but gives little attention to the moral and cultural biases that militate against their successes.

24. In *Liberating Feminism* (1976).

25. Beth Belton, "Workers Less Secure," *U.S.A. Today*, Aug. 29, 1997, p. 1.

26. *Ibid.*

27. Cited by Beth Belton, "Workers Less Secure."

28. Restructuring costs of the merger of over a billion dollars are likely to be passed on to the federal government, and thus to the taxpayers. See William Hartung, "Military Monopoly," *The Nation*, Jan. 13/20, 1997.

29. Sebastian de Grazia, *Time, Work and Leisure* (1962). Stanley Parker argues for more public and active forms of leisure in his *The Future of Work and Leisure* (1971), while Joffre Dumazedier promotes the influence that leisure policy can have on securing democracy in his *Towards a Society of Leisure* (1967). See also T. Goodale and G. Godbey, *The Evolution of Leisure* (1988), and Max Kaplan and Phillip Bosserman, eds., *Technology, Human Values, and Leisure* (1971).

30. Low rates of electoral participation, hovering at about 50 percent in American Presidential elections, and descending from higher levels in Europe, are apparent in the analysis of aggregate data. When disaggregated, the data show that the poor, young, and marginalized (people of color in the United States) participate even less. Only one out of five young people between eighteen and twenty-five, for example, vote in elections.

31. This is the true promise of what Harry Boyte calls "public work" in Boyte and Kari, *Building America: The Democratic Promise of Public Work* (1997).

32. See Bruce Ackerman, *The Stakeholder Society* (1998), and Tony Atkinson, *Public Economics at Work* (1997).

33. Lester C. Thurow, in the compendium of op-ed views gathered together in "What's Ahead for Working Men and Women," *The New York Times*, Aug. 31, 1997, p. E9.

34. Just how difficult the task will be is suggested by the skepticism that many theorists express about linking leisure and citizenship. Kenneth Roberts is typical when he writes, "Leisure has not unleashed a flood of effort and commitment into civic organizations . . . participation carries few intrinsic rewards . . . [for] civic participation is not among the most rewarding leisure activities for the mass of people." Roberts' conclusion is our challenge: "The growth of leisure has not produced and remains unlikely to produce a new type of participant democracy." Kenneth Roberts, *Contemporary Society and the Growth of Leisure* (1978), pp. 145–46.

■ *QUESTIONS FOR MAKING CONNECTIONS WITHIN THE READING* ■

1. What might Barber mean by "civil society"? Although most dictionaries will provide a standard definition, use cues from Barber's writing to devise a text-specific explanation of the term. Why doesn't Barber simply call it "society" or "the government"? Is there any important difference between our *civil* society and, say, Americans in general. Is there a difference between civil society and the formal institutions of the state—the legislatures, the courts, federal agencies, and so on?

2. Explain what Barber means by "the ideology of work." Why doesn't he use the more familiar term, "the work *ethic*"? What's the difference between an "ethic" and an "ideology"? What, according to Barber, is the history behind the ideology of work? Why does he view the celebration of work as damaging rather than redemptive?

3. Why does Barber object to the linkage between economic power and political power? What does this objection suggest about his conception of democracy and the proper place of the economic sphere? If money should not be the prerequisite for participation in political life, what prerequisites does Barber think should take its place?

■ *QUESTIONS FOR WRITING* ■

1. Many economists have argued that the market—our economic system—takes its orders from the humble consumer. Some have even argued that the market responds to the popular will much more directly and completely than does our political system. What might Barber say in response to this view? Is Barber fair to the market? Does he recognize its strengths as well as its weaknesses? By extension, does he overestimate the power of politics? Should decisions about wages be made by political means rather than by following the law of supply and demand?

2. If Barber's proposal were put into effect—if people were paid to work less or not at all—would this change result in more widespread participation in politics, or would it create a two-tier society with a working class and a dependent class? On the basis of the evidence that Barber provides, do you feel that a change in our attitudes toward leisure is an adequate remedy for the problem of the "jobless future"? If not, what alternatives can you imagine?

■ *QUESTIONS FOR MAKING CONNECTIONS BETWEEN READINGS* ■

1. What responsibility does civil society have for those who refuse to work? For those who elect not to pursue professional success? For those who

can't work? Jon Krakauer recounts Chris McCandless's flight from the world of work and leisure that Barber describes in his essay. Is McCandless's journey into the wild evidence that Barber's assessment of the American work ethic is correct? Should civil society be concerned with those who do not or cannot conform to its norms and expectations? How does one determine membership in civil society?

2. Is the fast-food industry a threat to civil society? Are agribusiness and biogenetic engineering? Is civil society possible without corporate success? Does globalization extend or curtail the influence of civil society? Drawing on either Eric Schlosser's "Global Realization" or Michael Pollan's "Playing God in the Garden," consider the relationship between corporations and civil society, as Barber has defined it.

For additional suggestions about making connections between readings, visit the Link-O-Mat and More Sample Assignments at <www.newhum.com>.

JASPER BECKER

IN THE MEDIA AGE, when images and information can be dispersed rapidly around the globe, all governments are concerned with exercising some control over how they are represented to their citizens and to the rest of the world. This concern is only heightened during times of war, when the survival of a nation may partially rest on how well the government regulates the flow of images and information about itself and its enemies. In his award-winning book, *Hungry Ghosts: Mao's Secret Famine*, Jasper Becker details Mao's efforts to control scientific research in China and the disastrous consequences this had for China and its people.

Becker focuses on the unreported famine that followed the Great Leap Forward, Mao's ambitious plan to revolutionize farming and industry in China during the late 1950s. News of the famine did not reach the West until the 1980s, when demographers working with population statistics that had been released at the beginning of China's open-door policy began to piece together the magnitude of this human catastrophe. As Becker describes it in the foreword to *Hungry Ghosts*, "[The demographers'] conclusion was startling: at least 30 million people had starved to death, far more than anyone, including the most militant critics of the Chinese Communist Party, had ever imagined. Why, and how, did such a cataclysm take place? Who was to blame? How was it kept secret for so long? And what was life like in the countryside? How did people behave and how did they survive?"

Jasper Becker is a British journalist who has served as the Asian Affairs Analyst for the BBC World Service and for the Royal Institute of International Affairs in London. He is a contributing writer for *The Guardian, The Spectator*, and *The Economist*. Becker presently lives in Beijing and is the bureau chief for the *South China Morning Post*. During the past two decades he has reported on the Tiananmen Square Massacre, the colossal Three Gorges Dam project, the rise of Falun Gong, and China's vexed relations with Tibet.

Becker, Jasper. "False Science, False Promises" and "How Many Died?" *Hungry Ghosts: Mao's Secret Famine.* New York: The Free Press, 1996. 58–82; 266–274, + Notes.
Biographical information drawn from the Henry Holt and Company Web site <http://216.247.214.252/98-1owl/hungryghosts.htm> and the Pioom Award Web site <http://www.fsw.leidenuniv.nl/www/w3_liswo/Newsletter81/Pioom_award_1997.htm>.

To learn more about Jasper Becker and the Great Leap Forward, visit the Link-O-Mat at <www.newhum.com>.

■ ■

Selections from

Hungry Ghosts: Mao's Secret Famine

False Science, False Promises

'Practical success in agriculture is the
ultimate criterion of truth.'
Stalin

'Seeing all men behaving like drunkards,
how can I alone remain sober?'
Tang dynasty poem

To launch the Great Leap Forward, Mao whipped up a fever of expectation all over China that amounted to mass hysteria. Mao the infallible, the 'great leader,' the 'brilliant Marxist,' the outstanding thinker and genius, promised that he would create a heaven on earth. Even in the 1940s, the Party had encouraged a personality cult around Mao but now this reached new and grotesque heights: Mao was an infallible semi-divine being. The nation's poets, writers, journalists and scientists, and the entire Communist Party, joined him in proclaiming that Utopia was at hand. Out of China, the land of famine, he would make China, the land of abundance. The Chinese would have so much food they would not know what to do with it, and people would lead a life of leisure, working only a few hours a day. Under his gifted leadership, China would enter the final stage of Communism, ahead of every other country on earth. If the Soviets said they would reach Communism in ten or twenty years, Mao said the Chinese could get there in a year or two. In fact, he promised that within a year food production would double or triple. Even Liu Shaoqi entered into the spirit of things by coining the slogan 'Hard work for a few years, happiness for a thousand.'[1]

The Great Leap Forward was preceded by a new campaign to raise Mao's personality cult to a level rivaling that of Stalin. From the end of 1957, his portraits, large and small, began appearing everywhere. Mao was compared to the sun and people declared that the era of Mao was already like heaven on earth. The *China Youth Daily* wrote that 'the dearest people in the world are our parents, yet they cannot be compared with Chairman Mao.' In songs, too, Mao was eulogized:

Chairman Mao is infinitely kind,
Ten thousand songs are not enough to praise him.
With trees as pens, the sky as paper
And an ocean of ink,
Much would be left unwritten.[2]

Officials toured the country in 1958 describing what happiness and bliss were at hand. Tan Chen Lin, the Minister of Agriculture, painted a fantasy of peasants jumping in one leap from mud huts to skyscrapers, travelling not on donkeys but in aeroplanes.

After all, what does Communism mean? . . . First, taking good food and not merely eating one's fill. At each meal one enjoys a meat diet, eating chicken, pork, fish or eggs . . . delicacies like monkey brains, swallows' nests, white fungi are served to each according to his needs . . .

Second, clothing. Everything required is available. Clothing of various designs and styles, not a mass of black garments or a mass of blue outfits. After working hours, people will wear silk, satin and woollen suits . . . Foxes will multiply. When all people's communes raise foxes, there will be overcoats lined with fox furs . . .

Third, housing. Housing is brought up to the standard of modern cities. What should be modernised? People's communes. Central heating is provided in the north and air-conditioning in the south. All will live in high buildings. Needless to say, there are electric lights, telephones, piped water, receiving sets and TV . . .

Fourth, communications. Except for those who take part in races, all travellers and commuters will use transport. Air services are opened in all directions and every *xian* [county] has an airport . . . The time is not remote when each will have an aeroplane.

Fifth, higher education for everyone and education is popularised. Communism means this: food, clothing, housing, transportation, cultural entertainment, science institutes, and physical culture. The sum total of these means Communism.[3]

This fantasy of American life was repeated even to peasants in faraway Tibet where people had never even seen an aeroplane or heard of a skyscraper: 'Everyone would live in one big family . . . We would have no worries about food, clothing and housing as everyone would wear the same clothes, eat the same food and live in the same houses . . . practically everything would be done by machines. In fact a time would come when our meals would be brought by machines right up to our mouths.'[4]

Such fairy-tales of overnight prosperity had been spread as early as 1956. One interviewee, a former journalist from Shaanxi, recalled going to a meeting of propaganda chiefs in 1956 and hearing Mao say that after three years of hard work, China would enjoy such prosperity that no one would need to work hard, or grow much, yet all would live in great luxury.

Writers, too, were busy painting pictures of this happiness. A character in Qin Chaoyang's *Village Sketches* described what would happen:

> Socialism means that our mountain district will be clothed with trees, that our peach blossom and pear blossom will cover the hillsides. Lumber mills will spring up in our district, and a railway too, and our trees will be sprayed by insecticide from aeroplanes, and we will have a big reservoir . . .
>
> Can we cover more and more of the mountains in the whole district with green trees, and make the streams clearer each year? Can we make the soil more fertile and make the faces of the people in every village glow with health? Can we make this mountain district of ours advance steadily on the path to socialism? If you ask me, I tell you it can be done! We have the heart, and we have the hands! It can be done!

Another novel, *Great Changes in a Mountain Village* by Zhou Libo, describes how the secretary of a village youth league envisages a future with all modern conveniences:

> It'll be soon, we won't have to wait for ten or even five years. Then we'll use some of the co-operative's accumulated funds to buy a lorry and when you women go to the theatre in the town, you can ride a lorry. With electric light, telephones, lorries and tractors we shall live more comfortably than they do in the city, because we have the beautiful landscape and the fresh air. There'll be flowers all the year round and wild fruit, more than we can eat: chinquapins [dwarf chestnuts] and chestnuts all over the hills.[5]

Naturally enough, peasants all over China began to ask when they would get to Communism and were told soon, very soon. Such fantastic optimism was based on Mao's fundamental ignorance of modern science. Although he had barely ventured outside China and had never studied Western science, Mao believed that science could make his dreams come true. While in the remote hills of Yanan, Mao and his colleagues carefully studied Moscow's propaganda works eulogizing the great achievements of such Soviet scientists as Pavlov, Lysenko and others, and became convinced that they were genuine.

Marxism claims, above all, to be a 'scientific' philosophy, one which applies the principles of science to politics and society. In like manner, Mao believed, modern science could transform the lives of those millions of ignorant peasants sunk in the mire of centuries of feudal superstition. There was no time to wait for them to become convinced, they would have to be forcibly dragged into the twentieth century. Everything connected with traditional beliefs was smashed in the Great Leap Forward (although many observers tend to assume that this happened later, in the Cultural Revolution) but, ironically, what Mao put in place of these beliefs was a pseudo-science, a fantasy that could not be validated by science, or stand up to rational examination, any more than could the peasant superstitions which the Party ridiculed.

Kang Sheng, Mao's loyal henchman, exemplified this casual approach to facts: 'We should be like Marx, entitled to talk nonsense,' he told everyone, and he toured the country lecturing about the need to add imagination to science. 'What is science?' he asked teachers in Zhengzhou, Henan province, in 1958. 'Science is simply acting daringly. There is nothing mysterious about it.' In Hefei, Anhui province, he continued on the same theme: 'There is nothing special about making nuclear reactors, cyclotrons or rockets. You shouldn't be frightened by these things: as long as you act daringly you will be able to succeed very quickly . . . You need to have spirit to feel superior to everyone, as if there was no one beside you . . . You shouldn't care about any First Machine Building Ministry, Second Machine Building Ministry, or Qinghua University, but just act recklessly and it will be all right.'[6]

In Shanghai that year he told cadres that 'if by national day next year, Shanghai's schools are able to launch a third-grade rocket to an altitude of 300 kilometres, they should get three marks . . . A third-grade rocket with a satellite should get five marks. This is very easy. At New Year, the [ordinary] Shanghainese fire rockets, so surely the schools can launch [real] rockets!'[7]

Trained scientists such as Professor Qian Xusen, the American nuclear physicist who returned to serve Mao and help build China's nuclear bomb, gave credibility to this optimism. He wrote articles and gave lectures to agricultural experts stating that it was quite realistic to increase crop yields ten or a hundred times. Qian said that one small plot of land could yield over a dozen tonnes of grain if just a small percentage of the energy from sunlight were properly utilized.[8]

Such carelessness with the truth shocked even visiting Soviet scientists like Mikhail Klochko. He discovered first-year chemistry students at a teacher training school rewriting their organic chemistry textbooks as they went along. For example, the students had decided they would only learn about copper, because they lived in Yunnan province which is rich in copper ore, so there was no need to bother with the other metals and elements.[9] This approach to science mirrored that in Soviet Russia when Stalin launched his first five-year plan. Then, the message of countless books and articles was the same: the impossible could only be achieved by ignoring the advice of timid experts, the 'bourgeois specialists' who lived in ivory towers, pedantically inching their way forward. True scientists were peasants filled with intuitive knowledge and led by Party members driven by revolutionary fervour—that was how miracles were achieved. The Soviet novel *Izbrannoe (The Select)* by I. Babel, for example, contains a discussion in which a noted oil expert is reprimanded by a young Party member who says: 'We do not doubt the knowledge or goodwill of the professor . . . but we reject the fetishism of figures which hold us in thrall . . . We reject the multiplication table as the basis for policy.'

In the Great Leap Forward, much the same happened in China, only in real life. The *People's Daily* reported how students in one faculty of science and mathematics showed their disdain for basic theory by putting decimal points in the wrong place while others deliberately made mistakes when calculating square roots.[10] Still worse, the message was put out that science was so simple, even a child could excel at it. A propaganda book, *They Are Creating Miracles*, described how children at a primary school 'developed ten more new crops on its experimental plot,' a feat presented as hard fact: 'It's a story out of a science-fiction book! But, no, my young friends, it is not! This is a true story. There are no fairy-tale magicians, no white-bearded wizards of never-never land. The heroes of our story are a group of Young Pioneers studying in an ordinary village primary school.'[11]

All over China in 1958, the Party created thousands of new colleges, universities and research institutes, while real scientists were imprisoned or sent to do manual labour. In their place, thousands of untrained peasants carried out 'scientific research'. Many kinds of miracles were announced but the Great Leap Forward was above all about creating huge increases in grain and steel production. These were the 'two generals' that Mao said would modernize China.

Just as Stalin saw a huge increase in steel production as the cornerstone of his crash industrialization programme, Mao envisaged a doubling or tripling of steel output within a year. The entire country, from peasants in remote villages on the Tibetan plateau to top Party officials in Zhongnanhai in Beijing, set up smelters in 1958 and 1959 to create 'steel' in backyard furnaces. Everyone had to meet a quota by handing over their metal possessions. People handed in bicycles, railings, iron bedsteads, door knobs, their pots and pans and cooking grates. And to fire the furnaces, huge numbers of trees were cut down. In the countryside people worked day and night fuelling these furnaces. While they did so, they could eat as much as they wanted out of the communes' collective food stores. The lumps of useless metal that emerged were supposed to be used in the mechanization of agriculture. Had China really produced a lot more steel then it could have been used to make the necessary tractors, ploughs, threshing machines, trucks, diesel engines and pumps. Instead the peasants relied on *tu fa*—literally 'earth methods'—to mechanize their work by inventing hundreds of Heath Robinson-type contraptions of pulleys, ropes and cogs, all made out of wood, not steel. Propaganda photographs showed wooden conveyor belts, wooden threshing machines, wooden automatic compost-appliers—a sort of wheelbarrow with a box on top—wooden rail tracks, wooden railcars, wooden rice-planting machines, wooden wheat harvesters, wooden jute harvesters and, in Shandong, a whole truck made of wood. They were all a great credit to the considerable ingenuity of the Chinese peasant but, in the end, perfectly worthless. Not one has survived in use. Yet, for all the waste and folly of the backyard furnace campaign, it was never more than a minor contributory factor to the starvation that was to result from the Great Leap Forward.

Rather, it was the half-baked ideas on growing more grain, Mao's second 'general,' which he insisted the nation should follow, that led to a substantial decline in grain yields. Many Chinese believe his ideas were rooted in traditional Chinese peasant lore, but though this may explain their appeal to a peasant's son like Mao, in fact he merely adopted them from the Soviet Union. To understand what happened in China, therefore, one must first step back in time to the Stalin years and examine the theories of such pseudo-scientists as Lysenko, Michurin and Williams.

For twenty-five years Trofim Denisovitch Lysenko ruled over Soviet agricultural scientists as a dictator. Those who opposed him were shot or perished in labour camps, and his victims were not rehabilitated until 1986 when Mikhail Gorbachev came to power.[12] Until then, Lysenko's portrait hung in all scientific institutions. At the height of his personality cult, art stores sold busts and bas-reliefs of him, and cities erected statues in his honour. When he gave a lecture, he was preceded by a brass band and people sang songs in his honour:

> Merrily play one, accordion,
>
> With my girlfriend let me sing
> Of the eternal glory of Academician Lysenko.

Lysenko dismissed the developing science of genetics as an 'expression of the senile decay and degradation of bourgeois culture'. Instead, he advocated a mumbo-jumbo of his own which muddled up Darwin's theories on evolution and the competition in nature between different species and among members of the same species. His school rejected the 'fascist' theories that plants and animals have inherited characteristics which selective breeding can develop. Lysenkoists believed that, on the contrary, environmental factors determine the characteristics of plants and animals. Just as Communists thought that people could be changed by altering their surroundings, so Lysenko held that plants acquire new characteristics when their environment is changed and that these changes are transmitted to the next generation. As one observer pointed out, this was tantamount to saying that lambs would be born without tails just because you cut off their mother's tail. Yet Lysenko asserted that he could make orange trees flourish in Siberia, or change them into apple trees, not by selective breeding but by following Stalin's unintelligible teachings on evolution. As the Lysenkoist journal *Agrobiologiya* put it: 'Stalin's teachings about gradual, concealed, unnoticeable quantitative changes leading to rapid, radical qualitative changes permitted Soviet biologists to discover in plants the realisation of such qualitative transitions that one species could be transformed into another.'

Lysenko was a semi-literate peasant from Azerbaijan whom *Pravda* praised in 1927 as a 'barefoot scientist' after he claimed to have found a way of growing peas in winter. These peas, he said, would green the mountains of the Caucasus in winter and solve the problem of winter forage. His next, and equally bogus, achievement went under the name of 'vernalization' (from the Latin, *vernalis,* for spring). Most Russian wheat is sown in winter but the seeds are sometimes damaged by severe weather. The yield from spring wheat is higher so when Lysenko claimed he could turn winter wheat seeds into spring seeds, he was promising to raise yields in many parts of the Soviet Union. His method was simple: change the environment of the seeds by soaking them in very cold water and they themselves would change.

The second verse of the Lysenko song, quoted above, also commemorates another Soviet hero, Michurin:

> He walks the Michurin path
> With firm tread.
> He protects us from being duped
> By Mendelist-Morganists.

If the Austrian monk Gregor Mendel and the American scientist Thomas Morgan are the fathers of genetics, then I.V. Michurin, an impoverished nobleman turned tree-grafter, is the true founder of Lysenkoism. He first rose to fame in the early 1920s when a Soviet leader praised his hybrid creations, including a part melon, part squash vegetable, on show at the First All Russian Agricultural Exhibition. Michurin claimed to have created hundreds of hybrid fruit trees, and because he had received only primary education, he qualified as a genuine peasant hero. The whole nation had to follow his methods, although he insisted that 'intuition' was as vital an element in matching his success as his theories. Michurin dismissed real scientists as 'the caste priests of jabberology,' especially those who espoused the theories of Mendel.

Although Michurin was later conclusively shown to be a fraud, he was hailed during Stalin's first five-year plan as an example of what could be done with the correct attitude to science. The daring, untrammelled spirit of his thinking was evoked in this call to arms published in the magazine *October*: 'Knock out sleepiness with punches, with demands, with insistence, with daring. With daring to master and transform the earth, nature, fruit. Is it not daring to drive the grape into the tundra? Drive! Drive! Drive! Into the

furrows, into the gardens, into the orchards, into the machines of jelly factories . . . Faster, faster, faster, comrade agronomists!'

Another hero of the Lysenko school was the son of an American engineer, Vasily Williams, who became a professor at the Moscow Agricultural
Academy. Williams thought that capitalism and American-style commercial
farming based on the application of chemical fertilizers were taking the
world to the brink of catastrophe. This was in the early 1930s when American farmers in Oklahoma saw their fields turn to dust. Williams believed
that the answer was to rotate fields as medieval peasants had done, growing
grain only every third year. The rest of the time the fields would be left fallow, allowing nitrogen to accumulate in the roots of clover and other grasses
which would enrich the soil. He was opposed by other experts, among them
Pryanishnikov, who stressed the importance of mineral fertilizers and shallow ploughing, but Williams dubbed them 'wreckers of socialist agriculture.' Khrushchev later explained: 'The debate was essentially decided on
the basis of capital investments. Pryanishnikov's theory of mineral fertilizers would have required enormous capital investments in order to build fertilizer plants and new machinery. We were short of capital at that time and
so Williams' theory was more attractive. That is how Williams' grasslands
theory came to reign supreme.'[13]

Khrushchev was one of those who supported Williams, but he admits in
his memoirs that 'the fact of the matter is that Williams' system didn't work.
Even after it had been consistently implemented throughout the Ukraine,
there was no improvement in our agricultural production.'

Stalin also turned to the ideas of Terenty Maltsev, a pupil of Williams,
who recommended ploughing furrows four or five feet deep as a way of improving the soil texture and obtaining higher yields. New ploughs to do this
were designed and manufactured and Stalin gave Maltsev the Lenin prize
for science.

All these ideas helped transform a rich farming nation into one beset by
permanent food shortages. On the collectives, farmers could use neither
chemical fertilizers nor the hybrid corn that America was using to boost
yields by 30 percent. Furthermore, their fields were left fallow most of the
time, and when the crops were sown, the 'vernalized' wheat did not sprout;
nor did Lysenko's frost-resistant wheat and rye seeds, nor the potatoes
grown in summer and the sugar beet planted in the hot plains of Central
Asia. They all rotted. One year, Lysenko even managed to persuade the government to send an army of peasants into the fields with tweezers to remove
the anthers from the spikes of each wheat plant because he believed that his
hybrids must be pollinated by hand. Under banners proclaiming 'Greater
harvests with less dung,' Soviet farmers also had to create artificial manure
by mixing humus with organic mineral fertilizers in a rotating barrel. This
method removed the phosphate and nitrogen, and when the muck was
spread on the fields, it was useless. Ignoring Lysenko's repeated failures, the

Soviet press continued to trumpet his endless successes: cows which produced only cream, cabbages turned into swedes, barley transformed into
oats, and lemon trees which blossomed in Siberia.

Lysenko's greatest triumphs came after the Second World War when he
dreamt up the 'Great Stalin Plan for the Transformation of Nature.' To create
a new and warmer climate in the vast lands of Siberia, Lysenko proposed
planting millions of trees. The peasants had to plant the seeds and saplings
close together because, according to Lysenko's 'law of the life of species,' individuals of the same species do not compete but help each other survive.
Naturally all the seedlings died but not before the composer Shostakovich
had written his choral symphony, *The Song of the Trees*, and Bertolt Brecht
had penned this poem:

> So let us with ever newer arts
> Change this earth's form and operation.
> Gladly measure thousand-year-old wisdom
> By new wisdom one year old.
> Dreams! Golden if!
> Let the lovely flood of grain rise higher!

In China, Mao became greatly taken with the theories of Williams, Lysenko and Michurin. He read Williams' book on soil while still in Yanan and
later frequently quoted both him and Lysenko. Mao, too, wanted the Chinese
to plant seeds close together because, as he told colleagues, 'with company
they grow easily, when they grow together they will be comfortable.'[14] Lysenko's theories meshed perfectly with Mao's obsession with class struggle.
He readily believed that plants from the same 'class' would never compete
against each other for light or food. While the Chinese Communists were still
in Yanan, the chief Chinese Lysenkoist, Luo Tianyu, propagated the Soviet
teachings: and in the 1942 rectification movement, a purge of Party members,
Luo enthusiastically persecuted those who believed in genetics.[15]

After the Communist victory in 1949, Luo was put in charge of the new
Beijing Agricultural University and Soviet-style science now reigned
supreme. In the 1950s, all Soviet methods, textbooks and ideas had to be followed, while Western-trained scientists were either arrested or forced publicly to disown their 'fascist eugenics' theories. All research in genetics came
to a stop. Lysenko's Soviet disciples toured China giving lectures, and Chinese peasants studied his theories at Michurin societies. China had her own
Michurin, a peasant called Shi Yiqian who became a professor at the Henan
Agricultural College after he grew grapes on a persimmon tree, and apples
on a pear tree. In schools, children also set up a Michurin corner in their
classrooms to study how to create such hybrids. Some reportedly managed
not only to graft one vegetable on to another but also to cross-breed animals
such as rabbits and pigs.

Soviet ideas also dominated other fields, notably that of medicine. Perhaps the most absurd notion introduced to the Chinese was the work of Olga Lepeshenskaya, who supposedly proved that living cells could be created from non-living organic material.[16] None of this could be challenged, as a former doctor in Beijing explained:

> We were told the Soviets had discovered and invented everything, even the aeroplane. We had to change textbooks and rename things in Lysenko's honour. So the Harving Cushing Syndrome—a disease of the adrenalin gland—became Lysenko's Syndrome to show it had been discovered by him. Since genetics did not exist, we were forbidden to talk about inherited diseases such as sickle cell anaemia, even to students. This meant that all through Mao's lifetime there was no policy to stop people in the same family marrying each other and passing down their genes. A lot of idiots were born as a result.[17]

Adherence to Lysenkoism meant that when a potato virus struck large areas of China in the 1950s, nothing could be done because, as in the Soviet Union, the changes had to be attributed to environmental factors. Chinese scientists who had invested years of research into the blight were ignored, and their work was not published until 1979. Some believe that potato output in the Mao era was half what it might have been had the cause of the problem been correctly identified.

Lysenkoism reached its apogee in the Great Leap Forward when in 1958 Mao personally drew up an eight-point Lysenkoist blueprint for all Chinese agriculture. Every farmer in every commune in the country had to follow it. The eight elements of this 'constitution,' as it was called, were:

1. The popularization of new breeds and seeds
2. Close planting
3. Deep ploughing
4. Increased fertilization
5. The innovation of farm tools
6. Improved field management
7. Pest control
8. Increased irrigation

The Popularization of New Breeds and Seeds

All over the country in 1958 people began to announce remarkable achievements like those of China's Michurin, Shi Yiqian. In Guangzhou, children and teachers crossed a pumpkin with a papaya, and runner beans with soybeans. In Henan, they produced sunflowers crossed with artichokes. In Beijing, scientists crossed tomatoes with aubergines, corn with rice, and sorghum with rice. One of the most glorious claims was a cross between a cotton plant and a tomato—the result red cotton! [18]

In addition to these vegetable freaks, the New China (Xinhua) News Agency also trumpeted claims that peasants were growing super-big plants—pumpkins weighing not 13 lbs, but 132 lbs, wheat with extra-large ears, and rice of exceptional weight. The country's top national agricultural worker, Yang Guangbo, set the pace by growing paddy rice with 150 grains per ear instead of 100. Others, too, were held up for emulation, amongst them Jiang Shaofang of the Yuli Botanical Normal School in Guangxi province whose achievements were described in *China Youth News*:

> The grains of sorghum are as big as those of corn, one full spike weighing as much as one pound, and one stalk may have several ears of corn giving a yield much greater than normal corn . . . Jiang Shaofang now plans by cross-breeding and grafting sorghum and corn and sugar cane to produce a plant that will be all three—sorghum, corn and sugar cane. He is also preparing next year to plant a high-yield field of wet rice that will produce 600–1,000 lbs per 0.04 acre.[19] The methods he plans to use will be a) to breed a very high yield of wet rice and b) to apply highly advanced agricultural techniques.

Specimens of these miraculous plants appeared at exhibitions or on giant pictures paraded through every city. The Chinese also claimed to produce extraordinary animals. The Ministry of Agriculture boasted in 1960 how peasants at the Golden Dragon Commune near Chongqing had been the first in the world to cross a Yorkshire sow with a Holstein Friesian cow using artificial insemination. The Xinhua News Agency described how after a year the litter was still thriving: some of these curious creatures were white but others were patched like the Holstein and 'in general they had shorter snouts and sturdier legs than ordinary pigs.'[20]

These fantasies were not without consequences in the real world. One interviewee, condemned as a 'rightist,' was sent to a farm near Shanghai where he ran the pig pen. Cadres ordered him to start the pigs breeding prematurely. Normally, pigs do not breed before they are a year old and weigh at least 160 lbs. Instructions came down from above first to start breeding when the pigs weighed 66 lbs and later to start when the piglets were just four months old and weighed only 33 lbs. There was also a scheme to cross Chinese pigs, which produce small litters of two or three piglets, with much bigger Russian sows which have up to fourteen piglets in a litter. The result was indeed larger litters but all the piglets died because the sow could not produce enough milk to feed them. The interviewee said he tried but failed to save the piglets by bottlefeeding them. Attempts in Inner Mongolia and Tibet to crossbreed local sheep and goats with Ukrainian breeds were no more successful because the offspring, ill-adapted to the harsher climate, died in the first winter.

Close Planting

Mao's faith in high-density planting led nearly every commune in China to start an experimental field growing grain in this way. These experimental fields were begun in 1958 and in many places were retained until 1980. In some provinces, like Guangdong, close planting was initially obligatory in all fields. A density of 1.5 million seedlings per 2.5 acres is usually the norm in the south, but in 1958 peasants were ordered to plant 6–7.5 million seedlings and the next year 12–15 million per 2.5 acres. The same close planting was done throughout China with wheat, cotton, sorghum, millet and every other important crop: the results were identical—the seedlings died. Yet the press published photographs apparently showing wheat growing so densely that children could sit on top of it. A retired Xinhua photographer later told the author that the pictures were faked by putting a bench underneath the children.

Fortunately, in most places the peasants knew that close planting was dangerous nonsense and avoided carrying it out on a large scale, otherwise there would have been no food at all in China. Party officials knew this too. One interviewee recalled that before Mao visited the Xinli experimental field in the suburbs of Tianjin in 1958, the cadres brought rice plants from other fields and pushed them close together by hand. 'They were so close together, you really could walk across them,' the interviewee remembered. When Mao left, the cadres immediately removed and replanted the shoots. Mao's doctor, Li Zhisui, recalls how the same thing happened in Hubei: 'Party Secretary Wang Renzhong ordered the peasants to remove rice plants from away fields and transplant them along Mao's route to give the impression of a wildly abundant crop . . . All of China was a stage, all the people performers in an extravaganza for Mao.'

Deep Ploughing

Mao took the idea of deep ploughing to even greater extremes than had Stalin, in the belief that if it was good to plough deep, it was better to plough deeper still. In some places furrows dug by hand were ten feet deep although generally they were around three to four feet. The exhausting, backbreaking work was often done by crack teams of peasants who sweated around the clock. In 1958 Liaoning province's Governor, Huang Oudong, ordered 5 million people with tens of thousands of animals to toil non-stop for forty-five days to deep-plough 3 million hectares of land. Where the top soil was too shallow, he instructed the peasants to transport soil from fields elsewhere. All this was intended to treble yields in Liaoning.[21] In Heilongjiang in the far north, where for part of the year the soil is frozen solid, peasants blasted open furrows with dynamite. In labour camps on the high plateaux and mountains of Qinghai, the inmates tried to soften the iron-hard soil by digging little holes and filling them with straw and grass which were set on fire. In the rice fields of the south, peasant women waded through the deep paddies up to their waists and many caught infections as a result. In Anhui, where the soil is thin, the deep ploughing destroyed the fertility of the fields for many years to come. In some regions, fields were excavated to a depth of thirteen feet.[22] Indeed, in Guizhou province the trenches were so deep that peasants had to tie ropes around their waists to prevent themselves from drowning. Later, the same province claimed to have the biggest yield in the entire country, an absurd 130,000 *jin*, or 65 tonnes per 0.17 acres.[23]

Of course, there was never any real proof that any of this was effective, but agricultural halls displayed exhibits showing how much taller wheat plants grew the deeper they were planted. In February 1959, agronomists in Anguo county reportedly dug up wheat plants to prove that deep plough-ing worked: 'Land ploughed 5 inches had roots only 13 inches long after two months' growth. Land ploughed 5 feet had roots 5 feet long and wheat plants growing in land ploughed 8 feet deep had roots 7 feet 8 inches long.'[24] The deep ploughing was not practised everywhere all of the time, but in some places peasants kept it up for three years or more.

Increased Fertilization

Lysenkoist agrobiology ruled out the use of chemical fertilizers so the Chinese government halted investment in chemical plants and, instead, instructed peasants to use a new method to replace lost nutrients. The Russians claimed that earth when mixed with manure would acquire the qualities of manure and recommended a ratio of 10 per cent manure to 90 per cent earth. So all over China millions of peasants started mixing all sorts of earth and rubbish with real manure and laboriously hauled this to their fields and spread it. To ease the transport of massive amounts of this 'fertil-izer', peasants build carts running on wooden rails to carry it to the fields.

The most extraordinary rubbish was thrown onto the fields as fertilizer. People in Guangzhou took their household rubbish to the outskirts of the city where it was buried for several weeks before being put on the fields. Near Shanghai peasants dumped so much broken glass that they could not walk in the fields in bare feet. Others broke up the mud floors of their huts and their brick stoves and even pulled down their mud walls to use as fertil-izer. Elsewhere people tried to turn ordinary soil into manure by heating and smoking it for ten days. Some tried to collect manure by dragging riverbeds for the rich mud and weeds. An article in the *People's Daily* ex-plained that, thanks to the Communists, China was now no longer short of fertilizer:

> Chinese scientists have said that in the past, many people only considered
> the mineral plant nutrients, that is the amount of nitrogen, phosphorus and

potassium in the fertilizer and their relative proportions. They neglected the experience of the Chinese peasants over thousands of years in using organic fertilizer whose application in massive quantities produces high yields. Agronomists proved last year that they could supply the nutrients continuously and improve the physical properties of the soil.[25]

The Research Institute of Hydrobiology also claimed to have invented 'an everlasting fertilizer,' described as a blue-green algae which assimilates nitrogen. *China Pictorial* boasted that when planted in a paddy field 'it is the equivalent of a permanent nitrogenous fertilizer.' Peasant scientists such as He Wenyi, 'who could neither recognize chemical symbols, nor understand laboratory reports, nor remember lists of ingredients,' were also said to have invented a method for producing fertilizer from bacteria.

The Innovation of Farm Tools

Some of these incredible Heath Robinson inventions made of wood instead of steel have already been described. China also experienced major setbacks when she tried to mass-produce and use machinery based on impractical designs. One example was a rice planter designed to automate the delicate and back-breaking task of planting rice shoots which proved useless because it could handle only one variety at a fixed spacing. Another was a special Soviet plough designed for deep ploughing. The Chinese version, the double-share plough, cost ten times as much as a traditional plough but proved unsuitable for the terraces and paddy fields of southern China: 700,000 had to be withdrawn from use and melted down again. In addition, the Chinese began to manufacture big, heavy Soviet tractors and rejected the small walking tractors which were then helping Japanese farmers to reap record yields on their small plots. In the 1980s, these small tractors were produced in large numbers and were credited with transforming the work of Chinese peasants.

Improved Field Management

Improved field management referred to the field rotation system advanced by Williams. A communiqué issued at a high-level meeting at Wuhan in 1958 summarized its aims: 'We should try to reduce the area sown to various crops to about one-third the present acreage. Part of the land so saved can be left fallow or used for pasturage and the growing of grass fertilizers: the rest can be used for afforestation, reservoirs and the extensive cultivation of flowers, shrubs and trees to turn the whole land with its plains, hills, and waters into a garden.'[26]

Though most provinces were not so foolish as to remove two-thirds of their fields from production, Mao's slogan of 'Plant less, produce more, harvest less' could not be completely ignored. Henan province reported cutting the area sown to grain by 14 per cent and Inner Mongolia and Qinghai by 21 per cent, while Shaanxi stated that it was allowing a third of its arable land to lie fallow.[27]

At the same time, the intensive effort put into those areas which were sown with grain sometimes had disastrous results. In provinces such as Hunan which normally grows two crops of rice, peasants were ordered to grow three. Farmers who had poor land were ordered to switch to growing crops which promised a higher yield but exhausted the soil. As a result, in northern Anhui the peasants planted maize in the summer, and in Shaanxi they had to grow corn instead of millet. Since the only crop that mattered to Mao was grain, the acreage devoted to cash crops was in some places reduced. And in Fujian, where China's best tea is grown, tea bushes were ripped out to make way for grain.

Pest Control

In the interests of pest control a new campaign to exterminate the 'four evils'—birds, rats, insects and flies—was launched in 1958. The whole country was turned out to make a noise, beating drums and pans to prevent sparrows from landing anywhere until they fell down dead with exhaustion. The war against the sparrows, as it was termed, was only called off in April 1960 and the birds were replaced on the list by bedbugs.[28] Without the birds to prey on them, insects multiplied, causing damage to crops. Peasants tried to kill the insects at night by setting up huge lamps in the middle of the fields so that the insects would fly around them until they dropped down dead. Everywhere people were ordered to fulfil a quota by catching and killing flies. The same had to be done with rats and field mice. Since Tibetans regarded the killing of a living animal as a grave sin, some imprisoned lamas killed themselves rather than meet their daily quotas. This campaign was also accompanied by an intensive hygiene campaign. Even at the height of the famine people's houses were still being inspected for cleanliness.

Increased Irrigation

At the same time, every county in China was ordered to construct a water reservoir by building a dam and water channels. A series of gigantic schemes were also conceived and the construction of those already under way, like the Sanmenxia Dam on the Yellow River, was speeded up. Almost without exception, the engineering schemes of this period neither worked nor lasted. A senior Ministry of Agriculture official speaking in the 1990s simply dismissed all the small reservoirs as 'completely worthless.'[29] Most of the county dams had collapsed within two or three years and the dam on the Yellow River quickly filled up with silt, rendering it next to useless.[30] Even today it barely functions. A few medium-scale dams did survive, only to collapse later with terrible results. In the worst dam disaster in history, the Banqiao and Shimantan dams at Zhumadian in Henan province burst after heavy rainfall in August 1975, releasing a wall of water which killed 240,000 people.[31]

The labour put into the construction of these dams was stupendous. Nearly all the construction work was performed by people using the simplest tools who worked day and night in shifts, living in makeshift tents and being fed only when they worked. The peasant labourers were organized in military units and marched to work following flags, with martial music blaring from loudspeakers. On the larger projects, tens of thousands were conscripted as labourers and paid nothing.

To make room for the reservoirs, uncounted numbers of people were evicted from their villages and forcibly relocated. In 1958, when the Xin'anjiang reservoir was built in northern Zhejiang province, 300,000 people were transferred *en masse,* and from one county alone, Chun An, 137,000 people were evacuated:

> Along the road, many of the evacuated families had to eat and sleep in the open air or in rough tents. Freezing and starving, they ate uncooked grain to fend off hunger. People collapsed with illness on the roadside, some even died; pregnant women had to give birth during the journey. According to an old cadre who took part in the relocation work, the marching peasants resembled wartime columns of refugees.[32]

Inspired by the gigantic dams in the Soviet Union, such as that on the Dnieper, and schemes like the Volga-White Sea canal, the Chinese also planned 'the greatest construction undertaking in history.' This was a project to divert surplus water from the Yangtze to the Yellow River in the north. The water would be taken through a huge interlocking system of deep canals, dams, tunnels, ravines and lakes. Work began during the Great Leap Forward and it was envisaged that it would take millions of men seven years to complete it. As it was, the Xinhua News Agency reported that throughout China the peasants had shifted more rock and earth in a single day than had the builders of the Panama Canal in a whole decade: 'A total of 6,560 million cubic feet was excavated in the week ending December 12, 1959. This is more than 12 times the amount shifted for the building of the Panama Canal.'[33] The Party also planned to water the deserts of western China and plant millions of trees by melting the glaciers of the Tianshan mountains. Propaganda photographs even showed scientists dropping materials from aeroplanes to melt the ice.

In the countryside, the dams collapsed because they were made of earth not concrete, and were designed not by engineers but by untrained peasants. The Party took a peculiar pride in defying 'book learning.' One article in *China Pictorial* eulogized Le Heyun, a water conservancy engineer of peasant origin, as a 'bold innovator' and 'advanced worker': 'In 1959, when the construction of the county's Huangtan reservoir was in progress, he suggested that the culvert and conduit should be built of substitutes instead of reinforced concrete as originally planned, thereby saving 7,000 yuan.' Interviewees said concrete was rarely used and this explained why none of the dams lasted more than a year or two. Without a functioning reservoir, the canals and irrigation ditches were rendered equally useless. In later years a few were rebuilt using concrete and one in Sichuan now serves as a boating lake.

Even when the famine was over, Mao's faith in his agricultural methods does not appear to have been shaken in the slightest by their evident failure. On the contrary, in 1964, Mao established at Dazhai in Shanxi province a working model of his eight-point 'constitution.' Millions of visitors, both domestic and foreign, would be taken around Dazhai and told of the wonders of its amazing peasant scientists, their nitrogen-fixing bacteria, the splendid new varieties of plants, the home-made dams, and so on. Perhaps Mao's vanity prevented him from realizing what a fool he had made of himself.

Certainly, in 1958 and 1959, Mao seemed immune to any doubts, believing he had personally witnessed proof that his methods were succeeding beyond even *his* expectations. As a peasant song put it, the grain reached to the sky and paradise was at hand. For example, in 1958 he visited Xushui, one of the model communes, a convenient train ride away from the capital in Hebei province. As he was driven up to the commune centre, his car passed piles of vegetables, turnips, cabbages and carrots laid out for half a mile along the roadside.[34] Officials told him that the peasants had dumped the vegetables because they had grown so much food they did not know what to do with it. At the commune headquarters, the Party secretary told him that they were eating five meals a day free of charge and the autumn grain harvest had quadrupled to half a million tonnes. Mao was reportedly so staggered by this that he pushed up his cap and asked: 'How can you consume all this food? What are you going to do with the surplus?'

The *People's Daily* even started a debate on how China should cope with its food surplus.[35] Everywhere Mao went, Party officials told him of astounding successes: fields which did not produce 330 lbs of grain—the average before the Great Leap Forward—but 49,500 lbs or even 53,000 lbs per 0.17 acres. In fact, there was no way of knowing the real size of the harvest since the State Statistical Bureau had been dismantled and its local offices replaced by 'good news reporting stations.' Yet the propaganda machine churned out one triumphant claim after another. China had outstripped the United States in wheat and cotton production, she had beaten

Japan in per unit yields of rice, and she had bettered the United Sates in cotton yields.

Mao was not alone in believing this nonsense. Liu Shaoqi, formerly an advocate of gradual progress, and his wife, Wang Guangmei, applied to join the Xushui model commune. Its 1958 harvest was double that of 1957, Liu asserted, and he urged the country to 'go right ahead and realize Communism. We must not think that Communism will only be realized very slowly. So long as we work properly, it will be very soon.'

Deng Xiaoping was equally optimistic. He expected per capita grain distribution in 1958 to be 1,375 lbs on the strength of a peasant's assurance that by using Mao's agricultural methods he had produced 77,000 lbs per 0.17 acres on an experimental field. Deng calculated that at this rate yields in 1959 would rise to 231,000 lbs per 0.17 acres and would by 1962 stand at 2.5 tonnes. 'We can all have as much as we want,' he concluded.[36] At Ya'an, in Deng's home province of Sichuan, people showed how much food they had to eat by leaving pots of cooked food on the roadside from which any passer-by could help himself.[37] Chen Boda, one of Mao's cronies, went so far as to declare that the time had come to abolish money; from now on not only should food be free but also clothing, haircuts and everything else.

Mao felt such achievements trumped those of the Soviet Union which had in 1957 launched the first satellite in space. The breaking of such records was therefore called 'launching a satellite' or 'launching a sputnik.' He also declared that China was achieving such success that she was overtaking the Soviet Union on the road to Communism. No one dared challenge these bogus claims directly and later every senior official would explain that, like Deng, they had been innocently duped by the peasants.

In the belief that China was awash with food, everyone in the autumn of 1958 was encouraged to eat as much as they wanted, and for free. In Jiangsu province the slogan was 'Eat as much as you can and exert your utmost in production.' In Guangdong, the Party Secretary Tao Zhu urged everyone to 'eat three meals a day.'[38] In Zengu village, peasants later told American anthropologists what it was like: 'Everyone irresponsibly ate whether they were hungry or not, and in 20 days they had finished almost all the rice they had, rice which should have lasted six months.'[39] In Shanxi, the American William Hinton heard the same thing: 'If there was one facet of the Great Leap Forward that everyone remembers, it was the food. "We lived well," said Wei-de. "We ate a lot of meat. It was considered revolutionary to eat meat. If you didn't eat meat, it wouldn't do . . . People even vied with each other to see who could eat the most . . ."'[40]

What was happening in China was almost identical to what had happened in the Soviet Union during Stalin's collectivization movement. In his semi-fictional novel *The Soil Upturned*, Sholokhov describes a similar scene: 'They ate until they could eat no more. Young and old suffered from stomach-ache. At dinner-time, tables groaned under boiled and roasted meat. At dinner-time everyone had a greasy mouth, everyone hiccupped as if at a wake. Everyone blinked like an owl as if drunk from eating.'

In China, where there had never been enough food for all, people ate so much that by the winter of 1958–9, the granaries were bare. Some far-sighted rural Party secretaries saved their communities by planting sweet potatoes but elsewhere people trusted that they, like the city folk, would under Communism be provided for out of the state granaries. Yet Mao refused to accept that there was a shortage and, since he was convinced that the peasants were hiding their grain, he refused to open the state granaries. Even worse, over the three years from 1958 China doubled her grain exports and cut her imports of food. Exports to the Soviet Union rose by 50 percent and China delivered grain *gratis* to her friends in North Korea, North Vietnam and Albania.[41] This generosity spelt death to many in China.

The Chinese are still suffering from the greatest and most far-reaching consequence of Mao's illusions. Convinced that China had entered an era of unprecedented abundance, Mao rejected any thought of China limiting her population growth. The country's most prominent advocate of birth control was Ma Yinchu, the Chancellor of Beijing University. In 1958, he was dismissed and condemned as a Malthusian. Only a year earlier he had warned of the consequences if no limits were set on population growth. As with so many things, Mao took an orthodox Leninist view. From early on Communists had believed that modern science was the key to a limitless expansion of food supplies. In 1913 Lenin had declared that 'we are the implacable enemy of the neo-Malthusian theory' which he described as 'reactionary' and 'cowardly.' Mao repeatedly attacked the warnings not just of experts like Professor Ma but also of foreigners such as Professor Lossing Buck and the US Secretary of State, Dean Acheson, who feared that China's population growth would outpace any increase in her food supply. In the early 1960s, as China was starving, Mao wrote in yet another criticism of Acheson that: 'Among all things on earth man is the most precious. Under the leadership of the Communist Party miracles can be wrought as long as there are men. We are against Acheson's counter-revolutionary theory. We believe that revolution can change everything. China's big population is a very good thing.'[42]

Mao even feared that there would be a labour shortage. In December 1958, following a meeting of Chinese leaders at Wuchang, a communiqué was issued claiming that 'it will be found that the amount of arable land is not too little but quite a lot and it is not a question of overpopulation but rather a shortage of manpower.' So, from the start of the Great Leap Forward, the Chinese peasants were encouraged to have as many children as possible because, as Mao liked to remind listeners, 'with every stomach comes another pair of hands.' Within a generation, China's population would double to 1.2 billion.

In the winter of 1958–9, people in China began to starve in large numbers but another two years would pass before the Party would come to grips with the terrible disaster. Within the Party leadership, however, a struggle over Mao's policies was about to begin.

How Many Died?

'Any society that is alive is a society with a *history*.'

Vaclav Havel

China has never officially acknowledged that the famine took place nor published an estimate of the death toll. The results of any internal investigations are a state secret and no public discussion of the famine is permitted.

Western experts made the first estimates of the death toll in the early 1980s, nearly a quarter of a century after the famine had taken place, and these calculations are only educated guesses, carried out on the basis of limited information. Yet given that the number of victims of the Holocaust and the Ukrainian famine are still being debated even though far more is known about them, such uncertainty over the death toll in China is hardly surprising. Moreover, in China the Party responsible for the famine is still in power and venerates the memory of Mao. Even in Russia, where the Communists have lost power, it is still proving difficult to determine how many died in Stalin's purges, the famines or the Second World War. Nor have the internal records of Mao's regime been scrutinized by an occupying power in the way the Allies were able to examine those of Nazi Germany.

However, reaching a reliable figure about a famine which lasted for years and extended over such a large country would be difficult even if China were to open all her archives. Many records were lost during the Cultural Revolution and a great deal of other evidence has been deliberately destroyed. In addition, only three censuses were taken in China between 1949 and 1982, one in 1953, another in 1964 and the third in 1982. And, as will be seen, data from that of 1964 must be treated with considerable caution.

During the Great Leap Forward, the State Statistical Bureau, set up in 1952 and modelled on its Soviet equivalent, simply did not function. Professional statisticians were relegated to other work and were only reappointed in July 1961. And only in the following year, on the instructions of Liu Shaoqi and Zhou Enlai, were plans drawn up for the establishment of a powerful, centralized and unified statistics system. At the same time, Party and government departments were forbidden to change statistical figures.[1]

Provisional regulations governing statistical work were issued in 1963 but the newly reconstituted bureau functioned only for another four years or so. On the eve of the Cultural Revolution, Wang Sihua, head of the State Statistical Bureau, was arrested and accused of implementing a revisionist line, 'seizing power from the Party' and 'asserting his independence.' At the same time, large quantities of material from the bureau were burnt. Wang had been in charge of organizing China's second national population census completed in 1964. The census had been conducted amid such secrecy that the outside world was unaware of it, and Mao refused to publish the results. Details of the 1964 census were only published in 1980. Thus for nearly a quarter of a century there was an effective blackout on all Chinese population statistics.[2]

These circumstances parallel those during collectivization and the ensuing famine in the Soviet Union. Stalin had ordered a new census in 1937 but its results were never released and lay buried in the central national archives for half a century. The director of the Census Bureau, O.A. Kvitkin, was dismissed and later shot. Stalin had estimated that the Soviet Union had a population of around 170 million people. However, the census itself counted only 162 million people, clearly showing that 7 million or more people had starved to death in the Ukraine and the northern Caucasus.

The parallels with China do not end there. Researchers have discovered that the Soviet Central Office of Statistics produced two sets of demographic statistics, one for internal use and one for publication. During the Mao era, China appears to have done much the same, at least as far as meteorological data is concerned. During the Great Leap Forward, the Central Meteorological Office continued to function accurately but the information it produced was restricted to senior levels of the Party. The meteorologists reported that there was no unusually bad weather or natural disasters in 1959, 1960 or 1961; indeed the weather was rather good. However, the official media reported claims by Mao and others that China had in this period experienced the worst natural disasters for a century. Official news reports even quoted experts as saying that China's climate had changed. In fact, the worst years since 1949 have been 1954 and 1980–1 when there was neither a severe grain shortage nor a nationwide famine.[3]

However, even if one is prepared to accept that the statistics released by China after 1980 were undoctored, there are doubts as to whether in the midst of a ruthless political struggle, an accurate census was taken in 1964. The count must have been made at the provincial level with the cooperation of the local Party organization and the results passed on to the centre only with the approval of the provincial Party Secretaries. In many provinces, the same officials who were responsible for the famine were still in power and would have had every reason to censor damaging information. In Sichuan, for example, Li Jingquan was still in power in 1964: the census would have revealed his responsibility for 7–9 million deaths. Nonetheless, the data from the 1964 census is crucial to making a proper estimate of the death toll for, without it, one is faced with a gap of twenty-nine years between the first census in 1953 and the third in 1982.

China began to publish a flood of statistical and demographic data after 1980, when the State Statistical Bureau was re-established and the country's few remaining statisticians returned from long years of physical labour in the countryside. It is now possible, using the data from 1953, 1964 and 1982, to track the progress of each age cohort from census to census and therefore establish how many of those born in 1950 survived until 1964 and then 1982. However, two factors in particular hinder a demographer from making a definitive study of the death toll during the famine—internal migration and the number of children who were born and died between 1958 and 1962.

In a famine people flee their homes and often do not return, but a census count does not show whether they have starved to death or whether they have moved away and failed to register elsewhere. Census figures for Shanghai, for example, show that 950,000 people left Shanghai between 1953 and 1964, but they do not reveal what happened to these people or where they went. During the famine, uncounted numbers fled the worst-hit regions, over 10 million settling in Manchuria and Inner Mongolia alone.

The other great challenge is to try and guess how many children were born during the famine years and, of these, how many died. This is not revealed by the 1953 and 1964 censuses although experts can make educated guesses based on birth rates and infant mortality rates before and after the famine. On the other hand, pre-famine trends are not a strong guide because it is clear that fewer babies are born in a famine. Many women stop ovulating altogether, and if they do give birth, they produce less milk and infant mortality rises sharply. One expert has calculated that Anhui suffered a fertility crisis for as long as two years during the famine but obviously the scale of the crisis varied from province to province.[4] With a population the size of China's, the margin for error is fairly high. Under normal conditions, China might in the late 1950s and early 1960s have seen around 25 million births a year. Even in famine conditions, the number of births might still have been 14 million a year. Thus in the four years from 1958 to 1962, the number of births could have ranged from a low of 56 million to a maximum of 100 million.

The censuses are not the sole guide to calculating the death toll in China because the local authorities also maintain registers of births and deaths. Given the rationing system which existed during this period, a careful record would have been made at times of the number of mouths to feed. On the other hand, at the height of the famine in the countryside, no one was burying the dead, let alone recording the number of deaths. The births and deaths of small children, in particular, would often have passed almost unnoticed. Nor would officials have kept track of those who fled and managed to survive or of those who died on the roads. And there is another, final question-mark about Chinese figures: how were the inmates of the labour camps and prisons recorded? And the millions in the armed forces? Generally, both groups are excluded from provincial population figures but during the famine there were perhaps as many as 10 million prisoners and the death rate in the camps was exceptionally high, on average 20 percent and often far higher.

In the early 1980s, Dr. Judith Banister undertook a major investigation of China's population statistics which was published in *China's Changing Population*. Taking all the above factors into account, she reached the following conclusion:

Assuming that without the Great Leap Forward policies and experiences China would have maintained its claimed 1957 death rate of 10.8 during the years 1958–1961, the official data imply that those four years saw over 15 million excess deaths attributable to the Great Leap Forward in combination with poor weather conditions. The computerized reconstruction of China's population trends utilized in this book, which assumes under-reporting of deaths in 1957, as well as in all the famine years, results in an estimated 30 million excess deaths during 1958–1961.[5]

This figure, arrived at in 1984, is the most reliable estimate we have but it is not the only one.

While China has never formally rejected this total or put forward an alternative, a wealth of statistical information has been published which amounts to quasi-official recognition that millions did die of famine. One such work, *Contemporary Chinese Population* published in 1988, goes further by explicitly stating that the official data disguises the extent of the death toll. Official figures show that between 1959 and 1961, the population fell by 13.48 million but the authors say: 'The problem is that there are false figures and 6.03 million people during the three years of difficulty were not taken into account when the calculations were made . . . If we take this into account, the death rate in 1960 should be 1 percent higher at 3.85 percent. So out of a population of 500 million, there were 19.5 million deaths in the countryside.'[6]

The authors also substantiate anecdotal evidence that large numbers of girls were allowed to die or were killed during the famine. According to the 1964 census, 0.5 percent more boys than girls aged 5–9 and 0.4 percent more males than females aged 9–14 years survived the famine. Generally, even in normal times a higher proportion of male infants than female infants survive in China but the 1982 census indicates that the normal difference is only about 0.1 percent. This means that during the famine 4.7 million fewer girls survived than would have done so in normal years. In other words, nearly a quarter of the 19.5 million famine victims were peasant girls, who appear to have been deliberately allowed to starve to death or were killed by their parents.

Articles published by some experts in China and by exiled dissidents claim that the death toll is far higher even than Banister's estimate. In 1993, a Chinese scholar writing under the pen-name Jin Hui published an article in a Shanghai academic journal, *Society*, which was later withdrawn. The author looked at inconsistencies in official statistics on birth and death rates, sex ratios, rural and urban populations and provincial and national figures, and concluded that the figures had been falsified to hide a death toll of at least 40 million. Unfortunately, it is also true that Chinese statistics about any subject are rarely internally consistent so it is hard to know how significant these discrepancies are. Whether or not this figure of 40 million is to be trusted, it is now used, almost casually, by various authors inside China who lump deaths and the reduction in births together. Cong Jin of the National

Defence University writes in *China 1949–1989: The Zig-zag Development Era* that 'From 1959 to 1961 the abnormal deaths plus the reduction of births reached about 40 million.'[7] Another book, *Leftism in China* by Wen Yu, published in 1993, claims that 'from 1959 to 1961, the abnormal deaths plus the reduction of births reached altogether more than 40 million with direct economic losses of 120 billion yuan.'[8]

The estimates of American demographers are also challenged by Chen Yizi, a senior Chinese Party official who fled to America after the crackdown that followed the 1989 Tiananmen pro-democracy demonstrations. After 1979, Chen played an important role in the rural reforms as a member of a think-tank called the *Tigaisuo* or System Reform Institute patronized by Zhao Ziyang, then Premier and later Party General Secretary. The new Chinese leadership wanted to find out what had really happened under Mao, and one of the institute's first tasks was to draw up a picture of rural China. Chen was part of a large team of 200 officials who visited every province and examined internal Party documents and records. The institute's report concluded that between 43 and 46 million people had died during the famine and several sources said that an even larger figure of 50 and 60 million deaths were cited at internal meetings of senior Party officials.

The institute's report has never been released but in an interview Chen recalled the death toll for a number of provinces:

Henan	7.8 million
Anhui	8 million
Shandong	7.5 million
Sichuan	9 million
Qinghai	900,000

Thus, in these five provinces alone, 33.2 million people died. Chen argues that these figures are reliable because each province compiled detailed statistics on its population. In normal times, Chinese local officials keep records of household registration and these were particularly important when the commune system operated because with all food rationed, great care was taken in counting the number of mouths.

That such detailed records were kept is clear from the report on Fengyang county in Anhui. Such figures were also used when the Party compiled reports on the famine in each province at the end of 1960; and in places like Gansu officials kept a record of famine deaths as well as the number of mouths to feed. However, while it is clear that Beijing was aware of the scale of the disaster, the reliability of such figures is hard to ascertain. In addition, there is an added complication, because evidence suggests that the Party often produced different versions of the same report. Lower figures were released to lower-ranking officials. Until these internal reports are made public, we cannot be sure that they exist or, if they do, whether they take into account such factors as internal migration or include normal deaths in the totals.

From a moral perspective, the debate is meaningless. Whether 30 or over 40 million perished, China managed to hide the largest famine in history for twenty years. In terms of sheer numbers, no other event comes close to this. Until the Great Leap Forward, the largest famine on record took place in China between 1876 and 1879 when 9–13 million died.

In other great historical famines, a higher proportion of the population died than in China in 1958–61. At the start of the great Irish potato famine in 1845, Ireland had a population of about 8.5 million of whom around 1 million died of hunger and 1.5 million emigrated. Most historians recognize that the Irish famine was caused by a blight which destroyed the potato harvest on which the population depended for most of its food. Relief efforts were undermined by the slowness of communications and transport, and when grain was shipped from North America it did not relieve the hunger. The Irish economy was so dependent on the potato that it was not equipped to process the grain for human consumption. Indeed, before the famine bread was seldom seen and ovens virtually unknown. Even so, the British government still stands accused of acting with indifference to a subject people.

In more recent times, except during war, famines have become rarer. China is often compared to India but in this century India has not suffered a famine of comparable dimensions. India's largest famine in modern times took place between 1896 and 1897 when drought led to 5 million deaths. The Bengal famine of 1942, when around 1.5 million died, was caused by the Japanese invasion of Burma which cut off rice imports.

What sets Mao's famine apart from those in Ireland and India is that it was entirely man-made. China was at peace. No blight destroyed the harvest. There were no unusual floods or droughts. The granaries were full and other countries were ready to ship in grain. And the evidence shows that Mao and the Chinese bureaucracy were in full control of the machinery of government.

The event which most resembles Mao's famine is that in the Ukraine in 1932–3 where circumstances were almost identical [. . .]. A slightly larger proportion of China's population died in the Great Leap Forward than in the Soviet Union—4.6 percent (if one accepts a figure of 30 million out of a total population of 650 million) compared to 4.11 percent (7 million out of 170 million). In China, deaths were concentrated among the rural population, so out of a maximum 550 million peasants 5.45 percent died, one in twenty. Around a quarter of the population of the Ukraine perished in the famine there, largely in one year, 1933. However, in parts of China such as Anhui, it is likely that a quarter of the rural population died just as in the Ukraine.[9]

One can also compare China with Cambodia under Pol Pot. Inspired by Mao, the Khmer Rouge collectivized the entire population in the 1970s and it is reckoned that out of 8 million people, 1 million died. However, this number also includes the victims of a civil war and a war with Vietnam, so the extent of deaths due to famine alone is unclear.

If we look at Mao's famine as a deliberate act of inhumanity, then his record can also be measured against that of Hitler and Stalin. Some 12 million died in the Nazi concentration camps and a further 30 million were killed during the Second World War. Stalin is thought to have allowed 20 million to die in the gulags and overall he is believed to have been responsible for between 30 and 40 million deaths. However, an investigation into Mao's record by Daniel Southerland in the *Washington Post* suggests that Mao exceeded even these ghastly totals:

> While most scholars are reluctant to estimate a total number of 'unnatural deaths' in China under Mao, evidence shows that he was in some way responsible for at least 40 million deaths and perhaps 80 million or more. This includes deaths he was directly responsible for and deaths resulting from disastrous policies he refused to change. One government document that has been internally circulated and seen by a former Communist Party official now at Princeton University [Chen Yizi] says that 80 million died unnatural deaths—most of them in the famine following the Great Leap Forward.[10]   ∎

NOTES FOR "FALSE SCIENCE, FALSE PROMISES"

1. Edward Friedman, Paul G. Pickowicz and Mark Selden, *Chinese Village, Socialist State*, pp. 216–217.
2. Quoted in Klaus Mehnert, *Peking and Moscow*, p. 356. Mehnert also describes how during the Great Leap Forward, Shanghai writers undertook to produce 3,000 literary works in two years. Soon they had far exceeded their plan: one single evening three thousand Shanghai workers and soldiers 'produced' 3,000 poems and 360 songs. One of the poems awarded a special prize was 'Ode to the Red Sun':
   'When Chairman Mao comes forth,
   The East shines Red.
   All living things prosper,
   The Earth is "red".
   Six hundred million, peony bright:
   Each one is "red".'
   For all our beautiful hills and streams,
   Eternal time is "red".'
3. Quoted from a Red Guard magazine in Roderick MacFarquhar, *The Origins of the Cultural Revolution*, p. 84.
4. Dawa Norbu, *Red Star over Tibet*, p. 129.
5. Zhou Libo, *Great Changes in a Mountain Village*, was translated by Derek Bryan and published by the Foreign Languages Press in 1961. Quoted in *A Chinese View of China* by John Gittings, p. 139.
6. John Byron and Robert Pack, *The Claws of the Dragon: Kang Sheng*, p. 234.
7. John Byron and Robert Pack, *The Claws of the Dragon: Kang Sheng*, p. 234.
8. Li Rui, *A True Account of the Lushan Meeting*, p. 8.
9. Mikhail Klochko, *Soviet Scientist in China*, pp. 139–140.
10. *People's Daily*, 1958.

11. *They Are Creating Miracles*, Foreign Languages Press, 1960. The Chinese edition appeared earlier.

12. For a detailed account of Lysenko see Zhores A. Medvedev, *The Rise and Fall of T.D. Lysenko*, translated by I. Michael Wermner, Columbia University Press, 1969; and David Joravsky, *The Lysenko Affair*, University of Chicago Press, 1970.

13. Nikita Khrushchev, *Khrushchev Remembers*, p. 13.

14. Roderick MacFarquhar, Timothy Cheek and Eugene Wu (eds.), *The Secret Speeches of Chairman Mao*, p. 450.

15. Denis Fred Simon and Merle Goldman (eds.), *Science and Technology in Post-Mao China*, p. 48.

16. Denis Fred Simon and Merle Goldman (eds.), *Science and Technology in Post-Mao China*, p. 53.

17. Interview with the author.

18. British United Press, printed in the *Guardian*, 24 March 1960.

19. The Chinese measure of land is the *mu*, eqivalent to 0.17 acres.

20. Reported in the *Sunday Times* by Richard Hughes, June 1960.

21. Alfred L. Chan, 'The Campaign for Agricultural Development in the Great Leap Forward: A Study of Policy-making and Implementation in Liaoning', *China Quarterly*, No. 129 (March 1992), pp. 68–69.

22. Bo Yibo, *Retrospective of Several Big Decisions and Incidents*, Central Party School, 1993.

23. Interview with Chen Yizi.

24. *China Pictorial*, 1959.

25. *Far Eastern Economic Review*, February 1959.

26. *Far Eastern Economic Review*, 10 December 1958.

27. Roderick MacFarquhar, *The Origins of the Cultural Revolution*.

28. Reuters, 7 April 1960.

29. Interview with the author.

30. Vaclav Smil, *The Bad Earth: Environmental Degradation in China*.

31. *Human Rights Watch Asia Report*, February 1995, pp. 37–44.

32. Dai Qing (ed.), *Changjiang Yimin (Population Transfer on the Yangzi River)*, a documentary anthology.

33. Richard Hughes, *The Chinese Communes*, p. 69.

34. Interview with the author.

35. Jung Chang, *Wild Swans*, p. 226.

36. Roderick MacFarquhar, *The Origins of the Cultural Revolution*, p. 121.

37. Interview with the author.

38. Roderick MacFarquhar, *The Origins of the Cultural Revolution*, p. 139.

39. Jack Potter and Sulamith Heins Potter, *China's Peasants—The Anthropology of a Revolution*, p. 73.

40. William Hinton, *Shenfan*, p. 218.

41. Denis Twitchett and John K. Fairbank (eds.), *Cambridge History of China*, vol. 14, pp. 378–386.

42. *Far Eastern Economic Review*, 11 August 1960.

NOTES FOR "HOW MANY DIED"

1. Judith Banister, *China's Changing Population*, p. 13.
2. Judith Banister, *China's Changing Population*, pp. 2–26.
3. Interview with Chinese officials. The worst fear for droughts and floods was 1954 according to tables produced by the Chinese Central Meteorological Centre. Both 1960 and 1961 had fewer floods and droughts than 1958 which was publicly hailed as an outstanding year.
4. Peng Xizhe, 'Demographic Consequences of the Great Leap Forward in China's Provinces,' *Population and Development Review*, Vol. 3, No. 4, December 1987, p. 641.
5. Banister (p. 85) draws on work on Chinese population figures by John S. Aird, Ansley J. Coale and other authorities in the United States.
6. Wang Weizhi, *Contemporary Chinese Population*, edited by Xu Dixin, p. 9.
7. Cong Jin, *China, 1949–1989: The Zig-zag Development Era*, p. 272.
8. Wen Yu, *Disasters of Leftism in China*, p. 280.
9. See also Nicholas R. Lardy, 'The Chinese Economy under Stress, 1958–1965' in *The Cambridge History of China*, Vol. 14, which looks at mortality and compares China's famine with that in the Soviet Union.
10. Daniel Southerland in *Washington Post*, 18 July 1994. Chen Yizi is now President of the Center for Modern China at Princeton University.

■ QUESTIONS FOR MAKING CONNECTIONS WITHIN THE READING ■

1. In order to follow Jasper Becker's argument about the relationship between science and politics during Mao's reign, you need to be able to distinguish between the genetic theories of Mendel, Lysenko, and Michurin and be able to summarize the agricultural innovations made by Vasily Williams and Terenty Maltsev. What did each of these scientists believe about how best to improve the productivity of plants? Why were Lysenko and Michurin hailed by Mao and Stalin?

2. Becker's analysis of Mao's eight-point agricultural "constitution" is hardly neutral: he describes the approaches as "fantasies" and "dangerous nonsense." What is it that enables Becker to see the problems with Mao's plan? Could the failure of this plan have been predicted at the time? Could it have been prevented without sacrificing Mao's larger vision of how society should work?

3. What is Becker trying to accomplish in "How Many Died?" What does he want his readers to see about Mao's role in the Great Famine? And what are his readers supposed to do once they understand this point?

■ QUESTIONS FOR WRITING ■

1. One could argue that Becker is able to see the problems with the Great Leap Forward because he has the luxury of hindsight. Now that so much

more is known about how to increase agricultural productivity, the argument goes, the failings of earlier approaches are obvious. How would Becker respond to this argument? What is to be gained by pursuing this kind of historical research? What might a reader be expected to do after reading the results of Becker's research? What purpose is served by cataloging "how many died"?

2. Becker explores how the relationship between the scientific community and the government played out in China, and in so doing he suggests that there is a better alternative. In our own time, the scientific community regularly reveals insights and advocate products and practices that have profound social consequences, as with the advent of the birth-control pill, the morning-after pill, cloning, and stem cell research. While it is relatively easy to say that Mao abused his power by redefining science to meet his political ends, it is more difficult to say what the appropriate relationship between the government and the scientific community should be. Does Becker's work provide us with direction as to how this relationship should be worked out?

■ *QUESTIONS FOR MAKING CONNECTIONS BETWEEN READINGS* ■

1. Jasper Becker has cataloged the consequences of Mao's belief that nature could be bridled to serve his political philosophy. Are those scientists currently engaged in the work of genetic engineering, as described in Michael Pollan's "Playing God in the Garden," suffering from similar delusions about their own powers? Is it conceivable that fifty years from now another scholar will write a similar book about the blind faith that Americans had in science and the devastating consequences this had on our food supply? Or are there aspects of the democratic and capitalist systems that ensure that no similar "manmade" disaster will happen here?

2. In "To Engineer Is Human," Henry Petroski writes candidly about the role that structural failure plays in the process of design, and he refers to examples where these failures have resulted in the loss of life and capital. With this in mind, one might say that Mao was engaged in the process of "social engineering," experimenting with alternate ways of organizing social relations, and that the failure of the structure he designed was just part of the design process. If Petroski is correct that humans learn by playing, testing limits, and improving on failures, is Mao simply an example of someone who used human beings as his building materials? If there's acceptable risk in engineering, is there also acceptable risk in the creation of social organizations?

For additional suggestions about making connections between readings, visit the Link-O-Mat and More Sample Assignments at <www.newhum.com>.

JONATHAN BOYARIN

JONATHAN BOYARIN is an anthropologist and an ethnographer who has studied the lifestyle and culture of Jews the world over. Although anthropology originally emerged as a way for outsiders to study and understand foreign cultures, the anthropology that Boyarin practices is of a different sort: he provides an insider's view of cultures and traditions that are, in some ways, his own.

Thus, in pursuing his fieldwork, Boyarin has been concerned not only with describing Jewish identity in Paris, New York, and Jerusalem, but also with contributing to the broader project of preserving Jewish culture. This approach to anthropology has helped Boyarin invent for himself a "funky Orthodox" Jewish identity, as "Waiting for a Jew" chronicles.

Considered one of America's most original thinkers about Jewish culture, Boyarin has written extensively about the roles that history, memory, and geography have played in the formation of Jewish identity. In *A Storm from Paradise: The Politics of Jewish Memory* (1992), *Palestine and Jewish History: Criticism at the Borders of Ethnography* (1996), and *Thinking in Jewish* (1996), Boyarin asks his readers to consider whether there is such a thing as an "essential" Jewish identity. While the notion that there is an essential, unchanging self at the core of every human being has fallen out of favor in academic circles, Boyarin bids his readers to recognize that identity does not serve the same function for marginalized groups that it serves for dominant groups. As Boyarin puts it in *Remapping Memory: The Politics of TimeSpace* (1994), "For people who are somehow part of a dominant group, any assertions of essence are ipso facto products and reproducers of the system of domination. For subaltern groups, however, essentialism is resistance, the insistence on the 'right' of the group actually to exist." As "Waiting for a Jew" documents, answering the question "Who are you?" is not as simple as it might seem, for the answer requires that one first consider the histories, traditions, and communal life experiences that have made the notions of "an identity" and "one's own identity" possible.

To learn more about Jonathan Boyarin and the construction of Jewish identity, visit the Link-O-Mat at <www.newhum.com>.

Boyarin, Jonathan. "Waiting for a Jew." *Thinking in Jewish*. Chicago: The University of Chicago Press, 1996. 8–34.

Waiting for a Jew
Marginal Redemption at the Eighth Street Shul

My story begins in a community, with an illusion of wholeness. I am between the age when consciousness begins and the age of ten, when my family leaves the community and my illusion is shattered. Our family lives on the edge of the Pine Barrens in Farmingdale, New Jersey, along with hundreds of other families of Jewish chicken farmers who have come from Europe and New York City in several waves, beginning just after World War I.

Among the farmers are present and former Communists, Bundists, Labor Zionists, German refugees who arrived in the 1930s, and Polish survivors of concentration camps. These, however, are not the distinctions I make among them as a child. Johannes Fabian has shown us that when we write ethnography we inevitably trap those about whom we write into a hypostatic, categorical, grammatical "present" (Fabian 1983). An autobiographer has the same power over the memory of himself and those he knew in prior times as the fieldworker who later obliterates the narrative aspect of his encounter with his subjects—the power to deny their autonomy in hindsight.[1] Those of the farming community whom I will later remember, I know therefore by their own names and places: my grandparents closer to Farmingdale proper; the Silbers off on Yellowbrook Road, with a tree nursery now instead of chickens; the Lindauers, stubbornly maintaining an egg-packing and -distribution business, while others find different ways to earn a living.

My child's world is not exclusively Jewish, nor am I brought up to regard it as such. Across our road and down a few hundred yards is a tiny house built by Jewish farmers when they first came to settle here. It is now, incredibly, occupied by a black family of ten. Next to them lives an equally poor and large white family. Shortly before we leave Farmingdale, the old Jew in the farm next to ours passes away, and the property passes to a Japanese businessman. The young men he hires live in the farmhouse, growing oriental vegetables on the open field and bonsai in a converted chicken coop, and they introduce me to the game of Go. The nearest Jewish household is that of my great-uncle Yisroel and his wife Helen, the third house to the right of ours.

Yet we are near the heart of Jewish life in Farmingdale. Half a mile—but no, it must be less—down Peskin's Lane (the name my grandfather Israel Boyarin gave to what was a dirt road in the 1930s) is the Farmingdale Jewish Community Center, on the next plot of land after Uncle Yisroel's house.

Just past the community center is the farm that once belonged to my father's uncle Peskin, the first Jew in Farmingdale. Fifteen years after Peskin's death, the bodies of two gangsters were found buried on the farm. The local papers noted: "Mr. Peskin was not available for comment."

Our own farm consists of eleven acres. Facing the road is the house my grandfather built, with a large front lawn and an apple tree in back. Farther back, four large chicken coops mark the slope of a hill ending in our field, behind which woods conceal the tiny Manasquan River. The field, well fertilized by chickens allowed to scratch freely on it during the day, is leased each summer by a dirt farmer who grows corn. My father has joined the insurance agency begun by my mother, and they have gotten rid of the birds. The coops stand empty by my fourth birthday. One day, though, while a friend and I chase each other through the coops in play, we are startled by a pair of chickens. Their presence in the stillness and the faint smell of ancient manure is inexplicable and unforgettable. Thus, on the abandoned farm, my first memories are tinged with a sense of traces, of mystery, of loss. Do all who eventually become anthropologists have this experience in some form, at some time in their early lives?

My mother's turn to business is wise: chicken farming as the basis for the community's livelihood is quickly becoming untenable. Nor is it surprising, as she had given up a career as a chemist to come live with my father on the farm—thus taking part in the process of Jewish dispersal from the immigrants' urban centers, which in the last quarter of the century would be mirrored by a shrinking of Jewish communities in small towns and a reconsolidation of the Orthodox centers. My mother's father, an Orthodox Jew from a leading Lithuanian rabbinical family, has struggled to learn English well and has gone into the insurance business himself. After his death, my mother tells me that he had originally resisted her desire to marry the son of a Jewish socialist, but he consented when he met my father's father's father, a Lubavitcher Hasid named Mordechai.

My grandfather's concern for his daughter's future as an observant Jew was well founded. The Sabbath is marked in our family only on Friday nights: by my mother's candle-lighting, and her chicken soup in winter; by the challah; by the presence of my grandfather. We do not keep kosher, nor do we go to shul on *shabbes*.

The Jewish Community Center—with its various functions as social and meeting hall, synagogue, and school—is nevertheless a focus of our family's life. Most of the ten or so other children in these classes I see at other times during the week as well, either in public school or playing at one another's homes. I am there three times each week, first for Sunday school, and then for Hebrew school on Tuesday and Thursday afternoons. This odd distinction is no doubt a practical one, since some parents do not choose to send their children three times a week. But since Sunday school was first a Christian institution, it also reflects an accommodation to Christian church patterns, as evidenced by the fact that Sundays are devoted to teaching stories of the Bible. One Sunday school teacher we have in our kindergarten year captivates me with his skill in making these stories come to life, as when he imitates the distress of an Egyptian waking up to find his bed covered with frogs.

Another teacher, a young woman with a severe manner and a heavy black wig, the wife of a member of the Orthodox yeshiva in Lakewood, later causes general misery because of her inability to understand children, although I will eventually appreciate the prayers she teaches us to read. One time I come in to Hebrew school immediately after yet another in a series of martyred family dogs has been run over in front of our house. Her attempt to comfort me is like some malicious parody of Talmudic reasoning: "You shouldn't be so upset about an animal. If a chicken and a person both fell down a well, which one would you save first?"

In addition to this somewhat haphazard religious training, there is the local chapter of Habonim, the Labor Zionist Youth Organization, to which my older brother and sister belong. I tag along and am tolerated by their peers. Once I am given a minor role in a stage performance by the chapter. Though I am too young to remember quite what it is about, the phrase *komets-aleph:aw* stands in my memory.

Later I will learn that this phrase occurs in a famous and sentimental Yiddish folksong. It is the first letter of the Hebrew alphabet, the first thing countless generations of Jewish children have been taught. Here is an unusual case in which a traditional lesson—how to pronounce the alphabet—is successfully inculcated in the secularized framework of a dramatic performance about the traditional setting. Perhaps this is because of the necessary rehearsals, in which I must have heard, as the song puts it, "once more, over and over again, *komets-aleph:aw*." The memory reinforces my later preference for this older, European pronunciation of the Hebrew vowels, my sense of the Israeli *komets-aleph:ah* as inauthentic.

Also memorable at the Jewish Community Center is the annual barbecue run by the Young Couples' Club. Though my father will assure me in an interview years later that its association with the Fourth of July was purely a matter of convenience, the atmosphere is certainly one of festival, even including "sacrifices" and "altars": My father and his friends set up huge charcoal pits with cement blocks, and broil vast amounts of chicken; corn is boiled in aluminum garbage cans to go with it.[2] For the children, a Purim-like element of riotous excess is added: This one time each year, we are allowed to drink as much soda as we want. One year "wild," blond-haired Richie L., whose parents have a luncheonette booth for a kitchen table and an attic filled with antiques, claims to drink fourteen bottles, thus adding to the mystique he holds for me.

But it is the days when the Community Center becomes a synagogue that leave the strongest impression on my memory. There must be services every Saturday morning, but I am completely unaware of them. What I will remember are the holidays: Purim, Rosh Hashanah, Yom Kippur, Simchas Torah, and a crowd of people who just a few years later will never be there again. On the fall holidays, the shul is full of movement, impatience, noise, and warmth. Except for a few moments such as the shofar blowing, we children are free to come and go: By the steps in front, tossing the juicy, poisonous red berries of a yew that was planted, I am told, in memory of my brother Aaron, whom I never knew; inside the main doors, to look left at Walter Tenenbaum wrapped in a *tallis* that covers his head, standing at a lectern by the Ark of the Torah as he leads the service, or to look right, along the first long row of folding chairs for our fathers; thence a few rows back to where our mothers sit separately from the men, although unlike most synagogues that look and sound as traditional as this one, there is no *mekhitse*, no barrier between women and men; and finally out through the side door and down a flight of wooden steps to the monkey bars, into the ditch where one miraculous day we found and drank an intact bottle of orange soda, or into the kitchen, social room, and classroom in the basement. Once each year we children are the center of attention, as we huddle under a huge tallis in front of the Ark on Simchas Torah to be blessed.

In classic ethnographies of hunting-and-gathering groups, landscapes are described as personalized, integral elements of culture. This was true of the landscape of my childhood friendships, which today is as obliterated as any *shtetl* in Eastern Europe. Any marginal group in mass society may be subject without warning to the loss of its cultural landscape, and therefore those who are able to create portable landscapes for themselves are the most likely to endure.

The Jews have been doing so for thousands of years; the Simchas Torah tallis can stand in front of any Ark, and the original Ark, in the biblical account, was itself transported from station to station in the desert. Yet the members of a community are orphaned when the naïve intimacy of a living environment is torn away from them. Such a break appears often in Jewish literature—significantly with the emphasis not forward on the beginning of adulthood, as in the European *Bildungsroman*, but rather on the end of childhood.[3]

I suddenly discover the distance between the world and myself at the end of August in 1966. When my parents pick me up from camp, they take me to a new house. For the last time, we attend high holiday services in Farmingdale. It is the only time we will ever drive there, and our family's friends no longer join us during the afternoon break on Yom Kippur for a surreptitious glass of tea and a slice of challah. Farmingdale is no longer home, and though our new house is only ten miles away, it is another world.

We live now in an almost exclusively white, middle-class suburb with many Jews, but our older, brick house is isolated on a block of working-class cubes. While neighbors my age play football in our yard, I often retreat to my room and console myself with sports books for preadolescents. My new and bewildering sense of marginality leads me to develop an exquisite self-consciousness. It is manifested in an almost constant internal dialogue, which keeps me company and will interfere with my adolescent sexuality.

Ostracism is often the fate of a new kid on the block, and it may last longer when his family is Jewish and his home better than those on either side. There is a custom in this part of New Jersey of tolerating petty vandalism on "mischief night," the night before Halloween. Pumpkins are smashed, and we, along with other unpopular families on the block, have the windows of our cars and house smeared with soap. One Halloween I wake up to see graffiti chalked in bold letters on the sidewalk in front of our house: "Jon the Jew, a real one too." My father summons the kids next door—whom we suspect of being the authors—to scrape the words off the sidewalk, as I burn with shame.

He and I never discuss the incident, but later I will compare it with a memory of Freud's: As a child, he was walking with his father, when a gentile knocked his father's hat off. Rather than confronting the man, Freud's father meekly bent over to pick up the hat, and his son's humiliation persisted into adulthood (Bakan 1958; D. Boyarin 1997). The moral is that a victim is likely to view any response as adding insult to injury. In my case, as my father asserts the American principle of equality and "teaches a lesson" to my occasional and vindictive playmates by forcing them to erase what they have written, I feel as though he is inviting them to write the words again, this time making me watch my own degradation.

The new synagogue my parents join is only a partial refuge. It exemplifies the difference between a shul and a temple. Everything in Farmingdale had faced inward: little concern was paid for praying in unison, and though the *shammes* would bang his hand on the table for silence, he was seldom heeded; even the cantor was alone with God, facing away from everyone else, rather than performing for the congregation. Calling a synagogue a temple, by contrast, is doubly revealing. On the one hand, it indicates a striving for the majesty of the ancient House in Jerusalem. On the other hand, just like the English term used to designate it, its trappings are borrowed from the Christian world, down to the black robes worn by the rabbi and cantor.

These robes lack the warm mystery of Walter Tenenbaum's tallis. The responsive readings of Psalms in English seem ridiculously artificial to me from the first. And my mother, who still comes only on the holidays though I sometimes drag my father to temple on Friday nights, complains of the rabbi's long-winded sermons and yearns aloud for the intimate conversations along the back wall of the Farmingdale Jewish Community Center.

Unlike some, I do not leave the synagogue immediately after my bar mitzvah. I teach the blessings of the Haftorah to two reluctant boys a year younger than me. I briefly experience religious inspiration, and for perhaps two weeks put on *tefillin* every morning. But the atmosphere is hollow, and the emptiness breeds cynicism in me in my teens.

The coldness of the building itself is symptomatic of the lack of sustenance I sense there. The pretense and bad taste of modern American synagogues are well-known yet puzzling phenomena that deserve a sociological explanation of their own. Even the walls of the temple are dead concrete blocks, in contrast to the wood of the Farmingdale Jewish Community Center. Services are held in a "sanctuary," unlike the room at the Community Center where activities as varied as dances and political meetings were conducted when services were not being held. Aside from any question of Jewish law, there is a loss of community marked by the fact that everyone drives to the temple rather than walking. It is a place separated from the home, without the strong and patient webs spun by leisurely strolling conversations to and from a shul.

Most generally, the temple is victim to the general alienation of the suburbs. What happens or fails to happen there is dependent on what the people who come there expect from each other. Those who belong (there are vastly more "members" than regular attendees) seem bound primarily by a vague desire to have Jewish grandchildren. The poor rabbi, typical of Conservative congregations, seems hired to be a stand-in Jew, to observe all the laws and contain all the knowledge they don't have the time for. They are not bound to each other by Jewish religious ways, nor do they share the common interests of everyday life—the same livelihood or language—that helped to make a complete community in Farmingdale.

I go off to college and slowly discover that my dismissal of Judaism leaves me isolated, with few resources. I had realized my individual difference on leaving Farmingdale. Now, much more removed from a Jewish environment than ever before, I become aware of my inescapable Jewishness. In the small northwestern college of my dreams, everyone around me seems "American" and different, though I have never thought of myself as anything but American. Even in the humanities curriculum on which the school prides itself, Jewish civilization is absent. It is as though Western cultural history were just a triumphant straight line from the Greeks to Augustine and Michelangelo (with his horned Moses and uncircumcised David), confusion setting in at last only with Marx and Freud.

Five years too late to benefit me, a Jewish Studies position will in fact be established at the college. Such positions are usually funded by Jewish individuals or organizations, and hence they represent the growing acculturation (not assimilation) of Jews into American academic life. The fact that they are regarded as legitimate by the academic community, however, is part of a reintegration of Jewish thought into the concept of Western humanities. Jewish ethnographers can contribute to this movement—for example, by elucidating the dialectic of tradition and change as worked out in communities facing vastly different historical challenges. We may then move beyond efforts to explain the explosive presence of Jews in post-Enlightenment intellectual life as a result of their "primitive" encounter with "civility" (Cuddihy 1974) to explore how the Jewish belief that "Creation as the (active) speech or writing of God posits first of all that the Universe is essentially intelligible" (Faur 1986:7) provided a pathway from Torah to a restless, unifying modern impulse in the natural and social sciences.

Such notions are far beyond me as an undergraduate. At my college in the 1970s, the social scientists in their separate departments strive to separate themselves from their "objects of study"; the humanists treasure the peace of their cloisters; the artists, knowing they are intellectually suspect, cultivate a cliquish sense of superiority; and there is none of the give-and-take between learning and everyday experience that I have come to associate with the best of Jewish scholarship.

I find a friend, a Jew from Long Island, and we begin to teach each other that we need to cultivate our Jewishness. We discuss the "Jewish mentality" of modern thinkers, and paraphrasing Lenny Bruce's category of the *goyish*, sarcastically reject all that is "white." "I am not 'white,' " my friend Martin proudly postures, "I am a Semite." Meanwhile, reflecting on my own dismissal of suburban Judaism, I decide not to end willingly an almost endless chain of Jewish cultural transmission. I stake my future on the assumption that a tradition so old and varied must contain the seeds of a worthwhile life for me, and decide to begin to acquire them through study.

Besides, my reading as a student of anthropology leads me to reason that if I concentrate on Jewish culture, no one will accuse me of cultural imperialism (see Gough 1968). No doubt others in my generation who choose to do fieldwork with Jews are motivated by similar considerations. Jewish anthropologists as a class are privileged to belong to the world of academic discourse, and to have an entrée into a variety of unique communities that maintain cultural frameworks in opposition to mass society.

Something deeper than Marxist critiques of anthropology draws me to Yiddish in particular. Before I left Farmingdale, my best friend had been a child of survivors from Lemberg. I remember being at his house once, and asking with a sense of wonder: "Ralph, do you really know Yiddish?"

Ralph told me that although he understood the language—which his parents still spoke to him—he had never learned to speak it. Still, I was impressed that he knew this secret code. And now that I am finished with college and looking to find my own way home, Yiddish seems to be the nearest link to which I can attach myself. It is the key to a sense of the life of the *shtetl*, that Jewish dreamtime that I inevitably associate with my lost Farmingdale.

The Farmingdale community has, by this point, completely disintegrated: Virtually no Jews in that part of New Jersey earn their living as chicken farmers anymore. Many of those who have gone into business have moved to nearby towns like Lakewood. The Torah scrolls of the Community Center have been ceremoniously transferred to a new synagogue near housing developments on the highway between Farmingdale and Lakewood. I have never considered becoming a chicken farmer myself.

So, when I finish my college courses, without waiting for graduation, I flee back to New York. "Flee": No one chases me out of Portland, Oregon,

God forbid! "Back": The city, though a magnet and a refuge, has never been my home before. Yet for three years I have shaped my identity in opposition to the "American" world around me, and I have reverted, along with my close friends, to what we imagine is an authentic New York accent—the "deses" and "doses" that were drilled out of my parents' repertoire in the days when New York public school teachers had to pass elocution exams.

Rejecting suburban Judaism, belatedly pursuing the image of the sixties' counterculture to the Pacific Northwest, and self-consciously affecting a "New York Jew" style were all successive attempts to shape a personal identity. In each case, the identity strategy was in opposition to the prevailing conventions of the immediate social order. Similarly, opposition to their parents' perceived bourgeois complacency may underlie the involvement of young people with Judaism. Yet as Dominique Schnapper has noted (1983), for young, intellectual Jews becoming involved in Jewish religion, politics, or culture, there can be no question of canceling out prior experience and "becoming traditional." In fact, this is true even of the most seemingly Orthodox and insular Jewish communities. There is a difference between learning about great rabbis of the past through meetings with Jewish graybeards who knew them, and through reading about their merits in the Williamsburg newspaper *Der Yid*.

Of course, not only Jews are in the position of reconstituting interrupted tradition (cf. Clifford 1986: 116 ff.). But since they have been in the business of reshaping tradition in a dialogue with written texts for thousands of years, Jews may benefit more directly than others from learning about what other Jews are doing with their common tradition. It is conceivable that individuals may choose to adopt traits from other communities or even join those communities based on what they read in ethnographies. Whether such cultural borrowings and recombinations are effected in an "authentic" manner will depend less on precedent than on the degree of self-confident cultural generosity that results.

Arriving in New York, I adopt a knitted yarmulke, although my hair still falls below my shoulders. I immediately begin a nine-week summer course in Yiddish at Columbia, and it seems as though the language were being brought out from deep inside me. When I go to visit my parents on weekends, my father remembers words he'd never noticed forgetting. When I take the IRT after class back down to the Village, it seems as if everybody on the train is speaking Yiddish. Most important for my sense of identity, phrases here and there in my own internal dialogue are now in Yiddish, and I find I can reflect on myself with a gentle irony that was never available to me in English.

Then, after my first year in graduate school, I am off to Europe the following summer, courtesy of my parents. I arrive at the Gare du Nord in Paris with the address of a friend and without a word of French. I am spotted wearing my yarmulke by a young North African Jew who makes me understand, in broken English, that he studies at the Lubavitch yeshiva in

Paris. He buys me a Paris guidebook and sets me on my way in the Metro. At the end of the summer, this meeting will stand as the first in a set of Parisian reactions to my yarmulke which crystallize in my memory:

—The reaction of the generous young Trotskyist with whom my friend had grown close and with whom I stayed for two weeks: She could see the yarmulke only as a symbol of Jewish nationalism and argued bitterly that it was inherently reactionary;

—Of a young North African Jew, selling carpets at the flea market at Clignoncourt, who grabbed my arm and cried, "*Haver! Haver!* Brother Jew!";

—Of another young man, minding a booth outside one of the great department stores, who asked me if I were Orthodox, and interrupted my complicated response to explain that, although he was Orthodox himself, he was afraid to wear a yarmulke in the street;

—Of an old man at the American Express office who spoke to me in Yiddish and complained that the recent North African migrants dominated the Jewish communal organizations, and that there was no place for a Polish Jew to go.

Those first, fragmentary encounters are my fieldwork juvenilia. In assuming the yarmulke, I perhaps do not stop to consider that neither my actions nor my knowledge match the standards that it symbolically represents. But it works effectively, almost dangerously, as a two-way sensor, inducing Jews to present themselves to me and forcing me to try to understand how I am reflected in their eyes.

Externally, I learn many things about the situation of French Jewry. From the patent discomfort my non-Jewish Trotskyist friend feels at my display of Jewish specificity, I gain some sense of the conflicts young French Jews—coming out of the universalist, antihistorical revolutionary apogee of May 1968—must have felt years later when they first began to distinguish themselves from their comrades and view the world from the vantage point of their specific history. From the young street peddlers, I learn about how much riskier public proclamation of oneself as a Jew is perceived as being in Paris than in New York, and a concomitant depth of instant identification of one Jew with another. My meeting with the old Polish Jew at the American Express office hints at the dynamics of dominant and declining ethnic groups within the Jewish community, so vastly different from those dynamics in the United States.

Internally, I begin to understand that an identifiably Jewish headcovering places its own claims on the one who wears it. The longer it stays put, the more its power to keep him out of non-kosher restaurants grows. More important, people want to know who he is as a Jew. And if he does not know, the desire for peace of mind will spur further his effort to shape an identity.

Returning from Paris, I find an apartment at Second Avenue and Fifth Street in Manhattan. I tell people, "After three generations, my family has finally made it back to the Lower East Side." In fact, none of my grandparents lived on the East Side for a long time after immigrating, even though my mother tells me she regrets having missed the Yiddish theater on Second Avenue during her girlhood. By the time I move in, there is no Yiddish theater left. The former Ratner's dairy restaurant on Second Avenue, where, I'm told, Trotsky was a lousy tipper, is now a supermarket. Though sometimes one still sees a white newspaper truck with the word *Forverts* in lovely blue Hebrew letters on its side drive by late at night, this neighborhood has been the East Village since the sixties, and I think of it as such.

A new friend, who devotes his time to a frustrating effort to rescue Lower East Side synagogues, tells me of a shul still in use on an otherwise abandoned block east of Tompkins Square Park. Though my friend has never been inside, he is sure that I will be welcomed, since such an isolated congregation must be looking for new blood.

The place is called the Eighth Street Shul, but its full name is Kehilas Bnei Moshe Yakov Anshei Zavichost veZosmer—Congregation Children of Moses and Jacob, People of Zavichost and Zosmer. It is owned by a *landsmanshaft* (hometown society) founded by émigrés and refugees from two towns in south central Poland. No one born in either town prays regularly at the shul now, and only one or two of the congregants are actually members of the society.

The shul is located in the center of what New York Latinos call "Loisaida"—an area bounded by Avenue A on the east, Avenue D on the west, Houston Street on the south, and Fourteenth Street on the north. Once the blocks up to Tenth Street were almost exclusively Jewish, and on nearly every one stood a synagogue or a religious school. Now two of those former synagogues stand abandoned, several more have become churches, and the rest have disappeared.

Eighth Street is a typical and not especially distinguished example of turn-of-the-century Lower East Side synagogue architecture.[4] It consists of five levels. The lowest contains a cranky and inadequate boiler. The second is the *besmedresh* or study room, which was destroyed by a suspicious fire in August 1982. The third level is the main sanctuary, long and narrow like the tenements among which it was tucked when it was built. Two rows of simple pews are separated by an aisle, which is interrupted in the center of the room by the raised table from which the weekly Torah portion is read. At the very front is the Ark, surrounded by partially destroyed wooden carvings that are the most artistic aspect of the shul. The walls are decorated with representations of the traditional Jewish signs for the zodiac; the two in front on the left have been obliterated by water damage from the leaky roof. Covering most of this level, with roughly an eight-foot opening extending toward the back, is the women's gallery. The gallery is constructed in such a way that it is easier for women sitting on opposite sides of the opening to converse with one another than to see what the men are doing downstairs. Finally, upstairs from the women's gallery is an unused and cramped apartment that was once occupied by the shul's caretaker. In the roof behind it, an opening that was a skylight until there was a break-in is now covered with a solid wooden framework, allowing neither light nor vandals to enter.

Avenues B and C, which mark off the block, were once lively commercial streets with mostly Jewish storekeepers. There were also several smaller streets lined with tenements, right up to the edge of the East River. When the FDR Drive was built along the river, all the streets east of Avenue D disappeared, the tenements on the remaining available land were replaced by municipal housing, and the stores declined rapidly. During the same years, a massive middle-class housing cooperative, funded by a government mortgage, was built along Grand Street one mile to the south. Many of the remaining Jewish families moved into those houses, leaving virtually no Jews in the immediate area of the Eighth Street Shul.

Yet a minyan has continued to meet there every Saturday morning, with virtually no interruptions, throughout the years of the neighborhood's decline, while the block served as the Lower East Side's heaviest "shopping street" for hard drugs. It has lasted into the present, when buildings all around it are being speculated upon and renovated by both squatters and powerful real estate interests. It appears that until recently the main reason for this continuity was a felicitous rivalry between two men who were unwilling to abandon the synagogue because their fathers had both been presidents of it at one time. Perhaps if there had been only one, he would have given up and made peace with his conscience. Perhaps if the two men had naturally been friends they could have agreed to sell the building and officially merge their society with another still functioning further south in the neighborhood. If they had been able to agree on anything besides continuing to come to the shul, the shul might not have survived this long.

The first time I walk in, a clean-shaven, compact man in his sixties—younger than several of the congregants, who number perhaps seventeen in all—hurries forward to greet me. What's my name? Where do I live? Where am I from originally? And where do I usually go to pray on shabbes? His name is Moshe Fogel, and he sees to it that I am called to the Torah, the honor accorded any guest who comes for the first time, without asking any questions as to his level of religious observance. Later, an older member explains to me: "Once upon a time, you wouldn't get called to the Torah unless you kept kosher and observed shabbes." Now, Moish prefers simply to leave those matters undiscussed.

The history of the East Side as a place where all types of Jews have lived together reinforces his discretion. Externalities such as proper or improper clothing are not essential criteria for participation. This is true of the entire Orthodox community on the East Side and has even become part of its mystique. Rabbi Reuven Feinstein, head of the Staten Island branch of the East Broadway-based yeshiva, Tifereth Jerusalem, noted in a recent speech the common reaction in Boro Park and other thriving Orthodox centers to the nonconformist dress of East Side visitors: "It's okay, you're from the East

Side." The president at Eighth Street still wears a traditional *gartl* when he prays, a belt worn over his jacket to separate the pure from the base parts of his body, and no one has suggested that such old customs are out of place today. But partly because the older members at the Eighth Street Shul walked through the East Village in the 1960s and knew there were many young Jews among the longhairs—even if they were horrified at the thought—they were willing to include in the minyan a young man in the neighborhood who, when he first came, wore dreadlocks under a Rastafarian-style knitted cap. It is also doubtless true that at that time there was no other Orthodox synagogue anywhere that he would have contemplated entering.

By contrast, it is impossible for any Jew raised in the middle of secular society (including a Jewish anthropologist) to join a traditionalist community without giving up major parts of his or her identity. The ways in which a researcher of contemporary Hasidic life "becomes a Hasid" are much more dramatic than the way in which one becomes a regular at Eighth Street—but they are probably more transient as well. In order to gain the confidence of the traditionalist communities, the fieldworker has to give the impression, whether implicitly or explicitly, that he or she is likely eventually to accept their standards in all areas of life (Belcove-Shalin 1988). All one has to do at Eighth Street is agree to come back—"a little earlier next time, if possible."

Two things will draw me back to join this congregation, occasionally referred to as "those holy souls who *daven* in the middle of the jungle." The first pull is the memory of Farmingdale: the Ashkenazic accents and melodies (though here they are Polish, whereas Walter Tenenbaum had prayed in his native Lithuanian accent); the smell of herring on the old men's breath and hands; the burning sensation of whiskey, which I must have tasted surreptitiously at the conclusion of Yom Kippur one year in Farmingdale.

The second thing that draws me, though I do not come every week, is a feeling that I am needed and missed when I am absent. It's hard for me to get up early on Saturday mornings, after being out late Friday nights. It still seems like a sacrifice, as though I were stealing part of my weekend from myself. If I arrive in time for the *Shema*, about half an hour into the service, I congratulate myself on my devotion. The summer before I marry, in 1981, I hardly come at all. When I go with my brother to meet Moshe Fogel at the shul and give him the provisions for the kiddush I am giving to celebrate my upcoming wedding, I tell Dan that I usually arrive "around nine-thirty," to which Moish retorts: "Even when you used to come, you didn't show up at nine-thirty!" Though he says it with a smile, a message comes through clearly: If I want to claim to belong, I should attend regularly and arrive on time. Although I am always welcome, only if I can be counted on am I part of the minyan. The dependence of Jews on each other—a theme running through biblical and rabbinic literature—is pressingly literal at Eighth Street.

Meanwhile, my feelings about Paris coalesce into a plan. I know I want to live there for a time, but only if I will be among Jews. Since I am at the point in my graduate school career when I must find a dissertation topic, I decide to look for fieldwork situations with Jews in Paris. I make an exploratory visit with my fiancée, Elissa. Will she agree to a pause in her own career to follow me on this project? Will the organizations of Polish Jewish immigrants whom I have chosen to study be willing to have me study them?

The answer is yes to both questions. Speaking Yiddish and appearing as a nice young Jewish couple seem to be the critical elements in our success. We are invited to sit in on board meetings, negotiations aimed at the reunification of societies split by political differences for over half a century. I am struck by the fact that these immigrants seem so much more marked by their political identification than the East European Jews I've met in New York. Also, I am impressed at the number of societies remaining in a country that has suffered Nazi occupation and that historically has shown little tolerance for immigrant cultural identifications.

But I am drawn not so much by the differences between these Yiddish speakers and those I know in New York as by encountering them in an environment that is otherwise so foreign. Speaking Yiddish to people with whom I have no other common language confirms its legitimacy and reinforces the sense of a distinctive Jewish identity that is shared between generations. I go for a trial interview of one activist, who is disappointed that I didn't bring "the girl," Elissa, along with me. When he discovers to my embarrassment that I have been secretly taping the interview, he is flattered.

Just before leaving Paris, Elissa and I climb the steps of Sacré Coeur. The cathedral itself is an ungracious mass, and the city looks gray and undifferentiated below us. I experience a moment of vertigo, as if I could tumble off Montmartre and drown. Part of my dream of Paris, "capital of the nineteenth century," is an infantile fantasy of becoming a universal intellectual—to be free both of the special knowledge and of the limitations of my knowledge that follow on my personal history. Yet I know I cannot come to Paris and immediately move among its confident, cliquish intellectual elite. Even less will I ever have contact with that "quintessentially French" petite bourgeoisie typified by the stolid Inspector Maigret. My first place will be with the immigrants, whose appearance, strange language, and crowded quarters provided material for unkind portraits by Maigret's creator, Simenon, in the 1930s.[5] If I am unable to come to see Paris as they have seen it, if I cannot make out of a shared marginality a niche in the city for myself, I will be lost, as much as the "lost generation," and in a most unromantic way.

During the two years between our decision to spend a year in Paris and the beginning of that year, I attend the Eighth Street Shul more and more regularly, and Elissa occasionally joins me. Gradually, my feelings when I miss a week shift from guilt to regret. One shabbes, waking up late but not wanting to miss attending altogether, I arrive just in time for the kiddush, to the general amusement of the entire minyan. One February morning I wake up to see snow falling and force myself to go outside against my will, knowing that on a day like this I am truly needed.

Other incidents illustrate the gap in assumptions between myself and the other congregants. I try to bring friends into the shul, partly because it makes me more comfortable, and partly to build up the congregation. A friend whose hair and demeanor reflect his love of reggae music and his connections with Jamaican Rastafarians comes along one Yom Kippur. We reach the point in the service when pious men, remembering the priests in the days of the Temple, descend to their knees and touch their foreheads to the floor. Since no one wants to soil his good pants on the dirty floor, sheets of newspaper are provided as protection. Reb Simcha Taubenfeld, the senior member of the congregation, approaches my friend with newspaper in hand and asks in his heavy Yiddish accent: "Do you fall down?" The look of bewilderment on my friend's face graphically illustrates the term "frame of reference."

Another week, the same friend, failing to observe the discretion with regard to the expression of political opinions that I have learned to adopt at shul, gets into a bitter argument over the Palestinian question. Fishel Mandel, a social worker and one of the younger members of the congregation, calls me during the week to convey the message that "despite our political differences, your friend is still welcome."

After our wedding, I attend virtually every week. When Elissa comes, she is doubly welcome, since the only other woman who attends regularly is Goldie Brown, Moish Fogel's sister. Though Goldie doesn't complain about being isolated in the women's gallery one flight above the men, she seconds Elissa's suggestion that a mekhitse be set up downstairs. The suggestion gets nowhere, however: It would entail displacing one of the regular members of the congregation from his usual seat, and though there is no lack of available places (I myself usually wander from front to back during the course of the service), he refuses to consider moving.

I reason that I will have more of a voice concerning questions such as the seating of women if I formalize my relationship to the shul by becoming a member. My timid announcement that I would like to do so meets with initial confusion on the part of the older members of the society present. Then Fishel, ever the mediator and interpreter, explains to me that the shul is not organized like a suburban synagogue: "There's a *chevra*, a society, that owns the shul. In order to join, you have to be *shomer mitzves*, you have to keep kosher and strictly observe the Sabbath."

I drop my request. Shiye the president reassures me with a speech in his usual roundabout style to the effect that belonging to the chevra is a separate question from being a member of the minyan: "They send their money in from New Jersey and Long Island, but the shul couldn't exist without the people that actually come to pray here."

Meanwhile, our plans to go to Paris proceed. Our travel plans become a topic for discussion over kiddush at shul. One of the older, Polish-born members tells us for the first time that he lived in Paris for nine years after the war. We ask him why he came to America, and he answers, "*Vern a frantsoyz iz shver* [It's hard to become a Frenchman]," both to obtain citizenship and to be accepted by neighbors.

At the end of the summer, we expect to give a farewell kiddush at the shul. A few days before shabbes, I get a phone call from Moish Fogel: "Don't get things for kiddush. We won't be able to daven at Eighth Street for a while. There's been a fire. Thank God, the Torah scrolls were rescued, but it's going to take a while to repair the damage." It is two weeks after Tisha B'Av, the fast commemorating the destruction of the Temple in Jerusalem.

Leaving New York without saying goodbye to the shul and its congregation, we fly overnight to Brussels and immediately *shlep* (the word "drag" would not do the burden justice) our seven heavy suitcases onto a Paris train. Arriving again at the Gare du Nord, I think of the thousands of Polish Jews who were greeted at the station in the twenties and thirties by fellow immigrants eager to hire workers. As soon as we get off the train, Elissa immediately "gets involved," demanding the credentials of two men who claim to be policemen and attempt to "confiscate" a carpet two Moroccan immigrants are carrying. Upon Elissa's challenge, the "policemen" demur.

We practice our French on the cab driver: I explain to him why we've come to Paris. He warns us that we shouldn't tell strangers we're Jewish. It is only a few weeks since the terrorist attack on Goldenberg's restaurant, and no one knows when the next anti-Semitic attack may come. I reply that if I hadn't said we were Jewish, we wouldn't have found out he was a Jew as well, adding that in New York the names of taxi drivers are posted inside the cabs. He says he wouldn't like that at all.

So we receive an early warning that ethnicity in Paris is not celebrated publicly as it is in New York, nor are ethnic mannerisms and phrases so prevalent as a deliberate element of personal style. This is the repressive underside of marginality. It appears wherever the individual or community think it is better not to flaunt their distinctiveness, even if they cannot fully participate in the host culture. It leads to suspicion and silence, to the taxi driver's desire for anonymity.

Arriving at our rented apartment, we meet our neighbor Isabel, who will be our only non-Jewish friend during the year in Paris, and who later explains that meeting us has helped dispel her prejudices about Jews. Over the next few days, we introduce ourselves to Jewish storekeepers in the neighborhood: Guy, the Tunisian kosher butcher; Chanah, the Polish baker's wife; Leon, the deli man from Lublin, who insists he didn't learn Yiddish until he came to Paris.

We have a harder time finding a synagogue where we feel at home. For Rosh Hashanah and Yom Kippur, we have purchased tickets at one of the "official" synagogues run by the Consistoire, the recognized religious body of French Jewry set up under Napoleon. Most synagogues run by the Consistoire are named after the streets on which they're located. Meeting a Hasid on the street, I ask him whether he happens to know when Rosh

Hashanah services begin at "Notre Dame de Nazareth." He grimaces and makes as if spitting: "Don't say that name, *ptu ptu ptu!*"

The synagogue is strange to us as well. Most of the crowd seems if anything more secular than most American Jews, who go to the synagogue only on the high holidays. Many teenagers wear jeans or miniskirts. Because of the fear of terrorism, everyone is frisked on entering. Inside, the synagogue is picturesque with its nineteenth-century pseudo-Moorish motifs; when it was built, Offenbach was the choirmaster. Yet it is as religiously dissatisfying as the suburban American temple I used to attend. The services seem to be conducted in a traditional manner, but it is hard to tell from among the noisy throng in back. The shammes, as a representative of the government, wears a Napoleonic hat, and the rabbi delivers his sermon from a high pulpit.

After Yom Kippur, I think idly about the need to find a more comfortable shul, and when I hear about an East European-style minyan within walking distance, I consider going on Simchas Torah. Watching television reports of terrorist attacks on Simchas Torah in other European capitals, I am consumed with shame at my own apathy, and thus I walk a kilometer or two to find the synagogue on the rue Basfroi the following shabbes.

Going in, I am first shown into a side room, where men are reciting incomprehensible prayers with strange and beautiful melodies. Eventually I realize that they are North African Jews, and I venture into the main room to ask, "Is there an Ashkenazic minyan here?"

The man I ask replies in French, "We're not racists here! We're all Jews!" at which his friend points out:

"The young man spoke to you in Yiddish!" Continuing in Yiddish, he explains that while everyone is welcome in the main synagogue, the services there are in fact Ashkenazic, and so some of the North African men prefer to pray in their own style in the smaller room.

Gradually I settle in, though I have trouble following the prayers in the beginning. Remembering a particular turn in the melody for the reader's repetition of the Amidah that the president at Eighth Street uses, I listen for it from the cantor here at the rue Basfroi, and hear a satisfying similarity in his voice. I feel like a new immigrant coming to his landsmanshaft's shul to hear the melodies from his town.

Throughout our year in Paris, I attend this synagogue about as frequently as I had gone to Eighth Street at first. Although the congregation is not unfriendly, no one invites me home for lunch, partly out of French reserve, and perhaps also because it is clear that I'm not very observant. I feel "unobservant" here in another sense: I do not register the vast store of information obviously available here about the interaction of religious Jews from different ethnic backgrounds. It escapes me, as though I were "off duty." In contrast to my feelings at Eighth Street, I am not motivated by the desire to make myself a regular here. And this is not my fieldwork situation: Nothing external moves me to push my way through socially, to find out who these people really are and let them see me as well.

The Jews I encounter in the course of my research belong to an entirely different crowd. The landsmanshaftn to which they belong are secular organizations. If I wanted to observe the Sabbath closely, it would be difficult for me to do my fieldwork. The immigrants hold many meetings on Saturdays, including a series of *shabbes-shmuesn*, afternoon discussions at which the main focus this year is the war in Lebanon.

I mention to one of my informants that I sometimes go to the synagogue. "I admire that," he responds. "I can't go back to the synagogue now. I've been away too long; it's too late for me." Toward the end of the year, we invite an autodidact historian of the immigrant community to dinner on Friday night and ask him to say the blessing over the challah. "I can't," he refuses, and will not explain further. Though his intellectual curiosity has led him to become friendly with us, and he is considering doing research on the resurgence of Orthodoxy among French Jews, his critical stance vis-à-vis his own secularist movement is insufficient to allow him to accept this religious honor. Enjoying the possibilities offered by marginality is sometimes impossible for those who are neither young nor well educated and who have often been deceived in their wholehearted commitments.

Throughout the year, Elissa has been growing stricter regarding *kashres*. She refuses to eat nonkosher meat and will order only fish in restaurants. She articulates our shared impression that Jewish secularism has failed to create everyday lifeways that can be transmitted from generation to generation, and that any lasting Judaism must be grounded in Jewish law and learning. Before parting for the summer—she to study Yiddish at Oxford, I to Jerusalem, to acquire the Hebrew that I will need to learn about Jewish law—we discuss the level of observance we want to adopt on our return to New York, but we come to no decision.

Elissa and I meet at the end of the summer in Los Angeles, for the bar mitzvah of her twin cousins. I am uncomfortable riding on shabbes; after spending an entire summer in Jerusalem, for the first time, it seems like a violation of myself. The roast beef sandwich I eat at the reception is the first nonkosher food I've eaten since leaving Paris.

Thus, without having made a formal declaration, I join Elissa in observing kashres (save for occasional lapses that I call my "*treyf* of the month club" and that become less and less frequent), and she joins me in keeping shabbes, albeit with some reluctance. Preparing to fulfill a promise made in a dream I had while in Paris, I take a further step: At the beginning of November, I begin attending daily services at another East Side shul and thus putting on tefillin again. One of my mother's cousins at the Telshe Yeshiva in Cleveland—whom I have never met—told me in the dream that I would always be welcome there, and I responded that if I got there, I would put on tefillin every day from then on. Later in November, Elissa and I fly to Cleveland for the weekend. Though we are welcomed warmly, it is clear that the rabbis and *rebetsins* at the yeshiva hoped for something more

Jewish from me, the great-grandson of the Rosh Yeshiva's second wife, Miriam.

We return to the Eighth Street Shul as well, which has been secured and repaired sufficiently to make it usable once again. There are changes. Old Mr. Klapholz, with whom I hardly had exchanged a word, has passed away. Fishel's uncle Mr. Hochbaum, a congregant for half a century, no longer attends, since he is unable to walk all the way from Grand Street. On the other hand, my long-haired friend has moved into the neighborhood and attends regularly. Two of the younger members of the congregation have small children now, and they must go to a shul where there are other children for their son and daughter to play with. In February, our oldest member passes away, and after Shavuot, another member moves to Jerusalem. Two more young men eventually begin coming regularly and bring along their infant children. Now, in June 1986, the shul has thirteen regular male attendees. I am no longer free to sleep late on Saturday mornings, and fortunately I no longer want to.

All of this, to the extent it is of my own making, is the result of a search to realize that fragile illusion of wholeness which was destroyed when my family and almost all the others left Farmingdale. I will hazard a guess that Jewish anthropologists—perhaps anthropologists in general—are motivated by a sense of loss. Yet the seamless image of community is inevitably a child's image. We cannot regain what is lost, if only because it never existed as we remember it. Nothing in society is quite as harmonious as it seemed to me then, and I later learned about bitter political struggles that had taken place in Farmingdale, just as they had among the immigrants in Paris.

Our strategy, rather, should be to attempt to understand what it is we miss and need, which is available in still-living communities in another form. The image of wholeness which we share is foreshadowed by communities all of us stem from, however many generations back, and it can serve as a guide in the search for the reciprocal relationships of autonomous adulthood.

Anthropology is a tool for mediating between the self and the community. It has helped me to come to belong at the Eighth Street Shul: to withhold my opinions when it seems necessary, without feeling the guilt of self-compromise; to accept instruction and gentle reprimands with good humor; to believe it is worthwhile preserving something that might otherwise disappear. But belonging at Eighth Street does not mean that I have dissolved myself into an ideal Orthodox Jew. If I attempted to do so, I would be unable to continue being an anthropologist. If I fit into any category, it may be what my friend Kugelmass calls the "funky Orthodox": that is, those who participate in the community but whose interests and values are not confined to the Orthodox world. In fact, there are no ideal Orthodox Jews at Eighth Street; it is our respective quirks that provide the *raison d'être* of this haphazard but now intentional once-a-week community.

The fact that I have found a religious community that needs me because of its marginality and will tolerate me because of a generosity born of tradition is what I mean by the marginal redemption of one Jew. Likewise, if the shul survives, it will be because of its very marginality, because of the many individuals who have recognized the creative possibilities of a situation that demands that they create a new unity, while allowing each of them to retain their otherness. Isn't this the dream of anthropologists? Whether attempting to communicate knowledge between different Jewish communities, or between communities much more distant in tradition and empathy, we are messengers. We spend our own lives in moving back and forth among the worlds of others. As we do so, in order to avoid getting lost along the way we must become cultural pioneers, learning to "get hold of our *trans*cultural selves" (Wolff 1970: 40). Communities on the edge of mass society, or even on the fringes of ethnic enclaves, seem to be among the most congenial fields in which to do so.

Let me finish with a parable:

Two Jews can afford to be fastidious about the dress, comportment, and erudition of a third. It gives them something to gossip about and identify against. Ten healthy Jews can have a similar luxury; an eleventh means competition for the ritual honors. It's nine Jews who are the most tolerant, as I learned one forlorn shabbes at Eighth Street. It was almost ten o'clock, and there was no minyan. Since everyone seemed content to wait patiently, I assumed that someone else had promised to come, and asked, "Who are we waiting for?"

"A *yid*," our oldest member replied without hesitation.

Eventually a Jew came along.   ■

NOTES

1. Compare Pierre Bourdieu's critique of the structuralist theory of "reciprocal" gift exchange: "Even if reversibility [i.e., the assumption that gifts entail counter-gifts of equivalent value] is the objective truth of the discrete acts which ordinary experience knows in discrete form and calls gift exchanges, it is not the whole truth of a practice which could not exist if it were consciously perceived in accordance with the model. The temporal structure of gift exchange, which objectivism ignores, is what makes possible the coexistence of two opposing truths, which defines the full truth of the gift" (1977:6).

    Similarly, in a narrative such as this one, because I, as author, already know the ending, it may seem as though each successive element fits into those that precede and follow it in such a way that their necessity is perfectly known. Actually my aim is to show how the background that nurtured me shaped in part my unpredictable responses to situations that in themselves were historically rather than culturally determined. See my conclusion, where I refer to one of the communities I now participate in as "haphazard but intentional."

2. Even if it was no more than a matter of convenience, this annual event demonstrates Jonathan Woocher's point that American Jewish "civil religion expects Jews to take advantage of the opportunities which America provides, and to use them to help fulfill their Jewish responsibilities" (1985:161).

3. This may seem an outrageously loose claim, and I am quite willing to be proven wrong by literary scholars. But compare the conclusion of James Joyce's *Portrait of the Artist as a Young Man:*

   > Mother is putting my new secondhand clothes in order. She prays now, she says, that I may learn in my own life and away from home and friends what the heart is and what it feels. Amen. So be it. Welcome, O life! I go to encounter for the millionth time the reality of experience and to forge in the smithy of my soul the uncreated conscience of my race. (1968:252–53)

   with the end of Moshe Szulsztein's memoir of a Polish Jewish childhood:

   > When the truck was already fairly far along Warsaw Street and Kurow was barely visible, two more relatives appeared in a great rush, wanting to take their leave. These were my grandfather's pair of pigeons. The pigeons knew me, and I knew them. I loved them, and perhaps they loved me as well . . . But the truck is stronger than they are, it drives and drives further and further away from Kurow. My poor pigeons can't keep up, they remain behind . . . Before they disappear altogether from my view I still discern them within the distant evening cloud, two small flying silver dots, one a bit behind the other. That, I know, is the male, and the second, a bit in front, is the female. (1982:352)

4. For photographs of Eighth Street and other Lower East Side shuls, both surviving and abandoned, see Fine and Wolfe (1978).

5. "In every corner, in every little patch of darkness, up the blind alleys and the corridors, one could sense the presence of a swarming mass of humanity, a sly, shameful life. Shadows slunk along the walls. The stores were selling goods unknown to French people even by name" (Simenon 1963: 45).

REFERENCES

Bakan, David. 1958. *Sigmund Freud and the Jewish Mystical Tradition.* Princeton, N.J.: Van Nostrand.

Belcove-Shalin, Janet. 1988. "Becoming More of an Eskimo." In *Between Two Worlds: Ethnographic Essays on American Jews.* Pp. 77–98. Ithaca, N.Y.: Cornell University Press.

Bourdieu, Pierre. 1977. *Outline of a Theory of Practice.* Cambridge University Press.

Boyarin, Daniel. 1997. *Judaism as a Gender.* Berkeley and Los Angeles: University of California Press.

Clifford, James. 1986. "On Ethnographic Allegory." In *Writing Culture: The Poetics and Politics of Ethnography,* edited by James Clifford and George Marcus. Pp. 98–121. Berkeley and Los Angeles: University of California Press.

Cuddihy, John. 1974. *The Ordeal of Civility: Freud, Marx, Lévi-Strauss and the Jewish Struggle with Modernity.* New York: Basic Books.

Fabian, Johannes. 1983. *Time and the Other.* New York: Columbia University Press.

Faur, José. 1986. *Golden Doves with Silver Dots.* Bloomington: Indiana University Press.

Fine, Jo Renée and Gerard Wolfe. 1978. *The Synagogues of New York's Lower East Side.* New York: Washington Mews Books.

Gough, Kathleen. 1968. "Anthropology and Imperialism." *Monthly Review* 19: 12–27.

Joyce, James. 1968 (1916). *Portrait of the Artist as a Young Man.* New York: Viking Press.

Schnapper, Dominique. 1983. *Jewish Identities in France: An Analysis of Contemporary French Jewry,* translated by Arthur Goldhammer. Chicago: University of Chicago Press.

Simenon, Georges. 1963. *Maigret and the Enigmatic Lett,* edited by Daphne Woodward. New York: Penguin Books.

Szulsztein, Moshe. 1982. *Dort vu mayn vig iz geshtanen.* Paris: Published by a Committee.

Wolff, Kurt. 1970. "The Sociology of Knowledge and Sociological Theory." In *The Sociology of Sociology,* edited by Larry T. Reynolds and Janice M. Reynolds. Pp. 31–67. New York: David McKay.

Woocher, Jonathan. 1985. "Sacred Survival." *Judaism* 34 (2):151–62.

▦ QUESTIONS FOR MAKING CONNECTIONS WITHIN THE READING ▦

1. As Jonathan Boyarin describes his childhood in Farmingdale, New Jersey, he takes us into a world of Jewish traditions and references that may be unfamiliar to some readers: indeed, Boyarin's essay is concerned, in part, with tracing the author's efforts to grow more familiar with and gain a greater understanding of his own traditions. In the process, he describes many different kinds of Jews: an Orthodox Jew, a Jewish socialist, a Lubavitcher Hasid, an observant Jew, Zionists, Jews who have been acculturated into American academic life, to name a few. What is the difference between the groups that Boyarin identifies? Why is he drawn to one group more than another?

2. "Waiting for a Jew" opens with the statement, "My story begins in a community . . .". What is the difference between an essay and a story? Why has Boyarin elected to tell his fellow anthropologists a story? What are the major events or pieces of this story? Is this a story that has a point? A moral? An argument?

3. The subtitle Boyarin has selected for his essay is "Marginal Redemption at the Eighth Street Shul." What is "marginal redemption"? What is it that gets redeemed in "Waiting for a Jew"?

▦ QUESTIONS FOR WRITING ▦

1. "[O]n the abandoned farm," Boyarin writes, "my first memories are tinged with a sense of traces, of mystery, of loss. Do all who eventually become anthropologists have this experience in some form, at some time in their early lives?" In posing this question, Boyarin suggests that there

might be a connection between anthropology and a sense of loss. What might this connection be? In what ways has Boyarin's own research been shaped by this sense of loss?

2. Boyarin believes that "[a]ny marginal group in mass society may be subject without warning to the loss of its cultural landscape, and therefore those who are able to create portable landscapes for themselves are the most likely to endure." What is the difference between a "cultural landscape" and a "portable landscape"? At the end of Boyarin's story, what kind of landscape does he inhabit?

■ *QUESTIONS FOR MAKING CONNECTIONS BETWEEN READINGS* ■

1. Lila Abu-Lughod, an anthropologist of Arab descent, and Jonathan Boyarin, a Jewish anthropologist, can be considered "insiders," part of the very cultures they are studying. What difference does it make whether a culture is studied by insiders or outsiders? Who benefits from such work? And how does one determine whether such work has been successful or not?

2. Boyarin and Jan Willis both recount how they came to decide to join religious communities. Did they make the same decision? Do such decisions involve realizing who one is at some fundamental level? Do they involve transforming who one is at some fundamental level? Do they involve inventing who one would like to be? Can anyone make such decisions?

For additional suggestions about making connections between readings, visit the Link-O-Mat and More Sample Assignments at <www.newhum.com>.

PETER HO DAVIES

IT IS EASY ENOUGH to predict how the media will respond when the next school shooting occurs: there will be interviews with distraught parents, indictments of confused and harried administrators, glimpses of tearful students placing cards and bouquets at hastily assembled memorials. These stock images succeed in providing a visual record of how people respond to such tragedies; what they can't do, however, is offer a more complex account of the emotions that are evoked when violence enters the schools and the media comes to town in search of a story. Peter Ho Davies, the author of two collections of short stories, *The Ugliest House in the World* (1998) and *Equal Love* (2000), uses fiction to explore this issue in his story, "What You Know," in which a teacher struggles to understand what motivated one of his students to go on a suicidal shooting spree.

Davies has said, "One of the things I enjoy about fiction is its slyness. The ability to slip things in. Working with historical material, where there's already some factual basis, accentuates that slyness for me. It spurs my imagination. I tend to find that I'll come up with two or three facts and then I'll be inspired to join the dots between them with my fictional imagination." In "What You Know," Davies starts with "two or three facts" about a schoolyard shooting and then uses his imagination to tell a story that poses a series of pointed questions: What would you need to do to understand another person's motives? What does it take to make violence and suicide seem like appealing options? What is it that teachers know about their students? What can they know?

In her review of *Equal Love*, Jacqueline Carey claims that what makes Davies' stories remarkable is that they arise out of Davies' "profound respect for the power and vitality of human connections, however complicated. He captures these connections with economy and steely grace." Davies' own history is marked by the complicated connections he explores in his fiction. Born to Welsh and Chinese parents, Davies grew up in Britain before moving to the United

Davies, Peter Ho. "What You Know." *Harper's,* vol. 302, no. 1808, (January 2001): 82–89.
Quotations from Katie Bolick, "On the Sly: An Interview with Peter Ho Davies," *Atlantic Unbound,* December 16, 1998, <http://www.theatlantic.com/unbound/factfict/ff9812.htm>, Jacqueline Carey, "Ties That Grind," review of *Equal Love,* by Peter Ho Davies, *New York Times Book Review,* 19 March 2000.

States. He holds bachelor's degrees in both physics and English from the University of Manchester England and a master's degree in creative writing from Boston University. Currently, Davies is a member of the faculty of the Department of English at the University of Michigan.

To learn more about Peter Ho Davies and the history of school violence in the United States, visit the Link-O-Mat at <www.newhum.com>.

What You Know

People suddenly want to know all about my students, what they're like. What do I know? I want to say. I'm just a writer, a writer-in-the-schools. All I see is their writing.

So what are they like as writers?

They're shocking. Appalling, in fact. Indescribably awful (and when a writer, even one of my low self-esteem, says that, you know it's serious). The good ones are bad, and the bad ones are tragic.

When at the start of each class I ask them their favorite books, their fifteen-year-old faces are as blank as paper. The better students struggle to offer a "right" answer: *Catcher, Gatsby,* the Bible(!). The honest ones, the stupid, arrogant honest ones, tell me, *For the Love of the Game* by Michael Jordan, or the latest Dean Koontz.

The most voracious readers among them are the science-fiction fans, the genre nerds, the heavy-duty bookworms (all those sequels and prequels, trilogies and tetralogies), but none of them are deterred for a nanosecond when I tell them that good science fiction is one of the hardest things to write. After all, they're thinking—I can see it in their eyes—it's just a matter of taste, isn't it?

As a matter of fact, no. I believe in the well-made story. Have your character want something, I tell them. Have a conflict. Have the character change. Learn these simple rules, and you can spend the rest of your life breaking them.

But most of the time I find myself telling them what not to write. All the narrative clichés. No stories about suicide. No flashbacks longer than a page. No narrators from beyond the grave. No "And then I woke up" endings. No "I woke up and then . . ." beginnings. No psychedelic dream sequences. The list of boringly bad stories ("But it's supposed to be boring, life is boring") goes on and on.

"No suicides?" they say in their flat, whiny voices, as if there is nothing else, nothing better. "How can suicide be boring?"

Maybe not in life, I explain quickly, but in fiction? Sure. It's a cruel world of readers out there—callous, heartless, *commuting* readers—who've been there, seen that, read it all before. "I'm not saying you can't try to write about suicide," I console them. "I'm just saying it's hard to do well, that you owe it to the material to do it justice, to find a way of making it real and raw for readers again."

Writers aren't godlike, I tell them, readers are. Writers only create; readers judge.

They nod in complete incomprehension. Yes, they're saying. Yes, we see now that there is absolutely no chance we'll understand a word you say. We're just here for the extra credit. It's the nod you give a crazy man, a lunatic with a gun.

What redeems it? My love of teaching? I do love teaching, but for all the wrong reasons. I love the sound of my own voice. I love to pontificate about writing, get excited about it, argue about it (and usually win) with people who have to listen to me, more or less (unlike my parents, my friends, my wife). But always, behind their acquiescence, behind the fact that however bad my taste I'm still the coolest teacher they have (the competition is not stiff), lie the awful, numbing questions: "What have you published? Why haven't we heard of you?"

What really redeems it are the laughs. The laughable badness of their prose. The moose frozen like a *dear* in the headlights. The cop slapping on the *cuff links*. The *viscous* criminal. The *escape* goat.

It's as if they're hard of hearing, snatching up half-heard, half-comprehended phrases, trusting blindly in their spell checkers to save them. (Think! Think who designs spell checkers for a moment. Were these people ever good spellers?)

I once had a heated argument with one student about the death knoll.

"Knell," I said.

"Knoll," he insisted with vehemence, until finally we determined that he was thinking of the *grassy* knoll. My way might be right, he conceded grudgingly, but his way made more sense. We took a vote in class (they love democracy) and the majority agreed. And perhaps this is the way that language, meaning, evolves before our very eyes and ears. "It's the death mole of literacy," I told them, but they didn't get it. Sometimes, I despair of language. If only there was some way for what I know to just appear, instantaneously, in their heads.

So *that*, if you really want to know, is what my students are like. Does any of it explain why one of them last week shot his father in the head across the breakfast nook, rode the bus to school with a pistol in his waistband, emptied it in his homeroom, killing two and wounding five, before putting the gun in his mouth and splashing his brains all over the whiteboard?

No stories about suicide?
No viscous criminals?

In the moments after the crisis no one thinks to call me—as the other staff, the *full-time* staff, are called—to warn me not to talk to the media. No one, in fact, calls me *apart* from the media. "It's CNN," my wife says, passing me the phone, then stepping back as if I hold a snake in my hands. But we're *watching* CNN, I want to say. I look at her and she mimes helplessness. It never occurs to me that all my fellow teachers have been asked to say nothing to the media, that this is why some bright spark in Atlanta after trying five or six names and getting the same response has slid his finger down the faxed list before him to "Other" and found me, not quite a teacher, but better than a janitor.

What he wants to know is if I had taught the killer, the dead boy, Clark, and when I admit, and it feels like an admission, nothing to be proud of, that yes I have, I have him—*had him* (watch those tense changes)—in a writing workshop, I can hear the reporter lean forward in his chair, cup his hand around the mouthpiece. I wonder for a second about him, this young journalist, probably around my age, looking for his big break. This could be it, I realize, and I feel an odd vertiginous jealousy, almost wanting to hold back. But later, listening to my voice over and over on national TV—a grainy photo from the latest yearbook and a caption identifying me as a writer floating over a live shot of the blank school buildings—I'm glad I talked to him, glad I didn't say anything stupid, that I come across as dignified and responsible. I answer all his questions in the first person plural. "We're shocked and appalled. We'll all be doing our best to help our students through this awful period. Our hearts go out to the families in the tragedy." Later my mother will call from Arizona, then my colleagues, even the principal with a warning not to say anything else, but an off-the-record pat on the back for "our unofficial spokesman." "A way with words," my mother will say. "You always had a way with words." Even though she's never read a single one of my stories. I tell her it was easy and it was. It comes naturally. For months now I've been talking in the first person plural. We're pregnant, my wife and I. We're expecting. We're about to be parents ourselves.

"CNN," my wife says, touching her stomach. "Something to tell the kid." It's not often she's proud of me, and I'm pleased, even though I despise the network, its incompetent staff. I heard one anchor a couple of years back talking about a first in the "anals" of country music. Another time I caught a piece in which the President was described as being "salt and peppered" with questions at a news conference. Someone wrote that, was paid to. "I suppose I should be grateful," I tell my wife. "My caption could have read 'waiter,' not 'writer.'" And she smiles uncertainly, not sure who this particular joke is on.

What I tell no one, though, not even my wife, is the reporter's last question, off air, quietly into my ear after he has thanked me and double-checked the spelling of my name. Only the tone alerted me, otherwise this could have been the same as any of the previous questions—"Was he a good student? What was he like?" This final shot: "Do you have anything he wrote for you? A poem or a story?"

I said, "No," but something in my voice must have made him wonder because he added softly, "It could be worth a great deal." So I said, "No" again, more forcefully, and then, "I'm sorry," and hung up.

Why was I sorry? Easier to explain why I said, "No," with that catch of hesitation. Because I couldn't remember, that's why. I had work upstairs, ungraded stories, the response to an exercise: "Write about a moment of extreme emotion—fear, hate, love, joy, laughter." The idea is to have them write about a true emotion and use this as a benchmark against which to compare the emotions of their fictional characters. Something by Clark might be there, if he'd done the assignment. They often didn't. And, indeed, when I look there's nothing, just a note—brief—he'd been sick, and below his own signature, another—larger, flowing. It takes me a second to realize; it's his father's.

So why was I sorry? Because I'm a writer-in-the-schools. I earn $8,000 a year ($6,000 less than my wife's bookstore job pays) and we are pregnant. I was sorry I hadn't had the nerve to say: "How much?" He might have even been bullshitting me, the reporter. CNN would never do business like that, right? But something in his voice, the shift of register, made me think he might have just slipped into freelance mode. The phone was hot where I was pressing it against my head, but for a second I could have sworn it was his warm breath in my ear. Now I wondered—$1,000, $5,000, $10,000? Who knew? I was only sure it would be more than anything I'd ever gotten for my own work. And out of this irony, of course, came this idea. I could write a piece by Clark. *I* could write it and sell it. I could. His letter was typed, printed. He was a loner, without friends. His father was dead. He was dead. Who would know?

No narrators from beyond the grave?
Have your character want something.
Ten thousand big ones.

As a plan it seemed so simple at first, at least if you separate it from the issue of morality. And separating from that issue is something I teach my students. Don't stop yourselves writing something because it might hurt someone—your family, your friends. Don't stop yourself writing it because you think it's too personal, sexual, violent. Don't censor yourselves, I tell them, at least not alone when it's just you and the paper.

Oddly, they're prudish. Reluctant to write about feelings, except in the safest, most clichéd terms. Love, sex especially, makes them sneer with embarrassment, while violence is simply comic.

"But what's the point?" I remember one of them asking (I wish I could say it was Clark, but I can't picture him any more than I can bring to mind the faces of three or four other boys who sit in the back row with their baseball caps pulled low over their eyes), "What's the point writing it if you're not going to show it to someone?" And I have sympathy with this. I believe in writing for an audience. Writing fiction is an act of communication—not just facts or opinions like a newspaper, but emotions. I tell them this. And in truth once something is written, actually expressed, showing it to someone—the desire to do that—is hard to escape. It's the momentum of the act. So I tell myself that writing a piece as Clark isn't the same as passing it off to others as Clark's, but once you've got it—especially if it's good—what else is there to do with it? So perhaps the moral problem does lie behind this practical one: it should be easy to write this piece—it doesn't have to be *good*, after all; it needs, in fact, to be bad to be good—yet, after all the mockery I've heaped on their work, I can't do it. I can't imitate my students.

God help me, I'm blocked.

Here's the trouble. If I'm to write this and overcome the lie of it I need it to mean something, to explain something. I want to offer, coded, buried, subtly perhaps, an answer, a psychological, sociological subtext, that will explain these deaths, and in explaining offer some hope or comfort to us all. It may not be *the* meaning, but surely any meaning, even a sniff of meaning, is what we want. It is the writer's instinct to offer these things, and, beyond mere morality, I can't quite shrug off this duty to, of all things, art.

Which is why I find myself in my 1988 Subaru wagon, driving out to a gun range on the interstate called the Duke's Den. I have never fired a gun before and I decide that this—everything else notwithstanding—is the problem. If I want to understand Clark, take on his voice, I should at least try to understand how he expressed himself.

And this, too, is what I teach them. Show don't tell. Write what you know. Did Clark's baseball cap bob at that one? Did he take notes? Some of them do and it still amazes me, makes me think they're making fun, when in truth they only set down what they don't understand. "Show," they write carefully, "and Tell."

Write what you know is even worse. They look at me as if I've asked them to raise the dead, as if they know nothing or everything. Some I have to persuade that their lives are important enough; others that they're not quite as important as they think. But either way, what most of them know is deadly—not the stories themselves, or their lives as such, but how they live them, think about them. The best ones, they know this already. Know it like an instinct. Write what they know? Not yet. Not until they know what they know. But the worst ones? They don't even want to know what they know.

"So is that why we can't write about suicide? Because if you know it, you're, like, dead?"

"Yeah, and there're no narrators from beyond the grave, right?"

They look at me, so pleased, so earnest, as if they've figured it out, and I feel my heart clench. I think about explaining that the rule really ought to be: "Write whatever you know just a little more about than your reader." But truly what I want to tell them is that these rules aren't, after all, rules for writers; they're rules for people who are trying to be writers but won't ever make it.

So I don't get any suicide stories (though as one bright spark recently pointed out: "It's ironic, don't you think? Considering how many writers kill themselves"). Instead, I get first-kiss stories, first-joint stories, the death of pets, the death of grandparents, sad fat girls, thin sad girls. The tone is always the same—life is tragic; tragically small or epically tragic (the chasm, come to think of it, that suicide bridges).

Lighten up, I want to tell them. It's not the end of the world. You've got your whole lives before you. All the lines my father taught me when I was their age and deciding to become a writer, all the lines I've taught them to recognize as clichés. Except, as they like to remind me, that doesn't mean they can't still be true. Some people do have apple cheeks or strawberry hair or cherry lips (the fruit-salad style of physical description). Don't clichés, in fact, have to be true to become clichés? No, I tell them, we just have to want them to be true.

What else do I teach them? Certainly not how to be creative. I'm not into breathing exercises, or free writing, or journaling. Sucking up to the muse. Nor even how to write correctly—I'm no grammar maven. "How to tell stories" is what I told CNN, though the line never aired, and that's closer to the truth.

I teach them what Forster says: that there are stories and there are plots. That stories are simple sequences of events (this happened and then this and then that), but that plots are about causes, motivation (this happened because of this, on account of that). Plots are what stories mean. And the truth is that life is all stories and fiction is all plots, and what we're looking for in Clark's story is the plot that makes sense of it. Which is why it has to be someone's fault—his, his father's, the NRA, Nintendo, Hollywood, all the escape goats—doesn't it? This happened because of that or that or that. Or all of them.

So I teach them how to tell stories, or (since we're all storytellers every time we open our mouths) how to tell them better, which is to say I try to teach them to make sense of their stories, to figure out what they mean if they mean anything. Because the way we tell stories explains them.

Write what they know? Mostly, I just try to help them know what they write.

So that's what I teach them: how to plot.

And if that's beyond them, what I try to leave them with is this: when in doubt, when stuck, blocked, or fucked, to always ask themselves, "What if?" (Even if their instinct is to ask, "So what?")

What if I pick up a gun and fire it?

The range is quiet. It's the weekend after the shooting, we're still in shock. I show my driver's license and join for $25, which entitles me to rent guns from behind the counter for $5 an hour. It seems so cheap—what can you get for five bucks?—but as I buy ammunition for my choice, a .38 caliber revolver (I just pointed to the first gun I recognized from TV), I realize that this is what costs. Guns are just game consoles, VCRs; it's what you put in them that costs. The man behind the counter is unfailingly polite and helpful. He reminds me of a hardware salesman, the kind of guy in a brown apron who'll show you how to use a tool, dig out exactly the right size of wrench or washer for your job. The kind of guy who loves what he does and who'll tell you all about it if you're not careful. His name is Vern, and above his head, hanging up like so many hammers and saws on a workshop wall, are all manner of guns, not just pistols but rifles, even a replica tommy gun, the kind of thing Al Capone might have used. There's an air of fancy dress about the display; an air of the toy store, the magic trick. On a ledge at the very top of the display is a line of model railway rolling stock. Vern is a train enthusiast, a hobbyist.

After the gun and the shells—they come in a plastic rack, not the waxed paper box I expect—he hands over a pair of ear defenders and then asks, "Target?" I must look puzzled, because he repeats himself. "What kind of target?"

"What kinds do you have?"

He grins, glad I asked, and starts to show me. There's a simple roundel, each ring marked with a score, a sheet covered in playing cards for "shooting poker," the "classic" silhouette, a double one—of a gunman and a woman, his hostage—and finally a set of caricature targets of everyone from Saddam Hussein to Barney. I take the classic silhouette, and Vern rolls it for me and secures it with a rubber band. He hands me the lot—gun, shells, target, ear defenders in an EZ-carry plastic tray—and points me back toward the range, which is separated from the shop by double glazing. Through the glass I can see one man, broad shouldered, graying, balding, firing. "You put your headset on in the booth," Vern tells me, indicating the double set of doors between the shop and the range. "Take lane three."

Inside, with the ear defenders pinching my skull, the shots from the other man in the range sound like a distant hammering pulse. I set up in the lane beside him. Place the gun on the counter and the shells beside it, work the toggle switch that brings the target toward me on a wire. All this is familiar from the movies. When the target board arrives I'm momentarily at a loss as to how to fix the silhouette to it. I look around and there's Vern on the other side of the glass pointing, and when I look again I see a tape dispenser mounted to the wall.

I run the target back about halfway to the rear concrete wall. It's ridged, corrugated, and it takes me a slow moment to realize that this is to prevent ricochets. The concrete makes the range cooler than the shop, like a bunker, and it smells, but only faintly, of the Fourth of July, fireworks. And this creeping nostalgia, the insulation of the ear defenders, the odd underground cool, give the experience an air of unreality.

The target jumps about on the wire for a few seconds like a puppet, and I wait until it's still before turning to the gun. Vern has taught me how to load it, flipping out the cylinder and dropping in the shells. It's a six-shooter, but he warned me to put five shots in and leave the chamber under the hammer empty, "to save your toes." The bullets go in very easily and quickly—the whole thing feels well made in a way that very few things do these days—and I slide the cylinder back into the gun. I hold it away from me and down and then slowly raise it. Vern has shown me how to cock the hammer and fire or how to pull the trigger all the way back. He has advised me to keep my trigger finger outside the guard until I'm ready to shoot. I'm frightened of it going off before I'm ready, of seeming dangerous. But once I have it in position cocking it is simple, and when I fire my first shot I'm surprised how easy it comes. (Vern is a good teacher.) There's a crack and a small flash from the gun, but the recoil is almost playful in the way it bats my hand up. I've hit serves that jarred worse. I look last at the target and see a small neat puncture in the shoulder of my silhouette. Almost too neat, but for the slight tearing of the paper. I fire again. And again and again and again. Because, after all, what else is there to do? By my fifth shot I'm not cocking but experimenting with pulling the trigger back. Two of my shots score tens in the target's chest. With my next set I take aim at the head and put all five on target. I feel like Dirty Harry or Steve McGarrett. Just not Clark.

Beside me as I'm loading again, the other shooter reels in his target, unrolls another, and tapes it up. He's old, grandfatherly, dressed in polyester, metallic-blue Sansabelt pants and a teal polo shirt. He nods and I nod back. He looks like a bowler, and I realize that's exactly what this experience is reminding me of, bowling. I'd laugh at him rather than nod back, that slightly too portentous nod, except that he has a loaded weapon on the counter before him, a tool with which he could kill me. It occurs to me that if he took that into his head the only thing stopping him would be the fact that I might shoot back.

I try to ask myself what this might have meant to Clark, but I can't guess. The experience isn't inspiring, just deadening, mechanical. I feel the panic rising again, the greed. We need the money. I think of my own son, my unborn son (I wanted to know the sex; not for me the surprise ending), for whom I'm doing this, and I wonder what might possibly ever drive him to kill me. I know I thought about killing him. We talked about it, about a termination, an abortion. We hadn't planned on this. I kept thinking something would come up—a new job, a major publication. I had a story with one of the slick magazines, and they had held it for weeks, months, so long my hopes were rising day by day. A score like that—thousands of dollars—could change our lives. I found myself putting my imaginative energy not into new work but into visualizing that moment, the letter in the mail, not in my own self-addressed envelope but the magazine's embossed one, telling me blah, blah, blah, *delighted*. I didn't say so, but I think I'd decided we'd keep the baby if I sold the story. When the rejection letter ("too familiar") finally came, with that sudden rushing inevitability they all have, I couldn't stop shaking. My wife, used to rages or resignation, was speechless. But later, lying in bed, I realized, *how insane*. In the morning we talked it through again and I told my wife I thought we should go ahead and she cried and held me and I felt saved.

So the thought that one day in some world this child might kill me, might shoot me in the face, who wants to imagine that? And yet, and yet, when I think of my own father, there have been . . . moments. If I'd had a gun, known how to use one. Oh yes. But petty reasons, anger over a grounding, over using the car, disappointing him. Not worth killing for. Not worth going out and buying a gun and laying in ambush for. But if the gun were at hand? Not worth running upstairs for, perhaps, not worth crossing the hall for, but if it were on the counter (what the fuck would it be doing on the counter? but just suppose), on the table, in my hand. I did punch my father once. I'd come in late and he waited up, barred the door to my room. We yelled at each other and I raised a fist. There was a moment when I could have lowered it, merely threatened, but having made it I couldn't stop. I hit him and he took a step back, out of surprise, I think. "Do that again," he told me when he'd recovered himself, and I did—bowing to that curious complicit male desire to make a bad thing worse, to transform an accident, a mistake, into a tragedy, to render ourselves not hapless, not foolish and vain, but heroic, grand, awesome. And he took the next shot too, and then he beat me unconscious (in fact, he only raised his own fist, and I took a step back, fell down the stairs, and knocked myself cold—so close is tragedy to farce—but the first version makes a better story). Except if it hadn't been a fist, if it had been a gun I'd raised, he wouldn't have had the chance, would he? And all over nothing.

He's dead now, my father, and as I empty the gun I'm thinking of naming my son after him.

Shooting is actually duller than bowling, I'm finding, duller and easier. I can daydream while doing it. There's something effortless and magical in the seemingly instantaneous bang and the appearance yards away of a small hole. I fire another twenty rounds. I move the target back, forward. I shoot to kill, I shoot to wound, I shoot from the hip. I suddenly understand why someone might rent a machine gun. What I want most in the world I realize is a moving target, a more interesting target. The idea on the range is marksmanship, but there's no real challenge here. I look down the barrel of my gun but watch the shots of the man next to me. He doesn't seem much better, and I've only been shooting for twenty minutes. I watch him cluster his shots in the high-scoring body of the target—one, two, three, four. Nothing. And something about the rhythm, my focus on his target, makes me swing my gun over and put a fifth shot into the face of his target. Perhaps because of the angle I'm firing from, the bullet makes a ragged hole, tearing loose a strip of paper that curls slightly, flaps like a tongue. I hold my breath, horrified. I keep the gun raised, keep sighting down it. I can't hear anything from my neighbor behind his screen. Perhaps he's reloading, hasn't noticed. The pause goes on, and eventually I empty my revolver, slowly and methodically into my target. When I'm done and my gun is down and I'm pushing out the shells, I feel a heavy tap on my shoulder. It's him. He's waited for me to empty.

Have some conflict.

He mouths something, and I shake my head, lift an ear cup.

"What the hell was that back there?" he asks again, gesturing toward the target without taking his eyes off me. His hand is huge and mottled red and white where he's been gripping his gun. His other hand is out of sight.

"Sorry," I tell him, and it sounds as if I'm speaking in slow motion. "A. Mis. Fire?"

He looks at me for a long moment, waits for my eyes to meet his, the dark muzzles of his pupils behind their yellow protective goggles. It occurs to me that they are the exact same shade as my computer screen, and I imagine my precious last words drifting across them, the letters springing into existence under the beating cursor: "like a dear in the headlights." Finally, he nods and says, "All right, then," vanishes back behind his booth.

I reload, pressing the shells home, letting their snug fit steady me, and wait for him to start firing again. And wait and wait and wait until my hand begins to tremble, and finally I can't not fire. The gap between thought and action is so fine. It's like standing on a cliff, the way the fear of falling makes you want to end the tension, take control, jump before you fall. I felt the death mole, if you like. I felt it burrowing forward, undermining me.

Only when I'm empty do I see my neighbor's target beside me jerk finally. He puts five rounds into the head of his target in a tight fist, then draws it toward him, packs up, and leaves. I still have ammo left. Unfinished business, like a chore. I pick the gun back up and fire round after round after round like hammering nails.

Sometime in there—after the fear wears off and then the elation, and the boredom sets in—I realize there's nothing to learn here. This won't tell me anything about Clark. And the thought of continuing failure fills me with sudden despair. I put the gun down for a moment, afraid of it. I have about one suicidal thought a year, but this isn't a good time to be having it. And then the moment passes, because I know with an adrenaline-fueled clarity that killing myself won't make any kind of difference. I know my wife will go on, my son will be born. My work won't suddenly be discovered. There's no point. And it's a crushing feeling. Knowing that the ultimate gesture, the very worst thing you can do, is nothing special, a failure of imagination.

I fire five more times, reel in my target, roll it up in a tight tube.

When I return my gun and pay, Vern gives my credit card a long look.

"I thought I knew you. You're the teacher from that school. You were on TV." He shakes his head sadly, and for a second I think it's a moment of contrition, and then he says, "What are you teaching those kids anyway?"

I pass behind school on my way home, and I have to stop, I'm shaking so much. It's in my bones now, the distant ringing shudder of the gun. My hands smell of powder, my hair, my shirt, and I clamber out of the car so I won't gag. There's an old pack of Marlboro Lights in the glove box from before my wife got pregnant, and I fumble for a cigarette, suck on it until all I can taste is tobacco smoke. The storm fence here has been festooned with tokens—flowers, cards, soft toys, hang from the wire. Damp from the dew, a little faded already, they ripple in the breeze, fluttering and twisting against the chain-link as if caught in a net. I lean on my hood, watching the twilight seep up out of the earth toward the still bright sky.

Have your character change.

What do I teach them? I teach them that telling stories is the easiest and hardest thing in the world, and among the looks of disbelief and confusion there's always one who nods, who gets it, like the teenage fatalist who asked me once, "Because there are only so many stories, right? Like seven or something." Seven, or ten, or a dozen, though no one can agree what they are and there are countless ways of telling them wrong. But the theory feels right. A finite number of stories, which writers try to tell over and over again. So suicide is boring? Then how do you make it not boring? How do you make it exciting? How do you make it new? So fresh, so vital, so original, that it speaks to an audience?

Before the light fades completely, I step up to the fence to read the messages. The first moves me close to tears, and I sag against the wire. It's such a relief. I read another and another, hungrily, but by the time I've read a dozen my eyes are dry as stone. I snatch at them, plucking them down, the ribbon and colored wool they dangle from gouging through the soft card. Taken together they're clichéd, mawkish, misspelled. There are hundreds of them stretching forty, fifty yards in each direction, as far as I can see in the gloom, like so much litter swept here by the wind. And I want to tear them all down, I want to rip them to shreds. Every awful word. ∎

■ *QUESTIONS FOR MAKING CONNECTIONS WITHIN THE READING* ■

1. The narrator of "What You Know" advises his students to avoid "narrative clichés." What are clichés? Does Davies himself avoid producing such clichés in his own story?

2. What are the emotional states the narrator moves through over the course of this story? How does the narrator feel about Clark's suicide at the beginning of the story, at the middle, and at the end? The narrator says, "Writers only create; readers judge." How do you judge this story?

3. The narrator describes his teaching practice this way: "I teach them what Forster says: that there are stories and there are plots." What is the difference between a story and a plot? What is the plot of "What You Know"?

■ *QUESTIONS FOR WRITING* ■

1. "What You Know," the title that Peter Ho Davies selected for his short story, bids his readers to consider what they know and how they know it. One way that we come to know the world is through the media; another way is through what our teachers tell us; other ways involve writing, thinking, and using our imaginations. What is the difference between these ways of knowing? Is there anything you can't know? Will never know?

2. Some readers find Davies' short story disturbing because the narrator is callous, calculating, desperate. Davies has this narrator explain to his students the difference between a "story" and a "plot": the former is just a list of what happens, the latter is what a story means. Why has Davies presented us with this unflattering account of the inner life of a creative-writing teacher? What does his story mean?

■ *QUESTIONS FOR MAKING CONNECTIONS BETWEEN READINGS* ■

1. Davies tells a fictional story about an act of violence and its consequences; Beth Loffreda explores the stories that the media and local townspeople told each other after the real-life murder of Matthew Shepard. Both authors are trying to get at some truth that the media can't represent: What is this truth? Is it the same truth for both authors? In what ways would the media have to change if they were going to try to tell the kinds of stories that interest Davies and Loffreda?

2. In "The Wreck of Time," Annie Dillard proposes to "take the measure" of the past century which, she says, some find special because of "its nuclear bombs, its unique and unprecedented Holocaust, its serial exterminations and refugee populations. . . ." What has Davies taken the measure of with his short story? With Dillard and Davies in mind, what would you say is the most useful response to random acts of violence?

For additional suggestions about making connections between readings, visit the Link-O-Mat and More Sample Assignments at <www.newhum.com>.

Annie Dillard

ANNIE DILLARD, poet, essayist, novelist, and writing teacher, won a Pulitzer Prize for her book of naturalist reflections, *Pilgrim at Tinker Creek* (1973), when she was just twenty-nine years old. In this, her first book, Dillard describes the life she elected to live in a remote part of the Blue Ridge Mountains after she had survived a near-fatal bout of pneumonia. Weaving together observations of her surroundings with mystical longings and theological reflections on the violence and the beauty that coexist in the natural world, Dillard set out, in her own words, "to learn, or remember, how to live. . . . I don't think I can learn from a wild animal how to live in particular . . . but I might learn something of mindlessness, something of the purity of living in the physical senses and the dignity of living without bias or motive."

In the many books that have followed, including *Teaching a Stone to Talk* (1982), her autobiographical musings in *An American Childhood* (1987), and her novel, *The Living* (1992), Dillard has continued to ruminate on the power of nature and to wonder about the place of humanity in the cosmos. For Dillard, the enduring appeal and importance of such a spiritual project is self-evident: "In nature I find grace tangled in a rapture with violence; I find an intricate landscape whose forms are fringed in death; I find mystery, newness, and a kind of exuberant, spendthrift energy."

"The Wreck of Time" includes passages that appear in *For the Time Being* (2000), Dillard's most recent effort to define a spiritual vision that embraces a cosmos where grace "is tangled in a rapture with violence."Although Dillard was raised a Presbyterian, she converted to Catholicism in her twenties and now describes herself as a "Hasidic Christian," her meditations on the natural world having led her to unite Jewish mysticism with Christian spirituality. "The world is as glorious as ever, and exalting," Dillard announces at the beginning of *For the Time Being*, "but for credibility's sake let's start with the bad news." If one starts with the

---

Dillard, Annie. "The Wreck of Time." *Harper's*, vol. 296, no. 1772 (January 1998): 51–56.

Quotations from Annie Dillard, *Pilgrim at Tinker Creek*, HarperPerennial, 1973; Annie Dillard, interview by Grace Suh, The Yale Herald, 4 October 1996, <http://www.yaleherald.com/archive/xxii/10.4.96/ae/dillard.html>; Annie Dillard, *For the Time Being*, Vintage Books, 2000.

bad news, as Dillard does in "The Wreck of Time," is it possible to recover a sense that "the world is as glorious as ever"? That the future is bright? These are the questions that Dillard wrestles with—and asks her readers to wrestle with, as well.

To learn more about Annie Dillard and the study of time, visit the Link-O-Mat at <www.newhum.com>.

■ ■

The Wreck of Time
Taking Our Century's Measure

Ted Bundy, the serial killer, after his arrest, could not fathom the fuss. What was the big deal? David Von Drehle quotes an exasperated Bundy in *Among the Lowest of the Dead*: "I mean, there are *so* many people."

One R. Houwink, of Amsterdam, uncovered this unnerving fact: The human population of earth, arranged tidily, would just fit into Lake Windermere, in England's Lake District.

Recently in the Peruvian Amazon a man asked the writer Alex Shoumatoff, "Isn't it true that the whole population of the United States can be fitted into their cars?"

How are we doing in numbers, we who have been alive for this most recent installment of human life? How many people have lived and died?

"The dead outnumber the living, in a ratio that could be as high as 20 to 1," a demographer, Nathan Keyfitz, wrote in a 1991 letter to the historian Justin Kaplan. "Credible estimates of the number of people who have ever lived on the earth run from 70 billion to over 100 billion." Averaging those figures puts the total persons ever born at about 85 billion. We living people now number 5.8 billion. By these moderate figures, the dead outnumber us about fourteen to one. The dead will always outnumber the living.

Dead Americans, however, if all proceeds, will not outnumber living Americans until the year 2030, because the nation is young. Some of us will be among the dead then. Will we know or care, we who once owned the still bones under the quick ones, we who spin inside the planet with our heels in the air? The living might well seem foolishly self-important to us, and overexcited.

We who are here now make up about 6.8 percent of all people who have appeared to date. This is not a meaningful figure. These our times are, one might say, ordinary times, a slice of life like any other. Who can bear to hear this, or who will consider it? Are we not especially significant because our century is—our century and its nuclear bombs, its unique and unprecedented Holocaust, its serial exterminations and refugee populations, our century and its warming, its silicon chips, men on the moon, and spliced genes? No, we are not and it is not.

Since about half of all the dead are babies and children, we will be among the longest-boned dead and among the dead who grew the most teeth—for what those distinctions might be worth among beings notoriously indifferent to appearance and all else.

In Juan Rulfo's novel *Pedro Páramo*, a dead woman says to her dead son, "Just think about pleasant things, because we're going to be buried for a long time."

II

On April 30, 1991—on that one day—138,000 people drowned in Bangladesh. At dinner I mentioned to my daughter, who was then seven years old, that it was hard to imagine 138,000 people drowning.

"No, it's easy," she said. "Lots and lots of dots, in blue water."

The paleontologist Pierre Teilhard de Chardin, now dead, sent a dispatch from a dig. "In the middle of the tamarisk bush you find a red-brick town, partially exposed. . . . More than 3,000 years before our era, people were living there who played with dice like our own, fished with hooks like ours, and wrote in characters we can't yet read."

Who were these individuals who lived under the tamarisk bush? Who were the people Ted Bundy killed? Who was the statistician who reckoned that everybody would fit into Lake Windermere? The Trojans likely thought well of themselves, one by one; their last settlement died out by 1,100 B.C.E. Who were the people Stalin killed, or any of the 79.2 billion of us now dead, and who are the 5.8 billion of us now alive?

"God speaks succinctly," said the rabbis.

Is it important if you have yet died your death, or I? Your father? Your child? It is only a matter of time, after all. Why do we find it supremely pertinent, during any moment of any century on earth, which among us is topsides? Why do we concern ourselves over which side of the membrane of topsoil our feet poke?

"A single death is a tragedy, a million deaths is a statistic." Joseph Stalin, that connoisseur, gave words to this disquieting and possibly universal sentiment.

How can an individual count? Do we individuals count only to us other suckers, who love and grieve like elephants, bless their hearts? Of Allah, the Koran says, "Not so much as the weight of an ant in earth or heaven escapes from the Lord." That is touching, that Allah, God, and their ilk care when one ant dismembers another, or note when a sparrow falls, but I strain to see the use of it.

Ten years ago we thought there were two galaxies for each of us alive. Lately, since we loosed the Hubble Space Telescope, we have revised our figures. There are nine galaxies for each of us. Each galaxy harbors an average of 100 billion suns. In our galaxy, the Milky Way, there are sixty-nine suns for each person alive. The Hubble shows, says a report, that the universe "is at least 15 billion years old." Two galaxies, nine galaxies . . . sixty-nine suns, 100 billion suns—

These astronomers are nickel-and-diming us to death.

III

What were you doing on April 30, 1991, when a series of waves drowned 138,000 people? Where were you when you first heard the astounding, heartbreaking news? Who told you? What, seriatim, were your sensations? Who did you tell? Did you weep? Did your anguish last days or weeks?

All my life I have loved this sight: a standing wave in a boat's wake, shaped like a thorn. I have seen it rise from many oceans, and I saw it rise from the Sea of Galilee. It was a peak about a foot high. The standing wave broke at its peak, and foam slid down its glossy hollow. I watched the foaming wave on the port side. At every instant we were bringing this boat's motor, this motion, into new water. The stir, as if of life, impelled each patch of water to pinch and inhabit this same crest. Each crest tumbled upon itself and released a slide of white foam. The foam's bubbles popped and dropped into the general sea while they were still sliding down the dark wave. They trailed away always, and always new waters peaked, broke, foamed, and replenished.

What I saw was the constant intersection of two wave systems. Lord Kelvin first described them. Transverse waves rise abaft the stern and stream away perpendicular to the boat's direction of travel. Diverging waves course out in a V shape behind the boat. Where the waves converge, two lines of standing crests persist at an unchanging angle to the direction of the boat's motion. We think of these as the boat's wake. I was studying the highest standing wave, the one nearest the boat. It rose from the trough behind the stern and spilled foam. The curled wave crested over clear water and tumbled down. All its bubbles broke, thousands a second, unendingly. I could watch the present; I could see time and how it works.

On a shore, 8,000 waves break a day. James Trefil, a professor of physics, provides these facts. At any one time, the foam from breaking waves covers between 3 and 4 percent of the earth's surface. This acreage of foam is equal to the entire continent of North America. By coincidence, the U.S. population bears nearly the same relation to the world population: 4.6 percent. The U.S. population, in other words, although it is the third largest population among nations, is as small a portion of the earth's people as breaking waves' white foam is of the sea.

"God rises up out of the sea like a treasure in the waves," wrote Thomas Merton.

We see generations of waves rise from the sea that made them, billions of individuals at a time; we see them dwindle and vanish. If this does not astound you, what will? Or what will move you to pity?

IV

One tenth of the land on earth is tundra. At any time, it is raining on only 5 percent of the planet's surface. Lightning strikes the planet about a hundred times every second. The insects outweigh us. Our chickens outnumber us four to one.

One fifth of us are Muslims. One fifth of us live in China. And every seventh person is a Chinese peasant. Almost one tenth of us live within range of an active volcano. More than 2 percent of us are mentally retarded. We humans drink tea—over a billion cups a day. Among us we speak 10,000 languages.

We are civilized generation number 500 or so, counting from 10,000 years ago, when we settled down. We are *Homo sapiens* generation number 7,500, counting from 150,000 years ago, when our species presumably arose; and we are human generation number 125,000, counting from the earliest forms of *Homo*.

Every 110 hours a million more humans arrive on the planet than die into the planet. A hundred million of us are children who live on the streets. Over a hundred million of us live in countries where we hold no citizenship. Twenty-three million of us are refugees. Sixteen million of us live in Cairo. Twelve million fish for a living from small boats. Seven and a half million of us are Uygurs. One million of us crew on freezer trawlers. Nearly a thousand of us a day commit suicide.

HEAD-SPINNING NUMBERS CAUSE MIND TO GO SLACK, the *Hartford Courant* says. But our minds must not go slack. How can we think straight if our minds go slack? We agree that we want to think straight.

Anyone's close world of family and friends composes a group smaller than almost all sampling errors, smaller than almost all rounding errors, a group invisible, at whose loss the world will not blink. Two million children die a year from diarrhea, and 800,000 from measles. Do we blink? Stalin starved 7 million Ukrainians in one year, Pol Pot killed 1 million Cambodians, the flu epidemic of 1918 killed 21 or 22 million people . . . shall this go on? Or do you suffer, as Teilhard de Chardin did, the sense of being "an atom lost in the universe"? Or do you not suffer this sense? How about what journalists call "compassion fatigue"? Reality fatigue? At what limit for you do other individuals blur? Vanish? How old are you?

V

Los Angeles airport has 25,000 parking spaces. This is about one space for every person who died in 1985 in Colombia when a volcano erupted. This is one space for each of the corpses of more than two years' worth of accidental killings from leftover land mines of recent wars. At five to a car, almost all the Inuit in the world could park at LAX. Similarly, if you propped up or stacked four bodies to a car, you could fit into the airport parking lot all the corpses from the firestorm bombing of Tokyo in March 1945, or the corpses of Londoners who died in the plague, or the corpses of Burundians killed in civil war since 1993. But you could not fit America's homeless there, not even at twenty to a car.

Since sand and dirt pile up on everything, why does the world look fresh for each new crowd? As natural and human debris raises the continents, vegetation grows on the piles. It is all a stage—we know this—a temporary stage on top of many layers of stages, but every year a new crop of sand, grass, and tree leaves freshens the set and perfects the illusion that ours is the new and urgent world now. When Keats was in Rome, I read once, he saw pomegranate trees overhead; they bloomed in dirt blown onto the Colosseum's broken walls. How can we doubt our own time, in which each bright instant probes the future? In every arable soil in the world we grow grain over tombs—sure, we know this. But do not the dead generations seem to us dark and still as mummies, and their times always faded like scenes painted on walls at Pompeii?

How can we see ourselves as only a new, temporary cast for a long-running show when a new batch of birds flies around singing and new clouds move? Living things from hyenas to bacteria whisk the dead away like stagehands hustling between scenes. To help a living space last while we live on it, we brush or haul away the blowing sand and hack or burn the greenery. We are mowing the grass at the cutting edge.

VI

In northeast Japan, a seismic sea wave killed 27,000 people on June 15, 1896. Do not fail to distinguish this infamous wave from the April 30, 1991, waves that drowned 138,000 Bangladeshi. You were not tempted to confuse, conflate, forget, or ignore these deaths, were you?

On the dry Laetoli plain of northern Tanzania, Mary Leakey found a trail of hominid footprints. The three barefoot people—likely a short man and woman and child *Australopithecus afarensis*—walked closely together. They walked on moist volcanic tuff and ash. We have a record of those few seconds from a day about 3.6 million years ago—before hominids even chipped stone tools. More ash covered their footprints and hardened. Ash also preserved the pockmarks of the raindrops that fell beside the three who walked; it was a rainy day. We have almost ninety feet of the three's steady footprints intact. We do not know where they were going or why. We do not know why the woman paused and turned left, briefly, before continuing. "A remote ancestor," Leakey said, "experienced a moment of doubt." Possibly they watched the Sadiman volcano erupt, or they took a last look back before they left. We do know we cannot make anything so lasting as these three barefoot ones did.

After archeologists studied this long strip of record for several years, they buried it again to save it. Along one preserved portion, however, new tree roots are already cracking the footprints, and in another place winds threaten to sand them flat; the preservers did not cover them deeply enough. Now they are burying them again.

Jeremiah, walking toward Jerusalem, saw the smoke from the Temple's blaze. He wept; he saw the blood of the slain. "He put his face close to the ground and saw the footprints of sucklings and infants who were walking into captivity" in Babylon. He kissed the footprints.

Who were these individuals? Who were the three who walked together and left footprints in the rain? Who was that eighteenth-century Ukrainian peasant the Baal Shem Tov, the founder of modern Hasidism, who taught, danced, and dug clay? He was among the generations of children of Babylonian exiles whose footprints on the bare earth Jeremiah kissed. Centuries later the Emperor Hadrian destroyed another such son of exile in Rome, Rabbi Akiba. Russian Christians and European Christians tried, and Hitler tried, to wipe all those survivors of children of exile from the ground of the earth as a man wipes a plate—survivors of exiles whose footprints on the ground I kiss, and whose feet.

Who and of what import were the men whose bones bulk the Great Wall, the 30 million Mao starved, or the 11 million children under five who die each year now? Why, they are the insignificant others, of course; living or dead, they are just some of the plentiful others. And you?

Is it not late? A late time to be living? Are not our current generations the important ones? We have changed the world. Are not our heightened times the important ones, the ones since Hiroshima? Perhaps we are the last generation—there is a comfort. Take the bomb threat away and what are we?

We are ordinary beads on a never-ending string. Our time is a routine twist of an improbable yarn.

We have no chance of being here when the sun burns out. There must be something ultimately heroic about our time, something that sets it above all those other times. Hitler, Stalin, Mao, and Pol Pot made strides in obliterating whole peoples, but this has been the human effort all along, and we have only enlarged the means, as have people in every century in history. (That genocides recur does not mean that they are similar. Each instance of human evil and each victim's death possesses its unique history and form. To generalize, as Cynthia Ozick points out, is to "befog" evil's specificity.)

Dire things are happening. Plague? Funny weather? Why are we watching the news, reading the news, keeping up with the news? Only to enforce our fancy—probably a necessary lie—that these are crucial times, and we are in on them. Newly revealed, and I am in the know: crazy people, bunches of them! New diseases, sways in power, floods! Can the news from dynastic Egypt have been any different?

As I write this, I am still alive, but of course I might well have died before you read it. Most of the archeologists who reburied hominid footprints have likely not yet died their deaths; the paleontologist Teilhard is pushing up daisies.

Chinese soldiers who breathed air posing for 7,000 individual clay portraits—twenty-two centuries ago—must have thought it a wonderful difference that workers buried only their simulacra then so that their sons could bury their flesh a bit later. One wonders what they did in the months or years they gained. One wonders what one is, oneself, up to these days.

VII

Was it wisdom Mao Tse-tung attained when—like Ted Bundy—he awakened to the long view?

"The atom bomb is nothing to be afraid of," Mao told Nehru. "China has many people. . . . The deaths of ten or twenty million people is nothing to be afraid of." A witness said Nehru showed shock. Later, speaking in Moscow, Mao displayed yet more generosity: he boasted that he was willing to lose 300 million people, half of China's population.

Does Mao's reckoning shock me really? If sanctioning the death of strangers could save my daughter's life, would I do it? Probably. How many others' lives would I be willing to sacrifice? Three? Three hundred million?

An English journalist, observing the Sisters of Charity in Calcutta, reasoned: "Either life is always and in all circumstances sacred, or intrinsically of no account; it is inconceivable that it should be in some cases the one, and in some the other."

One small town's soup kitchen, St. Mary's, serves 115 men a night. Why feed 115 individuals? Surely so few people elude most demographics and achieve statistical insignificance. After all, there are 265 million Americans, 15 million people who live in Mexico City, 16 million in greater New York, 26 million in greater Tokyo. Every day 1.5 million people walk through Times Square in New York; every day almost as many people—1.4 million—board a U.S. passenger plane. And so forth. We who breathe air now will join the already dead layers of us who breathed air once. We arise from dirt and dwindle to dirt, and the might of the universe is arrayed against us.   ■

■ *QUESTIONS FOR MAKING CONNECTIONS WITHIN THE READING* ■

1. "The Wreck of Time" is divided into seven sections. What is each section about? How are the sections connected? Is there an argument that develops over the course of the seven sections? Are there themes that are repeated across the sections? What is it that Dillard would like her readers to see or understand when they've completed her essay?

2. In the third section of "The Wreck of Time," Dillard describes how a boat creates a standing wave. At the end of her description, she writes that watching such waves allowed her to "see time and how it works." How does time work? What does her vision of the standing wave have to do with the other images she details in her essay?

3. When Dillard's essay first appeared in *Harper's,* a series of images were interspersed throughout the text. What images do you think would be appropriate for this essay? Bring to class an image or series of images that you feel illustrates or comments on the argument Dillard is making in "The Wreck of Time." Be prepared to discuss why the image you've selected is appropriate.

■ *QUESTIONS FOR WRITING* ■

1. In many ways, Annie Dillard's "The Wreck of Time" defies our common expectations about what a piece of writing *should* do: the essay has no clear thesis statement; it has no marked transitions between the paragraphs; it provides no obvious connection between its various subsections. Indeed, on first reading Dillard's piece, one might be tempted to conclude that it's little more than the recitation of a series of unrelated statistics and the posing of a series of unanswered questions. What is the relationship between the way that Dillard has written this piece and what she has to say in the piece? What is it that Dillard wants us to think about while reading her essay?

2. "We who are here now make up about 6.8 percent of all people who have appeared to date," Dillard writes; "This is not a meaningful figure." "The Wreck of Time" is filled with statistics about world population, the size of the universe, natural and man-made disasters. Are any of these figures "meaningful"? Can such figures be invested with meaning?

▪ *QUESTIONS FOR MAKING CONNECTIONS BETWEEN READINGS* ▪

1. At the end of "Does God Have a Future?" Karen Armstrong asserts, "Human beings cannot endure emptiness and desolation; they will fill the vacuum by creating a new focus of meaning." Does Annie Dillard do this? What philosophical, religious, or moral system emerges from the vision Dillard has provided in "The Wreck of Time"?

2. Given the argument that Dillard makes in "The Wreck of Time," does it make sense to pursue a project like cleaning up the Ganges River that Alexander Stille describes? Is Dillard's view of the natural world consonant with Mishra's? Will the notion of "the sacred" last into the next century, or will it be replaced by science and information?

For additional suggestions about making connections between readings, visit the Link-O-Mat and More Sample Assignments at <www.newhum.com>.

ELLEN DISSANAYAKE

ELLEN DISSANAYAKE [Diss-an-'eye-a-ka] is an independent scholar and lecturer who brings together theories about aesthetics, human development, psychology, and evolutionary biology in order to understand why humans have an "aesthetic imagination." Arguing that there are fundamental similarities between play, ritual, fantasy, and the more highly valued activity of "art-making," Dissanayake maintains that all of these behaviors of "making special" have an essential evolutionary value. In so doing, she argues that the humanities are not separate from but, rather, are a part of, the human sciences.

Dissanayake's interest in the relationship between science, evolution, and art came together during more than fifteen years she spent living in Sri Lanka. After having grown up and gone to college in Washington State in the 1950s, Dissanayake fell in love with how the arts are integrated into the daily lives of the Sri Lankans, and she began to wonder about the role the arts play in improving the chances of the survival of the human species. Noting that humans the world over engage in the activity of art-making, Dissanayake began to rethink the idea that life in Sri Lanka was somehow fundamentally different from life in Washington: as she explains it in *Art and Intimacy*, "My intimate life with Sri Lankans made me the opposite of a fanatical cultural relativist: I have in fact become more impressed with the deeper human similarities that underlie cultural difference."

Her three books, *What Is Art For* (1988), *Homo Aestheticus: Where Art Comes From and Why* (1995), and *Art and Intimacy: How the Arts Began* (2000), explore the consequences of the argument she makes in "The Core of Art," that the need to "make special" is part of humanity's genetic profile. Declared "a true pioneer" by Edward O. Wilson and "ahead of her time" by Steven Pinker, Dissanayake asks her readers to rethink the place of art in their lives and to consider the possibility that the ongoing survival of the species may depend on the ability of its members to "make special."

Dissanayake, Ellen. "The Core of Art: Making Special." *Homo Aestheticus: Where Art Comes From and Why*. New York: The Free Press, 1995. 39–63.

Biographical information and quotations from Caleb Crain, "The Artistic Animal," *Lingua Franca* 11, (2001) <http://www.linguafranca.com/print/0110/cover.html>.

To learn more about Ellen Dissanayake, evolutionary theory, and aesthetics, visit the Link-O-Mat at <www.newhum.com>.

The Core of Art

Making Special

When contemporary philosophers of art make the radical and rather astonishing statement that art has existed for only two centuries,[1] they are referring to the insufficiently appreciated fact that the abstract concept "art" is a construction of Western culture and in fact has a discernible historical origin.[2] It was only in the late eighteenth century—in Enlightenment England and Germany—and subsequently, that the subject of aesthetics was named and developed, that "the aesthetic" came to be regarded as a distinctive kind of experience, and that an art world of academies, museums, galleries, dealers, critics, journals, and scholars arose to address a type of human artifact that was made primarily and often specifically for acquisition and display. At the same time ideas of genius, creative imagination, self-expression, originality, communication, and emotion, having originated in other contexts, became increasingly and even primarily or exclusively associated with the subject of "art." The concepts "primitive" and "natural" [. . .] also developed at this time to become part of modern Western cultural consciousness.

Previously, the sorts of objects that in the post-eighteenth century West came to be called art—paintings, sculptures, ceramics, music, dance, poetry, and so forth—were made to embody or to reinforce religious or civic values, and rarely, if ever, for purely aesthetic purposes. Paintings and sculptures served as portraits, illustrations, interior or exterior decoration; ceramics were vessels for use; music and dance were part of a ceremonial or special social occasion; poetry was storytelling or praise or oratory to sway an audience. Even when beauty, skill, or ostentation were important qualities of an object, they did not exist "for their own sake," but as an enhancement of the object's ostensible if not actual use. This enhancement would be called beautification or adornment, not art. The word *art* as used before the late eighteenth century meant what we would today call "craft" or "skill" or "well-madeness," and could characterize any object or activity made or performed by human (rather than natural or divine) agency—for example, the art of medicine, of retailing, of holiday dining.

It may be a surprise to realize how peculiar our modern Western notion of art really is—how it is dependent on and intertwined with ideas of commerce, commodity, ownership, history, progress, specialization, and individuality—and to recognize the truth that only a few societies have thought of it even remotely as we do (Alsop 1982). Of course, in the preindustrial West and elsewhere, people had and continue to have "aesthetic" ideas—notions of what makes something beautiful or excellent-of-its-kind—but such ideas can be held without tacitly assuming that there is a superordinate abstract category, Art, to which belong *some* paintings, drawings, or carvings and not *other* paintings, drawings, or carvings.[3]

As Western aesthetics developed, something was assigned to the category of genuine art if it was deemed capable of providing and sustaining genuine aesthetic experience. Genuine aesthetic experience was defined as something one experienced when contemplating genuine art. Note the circularity of this argument. Moreover, difficulties arose in specifying the cause or location of this genuineness (in the face of differences of opinion about the validity of individual works or responses). People should have recognized that these difficulties threw the concept of a pure or singular art itself into doubt.

To be sure, philosophers and artists in the past (for example, Aristotle, Saint Thomas Aquinas, Leonardo da Vinci) had proposed criteria for beauty or excellence, for example, fitness, clarity, harmony, radiance, a mirror held up to nature. Nineteenth- and twentieth-century thinkers proposed other criteria, such as truth, order, unity in variety, and significant form, as being the defining feature of this mysterious entity "Art."

But, as every first-year student of Western aesthetics learns, determining what is beauty or truth, not to mention significance or harmony, is no less difficult than defining art in the first place. And in any case, since the romantic period artists themselves (influenced by the ever-growing Western cultural emphasis on individualism and originality) have deliberately flouted and contradicted the canonic aesthetic features, as they were described or proposed by philosophers, critics, and other thinkers, as if to demonstrate that art, whatever its essence or validity, is protean, undefinable, and irreducible.

Hence the search for a common denominator, some quality or feature that characterizes all instances of art, that *makes* something "Art," gradually became both outmoded and a lost cause. Today's philosophers of art have totally abandoned trying to define the word or the concept. Looking at the plural and radical nature of the arts in our time, aware of the economic ramifications where canvases may be "worth" millions of dollars and where critics, dealers, and museum directors rather than artists or publics largely decide this value, philosophers concerned with art have concluded that art no longer exists (if it ever did) in a vacuum or ideal realm for its own sake, with its sacred essence waiting to be discovered, but must be considered as it appears in and is dependent on a particular social context. In a postindustrial, postmodern society, an art world (or "artworld") determines what "Art" is and what is "Art." It exists, if at all, only as a socially and historically conditioned label.

The reader must recognize, however, that this position arises from contemporary postmodern Western society, which despite our natural ethnocentrism [. . .] is not, of course, the apogee of humankind's enterprise and wisdom nor its ultimate destiny. We must not forget that although "Art" as a concept seems to have been born of and continues to be sustained by a commercial society, is therefore only roughly two centuries old, and hence is relative, even discardable, *the arts* have always been with us. And so have ideas of beauty, sublimity, and transcendence, along with the verities of the human condition: love, death, memory, suffering, power, fear, loss, desire, hope, and so forth. These have been the subject matter of and occasion for the arts throughout human history. Thus when contemporary theory accepts that art is contingent and dependent on "a particular social context," the mistake should not be made of assuming that the abiding human concerns and the arts that have immemorially been their accompaniment and embodiment are themselves contingent and dependent.

The species-centric view of art recognizes and proclaims as valid and intrinsic the association between what humans have always found to be important and certain ways—called "the arts"—that they have found to grasp, manifest, and reinforce this importance. That the arts in postmodern society do not perform these functions, at least to the extent that they do in premodern societies, is not because of some deficiency or insubstantiality of an abstract concept but because their makers inhabit a world—unprecedented in human history—in which these abiding concerns are artificially disguised, denied, trivialized, ignored, or banished.

An ethological view of art, then, departs from the entrenched position of contemporary aesthetics and reinstates the search for a "common denominator," although in a manner never dreamed of by philosophers of art. In order to show that a behavior of art is universal and indelible, *it is necessary to identify a core behavioral tendency upon which natural selection could act.*

In trying to uncover this deep marrow of a behavior of art, we will not be primarily concerned with contemporary society, not even with earlier civilizations or with traditional or what used to be called "primitive" societies. Rather, we must look for a behavioral tendency that could have been possessed by protohumans, the early hominids who existed one to four million years ago. These, our ancestors, were creatures who walked on two legs and lived in small, nomadic bands on the African savannah. They hunted, foraged, scavenged, and gathered their food, as hominids did until about 10,000 B.C. when settled agricultural communities began to establish themselves in certain parts of the world. Somewhere in this continuum of hominid evolution will have arisen a behavioral tendency that helped individuals who possessed it (and by extension a social group whose members had it) to survive better than individuals and groups who lacked the tendency. This core or common denominator of art will, however, be a behavioral tendency that is not incompatible with art today and elsewhere, yet can also characterize creatures such as these, our hominid ancestors.

The Extra-Ordinary

In my view, the biological core of art, the stain that is deeply dyed in the behavioral marrow of humans everywhere, is something I have elsewhere called "making special." Like other key phrases used to name or summarize a complex concept ("pleasure principle," "survival of the fittest"), "making special" can without elaboration or context sound trivial or woolly. Before describing it in more detail, [. . .] I would like to recount briefly the background of my search for this core tendency that I believe lies behind or within what is today considered to be the impulse toward (the behavioral tendency of) art.

Play and Ritual

My own earliest attempts to approach art as a behavior began when I first read ethological accounts of play. Play in animals (including humans) is an appealing and quite mysterious behavior. It occurs in many species in which animals play naturally, without being taught. Yet, unlike other behaviors, play seems to be, at the time of playing at least, biologically purposeless and even disadvantageous. The players do not gain a life-serving goal, as they do in other behaviors where they find food, mate, repel an intruder, rest, and so on. In fact, animals at play seem to expend a lot of energy for no useful purpose and risk hurting themselves, attracting predators, or otherwise decreasing their chances of survival. Yet young animals will play indefatigably. They seem to play for play's sake, for sheer enjoyment and intrinsic reward. Thus it would seem that play has hidden survival benefits that outweigh the costs of its energy expenditure and risks.

In play, novelty and unpredictability are actively sought, whereas in real life we do not usually like uncertainty. Wondering whether an untried shortcut will take us to the bank before it closes on the day before a holiday is different from choosing an unknown path just to see where it will lead while on holiday.

Play can be said to be "extra," something outside normal life. At least normal constraints do not hold. At play, you can be a princess, a mother, or a horse. You can be strong and invincible. You can act *like*, be *like*, a desperado or a soldier. You pretend to fight or pretend to have a tea party, but these are "not for real." Real weapons (like loaded guns or unsheathed claws) are not used; the teacups may be empty.

But play is marked by constraints nevertheless. One generally finds, even in animals, "rules" of play: special signals (such as wagging the tail or not using claws), postures, facial expressions, and sounds that mean "This is make-believe." Often special places are set aside for playing: a stadium, a gymnasium, a park, a recreation room, a ring or circle. There are special times, special clothes, a special mood for play—think of holidays, festivals, vacations, weekends.

As I read about play, its similarities to art became obvious. Art, as I knew it from aesthetics and art history classes, is "nonutilitarian," "for its own sake": Cellini's saltcellar was art, but not because it held salt better than a clay or glass container. Art, like play, was not "real" but pretend: the actor playing Hamlet did not really stab the actor playing Polonius. Art made exquisite use of surprise and ambiguity. There were special places like museums and concert halls set aside for art, special times, even special clothes for it—such as dark attire for symphony musicians. And there was especially a special mood, which I had learned to describe as "disinterested contemplation": one *did not* rush up on stage to help the hero overcome the villain, one *did* contemplate the skill and subtlety of the actors, the craft and language of the playwright. Art, like play, was something extra, an embellishment, an enhancement to life.

As I looked further into the subject, I discovered I was only the latest in a long lineage to have noticed the resemblance between play and art and to have gone on to conclude that art was a derivative of play.[4] The new contribution I hoped to offer was making this conclusion plausible by means of ethological (rather than, as others had done, from psychological or historical or metaphysical) evidence. I thought that the "metaphorical" nature of both art and play, the make-believe aspect where something is, in reality, something else, was the salient core feature.

For an ethologist, the apparent absence of evolutionary purpose is a problem both for play and for art. Because humans everywhere avidly engage in both playful and artistic pursuits, these must serve some purpose, even if it is not immediately evident.

With regard to play, it is generally agreed that although there might not be immediate survival benefits associated with play, young animals in play are practicing (in situations that are not yet "for keeps") skills that eventually enable them to find food, defend themselves, and mate, among other adult necessities. Also—importantly—in play, they learn how to get along with others. Individuals who play, and thereby learn practical and social skills, survive better than individuals who are not inclined to play or who are deprived of play and therefore lack practice with these essential things. As with an insurance policy, the benefits of play are deferred.

Looking at art, I was aware that it consisted of more than exercise, practice, or socialization. But what? Freud claimed that the function of both play and art was therapy. They allowed for fantasy, for the sublimation or fulfillment of hidden wishes that in real life were denied or tabooed: if you can't get the girl, dream or fantasize or write a story or paint a picture about getting her. As I considered the problem from an ethological point of view, I concluded that art in human evolution must have done something more than give fantasy free rein. How much fantasy did our hominid ancestors practice anyway? Did they need more make-believe than they acquired from play? (It is almost certain that early hominids, like all primates, must have played.) Was it not more important that they accept and comply with *reality:* the daily "business" of meals, safety, cooperation?[5] Fantasy and make-believe may well be important safety valves for modern humans mired in the discontents of civilization, but I hoped to find a more plausible reason to explain why early hominids would have developed art *as well as* or in addition to play. Practice, socialization, recreation, wish-fulfillment—these goals could have been satisfied by play without necessitating another sort of behavior that accomplished the same ends. Unless I were willing to accept the idea that art was simply a variety of play, which seemed an inadequate explanation, I had to look further into the matter of its ethological origin, nature, and probable selective value.

During the years that I lived in Sri Lanka, the small Buddhist country formerly known as Ceylon, I became acquainted with what sociologists call a traditional society. In such societies, modern technology is still relatively undeveloped: at building sites, for example, scaffoldings are made of bamboo tied together, and people rather than backhoes and bulldozers move the earth. Many families still live on the land and are relatively self-sufficient; village houses and utensils are largely made by hand from local materials and food is grown in the family garden. Custom and authority continue to provide the boundaries within which people lead their lives and find their satisfactions—most marriages are arranged by parents or other relatives, for example, and it is not considered unusual for important decisions to be made only after consulting an astrologer.

People living in traditional societies seem much closer to the verities of life than people living in highly technological societies like our own. Because they have known each other's families for generations, events like weddings and funerals—matters of life and death—are important occasions for socializing. I attended my first funeral and saw a dead body for the first time while in Sri Lanka, and I was initially amazed that babies and small children were also in attendance.

Traditional ceremony and custom thus play a much larger part in the life of a Sri Lankan than in ours. After a person dies in Sri Lanka, the mourners arrive during the course of the day at the home where the deceased is lying in an open coffin on a table in the living room, surrounded by flowers. The bereaved family members greet each visitor at the door, breaking down in sobs with each new arrival as they talk about the circumstances of the death and the merits of the deceased. The guest enters the house and joins other guests; they chat quietly with each other about any subject (I heard discussions about movies, business, and political matters); and after a decent interval they leave. Eventually the family and close friends go to the place of cremation or burial where Buddhist monks join them and recite the appropriate Pali texts—reflections on birth, death, decay, and reincarnation. Three days after the disposition of the body the family and priests hold an almsgiving ceremony; other almsgivings in memory of the deceased occur after three months, one year, and at yearly intervals thereafter.

I realized that this kind of formalized handling of grief, with regular, community-sanctioned opportunities to weep and express one's loss at greater and greater intervals of time, gave to the bereaved a sort of patterned program to follow, a form that could shape and contain their feelings. Instead of having to suppress their grief and sense of loss in the interests of being brave or "realistic," or having to release it haphazardly or in solitude, the bereaved is enabled—compelled—by the ritual of mourning to acknowledge and express it publicly, over and over again, within a preordained structure. The temporal structure of the mourning ritual, simple as it is, assures that thoughts and feelings about one's loss will be reiterated at prescribed times. Even if one might not consciously have proper mournful feelings, the custom of successive almsgivings ensures that these feelings are elicited. The prescribed formal ceremonies become the occasion for and even the cause of individuals feeling and publicly expressing their sorrow.[6]

It occurred to me that in a very similar way, the arts also are containers for, molders of feeling. The performance of a play, a dance, or a musical composition manipulates the audience's response: expands, contracts, excites, calms, releases. The rhythm and form of a poem do the same thing. Even nontemporal arts, like painting, sculpture, and architecture, structure the viewer's response and give a form to feeling.

It is well known that in most societies the arts are commonly associated with ceremonial contexts, with rituals. So next I began to try to discover what art and ritual had in common. It was intriguing to learn that "ritualized behavior" in animals, like play, was an important ethological subject and that at least some anthropologists noted real, not just superficial, parallels between ritualized behavior in animals and ceremonial rituals in humans (Huxley 1966; Turner 1983). Perhaps like ritual (and play), one could call art "a behavior" also.

As I had suspected and hoped, the similarities between ceremonial ritual and art were provocative. For example, both ritual and art are *compelling*. They use various effective means to arouse, capture, and hold attention. Both are fashioned with the intent to affect individuals emotionally—to bring their feelings into awareness, to display them. A large part of the compelling nature of rituals and art is that they are deliberately *nonordinary*. In Sri Lankan—and our own—funeral services, for example, unusual language is used: ancient religious works with their archaic and poetic vocabulary and word order serve as texts for the services, and these texts are intoned or

Crowd of devotees at Hemis Festival, Ladakh, Kashmir
Ritual occasions may bring together and unify great numbers of people through their common participation in extraordinary and compelling experiences. © Ernest Haas/ Hulton Archive—Getty Images

chanted in a voice unlike that employed in normal discourse. Other nonordinary devices for making ritual (and art) compelling include exaggeration (the rhythm of funeral processions may be unusually slow and deliberate), repetition (the Sri Lankan funeral ritual punctuates time with repeated almsgivings), and elaboration (the profusion of flowers, the wearing of special clothing, other extravagances like the gathering of unusually large numbers of people).

The *stylization* of ritual and art also adds to their nonordinary aspect. They are self-consciously performed as if acted. During the ceremonial signing of a bill, the president of the United States speaks highly rhetorical phrases sanctified by use reaching back two hundred years, things like "Thereunto I set this seal." The ballerina or opera singer makes a ritualized—exaggerated, elaborated, formalized—series of bows to acknowledge the applause at the end of her performance (which itself was composed of exaggerated, elaborated, and formalized movements or vocalizations).

Thus, in general, both rituals and art are *formalized*. Movements—what people do—are prescribed, the order of events is structured, and the individual participants' perceptions, emotions, and interpretations are thereby shaped.

Ritual ceremonies and the arts are *socially reinforcing*, uniting their participants and their audiences in one mood. They both provide an occasion for feelings of individual transcendence of the self—what Victor Turner (1969) calls *communitas* and Mihaly Csikszentmihalyi (1975) calls "flow"—as everyone shares in the same occasion of patterned emotion. For a time, the hard edges of their customary isolation from each other are softened or melted together or their everyday taken-for-granted comradeship is reinforced.

Rituals and the arts are *bracketed*, set off from real or ordinary life. A stage of some kind—a circle, a demarcated area, a museum, or platform— sets off the holy from the profane, the performers from the audience, the extra-ordinary from the everyday. And both rituals and the arts make conspicuous *use of symbols*: things have hidden or arcane meanings, reverberations beyond their apparent surface significance.

Ritual ceremonies are universal, found in every human society. They serve numerous social purposes: they state and publicly reinforce the values of a group of people; they unite it in common purpose and belief; they "explain" the inexplicable—birth, death, illness, natural disaster—and attempt to control it and make it bearable. From the ethological perspective, people in social groups that did not have ceremonial rituals would not survive as well as those who did have them. They would be less cohesive and cooperative; they would respond to adversity in individualized, fragmented, unfocused, and ultimately less satisfactory ways.

Apart from the many similarities that ritual and art share as general "behaviors," they are virtually always linked together in practice. During ritual ceremonies one invariably finds the arts: the use of beautiful or arresting objects, the wearing of specially decorated attire, music, visual display, poetic language, dance, performances. It seemed nondebatable to me that an understanding of ceremonial ritual was relevant, even critical, to an ethological understanding of art.

Because of the many close connections between art and ritual, I first wondered whether art could be considered as a derivative of ritual, much as I had earlier thought of art as a kind of play.[7] After struggling to make sense of how and why this might have happened, an idea came to me: art was not a variety of play or ritual, but like them it was concerned with a special order, realm, mood, state of being. In play, ritual, *and* art things were not ordinary—they are less real or more real than everyday reality. I decided to try looking there for the behavioral core of art.

Differentiating Ordinary from Extra-Ordinary

My thesis that the evolution and selective value of a behavior of art arises from a tendency to make special rests on the claim that humans everywhere, in a manner that is unlike that of other animals, differentiate between an order, realm, mood, or state of being that is mundane, ordinary, or "natural," and one that is unusual, extra-ordinary, or "super-natural."

But is this a justifiable claim? In some premodern societies the former and the latter appear to interpenetrate. According to Robert Tonkinson

(1978, 96), the Mardudjara, an Australian aboriginal group, make no clear distinction between natural and spiritual realms, considering themselves and nonhuman entities and forces to be all equally real inhabitants of their cosmic order.[8] Other peoples, in Australia and elsewhere, similarly find "natural" and "spiritual" to be more continuous than we do—to consider the spiritual *as* natural. One might wonder whether an "obvious" separation between ordinary and extra-ordinary, like that between profane and sacred, natural and super-natural, nature and culture, body and soul, flesh and spirit, is to be traced to the discontents and artificialities of civilization.

I am prepared to claim, however, that making such a distinction is a characterizing universal predisposition of human behavior and mentality. Moreover, I would argue that it is in this predisposition that we are to look for the core of a behavior of art. Even in human groups that do not articulate an explicit separation between extra-ordinary and ordinary, their actions demonstrate such an awareness. Tonkinson himself says of the Mardudjara: "the Dreamtime [the spiritual dimension or domain in which ancestral beings have their existence] is crucial because it is held to be the source of all power, given in response to ritual performance, but also available to individuals when they are able *briefly to transcend their humanity and tap this reservoir (for example, during dance, trance, visions, dreams, and heightened emotional and religious states.*" (Tonkinson 1978, 16; my italics).

Many anthropological studies describe "other worlds": the mysterious permanent dimension of reality that the Yoruba call *iron* (Drewal and Drewal 1983); the spirit of the forest of the Ituri forest pygmies (Turnbull 1961); the *engang*, or unseen world of dead spirits, of the Fang of Gabon (Fernandez 1973); the Eskimo *sila* or "life force" (Birket-Smith 1959); the *kore* ("wilderness") of the Gimi, otherworldly compared to *dusa*, the domesticated forms of plants and animals and the constraints of human social existence (Gillison 1980, 144); the transcendent reality of the Umeda which is grasped only through rituals that are the antithesis or opposite of what usually is (Gell 1975); the "underneath" side of things and words of the Kaluli (Feld 1982); the hyperanimacy of the powerful beings that the Kalapalo communally sing into being (Basso 1985); the *kia* experience of Bushmen (Katz 1982)—one would be hard-pressed to find an anthropological monograph about a people that did not recognize or manifest by their actions the recognition of a nonordinary if not sacred dimension along with everyday reality.

How and why would evolving humans perceive or create "other worlds" apart from the everyday? As I pointed out in the previous section, the penchant for acknowledging an extra-ordinary realm is inherent in the behavior of play, where actions are "not for real." The "as-ifness" of play, then, can be thought of as a reservoir from which more flexible, imaginative, innovative behaviors can arise—as when we "play around with" an idea. And in ritual also (both the ritualized behaviors of animals and human ritual ceremonies), ordinary behavior is formalized and exaggerated, thereby (particularly in humans) acquiring a meaning and weight that makes it different from what it usually is: it becomes extra-ordinary. It seems undeniable that at some point, evolving hominids, being acquainted in their daily lives with play and ritual, would have been predisposed (as individuals and eventually as a species) to recognize and even create "meta-" or "as-if" realities.

Yet it must be admitted that at the most fundamental level, being able to distinguish between ordinary and extra-ordinary is not a particularly remarkable ability at all. Every animal is equipped to differentiate the normal from the abnormal, the neutral from the extreme. A salamander or mosquito, as well as more complex forms of life, will know when there is a change that suggests something out of the ordinary might occur: a sudden shadow, a sharp noise, an unexpected movement. Life, after all, depends on reacting (or being ready to react) to changes in habitual existence. Moreover, many nonhuman animals also play, but did not go on to invent arts or imaginative works of any kind. And formalized, ritualized behaviors, analogous to ritual ceremonies in humans in their use of rare and extra-ordinary postures, odors, sounds, and movements (Geist 1978), are also widespread in other animals but have not given rise in them to anything we can justifiably call art. What was it about humans that provoked or permitted them to recognize and then proceed to further elaborate "other" worlds, special fanciful worlds like those invented in play, invoked in ritual, or fabricated in the arts?

The evolving hominids we are concerned with—say, a quarter of a million years ago—were more intelligent and resourceful than other animals. Their brains were larger and more intricately composed, and the mental and emotional complexity this endowment permitted led to a wider range of thought and feeling. Whereas other animals can be assumed to inhabit a continuous present, generally unconcerned with what happened yesterday and what might happen tomorrow, gradually during the Middle or Early Upper Paleolithic, humans must have become, as Walter Burkert (1987, 172) has remarked with regard to the biological origins of religion, "painfully aware of past and future."

I suggest that the standard and unexceptional animal inclination to differentiate ordinary from extra-ordinary, to recognize specialness, would have been developing over tens of thousands of years, along with other higher-level cognitive abilities that were also evolving, such as planning ahead or assessing causes and their consequences.[9] At some point in their evolution, humans began deliberately to set out to *make things special* or extra-ordinary, perhaps for the purpose of influencing the outcome of important events that were perceived as uncertain and troubling, requiring action beyond simple fight or flight, approach or avoidance.[10]

A Closer Look at Making Special

In *What Is Art For?* I proposed that we could understand the arts ethologically by considering them as ways of making important things and activities "special." That is to say, I emphasized the "behavior" or activity [. . .] rather than, as other art theorists have done, the results: the things and activities themselves as "works of art."

I suggested that elements of what we today call the arts (e.g., pattern, vividness) would have existed first in nonaesthetic contexts. But because these elements were inherently gratifying (perceptually, emotionally, cognitively) to humans, humans who had an inherent proclivity for making special would use them—not for their own sake, but instead, in ethological terms, as "enabling mechanisms"—in the performance of other selectively valuable behaviors.

To begin with, I thought that the reason making special first occurred might have been to persuade oneself and others that what was being done was worthwhile and effective. This is a reason for embellishment in other species—notably, songbirds, who elaborate their songs much more than is necessary simply to advertise their presence or individuality. My reasoning went something like this. If you are an early human who wants to achieve a goal—to kill an animal, for example, or to cure a sickness—you will take pains, take the activity seriously. If you accidentally or deliberately say or do something extra, and are successful, you may well remember to do the extra something again the next time, just in case, as when a baseball player touches his cap and ear in a certain way before throwing a pitch, or a performer or pilot always carries a particular trinket that has in the past brought her or him good luck.

It is clear that taking serious and important activities seriously should be of immense survival value. Every bit of psychological reinforcement would count, for yourself as well as for the others who observe you. (As I pointed out, people who spent time and trouble to reinforce and elaborate deleterious things would not have survived.)

The idea of making special as persuasion or rhetoric seemed promising. Making life-serving implements (tools, weapons) special both expressed and reinforced their importance to individuals and would have assured their more careful manufacture and use. But equally or more important would have been the contribution of making special to ritual ceremonies. When language was used poetically (with stress, compelling rhythm, rhyme, noteworthy similes or word choice); when costumes or decor were striking and extravagant; when choruses, dances, and recitations allowed vicarious or actual audience participation, the content of the ceremonies would have been more memorable than when left "untreated." Whatever message the ceremony intended to communicate ("In union is strength"; "Death is an end and a beginning"; "We are the best"; "Transitions are scary but unavoidable"; "We need food for the coming season") would be first engendered and then reinforced, acquiring special import by virtue of the special effort and attention expended upon it. At the same time, the fellow-feeling arising from the mutual participation and shared emotion was a microcosmic acting out of the general cooperation and coordination that was essential for small groups to survive in a violent, unpredictable world.[11] Groups whose individual members had the tendency to make things special would have had more unifying ritual ceremonies, and thus these individuals and groups would have survived better than individuals and groups that did not.

In ritual ceremonies, then, one can see that making special could acquire even more import than in individual occurrences. Because it is used to articulate substantive and vital concerns, it is drawn from, expresses, and engages one's deepest and strongest feelings.[12] [. . .]

The Relationship of Making Special and Art

[. . .] I was first led to develop the concept of making special because of my dissatisfaction with Western culture's general perplexity surrounding the notion of art and, reflecting this confusion, the inadequacy of the available speculations about the role of the arts in human evolution. It seemed to me that if evolutionists did not recognize *Homo aestheticus*, that is, could not satisfactorily explain how and why art was a human universal and could view it only as an epiphenomenon, their concept of art itself must be aberrant. Something so widespread, pleasurable, and obviously important to those who did it should not be so inexplicable.

Trapped in the confines and presuppositions of my culture's concepts and attitudes regarding art, I too floundered and took circuitous detours around the subject, as when I tried for a time to derive art from play or art from ritual. I continually returned to the quality in the arts of all times and places of being *extra-ordinary*, outside the daily routine and not strictly utilitarian (in a materialistic, ultimate sense)—even when considered "necessary" to their practitioners. That was where evolutionary explanations always broke down because something "nonutilitarian" should not have been selected for. Yet nonetheless it existed.

The best word for this characteristic of the arts seemed to be *special*. *Extra-ordinary* with a hyphen might have served, but it is too easily read as "astonishing" or "remarkable"—that is, as a synonym for nonhyphenated *extraordinary*. *Unnecessary* and *nonutilitarian* emphasize what the arts are not, and also smack too much of Western ideas of art-for-art's-sake. *Elaboration* used alone disregards the importance of shaping, and like *enhance* suggests, in Western culture at least, the superficial or merely added. While "special" might seem too imprecise and naively simple, or suggest mere decoration, it easily encompassed an array of what is done in making the arts that is generally different from making nonarts: embellishing, exaggerating, patterning, juxtaposing, shaping, and transforming.

"Special" also denotes a positive factor of care and concern that is absent from the other words. It thus suggests that the special object or activity appeals to emotional as well as perceptual and cognitive factors—that is, to all aspects of our mental functioning. Even though all three are inseparable, [. . .] the usual aesthetic nomenclature ("for its own sake," "beauty," "harmony," "contemplation") tends to emphasize calm or abstract intellectual satisfactions at the expense of sensory/emotional/physical/pleasurable ones. Hence "special" can indicate that not only are our senses arrested by a thing's perceptual strikingness (specialness), and our intellects intrigued and stimulated by its uncommonness (specialness), but that we make something special because doing so gives us a way of expressing its positive emotional valence for us, and the ways in which we accomplish this specialness not only reflect but give unusual or special gratification and pleasure (i.e., are aesthetic).

It is important to recognize that the elements used for making something aesthetically special are normally themselves inherently pleasing and gratifying to humans and thus can be called "aesthetic" or "protoaesthetic" even when they occur naturally in nonaesthetic contexts. These pleasing characteristics are those that would have been selected-for in human evolution as indicating that something is wholesome and good: for example, visual signs of health, youth, and vitality such as smoothness, glossiness, warm or true colors, cleanness, fineness, or lack of blemish, and vigor, precision, and comeliness of movement.

Thus we find that most, if not all, societies value agility, endurance, and grace in dance; sonority, vividness, and rhythmic or phonic echoing (rhyme and other poetic devices) in language; and resonance and power in percussion. The Wahgi of Papua New Guinea's Western Highlands, for example, explicitly judge body decoration, dancing, drumming, and ensemble performance in terms of their being rich, glossy, glinting, fiery, slashing, shining, flaming, that is, as the converse of dull, dry, flaky, matte, and lusterless (O'Hanlon 1989).

In the arts of the West, high value has also been given to skillfully made polished marble statuary, implements and ornaments of burnished metal, vivid glowing tempera and oil paintings, and ornately sumptuous or softly diaphanous textiles. Indeed, it is the obvious lack of these inherently pleasurable or "beautiful" features that has made it so difficult for unsophisticated people to accept certain works of art made during the past century or so as "art," for the artists' deliberate choices to defy traditional expectations regarding pleasing characteristics have set their works outside the pale of "recognizable" art.

In addition to elements that appeal to the senses, particularly vision and hearing, there are others that are pleasing to the cognitive faculties: repetition, pattern, continuity, clarity, dexterity, elaboration or variation of a theme, contrast, balance, proportion. These qualities have to do with comprehension, mastery, and hence security, and thus they are recognized as "good," when used outside a utilitarian context, to make something special. Visual prototypes (e.g., fundamental geometric shapes such as circles or other mandala forms like diagonal or upright crosses) also clarify and control untidiness and are thought and felt to be satisfying and good. [. . .]

The responses to "specialness" in the aesthetic sense—"This is (sensorily and emotionally as well as intellectually) gratifying and special"—presumably evolved alongside other responses to "specialness"—"This is dangerous, unprecedented, needs to be dealt with." As I suggested in speaking of salamanders and mosquitoes, not all specialness engenders or results from gratifying "aesthetic" acts or responses.

"Marking" of any kind for utilitarian identification, for example, the X's made by Hindus on the doors of railway cars that carried Moslems during the Indian-Pakistani conflicts after independence, is, strictly speaking, making something special, as is the construction by a state security police department of a special room, in a special place, without windows and with unusual equipment, in which to extract confessions from prisoners. But these unpleasant examples of "specialness" should not be included in the notion I am developing here of aesthetic specialness: the intention to appeal to (that is, to attract and, if successful, to satisfy) another's faculty for apprehending and appreciating a specialness that is more than what is necessary to fulfill a practical end. Additionally, the "artist" takes the protoaesthetic elements out of their "natural" context of indicating vitality and goodness, and "domesticates" them—deliberately using them in aesthetic making special. [. . .]

Thus, in order to be "aesthetically special," the X's made by the Hindus would have to have been made with care as to their proportion, color, and spatial relationship to the size of the door; and the room constructed by the security police would have to be arranged with an eye for visual relationship among the objects in the room, color coordination, or accent—that is, with a sensory/emotional component that originally evolved for enhancement, pleasure, and gratification over and above (or along with) the sheerly informational or purposeful aspects which, in an academic or analytic sense, we can isolate and separate out.

To evolving humans, as to those living in premodern societies today, the "aesthetic pleasure" derived from making special is not perhaps so easily separated from the "message" it packages as it has become in Western art today. Although contemporary aesthetic (and evolutionary) theory considers making and responding to aesthetic specialness to be nonutilitarian or "more than necessary" (hence not understandable as a selectively valuable behavioral tendency in human evolution), in its original context it *was* necessary and utilitarian. To adapt an anthropological truism, the obligatory was converted—by making it special—into the desirable, and hence it was willingly done.[13]

But even after establishing that aesthetic making special (in the sense of being sensorily and emotionally gratifying and more than strictly necessary) can be differentiated from nonaesthetic making special such as marking or intimidating, it still remains true that even though all art can be included as aesthetic making special, not all aesthetic making special is art. In ritual and play everyday reality is transformed, as in art, in emotionally and sensorily gratifying ways, and thus can be appreciated apart from use or practical function. I have not always been able to separate instances of making special in "art" from those in "ritual" and "play," as from X's on doors or torture chambers.

I do not think, however, that this difficulty seriously jeopardizes the attempt to treat art—in the sense of making special—as a human behavior. For if we step outside our blinkered Western modernist and post-modernist paradigms where art is either grand, rare, and intimidating, or socially constructed, slick, and provocative, it should be possible to accept the larger, more inclusive entity, making special (including art, ritual, and play) as a universal behavior. That is, by expanding our notion from "art" or even "art as making special" to "the faculty for making and expressing specialness," we can understand in a humanly grounded and relevant way how "the arts" (instances of making special) originally arose and why they not only enhance our individual lives as *Homo aestheticus*, but have been essential for our evolution as a species.

The radical position that I offer here as a species-centered view of art is that *it is not art (with all its burden of accreted connotations from the past two centuries) but making special that has been evolutionarily or socially and culturally important.* That is to say, until recent times in the West, what has been of social, cultural, and individual evolutionary importance in any art or "work of art" has been its making something special that is important to the species, society, or culture.

There is no need to decide whether a theater or concert performance is "play," "ritual" or "art." The three often interpenetrate, since "metareality" and "specialness" generally presuppose the freedom, unpredictability, make-believe, imagination, and delight that are associated with play (and art), or the formality, stylization, elaboration, and entrancement that characterize ritual (and art).

In *What Is Art for?* (59) I likened the modern Western concept of art to the Victorian notion of "vapours," an ambiguous ailment that has long since disappeared, or rather has been replaced by a number of particular named

Village women of Zisgre singing and dancing to greet a foreigner. Upper Volta, 1980 Should we call these women's activity ritual, play, or art? United Nations Photo 148530, by Carolyn Redenius. Photo provided by UN/DPI.

maladies: depression, premenstrual syndrome, hypochondria, flu, bad cold, and so forth. The analogy may have appeared to be merely an amusing aside, but I think it deserves further attention. Indeed, I think our understanding of art as a human behavior would improve if we altogether banned the word *art* in its singular, conceptual form, just as we no longer find it useful to invoke a broad term, *vapours*, for diverse complaints that gain nothing by being clumped together.

Postmodernists, who claim that art is in any case only two centuries old, should have little theoretical difficulty abandoning the word *art*, although to be sure it has permeated our thought from a practical point of view and is probably impossible to eliminate. The reader should try to remember, however, that henceforth in this book, reference to a "behavior of art" means "aesthetic making special" as elucidated in this section, which is a broader concept of "art" than is usual.

[Elsewhere], I will describe in more detail how a behavior of art could have developed from the tendency to recognize an extra-ordinary dimension of experience—that is, I will examine what circumstances in the human evolutionary environment could have called forth and refined such a behavioral tendency and hence why it should have been selected-for. Before ending the discussion of making special, however, I think it would be useful to summarize some of its implications for aesthetic theory today.

Implications of Making Special

The concept of making special, in the biobehavioral view of its being the core defining feature of a behavior of art, casts a new light on previously troublesome questions about the nature, origin, purpose, and value of art, and its place in human life.

1. It explains how a concept of art can comprise such variety, even contradiction. Art may be rare and restricted, as modernists believed, or liberating and problematizing, as postmodernists argue. It may be well or poorly done; it may be an individual original creation or a manifestation of a codified historical or regional tradition. It may require talent and long specialized training or be something everyone does naturally much as they learn to swim or cook or hunt. It may be used for anything, and anything can become an occasion for art. It may or may not be beautiful; although making special often results in "making beautiful," specialness also may consist of strangeness, outrageousness, or extravagance. As making special is protean and illimitable, so is art.

Toast to Old Glory, 1989, from an exhibition inspired by the public controversy over burning the American flag.
Specialness may be strangeness, outrageousness, or extravagance. Don Mohr, artist, Anchorage. Photo © Don Mohr

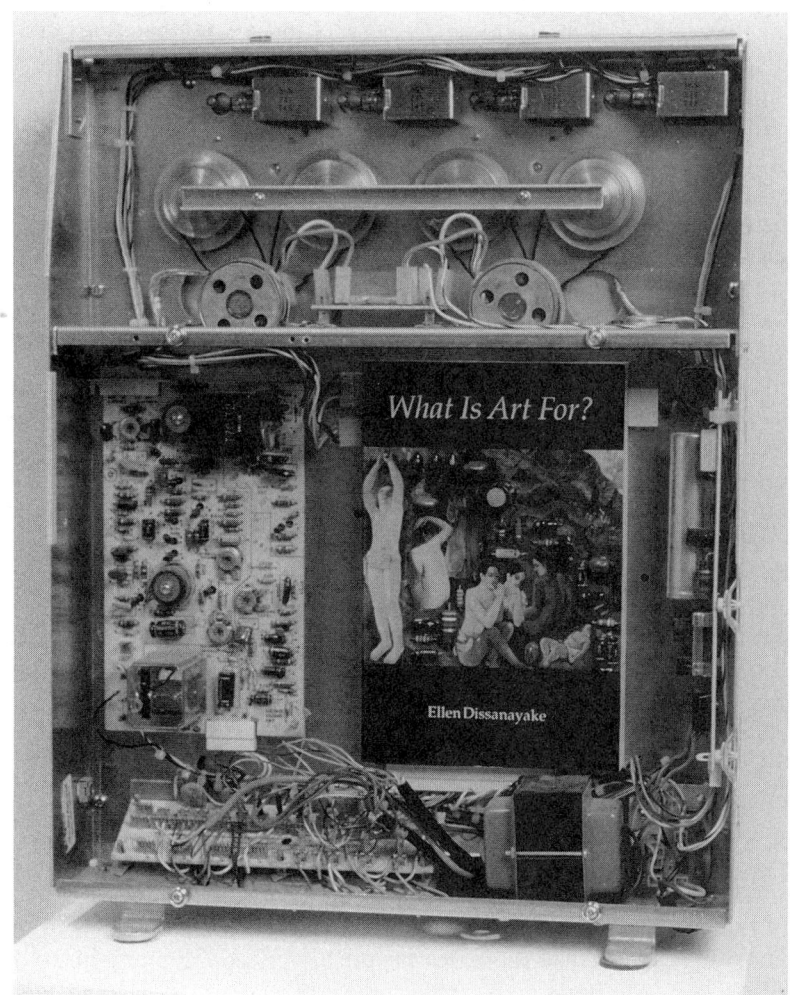

Manifestations of What Might Be Art, 1990, from an exhibition called "What Is Art For?" using books and other found objects, with titles drawn from phrases in book. Art may be used for anything and anything can become an occasion for art. Don Mohr, artist, Anchorage. Photo © Don Mohr

2. If the essential behavioral core is making special, a concern about whether one or another example of it is or is not "art" becomes irrelevant. One can, of course, ask whether one personally wants to take the time and trouble to appreciate or attempt to appreciate its specialness. Funding agencies will no doubt continue to debate whether certain Robert Mapplethorpe photographs, for example, are or are not "art" in some restricted culture-centered sense. But from the species-centered perspective with which [I am] concerned, what is relevant is that *Homo aestheticus* "needs" to

make special and appreciate specialness. Humans and their societies provide the means and parameters within which to do (or not do) this and within which to evaluate the results.

3. At the same time, the idea of making special would not allow the loose declaration (sometimes heard from postmodernist artists, composers, and critics) that art is everything and everything is art. It may be the case that anything is *potentially* art, but in order to *be* art, there is a requirement, first, of aesthetic intention or regard and secondly, of fashioning in some way—actively making special or imaginatively treating as special. If art is everything and everything is art, or sound is music and music is sound, as I have heard it said, why distinguish these activities by calling them "art" or "music"?

4. Making special emphasizes the idea that the arts, biologically endowed predispositions, have been physically, sensuously, and emotionally satisfying and pleasurable to humans. By using elements that pleased and gratified human senses—elements that themselves arose in nonaesthetic contexts: bright colors; appealing shapes and sounds; rhythmic movement; aural, gestural, and visual contours with emotional significance[14]—and arranging and patterning these elements in unusual, "special" ways, early humans assured the willing participation in, and accurate performance of, ceremonies that united them. The arts "enabled" ceremonies because they made ceremonies feel good. Before they were ever consciously used to make things special, the satisfactions of rhythm, novelty, order, pattern, color, bodily movement, and moving in synchrony with others were fundamental animal pleasures, essential ingredients of life. Using these bodily pleasurable elements to make ceremonies special—elaborating and shaping them—the arts, and art, were born.

5. My theory recognizes that art, or, more accurately, the desire to make some things special, is a biologically endowed need. The impetus to mark as "special" an expression or artifact, even our bodies, is deep-seated and widespread. Quite naturally we exaggerate, pattern, and otherwise alter our movements or voices or words to indicate that what we are doing is set apart from ordinary movement, intonation, and speech.[15] More essential than the result (the "work of art," which can be striking or dull, achieved or abandoned) is the behavior or the activity, and more interesting, for our purposes, is the impetus that animates the behavior or activity. Not all things are made special and those that are chosen are usually made special for a reason. That reason throughout our unrecorded evolutionary history, and also for most of recorded human history, was different, more serious and emotionally involving, than the reason or reasons involved with making special in the modern, industrialized, Western or Western-influenced world.

6. My theory reminds us that the desire or need to make special has been throughout human history, until quite recently, primarily in the service of abiding human concerns—ones that engage our feelings in the most profound ways. Until recently, the arts—when they were not play or entertainment (which are legitimate and age-old ways of making human life more than ordinary)—were used to address or at least to suggest or intimate serious and vital concerns. We moderns feel "art" to be a private compulsion, a personal desire to mold or make something out of one's individual experience. But art actually originated and thrived for most of human history as a communal activity: in the smaller and more interdependent and like-minded societies in which humans evolved, the need to make sense of experience was satisfied in communally valued and validated activities. Much art today is rather like the display of a captive, lone peacock vainly performed for human (not peahen) spectators, or the following by baby geese of a bicycle wheel instead of their mother. When an animal is removed from its natural milieu and deprived of the cues and circumstances to which it is designed by nature to respond, it will respond and behave as best it can but probably in aberrant ways or with reference to aberrant cues and circumstances.

The principal evolutionary context for the origin and development of the arts was in activities concerned with survival. As we look back through the eons, we see abundant evidence of humans making things or experience special. Overwhelmingly what was chosen to be made special was what was considered important: objects and activities that were parts of ceremonies having to do with important transitions, such as birth, puberty, marriage, and death; finding food, securing abundance, ensuring fertility of women and of the earth; curing the sick; going to war or resolving conflict; and so forth. In the past things were made special because they were perennially important, while today we consider something (anything) momentarily important because it has been made flashily if transiently special.

This is an important difference and points up, I think, why in the contemporary West we have been so preoccupied with and confused about art, seduced by it, expecting miracles from it, alternately feeling elevated or dispirited by it, feeling somewhat betrayed if not altogether scorned by it.

In Wallace Stevens's poem "Anecdote of the Jar" a round jar is placed on a hill in Tennessee and the "slovenly wilderness" surrounding it immediately seems to fall into place. The jar becomes a kind of focus or center—"it took dominion everywhere"—that gives meaning or relevance to what before was wild, haphazard, and insignificant. In my ethological terms, placing the jar in that unlikely place was "making it special": an instance, if you will, of artistic behavior. Stevens's poem that tells the story also makes the deed (real or imagined) special by choosing unusual word order ("and

round it was upon that hill"), strange phrases ("and of a port in air," "it did
not give of bird or bush"), and rhyme (round/ground; air/bare/where) for
the telling. A beautiful and successful poem in the high modernist tradition,
"Anecdote of the Jar" is an exemplum of what a modern or postmodern
painter or sculptor does when she or he chooses a subject and material and
shapes and elaborates them, making special what before her or his action
and vision would have been ordinary and unremarkable.

Yet in premodern society, the hill, though slovenly and wild, would
most likely have been already somehow important: it would have been
the abode of a spirit, or the place where a valued person was killed, or the
site where a vision had occurred. Or perhaps the jar itself would have
been important—because of some sacredness involved in its making or
some magical marks added to its surface—so that placing it on the hill
would have been a way of bringing human or divine presence to the hill
or imparting a power to it. While such motives may still be the impetus
behind some artistic acts today, they need not be. The act alone, for its
own sake, is enough and we have learned to respond to the act and its result quite apart from the intention or idea that gave rise to the act.

Human evolution may have involved gratuitous acts of making
special, but it is difficult to see how these would have made sufficient difference to the survival of individuals or groups to have been retained by
natural selection as a genetic predisposition (except perhaps insofar as
they are considered part of the general behavior of play, whose motivation is quite different from acknowledging or creating or celebrating
importance). I admit that making special manifested as playfulness or
idiosyncrasy can be pleasurable and rewarding, but I doubt whether in
themselves they would have led before modern times to the creations that
have been enshrined as our most representative examples of "art."

7. To suggest that making important things special was the original impetus
for a "behavior of art" accounts for the close association in historic times
as well as in prehistory between the arts and religion—more accurately,
the ritual expression of religion.

The earliest anthropological observers noted the importance of religion in human societies everywhere. Emile Durkheim, the great French
founder of sociology, called religion a unified system of beliefs and practices related to sacred things—things set apart and forbidden (1964, 62).
These beliefs, practices, and things belong to a realm called by different
authors the numinous (Dodds 1973), the serious (Shils 1966), the supernatural—all suggesting the extra-ordinary, outside ordinary life.

[Elsewhere,] I will show that the origins of religious beliefs and practices and the arts must have been inseparable and that the ceremonies
that have arisen in every human society for the purpose of dealing with
vital, emotionally significant, archetypal concerns expressed these by

means of arts. Yet before doing this I should remind the reader that today in the modern West very little is, in Durkheim's words, set apart or forbidden. Indeed, being considered forbidden or taboo seems cause and justification for being openly discussed and displayed.[16]

What is more, in the modern world, as Kaplan (1978, 86) has pithily remarked, the interesting is no longer important, and the important is no longer interesting. It seems worth asking whether the confusing and unsatisfying state of art in our world has anything to do with the fact that we no longer care about important things. In our predominantly affluent and hedonistic society survival is no longer paramount for most of us, and spiritual concerns, while perhaps given public lip service, are less and less privately validated. Our experience of the extra-ordinary tends to be an ever-growing involvement with such things as gambling, violent films, and mood-altering drugs. Caring deeply about vital things is out of fashion, and, in any case, who has the time (or allows the time) to care and to mark one's caring?[17] Human history has demonstrated that people can endure surprising amounts of hardship and suffering—conditions that usually elicit a serious and religious attitude toward life. Whether people are as well equipped to thrive under conditions of unprecedented leisure, comfort, and plenty is a question that is being tested on a large scale in our present circumstances: the answer does not appear to be promising.   ■

NOTES

1. Paul Mattick, comment made during presentation in panel entitled "The Institutions of Art/2" (forty-seventh Annual Meeting of the American Society for Aesthetics, 25–28 October 1989, New York City).

2. My account concerns Western aesthetics and does not attempt to address aesthetic concepts in other civilizations or how they relate to those in the West.

3. While my discussion in the text uses examples primarily from the visual arts, the history, criticism, and theory of the other arts are much the same. For example, Lydia Goehr (1989) makes a point similar to mine in her analysis of the development of an abstract concept of a musical "work."

4. "Play" theories of art are most commonly associated with Friedrich Schiller (1795/1967), Herbert Spencer (1880–82), Sigmund Freud (1907/1959), and Johan Huizinga (1949).

5. Richard Alexander (1989) explains human social play as leading "to an expanding ability and tendency to elaborate and internalize social-intellectual-physical scenarios," which itself underlies the evolutionary development of the human psyche—a neat combination of the human appreciation of fantasy and reality. [. . .]

6. Radcliffe-Brown (1922/1948) in his monograph on the Andaman Islanders, stresses that ceremonies produce changes in or structure feelings. They "maintain and transmit from one generation to another the *emotional dispositions on which the society depends for its existence*" (234, my italics). Being obligatory, they compel participants to

act as though they felt certain emotions and thereby to some extent actually serve to induce those emotions in them. [. . .]

7. It was also intriguing for me to realize that play is often ritualized, as in sport, with its special arena, costumes, ways of behaving, structure in time. In rituals people often pretend (play or act "as if"): Australian aborigines, for example, imitate animals or pretend to kill them, and the Yanomamo Indians of South America do battle with spirits. Our "plays," and performances in general, can be considered simultaneously as art, as ritual, and as play.

8. Peter Sutton (1988, 18–19) also states that in traditional Aboriginal thought, there is no nature without culture. He quotes W. E. H. Stanner (*On Aboriginal Religion* [1963, 227]): "Anyone who . . . has moved in the Australian bush with Aboriginal associates becomes aware . . . [that he] moves not in a landscape but in a humanized realm saturated with significations."

9. Evidence of deliberate foresight and planning has been claimed for Middle Paleolithic early *sapiens* hominids more than 100,000 years ago in their cooperative hunting strategies (Chase 1989); in their hafting of stone tools, which implies the ability to predict the likelihood of recurring tasks requiring a particular tool (Shea 1989); and in their transporting artifactual material from afar to be used at home (Deacon 1989). Hayden and Bonifay (1991, 6) marshal data that "provide overwhelming support for the notion that Neanderthals were curating lithic tools, exhibiting planning and foresight similar to upper Paleolithic people, and acting in economically rational fashions."

10. The earliest archaeological evidence for body ornaments seems to date from the transition from the Middle Paleolithic to the Upper Paleolithic, that is, from around 35,000 B.P. It is interesting that these ornaments were made primarily from exotic (i.e., "special") materials, such as shell, soft stone, teeth, and tusks, that had been brought sometimes from hundreds of kilometers away from where they were excavated. Randall White (1989) suggests that the ornaments were used for social display and were perhaps symbolic of social distinctions. Whatever their use or significance, it is interesting to see that when making themselves special, individuals also used special materials.

11. In *The Creative Explosion* (1982), John Pfeiffer presented a similar reconstruction of art and ceremony in the Upper Paleolithic. His concern was to elucidate the remarkable flowering of cultural behavior at that time, and not to address ethologically art's earlier origins and putative selective value.

12. It was both amusing and gratifying to later discover that Arthur Danto (1986, 21), who was not concerned with selective value or ethology, argued that "the structure of artworks is of a piece with the structure of rhetoric," and that "it is the office of rhetoric to modify the minds and then the actions of men and women by coopting their feelings." Danto's idea of "the transfiguration of the commonplace" in contemporary Western art (1981) is also congruent with a notion of making the ordinary extraordinary or "making special."

13. See note 6. In his classic monograph (1922/1948), Radcliffe-Brown explicitly states that ceremonies (in which, of course, objects and activities are made special) transmit feelings. More recent anthropologists have been generally concerned with ceremonies primarily as a means of transmitting information, traditions, and symbols.

14. See Eibl-Eibesfeldt (1989a, 1989b) for additional and fascinating examples of appealing and arresting bioaesthetic elements arising from human perception and behavior.

15. Even in the gestural sign language of the deaf, poetic statements are signed in a different manner than everyday conversation. Rather than using a dominant hand, the two hands are balanced; a smoothness of movement is imposed on the signs; and they are given a rhythmic temporal pattern and an enlarged "designed" spatial pattern, with exaggerations of representational or pantomime aspects (Klima and Bellugi 1983).

16. In some areas of modern life disclosure and open discussion are still frowned upon— e.g., military, government, and industrial affairs—but the information associated with these realms does not really correspond to the kinds of information formerly considered numinous. Revealing military or industrial secrets is considered far more deplorable than exposing personal emotional or spiritually significant matters.

17. It is not only that we are too "busy" or sated to care. Caring usually involves acting upon what one cares about. In our pluralistic and impersonal society, we cannot usually affect change, or by trying to do so we may at the same time be going against other important personal or group interests. Thus not caring is self-protective and a way of coping with impotence.

REFERENCES

Alexander, Richard D. 1989. The evolution of the human psyche. In Mellars, Paul, and Chris Stringer, eds., 455–513.

Alsop, Joseph. 1982. *The rare art traditions: The history of art collecting and its linked phenomena.* New York: Harper and Row.

Basso, Ellen B. 1985. *A musical view of the universe: Kalapalo myth and ritual performances.* Philadelphia: University of Pennsylvania Press.

Birket-Smith, Kaj. 1959. *The Eskimos.* London: Methuen. (Original work published 1927.)

———. 1987. The problem of ritual killing. In Hamerton-Kelly, Robert G., ed., *Violent origins: Ritual killing and cultural formation,* 149–76. Palo Alto: Stanford University Press.

Chase, Philip G. 1989. How different was Middle Palaeolithic subsistence? A zooarchaeological perspective on the Middle to Upper Palaeolithic transition. In Mellars, Paul, and Chris Stringer, eds., 321–37.

Csikszentmihalyi, Mihaly. 1975. *Beyond boredom and anxiety.* San Francisco: Jossey-Bass.

Danto, Arthur. 1981. *The transfiguration of the commonplace.* Cambridge: Harvard University Press.

———. 1986. *The philosophical disenfranchisement of art.* New York: Columbia University Press.

Deacon, H. J. 1989. Late Pleistocene palaeontology and archaeology in the Southern Cape, South Africa. In Mellars, Paul, and Chris Stringer, eds., 547–64.

Dissanayake, Ellen. 1988. *What is art for?* Seattle: University of Washington Press.

———. 1990. Of transcribing and superliteracy. *The World & I.,* October, 575–87.

Dodds, E. R. 1973. *The Greeks and the irrational.* Berkeley and Los Angeles: University of California Press. (Original work published 1951.)

Drewal, Henry John, and Margaret Thompson Drewal. 1983. *Gélédé: Art and female power among the Yoruba.* Bloomington: University of Indiana Press.

Durkheim, Emile. 1964. The dualism of human nature and its social conditions. In *Essays on sociology and philosophy by Emile Durkheim et al.,* 325–40. Edited by Kurt H. Wolff. Translated by Charles Blend. New York: Harper and Row. (Original work published 1914.)

Eible-Eibesfeldt, I. 1989a. *Human ethology*. Translated by Pauline Wiessner-Larsen and Anette Heunemann. New York: Aldine de Gruyter.

———. 1989b. The biological foundation of aesthetics. In Rentschler, I., B. Herzberger, and D. Epstein, eds., *Beauty and the brain: Biological aspects of aesthetics*, 29–68. Basel, Switzerland: Birkhauser.

Feld, Steven. 1982. *Sound and sentiment: Birds, weeping, poetics, and song in Kaluli expression*. Philadelphia: University of Pennsylvania Press.

———. 1973. The exposition and imposition of order: Artistic expression in Fang culture. In d'Azevedo, Warren L., ed., 194–220.

Freud, Sigmund. 1959. Obsessive acts and religious practices. In Strachey, James, ed. and trans., *The standard edition of the complete psychological works of Sigmund Freud*, 9: 117–27. (Original work published 1907.)

Geist, Valerius. 1978. *Life strategies, human evolution, environmental design*. New York: Springer.

Gell, Alfred. 1975. *Metamorphosis of the Cassowaries*. London: Athlone.

Gillison, Gillian. 1980. Images of nature in Gimi thought. In MacCormack, Carol P., and Marilyn Strathern, eds., 143–173.

Goehr, Lydia. 1989. Being true to the work. *Journal of Aesthetics and Art Criticism* 47, no. 1: 55–67.

Hayden, Brian, and Eugene Bonifay, 1991. *The Neanderthal nadir*. (Unpublished manuscript.)

Huxley, Julian, ed. 1966. *A discussion on ritualization of behaviour in animals and man*. Philosophical Transactions of the Royal Society of London. Series B: Biological Sciences, 251: 247–526. December.

Kaplan, Stephen. 1978. Attention and fascination: The search for cognitive clarity. In Kaplan, Stephen, and Rachel Kaplan, eds., *Humanscape: Environments for people*, 84–90. North Scituate, Mass.: Duxbury Press.

Katz, Richard. 1982. *Boiling energy: Community healing among the Kalahari Kung*. Cambridge: Harvard University Press.

Klima, Edward S., and Ursula Ballugi. 1983. Poetry without sound. In Rothenberg, Jerome, and Diane Rothernberg, eds., 291–302.

O'Hanlon, Michael. 1989. *Reading the skin: Adornment, display, and society among the Wahgi*. London: British Museum Publications.

Pfeiffer, John E. 1982. *The creative explosion*. New York: Harper and Row.

Radcliffe-Brown, A. R. 1948. *The Andaman Islanders*. Glencoe, Ill.: Free Press. (Original work published 1922.)

Schiller, Friedrich, 1967. Fourteenth Letter. In *Letters on the aesthetic education of man*. Edited by Wilkinson, E. H., and L. A. Willoughby. Oxford: Oxford University Press. (Original work published 1795.)

Shea, John J. 1989. A functional study of the lithnic industries associated with hominid fossils in the Kebara and Qafzeh caves, Israel. In Mellars, Paul, and Chris Stringer, eds., 611–25.

Shils, Edwin. 1966. Ritual crisis. In Huxley, Julian, ed., 447–50.

Spencer, Herbert. 1880–82. The aesthetic sentiments. In *Principles of psychology*, 2:2. London: Williams and Norgate.

Sutton, Peter, ed. 1988. *Dreamings: The art of aboriginal Australia*. New York: Braziller.

Tonkinson, Robert. 1978. *The Mardudjara aborigines: Living the dream in Australia's desert*. New York: Holt, Rinehart and Winston.

Turnbull, Colin M. 1961. *The forest people.* London: Chatto and Windus.

Turner, Victor. 1969. *The ritual process: Structure and anti-structure.* London: Routledge and Kegan Paul.

———. 1983. Body, brain, and culture. *Zygon* 18 (September), 221–45.

White, Randall. 1989a. Production complexity and standardization in early Aurignacian bead and pendant manufacture: Evolutionary implications. In Mellars, Paul, and Chris Stringer, eds., 366–90.

■ *QUESTIONS FOR MAKING QUESTIONS WITHIN THE READING* ■

1. What does Dissanayake mean when she writes that "in the contemporary West" we have been "preoccupied with and confused about art, seduced by it, expecting miracles from it, alternately feeling elevated or dispirited by it, feeling somewhat betrayed if not altogether scorned by it"? What is an "ethological view," and how might it alter our thinking about art?

2. Dissanayake contrasts traditional societies to their postmodern, post-industrial counterparts. Why might the arts play such different roles in the two? What conclusions have philosophers and theorists drawn on the basis of these differences? What conclusions has Dissanayake drawn?

3. One popular school of thought in our time is known as "sociobiology," which holds that human behavior can be explained in strictly biological terms. For many sociobiologists, the real purpose of all human behavior is the perpetuation of our genes, while our personal aspirations and cultural values have a secondary importance. Given this definition, does Dissanayake qualify as a sociobiologist? How does she view the relation between biological forces and human culture?

■ *QUESTIONS FOR WRITING* ■

1. On the basis of your own experience and background knowledge, what assumptions about "art" and "artists" do we ordinarily make? Are these assumptions closer to the outlook held by specialized philosophers of the arts, or do they come closer to "ethological view" that Dissanayake explores in her book?

2. For the last two hundred years, philosophers of aesthetics have emphasized the purposeless and playful character of art—art for art's sake. Why does this way of thinking pose a problem for those, like Dissanayake, who view human behavior from the standpoint of the natural sciences? What difference does it make which view of art one takes? That is, what are the consequences of accepting one version of art's purpose rather than another?

■ *QUESTIONS FOR MAKING CONNECTIONS BETWEEN READINGS* ■

1. What is play and why do humans engage in it? If play is as instructive as Petroski claims and as essential to creativity as Dissanayake claims, why does it occupy such a limited place in the educational system? Can one engage in play while thinking? Can we be taught to play? To be creative? Drawing on the work of Henry Petroski and Dissanayake, discuss the role of play in human development.

2. Are the Bedouin, as described by Lila Abu-Lughod in "Honor and Shame," an example of a "traditional society" in Dissanayake's terms? Does Abu-Lughod's account call into question Dissanayake's largely positive assessment of traditional societies? What losses follow from the passing of traditional societies? What gains have followed? By self-consciously changing the course of her life in "Honor and Shame," is Kamla participating in the activity of "making special," or is she just giving in to the attractions of the material world?

For additional suggestions about making connections between readings, visit the Link-O-Mat and More Sample Assignments at <www.newhum.com>.

Peter F. Drucker

Peter F. Drucker, considered the founder of modern managerial theory, has spent the past sixty years writing about alternatives to the Taylorist model for maximizing efficiency in the work place, alternatives that seek to provide working conditions that allow all employees to realize their potential. In the words of Scott Stossel, executive editor of *The American Prospect*, "Many of the terms and metaphors by which we apprehend contemporary society—Global Economy, Knowledge Worker, Information Society, Postmodern—are concepts conceived of or developed by Drucker. Indeed, even the invention of 'management' as the self-conscious art and science of governing our companies, our institutions, and ourselves is generally credited" to Drucker.

Born in Vienna in 1909, Drucker worked as a journalist before moving to the United States in 1937. Convinced that corporations could serve as a powerful force for creating citizens and for fostering the economic conditions that stave off totalitarianism, Drucker spent the World War II years producing a report on the managerial practices of General Motors, *Concept of the Corporation,* which became an instant classic. In the many books that have followed, Drucker has demonstrated a knack for being the first to discern major trends in the business industry, including the rise of the knowledge worker, which he discusses in "The Age of Social Transformation." And, despite sustained criticism in the business community that management must be concerned first and foremost with the bottom line, Drucker has consistently maintained that creating democratic workplaces with egalitarian pay structures is the best way to promote corporate profitability and global economic health.

Currently the Marie Rankin Clarke Professor of Social Science and Management and the Dean of the Peter F. Drucker School of Graduate Management at Claremont Graduate University, Drucker continues to lead seminars for advanced graduate students and executives that explore the role of corporations in

Drucker, Peter. "The Age of Social Transformation." *The Atlantic Monthly*, vol. 274, no. 5 (November) 1994: 53–69.

Quotations from Scott Stossel, "The Author of Modernity," interview by Jack Brady, *The Atlantic Monthly*, 29 January 1998. *Atlantic Unbound* <http://www.theatlantic.com/unbound/bookauth/jbint.htm>.

contemporary society. And, recognizing the importance of lifelong learning and of the necessity of getting corporations to fulfill their obligation to improve the quality of life in the local community and more generally, Drucker established the Peter F. Drucker Foundation for Nonprofit Management in 1990, which provides a venue for executives and policymakers to ask the question: Can the business community, its managers, and its investors find ways to advance the social good, or does the corporate commitment to profit at any cost rule out such ventures?

To learn more about Peter F. Drucker and management theory, visit the Link-O-Mat at <www.newhum.com>.

The Age of Social Transformation

No century in recorded history has experienced so many social transformations and such radical ones as the twentieth century. They, I submit, may turn out to be the most significant events of this, our century, and its lasting legacy. In the developed free-market countries—which contain less than a fifth of the earth's population but are a model for the rest—work and work force, society and polity, are all, in the last decade of this century, qualitatively and quantitatively different not only from what they were in the first years of this century but also from what has existed at any other time in history: in their configurations, in their processes, in their problems, and in their structures.

Far smaller, and far slower social changes in earlier periods triggered civil wars, rebellions, and violent intellectual and spiritual crises. The extreme social transformations of this century have caused hardly any stir. They have proceeded with a minimum of friction, with a minimum of upheavals, and, indeed, with a minimum of attention from scholars, politicians, the press, and the public. To be sure, this century of ours may well have been the cruelest and most violent in history, with its world and civil wars, its mass tortures, ethnic cleansings, genocides, and holocausts. But all these killings, all these horrors inflicted on the human race by this century's murderous "charismatics," hindsight clearly shows, were just that: senseless killings, senseless horrors, "sound and fury, signifying nothing." Hitler, Stalin, and Mao, the three evil geniuses of this century, destroyed. They created nothing.

Indeed, if this century proves one thing, it is the futility of politics. Even the most dogmatic believer in historical determinism would have a hard time explaining the social transformations of this century as caused by the headline-making political events, or the headline-making political events as caused by the social transformations. But it is the social transformations, like ocean currents deep below the hurricane-tormented surface of the sea, that have had the lasting, indeed the permanent, effect. They, rather than all the violence of the political surface, have transformed not only the society but also the economy, the community, and the polity we live in. The age of social transformation will not come to an end with the year 2000—it will not even have peaked by then.

The Social Structure Transformed

Before the First World War, farmers composed the largest single group in every country. They no longer made up the population everywhere, as they had from the dawn of history to the end of the Napoleonic Wars, a hundred years earlier. But farmers still made up a near-majority in every developed country except England and Belgium—in Germany, France, Japan, the United States—and, of course, in all underdeveloped countries, too. On the eve of the First World War it was considered a self-evident axiom that developed countries—the United States and Canada being the only exceptions— would increasingly have to rely on food imports from nonindustrial, nondeveloped areas.

Today only Japan among major developed free-market countries is a heavy importer of food. (It is one unnecessarily, for its weakness as a food producer is largely the result of an obsolete rice-subsidy policy that prevents the country from developing a modern, productive agriculture.) And in all developed free-market countries, including Japan, farmers today are at most five percent of the population and work force—that is, one tenth of the proportion of eighty years ago. Actually, productive farmers make up less than half of the total farm population, or no more than two percent of the work force. And these agricultural producers are not "farmers" in most senses of the word; they are "agribusiness," which is arguably the most capital-intensive, most technology-intensive, and most information-intensive industry around. Traditional farmers are close to extinction even in Japan. And those that remain have become a protected species kept alive only by enormous subsidies.

The second-largest group in the population and work force of every developed country around 1900 was composed of live-in servants. They were considered as much a law of nature as farmers were. Census categories of the time defined a "lower middle class" household as one that employed fewer than three servants, and as a percentage of the work force domestics grew steadily up to the First World War. Eighty years later live-in domestic servants scarcely exist in developed countries. Few people born since the

Second World War—that is, few people under fifty—have even seen any except on the stage or in old movies.

In the developed society of 2000 farmers are little but objects of nostalgia, and domestic servants are not even that.

Yet these enormous transformations in all developed free-market countries were accomplished without civil war and, in fact, in almost total silence. Only now that their farm population has shrunk to near zero do the totally urban French loudly assert that theirs should be a "rural country" with a "rural civilization."

The Rise and Fall of the Blue-Collar Workers

One reason why the transformations caused so little stir (indeed, the main reason) was that by 1900 a new class, the blue-collar worker in the manufacturing industry—Marx's "proletarian"—had become socially dominant. Farmers were loudly adjured to "raise less corn and more hell," but they paid little attention. Domestic servants were clearly the most exploited class around. But when people before the First World War talked or wrote about the "social question," they meant blue-collar industrial workers. Blue-collar industrial workers were still a fairly small minority of the population and work force—right up to 1914 they made up an eighth or a sixth of the total at most—and were still vastly outnumbered by the traditional lower classes of farmers and domestic servants. But early twentieth-century society was obsessed with blue-collar workers, fixated on them, bewitched by them.

Farmers and domestic servants were everywhere. But as classes, they were invisible. Domestic servants lived and worked inside individual homes or on individual farms in small and isolated groups of two or three. Farmers, too, were dispersed. More important, these traditional lower classes were not organized. Indeed, they could not be organized. Slaves employed in mining or in producing goods had revolted frequently in the ancient world—though always unsuccessfully. But there is no mention in any book I ever read of a single demonstration or a single protest march by domestic servants in any place at any time. There have been peasant revolts galore. But except for two Chinese revolts in the nineteenth century—the Taiping Rebellion, in midcentury, and the Boxer Rebellion, at the century's end, both of which lasted for years and came close to overturning the regime—all peasant rebellions in history have fizzled out after a few bloody weeks. Peasants, history shows, are very hard to organize and do not stay organized—which is why they earned Marx's contempt.

The new class, industrial workers, was extremely visible. This is what made these workers a "class." They lived perforce in dense population clusters and in cities—in St. Denis, outside Paris; in Berlin's Wedding and Vienna's Ottakring; in the textile towns of Lancashire; in the steel towns of

America's Monongahela Valley; and in Japan's Kobe. And they soon proved eminently organizable, with the first strikes occurring almost as soon as there were factory workers. Charles Dickens's harrowing tale of murderous labor conflict, *Hard Times,* was published in 1854, only six years after Marx and Engels wrote *The Communist Manifesto.*

By 1900 it had become quite clear that industrial workers would not become the majority, as Marx had predicted only a few decades earlier. They therefore would not overwhelm the capitalists by their sheer numbers. Yet the most influential radical writer of the period before the First World War, the French ex-Marxist and revolutionary syndicalist Georges Sorel, found widespread acceptance for his 1906 thesis that the proletarians would overturn the existing order and take power by their organization and in and through the violence of the general strike. It was not only Lenin who made Sorel's thesis the foundation of his revision of Marxism and built around it his strategy in 1917 and 1918. Both Mussolini and Hitler—and Mao, ten years later—built their strategies on Sorel's thesis. Mao's "power grows out of the barrel of a gun" is almost a direct quote from Sorel. The industrial worker became the "social question" of 1900 because he was the first lower class in history that could be organized and could stay organized.

No class in history has ever risen faster than the blue-collar worker. And no class in history has ever fallen faster.

In 1883, the year of Marx's death, "proletarians" were still a minority not just of the population but also of industrial workers. The majority in industry were then skilled workers employed in small craft shops, each containing twenty or thirty workers at most. Of the anti-heroes of the nineteenth century's best "proletarian" novel, *The Princess Casamassima,* by Henry James—published in 1886 (and surely only Henry James could have given such a title to a story of working-class terrorists!)—one is a highly skilled bookbinder, the other an equally skilled pharmacist. By 1900 "industrial worker" had become synonymous with "machine operator" and implied employment in a factory along with hundreds if not thousands of people. These factory workers were indeed Marx's proletarians—without social position, without political power, without economic or purchasing power.

The workers of 1900—and even of 1913—received no pensions, no paid vacation, no overtime pay, no extra pay for Sunday or night work, no health or old-age insurance (except in Germany), no unemployment compensation (except, after 1911, in Britain); they had no job security whatever. Fifty years later, in the 1950s, industrial workers had become the largest single group in every developed country, and unionized industrial workers in mass-production industry (which was then dominant everywhere) had attained upper-middle-class income levels. They had extensive job security, pensions, long paid vacations, and comprehensive unemployment insurance or "lifetime employment." Above all, they had achieved political power. In Britain the labor unions were considered to be the "real government," with greater power than the Prime Minister and Parliament, and much the same was true elsewhere. In the United States, too—as in Germany, France, and Italy—the labor unions had emerged as the country's most powerful and best organized political force. And in Japan they had come close, in the Toyota and Nissan strikes of the late forties and early fifties, to overturning the system and taking power themselves.

Thirty-five years later, in 1990, industrial workers and their unions were in retreat. They had become marginal in numbers. Whereas industrial workers who make or move things had accounted for two fifths of the American work force in the 1950s, they accounted for less than one fifth in the early 1990s—that is, for no more than they had accounted for in 1900, when their meteoric rise began. In the other developed free-market countries the decline was slower at first, but after 1980 it began to accelerate everywhere. By the year 2000 or 2010, in every developed free market country, industrial workers will account for no more than an eighth of the work force. Union power has been declining just as fast.

Unlike domestic servants, industrial workers will not disappear—any more than agricultural producers have disappeared or will disappear. But just as the traditional small farmer has become a recipient of subsidies rather than a producer, so will the traditional industrial worker become an auxiliary employee. His place is already being taken by the "technologist"— someone who works both with hands and with theoretical knowledge. (Examples are computer technicians, x-ray technicians, physical therapists, medical-lab technicians, pulmonary technicians, and so on, who together have made up the fastest-growing group in the U.S. labor force since 1980.) And instead of a class—a coherent, recognizable, defined, and self-conscious group—industrial workers may soon be just another "pressure group."

Chroniclers of the rise of the industrial worker tend to highlight the violent episodes—especially the clashes between strikers and the police, as in America's Pullman strike. The reason is probably that the theoreticians and propagandists of socialism, anarchism, and communism—beginning with Marx and continuing to Herbert Marcuse in the 1960s—incessantly wrote and talked of "revolution" and "violence." Actually, the rise of the industrial worker was remarkably nonviolent. The enormous violence of this century—the world wars, ethnic cleansings, and so on—was all violence from above rather than violence from below; and it was unconnected with the transformations of society, whether the dwindling of farmers, the disappearance of domestic servants, or the rise of the industrial worker. In fact, no one even tries anymore to explain these great convulsions as part of "the crisis of capitalism," as was standard Marxist rhetoric only thirty years ago.

Contrary to Marxist and syndicalist predictions, the rise of the industrial worker did not destabilize society. Instead it has emerged as the century's most stabilizing social development. It explains why the disappearance of the farmer and the domestic servant produced no social crises. Both the flight from the land and the flight from domestic service were voluntary. Farmers and maids were not "pushed off" or "displaced." They went into industrial employment as fast as they could. Industrial jobs required no skills they did not already possess, and no additional knowledge. In fact, farmers on the whole had a good deal more skill than was required to be a machine operator in a mass-production plant—and so did many domestic servants. To be sure, industrial work paid poorly until the First World War. But it paid better than farming or household work. Industrial workers in the United States until 1913—and in some countries, including Japan, until the Second World War—worked long hours. But they worked shorter hours than farmers and domestic servants. What's more, they worked specified hours: the rest of the day was their own, which was true neither of work on the farm nor of domestic work.

The history books record the squalor of early industry, the poverty of the industrial workers, and their exploitation. Workers did indeed live in squalor and poverty, and they were exploited. But they lived better than those on a farm or in a household, and were generally treated better.

Proof of this is that infant mortality dropped immediately when farmers and domestic servants moved into industrial work. Historically, cities had never reproduced themselves. They had depended for their perpetuation on constant new recruits from the countryside. This was still true in the mid-nineteenth century. But with the spread of factory employment the city became the center of population growth. In part this was a result of new public-health measures: purification of water, collection and treatment of wastes, quarantine against epidemics, inoculation against disease. These measures—and they were effective mostly in the city—counteracted, or at least contained, the hazards of crowding that had made the traditional city a breeding ground for pestilence. But the largest single factor in the exponential drop in infant mortality as industrialization spread was surely the improvement in living conditions brought about by the factory. Housing and nutrition became better, and hard work and accidents came to take less of a toll. The drop in infant mortality—and with it the explosive growth in population—correlates with only one development: industrialization. The early factory was indeed the "Satanic Mill" of William Blake's great poem. But the countryside was not "England's green and pleasant Land" of which Blake sang; it was a picturesque but even more satanic slum.

For farmers and domestic servants, industrial work was an opportunity. It was, in fact, the first opportunity that social history had given them to better themselves substantially without having to emigrate. In the developed free-market countries over the past 100 or 150 years every generation has been able to expect to do substantially better than the generation preceding it. The main reason has been that farmers and domestic servants could and did become industrial workers.

Because industrial workers are concentrated in groups, systematic work on their productivity was possible. Beginning in 1881, two years before Marx's death, the systematic study of work, tasks, and tools raised the productivity of manual work in making and moving things by three to four percent compound on average per year—for a fiftyfold increase in output per worker over 110 years. On this rest all the economic and social gains of the past century. And contrary to what "everybody knew" in the nineteenth century—not only Marx but all the conservatives as well, such as J.P. Morgan, Bismarck, and Disraeli—practically all these gains have accrued to the industrial worker, half of them in the form of sharply reduced working hours (with the cuts ranging from 40 percent in Japan to 50 percent in Germany), and half of them in the form of a twenty-five fold increase in the real wages of industrial workers who make or move things.

There were thus very good reasons why the rise of the industrial worker was peaceful rather than violent, let alone revolutionary. But what explains the fact that the fall of the industrial worker has been equally peaceful and almost entirely free of social protest, of upheaval, of serious dislocation, at least in the United States?

The Rise of the Knowledge Worker

The rise of the class succeeding industrial workers is not an opportunity for industrial workers. It is a challenge. The newly emerging dominant group is "knowledge workers." The very term was unknown forty years ago. (I coined it in a 1959 book, *Landmarks of Tomorrow*.) By the end of this century knowledge workers will make up a third or more of the work force in the United States—as large a proportion as manufacturing workers ever made up, except in wartime. The majority of them will be paid at least as well as, or better than, manufacturing workers ever were. And the new jobs offer much greater opportunities.

But—and this is a big but—the great majority of the new jobs require qualifications the industrial worker does not possess and is poorly equipped to acquire. They require a good deal of formal education and the ability to acquire and to apply theoretical and analytical knowledge. They require a different approach to work and a different mind-set. Above all, they require a habit of continuous learning. Displaced industrial workers thus cannot simply move into knowledge work or services the way displaced farmers and domestic workers moved into industrial work. At the very least they have to change their basic attitudes, values, and beliefs.

In the closing decades of this century the industrial work force has shrunk faster and further in the United States than in any other developed country—while industrial production has grown faster than in any other developed country except Japan.

The shift has aggravated America's oldest and least tractable problem: the position of blacks. In the fifty years since the Second World War the economic position of African-Americans in America has improved faster than that of any other group in American social history—or in the social history of any country. Three fifths of America's blacks rose into middle class incomes; before the Second World War the figure was one twentieth. But half that group rose into middle-class incomes and not into middle class jobs. Since the Second World War more and more blacks have moved into blue-collar unionized mass-production industry—that is, into jobs paying middle-class and upper-middle-class wages while requiring neither education nor skill. These are precisely the jobs, however, that are disappearing the fastest. What is amazing is not that so many blacks did not acquire an education but that so many did. The economically rational thing for a young black in postwar America was not to stay in school and learn; it was to leave school as early as possible and get one of the plentiful mass-production jobs. As a result, the fall of the industrial worker has hit America's blacks disproportionately hard—quantitatively, but qualitatively even more. It has blunted what was the most potent role model in the black community in America: the well-paid industrial worker with job security, health insurance, and a guaranteed retirement pension—yet possessing neither skill nor much education.

But, of course, blacks are a minority of the population and work force in the United States. For the overwhelming majority—whites, but also Latinos and Asians—the fall of the industrial worker has caused amazingly little disruption and nothing that could be called an upheaval. Even in communities that were once totally dependent on mass-production plants that have gone out of business or have drastically slashed employment (steel cities in western Pennsylvania and eastern Ohio, for instance, or automobile cities like Detroit and Flint, Michigan), unemployment rates for nonblack adults fell within a few short years to levels barely higher than the U.S. average—and that means to levels barely higher than the U.S. "full-employment" rate. Even in these communities there has been no radicalization of America's blue-collar workers.

The only explanation is that for the nonblack blue-collar community the development came as no surprise, however unwelcome, painful, and threatening it may have been to individual workers and their families. Psychologically—but in terms of values, perhaps, rather than in terms of emotions— America's industrial workers must have been prepared to accept as right and proper the shift to jobs that require formal education and that pay for knowledge rather than for manual work, whether skilled or unskilled.

In the United States the shift had by 1990 or so largely been accomplished. But so far it has occurred only in the United States. In the other developed free-market countries, in western and northern Europe and in Japan, it is just beginning in the 1990s. It is, however, certain to proceed rapidly in these countries from now on, perhaps faster than it originally did in the United States. The fall of the industrial worker in the developed free-market countries will also have a major impact outside the developed world. Developing countries can no longer expect to base their development on their comparative labor advantage—that is, on cheap industrial labor.

It is widely believed, especially by labor-union officials, that the fall of the blue-collar industrial worker in the developed countries was largely, if not entirely, caused by moving production "offshore" to countries with abundant supplies of unskilled labor and low wage rates. But this is not true.

There was something to the belief thirty years ago. Japan, Taiwan, and, later, South Korea did indeed (as explained in some detail in my 1993 book *Post-Capitalist Society*) gain their initial advantage in the world market by combining, almost overnight, America's invention of training for full productivity with wage costs that were still those of a pre-industrial country. But this technique has not worked at all since 1970 or 1975.

In the 1990s only an insignificant percentage of manufactured goods imported into the United States are produced abroad because of low labor costs. While total imports in 1990 accounted for about 12 percent of the U.S. gross personal income, imports from countries with significantly lower wage costs accounted for less than three percent—and only half of those were imports of manufactured products. Practically none of the decline in American manufacturing employment from some 30 or 35 percent of the work force to 15 or 18 percent can therefore be attributed to moving work to low-wage countries. The main competition for American manufacturing industry—for instance, in automobiles, in steel, and in machine tools—has come from countries such as Japan and Germany, where wage costs have long been equal to, if not higher than, those in the United States. The comparative advantage that now counts is in the application of knowledge—for example, in Japan's total quality management, lean manufacturing processes, just-in-time delivery, and price-based costing, or in the customer service offered by medium-sized German or Swiss engineering companies. This means, however, that developing countries can no longer expect to base their development on low wages. They, too, must learn to base it on applying knowledge—just at the time when most of them (China, India, and much of Latin America, let alone black Africa) will have to find jobs for millions of uneducated and unskilled young people who are qualified for little except yesterday's blue-collar industrial jobs.

But for the developed countries, too, the shift to knowledge-based work poses enormous social challenges. Despite the factory, industrial society was still essentially a traditional society in its basic social relationships of production. But the emerging society, the one based on knowledge and knowledge workers, is not. It is the first society in which ordinary people—and that means most people—do not earn their daily bread by the sweat of their brow. It is the first society in which "honest work" does not mean a callused hand. It is also the first society in which not everybody does the same work, as was the case when the huge majority were farmers or, as seemed likely only forty or thirty years ago, were going to be machine operators.

This is far more than a social change. It is a change in the human condition. What it means—what are the values, the commitments, the problems of the new society—we do not know. But we do know that much will be different.

The Emerging Knowledge Society

Knowledge workers will not be the majority in the knowledge society, but in many if not most developed societies they will be the largest single population and work-force group. And even where outnumbered by other groups, knowledge workers will give the emerging knowledge society its character, its leadership, its social profile. They may not be the ruling class of the knowledge society, but they are already its leading class. And in their characteristics, social position, values, and expectations, they differ fundamentally from any group in history that has ever occupied the leading position.

In the first place, knowledge workers gain access to jobs and social position through formal education. A great deal of knowledge work requires highly developed manual skill and involves substantial work with one's hands. An extreme example is neurosurgery. The neurosurgeon's performance capacity rests on formal education and theoretical knowledge. An absence of manual skill disqualifies one for work as a neurosurgeon. But manual skill alone, no matter how advanced, will never enable anyone to be a neurosurgeon. The education that is required for neurosurgery and other kinds of knowledge work can be acquired only through formal schooling. It cannot be acquired through apprenticeship.

Knowledge work varies tremendously in the amount and kind of formal knowledge required. Some jobs have fairly low requirements, and others require the kind of knowledge the neurosurgeon possesses. But even if the knowledge itself is quite primitive, only formal education can provide it.

Education will become the center of the knowledge society, and the school its key institution. What knowledge must everybody have? What is "quality" in learning and teaching? These will of necessity become central concerns of the knowledge society, and central political issues. In fact, the acquisition and distribution of formal knowledge may come to occupy the place in the politics of the knowledge society which the acquisition and distribution of property and income have occupied in our politics over the two or three centuries that we have come to call the Age of Capitalism.

In the knowledge society, clearly, more and more knowledge, and especially advanced knowledge, will be acquired well past the age of formal schooling and increasingly, perhaps, through educational processes that do not center on the traditional school. But at the same time, the performance of the schools and the basic values of the schools will be of increasing concern to society as a whole, rather than being considered professional matters that can safely be left to "educators."

We can also predict with confidence that we will redefine what it means to be an educated person. Traditionally, and especially during the past 300 years (perhaps since 1700 or so, at least in the West, and since about that time in Japan as well), an educated person was somebody who had a prescribed stock of formal knowledge. The Germans called this knowledge *allgemeine Bildung,* and the English (and, following them, the nineteenth century Americans) called it the liberal arts. Increasingly, an educated person will be somebody who has learned how to learn, and who continues learning, especially by formal education, throughout his or her lifetime.

There are obvious dangers to this. For instance, society could easily degenerate into emphasizing formal degrees rather than performance capacity. It could fall prey to sterile Confucian mandarins—a danger to which the American university is singularly susceptible. On the other hand, it could overvalue immediately usable, "practical" knowledge and underrate the importance of fundamentals, and of wisdom altogether.

A society in which knowledge workers dominate is under threat from a new class conflict: between the large minority of knowledge workers and the majority of people, who will make their living traditionally, either by manual work, whether skilled or unskilled, or by work in services, whether skilled or unskilled. The productivity of knowledge work—still abysmally low—will become the economic challenge of the knowledge society. On it will depend the competitive position of every single country, every single industry, every single institution within society. The productivity of the nonknowledge, services worker will become the social challenge of the knowledge society. On it will depend the ability of the knowledge society to give decent incomes, and with them dignity and status, to nonknowledge workers.

No society in history has faced these challenges. But equally new are the opportunities of the knowledge society. In the knowledge society, for the first time in history, the possibility of leadership will be open to all. Also, the possibility of acquiring knowledge will no longer depend on obtaining a prescribed education at a given age. Learning will become the tool of the individual—available to him or her at any age—if only because so much skill and knowledge can be acquired by means of the new learning technologies.

Another implication is that how well an individual, an organization, an industry, a country, does in acquiring and applying knowledge will become the key competitive factor. The knowledge society will inevitably become far more competitive than any society we have yet known—for the simple reason that with knowledge being universally accessible, there will be no excuses for nonperformance. There will be no "poor" countries. There will only be ignorant countries. And the same will be true for companies, industries, and organizations of all kinds. It will be true for individuals, too. In fact, developed societies have already become infinitely more competitive for individuals than were the societies of the beginning of this century, let alone earlier ones.

I have been speaking of knowledge. But a more accurate term is "knowledges," because the knowledge of the knowledge society will be fundamentally different from what was considered knowledge in earlier societies— and, in fact, from what is still widely considered knowledge. The knowledge of the German *allgemeine Bildung* or of the Anglo-American liberal arts had little to do with one's life's work. It focused on the person and the person's development, rather than on any application—if, indeed, it did not, like the nineteenth-century liberal arts, pride itself on having no utility whatever. In the knowledge society knowledge for the most part exists only in application. Nothing the x-ray technician needs to know can be applied to market research, for instance, or to teaching medieval history. The central work force in the knowledge society will therefore consist of highly specialized people. In fact, it is a mistake to speak of "generalists." What we will increasingly mean by that term is people who have learned how to acquire additional specialties rapidly in order to move from one kind of job to another—for example, from market research into management, or from nursing into hospital administration. But "generalists" in the sense in which we used to talk of them are coming to be seen as dilettantes rather than educated people.

This, too, is new. Historically, workers were generalists. They did whatever had to be done—on the farm, in the household, in the craftsman's shop. This was also true of industrial workers. But knowledge workers, whether their knowledge is primitive or advanced, whether there is a little of it or a great deal, will by definition be specialized. Applied knowledge is effective only when it is specialized. Indeed, the more highly specialized, the more effective it is. This goes for technicians who service computers, x-ray machines, or the engines of fighter planes. But it applies equally to work that requires the most advanced knowledge, whether research in genetics or research in astrophysics or putting on the first performance of a new opera.

Again, the shift from knowledge to knowledges offers tremendous opportunities to the individual. It makes possible a career as a knowledge worker. But it also presents a great many new problems and challenges. It demands for the first time in history that people with knowledge take responsibility for making themselves understood by people who do not have the same knowledge base.

How Knowledges Work

That knowledge in the knowledge society has to be highly specialized to be productive implies two new requirements: that knowledge workers work in teams, and that if knowledge workers are not employees, they must at least be affiliated with an organization.

There is a great deal of talk these days about "teams" and "teamwork." Most of it starts out with the wrong assumption—namely, that we have never before worked in teams. Actually people have always worked in teams; very few people ever could work effectively by themselves. The farmer had to have a wife, and the farm wife had to have a husband. The two worked as a team. And both worked as a team with their employees, the hired hands. The craftsman also had to have a wife, with whom he worked as a team—he took care of the craft work, and she took care of the customers, the apprentices, and the business altogether. And both worked as a team with journeymen and apprentices. Much discussion today assumes that there is only one kind of team. Actually there are quite a few. But until now the emphasis has been on the individual worker and not on the team. With knowledge work growing increasingly effective as it is increasingly specialized, teams become the work unit rather than the individual himself.

The team that is being touted now—I call it the "jazz combo" team—is only one kind of team. It is actually the most difficult kind of team both to assemble and to make work effectively, and the kind that requires the longest time to gain performance capacity. We will have to learn to use different kinds of teams for different purposes. We will have to learn to understand teams—and this is something to which, so far, very little attention has been paid. The understanding of teams, the performance capacities of different kinds of teams, their strengths and limitations, and the trade-offs between various kinds of teams will thus become central concerns in the management of people.

Equally important is the second implication of the fact that knowledge workers are of necessity specialists: the need for them to work as members of an organization. Only the organization can provide the basic continuity that knowledge workers need in order to be effective. Only the organization can convert the specialized knowledge of the knowledge worker into performance.

By itself, specialized knowledge does not yield performance. The surgeon is not effective unless there is a diagnosis—which, by and large, is not the surgeon's task and not even within the surgeon's competence. As a loner in his or her research and writing, the historian can be very effective. But to educate students, a great many other specialists have to contribute—people whose specialty may be literature or mathematics, or other areas of history. And this requires that the specialist have access to an organization.

The access may be as a consultant, or it may be as a provider of specialized services. But for the majority of knowledge workers it will be as employees, full-time or part-time, of an organization, such as a government agency, a hospital, a university, a business, or a labor union. In the knowledge society it is not the individual who performs. The individual is a cost center rather than a performance center. It is the organization that performs.

What Is an Employee?

Most knowledge workers will spend most if not all of their working lives as "employees." But the meaning of the term will be different from what it has been traditionally—and not only in English but in German, Spanish, and Japanese as well.

Individually, knowledge workers are dependent on the job. They receive a wage or salary. They have been hired and can be fired. Legally each is an employee. But collectively they are the capitalists; increasingly, through their pension funds and other savings, the employees own the means of production. In traditional economics—and by no means only in Marxist economics—there is a sharp distinction between the "wage fund," all of which goes into consumption, and the "capital fund," or that part of the total income stream that is available for investment. And most social theory of industrial society is based, one way or another, on the relationship between the two, whether in conflict or in necessary and beneficial cooperation and balance. In the knowledge society the two merge. The pension fund is "deferred wages," and as such is a wage fund. But it is also increasingly the main source of capital for the knowledge society.

Perhaps more important, in the knowledge society the employees—that is, knowledge workers—own the tools of production. Marx's great insight was that the factory worker does not and cannot own the tools of production, and therefore is "alienated." There was no way, Marx pointed out, for the worker to own the steam engine and to be able to take it with him when moving from one job to another. The capitalist had to own the steam engine and to control it. Increasingly, the true investment in the knowledge society is not in machines and tools but in the knowledge of the knowledge worker. Without that knowledge the machines, no matter how advanced and sophisticated, are unproductive.

The market researcher needs a computer. But increasingly this is the researcher's own personal computer, and it goes along wherever he or she goes. The true "capital equipment" of market research is the knowledge of markets, of statistics, and of the application of market research to business strategy, which is lodged between the researcher's ears and is his or her exclusive and inalienable property. The surgeon needs the operating room of the hospital and all its expensive capital equipment. But the surgeon's true capital investment is twelve or fifteen years of training and the resulting knowledge, which the surgeon takes from one hospital to the next. Without that knowledge the hospital's expensive operating rooms are so much waste and scrap.

This is true whether the knowledge worker commands advanced knowledge, like a surgeon, or simple and fairly elementary knowledge, like a junior accountant. In either case it is the knowledge investment that determines whether the employee is productive or not, more than the tools, machines, and capital furnished by an organization. The industrial worker needed the capitalist infinitely more than the capitalist needed the industrial worker—the basis for Marx's assertion that there would always be a surplus of industrial workers, an "industrial reserve army," that would make sure that wages could not possibly rise above the subsistence level (probably Marx's most egregious error). In the knowledge society the most probable assumption for organizations—and certainly the assumption on which they have to conduct their affairs—is that they need knowledge workers far more than knowledge workers need them.

There was endless debate in the Middle Ages about the hierarchy of knowledges, with philosophy claiming to be the "queen." We long ago gave up that fruitless argument. There is no higher or lower knowledge. When the patient's complaint is an ingrown toenail, the podiatrist's knowledge, not that of the brain surgeon, controls—even though the brain surgeon has received many more years of training and commands a much larger fee. And if an executive is posted to a foreign country, the knowledge he or she needs, and in a hurry, is fluency in a foreign language—something every native of that country has mastered by age three, without any great investment. The knowledge of the knowledge society, precisely because it is knowledge only when applied in action, derives its rank and standing from the situation. In other words, what is knowledge in one situation, such as fluency in Korean for the American executive posted to Seoul, is only information, and not very relevant information at that, when the same executive a few years later has to think through his company's market strategy for Korea. This, too, is new. Knowledges were always seen as fixed stars, so to speak, each occupying its own position in the universe of knowledge. In the knowledge society knowledges are tools, and as such are dependent for their importance and position on the task to be performed.

Management in the Knowledge Society

One additional conclusion: Because the knowledge society perforce has to be a society of organizations, its central and distinctive organ is management.

When our society began to talk of management, the term meant "business management"—because large-scale business was the first of the new organizations to become visible. But we have learned in this past half century that management is the distinctive organ of all organizations. All of them require management, whether they use the term or not. All managers do the same things, whatever the purpose of their organization. All of them have to bring people—each possessing different knowledge—together for joint performance. All of them have to make human strengths productive in performance and human weaknesses irrelevant. All of them have to think through what results are wanted in the organization—and have then to define objectives. All of them are responsible for thinking through what I call the theory of the business—that is, the assumptions on which the organization bases its performance and actions, and the assumptions that the organization has made in deciding what not to do. All of them must think through strategies—that is, the means through which the goals of the organization become performance. All of them have to define the values of the organization, its system of rewards and punishments, its spirit and its culture. In all organizations managers need both the knowledge of management as work and discipline and the knowledge and understanding of the organization itself—its purposes, its values, its environment and markets, its core competencies.

Management as a practice is very old. The most successful executive in all history was surely that Egyptian who, 4,500 years or more ago, first conceived the pyramid, without any precedent, designed it, and built it, and did so in an astonishingly short time. That first pyramid still stands. But as a discipline management is barely fifty years old. It was first dimly perceived around the time of the First World War. It did not emerge until the Second World War, and then did so primarily in the United States. Since then it has been the fastest-growing new function, and the study of it the fastest-growing new discipline. No function in history has emerged as quickly as has management in the past fifty or sixty years, and surely none has had such worldwide sweep in such a short period.

Management is still taught in most business schools as a bundle of techniques, such as budgeting and personnel relations. To be sure, management, like any other work, has its own tools and its own techniques. But just as the essence of medicine is not urinalysis (important though that is), the essence of management is not techniques and procedures. The essence of management is to make knowledges productive. Management, in other words, is a social function. And in its practice management is truly a liberal art.

The Social Sector

The old communities—family, village, parish, and so on—have all but disappeared in the knowledge society. Their place has largely been taken by the new unit of social integration, the organization. Where community was fate, organization is voluntary membership. Where community claimed the entire person, organization is a means to a person's ends, a tool. For 200 years a hot debate has been raging, especially in the West: are communities "organic" or are they simply extensions of the people of which they are made? Nobody would claim that the new organization is "organic." It is clearly an artifact, a creation of man, a social technology.

But who, then, does the community tasks? Two hundred years ago whatever social tasks were being done were done in all societies by a local community. Very few if any of these tasks are being done by the old communities anymore. Nor would they be capable of doing them, considering that they no longer have control of their members or even a firm hold over them. People no longer stay where they were born, either in terms of geography or in terms of social position and status. By definition, a knowledge society is a society of mobility. And all the social functions of the old communities, whether performed well or poorly (and most were performed very poorly indeed), presupposed that the individual and the family would stay put. But the essence of a knowledge society is mobility in terms of where one lives, mobility in terms of what one does, mobility in terms of one's affiliations. People no longer have roots. People no longer have a neighborhood that controls what their home is like, what they do, and, indeed, what their problems are allowed to be. The knowledge society is a society in which many more people than ever before can be successful. But it is therefore, by definition, also a society in which many more people than ever before can fail, or at least come in second. And if only because the application of knowledge to work has made developed societies so much richer than any earlier society could even dream of becoming, the failures, whether poor people or alcoholics, battered women or juvenile delinquents, are seen as failures of society.

Who, then, takes care of the social tasks in the knowledge society? We cannot ignore them. But the traditional community is incapable of tackling them.

Two answers have emerged in the past century or so—a majority answer and a dissenting opinion. Both have proved to be wrong.

The majority answer goes back more than a hundred years, to the 1880s, when Bismarck's Germany took the first faltering steps toward the welfare state. The answer: the problems of the social sector can, should, and must be solved by government. This is still probably the answer that most people accept, especially in the developed countries of the West—even though most people probably no longer fully believe it. But it has been totally disproved. Modern government, especially since the Second World War, has everywhere become a huge welfare bureaucracy. And the bulk of the budget in every developed country today is devoted to *Entitlements*—to payments for all kinds of social services. Yet in every developed country society is becoming sicker rather than healthier, and social problems are multiplying. Government has a big role to play in social tasks—the role of policymaker, of standard setter, and, to a substantial extent, of paymaster. But as the agency to run social services, it has proved almost totally incompetent.

In my *The Future of Industrial Man* (1942), I formulated a dissenting opinion. I argued then that the new organization—and fifty years ago that meant the large business enterprise—would have to be the community in which the individual would find status and function, with the workplace community becoming the one in and through which social tasks would be organized. In Japan (though quite independently and without any debt to me) the large employer—government agency or business—has indeed increasingly attempted to serve as a community for its employees. Lifetime employment is only one affirmation of this. Company housing, company health plans, company vacations, and so on all emphasize for the Japanese employee that the employer, and especially the big corporation, is the community and the successor to yesterday's village—even to yesterday's family. This, however, has not worked either.

There is need, especially in the West, to bring the employee increasingly into the government of the workplace community. What is now called empowerment is very similar to the things I talked about fifty years ago. But it does not create a community. Nor does it create the structure through which the social tasks of the knowledge society can be tackled. In fact, practically all these tasks—whether education or health care; the anomies and diseases of a developed and, especially, a rich society, such as alcohol and drug abuse; or the problems of incompetence and irresponsibility such as those of the underclass in the American city—lie outside the employing institution.

The right answer to the question Who takes care of the social challenges of the knowledge society? is neither the government nor the employing organization. The answer is a separate and new social sector.

It is less than fifty years, I believe, since we first talked in the United States of the two sectors of a modern society—the "public sector" (government) and the "private sector" (business). In the past twenty years the United States has begun to talk of a third sector, the "nonprofit sector"—those organizations that increasingly take care of the social challenges of a modern society.

In the United States, with its tradition of independent and competitive churches, such a sector has always existed. Even now churches are the largest single part of the social sector in the United States, receiving almost half the money given to charitable institutions, and about a third of the time volunteered by individuals. But the nonchurch part of the social sector has been the growth sector in the United States. In the early 1990s about a million organizations were registered in the United States as nonprofit or charitable organizations doing social-sector work. The overwhelming majority of these, some 70 percent, have come into existence in the past thirty years. And most are community services concerned with life on this earth rather than with the Kingdom of Heaven. Quite a few of the new organizations are, of course, religious in their orientation, but for the most part these are not churches. They are "parachurches" engaged in a specific social task, such as the rehabilitation of alcohol and drug addicts, the rehabilitation of criminals, or elementary school education. Even within the church segment of the social sector the organizations that have shown the capacity to grow are radically new. They are the "pastoral" churches, which focus on the spiritual needs of individuals, especially educated knowledge workers, and then put the spiritual energies of their members to work on the social challenges and social problems of the community—especially, of course, the urban community.

We still talk of these organizations as "nonprofits." But this is a legal term. It means nothing except that under American law these organizations do not pay taxes. Whether they are organized as nonprofit or not is actually irrelevant to their function and behavior. Many American hospitals since 1960 or 1970 have become "for-profits" and are organized in what legally are business corporations. They function in exactly the same way as traditional "nonprofit" hospitals. What matters is not the legal basis but that the social-sector institutions have a particular kind of purpose. Government demands compliance; it makes rules and enforces them. Business expects to be paid; it supplies. Social-sector institutions aim at changing the human being. The "product"of a school is the student who has learned something. The "product"of a hospital is a cured patient. The "product" of a church is a church-goer whose life is being changed. The task of social-sector organizations is to create human health and well being.

Increasingly these organizations of the social sector serve a second and equally important purpose. They create citizenship. Modern society and modern polity have become so big and complex that citizenship—that is, responsible participation—is no longer possible. All we can do as citizens is to vote once every few years and to pay taxes all the time.

As a volunteer in a social-sector institution, the individual can again make a difference. In the United States, where there is a long volunteer tradition because of the old independence of the churches, almost every other adult in the 1990s is working at least three—and often five—hours a week as a volunteer in a social-sector organization. Britain is the only other country with something like this tradition, although it exists there to a much lesser extent (in part because the British welfare state is far more embracing, but in much larger part because it has an established church—paid for by the state and run as a civil service). Outside the English-speaking countries there is not much of a volunteer tradition. In fact, the modern state in Europe and Japan has been openly hostile to anything that smacks of volunteerism—most so in France and Japan. It is ancien regime and suspected of being fundamentally subversive.

But even in these countries things are changing, because the knowledge society needs the social sector, and the social sector needs the volunteer. But knowledge workers also need a sphere in which they can act as citizens and create a community. The workplace does not give it to them. Nothing has been disproved faster than the concept of the "organization man," which was widely accepted forty years ago. In fact, the more satisfying one's knowledge work is, the more one needs a separate sphere of community activity.

Many social-sector organizations will become partners with government—as is the case in a great many "privatizations," where, for instance, a city pays for street cleaning and an outside contractor does the work. In American education over the next twenty years there will be more and more government-paid vouchers that will enable parents to put their children into a variety of different schools, some public and tax supported, some private and largely dependent on the income from the vouchers. These social-sector organizations, although partners with government, also clearly compete with government. The relationship between the two has yet to be worked out—and there is practically no precedent for it.

What constitutes performance for social-sector organizations, and especially for those that, being nonprofit and charitable, do not have the discipline of a financial bottom line, has also yet to be worked out. We know that social-sector organizations need management. But what precisely management means for the social-sector organization is just beginning to be studied. With respect to the management of the nonprofit organization we are in many ways pretty much where we were fifty or sixty years ago with respect to the management of the business enterprise: the work is only beginning.

But one thing is already clear. The knowledge society has to be a society of three sectors: a public sector of government, a private sector of business, and a social sector. And I submit that it is becoming increasingly clear that through the social sector a modern developed society can again create responsible and achieving citizenship, and can again give individuals—especially knowledge workers—a sphere in which they can make a difference in society and re-create community.

The School as Society's Center

Knowledge has become the key resource, for a nation's military strength as well as for its economic strength. And this knowledge can be acquired only through schooling. It is not tied to any country. It is portable. It can be created everywhere, fast and cheaply. Finally, it is by definition changing. Knowledge as the key resource is fundamentally different from the traditional key resources of the economist—land, labor, and even capital.

That knowledge has become the key resource means that there is a world economy, and that the world economy, rather than the national economy, is in control. Every country, every industry, and every business will be in an increasingly competitive environment. Every country, every industry, and every business will, in its decisions, have to consider its competitive standing in the world economy and the competitiveness of its knowledge competencies.

Politics and policies still center on domestic issues in every country. Few if any politicians, journalists, or civil servants look beyond the boundaries of their own country when a new measure such as taxes, the regulation of business, or social spending is being discussed. Even in Germany—Europe's most export-conscious and export-dependent major country—this is true. Almost no one in the West asked in 1990 what the government's unbridled spending in the East would do to Germany's competitiveness.

This will no longer do. Every country and every industry will have to learn that the first question is not Is this measure desirable? but What will be the impact on the country's, or the industry's, competitive position in the world economy? We need to develop in politics something similar to the environmental-impact statement, which in the United States is now required for any government action affecting the quality of the environment: we need a competitive-impact statement. The impact on one's competitive position in the world economy should not necessarily be the main factor in a decision. But to make a decision without considering it has become irresponsible.

Altogether, the fact that knowledge has become the key resource means that the standing of a country in the world economy will increasingly determine its domestic prosperity. Since 1950 a country's ability to improve its position in the world economy has been the main and perhaps the sole determinant of performance in the domestic economy. Monetary and fiscal policies have been practically irrelevant, for better and, very largely, even for worse (with the single exception of governmental policies creating inflation, which very rapidly undermines both a country's competitive standing in the world economy and its domestic stability and ability to grow).

The primacy of foreign affairs is an old political precept going back in European politics to the seventeenth century. Since the Second World War it has also been accepted in American politics—though only grudgingly so, and only in emergencies. It has always meant that military security was to be given priority over domestic policies, and in all likelihood this is what it will continue to mean, Cold War or no Cold War. But the primacy of foreign affairs is now acquiring a different dimension. This is that a country's competitive position in the world economy—and also an industry's and an organization's—has to be the first consideration in its domestic policies and strategies. This holds true for a country that is only marginally involved in the world economy (should there still be such a one), and for a business that is only marginally involved in the world economy, and for a university that sees itself as totally domestic. Knowledge knows no boundaries. There is no domestic knowledge and no international knowledge. There is only knowledge. And with knowledge becoming the key resource, there is only a world economy, even though the individual organization in its daily activities operates within a national, regional, or even local setting.

How Can Government Function?

Social tasks are increasingly being done by individual organizations, each created for one, and only one, social task, whether education, health care, or street cleaning. Society, therefore, is rapidly becoming pluralist. Yet our social and political theories still assume that there are no power centers except government. To destroy or at least to render impotent all other power centers was, in fact, the thrust of Western history and Western politics for 500 years, from the fourteenth century on. This drive culminated in the eighteenth and nineteenth centuries, when, except in the United States such early institutions as still survived—for example, the universities and the churches—became organs of the state, with their functionaries becoming civil servants. But then, beginning in the mid nineteenth century, new centers arose—the first one, the modern business enterprise, around 1870. And since then one new organization after another has come into being.

The new institutions—the labor union, the modern hospital, the mega church, the research university—of the society of organizations have no interest in public power. They do not want to be governments. But they demand—and, indeed, need—autonomy with respect to their functions. Even at the extreme of Stalinism the managers of major industrial enterprises were largely masters within their enterprises, and the individual industry was largely autonomous. So were the university, the research lab, and the military.

In the "pluralism" of yesterday—in societies in which control was shared by various institutions, such as feudal Europe in the Middle Ages and Edo Japan in the seventeenth and eighteenth centuries—pluralist organizations tried to be in control of whatever went on in their community. At least, they tried to prevent any other organization from having control of any community concern or community institution within their domain. But in the society of organizations each of the new institutions is concerned only with its own purpose and mission. It does not claim power over anything else. But it also does not assume responsibility for anything else. Who, then, is concerned with the common good?

This has always been a central problem of pluralism. No earlier pluralism solved it. The problem remains, but in a new guise. So far it has been seen as imposing limits on social institutions—forbidding them to do things in the pursuit of their mission, function, and interest which encroach upon the public domain or violate public policy. The laws against discrimination—by race, sex, age, educational level, health status, and so on—which have proliferated in the United States in the past forty years all forbid socially undesirable behavior. But we are increasingly raising the question of the social responsibility of social institutions: What do institutions have to do—in addition to discharging their own functions—to advance the public good? This, however, though nobody seems to realize it, is a demand to return to the old pluralism, the pluralism of feudalism. It is a demand that private hands assume public power.

This could seriously threaten the functioning of the new organizations, as the example of the schools in the United States makes abundantly clear. One of the major reasons for the steady decline in the capacity of the schools to do their job—that is, to teach children elementary knowledge skills—is surely that since the 1950s the United States has increasingly made the schools the carriers of all kinds of social policies: the elimination of racial discrimination, of discrimination against all other kinds of minorities, including the handicapped, and so on. Whether we have actually made any progress in assuaging social ills is highly debatable; so far the schools have not proved particularly effective as tools for social reform. But making the school the organ of social policies has, without any doubt, severely impaired its capacity to do its own job.

The new pluralism has a new problem: how to maintain the performance capacity of the new institutions and yet maintain the cohesion of society. This makes doubly important the emergence of a strong and functioning social sector. It is an additional reason why the social sector will increasingly be crucial to the performance, if not to the cohesion, of the knowledge society.

Of the new organizations under consideration here, the first to arise, 120 years ago, was the business enterprise. It was only natural, therefore, that the problem of the emerging society of organizations was first seen as the relationship of government and business. It was also natural that the new interests were first seen as economic interests.

The first attempt to come to grips with the politics of the emerging society of organizations aimed, therefore, at making economic interests serve the political process. The first to pursue this goal was an American, Mark Hanna, the restorer of the Republican Party in the 1890s and, in many ways, the founding father of twentieth-century American politics. His definition of politics as a dynamic disequilibrium between the major economic interests—farmers, business, and labor—remained the foundation of American politics until the Second World War. In fact, Franklin D. Roosevelt restored the Democratic Party by reformulating Hanna. And the basic political position of this philosophy is evident in the title of the most influential political book written during the New Deal years—*Politics: Who Gets What, When, How* (1936), by Harold D. Lasswell.

Mark Hanna in 1896 knew very well that there are plenty of concerns other than economic concerns. And yet it was obvious to him—as it was to Roosevelt forty years later—that economic interests had to be used to integrate all the others. This is still the assumption underlying most analyses of American politics—and, in fact, of politics in all developed countries. But the assumption is no longer tenable. Underlying Hanna's formula of economic interests is the view of land, labor, and capital as the existing resources. But knowledge, the new resource for economic performance, is not in itself economic.

It cannot be bought or sold. The fruits of knowledge, such as the income from a patent, can be bought or sold; the knowledge that went into the patent cannot be conveyed at any price. No matter how much a suffering person is willing to pay a neurosurgeon, the neurosurgeon cannot sell to him—and surely cannot convey to him—the knowledge that is the foundation of the neurosurgeon's performance and income. The acquisition of knowledge has a cost, as has the acquisition of anything. But the acquisition of knowledge has no price.

Economic interests can therefore no longer integrate all other concerns and interests. As soon as knowledge became the key economic resource, the integration of interests—and with it the integration of the pluralism of a modern polity—began to be lost. Increasingly, non-economic interests are becoming the new pluralism—the special interests, the single-cause organizations, and so on. Increasingly, politics is not about "who gets what, when, how" but about values, each of them considered to be an absolute. Politics is about the right to life of the embryo in the womb as against the right of a woman to control her own body and to abort an embryo. It is about the environment. It is about gaining equality for groups alleged to be oppressed and discriminated against. None of these issues is economic. All are fundamentally moral.

Economic interests can be compromised, which is the great strength of basing politics on economic interests. "Half a loaf is still bread" is a meaningful saying. But half a baby, in the biblical story of the judgment of Solomon, is not half a child. No compromise is possible. To an environmentalist, half an endangered species is an extinct species.

This greatly aggravates the crisis of modern government. Newspapers and commentators still tend to report in economic terms what goes on in Washington, in London, in Bonn, or in Tokyo. But more and more of the lobbyists who determine governmental laws and governmental actions are no longer lobbyists for economic interests. They lobby for and against measures that they—and their paymasters—see as moral, spiritual, cultural. And each of these new moral concerns, each represented by a new organization, claims to stand for an absolute. Dividing their loaf is not compromise; it is treason.

There is thus in the society of organizations no one integrating force that pulls individual organizations in society and community into coalition. The traditional parties—perhaps the most successful political creations of the nineteenth century—can no longer integrate divergent groups and divergent points of view into a common pursuit of power. Rather, they have become battlefields between groups, each of them fighting for absolute victory and not content with anything but total surrender of the enemy.

The Need for Social and Political Innovation

The twenty-first century will surely be one of continuing social, economic, and political turmoil and challenge, at least in its early decades. What I have called the age of social transformation is not over yet. And the challenges looming ahead may be more serious and more daunting than those posed by the social transformations that have already come about, the social transformations of the twentieth century.

Yet we will not even have a chance to resolve these new and looming problems of tomorrow unless we first address the challenges posed by the developments that are already accomplished facts, the developments reported in the earlier sections of this essay. These are the priority tasks. For only if they are tackled can we in the developed democratic free market countries hope to have the social cohesion, the economic strength, and the governmental capacity needed to tackle the new challenges. The first order of business—for sociologists, political scientists, and economists; for educators; for business executives, politicians, and nonprofit-group leaders; for people in all walks of life, as parents, as employees, as citizens—is to work on these priority tasks, for few of which we so far have a precedent, let alone tested solutions.

We will have to think through education—its purpose, its values, its content. We will have to learn to define the quality of education and the productivity of education, to measure both and to manage both.

We need systematic work on the quality of knowledge and the productivity of knowledge—neither even defined so far. The performance capacity, if not the survival, of any organization in the knowledge society will come increasingly to depend on those two factors. But so will the performance capacity, if not the survival, of any individual in the knowledge society. And what responsibility does knowledge have? What are the responsibilities of the knowledge worker, and especially of a person with highly specialized knowledge?

Increasingly, the policy of any country—and especially of any developed country—will have to give primacy to the country's competitive position in an increasingly competitive world economy. Any proposed domestic policy needs to be shaped so as to improve that position, or at least to minimize adverse impacts on it. The same holds true for the policies and strategies of any institution within a nation, whether a local government, a business, a university, or a hospital.

But then we also need to develop an economic theory appropriate to a world economy in which knowledge has become the key economic resource and the dominant, if not the only, source of comparative advantage.

We are beginning to understand the new integrating mechanism: organization. But we still have to think through how to balance two apparently contradictory requirements. Organizations must competently perform the one social function for the sake of which they exist—the school to teach, the hospital to cure the sick, and the business to produce goods, services, or the capital to provide for the risks of the future. They can do so only if they single-mindedly concentrate on their specialized mission. But there is also society's need for these organizations to take social responsibility—to work on the problems and challenges of the community. Together these organizations are the community. The emergence of a strong, independent, capable social sector—neither public sector nor private sector—is thus a central need of the society of organizations. But by itself it is not enough—the organizations of both the public and the private sector must share in the work.

The function of government and its functioning must be central to political thought and political action. The megastate in which this century indulged has not performed, either in its totalitarian or in its democratic version. It has not delivered on a single one of its promises. And government by countervailing lobbyists is neither particularly effective—in fact, it is paralysis—nor particularly attractive. Yet effective government has never been needed more than in this highly competitive and fast-changing world of ours, in which the dangers created by the pollution of the physical environment are matched only by the dangers of worldwide armaments pollution. And we do not have even the beginnings of political theory or the political institutions needed for effective government in the knowledge-based society of organizations.

If the twentieth century was one of social transformations, the twenty-first century needs to be one of social and political innovations, whose nature cannot be so clear to us now as their necessity.   ■

■ *QUESTIONS FOR MAKING CONNECTIONS WITHIN THE READING* ■

1. To understand Drucker's argument, it is useful to make a chart of the changes he is describing. What kind of jobs dominated at the beginning of the twentieth century, at the middle, and at the end? How do the societies founded on these jobs differ?

2. In presenting his theory about how the structure of society underwent a major transformation during the twentieth century, Drucker is implicitly arguing against other ways of explaining the changes that took place during this time. As he puts it, "if this century proves one thing, it is the futility of politics." What is Drucker's view of how societies are changed and what are the alternate views that he is rejecting?

3. As Drucker looks to the future, he writes, "We can also predict with confidence that we will redefine what it means to be an educated person." What did it mean to be an educated person a hundred years ago? What does it mean to be an educated person now? And what will it mean twenty years from now?

■ *QUESTIONS FOR WRITING* ■

1. In "The Age of Social Transformation," Peter F. Drucker describes the rise of what he terms "the knowledge society." The essence of this new society, Drucker believes, is mobility—"mobility in terms of where one lives, mobility in terms of what one does, mobility in terms of one's affiliations."

Discuss the problems and the opportunities that are created for society as a whole by the mobility of the knowledge worker.

2. As Drucker describes it, the knowledge society is fundamentally different from the societies that preceded it because its key resource, knowledge, is "fundamentally different from the traditional key resources of the economist—land, labor, and even capital." What problems does this pose for governments and nations? What social and political innovations might we see in the twenty-first century as governments and nations attempt to respond to the emergence of the knowledge society?

■ *QUESTIONS FOR MAKING CONNECTIONS BETWEEN READINGS* ■

1. Drucker argues in "The Age of Social Transformation" that the emergence of the knowledge society requires that we "redefine what it means to be an educated person." Deborah Tannen, in "The Roots of Debate in Education and the Hope of Dialogue," provides an overview of what it has meant to be an educated person in the American school system up to the present time. With the arguments made by Drucker and Tannen in mind, discuss how the educational system might be reformed in the twenty-first century. How would the curriculum have to change? The teaching practices? And how would students themselves have to change?

2. What follows from claiming, as Drucker does, that the last century has demonstrated "the futility of politics"? Does it mean, for example, that there's no need to transform the system for representing the needs and concerns of the governed, as called for by Lani Guinier? If politics is futile, what role are the governed to play in the knowledge society? Are efforts, like Guinier's, to improve the political system just a waste of time? Does the rise of the knowledge worker require that the ideals of democracy be transformed, abandoned, or left unchanged?

For additional suggestions about making connections between readings, visit the Link-O-Mat and More Sample Assignments at <www.newhum. com>.

SUSAN FALUDI

PULITZER-PRIZE WINNING journalist Susan Faludi first became interested in writing about feminism in the fifth grade when she polled her classmates to determine their feelings about the Vietnam War and legalized abortion. In the furor that followed Faludi's release of her data demonstrating the liberal attitudes of her peers, Faludi came to realize, as she put it in a recent interview, "the power that you could have as a feminist writer. Not being the loudest person on the block, not being one who regularly interrupted in class or caused a scene, I discovered that through writing I could make my views heard, and I could actually create change."

The daughter of a homemaker and a Hungarian Holocaust survivor, Faludi was raised in Queens, New York, and attended Harvard University, where she studied literature and American history. After graduating in 1981, Faludi worked for a number of newspapers, including the *New York Times* and the *Wall Street Journal*, before devoting her time to writing *Backlash: The Undeclared War Against American Women* (1991), a study of the media's assault on feminism. *Backlash* won the National Book Critics Circle Award for general nonfiction in 1992 and made Faludi a household name—she appeared on the cover of *Time* magazine alongside Gloria Steinem and, almost overnight, became a national spokesperson on women's rights and the future of feminism.

While doing research for *Backlash,* Faludi began to wonder why the men who opposed women's progress were so angry. In setting out to understand this anger, Faludi interviewed fundamentalists, sex workers in the pornography industry, union members, the unemployed, and other disenfranchised males. "The Citadel," which presents Faludi's investigation into why male cadets were so enraged by the admission of women into the military academy, is one part of this project and has since been incorporated into Faludi's second book, *Stiffed: The Betrayal of the American Man* (1999). The surprising thesis of *Stiffed* is that men,

Faludi, Susan. "The Naked Citadel." *New Yorker.* 5 September 1994. 62–81.

Quotations and biographical information from Susan Faludi, interview by Brian Lamb, Booknotes, 25 October 1992 <http://www.booknotes.org/Transcript/?ProgramID=1121>; Susan Faludi, "Feminist Author Susan Faludi Preaches Male Inclusion," interview by Kate Melloy <http://www.kollegeville.com/kampus/faludi.htm>; *Stiffed: The Betrayal of the American Man.* New York: W. Morrow & Co., 1999.

too, have suffered during the recent social upheavals because "working with others anonymously and loyally to build something larger than yourself is no longer seen as glorious." While Faludi holds out the hope for a society where men and women can work together cooperatively, she also believes that "[t]o revive a genuine feminism, we must disconnect feminism from the individual pursuit of happiness and reconnect it with the individual desire for social responsibility: the basic human need and joy to be part of a larger, meaningful struggle, which engages the entire society."

To learn more about Susan Faludi and the Citadel, visit the Link-O-Mat at <www.newhum.com>.

■ ■

The Naked Citadel

Along the edges of the quad, in the gutters, the freshman cadets were squaring their corners. The "knobs," as they are called for their nearly hairless doorknob pates, aren't allowed to step on the lawn of the broad parade ground, which is trimmed close, as if to match their shorn heads. Keeping off the grass is one of many prohibitions that obtain at The Citadel, a public military college on Charleston's Ashley River. Another is the rule that so many of the cadets say brought them to this Moorish-style, gated campus: Girls keep out.

The campus has a dreamy, flattened quality, with its primary colors, checkerboard courtyards, and storybook-castle barracks. It feels more like an architect's rendering of a campus—almost preternaturally clean, orderly, antiseptic—than the messy real thing. I stood at the far end of the quad, at the academic hall's front steps, and watched the cadets make their herky-jerky perpendicular turns as they drew closer for the first day of class. They walked by stiffly, their faces heat-blotched and vulnerable, and as they passed each in turn shifted his eyes downward. I followed one line of boys into a classroom, a Western Civ class—except, of course, they weren't really boys at all. These were college men, manly recruits to an elite military college whose virile exploits were mythicized in best-selling novels by Calder Willingham and Pat Conroy, both Citadel alumni. So why did I expect their voices to crack when they spoke for the first time? Partly, it was the grammar-schoolish taking of attendance, compulsory at The Citadel. Multiple absences can lead to "tours," hours of marching back and forth in the courtyard with a pinless rifle over one shoulder; or to "cons," confinement to one's room.

But mostly it was the young men themselves, with their doughy faces and twitching limbs, who gave me the urge to babysit. Despite their enrollment in a college long considered "the big bad macho school" (as a former R.O.T.C. commander, Major General Robert E. Wagner, once put it), the cadets lacked the swagger and knowingness of big men on campus. They perched tentatively on their chairs, their hands arranged in a dutiful clasp on their desktops, as if they were expecting a ruler slap to the knuckles. A few dared to glance over at the female visitor, but whenever they made eye contact they averted their gaze and color stained their cheeks.

"As many of you probably know," their teacher said, "this was almost the day the first woman joined The Citadel." The cadets continued to study their polished shoes. "How do you, in fact, feel about whether women should be allowed to attend?"

Silence reigned. Maybe the cadets felt the question put them in an awkward spot. Not only was their teacher in favor of admitting women to The Citadel's Corps of Cadets, the teacher *was* a woman. Indeed, Professor Jane Bishop seemed to be in the strange situation of calling in an air strike on her own position. It was the first day of fall classes in the 1993–94 academic year at The Citadel, and she was broaching the question of the hour. But this incongruity wasn't limited to her classroom. From the moment I stepped onto the school's campus, I had been struck by an unexpected circumstance: though an all-male institution—an institution, moreover, whose singular mission was "making men"—The Citadel was by no means free of women. Female teachers were improving cadets' minds, female administrators were keeping their records, and an all-female (and all-black) staff served the meals in the mess hall. There was also the fact that female students made up seventy-seven percent of the enrollment of the evening school, and many other female students attended summer school with the cadets. What about them? Of course, summer school and evening school aren't part of the military college proper. Cadets don't attend the evening school; and as Major Rick Mill, The Citadel's public-relations director, notes, those cadets who attend the summer school "aren't wearing their uniforms."

Today they were, and so was their teacher. All permanent instructors, regardless of their sex (about fifteen percent are women), wear uniforms as part of their required affiliation with a largely ceremonial outfit once known as the South Carolina Unorganized Militia, and still called by the unfortunate acronym SCUM. Bishop wore hers with what seemed like a deliberate air of disarray.

The cadets' uniforms were considerably tidier—testament to the efficacy of the famous cadet shirt tuck, a maneuver akin to hospital-corners bedmaking and so exacting a cadet cannot perform it without assistance. Even so, the gray cadet uniform, with the big black stripe down the side of the pants

Freshmen are in the "fourth-class system," a regimen to "strip" each recruit of his identity and remold him into the "Whole Man." Illustration by Mark Zingarelli, originally published in *The New Yorker*

and the nametag above the left breast, is the sort more often seen on high-school band members than on fighting soldiers.

"Remember," Bishop prodded them, "speech is free in the classroom."

At last, a cadet unclasped and raised a hand. "Well, I'd have no problem with her in the day program, but she can't join the Corps."

"She," as everyone there knew, was Shannon Faulkner, the woman who had challenged the school's hundred-and-fifty-year-old all-male policy by omitting reference to her sex from her application and winning acceptance to the Corps of Cadets earlier that year—acceptance that was rescinded once the administrators discovered their error. Faulkner's attempt to gain entrance then shifted from the admissions office to the courts. She was allowed under court order to attend day classes during the spring semester of 1994, the first woman to do so. On July 22nd, a United States District Court ruled that The Citadel must admit Faulkner into the Corps of Cadets proper; three weeks later, the Fourth United States Circuit Court of Appeals granted The Citadel a stay pending appeal.

Yet why shouldn't she be permitted into the Corps, Bishop pressed. One of her students recited the fitness requirement—forty-five pushups and fifty-five sit-ups in two-minute sets, and a two-mile run in sixteen minutes. But the administration made passing the fitness test a requirement for graduation only *after* Shannon Faulkner filed suit. An alumnus recounted in court that many upperclassmen he knew who had failed the test skipped the punitive morning run and "sat around and ate doughnuts." Another of Bishop's students cited the shaved-head rule. But this, too, seemed a minor point. A woman cadet could conceivably get a buzz cut. Sinéad O'Connor had done it, Bishop pointed out, without undue injury to her career. And, anyway, after freshman year the men no longer get their heads shaved. Other deprivations of freshman year were invoked: having to "brace" on demand—that is, assume a stance in which a knob stands very erect and tucks in his chin until it puckers up like a rooster's wattle—and having to greet every upperclassman's bellowed command and rebuke with "Sir, yes sir!" or "Sir, no sir!" or "Sir, no excuse sir!" But women, obviously, aren't incapable of obeisance; one might even say they have a long history of it.

Weighing heaviest on the cadets' minds, it turned out, was the preservation of the all-male communal bathroom. The sharing of the stall-less showers and stall-less toilets is "at the heart of the Citadel experience," according to more than one cadet. The men bathe as a group; they walk to the shower down the open galleries, in full view of the courtyard below, and do so, one cadet said, in "nothing but our bathrobes" or "even without any clothes." Another cadet said, "I know it sounds trivial, but all of us in one shower, it's like we're all one, we're all the same, and—I don't know—you feel like you're exposed, but you feel safe. You know these guys are going to be your friends for life." His voice trailed off. "I just can't explain it but when they take that away, it's over. This place will be ruined."

"If women come here, they'll have to put up window shades in all the rooms," a cadet said. "Think of all the windows in the barracks. That could be eight thousand, nine thousand dollars. You've got to look at the costs."

At the end of the hour, the cadets filed out and resumed their double-time jog along the gutters—and their place in the "fourth-class system." This "system" is a nine-month regimen of small and large indignities intended to "strip" each young recruit of his original identity and remold him into the "Whole Man," a vaguely defined ideal, half Christian soldier, half Dale Carnegie junior executive. As a knob explained it to me, "We're all suffering together. It's how we bond." Another knob said, "It's a strange analogy, but it's almost like a P.O.W. camp."

One cadet dawdled, glancing nervously around, then sidled up to me. He spoke in a near whisper, and what he had to say had nothing to do with lavatory etiquette or military tradition. "The great majority of the guys here are very misogynistic," he said. "All they talk about is how girls are pigs and sluts."

I asked him to explain at greater length. He agonized. "I have to keep quiet," he said, but he finally agreed to meet me later, in an out-of-the-way spot on the upper floor of the student-activities center. He rejoined his class-mates with that distinctive knob march, "the march of the puppets," as a professor described it to me later. It was a gait caused in some cases, I was told, by the most conscientious cadets' efforts to keep their shirts perfectly straight with the help of garters—one end of the garter clipped to the shirt-tail, the other end to the socks.

As I waited for my cadet informant, I decided to kill an hour on the vast parade ground, where the Corps of Cadets marches every Friday afternoon in full dress uniforms, and where, according to an old school brochure, "manhood meets mastery." This is a paramilitary display, not a military one. Despite the regalia and officer ranks, and despite its notoriously fierce military discipline ("To discipline is to teach" is the motto emblazoned on one of the school's books of regulations), this is a military academy by self-designation only. Unlike the federal service academies—West Point, An-napolis, the Air Force Academy—The Citadel has no connection with the United States Armed Forces (other than its R.O.T.C. program and its em-ployment of some active and retired officers). Its grounds are adorned with dusty and decommissioned military hardware—a Sherman tank, a subma-rine's torpedo-loading hatch, a Phantom jet named Annette, two cannons named Betsy and Lizzie. In most cases, the weapons, including the pinless M-14s the cadets carry, are inoperative. The mouths of the various cannons are stuffed with cement—all except those of Betsy and Lizzie, which are fired during parades, but carefully aimed high enough so that their powder does not dust the crenellated barracks. The over-all effect is that of a theme park for post–Cold War kids.

The hokeyness and childlike innocence of the scene—the stage-prop artillery, the toy-soldier clip-clop of the cadets as they squared their corners—were endearing, in a Lost Boys sort of way, and I strolled over to the student-activities center for my rendezvous with my cadet informant thinking that The Citadel's version of martial culture was not so menacing after all. The cadet was not in evidence. I spent the next thirty minutes prowling the halls, which were lined with portraits of stern-faced "generals" (I couldn't tell which were United States military and which were SCUM), and examining ads on the student bulletin board for items like "Save the Males" bumper stickers. I tried to reach the cadet's room by phone—women aren't admitted into the barracks—but he was not there. A bit thoughtlessly, I left a message with an upper-classman and headed toward town.

At my hotel, the receptionist handed me a message from my vanished cadet. "Please, don't ever call here again!" it read. The phone clerk peered at me curiously. "Sorry about that exclamation mark, but he seemed quite distraught," she said. "His voice was shaking."

What brought a young man to an all-male preserve in the last decade of the twentieth century, anyway? What was going on outside the academy gates that impelled thousands of boys, Southern and Northern alike (about a fifth of its student body of about two thousand are Yankees), to seek refuge behind a pair of corroding cannons?

"The forces arrayed against us," an attorney named Robert Patterson declared in a February, 1994, court hearing, consider his military academy to be "some big-game animal to be hunted down, tracked, caught, badgered, and killed so that some lawyer or some organization can go back up and hang a trophy on a wall in an office." Patterson was defending not The Citadel but the Virginia Military Institute, which is the only other public military academy in the United States that does not admit women, and which was involved in a similar sex-discrimination suit. (Three months later, Patterson, a V.M.I. alumnus, returned to court to defend The Citadel.) "I will say this, Your Honor," he went on. "This quest by these people constitutes the longest and most expensive publicly financed safari in the annals of big-game hunting."

The Citadel's administration has fought the female hunters with a legal arsenal of nearly a million dollars and with dour, tight-lipped determination, which has only increased with time. The Citadel's president, Claudius Elmer (Bud) Watts III, who is a retired Air Force lieutenant general and a second-generation Citadel alumnus, views Shannon Faulkner's legal efforts as an enemy invasion, placing his young troops "under attack." "The Citadel is in this to the end," he pronounced at a press conference held in the spring of 1994 on the parade ground, his feet planted between Betsy and Lizzie, his uniform decked with ribbons, and his chin tucked in, as is his custom, as if in a permanent brace position.

Later, in his living room, surrounded by coffee-table books on football, Watts told me firmly, "You cannot put a male and a female on that same playing field," though he couldn't say exactly why. Of his own Citadel years he conceded, "I've not the foggiest notion if it would have been different" had women attended. He was just glad there were no female cadets then; otherwise, he said, the cadets would have faced "a different form of intimidation—not wanting to be embarrassed in front of a girl."

Faulkner has been opposed not only by many Citadel staff and alumni but—at least, publicly—by almost all the current cadets. They say that her presence in the Corps would absolutely destroy a basic quality of their experience as Citadel men. She would be what one Citadel defender called in his court deposition "a toxic kind of virus." Tellingly, even before the United States District Court judge enjoined The Citadel to admit Faulkner to the Corps of Cadets for the fall of 1994, and before the injunction was set aside, the administration announced its selection of her living quarters: the infirmary.

Cadets cite a number of reasons that women would have a deleterious effect on the Corps of Cadets, and the reasons are repeated so often as to be easily predictable, though their expression can be novel. "Studies show—I can't cite them, but studies show that males learn better when females aren't there," one cadet explained to me (a curious sentiment at a school where a knob motto about grades is "2.0 and Go"). "If a girl was here, I'd be concerned not to look foolish. If you're a shy student, you won't be as inhibited." Another cadet said, "See, you don't have to impress them here. You're free." From a third: "Where does it end? Will we have unisex bathrooms?" But among the reasons most frequently heard for repelling Faulkner at the gate is this: "She would be destroying a long and proud tradition."

The masculine traditions of West Point and Annapolis were also closely guarded by their male denizens, but the resistance to women joining their ranks was nowhere near as fierce and filled with doomsday rhetoric as The Citadel's efforts to repel feminine interlopers. At Norwich University, a private military college in Northfield, Vermont, that voluntarily opened its barracks to women in 1974, two years before the federal service academies, the administration actually made an effort to recruit and accommodate women. "There was no storm of protest," said a Norwich spokeswoman, Judy Clauson. But then, "it was a time when there were so many rules that were being loosened." The Air Force veteran Linnea Westberg, who was one of the eight women in Norwich's first coed class, recalled, of her integration into its corps, that "ninety-five percent of the male cadets were fine, especially the freshmen, who didn't know any different." Westberg said she was baffled by the intensity of The Citadel's opposition to women in its corps. "It's hard for me to believe it's still an issue."

"The Citadel is a living museum to the way things used to be," John Drennan, a Citadel graduate and a public defender in Charleston, told me one day during The Citadel's legal proceedings. But how, exactly, did things use to be? The cadets and the alumni of the school, along with those protesting against its exclusionary policies, envision its military tradition above all. And The Citadel once did have a strong military aspect: it was formed as an arsenal in 1822 in response to a slave revolt purportedly planned by the freed Charleston slave Denmark Vesey, which, though it was foiled, aroused widespread alarm in the region. Yet twenty years later the guns and the gold braid became mere adornment as The Citadel turned into an industrial school of domestic and practical skills. Union troops shut down The Citadel at the end of the Civil War, but it was reinvented and reopened in 1882, after the Union's Reconstruction officials had thoroughly stripped the school of all military muscle. Its new mission was to reinvigorate the masculinity of the South by showing its men how to compete with the business and industrial skills of the Yankee carpetbaggers, who were believed to be much better prepared than the sons of Dixie to enter the Darwinian fray of modern commerce. John Peyre Thomas, who ran The Citadel from 1882 to 1885, wrote of the need to teach spoiled plantation boys the rudiments of self-reliance. "It must be admitted that the institution of African slavery, in many respects, affected injuriously the white youth of the South," he wrote. "Reared from infancy to manhood with servants at his command to bring his water, brush his shoes, saddle his horse, and, in fine, to minister to his personal wants, the average Southern boy grew up in some points of character dependent, and lazy, and inefficient. He was found, too, wanting in those habits of order and system that come from the necessity, in man, to economize time and labor."

What makes the school's Reconstruction-era mission important is that in so many ways it remains current; the masculine and industrial culture of our age and that of the conquered South may have more in common than we care to imagine. Again, we are at a psychic and economic crisis point for manhood. And, again, the gun issues hide the butter issues: the bombast masks a deep insecurity about employment and usefulness in a world where gentleman soldiers are an anachronism and a graduate with gentleman's C's may find himself busing tables at Wendy's.

The uncertain prospects of Citadel graduates are worsened by military downsizing. Only about a third of recent graduates entered the military—a figure that has fallen steeply since the mid-seventies, when half of The Citadel's graduating class routinely took a service commission. News of Shannon Faulkner's court case competed in the Charleston *Post & Courier* with news of the shutting down of the local shipyards and decommissionings from the local military installations.

The night before the closing arguments in Faulkner's suit, I had dinner at the on-campus home of Philippe and Linda Ross, who have both taught at The Citadel. Philippe, the head of the Biology Department, had just completed his first round of moonlighting as a "retraining" instructor at the Charleston Naval Shipyard. He had been prepping laid-off nuclear engineers to enter one of the few growth industries in the area—toxic-waste management. Facing a room filled with desperate men each day had been a dispiriting experience, he said. He recalled the plea of a middle-aged engineer, thrust out of the service after twenty-six years: "All I want to do is work." Linda Ross, who was then teaching psychology at The Citadel, looked across the table with a pained expression. "That whole idea that if a young man went to college he could make a decent living and buy a house, and maybe even a boat, just does not hold anymore," she said softly. "There's a Citadel graduate working as a cashier at the grocery store. And the one thing these young men felt they could count on was that if things got hard they could always go into the military. No more. And they are bitter and angry."

In the fall of 1991, Michael Lake, a freshman, decided to leave The Citadel. He had undergone weeks of bruising encounters with upperclassmen—encounters that included being knocked down with a rifle butt and beaten in the dark by a pack of cadets. Incidents of hazing became so violent that, in a school where publicly criticizing the alma mater is virtually an act of treason, several athletes told their stories to *Sports Illustrated*. Much of the violence was aimed at star freshman athletes: a member of the cycling team was forced to hang by his fingers over a sword poised two inches below his testicles; a placekicker had his head dunked in water twenty times until he was unconscious; a linebacker was forced to swallow his chewing tobacco and tormented until, he said later, "I was unable even to speak clearly in my classes." It was a time when the Churchill Society, a literary club reportedly containing a white-supremacist faction, was organized on campus. It was a time when the local chapter of the National Association for the Advancement of Colored People urged a federal investigation into a pair of racial incidents on the school's campus: the appearance of a noose over the bed of a black freshman who had earlier refused to sing "Dixie," and the shooting and wounding of a black cadet by a sniper who was never identified. (A few years earlier, upperclassmen wearing Klan-like costumes left a charred paper cross in the room of a black cadet.) And it was a time when a leader of the Junior Sword Drill, a unit of cadet sword-bearers, leaped off a five-foot dresser onto the head of a prostrate cadet, then left him in a pool of blood in a barracks hall. According to one cadet, a lacrosse-team member returning from an away game at three in the morning stumbled upon the victim's unconscious body, his face split open, jaw and nose broken, mouth a jack-o'-lantern of missing teeth.

One night, at about 2 A.M., high-ranking cadets trapped a raccoon in the barracks and began to stab it with a knife. Beau Turner, a student at the school, was awakened by the young men's yelling. "My roommate and I went out there to try and stop it," Turner recalled, "but we were too late." Accounts of the episode vary. In a widely circulated version (which was referred to in a faculty member's testimony), the cadets chanted, "Kill the bitch! Kill the bitch!" as they tortured the raccoon to death.

In October, 1993, two upperclassmen burst into the room of two freshmen and reportedly kneed them in the genitals, pulled out some of their chest hair, and beat them up. They were arrested on charges of assault and battery, and agreed to a program of counselling and community service, which would wipe clean their records. They withdrew from The Citadel, in lieu of expulsion, the spokesman Major Rick Mill said.

One of the offending cadets, Adrian Baer, told me that he and the other accused sophomore, Jeremy Leckie, did indeed come back from drinking, burst into the knobs' room after 10 P.M., and "repeatedly struck them in the chest and stomach" and bruised one of them in the face, but he denied having kicked them in the groin and yanked out chest hair. He said that what he did was common procedure—and no different from the "motivational" treatment he had received as a knob at the hands of a senior who came into *his* room. They entered the freshmen's room, Baer explained, because they viewed one of the occupants as "a problem" knob who "needed some extra motivation." Baer elaborated: "His pinkie on his right hand wouldn't completely close when he went to salute. He caught a lot of heat for that, of course, because it's a military school; it's important to salute properly." The strict rule that upperclassmen not fraternize with knobs, he said, meant that they couldn't simply counsel the freshman kindly. "If we just sat down and said, 'Listen, guy, we have a little problem,' that would be fraternization. And more important, knobs would lose respect for upperclassmen. It's a lot of denial on the part of officials at The Citadel about hazing," Baer said. "They don't want to believe it goes on." Leckie's father, Timothy Rinaldi, said that while he believed his son "was definitely in the wrong," he felt The Citadel's fourth-class system bred such behavior. "They help build this monster," he said of The Citadel, "the monster gets up off the table and starts walking through town—and now Dr. Frankenstein wants to shoot it."

Needless to say, not every cadet embraces the climate of cruelty; the nocturnal maulings likely frighten as many cadets as they enthrall. But the group mentality that pervades The Citadel assures that any desire on the part of a cadet to speak out about the mounting violence will usually be squelched by the threat of ostracism and shame. While group rule typifies many institutions, military and civilian, that place a premium on conformity, the power and authoritarianism of the peer group at The Citadel is exceptional, because the college gives a handful of older students leave to "govern" the others as they see fit. (A lone officer provided by the military, who sleeps in a wing off one of the dorms, seldom interferes.) This is a situation that, over the years, an occasional school official has challenged, without success. A former assistant commandant for discipline, Army Lieutenant Colonel T. Nugent Courvoisie, recalled that he "begged" the school's president back in the sixties to place more military officers—and ones who were more mature—in the barracks, but his appeals went unheeded. Discipline and punishment in the dorms is in the hands of the student-run regimental command, and ascendancy in this hierarchy is not always predicated on compassion for one's fellow-man. In consequence, the tyranny of the few buys the silence of the many.

This unofficial pact of silence could, of course, be challenged by the Citadel officialdom. On a number of occasions over the past three decades— most recently when some particularly brutal incidents found their way into the media—The Citadel has commissioned "studies." But when the administration does go on the offensive, its animus is primarily directed not at miscreant cadets but at the "unfair" media, which are "victimizing" the institution by publicizing the bad behavior of its boys.

In recent years, enough bad news leaked out locally to become a public-relations nightmare, and the school appointed a committee of Citadel loyalists to assess the situation. Even the loyalists concluded, in a January, 1992, report, that the practice of physical abuse of freshmen, along with food and sleep deprivation, had got out of hand. As a result, Major Mill told me, The Citadel ordered upperclassmen to stop using pushups as a "disciplinary tool" on individual cadets. "That was the most important one" of the reforms prompted by the report, Mill said. Other reforms were adopted: for example, freshmen would no longer be compelled to deliver mail to upperclassmen after their evening study hours, thus reducing opportunities for hazing; freshmen would—at least officially—no longer be compelled to "brace" in the mess hall. At the same time, the report declared that it "wholeheartedly endorses the concept of the fourth-class system," which it called "essential to the attainment of college objectives and the development of the Citadel man."

Institutions that boast of their insularity, whether convents or military academies, are commonly pictured in the public imagination as static, unchanging abstractions, isolated from the ebb and flow of current events. But these edifices are rarely as otherworldly as their guardians might wish; indeed, in the case of The Citadel, its bricked-off culture has functioned more as a barometer of national anxieties than as a garrison against them. The militaristic tendencies within the Corps seem to vary inversely with the esteem in which the American soldier is held in the larger society. In times when the nation has been caught up in a socially acceptable conflict, one in which its soldiers return as heroes greeted by tickertape parades, The Citadel has loosened its militaristic harness, or even removed it altogether. Thus, during perhaps the most acceptable war in American history, the Second World War, the fourth-class system of knob humiliation was all but discontinued. Upperclassmen couldn't even order a knob to brace. The changes began largely in response to the demands of the real military for soldiers they could use in a modern war. "The War Department and the Navy Department were asking R.O.T.C. to do less drilling, more calculus," Jamie Moore, a professor of history at The Citadel and a former member of the United States Army's Historical Advisory Committee, told me. "The Citadel dismantled its fourth-class system because it was getting in the way of their military training." The changes didn't seem to interfere with the school's production of Whole Men; on the contrary, an extraordinary percentage of The Citadel's most distinguished graduates come from these years, among them United States Senator Ernest (Fritz) Hollings; Alvah Chapman, Jr., the former chief executive of Knight-Ridder; and South Carolina's former governor John C. West.

The kinder, gentler culture of the Second World War–era Citadel survived well into the next decade. Although a new fourth-class system was soon established, it remained relatively benign. "We didn't have the yelling we have today," Colonel Harvey Dick, class of '53 and now a member of The Citadel's governing body, recalled. "They didn't even shave the freshmen's heads."

The postwar years also brought the admission of women to the summer program, and without the hand-wringing provoked by Shannon Faulkner's application. "WOMEN INVADE CITADEL CLASSES FIRST TIME IN SCHOOL'S HISTORY," the Charleston daily noted back on page 16 of its June 21, 1949, edition. "Most male students took the advent of the 'amazons' in their stride," the paper reported cheerfully. "Only the younger ones seemed at all uneasy. Professors and instructors were downright glad to see women in their classes."

The Vietnam War, needless to say, did not inspire the same mood of relaxation on campus. "The fourth-class system was very physical," Wallace West, the admissions director, who was an undergraduate at The Citadel during the Vietnam War years, said. "When I was there, there was no true emphasis on academics, or on positive leadership. It was who could be worked to physical exhaustion." Alumni from those years recounted being beaten with sticks, coat hangers, and rifle butts. That was, of course, the era that inspired Pat Conroy's novel "The Lords of Discipline," a tale of horrific hazing, directed with special virulence against the school's first African-American cadet. "They just tortured us," Conroy recalled from his home, in Beaufort, South Carolina. "It taught me the exact kind of man I didn't want to be," he added.

In 1968, the administration appointed a committee to investigate the violence. The committee issued a report that, like its 1992 successor, concluded "there have been significant and extensive abuses to the [fourth-class] system." And, with its strong recommendation that hazing result in expulsion, the report seemed to promise a more pacific future on campus.

In the past decade and a half, however, the record of violence and cruelty at The Citadel has attracted increasing notice, even as the armed forces have been racked by downsizing and scandal. The Citadel president during much of this era, Major General James A. Grimsley, Jr., declined to discuss this or any other aspect of campus life during his tenure. "I don't do interviews," he said. "Thank you for calling, young lady." He then hung up. Others have been less reticent.

Thirteen years before Vice-Admiral James B. Stockdale consented to be Ross Perot's running mate, he took on what turned out to be an even more thankless task: fighting brutal forms of hazing at The Citadel. In 1979, Stockdale, who had graduated from Annapolis, was chosen to be The Citadel's president because of his status as a genuine military hero: he had survived eight years as a P.O.W. in Vietnam. This hero failed to see the point of manufactured adversity. In an afterword to the book "In Love and War," a collaboration between Stockdale and his wife, Sybil, he wrote that there was "something mean and out of control about the regime I had just inherited."

On his first day in the president's office, Stockdale opened a desk drawer and discovered "what turned out to be Pandora's box," he wrote. "From the top down, what was written on the papers I took out of the desk drawers—and conversations with some of their authors—was enough to break anybody's heart." Among them was a letter from an infuriated father who wanted to know what had happened to his son "to change him from a levelheaded, optimistic, aggressive individual to a fatigued, irrational, confused and bitter one." He also found copies of memos from The Citadel's staff physician complaining repeatedly of (as Stockdale recalled) "excessive hospitalization"—such as the case of a knob who had suffered intestinal bleeding and was later brought back to the infirmary, having been exercised to unconsciousness. Stockdale sought to reform the system, but he was stymied at every turn. He clashed with The Citadel's powerful Board of Visitors, an eleven-member committee of alumni that sets school policy. The Board of Visitors overruled his expulsion of a senior cadet who had reportedly been threatening freshmen with a pistol. A year into his presidency, Stockdale submitted his resignation. After he left, the board reinstated an avenging friend of the senior cadet who, according to Stockdale, had attempted to break into his house one evening. (The then chairman of the Board of Visitors maintains that the cadet was drunk and looking for the barracks.)

"They thought they were helping people into manhood," Stockdale recalled, from a more serene post, in Palo Alto, California, where he is a scholar at Stanford's Hoover Institution on War, Revolution, and Peace. "But they had no idea what that meant—or who they were."

After Watts became president, in 1989, some faculty members began to observe a creeping militarization imposed by the administration upon the Corps's already drill-heavy regimen. Four special military days were added to the academic year. At the beginning of one semester, President Watts held a faculty meeting in a room above the mess hall."Watts had these soldiers standing around the room with their hands behind them," Gardel Feurtado, a political-science professor and one of only two African-American professors, recalled. Watts, he said, lectured the faculty for about three hours. "He didn't talk about academics or educational goals. He just talked about cadets' training, and he showed us a film of it," Feurtado told me. According to Feurtado, Watts told the faculty to line up in groups behind the soldiers for a tour of the barracks. "I said, 'Enough of this,' and I started to walk out. And this soldier stopped me and said, 'Where do you think you're going, sir?' and I said, 'You do realize that I am not in the military?'" Feurtado had to push by him to leave.

Illustration by Mark Zingarelli, originally published in *The New Yorker*

When Michael Lake looked back on the abuse he suffered during his abbreviated knob year of '91, he could now see before him, like the emergence of invisible ink on what appeared to be a blank piece of paper, the faint outlines of another struggle. What he saw was a submerged gender battle, a bitter but definitely fixed contest between the sexes, concealed from view by the fact that men played both parts. The beaten knobs were the women, "stripped" and humiliated, and the predatory upperclassmen were the men, who bullied and pillaged. If they couldn't re-create a male-dominant society in the real world, they could restage the drama by casting male knobs in all the subservient feminine roles.

"They called you a 'pussy' all the time," Lake recalled. 'Or a 'fucking little girl.'" It started the very first day they had their heads shaved, when the upperclassmen stood around and taunted. 'Oh, you going to get your little girlie locks cut off?" When they learned that Lake would be playing soccer that fall, their first response was "What is that, a girl's sport?" Another former cadet said that he had withstood "continual abuse," until he found himself thinking about jumping out the fourth-story window of the barracks—and quit. He reported an experience similar to Lake's. Virtually every taunt equated him with a woman: whenever he showed fear, they would say, "You look like you're having an abortion," or "Are you menstruating?" The knobs even experienced a version of domestic violence. The upperclassmen, this cadet recalled, "would go out and get drunk and they would come home and haze, and you just hoped they didn't come into your room."

"According to the Citadel creed of the cadet," Lake said, "women are objects, they're things that you can do with whatever you want to." In order to maintain this world view, the campus has to be free of women whose status might challenge it—a policy that, of course, is rarely enunciated. The acknowledged policy is that women are to be kept at a distance so they can be "respected" as ladies. Several months before Faulkner's lawsuit came to trial, I was sitting in the less than Spartan air-conditioned quarters of the senior regimental commander, Norman Doucet, the highest-ranking cadet, who commanded the barracks. Doucet, who was to be The Citadel's star witness at the Faulkner trial, was explaining to me how excluding women had enhanced his gentlemanly perception of the opposite sex. "The absence of women makes us understand them better," Doucet said. "In an aesthetic kind of way, we appreciate them more—because they are not there."

Women at less of a remove fare less well. In The Citadel's great chain of being, the "waitees"—as many students call that all-black, all-female mess-hall staff—rate as the bottom link. Some upperclassmen have patted them on their rear ends, tried to trip them as they pass the tables, or hurled food at their retreating backs. Cadets have summoned them with "Come here, bitch," or addressed one who dropped a plate or forgot an order as "you stupid whore." The pages of the *Brigadier,* the school's newspaper, bear witness to the cadets' contempt for these women. Gary Brown, now the editor-in-chief of the *Brigadier,* once advised fellow-cadets to beware of "waitee" food contamination—"the germ filled hands, the hair follicles, and other unknown horrors." Not only was he dismayed by "wavy little follicles in my food" but he found the women insufficiently obedient. "Duty is certainly not the sublimest word in the Waitee language," he wrote. In a letter to the editor, Jason S. Pausman, class of '94, urged fellow-cadets to demand "waitees without chronic diseases that involve sneezing, coughing or wiping of body parts. . . . The reality is simple, we CANNOT sit by and let the waitees of this school control us."

Some women faculty members report similarly resentful responses to their presence, despite—or because of—their positions of authority. Angry messages on a professor's door are one tactic. When Jane Bishop recently posted on her office door a photocopy of a *New York Times* editorial supporting women's admission to the Corps of Cadets, she found it annotated with heated rejoinders in a matter of days. "Dr. Bishop, you are a prime example of why women should not be allowed here," one scribble read. Another comment: "Women will destroy the world."

The Citadel men's approach to women seems to toggle between extremes of gentility and fury. "First, they will be charming to the women to get their way," Linda Ross said. "But if that doesn't work they don't know any other way. So then they will get angry." It's a pattern that is particularly evident in some cadets' reaction to younger faculty women.

December Green joined The Citadel's Political Science Department in 1988, the first woman that the department had ever hired for a tenure-track position. She was twenty-six and attractive—"someone the cadets might fantasize about," a colleague recalled. They were less enchanted, however, by her left-leaning politics. She soon found herself getting obscene phone calls in the middle of the night. Then obscenities began appearing on her office door. "Pussy" is the one that sticks in her mind.

Though Green's work at The Citadel was highly praised—she received an award for teaching, research, and service—she said that no one in the administration tried to stop her when she left in 1992, in despair over her in-

The legendary Citadel elder known as the Boo, who oversaw racial integration at The Citadel in the sixties, says, "With women, there's going to be sexual harassment." His wife, Margaret, counters, "Oh, honey, those cadets are harassing each other right now." "That's different," he says. "That's standard operating procedure."
Illustration by Mark Zingarelli, originally published in *The New Yorker*

ability to contain the cadets' fury. Nor, apparently, had anyone responded to her appeals to correct the situation. "A lot of terrible things happened to me there," Green, who is now teaching in Ohio, said, reluctant to revisit them. The hostility ranged from glowering group stares in the hallway to death threats—some of which appeared on the cadets' teacher-evaluation forms. The male faculty offered little support. Green recalls the department chairman instructing her to "be more maternal toward the students" when a cadet lodged a complaint about her (she had challenged his essay in which he praised apartheid). And a professor who stood by one day while his students harassed her and another woman informed her, "You get what you provoke."

Green said she eventually had to get an unlisted number to stop the obscene calls, and also moved, in part out of fear of the cadets' vengeance. The last straw, however, came when she submitted the written threats she had received to her chairman, who passed them on to the dean of undergraduate studies, in hopes of remedial action. The dean, she said, did nothing for some months, then, after she inquired, said he had "misplaced" the offending documents.

The dean, Colonel Isaac (Spike) Metts, Jr., told me he didn't recall saying he misplaced the documents but "I might have said it's not on my desk at that time and I don't know where it is." He added that Green was a "very valuable" professor. "I don't know what else we could've done," Metts said. In any event, soon after submitting the threatening notes to the dean Green gave up. At her exit interview, she recalled, President Watts told her he didn't understand why she had been upset by the cadet harassment. "It's just a bunch of kid stuff," another male colleague said. (Lewis Spearman, the assistant to the president, said that, because of federal privacy law, Watts would have no response to Green's version of events.)

The remaining category of women that cadets have to deal with is "the dates," as the young women they socialize with are generally called. (There are no wives; Citadel policy forbids cadets to marry, and violators are expelled.) In some respects, these young women are the greatest challenge to the cadet's sense of gender hierarchy. While the "waitees" can be cast as household servants and the female teachers as surrogate mothers, the dates are more difficult to place. Young women their age are often college students, with the same aspirations as the cadets, or even greater ones. The cadets deal with young women's rising ambitions in a number of ways. One is simply to date high-school girls, an option selected by a number of cadets. Another strategy, facilitated by The Citadel, is to cast the young women who are invited on campus into the homecoming-queen mold. The college holds a Miss Citadel contest each year, and Anne Poole, whose husband, Roger, is the vice-president of academic affairs and the dean of the college, has sat on the judging panel. Each cadet company elects a young woman mascot from a photograph competition, and their faces appear in the yearbook.

The school also sends its young men to an in-house etiquette-training seminar, in which the Citadel "hostess," a pleasant woman in her forties named Susan Bowers, gives them a lecture on how "to act gentlemanly with the girls." She arms cadets with "The Art of Good Taste," a do's-and-don'ts manual with a chapter entitled "Helping the Ladies." The guidebook outlines the "correct way of offering an arm to a lady . . . to help her down the steps," and the best method for assisting "a lady in distress." (The example of distress provided involves an elderly woman trying to open a door when her arms are full of shopping bags.) Such pointers are illustrated with pictures of fifties-style coeds sporting Barbie-doll hair flips and clinging to the arms of their cadets, who are escorting them to "the Hop." The manual's preface states emphatically, "At all times [ladies] must be sheltered and protected not only from the elements and physical harm but also from embarrassment, crudity, or coarseness of any sort."

Susan Bowers explained the duties of her office: "At the beginning of the year, we do 'situation cards' for the freshmen. And we'll bring in cheerleaders and use them as props. . . . We show cadets how to go through the receiving line, how to introduce your date, and what to say to them. In the past, we didn't have the cheerleaders to use, so they dressed up some of the guys as girls." Bowers said she felt bad for the cadets, who often come to her seeking maternal consolation. "They are very timid—afraid, almost," she said. "They are so lost, and they need a shoulder."

"The Art of Good Taste" is silent on the subject of proper etiquette toward women who require neither deference nor rescue. And, as Linda Ross observed, when the gentlemanly approach fails them cadets seem to have only one fallback—aggression. Numerous cadets spoke to me of classmates who claimed to have "knocked around" uncompliant girlfriends. Some of those classmates, no doubt, were embellishing to impress a male audience, but not always. "I know lots of stories where cadets are violent toward women," a 1991 Citadel graduate named Ron Vergnolle said. He had witnessed cadets hitting their girlfriends at a number of Citadel parties—and observed one party incident in which two cadets held down a young woman while a third drunken cadet leaned over and vomited on her. Vergnolle, a magna-cum-laude graduate of the Citadel class of '91, recounted several such stories to me, and added that bragging about humiliating an ex-girlfriend is a common practice—and the more outrageous the humiliation, the better the story, as far as many cadets are concerned. Two such cadet storytellers, for example, proudly spread the word of their exploits on Dog Day, a big outdoor party sponsored by The Citadel's senior class. The two cadets told about the time they became enraged with their dates, followed them to the Portosans, and, after the women had entered, pushed the latrines over so they landed on the doors, trapping the occupants. The cadets left them there. Another cadet told Vergnolle that he had tacked a live hamster to a young woman's door. There was also the cadet who boasted widely that, as vengeance against an uncooperative young woman, he smashed the head of her cat against a window as she watched in horror. "The cat story," Vergnolle noted, "that was this guy's calling card."

Something of these attitudes shows up even in the ditties the cadets chant during their daily runs. Many of the chants are the usual military "jodies," well known for their misogynistic lyrics. But some are vintage Citadel, and include lyrics about gouging out a woman's eyes, lopping off body parts, and evisceration. A cadence remembered by one Citadel cadet, sung to the tune of "The Candy Man," begins, "Who can take two jumper cables/Clip 'em to her tit/Turn on the battery and watch the bitch twitch." Another verse starts with "Who can take an ice pick . . ." and so on.

The day after last Thanksgiving, the phone rang at one-thirty in the morning in the home of Sandy and Ed Faulkner, in Powdersville, South Carolina, a tiny community on the outskirts of Greenville. The caller was a neighbor. They had better come outside, he said—a car had been circling their block. Sandy and Ed, the parents of Shannon Faulkner, went out on their front lawn and looked around. At first, they saw nothing. Then, as they turned back to the house, they saw that across the white porch columns and along the siding of the house, painted in gigantic and what Sandy later recalled as "blood-red" letters, were the words, "Bitch," "Dyke," "Whore," and "Lesbo." Ed got up again at 6 A.M.. and, armed with a bucket of white paint, hurried to conceal the message from his daughter.

A few days after the judge ordered The Citadel to admit Faulkner to the Corps of Cadets, morning rush-hour drivers in Charleston passed by a huge portable sign that read "Die Shannon." At least this threat wasn't home delivered. In the past year, instances of vandalism and harassment have mounted at the Faulkner home. Someone crawled under the house and opened the emergency exhaust valve on the water heater. The gas tank on Sandy's car was pried open. Someone driving a Ford Bronco mowed down the mailbox. Another motorist "did figure-eights through my flower bed," Sandy said. "This year, I didn't even plant flowers, because I knew they would just tear them up." And someone with access to Southern Bell's voice-mail system managed, twice, to tap into their voice mail and change their greeting, both times to a recording featuring rap lyrics about a "bitch" with a "big butt." Callers phoned in the middle of the night with threatening messages. Sandy called the county sheriff's department about the vandalism, but in Anderson county, which has been home to many Citadel's graduates, the deputy who arrived was not particularly helpful. He told them, Sandy recalled, "Well, if you're going to mess with The Citadel, you're just going to have to expect that."

Every trial has its rare moments of clarity, when the bramble of admissibility arguments and technicalities is cut away and we see the actual issue in dispute. One such moment came toward the end of the Faulkner-Citadel trial, when Alexander Astin, the director of the Higher Education Research Institute at the University of California at Los Angeles, took the stand. Astin, who is widely viewed as a leading surveyor of college-student performance and attitudes, found no negative effects on male students in nineteen all-male colleges he had studied which had gone coeducational.

"Can you tell me what kind of woman you would think would want to attend a coeducational Citadel?" Robert Patterson, the Citadel attorney who had previously represented V.M.I, asked Astin, his voice full of unflattering insinuation about the kind of woman he imagined her to be.

ASTIN: I suppose the same as the kind of men who want to go there.

PATTERSON: Would it be a woman that would not be all that different from men?

ASTIN: Yes.

To Patterson, this was a triumphant moment, and he closed on it: he had forced the government's witness to admit that a woman like Shannon Faulkner would have to be a mannish aberration from her gender. But in fact Astin's testimony expressed the precise point that the plaintiff's side had been trying to make all along, and that The Citadel strenuously resisted: that the sexes were, in the end, not all that different.

"I was considered the bitch of the band," Shannon Faulkner said, without embarrassment, of her four years in her high school's marching band—just stating a fact. She was lounging on the couch in her parents' living room, comfortable in an old T-shirt and shorts, one leg swung over an arm of the couch. "That's because I was the one who was mean and got it done." The phone rang, for the millionth time—another media call. "I'm not giving statements to the press right now," she said efficiently into the phone, and hung up. She did not apologize for her brusqueness, as I was half expecting her to do, after she put down the receiver. There is nothing of the good girl about her. Not that she is disagreeable; Shannon Faulkner just doesn't see the point in false deference. "I never let anyone push me around, male or female," Faulkner said, and that fact had been exasperatingly obvious to reporters who covered the trial: they found that all the wheedling and cheap flatteries that usually prompt subjects to say more than they should didn't work with Faulkner.

One could scrounge around in Faulkner's childhood for the key to what made her take on The Citadel. You could say that it was because she was born six weeks premature, and her fierce struggle to live forged a "survivor." You could cite her memory that as a small child she preferred playing outside with the boys to playing with certain girls whom she deemed "too prissy." You could point to her sports career in high school and junior high: she lettered in softball for four years and kept stats for three of the schools' four basketball teams. You could note her ability to juggle tasks: she edited the yearbook, wrote for the school paper, and graduated with a 3.48 grade-point average. And you could certainly credit the sturdy backbone and outspokeness of both her mother and her maternal grandmother; this is a family where the women talk and the men keep a low profile. Her father, Ed, owns a small fence-building business. At thirty, a few years after Shannon's birth, Sandy returned to college to get her degree, a double major in psychology and education, and became a high-school teacher of psychology, sociology, United States history, and minority cultures. When a male professor had complained about certain "older women" in his class who asked "too many questions," Sandy hurled one of her wedge-heeled sandals at him. "I said, 'I'm paying for this class, and don't you ever tell me what I can ask.'" Shannon's maternal grandmother, sixty-seven-year-old Evelyn Richey, was orphaned at six and worked most of her life in textile factories, where, she noted, "women could do the job and men got the pay." Of her granddaughter's suit she said, "Women have got to come ahead. I say, let's get on with the show."

But there's little point in a detailed inspection of family history, because there's no real mystery here. What is most striking about Shannon herself is that she's not particularly unusual. She reads novels by Tom Clancy and

John Grisham, has worked in a local day-care center, is partial to places like Bennigan's. She wants a college education so she can support herself and have a career as a teacher or a journalist—she hasn't yet decided which. She might do a stint in the military, she might not. She is in many ways representative of the average striving lower-middle-class teenage girl, circa 1994, who intends to better herself and does not intend to achieve that betterment through a man—in fact, she has not for a moment entertained such a possibility.

Throughout the trial, cadets and Citadel alumni spoke of a feminist plot: she is "a pawn" of the National Organization for Women, or—a theory repeatedly posited to me by cadets—"Her mother put her up to it." Two Citadel alumni asked me in all seriousness if feminist organizations were paying Shannon Faulkner to take the stand. In truth, Shannon makes an unlikely feminist poster girl. She prefers to call herself "an individualist" and seems almost indifferent to feminist affairs; when I mentioned Gloria Steinem's name once in conversation, Shannon asked me, "Who's that?" After the judge issued his decision to admit her to the Corps, she told the *New York Times* that she didn't consider the ruling a victory "just for women"—only a confirmation of her belief that if you want something, "go for it." Shannon Faulkner's determination to enter The Citadel's Corps of Cadets was fuelled not so much by a desire to trailblaze as by a sense of amazement and indignation that this trail was barricaded in the first place. She had never, she told the court, encountered such a roadblock in all her nineteen years—a remark that perhaps only a young woman of her fortunate generation could make without perjuring herself.

Shannon Faulkner got the idea of attending The Citadel back in December of 1992. She was taking a preparatory education course at Wren High School, the local public school. Mike Hazel, the teacher, passed out articles for them to read and discuss, and Faulkner picked the article in *Sports Illustrated* about hazing at The Citadel. "It was almost as accidental as Rosa Parks," Hazel recalled. "I just held up *Sports Illustrated* and asked, 'Who wants to do this?'"

Faulkner told me she'd selected the article because "I had missed that issue." During the ensuing discussion, the class wandered off the subject of hazing and onto the question of what, exactly, a public state institution was doing barring women from its classrooms. After a while, Faulkner got up and went down to the counselor's office, and returned with an application form from The Citadel. "I said, 'Hey, it doesn't even say 'Male/Female,'" she recalled. While she was sitting in class, she filled it out. "I didn't really make a big to-do about it."

Two weeks after Faulkner received her acceptance letter, The Citadel got word she was a woman and revoked her admission, and in August of 1993 she went off to spend a semester at the University of South Carolina at Spartanburg while the courts thrashed out the next move. As the lawyers filed papers, The Citadel's defenders delivered their own increasingly agitated personal beliefs to the plaintiff herself. Faulkner worked evenings as a waitress in a local bar called Chiefs Wings and Firewater until the nightly tirades from the many drunk Citadel-graduate customers got to be too much. Actually, Faulkner said, she wouldn't have quit if some of her male college friends hadn't felt the need to defend her honor. "I didn't want them getting hurt," she said. Her manner of dealing with the Citadel crowd was more good-humored. One day at the bar, she recalled, "a guy came up to me. 'Are you Shannon Faulkner?' he asked, and I said, 'Why?'—very casual. Then he got real huffy-puffy, madder and madder." Finally, she said, he stuck his ring in her face, then slammed his hand down on the table. "You will never wear *that!*" he yelled. Shannon saw him a few times in the bar after that, scowling at her from a far table. To lighten the mood, she once had the bartender send him a beer. He wouldn't drink it.

"I never show my true emotions in public," Shannon said. "I consider that weak." She can laugh at the cadets' threats, even when they turn ugly, because she doesn't see the reason for all the fuss. Whenever she is asked to sign the latest T-shirt inspired by the controversy, which depicts a group of male bulldogs (The Citadel's mascot) in cadet uniforms and one female bulldog in a red dress, above the caption "1,952 Bulldogs and 1 Bitch," Faulkner told me, "I always sign under the 'Bitch' part."

The first day that Shannon Faulkner attended classes, in January, 1994, the cadets who had lined up by the academic building told the media the same thing over and over. "We were trained to be gentlemen, and that's what we'll be." But in Shannon's first class, biology, all three cadets assigned to sit in her row changed their seats. The teacher, Philippe Ross, had to threaten to mark them absent to get them to return to their places. (More than twenty unexcused absences a semester is grounds for failure). Shortly thereafter, a rumor began to circulate that Faulkner was using a fake I.D. in the local bars. This summer, talk of a plot against Faulkner surfaced—to frame her, perhaps by planting drugs in her belongings. The threat seemed real enough for Faulkner to quit her summer job, in the Charleston area, and return home.

The *Brigadier's* column "Scarlet Pimpernel" took up the anti-Shannon cause with a vengeance. The columnist dubbed her "the divine bovine," likening her to a plastic revolving cow at a nearby mall (the mounting of which is a cadet tradition). The "Pimpernel" comments on an incident that occurred on Faulkner's first day were particularly memorable. An African-American cadet named Von Mickle dared to shake her hand in front of the media and say, "It's time for women," and compared the exclusion of women to that of blacks. For this lone act, he was not only physically threatened by classmates but derided in the "Pimpernel." "The PIMP doth long to tame the PLASTIC COW on this most wondrous of nights," the anonymous author wrote, with the column's unusual antique-English flourishes and coded references. "But it seems that we will have a live specimen, a home grown DAIRY QUEEN from the stables of Powerville. Perhaps NON DICKLE will be the first to saddle up. He is DIVINE BOVINE'S best friend after all."

More disturbing were cadet writings on Faulkner that were not for public consumption. Tom Lucas, a graduate student in The Citadel's evening program, told me about some "very harsh" graffiti that he'd found over one of the men's rooms in The Citadel's academic building. The inscription that most stuck in his mind: "Let her in—then fuck her to death."

On the whole, The Citadel administrators to whom I spoke were defensive, evasive, or dismissive of the cadets' hostile words and deeds toward Faulkner. When I asked Citadel officials to respond to reports of barracks violence, harrassment of women on staff, or verbal abuse of Faulkner, the responses were dismaying. Cases of violence and abuse were "aberrations"; cadets who spoke up were either "troublemakers" or "mama's boys"; and each complaint by a female faculty member was deemed a "private personnel matter" that could not be discussed further.

Certainly the administrators and trustees themselves are less than enthusiastic about Faulkner's arrival. William F. Prioleau, Jr., until recently a member of the Board of Visitors, implied in a radio talk show that abortions would go up as a result of the female invasion, as he claimed had happened at West Point. Meanwhile, in The Citadel's Math Department, all that was going up as a result of Shannon Faulkner's presence was the grade-point average. Faulkner's highest mark at the semester's end was in calculus, where she earned an A (prompting a surprised Dean Poole to comment to her that she was "certainly not a stereotypical woman"). The Math Department has in recent years invited A students to an annual party. But rather than include Faulkner, the department limited the guest list to math majors. Math professor David Trautman, who was in charge of invitations to the party, explained in an E-mail message to colleagues, "Her presence would put a damper on the evening."

Linda Ross, then a professor at The Citadel, was speaking one day with a seventy-six-year-old alumnus, and the talk turned to Faulkner's lawsuit. He asked her if she thought it possible that this young woman might prevail. "Well, it's probably an inevitable turning of the tide," Ross said, shrugging. To her amazement, the alumnus began to cry.

"I have the worst chance in society of getting a job, because I'm a white male," William H. Barnes, the senior platoon leader, shouted at me over the din in The Citadel's mess hall, a din created by the upperclassmen's tradition of berating knobs at mealtime. "And that's the major difference between me and my father." In a society where, at least since the Second World War, surpassing one's father has been an expected benchmark of American manhood, Barnes's point is a plangent one. But it's hard to say which Citadel generation is more undone by the loss of white male privilege—the young men who will never partake of a dreamed world of masculine advantage or the older men who are seeing that lived world split apart, shattered.

"I was in Vietnam in '63, and I'll defy you or Shannon or anyone else to hike through the rice paddies," the usually genial Colonel Harvey Dick, sixty-seven, a Board of Visitors member, an ex-marine, and an Army lieutenant colonel, was practically shouting from his recliner armchair in his Charleston home. He popped a Tums in his mouth. "There's just no way you can do that. . . . You can't pick up a ninety-five-pound projectile. There are certain things out there that are differences." On the wall above his head were seven bayonets. He was wearing his blue Citadel T-shirt, which matched the Citadel mementos that overwhelmed his den—Citadel mugs, hats, footballs, ceramic bulldogs. It was a room known in the Dick household as "Harvey's 'I Love Me' Room." Dick treated it as his command post—whenever the phone rang, he whipped it off the cradle and barked "Colonel Dick!"—but what he was commanding was unclear; he retired in 1993 from a sixteen-year stint as The Citadel's assistant commandant. Still, he at least knew that he was once in charge, that he once enjoyed lifetime job security as a career military man. This was something his son couldn't say: Harvey Dick II, a nuclear pipe fitter, had recently been laid off at the Charleston Naval Shipyard.

Colonel Dick wanted it known that he wasn't "one of those male-chauvinist pigs"; in fact, he believes that women are smarter than men. "Women used to let the men dominate," he said. "Maybe we need a male movement, since evidently we're coming out second on everything." He slipped another Tums from an almost empty roll. The sun was dropping as we spoke, and shadows fell across the Citadel hats and figurines in his room. "Go back and look at your Greek and Roman empires and why they fell," he said.

His wife cleared her throat. "This doesn't have anything to do with male-female," she said.

"I see a decline in this great nation of ours," Dick said. He crossed his arms and stared into the gathering darkness of the late summer afternoon. After a while, he said, "I guess I sound like a buffoon."

Unlike the cadets, the older male Citadel officials often have to face dissent from wives or daughters whose views and professional aspirations or accomplishments challenge their stand on women's proper place. Lewis Spearman, the assistant to the president, recently remarried, and his wife is a feminist paralegal who is now getting her master's degree in psychology. She says she engaged for more than a year in "shriekfests" with him over the Shannon Faulkner question before she halfheartedly came around to the Citadel party line on barring women. And, while the wife of Dean Poole may have sat on the Miss Citadel judging panel, their daughter, Mindy, had loftier ambitions. Despite the fact that she suffered from cystic fibrosis, she was an ardent skier, horseback rider, and college athlete, rising at 5 A.M. daily with her crew-team members at the University of Virginia. And, despite a double lung transplant during her junior year, she graduated in 1991 with honors and won a graduate fellowship. "She was an outstanding young lady," Poole said. "I was very proud of her." His eyes clouding over at the memory, he recalled that she had made him promise to take her to the big Corps Day parade on The Citadel's sesquicentennial. The day the father and daughter were to attend the parade was the day she died. "Sort of an interesting footnote," he said, wiping at his moist eyes. What if she had wanted to go to The Citadel? Well, actually, Poole said, she *had* talked about it. If she had persisted he would have tried to change her mind, he said, but he added, "I would never have stopped her from doing something she wanted to do."

One of the biggest spousal battles over Shannon Faulkner is waged nightly at the home of a man who might seem the least likely figure at The Citadel to wind up with a feminist wife. Probably The Citadel's most legendary elder, thanks to Pat Conroy's thinly veiled and admiring portrait of him in "The Lords of Discipline," is Lieutenant Colonel T. Nugent Courvoisie, who, as an assistant commandant in the sixties, oversaw the admission of the first African-American cadet to The Citadel. A gravelly-voiced and cigar-chomping tender tyrant, Courvoisie—or the Boo, as he is known, for obscure reasons—was a fixture at the school for more than two decades. There are two Citadel scholarships in his family name, and his visage peers down from two portraits on campus.

A courtly man, and still dapper at seventy-seven, the Boo, who has since given up cigars, insisted on picking me up at my hotel and driving me to his home, though I had a rental car sitting in the parking lot. On the drive over, he ticked off the differences between the sexes which he believed made it impossible for The Citadel to admit women—differences such as that "the average female is not as proficient athletically as the average male." When we were settled in the living room, the Boo on his recliner and his second wife, Margaret, who is also seventy-seven, in a straight-back chair, the subject of Shannon Faulkner was revisited. The first words out of Margaret's mouth were "The Citadel wants to chop the head off women." A low growl emanated from the Boo's corner. He lowered the recliner a notch. "We don't talk about it here," Margaret said—an obvious untruth. "We haven't come to blows yet, but—"

The Boo interrupted, "I have the correct view."

She retorted, "No one has the *correct* view." She turned and addressed me. "You have to understand him," she said of her husband of nine years. "This is a man who went to military prep schools and a church that was male-dominated, naturally."

The Boo interrupted, "J.C. picked twelve *men* as his disciples," he said.

Margaret rolled her eyes. "See? He even takes it into the church—and he's on such familiar ground with Christ he calls him J.C."

The Boo said, "J.C. never picked a woman, except his mother."

Margaret said, "Oh God, see, this is why we don't go into it."

But, as usual, go into it they did. As the words got batted back and forth, with Margaret doing most of the batting, the Boo levered his recliner progressively lower, until all I could see of him were the soles of his shoes.

MARGARET: You had plenty of good women soldiers in Saudi Arabia.

BOO: Plenty of pregnant ones . . .

MARGARET: What, do you think [the cadets] didn't get girls pregnant before? There've been plenty of abortions. And I know of a number of cases that, by the time [a cadet] graduated, there were four or five kids.

BOO: That's an exaggeration. Maybe two or three . . . With women, there's going to be sexual harassment.

MARGARET: Oh, honey, those cadets are harassing each other right now, all the time.

BOO: That's different. That's standard operating procedure.

In the nineteen-sixties, Margaret worked in the library at The Citadel, where she would often see Charles Foster, the first African-American cadet (who died a few years ago) alone at one of the library desks. "He would just come to the library and sit there a lot. It's hard to be the only one, to be the groundbreaker. That's why I admire this girl."

Boo's voice boomed from the depths of his recliner: "But there's no need for her. She's ruining a good thing."

Margaret gave a mock groan. "This is the last vestige of male bastionship," she said, "and it's going to kill 'em when it crumbles." Boo raised his chair halfway back up and considered Margaret. "She has a good mind," he told me after a while.

Margaret smiled. "I'm a new experience for him. He's always been military. People didn't disagree with him."

The Boo showed the way upstairs, to the attic, where he has his own "Citadel room"—a collection of Citadel memorabilia vaster than but almost identical to Dick's. Around the house, there were sketches of Boo at various points in his Citadel career. He told me that, before he retired, the cadets commissioned a portrait of him that hangs in Jenkins Hall. "Man, I looked good in that," he said. "Like a man. A leader."

Margaret didn't think so. "No, it was horrible," she said. "It didn't look like you."

"If Shannon were in my class, I'd be fired by March for sexual harassment," Colonel James Rembert, an English professor, was saying as we headed toward his classroom. He had a ramrod bearing and a certain resemblance to Ted Turner (who, it happens, sent all three of his sons to The Citadel—Beau Turner among them—and donated twenty-five million dollars to the school earlier this year). The Colonel identifies himself as one of "the last white Remberts" in South Carolina, the Remberts being a Huguenot family of

Dependency is a main theme in cadet relationships. Colonel James Rembert says that the cadets' intimate bond is "like a true marriage."
Illustration by Mark Zingarelli, originally published in *The New Yorker*

sufficiently ancient lineage to gain him admission to the St. John's Hunting Club, of South Carolina—an all-male society chaired by a Citadel alumnus. Rembert, who has a Cambridge University doctorate and wrote a book on Jonathan Swift, said he preferred the company of men, in leisure and in learning. "I've dealt with young men all my life," he went on. "I know how to play with them. I have the freedom here to imply things I couldn't with women. I don't want to have to watch what I say."

The literary work under discussion that day was "Beowulf," and the cadets agreed that it was all about "brotherhood loyalty" and, in the words of one student, "the most important characteristics of a man—glory and eternal fame." Then they turned to their papers on the topic.

"Mr. Rice," Rembert said in mock horror. "You turned in a single-spaced paper." This was a no-no. Rembert instructed him to take a pencil and "pen-e-trate"—Rembert drew the syllables out—the paper with the point. He shook his head. "What a pansy!" Rembert said. "Can't catch, can't throw, can't write." Another student was chastised for the use of the passive voice. "Never use the passive voice—it leads to effeminacy and homosexuality," Rembert told the class. "So next time you use the passive voice I'm going to make you lift up your limp wrist." Literary pointers concluded, Rembert floated the subject of Shannon Faulkner. The usual objections were raised. But then the class wandered into more interesting territory, provoked by a cadet's comment that "she would change the relationship between the men here." Just what is the nature of that relationship?

"When we are in the showers, it's very intimate," a senior cadet said. "We're one mass, naked together, and it makes us closer. . . . You're shaved, you're naked, you're afraid together. You can cry." Robert Butcher, another senior, said that the men take care of each classmate. "They'll help dress him, tuck in his shirt, shine his shoes." You mean like a mother-child relationship? I asked.

"That *is* what it is," another cadet said. "It's a family, even the way we eat—family style." A fourth cadet said, "Maybe it's a Freudian thing, but males feel more affection with each other when women are not around. Maybe we're all homosexuals."

The class groaned. "Speak for yourself, buddy," a number of cadets said, almost in a chorus.

Rembert said, "With no women, we can hug each other. There's nothing so nurturing as an infantry platoon."

The hooted-down cadet weighted in again: "When I used to wrestle in high school, we had this great tradition. Right before the game, the coach, he'd slap us really hard on the butt."

Rembert, a onetime paratrooper, said he and his skydiving buddies did that, too, right before they jumped. "First man out gets a pat right there."

Over lunch, Rembert returned to the theme of manly nurturance among Citadel men. "We hug each other," he said. One of his colleagues, "always kisses me on the cheek," he went on. "It's like a true marriage. There's an affectionate intimacy that you will find between cadets. With this security they can, without being defensive, project tenderness to each other."

Months later, I was sitting in court watching Norman Doucet, the cadet regimental commander, testify. He was showing the judge a video of the Citadel experience and explaining the various scenes. First we were shown "one of the great parts" of a knob's first day—the mothers looking weepy at the gate as their sons were led away. Doucet lingered over the head-shaving science. "This is what does it, right here," he said. "Mothers can't even tell their sons apart after this." Thus shielded from the prying maternal eye, the cadets began their new life, and the video action shifted to a typical day in the life of the Corps. But the editing made it a day as heavy on early-morning domestic chores as it was on martial activity. Much of the film was devoted to housekeeping: scenes of cadets making beds, dressing each other, sweeping, taking out the trash, all of which Doucet described as "like some kind of a ballet or a dance that's going on." This is a dance where the most important moves took place before the show, in the dressing room. "What they are doing here is the Citadel shirt tuck," Doucet said. The tuck requires that a cadet unzip his pant halfway and fold down his waistband, then stand still while his helper approaches him from the back, puts his arms around the cadet's waist, pulls the loose shirt material firmly to the back, jams it as far down in the pants as he can, and then pulls the cadet's pants up. "If you watch closely right here, this is what the fourth-class system is all about," Doucet continued. "In order to get a proper shirt tuck, you can't do it yourself—you need your classmates to do it for you. There's really a lot of dependence upon your classmates." But, as Doucet's account suggested, cadets can experience that dependence only in concealment, away from mothers, away from all women.

When a Citadel attorney asked Doucet why female cadets would pose a problem on the campus, the only issue he raised was the humiliation that cadets feel if women observed the cadets' on-campus interactions. He spoke of the shame that knobs feel when, on occasion, a woman happened to be on the parade ground while upperclassmen were disciplining them. The cadets observing in the courtroom nodded in agreement.

It may seem almost paradoxical that the fourth-class system should be so solicitous of the emotional vulnerability of its wards—the same wards it subjects to such rigors. And yet the making of Whole Men evidently requires an initial stage of infantilization. Indeed, the objective of recapitulating childhood development is plainly spelled out in The Citadel's yearbook, known as "the Sphinx." The 1990 "Sphinx" explained, "As a freshman enters, he begins to release his childhood and takes the first steps to becoming a 'Citadel Man.' . . . As a 'knob,' every aspect of life is taught, a new way to walk. . . . Knobs are told how, where, and when to walk." Reentrance into manhood for the toddling knobs occurs on Recognition Day, when the upper-classmen force the knobs to do calisthentics until they drop, then gently lift up their charges and nurse them with cups of water. At that moment, for the first time in nine months, the older cadets call the knobs by their first names and embrace them.

The relationship between knobs and upperclassmen following Recognition Day, as they are integrated into the Corps, shifts from maternal to matrimonial. The yearbooks of the last several years picture Citadel men spending a lot of time embracing and kissing. Of course, this impulse, when it is captured on film, is always carefully disarmed with a jokey caption.

One afternoon, a group of cadets recounted for me the campus's many "nudity rituals," as they jokingly called them. There's "Senior Rip-Off Day," a spring rite in which three hundred seniors literally rip each other's clothes off, burn them in a bonfire, and hug and wrestle on the ground. There's "Nude Platoon," in which a group of juniors, unclad except for their cross-webbing, run around the quad yelling, "We love the Nude Platoon!" And there's the birthday ritual, in which the birthday boy is stripped, tied to a chair, and covered with shaving cream, while his groin is coated in liquid shoe polish.

During the fall semester before graduation, the seniors receive their "band of gold" (as it is called) in the Ring Ceremony. The chaplain blesses each class ring. (Receiving the ring, which I was constantly reminded is "the biggest class ring of any college," is a near-sacrament, and the yearbooks are filled with pictures of young men holding up their rings in fervor, as if clutching a crucifix before a vampire.) Then each senior walks through a ten-foot replica of the class ring with his mother on one arm and his "date" on the other. In a sort of reverse marriage ceremony, the mother gives the cadet away. Mother and date accompany him through the towering ring; then he kisses Mother farewell and marches under the arched swords of the Junior Sword Drill, a new bride of the Corps. Several cadets and alumni told me that when a Citadel graduate marries, it is a tradition to slide the class ring over the wedding band. Indeed, I saw such an ordering of priorities on the fingers of a number of Citadel men in the courtroom.

In the late-twentieth-century setting of The Citadel, in a time when extreme insecurity and confusion about masculinity's standing run rampant, the Corps of Cadets once again seeks to obscure a domestic male paradise with an intensifying of virile showmanship and violence. The result is a ruthless intimacy, in which physical abuse stands in for physical affection, and every display of affection must be counterbalanced by a display of sadism. Knobs told me that they were forced to run through the showers while the upper-classmen "guards" knocked the soap out of their hands and, when the knobs leaned over to retrieve it the upperclassmen would unzip their pants and yell, "Don't pick it up, don't pick it up! We'll use you like we used those girls!" A former Citadel Halloween tradition, of upper-classmen dressing up—mostly in diapers and women's clothes—and collecting candy treats from knobs, has given way to "tricks" of considerable violence. (One upperclassman told me of cadets who knocked dressers over on candy-dispensing cadets and then walked on top of them.) The administration tried, unsuccessfully, to put a stop to the whole affair; too many freshmen were getting injured. And the playful pat on the butt that served to usher cadets into the brotherhood has degenerated into more invasive acts. According to a recent graduate one company of cadets recently devised a regimen in which the older cadets tested sophomores nightly with increasingly painful treatments—beatings and stompings and so forth. The process, which they dubbed "Bananarama," culminated on a night in which an unpeeled banana was produced—and shoved into a cadet's anus.

Given this precarious dynamic, it is not surprising that in the past few years at The Citadel social rage has been directed toward any men who were perceived to be gay. Several young men who were suspected of homosexual inclinations were hounded out of the school. One cadet, Herbert Parker, who said that he was falsely accused of having a sexual encounter with a male janitor, recalled a year of total isolation—cadets refused to sit near him in the mess hall or in classes—and terror: incessant threatening phone calls and death threats. The cadets and the administration—which had responded to the report of his encounter by sending out a campus-security police car with lights flashing to question him—acted "like I had murdered someone."

The scapegoating reached such brutal proportions that the counselling center recently set up a sort of group-therapy session for the targeted young men, who are known as It, as in the game of tag.

One evening after the trial, I went over to the Treehouse, a "mixed" bar in Charleston, with an upstairs gay bar and nightly drag shows on the weekends. My intention was to ask about cadet violence against gay men. I presumed that on a campus where every second epithet was "faggot" such hate crimes were all but inevitable. There were indeed a few such cases, I learned, but the circumstances were different from what I had imagined. Nor were those cases the essence of my findings that evening.

"The proper terminology for The Citadel," a customer at the bar named Chris said, "is The Closet." Up and down the bar, heads bobbed in agreement. "They love faggots like me." What he meant by "like me," however, was not that he was gay. That night, he looked like a male model—sleek black hair and a handsome, chiselled face. But on the nights he was dressed for a performance he could pass for a woman. Arching an eyebrow, Chris said, "The cadets go for the drag queens."

Chris's observation was echoed in ensuing conversations in the bar. There are thousands of cadets, presumably, who have not dated drag queens, but in two visits to the Treehouse I could find only two drag queens, out of maybe a dozen, who did not tell me of dating a cadet—and that was only because these two found Citadel men "too emotional." Cadets can also occasionally be dangerous, Chris told me. "You can get the ones who are violent. They think they want it, then afterwards they turn on you, like you made them do it." Nonetheless, a drag queen who called himself Holly had been happily involved with a cadet for three years now. Marissa, another drag queen, the reigning "Miss Treehouse, 1993–94," had gone out with one cadet, broken up, and was now in the throes of a budding romance with another. A third drag queen, who asked to be identified as Tiffany, was known to be a favorite of cadets.

As Chris and I were talking that first night, a drag queen called Lownie wandered in and settled on a bar stool. Lownie delighted in the Corps of Cadets pageantry—especially the Friday dress parades. "The parades are a big thing with the queers in Charleston," he said. "We'll have a cocktail party and go over and watch the boys. It's a very Southern-'lady' thing to do." Years ago, Lownie had been a student at the College of Charleston when he met *his* Citadel lover, and they had begun covert assignations—communicating through notes slipped in little-used books in the Citadel library. The only drawback, Lownie said, was dealing with his lover's constant emotional anxiety over making the grade at The Citadel. He was, in fact, a model macho cadet: a Junior Sword Drill member, a regimental officer, and a "hang king," who could dangle interminably from a closet rack by his fingertips. Lownie, who found such records more amusing than impressive, grinned, and said, "I used to make him wear his shako"—The Citadel's military cap—"when we were having sex. It's manhood at its most."

Lownie said he could begin to fathom his cadet's intense attachment to The Citadel—an emotion that he likened to a love affair—because he himself had spent four years in the Air Force. "The day-to-day aspect of being in a military environment is that you run around in a little bit of clothing and you are being judged as to how good a man you are by doing women's work—pressing pants, sewing, polishing shoes. You are a *better* man if you have mastery of womanly arts. . . . The camaraderie doesn't get any stronger than when you are in the barracks, sitting around at the end of the day in your briefs and T's and dogtags—like a bunch of hausfraus, talking and gossiping." The military stage set offers a false front and a welcome trapdoor—an escape hatch from the social burdens of traditional masculinity. Behind the martial backdrop, Lownie said, "you don't have to be a breadwinner. You don't have to be a leader. You can play back seat. It's a great relief. You can act like a human being and not have to act like a man."

"You know what the [cadet] I'm seeing now said to me?" Tiffany said. We were sitting in the dressing room a couple of hours before the night's performance, and as Tiffany spoke he peered into an elaborate mirror set illuminated with miniature movie-star lights, applying layer after layer of mascara and eyeliner with expert precision. "He said, 'You're more of a woman than a woman is.' And that's an exact quote." Tiffany stood up and struck a Southern belle pose by way of illustration. "I overexemplify everything a female is—my breasts, my hair, the way I hold myself." And who could better complete the hoopskirts picture than a fantasy gentleman in uniform?

Marissa, Miss Treehouse, looked up from his labors, painting row after row of fake nails with pink polish. "I love how they wear their caps slung low so you can't quite see their eyes," he said. "It's like all of us are female illusionists and they are male illusionists. A man in a uniform is a kind of dream."

Tiffany said, "For Halloween, you know what my cadet boyfriend wanted to dress as? A cadet."

The dressing-room scene before me, of a group of men tenderly helping each other get ready for the evening—an elaborate process of pinning and binding and stuffing—was not very different, in its way, from the footage in Norman Doucet's video of the cadets tucking in each other's shirts. As the drag queens conversed, they tossed stockings and Ace bandages and cosmetic bags back and forth. "Has anyone seen my mascara wand?" "O.K., who has the blush?" There was a homey comfort that reminded me of slumber parties when I was a girl, where we would put big pink spongy rollers in each other's hair and screech with laughter at the results. And suddenly it became obvious to me what was generating that void, that yearning, in the cadets' lives—and maybe in the lives of many American men. What was going on here was play—a kind of freedom and spontaneity that, in this culture, only women are permitted.

No wonder men found their Citadels, their Treehouses, where the rules of gender could be bent or escaped. For the drag queens of the Treehouse, the distinctions between the sexes are a goof, to be endlessly manipulated with fun-house-mirror glee. For cadets, despite the play set of The Citadel and the dress-up braids and ribbons, the guarding of their treehouse is a dead-serious business. Still, undercover at The Citadel, the cadets have managed to create for themselves a world in which they get half the equation that Lownie described: they can "act like human beings" in the safety of the daily domestic life of the barracks. But, in return, the institution demands that they never cease to "act like a man"—a man of cold and rigid bearing, a man no more male than Tiffany's Southern belle is female, a man that no one, humanly, can be. That they must defend their inner humanity with outer brutality may say as much about the world outside The Citadel walls as about the world within them. The cadets feel called to defend those walls. Never mind that their true ideal may not be the vaunted one of martial masculinity, just as their true enemy is not Shannon Faulkner. The cadets at The Citadel feel that something about their life and routine is worthy on its merits and is endangered from without. And in that they may be right.   ∎

■ *QUESTIONS FOR MAKING CONNECTIONS WITHIN THE READING* ■

1. In "The Naked Citadel," Susan Faludi provides a series of vignettes that describe life at the military school. Why does she present the vignettes in the order she does? Why does she start her article in Jane Bishop's classroom? Why does she then move to the courtroom? Make a chart that tracks the organization of Faludi's essay. What is the argument that Faludi is making by telling these vignettes in this order?

2. The sociologist Erving Goffman coined the term "total institutions" to describe places that become almost entirely self-enclosed and self-referential in their values and behaviors. Goffman's principal example was the mental asylum. Can we describe The Citadel accurately as a "total institution"? Are its values the product of its isolation, or does Faludi's account furnish evidence that the attitudes holding sway in The Citadel also persist outside the institution as well? Is The Citadel just an aberration, or does it tell us certain truths about our own society?

3. Faludi offers this overview of The Citadel

> In the late-twentieth-century setting of The Citadel, in a time when extreme insecurity and confusion about masculinity's standing run rampant, the Corps of Cadets once again seeks to obscure a domestic male paradise with an intensifying of virile showmanship and violence. The result is a ruthless intimacy, in which physical abuse stands in for physical affection, and every display of affection must be counterbalanced by a display of sadism.

   On the basis of the evidence Faludi provides, is this a fair assessment of the culture of The Citadel? What evidence confirms this assessment? What evidence might be said to complicate or even contradict it? What other explanations might we offer for events at The Citadel? Does masculinity have to occupy the central place in our analysis, or might other factors be more important?

■ *QUESTIONS FOR WRITING* ■

1. In what sense is Susan Faludi a feminist? If we define a feminist as someone who is specifically concerned with defending the rights of women, does she qualify? Does she regard the rights of women as practically or theoretically distinct from the rights of men? How about the needs and aspirations of women? Are these fundamentally different from the needs and aspirations of men? Does Faludi see men as "oppressors of women"? Does she imply that our society systematically empowers men while systematically disempowering women, or does disempowerment cross gender lines?

2. "The Naked Citadel" might be described as a case study of the relations between sexuality and social structures. In what ways do social structures shape sexuality at The Citadel? Does Faludi's account call into question the belief in a single, natural form of male sexual expression? Is the problem with The Citadel that natural sexuality has been perverted by linking it to relations of power? Can sexuality and power ever be separated?

▪ QUESTIONS FOR MAKING CONNECTIONS BETWEEN READINGS ▪

1. Faludi and Martha Nussbaum are both considered feminists, but are they feminists of the same kind? Do they share the same understanding of women, of women's dilemmas, and of the solutions to those dilemmas? In what ways do their feminisms intersect with other more general issues, such as the struggle for human rights? Is it possible that the degradation of different women in different contexts requires different approaches? Should we discuss *women's* rights at all, or should we concern ourselves primarily with *human* rights?

2. Like The Citadel, the People's Republic of China during Mao's later years might be described as an authoritarian society—a society that offers ordinary people little personal freedom and control over their own lives. On the basis of your reading Faludi's "The Naked Citadel" and the selections from Jasper Becker's *Hungry Ghosts*, make an argument about the origins of authoritarianism. Is it fair to say that authoritarian regimes are generally the product of evil geniuses—like Hitler and Saddam Hussein—who drag along everyone else? Do authoritarian societies maintain control over the populace simply by the exercise of brute force, or do good and well-meaning people participate in such societies willingly? If authoritarian societies are not created by evil geniuses or by the exercise of brute force, how do they come into existence?

For additional suggestions about making connections between readings, visit the Link-O-Mat and More Sample Assignments at <www.newhum.com>.

MALCOLM GLADWELL

HOW DO CULTURES CHANGE? Is it possible to control and direct cultural change? These are the questions that most interest Malcolm Gladwell, author of the best-selling book, *The Tipping Point: How Little Things Can Make a Big Difference* (2000). Gladwell first became interested in the notion that ideas might spread through culture like an epidemic while he was covering the AIDS epidemic for the *Washington Post*. In epidemiology the phrase "the tipping point" is used to describe that moment when a virus reaches critical mass, and, as Gladwell learned while doing his research, AIDS reached its tipping point in 1982, "when it went from a rare disease affecting a few gay men to a worldwide epidemic." Fascinated by this medical fact, Gladwell found himself wondering whether it also applied to the social world. That is, is there some specific point at which a fad becomes a fashion frenzy? When delinquency and mischief turn into a crime wave? When repetition leads to understanding?

The Tipping Point is the result of Gladwell's effort to understand why some ideas catch on and spread like wildfire, and others fail to attract widespread attention and wither on the vine. Drawing on work in psychology, sociology, and epidemiology, Gladwell examines events as diverse as Paul Revere's ride and the success of *Sesame Street* and *Blue's Clues* and the precipitous decline of the crime rate in New York City, which is discussed in "The Power of Context," the chapter included here. Working across these wide-ranging examples, Gladwell develops an all-encompassing model for how cultural change occurs, a model that highlights the influential role that context plays in shaping and guiding human acts and intentions.

Gladwell was born in 1963 in England and grew up in Canada. He graduated from the University of Toronto with a degree in history in 1984. Currently the Critic at Large for the *New Yorker*, Gladwell sees himself as "a kind of translator between the academic and non-academic worlds. There's just all sorts of

Gladwell, Malcolm. "The Power of Context: Bernie Goetz and the Rise and Fall of New York City Crime," *The Tipping Point: How Little Things Can Make a Big Difference.* Boston: Little, Brown, 2000. 133–168.

Quotations and biographical information from Author Q&A <http://www.gladwell.com/books2.html> and Malcolm Gladwell, interview by Toby Lester, *The Atlantic Unbound* <http://www.theatlantic.com/unbound/interviews/ba2000-03-29.htm>.

fantastic stuff out there, but there's not nearly enough time and attention paid to that act of translation. Most people leave college in their early twenties, and that ends their exposure to the academic world. To me that's a tragedy."

To learn more about Malcolm Gladwell and the role that context plays in cultural change, visit the Link-O-Mat at <www.newhum.com>.

The Power of Context
Bernie Goetz and the Rise and Fall
of New York City Crime

On December 22, 1984, the Saturday before Christmas, Bernhard Goetz left his apartment in Manhattan's Greenwich Village and walked to the IRT subway station at Fourteenth Street and Seventh Avenue. He was a slender man in his late thirties, with sandy-colored hair and glasses, dressed that day in jeans and a windbreaker. At the station, he boarded the number two downtown express train and sat down next to four young black men. There were about twenty people in the car, but most sat at the other end, avoiding the four teenagers, because they were, as eyewitnesses would say later, "horsing around" and "acting rowdy." Goetz seemed oblivious. "How are ya?" one of the four, Troy Canty, said to Goetz, as he walked in. Canty was lying almost prone on one of the subway benches. Canty and another of the teenagers, Barry Allen, walked up to Goetz and asked him for five dollars. A third youth, James Ramseur, gestured toward a suspicious-looking bulge in his pocket, as if he had a gun in there.

"What do you want?" Goetz asked.

"Give me five dollars," Canty repeated.

Goetz looked up and, as he would say later, saw that Canty's "eyes were shiny, and he was enjoying himself. . . . He had a big smile on his face," and somehow that smile and those eyes set him off. Goetz reached into his pocket and pulled out a chrome-plated five-shot Smith and Wesson .38, firing at each of the four youths in turn. As the fourth member of the group, Darrell Cabey, lay screaming on the ground, Goetz walked over to him and said, "You seem all right. Here's another," before firing a fifth bullet into Cabey's spinal cord and paralyzing him for life.

In the tumult, someone pulled the emergency brake. The other passengers ran into the next car, except for two women who remained riveted in panic. "Are you all right?" Goetz asked the first, politely. Yes, she said. The second woman was lying on the floor. She wanted Goetz to think she was dead. "Are you all right?" Goetz asked her, twice. She nodded yes. The conductor, now on the scene, asked Goetz if he was a police officer.

"No," said Goetz. "I don't know why I did it." Pause. "They tried to rip me off."

The conductor asked Goetz for his gun. Goetz declined. He walked through the doorway at the front of the car, unhooked the safety chain, and jumped down onto the tracks, disappearing into the dark of the tunnel.

In the days that followed, the shooting on the IRT caused a national sensation. The four youths all turned out to have criminal records. Cabey had been arrested previously for armed robbery, Canty for theft. Three of them had screwdrivers in their pockets. They seemed the embodiment of the kind of young thug feared by nearly all urban-dwellers, and the mysterious gunman who shot them down seemed like an avenging angel. The tabloids dubbed Goetz the "Subway Vigilante" and the "Death Wish Shooter." On radio call-in shows and in the streets, he was treated as a hero, a man who had fulfilled the secret fantasy of every New Yorker who had ever been mugged or intimidated or assaulted on the subway. On New Year's Eve, a week after the shooting, Goetz turned himself in to a police station in New Hampshire. Upon his extradition to New York City, the *New York Post* ran two pictures on its front page: one of Goetz, handcuffed and head bowed, being led into custody, and one of Troy Canty—black, defiant, eyes hooded, arms folded—being released from the hospital. The headline read, "Led Away in Cuffs While Wounded Mugger Walks to Freedom." When the case came to trial, Goetz was easily acquitted on charges of assault and attempted murder. Outside Goetz's apartment building, on the evening of the verdict, there was a raucous, impromptu street party.

1.

The Goetz case has become a symbol of a particular, dark moment in New York City history, the moment when the city's crime problem reached epidemic proportions. During the 1980s, New York City averaged well over 2,000 murders and 600,000 serious felonies a year. Underground, on the subways, conditions could only be described as chaotic. Before Bernie Goetz boarded the number two train that day, he would have waited on a dimly lit platform, surrounded on all sides by dark, damp, graffiti-covered walls. Chances are his train was late, because in 1984 there was a fire somewhere on the New York system every day and a derailment every other week. Pictures of the crime scene, taken by police, show that the car Goetz sat in was filthy, its floor littered with trash and the walls and ceiling thick with graffiti, but that wasn't unusual because in 1984 every one of the 6,000 cars in the Transit Authority fleet, with the exception of the midtown shuttle, was covered with graffiti—top to bottom, inside and out. In the winter, the cars were cold because few were adequately heated. In the summer, the cars were stiflingly hot because none were air-conditioned. Today, the number two train accelerates to over 40 miles an hour as it rumbles toward the Chambers Street express stop. But it's doubtful Goetz's train went that fast. In 1984, there were 500 "red tape" areas on the system—places where track damage had made it unsafe for trains to go more than 15 miles per hour. Fare-beating was so commonplace that it was costing the Transit Authority as much as $150 million in lost revenue annually. There were about 15,000 felonies on the system a year—a number that would hit 20,000 a year by the end of the decade—and harassment of riders by panhandlers and petty criminals was so pervasive that ridership of the trains had sunk to its lowest level in the history of the subway system. William Bratton, who was later to be a key figure in New York's successful fight against violent crime, writes in his autobiography of riding the New York subways in the 1980s after living in Boston for years, and being stunned at what he saw:

> After waiting in a seemingly endless line to buy a token, I tried to put a coin into a turnstile, and found it had been purposely jammed. Unable to pay the fare to get into the system, we had to enter through a slam gate being held open by a scruffy-looking character with his hand out; having disabled the turnstiles, he was now demanding that riders give him their tokens. Meanwhile, one of his cohorts had his mouth on the coin slots, sucking out the jammed coins and leaving his slobber. Most people were too intimidated to take these guys on: Here, take the damned token, what do I care? Other citizens were going over, under, around, or through the stiles for free. It was like going into the transit version of Dante's *Inferno.*

This was New York City in the 1980s, a city in the grip of one of the worst crime epidemics in its history. But then, suddenly and without warning, the epidemic tipped. From a high in 1990, the crime rate went into precipitious decline. Murders dropped by two-thirds. Felonies were cut in half. Other cities saw their crime drop in the same period. But in no place did the level of violence fall farther or faster. On the subways, by the end of the decade, there were 75 percent fewer felonies than there had been at the decade's start. In 1996, when Goetz went to trial a second time, as the defendant in a civil suit brought by Darrell Cabey, the case was all but ignored by the press, and Goetz himself seemed almost an anachronism. At a time when New York had become the safest big city in the country, it seemed hard to remember precisely what it was that Goetz had once symbolized. It was simply inconceivable that someone could pull a gun on someone else on the subway and be called a hero for it. . . .

3.

During the 1990s violent crime declined across the United States for a number of fairly straightforward reasons. The illegal trade in crack cocaine, which had spawned a great deal of violence among gangs and drug dealers, began to decline. The economy's dramatic recovery meant that many people who might have been lured into crime got legitimate jobs instead, and the general aging of the population meant that there were fewer people in the age range—males between eighteen and twenty-four—that is responsible for the majority of all violence. The question of why crime declined in New York City, however, is a little more complicated. In the period when the New York epidemic tipped down, the city's economy hadn't improved. It was still stagnant. In fact, the city's poorest neighborhoods had just been hit hard by the welfare cuts of the early 1990s. The waning of the crack cocaine epidemic in New York was clearly a factor, but then again, it had been in steady decline well before crime dipped. As for the aging of the population, because of heavy immigration to New York in the 1980s, the city was getting younger in the 1990s, not older. In any case, all of these trends are long-term changes that one would expect to have gradual effects. In New York the decline was anything but gradual. Something else clearly played a role in reversing New York's crime epidemic.

The most intriguing candidate for that "something else" is called the Broken Windows theory. Broken Windows was the brainchild of the criminologists James Q. Wilson and George Kelling. Wilson and Kelling argued that crime is the inevitable result of disorder. If a window is broken and left unrepaired, people walking by will conclude that no one cares and no one is in charge. Soon, more windows will be broken, and the sense of anarchy will spread from the building to the street on which it faces, sending a signal that anything goes. In a city, relatively minor problems like graffiti, public disorder, and aggressive panhandling, they write, are all the equivalent of broken windows, invitations to more serious crimes:

> Muggers and robbers, whether opportunistic or professional, believe they reduce their chances of being caught or even identified if they operate on streets where potential victims are already intimidated by prevailing conditions. If the neighborhood cannot keep a bothersome panhandler from annoying passersby, the thief may reason, it is even less likely to call the police to identify a potential mugger or to interfere if the mugging actually takes place.

This is an epidemic theory of crime. It says that crime is contagious—just as a fashion trend is contagious—that it can start with a broken window and spread to an entire community. The Tipping Point in this epidemic, though, isn't a particular kind of person. . . . It's something physical like graffiti. The impetus to engage in a certain kind of behavior is not coming from a certain kind of person but from a feature of the environment.

In the mid-1980s Kelling was hired by the New York Transit Authority as a consultant, and he urged them to put the Broken Windows theory into practice. They obliged, bringing in a new subway director by the name of David Gunn to oversee a multibillion-dollar rebuilding of the subway system. Many subway advocates, at the time, told Gunn not to worry about graffiti, to focus on the larger questions of crime and subway reliability, and it seemed like reasonable advice. Worrying about graffiti at a time when the entire system was close to collapse seems as pointless as scrubbing the decks of the *Titanic* as it headed toward the icebergs. But Gunn insisted. "The graffiti was symbolic of the collapse of the system," he says. "When you looked at the process of rebuilding the organization and morale, you had to win the battle against graffiti. Without winning that battle, all the management reforms and physical changes just weren't going to happen. We were about to put out new trains that were worth about ten million bucks apiece, and unless we did something to protect them, we knew just what would happen. They would last one day and then they would be vandalized."

Gunn drew up a new management structure and a precise set of goals and timetables aimed at cleaning the system line by line, train by train. He started with the number seven train that connects Queens to midtown Manhattan, and began experimenting with new techniques to clean off the paint. On stainless-steel cars, solvents were used. On the painted cars, the graffiti were simply painted over. Gunn made it a rule that there should be no retreat, that once a car was "reclaimed" it should never be allowed to be vandalized again. "We were religious about it," Gunn said. At the end of the number one line in the Bronx, where the trains stop before turning around and going back to Manhattan, Gunn set up a cleaning station. If a car came in with graffiti, the graffiti had to be removed during the changeover, or the car was recoved from service. "Dirty" cars, which hadn't yet been cleansed of graffiti, were never to be mixed with "clean" cars. The idea was to send an unambiguous message to the vandals themselves.

"We had a yard up in Harlem on one hundred thirty-fifth Street where the trains would lay up over night," Gunn said. "The kids would come the first night and paint the side of the train white. Then they would come the next night, after it was dry, and draw the outline. Then they would come the third night and color it in. It was a three-day job. We knew the kids would be working on one of the dirty trains, and what we would do is wait for them to finish their mural. Then we'd walk over with rollers and paint it over. The kids would be in tears, but we'd just be going up and down, up and down. It was a message to them. If you want to spend three nights of your time vandalizing a train, fine. But it's never going to see the light of day."

Gunn's graffiti cleanup took from 1984 to 1990. At that point, the Transit Authority hired William Bratton to head the transit police, and the second stage of the reclamation of the subway system began. Bratton was, like Gunn, a disciple of Broken Windows. He describes Kelling, in fact, as his intellectual mentor, and so his first step as police chief was as seemingly quixotic as Gunn's. With felonies—serious crimes—on the subway system at an all-time high, Bratton decided to crack down on fare-beating. Why? Because he believed that, like graffiti, fare-beating could be a signal, a small expression of disorder that invited much more serious crimes. An estimated

170,000 people a day were entering the system, by one route or another, without paying a token. Some were kids, who simply jumped over the turnstiles. Others would lean backward on the turnstiles and force their way through. And once one or two or three people began cheating the system, other people—who might never otherwise have considered evading the law—would join in, reasoning that if some people weren't going to pay, they shouldn't either, and the problem would snowball. The problem was exacerbated by the fact fare-beating was not easy to fight. Because there was only $1.25 at stake, the transit police didn't feel it was worth their time to pursue it, particularly when there were plenty of more serious crimes happening down on the platform and in the trains.

Bratton is a colorful, charismatic man, a born leader, and he quickly made his presence felt. His wife stayed behind in Boston, so he was free to work long hours, and he would roam the city on the subway at night, getting a sense of what the problems were and how best to fight them. First, he picked stations where fare-beating was the biggest problem, and put as many as ten policemen in plainclothes at the turnstiles. The team would nab fare-beaters one by one, handcuff them, and leave them standing, in a daisy chain, on the platform until they had a "full catch." The idea was to signal, as publicly as possible, that the transit police were now serious about cracking down on fare-beaters. Previously, police officers had been wary of pursuing fare-beaters because the arrest, the trip to the station house, the filling out of necessary forms, and the waiting for those forms to be processed took an entire day—all for a crime that usually merited no more than a slap on the wrist. Bratton retrofitted a city bus and turned it into a rolling station house, with its own fax machines, phones, holding pen, and fingerprinting facilities. Soon the turnaround time on an arrest was down to an hour. Bratton also insisted that a check be run on all those arrested. Sure enough, one out of seven arrestees had an outstanding warrant for a previous crime, and one out of twenty was carrying a weapon of some sort. Suddenly it wasn't hard to convince police officers that tackling fare-beating made sense. "For the cops it was a bonanza," Bratton writes. "Every arrest was like opening a box of Cracker Jack. What kind of toy am I going to get? Got a gun? Got a knife? Got a warrant? Do we have a murderer here? . . . After a while the bad guys wised up and began to leave their weapons home and pay their fares." Under Bratton, the number of ejections from subway stations—for drunkenness, or improper behavior—tripled within his first few months in office. Arrests for misdemeanors, for the kind of minor offenses that had gone unnoticed in the past, went up fivefold between 1990 and 1994. Bratton turned the transit police into an organization focused on the smallest infractions, on the details of life underground.

After the election of Rudolph Giuliani as mayor of New York in 1994, Bratton was appointed head of the New York City Police Department, and he applied the same strategies to the city at large. He instructed his officers to crack down on quality-of-life crimes: on the "squeegee men" who came up to drivers at New York City intersections and demanded money for washing car windows, for example, and on all the other above-ground equivalents of turn-stile-jumping and graffiti. "Previous police administration had been hand-cuffed by restrictions," Bratton says. "We took the handcuffs off. We stepped up enforcement of the laws against public drunkenness and public urination and arrested repeat violators, including those who threw empty bottles on the street or were involved in even relatively minor damage to property. . . . If you peed in the street, you were going to jail." When crime began to fall in the city—as quickly and dramatically as it had in the subways—Bratton and Giu-liani pointed to the same cause. Minor, seemingly insignificant quality-of-life crimes, they said, were Tipping Points for violent crime.

Broken Windows theory and the Power of Context are one and the same. They are both based on the premise that an epidemic can be reversed, can be tipped, by tinkering with the smallest details of the immediate environment. This is, if you think about it, quite a radical idea. Think back, for instance, to the encounter between Bernie Goetz and those four youths on the subway: Allen, Ramseur, Cabey, and Canty. At least two of them, according to some reports, appear to have been on drugs at the time of the incident. They all came from the Claremont Village housing project in one of the worst parts of the South Bronx. Cabey was, at the time, under indictment for armed robbery. Canty had a prior felony arrest for possession of stolen property. Allen had been previously arrested for attempted assault. Allen, Canty, and Ramseur also all had misdemeanor convictions, ranging from criminal mischief to petty larceny. Two years after the Goetz shooting, Ramseur was sentenced to twenty-five years in prison for rape, robbery, sodomy, sexual abuse, assault, criminal use of a firearm, and possession of stolen property. It's hard to be sur-prised when people like this wind up in the middle of a violent incident.

Then there's Goetz. He did something that is completely anomalous. White professionals do not, as a rule, shoot young black men on the subway. But if you look closely at who he was, he fits the stereotype of the kind of person who ends up in violent situations. His father was a strict disciplinar-ian with a harsh temper, and Goetz was often the focus of his father's rage. At school, he was the one teased by classmates, the last one picked for school games, a lonely child who would often leave school in tears. He worked, after graduating from college, for Westinghouse, building nuclear submarines. But he didn't last long. He was constantly clashing with his superiors over what he saw as shoddy practices and corner-cutting, and sometimes broke company and union rules by doing work that he was con-tractually forbidden to do. He took an apartment on Fourteenth Street in Manhattan, near Sixth Avenue, on a stretch of city block that was then heavy with homelessness and drug dealing. One of the doormen in the building, with whom Goetz was close, was beaten badly by muggers. Goetz became obsessed with cleaning up the neighborhood. He complained endlessly about a vacant newsstand near his building, which was used by vagrants as a trash bin and stank of urine. One night, mysteriously, it burned down, and the next day Goetz was out on the street sweeping away the debris. Once at a community meeting, he said, to the shock of others in the room, "The only way we're going to clean up this street is to get rid of the spics and niggers." In 1981, Goetz was mugged by three black youths as he entered the Canal Street station one afternoon. He ran out of the station with the three of them in pursuit. They grabbed the electronics equipment he was carrying, beat him, and threw him up against a plate-glass door, leaving him with permanent damage to his chest. With the help of an off-duty sanitation worker, Goetz managed to subdue one of his three attackers. But the experience left him embittered. He had to spend six hours in the station house, talking to police, while his assailant was released after two hours and charged, in the end, with only a misdemeanor. He applied to the city for a gun permit. He was turned down. In September 1984, his father died. Three months later, he sat down next to four black youths on the subway and started shooting.

Here, in short, was a man with an authority problem, with a strong sense that the system wasn't working, who had been the recent target of humiliation. Lillian Rubin, Goetz's biographer, writes that his choice to live on Fourteenth Street could hardly have been an accident. "For Bernie," she writes, "there seems to be something seductive about the setting. Precisely because of its deficits and discomforts, it provided him with a comprehensible target for the rage that lives inside him. By focusing it on the external world, he need not deal with his internal one. He rails about the dirt, the noise, the drunks, the crime, the pushers, the junkies. And all with good reason." Goetz's bullets, Rubin concludes, were "aimed at targets that existed as much in his past as in the present."

If you think of what happened on the number two train this way, the shooting begins to feel inevitable. Four hoodlums confront a man with apparent psychological problems. That the shooting took place on the subway seems incidental. Goetz would have shot those four kids if he had been sitting in a Burger King. Most of the formal explanations we use for criminal behavior follow along the same logic. Psychiatrists talk about criminals as people with stunted psychological development, people who have had pathological relationships with their parents, who lack adequate role models. There is a relatively new literature that talks about genes that may or may not dispose certain individuals to crime. On the popular side, there are endless numbers of books by conservatives talking about crime as a consequence of moral failure—of communities and schools and parents who no longer raise children with a respect for right and wrong. All of those theories are essentially ways of saying that the criminal is a personality type—a personality type distinguished by an insensitivity to the norms of normal society. People with stunted psychological development don't understand how to conduct healthy relationships. People with genetic predispositions to violence fly off the handle when normal people keep their cool. People who aren't taught right from wrong are oblivious to what is and what is not appropriate behavior. People who grow up poor, fatherless, and buffeted by racism don't have the same commitment to social norms as those from healthy middle-class homes. Bernie Goetz and those four thugs on the subway were, in this sense, prisoners of their own, dysfunctional, world.

But what do Broken Windows and the Power of Context suggest? Exactly the opposite. They say that the criminal—far from being someone who acts for fundamental, intrinsic reasons and who lives in his own world—is actually someone acutely sensitive to his environment, who is alert to all kinds of cues, and who is prompted to commit crimes based on his perception of the world around him. That is an incredibly radical—and in some sense unbelievable— idea. There is an even more radical dimension here. The Power of Context is an environmental argument. It says that behavior is a function of social context. But it is a very strange kind of environmentalism. In the 1960s, liberals made a similar kind of argument, but when they talked about the importance of environment they were talking about the importance of fundamental social factors: crime, they said, was the result of social injustice, of structural economic inequities, of unemployment, of racism, of decades of institutional and social neglect, so that if you wanted to stop crime you had to undertake some fairly heroic steps. But the Power of Context says that what really matters is little things. The Power of Context says that the showdown on the subway between Bernie Goetz and those four youths had very little to do, in the end, with the tangled psychological pathology of Goetz, and very little as well to do with the background and poverty of the four youths who accosted him, and everything to do with the message sent by the graffiti on the walls and the disorder at the turnstiles. The Power of Context says you don't have to solve the big problems to solve crime. You can prevent crimes just by scrubbing off graffiti and arresting fare-beaters. . . . This is what I meant when I called the Power of Context a radical theory. Giuliani and Bratton—far from being conservatives, as they are commonly identified—actually represent on the question of crime the most extreme liberal position imaginable, a position so extreme that it is almost impossible to accept. How can it be that what was going on in Bernie Goetz's head doesn't matter? And if it is really true that it doesn't matter, why is that fact so hard to believe?

4.

[Elsewhere], . . . I talked about two seemingly counterintuitive aspects of persuasion. One was the study that showed how people who watched Peter Jennings on ABC were more likely to vote Republican than people who watched either Tom Brokaw or Dan Rather because, in some unconscious way, Jennings was able to signal his affection for Republican candidates. The second study showed how people who were charismatic could—without saying anything and with the briefest of exposures—infect others with their emotions. The implications of those two studies go to the heart of the Law of the Few, because they suggest that what we think of as inner states—preferences and emotions—are actually powerfully and imperceptibly influenced by seemingly inconsequential personal influences, by a newscaster we watch for a few minutes a day or by someone we sit next to, in silence, in a two-minute experiment. The essence of the Power of Context is that the same thing is true for certain kinds of environments—that in ways that we don't necessarily appreciate, our inner states are the result of our outer circumstances. The field of psychology is rich with experiments that demonstrate this fact. . . .

In the early 1970s, a group of social scientists at Stanford University, led by Philip Zimbardo, decided to create a mock prison in the basement of the university's psychology building. They took a thirty-five-foot section of corridor and created a cell block with a prefabricated wall. Three small, six- by nine-foot cells were created from laboratory rooms and given steel-barred, black-painted doors. A closet was turned into a solitary confinement cell. The group then advertised in the local papers for volunteers, men who would agree to participate in the experiment. Seventy-five people applied, and from those Zimbardo and his colleagues picked the 21 who appeared the most normal and healthy on psychological tests. Half of the group were chosen, at random, to be guards, and were given uniforms and dark glasses and told that their responsibility was to keep order in the prison. The other half were told that they were to be prisoners. Zimbardo got the Palo Alto Police Department to "arrest" the prisoners in their homes, cuff them, bring them to the station house, charge them with a fictitious crime, fingerprint them, then blindfold them and bring them to the prison Psychology Department basement. Then they were stripped and given a prison uniform to wear, with a number on the front and back that was to serve as their only means of identification for the duration of their incarceration.

The purpose of the experiment was to try to find out why prisons are such nasty places. Was it because prisons are full of nasty people, or was it because prisons are such nasty environments that they make people nasty? In the answer to that question is obviously the answer to the question posed by Bernie Goetz and the subway cleanup, which is how much influence does immediate environment have on the way people behave? What Zimbardo found out shocked him. The guards, some of whom had previously identified themselves as pacifists, fell quickly into the role of hard-bitten disciplinarians. The first night they woke up the prisoners at two in the morning and made them do pushups, line up against the wall, and perform other arbitrary tasks. On the morning of the second day, the prisoners rebelled. They ripped off their numbers and barricaded themselves in their cells. The guards responded by stripping them, spraying them with fire extinguishers, and throwing the leader of the rebellion into solitary confinement. "There were times when we were pretty abusive, getting right in their faces and yelling at them," one guard remembers. "It was part of the whole atmosphere of terror." As the experiment progressed, the guards got systematically crueler and more sadistic. "What we were unprepared for was the intensity of the change and the speed at which it happened," Zimbardo says. The guards were making the prisoners say to one another they loved each other, and making them march down the hallway, in handcuffs, with paper bags over their heads. "It was completely the opposite from the way I conduct myself now," another guard remembers. "I think I was positively creative in terms of my mental cruelty." After 36 hours, one prisoner began to get hysterical, and had to be released. Four more then had to be released because of "extreme emotional depression, crying, rage, and acute anxiety." Zimbardo had originally intended to have the experiment run for two weeks. He called it off after six days. "I realize now," one prisoner said after the experiment was over, "that no matter how together I thought I was inside my head, my prisoner behavior was often less under my control than I realized." Another said: "I began to feel that I was losing my identity, that the person I call ———, the person who volunteered to get me into this prison (because it was a prison to me, it still is a prison to me, I don't regard it as an experiment or a simulation . . .) was distant from me, was remote, until finally I wasn't that person. I was 416. I was really my number and 416 was really going to have to decide what to do."

Zimbardo's conclusion was that there are specific situations so powerful that they can overwhelm our inherent predispositions. The key word here is situation. Zimbardo isn't talking about environment, about the major external influences on all of our lives. He's not denying that how we are raised by our parents affects who we are, or that the kinds of schools we went to, the friends we have, or the neighborhoods we live in affect our behavior. All of these things are undoubtedly important. Nor is he denying that our genes play a role in determining who we are. Most psychologists believe that nature—genetics—accounts for about half of the reason why we tend to act the way we do. His point is simply that there are certain times and places and conditions when much of that can be swept away, that there are instances where you can take normal people from good schools and happy families and good neighborhoods and powerfully affect their behavior merely by changing the immediate details of their situation. . . .

The mistake we make in thinking of character as something unified and all-encompassing is very similar to a kind of blind spot in the way we process information. Psychologists call this tendency the Fundamental Attribution Error (FAE), which is a fancy way of saying that when it comes to interpreting other people's behavior, human beings invariably make the mistake of overestimating the importance of fundamental character traits and underestimating the importance of the situation and context. We will always reach for a "dispositional" explanation for events, as opposed to a contextual explanation. In one experiment, for instance, a group of people are told to watch two sets of similarly talented basketball players, the first of whom are shooting baskets in a well-lighted gym and the second of whom are shooting baskets in a badly lighted gym (and obviously missing a lot of shots). Then they are asked to judge how good the players were. The players in the well-lighted gym were considered superior. In another example, a group of people are brought in for an experiment and told they are going to play a quiz game. They are paired off and they draw lots. One person gets a card that says he or she is going to be the "Contestant." The other is told he or she is going to be the "Questioner." The Questioner is then asked to draw up a list of ten "challenging but not impossible" questions based on areas of particular interest or expertise, so someone who is into Ukrainian folk music might come up with a series of questions based on Ukrainian folk music. The questions are posed to the Contestant, and after the quiz is over, both parties are asked to estimate the level of general knowledge of the other. Invariably, the Contestants rate the Questioners as being a lot smarter than they themselves are.

You can do these kinds of experiments a thousand different ways and the answer almost always comes out the same way. This happens even when you give people a clear and immediate environmental explanation of the behavior they are being asked to evaluate: that the gym, in the first case, has few lights on; that the Contestant is being asked to answer the most impossibly biased and rigged set of questions. In the end, this doesn't make much difference. There is something in all of us that makes us instinctively want to explain the world around us in terms of people's essential attributes: he's a better basketball player, that person is smarter than I am.

We do this because . . . we are a lot more attuned to personal cues than contextual cues. The FAE also makes the world a much simpler and more understandable place. . . . The psychologist Walter Mischel argues that the human mind has a kind of "reducing valve" that "creates and maintains the perception of continuity even in the face of perpetual observed changes in actual behavior." He writes:

> When we observe a woman who seems hostile and fiercely independent some of the time but passive, dependent and feminine on other occasions, our reducing valve usually makes us choose between the two syndromes. We decide that one pattern is in the service of the other, or that both are in the service of a third motive. She must be a really castrating lady with a façade of passivity—or perhaps she is a warm, passive-dependent woman with a surface defense of aggressiveness. But perhaps nature is bigger than our concepts and it is possible for the lady to be a hostile, fiercely independent, passive, dependent, feminine, aggressive, warm, castrating person all-in-one. Of course which of these she is at any particular moment would not be random or capricious—it would depend on who she is with, when, how, and much, much more. But each of these aspects of her self may be a quite genuine and real aspect of her total being.

Character, then, isn't what we think it is or, rather, what we want it to be. It isn't a stable, easily identifiable set of closely related traits, and it only seems that way because of a glitch in the way our brains are organized. Character is more like a bundle of habits and tendencies and interests, loosely bound together and dependent, at certain times, on circumstance and context. The reason that most of us seem to have a consistent character is that most of us are really good at controlling our environment. . . .

5.

Some years ago two Princeton University psychologists, John Darley and Daniel Batson, decided to conduct a study inspired by the biblical story of the Good Samaritan. As you may recall, that story, from the New Testament Gospel of Luke, tells of a traveler who has been beaten and robbed and left for dead by the side of the road from Jerusalem to Jericho. Both a priest and a Levite—worthy, pious men—came upon the man but did not stop, "passing by on the other side." The only man to help was a Samaritan—the member of a despised minority—who "went up to him and bound up his wounds" and took him to an inn. Darley and Batson decided to replicate that study at the Princeton Theological Seminary. This was an experiment very much in the tradition of the FAE, and it is an important demonstration of how the Power of Context has implications for the way we think about social epidemics of all kinds, not just violent crime.

Darley and Batson met with a group of seminarians, individually, and asked each one to prepare a short, extemporaneous talk on a given biblical theme, then walk over to a nearby building to present it. Along the way to the presentation, each student ran into a man slumped in an alley, head down, eyes closed, coughing and groaning. The question was, who would stop and help? Darley and Batson introduced three variables into the experiment, to make its results more meaningful. First, before the experiment even started, they gave the students a questionnaire about why they had chosen to study theology. Did they see religion as a means of personal and spiritual fulfillment? Or were they looking for a practical tool for finding meaning in everyday life? Then they varied the subject of the theme the students were asked to talk about. Some were asked to speak on the relevance of the professional clergy to the religious vocation. Others were given the parable of the Good Samaritan. Finally, the instructions given by the experimenters to each student varied as well. In some of the cases, as he sent the students on their way, the experimenter would look at his watch and say, "Oh, you're late. They were expecting you a few minutes ago. We'd better get moving." In other cases, he would say, "It will be a few minutes before they're ready for you, but you might as well head over now."

If you ask people to predict which seminarians played the Good Samaritan (and subsequent studies have done just this) their answers are highly consistent. They almost all say that the students who entered the ministry to help people and those reminded of the importance of compassion by having just read the parable of the Good Samaritan will be the most likely to stop. Most of us, I think, would agree with those conclusions. In fact, neither of those factors made any difference. "It is hard to think of a context in which norms concerning helping those in distress are more salient than for a person thinking about the Good Samaritan, and yet it did not significantly increase helping behavior," Darley and Batson concluded. "Indeed, on several occasions, a seminary student going to give his talk on the parable of the

Good Samaritan literally stepped over the victim as he hurried on his way." The only thing that really mattered was whether the student was in a rush. Of the group that was, 10 percent stopped to help. Of the group who knew they had a few minutes to spare, 63 percent stopped.

What this study is suggesting, in other words, is that the convictions of your heart and the actual contents of your thoughts are less important, in the end, in guiding your actions than the immediate context of your behavior. The words "Oh, you're late" had the effect of making someone who was ordinarily compassionate into someone who was indifferent to suffering— of turning someone, in that particular moment, into a different person. Epidemics are, at their root, about this very process of transformation. When we are trying to make an idea or attitude or product tip, we're trying to change our audience in some small yet critical respect: we're trying to infect them, sweep them up in our epidemic, convert them from hostility to acceptance. That can be done through the influence of special kinds of people, people of extraordinary personal connection. That's the Law of the Few. It can be done by changing the content of communication, by making a message so memorable that it sticks in someone's mind and compels them to action. That is the Stickiness Factor. I think that both of those laws make intuitive sense. But we need to remember that small changes in context can be just as important in tipping epidemics, even though that fact appears to violate some of our most deeply held assumptions about human nature.

This does not mean that our inner psychological states and personal histories are not important in explaining our behavior. An enormous percentage of those who engage in violent acts, for example, have some kind of psychiatric disorder or come from deeply disturbed backgrounds. But there is a world of difference between being inclined toward violence and actually committing a violent act. A crime is a relatively rare and aberrant event. For a crime to be committed, something extra, something additional, has to happen to tip a troubled person toward violence, and what the Power of Context is saying is that those Tipping Points may be as simple and trivial as everyday signs of disorder like graffiti and fare-beating. The implications of this idea are enormous. The previous notion that disposition is everything— that the cause of violent behavior is always "sociopathic personality" or "deficient superego" or the inability to delay gratification or some evil in the genes—is, in the end, the most passive and reactive of ideas about crime. It says that once you catch a criminal you can try to help him get better—give him Prozac, put him in therapy, try to rehabilitate him—but there is very little you can do to prevent crime from happening in the first place. . . .

Once you understand that context matters, however, that specific and relatively small elements in the environment can serve as Tipping Points, that defeatism is turned upside down. Environmental Tipping Points are things that we can change: we can fix broken windows and clean up graffiti and change the signals that invite crime in the first place. Crime can be more than understood. It can be prevented. There is a broader dimension to this.

Judith Harris has convincingly argued that peer influence and community influence are more important than family influence in determining how children turn out. Studies of juvenile delinquency and high school drop-out rates, for example, demonstrate that a child is better off in a good neighborhood and a troubled family than he or she is in a troubled neighborhood and a good family. We spend so much time celebrating the importance and power of family influence that it may seem, at first blush, that this can't be true. But in reality it is no more than an obvious and commonsensical extension of the Power of Context, because it says simply that children are powerfully shaped by their external environment, that the features of our immediate social and physical world—the streets we walk down, the people we encounter—play a huge role in shaping who we are and how we act. It isn't just serious criminal behavior, in the end, that is sensitive to environmental cues, it is all behavior. Weird as it sounds, if you add up the meaning of the Stanford prison experiment and the New York subway experiment, they suggest that it is possible to be a better person on a clean street or in a clean subway than in one littered with trash and graffiti.

"In a situation like this, you're in a combat situation," Goetz told his neighbor Myra Friedman, in an anguished telephone call just days after the shooting. "You're not thinking in a normal way. Your memory isn't even working normally. You are so hyped up. Your vision actually changes. Your field of view changes. Your capabilities change. What you are capable of changes." He acted, Goetz went on, "viciously and savagely. . . . If you corner a rat and you are about to butcher it, okay? The way I responded was viciously and savagely, just like that, like a rat."

Of course he did. He was in a rat hole.   ■

■ *QUESTIONS FOR MAKING CONNECTIONS WITHIN THE READING* ■

1 "The Power of Context" is one of the middle chapters in Malcolm Gladwell's book, *The Tipping Point: How Little Things Can Make a Big Difference.* In "The Power of Context," Gladwell refers to the three principles that govern what he calls "the epidemic transmission" of an idea: the Law of the Few, the Stickiness Factor, and the Power of Context. He provides thumbnail sketches of the first two principles in this chapter, along with an elaboration of the Power of Context. What is "the law of the few? What is "the Stickiness Factor"? How much can you piece together about the first two principles from what Gladwell presents in "The Power of Context"?

2. Gladwell states that the "Broken Windows theory and the Power of Context are one and the same." What is the "Broken Windows theory" of crime? How would one go about testing this theory? What other theories are available to explain the cause of crime? Does it matter which theory one accepts?

3. Why is it a mistake to think of "character as something unified and all-encompassing"? If we accept the alternative, namely, that character is

fragmented and situation specific, what follows? How is this meant to change one's understanding of criminals and their behavior? Of law-abiding citizens and their behavior?

■ QUESTIONS FOR WRITING ■

1. Toward the end of "The Power of Context," Gladwell asserts that his discussion of the relationship between criminal activity and local context has implications that "are enormous." Gladwell leaves it to his readers to spell out these implications. How would our social structure, our criminal system, our modes of education have to change if we abandoned what Gladwell terms our "most passive and reactive ideas about crime"?

2. Gladwell argues that "small changes in context" can play a major role in determining whether an idea takes off or disappears without a trace. This fact, he goes on, "appears to violate some of our most deeply held assumptions about human nature." What does "human nature" mean, if one accepts the argument Gladwell makes in "The Power of Context"? Is it possible to create any form of human behavior just by manipulating the contextual background? Does Gladwell's view suggest that humans are freer than previously thought or that their behavior is more fully determined than previously thought possible?

■ QUESTIONS FOR MAKING CONNECTIONS BETWEEN READINGS ■

1. "Down with Dualism" concludes with Frans de Waal's assertion "that distress at the sight of another's pain is an impulse over which we exert no control." Is compassion an intrinsic part of humans, or is it subject to the "power of context" that Gladwell has described? Does Gladwell's discussion of human character reinforce de Waal's argument about human evolution, or does it call that argument into question? Does sensitivity to context have any necessary selective value for the evolution of the species?

2. In "The Naked Citadel," Susan Faludi provides a rich description of how lives are lived in an alternate social structure—the military academy. Does Malcolm Gladwell's account help to explain why Shannon Faulkner wasn't welcomed into the academy? Did Faulkner's appearance cause the academy to "tip"? Does Gladwell's theory have any predictive value? That is, could it tell us, ahead of time, whether the academy would be transformed by being required to admit women?

For additional suggestions about making connections between readings, visit the Link-O-Mat and More Sample Assignments at <www.newhum.com>.

JANE GOODALL

JANE GOODALL is an internationally renowned primatologist and conservationist who has spent more than twenty-five years living in the jungles of Tanzania studying chimpanzees and now travels the world speaking on behalf of animal rights. Goodall first arrived in Kenya in 1957 and sought out the famous anthropologist Louis Leakey in hopes of getting a job studying animals. Leakey, seeing Goodall's lack of a college education as an advantage, since it meant that her mind was "uncluttered by academia," allowed her to assist him with his work and eventually encouraged her to devote all her energies to studying chimpanzees in the Gombe, a rugged, mountainous region in Tanzania. Although many people at the time doubted that a woman living on her own in the wild could survive, let alone complete a scientifically significant project, Goodall revolutionized the study of primates through her unorthodox approach to observation in the wild and successfully established the longest running field study of animals in their natural habitat.

In her years in the wild, Goodall came to see that chimpanzees are highly intelligent, emotional creatures who live in complex social groups. She also discovered that chimpanzees make and use tools, a skill long assumed to be possessed by only humans. While this research has compelled the scientific community to reassess how primates should be studied, Goodall's larger project has become helping the general public recognize that there are environmental, psychic, and spiritual consequences that follow from treating animals inhumanely and from not living in harmony with the natural world. Thus, while the scientific community continues to rely on chimpanzees to pursue medical research, Goodall insists that we recognize that "it isn't only human beings who have personality, who are capable of rational thought [and] emotions like joy and sorrow." It is Goodall's many years in the Gombe that have shown her the perils of allowing the abuse of animals and the destruction of their natural habitats to continue: "Living under the

Goodall, Jane. Selections from *Through a Window: My Thirty Years with the Chimpanzees of Gombe*, "The Mind of the Chimpanzee," 12–23; "Bridging the Gap," 206–216. Boston: Houghton Mifflin Company, 2000.

Biographical information and quotations from the Jane Goodall Institute <http://www.janegoodall.org/index.html> and "Jane Goodall's Wild Chimpanzees," PBS Nature series, <http://www.pbs.org/wnet/nature/goodall/story.html>.

skies, the forest is for me a temple, a cathedral made of tree canopies and dancing light, especially when it's raining and quiet. That's heaven on earth for me. I can't imagine going through life without being tuned into the mystical side of nature."

To learn more about Jane Goodall and her conservation efforts, visit the Link-O-Mat at <www.newhum.com>.

Selections from
Through a Window
My Thirty Years with the Chimpanzees of Gombe

The Mind of the Chimpanzee

Often I have gazed into a chimpanzee's eyes and wondered what was going on behind them. I used to look into Flo's, she so old, so wise. What did she remember of her young days? David Greybeard had the most beautiful eyes of them all, large and lustrous, set wide apart. They somehow expressed his whole personality, his serene self-assurance, his inherent dignity—and, from time to time, his utter determination to get his way. For a long time I never liked to look a chimpanzee straight in the eye—I assumed that, as is the case with most primates, this would be interpreted as a threat or at least as a breach of good manners. Not so. As long as one looks with gentleness, without arrogance, a chimpanzee will understand, and may even return the look. And then—or such is my fantasy—it is as though the eyes are windows into the mind. Only the glass is opaque so that the mystery can never be fully revealed.

I shall never forget my meeting with Lucy, an eight-year-old home-raised chimpanzee. She came and sat beside me on the sofa and, with her face very close to mine, searched in my eyes—for what? Perhaps she was looking for signs of mistrust, dislike, or fear, since many people must have been somewhat disconcerted when, for the first time, they came face to face with a grown chimpanzee. Whatever Lucy read in my eyes clearly satisfied her for she suddenly put one arm round my neck and gave me a generous and very chimp-like kiss, her mouth wide open and laid over mine. I was accepted.

For a long time after that encounter I was profoundly disturbed. I had been at Gombe for about fifteen years then and I was quite familiar with chimpanzees in the wild. But Lucy, having grown up as a human child, was like a changeling, her essential chimpanzeeness overlaid by the various human behaviours she had acquired over the years. No longer purely chimp yet eons away from humanity, she was man-made, some other kind of being. I watched, amazed, as she opened the refrigerator and various cupboards, found bottles and a glass, then poured herself a gin and tonic. She took the drink to the TV, turned the set on, flipped from one channel to another then, as though in disgust, turned it off again. She selected a glossy magazine from the table and, still carrying her drink, settled in a comfortable chair. Occasionally, as she leafed through the magazine she identified something she saw, using the signs of ASL, the American Sign Language used by the deaf. I, of course, did not understand, but my hostess, Jane Temerlin (who was also Lucy's 'mother'), translated: 'That dog,' Lucy commented, pausing at a photo of a small white poodle. She turned the page. 'Blue,' she declared, pointing then signing as she gazed at a picture of a lady advertising some kind of soap powder and wearing a brilliant blue dress. And finally, after some vague hand movements—perhaps signed mutterings—'This Lucy's, this mine,' as she closed the magazine and laid it on her lap. She had just been taught, Jane told me, the use of the possessive pronouns during the thrice weekly ASL lessons she was receiving at the time.

The book written by Lucy's human 'father,' Maury Temerlin, was entitled *Lucy, Growing Up Human*. And in fact, the chimpanzee is more like us than is any other living creature. There is close resemblance in the physiology of our two species and genetically, in the structure of the DNA, chimpanzees and humans differ by only just over one percent. This is why medical research uses chimpanzees as experimental animals when they need substitutes for humans in the testing of some drug or vaccine. Chimpanzees can be infected with just about all known human infectious diseases including those, such as hepatitis B and AIDS, to which other nonhuman animals (except gorillas, orangutans and gibbons) are immune. There are equally striking similarities between humans and chimpanzees in the anatomy and wiring of the brain and nervous system, and—although many scientists have been reluctant to admit to this—in social behaviour, intellectual ability, and the emotions. The notion of an evolutionary continuity in physical structure from pre-human ape to modern man has long been morally acceptable to most scientists. That the same might hold good for [the] mind was generally considered an absurd hypothesis—particularly by those who used, and often misused, animals in their laboratories. It is, after all, convenient to believe that the creature you are using, while it may react in disturbingly human-like ways, is, in fact, merely a mindless and, above all, unfeeling, 'dumb' animal.

When I began my study at Gombe in 1960 it was not permissible—at least not in ethological circles—to talk about an animal's mind. Only humans had minds. Nor was it quite proper to talk about animal personality. Of course everyone knew that they *did* have their own unique characters—everyone who had ever owned a dog or other pet was aware of that. But ethologists, striving to make theirs a 'hard' science, shied away from the task of trying to explain such things objectively. One respected ethologist, while acknowledging that there was 'variability between individual animals,' wrote that it was best that this fact be 'swept under the carpet.' At that time ethological carpets fairly bulged with all that was hidden beneath them.

How naïve I was. As I had not had an undergraduate science education I didn't realize that animals were not supposed to have personalities, or to think, or to feel emotions or pain. I had no idea that it would have been more appropriate to assign each of the chimpanzees a number rather than a name when I got to know him or her. I didn't realize that it was not scientific to discuss behaviour in terms of motivation or purpose. And no one had told me that terms such as *childhood* and *adolescence* were uniquely human phases of the life cycle, culturally determined, not to be used when referring to young chimpanzees. Not knowing, I freely made use of all those forbidden terms and concepts in my initial attempt to describe, to the best of my ability, the amazing things I had observed at Gombe.

I shall never forget the response of a group of ethologists to some remarks I made at an erudite seminar. I described how Figan, as an adolescent, had learned to stay behind in camp after senior males had left, so that we could give him a few bananas for himself. On the first occasion he had, upon seeing the fruits, uttered loud, delighted food calls: whereupon a couple of the older males had charged back, chased after Figan, and taken his bananas. And then, coming to the point of the story, I explained how, on the next occasion, Figan had actually suppressed his calls. We could hear little sounds, in his throat, but so quiet that none of the others could have heard them. Other young chimps, to whom we tried to smuggle fruit without the knowledge of their elders, never learned such self-control. With shrieks of glee they would fall to, only to be robbed of their booty when the big males charged back. I had expected my audience to be as fascinated and impressed as I was. I had hoped for an exchange of views about the chimpanzee's undoubted intelligence. Instead there was a chill silence, after which the chairman hastily changed the subject. Needless to say, after being thus snubbed, I was very reluctant to contribute any comments, at any scientific gathering, for a very long time. Looking back, I suspect that everyone was interested, but it was, of course, not permissible to present a mere 'anecdote' as evidence for anything.

The editorial comments on the first paper I wrote for publication demanded that every *he* or *she* be replaced with *it*, and every *who* be replaced with *which*. Incensed, I, in my turn, crossed out the *its* and *whichs* and scrawled back the original pronouns. As I had no desire to carve a niche for myself in the world of science, but simply wanted to go on living among and learning about chimpanzees, the possible reaction of the editor of the learned journal did not trouble me. In fact I won that round: the paper when finally published did confer upon the chimpanzees the dignity of their appropriate genders and properly upgraded them from the status of mere 'things' to essential Being-ness.

However, despite my somewhat truculent attitude, I did want to learn, and I was sensible of my incredible good fortune in being admitted to Cambridge. I wanted to get my PhD, if only for the sake of Louis Leakey and the other people who had written letters in support of my admission. And how lucky I was to have, as my supervisor, Robert Hinde. Not only because I thereby benefited from his brilliant mind and clear thinking, but also because I doubt that I could have found a teacher more suited to my particular needs and personality. Gradually he was able to cloak me with at least some of the trappings of a scientist. Thus although I continued to hold to most of my convictions—that animals had personalities; that they could feel happy or sad or fearful; that they could feel pain; that they could strive towards planned goals and achieve greater success if they were highly motivated—I soon realized that these personal convictions were, indeed, difficult to prove. It was best to be circumspect—at least until I had gained some credentials and credibility. And Robert gave me wonderful advice on how best to tie up some of my more rebellious ideas with scientific ribbon. 'You can't *know* that Fifi was jealous,' he admonished on one occasion. We argued a little. And then: 'Why don't you just say *If Fifi were a human child we would say she was jealous.*' I did.

It is not easy to study emotions even when the subjects are human. I know how I feel if I am sad or happy or angry, and if a friend tells me that he is feeling sad, happy or angry, I assume that his feelings are similar to mine. But of course I cannot know. As we try to come to grips with the emotions of beings progressively more different from ourselves the task, obviously, becomes increasingly difficult. If we ascribe human emotions to non-human animals we are accused of being anthropomorphic—a cardinal sin in ethology. But is it so terrible? If we test the effect of drugs on chimpanzees because they are biologically so similar to ourselves, if we accept that there are dramatic similarities in chimpanzee and human brain and nervous system, is it not logical to assume that there will be similarities also in at least the more basic feelings, emotions, moods of the two species?

In fact, all those who have worked long and closely with chimpanzees have no hesitation in asserting that chimps experience emotions similar to those which in ourselves we label pleasure, joy, sorrow, anger, boredom and so on. Some of the emotional states of the chimpanzee are so obviously similar to ours that even an inexperienced observer can understand what is going on. An infant who hurls himself screaming to the ground, face contorted, hitting out with his arms at any nearby object, banging his head, is clearly having a tantrum. Another youngster, who gambols around his mother, turning somersaults, pirouetting and, every so often, rushing up to her and tumbling into her lap, patting her or pulling her hand towards him in a request for tickling, is obviously filled with *joie de vivre*. There are few observers who would not unhesitatingly ascribe his behaviour to a happy, carefree state of well-being. And one cannot watch chimpanzee infants for long without realizing that they have the same emotional need for affection and reassurance as human children. An adult male, reclining in the shade after a good meal, reaching benignly to play with an infant or idly groom an adult female, is clearly in a good mood. When he sits with bristling hair, glaring at his subordinates and threatening them, with irritated gestures, if they come too close, he is clearly feeling cross and grumpy. We make these judgements because the similarity of so much of a chimpanzee's behaviour to our own permits us to empathize.

It is hard to empathize with emotions we have not experienced. I can imagine, to some extent, the pleasure of a female chimpanzee during the act of procreation. The feelings of her male partner are beyond my knowledge— as are those of the human male in the same context. I have spent countless hours watching mother chimpanzees interacting with their infants. But not until I had an infant of my own did I begin to understand the basic, powerful instinct of mother-love. If someone accidentally did something to frighten Grub, or threaten his well-being in any way, I felt a surge of quite irrational anger. How much more easily could I then understand the feelings of the chimpanzee mother who furiously waves her arm and barks in threat at an individual who approaches her infant too closely, or at a playmate who inadvertently hurts her child. And it was not until I knew the numbing grief that gripped me after the death of my second husband that I could even begin to appreciate the despair and sense of loss that can cause young chimps to pine away and die when they lose their mothers.

Empathy and intuition can be of tremendous value as we attempt to understand certain complex behavioural interactions, provided that the behaviour, as it occurs, is recorded precisely and objectively. Fortunately I have seldom found it difficult to record facts in an orderly manner even during times of powerful emotional involvement. And 'knowing' intuitively how a chimpanzee is feeling—after an attack, for example—may help one to understand what happens next. We should not be afraid at least to try to make use of our close evolutionary relationship with the chimpanzees in our attempts to interpret complex behaviour.

Today, as in Darwin's time, it is once again fashionable to speak of and study the animal mind. This change came about gradually, and was, at least in part, due to the information collected during careful studies of animal societies in the field. As these observations became widely known, it was impossible to brush aside the complexities of social behaviour that were revealed in species after species. The untidy clutter under the ethological carpets was brought out and examined, piece by piece. Gradually it was realized that parsimonious explanations of apparently intelligent behaviours were often misleading. This led to a succession of experiments that, taken together, clearly prove that many intellectual abilities that had been thought unique to humans were actually present, though in a less highly developed form, in other, non-human beings. Particularly, of course, in the non-human primates and especially in chimpanzees.

When first I began to read about human evolution, I learned that one of the hallmarks of our own species was that we, and only we, were capable of making tools. *Man the Toolmaker* was an oft-cited definition—and this despite the careful and exhaustive research of Wolfgang Kohler and Robert Yerkes on the tool-using and tool-making abilities of chimpanzees. Those studies, carried out independently in the early twenties, were received with skepticism. Yet both Kohler and Yerkes were respected scientists, and both had a profound understanding of chimpanzee behaviour. Indeed, Kohler's descriptions of the personalities and behaviour of the various individuals in his colony, published in his book *The Mentality of Apes,* remain some of the most vivid and colourful ever written. And his experiments, showing how chimpanzees could stack boxes, then climb the unstable constructions to reach fruit suspended from the ceiling, or join two short sticks to make a pole long enough to rake in fruit otherwise out of reach, have become classic, appearing in almost all textbooks dealing with intelligent behaviour in non-human animals.

By the time systematic observations of tool-using came from Gombe those pioneering studies had been largely forgotten. Moreover, it was one thing to know that humanized chimpanzees in the lab could use implements: it was quite another to find that this was a naturally occurring skill in the wild. I well remember writing to Louis about my first observations, describing how David Greybeard not only used bits of straw to fish for termites—but actually stripped leaves from a stem and thus *made* a tool. And I remember too receiving the now oft-quoted telegram he sent in response to my letter: 'Now we must redefine *tool,* redefine *Man,* or accept chimpanzees as humans.'

There were, initially, a few scientists who attempted to write off the termiting observations, even suggesting that I had taught the chimps! By and large, though, people were fascinated by the information and by the subsequent observations of the other contexts in which the Gombe chimpanzees used objects as tools. And there were only a few anthropologists who objected when I suggested that the chimpanzees probably passed their tool-using traditions from one generation to the next, through observations, imitation and practice, so that each population might be expected to have its own unique tool-using culture. Which, incidentally, turns out to be quite true. And when I described how one chimpanzee, Mike, spontaneously solved a new problem by using a tool (he broke off a stick to knock a banana to the ground when he was too nervous to actually take it from my hand) I don't believe there were any raised eyebrows in the scientific community. Certainly I was not attacked viciously, as were Kohler and Yerkes, for suggesting that humans were not the only beings capable of reasoning and insight.

The mid-sixties saw the start of a project that, along with other similar research, was to teach us a great deal about the chimpanzee mind. This was Project Washoe, conceived by Trixie and Allen Gardner. They purchased an infant chimpanzee and began to teach her the signs of ASL, the American Sign Language used by the deaf. Twenty years earlier another husband and wife team, Richard and Cathy Hayes, had tried, with an almost total lack of success, to teach a young chimp, Vikki, to talk. The Hayes's undertaking taught us a lot about the chimpanzee mind, but Vikki, although she did well in IQ tests, and was clearly an intelligent youngster, could not learn human speech. The Gardners, however, achieved spectacular success with their pupil, Washoe. Not only did she learn signs easily, but she quickly began to string them together in meaningful ways. It was clear that each sign evoked, in her mind, a mental image of the object it represented. If, for example, she was asked, in sign language, to fetch an apple, she would go and locate an apple that was out of sight in another room.

Other chimps entered the project, some starting their lives in deaf signing families before joining Washoe. And finally Washoe adopted an infant, Loulis. He came from a lab where no thought of teaching signs had ever penetrated. When he was with Washoe he was given no lessons in language acquisition—not by humans, anyway. Yet by the time he was eight years old he had made fifty-eight signs in their correct contexts. How did he learn them? Mostly, it seems, by imitating the behaviour of Washoe and the other three signing chimps, Dar, Moja and Tatu. Sometimes, though, he received tuition from Washoe herself. One day, for example, she began to swagger about bipedally, hair bristling, signing *food! food! food!* in great excitement. She had seen a human approaching with a bar of chocolate. Loulis, only eighteen months old, watched passively. Suddenly Washoe stopped her swaggering, went over to him, took his hand, and moulded the sign for *food* (fingers pointing towards mouth). Another time, in a similar context, she made the sign for *chewing gum*—but with *her* hand on *his* body. On a third occasion Washoe, apropos of nothing, picked up a small chair, took it over to Loulis, set it down in front of him, and very distinctly made the *chair* sign three times, watching him closely as she did so. The two food signs became incorporated into Loulis's vocabulary but the sign for chair did not. Obviously the priorities of a young chimp are similar to those of a human child!

When news of Washoe's accomplishments first hit the scientific community it immediately provoked a storm of bitter protest. It implied that chimpanzees were capable of mastering a human language, and this, in turn, indicated mental powers of generalization, abstraction and concept-formation as well as an ability to understand and use abstract symbols. And these intellectual skills were surely the prerogatives of *Homo sapiens*. Although there were many who were fascinated and excited by the Gardners' findings, there were many more who denounced the whole project, holding that the data was suspect, the methodology sloppy, and the conclusions not only misleading, but quite preposterous. The controversy inspired all sorts of other language projects. And, whether the investigators were sceptical to start with and hoped to disprove the Gardners' work, or whether they were attempting to demonstrate the same thing in a new way, their research provided additional information about the chimpanzee's mind.

And so, with new incentive, psychologists began to test the mental abilities of chimpanzees in a variety of different ways; again and again the results confirmed that their minds are uncannily like our own. It had long been held that only humans were capable of what is called 'cross-modal transfer of information'—in other words, if you shut your eyes and someone allows you to feel a strangely shaped potato, you will subsequently be able to pick it out from other differently shaped potatoes simply by looking at them. And vice versa. It turned out that chimpanzees can 'know' with their eyes what they 'feel' with their fingers in just the same way. In fact, we now know that some other non-human primates can do the same thing. I expect all kinds of creatures have the same ability.

Then it was proved, experimentally and beyond doubt, that chimpanzees could recognize themselves in mirrors—that they had, therefore, some kind of self-concept. In fact, Washoe, some years previously, had already demonstrated the ability when she spontaneously identified herself in the mirror, staring at her image and making her name sign. But that observation was merely anecdotal. The proof came when chimpanzees who had been allowed to play with mirrors were, while anaesthetized, dabbed with spots of odourless paint in places, such as the ears or the top of the head, that they could see only in the mirror. When they woke they were not only fascinated by their spotted images, but immediately investigated, with their fingers, the dabs of paint.

The fact that chimpanzees have excellent memories surprised no one. Everyone, after all, has been brought up to believe that 'an elephant never forgets' so why should a chimpanzee be any different? The fact that Washoe spontaneously gave the name-sign of Beatrice Gardner, her surrogate mother, when she saw her after a separation of eleven years was no greater an accomplishment than the amazing memory shown by dogs who recognize their owners after separations of almost as long—and the chimpanzee has a much longer life span than a dog. Chimpanzees can plan ahead, too, at least as regards the immediate future. This, in fact, is well illustrated at Gombe, during the termiting season: often an individual prepares a tool for use on a termite mound that is several hundred yards away and absolutely out of sight.

This is not the place to describe in detail the other cognitive abilities that have been studied in laboratory chimpanzees. Among other accomplishments chimpanzees possess pre-mathematical skills: they can, for example, readily differentiate between *more* and *less*. They can classify things into specific categories according to a given criterion—thus they have no difficulty in separating a pile of food into *fruits* and *vegetables* on one occasion, and, on another, dividing the same pile of food into *large* versus *small* items, even though this requires putting some vegetables with some fruits. Chimpanzees who have been taught a language can combine signs creatively in order to describe objects for which they have no symbol. Washoe, for example, puzzled her caretakers by asking, repeatedly, for a *rock berry.* Eventually it transpired that she was referring to Brazil nuts which she had encountered for the first time a while before. Another language-trained chimp described a cucumber as a *green banana,* and another referred to an Alka-Seltzer as a *listen drink.* They can even invent signs. Lucy, as she got older, had to be put on a leash for her outings. One day, eager to set off but having no sign for *leash,* she signalled her wishes by holding a crooked index finger to the ring on her collar. This sign became part of her vocabulary. Some chimpanzees love to draw, and especially to paint. Those who have learned sign language sometimes spontaneously label their works, 'This [is] apple'—or bird, or sweetcorn, or whatever. The fact that the paintings often look, to our eyes, remarkably unlike the objects depicted by the artists either means that the chimpanzees are poor draughtsmen or that we have much to learn regarding ape-style representational art!

People sometimes ask why chimpanzees have evolved such complex intellectual powers when their lives in the wild are so simple. The answer is, of course, that their lives in the wild are not so simple! They use—and need—all their mental skills during normal day-to-day life in their complex society. They are always having to make choices—where to go, or with whom to travel. They need highly developed social skills—particularly those males who are ambitious to attain high positions in the dominance hierarchy. Low-ranking chimpanzees must learn deception—to conceal their intentions or to do things in secret—if they are to get their way in the presence of their superiors. Indeed, the study of chimpanzees in the wild suggests that their intellectual abilities evolved, over the millennia, to help them cope with daily life. And now, the solid core of data concerning chimpanzee intellect collected so carefully in the lab setting provides a background against which to evaluate the many examples of intelligent, rational behaviour that we see in the wild.

It is easier to study intellectual prowess in the lab where, through carefully devised tests and judicious use of rewards, the chimpanzees can be encouraged to exert themselves, to stretch their minds to the limit. It is more meaningful to study the subject in the wild, but much harder. It is more meaningful because we can better understand the environmental pressures that led to the evolution of intellectual skills in chimpanzee societies. It is harder because, in the wild, almost all behaviours are confounded by countless variables; years of observing, recording and analysing take the place of contrived testing; sample size can often be counted on the fingers of one hand; the only experiments are nature's own, and only time—eventually—may replicate them.

In the wild a single observation may prove of utmost significance, providing a clue to some hitherto puzzling aspect of behaviour, a key to the understanding of, for example, a changed relationship. Obviously it is crucial to see as many incidents of this sort as possible. During the early years of my study at Gombe it became apparent that one person alone could never learn more than a fraction of what was going on in a chimpanzee community at any given time. And so, from 1964 onwards, I gradually built up a research team to help in the gathering of information about the behaviour of our closest living relatives.

Bridging the Gap

Louis Leakey sent me to Gombe in the hope that a better understanding of the behaviour of our closest relatives would provide a new window onto our own past. He had amassed a wealth of evidence that enabled him to reconstruct the physical characteristics of early humans in Africa, and he could speculate on the use of the various tools and other artifacts found at their living floors. But behaviour does not fossilize. His curiosity about the great apes was due to his conviction that behaviour common to modern man and modern chimpanzee was probably present in our common ancestor and, therefore, in early man himself. Louis was way ahead of most of his contemporaries in his thinking, and today his approach seems even more worthwhile in view of the surprising discovery that, as mentioned, human DNA differs from chimpanzee DNA by only just over one percent.

There are many similarities in chimpanzee and human behaviour—the affectionate, supportive and enduring bonds between family members, the long period of childhood dependency, the importance of learning, nonverbal communication patterns, tool-using and tool-making, cooperation in hunting, sophisticated social manipulations, aggressive territoriality, and a variety of helping behaviours, to name but a few. Similarities in the structure of the brain and central nervous system have led to the emergence of similar intellectual abilities, sensibilities and emotions in our two species. That this information concerning the natural history of chimpanzees has been helpful to those studying early man is demonstrated, again and again, by the frequency with which anthropological textbooks refer to the behaviour of the Gombe chimpanzees. Of course, theories regarding the behaviour of early man can never be anything but speculative—we have no time-machine, we cannot project ourselves back to the dawn of our species to watch the behaviour and follow the development of our forebears: if we seek to understand these things a little we must do the best we can with the flimsy evidence available. So far as I am concerned, the concept of early humans poking for insects with twigs and wiping themselves with leaves seems entirely sensible. The thought of those ancestors greeting and reassuring one another with kisses or embraces, cooperating in protecting their territory or in hunting, and sharing food with each other, is appealing. The idea of close affectionate ties within the Stone Age family, of brothers helping one another, of teenage sons hastening to the protection of their old mothers, and of teenage daughters minding the babies, for me brings the fossilized relics of their physical selves dramatically to life.

But the study at Gombe has done far more than provide material upon which to base our speculations of prehistoric human life. The opening of this window onto the way of life of our closest living relatives gives us a better understanding not only of the chimpanzee's place in nature, but also of *man's* place in nature. Knowing that chimpanzees possess cognitive abilities once thought unique to humans, knowing that they (along with other 'dumb' animals) can reason, feel emotions and pain and fear, we are humbled. We are not, as once we believed, separated from the rest of the animal kingdom by an unbridgeable chasm. Nevertheless, we must not forget, not for an instant, that even if we do not differ from the apes in kind, but only in degree, that degree is still overwhelmingly large. An understanding of chimpanzee behaviour helps to highlight certain aspects of human behaviour that *are* unique and that *do* differentiate us from the other living primates. Above all, we have developed intellectual abilities which dwarf those of even the most gifted chimpanzees. It was because the gap between the human brain and that of our closest living relative, the chimpanzee, was so extraordinarily large, that palaeontologists for years hunted for a half-ape, half-human skeleton that would bridge this human/non-human gap. In fact, this 'missing link' is comprised of a series of vanished brains, each more complex than the one before: brains that are for ever lost to science save for a few faint imprints on fossil craniums; brains that held, in their increasingly intricate convolutions, the dramatic serial story of developing intellect that has led to modern man.

Of all the characteristics that differentiate humans from their non-human cousins, the ability to communicate through the use of a sophisticated spoken language is, I believe, the most significant. Once our ancestors had acquired that powerful tool they could discuss events that had happened in the past and make complex contingency plans for both the near and the distant future. They could teach their children by explaining things without the need to demonstrate. Words gave substance to thoughts and ideas that, unexpressed, might have remained, forever, vague and without practical value. The interaction of mind with mind broadened ideas and sharpened concepts. Sometimes, when watching the chimpanzees, I have felt that, because they have no human-like language, they are trapped within themselves. Their calls, postures and gestures, together, add up to a rich repertoire, a complex and sophisticated method of communication. But it is nonverbal. How much more they might accomplish if only they could talk to each other. It is true that they can be taught to use the signs or symbols of a human-type language. And they have cognitive skills to combine these signs into meaningful sentences. Mentally, at least, it would seem that chimpanzees stand at the threshold of language acquisition. But those forces that were at work when humans began to speak have obviously played no role in shaping chimpanzee intellect in this direction.

Chimpanzees also stand at the threshold of another uniquely human behaviour—war. Human warfare, defined as *organized armed conflict between groups*, has, over the ages, had a profound influence on our history. Wherever there are humans they have, at one time or another, waged some sort of war. Thus it seems most likely that primitive forms of warfare were present in our earliest ancestors, and that conflict of this sort played a role in human evolution. War, it has been suggested, may have put considerable selective pressure on the development of intelligence and of increasingly sophisticated cooperation. The process would have escalated—for the greater the intelligence, cooperation and courage of one group, the greater the challenge to its enemies. Darwin was among the first to suggest that warfare may have exerted a powerful influence on the development of the human brain. Others have postulated that warfare may have been responsible for the huge gap between the human brain and that of our closest living relatives, the great apes: hominid groups with inferior brains could not win wars and were exterminated.

Thus it is fascinating as well as shocking to learn that chimpanzees show hostile, aggressive territorial behaviour that is not unlike certain forms of primitive human warfare. Some tribes, for example, carry out raids during which 'they stalk or creep up to the enemy, using tactics reminiscent of hunting'—thus writes Renke Elbi-Elbesfeldt, an ethologist who has studied aggression in peoples around the world. Long before sophisticated warfare evolved in our own species, prehuman ancestors must have shown preadaptations similar—or identical—to those shown by the chimpanzees today, such as cooperative group living, cooperative territoriality, cooperative hunting skills, and weapon use. Another necessary preadaptation would have been an inherent fear or hatred of strangers, sometimes expressed by aggressive attacks. But attacking adult individuals of the same species is always a dangerous business and, in human societies, in historical times, it has been necessary to train warriors by cultural means such as glorifying their role, condemning cowardice, offering high rewards for bravery and skill on the battle field, and emphasizing the worthiness of practising 'manly' sports during childhood. Chimpanzees, however, particularly young adult males, clearly find inter-group conflict attractive, despite the danger. If young male prehumans also found excitement in encounters of this sort, this would have provided a firm biological basis for the glorification of warriors and warfare.

Among humans, members of one group may see themselves as quite distinct from members of another, and may then treat group and non-group individuals differently. Indeed, non-group members may even be 'dehumanized' and regarded almost as creatures of a different species. Once this happens people are freed from the inhibitions and social sanctions that operate within their own group, and can behave to non-group members in ways that would not be tolerated amongst their own, This leads, among other things, to the atrocities of war. Chimpanzees also show differential behaviour towards group and non-group members. Their sense of group identity is strong and they clearly know who 'belongs' and who does not: non-community members may be attacked so fiercely that they die from their wounds. And this is not simple 'fear of strangers'—members of the Kahama community were familiar to the Kasakela aggressors, yet they were attacked brutally. By separating themselves, it was as though they forfeited their 'right' to be treated as group members. Moreover, some patterns of attack directed against non-group individuals have never been seen during fights between members of the same community—the twisting of limbs, the tearing off of strips of skin, the drinking of blood. The victims have thus been, to all intents and purposes, 'dechimpized,' since these are patterns usually seen when a chimpanzee is trying to kill an adult prey animal—an animal of another species.

Chimpanzees, as a result of an unusually hostile and violently aggressive attitude towards non-group individuals, have clearly reached a stage where they stand at the very threshold of human achievement in destruction, cruelty and planned inter-group conflict. If ever they develop the power of language, might they not push open the door and wage war with the best of us?

What of the other side of the coin? Where do the chimpanzees stand, relative to us, in their expression of love, compassion and altruism? Because violent and brutal behaviour is vivid and attention-catching, it is easy to get the impression that chimpanzees are more aggressive than they really are. In fact, peaceful interactions are far more frequent than aggressive ones; mild threats are more common than vigorous ones; threats per se are much more frequent than fights; and serious, wounding conflicts are rare compared to brief, relatively mild ones. Moreover, chimpanzees have a rich repertoire of behaviours that serve to maintain or restore social harmony and promote cohesion among community members. The embracing, kissing, patting and holding of hands that serve as greetings after separation, or are used by dominant individuals to reassure their subordinates after aggression. The long, peaceful sessions of relaxed social grooming. The sharing of food. The concern for the sick or wounded. The readiness to help companions in distress, even when this means risking life or limb. All these reconciliatory, friendly, and helping behaviours are, without doubt, very close to our own qualities of compassion, love and self-sacrifice.

At Gombe care of the sick is not a helping behaviour common among unrelated chimpanzees. Indeed, a badly injured individual is sometimes shunned by non-family members. When Fifi, who had a gaping wound in her head, repeatedly solicited grooming from others in her group, they peered at the injury (where some fly maggots could be seen) then moved hastily away. But her infant son groomed carefully around the edges of the lesion and sometimes licked it. And when old Madam Bee lay dying, after the assault by the Kasakela males, Honey Bee spent hours each day grooming her mother and keeping the flies away from her terrible wounds. In groups of captive chimpanzees, individuals who have been raised together, and who are as familiar as close kin in the wild, will zealously squeeze or poke pus from one another's wounds and remove splinters. One took a speck of grit from his companion's eye. A young female developed the habit of cleaning her companion's teeth with twigs. She found this particularly fascinating when their milk teeth were loose and wiggly, and she even performed a couple of extractions! Such manipulations are for the most part due to a fascination for the activity itself, and almost certainly derive from social grooming. The results, however, are sometimes beneficial to the recipients and, coupled with the concern so often shown for family members, the behaviour provides a biological base for the emergence of compassionate health care in man.

Among non-human primates in the wild it is rare for adults to share food with each other, although mothers will typically share with their young. In chimpanzee society, however, even non-related adults frequently share with each other, although they are more likely to do so with kin and close friends. At Gombe sharing among adults is seen most often during meat eating when, in response to an outstretched hand or other begging gesture, the possessor may allow a portion of the flesh to be taken—or may actually tear off a piece and hand it to the supplicant. Some individuals are much more generous than others in this respect. Sometimes other foods in short supply are shared, too—such as bananas. A good deal of sharing is seen among captive chimps. Wolfgang Kohler, 'in the interests of science,' once shut the young male Sultan into his cage without his supper, while feeding the old female Tschego outside. As she sat eating her meal, Sultan became increasingly frenzied in his appeals to her, whimpering, screaming, stretching his arms towards her, and even throwing bits of straw in her direction. Eventually (when, presumably, she had taken the edge off her own hunger) she gathered a pile of food together and pushed it into his cage.

Food sharing among chimpanzees is usually explained away by scientists as being merely the best way of getting rid of an irritation—the begging of a companion. Sometimes this is undoubtedly true, for begging individuals can be extraordinarily persistent. Yet often the patience and tolerance of the individual who has possession of the desired object is remarkable. There was, for example, the occasion when old Flo wanted the piece of meat that Mike was chewing. She begged with both hands cupped around his muzzle, for well over a minute. Gradually she moved her pouted lips closer and closer until they were within an inch of Mike's. In the end he rewarded her, pushing the morsel (well chewed by then) directly from his mouth into hers. And what of Tschego's feeding of young Sultan? Admittedly she may have been irritated by his noisy tantrum—but she could have walked away to the far corner of her enclosure. Robert Yerkes tells of a female who was offered fruit juice from a cup through the bars of her cage. She filled her mouth and then, in response to pleading whimpers from the next cage, walked over and transferred the juice into her friend's mouth. She then returned for another mouthful which she delivered in the same manner. And so it continued until the cup was empty.

Towards the end of Madam Bee's life there was an unusually dry summer at Gombe, and the chimpanzees had to travel long distances between one food source and the next. Madam Bee, old and sick, sometimes got so tired during these journeys that she had no energy to climb for food upon arrival. Her two daughters would utter soft calls of delight and rush up to feed, but she simply lay below, exhausted. On three quite separate occasions Little Bee, the elder daughter, after feeding for about ten minutes, climbed down with food in her mouth and food in one hand, then went and placed the food from her hand on the ground beside Madam Bee. The two sat side by side, eating companionably together. Little Bee's behaviour was not only a demonstration of entirely voluntary giving, but it also showed that she understood the needs of her old mother. Without understanding of this sort there can be no empathy, no compassion. And, in both chimpanzees and humans, these are the qualities that lead to altruistic behaviour and self-sacrifice.

In chimpanzee society, although most risk-taking is on behalf of family members, there are examples of individuals risking injury if not their lives to help non-related companions. Evered once risked the fury of adult male baboons to rescue adolescent Mustard, pinned down and screaming, during a baboon hunt. And when Freud was seized during a bushpig hunt by an enraged sow, Gigi risked her life to save him. The pig had seized him from behind, and Freud, dropping his piglet, was screaming and struggling to escape, when Gigi raced up, hair bristling. The sow wheeled to charge Gigi, and Freud, bleeding heavily, was able to escape up a tree.

In some zoos, chimpanzees are kept on man-made islands, surrounded by water-filled moats. There are tales of heroism from there, too. Chimpanzees cannot swim and, unless they are rescued, will drown if they fall into deep water. Despite this, individuals have sometimes made heroic efforts to save companions from drowning—and were sometimes successful. One adult male lost his life as he tried to rescue a small infant whose incompetent mother had allowed it to fall into the water.

In all those animal species in which parents devote time and energy to the raising of their young they will, when occasion demands, risk life and limb in defence of their offspring. It is much more unusual for an adult to show altruistic behaviour towards an individual who is not closely related. After all, if you help your kin, all of whom bear some of the same genes as yourself, then your action will still be of some benefit to your clan in its struggle to survive—even if you yourself get harmed in the process. From these basically selfish roots sprang the most rarified form of altruism—helping another even when you stand to gain nothing for yourself or your kin.

As the ancestors of chimpanzees (and, incidentally, ourselves) gradually evolved more complex brains, so the period of childhood dependency became longer and mothers were forced to expend more and more time and energy in raising their families. Mother-offspring bonds became ever more enduring. The offspring of the most caring, supportive and successful mothers thrived and became themselves good and caring mothers who tended to produce many offspring. Youngsters who were less well cared for were less likely to survive, and those that did were often relatively poor mothers themselves and were less likely to produce large families. Loving and nurturing characteristics thus competed successfully, in the genetic sense, with more selfish behaviours. Over the eons, tendencies to help and protect, which were originally developed for the successful raising of young, gradually infiltrated the genetic make-up of chimpanzees. Today we observe, again and again, that the distress of a non-related but well-known community member may elicit genuine concern in a companion, and a desire to help.

Compassion and self-sacrifice are two of the qualities we value most in our own western society. In some cases—as when someone risks his or her life to save another—the altruistic act is probably motivated by the same inherent complex of helping behaviours that cause a chimpanzee to aid a companion. But there are countless instances when the issue is clouded by cultural factors. If we know that another, especially a close relative or friend, is suffering, then we ourselves become emotionally disturbed, sometimes to the point of anguish. Only by helping (or trying to help) can we hope to alleviate our own distress. Does this mean, then, that we act altruistically only to soothe our own consciences? That our helping, in the final analysis, is but a selfish desire to set our minds at rest? One can speculate endlessly on human motives for helping others. Why do we send money to starving children in the Third World? Because others will applaud and our reputation will be enhanced? Or because starving children evoke in us a feeling of pity which makes us uncomfortable? If our motive is to advance our social standing, or even to alleviate our own mental discomfort, is not our action basically selfish? Perhaps, but I feel strongly that we should not allow reductionist arguments of this sort to detract from the inspirational nature of many human acts of altruism. The very fact that we feel distressed by the plight of individuals we have never met, says it all.

We are, indeed, a complex and endlessly fascinating species. We carry in our genes, handed down from our distant past, deep-rooted aggressive tendencies. Our patterns of aggression are little changed from those that we see in chimpanzees. But while chimpanzees have, to some extent, an awareness of the pain which they may inflict on their victims, only we, I believe, are capable of real cruelty—the deliberate infliction of physical or mental pain on living creatures despite, or even because of, our precise understanding of the suffering involved. Only we are capable of torture. Only we, surely, are capable of evil.

But let us not forget that human love and compassion are equally deeply rooted in our primate heritage, and in this sphere too our sensibilities are of a higher order of magnitude than those of chimpanzees. Human love at its best, the ecstasy deriving from the perfect union of mind and body, leads to heights of passion, tenderness and understanding that chimpanzees cannot experience. And while chimpanzees will, indeed, respond to the immediate need of a companion in distress, even when this involves risk to themselves, only humans are capable of performing acts of self-sacrifice with *full* knowledge of the costs that may have to be borne—not only at the time, but also, perhaps, at some future date. A chimpanzee does not have the conceptual ability to become a martyr, offering his life for a cause.

Thus although our 'bad' is worse, immeasurably worse, than the worst conceivable actions of our closest living relatives, let us take comfort in the knowledge that our 'good' can be incomparably better. Moreover we have developed a sophisticated mechanism—the brain—which enables us, if we will, to control our inherited aggressive hateful tendencies. Sadly, our success in this regard is poor. Nevertheless, we should remember that we alone among the life forms of this planet are able to overcome, by conscious choice, the dictates of our biological natures. At least, this is what I believe.

And what of the chimpanzees? Are they at the end of their evolutionary progression? Or are there pressures in their forest habitat that might, given time, push them further along the path taken by our own prehistoric ancestors, producing apes that would become ever more human? It seems unlikely; evolution does not often repeat itself. Probably chimpanzees would become ever more *different*—they might, for example, develop the right side of the brain at the expense of the left.

But the question is purely academic. It could not be answered for countless thousands of years, and even *now* it is clear that the days of the great African forests are numbered. If the chimpanzees themselves survive in freedom, it will be in a few isolated patches of forest grudgingly conceded, where opportunities for genetic exchange between different social groups will be limited or impossible. And, unless we act soon, our closest relatives may soon exist only in captivity, condemned, as a species, to human bondage. ■

■ *QUESTIONS FOR MAKING CONNECTIONS WITHIN THE READING* ■

1. Clearly, Jane Goodall draws on scientific research, but she does not make her case on strictly scientific grounds or in the format of a scientific article. What different kinds of evidence does Goodall offer in support of her argument for the existence of "animal minds"? Notice that she refers not simply to different writers but also to *sources* of knowledge other than written ones. Why might she have chosen this eclectic approach?

2. How would you characterize Goodall's attitude toward the scientific community? Is it simply negative—the perspective of a disappointed former member? Or is it more complex and more nuanced than that? Does Goodall believe that science should attempt to include emotions and experience as legitimate forms of evidence? If scientists attempted to include them, what might be the consequences?

3. Goodall's second chapter, "Bridging the Chasm," ends on a rather ominous note. "[U]nless we act soon," she warns, "our closest relatives may soon exist only in captivity, condemned, as a species, to human bondage." Here Goodall's argument extends beyond chimpanzees to our relationship with the natural world in general. Why might existence in captivity do harm to chimpanzees? What's wrong with "human bondage"? Does she mean that we should view animals as our equals in some respect, with the rights we might afford other human beings?

■ *QUESTIONS FOR WRITING* ■

1. Is Goodall a scientist? Can one be a scientist and an activist at the same time? Is science by definition committed to improving the human condition? To the pursuit of truth? To understanding the nature of reality? Define science and discuss whether Goodall's methods for studying the natural world meet your definition.

2. Toward the end of her argument, Goodall makes the following observation: "only humans are capable of performing acts of self-sacrifice with *full* knowledge of the costs that may have to be borne—not only at the time, but also, perhaps, at some future date." In this passage, does Goodall reinforce the great divide between humans and other animals after arguing for so many pages about their profound similarities? Given all that Goodall tells us about our kinship with chimpanzees, do you believe that it is really possible for us to "overcome," as Goodall says, "the dictates of our biological natures"? Is it merely human arrogance to think that we can have a "*full* knowledge" of anything?

■ *QUESTIONS FOR MAKING CONNECTIONS BETWEEN READINGS* ■

1. Goodall describes chimpanzees as "more like us than is any other living creature." But if Ian Wilmut and his colleagues are successful in creating animals who can generate donor organs for humans, will Goodall's statement be true any longer? How is one to decide when using animals to improve the quality of life for humans is acceptable? Is this a moral decision, an ethical choice, or something one comes to through reasoned argument?

2. Has evolution decreed our superiority over all animals, or do we misuse the language of biology when we speak in this way? Drawing on Stephen Jay Gould's essay, "What Does the Dreaded 'E' Word *Mean*, Anyway?", discuss what Goodall's research suggests about the role humans have to play in the evolutionary process.

For additional suggestions about making connections between readings, visit the Link-O-Mat and More Sample Assignments at <www.newhum.com>.

STEPHEN JAY GOULD

PERHAPS MORE THAN any other contemporary American scientist, Stephen Jay Gould has committed himself to communicating the goals, processes, and achievements of science to the public. Gould's high visibility, distinctive critical voice, and marked enthusiasm for making science accessible to the general public have led him to contribute to debates concerning Creationist science, evolutionary psychology, and biological determinations of race and intelligence. The essay included here, "What Does the Dreaded 'E' Word *Mean*, Anyway?" continues Gould's lifelong project of explaining Darwin's evolutionary theory, a project that involves clarifying what "survival of the fittest" means and addressing the notion that evolutionary development involves progress toward perfection. As Gould's opening discussion of the Kansas school board's treatment of evolutionary theory shows, Darwin's ideas and their significance remain largely misunderstood to this day, more than 150 years after they were first voiced.

A prolific writer, Gould has published more than twenty books, including *The Mismeasure of Man* (1982), which criticized pseudoscientific justifications for racism and won a National Book Critics Circle Award; *The Panda's Thumb* (1980), which won the American Book Award; and *Wonderful Life: The Burgess Shale and the Nature of History* (1990), which was a finalist for the Pulitzer Prize and winner of the Science Book Prize. Professor of Geology and Zoology at Harvard University and curator of the Invertebrate Paleontology collection at Harvard's Museum of Comparative Zoology, Gould is also the recipient of many academic awards and distinctions, including a MacArthur "Genius Grant," the Glenn T. Seaborg Award for contribution to public interest in science, the Distinguished Service Award from the National Association of Biology Teachers, and the Distinguished Service Award from the American Humanists Association.

Gould has written that "humans are not the end result of predictable evolutionary progress, but rather a fortuitous cosmic afterthought, a tiny little twig on the enormously arborescent bush of life, which if replanted from seed, would

Gould, Stephen Jay. "What Does the Dreaded 'E' Word *Mean*, Anyway? A Reverie for the Opening of the New Hayden Planetarium." *Natural History.* February 2000. 28–44.

Quotation and biographical information from Stephen Jay Gould, interview by AnnOnLine, 9 October 1996 <http://www.annonline.com/interviews/961009/>.

almost surely not grow this twig again." While such a world view may seem bleak and uninviting, for Gould, it provides an opportunity to read, write, and think more deeply about the geological, biological, and evolutionary events that gave rise to the "fortuitous cosmic afterthought" that is humanity.

To learn more about Stephen Jay Gould and the evolutionary process, visit the Link-O-Mat at <www.newhum.com>.

What Does the Dreaded "E" Word *Mean,* Anyway?

A Reverie for the Opening of the New Hayden Planetarium

Evolution posed no terrors in the liberal constituency of New York City when I studied biology at Jamaica High School in 1956. But our textbooks didn't utter the word either—a legacy of the statutes that had brought William Jennings Bryan and Clarence Darrow to legal blows at Tennessee's trial of John Scopes in 1925. The subject remained doubly hidden within my textbook—covered only in chapter 63 (of 66) and described in euphemism as "the hypothesis of racial development."

The antievolution laws of the Scopes era, passed during the early 1920s in several southern and border states, remained on the books until 1968, when the Supreme Court declared them unconstitutional. The laws were never strictly enforced, but their existence cast a pall over American education, as textbook publishers capitulated to produce "least common denominator" versions acceptable in all states—so schoolkids in New York got short shrift because the statutes of some distant states had labeled evolution dangerous and unteachable.

Ironically, at the very end of this millennium (I am writing this essay in late November 1999), demotions, warnings, and anathemas have again come into vogue in several regions of our nation. The Kansas school board has reduced evolution, the central and unifying concept of the life sciences, to an optional subject within the state's biology curriculum—an educational ruling akin to stating that English will still be taught but that grammar may henceforth be regarded as a peripheral frill, permitted but not mandated as a classroom subject. Two states now require that warning labels be pasted (literally) into all biology textbooks, alerting students that they might wish to consider alternatives to evolution (although no other well-documented scientific concept evokes similar caution). Finally, at least two states have retained all their Darwinian material in official pamphlets and curricula but have replaced the dreaded "e" word with a circumlocution, thus reviving the old strategy of my high school text.

As our fight for good (and politically untrammeled) public education in science must include our forceful defense of a key word—for inquisitors have always understood that an idea can be extinguished most effectively by suppressing all memory of a defining word or an inspirational person—we might consider an interesting historical irony that, properly elucidated, might even aid us in our battle. We must not compromise *our* showcasing of the "e" word, for we give up the game before we start if we grant our opponents control over basic terms. But we should also note that Darwin himself never used the word "evolution" in his epochal book of 1859. In *Origin of Species*, he calls this fundamental biological process "descent with modification." Darwin, needless to say, did not shun "evolution" from motives of fear, conciliation, or political savvy but rather for an opposite and principled reason that can help us appreciate the depth of the intellectual revolution that he inspired and some of the reasons (understandable if indefensible) for the persistent public unease.

Pre-Darwinian terminology for evolution—a widely discussed, if unorthodox, view of life in early nineteenth-century biology—generally used such names as transformation, transmutation, or the development hypothesis. In choosing a label for his own, very different account of genealogical change, Darwin would never have considered "evolution" as a descriptor, because that vernacular English word implied a set of consequences contrary to the most distinctive features of his proposed revolutionary mechanism of change.

"Evolution," from the Latin *evolvere*, literally means "an unrolling"—and clearly implies an unfolding in time of a predictable or prepackaged sequence in an inherently progressive, or at least directional, manner (the "fiddlehead" of a fern unrolls and expands to bring forth the adult plant—a true evolution of preformed parts). The *Oxford English Dictionary* traces the word "evolution" to seventeenth-century English poetry. Here the word's key meaning—the sequential exposure of prepackaged potential—inspired the first recorded usages in our language. For example, Henry More (1614–87), the British philosopher responsible for several of the seventeenth-century citations in the *OED* entry, stated in 1664, "I have not yet evolved all the intangling superstitions that may be wrapt up."

The few pre-Darwinian English citations of genealogical change as "evolution" all employ the word as a synonym for predictable progress. For example, in describing Lamarck's theory for British readers (in the second volume of his *Principles of Geology*, 1832), Charles Lyell generally uses the neutral term "transmutation"—except in one passage, where he wishes to highlight a claim for progress: "The testacea of the ocean existed first, until some of them by gradual evolution were improved into those inhabiting the land."

Although the word "evolution" does not appear in the first edition of *Origin of Species*, Darwin does use the verbal form "evolved," clearly in the vernacular sense and in an especially crucial spot: the very last word of the book! Most students have failed to appreciate the incisive and intended "gotcha" of these closing lines, which have generally been read as a poetic reverie, a harmless linguistic flourish essentially devoid of content, however rich in imagery. In fact, the canny Darwin used this maximally effective location to make a telling point about the absolute glory and comparative importance of natural history as a calling.

We usually regard planetary physics as the paragon of rigorous science, while dismissing natural history as a lightweight exercise in dull, descriptive cataloging that any person with sufficient patience might accomplish. But Darwin, in his closing passage, identified the primary phenomenon of planetary physics as a dull and simple cycling to nowhere, in sharp contrast with life's history, depicted as a dynamic and upwardly growing tree. The Earth *revolves* in uninteresting sameness, but life *evolves* by unfolding its potential for ever expanding diversity along admittedly unpredictable, but wonderfully various, branchings:

> Whilst this planet has gone cycling on according to the fixed law of gravity, from so simple a beginning endless forms most beautiful and most wonderful have been, and are being, evolved.

But Darwin could not have described the process regulated by his mechanism of natural selection as "evolution" in the vernacular meaning then conveyed by the word. For the mechanism of natural selection yields only increasing adaptation to changing local environments, not predictable progress in the usual sense of cosmic or general betterment expressed as growing complexity, augmented mentality, or whatever. In Darwin's causal world, an anatomically degenerate parasite, reduced to a formless clump of feeding and reproductive cells within the body of a host, may be just as well adapted to its surroundings, and just as well endowed with prospects for evolutionary persistence, as is the most intricate creature, exquisitely adapted in all parts to a complex and dangerous external environment. Moreover, since natural selection can adapt organisms only to local circumstances, and since local circumstances change in an effectively random manner through geological time, the pathways of adaptive evolution cannot be predicted.

Thus, on these two fundamental grounds—lack of inherent directionality and lack of predictability—the process regulated by natural selection could scarcely have suggested, to Darwin, the label "evolution," an ordinary English word for sequences of predictable and directional unfolding. We must then, and obviously, ask how "evolution" achieved its coup in becoming the name for Darwin's process—a takeover so complete that the word has now almost (but not quite, as we shall soon see) lost its original English meaning of "unfolding" and has transmuted (or should we say "evolved"?) into an effective synonym for biological change through time.

This interesting shift, despite Darwin's own reticence, occurred primarily because a great majority of his contemporaries, while granting the overwhelming evidence for evolution's factuality, could not accept Darwin's radical views about the causes and patterns of biological change. Most important, they could not bear to surrender the comforting and traditional view that human consciousness must represent a predictable (if not a divinely intended) summit of biological existence. If scientific discoveries enjoined an evolutionary reading of human superiority, then one must bow to the evidence. But Darwin's contemporaries (and many people today as well) would not surrender their traditional view of human domination, and therefore could conceptualize genealogical transmutation only as a process defined by predictable progress toward a human acme—in short, as a process well described by the term "evolution" in its vernacular meaning of "unfolding an inherent potential."

Herbert Spencer's progressivist view of natural change probably exerted the greatest influence in establishing "evolution" as the general name for Darwin's process, for Spencer held a dominating status as Victorian pundit and grand panjandrum of nearly everything conceptual. In any case, Darwin had too many other fish to fry and didn't choose to fight a battle about words rather than things. He felt confident that his views would eventually prevail, even over the contrary etymology of a word imposed upon his process by popular will. (He knew, after all, that meanings of words can transmute within new climates of immediate utility, just as species transform under new local environments of life and ecology!) Darwin never used the "e" word extensively in his writings, but he did capitulate to a developing consensus by referring to his process as evolution for the first time in *Descent of Man,* published in 1871. (Still, Darwin never used the word "evolution" in the title of any book—and he chose, in his book on human history, to emphasize the genealogical "descent" of our species, not our "ascent" to higher levels of consciousness.)

When I was a young boy, growing up on the streets of New York City, the American Museum of Natural History became my second home and inspiration. I loved two exhibits most of all—the *Tyrannosaurus* skeleton on the fourth floor and the star show at the adjacent Hayden Planetarium. I juggled these two passions for many years and eventually became a paleontologist; Carl Sagan, my near-contemporary from the neighboring neverland of Brooklyn (I grew up in Queens) weighed the same two interests in the same building but opted for astronomy as a calling. (I have always suspected a basic biological determinism behind our opposite choices. Carl was tall and looked up toward the heavens; I am shorter than average and tend to look down at the ground.)

My essays may be known for their tactic of selecting odd little tidbits as illustrations of general themes. But why, to mark the reopening of the Hayden Planetarium, would I highlight such a quirky and apparently irrelevant subject as the odyssey of the term "evolution" in scientific, and primarily biological, use—thus seeming, once again, to reject the cosmos in favor of the dinosaurs? Method does inhere in my apparent madness (whether or not I succeed in conveying this reasoning to my readers). I am writing about the term "evolution" in the domain I know in order to explicate its strikingly different meaning in the profession that I put aside but still love avocationally. A discussion of the contrast between biological evolution and cosmological evolution might offer some utility as a commentary about alternative worldviews and as a reminder that many supposed debates in science arise from confusion engendered by differing uses of words and not from deep conceptual muddles about the nature of things.

Interdisciplinary unification represents a grand and worthy goal of intellectual life, but greater understanding can often be won by principled separation and mutual respect, based on clear definitions and distinctions among truly disparate processes, rather than by false unions forged with superficial similarities and papered over by a common terminology. In our understandable desire to unify the sciences of temporal change, we have too often followed the Procrustean strategy of enforcing a common set of causes and explanations upon the history of a species and the life of a star—partly, at least, for the very bad reason that both professions use the term "evolution" to denote change through time. In this case, the fundamental differences trump the superficial similarities—and true unity will be achieved only when we acknowledge the disparate substrates that, taken together, probe the range of possibilities for theories of historical order.

The Darwinian principle of natural selection yields temporal change—evolution in the biological definition—by the twofold process of producing copious and undirected variation within a population and then passing along only a biased (selected) portion of this variation to the next generation. In this manner, the variation within a population at any moment can be converted into differences in mean values (average size, average braininess) among successive populations through time. For this fundamental reason, we call such theories of change *variational* as opposed to the more conventional, and more direct, models of *transformational* change imposed by natural laws that mandate a particular trajectory based on inherent (and therefore predictable) properties of substances and environments. (A ball rolling down an inclined plane does not reach the bottom because selection has favored the differential propagation of moving versus stable elements of its totality but because gravity dictates this result when round balls roll down smooth planes.)

To illustrate the peculiar properties of variational theories like Darwin's in an obviously caricatured, but not inaccurate, description: Suppose that a population of elephants inhabits Siberia during a warm interval before the advance of an ice sheet. The elephants vary, at random and in all directions, in their amount of body hair. As the ice advances and local conditions become colder, elephants with more hair will tend to cope better, by the sheer good fortune of their superior adaptation to changing climates—and they will leave more surviving offspring on average. (This differential reproductive success must be conceived as broadly statistical and not guaranteed in every case: in any generation, the hairiest elephant of all may fall into a crevasse and die.) Because offspring inherit their parents' degree of hairiness, the next generation will contain a higher proportion of more densely clad elephants (who will continue to be favored by natural selection as the climate becomes still colder). This process of increasing average hairiness may continue for many generations, leading to the evolution of woolly mammoths.

This little fable can help us understand how peculiar and how contrary to all traditions of Western thought and explanation of the Darwinian theory of evolution, and variational theories of historical change in general, must sound to the common ear. All the odd and fascinating properties of Darwinian evolution—the sensible and explainable but quite unpredictable nature of the outcome (dependent upon complex and contingent changes in local environments), the nonprogressive character of the alteration (adaptive only to these unpredictable local circumstances and not inevitably building a "better" elephant in any cosmic or general sense)—flow from the variational basis of natural selection.

Transformational theories work in a much simpler and more direct manner. If I want to go from A to B, I will have so much less conceptual (and actual) trouble if I can postulate a mechanism that will just push me there directly than if I must rely upon the selection of "a few good men" from a random cloud of variation about point A, then constitute a new generation around an average point one step closer to B, then generate a new cloud of random variation about this new point, then select "a few good men" once again from this new array—and then repeat this process over and over until I finally reach B.

When one adds the oddity of variational theories in general to our strong cultural and psychological resistance against their application to our own evolutionary origin (as an unpredictable and not necessary progressive little twig on life's luxuriant tree), then we can better understand why Darwin's revolution surpassed all other scientific discoveries in reformatory power and why so many people still fail to understand, and may even actively resist, its truly liberating content. (I must leave the issue of liberation for another time, but once we recognize that the specification of morals and the search for a meaning to our lives cannot be accomplished by scientific study in any case, then Darwin's variational mechanism will no longer seem threatening and may even become liberating in teaching us to look within ourselves for answers to these questions and to abandon a chimerical search for the purpose of our lives, and for the source of our ethical values, in the external workings of nature.)

These difficulties in grasping Darwin's great insight became exacerbated when our Victorian forebears made their unfortunate choice of a defining word—"evolution"—with its vernacular meaning of "directed unfolding." We would not face this additional problem today if "evolution" had undergone a complete transformation to become a strict and exclusive definition of biological change—with earlier and etymologically more appropriate usages then abandoned and forgotten. But important words rarely undergo such a clean switch of meaning, and "evolution" still maintains its original definition of "predictable unfolding" in several nonbiological disciplines—including astronomy.

When astronomers talk about the evolution of a star, they clearly do not have a variational theory like Darwin's in mind. Stars do not change through time because mama and papa stars generate broods of varying daughter stars, followed by the differential survival of daughters best adapted to their particular region of the cosmos. Rather, theories of stellar "evolution" could not be more relentlessly transformational in positing a definite and predictable sequence of changes unfolding as simple consequences of physical laws. (No biological process operates in exactly the same manner, but the life cycle of an organism certainly works better than the evolution of a species as a source of analogy.)

Ironically, astronomy undeniably trumps biology in faithfulness to the etymology and the vernacular definition of "evolution"—even though the term now holds far wider currency under the radically altered definition of the biological sciences. In fact, astronomers have been so true to the original definition that they confine "evolution" to historical sequences of predictable unfolding and resolutely shun the word when describing cosmic changes exhibiting the key features of biological evolution—unpredictability and lack of inherent directionality.

As an illustration of this astronomical usage, consider the most standard and conventional of all sources—the *Encyclopedia Britannica* article "Stars and Star Clusters" (15th edition, 1990 printing). The section entitled "Star Formation and Evolution" begins by analogizing stellar "evolution" to a preprogrammed life cycle, with the degree of evolution defined as the position along the predictable trajectory:

> Throughout the Milky Way Galaxy . . . astronomers have discovered stars that are well evolved or even approaching extinction, or both, as well as occasional stars that must be very young or still in the process of formation. Evolutionary effects on these stars are not negligible.

The fully predictable and linear sequence of stages in a stellar lifetime (evolution, to astronomers) records the consequences of a defining physical process in the construction and history of stars: the conversion of mass to energy by nuclear reactions deep within stars, leading to the transformation of hydrogen into helium.

> The spread of luminosities and colors of stars within the main sequence can be understood as a consequence of evolution . . . As the stars evolve, they adjust to the increase in the helium-to-hydrogen ratio in their cores . . . When the core fuel is exhausted, the internal structure of the star changes rapidly; it quickly leaves the main sequence and moves towards the region of giants and supergiants.

The same basic sequence unfolds through stellar lives, but the rate of change (evolution, to astronomers) varies as a predictable consequence of differences in mass:

> Like the rate of formation of a star, the subsequent rate of evolution on the main sequence is proportional to the mass of the star; the greater the mass, the more rapid the evolution.

More complex factors may determine variation in some stages of the life cycle, but the basic directionality (evolution, to astronomers) does not alter, and predictability from natural law remains precise and complete:

> The great spread in luminosities and colors of giant, supergiant, and subgiant stars is also understood to result from evolutionary events. When a star leaves the main sequence, its future evolution is precisely determined by its mass, rate of rotation (or angular momentum), chemical composition, and whether or not it is a member of a close binary system.

In the most revealing verbal clue of all, the discourse of this particular scientific culture seems to shun the word "evolution" when historical sequences become too meandering, too nondirectional, or too complex to explain as simple consequences of controlling laws—even though the end result may be markedly different from the beginning state, thus illustrating significant change through time. For example, the same *Britannica* article on stellar evolution notes that one can often reach conclusions about the origin of a star or a planet from the relative abundance of chemical elements in its present composition.

Earth, however, has become so modified during its geological history that we cannot use this inferential method to reconstruct the initial state of our own planet. Because the current configuration of Earth's surface developed through complex contingencies and could not have been predicted from simple laws, this style of change apparently does not rank as evolution—but only, in astronomical parlance, as being "affected."

The relative abundances of the chemical elements provide significant clues regarding their origin. The Earth's crust has been affected severely by erosion, fractionation, and other geologic events, so that its present varied composition offers few clues as to its early stages.

I don't mention these differences to lament, to complain, or to criticize astronomers in any way. After all, their use of "evolution" remains more faithful to etymology and the original English definition, whereas our Darwinian reconstruction has virtually reversed the original meaning. In this case, since neither side will or should give up its understanding of "evolution" (astronomers because they have retained an original and etymologically correct meaning, and evolutionists because their redefinition expresses the very heart of their central and revolutionary concept of life's history), our best solution lies simply in exposing the legitimate differences and explaining the good reasons behind the disparity in usage.

In this way, at least, we may avoid confusion and also the special frustration generated when prolonged wrangles arise from misunderstandings of words rather than from genuine disputes about things and causes in nature. We evolutionary biologists must remain especially sensitive to this issue, because we still face considerable opposition, based on conventional hopes and fears, to our insistence that life evolves in unpredictable directions, with no inherent goal. Since astronomical evolution upholds both contrary positions—predictability and directionality—evolutionary biologists need to emphasize their own distinctive meaning, especially since the general public feels much more comfortable with the astronomical sense and will therefore impose this more congenial definition upon the history of life if we do not clearly explain the logic, the evidence, and the sheer fascination of our challenging conclusion.

Two studies published within the past month led me to this topic, because each discovery confirms the biological, variational, and Darwinian "take" on evolution while also, and quite explicitly, refuting a previous, transformational interpretation—rooted in our culturally established prejudices for the more comforting, astronomical view—that had blocked our understanding and skewed our thoughts about an important episode in life's history:

1. *Vertebrates "all the way down."* In one of the most crucial and enigmatic episodes in the history of life—and a challenge to the older, more congenial idea that life has progressed in a basically stately, linear manner through the ages—nearly all animal phyla made their first appearance in the fossil record at essentially the same time, an interval of some 5 million years (about 525 million to 530 million years ago) called the Cambrian explosion. (Geological firecrackers have long fuses when measured by the inappropriate scale of human time.) Only one major phylum with prominent and fossilizable hard parts did not appear in this incident or during the Cambrian

period at all—the Bryozoa, a group of colonial marine organisms unknown to most nonspecialists today (although still relatively common in shallow oceanic waters) but prominent in the early fossil record of animal life.

One other group, until last month, also had no record within the Cambrian explosion, although late Cambrian representatives (well after the explosion itself) have been known for some time. Whereas popular texts have virtually ignored the Bryozoa, the absence of this other group has been prominently showcased and proclaimed highly significant. No vertebrates had ever been recovered from deposits of the Cambrian explosion, although close relatives within our phylum (the Chordata), if not technically vertebrates, had been collected (the Chordata includes three major subgroups: the tunicates, *Amphioxus* and its relatives, and the vertebrates proper).

This absence of vertebrates from strata bearing nearly all other fossilizable animal phyla provided a strong ray of hope for people who wished to view our own group as "higher" or more evolved in a more predictable direction. If evolution implies linear progression, then later is better—and uniquely later (or almost uniquely, given those pesky bryozoans) can only enhance the distinction. But the November 4, 1999, issue of *Nature* includes a persuasive article ("Lower Cambrian Vertebrates from South China," by D-G. Shu, H-L. Luo, S. Conway Morris, X-L. Zhang, S-X. Hu, L. Chen, J. Han, M. Zhu, Y. Li, and L-Z. Chen) reporting the discovery of two vertebrate genera within the Lower Cambrian Chengjiang formation of southern China, right within the temporal heart of the Cambrian explosion. (The Burgess Shale of western Canada, the celebrated site for most previous knowledge of early Cambrian animals, postdates the actual explosion by several million years. The recently discovered Chengjiang fauna, with equally exquisite preservation of soft anatomy, has been yielding comparable or even greater treasures for more than a decade. See "On Embryos and Ancestors," *Natural History*, July–August 1998.)

These two creatures—each only an inch or so in length and lacking both jaws and a backbone and in fact possessing no bony skeleton at all—might not strike a casual student as worthy of inclusion within our exalted lineage. But these features, however much they may command our present focus, arose later in the history of vertebrates and do not enter the central and inclusive taxonomic definition of our group. The vertebrate jaw, for example, evolved from hard parts that originally fortified the gill openings and then moved forward to surround the mouth. All early fishes—and two modern survivors of this initial radiation, the lampreys and the hagfishes—lacked jaws.

The two Chengjiang genera possess all the defining features of vertebrates: the stiff dorsal supporting rod, or notochord (subsequently lost in adults after the vertebal column evolved); the arrangement of flank musculature in a series of zigzag elements from front to back; the set of paired openings piercing the pharynx (operating primarily as respiratory gills in later fishes but used mostly for filter feeding in ancestral vertebrates). In fact, the best reconstruction of branching order on the vertebrate tree places the origin of these two new genera after the inferred ancestors of modern hagfishes but before the presumed forebears of lampreys. If this inference holds, then vertebrates already existed in substantial diversity within the Cambrian explosion. In any case, we now have two distinct and concrete examples of vertebrates "all the way down"—that is, in the very same strata that include the first known fossils of nearly all phyla of modern multicellular animals. We vertebrates do not stand higher and later than our invertebrate cousins, for all "advanced" animal phyla made their first appearance in the fossil record at essentially the same time. The vaunted complexity of vertebrates did not require a special delay to accommodate a slow series of progressive steps, predictable from the general principles of evolution.

2. *An ultimate parasite, or "how are the mighty fallen."* The phyla of complex multicellular animals enjoy a collective designation as Metazoa (literally, "higher animals"). Mobile, single-celled creatures bear the name Protozoa ("first animals"—actually a misnomer, since many of these creatures, in terms of genealogical branching, rank as close to multicellular plants and fungi as to multicellular animals). In a verbal in-between stand the Mesozoa ("middle animals"). Many taxonomic and evolutionary schemes for the organization of life rank the Mesozoa by the literal implication of their name—that is, as a persistently primitive group intermediate between the single-celled and the multicellular animals and illustrating a necessary transitional step in a progressivist reading of life's history.

But the Mesozoa have always been viewed as enigmatic, primarily because they live as parasites within truly multicellular animals, and parasites often adapt to their protected surroundings by evolving an extremely simplified anatomy, sometimes little more than a glob of absorptive and reproductive tissue cocooned within the body of a host. Thus, the extreme simplicity of parasitic anatomy could represent the evolutionary degeneration of a complex, free-living ancestor rather than the maintenance of a primitive state.

The major group of mesozoans, the Dicyemida, live as microscopic parasites in the renal organs of squid and octopuses. Their adult anatomy could hardly be simpler: a single axial cell (which generates the reproductive cells) in the center, enveloped by a single layer of ciliated outer cells (some ten to forty in number) arranged in a spiral around the axial cell, except at the front end [. . .].

The zoological status of the dicyemids has always been controversial. Some scientists, including Libbie H. Hyman, who wrote the definitive, multivolume text on invertebrate anatomy for her generation, regarded their simplicity as primitive and their evolutionary status as intermediate in the rising complexity of evolution. As she noted in 1940, "Their characters are in the main primitive and not the result of parasitic degeneration." But even those researchers who viewed the dicyemids as parasitic descendants of more complex free-living ancestors never dared to derive these ultimately simple multicellular creatures from a very complex metazoan. For example, Horace W. Stunkard, the leading student of dicyemids in the generation of my teachers, thought that these mesozoans had descended from the simplest of all Metazoa above the grade of sponges and corals—the platyhelminth flatworms.

Unfortunately, the anatomy of dicyemids has become so regressed and specialized that no evidence remains to link them firmly with other animal groups, so the controversy of persistently primitive versus degeneratively parasitic could never be settled until now. But newer methods of gene sequencing can solve this dilemma, because even though visible anatomy may fade or transform into something unrecognizable, evolution can hardly erase all traces of complex gene sequences. If genes known only from advanced Metazoa—and known to operate only in the context of organs and functions unique to Metazoa—also exist in dicyemids, then these creatures are probably degenerated metazoans. But if, after extensive search, no sign of distinctive metazoan genomes can be detected in dicyemids, then the Mesozoa may well be intermediate between single and multicelled life after all.

In the October 21, 1999, issue of *Nature*, M. Kobayashi, H. Furuya, and P.W.H. Holland present an elegant solution to this old problem ("Dicyemids Are Higher Animals"). These researchers located a *Hox* gene—a member of a distinctive subset known only from metazoans and operating in the differentiation of body structures along the antero-posterior (front to back) axis—in *Dicyema orientale*. These particular *Hox* genes occur only in triploblastic, or "higher," metazoans with body cavities and three cell layers, and not in any of the groups (such as the Porifera, or sponges, and the Cnidaria, or corals and their relatives) traditionally placed "below" triploblasts. Thus, the dicyemids are descended from "higher," triploblastic animals and have become maximally simplified in anatomy by adaptation to their parasitic lifestyle. They do not represent primitive vestiges of an early stage in the linear progress of life.

In short, if the traditionally "highest" of all triploblasts—the vertebrate line, including our exalted selves—appears in the fossil record at the same time as all other triploblastic phyla in the Cambrian explosion, and if the most anatomically simplified of all parasites can evolve (as an adaptation to local ecology) from a free-living lineage within the "higher," triploblastic phyla, then the biological, variational, and Darwinian meaning of "evolution" as unpredictable and nondirectional gains powerful support from two cases that, in a former and now disproven interpretation, once bolstered an opposite set of transformational prejudices.

As a final thought to contrast the predictable unfolding of stellar evolution with the contingent nondirectionality of biological evolution, I should note that Darwin's closing line about "this planet . . . cycling on according to the fixed law of gravity," while adequate for now, cannot hold for all time. Stellar evolution will, one day, enjoin a predictable end, at least to life on Earth. Quoting one more time from *Britannica*:

The Sun is destined to perish as a white dwarf. But before that happens, it will evolve into a red giant, engulfing Mercury and Venus in the process. At the same time, it will blow away the earth's atmosphere and boil its oceans, making the planet uninhabitable.

The same predictability also allows us to specify the timing of this catastrophe—about 5 billion years from now! A tolerably distant future, to be sure, but consider the issue another way, in comparison with the very different style of change known as biological evolution. Earth originated about 4.6 billion years ago. Thus, half of our planet's potential history unfolded before contingent biological evolution produced even a single species with consciousness sufficient to muse over such matters. Moreover, this single lineage arose within a marginal group of mammals—the primates, which include about 200 of the 4,000 or so mammalian species. By contrast, the world holds at least half a million species of beetles. If a meandering process consumed half of all available time to build such an adaptation even once, then mentality at a human level certainly doesn't seem to rank among the "sure bets," or even the mild probabilities, of history.

We must therefore contrast the good fortune of our own evolution with the inexorable evolution of our nurturing Sun toward a spectacular climax that might make our further evolution impossible. True, the time may be too distant to inspire any practical concern, but we humans do like to muse and to wonder. The contingency of our evolution offers no guarantees against the certainties of the Sun's evolution. We shall probably be long gone by then, perhaps taking a good deal of life with us and perhaps leaving those previously indestructible bacteria as the highest mute witnesses to a stellar expansion that will finally unleash a unicellular Armageddon. Or perhaps we, or our successors, will have colonized the universe by then and will shed only a brief tear for the destruction of a little cosmic exhibit entitled "the museum of our geographic origins." Somehow I prefer the excitement of wondering and cogitation—not to mention the power inherent in acting upon things that *can* be changed—to the certainty of distant dissolution.   ■

■ *QUESTIONS FOR MAKING CONNECTIONS WITHIN THE READING* ■

1. What is at stake in changing the meaning of the word *evolution*? What does the word mean to the Kansas school board? To biologists? To astronomers? To nonscientists?

2. Gould states that, "All the odd and fascinating properties of Darwinian evolution . . . flow from the variational basis of natural selection." What is the "variational basis"? What are the "odd and fascinating properties" that it gives to Darwinian evolution?

3. Gould makes the following observation:

> once we recognize that the specification of morals and the search for a meaning to our lives cannot be accomplished by scientific study in any case, then Darwin's variational mechanism will no longer seem threatening and may even become liberating in teaching us to look within ourselves for answers to these questions and to abandon a chimerical search for the purpose of our lives, and for the source of our ethical values, in the external workings of nature.

Is Gould's point that life has no purpose or meaning? What does he consider to be the appropriate relation between moral and ethical questions and scientific research? Do these observations have anything to do with the history surrounding the idea of evolution? How about with events like the decision by the Kansas school board?

▪ QUESTIONS FOR WRITING ▪

1. Is it really possible for ordinary people to take science into account when posing ethical and moral questions? How can we believe in human moral or technological progress, for example, if we believe that biological life "evolves in unpredictable directions, with no inherent goal"? If people generally believed that life has no inherent goal, would this necessarily have destructive consequences? Does society have a right to protect itself from destructive values even when these values have their basis in good science?

2. Some recent thinkers have argued that words predetermine what we see and say. According to these thinkers, we can never know the world directly but must always view it through the "screen" of language. The only way to learn anything new is to change our use of words, and only after we have changed them can changes on the level of experience take place. When we look at snow, for example, we see only one thing because we have only one word. But when Inuit from the Arctic Circle look at snow, they may see more than twenty different kinds of things because their language has more than twenty different words for the single item we call *snow*. Does Gould's historical account of the term *evolution* confirm, contradict, or complicate this view?

▪ QUESTIONS FOR MAKING CONNECTIONS BETWEEN READINGS ▪

1. If we accept Gould's argument, does it make sense to view Peter F. Drucker's "knowledge society" as an example of genuine progress? Can we say that the rise of this new society has been in some sense preor-

dained by natural laws? Does Drucker himself imply the existence of an evolutionary *telos* in human history? Which approach to evolution makes more sense in discussing social, cultural, and economic change—the definition used by biological scientists or the one used by astronomers? If neither approach is appropriate, is the word *evolution* ever appropriate in discussions of human affairs?

2. Would Ellen Dissanayake agree with Gould's views on the proper relation between human values and scientific discoveries? If not, does her approach directly contradict Gould's position, or does it seem to represent an alternative he failed to consider but of which he might approve?

For additional suggestions about making connections between readings, visit the Link-O-Mat and More Sample Assignments at <www.newhum.com>.

LANI GUINIER

LANI GUINIER [gwen-'ēr] rose to national prominence in 1993 when she was nominated by President Bill Clinton to fill the post of Assistant Attorney General for Civil Rights in the U.S. Justice Department. At the time of her nomination, Guinier was a professor at the University of Pennsylvania Law School and was primarily known in academic circles for having written extensively on how the electoral system might be reformed to better represent all of the nation's citizens in local, state, and national governing bodies. Within weeks of being nominated, however, Guinier found herself regularly pilloried in the press as the "quota queen" and, eventually, had her nomination withdrawn by Clinton who declared her ideas to be "undemocratic."

In an interview that followed shortly afterward, Guinier reflected back on the experience of having had her ideas distorted and of having been deprived a chance to defend her positions: "I would like to think that I stood on principle and that I didn't lose. I lost a job, . . . but I have a job for life [as a professor with tenure]. So [having the nomination withdrawn] really wasn't about my personal story but about the larger story of what my experience meant for the American people and our inability to have a genuine, meaningful conversation about race without name-calling and finger-pointing." Guinier has subsequently published a series of books that outline her commitment to what she terms in "Second Proms and Second Primaries" "the ideal of democracy," including *The Tyranny of the Majority: Fundamental Fairness in Representative Democracy* (1995); *Lift Every Voice: Turning a Civil Rights Setback into a New Vision of Social Justice* (1998); and with Gerald Torres, *The Miner's Canary: Enlisting Race, Resisting Power, Transforming Democracy* (2002).

Guinier, Lani. "Second Proms and Second Primaries: The Limits of Majority Rule," *Boston Review*. Oct/Nov 1992. 32–34.

Quotations and biographical information from Lani Guinier, "An Interview with Brian Lamb," 26 June 1994. <http://www.booknotes.org/transcripts/10199.htm>; Lani Guinier, "A 'Commonplace' Conversation with Lani Guinier," interview by Lise Funderburg. *African American Review*, 30(1996):196–204.

The first African American woman to be appointed to the faculty at Harvard University Law School, Guinier is particularly sensitive to the limits of a political system that embraces "the worst excesses of the adversarial model of litigation, the 'winner take all' model of sports, and the 'only one of you is going to be left standing' model of war." By focusing on race, voting rights, and representation, Guinier has sought to revive national discussion about the meaning of democracy in an increasingly heterogenous world: What is the meaning of democracy, Guinier asks, if voting minorities have no way to make their voices heard?

To learn more about Lani Guinier and the Civil Rights movement, visit the Link-O-Mat at <www.newhum.com>.

Second Proms and Second Primaries: The Limits of Majority Rule

Brother Rice High School held two senior proms last spring. It was not planned that way. The members of the prom committee at Brother Rice, a boy's Catholic high school in Chicago, expected just one prom when they hired a disc jockey, picked a rock band, and selected music for the prom by consulting student preferences. Each senior was asked to list his three favorite songs, with the understanding that the band would play the songs that appear most frequently on the lists.

Sounds attractively democratic. But Brother Rice is predominantly white, and last year's senior prom committee was all white. That's why they ended up with two proms. The black seniors at Brother Rice felt so shut out by the "democratic process" that they organized their own prom. As one black student put it: "For every vote we had, there were eight votes for what they wanted. . . . [W]ith us being in the minority we're always outvoted. It's as if we don't count." Some embittered white seniors saw things differently. They complained that the black students should have gone along with the majority: "The majority makes a decision. That's the way it works."

In a way, both groups were right: with majority rule and a racially organized majority, "we don't count" is the "way it works" for minorities. In a racially divided society majority rule is not a reliable instrument of democracy. That's a large claim, and one I don't base solely on the actions of the prom committee in one Chicago high school.

In a recent voting rights suit in Arkansas, I represented some black plaintiffs in a case that turned, in the end, less on legal technicalities than on the relationship between democracy and majority rule. The failure to challenge traditional assumptions about that relationship—to show that majority rule is sometimes unfair—sealed the defeat of the plaintiffs. With the Arkansas case as background, I will discuss the standard remedy that courts use when black plaintiffs win in voting rights cases—to establish a majority black electoral district. This strategy of "race conscious districting" is, I believe, an inadequate method for representing minority interests.

But if a group is unfairly treated when it forms a racial minority within a single district, and, if we cannot combat the unfairness by setting up a new district in which the racial minority is now a majority, then what is to be done? The answer is that we need an alternative to majoritarianism: a "principle of proportionality" that transcends winner-take-all majority rule and better accommodates the values of self-government, fairness, deliberation, compromise, and consensus that lie at the heart of the democratic ideal.

The Case of the Majority Vote Run-off

Phillips County is a predominantly rural, economically depressed county in Arkansas. Majority black in population, it is majority white both in voting age population and in registered voters. According to the 1980 census, 53 percent of the 34,772 residents are black; but blacks constitute only 47 percent of the county voting age population. Despite this representation in the population, blacks in the county have never had much political power. In fact, since Reconstruction, no black has ever been nominated to any county-wide office in Phillips County.

According to Sam Whitfield and the other plaintiffs in the case of *Whitfield, et al.* vs. *State Democratic Party*, the Arkansas law regulating primary elections bears a significant share of the responsibility for the lack of black political power. The law requires that a candidate receive a "majority of all the votes cast for candidates for the office" in order to win the party's nomination. If no candidate wins a majority in the first round of primaries, then the two leading candidates face each other in a run-off election two weeks later. The plaintiffs alleged that the majority requirement deprived black voters in Phillips County of an equal opportunity to elect the candidates of their choice—a violation of Section 2 of the Voting Rights Act of 1965 (as amended in 1982).

The cornerstone of their argument was the historical pattern of racially polarized voting in Phillips County: white voters vote exclusively for white candidates and black voters for black candidates. So if more than one white candidate sought a nomination, the white vote would be divided and the black candidate might win the support of a plurality by winning all the votes cast by black voters. But there would be no chance for a black candidate to win a majority of the votes for nomination. The majority requirement would, then, force a run-off two weeks later. And in the run-off, the whites would close ranks and defeat the black candidate.

In 1986 and 1988, for example, four blacks came in first as plurality winners in preferential primaries, only to be defeated by racially polarized voting in run-offs. In neither the first or second primary did any white person publicly support or endorse a black candidate. In fact, Rev. Julius McGruder, black political candidate and former school board member, testified on the basis of 15 years working in elections that "no white candidate or white person has came out and supported no black." When Sam Whitfield won a first primary and requested support from Kenneth Stoner, a white candidate he defeated in the first round, Stoner told him that "He could not support a black man. He lives in this town. He is a farmer. His wife teaches school here and that there is just no way that he could support a black candidate."

But racially polarized voting is only one of the political disadvantages for blacks in Phillips County. Blacks also suffer disproportionately from poverty, and that poverty works to impede their effective participation in the run-off primary. For example, 42 percent of blacks lack any vehicle, while only nine percent of the white population are similarly handicapped; and 30 percent of blacks—compared to 11 percent of whites—have no telephone. Isolated by this poverty, black voters are less able to maneuver around such obstacles as frequent, last minute changes in polling places—moving them to locations up to twelve to fifteen miles away, over dirt and gravel roads. Moreover, because of the number of blacks without cars, the lack of public transportation in the county, and the expense of taxis, the run-off election campaigns of black candidates must include "a get-out-and-vote kind of funding effort where we try to have cars to drive people to the polls."

Getting people to the polls a second time within a two-week period severely limits the resources of black candidates, who have difficulty raising money a second time, paying for advertisements, notifying their supporters of the run-off election, and then convincing their supporters to go back to the polls a second time. Rev. McGruder testified that the run-off "just kill[s] all of the momentum, all of the hope, all of the faith, the belief in the system." According to McGruder, many voters "really can't understand the situation where you say 'You know, Brother Whitfield won last night' and then come up to a grandma or my uncle, auntie and say 'Hey, you know, we're going to have to run again in the next 10 days and—because we've got a run-off.'"

In fact, between the first and second primary, turn-out drops precipitously, so that the so-called majority winner in the run-off may receive fewer votes than the black plurality winner in the first primary. For example, 1,893 fewer people voted in the run-off for County Judge in 1986 than in the first primary; and 1,725 fewer people voted in the 1986 circuit clerk run-off. In fact, in all three black/white run-off contests in 1986, the white run-off victor's majority occurred only because the number of people who came out to vote in the second primary went down.

The District Court that heard the 1988 challenge to the Arkansas law did not dispute the facts: that no black candidate had ever been elected to county-wide or state legislative office from Phillips County, and that "race has frequently dominated over qualifications and issues" in elections. Nevertheless, the court rejected the challenge to the majority requirement.

In the first place, the Court argued that the run-off requirement could not itself be blamed for the dilution of black voting strength. To be sure, bloc-voting by the white majority consistently prevented a relatively cohesive black population from nominating or electing their chosen representatives. But, the Court argued, that problem could not be solved by eliminating the run-off. On the contrary, if white candidates were stripped of the protection provided by the run-off, they would simply limit their numbers in the first round, self-selecting one white to run head-to-head against a black. So eliminating the run-off would "tend to perpetuate racial polarization and bloc-voting."

More fundamentally, however, the Court's decision was based more on its enthusiasm for the majority vote requirement than on its skepticism about the benefits of removing that requirement. Majority rule lies at "the very heart of our political system"; the requirement in the primaries was "not tenuous but, to the contrary, strong, laudable, reasonable, and fair to all." For a court to invalidate a majority vote requirement would undermine the operation of democratic systems of representation because "Americans have traditionally been schooled in the notion of majority rule. . . . [A] majority vote gives validation and credibility and invites acceptance; a plurality vote tends to lead to a lack of acceptance and instability."

The central place of majoritarianism in the Court's perception of the case can be highlighted with one more piece of background. Courts do, of course, sometimes invalidate voting schemes on the ground that those schemes deny a minority "an equal opportunity" to nominate or elect "candidates of their choice." In such cases, the court aims to ensure that all groups have some opportunity to have their interests represented in the governing body. For example, when an existing district has a black minority the standard remedy is to establish a subdistrict with a black majority in which blacks can elect representatives of their choice. By creating pockets in which minorities are majorities, race conscious districting provides a remedy for underrepresentation that respects the concerns of minorities while affirming the dominance of the majority principle.

But there was a problem with the standard remedy in Phillips County: the majority vote requirement applied to elections for seven county-wide positions. So each position represented the *entire* electorate. In such a circumstance, several courts have said that the statute does not apply. There can be no equal opportunity to elect because there is "no share" of a single-person office. Modifying an electoral structure to create alternative subdistrict majorities is not plausible where the majority vote rule applies to single-person offices.

With subdistricting ruled out, the only possible remedy then, would have been for the court to require the replacement of the majority requirement with a plurality system. And that is precisely what the plaintiffs asked the Court to do. But—and here we return to the main point—the Court would not require a plurality scheme because of its own conception of the central place of majoritarianism in democracy. While a plurality win in many cases is quite conventional, to order it as a remedy opened up possibilities of non-majoritarianism that the Court found quite threatening. With a plurality system unacceptable, and subdistricting unavailable, the court had no remedy for the plaintiffs. Absent a remedy, the Court found no violation.

At bottom then, the case was about democracy and majority rule. The Court denied relief because it identified democracy with majority rule. In fact, the Court actually suggested that if plaintiffs lost an election, their interpretation of the Act would require the Court simply to suspend elections. Where the Court saw democracy, however, the plaintiffs saw rule by a white numerical majority. As a numerical and stigmatized minority, they regarded the majority vote requirement as simply a white tool to "steal the election"— a tool that had the effect of demobilizing black political participation, enhancing polarization rather than fostering debate and, in general, excluding black interests from the political process.

In short, the Court's conclusions were supported less by the evidence in Phillips County than by the Court's own majoritarian conception of democracy. To win the case then, the plaintiffs needed directly to challenge this premise about the intimate link between majority rule and democracy.

For example, they might have argued that majority rule is legitimate only when it is fair, and not simply because it is desirable to make decisions whose supporters outnumber their opponents. The conventional case for the fairness of majority rule, however, is that it is not really the rule of a fixed group—The Majority—on all issues; instead it is the rule of shifting majorities, as the losers at one time or on one issue join with others and become part of the governing coalition at another time or on another issue. So the argument for the majority principle connects it with the value of reciprocity: you cooperate when you lose in part because members of the current majority will cooperate when you win and they lose. The result will be a fair system of mutually beneficial cooperation.

But when a prejudiced majority excludes, refuses to inform itself about, or even seeks to thwart the preferences of the minority, then majority rule loses its link with the ideal of reciprocity, and so its moral authority. As the plaintiffs' evidence conclusively demonstrated, this was precisely the situation in Phillips County, where the fairness of the majority requirement was destroyed by the extreme racial polarization, the absence of reciprocity, and the artificial majorities created in the run-offs.

Racial Districting

Under conditions of sharp racial division then, majority rule can serve as an instrument to suppress a minority. It is not a fair way to resolve disagreements because it no longer promises reciprocity. That is what we learn from Brother Rice High School and Phillips County, Arkansas.

How can this unfairness be remedied? Perhaps through a more vigorous application of the conventional remedy of race-conscious districting. As indicated earlier, this remedy is not applied when—as in Phillips County—there is a system of district-wide, single-person offices rather than a collective decision-making body with multiple seats. But in the face of evidence of racial subordination, courts could simply reject such arrangements, require a system of subdistricts, and then ensure that some subdistricts have, for example, a black majority.

This strategy of judicially imposing alternative electoral constituencies is in fact consistent with some understandings of the Voting Rights Act. But instead of dwelling on legal issues, since race-conscious districting is, like any system of winner-take-all, flawed as a method for ensuring a fair system of political representation—I'll argue and evaluate the conventional remedy on three tests of political fairness from the perspective of minority interests: Does a system mobilize or discourage participation? Does it encourage genuine debate or foster polarization? Does it promise real inclusion or only token representation? Race-conscious districting does not do well on any of these three dimensions. While it may be true that no election structure alone can do all that I envision, we need to consider alternatives to single-member districts—in particular, to consider systems of proportional representation, which promise politically cohesive minorities both potential electoral success *and proportionate influence* throughout the extended political process. But I'm jumping ahead. First we need to see the problems with establishing geographically defined, race-conscious districts, each of which elects a single member to a representative body.

Firstly, *districting fails to mobilize sustained voter participation.* Districting systems rely on geography as a tool for identifying voter interests. Voters are assigned to territorial constituencies, the assumption being that territorial contiguity is associated with a community of interest.

Moreover, districting assumes that smaller political units best fulfill the political empowerment and equality norms of American constitutional jurisprudence. With smaller units, it's easier for constituents to identify political leaders, easier to recognize communities of interest, and easier to participate. Also, safe black districts enable blacks to get elected and then re-elected leading to positions of seniority and status within the elected body.

At the same time, however, single member districts emphasize individual candidacies, and for this reason may demobilize poor black and Latino voters. Turn-out generally goes up in response to first time election opportunities for the candidate of choice of the minority community. But the mobilization efforts for these break-through elections are generally not repeated. As the black pioneer becomes the incumbent, turn-out drops.

Moreover, politics in geographically organized, winner-take-all electoral districts tend to develop an exclusively electoral focus. The result is that the core constituency becomes alienated given the absence of local, alternative community organizations to educate and mobilize constituent participation outside of elections. Indeed, once elected, incumbents may demobilize constituents by not maintaining a genuine, community-based political organization to provide feedback, ideas, and reinforcement to the elected official while in office.

Furthermore, given racially-polarized voting, single-member districts give rise to real gains only to the extent there is substantial residential segregation at the appropriate geographic scale. Thus, for Latinos who live in dispersed barrios, districting does not capture either their real or potential power. In addition, it may exacerbate intergroup conflict as minorities are pitted against each other in a fight to be "the group" who gets the district. In jurisdictions with a complicated racial, ethnic, and linguistic mix, the redistricting struggle often becomes a source of conflict between blacks and other minority voters. These groups may compete over how many minority districts should be created and who should control them. Each group is encouraged to assert its superior moral, historic, and pragmatic claim. But in the lottery of competing oppression, no one wins.

Single-member districts also tend to under-represent minority voters, even where some race-conscious districts are created. Unless minority voters are both large enough and concentrated "just right," they will not enjoy representation in proportion to their presence in the population. Thus after a decade of race-conscious districting, blacks are not proportionately represented in any of the Southern legislatures.

Districting then, is limited as a strategy of empowerment. It is also troubling because it denies the connection between empowerment and voluntary participation. Districts are drawn by professionals without any involvement by voters. The presumption is that their political interests can be identified by their residential choices. The process of creating districts, which may be accompanied by extensive but perfunctory public hearings, is dominated by incumbent self-interest or court-appointed experts with no particular tie to grassroots concerns. By removing the issue from the voter, the districting process is antithetical to empowerment strategies based on voter participation and voter choice.

Furthermore, districting assumes that even where voters' interests are not represented by the ultimate district winner, their real interests will somehow indirectly get represented. Consider an earlier Supreme Court case, *UJO v. Carey*. Hasidic Jews in Brooklyn challenged a legislative plan on the grounds that it discriminated against them by employing race-conscious districting. The Court denied the claim, holding that the challenged plan conveyed no stigma or disadvantage and so was not unconstitutional. In arriving at this conclusion, the Court in effect treated the Hasidim as just another group of white voters. The Court argued that white voters were proportionately represented state-wide, so drawing districts to represent blacks did not disadvantage whites—even a white, Hasidic minority within a majority black district. This argument assumes that voters are interchangeable, that the courts can override voters' self-categorizations, and that the courts know better than the voters when their real interests are represented.

Secondly, *districting fails to foster genuine debate about issues.* In geographic districts, the threshold of representation is put close to 50 percent because districts are winner-take-all. The idea is that the winning candidate must demonstrate significant support to justify gaining *all* the power, but this pushes candidates toward the middle of the political spectrum where most of the votes are. The focus on developing consensus prior to the election means that issues are often not fully articulated or debated. Candidates avoid controversial positions and instead offer palliatives designed to offend no one.

Furthermore, the fact that interests within the district are only represented to the extent they garner majority support dooms third political parties to perpetual defeat. Because parties only win anything if they win a majority, and because it is difficult for a third party to win a majority, voters are reluctant to "throw away" their votes on third party candidates. And this in turn narrows the scope of political debate.

By promoting only two real choices, winner-take-all districting also has created an environment conducive to negative campaigning. A system that fosters two-way races is the "basis for such tried-and-true strategies as driving up the negatives of [an opponent] without worrying that the defecting voters will turn to a relatively unsullied third candidate," a common occurrence in three-way races. Negative campaign tactics contribute to voter alienation and apathy.

And thirdly, *districting fails to promote opportunities for more than token inclusion.* Proponents of race-conscious districting believe that separate can be made equal, or at least that poor blacks are empowered when provided a choice to elect a representative accountable only to them. Thus, they assume that electoral control works as a proxy for interest.

Creating majority black, predominantly poor districts is one way to ensure at least physical representation of black interests. This makes sense to the extent that electoral control insures accountability and influence. But racial districting also means that the electoral success of white legislators in white districts is not dependent on black votes. The direct consequence of majority black districts is that fewer white legislators are directly accountable to black interests. In this way, districting may reproduce within the legislature the polarization experienced at the polls; token electoral presence is replaced by token legislative presence.

Where blacks and whites are geographically separate, race-conscious districting isolates blacks from potential white allies—for example, white women—who are not geographically concentrated. It "wastes" the votes of white liberals who may be submerged within white, Republican districts. Thus it suppresses the potential development of issue-based campaigning and cross-racial coalitions.

As a consequence, race-conscious districting does not give blacks proportional legislative influence. Because majority black districts are necessarily accompanied by majority white districts, black representatives may be isolated in the governing body. Some conservative critics of race-conscious districting argue that such districts quarantine poor blacks in inner-city ghettoes. For example, critics of newly-drawn majority black congressional districts claim that the districts ultimately benefit white Republicans. In Alabama, for example, one critic claims such a district "yokes together by violence" areas as geographically different but racially similar as a large section of industrial Birmingham and vast expanses of the rural Black Belt, thus leaving other districts whiter and more Republican.

What these and related difficulties underscore is that proportionate influence requires something that winner-take-all districts simply cannot provide to numerically-weak minority voters: a basis of inclusion and representation that does not require winning more than 50 percent of the votes in a politically-imposed and geographically-defined constituency.

Proportionality

Let's now consider a system of proportional representation that drops the majority requirement. There are many such systems, but here I will focus on a scheme used in corporate governance called "cumulative voting." Under cumulative voting, voters cast multiple votes up to the number fixed by the number of open seats. If there are five seats on the city council, then each voter gets to cast five votes; if there are thirty songs at the senior prom, then each senior gets thirty votes. But they may choose to express the intensity of their preferences by concentrating all of their votes on a single candidate or a single song.

Let's return now to the three tests sketched earlier, and consider how cumulative voting fares in mobilizing participation, encouraging debate, and fostering inclusion.

Cumulative Voting and Participation. If voting is polarized along racial lines, as voting rights litigation cases hypothesize, then a system of cumulative voting would likely operate to provide at least a minimal level of minority representation. Unlike race-conscious districting, however, cumulative voting allows minority group members to identify their own allegiances and their preferences based on their strategic use of multiple voting possibilities. Instead of having the government authoritatively assign people to groups and districts, cumulative voting allows voluntary interest constituencies to form and regroup at each election; voters in effect "redistrict" themselves at every election. By abandoning geographic districting, it also permits a fair representation of minority voters who do not enjoy the numerical strength to become a district electoral majority or who—as in my earlier example of Latinos living in dispersed barrios—are so geographically separated within a large metropolitan area that their strength cannot be maximized within one or more single-member districts.

In all of these ways, cumulative voting would likely encourage greater electoral participation.

Cumulative Voting and Political Debate. Cumulative voting also looks good as a way to encourage genuine debate rather than foster polarization. Cumulative voting lowers the barriers to entry for third parties since supporters of such parties can concentrate all their votes on the candidates from their party. With those barriers reduced, minority political parties might reclaim, at a newly invigorated grassroots level, the traditional party role of mobilizing voter participation, expanding the space of organized alternatives, and so stretching the limits of political debate. Additionally, locally-based political parties might then organize around issues or issue-based coalitions. Since the potential support for the minority political party is not confined by a geographic or necessarily racial base, cross-racial coalitions are possible.

Cumulative Voting and Inclusion. Cumulative voting is more inclusive than winner-take-all race-conscious districting. Cumulative voting begins with the proposition that a consensus model of power sharing is preferable to a majoritarian model of centralized, winner-take-all accountability and popular sovereignty. It takes the idea of democracy by consensus and compromise and structures it in a deliberative, collective decision-making body in which the prejudiced white majority is "disaggregated." The majority is disaggregated both because the threshold for participation and representation is lowered to something less than 51 percent and because minorities are not simply shunted into "their own districts." These changes would encourage and reward efforts to build electoral alliances with minorities.

To get the full benefits of cumulative voting, however, it would also be necessary to change the process of governmental decision-making itself, away from a majoritarian model toward one of proportional power. In particular, efforts to centralize authority in a single executive would be discouraged in favor of power-sharing alternatives that emphasize collective decision-making. Within the legislature, rules would be preferred that require super-majorities for the enactment of certain decisions so that minority groups have an effective veto, thus forcing the majority to bargain with them and include them in any winning coalition, and with other devices for minority incorporation such as rotation in legislative office. Other electoral and legislative decision-making alternatives also exist such as legislative cumulative voting, that are fair and legitimate and that preserve representational authenticity, yet are more likely than current practices to promote just results.

The principle of proportionality is molded by the hope that a more cooperative political style of deliberation and ultimately a more equal basis for preference satisfaction is possible when authentic minority representatives are reinforced by structures to empower them at every stage of the political process. Ultimately however, representation and participation based on principles of proportionality are also an attempt to reconceptualize the ideal of political equality, and so the ideal of democracy itself.

The aim of that reconstruction should be to re-orient our political imagination away from the chimera of achieving a physically integrated legislature in a color-blind society and toward a clearer vision of a fair and just society. In the debate over competing claims to democratic legitimacy based on the value of minority group representation, I side with the advocates of an integrated, diverse legislature. A homogeneous legislature in a heterogeneous society is simply not legitimate.

But while black legislative visibility is an important measure of electoral fairness, taken by itself it represents an anemic approach to political fairness and justice. A vision of fairness and justice must begin to imagine a full and effective voice for disadvantaged minorities, a voice that is accountable to self-identified community interests, a voice that persuades, and a voice that is included in and resonates throughout the political process. That voice will not be achieved by majoritarian means or by enforced separation into winner-take-all racial districts. For in the end democracy is not about rule by the powerful—even a powerful majority—nor is it about arbitrarily separating groups to create separate majorities in order to increase their share. Instead, the ideal of democracy promises a fair discussion among self-defined equals about how to achieve our common aspirations. To redeem that promise, we need to put the idea of proportionality at the center of our conception of representation.   ∎

▪ QUESTIONS FOR MAKING CONNECTIONS WITHIN THE READING ▪

1. Lani Guinier distinguishes among three different models for governance: the winner-take-all majority rule; an electoral system that awards victory to the candidate who has received a plurality of the votes; and, finally, a system based on a "principle of proportionality." What are the differences among these three systems? Is one system more democratic than the others? More fair? More just? Are these terms interchangeable?

2. The primary solution to the problem of minority underrepresentation in the political process has been to redraw the lines that establish voting

districts. What's wrong with this as a solution? Why can't redistricting lead to the kind of proportional representation that Guinier favors?

3. At the end of her essay, Guinier calls for us to move "away from the chimera of achieving a physically integrated legislature in a color-blind society and toward a clearer vision of a fair and just society." Why is "achieving a physically integrated legislature in a color-blind society" a "chimera"? And what would a "fair and just society" look like if it abandoned this chimera? How would it differ from the society we have today?

■ *QUESTIONS FOR WRITING* ■

1. Lani Guinier sets out, in "Second Proms and Second Primaries," to redefine democracy. What is the difference between her vision of democracy and a democracy based on majoritarianism? How do fairness and justice get defined in each of these understandings of democracy? What are the dangers you see in each of these understandings?

2. "[W]hen a prejudiced majority excludes, refuses to inform itself about, or even seeks to thwart the preferences of the minority," Guinier writes, "then majority rule loses its link with the ideal of reciprocity, and so its moral authority." Why is Guinier concerned with reciprocity and moral authority? What do these ideas have to do with elections and the democratic process? Does democracy depend on the ideal of reciprocity?

■ *QUESTIONS FOR MAKING CONNECTIONS BETWEEN READINGS* ■

1. Guinier argues that "[a] homogenous legislature in a heterogeneous society is simply not legitimate." Both Lani Guinier and Benjamin R. Barber describe democracy as a system that is in crisis. What changes would need to take place to establish a democratic system that would be recognized as both legitimate and successful by these two authors?

2. Throughout "Second Proms and Second Primaries," Guinier argues that changing the electoral process will improve the quality of communication between the races, between constituencies, and across parties. What would Deborah Tannen make of Guinier's call to "encourage genuine debate"? Is the ideal of democracy that Guinier refers to approached through dialogue, debate, or some other mode of communication? What is the best way for citizens in a democracy to resolve their disagreements?

For additional suggestions about making connections between readings, visit the Link-O-Mat and More Sample Assignments at <www.newhum.com>.

STEPHEN S. HALL

THOSE WHO WORK in the pharmaceutical industry are regularly confronted with ethical questions that have life-or-death consequences. On the one hand, the industry is charged with creating and testing the medicinal drugs that ensure the public's health. On the other hand, the industry profits from the illness and suffering of others. Consequently, when those who work in the industry decide which drugs to develop and how much they should cost, their choices inevitably influence public health, the economy, and even, as was made clear after the anthrax attacks in the United States in 2001, national security. How are such decisions made? Why does the pharmaceutical industry elect to test and market one drug rather than another? What, if anything, does the industry do to ensure that real people aren't sacrificed during the pursuit of potential profit? These are the questions that Stephen Hall takes up in "Prescription for Profit," in which he examines the marketing of the antihistamine Claritin and the roles that doctors, scientists, and government regulators have played in making this the best-selling prescription drug of all time.

Hall has written extensively about scientific culture and scientific efforts to discover, explore, and create new knowledge. The author of *Invisible Frontiers: The Race to Synthesize a Human Gene* (1987), which describes the mapping of the human genome, and *A Commotion in the Blood: Life, Death, and the Immune System* (1998), which chronicles the medical community's attempts to cure cancer, Hall has tried to advance the public's understanding of the ethical perils and world-altering opportunities afforded by current scientific research projects. Hall has said, though, that he prefers not to be called a "science writer," but rather "a writer who happens to write about science." The distinction reflects Hall's overriding interest in telling stories and his belief that "science offers some of the most interesting stories, not merely in terms of personalities and individuals,

Hall, Stephen. "Prescription for Profit." *New York Times Magazine.* 11 March 2001. 41–100.

Quotations from Stephen Hall, interview, Winding Your Way through DNA Symposium, University of California, San Francisco, Fall 1992 <http://www.accessexcellence.com/AB/CC/hall.html>.

Note: Schering-Plough has denied permission to reprint the Claritin ads that accompanied the original version of this article.

but [also because] it is really one of the last cultures in this century of exploration and discovery." With his "biography" of Claritin, Hall gives his readers
access to the day-to-day workings, the moral tensions, and the financial concerns of this thriving, and sometimes threatening, culture.

To learn more about Stephen Hall and the pharmaceutical industry, visit the
Link-O-Mat at <www.newhum.com>.

Prescription for Profit

It had been yet another miserable, nose-dripping, red-eyed spring a couple
of years ago, when I finally went to see an allergy specialist. I've been battered by seasonal allergies all my life but relied on family doctors and, more
recently, "primary-care physicians" for relief. In a kind of a pharmaceutical
version of playing catch with Dad, my father and I shared his hay-fever pills
when I was growing up. They were smooth, round yellow tablets, etched
with a tiny red corporate symbol that was as delicate as a Chinese ideograph.
At a time before people routinely gobbled down a half dozen medicines a
day, those pills held a kind of mythic power for me, not only because they
could make the misery of allergies disappear but also because they were *prescription* drugs—inherently more powerful, more inaccessible, more special.

Those yellow pills were called Chlor-Trimeton, manufactured by the
Schering-Plough Corporation, first as a prescription drug and then, after
1976, as an over-the-counter medication. It definitely worked, but it knocked
me out. I remember days when I felt glazed by sleepiness. Even as the high
tide in my nose and throat subsided, I felt mentally waterlogged.

For the most part, I managed to get by with over-the-counter medications until that spring in 1999, when I decided I needed something stronger.
After rummaging through a cabinet in the examining room, my new allergist handed me a week's supply of Claritin, also made by Schering-Plough.
Claritin was, and still is, the most frequently dispensed drug sample in the
United States, part of the nearly $8 billion worth of free drug samples that
pharmaceutical companies distribute to doctors annually. I had seen the ads
on TV—who hadn't? I figured I'd give it a try.

Claritin had several other distinctions: it was by then the best-selling antihistamine in the United States, indeed the most profitable antihistamine of
all time, with annual sales of more than $2 billion. And it was the most ag-
gressively marketed drug to American consumers. Claritin is a drug for our
time: designed to relieve symptoms and improve "quality of life," hardly

lifesaving or even curative, expensive as hell. A month's supply of Claritin currently costs about $80 or $85 in the United States, even though it is an over-the-counter drug in many other countries, where it usually costs $10 or $15. The high domestic price is paired with an enormous potential market: an estimated 35 million Americans suffer seasonal allergies, and many of us will be feeling that first tickle of dread [in late March], when spring tree pollen begins to barge into our air passages like molecular roustabouts.

So I went home and tried it. The little white pill was easy to swallow and had to be taken only once a day. There was just one problem: it didn't work. It didn't relieve my runny nose and red-rimmed, gunked-up eyes. When I told my allergist, he didn't seem particularly surprised. Only about 30 to 40 percent of his patients, he said, found the drug helpful. And, he added, that estimate was "generous." I was surprised, perhaps naïvely, by this remark. I figured a "blockbuster" drug would be efficacious in more than 50 percent of the people who took it. The percentage he mentioned, incidentally, is certainly debatable; in fact a debate broke out later between my allergist and his partner, who thought 50 or 55 percent was more like it. Even so, it made me wonder: $80 for a drug that works only half the time?

Claritin has been singled out as a prime example of greed by the American pharmaceutical industry, notably [in summer of 2000] by Al Gore during his presidential campaign, and there has been a constant stream of negative press about Schering-Plough's efforts to get the basic patent on Claritin extended beyond its 2002 expiration. Schering-Plough has argued that the patent should be extended because the Food and Drug Administration review of Claritin was unusually "protracted" (which, in fact, it was). To press its case in Washington, the company has paid millions of dollars in political contributions and assembled a high-powered, strange-bedfellows team of lobbyists (including the former senators Howard Baker and Dennis DeConcini, the Gore confidant Peter Knight and Linda Daschle, wife of the Senate minority leader, Tom Daschle); it has also encouraged repeated attempts by Congressional supporters to insert language favorable to Schering into legislation at the last instant.

Claritin's 77-month odyssey through the F.D.A. approval process was indeed lengthy, as a General Accounting Office report, issued [in August 2000], documents. That report prompted me to read through the transcripts of old F.D.A. meetings, obtain other documents through Freedom of Information requests and speak to doctors about allergy medications in general. As I learned more about the approval of Claritin, I realized that the biography of this one drug reveals a great deal about why prescription drugs cost so much to bring to market, and also why health-care economists like Uwe E. Reinhardt of Princeton University argue that we are paying premium prices for new drugs like these without actually knowing if they are better than the drugs they've replaced. The Claritin story is an unauthorized biography, in the sense that Schering-Plough declined to grant any interviews and responded only to written questions.

It is above all a case study of how a drug company creates a blockbuster. There are no villains, no broken laws—just an enormous expenditure of money, a highly sophisticated understanding of food and drug laws, daring marketing, a great deal of luck. Making it all possible is a financial system that ultimately passes along the high price of a modest drug to third-party payers—and you.

Claritin's journey from lab bench to marketplace was nearly epic in the time it took, the vicissitudes encountered and the plot twists along the way. In June 1980, when Schering filed a patent for the group of chemical compounds that included the drug that would eventually be known as Claritin, the world of drug development was quite different. It typically cost a pharmaceutical company roughly $200 million to $250 million to develop a new drug; that cost is estimated to be closer to $500 million today, a figure that also accounts for failures along the way. A patent lasted 17 years from the date it was issued; it now lasts 20 years from the date the application is filed. And the effective patent life of a new drug—the amount of time a company can expect to enjoy an exclusive run in the marketplace—was about eight years; the average effective patent life of a drug has nearly doubled since then. The Schering patent, issued Aug. 4, 1981, stated that the compounds, including the future Claritin, were "useful as antihistamines with little or no sedative effects." Pharmaceutical companies rarely disclose the cost of bringing a specific drug to market, but it's a safe bet that it took at least several hundred million dollars to deliver on the promise of those nine words.

Loratadine (pronounced "low-RAT-a-deen")—the generic name for Claritin—was one of several second-generation antihistamines that emerged from drug-company laboratories in the 1980's. They worked by essentially the same simple mechanism as the first-generation antihistamines developed immediately after World War II, like Chlor-Trimeton. When pollen bumps into certain immune-system cells just beneath the lining of the nose, eyes or respiratory passages, it provokes an immunological overreaction in susceptible people. Thus perturbed, these "mast cells" shudder with the molecular equivalent of uncontrollable weeping; they churn out at least 15 different inflammatory molecules, many of which contribute to the allergic reaction. One of those molecules, unleashed instantaneously, is called histamine.

When these roving histamine molecules attach to receptors on nearby nerve cells, you feel an itch or a sneeze or a scratchy, ticklish palate. When they dock onto receptors in nearby blood vessels, the vessels become porous and leaky, and fluids begin to ooze into the tissues of your nose and eyes. Antihistamine drugs work because the active ingredient is a molecule that fits like a cap onto the histamine receptor, blocking the signal that causes itchy, watery symptoms.

Everyone agrees these drugs are effective, but just how effective is very difficult to say. All the antihistamine drugs, new and old, are plagued by high placebo effects. "It's a question of how bad a placebo effect you have," says Dr. Peter S. Creticos, head of the allergy and clinical immunology division at the Johns Hopkins University School of Medicine. "The placebo effect can be anywhere from 20 to 40 percent."

Complicating the process of determining efficacy is how the data are gathered: patients in these trials typically assess their own degree of symptom relief, which many allergists concede makes the data somewhat subjective.

Then there's the sponsorship of the science. Because the placebo effect is so high, large numbers of patients must be enlisted in chemical trials to achieve a robust, or statistically "significant," result, which means that only drug companies can afford the expense. Studies sponsored by drug companies tend to show an advantage for the company's own products. Zyrtec, an antihistamine produced by Pfizer, for example, has been shown to be more potent than other drugs in its antihistamine effect—in a study sponsored by Pfizer. Desloratadine, currently awaiting F.D.A. approval as the next generation "super-Claritin," is said to relieve nasal stuffiness, unlike other antihistamines—in a study done by Schering. And Allegra, produced by Aventis, was recently shown to be equal to Zyrtec—in a study sponsored by Aventis. "They're going to take that study all the way to the bank," one academic allergist chuckled. Which is precisely the point. Scientific studies of these drugs serve as marketing tools, providing drug-company salesmen with their best lines.

The first-generation antihistamines, now sold over the counter as Chlor-Trimeton, Benadryl, Tavist and others, are still considered pretty effective medicines. In fact, many allergists told me that they are at least equivalent in medical potency to newer drugs like Claritin and Allegra. But the first-generation molecules cross the blood-brain barrier and get into the central nervous system, causing drowsiness. The second-generation drugs have been medicinally engineered to stay out of the brain. As a result, they cause little or no sedation.

A nonsedating antihistamine was clearly a desirable drug, and Schering-Plough had been looking for one since the 1960's. In fact, the company thought it had one in a compound called azatadine. The drug is still sold as Optimine, and if you've never heard of it, that's because the compound looked deceptively nonsedating when it was tested in cats and showed its true, somnolent colors only during human testing. Next came loratadine. Following years of testing, Schering formally submitted what is known as a New Drug Application, or N.D.A., to the Food and Drug Administration on Oct. 31, 1986, seeking approval of loratadine.

Schering was not the first company to knock on the F.D.A.'s door with a nonsedating antihistamine. Seldane (terfenadine), manufactured by Marion Merrell Dow, had been approved the year before, and Hismanal (astemizole) was already under F.D.A. review. Because a similar nonsedating antihistamine was already on the market, the F.D.A. assigned Claritin its lowest priority for review—it was considered, according to an F.D.A. classification system no longer in use, a drug that "essentially duplicates in medical importance and therapeutic usage one or more already marketed drugs, offering little or no therapeutic gain over existing therapies." Technically, Claritin started out as a "me too" drug.

Schering-Plough doggedly pursued the approval of Claritin, spurred, no doubt, by the phenomenal success of Seldane. But it wasn't easy. Over six and a half years, Schering filed 37 major amendments to its application. The company decided to switch the formulation from capsules to tablets, and it took more than two years to show that the capsules used in clinical trials were pharmacologically identical to the tablets it intended to sell. Among the many obstacles Schering had to overcome, the first was to convince F.D.A. reviewers of the drug's main selling point: that it could be effective without causing drowsiness.

To approve a new drug, the F.D.A. must be convinced that it is both safe and effective. As a practical matter, that often means arriving at a balance between potency and side effects. Drug companies routinely submit notebooks of dictionary girth full of experimental results establishing a drug's safety profile, first in animals and then in human subjects. In establishing the effectiveness of a new drug, however, a company has only to show in well-designed trials that a drug is more effective than a sugar pill, and if there is already an equivalent drug on the market for the same use, that it is at least equally effective.

The effectiveness of loratadine had been an area of F.D.A. concern as early as January 1987, just months after Schering filed its application. Dr. Sherwin D. Straus, the F.D.A. medical officer assigned to review the drug, told the company that a 10-milligram dose of Claritin—the amount marketed today—did not appear to be very effective. He reiterated that point in public on Oct. 23, 1987, when the F.D.A.'s Pulmonary-Allergy Drugs Advisory Committee met at the agency headquarters in Rockville, Md., to consider Schering's application for loratadine. (This panel of outside experts doesn't formally approve new drugs, but makes influential recommendations to the agency.)

Establishing a drug's safety and efficacy is not a pretty business. A parade of Schering representatives described a staggering amount of data from animal tests in mice, rats, guinea pigs, cats and monkeys, including the "mouse-paw edema test" (in which mice have their paws cut off and weighed to see how successfully an antihistamine inhibits swelling). In several studies, extremely high doses of the drug, consumed daily for up to two years, produced borderline evidence of liver-tumor formation in rats and male mice, but otherwise loratadine appeared very clean. Indeed, the company maintains that the drug's "excellent safety profile is well established" by 10 billion "patient days" of experience in the marketplace.

After preclinical animal tests, Schering began to test loratadine in thousands of human patients, first to establish its safety and then to prove its effectiveness. The company ultimately submitted three so-called "pivotal" clinical trials to support the drug's safety and efficacy. Schering conducted what is considered the gold standard in drug testing—randomized, double-blind trials pitting Claritin against both placebo and one of several already approved antihistamines—and the results reveal just how vexing the placebo effect can be. In one study, for example, people taking Claritin experienced a 46 percent improvement in symptoms at the end of the trial; patients taking a placebo reported 35 percent improvement. In another trial, Claritin produced 43 percent improvement versus 32 percent on placebo. As part of these same studies, physicians examined the patients and, unaware of which treatment each had received, assessed their condition; these doctors concluded that anywhere from 37 to 47 percent of patients taking the sugar pill showed a "good or excellent response to treatment."

When it was his turn to speak, Straus engaged in a little bureaucratic soft-shoe, complimenting the Schering team's presentations as "a tough act to follow." Then he tried to demolish the heart of Schering's application. Straus didn't doubt that loratadine worked as an antihistamine, he said; he just doubted that it worked at the 10-milligram dose. In fact, at one point he claimed that "10 milligrams is not very different than placebo clinically." The reason the dose was so low, he argued, is that evidence of sedation began to crop up at higher, more effective doses.

What he didn't say—but what everyone understood—is that using a higher, more effective dose of Claritin would affect how the drug was described on the label. The term "nonsedating" was considered a critical marketing point. A single adjective or phrase contained in the F.D.A.-approved label—"no more sedating than a sugar pill," for example—can form the basis of claims made by company salesmen to doctors, the basis of words that throb in the bold type of advertisements, even the basis of lawsuits filed against competitors. Those seemingly eye-glazing, hairsplitting distinctions provide the foundation for multimillion-dollar marketing campaigns.

The clash over effectiveness was crystallized in one edgy exchange between Straus and Dr. Anthony Nicholson, a British neuroscientist, one of the Schering-sponsored clinical researchers, over the interpretation of a study that compared loratadine to a sedating antihistamine called tripolidine. "We are not actually in the business of saying one drug is better than the other," Nicholson told Straus. "We are in the business of saying whether a drug is acceptable in terms of its performance profile."

"But how can you say it is acceptable in terms of its performance profile," Straus replied, "without comparing it to what else is out there?"

"We compare it with placebo," Nicholson said.

"So you compare it to nothing."

"Yes."

"And it is better than nothing."

"Yes."

"All right," Straus said. "I can't argue with that."

The Schering representatives gave as good as they got. One suggested that Straus was guilty of statistical mischief; he had selectively looked at variables, subsets and time points, "and this is, as I am sure everybody in this audience knows, the perfect method of proving any claim one wants." Dr. William Darrow, a senior vice president at Schering, acknowledged that Straus's concerns were legitimate, "but for us the question is whether we have demonstrated consistently superiority and adequate efficacy over placebo by the 10-milligram dose. And we stand on our data there."

In a sense, they were both right. Schering had shown, according to the requirements of the law, that a 10-milligram dose of loratadine was more effective, and no more sedating, than placebo. And Straus had argued, to the satisfaction of at least some people on the committee, that while the drug might be more effective than placebo, it was not a whole lot more effective.

Perhaps the most startling assertion made at that 1987 meeting came not from Straus, however, but from Leslie Hendeles, a pharmacology professor at the University of Florida, and it is as relevant to allergy sufferers today as it was back then. He suggested that most of the patients in Schering's Claritin studies would have been better off being treated with a different class of allergy medication altogether—steroid nasal sprays. "Certainly, in this kind of patient that was selected for this study," he said to the gathering, "most clinicians would probably use intranasal steroids to provide very prompt and sustained relief, rather than antihistamines." To treat full-blown allergy symptoms with an antihistamine, he continued, was "pharmacologically irrational."

Hendeles and other experts made a similar point to me recently: steroid nasal sprays, like Flonase and Schering's own Nasonex, shut off an allergic reaction that's already under way. In 1998, the *Annals of Allergy, Asthma and Immunology* published treatment guidelines stating that these nasal sprays "are the most effective medication class for controlling symptoms" of allergies. The popular antihistamines are valuable at preventing an allergy attack from getting under way if taken ahead of time and seem to be effective against eye symptoms, but they rarely bring quick and substantial relief of nasal symptoms once histamine has already begun to wreak havoc. "We don't use these medicines correctly," said Peter Creticos of Johns Hopkins. "As I tell patients, by the time the process starts, the horse is already out of the barn in terms of the antihistamines. You turn the process off by using a nasal steroid."

Although the F.D.A. advisory committee recommended approval of loratadine, Straus remained skeptical. In the conclusions of a 321-page "medical officer review" dated Nov. 9, 1987, he described the proposed 10-milligram dose of Claritin as "minimally effective versus placebo" and added that 40 milligrams appeared to be "the minimum effective dose." He also argued that the label "must include sedation as an adverse reaction and include warnings to this effect." A former F.D.A. official, who requested anonymity, said that the agency informally asked Schering to test a higher dose of loratadine but lacked the regulatory authority to mandate it.

By May 1988, however, the F.D.A. had come to the conclusion that the 10-milligram dose was no more sedating than a placebo pill, and by July 1989, as the General Accounting Office report puts it, "a consensus had developed at F.D.A. that 10 milligrams was effective." It is impossible to determine whether Sherwin Straus had changed his mind. Around the time he was assessing loratadine, according to former colleagues, he developed multiple sclerosis and became seriously ill, eventually dying of the disease.

"Schering-Plough always believed that loratadine was safe and effective at the 10-milligram dose," William O'Donnell, a company spokesman, wrote in reply to a question, "and felt that the clinical studies that were done fully supported that conclusion."

Pharmaceutical executives rarely talk about luck as a feature in the process of drug development, but in 1989 alone, Claritin's fortunes were buffeted like a grain of pollen in an early spring breeze. In September of that year, the acting division director at the F.D.A., reviewing the drug's status, concluded that all outstanding issues regarding safety, efficacy and the equivalence of tablets and capsules had been resolved. Claritin should have been nearing approval. But earlier in the year, as part of an F.D.A. reorganization, the Claritin application was transferred to a different division within the F.D.A.; with the transfer came a new pharmacology reviewer. This reviewer revisited some toxicology issues Schering thought had been settled.

Around this time, according to Schering, tests on other products being conducted at the F.D.A.'s National Center for Toxicological Research in Jefferson, Ark., were showing that high doses of doxylamine, an antihistamine and sleep aid, produced liver tumors in rodents. These findings apparently prompted the F.D.A. to reconsider results of animal experiments with both loratadine and cetinizine (the active ingredient in Zyrtec); they, too, had shown increases in liver adenomas, abnormal growths that were then considered to be a "larval" form of malignant tumor.

The stakes for Claritin were high. If a prescription drug caused cancer in animals but was of medical importance, and if no satisfactory alternative existed, the usual procedure would be to approve the drug and describe the findings on the drug's label, said Paula Botstein, then a deputy F.D.A. director, at a 1991 meeting. But if similar drugs were already on the market and were not carcinogens, she said, the F.D.A. would "ordinarily" not approve a new drug if it caused cancer in animals. Both Seldane and Hismanal were already on the market, and neither caused cancer in animals. Because of this situation, said a former F.D.A. official who asked not to be named, the Claritin approval was "certainly" in doubt—even after an advisory panel concluded that it was unlikely to pose a cancer risk to humans. (The other two drugs, doxylamine and cetirizine, were also cleared of suspicion.) Nevertheless, the F.D.A. still insisted on further tests, which eventually convinced agency officials that the drug was safe. Schering-Plough has always insisted that Claritin is not a carcinogen.

While these safety concerns were being investigated, a fateful new chapter in the Claritin story began to unfold. On a night in November 1989, in what first looked like an unrelated event, a 39-year-old woman was brought to the National Naval Medical Center in Bethesda, Md., after fainting while driving on the Washington Beltway. She had lost consciousness four times in a two-day period. She was taking the antihistamine Seldane (not for allergies but for a sinus condition) and then began using an antifungal drug, ketoconazole, to prevent a vaginal yeast infection. "And that turned out to be a deadly combination," recalled Dr. Brian P. Monahan, who treated the woman for potentially fatal cardiac arrhythmias.

As doctors investigated this unusual case, they uncovered previous reports of dangerous irregularities in heartbeat among Seldane patients. Later they found that risk in Seldane patients to be associated with ketoconazole or erythromycin, a widely used antibiotic. In August 1990, at the F.D.A.'s urging, Seldane's manufacturer, Marion Merrell Dow, sent letters to doctors warning of these potentially fatal drug interactions, and in 1992 the F.D.A. ordered warning statements, outlined by a prominent black box, to appear at the top of the label and packaging on Seldane and Hismanal.

This turned out to be very good news for Claritin. Because of growing concerns about the two other nonsedating antihistamines, the F.D.A. "started to believe that it would be beneficial to have Claritin for sale," according to G.A.O. investigators. (Schering said in a statement, "We do not believe that loratadine was the result of a balancing of product-safety issues.")

In the span of several years, therefore, Claritin had gone from being a me-too drug, to one that looked possibly unapprovable, to the only game in town. This regulatory roller coaster finally came to a rest in April 1993 when, 77 months after Schering applied, the F.D.A. approved loratadine.

At least one analyst, Mara Goldstein of C.I.B.C. World Markets, estimates that Schering-Plough lost $4 billion in revenues because of the delay. But I heard a different view from a pharmacologist who, although insisting on anonymity, was familiar with these unfolding events. "I think they've grossly benefited from the delay at the agency," this researcher told me. "Because terfenadine"—the generic name for Seldane—"was getting blasted, they looked like a good alternative, and I think they actually got a much larger share when they hit the market because of it."

Since Claritin's approval, the marketing campaign for the drug has rewritten the rules for pharmaceutical promotion. The brand is ubiquitous: watching the World Series in 1999, viewers frequently saw Claritin proclaimed the "official allergy medication of Major League Baseball"; the bag the pharmacist gives you when you fill almost any prescription suggests that you "ask your pharmacist about Claritin-D 24 Hour."

The direct-to-consumer ads seen on TV and in magazines are only the tip of the iceberg. The bulk of pharmaceutical marketing goes on behind closed doors, where drug salesmen tout their products to doctors, and pharmaceutical companies now spend more than $13 billion a year on such promotion, according to I.M.S. Health, a company that tracks the pharmaceutical business. The language of those presentations is constrained by the language on the F.D.A.-approved label—in other words, all the battles over efficacy and sedation at those obscure F.D.A. meetings in the 1980's define the sales vocabulary of the 1990's.

Once again, Claritin was the beneficiary of some lucky timing. In August 1997, the F.D.A. relaxed its rules governing television advertising; rather than having to run the same fine print required in magazine ads, commercials could satisfy F.D.A. rules by giving a toll-free number, mentioning a magazine advertisement and instructing viewers to "ask your doctor" for more information. In a daring move closely watched by the rest of the industry, Schering-Plough poured $322 million into pitching Claritin to consumers in 1998 and 1999, far more than any other brand, according to the National Institute for Health Care Management Foundation, a nonprofit group in Washington.

"That campaign was a landmark," says the group's Steven D. Findlay. "The Claritin campaign, along with Viagra, Prilosec and a few other high-profile drugs, was very influential. Claritin was clearly the most visible, the most expensive and skillfully executed, and the bottom-line results were immediately apparent. It had a huge impact, because everybody is watching everybody else very closely." Drug companies spent an estimated $2.5 billion on consumer advertising in 2000; these ads may have brought in as much as a $5-to-$6 return for each dollar spent.

Yet critics point out that direct-to-consumer advertising illustrates an embarrassing paradox: marketing may be most indispensable in categories where new drugs may actually be less innovative. "Marketing is meant to sell drugs," Marcia Angell wrote in an editorial in *The New England Journal of Medicine* last June, "and the less important the drug, the more marketing it takes to sell it. Important new drugs do not need much promotion. Me-too drugs do."

But promotion works. Sales in the United States of the entire Claritin family—not just the 10-milligram tablets, but a syrup, quick-dissolving Redi-Tabs and both 12-hour and 24-hour Claritin-D versions with a decongestant—which stood at $1.4 billion in 1997, jumped to $2.6 billion by 2000. It accounts for nearly 30 percent of Schering-Plough's annual revenues.

Schering had a magnificent cash cow. Now the trick was to milk it as long as possible.

* * *

Almost from the moment Claritin was approved in 1993, with only five years remaining on its basic patent at the time, Schering-Plough and its competitors began to tussle over the drug's afterlife—and, more important, when it would begin. Generic drug companies typically gear up to produce a cheap version of a drug about five to seven years before a patent is due to expire. Schering, at that same time, began to mount its expensive legislative campaign to extend Claritin's patent. This fundamental conflict, played out in Congress and in court, is shaping the golden years of Claritin's already eventful career as a drug.

The Claritin patent has been extended several times already, each extension reflecting laws passed by Congress in the last two decades that have modernized the F.D.A. review process and significantly extended the effective life of drug patents. The extensions began with the Drug Price Competition and Patent Term Restoration Act of 1984, known informally as the Hatch-Waxman Act. Despite its dense legal provisions, Hatch-Waxman is an essential element of any conversation about drug prices in this country. The law was a legislative high-wire act designed to reward innovation at major pharmaceutical companies and protect intellectual property, while at the same time promoting lower drug costs, primarily by making it easier for generic drug makers to get to the American marketplace. As part of Hatch-Waxman, new drugs being developed after the law was enacted in 1984 could receive automatic patent extensions of five years. More than 100 drugs, including Claritin, were already in development when the law was passed; these products, known as "pipeline" drugs, were eligible for only two years. That reset the clock for Claritin's patent expiration to the summer of 2000.

In 1994, the Uruguay Round Agreements Act, an obscure addendum to the GATT treaty, added 22 months to the patent life of Claritin, pushing the expiration back to June 2002. And [in August 2000], the basic patent on Claritin was extended yet another six months, to December 2002, because Schering-Plough conducted pediatric trials of the drug. If six months doesn't sound like a lot, consider the economic incentive here: for the price of a modest clinical trial in children (costing at most $3 million), Schering can extend the life of its basic patent half a year and earn close to $1 billion. By one unofficial estimate, these three patent extensions will ultimately translate into additional Claritin revenues totaling about $13 billion.

Since 1996, there have been at least a half dozen attempts to extend Claritin's patent life even more. There was an attempt, for instance, in the summer of 2000 to slip language at the last minute into a military-appropriations bill. Schering's lobbying efforts have not been the most persistent, "just the crudest," according to Bruce Downey, C.E.O. of Barr Laboratories, a generic drug maker based in Pomona, N.Y., who has also testified against extending the Claritin patent.

Representative Waxman has derided the legislation proposed to provide Schering relief as the "Claritin Monopoly Relief Act." But the case for some of the pipeline drugs may not be as outrageous as some critics have suggested. Peter Barton Hutt, the former chief counsel at the F.D.A. and now a lawyer at the Washington firm Covington & Burling, has argued that limiting loratadine and several other pipeline drugs to a two-year extension was "completely arbitrary" and assumed much speedier approval.

As has been true of so much of this drug's history, however, timing is everything, and Schering-Plough's efforts to extend its monopoly [have] coincided with surging public discontent about the cost of drugs. As a result, each attempt by the company to get Congressional patent relief has become a rallying cry for opponents, including consumer watchdogs, health insurers and generic drug makers. Since the 1996 election, Schering has spent $19.9 million on lobbying and campaign contributions, according to the watchdog group Public Citizen. Yet the most tangible achievement to date of that $20 million lobbying campaign may be the way that it has galvanized the generic drug industry and attracted the attention of lawmakers. [In fall 2000], Senators John McCain and Charles Schumer introduced legislation designed to close loopholes in Hatch-Waxman.

For all the closed-door maneuvering in Washington, an equally revealing pharmaceutical endgame has been playing out, slowly, in a courtroom in New Jersey.

A chilly day in January, about two dozen dark-suited patent attorneys gathered in the United States District Court in Newark, in what has become a typical chain of events toward the end of a prescription drug's life: patent litigation. Unlike the arguments made by Schering-Plough's lobbyists in Washington, however, those made by its lawyers in court documents maintain that Claritin's patent protection extends beyond 2002.

[In August 2000], Teva Pharmaceuticals became the first company to receive tentative approval from the F.D.A. to market a generic version of Claritin. The key word here is "tentative." Teva must wait for the basic loratadine patent to expire [in June 2002]. It must wait for the resolution of a lawsuit filed against it by Schering, which could conceivably stretch into 2003. And it must wait for Geneva Pharmaceuticals, a generic company based in Broomfield, Colo., to bring *its* version of Claritin to market; Geneva is entitled to an exclusive 180-day run as the only generic in the market, a monopoly that the company receives as Hatch-Waxman's reward for being the first generic drug maker to challenge a brand drug's patent. The moment the first generic enters the market, industry experts estimate, the cost of generic Claritin will drop to about 80 percent of current prices. When everyone else jumps in six months later, the price will fall off a cliff. "With so many competitors," one generic executive told me, "the price will drop to $10 very quickly."

Generic companies fill about 42 percent of all drug prescriptions in this country, but the price disparity with brand-name drugs is striking. That market share accounted for slightly less than $20 billion in drug sales in

1999; brand company sales accounted for more than $90 billion. Industry advocates claim that if generic sales inched up to 52 percent, American consumers would save an estimated $11 billion a year in drug costs. If the generic industry is beginning to mature, as some maintain, one of the main factors in that process has been, oddly, Schering-Plough. "I think loratadine is one of the first examples," said Dr. Carole BenMaimon, head of the Generic Pharmaceutical Industry Association and until recently a vice president at Teva. "We were really able to make it an issue."

Much of the industry's current disgruntlement involves patent litigation—or as George S. Barrett, president and C.E.O. of Teva USA puts it, "the way the patent system has just been abused." When Congress devised the language of Hatch-Waxman back in 1984, the notion of a drug coming "off patent" was as simple as it sounds: once the patent for a basic compound expired, other companies were free to enter the market. But it's not that simple anymore, said BenMaimon, a physician who now heads a research division at Barr.

Brand companies now patent the process of manufacturing the raw material. They patent the medical uses to which the drug can be applied. They patent the formulation of the medicine (the other ingredients used to stabilize the drug). They can patent what's known in the industry as "trade dress"—the color, size and shape of the pill. They patent metabolites—the chemicals into which a drug breaks after being metabolized by the human body.

So drugs don't come "off patent" the way the 1984 law envisioned; they come off as a series of strategically staggered patents, a practice known as layering. And here's where Hatch-Waxman has inadvertently turned into a playbook for complicated, time-consuming—and, according to generic drug makers, frivolous—patent litigation.

On Feb. 5, 1998, Geneva Pharmaceuticals filed what's known as an abbreviated new drug application, or ANDA, seeking F.D.A. permission to sell a generic version of Claritin. Several days later, as obliged by Hatch-Waxman, Geneva notified the patent holder, Schering, of its plans. On March 19, Schering-Plough sued Geneva and its parent corporation, Novartis, claiming that two of its Claritin patents had been infringed. Since then, seven other drug makers—Zenith Goldline, Teva Pharmaceuticals, Mylan, Andrx, Impax, American Home Products and Apotex-Novex—have gone to the F.D.A. seeking approval to sell generic versions of Claritin. Although the issues vary from case to case, Schering has sued all of them.

Some critics make the case that since Hatch-Waxman, an inordinate amount of innovation has been displaced from research to litigation strategies. A lawsuit is far cheaper (about $5 million per case) and less risky than research, and the return on investment can be very high. "It's always cheaper to litigate than to lose market share," said a former top-level F.D.A. official who asked not to be named. "If you can keep a generic off the market for one day, three days, five days, two months or two years, that's a lot of revenue. Certainly a lot more than it would cost to pay your lawyers." A Schering spokesman says, "Schering-Plough believes that its patents are valid and enforceable."

William Fletcher, president of Teva North America, knows how frustrating this can be. "You know, people here have asked us several times, 'Why bother doing Claritin?'" he said. "There are going to be at least 10 competitors out there. The price is going to be, you know, 5 percent of Claritin. Why bother doing it? One reason is that we are a broad-line supplier, and we have to have every product in our line. The other reason is that we're just bloody-minded about it, quite frankly. Stubborn. You know, you're damned if you're going to let Schering-Plough get away with it!"

There's a larger game in play in the Newark courtroom, too, according to the generic companies, and it became more interesting a few weeks ago. As Schering-Plough holds the generics at bay with one hand, it had hoped to receive F.D.A. approval in time to introduce desloratadine, its second-generation version of Claritin that [was] marketed as Clarinex, [beginning in spring 2001]. "The longer the litigation is dragged out," says Elliot F. Hahn, president of Andrx, "the more opportunity they have to market desloratadine to physicians and switch them from the Claritin line to the desloratadine line." But that plan ran into a major snag in mid-February, when Schering-Plough revealed that the approval of desloratadine was being held up until the company corrects manufacturing deficiencies cited by the F.D.A. at four of its plants.

What to do in a crisis? Market! Several days later, as the company's stock plunged and attorneys hustled to organize shareholder lawsuits, Schering-Plough announced big new "consumer education" and pharmacy programs for Claritin—the "largest and most comprehensive allergy initiative of its kind." The company plans to distribute 35 million free drug samples to doctors, 6 million allergy brochures, 65,000 drugstore displays and, yes, 350 million more of those little blue pharmacy bags.

Finally, an edifying case of sticker shock. Late [in fall 2000], my allergist prescribed a month's supply of Claritin-D to clear up some congestion before I started my first round of allergy desensitization shots. The pharmacy had misplaced my insurance number, so when I went to pick up the prescription, the clerk handed me a bill for $103. This is the consumer's trickle-down tab for the roughly $250 million in drug development, more than $100 million a year in consumer advertising, many millions in closed-door marketing, $20 million in lobbying and political contributions, $5 million a year for litigation. I was stunned that it was so expensive, and I asked myself a question that is a normal part of every marketplace but health care. If I had to pay $103 out of my own pocket, would I buy this medicine? Was it worth it?

With the exception of elderly people on Medicare and the uninsured, most of us never ask that question. In a recent conversation, Gillian Shepherd, a Manhattan allergy specialist, addressed the same point, noting that antihistamines like Claritin and Allegra are about equal in potency to over-the-counter drugs like Chlor-Trimeton. And while some patients experience sedation with these drugs, many do not. "Fifty percent of the population can tolerate most of them without any sedation," she explained. "The feeling is that if there's a chance of sedation and third parties are paying, why not use the nonsedating drugs? If people were paying out of pocket, the story would be completely different."

As I labored to sort through all the clinical data and all the confusing advertising, I found myself wishing that we had reviewers who would talk bluntly about new drugs, who could discuss efficacy, safety and value from the consumer's point of view, who could deconstruct the advertising, who would include cost as a criterion. But those are medical judgments, some would say, and only doctors should dispense them. True, but many doctors, it turns out, have largely abdicated that responsibility—they rarely know what a drug costs, and as Shepherd mentioned, many learn about the properties of a given drug not from the medical literature but from company salesmen, who are paid to tell one-sided stories.

And so what? Richard Kogan, Schering's C.E.O., testified before Congress [in 1999] that drug companies need constant and ample revenue streams to support their enormous and dicey R&D enterprise, and he's right. In order to be competitive in this post-genomic era, large pharmaceutical companies need to spend $2 billion to $4 billion a year on research to develop new drugs. The industry has developed many remarkable medicines, and more are on the way.

But if high drug prices are a kind of innovation tax for American consumers, we should at least demand innovation in return. Many high-priced, successful drugs, like Zyrtec, are developed overseas and simply marketed here by American companies. Moreover, a significant amount of pharmaceutical innovation currently occurs in the biotech sector, where small, cutting-edge companies typically license their discoveries to big pharma, which has the marketing expertise. What innovative new drugs does Schering, for example, have in the pipeline, subsidized by the billions of dollars earned from Claritin? Financial analysts are mixed on the company's potential treatments—for cancer, asthma, high cholesterol and several other major diseases—but a leading candidate for future blockbuster status is . . . desloratadine, the chemical that is the principal metabolite, or breakdown product, of Claritin. Anyone who has taken Claritin has already had desloratadine in his or her body.

No one has seen much clinical data on the new drug, but many pharmacologists told me that metabolites rarely possess significantly more potency than their parent compounds, and one allergist confided, not for attribution: "The only reason I can see scientifically for bringing this out is that their patent is about to expire. There have been about 20 abstracts published for desloratadine, all from Schering and all saying there's a little edge here, a little edge there, none of which strike me as terribly important." But then, as the Claritin story makes clear, it's not always about innovation but rather about finding little edges here and there and then marketing the hell out of them.

Meanwhile, the laboratory of Raymond Woosley of Georgetown University has done research on an over-the-counter antihistamine, Schering's own Chlor-Trimeton—the same one my father shared with me decades ago. The lab has shown through sophisticated molecular-binding experiments that Chlor-Trimeton is more potent at grabbing and hanging onto the histamine receptor than any other antihistamine it has tested. For several years, the lab has wanted to test a lower—and possibly nonsedating—dose of the drug, to no avail. "We did a grant for four years for the N.I.H., and we didn't get it funded," Woosley said. "We assumed the innovator company didn't want to do it because they were making Claritin, and the generic companies didn't want to do it because it would cut into their profit margins even more."

Woosley's study might work; it might not. The issue is that our healthcare system has evolved to the point where there is no economic incentive even to try. For an industry that prides itself on taking risk, the risk of discovering that cheaper, older medicines might be just as good, and perhaps even better, than expensive new versions is apparently one risk too great to take. ∎

■ *QUESTIONS FOR MAKING CONNECTIONS WITHIN THE READING* ■

1. In order to follow the argument in "Prescription for Profit," one needs to have a general understanding of what an antihistamine is and how it works. In your own words, describe what an antihistamine is for, who uses it, and how it works.

2. Stephen Hall's argument includes lots of numbers; indeed, to understand the argument that he is making, you need to be able to identify which numbers are important and to be able to explain why those numbers are important. What would you say are the three most important figures that appear in Hall's argument? What makes the figures you've selected more important than the other figures in "Prescription for Profit"? How did you decide which figures to pick?

3. The title for Hall's article, "Prescription for Profit," seems a clever play on words: the article describes how Claritin became successful and, in so doing, appears to prescribe the approach to creating a profitable prescription drug. What is the difference between description and prescription? If one wished to successfully market a pharmaceutical drug, what are the prescribed steps that are "recommended" here?

■ *QUESTIONS FOR WRITING* ■

1. Stephen Hall describes Claritin as "a drug for our time" and he says his goal in "Prescription for Profit" is to provide "the biography" of this drug. What does the success of Claritin tell us about our time, exactly? Does the success of this drug suggest that health-care reform is necessary, or does it establish that our health-care system is working effectively as is? Can one have a first-rate health-care system without a commitment to profit?

2. Hall writes, "Establishing a drug's safety and efficacy is not a pretty business." The problem with determining whether a drug is safe and efficacious, according to Hall, is that all the research that is done to answer such questions is carried out by corporate scientists. If this is the problem, what is the solution? What is done currently to ensure that the health and welfare of those who use prescription drugs is protected? What other measures might be adopted?

■ *QUESTIONS FOR MAKING CONNECTIONS BETWEEN READINGS* ■

1. In "Science in the Courtroom: Opinions Without Evidence," Marcia Angell describes the problems that arise when scientists are called into court to testify on behalf of parties who pay their salaries. What does Stephen Hall's account suggest about the objectivity of science outside the courtroom? Where might one find scientific research that is objective? Is such neutral research an achievable goal, or is it simply a professional ideal?

2. Can Malcolm Gladwell's theory about the importance of context accommodate the roles that chance and marketing have played in Claritin's success, or do we need some other theory to explain why some approaches to treating physical discomfort succeed and others fail? That is, did Claritin "tip" because of how it was marketed, because of its innate value to consumers, or for some other reason altogether?

For additional suggestions about making connections between readings, visit the Link-O-Mat and More Sample Assignments at <www.newhum.com>.

HAZEL HENDERSON

THE ARGUMENT CAN be made that politics is the greatest casualty of our educational system. We study economics in economics classes, science in departments of biology and chemistry, and political science as a specialized discipline much like all the others. We seldom have the chance, though, to explore the connections between business trends and legislation, or between the environment and federal policy. Because we often think of politics as separate from the other aspects of our lives, few people have considered the possibility that the information revolution might also pave the way for a profound change in our political processes.

One person who has written thoughtfully about this subject is the independent scholar Hazel Henderson, who is most widely known for her work on the environment, communications, and global economics. Early in her career, Henderson became intrigued by the failures of economic and technological modernization in the Third World or Least Developed Countries (LDCs). In a series of books and articles, including *Creating Alternative Futures: The End of Economics* (1978), *Building a Win-Win World: Life Beyond Global Economic Warfare* (1996), and *Beyond Globalization: Shaping a Sustainable Global Economy* (1999), Henderson questioned the widely held assumption that modernization was simply a matter of importing scientific know-how and attracting adequate investment. Arguing that cultural, historical, and environmental factors had been fatally overlooked in efforts to offer international assistance, Henderson became a voice in the world community for "sustainable development," development designed to preserve or enhance the social and ecological health of local communities, as well as their political autonomy. In "Perfecting Democracy's Tools," Henderson considers how advances in communications technology might serve to make participatory democracy possible.

In order to appreciate the argument that follows, readers need to understand the kind of work that Henderson typically does. We might think of her as

---

Henderson, Hazel. "Perfecting Democracy's Tools." *Building a Win-Win World: Life Beyond Global Economic Warfare.* San Francisco: Berrett Koehler Publishers, 1996. 247–268.

Biographical information and illustration from Hazel Henderson's home page <http://www.hazelhenderson.com/>.

a "connector," to use Malcolm Gladwell's term. While some writers are widely
known for developing new and often specialized paradigms, others play an
equally important role by bringing together many different paradigms in original ways. Although Henderson has certainly done specialized work of her own,
much of her writing is primarily connective. Here she provides her readers with
the "tools" they will need in reconsidering the possibilities for direct democracy.

To learn more about Hazel Henderson and direct democracy, visit the Link-
O-Mat at <www.newhum.com>.

■ ■

Perfecting Democracy's Tools

. . .To steer today's complex societies, democracy now requires systemic, cy-
bernetic models, self-regulated by thousands of feedback loops at all levels.
As systems theorists know, the more complex a system, the more feedback
loops are required. Living systems, such as cities, corporations, nations, and
the United Nations, are the most complex of all. Thus it has been a triumph
of common sense that so many politicians, regardless of ideology and tradition, have begun moving toward democratization and markets, amplified
by freeing mass media to help guide inevitable restructurings.

A new danger is in simply *equating* democracy with other forms of de-
centralization, privatization, and markets. There is also widening confusion
between the two key individual signals from people to their decision makers in government and business—*votes* and *prices*—as feedbacks to guide
and correct decisions. These two vital forms of feedback are failing to deliver
enough timely information on the effects of policies and multiple restructurings to adequately guide and correct decisions. Votes every two or four
years are too slow and cannot refine voters' feedbacks on multiple issues,
while prices cannot guide markets without incorporating the fuller social
and environmental costs of products and services.

In the United States, democracy has atrophied. Over two hundred years
of experience with both votes and prices has not advanced the model of democratic, privately driven, self-organizing processes. In *Creating Alternative
Futures* (1978, 1996), I noted that the two hundredth birthday of the United
States in 1976 was a good time for us to examine the state of our lives, our
beliefs, and our values, so as to illuminate which were deep—even eternal—
and which were transient or merely fashionable. What might be "excess bag-
gage" and what would we continue to cherish and carry with us into our

third century? Could we clarify the cultural confusion over rights and responsibilities, preserving individual freedom in relationship to family values, our desire for community, and a broader national identity?

At the time of the U.S. bicentennial, expectations were high that all these problems could be addressed through the institutions inherited since the country's founding. In 1976 most U.S. citizens saw their country continuing to grow richer—with each generation aspiring to achieve better living standards that those of their forebears. The American Dream, however, sparked similar dreams via movies, TV, and radio all over the world. In the mid-1990s, the United States also encountered the hurricane change unleashed by the great globalization forces. There were increasing disagreements over priorities in budgeting and even over constitutional rights to "life, liberty, and the pursuit of happiness" under the rapidly changing conditions. Yet . . . technologies to help perfect U.S. democracy—high-speed data processing, electronic communications, call-in radio, TV, electronic town meetings, polling—had all been available . . . for over two decades. Well-grounded fears of misuses of such instantaneous forms of democracy had stifled the debate on how to design these potential tools of democratic participation so as to avoid abuse and new forms of totalitarianism.

How can we humans shape *hardware* technologies that have shrunk our world by consciously designing the needed *software* and social innovations now vital for our survival and cultural evolution? This developmental lag in social software and architecture can be seen in the twentieth century's triumphant political model: democracy. Nation after nation has come to acknowledge democracy as a necessary component for managing complex, modern social and political structures. South Africa, now an emerging powerhouse of leadership on that continent, has made a historic transition to democracy. Mechanistic models of eighteenth-century representative democracy, however, can no longer solve our ever-more-complex web of social, cultural, political, and economic problems.

First, we must accept that electronic hardware (largely developed for commercial markets and research *about* and their habits) will continue to be used and abused. We cannot repeal these technologies. We can redesign and adapt them from elitist to populist purposes (1) to help people understand more about their societies and the new threats and opportunities in today's global village; and (2) to collect and steer feedback and informed consent or opposition back to all decision-making levels: community groups; school boards; local, state, and national governments; and international bodies.

The challenge, as usual, is in designing the software to manage these potential feedback technologies. We must restructure their manipulative, top-down, "big-brother" aspects, which currently reinforce hierarchical institutions in both public and private sectors, as well as today's mindless mediocracy politics. The design principles we need to follow to gear the technologies to encourage the evolution of democracy include *prevention* (foresight); *coop-*

eration (finding consensus and balancing markets' emphases on competition); *acceptance of diversity* (a basic principle of living systems); and *clarification of underlying assumptions* (beliefs, goals, values) as the first step in the search for unifying global concerns and ethics. Emerging global ethics include respect for life, fairness and equity, aspirations for future generations, openness and freedom of information, and a love of one's homeland as part of the Earth (rather than mere allegiance to nations, leaders, or flags).

Genuine democracy must close the gap between elitism and populism and embrace a commitment to the proposition that people *can* govern themselves. Deeply held views about human nature color politics: whether humans are viewed as basically untrustworthy and morally flawed or whether they are deemed intrinsically good. This kind of deeply rooted either/or polarization plays out as either conservative, authoritarian, benevolent, or dictatorial elitism, or visionary idealism, populism, democracy, or anarchy. The wretched "Law of the Excluded Middle" (i.e., A cannot equal Not-A) that Western societies inherited from the Greeks still underlies our language and polarized, gridlocked politics.

My view is that human nature has equally positive and negative aspects. Thus the good-natured, life-affirming tendencies *and* the bad-tempered, selfish, greedy ones are reinforced (for better or worse) by feedbacks from family and community relationships, economic rules, and social and cultural life as well as the politics of nationals. As Western societies have become more technologically complex and interdependent, the simple either/or, conservative/liberal polarity and its familiar two-party politics, such as in the United States, cannot channel the multiplicity of issues and multidimensional debates that are necessary. I theorized in *Creating Alternative Futures* and *The Politics of the Solar Age* (1981, 1988) why the protest movements of the 1960s could not find expression in U.S. politics via the traditional transmission belts of the two parties. I diagrammed U.S. political movements of that time, not on a polarized single axis from "left to right," but as a spectrum. The movements of the sixties and the seventies encompassed multidimensional issues, crosscut by concerns about centralization and devolution, globalism and localism. On this political spectrum, grassroots anarchists were comfortably akin to conservative libertarians. This spectrum, in reality a hologram, persists today. [see illustration].

Either/or, two-party politics are beloved by industrial era political theorists. Their simple mechanical models are reminiscent of Isaac Newton's clockwork universe. But as the complexities and interdependencies of postindustrial societies in the twentieth century have grown, inevitably, two-party politics has not been able to reflect the range of new issues. As mediocracies developed in the 1980s and 1990s, political parties were simply bypassed by mass media and shrank in number and significance. Both parties are about money. In the United States, for example, Republican and Democratic politicians in these "pork and bacon" parties became the "political entrepreneurs" we are familiar with today: wheeling, dealing, fund raising

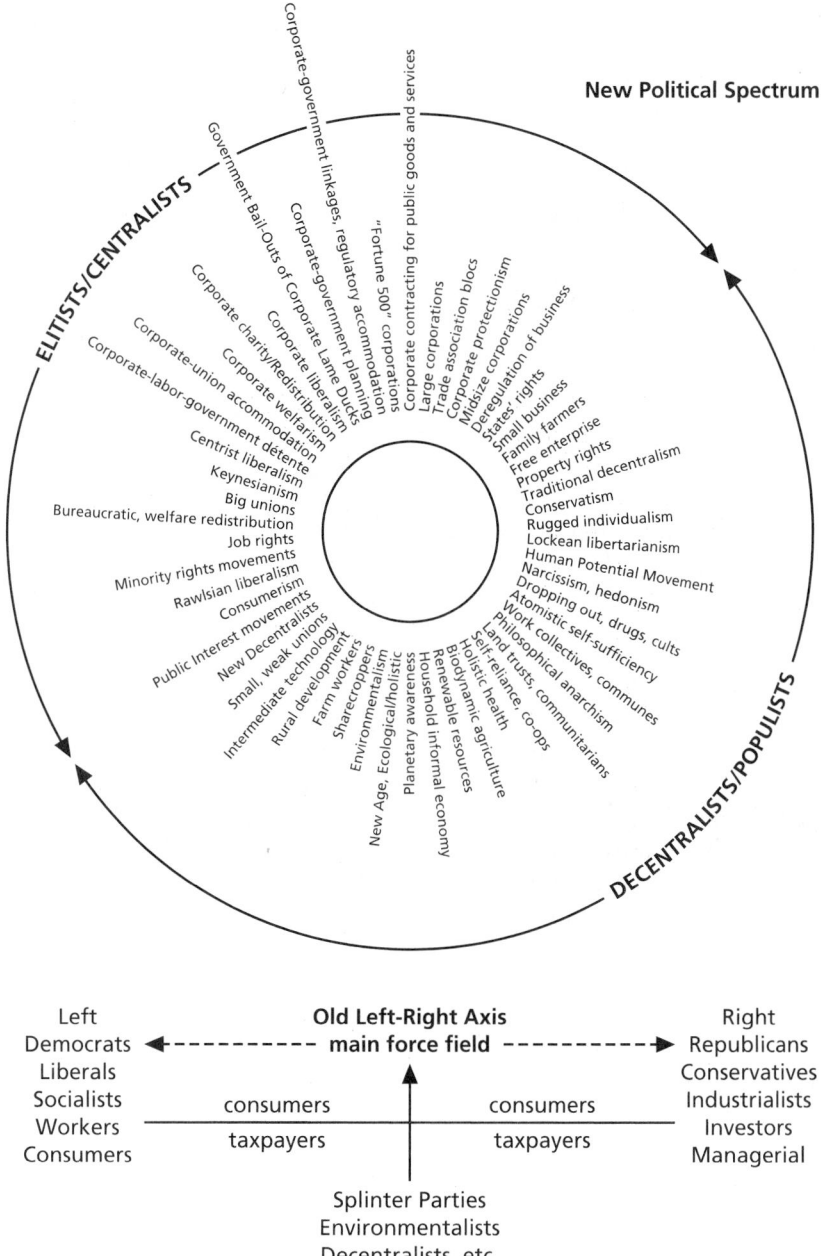

New Political Spectrum

ELITISTS/CENTRALISTS

Corporate-government linkages, regulatory accommodation
Government Bail-Outs of Corporate Lame Ducks
Corporate-government planning
Corporate charity/Redistribution
Corporate liberalism
Corporate welfarism
Corporate-union accommodation
Corporate-labor-government détente
Centrist liberalism
Keynesianism
Big unions
Bureaucratic, welfare redistribution
Job rights
Minority rights movements
Rawlsian liberalism
Consumerism
Public Interest movements
New Decentralists
Small, weak unions
Intermediate technology
Rural development
Farm workers
Sharecroppers
Environmentalism
New Age, Ecological/holistic
Planetary awareness
Household informal economy
Renewable resources
Biodynamic agriculture
Holistic health
Self-reliance, co-ops
Land trusts, communitarians
Work collectives, communes
Philosophical anarchism
Atomistic self-sufficiency
Dropping out, drugs, cults
Narcissism, hedonism
Human Potential Movement
Lockean libertarianism
Rugged individualism
Conservatism
Traditional decentralism
Property rights
Free enterprise
Family farmers
Small business
States' rights
Deregulation of business
Corporate protectionism
Midsize corporations
Trade association blocs
Large corporations
Corporate contracting for public goods and services
"Fortune 500" corporations

DECENTRALISTS/POPULISTS

Left	Old Left-Right Axis	Right
Democrats	◄--------- main force field ---------►	Republicans
Liberals		Conservatives
Socialists	consumers consumers	Industrialists
Workers	———————————— ————————————	Investors
Consumers	taxpayers taxpayers	Managerial

Splinter Parties
Environmentalists
Decentralists, etc.

Changing political configurations (from Hazel Henderson, *The Politics of the Solar Age: Alternatives to Economics.* Garden City, N.Y.: Anchor Press/Doubleday, 1981. 23.) Reprinted with permission of the publisher. From *Building A Win-Win World,* copyright © 1988 by Hazel Henderson. Berrett-Koehler Publishers, Inc., San Francisco, CA. All rights reserved. www.bkconnection.com

with interest groups and lobbyists for their own accounts and to advance their individual careers.

This view of politicians reflects the conservative viewpoint taught in law and economics departments at the University of Chicago and elsewhere, but also captures and reinforces today's cynicism. One result of this type of thinking has been the polarization of politics and issues in ever more simplistic ways, which politicians see as their only recourse. They have resorted to sloganeering, sound bytes, and flowery rhetoric—casting complex issues in terms of fundamental principles and values. This has only served to polarize media editors and talk-show hosts in the "Crossfire"-type formats that copycat the popular "left/right" programs on CNN. Mainstream media were shocked by the new angry populism and its some six hundred radio outlets in 1995.[1]

All this further polarizes voters, who became even more angry and cynical. [. . .] This, in turn, opens up possibilities for a third party to organize the 35 percent of the disgusted U.S. electorate that call themselves "Independents." These are the voters who deposed George Bush in 1992 by casting almost 20 percent of the swing votes for Ross Perot, and in 1994 turned their wrath on Bill Clinton. By contrast, in coalition governments with multiparty systems such as are common in Europe (particularly the Nordic countries and the Netherlands), issues are always in dynamic play and can be triangulated, shaped, and reshaped to achieve multiparty coalition governments and much wider consensus. Citizen movements and pressure groups have much less difficulty in achieving parliamentary representation for their views, as occurred with the rise of the Greens in Germany leading to Europe's now flourishing green parties.[2] Lack of proportional representation in Britain and the obsolete electoral college in the United States crippled budding green parties, which are still condemned by the U.S. political structure and its money-dominated politics to remain a movement.

As all countries restructure under globalization pressures, two-party politics will increasingly give way to coalitions and new parties as the old centers cannot hold. All three political parties in Britain, combined, have fewer members than the Royal Society for the Protection of Birds. Britain's Citizen's Charter, created to woo voters and hear complaints, was judged in a 1995 MORI (Market and Research International) poll, which found that less than 25 percent of petitioners even received apologies for deficient public services.[3] Governments began calling in management gurus as they experimented with reorganization—but soon learned that politics and government are very different in nature and goals from business.

Democracy's Future: Citizens Want to Set Priorities

The abortive 1992 U.S. Presidential candidacy of Ross Perot was a dress rehearsal for raising all the right questions about democracy's future. Yet in the millions of words written on the Perot phenomenon, few examined his-torical experience with electronic town meetings (ETMs) and public opinion polling, or efforts already under way to prevent abuses and perfect such new feedback channels provided by technology. Much has already been learned from ETM experiments in New Zealand in 1980 to clarify that coun-try's goals and values as well as similar electronic referenda conducted in Hawaii by political scientist Theodore Becker. [. . .]

Professors Becker and Slaton, based at Auburn University in Alabama, reported in 1995 in "Teledemocracy Action News + Network" that little progress had been made [. . .] in this area in the United States. Nothing had advanced citizen empowerment even though some attention had been given to creating "pressure valves" to relieve citizen frustration. An example was the U.S. version of University of Texas Professor James Fishkin's 1994 and 1995 series of TV programs on Britain's Channel 4, a process he called "De-liberative Polling." Fishkin teamed up with the U.S. Public Broadcasting System, which convened a representative sample of six hundred U.S. citi-zens who were exposed to presentations of two or three issues by experts—with polls taken before and afterward. These formats are a pale imitation of what is technologically possible, and the results are highly sensitive to the way the issues are framed. The Kettering and Public Agenda Foundations suffer similar problems from rigid "containment" of the issues. Indeed, they trivialized the process by fragmenting the debate into such rigid Cartesian boxes as health care, environment, and so on, rather than choosing a holistic crosscut, such as the Federal Budget, which would allow participants to *set priorities* across the entire range of issues.

The opportunity to set priorities is what a majority of U.S. citizens want, as the consensus locator survey method of the Americans Talk Issues Foun-dation (ATIF) determined. When ATIF asked if citizens would like to have sent to them, along with their income tax forms, a questionnaire on how they would like government to spend their tax dollars (i.e., a de facto non-binding referendum on overall priorities), 79 percent approved.[4] The Clin-ton administration considered experimenting with a small sample of tax returns—they opted out because "the administration might lose control of the budget process."[5] This, of course, was the idea.

Professor Becker reported an advance in Canada, where the Reform Party captured 16 percent of the 295 seats in the Parliament after the 1993 rout of Mulroney's conservatives. The Reform Party, in 1994 via an ETM, had sampled districts in Calgary on the issue of physician-assisted suicide, which the party opposed. They promised to abide by an electronic referen-dum where voters with PIN numbers called in massively in favor. The party changed its position and supported physician-assisted suicide. In Nova Scotia and British Columbia, some parties elect their leaders by phone. Similar projects have been conducted in Finland, while Oregonians vote by mail.

Another useful form of anticipatory democracy is the "futures search" conference, pioneered by Eric Trist and Fred Emery and described by practitioners Marvin R. Weisbord and Sandra Janoff in *Future Search* (1995). Search conferences were originally used by organizations, but their application to cities, counties, and states was fostered by the Washington-based Institute for Alternative Futures, and many local efforts have been documented by its founder Clement Bezold. Another approach is that of the Idaho Centennial Conference and Survey *Visualizing the Future: Idaho's Second Century*, which surveyed voters' quality-of-life preferences on a broad range of issues in 1990.[6]

Building on his research in designing communication systems, mathematician/entrepreneur Alan F. Kay has also broken new ground in public-opinion surveying on policy issues. Kay's Americans Talk Issues Foundation (ATIF), founded in 1987, discovered that scientifically random telephone polls sampling a national statistical cross section of one thousand Americans can often identify a genuine "wisdom of the people" on many complex issues. Often the public chooses farsighted, globally aware policy alternatives not offered by either political party or any mainstream political figures, experts, or pundits. ATIF's method is in fact a social innovation, far less expensive than ETMs, and can be used to prevent abuses in town-meetings and call-in programs. The opinion surveys are nonpartisan, designed to broaden the range of policy alternatives offered, and provide essential, unbiased information on each policy issue, prepared by many experts on all sides. Questions often range well beyond the current debate.

A 1991 survey broke ground on issues of globalization. One of its fifty questions was, "Would you support a proposal for the UN to monitor and tax international arms sales with the money going to famine relief and humanitarian aid?" Even after hearing arguments against as well as for the proposal (another ATIF method), an average of almost 70 percent remained unshakably in favor of this proposal in a series of seven polls from 1991 through 1995, where this question was included.

Many rules emerge from experiments in gathering such data, including the vital need to randomize all feedback, whether in opinion polls, via studio audiences, or on electronic town-hall-type programs. Similarly, such randomized feedback can balance incoming phone calls to call-in radio and television shows (which are always biased) by comparing the calls registering crude yes or no votes with a scientific, random sampling of all Americans. Indeed, this randomizing feedback rule is one of the reasons why we should trust the general public *more* than leaders, politicians, and elites. The U.S. Congress is gridlocked by special interests, political action committees (PACs), and other campaign donors, and by limited information from biased lobbyists. ATIF random-sampling feedback from all Americans can "damp out" such distortions and often identify common-ground solutions.

We also need more democratic access to TV, radio, and print media, now dangerously concentrated in commercial, and increasingly global, corporate ownership. The hope that cable would open up TV channels died in a plethora of old movies and sitcom reruns. Public Access TV, hard won by activists in the 1960s, has been frittered away by cities and communities unaware of its political potential. The Perot movement, United We Stand America (UWSA), is about taming Washington's arrogance; "restoring the United States to its rightful owners: the people"; access to media; and fuller participation in politics.[7] Perot demonstrated the possibilities in the new communications technologies for end-running the political parties and short-circuiting the old electoral process. Yet Perot, too, became manipulative. His March 1993 "electronic town meeting" turned out to be a half-hour infomercial (i.e., a paid political or commercial program). It starred Perot asking seventeen simple yes/no questions and urging people to call in or write to him at UWSA. [. . .]

Today's frustrated efforts to redesign and expand democracy must now be channeled by every means possible at all levels, so that viable third parties and broader coalitions can emerge to break the stranglehold of special interest on the majority parties. In 1995, the University of California at Berkeley's Center for Community Economic Research introduced a new computer simulation game on its Internet Web page: Balance the Federal Budget. The game allows users to play a congress member's role and prioritize, cut, add, or otherwise balance the U.S. budget. Twelve hundred users logged on, including one from the White House.[8] A radical reform proposed by Ernest Callenbach and Michael Phillips in *A Citizen Legislature* (1985) would overcome special interests by random selection of congressional members in the same way that juries are selected. In all the restructuring between levels of governance, the overarching principle for the new democracies is that articulated in the European Union (EU): *subsidiary,* i.e., policy making as close to the people as feasible. Feedback from the grassroots is, at last, reclaiming issues and problem solving from distant, indifferent, or uninformed elites, as feisty, intelligent Danes demonstrated in refusing to ratify the EU's Treaty of Maastricht.

Another democratic principle: transparency underlies efforts to redesign the too-highly averaged statistics of macroeconomics, which has allowed political issues and vital clarification of values to be obscured by cost- and risk-benefit analyses, i.e., portrayed as technical or economic matters on which the public was deemed "unqualified" to comment. Broader, quality-of-life indicators for health care, literacy, air and water quality, cultural amenities, democratic participation, and human rights are becoming essential tools of democracy, as well as better predictors of truly human development.

The nature of computer and communications systems makes them ideally suited to collecting, analyzing, and delivering the "feedback" of voters' viewpoints to the political system. As the voter becomes more dissatisfied with outmoded hand tools for political expression—the ballot, the pen, and the periodic election of representatives—we are seeing evidence of the short-circuiting of these traditional methods by the use of highly simplistic, partisan polls to take the voters' pulse on current issues. Yet as *The Economist* has editorialized, "the opinion poll is, in a sense, a prototype for interactive politics.[9] An ATIF poll on "Improving Democracy in America," April 3, 1993, found U.S. citizens favored by 70 percent the following statement: "Require Congress to fund an independent office, set up to conduct scientific, nonpartisan, large-sample surveys of public opinion on all important national issues AND to promptly release the results to the media so that Congress and the public will know what most Americans want for legislation." This survey was part of the reason Congressman Ron Klink introduced a bill that would set up such a Congressional Office of Public Opinion Research and Assessment (COPORA).

The instant electronic referendum is already technically possible and the hardware, the television set as the citizen's information-receiving device and the telephone as the political-input unit, is already in place in almost every home. ATIF Survey #24, "Steps for Democracy: The Many Versus the Few," March 25, 1994, found 70 percent of U.S. citizens favored national referenda *binding* on Congress—while only 59 percent favored nonbinding referenda. As *The Economist* rightly notes, referenda may be a better way to deal with lobbying and special interest—since the people rather than politicians must be lobbied.[10] Yet the referenda process is often corrupted by money, special interests, and media campaigns such as those of the tobacco lobby and the interests that defeated the 1990 California environmental referendum: Big Green.[11]

Before we are overwhelmed by fears of the tyranny of the majority, let us clarify two U.S. beliefs: (1) citizens should participate in social decision making in a democratic society; and (2) voters must communicate their views to one another, to the organizations in which they are involved, and to elected government officials. The rationale lies deep in U.S. history in the ever-more-liberally interpreted premise of its great social experiment: wisdom, creativity, and common sense are qualities distributed quite randomly throughout our population. Biology has not found us mistaken in this belief. This central premise, that an informed citizenry is capable of self-government, is not to say that the citizen will have all, or even some, of the answers to often complex, technical issues. But nonspecialized viewpoints can discipline technocrats by raising broad, humanistic questions, thereby helping experts structure problems, justify their projects, and think through long-range consequences more carefully.

Opening up existing and new channels of communication in commercial and noncommercial mass media is the key to assuring that citizens are sufficiently enlightened to vote wisely. Already U.S. citizens and those of other OECD countries are the most broadly educated populations in world history—and mass communications can raise this level even further. More continuous public affairs programming, such as on Britain's BBC and C-SPAN in the United States, is essential. Free, equitably apportioned time for political candidates and public and private officials is also vital and available in many OECD countries. By contrast in the United States, this free and equal time provision as well as the Fairness Doctrine were repealed, as mentioned, by pressure from commercial broadcast lobbies. While speaking on a platform with him, I asked New Jersey Senator Bill Bradley about reinstating these former provisions of the Federal Communications Commission. Bradley ducked this issue and said that he favors a constitutional amendment to limit campaign donations.

Higher education could be available to all via the airwaves, as in Britain's Open University. Education no longer needs buildings, only the voluntary communion of the minds of our greatest teachers and of all who thirst for knowledge and understanding.[12] Indeed, in the past two decades highly educated citizen groups, with their academic advisors in tow, forced onto national agendas: (1) energy efficiency standards, conservation, and renewable energy sources (solar, wind power, etc.); (2) recognition of biodiversity as a fundamental natural resource; (3) self-determination for the world's indigenous peoples; (4) human rights; (5) equitable, resource-efficient, sustainable forms of development mindful of future generations; (6) restructuring of the World Bank and the IMF; and (7) overhauling of the gross national product (GNP) to deduct social and environmental costs.

Collecting and analyzing individual viewpoints is already common practice in the commercial world; it's done by market sampling of consumer preferences and by use of data banks containing credit information or medical histories. We see it too in the statistical studies so prevalent in the behavioral sciences, and of course in the increasing use that politicians make of opinion polls. Yet the private use of information-gathering on credit or medical record has itself become a threat—with individuals' rights to challenge or correct erroneous data now protected by law. In the United States, commercial Neilsen ratings of audience size have been disastrous for quality television. Such methods tend to screen out of consideration new or random ideas, which are a vital component of an innovative society—just as money corrupts politics. [. . .]   ■

NOTES

1. See, for example, *Business Week,* "Populism: A Diverse Movement Is Shaking America and May Imperil Its Role in the Global Economy," 13 March 1995, 73; and "Who Speaks for America?" 8 May 1995, 90.

2. "Green Swingers," *The Economist,* 20 May 1995, 49.

3. *The Economist,* 15 July 1995, 41.

4. Americans Talk Issues Foundation, *"Interviews with the Public Guide Us . . . on the Road to Consensus"* (April 1994). For copies of all surveys write to Americans Talk Issues Foundation, 10 Carrera St., St. Augustine, Florida 32084.

5. Alan F. Kay, "Revealed in ATIF Survey #28: Important Stories Leaders Won't Mention and the Press Ignores." Unpublished paper, Americans Talk Issues Foundation, Washington D.C., 12 September 1995, 6.

6. Conducted by the Survey Research Center, School of Social Sciences and Public Affairs, Boise State University, 1990. Sponsored by and available from the Idaho Centennial Commission, 217 West State Street, Boise, Idaho 83702.

7. Ross Perot, *United We Stand* (New York: Hyperion, 1992) 2–4.

8. "If You're So Smart, You Cut the Deficit," *Business Week*, 19 June 1995, 6.

9. "Democracy and Technology," *The Economist*, 17 June 1995, 22.

10. Ibid.

11. See, for example, "Full-Flavored, Unfiltered State House Shenanigans," *Business Week*, 22 May 1995.

12. Samuel Dunn, "The Challenge of the '90s in Higher Education," *Futures Research Quarterly* (fall 1994): 34–35.

■ *QUESTIONS FOR MAKING CONNECTIONS WITHIN THE READING* ■

1. In direct democracies like the ancient city-state of Athens and the cantons of the Swiss Confederation, ordinary people can vote directly on the laws that they themselves propose. In a representative system, like ours in the United States, democracy is indirect: the people elect representatives and these representatives actually make the laws ordinary citizens must obey. What groups in America might be expected to oppose Henderson's call to make the American system more directly democratic?

2. According to Henderson, what role do "elites" play in American politics? Are they necessary and beneficial in some ways? What problems do they pose for a democracy like the one we have in the United States? Does Henderson foresee the disappearance of elites, or will the changes she proposes simply produce elites of a new kind?

3. Henderson puts great faith in communications technology. Why has this technology so far failed to produce a greater degree of public participation in American political life? Do we really need new technology to bring about the changes she envisions? Is a greater degree of citizen participation simply a matter of political will—of the citizens themselves deciding to make it happen? Or has the size and complexity of the United States made direct democracy impossible until now?

■ *QUESTIONS FOR WRITING* ■

1. In what ways are political problems actually technological problems? Why is it that we tend to separate politics from technology, economics, and culture? Does democracy become impossible in the absence of certain

technological, economic, and cultural conditions? What changes in our economic system, or in our system of values, might endanger the survival of democracy?

2. Is it possible that the information society might actually undermine our democratic traditions? How might that happen? Is Henderson overly optimistic about the liberating potential of the new technologies? Who controls those technologies? Will the people in control of them be willing to redistribute their own authority, power, and wealth?

■ *QUESTIONS FOR MAKING CONNECTIONS BETWEEN READINGS* ■

1. Henderson is a political *theorist*, that is, someone who formulates new paradigms for conceptualizing the life of our times. Theoretical reflection and its real-world implementation are often quite distinct, however. In what ways does Henry Petroski's practical perspective in the selections drawn from *To Engineer Is Human* complicate Henderson's ideas about the role that technology might play in transforming democracy? Is structural failure a necessary part of the democratic process? Can the kind of participatory democracy Henderson envisions be realized if structural failure is inevitable?

2. Do ordinary citizens possess the know-how required to function in the kind of democracy Henderson is calling for? If technological advances require new ways of reading, writing, and thinking, as Mitchell Stephens argues in "Thinking 'Above the Stream,'" do these new literacies help serve to advance the cause of participatory democracy, or do these new literacies further exclude ordinary citizens from civic participation?

For additional suggestions about making connections between readings, visit the Link-O-Mat and More Sample Assignments at <www.newhum.com>.

MARY KALDOR

FOLLOWING THE DESTRUCTION of the World Trade Center on September 11, 2001, people have come to understand the dangers posed by unofficial warfare—that is, conflicts not waged by governments but by paramilitary organizations that are often international and clandestine. While the dangers have become clear, the most effective ways to respond to this kind of warfare are far less obvious. Few writers in our time have addressed the problem more thoughtfully than Mary Kaldor. In the aftermath of September 11, Kaldor wrote in *The Nation* about just how different this new kind of warfare is: "What we have learned about this kind of war is that the only possible exit route is political. There has to be a strategy of winning hearts and minds to counter the strategy of fear and hate. There has to be an alternative politics based on tolerance and inclusiveness, which is capable of defeating the politics of intolerance and exclusion and capable of preserving the space for democratic politics. In the case of the current new war, what is needed is an appeal for global—not American—justice and legitimacy, aimed at establishing the rule of law in place of war and at fostering understanding between communities in place of terror."

Currently the director of the Program on Global Civil Society at the London School of Economics, Kaldor has spent her professional life studying globalization and the transformation of modern warfare. In the 1980s, she helped to co-found European Nuclear Disarmament (END), a nongovernmental organization dedicated to convincing Western European states to refuse to stockpile a nuclear arsenal. Subsequently, Kaldor cochaired the Helsinki Citizen's Assembly, an international consortium of nongovernmental organizations promoting global peace and human rights; she was also a member of the Independent International Commission to Investigate the Kosovo Crisis. The author of numerous books on global and European politics, her most recent work, *New and Old Wars:*

Kaldor, Mary. "Beyond Militarism, Arms Races, and Arms Control." Talk delivered at the Nobel Peace Prize Centennial Symposium, Oslo, Sweden, 6 December 2001.

Biographical Information from the London School of Economics and Political Science Web site <http://www.lse.ac.uk/experts/display?xml=experts.xml&xsl=experts.xsl&xslparam=person%3dm.h.kaldor>; quotation from "Wanted: Global Politics," The Nation, 5 November 2001 <http://www.thenation.com/doc.mhtml?i=20011105&s=kaldor>.

Organized Violence in a Global Era (1999), documents the shifts from an earlier form of warfare between armed combatants, where 80 percent of the casualties were soldiers, to the current form of organized violence, where 80 percent of the casualties are civilians. In the public talk reproduced here, Kaldor draws on this research to describe the challenges that unofficial warfare poses in the twenty-first century and to argue for the necessity of developing an international, humanitarian response to contain such conflicts.

To learn more about Mary Kaldor and the practice of unofficial warfare, please visit the Link-O-Mat at <www.newhum.com>.

Beyond Militarism, Arms Races, and Arms Control

Since the end of the Cold War, a profound restructuring of armed forces has taken place. During the Cold War period, armed forces tended to resemble each other all over the world. They were disciplined, hierarchical, and technology intensive. There were, of course, guerrilla and/or terrorist groups but they were considered marginal and their demand for weapons was small in relation to the overall demand for weapons.

The Cold War could be described as the final stage of what has come to be known as modernity, or to use Anthony Giddens' terminology, the final stages of the first phase of modernity. By *modernity,* I mean that period of human development that began somewhere between the fifteenth and the eighteenth centuries, characterized by the development of science and technology, the nation state, modern industry, and, I would argue, Clausewitzean[1] or modern war. By *modern war,* I mean war between states, fought by armed forces, for state interest; the type of war that was theorized so brilliantly by Clausewitz. The development of modern war cannot be disentangled from the development of modern states. It was in war that European states, which were to provide the model for other states, established their monopoly of organized violence within the territorial confines of the state; they eliminated competitors, centralized administration, increased taxation and forms of borrowing, and above all, created an idea of the state as the organization responsible for protection of borders against other states and for upholding a rule of law within the state. The sharp distinctions between the military and civilians, public and private, internal and external, are a product of these developments. As Charles Tilly put it in a famous phrase: "States made war and war made the state."

After 1945, the whole world was parceled up into individual states, each with their own currency and their own armed forces. Each state was a member of a bloc (West, East and non-aligned) and within each bloc, there were transfers of weapons and other types of military assistance according to a very similar model of warfare. The idea of war and of preparations for war was bound up with the ways in which states established their political legitimacy.

Since the end of the Cold War, military spending by governments has fallen substantially. But what we have witnessed is less a contraction of military forces than a restructuring and increased diversity of types of military forces. There is a parallel with the pre-modern period, which was also characterized by a diversity of military forces—feudal levies, citizens' militias, mercenaries, pirates, for example—and by a corresponding variety of types of warfare.

Two interlinked developments have been critical, in my view, in bringing about these changes. One is the sheer destructiveness of modern warfare. As all types of weapons have become more lethal and/or more accurate, decisive military victory has become more and more difficult. The scale of destruction in World War II (some 50 million dead) is almost unbearable to contemplate. The Cold War could be understood as a way of evading or psychologically suppressing the implications of that destructiveness. Through the system of deterrence, the idea of modern war was kept alive in the imagination and helped to sustain the legitimacy and discipline of modern states. The military planners and scenario builders imagined wars, even more destructive than World War II, and developed competitive new technologies that, in theory, would be used in such wars. There were, of course, real wars and some 5 million people have died in wars in every decade since 1945 but, among the dominant powers, these were regarded as 'not-war' or marginal to the main contingency—a global inter-state clash. With the end of the Cold War, we have to come to terms with the impossibility of wars of the modern type.

The second development is the process known as globalization. By *globalization*, I mean increasing interconnectedness, the shrinking of distance and time, as a result of the combination of Information and Communications Technology (ICT) and air travel. A central issue for theorists of globalization has to do with the implications for the modern state (Held, 1999). Some argue that the state has become an anachronism and that we are moving towards a single world community. Some take the opposite view, that globalization is an invention of the state and can easily be reversed. Yet others insist that globalization does not mean the end of the state but rather its transformation. I share the last position but I would argue that there is no single method of transformation. States are changing in a variety of ways and, moreover, these changes, I shall argue, are bound up with changes in the types of armed forces and the forms of warfare.

The terms *militarism, arms races,* and *arms control* are expressions drawn from the Cold War era and before. *Militarism* refers to excessive levels of military spending by the state and excessive influence of armed forces over civilian life. *Arms races* refer to the competition between similar types of military forces. *Arms control* refers to the process of treaty making between states based on the assumption that stability can best be preserved through a "balance of power (or terror)" between states.

In this essay, I shall distinguish between the different types of armed forces that are emerging in the post–Cold War world, only some of which can be characterized in terms of militarism and arms races, and discuss how they are loosely associated with different modes of state transformation and different forms of warfare. I have identified four different types of armed forces. They could be described as Weberian ideal types. They are probably not comprehensive, and no single example exactly fits a particular type. There is also a lot of overlap. The point is to provide a schematic account of what is happening in the field of warfare so as to be able to offer some new ways of thinking about the possibilities for controlling or limiting the means of warfare and why we need a new terminology beyond militarism, arms races, and arms control. I shall suggest that the emphasis that has been increasingly accorded to international law, particularly humanitarian law, offers a possible way forward.

Netforce: Informal or Privatized Armed Forces

A typical new phenomenon is armed networks of non-state and state actors. They include: para-military groups organized around a charismatic leader, warlords who control particular areas, terrorist cells, fanatic volunteers like the Mujahadeen, organized criminal groups, units of regular forces or other security services, as well as mercenaries and private military companies.

The form of warfare that is waged by these networks is what I call "new war" (Kaldor, 1999). New wars, which take place in the Balkans, Africa, Central Asia and other places, are sometimes called internal or civil wars to distinguish them from intra-state or Clausewitzean war. I think this terminology is inappropriate for a number of reasons. First, the networks cross borders. One of the typical features of the "new wars" is the key role played by Diaspora groups either far away (Sudanese or Palestinian workers in the Gulf states, former Yugoslav workers in Western Europe, immigrant groups in the new "melting pot" nations like North America or Oceania) or in neighboring states (Serbs in Croatia and Bosnia, Tutsis in Burundi or the DRC). Secondly, the wars involve an array of global actors—foreign mercenaries and volunteers, Diaspora supporters, neighboring states, not to mention the humanitarian actors such as aid agencies, NGOs or reporters.

And thirdly, and most importantly, the "new wars" tend to be concentrated in areas where the modern state is unraveling and where the distinctions between internal and external, public and private, no longer have the same meaning. Such areas are characterized by what are called frail or failing states, quasi or shadow states. These are states, formally recognized by the outside world, with some of the trappings of statehood—an incomplete administrative apparatus, a flag, sometimes a currency—but where those trappings do not express control over territory and where access to the state apparatus is about private gain not public policy. In particular these are states where the monopoly of legitimate organized violence is eroding.

In many of the areas where new wars take place, it is possible to observe a process that is almost the reverse of the process through which modern states were constructed. Taxes fall because of declining investment and production, increased corruption and clientilism, or declining legitimacy. The declining tax revenue leads to growing dependence both on external sources and on private sources, through, for example, rent seeking or criminal activities. Reductions in public expenditure as a result of the shrinking fiscal base as well as pressures from external donors for macro-economic stabilization and liberalization (which also may reduce export revenues) further erode legitimacy. A growing informal economy associated with increased inequalities, unemployment and rural-urban migration, combined with the loss of legitimacy, weakens the rule of law and may lead to the re-emergence of privatized forms of violence: organized crime and the substitution of "protection" for taxation; vigilantes; private security guards protecting economic facilities, especially international companies; or para-military groups associated with particular political factions. In particular, reductions in security expenditure, often encouraged by external donors for the best of motives, may lead to break away groups of redundant soldiers and policeman seeking alternative employment.

Of course, the networks that engage in new wars are not all to be found in these failing states. They include nodes in advanced industrial countries and, in the inner cities of the West, it is possible to observe gang warfare that has many of the characteristics of "new wars." Nevertheless, this type of state provides a fertile environment for these types of network.

There are three main characteristics of the "new wars." First of all, I use the term *war* to emphasize the political character of the new wars, even though they could also be described as organized crime (illegal or private violence) or as massive violations of human rights (violence against civilians). Because networks are loose horizontal coalitions, unlike vertical disciplined armies of the past, a shared narrative, often based on a common identity, ethnic or religious, is an important organizing mechanism. In the case of the netforce, the networks engaged in the new wars, what holds them together is generally an extreme political ideology based on the exclusive claim to state power on the basis of identity—ethnic chauvinism or religious communalism. I stress access to state power because these ideologies are not about substantive grievances, such as language rights or religious rights, although these may be indirectly important; rather they are about control of power and resources for an exclusively defined group of people.

I take the view that these ideologies are politically constituted. Even though they are based on pre-existing cleavages of tribe, nation and religion, and even though they may make use of memories and experiences of past injustices, they are constructed or accentuated for the purpose of political mobilization.

Modern communications are important for the new networks both as a way of organizing the network and as a form of mobilization. Constructions of the past are developed and disseminated through radio, videos and television. Thus hate radio was of key importance in Rwanda. In Serbia, television was effectively used to remind people of the injustices of the past—the defeat of the Serbs by the Turks in 1389 and the fascist Croat treatment of Serbs during World War II. In the Middle East, videocassettes of Bin Laden's speeches circulate widely. The effect of television and radio in speeding up mobilization especially in the countryside or among newly arrived urban migrants, who do not have the reading habit, should not be underestimated. There is an important contrast here with nineteenth century "imagined communities" which were propagated through the print media and involved the intellectual classes. The more populist electronic media are designed to appeal primarily to the least educated members of the public. In general, it is states that control the radio and television. But non-state groups can make use of other forms of media: Diaspora broadcasts through satellite television, which were important in Kosovo; the circulation of videos; or local radio in areas under political control.

A second characteristic of the "new wars" is that war itself is a form of political mobilization. In what I have called wars between states, the aim of war was, to quote Clausewitz, "to compel an opponent to fulfil our will." In general this was achieved through the military capture of territory and victory in battle. People were mobilized to participate in the war effort—to join the army or to produce weapons and uniforms. In the new wars, mobilizing people is the aim of the war effort; the point of the violence is not so much directed against the enemy; rather the aim is to expand the networks of extremism. Generally the strategy is to control territory through political means and military means are used to kill, expel, or silence those who might challenge control. This is why the warring parties use techniques of terror, ethnic cleansing, or genocide as deliberate war strategies. In the new wars, battles are rare and violence is directed against civilians. Violations of humanitarian and human rights law are not a side effect of war but the central methodology of new wars. Over 90 percent of the casualties in the new wars are civilian, and the number of refugees and displaced persons per conflict has risen steadily.

The strategy is to gain political power through sowing fear and hatred, to create a climate of terror, to eliminate moderate voices, and to defeat tolerance. The political ideologies of exclusive nationalism or religious communalism are generated through violence. It is generally assumed that extreme ideologies, based on exclusive identities—Serb nationalism, for example, or fundamentalist Islam—are the cause of war. Rather, the spread and strengthening of these ideologies are the consequence of war. "The war had to be so bloody," Bosnians will tell you, "because we did not hate each other; we had to be taught to hate each other."

A third characteristic of the new wars is the type of economy they generate. Because these networks flourish in states where systems of taxation have collapsed and where little new wealth is being created, and where the wars destroy physical infrastructure, cut off trade, and create a climate of insecurity that prohibits investment, they have to seek alternative, exploitative forms of financing. They raise money through loot and plunder, through illegal trading in drugs, illegal immigrants, cigarettes and alcohol, through "taxing" humanitarian assistance, through support from sympathetic states, and through remittances from members of the networks. All of these types of economic activity are predatory and depend on an atmosphere of insecurity. Indeed, the new wars can be described as a central source of the globalized informal economy—the transnational criminal and semi-legal economy that represents the underside of globalization.

The logical conclusion that can be drawn from these three characteristics is that the new wars are very difficult to contain and very difficult to end. They spread through refugees and displaced persons, through criminal networks, and through the extremist viruses they nurture. We can observe growing clusters of warfare in Africa, the Middle East, Central Asia or the Caucasus. The wars represent a defeat for democratic politics, and each bout of warfare strengthens those networks with a vested political and economic interest in continued violence. There are no clear victories or defeats because the warring parties are sustained both politically and economically by continuing violence. The wars speed up the process of state unraveling; they destroy what remains of productive activities, they undermine legitimacy, and they foster criminality. The areas where conflicts have lasted longest have generated cultures of violence, as in the jihad culture taught in religious schools in Pakistan and Afghanistan or among the Tamils of Sri Lanka, where young children are taught to be martyrs and where killing is understood as an offering to God. In the instructions found in the car of the hijackers in Boston's Logan Airport, it is written: "If God grants any one of you a slaughter, you should perform it as an offering on behalf of your father and mother, for they are owed by you. If you slaughter, you should plunder those you slaughter, for that is a sanctioned custom of the Prophet's."

It should be noted that there are other private or informal forces that do not correspond to this analysis. For example, in many of the new wars, villages or municipalities establish citizens' militias to defend local people—this was the case in among some groups in Rwanda and also in Tuzla and Zenica during the Bosnian war. There are also more traditional guerrilla groups, whose strategy is to gain political control through winning hearts and minds rather than through sowing fear and hatred; hence they attack agents of the state and not civilians, at least in theory. Finally, there are numerous private security companies, often established to protect multinational companies in difficult places, and mercenaries, who fight for money; tactics and forms of warfare, in these cases, depend largely on the paymasters.

The New American Militarism

It could be argued that if September 11 had not happened, the American military-industrial complex might have had to invent it. Indeed, what happened on September 11 could have come out of what seemed to be the wild fantasies of "asymmetric threats" that were developed by American strategic analysts as they sought a new military role for the United States after the end of the Cold War. A reporter for the *London Observer* claimed to have found in one of the headquarters for terrorist training in Afghanistan, a photocopy of the "terrorist cookbook" which circulates among the American fundamentalist right.

World military spending declined by one third in the decade after 1989. America military spending also declined but by less than the global average and began to rise again after 1998. As of the year 2000, American military spending in real terms is equivalent to its spending in 1980, just before the Reagan military build-up. More importantly, what took place during the 1990s was a radical shift in the structure of U.S. military expenditure. Spending on military research and development declined less than overall military spending and has increased faster since 1998. As of 2000, U.S. military R&D spending is 47 percent higher in real terms than in 1980 (SIPRI, 2001). Instead of ushering in a period of downsizing, disarmament and conversion (although some of that did take place at local levels in the U.S.), the end of the Cold War led to a feverish technological effort to apply information technology to military purposes, known as the Revolution in Military Affairs (RMA). . . .

The Gulf war provided a model for what can be described as casualty-free war—that is to say the use of high-technology either directly to attack an enemy or to support a proxy, say the KLA in Kosovo or the Northern Alliance in Afghanistan. The idea now is that this high-tech warfare can be used against "rogue states" sponsoring terrorists. The same techniques were used against Iraq in December 1998, in Yugoslavia in 1999 and now in Afghanistan. They satisfy a confluence of interests. They fulfill the needs of the scientists, engineers and companies that provide an infrastructure for the American military effort. They allow for a continuation of the imaginary war of the Cold War period from the point of view of Americans. They do not involve American casualties, and they can be watched on television and demonstrate the determination and power of the United States government—the "spectacles" as Der Derian has put it, that "serve to deny imperial decline." It is this imaginary character from an American perspective that explains Jean Baudrillard's famous remark that the Gulf War did not happen.

The program for national missile defense has to be understood in the same vein. Even if the system cannot work, it provides imaginary protection for the United States, allowing the United States to engage in casualty-free war without fear of retaliation. This notion is evident from the way in which Donald Rumsfeld, the U.S. defense secretary, talks about how NMD will enhance deterrence through a combination of defensive and offensive measures. The weakness of deterrence was always the problem of credibility; a problem that leads to more and more useable nuclear weapons. With casualty-free war, the credibility of U.S. action is more convincing; after all, it is said, that the attack on the World Trade Towers was equivalent to the use of a sub-strategic nuclear weapon. NMD, at least psychologically, extends the possibilities for casualty-free war.

However, from the point of view of the victims, these wars are very real and not so different from old wars. However precise the strikes, it is impossible to avoid "mistakes" or "collateral damage." It does not make civilian casualties any more palatable to be told they were not intended. Moreover, the destruction of physical infrastructure and the support for one side in the conflict, as in the case of proxies, results in many more indirect casualties. In the case of the Gulf War, direct Iraqi casualties can probably be numbered in the tens of thousands but the destruction of physical infrastructure and the ensuing wars with the Kurds and the Shiites caused hundreds of thousands of further casualties and seem to have entrenched the vicious and dangerous rule of Saddam Hussein. In the current war in Afghanistan, there have probably been thousands of casualties, both civilian and military, as well as thousands of people fleeing their homes and a humanitarian disaster because aid agencies have not been able to enter the country. The help provided to the hated Northern Alliance reduces the prospects of a broad-based Afghan government that might begin a process of stabilization. Far from extending support for democratic values, casualty-free war shows that American lives are privileged over the lives of others and contributes to a perception of the United States as a global bully.

Terms like *imperialism* are, however, misleading. The United States is best characterized not as an imperial power but as the "last nation state." It is the only state, in this globalized world, that still has the capacity to act unilaterally. Its behavior is determined less by imperial considerations than by concerns about its own domestic public opinion. Casualty-free war is also in a sense a form of political mobilization. It is about satisfying various domestic constituencies, not about influencing the rest of the world, even though such actions have a profound impact on the rest of the world.

Neo-Modern Militarism

Neo-modern militarism refers to the evolution of classical military forces in large transition states. These are states that are undergoing a transition from a centralized economy to a more internationally open market-oriented system and, yet, which are large enough to retain a sizeable state sector. Typical examples are Russia, India and China. They are not large enough to challenge the U.S. and they are constrained by many of the imperatives of globalization, subject to many of the pressures that are experienced by frail or failing states. They tend to adopt extreme ideologies that resemble the ideologies of the "new wars"—Russian or Hindu chauvinism, for example. And there are often direct links to and even co-operation with the shadier networks, especially in Russia. Israel should probably also be included in this category, although its capacity to retain a sizeable military sector is due less to its size than to its dependence on the United States.

These states have retained their military forces, including nuclear weapons. In the case of India, there has been a significant increase in military spending throughout the 1990s and it could be argued that the term *arms race* could be applied to India and Pakistan, especially after the 1998 nuclear tests. Pakistan, however, could be said to be closer to the networks of the new wars with its links to militants in Kashmir and Afghanistan; in other words somewhere between netforce and neo-modern militarism. In the case of Russia, there was a dramatic contraction of military spending after the break-up of the Soviet Union and a deep crisis in the military-industrial complex. But pressure to increase military spending has increased and the demands of the war in Chechnya are leading to a reassessment of the relative importance of conventional versus nuclear weapons. The proposed cuts in nuclear weapons discussed between Putin and Bush will release funds for conventional improvements. China is also engaged in military expansion, especially since 1998, when the military were prohibited from engaging in commercial activities. Given the reductions in Russian nuclear capabilities and the new generation of Chinese systems, China will come to look more like a competitor to Russia, especially in the nuclear field.

The type of warfare that is associated with neo-modern militarism is either limited inter-state warfare or counter-insurgency. These states envisage wars on the classic Clausewitzean model. They engage in counter-insurgency in order to defeat extremist networks as in Chechnya or Kashmir. Or they prepare for the defense of borders against other states, as in the case of the Kargil war between India and Pakistan in 1998. Unlike the United States, these states are prepared to risk casualties and, in the case of the Chechen war, Russian casualties have been extremely high. The typical tactics used against the networks are shelling from tanks, helicopters, or artillery, as well as population displacement to "clean" areas of extremists or "terrorists." The impact on civilians is thus very similar to the impact of the "new wars." Yet precisely because of the growing destructiveness of all types of weapons and the consequent difficulty of overcoming defensive positions, military victory against an armed opponent is very hard to achieve. Grozny has virtually been reduced to rubble. Yet still resistance persists.

The networks have understood that they cannot take territory militarily, only through political means, and the point of the violence is to contribute to those political means. The states engaged in neo-modern militarism are still under the illusion that they can win militarily. The consequence is either self-imposed limits, as in the case of inter-state war, or exacerbation of "new wars" as in the case of Kashmir, Chechnya or Palestine, where counter-insurgency merely contributes to the political polarizing process of fear and hate. In other words, the utility of modern military force, the ability to "compel an opponent to fulfill our will" is open to question nowadays.

Protectionforce: Peacekeeping/Peace-Enforcement

An important trend in the last decade has been the increase in peacekeeping operations. At the start of the decade, there were only eight United Nations peacekeeping operations; they involved some 10,000 troops. As of the end of 2000, there were fifteen United Nations operations involving some 38,000 military troops (Global Civil Society, 2001). In addition, a number of regional organizations were engaged in peacekeeping: NATO in Bosnia, Kosovo and Macedonia; the Commonwealth of Independent States (CIS), mainly Russia, in Tajikistan, Transdinestr, Abkhazia, and South Ossetia; the Economic Community of West African States (ECOWAS) in Sierra Leone, Liberia and Guinea.

Peacekeeping has not only increased in scale; there have been important changes in the tasks peacekeepers are asked to perform and in the way we think about peacekeeping. During the Cold War period, peacekeeping was based on the assumption that wars were of the Clausewitzean type. The job of peacekeepers was to separate the warring parties and to monitor cease-fires on the basis of agreements. Peacekeeping was sharply distinguished from peace enforcement, which was equated with war fighting, i.e., intervening in a war on one side, authorized under Chapter VIII of the UN Charter.

In terms of organization, peacekeeping has more in common with the networks than with classic military forces. Peacekeeping forces are generally loose transnational coalitions. Although they usually have a clearly defined multinational command system, peacekeepers are also subject to national commands, which erodes the vertical character of the command system. Because they are often far away from the decision-makers and because of the nature of their tasks, individual initiative is often more important than unquestioning obedience. Moreover, peacekeepers have to work together with a range of other agencies, international organizations like UNHCR or UNDP and also NGOs involved in humanitarian assistance or conflict resolution. A shared normative narrative based on humanitarian principles is critical in holding the networks together.

The new tasks for peacekeepers include the protection of safe havens, where civilians can find refuge, the protection of convoys delivering humanitarian assistance, disarmament and demobilization, providing a secure environment for elections or for the return of refugees and displaced persons, or capturing war criminals. These tasks reflect the changes in the nature of the warfare. New terms like *second-generation peacekeeping, wider peacekeeping* or *robust peacekeeping* have been used to describe these new roles. Peacekeepers nowadays operate in the context of continuing wars or insecure post-conflict situations, and they are more likely to risk casualties than were traditional peacekeepers.

A number of recent reports have emphasized that the new role of peacekeeping is, first and foremost, the protection of civilians since they are the main targets of the new wars (Brahimi, 2000). The new peacekeeping is indeed somewhere between traditional peacekeeping (separating sides) and peace enforcement (taking sides). I have argued that outright military victory is very very difficult nowadays, at least if we are unwilling to contemplate mass destruction. The job of the new protectionforce is not to defeat an enemy but to protect civilians and stabilize war situations so that non-extremist tolerant politics has space to develop. The task is thus more like policing than warfighting although it involves the use of military forces. Techniques like safe havens or humanitarian corridors are ways of protecting civilians and also increasing the international presence on the ground so as to influence political outcomes.

In practice, peacekeeping has not lived up to this description. Partly this is due to lack of resources. Not nearly enough has been invested in peacekeeping and in providing appropriate training and equipment. More importantly, international lives are still privileged over the lives of the civilians they are supposed to protect. OSCE monitors left Kosovo hurriedly when the bombing of Yugoslavia began, leaving behind a terrified population who had believed rightly or wrongly that the orange vans of the OSCE monitors were some protection; the local OSCE staff left behind were all killed. Likewise, Dutch peacekeepers handed over the 8000 men and boys of Srebrenica to Serb forces in July 1995 and they were all massacred. In Rwanda, UN forces were withdrawn just as the genocide of 800,000 Tutsis began, despite the impassioned plea of the Canadian UN Commander, General Dallaire, to establish safe havens. There are, of course, also moments of heroism, like the Ukrainian peacekeepers in Zepa or the British in Goradze, or the UN staff in East Timor who refused to evacuate their headquarters unless the people who had sought refuge there were also saved. But, as yet, these moments are insufficient to be seen to justify the commitment in resources and will that would be necessary for a serious and sustained use of peacekeeping.

Peacekeeping/peace-enforcement is associated with states that could be described as post-modern (Cooper, 2000) or globalizing (Clark, 1999). These are states that have come to terms with the erosion of their autonomy (their ability to retain control over what happens in their territory), in the context of growing interconnectedness. They have thus adopted a deliberate strategy of multilateralism, of trying to influence the formation of global rules and participating actively in the enforcement of those rules. The British Prime Minister Tony Blair attempted to articulate this position in his speech on the "Doctrine of the International Community" during the Kosovo war. "We are all internationalists now whether we like it or not," he told an audience in Chicago. "We cannot refuse to participate in global markets if we want to prosper. We cannot ignore new political ideas in other countries if we want to innovate. We cannot turn our backs on conflicts and the violation of human rights in other countries if we still want to be secure" (Blair, 1999).

The states that fit this category include most European states, Canada, South Africa, Japan, as well as a number of others. Of course, most states, including the United States and Russia, engage in this type of peace operation. But it is not viewed as the main contingency for which they prepare. The new globalizing states are reorienting their military doctrines along these lines. The wars in the Balkans have had a profound impact in Europe, where concern about Balkan stability and experience in the region is shaping military thinking.

Controlling War?

During the Cold War period, the main concern was how to prevent a war of global annihilation. Arms control was seen as one of the most important methods of prevention; it was a way of stabilizing the perception of a balance of power. A true balance of power is a war that no side can win. Because armed forces were roughly similar during the Cold War period, it was possible to estimate a surrogate balance of power based on quantitative estimates of military forces, which could be codified in arms control treaties. This surrogate balance of power was seen as a way of preventing perceptions of imbalance, which might have tempted one or other side to start a war. In practice, of course, numbers are irrelevant since any nuclear war is likely to lead to global annihilation but the exercise of measuring a balance of power shored up the notion of an imaginary war that could not be won.

The danger of a war of global annihilation has, thankfully, receded since the end of the Cold War. What we are now witnessing, however, is a series of real wars that cannot be won. There are no surrogate balances, except perhaps between the neo-modern military forces. The U.S. no longer has what is known in the jargon as a "peer competitor" and other types of armed forces are too varied to be compared. What I have tried to argue is that the first three types of armed forces (the networks, the new American military forces, and the neo-modern military forces) all engage in real wars with very similar consequences—indiscriminate suffering for civilians (even though the Americans claim that their greater precision and discriminateness minimizes such suffering). Nowadays, therefore, the emphasis of those who are concerned about such suffering has to be directly with the ways to control war. Limitations on weapons may be part of that wider goal but have to be viewed from a different perspective than in the Cold War period.

Perhaps the most hopeful approach to the contemporary problem of controlling war, nowadays, is not through arms control but through the extension and application of international humanitarian law (the "laws of war") and human rights law. During the 1990s, much greater importance was accorded to humanitarian norms—the notion that the international community has a duty to prevent genocide, violations of humanitarian law (war crimes) and massive violations of human rights (crimes against humanity). The idea of overriding state sovereignty in the case of humanitarian crises became much more widely accepted. The establishment of the Yugoslav and Rwanda Tribunals paved the way for the establishment of an International Criminal Court. The Pinochet and Ariel Sharon cases removed the principle of sovereign immunity.

Humanitarian law is not, of course, new. Its origins lie in the codification of "laws of war," especially under the auspices of the International Red Cross, in the late nineteenth century. The aim was to limit what we now call "collateral damage" or the side effects of war, above all, to prevent the indiscriminate suffering of civilians, and to ensure humane treatment for the wounded and for prisoners of war. These laws codified rules in Europe, which dated back to the Middle Ages and underlay a notion of "civilized" warfare, which was important in order to define the role of the soldier as the legitimate agent of the state, as a hero not a criminal. (Of course, these rules were not applied outside Europe against "barbarians" or the "rude nations").

Humanitarian law was greatly extended after World War II. The Nuremberg and Tokyo trials marked the first enforcement of war crimes and, indeed, crimes against humanity. The Genocide Convention of 1948 as well as further extension of the Geneva Conventions, and the newly developing human rights law all represented further strengthening of humanitarian law, albeit marginalized by the dominant Cold War confrontation.

What has changed in the last decades is the change in the nature of warfare, even though some aspects were presaged in the Holocaust and the bombing of civilians in the Second World War. As argued above, violations of humanitarian law and human rights law are no longer "side effects" of war, they represent the core of the new warfare. Therefore taking seriously humanitarian law is one way of controlling the new warfare.

This is the context in which the limitation of armaments should also be understood. Recent efforts to limit or eliminate categories of weapons, like the Land Mines Convention or the protocol to the Biological Weapons Convention, or the efforts to control small arms, are not based on the assumption of a balance between states. Rather they are the outcome of pressure by global civil society to uphold humanitarian norms and prevent indiscriminate harm to civilians. The 1996 International Court of Justice decision about nuclear weapons, as well as several recent cases in Scotland, is based on the same line of thinking.

Taken seriously, a humanitarian approach would outlaw netforce and would restructure legitimate, i.e., state, military forces from classic war-fighting tasks to a new and extended form of protectionforce. It would outlaw WMD as well as weapons like land mines that cause indiscriminate harm. Peacekeeping and peace-enforcement could be reconceptualized as humanitarian law enforcement, with appropriate equipment and training.

Such an approach would be consistent with the transformation of states along the lines of the post-modern or globalizing states. It would imply a strengthening of global rules and greater participation in the enforcement of rules. All three of the other types of warfare I have described are based on particularist assumptions about the need to protect particular communities, networks or states, and to privilege their lives over others. There is no reason why growing interconnectedness cannot be combined with particularism and fragmentation; indeed that is the characteristic of the contemporary world. But it is no longer possible to insulate particular communities or states; even the United States is now vulnerable to transnational networks. If we are to find ways to cope with the uneven impact of globalization and to deal with the criminal and violent underside of globalization, then the main task is to construct some form of legitimate set of global rules. This is not the same as a global state; rather it is about establishing a set of global regimes underpinned by states, international institutions and global civil society. The humanitarian regime would be at the heart of such a set of rules because of the legitimacy that derives from the assumption of human equality.

If the legitimacy of modern states derived from their ability to protect borders against external enemies and to uphold the law domestically, then the legitimacy of global governance is likely to be greatly enhanced by a humanitarian regime that takes ultimate responsibility for the protection of individuals and for upholding international law. I am not implying a single world security organization. Rather, I am talking about a collective commitment by states, international organizations, and civil society to act when individual states fail to sustain these norms and to do so within a framework of international law.

How would this approach have changed the reaction to the events of September 11? What happened on September 11 was a crime against humanity. It was interpreted, however, in the U.S. as an attack on the U.S. and a parallel has been repeatedly drawn with Pearl Harbour. Bush talks about a "war on terrorism" and has said that "you are either with us or with the terrorists." The approach of casualty-free war had been adopted, using high-tech strikes and a proxy, the Northern Alliance, to destroy the state sponsoring terrorism, the Taliban, and to destroy the Al-Qaeda network. (At the time of writing, some U.S. Special Forces and Marines have been deployed on the ground). We do not know how many people have died as a result of the strikes or have fled their homes but it undoubtedly numbers in hundreds if not thousands. The chances of stabilizing Afghanistan exist but are reduced by the dominant role played by the Northern Alliance. Most importantly, perhaps, the approach contributes to a political polarization between the West and the rest, both because of the privileging of American lives and the language in which the war is conducted. While the Taliban has been overthrown and, hopefully, bin Laden may be caught, there is unlikely to be any clear military victory. As I have argued, the political narrative, in this case of jihad against America, is central to the functioning of the network. Casualty-free war confirms the political narrative and sets up exactly the kind of war envisaged by the Al-Qaeda network.

A humanitarian approach would have defined September 11 as a crime against humanity. It would have sought United Nations authorization for any action and it would have adopted tactics aimed at increasing trust and confidence on the ground, for example through the establishment of safe havens in the North as well as humanitarian corridors. It would have established an International Court to try terrorists. It would have adopted some of the means already adopted to put pressure on terrorist networks through squeezing financial assets, for example, as well as efforts to catch the criminals. Such an approach would also have to eschew double standards. Catching Mladic and Karadic, the perpetrators of the Srebrenica massacre, is just as important as catching bin Laden. Human rights violations in Palestine and Chechnya are no less serious than in Kosovo or Afghanistan.

A humanitarian approach, of course, has to be part of a wider political approach. In wars, in which no military victory is possible, political approaches are key. An alternative political narrative, based on the idea of global justice, is the only way to minimize the exclusive political appeal of the networks. I am aware that all this sounds impossibly utopian. Unfortunately, the humanitarian approach may be seen in retrospect as a brief expression of the interregnum between the end of the Cold War and September 11, 2001. We are, I fear, on the brink of a global new war, something like the wars in the Balkans or the Israel-Palestine war, on a global scale with no outsiders to constrain its course. Sooner or later, the impossibility of winning such a war must become evident and that is why we need to keep the humanitarian approach alive. Even if it cannot solve these conflicts, it can offer some hope to those caught in the middle. ∎

NOTES

1. Carl Clausewitz (1780–1831) was a Prussian general who advocated "total war," which involved attacking the enemy's territory, property, and citizens.

REFERENCES

H. Anheier, M. Glasius, M. Kaldor (Eds.), *Global Civil Society 2001*, Oxford University Press, Oxford, England.

Blair, T. (1999), 'Doctrine of the International Community', (23 April), http://www.primeminister.gov.uk.

Brahimi (2000), *Report of the Panel on United Nations Peace Operations*, (UN Doc.A/55/305-S/2000/809, 21 August), New York, United Nations.

Clark, Ian (1999), *Globalisation and International Relations Theory*, Oxford, England, Oxford University Press.

Cooper, Robert (2000), *The Postmodern State and the World Order*, Demos/Foreign Policy Centre, London, 2nd edition.

Der Derian, J. and Shapiro, M. (1989) (Eds.), *International/Intertextual Relations: Postmodern Readings of World Politics*, Lexington, Mass.: Lexington Books.

Freedman, L. (1998), 'The Revolution in Strategic Affairs' *Adelphi Paper 318*, London, International Institute of Strategic Affairs.

Giddens, A. (1990), *The Consequences of Modernity*, Polity Press, 1990.

Held, David et al. (1999), *Global Transformations*, Polity Press, Cambridge.

Kaldor, M. (1999), *New and Old Wars: Organized Violence in a Global Era*, Cambridge, England: Polity Press.

SIPRI (2001), Stockholm International Peace Research Institute, *SIPRI Yearbook 2001: Armaments, Disarmament and International Security*, Oxford, England, Oxford University Press.

Tilly, C. (1992), *Coercion, Capital and European States AD 990-1992*, Blackwell, Oxford.

■ QUESTIONS FOR MAKING CONNECTIONS WITHIN THE READING ■

1. What does Charles Tilly mean when he writes, "States made war and war made the state"? Is it true that war is primarily what defines us as Americans today? How about in the past? In what ways have wars played a decisive role in shaping our national identity?

2. What forces are responsible for the idea of "casualty-free war"? Is the expectation on the part of Americans that war should be casualty free, or as close to this goal as possible, simply a consequence of technological innovations, or are there other causes as well? What kinds of wars do you feel that most Americans are prepared to support? What kinds might they object to?

3. Why doesn't Kaldor use the term *terrorism* to cover all forms of non-state-sponsored violence? In what ways does her alternative term, *new war*, complicate our thinking about "unofficial" conflicts? Would you say that her terminology runs the risk of legitimizing terrorism? Alternately, does it free us from the arbitrariness that some might see in the use of that term?

■ QUESTIONS FOR WRITING ■

1. Is there a contradiction between "the new American militarism" and Kaldor's view that "the most hopeful approach to the contemporary problem of controlling war . . . is not through arms control but through

the extension and application of international humanitarian law . . . and human rights law"? Does our country's "new militarism" contribute to, or detract from, the advancement of human rights and international order?

2. What is the difference between viewing the events of September 11 as an act of "terrorism" or "moral evil" and viewing them instead as "a political act"? What are the advantages and disadvantages of each approach to the event? Why, do you think, has a political interpretation of the events of September 11 received so little attention from the popular press? To say that readers and viewers "want something else" is not really an answer. Please consider the *culture* of the popular press: Does it rely on a nationalist perspective or globalist one?

■ *QUESTIONS FOR MAKING CONNECTIONS BETWEEN READINGS* ■

1. In her essay, "Perfecting Democracy's Tools," Hazel Henderson proposes a number of sweeping changes in American political life. How might these changes contribute to the fulfillment of Kaldor's "utopian" vision? How might such changes detract from the achievement of that goal? Do you think that most Americans are prepared to support a greater degree of international coorporation? Does globalization require the disappearance of the nation-state or its transformation instead?

2. Is Kaldor's view of human rights consistent with Martha Nussbaum's? If the United States were to adopt Nussbaum's ethical programs as the basis of its foreign policy, would the result be a higher level of integration between states, or an increased degree of international tension? In what ways might disagreements over basic moral issues stand in the way of global mechanisms for conflict resolution? Would the Taliban, for example, have bowed voluntarily to world pressure to improve the status of Afghan women? If globalization is inevitable, are wars over basic values inevitable as well, given the world's cultural diversity?

For additional suggestions about making connections between readings, visit the Link-O-Mat and More Sample Assignments at <www.newhum.com>.

JON KRAKAUER

JON KRAKAUER, a regular contributor to *Outside Magazine,* rose to national prominence with the publication of *Into the Wild,* his investigative account of the life
and death of Chris McCandless, a young man who disappeared after graduating from college in Georgia in the early 1990s and whose body was discovered
two years later in an abandoned school bus in the wilds of Alaska. In an interview, Krakauer explained why he was driven to pursue McCandless's story in
such detail:

> I was haunted by the particulars of the boy's starvation and by vague, unset-
> tling parallels between events in his life and those in my own. Unwilling to
> let McCandless go, I spent more than a year retracing the convoluted path
> that led to his death in the Alaskan taiga, chasing down details of his pere-
> grinations with an interest that bordered on obsession. In trying to under-
> stand McCandless, I inevitably came to reflect on other, larger subjects as
> well: the grip wilderness has on the American imagination, the allure high-
> risk activities hold for young men of a certain mind, the complicated, highly
> charged bond that exists between fathers and sons.

Retracing McCandless's journey, Krakauer meditates not only on what it
means to be a man at the end of the twentieth century but also, more generally,
on the place of the natural world in contemporary society.

After completing *Into the Wild,* Krakauer set off to study the tourist industry's guided climbs up Mount Everest. *Into Thin Air,* which also became an
instant bestseller, is Krakauer's firsthand account of his experiences on a disastrous trip up Mount Everest that left nine climbers dead. The fact that this
tragedy could easily have been avoided by staying down off the mountain has
not escaped Krakauer's attention: "[W]hen I got back from Everest, I couldn't
help but think that maybe I'd devoted my life to something that isn't just selfish

Krakauer, Jon. "The Alaska Interior" and "The Stampede Trail," *Into the Wild.* New York: Random House, 1996. 157–199.

Quotations from Jon Krakauer, "Everest a Year Later: Lessons in Futility," Outside Magazine,
May 1997 <http://www.outsidemag.com/magazine/0597/9705krakauer.html> and Jon
Krakauer's Author Introduction, Outside Magazine <http://www.outsidemag.com/disc/
guest/krakauer/bookintro.html>.

and vainglorious and pointless, but actually wrong. There's no way to defend it, even to yourself, once you've been involved in something like this disaster. And yet I've continued to climb." Why do people embark on such adventures? What are they looking for? What is it they hope to achieve? These are the questions that animate Krakauer's writing; they are also the questions that he continues to try to answer for himself.

To learn more about Jon Krakauer and adventure writing, visit the Link-O-Mat at <www.newhum.com>.

▬ ▬

Selections from
Into the Wild

The Alaska Interior

I wished to acquire the simplicity, native feelings, and virtues of savage life; to divest myself of the factitious habits, prejudices and imperfections of civilization; . . . and to find, amidst the solitude and grandeur of the western wilds, more correct views of human nature and of the true interests of man. The season of snows was preferred, that I might experience the pleasure of suffering, and the novelty of danger.

> *Estwick Evans,*
> A Pedestrious Tour, of Four Thousand Miles,
> Through the Western States and Territories,
> During the Winter and Spring of 1818

Wilderness appealed to those bored or disgusted with man and his works. It not only offered an escape from society but also was an ideal stage for the Romantic individual to exercise the cult that he frequently made of his own soul. The solitude and total freedom of the wilderness created a perfect setting for either melancholy or exultation.

> *Roderick Nash,*
> Wilderness and the American Mind

On April 15, 1992, Chris McCandless departed Carthage, South Dakota, in the cab of a Mack truck hauling a load of sunflower seeds. His "great Alaskan odyssey" was under way. Three days later he crossed the Canadian border at Roosville, British Columbia, and thumbed north through

Skookumchuck and Radium Junction, Lake Louise and Jasper, Prince George and Dawson Creek—where, in the town center, he took a snapshot of the signpost marking the official start of the Alaska Highway. MILE "0," the sign reads, FAIRBANKS 1,523 MILES.

Hitchhiking tends to be difficult on the Alaska Highway. It's not unusual, on the outskirts of Dawson Creek, to see a dozen or more doleful-looking men and women standing along the shoulder with extended thumbs. Some of them may wait a week or more between rides. But McCandless experienced no such delay. On April 21, just six days out of Carthage, he arrived at Liard River Hotsprings, at the threshold of the Yukon Territory.

There is a public campground at Liard River, from which a boardwalk leads half a mile across a marsh to a series of natural thermal pools. It is the most popular way-stop on the Alaska Highway, and McCandless decided to pause there for a soak in the soothing waters. When he finished bathing and attempted to catch another ride north, however, he discovered that his luck had changed. Nobody would pick him up. Two days after arriving, he was still at Liard River, impatiently going nowhere.

At six-thirty on a brisk Thursday morning, the ground still frozen hard, Gaylord Stuckey walked out on the boardwalk to the largest of the pools, expecting to have the place to himself. He was surprised, therefore, to find someone already in the steaming water, a young man who introduced himself as Alex.

Stuckey—bald and cheerful, a ham-faced sixty-three-year-old Hoosier—was en route from Indiana to Alaska to deliver a new motor home to a Fairbanks RV dealer, a part-time line of work in which he'd dabbled since retiring after forty years in the restaurant business. When he told McCandless his destination, the boy exclaimed, "Hey, that's where I'm going, too! But I've been stuck here for a couple of days now, trying to get a lift. You mind if I ride with you?"

"Oh, jiminy," Stuckey replied. "I'd love to, son, but I can't. The company I work for has a strict rule against picking up hitchhikers. It could get me canned." As he chatted with McCandless through the sulfurous mist, though, Stuckey began to reconsider: "Alex was clean-shaven and had short hair, and I could tell by the language he used that he was a real sharp fella. He wasn't what you'd call a typical hitchhiker. I'm usually leery of 'em. I figure there's probably something wrong with a guy if he can't even afford a bus ticket. So anyway, after about half an hour I said, 'I tell you what, Alex: Liard is a thousand miles from Fairbanks. I'll take you five hundred miles, as far as Whitehorse; you'll be able to get a ride the rest of the way from there.'"

A day and a half later, however, when they arrived in Whitehorse—the capital of the Yukon Territory and the largest, most cosmopolitan town on the Alaska Highway—Stuckey had come to enjoy McCandless's company so much that he changed his mind and agreed to drive the boy the entire distance. "Alex didn't come out and say too much at first," Stuckey reports.

"But it's a long, slow drive. We spent a total of three days together on those washboard roads, and by the end he kind of let his guard down. I tell you what: He was a dandy kid. Real courteous, and he didn't cuss or use a lot of that there slang. You could tell he came from a nice family. Mostly he talked about his sister. He didn't get along with his folks too good, I guess. Told me his dad was a genius, a NASA rocket scientist, but he'd been a bigamist at one time—and that kind of went against Alex's grain. Said he hadn't seen his parents in a couple of years, since his college graduation."

McCandless was candid with Stuckey about his intent to spend the summer alone in the bush, living off the land. "He said it was something he'd wanted to do since he was little," says Stuckey. "Said he didn't want to see a single person, no airplanes, no sign of civilization. He wanted to prove to himself that he could make it on his own, without anybody else's help."

Stuckey and McCandless arrived in Fairbanks on the afternoon of April 25. The older man took the boy to a grocery store, where he bought a big bag of rice, "and then Alex said he wanted to go out to the university to study up on what kind of plants he could eat. Berries and things like that. I told him, 'Alex, you're too early. There's still two foot, three foot of snow on the ground. There's nothing growing yet.' But his mind was pretty well made up. He was chomping at the bit to get out there and start hiking." Stuckey drove to the University of Alaska campus, on the west end of Fairbanks, and dropped McCandless off at 5:30 P.M.

"Before I let him out," Stuckey says, "I told him, 'Alex, I've driven you a thousand miles. I've fed you and fed you for three straight days. The least you can do is send me a letter when you get back from Alaska.' And he promised he would.

"I also begged and pleaded with him to call his parents. I can't imagine anything worse than having a son out there and not knowing where he's at for years and years, not knowing whether he's living or dead. 'Here's my credit card number,' I told him. '*Please* call them!' But all he said was 'Maybe I will and maybe I won't.' After he left, I thought, 'Oh, why didn't I get his parents' phone number and call them myself?' But everything just kind of happened so quick."

After dropping McCandless at the university, Stuckey drove into town to deliver the RV to the appointed dealer, only to be told that the person responsible for checking in new vehicles had already gone home for the day and wouldn't be back until Monday morning, leaving Stuckey with two days to kill in Fairbanks before he could fly home to Indiana. On Sunday morning, with time on his hands, he returned to the campus. "I hoped to find Alex and spend another day with him, take him sightseeing or something. I looked for a couple of hours, drove all over the place, but didn't see hide or hair of him. He was already gone."

After taking his leave of Stuckey on Saturday evening, McCandless spent two days and three nights in the vicinity of Fairbanks, mostly at the university. In the campus book store, tucked away on the bottom shelf of the Alaska section, he came across a scholarly, exhaustively researched field guide to the region's edible plants, *Tanaina Plantlore/Dena'ina K'et'una: An Ethnobotany of the Dena'ina Indians of Southcentral Alaska* by Priscilla Russell Kari. From a postcard rack near the cash register, he picked out two cards of a polar bear, on which he sent his final messages to Wayne Westerberg and Jan Burres from the university post office.

Perusing the classified ads, McCandless found a used gun to buy, a semiautomatic .22-caliber Remington with a 4-x-20 scope and a plastic stock. A model called the Nylon 66, no longer in production, it was a favorite of Alaska trappers because of its light weight and reliability. He closed the deal in a parking lot, probably paying about $125 for the weapon, and then purchased four one-hundred-round boxes of hollow-point long-rifle shells from a nearby gun shop.

At the conclusion of his preparations in Fairbanks, McCandless loaded up his pack and started hiking west from the university. Leaving the campus, he walked past the Geophysical Institute, a tall glass-and-concrete building capped with a large satellite dish. The dish, one of the most distinctive landmarks on the Fairbanks skyline, had been erected to collect data from satellites equipped with synthetic aperture radar of Walt McCandless's design. Walt had in fact visited Fairbanks during the start-up of the receiving station and had written some of the software crucial to its operation. If the Geophysical Institute prompted Chris to think of his father as he tramped by, the boy left no record of it.

Four miles west of town, in the evening's deepening chill, McCandless pitched his tent on a patch of hard-frozen ground surrounded by birch trees, not far from the crest of a bluff overlooking Gold Hill Gas & Liquor. Fifty yards from his camp was the terraced road cut of the George Parks Highway, the road that would take him to the Stampede Trail. He woke early on the morning of April 28, walked down to the highway in the predawn gloaming, and was pleasantly surprised when the first vehicle to come along pulled over to give him a lift. It was a gray Ford pickup with a bumper sticker on the back that declared, I FISH THEREFORE I AM. PETERSBURG, ALASKA. The driver of the truck, an electrician on his way to Anchorage, wasn't much older than McCandless. He said his name was Jim Gallien.

Three hours later Gallien turned his truck west off the highway and drove as far as he could down an unplowed side road. When he dropped McCandless off on the Stampede Trail, the temperature was in the low thirties—it would drop into the low teens at night—and a foot and a half of crusty spring snow covered the ground. The boy could hardly contain his excitement. He was, at long last, about to be alone in the vast Alaska wilds.

As he trudged expectantly down the trail in a fake-fur parka, his rifle slung over one shoulder, the only food McCandless carried was a ten-pound bag of long-grained rice—and the two sandwiches and bag of corn chips that Gallien had contributed. A year earlier he'd subsisted for more than a month beside the Gulf of California on five pounds of rice and a bounty of fish caught with a cheap rod and reel, an experience that made him confident he could harvest enough food to survive an extended stay in the Alaska wilderness, too.

The heaviest item in McCandless's half-full backpack was his library: nine or ten paperbound books, most of which had been given to him by Jan Burres in Niland. Among these volumes were titles by Thoreau and Tolstoy and Gogol, but McCandless was no literary snob: He simply carried what he thought he might enjoy reading, including mass-market books by Michael Crichton, Robert Pirsig, and Louis L'Amour. Having neglected to pack writing paper, he began a laconic journal on some blank pages in the back of *Tanaina Plantlore.*

The Healy terminus of the Stampede Trail is traveled by a handful of dog mushers, ski tourers, and snow-machine enthusiasts during the winter months, but only until the frozen rivers begin to break up, in late March or early April. By the time McCandless headed into the bush, there was open water flowing on most of the larger streams, and nobody had been very far down the trail for two or three weeks; only the faint remnants of a packed snow-machine track remained for him to follow.

McCandless reached the Teklanika River his second day out. Although the banks were lined with a jagged shelf of frozen overflow, no ice bridges spanned the channel of open water, so he was forced to wade. There had been a big thaw in early April, and breakup had come early in 1992, but the weather had turned cold again, so the river's volume was quite low when McCandless crossed—probably thigh-deep at most—allowing him to splash to the other side without difficulty. He never suspected that in so doing, he was crossing his Rubicon. To McCandless's inexperienced eye, there was nothing to suggest that two months hence, as the glaciers and snowfields at the Teklanika's headwater thawed in the summer heat, its discharge would multiply nine or ten times in volume, transforming the river into a deep, violent torrent that bore no resemblance to the gentle brook he'd blithely waded across in April.

From his journal we know that on April 29, McCandless fell through the ice somewhere. It probably happened as he traversed a series of melting beaver ponds just beyond the Teklanika's western bank, but there is nothing to indicate that he suffered any harm in the mishap. A day later, as the trail crested a ridge, he got his first glimpse of Mt. McKinley's high, blinding-white bulwarks, and a day after that, May 1, some twenty miles down the trail from where he was dropped by Gallien, he stumbled upon the old bus beside the Sushana River. It was outfitted with a bunk and a barrel stove, and previous visitors had left the improvised shelter stocked with matches, bug dope, and other essentials. "Magic Bus Day," he wrote in his journal. He decided to lay over for a while in the vehicle and take advantage of its crude comforts.

He was elated to be there. Inside the bus, on a sheet of weathered ply-wood spanning a broken window, McCandless scrawled an exultant decla-ration of independence:

*TWO YEARS HE WALKS THE EARTH. NO PHONE, NO POOL, NO PETS,
NO CIGARETTES. ULTIMATE FREEDOM. AN EXTREMIST. AN AES-
THETIC VOYAGER WHOSE HOME IS THE ROAD. ESCAPED FROM
ATLANTA. THOU SHALT NOT RETURN, 'CAUSE "THE WEST IS THE
BEST." AND NOW AFTER TWO RAMBLING YEARS COMES THE FINAL
AND GREATEST ADVENTURE. THE CLIMACTIC BATTLE TO KILL THE
FALSE BEING WITHIN AND VICTORIOUSLY CONCLUDE THE SPIRI-
TUAL PILGRIMAGE. TEN DAYS AND NIGHTS OF FREIGHT TRAINS
AND HITCHHIKING BRING HIM TO THE GREAT WHITE NORTH. NO
LONGER TO BE POISONED BY CIVILIZATION HE FLEES, AND WALKS
ALONE UPON THE LAND TO BECOME LOST IN THE WILD.*

Alexander Supertramp
May 1992

Reality, however, was quick to intrude on McCandless's reverie. He had difficulty killing game, and the daily journal entries during his first week in the bush include "Weakness," "Snowed in," and "Disaster." He saw but did not shoot a grizzly on May 2, shot at but missed some ducks on May 4, and finally killed and ate a spruce grouse on May 5; but he didn't shoot anything else until May 9, when he bagged a single small squirrel, by which point he'd written "4th day famine" in the journal.

But soon thereafter his fortunes took a sharp turn for the better. By mid-May the sun was circling high in the heavens, flooding the taiga with light. The sun dipped below the northern horizon for fewer than four hours out of every twenty-four, and at midnight the sky was still bright enough to read by. Everywhere but on the north-facing slopes and in the shadowy ravines, the snowpack had melted down to bare ground, exposing the previous sea-son's rose hips and lingonberries, which McCandless gathered and ate in great quantity.

He also became much more successful at hunting game and for the next six weeks feasted regularly on squirrel, spruce grouse, duck, goose, and por-cupine. On May 22, a crown fell off one of his molars, but the event didn't seem to dampen his spirits much, because the following day he scrambled up the nameless, humplike, three-thousand-foot butte that rises directly north of the bus, giving him a view of the whole icy sweep of the Alaska Range and mile after mile of uninhabited country. His journal entry for the day is char-acteristically terse but unmistakably joyous: "CLIMB MOUNTAIN!"

McCandless had told Gallien that he intended to remain on the move during his stay in the bush. "I'm just going to take off and keep walking west," he'd said. "I might walk all the way to the Bering Sea." On May 5, after pausing for four days at the bus, he resumed his perambulation. From the snapshots recovered with his Minolta, it appears that McCandless lost (or intentionally left) the by now indistinct Stampede Trail and headed west and north through the hills above the Sushana River, hunting game as he went.

It was slow going. In order to feed himself, he had to devote a large part of each day to stalking animals. Moreover, as the ground thawed, his route turned into a gauntlet of boggy muskeg and impenetrable alder, and McCandless belatedly came to appreciate one of the fundamental (if counterintuitive) axioms of the North: winter, not summer, is the preferred season for traveling overland through the bush.

Faced with the obvious folly of his original ambition, to walk five hundred miles to tidewater, he reconsidered his plans. On May 19, having traveled no farther west than the Toklat River—less than fifteen miles beyond the bus—he turned around. A week later he was back at the derelict vehicle, apparently without regret. He'd decided that the Sushana drainage was plenty wild to suit his purposes and that Fairbanks bus 142 would make a fine base camp for the remainder of the summer.

Ironically, the wilderness surrounding the bus—the patch of overgrown country where McCandless was determined "to become lost in the wild"— scarcely qualifies as wilderness by Alaska standards. Less than thirty miles to the east is a major thoroughfare, the George Parks Highway. Just sixteen miles to the north, beyond an escarpment of the Outer Range, hundreds of tourists rumble daily into Denali Park over a road patrolled by the National Park Service. And unbeknownst to the Aesthetic Voyager, scattered within a six-mile radius of the bus are four cabins (although none happened to be occupied during the summer of 1992).

But despite the relative proximity of the bus to civilization, for all practical purposes McCandless was cut off from the rest of the world. He spent nearly four months in the bush all told, and during that period he didn't encounter another living soul. In the end the Sushana River site was sufficiently remote to cost him his life.

In the last week of May, after moving his few possessions into the bus, McCandless wrote a list of housekeeping chores on a parchmentlike strip of birch bark: collect and store ice from the river for refrigerating meat, cover the vehicle's missing windows with plastic, lay in a supply of firewood, clean the accumulation of old ash from the stove. And under the heading "LONG TERM" he drew up a list of more ambitious tasks: map the area, improvise a bathtub, collect skins and feathers to sew into clothing, construct a bridge across a nearby creek, repair mess kit, blaze a network of hunting trails.

The diary entries following his return to the bus catalog a bounty of wild meat. May 28: "Gourmet Duck!" June 1: "5 Squirrel." June 2: "Porcupine, Ptarmigan, 4 Squirrel, Grey Bird." June 3: "Another Porcupine! 4 Squirrel, 2 Grey Bird, Ash Bird." June 4: "A THIRD PORCUPINE! Squirrel,

Grey Bird." On June 5, he shot a Canada goose as big as a Christmas turkey. Then, on June 9, he bagged the biggest prize of all: "MOOSE!" he recorded in the journal. Overjoyed, the proud hunter took a photograph of himself kneeling over his trophy, rifle thrust triumphantly overhead, his features distorted in a rictus of ecstasy and amazement, like some unemployed janitor who'd gone to Reno and won a million-dollar jackpot.

Although McCandless was enough of a realist to know that hunting game was an unavoidable component of living off the land, he had always been ambivalent about killing animals. That ambivalence turned to remorse soon after he shot the moose. It was relatively small, weighing perhaps six hundred or seven hundred pounds, but it nevertheless amounted to a huge quantity of meat. Believing that it was morally indefensible to waste any part of an animal that has been shot for food, McCandless spent six days toiling to preserve what he had killed before it spoiled. He butchered the carcass under a thick cloud of flies and mosquitoes, boiled the organs into a stew, and then laboriously excavated a burrow in the face of the rocky stream bank directly below the bus, in which he tried to cure, by smoking, the immense slabs of purple flesh.

Alaskan hunters know that the easiest way to preserve meat in the bush is to slice it into thin strips and then air-dry it on a makeshift rack. But McCandless, in his naïveté, relied on the advice of hunters he'd consulted in South Dakota, who advised him to smoke his meat, not an easy task under the circumstances. "Butchering extremely difficult," he wrote in the journal on June 10. "Fly and mosquito hordes. Remove intestines, liver, kidneys, one lung, steaks. Get hindquarters and leg to stream."

June 11: "Remove heart and other lung. Two front legs and head. Get rest to stream. Haul near cave. Try to protect with smoker."

June 12: "Remove half rib-cage and steaks. Can only work nights. Keep smokers going."

June 13: "Get remainder of rib-cage, shoulder and neck to cave. Start smoking."

June 14: "Maggots already! Smoking appears ineffective. Don't know, looks like disaster. I now wish I had never shot the moose. One of the greatest tragedies of my life."

At that point he gave up on preserving the bulk of the meat and abandoned the carcass to the wolves. Although he castigated himself severely for this waste of a life he'd taken, a day later McCandless appeared to regain some perspective, for his journal notes, "henceforth will learn to accept my errors, however great they be."

Shortly after the moose episode McCandless began to read Thoreau's *Walden*. In the chapter titled "Higher Laws," in which Thoreau ruminates on the morality of eating, McCandless highlighted, "when I had caught and cleaned and cooked and eaten my fish, they seemed not to have fed me essentially. It was insignificant and unnecessary, and cost more than it came to."

"THE MOOSE," McCandless wrote in the margin. And in the same passage he marked,

> *The repugnance to animal food is not the effect of experience, but is an instinct. It appeared more beautiful to live low and fare hard in many respects; and though I never did so, I went far enough to please my imagination. I believe that every man who has ever been earnest to preserve his higher or poetic faculties in the best condition has been particularly inclined to abstain from animal food, and from much food of any kind. . . .*
>
> *It is hard to provide and cook so simple and clean a diet as will not offend the imagination; but this, I think, is to be fed when we feed the body; they should both sit down at the same table. Yet perhaps this may be done. The fruits eaten temperately need not make us ashamed of our appetites, nor interrupt the worthiest pursuits. But put an extra condiment into your dish, and it will poison you.*

"YES," wrote McCandless and, two pages later, "*Consciousness* of food. Eat and cook with *concentration*. . . . Holy Food." On the back pages of the book that served as his journal, he declared:

> *I am reborn. This is my dawn. Real life has just begun.*
>
> <u>*Deliberate Living:*</u> *Conscious attention to the basics of life, and a constant attention to your immediate environment and its concerns, example* ➔ *A job, a task, a book; anything requiring efficient concentration (Circumstance has no value. It is how one <u>relates</u> to a situation that has value. All true meaning resides in the personal relationship to a phenomenon, what it means to you).*
>
> *The Great Holiness of* **<u>FOOD</u>**, *The Vital Heat.*
>
> <u>*Positivism*</u>, *the Insurpassable Joy of the Life Aesthetic.*
>
> *Absolute Truth and Honesty.*
>
> *Reality.*
>
> *Independence.*
>
> *Finality—Stability—Consistency.*

As McCandless gradually stopped rebuking himself for the waste of the moose, the contentment that began in mid-May resumed and seemed to continue through early July. Then, in the midst of this idyll, came the first of two pivotal setbacks.

Satisfied, apparently, with what he had learned during his two months of solitary life in the wild, McCandless decided to return to civilization: It was time to bring his "final and greatest adventure" to a close and get himself back to the world of men and women, where he could chug a beer, talk philosophy, enthrall strangers with tales of what he'd done. He seemed to have moved beyond his need to assert so adamantly his autonomy, his need to separate himself from his parents. Maybe he was prepared to forgive their imperfections; maybe he was even prepared to forgive some of his own. McCandless seemed ready, perhaps, to go home.

Or maybe not; we can do no more than speculate about what he intended to do after he walked out of the bush. There is no question, however, that he intended to walk out.

Writing on a piece of birch bark, he made a list of things to do before he departed: "Patch Jeans, Shave!, Organize pack. . . " Shortly thereafter he propped his Minolta on an empty oil drum and took a snapshot of himself brandishing a yellow disposable razor and grinning at the camera, clean-shaven, with new patches cut from an army blanket stitched onto the knees of his filthy jeans. He looks healthy but alarmingly gaunt. Already his cheeks are sunken. The tendons in his neck stand out like taut cables.

On July 2, McCandless finished reading Tolstoy's "Family Happiness," having marked several passages that moved him:

> *He was right in saying that the only certain happiness in life is to live for others. . . .*

> *I have lived through much, and now I think I have found what is needed for happiness. A quiet secluded life in the country, with the possibility of being useful to people to whom it is easy to do good, and who are not accustomed to have it done to them; then work which one hopes may be of some use; then rest, nature, books, music, love for one's neighbor—such is my idea of happiness. And then, on top of all that, you for a mate, and children, perhaps—what more can the heart of a man desire?*

Then, on July 3, he shouldered his backpack and began the twenty-mile hike to the improved road. Two days later, halfway there, he arrived in heavy rain at the beaver ponds that blocked access to the west bank of the Teklanika River. In April they'd been frozen over and hadn't presented an obstacle. Now he must have been alarmed to find a three-acre lake covering the trail. To avoid having to wade through the murky chest-deep water, he scrambled up a steep hillside, bypassed the ponds on the north, and then dropped back down to the river at the mouth of the gorge.

When he'd first crossed the river, sixty-seven days earlier in the freezing temperatures of April, it had been an icy but gentle knee-deep creek, and he'd simply strolled across it. On July 5, however, the Teklanika was at full flood, swollen with rain and snowmelt from glaciers high in the Alaska Range, running cold and fast.

If he could reach the far shore, the remainder of the hike to the highway would be easy, but to get there he would have to negotiate a channel some one hundred feet wide. The water, opaque with glacial sediment and only a few degrees warmer than the ice it had so recently been, was the color of wet concrete. Too deep to wade, it rumbled like a freight train. The powerful current would quickly knock him off his feet and carry him away.

McCandless was a weak swimmer and had confessed to several people that he was in fact afraid of the water. Attempting to swim the numbingly cold torrent or even to paddle some sort of improvised raft across seemed too risky to consider. Just downstream from where the trail met the river, the Teklanika erupted into a chaos of boiling whitewater as it accelerated through the narrow gorge. Long before he could swim or paddle to the far shore, he'd be pulled into these rapids and drowned.

In his journal he now wrote, "Disaster. . . . Rained in. River look impossible. Lonely, scared." He concluded, correctly, that he would probably be swept to his death if he attempted to cross the Teklanika at that place, in those conditions. It would be suicidal; it was simply not an option.

If McCandless had walked a mile or so upstream, he would have discovered that the river broadened into a maze of braided channels. If he'd scouted carefully, by trial and error he might have found a place where these braids were only chest-deep. As strong as the current was running, it would have certainly knocked him off his feet, but by dog-paddling and hopping along the bottom as he drifted downstream, he could conceivably have made it across before being carried into the gorge or succumbing to hypothermia.

But it would still have been a very risky proposition, and at that point McCandless had no reason to take such a risk. He'd been fending for himself quite nicely in the country. He probably understood that if he was patient and waited, the river would eventually drop to a level where it could be safely forded. After weighing his options, therefore, he settled on the most prudent course. He turned around and began walking to the west, back toward the bus, back into the fickle heart of the bush.

The Stampede Trail

Nature was here something savage and awful, though beautiful. I looked with awe at the ground I trod on, to see what the Powers had made there, the form and fashion and material of their work. This was that Earth of which we have heard, made out of Chaos and Old Night. Here was no man's garden, but the unhandselled globe. It was not lawn, nor pasture, nor mead, nor woodland, nor lea, nor arable, nor waste land. It was the fresh and natural surface of the planet Earth, as it was made forever and ever,—to be the dwelling of man, we say,—so Nature made it, and man may use it if he can. Man was not to be associated with it. It was Matter, vast, terrific,—not his Mother Earth that we have heard of, not for him to tread on, or to be buried in,—no, it were being too familiar even to let his bones lie there,—the home, this, of Necessity and Fate. There was clearly felt the presence of a force not bound to be kind to man. It was a place of heathenism and superstitious rites,— to be inhabited by men nearer of kin to the rocks and to wild animals than we. . . . What is it to be admitted to a museum, to see a myriad of particular things, compared with being shown some star's surface, some hard matter in its home! I stand in awe of my body, this matter to which I am bound has become so strange to me. I fear not spirits, ghosts, of which I am one,—that my body might,—but I fear bodies, I tremble to meet them. What is this Titan that has possession of me? Talk of mysteries! Think of our life in nature,—daily to be shown matter, to come in contact with it,—rocks, trees, wind on our cheeks! the solid earth! the actual world! the common sense! Contact! Contact! Who are we? where are we?

Henry David Thoreau, "Ktaadn"

A year and a week after Chris McCandless decided not to attempt to cross the Teklanika River, I stand on the opposite bank—the eastern side, the highway side—and gaze into the churning water. I, too, hope to cross the river. I want to visit the bus. I want to see where McCandless died, to better understand why.

It is a hot, humid afternoon, and the river is livid with runoff from the fast-melting snowpack that still blankets the glaciers in the higher elevations of the Alaska Range. Today the water looks considerably lower than it looks in the photographs McCandless took twelve months ago, but to try to ford the river here, in thundering midsummer flood, is nevertheless unthinkable. The water is too deep, too cold, too fast. As I stare into the Teklanika, I can hear rocks the size of bowling balls grinding along the bottom, rolled downstream by the powerful current. I'd be swept from my feet within a few yards of leaving the bank and pushed into the canyon immediately below, which pinches the river into a boil of rapids that continues without interruption for the next five miles.

Unlike McCandless, however, I have in my backpack a 1:63,360-scale topographic map (that is, a map on which one inch represents one mile). Exquisitely detailed, it indicates that half a mile downstream, in the throat of the canyon, is a gauging station that was built by the U.S. Geological Survey. Unlike McCandless, too, I am here with three companions: Alaskans Roman Dial and Dan Solie and a friend of Roman's from California, Andrew Liske. The gauging station can't be seen from where the Stampede Trail comes down to the river, but after twenty minutes of fighting our way through a snarl of spruce and dwarf birch, Roman shouts, "I see it! There! A hundred yards farther."

We arrive to find an inch-thick steel cable spanning the gorge, stretched between a fifteen-foot tower on our side of the river and an outcrop on the far shore, four hundred feet away. The cable was erected in 1970 to chart the Teklanika's seasonal fluctuations; hydrologists traveled back and forth above the river by means of an aluminum basket that is suspended from the cable with pulleys. From the basket they would drop a weighted plumb line to measure the river's depth. The station was decommissioned nine years ago for lack of funds, at which time the basket was supposed to be chained and locked to the tower on our side—the highway side—of the river. When we climbed to the top of the tower, however, the basket wasn't there. Looking across the rushing water, I could see it over on the distant shore—the bus side—of the canyon.

Some local hunters, it turns out, had cut the chain, ridden the basket across, and secured it to the far side in order to make it harder for outsiders to cross the Teklanika and trespass on their turf. When McCandless tried to walk out of the bush one year ago the previous week, the basket was in the same place it is now, on his side of the canyon. If he'd known about it, crossing the Teklanika to safety would have been a trivial matter. Because he had no topographic map, however, he had no way of conceiving that salvation was so close at hand.

Andy Horowitz, one of McCandless's friends on the Woodson High cross-country team, had mused that Chris "was born into the wrong century. He was looking for more adventure and freedom than today's society gives people." In coming to Alaska, McCandless yearned to wander uncharted country, to find a blank spot on the map. In 1992, however, there were no more blank spots on the map—not in Alaska, not anywhere. But Chris, with his idiosyncratic logic, came up with an elegant solution to this dilemma: He simply got rid of the map. In his own mind, if nowhere else, the *terra* would thereby remain *incognita.*

Because he lacked a good map, the cable spanning the river also remained incognito. Studying the Teklanika's violent flow, McCandless thus mistakenly concluded that it was impossible to reach the eastern shore. Thinking that his escape route had been cut off, he returned to the bus—a reasonable course of action, given his topographical ignorance. But why did he then stay at the bus and starve? Why, come August, didn't he try once more to cross the Teklanika, when it would have been running significantly lower, when it would have been safe to ford?

Puzzled by these questions, and troubled, I am hoping that the rusting hulk of Fairbanks bus 142 will yield some clues. But to reach the bus, I, too, need to cross the river, and the aluminum tram is still chained to the far shore.

Standing atop the tower anchoring the eastern end of the span, I attach myself to the cable with rock-climbing hardware and begin to pull myself across, hand over hand, executing what mountaineers call a Tyrolean traverse. This turns out to be a more strenuous proposition than I had anticipated. Twenty minutes after starting out, I finally haul myself onto the outcrop on the other side, completely spent, so wasted I can barely raise my arms. After at last catching my breath, I climb into the basket—a rectangular aluminum car two feet wide by four feet long—disconnect the chain, and head back to the eastern side of the canyon to ferry my companions across.

The cable sags noticeably over the middle of the river; so when I cut loose from the outcrop, the car accelerates quickly under its own weight, rolling faster and faster along the steel strand, seeking the lowest point. It's a thrilling ride. Zipping over the rapids at twenty or thirty miles per hour, I hear an involuntary bark of fright leap from my throat before I realize that I'm in no danger and regain my composure.

After all four of us are on the western side of the gorge, thirty minutes of rough bushwhacking returns us to the Stampede Trail. The ten miles of trail we have already covered—the section between our parked vehicles and the river—were gentle, well marked, and relatively heavily traveled. But the ten miles to come have an utterly different character.

Because so few people cross the Teklanika during the spring and summer months, much of the route is indistinct and overgrown with brush. Immediately past the river the trail curves to the southwest, up the bed of a fast-flowing creek. And because beavers have built a network of elaborate dams across this creek, the route leads directly through a three-acre expanse of standing water. The beaver ponds are never more than chest deep, but the water is cold, and as we slosh forward, our feet churn the muck on the bottom into a foul-smelling miasma of decomposing slime.

The trail climbs a hill beyond the uppermost pond, then rejoins the twisting, rocky creek bed before ascending again into a jungle of scrubby vegetation. The going never gets exceedingly difficult, but the fifteen-foot-high tangle of alder pressing in from both sides is gloomy, claustrophobic, oppressive. Clouds of mosquitoes materialize out of the sticky heat. Every few minutes the insects' piercing whine is supplanted by the boom of distant thunder, rumbling over the taiga from a wall of thunderheads rearing darkly on the horizon.

Thickets of buckbrush leave a crosshatch of bloody lacerations on my shins. Piles of bear scat on the trail and, at one point, a set of fresh grizzly tracks—each print half again as long as a size-nine boot print—put me on edge. None of us has a gun. "Hey, Griz!" I yell at the undergrowth, hoping to avoid a surprise encounter. "Hey, bear! Just passing through! No reason to get riled!"

I have been to Alaska some twenty times during the past twenty years—to climb mountains, to work as a carpenter and a commercial salmon fisherman and a journalist, to goof off, to poke around. I've spent a lot of time alone in the country over the course of my many visits and usually relish it. Indeed, I had intended to make this trip to the bus by myself, and when my friend Roman invited himself and two others along, I was annoyed. Now, however, I am grateful for their company. There is something disquieting about this Gothic, overgrown landscape. It feels more malevolent than other, more remote corners of the state I know—the tundra-wrapped slopes of the Brooks Range, the cloud forests of the Alexander Archipelago, even the frozen, gale-swept heights of the Denali massif. I'm happy as hell that I'm not here alone.

At 9:00 P.M. we round a bend in the trail, and there, at the edge of a small clearing, is the bus. Pink bunches of fireweed choke the vehicle's wheel wells, growing higher than the axles. Fairbanks bus 142 is parked beside a coppice of aspen, ten yards back from the brow of a modest cliff, on a shank of high ground overlooking the confluence of the Sushana River and a smaller tributary. It's an appealing setting, open and filled with light. It's easy to see why McCandless decided to make this his base camp.

We pause some distance away from the bus and stare at it for a while in silence. Its paint is chalky and peeling. Several windows are missing. Hundreds of delicate bones litter the clearing around the vehicle, scattered among thousands of porcupine quills: the remains of the small game that made up the bulk of McCandless's diet. And at the perimeter of this boneyard lies one much larger skeleton: that of the moose he shot, and subsequently agonized over.

When I'd questioned Gordon Samel and Ken Thompson shortly after they'd discovered McCandless's body, both men insisted—adamantly and unequivocally—that the big skeleton was the remains of a caribou, and they derided the greenhorn's ignorance in mistaking the animal he killed for a moose. "Wolves had scattered the bones some," Thompson had told me, "but it was obvious that the animal was a caribou. The kid didn't know what the hell he was doing up here."

"It was definitely a caribou," Samel had scornfully piped in. "When I read in the paper that he thought he'd shot a moose, that told me right there he wasn't no Alaskan. There's a big difference between a moose and a caribou. A real big difference. You'd have to be pretty stupid not to be able to tell them apart."

Trusting Samel and Thompson, veteran Alaskan hunters who've killed many moose and caribou between them, I duly reported McCandless's mistake in the article I wrote for *Outside*, thereby confirming the opinion of countless readers that McCandless was ridiculously ill prepared, that he had no business heading into any wilderness, let alone into the big-league wilds of the Last Frontier. Not only did McCandless die because he was stupid, one Alaska correspondent observed, but "the scope of his self-styled adventure was so small as to ring pathetic—squatting in a wrecked bus a few miles out of Healy, potting jays and squirrels, mistaking a caribou for a moose (pretty hard to do). . . . Only one word for the guy: incompetent."

Among the letters lambasting McCandless, virtually all those I received mentioned his misidentification of the caribou as proof that he didn't know the first thing about surviving in the back country. What the angry letter writers didn't know, however, was that the ungulate McCandless shot was exactly what he'd said it was. Contrary to what I reported in *Outside*, the animal was a moose, as a close examination of the beast's remains now indicated and several of McCandless's photographs of the kill later confirmed beyond all doubt. The boy made some mistakes on the Stampede Trail, but confusing a caribou with a moose wasn't among them.

Walking past the moose bones, I approach the vehicle and step through an emergency exit at the back. Immediately inside the door is the torn mattress, stained and moldering, on which McCandless expired. For some reason I am taken aback to find a collection of his possessions spread across its ticking: a green plastic canteen; a tiny bottle of water-purification tablets; a used-up cylinder of Chap Stick; a pair of insulated flight pants of the type sold in military-surplus stores; a paperback copy of the bestseller *0 Jerusalem!*, its spine broken; wool mittens; a bottle of Muskol insect repellent; a full box of matches; and a pair of brown rubber work boots with the name Gallien written across the cuffs in faint black ink.

Despite the missing windows, the air inside the cavernous vehicle is stale and musty. "Wow," Roman remarks. "It smells like dead birds in here." A moment later I come across the source of the odor: a plastic garbage bag filled with feathers, down, and the severed wings of several birds. It appears that McCandless was saving them to insulate his clothing or perhaps to make a feather pillow.

Toward the front of the bus, McCandless's pots and dishes are stacked on a makeshift plywood table beside a kerosene lamp. A long leather scabbard is expertly tooled with the initials R. F.: the sheath for the machete Ronald Franz gave McCandless when he left Salton City.

The boy's blue toothbrush rests next to a half-empty tube of Colgate, a packet of dental floss, and the gold molar crown that, according to his journal, fell off his tooth three weeks into his sojourn. A few inches away sits a skull the size of a watermelon, thick ivory fangs jutting from its bleached maxillae. It is a bear skull, the remains of a grizzly shot by someone who visited the bus years before McCandless's tenure. A message scratched in Chris's tidy hand brackets a cranial bullet hole: ALL HAIL THE PHANTOM BEAR, THE BEST WITHIN US ALL. ALEXANDER SUPERTRAMP, MAY 1992.

Looking up, I notice that the sheet-metal walls of the vehicle are covered with graffiti left by numerous visitors over the years. Roman points out a message he wrote when he stayed in the bus four years ago, during a traverse of the Alaska Range: NOODLE EATERS EN ROUTE TO LAKE CLARK 8/89. Like Roman, most people scrawled little more than their names and a date. The longest, most eloquent graffito is one of several inscribed by McCandless, the proclamation of joy that begins with a nod to his favorite Roger Miller song: TWO YEARS HE WALKS THE EARTH, NO PHONE, NO POOL, NO PETS, NO CIGA-RETTES. ULTIMATE FREEDOM. AN EXTREMIST. AN AESTHETIC VOYAGER WHOSE NAME IS THE ROAD. . . .

Immediately below this manifesto squats the stove, fabricated from a rusty oil drum. A twelve-foot section of a spruce trunk is jammed into its open doorway, and across the log are draped two pairs of torn Levi's, laid out as if to dry. One pair of jeans—waist thirty, inseam thirty-two—is patched crudely with silver duct tape; the other pair has been repaired more carefully, with scraps from a faded bedspread stitched over gaping holes in the knees and seat. This latter pair also sports a belt fashioned from a strip of blanket. McCandless, it occurs to me, must have been forced to make the belt after growing so thin that his pants wouldn't stay up without it.

Sitting down on a steel cot across from the stove to mull over this eerie tableau, I encounter evidence of McCandless's presence wherever my vision rests. Here are his toenail clippers, over there his green nylon tent spread over a missing window in the front door. His Kmart hiking boots are arranged neatly beneath the stove, as though he'd soon be returning to lace them up and hit the trail. I feel uncomfortable, as if I were intruding, a voyeur who has slipped into McCandless's bedroom while he is momentarily away. Suddenly queasy, I stumble out of the bus to walk along the river and breathe some fresh air.

An hour later we build a fire outside in the fading light. The rain squalls, now past, have rinsed the haze from the atmosphere, and distant, backlit hills stand out in crisp detail. A stripe of incandescent sky burns beneath the cloud base on the northwestern horizon. Roman unwraps some steaks from a moose he shot in the Alaska Range last September and lays them across the fire on a blackened grill, the grill McCandless used for broiling his game. Moose fat pops and sizzles into the coals. Eating the gristly meat with our fingers, we slap at mosquitoes and talk about this peculiar person whom none of us ever met, trying to get a handle on how he came to grief, trying to understand why some people seem to despise him so intensely for having died here.

By design McCandless came into the country with insufficient provisions, and he lacked certain pieces of equipment deemed essential by many Alaskans: a large-caliber rifle, map and compass, an ax. This has been regarded as evidence not just of stupidity but of the even greater sin of arrogance. Some critics have even drawn parallels between McCandless and the Arctic's most infamous tragic figure, Sir John Franklin, a nineteenth-century British naval officer whose smugness and hauteur contributed to some 140 deaths, including his own.

In 1819, the Admiralty assigned Franklin to lead an expedition into the wilderness of northwestern Canada. Two years out of England, winter overtook his small party as they plodded across an expanse of tundra so vast and empty that they christened it the Barrens, the name by which it is still known. Their food ran out. Game was scarce, forcing Franklin and his men to subsist on lichens scraped from boulders, singed deer hide, scavenged animal bones, their own boot leather, and finally one another's flesh. Before the ordeal was over, at least two men had been murdered and eaten, the suspected murderer had been summarily executed, and eight others were dead from sickness and starvation. Franklin was himself within a day or two of expiring when he and the other survivors were rescued by a band of métis.

An affable Victorian gentleman, Franklin was said to be a good-natured bumbler, dogged and clueless, with the naïve ideals of a child and a disdain for acquiring backcountry skills. He had been woefully unprepared to lead an Arctic expedition, and upon returning to England, he was known as the Man Who Ate His Shoes—yet the sobriquet was uttered more often with awe than with ridicule. He was hailed as a national hero, promoted to the rank of captain by the Admiralty, paid handsomely to write an account of his ordeal, and, in 1825, given command of a second Arctic expedition.

That trip was relatively uneventful, but in 1845, hoping finally to discover the fabled Northwest Passage, Franklin made the mistake of returning to the Arctic for a third time. He and the 128 men under his command were never heard from again. Evidence unearthed by the forty-odd expeditions sent to search for them eventually established that all had perished, the victims of scurvy, starvation, and unspeakable suffering.

When McCandless turned up dead, he was likened to Franklin not simply because both men starved but also because both were perceived to have lacked a requisite humility; both were thought to have possessed insufficient respect for the land. A century after Franklin's death, the eminent explorer Vilhjalmur Stefansson pointed out that the English explorer had never taken the trouble to learn the survival skills practiced by the Indians and the Eskimos—peoples who had managed to flourish "for generations, bringing up their children and taking care of their aged" in the same harsh country that killed Franklin. (Stefansson conveniently neglected to mention that many, many Indians and Eskimos have starved in the northern latitudes, as well.)

McCandless's arrogance was not of the same strain as Franklin's, however. Franklin regarded nature as an antagonist that would inevitably submit to force, good breeding, and Victorian discipline. Instead of living in concert with the land, instead of relying on the country for sustenance as the natives did, he attempted to insulate himself from the northern environment with ill-suited military tools and traditions. McCandless, on the other hand, went too far in the opposite direction. He tried to live entirely off the country—and he tried to do it without bothering to master beforehand the full repertoire of crucial skills.

It probably misses the point, though, to castigate McCandless for being ill prepared. He was green, and he overestimated his resilience, but he was sufficiently skilled to last for sixteen weeks on little more than his wits and ten pounds of rice. And he was fully aware when he entered the bush that he had given himself a perilously slim margin for error. He knew precisely what was at stake.

It is hardly unusual for a young man to be drawn to a pursuit considered reckless by his elders; engaging in risky behavior is a rite of passage in our culture no less than in most others. Danger has always held a certain allure. That, in large part, is why so many teenagers drive too fast and drink too much and take too many drugs, why it has always been so easy for nations to recruit young men to go to war. It can be argued that youthful derring-do is in fact evolutionarily adaptive, a behavior encoded in our genes. McCandless, in his fashion, merely took risk-taking to its logical extreme.

He had a need to test himself in ways, as he was fond of saying, "that mattered." He possessed grand—some would say grandiose—spiritual ambitions. According to the moral absolutism that characterizes McCandless's beliefs, a challenge in which a successful outcome is assured isn't a challenge at all.

It is not merely the young, of course, who are drawn to hazardous undertakings. John Muir is remembered primarily as a no-nonsense conservationist and the founding president of the Sierra Club, but he was also a bold adventurer, a fearless scrambler of peaks, glaciers, and waterfalls whose best-known essay includes a riveting account of nearly falling to his death, in 1872, while ascending California's Mt. Ritter. In another essay Muir rapturously describes riding out a ferocious Sierra gale, by choice, in the uppermost branches of a one-hundred-foot Douglas fir:

> [N]*ever before did I enjoy so noble an exhilaration of motion. The slender tops fairly flapped and swished in the passionate torrent, bending and swirling backward and forward, round and round, tracing indescribable combinations of vertical and horizontal curves, while I clung with muscles firm braced, like a bobolink on a reed.*

He was thirty-six years old at the time. One suspects that Muir wouldn't have thought McCandless terribly odd or incomprehensible.

Even staid, prissy Thoreau, who famously declared that it was enough to have "traveled a good deal in Concord," felt compelled to visit the more fearsome wilds of nineteenth-century Maine and climb Mt. Katahdin. His ascent of the peak's "savage and awful, though beautiful" ramparts shocked and frightened him, but it also induced a giddy sort of awe. The disquietude he felt on Katahdin's granite heights inspired some of his most powerful writing and profoundly colored the way he thought thereafter about the earth in its coarse, undomesticated state.

Unlike Muir and Thoreau, McCandless went into the wilderness not primarily to ponder nature or the world at large but, rather, to explore the inner country of his own soul. He soon discovered, however, what Muir and Thoreau already knew: An extended stay in the wilderness inevitably directs one's attention outward as much as inward, and it is impossible to live off the land without developing both a subtle understanding of, and a strong emotional bond with, that land and all it holds.

The entries in McCandless's journal contain few abstractions about wilderness or, for that matter, few ruminations of any kind. There is scant mention of the surrounding scenery. Indeed, as Roman's friend Andrew Liske points out upon reading a photocopy of the journal, "These entries are almost entirely about what he ate. He wrote about hardly anything except food."

Andrew is not exaggerating: The journal is little more than a tally of plants foraged and game killed. It would probably be a mistake, however, to conclude thereby that McCandless failed to appreciate the beauty of the country around him, that he was unmoved by the power of the landscape. As cultural ecologist Paul Shepard has observed,

> *The nomadic Bedouin does not dote on scenery, paint landscapes, or compile a nonutilitarian natural history. . . . [H]is life is so profoundly in transaction with*

nature that there is no place for abstraction or esthetics or a "nature philosophy" which can be separated from the rest of his life. . . . Nature and his relationship to it are a deadly-serious matter, prescribed by convention, mystery, and danger. His personal leisure is aimed away from idle amusement or detached tampering with nature's processes. But built into his life is awareness of that presence, of the terrain, of the unpredictable weather, of the narrow margin by which he is sustained.

Much the same could be said of McCandless during the months he spent beside the Sushana River.

It would be easy to stereotype Christopher McCandless as another boy who felt too much, a loopy young man who read too many books and lacked even a modicum of common sense. But the stereotype isn't a good fit. McCandless wasn't some feckless slacker, adrift and confused, racked by existential despair. To the contrary: His life hummed with meaning and purpose. But the meaning he wrested from existence lay beyond the comfortable path: McCandless distrusted the value of things that came easily. He demanded much of himself—more, in the end, than he could deliver.

Trying to explain McCandless's unorthodox behavior, some people have made much of the fact that like John Waterman, he was small in stature and may have suffered from a "short man's complex," a fundamental insecurity that drove him to prove his manhood by means of extreme physical challenges. Others have posited that an unresolved Oedipal conflict was at the root of his fatal odyssey. Although there may be some truth in both hypotheses, this sort of posthumous off-the-rack psychoanalysis is a dubious, highly speculative enterprise that inevitably demeans and trivializes the absent analysand. It's not clear that much of value is learned by reducing Chris McCandless's strange spiritual quest to a list of pat psychological disorders.

Roman and Andrew and I stare into the embers and talk about McCandless late into the night. Roman, thirty-two, inquisitive and outspoken, has a doctorate in biology from Stanford and an abiding distrust of conventional wisdom. He spent his adolescence in the same Washington, D.C., suburbs as McCandless and found them every bit as stifling. He first came to Alaska as a nine-year-old, to visit a trio of uncles who mined coal at Usibelli, a big strip-mine operation a few miles east of Healy, and immediately fell in love with everything about the North. Over the years that followed, he returned repeatedly to the forty-ninth state. In 1977, after graduating from high school as a sixteen-year-old at the top of his class, he moved to Fairbanks and made Alaska his permanent home.

These days Roman teaches at Alaska Pacific University, in Anchorage, and enjoys statewide renown for a long, brash string of backcountry escapades: He has—among other feats—traveled the entire 1,000-mile length of the Brooks Range by foot and paddle, skied 250 miles across the Arctic National Wildlife Refuge in subzero winter cold, traversed the 700-mile crest of the Alaska Range, and pioneered more than thirty first ascents of northern peaks and crags. And Roman doesn't see a great deal of difference between his own widely respected deeds and McCandless's adventure, except that McCandless had the misfortune to perish.

I bring up McCandless's hubris and the dumb mistakes he made—the two or three readily avoidable blunders that ended up costing him his life. "Sure, he screwed up," Roman answers, "but I admire what he was trying to do. Living completely off the land like that, month after month, is incredibly difficult. I've never done it. And I'd bet you that very few, if any, of the people who call McCandless incompetent have ever done it either, not for more than a week or two. Living in the interior bush for an extended period, subsisting on nothing except what you hunt and gather—most people have no idea how hard that actually is. And McCandless almost pulled it off.

"I guess I just can't help identifying with the guy," Roman allows as he pokes the coals with a stick. "I hate to admit it, but not so many years ago it could easily have been me in the same kind of predicament. When I first started coming to Alaska, I think I was probably a lot like McCandless: just as green, just as eager. And I'm sure there are plenty of other Alaskans who had a lot in common with McCandless when they first got here, too, including many of his critics. Which is maybe why they're so hard on him. Maybe McCandless reminds them a little too much of their former selves."

Roman's observation underscores how difficult it is for those of us preoccupied with the humdrum concerns of adulthood to recall how forcefully we were once buffeted by the passions and longings of youth. As Everett Ruess's father mused years after his twenty-year-old son vanished in the desert, "The older person does not realize the soul-flights of the adolescent. I think we all poorly understood Everett."

Roman, Andrew, and I stay up well past midnight, trying to make sense of McCandless's life and death, yet his essence remains slippery, vague, elusive. Gradually, the conversation lags and falters. When I drift away from the fire to find a place to throw down my sleeping bag, the first faint smear of dawn is already bleaching the rim of the northeastern sky. Although the mosquitoes are thick tonight and the bus would no doubt offer some refuge, I decide not to bed down inside Fairbanks 142. Nor, I note before sinking into a dreamless sleep, do the others. ∎

▪ QUESTIONS FOR MAKING CONNECTIONS WITHIN THE READING ▪

1. Jon Krakauer is telling the story of Chris McCandless, who was interested in, among other things, recording the adventures of "Alexander Supertramp." What is the relationship between McCandless and Supertramp? What does writing under a different name allow McCandless to do that he wouldn't otherwise be able to do?

2. Most everyone at one time or another has dreamed of getting away from it all. Chris McCandless actually did so. Would he have been able to have the adventure he was looking for if he'd done more research? Would his story be more or less compelling if he had brought along a map? If he had survived?

3. One of Krakauer's central concerns in *Into the Wild* is to determine what drove McCandless to embark on such a dangerous journey and to speculate on what McCandless's motives were when he sought to make his way back out of the wild. How does Krakauer go about trying to uncover the answers to these questions? What is his method? What counts as evidence for him? When does Krakauer know—or feel—that he has found what he was looking for?

■ *QUESTIONS FOR WRITING* ■

1. At the end of this reading, Krakauer asserts that one reason adults have so much difficulty understanding McCandless's actions is that they struggle "to recall how forcefully [they] were once buffeted by the passions and longings of youth." To understand this observation, one must be able to define what "the passions and longings of youth" are. What do these passions and longings have to do with escape? With the natural world? And if one can recall such passions and longings, how might this change one's understanding of the import of McCandless's death?

2. In providing a narrative of McCandless's journey, Krakauer draws on the writings Chris left behind in the blank pages and margins of his books and on the walls of the bus where he spent his final months. What does all this writing tell Krakauer about McCandless's motives for heading off into the wild? Is it possible to escape from civilization in the twenty-first century? Does it make sense to try?

■ *QUESTIONS FOR MAKING CONNECTIONS BETWEEN READINGS* ■

1. In "The Naked Citadel," Susan Faludi sets out to study how young men are turned into soldiers at a military academy and to record how this training process was upended when the academy was required to admit young women into its ranks. In detailing McCandless's journey into the wild, Krakauer provides a glimpse into another ritualized way of "becoming a man." Would you argue that McCandless's journey is consistent with The Citadel's efforts to create a certain kind of man? Or was McCandless's journey an attempt to escape from the masculine ideals embodied by the Citadel's students? What, if anything, do these two stories suggest

about how masculinity will be defined and experienced in the twenty-first century?

2. Toward the end of this reading, Krakauer cites the cultural ecologist Paul Shepard's observations about how the nomadic Bedouin relates to the natural world. According to Shepard: "The nomadic Bedouin does not dote on scenery, paint landscapes, or compile a nonutilitarian natural history . . . [H]is life is so profoundly in transaction with nature that there is no place for abstraction or esthetics or a 'nature philosophy' which can be separated from the rest of his life." This, Krakauer argues, is the kind of relationship with nature that McCandless achieved at the end of his travels. And yet, with Lila Abu-Lughod's depiction of Bedouin culture in mind, what are we to make of the fact that Chris fled the world that Kamla rushes to embrace? Is McCandless's view of the natural world a form of nostalgia only available to the privileged? Is Kamla's view of city life a fantasy only available to those on the margins?

For additional suggestions about making connections between readings, visit the Link-O-Mat and More Sample Assignments at <www.newhum.com>.

BETH LOFFREDA

HOW DOES THE MEDIA decide which stories to cover on any given day? And what gets left out when the stories that are chosen get transformed into a three-minute segment on the nightly news or into a column of print in the daily paper? These are some of the issues that Beth Loffreda takes up in *Losing Matt Shepard: Life and Politics in the Aftermath of Anti-Gay Murder,* her book-length study of how the residents of Wyoming responded when Shepard, a young gay student at the university in Laramie, was brutally beaten and left to die by the side of the road in fall 1998. Both an ethnographic study and a cultural critique, *Losing Matt Shepard* explores and carefully details the limits of the media's representation of the complexities of life in Wyoming after Shepard's highly publicized murder. In his review of *Losing Matt Shepard* for the *Lambda Book Report,* Malcolm Farley recommended that, "[a]nyone who cares about the gay experience in America—or about America in general—should read Loffreda's fiercely intelligent account of the causes and consequences of Matt Shepard's murder."

Beth Loffreda is an assistant professor of English and adjunct professor of women's studies at the University of Wyoming, where she also serves as an adviser to the university's gay, lesbian, bisexual, and transgendered student group. Since the publication of *Losing Matt Shepard,* which was selected as a finalist for the American Library Association's Gay, Lesbian, Bisexual, and Transgendered Round Table Award in 2000, Loffreda has become a national spokesperson in discussions about hate-crime legislation and gay rights. She was also recognized as one of the University of Wyoming's top teachers in 1999. In the selection from *Losing Matt Shepard* included here, Loffreda shows just how varied the response to Shepard's murder was at the University of Wyoming, in the surrounding communities of Laramie, and across the nation. As she does so, Loffreda asks her readers to consider the following question: Why it is that, when there are so many murders every year, this one in particular captured the nation's attention?

To learn more about Beth Loffreda and hate-crime legislation, visit the Link-O-Mat at <www.newhum.com>.

Loffreda, Beth. Selections from *Losing Matt Shepard: Life and Politics in the Aftermath of Anti-Gay Murder.* New York: Columbia University Press, 1–13.

Biographical information from Beth Loffreda, *Losing Matt Shepard.* New York: Columbia University Press, 2000.

Selections from
Losing Matt Shepard
Life and Politics in the Aftermath of Anti-Gay Murder

Perhaps the first thing to know about Laramie, Wyoming, is that it is beautiful. On most days the high-altitude light is so precise and clear that Laramie appears some rarefied place without need of an atmosphere. We were having a stretch of days like that in early October 1998, as the news began to trickle in that a man had been found beaten somewhere on the edge of town. We'd later sort out the key facts: that Matt Shepard had encountered Russell Henderson and Aaron McKinney late Tuesday night in the Fireside Bar; that he'd left with them; that they had driven him in a pickup truck to the edge of town; that Henderson had tied him to a fence there and McKinney had beaten him viciously and repeatedly with a .357 Magnum; that they had taken his shoes and wallet and intended to rob his apartment but instead returned to town and got into a fight with two other young men, Jeremy Herrera and Emiliano Morales (McKinney clubbed Morales on the head with the same gun, still covered in Matt's blood; Herrera retaliated by striking McKinney's head with a heavy stick); that the police, responding to the altercation, picked up Henderson—McKinney had fled—and saw the gun, Matt's credit card, and his shoes in the truck but didn't yet know the fatal meaning of those objects; that after being released later that night, Henderson and his girlfriend, Chasity Pasley, and McKinney and his girlfriend, Kristen Price, began to hatch their false alibis; and that through all this Matt remained tied to the fence and wouldn't be found until Wednesday evening, after an entire night and most of a day had passed. We'd learn all that, and learn that Matt's sexuality was woven through all of it. Those facts reached us swiftly, but making sense of them took much longer.

Jim Osborn, a recent graduate of the university's education program, was the chair of the Lesbian Gay Bisexual Transgender Association that October, a group that Matt, a freshman, had just recently joined. The LGBTA is the sole gay organization on campus and in Laramie itself. While students make up most of its membership, it welcomes university staff and townspeople as well, although only a few have joined. The group has been active since 1990; before that, another gay campus organization, Gays and Lesbians of Wyoming—GLOW—had an intermittent but vivid life in the 1970s and early 1980s. Women typically outnumber men at LGBTA meetings, although not by a significant margin; altogether, attendance on any given night usually hovers between ten and twenty members. The group's email list, however, reaches far more. There's no single reason for that discrepancy; it most likely arises from a combination of factors, including the familiar reluctance of many college students to join groups and, more specifically in this case, the anxiety some gay or questioning students might feel attending a public meeting.

The LGBTA gathers weekly in a nondescript, carpeted seminar room on the second floor of the university union. It has no office space of its own. (When hundreds of letters arrived after Matt's murder, the group stored them in the corner of the Multicultural Resource Center downstairs.) Meetings are usually hourlong sessions, punctuated by bursts of laughter, during which the group plans upcoming events—speakers, dances, potlucks. The LGBTA juggles numerous, sometimes contradictory roles as it tries to be a public face for gay and lesbian issues on campus (organizing events, running panels about sexuality for many courses) and at the same time create a comfortable, safe space for socializing in a town without a gay bar or bookstore. It also serves as something of a gay news exchange, sharing information about what teachers might be supportive or not, what places in town and elsewhere might be safe or not, what's happening that might not show up in the campus paper, *The Branding Iron*.

That last role mattered on Tuesday, October 6th. As the members handled the last-minute details of Gay Awareness Week, scheduled to begin the following Monday, Jim Osborn warned the group to be careful. The week before, he had been harassed while walking across campus. A young man—Jim thinks he was probably a university student—had come up behind him, said, "You're one of those faggots, aren't you?" and thrown a punch. Jim is a big, strapping white man from northern Wyoming; he blocked the punch and hit his attacker. They then took off in opposite directions. Jim didn't report the attack to the police but did want to alert members of the LGBTA that it had happened. Matt was among those there to hear Jim's story. After the meeting, members of the group, including Matt and Jim, went out for coffee at the College Inn, something of a Tuesday-night LGBTA tradition. Jim remembers that Matt sat at the other end of a crowded table. It was the last Jim would see of him.

Jim can talk an eloquent blue streak and is something of an organizational genius—at LGBTA meetings I've listened to him recall the minutiae of university regulations and budget protocols as if they were fond personal memories. He also has a staggeringly large network of friends and acquaintances. On Thursday morning, he got an email from Tina Labrie, a friend of his and Matt's; she had introduced them in August, when Matt, new to Laramie, wanted to learn about the LGBTA. The message said that Matt had been found near death the evening before and was hospitalized in Fort Collins, Colorado. (Matt had initially been taken to Ivinson Memorial Hospital in Laramie and was then transferred to Poudre Valley Hospital's more sophisticated trauma unit. While Matt was being treated in the Ivinson Memorial ER, McKinney was a few curtains down, admitted earlier for the head wound he had received from Herrera; like Matt, McKinney would also be transferred to Poudre Valley.) Horrified, Jim phoned Tina and learned that the police were trying to reconstruct Matt's whereabouts on Tuesday evening. When he called the Laramie Police to tell them what he knew, an officer informed him that Matt wasn't going to make it. Matt was suffering from hypothermia, and there was severe trauma to the brain stem. The officer told Jim that one side of Matt's head had been beaten in several inches and that the neurosurgeon was quite frankly surprised that he was still alive.

Bob Beck, news director for Wyoming Public Radio, also got word of the attack on Thursday. Beck has lived in Laramie since 1984; he's a tall, lanky midwesterner with a serious jones for Chicago Bulls basketball. On the radio he speaks in the sedated tones cultivated by NPR reporters everywhere, but in person he displays a vinegary wit and a likably aggravated demeanor. "It was a strange thing," he told me. "I teach a class, and one of my students called up and told me he needed to miss class that day because one of his friends had got beaten up very badly and was taken to the hospital in Fort Collins." That student was Phil Labrie, Tina's husband. Worried when they couldn't reach Matt, they had called the police on Wednesday, shortly after Matt was found, and learned what had happened. "[Phil] didn't tell me a lot of details because he said the cops had told him not to really tell anyone. But then he said I will know about it later and it will be a big story. . . . So I right away thought I better follow up on this immediately." He contacted the Albany County Sheriff's Office and learned that a press conference would be held later that day.

Beck attended the press conference that day—typically a routine exercise, but one that in this case would unexpectedly and profoundly shape public reaction to the attack. According to Beck, the sheriff

> indicated that there was a young man who had been very badly beaten, was on life support, had been taken to Poudre Valley Hospital. During the questioning, the sheriff at the time, Gary Puls, indicated that they thought he may have been beaten because he was gay. And when he described this situation to us he told us that [Shepard] was found by a mountain bike rider, tied to a fence like a scarecrow. My recollection is there was discussion of exactly what do you mean, "tied like a scarecrow," and I think every single one of us who were in the room got the impression certainly of being tied up spread-eagled, splayed out.

Matt hadn't actually been tied like a scarecrow; when he was approached first by the mountain biker, Aaron Kreifels, and then by Reggie Fluty, the sheriff's deputy who answered Kreifels's emergency call, Matt lay on his back, head propped against the fence, legs outstretched. His hands were lashed behind him and tied barely four inches off the ground to a fencepost.

In dramatic and widely reported testimony, Fluty would later state that at first she thought Matt could have been no older than thirteen, he was so small (Matt was only five feet two inches, barely over one hundred pounds). And when she described Matt's brutally disfigured face, she said that the only spots not covered in blood were the tracks cleansed by his tears—an enduring image that continues to appear in essays, poetry, and songs dedicated to Shepard. It is most likely that Kreifels was the source of Puls's press-conference description. Kreifels told police and reporters that he at first thought Matt was a scarecrow flopped on the ground, maybe some kind of Halloween joke staged a few weeks early. No matter its provenance, the notion that Matt had been strung up in something akin to a crucifixion became the starting point for the reporting and reaction to come.

Beck says, "I know that's how we all reported it, and that was never corrected."[1] The vicious symbolism of that image, combined with Puls's early acknowledgment that the beating might have been an anti-gay hate crime, drew instant attention. Attending the press conference were the Associated Press, members of the Wyoming and Colorado media, Beck, and two friends of Matt, Walt Boulden and Alex Trout. According to press reports, Boulden and Trout, afraid that the attack might go unnoticed, had already begun to alert the media earlier that day. Boulden had had plans with Matt for Tuesday night; Matt had canceled and later, apparently, had decided to head off to the Fireside alone. Boulden was not shy about seizing the attack as a political opportunity, linking the assault to the Wyoming legislature's failure to pass a hate crimes bill: he told reporters that "they said nothing like that happens in Wyoming because someone is gay, but we've always known someone would have to get killed or beaten before they finally listened. I just can't believe it happened to someone I cared so much about." By Friday morning, when the police already had McKinney, Henderson, Price, and Pasley in custody (Beck says "the investigation was one of the better I've seen"), the media interest, spurred by Thursday's press conference, had increased exponentially.

At the same time, Laramie's gay residents were learning what had happened. Stephanie and Lisa, a lesbian couple active in the LGBTA, heard the news from Jim on Thursday evening. Lisa, a striking redhead and a good friend of Jim's, talked to him first: "He told me Matt had been beaten. And I said, well, shit, how badly? Is he okay? And Jim said no—he's in critical condition, had to be airlifted to Poudre Valley." Both Stephanie and Lisa knew Matt only slightly, although Stephanie had expected to have the chance to grow closer. She had just agreed to be Matt's mentor in a program the LGBTA was considering as a way to welcome new students to the gay community. Like Lisa, Steph has an edgy, witty charisma, but it deserted her that night, as she, Lisa, and Jim watched the first TV news reports. "There was this horrifying feeling that we were standing on the brink of learning something really, really awful," she says of that Thursday. "Like the part in the horror movie just before she opens the closet and finds the dead cat. It was that moment. For a day. And then we got the facts . . . and everything started happening at this tremendous speed. The next day was the day the story broke. And there were newspaper reporters and cameras all over the place." Steph had called me early that Friday morning, spreading word of the attack and warning people associated with the LGBTA to watch their backs: "I can remember wanting to tell everybody, absolutely everybody, wanting to physically grab people by their lapels and make them listen."

An atmosphere of genuine shock permeated the university; most students and faculty I encountered that day wore stunned and distraught expressions that I imagine mirrored my own; they seemed absorbed simply in trying to understand how something so brutal could have happened within a short walk of their daily lives. Gay and lesbian members of the university that I spoke to felt a wrenching mix of fear and sadness; many, including Stephanie and Lisa, were also immediately and intensely angry. A number of students in my morning American Literature course, after a long discussion in which they sought answers for how to publicly express their repugnance for the crime, decided that the university's homecoming parade, coincidentally scheduled for the following morning, would be an ideal site for that response. Finding like-minded students in the United Multicultural Council, the LGBTA, and the student government, they began printing flyers, making hundreds of armbands, and arranging permits to join the parade.[2] Their unjaded eagerness to publicly involve themselves in the case contrasted sharply with the university administration's first official response, much of which had concerned itself with pointing out that the attack happened off campus and was committed by nonstudents.

On Friday afternoon—as Jim Osborn began to field what would eventually become an overwhelming flood of media requests for interviews—the four accused appeared in court for the first time. Bob Beck attended the initial appearance: "That's where you bring in the people, read them formal charges, and we then get their names, backgrounds—which is important for us." Beck had left for the courthouse a half hour early; initial appearances are typically held in a small room in the courthouse basement, and Beck thought it might be more full than usual. He was right. "It was sold out. It was wall-to-wall cameras." Residents of Laramie—professors and LGBTA members in particular—had also come to witness the proceedings. So many attended that the reading of the charges had to be delayed while everyone moved upstairs to the much larger district court. Beck remembers, "I went in—in fact it was so crowded I got shoved by where the jury box is located—and I stood behind the defendants when they came in. I got a really good look at everybody, and I was actually surprised at how young they looked, how scared they looked, and how little they were." Only Henderson, McKinney, and Chasity Pasley were charged that day; separate proceedings had been arranged for Kristen Price. Pasley wept throughout. She was

someone Jim Osborn knew well and liked. She worked in the campus activities center and had helped Jim countless times when the LGBTA needed
photocopying or assistance setting up for an event. "She was very supportive of the group," Jim says. Often when he saw her on a Wednesday, she'd
ask, "Hey, how'd it go last night?" In the past, he had seen her wearing one
of the group's "Straight But Not Narrow" buttons.

I was in the courtroom that afternoon and can remember the professional flatness with which the county judge, Robert Castor, read the charges
aloud. Castor had arrived in the courtroom to find a cameraman sitting at
the prosecution's table, an early symbol of the persistent media invasion,
Bob Beck believes, that frustrated the court and the prosecutor, Cal Rerucha,
and led them to sharply limit information about the case thereafter. Castor
charged McKinney and Henderson with three identical counts of kidnap-
ping, aggravated robbery, and attempted first-degree murder; Pasley he
charged with a count of accessory after the fact to attempted first-degree
murder (in addition to providing false alibis for their boyfriends, she and
Price had also helped dispose of evidence, including Henderson's bloody
clothing). After each count, Castor recited "the essential facts" supporting
the charge, in what became a truly grim ritual of repetition. In language I've
condensed from the court documents, the essential facts were these: "On or
between October 6, 1998, and the early morning hours of October 7, 1998,
Aaron McKinney and Russell Henderson met Matthew Shepard at the Fireside Bar, and after Mr. Shepard confided he was gay, the subjects deceived
Mr. Shepard into leaving with them in their vehicle to a remote area near
Sherman Hills subdivision in Albany County. En route to said location, Mr.
Shepard was struck in the head with a pistol." (McKinney, we'd later learn,
had apparently told Matt, "We're not gay, and you just got jacked," before
striking him.) "Upon arrival at said location, both subjects tied their victim
to a buck fence, robbed him, and tortured him, while beating him with the
butt of a pistol. During the incident, the victim was begging for his life. The
subjects then left the area, leaving the victim for dead." By the third time
Castor read that Matt had begged for his life, the courtroom had become
choked with sickness and grief. The true darkness of the crime had become
impossible to flee.

The next morning—Saturday—began with the university's homecoming parade. As the parade kicked off, one hundred students, university employees,
and townspeople lined up at the end of the long string of floats and marching bands. They had quietly gathered in the morning chill to protest the attack on Matt. The leaders of the march carried a yellow banner painted with
green circles, symbols of peace chosen by the UMC. They were followed by
a silent crowd wearing matching armbands and holding signs that read "No
Hate Crimes in Wyoming," "Is This What Equality Feels Like?" and
"Straight But Not Stupid." I walked a few yards from the front, watching

Carly Laucomer, a university student holding the middle of the banner, field questions from reporters walking backward a single pace in front of her. Beside me, Cat, another university student, muttered that she wished the marchers weren't so sparse. Cat, like Carly, was then a student in my American Literature course, a smart young woman usually prepared to be disappointed by the world around her. Laramie surprised her. As the march moved west down Ivinson Avenue, spectators began to join, walking off sidewalks into the street. By the time the march reached downtown (where a giant second-story banner proclaimed, "Hate Is Not a Wyoming Value") and circled back toward campus, it had swelled beyond even Cat's demanding expectations; final estimates ranged from five to eight hundred participants. It didn't seem like much—just a bunch of people quietly walking—but it was a genuinely spontaneous, grassroots effort to protest the attack and express the community's profound dismay, and in that sense it was unforgettable.

A very different sort of tribute to Matt appeared in the Colorado State University homecoming parade the same day in the city of Fort Collins. As Matt lay in the hospital just a few miles away, a float in the parade carried a scarecrow draped in anti-gay epithets. While the papers were reluctant to report the full range of insults, I heard that the signs read "I'm Gay" and "Up My Ass." Colorado State University acted quickly to punish the sorority and fraternity responsible for the float (the censured students blamed vandalism committed by an unknown third party), but still it is worth pausing for a moment to consider the degree of dehumanization such an act required, how much those responsible must have felt, however fleetingly or unconsciously, that Matt was not a fellow human being, their age, with his future torn away from him. Fort Collins is home to a visible and energetic community of gay activists, and the float was widely denounced. Still, a week later Fort Collins would vote down, by nearly a two-to-one margin, City Ordinance 22, a proposal to expand the city's antidiscrimination statute to include protections for gays and lesbians.

Later that Saturday, a moment of silence for Matt was held before the University of Wyoming's football game; players wore the UMC's symbols on their helmets. And, impossibly, the media presence continued to grow. Bob Beck, juggling requests for interviews with his own reporting, was in the thick of it and felt a growing frustration at the sloppiness of what he saw around him. "Right away it was horrible. Part of that, in fairness, was that we didn't have all the information we needed. While the sheriff was very up front at first, next thing you know, nobody's talking." City officials, naturally unprepared (in a town with barely a murder a year) for the onslaught, focused their resources on the investigation and, angry that Laramie was being depicted as a hate crimes capital, began to restrict press access. But the media, especially the TV tabloids, Beck says, needed to turn things around quickly, and since they were getting stonewalled by the city and by many

Laramie residents, "it seemed like the place they went to interview everybody was in bars. As we all know who are in the media, if you want to get
somebody to be very glib, give you a few quick takes, you want to go to a
bar. And you certainly are going to meet a segment of our population that
will have more interesting things to say." I remember watching for footage
of the Saturday morning march later that evening and seeing instead precisely the sort of bar interview Beck describes, a quick and dirty media tactic
I heard many residents mock in the coming months.

Beck also remembers one of the first television news reports he saw: "It
was this woman reporter outside the Fireside doing what we call a bridge, a
stand-up: 'Hate: it's a common word in Wyoming.'" Beck couldn't believe
it, but that mirrored precisely the assumptions of most of the media representatives he encountered that week. Journalists who interviewed him
began with comments like, "Well, this kind of thing probably happens a lot
up there," or, "You have that cowboy mentality in Wyoming, so this was
bound to happen." Reporters criticized Laramie, he says, for not having a
head trauma unit, not having gay bars, not pushing back homecoming. The
tone of the questioning was hostile; Jim Osborn, speaking to journalists from
locations as far-flung as Australia and the Netherlands, encountered it too.
Jim says the press he spoke to wanted to hear that this was a hateful, red-
neck town, that Wyoming was, in the inane rhyming of some commentators,
"the hate state." But Jim insisted on what he considered accurate: "Nobody
expects murder here—nobody. This is not a place where you kill your neighbor, and we see each other as neighbors. This is a good place."

But the crime, and Laramie, had already begun to take on a second life,
a broadcast existence barely tethered to the truths of that night or this place,
an existence nourished less by facts and far more by the hyperboles of
tabloid emotion. Such a development should be unsurprising to even the
most novice of cultural critics, yet to be in the middle of it, to watch rumor
become myth, to see the story stitched out of repetition rather than investigation, was something else entirely. Beck told me, "Right away I saw pack
journalism like I have not seen pack journalism in a while. It was really
something. I remember going to the courthouse, and somebody would say,
'Hey I understand he got burned'—which wasn't true by the way—'where
did he get burned?' And somebody would say, 'Oh, on his face,' and they're
all taking notes, and they were sources for each other. They would never say
where it came from or who had the information—it was just 'there were
burns on his face.'" As Beck watched, the mistakes multiplied. One journalist would announce, "'I did an interview with one of the deputies, and he
told me this,' and they would all go with it; no one [else] went and interviewed the deputy. Now part of this is that the deputies and other officials
weren't available to us . . . and the same stuff got continually reported." The
lead investigator on the case, Sergeant Rob DeBree of the Sheriff's Office,
held a press conference early on in an attempt to correct the errors, but, he

told me, it didn't seem to make much of a difference—the media had become a closed loop, feeding off their own energies.

As the fall wore on, the distance between Laramie and its broadcast image would become unbridgeable. The court increasingly limited press access to the case and eventually, in the spring, issued a gag order. In response, the Wyoming Press Association wrangled with the court throughout that year over access to hearings and records, suggesting that the court model its treatment of the media on press access guidelines in the Timothy McVeigh trial. Beck assessed Wyoming Public Radio's own performance for me: "I'm not saying we didn't make any mistakes, because we probably did. But I finally got so weary of it I said, 'You know what? If we can't confirm it ourselves, we don't go with it.' It was just too wild."

As the weekend continued, vigils for Matt were held across the nation. By the end of the week, we'd heard word of vigils in Casper, Cheyenne, and Lander (Wyoming towns), Colorado, Idaho, Montana, Iowa, Arizona, Rhode Island, and Pennsylvania. A memorial in Los Angeles attracted an estimated five thousand participants; a "political funeral" in New York City that ended in civil disobedience and hundreds of arrests, about the same. Several hundred mourners lit candles at a vigil outside Poudre Valley Hospital, and a Web site set up by the hospital to give updates about Matt's condition eventually drew over 815,000 hits from around the world.

In Laramie, we held two vigils of our own Sunday night. Jim spoke at the first, held outside the St. Paul's Newman Catholic Center. Father Roger Schmit, the organizer of the event, had contacted him earlier that weekend and asked him to speak. Jim remembers, "I'm sitting here thinking, 'Catholic Church . . . this is not exactly the scene I want to get into.'" But the priest told him, Jim says, "This is such a powerful opportunity—people need to hear from you, and it will help them." Jim thought, "I want to hate him, I want to disagree with him, but I can't." Indeed, such bedfellows would become less strange in the coming months. Matt's death triggered yearlong conversations in several Laramie churches; the Newman Center, the Episcopal church, and the Unitarian-Universalist Fellowship each began discussion groups devoted to questions of sexual orientation and religious doctrine. Father Schmit, the priest Jim regarded with such initial suspicion, would in particular become a vocal advocate for gay tolerance.

I attended that first vigil, which drew nearly one thousand people, a sizable fraction of Laramie's total population. As I crossed Grand Avenue, dodging traffic, the vigil already under way, I was struck by the size and murmurous intensity of the crowd. The speakers included friends of Matt, student leaders, and university officials. Father Schmit had also invited every religious leader in town but found many reluctant to come. The event was genuinely affecting and rightly given over to the desire, as Jim put it, to think of Matt "the person" and not the newly created symbol. While speakers did indeed condemn the homophobia that slid Matt from complicated human being to easy target, others, including Jim, also tried to rehumanize Matt by offering up small details—the nature of his smile, the clothes he liked to wear. The press was there too, of course, and—perhaps inevitably under such circumstances—a faint odor of PR hung in the air. University president Phil Dubois told the assembled, "Nothing could match the sorrow and revulsion we feel for this attack on Matt. It is almost as sad, however, to see individuals and groups around the country react to this event by stereotyping an entire community, if not an entire state."

Stephanie sensed another trouble, a hypocrisy, at work that night:

> There was a tremendous outpouring of support—the vigils, the parade—and a lot of those people—not all of them, not even a substantial portion, but some of those people—if they had known that Matt was gay while he was alive, would have spit on him. But now it was a cause, and that made me upset. Not that I think you can't grieve over this because you're straight or anything like that, but I just questioned the sincerity of some people. And I grew to be very angry at the vigil Sunday night, because it was so like the one I had attended for Steve.

She meant Steve Heyman, a gay man who had been a psychology professor and LGBTA faculty adviser at the university. Heyman was found dead on November 1, 1993, on the edge of Route 70 in Denver. He appeared to have been tossed from a moving car. The case was never solved. To Stephanie, who had known and adored Heyman, the coincidence was unbearable. "It was the same candles, the same fucking hymns. I will never sing 'We are a gentle, angry people' again, because it doesn't change anything. And I'm not going to sing 'We are not afraid today deep in my heart' because I am afraid, and I will always be afraid, and that's what they want, that's why they kill us."

Driven by that anger, Stephanie spoke at the second vigil that night. Much smaller—perhaps one hundred people were in attendance—it was held on the edge of town, at the Unitarian Fellowship. People who went that night tell me it was different from the first. Instead of a lengthy list of official speakers, community members were invited to testify to their mourning, and to their experiences of anti-gay discrimination in Laramie. It was more intense, more ragged, more discomfiting. But both vigils held the same fragile promise of a changed Laramie, a town that—whether it much wanted to or not—would think hard and publicly and not in unison about the gay men and women in its midst, about their safety and comfort and rights.

Later that Sunday night, as the participants in that second vigil left for home, thought about the events of the day, and got ready for bed, Matt Shepard's blood pressure began to drop. He died in the early hours of Monday, October 12th. It was the first day of Gay Awareness Week at the University of Wyoming.

* * *

Monday, flags were flown at half-staff on the university campus. Later that week, in Casper, flags were lowered on the day of Matt's funeral to signal a "day of understanding." (According to local newspapers, Wyoming governor Jim Geringer was criticized by the Veterans of Foreign Wars for not following "proper flag etiquette.") That Monday eight hundred people gathered for a memorial service held on Prexy's Pasture, a patch of green in the middle of campus encircled by parking spaces and university buildings and anchored by a statue of "the university family," a happy heterosexual unit of father, mother, and child that one lesbian student, in a letter to the student newspaper, longingly imagined detonating. The memorial service was another exercise in what was becoming a familiar schizophrenia for Laramie residents. Even the layout of the event expressed it: speakers stood in a small clump ringed by sidewalk; spread beyond them was the far larger, shaggy-edged group of listeners. In between the two was an encampment of reporters, flourishing microphones and tape recorders, pivoting cameras back and forth, capturing clips of the speakers and reaction shots of the crowd. It was hard to see past the reporters to the event that had drawn us in the first place, and it was hard to know to a certainty whether we were all there simply to mourn Matt or to make sure that mourning was represented. Not that the second urge was itself necessarily a hypocrisy or a contradiction of the first. It was instead an early manifestation of Laramie's new double consciousness. We didn't simply live here anymore: we were something transmitted, watched, evaluated for symbolic resonance; something available for summary. I suspect a few people naturally sought that televised attention, felt authenticated and confirmed, even thrilled, by the opportunity to be representative; and others seized it, as Walt Boulden had, as a chance to articulate political goals that might otherwise go unheard. Mostly, though, it just pissed people off. As the memorial drew to a close, I walked past satellite vans and the professional autism of TV reporters practicing their opening lines and switching on their solemn expressions and talking to no one in particular.

I was on my way to the first event of Gay Awareness Week. Shortly after the memorial, Leslea Newman, scheduled long before the murder to give the keynote talk, spoke about her gay-themed children's books, which include the oft-censored *Heather Has Two Mommies*. The week's events would be held despite Matt's death, but attendance that evening hadn't necessarily swelled in response—there were maybe seventy folks scattered around in the darkened auditorium. Newman spoke with a bracing, funny, New York brusqueness that scuffed up the audience as she briskly detailed her skirmishes with religious conservatives, and she spoke as well of her sorrow over Matt and her friends' fearful pleading that she cancel her visit to Laramie. They weren't alone in feeling that anxiety; many of the members of the LGBTA were tensed for a backlash as they passed out pro-gay trinkets and "heterosexual questionnaires" at the "Straight But Not Narrow" table in the student union during Awareness Week. They knew the statistics: that anti-gay violence tends to rise sharply in the aftermath of a publicized bashing. But instead, as consoling letters and emails flooded the offices of *The Branding Iron*, the LGBTA, and Wyoming newspapers, supporters flocking to the union tables quickly ran through the association's supplies of buttons and stickers.

As the week dragged on, Laramie residents hung in their windows and cars flyers decrying hate provided by the Wyoming Grassroots Project (a year and a half later, you can still find a few examples around town, stubbornly hanging on). Yellow sashes fluttered from student backpacks; local businesses announced, on signs usually reserved for information about nightly rates, indoor pools, and bargain lunches, their dismay with the crime. The Comfort Inn: "Hate and Violence Are Not Our Way of Life." The University Inn: "Hate Is Not a Laramie Value." Arby's: "Hate and Violence Are Not Wyoming Values 5 Regulars $5.95." Obviously, those signs suggested a typically American arithmetic, promiscuously mixing moral and economic registers. Underneath the sentiment lingered a question: what will his death cost us? But it would be wrong, I think, to see all those gestures as merely cynical calculation, a self-interested weighing of current events against future tourism. We were trying to shape the media summary of Laramie all right, but we were also talking to each other, pained and wondering, through such signs.

Late Monday, about the same time as the Prexy's Pasture memorial, the charges against McKinney, Henderson, and Pasley were upgraded in a closed hearing to reflect Matt's death. Price's charge, the same as Pasley's—accessory after the fact to first-degree murder—was announced at her individual arraignment on Tuesday. In a *20/20* interview that week, Price offered her defense of McKinney and Henderson. She claimed Shepard approached McKinney and Henderson and "said that he was gay and wanted to get with Aaron and Russ." They intended, she said, "to teach a lesson to him not to come on to straight people"—as if torture and murder were reasonable responses to the supposed humiliation of overtures from a gay man. McKinney's father, speaking to the *Denver Post,* argued that no one would care about the crime if his son had killed a heterosexual, which struck me as not exactly on point, even as a media critique. Wyoming's Libertarian gubernatorial candidate (it was an election year) had his own unique twist: he told reporters, "If two gays beat and killed a cowboy, the story would have never been reported by the national media vultures."

Fred Phelps, a defrocked minister, leader of the tiny Kansas Westboro Baptist Church, and author of the Internet site GodHatesFags.com, announced that Monday that he intended to picket Matthew's funeral, scheduled for the coming Friday at St. Mark's Episcopal Church in Casper. His Web site also promised a visit to Laramie on October 19th, but in the end he didn't show. Phelps had made a name for himself in the 1990s as a virulently anti-gay activist, notorious for protesting at the funerals of AIDS victims. Never one to shy from media attention, Phelps faxed reporters images of the signs he and his followers intended to carry at the funeral: "Fag Matt in Hell," "God Hates Fags," "No Tears for Queers." On his Web site, Phelps wrote that "the parents of Matt Shepard did not bring him up in the nature and admonition of the Lord, or he would not have been trolling for perverted sex partners in a cheap Laramie bar." He also, to the bitter laughter of members of the LGBTA, deemed the University of Wyoming "very militantly pro-gay." "The militant homosexual agenda is vigorously pursued" at the university, he proclaimed. At the time of Phelps's statement, the university's equal employment and civil rights regulations did not include sexual orientation as a protected category, nor did the university offer insurance benefits to same-sex partners. President Dubois and the board of trustees, in response to Matt's death, eventually rectified the former failure in September 1999; the latter still remains true to this day. Apparently none of that mattered much in Phelps's estimation, and he would become a familiar figure in Laramie in the months to come.

The Westboro Church's announcement was only one manifestation of the murder's parallel national life, its transmutation into political and religious currency. Matt himself might have been dead, but his image was resurrected by Phelps as well as by his antagonists, and those resurrections, while not invariably hypocritical or grotesque, nevertheless struck me as always risky. Not because we shouldn't talk about Matt, about the murder, looking hard at the facts of it, as well as at its contexts. The risk, it seemed to me, lay in what his image was so often used for in the coming months—the rallying of quick and photogenic outrage, sundered from the hard, slow work for local justice.

On Wednesday, October 14th, the national gay organization the Human Rights Campaign held a candlelight vigil on the steps of the U.S. Capitol, noteworthy if only for the incongruity of an event that paired the likes of Ted Kennedy and Ellen DeGeneres. Jim Osborn was also there—Cathy Renna, a member of GLAAD (Gay and Lesbian Alliance Against Defamation), who had arrived in Laramie the previous weekend to monitor events for her organization, had asked Jim to participate and taken him to Washington. That night, DeGeneres declared that "this is what she was trying to stop" with her television sitcom *Ellen*. The proportions of that statement—the belief that a sitcom could breathe in the same sentence as the brutal vortex of murder—seemed out of kilter to say the least, but it is the age of celebrity politics, after all: Elton John would send flowers to Matt's funeral, Barbara Streisand would phone the Albany County Sheriffs office to demand quick action on the case, and Madonna would call up an assistant to UW president Dubois to complain about what had happened to Matt. Jim Osborn remembers standing next to Dan Butler, an actor on *Frasier,* during the vigil; later, he spotted Kristen Johnston (of *Third Rock from the Sun*) smoking backstage. Attended by numerous federal legislators, the vigil was skipped by Wyoming's two senators, who had announced their sorrow and condemned intolerance in press releases the previous day. The disconnect worked both ways: the Human Rights Campaign, for all its sustained rallying on the national level, never, according to Jim, sent a representative to Laramie until the following summer.

Back in Laramie, on the same day as the D.C. vigil, the university initiated a three-day series of teach-ins on "prejudice, intolerance, and violence" to begin, according to the announcement, "the healing process." The ideas expressed that day were valuable, the sympathies genuine, but I remember feeling overloaded by premature talk of closure. It may have seemed easy for straight mourners to move so quickly, but as Stephanie told me that week, she'd barely begun to realize the extent of her anger. In the face of that, the swiftness of the official move to "healing" seemed at best a well-intended deafness, and indeed, in their outrage by proxy, denunciations of hatred, and exhortations for tolerance, most of the speakers seemed to be talking implicitly and exclusively to straight members of the audience who already agreed.

Many professors on campus also made time in their classes that week to let their students talk about Matt; the university provided a list of teachers willing to facilitate such discussions if individual faculty were uncomfortable raising such an emotionally fraught issue. It was indeed, as Jim Osborn put it, a "teachable moment," and those conversations undoubtedly did real good. One student, who spoke to me on the condition I didn't use his name, told me that before Matt's death he "straight-up hated fags." It hadn't occurred to him that there actually were any gays or lesbians around (a surprisingly common assumption at the university, not to mention in Wyoming generally)—"fag" was a word handy mainly for demeaning other guys in his dorm for "being pussy" (a typical but still depressing conflation of slurs). After seeing students cry in one of his classes as they discussed Matt's death, he had what he called, with a defensive grin, a real breakthrough: he felt a little sick, he told me, that he had thought things about gays that the two killers had probably been thinking about Shepard.

It's impossible to quantify such changes in attitude, but clearly they were happening in many classrooms around campus. Those developments were heartening, but it would be wrong to imply that the changes were immediate or seismic; several students in the coming weeks would describe to me overhearing others saying Matt "got what he deserved." One woman told me that during a class devoted to discussing the murder, "There was a really ugly incident with a couple of guys in the back who were like 'I hate gays and I'm not changing my opinion.'" "People really think that way here," she finished with a resigned expression. In the coming year students and faculty checking out books on gay topics sometimes found them defaced, and in the spring of 1999 vandals defecated on the university's copies of *The Advocate*, a gay magazine.

It would be wrong too to imply that the faculty were perfectly equipped to handle the events of October. When Matt died, there was only one openly gay faculty member on the university campus—Cathy Connelly, a professor of sociology. Since her arrival in 1991, Professor Connelly had periodically taught graduate courses on gay and lesbian issues, but other than Connelly and the small Safe Zone diversity-training group, the university had few resources in place to respond to what had happened. Troubling as well were the reactions of more than one professor I spoke to that week, whose primary responses were to comment on their own uselessness, their own irrelevance—as scholars of obscure fields of inquiry—to such primal issues of life and death. Academics tend to be fairly skilled at self-lacerating narcissism, but it seemed to me at the time an appalling luxury, an indulgence in a kind of intellectual self-pity at a moment when the basic skills of education—critical thinking, articulation, self-reflection—could be so concretely valuable. I wondered about that, and I wondered too when we'd stop talking about how we felt and begin talking about what to do.

Not that public political gestures are always more meaningful than private, emotional ones. On October 15th, the day before Shepard's funeral, the U.S. House of Representatives approved a resolution condemning the murder. Sponsored by Wyoming's sole representative, Barbara Cubin, it struck me as an essentially empty gesture. The nonbinding resolution stated that the House would "do everything in its power" to fight intolerance, and Cubin herself announced that "our country must come together to condemn these types of brutal, nonsensical acts of violence. We cannot lie down, we cannot bury our heads, and we cannot sit on out hands." Stirring stuff, but she also told reporters that day that she opposes federal hate crimes legislation and suggested such things be left up to individual states. So much for "our country coming together." Cubin was not alone, of course, in her contradictory patriotic embrace of Matt; flags were lowered, resolutions passed, in a nation otherwise happy to express its loathing of gays by closeting them in the military, refusing them antidiscrimination protection in most cities and states, repressing their presence in school curricula, faculty, and clubs, and denouncing them in churches. Meanwhile, back in Wyoming that afternoon, a bewildered and frustrated Casper City Council grappled with more concrete resolutions than those that faced the United States Congress. At an emergency meeting to address Phelps's intended picketing of Matt's funeral, the council decided that protesters must stay at least fifty feet from the church. Casper's SWAT team and the Street Drug Unit would be in attendance outside St. Mark's. Streets would be closed nearby the church, the Casper *Star-Tribune* reported, to allow "media satellite vehicles to position themselves."

The funeral on Friday unfurled as a heavy, wet snow fell on Casper. The storm ripped down power lines, cutting electricity in and around Casper;

hundreds of cottonwoods and elms lost their branches. Phelps and his handful of protesters (along with another anti-gay protester, W. N. Orwell of Enterprise, Texas) were penned inside black plastic barricades, taunting the huge crowd of mourners, which included strangers, gay and straight alike, drawn to the scene from Cheyenne, Denver, Laramie, and elsewhere. As Charles Levendosky put it a few days later in the *Star-Tribune*, "One thousand others from Wyoming and surrounding states flew or drove into Wyoming to mourn for Matt Shepard, the symbol." While a few mourners engaged in heated debate with the picketers—one carrying a sign reading "Get Back in Your Damn Closet"—most turned their backs to them, the umbrellas pulled out for the snow acting as a fortuitous blockade. To protect the Shepard family from hearing Phelps, the assembled crowd sang "Amazing Grace" to drown out his anti-gay preaching. (The family's loss would intensify that day—Shepard's great uncle suffered what would be a fatal heart attack in the church shortly before the service began.) The funeral inside St. Mark's remained restricted to friends and family of Matt, but a live audio feed carried the service to the First Presbyterian Church nearby. Outside St. Mark's, more mourners ("some wearing black leather," the *Star-Tribune* observed) listened to a KTWO radio broadcast of the service. At the funeral, Matt's cousin Ann Kirch, a minister in Poughkeepsie, New York, delivered the sermon. Emphasizing Matt's gentleness and desire "to help, to nurture, to bring joy to others," she echoed a statement made by Matt's father earlier in the day at a press conference outside city hall: "A person as caring and loving as our son Matt would be overwhelmed by what this incident has done to the hearts and souls of people around the world."

Three days later, the university held yet another memorial service. Around one thousand people heard songs by a multicultural chorus, psalms read by Geneva Perry of the university's Office of Minority Affairs, and statements by Tina Labrie, Jim Osborn, and Trudy McCraken, Laramie's mayor. Rounding out the service was university president Dubois, who made a passionate, personal plea for hate crimes legislation—the political issue that had already, only one week after his death, come to dominate discussions of Matt's murder. "No hate crime statute, even had it existed, would have saved Matt," Dubois read. "But Matt Shepard was not merely robbed, and kidnapped, and murdered. This was a crime of humiliation. This crime was all about being gay. . . . We must find a way to commemorate this awful week in a way that will say to the entire state and nation that we will not forget what happened here."

On Tuesday, October 20th, the Wyoming Lodging and Restaurant Association offered one such response to the nation by passing a resolution in favor of hate crimes legislation. The association was up front about its motivations: to curry favor among tourists who might seek recreation elsewhere. The director was quoted in the Casper *Star-Tribune*: "We want them to know this was an isolated case and could happen anywhere."

Could happen anywhere indeed. While that oft-repeated phrase was the quick defense offered by many who felt Laramie was being unfairly vilified, it also bumped up against an undeniable truth: in the late 1990s, homosexuality and vehement opposition to it were everywhere in American public culture and politics. Gays in the military, gays in the schools, gays in church, gays in marriage—the place of gay men and lesbians in American culture seemed to be debated in every way possible. For example, on October 14th, two days before Matt's funeral, the Supreme Court upheld a Cincinnati ordinance that denied gays and lesbians legal protection from discrimination in housing, employment, and other public accommodations. Later that autumn Ohio hosted a conference, organized by Focus on the Family, on how to prevent childhood homosexuality; one speaker there, John Paulk, became notorious during the summer of 1998 when he posed with his wife for national newspaper ads announcing that they were former homosexuals "cured" by their faith in God. About the same time the Supreme Court ruled on the city ordinance, the Roman Catholic Archdiocese of Cincinnati announced a deeply contradictory attempt to "reconcile church teachings that denounce homosexual sex as immoral but encourage the loving acceptance of gays." As long as they're celibate, that is—as long as they "live chaste lives." "Hate the sin, love the sinner"—that idea was invoked again and again in Laramie, in church congregations and letters to the editor. But it seems to me that in such visions sexuality slides so intimately close to identity itself that in the end such exhortations call for moral acrobatics requiring an impossible and fundamentally hypocritical kind of dexterity.

Religious justifications were everywhere, of course, in the attacks on homosexuality. Senate Majority Leader Trent Lott, in June 1998, said he learned from the Bible that "you should try to show them a way to deal with [homosexuality] just like alcohol . . . or sex addiction . . . or kleptomaniacs." Pat Robertson announced that "the acceptance of homosexuality is the last step in the decline of Gentile civilization." Bob Jones University in South Carolina instituted a rule banning gay alumni from returning to campus. The religious right boycotted Disney and American Airlines for having policies that refused to discriminate against gays and lesbians. Salt Lake City banned all student clubs rather than allow a gay-straight alliance to continue at one public high school. The Mormon Church donated roughly half a million dollars to supporters of Alaska's Proposition 2, an initiative banning same-sex marriage that succeeded in the fall of 1998. Bans on gay marriage would also pass in Hawaii, California, and West Virginia in the next year and a half. Vermont, with its legalization of gay "civil unions" early in 2000, would be one of the few bright spots.

That Matt's death occurred in the midst of such pervasive anxiety and upheaval might begin to explain why the nation paid attention, but it doesn't stretch very far—his was only one of thirty-three anti-gay murders that year, followed by, in the first months of 1999, a beheading in Virginia and a vicious beating in Georgia. Here in Laramie, we asked a version of that question too: Why Matt, when no one in the media seemed to take a second glance at the other truly awful recent murders we had the grim distinction of claiming? Why Matt, and not Daphne Sulk, a fifteen-year-old pregnant girl stabbed seventeen times and dumped in the snow far from town? Why Matt, and not Kristin Lamb, an eight-year-old Laramie girl who was kidnapped while visiting family elsewhere in Wyoming and then raped, murdered, and thrown in a landfill? Governor Geringer asked those very questions in an October 9th press release, and we asked them too, in Laramie—in letters to the editor, in private conversation. But we didn't always mean the same thing. To some, the media attention to Matt seemed to imply that his death was somehow worse than the deaths of the two girls, and such an implication was genuinely offensive. To some, like Val Pexton, a graduate student in creative writing, it had something to do with the politics of gender: "What happened to [Lamb] was certainly as violent, as hateful, as horrible; and I guess one of my first thoughts was, if [Henderson and McKinney] had done that to a woman, would this have made it into the news outside of Laramie, outside of Wyoming?" And to some, like Jim Osborn, the comparison of Matt to Kristin and Daphne sometimes masked a hostility to gays: "They became incensed—why didn't Kristin Lamb get this kind of coverage, why didn't Daphne Sulk get this kind of coverage? That was the way people could lash out who very much wanted to say, fuck, it was just a gay guy. But they couldn't say it was just a gay guy, so they said, what about these two girls?"

In some ways, it's easy to understand why the media industry seized upon Matt, and why so many responded to the image it broadcast (Judy Shepard, Matt's mother, told *The Advocate* magazine in March 1999 that the family had received "about 10,000 letters and 70,000 emails," as well as gifts, stuffed animals, blankets, and food). Matt was young (and looked younger), small, attractive; he had been murdered in a particularly brutal fashion. The mistaken belief that he had been strung up on the fence provided a rich, obvious source of symbolism: religious leaders, journalists, and everyday people saw in it a haunting image of the Crucifixion, and at the memorial services and vigils for Matt here and elsewhere, that comparison was often drawn. And while Matt had not in reality been put on display in that fashion, the idea that he had been resonated deeply with America's bitter history of ritual, public violence against minorities—many, including *Time* magazine, compared the attack to a lynching. But Matt seemed to provide a source of intense, almost obsessive interest whose explanation lies well beyond these considerations. Perhaps it was merely the insistent repetition of his image in those early days. In the few snapshots that circulated in the press, Matt appeared boyish, pensive, sweet, charmingly vulnerable in oversized wool sweaters—a boy who still wore braces when he died, a boy who looked innocent of sex, a boy who died because he was gay but whose unthreatening image allowed his sexuality to remain an abstraction for many. In my darker moods, I wonder too if Matt invited such sympathy and political outrage precisely because he was dead—if, for many of the straight people who sincerely mourned his murder, he would nevertheless have been at best invisible while alive. To Jim Osborn, the explanation was less dark and more simple: Matt was "someone we can identify with. Matt was the boy next door. He looked like everybody's brother and everybody's neighbor. He looked like he could have been anyone's son."

"He was the nuclear son of the nuclear family." Jay, a Shoshone-Northern Arapahoe-Navajo American Indian born on the Wind River Reservation in the center of Wyoming, is talking to me about the limits of identification. "If that was me hung on the fence, they'd just say, oh, another drunk Indian. No one would have paid much attention." Jay is gay (he uses the Navajo term *nádleeh*—which he translates as "one who loves his own kind"—to describe himself), and while he feels sympathy for Matt, he doesn't feel much kinship. To Jay, the reason why the nation seized upon Matt is just as simple as Jim Osborn's reason but radically different: to Jay, it was as if white, middle-class America finally had its own tragedy. His argument makes some undeniable sense: in a media culture consecrated to repetition, to the endless recopying of the supposed center of American life—white, moneyed, male—Matt did indeed fit the bill, did suit the recycled homogeneities of a still-myopic national culture. For Jay, the tremendous public outpouring of grief, no matter how sincere, remained essentially alienating. When I ask him how people he knows back on the reservation reacted to the murder, he sums up what he describes as a common response, which he himself shared: "Well, at least now one of them"—whites—"knows what we live through every day." Matt learned it, he says. "And one mother now knows, for a little while anyway, what our lives have always been." As he speaks, defiance, resignation, bitterness, and pride mingle in his voice. "Now people might know what our lives are like," what forms of violence—physical, political, cultural—native people experience in the still-hostile territories of the American West.

Jay's home on the reservation was without running water or electricity, but that never felt like deprivation or unusual circumstance to him—"it's just the way it was." When he was nine, Jay moved to Laramie with his family. They arrived after dark. "Laramie looked so beautiful—all these lights spread out—[it] seemed huge to me." He laughs as he describes how he has learned to love the materialism of life off the reservation—"I really, really like having things now," he admits in simultaneous mockery of himself and Anglo consumerism. When I ask him what white residents here don't know about their town, he replies that "Laramie's a nice town"—he likes life here fine—with a pointed caveat: "White people always say there's no bias in Laramie, no racism, but they just don't want to see." Jay has long black hair pulled back in a braid and a round, lived-in face; he's frequently mistaken for Hispanic. As a child, it didn't take him long to stumble across the racial fault lines he describes. In his first year in Laramie, as he walked home from school near the university campus, a college-aged man spit on him. And on the day we talked, a white woman hissed "spic" at Jay minutes before we met. A student at the university, Jay says there is a reason why the October vigils held for Matt were mostly attended by whites: when Matt died and then later, during the legal proceedings against Henderson and McKinney, Jay observes, "you never saw a minority alone on campus—they either left town, or stayed home, or walked in pairs or groups." They were, he and others say, afraid of a backlash—if "someone got killed for being gay, then someone might get killed for being black or Hispanic or native—that's how we felt." In Jay's opinion, the surprise and horror expressed at the vigils— not to mention simply attending them—was almost something of a white luxury: "They felt shock," Jay says, but "I wasn't shocked—I knew this was coming, since I was in high school, seeing the white and Hispanic kids fight. I knew sooner or later someone was going to die." To Jay, risk, the risk of visible difference, didn't seem all that unfamiliar.

Other minority students on campus confirm Jay's point, however melodramatic it might seem to some. Carina Evans, a young woman of Latino and African-American heritage, told me that when the minority community on campus heard that two Latino teenagers had also been attacked by Henderson and McKinney that night, "the immediate response was, oh my God, what about my safety? How safe am I here? And I think our way of dealing with it was just to not talk about it, because I think we figured the less we drew attention to ourselves, the less the chance that something else was going to happen. Which was a sorry response, but a lot of people left town, just did not feel safe, went away for the week or the weekend."[3] She and others thought, "I'm not going to make myself a target—I'm going to get out of here." No such retaliation was ever reported, but the fact that minority members of the community so feared its possibility that it felt logical to leave town—at the same time that so many white residents could unquestionably consider the attack an isolated incident—reveals something about the complexities of daily life in Laramie.

The divides that run through Jay's and Carina's lives became harder for many in Laramie to ignore in the aftermath of Matt's death. But it was nevertheless a town made defensive by such half-unearthed truths. "Hate is not a Wyoming value," residents kept telling each other, telling visitors, telling the press. "We really take care of each other here," a woman told me one day in a coffee shop, echoing a dearly held ethos I've heard from many in Laramie and that strikes me as generally true. That defensiveness intensified as it encountered the first, clumsy journalistic attempts to offer sociological explanations for the roots of Henderson and McKinney's violence, attempts that implied—to us here, anyway—that Laramie was to blame. Perhaps the most locally reviled version was an article written by Todd Lewan and

Steven K. Paulson for the Associated Press that appeared in October, an occasionally persuasive attempt at class analysis hamstrung by bad facts and a
love affair with the thuddingly clichéd symbolic density of the railroad
tracks that cut through town. Here is their Laramie:

> On the east side is the University of Wyoming's ivy-clad main campus,
> where students drive sports cars or stroll and bike along oak-shaded side-
> walks. On the opposite side of town, a bridge spans railroad tracks to an-
> other reality, of treeless trailer parks baking in the heavy sun, fenced-off
> half-acre lots, stray dogs picking for scraps among broken stoves, refrigera-
> tors, and junked pickups. Unlike the university students, youths on the
> west side have little in the way of entertainment: no malls, no organized
> dance troupes, no theater or playing fields.

Blowing holes in this picture is still a local sport, more than a year after
the murder. Bob Beck, for example, takes fairly comprehensive aim at the
story:

> They decided that the reason a murder like this happened was because
> those of us, including me, who live in west Laramie, the "other side of the
> tracks," are underprivileged, don't have benefits, all this stuff. Because
> we're over there, we're obviously looking to get even with the good side of
> the tracks and are going to commit a crime like this. [They] basically blamed
> the fact that some of us who live in west Laramie don't have a mall (mean-
> while there isn't a mall on the east side either); so we don't have a mall, we
> don't have paved streets, apparently don't have trees. And this is the rea-
> son for all this violence? That was one of the most damaging stories in ret-
> rospect, because it got picked up by just about every major paper. A lot of
> people got their impressions of the case from that.

The list of mistakes could continue: Henderson and McKinney didn't even
live in west Laramie; oaks rarely grow at seven thousand feet; and few university students drive fancy sports cars—more likely, like many of the students I've encountered, they're working fifteen to thirty hours a week to pay
their tuition, maybe at the same Taco Bell where Henderson worked as a
teenager. It's hard to choose, but my personal favorite is the anguished
handwringing over west Laramie's lack of organized dance troupes. Organized dance troupes?
    Plenty of folks I've spoken to volunteer that they live on the west side
and are quick to say they're "not trash," that they like the rustic character of
west Laramie's unpaved streets, that they don't necessarily feel excluded
from "Laramie proper," despite, for example, the west side's usual lack of
representation on the city council. And I've found few residents who
weren't offended by such shallow press characterizations of Laramie, who
didn't argue that status doesn't matter much here, that Laramie is friendly

and easygoing and safe, that most folks don't even bother to lock their doors. All their points of rebuttal are well taken, and indeed they're reasons why many love to live here. But nevertheless I think the eager rapidity with which so many of us rejected such examples of journalistic ineptitude masked at times a certain unease—and sometimes a hardworking amnesia—about the subtle realities of class, sexuality, and race here in Laramie. Those realities may be too complicated to sum up through the convenient shorthand of railroad tracks and trailer parks, but they still flow, hushed yet turbulent, beneath daily life in this town.   ■

NOTES

1. Melanie Thernstrom's essay on the murder in the March 1999 issue of *Vanity Fair* notes that Matt was not strung up, but only in a parenthetical remark near the end of the piece, and the article itself has the title "The Crucifixion of Matthew Shepard." JoAnn Wypijewski's tough-minded essay "A Boy's Life," which appeared in the September 1999 issue of *Harper's Magazine,* was the first thorough demystification of this myth in the national media, but many people still believe it. For example, Melissa Etheridge's song "Scarecrow" on her 1999 album *Breakdown* relies on it, as well as on other early misstatements of fact, including the false report that Shepard had been burned by his killers.

2. While the United Multicultural Council did good work that day, and while some strong connections have been made between the UMC and the LGBTA since Matt's death, it would be wrong to imply that those ties have been built without friction. Carina Evans, a university student who worked in the Minority Affairs Office that year, observed that at the time some members of the "diversity clubs" represented by the UMC "would not deal with the gay issue. The United Multicultural Council had no representation from the LGBTA, had no representation of openly gay students—and I think that's not at all multicultural. But they don't want to handle that. It's not like they're hostile about it, but they just don't encourage it." The tension flows both ways: Jay, a gay American Indian now active in the UMC, told me that some gay students of color he knows are uncomfortable attending LGBTA meetings because they feel that some members are not sensitive to racial differences.

3. A Mexican-American student, Lindsey Gonzales, spoke to me as well about the attack on Morales and Herrera. Lindsey knew Morales quite well (they'd hung out together in the past). She thinks neither the media nor the public cared much about the attack on Morales and Herrera compared to Matt because "they didn't die." But if they had, she speculates, people probably wouldn't have cared much more. When I ask her why, she says she's not sure, but she speculates that racial prejudice is simply more "familiar," something with a longer and better-known history in America, whereas "we're all just getting used to" homosexuality right now, and "that made it a big deal."

■*QUESTIONS FOR MAKING CONNECTIONS WITHIN THE READING* ■

1. As Beth Loffreda works to unpack the significance of Matt Shepard's murder, she finds herself confronting a wide array of prejudices, not only

about gays, but about Wyoming, the West, and Native Americans. Create a chart that details all of the prejudices that Loffreda uncovers. What are the relationships among these prejudices? Does Loffreda have any prejudices or is her view unbiased?

2. In detailing the responses to Shepard's murder, Loffreda refers to many different individuals by name. Who are the most important people in the story that Loffreda has to tell? Which responses had more weight at the time of the murder? Which responses have the most weight with Loffreda? With you?

3. How is this selection from *Losing Matt Shepard* organized? Is it a series of observations or an argument? Does it build to a point? Does it have a structure? How does the structure that Loffreda has chosen influence what she has to say?

▪ QUESTIONS FOR WRITING ▪

1. One of Loffreda's arguments in *Losing Matt Shepard* is that Matt Shepard, the individual, got lost in the media frenzy that followed his murder: part of the shock of Shepard's death, Loffreda reports, was "to watch rumor become myth, to see the story stitched out of repetition rather than investigation." If the media got Shepard's murder wrong, what are we to make of how and why they got it wrong? What would it take to provide "better coverage" of such tragedies? Are the print and visual media capable of providing nuanced understandings of unfolding events?

2. In describing how her colleagues at the University of Wyoming responded to Shepard's death, Loffreda records her own frustration at hearing teachers speak of their own "uselessness" and "irrelevance" in the face of such a tragedy. Such remarks struck Loffreda as "an appalling luxury, an indulgence in a kind of intellectual self-pity at a moment when the basic skills of education—critical thinking, articulation, self-reflection—could be so concretely valuable. I wondered about that, and I wondered too when we'd stop talking about how we felt and begin talking about what to do." What is it that teachers can or should do at such times? What role should secular institutions play in trying to shape the way their students see and understand the world?

▪ QUESTIONS FOR MAKING CONNECTIONS BETWEEN READINGS ▪

1. This selection from *Losing Matt Shepard* closes with Loffreda's discussion of what she terms "the limits of identification." In a sense, Susan Faludi's "The Naked Citadel" could also be described as a piece centrally concerned

with "the limits of identification." What are these limits? How are they discovered? Can they be changed?

2. In exploring the responses to Matt Shepard's murder, has Loffreda gained access to what James C. Scott terms "the hidden transcript," or are homophobia and its violent consequences better considered part of the nation's public transcript?

For additional suggestions about making connections between readings, visit the Link-O-Mat and More Sample Assignments at <www.newhum.com>.

MARTHA NUSSBAUM

MARTHA NUSSBAUM is the Ernst Freund Distinguished Service Professor of Law and Ethics at the University of Chicago, where she has appointments in the Philosophy department, the law school, the divinity school, and the Classics department. A philosopher, a critic, an activist, and a feminist, Nussbaum is equally at home discussing ancient Greek philosophy and contemporary moral and political philosophy. She has written at length about the connections between philosophy and literature, arguing that literature is the best means we have for exploring the consequences of moral choices. She has testified about homosexuality in Ancient Greece before the Supreme Court when it was deliberating a Colorado law that forbade extending civil rights to gays and lesbians. And, as a research adviser for the United Nation's World Institute for Development Economics Research for many years, she has committed herself to improving the status of women in the politics of international development.

Although Nussbaum has long had an interest in liberal education, it has been her work with the United Nations group researching the problems women face in developing countries that has most profoundly shaped her current thoughts about what education is for and what it takes to actually help people from other cultures. As she describes it, after joining this project, "I realized all of a sudden that my own education had not acquainted me at all with the fundamentals. . . . I knew nothing about Hinduism, nothing about Islam, nothing about Buddhism, nothing about the history of Africa or of India, so in short I was just very ill equipped to play the role that I was playing."

In learning more about these other cultures, traditions, and histories, Nussbaum came to see the needs of women in developing countries in a different light. While Nussbaum sees American academic feminists as largely satisfied by

Nussbaum, Martha. "Women and Cultural Universals." *Sex and Social Justice*. New York: Oxford University Press, 1999. 29–54.

Biographical information from Martha Nussbaum's home page at the University of Chicago Law School <http://www.law.uchicago.edu/faculty/nussbaum/>; quotations from Martha Nussbaum, interview by Barry Clark, for ABC's radio series, "Globally Speaking: The Politics of Globalization," on global citizenship <http://www.abc.net.au/global/radio/nussbaum.htm>.

449

playing games with language, she believes that international feminists must be committed to establishing the basic conditions for self-determination discussed in "Women and Cultural Universals." In order to act ethically in the global economy, Nussbaum argues, it is not sufficient just to learn some facts about other exotic cultures; it is necessary to cultivate "the ability to imagine what it might be like to be in the shoes of someone who's different from yourself." As Nussbaum sees it, her role as a teacher, scholar, and activist is to help foster such acts of critical imagination.

To learn more about Martha Nussbaum and women's rights in an international context, visit the Link-O-Mat at <www.newhum.com>.

Women and Cultural Universals

We shall only solve our problems if we see them as human problems arising out of a special situation; and we shall not solve them if we see them as African problems, generated by our being somehow unlike others.

Kwame Anthony Appiah,
Africa in the Philosophy of Cultures

Being a woman is not yet a way of being a human being.

Catharine MacKinnon

I. A Matter of Survival

"I may die, but still I cannot go out. If there's something in the house, we eat. Otherwise, we go to sleep." So Metha Bai, a young widow in Rajasthan, India, with two young children, described her plight as a member of a caste whose women are traditionally prohibited from working outside the home—even when, as here, survival itself is at issue. If she stays at home, she and her children may shortly die. If she attempts to go out, her in-laws will beat her and abuse her children. For now, Metha Bai's father travels from 100 miles away to plow her small plot of land. But he is aging, and Metha Bai fears that she and her children will shortly die with him.[1]

In this case, as in many others throughout the world, cultural traditions pose obstacles to women's health and flourishing. Depressingly, many traditions portray women as less important than men, less deserving of basic life support or of fundamental rights that are strongly correlated with quality of life, such as the right to work and the right to political participation. Sometimes, as in the case of Metha Bai, the women themselves resist these traditions. Sometimes, on the other hand, the traditions have become so deeply internalized that they seem to record what is "right" and "natural," and women themselves endorse their own second-class status.

Such cases are hardly confined to non-Western or developing countries. As recently as 1873, the U.S. Supreme Court upheld a law that forbade women to practice law in the state of Illinois, on the grounds that "[t]he constitution of the family organization, which is founded in the divine ordinance, as well as in the nature of things, indicates the domestic sphere as that which properly belongs to the domain and functions of womanhood." [2] And in 1993, a woman who was threatened and grossly harassed by her male coworkers, after becoming the first woman to work in the heavy metal shop in the General Motors plant in Indiana, was described by a federal district judge as having provoked the men's conduct by her "unladylike" behavior—behavior that consisted in using a four-letter word a few times in a five-year period. [3] Clearly our own society still appeals to tradition in its own way to justify women's unequal treatment.

What should people concerned with justice say about this? And should they say anything at all? On the one hand, it seems impossible to deny that traditions, both Western and non-Western, perpetrate injustice against women in many fundamental ways, touching on some of the most central elements of a human being's quality of life—health, education, political liberty and participation, employment, self-respect, and life itself. On the other hand, hasty judgments that a tradition in some distant part of the world is morally retrograde are familiar legacies of colonialism and imperialism and are correctly regarded with suspicion by sensitive thinkers in the contemporary world. To say that a practice endorsed by tradition is bad is to risk erring by imposing one's own way on others, who surely have their own ideas of what is right and good. To say that a practice is all right whenever local tradition endorses it as right and good is to risk erring by withholding critical judgment where real evil and oppression are surely present. To avoid the whole issue because the matter of proper judgment is so fiendishly difficult is tempting but perhaps the worst option of all. It suggests the sort of moral collapse depicted by Dante when he describes the crowd of souls who mill around in the vestibule of hell, dragging their banner now one way, now another, never willing to set it down and take a definite stand on any moral or political question. Such people, he implies, are the most despicable of all. They cannot even get into hell because they have not been willing to stand for anything in life, one way or another. To express the spirit of this chapter very succinctly, it is better to risk being consigned by critics to the "hell" reserved for alleged Westernizers and imperialists—however unjustified such criticism would in fact be—than to stand around in the vestibule waiting for a time when everyone will like what we are going to say. And what we are going to say is: that there are universal obligations to protect human functioning and its dignity, and that the dignity of women is equal to that of men. If that involves assault on many local traditions, both Western and non-Western, so much the better, because any tradition that denies these things is unjust. Or, as a young Bangladeshi wife said when local religious leaders threatened to break the legs of women who went to the literacy classes conducted by a local NGO (nongovernmental organization), "We do not listen to the *mullahs* any more. They did not give us even a quarter kilo of rice."[4]

The situation of women in the contemporary world calls urgently for moral standtaking. Women, a majority of the world's population, receive only a small proportion of its opportunities and benefits. According to the *Human Development Report,* in no country in the world is women's quality of life equal to that of men, according to a complex measure that includes life expectancy, educational attainment, and GDP (gross domestic product) per capita.[5] Some countries have much larger gender disparities than others. (Among prosperous industrial countries, for example, Spain and Japan perform relatively poorly in this area; Sweden, Denmark, and New Zealand perform relatively well.[6]) If we now examine the Gender Empowerment Measure, which uses variables chosen explicitly to measure the relative empowerment of men and women in political and economic activity,[7] we find even more striking signs of gender disparity. Once again, the Scandinavian nations do well; Japan and Spain do relatively poorly.[8]

If we turn our attention to the developing countries we find uneven achievements but, in the aggregate, a distressing situation. On average, employment participation rates of women are only 50% those of men (in South Asia 29%; in the Arab states only 16%).[9] Even when women are employed, their situation is undercut by pervasive wage discrimination and by long hours of unpaid household labor. (If women's unpaid housework were counted as productive output in national income accounts, global output would increase by 20–30%.) Outside the home, women are generally employed in a restricted range of jobs offering low pay and low respect. The percentage of earned income that goes to women is rarely higher than 35%. In many nations it is far lower: in Iran, 16%; Belize, 17%; Algeria, 16%; Iraq, 17%; Pakistan, 19%. (China at 38% is higher than Japan at 33%; highest in the world are Sweden at 45%, Denmark at 42%, and the extremely impoverished Rwanda at 41%, Burundi at 42%, and Mozambique at 42%.) The situation of women in the workplace is frequently undermined by sex discrimination and sexual harassment.

Women are much less likely than men to be literate. In South Asia, female literacy rates average around 50% those of males. In some countries the rate is still lower: in Nepal, 35%; Sierra Leone, 37%; Sudan, 27%; Afghanistan, 32%.[10] Two-thirds of the world's illiterate people are women. In higher education, women lag even further behind men in both developing and industrial nations.[11]

Although some countries allowed women the vote early in this century, some still have not done so. And there are many informal obstacles to women's effective participation in political life. Almost everywhere, they are underrepresented in government: In 1980, they made up only around 10% of the world's parliamentary representatives and less than 4% of its cabinet officials.[12]

As Metha Bai's story indicates, employment outside the home has a close relationship to health and nutrition. So too, frequently, does political voice. And if we now turn to the very basic issue of health and survival, we find compelling evidence of discrimination against females in many nations of the world. It appears that when equal nutrition and health care are present women live, on average, slightly longer than men—even allowing for a modest level of maternal mortality, Thus, in Europe the female/male ratio in 1986 was 105/100, in North America 104.7/100. [13] But it may be objected that for several reasons it is inappropriate to compare these developed countries with countries in the developing world. Let us, therefore, with Jean Drèze and Amartya Sen, take as our baseline the ratio in sub-Saharan Africa, where there is great poverty but little evidence of gender discrimination in basic nutrition and health.[14] The female/male ratio in 1986 was 102.2/100. If we examine the sex ratio in various other countries and ask the question, "How many more women than are now in country C would be there if its sex ratio were the same as that of sub-Sabaran Africa?," we get a number that Sen has graphically called the number of "missing women." The number of missing women in Southeast Asia is 2.4 million; in Latin America, 4.4; in North Africa, 2.4; in Iran, 1.4; in China, 44.0; in Bangladesh, 3.7; in India, 36.7; in Pakistan, 5.2.; in West Asia, 4.3. If we now consider the ratio of the number of missing women to the number of actual women in a country, we get, for Pakistan, 12.9%; for India, 9.5%; for Bangladesh, 8.7%; for China, 8.6%; for Iran, 8.5%; for West Asia, 7.8%; for North Africa, 3.9%; for Latin America, 2.2%; for Southeast Asia, 1.2%. In India, not only is the mortality differential especially sharp among children (girls dying in far greater numbers than boys), the higher mortality rate of women compared to men applies to all age groups until the late thirties.[15]

Poverty alone does not cause women to die in greater numbers than men. This is abundantly clear from comparative regional studies in India, where some of the poorest regions, for example, Kerala, have the most equal sex ratios, and some far richer regions perform very poorly.[16] When there is scarcity, custom and political arrangement frequently decree who gets to eat the little there is and who gets taken to the doctor. And custom and political arrangement are always crucial in deciding who gets to perform wage labor outside the home, an important determinant of general status in the family and the community. As Sen has argued, a woman's perceived contribution to the well-being of the family unit is often determined by her ability to work outside, and this determines, in turn, her bargaining position within the family unit.[17] Custom and politics decree who gets access to the education that would open job opportunities and make political rights meaningful. Custom and politics decree who can go where in what clothing in what company. Custom and politics decree who gets to make what sorts of protests against ill treatment both inside and outside the family and whose voice of protest is likely to be heard.

Customs and political arrangements, in short, are important causes of women's misery and death. It seems incumbent on people interested in justice, and aware of the information about women's status that studies such as the *Human Development Reports* present, to ask about the relationship between culture and justice and between both of these and legal-political arrangements. It then seems incumbent on them to try to work out an account of the critical assessment of traditions and political arrangements that is neither do-gooder colonialism or an uncritical validation of the status quo.

One might suppose that any approach to the question of quality of life assessment in development economics would offer an account of the relationship between tradition and women's equality that would help us answer these questions. But in fact such an account is sorely lacking in the major theoretical approaches that, until recently, dominated the development scene. (Here I do not even include what has been the most common practical approach, which has been simply to ask about GNP (gross national product) per capita. This crude approach does not even look at the distribution of wealth and income; far less does it ask about other constituents of life quality, for example, life expectancy, infant mortality, education, health, and the presence or absence of political liberties, that are not always well correlated with GNP per capita.[18] The failure to ask these questions is a particularly grave problem when it is women's quality of life we want to consider. For women have especially often been unable to enjoy or control the fruits of a nation's general prosperity.)

The leading economic approach to the family is the model proposed by Nobel Prize–winning economist Gary Becker. Becker assumes that the family's goal is the maximization of utility, construed as the satisfaction of preference or desire, and that the head of the household is a beneficent altruist who will adequately take thought for the interests of all family members.[19] In real life, however, the economy of the family is characterized by pervasive "cooperative conflicts," that is, situations in which the interests of members of a cooperative body split apart, and some individuals fare well at the expense of others.[20] Becker deserves great credit for putting these issues on the agenda of the profession in the first place. But his picture of male motivation does not fit the evidence, and in a way substantial enough to affect the model's predictive value—especially if one looks not only at women's stated satisfactions and preferences, which may be deformed by intimidation, lack of information, and habit,[21] but at their actual functioning.[22] Furthermore, the model prevents those who use it from even getting the information about individual family members on which a more adequate account might be based. [23]

Suppose we were to retain a utilitarian approach and yet to look at the satisfactions of all family members—assuming, as is standardly done in economics, that preferences and tastes are exogenous and independent of laws, traditions, and institutions rather than endogenously shaped by them. Such an approach—frequently used by governments polling citizens about well-being—has the advantage of assessing all individuals one by one. But the evidence of preference endogeneity is great, and especially great when we are dealing with people whose status has been persistently defined as second class in laws and institutions of various sorts. There are many reasons to think that women's perception even of their health status is shaped by traditional views, such as the view that female life is worth less than male life, that women are weaker than men, that women do not have equal rights, and so forth. In general, people frequently adjust their expectations to the low level of well-being they think they can actually attain.[24] This approach, then, cannot offer a useful account of the role of tradition in well-being, because it is bound by its very commitments to an uncritical validation of the status quo.

More promising than either Becker's model or the standard utilitarian approach is one suggested by John Rawls's liberalism, with its account of the just distribution of a small list of basic goods and resources.[25] This approach does enable us to criticize persistent inequalities, and it strongly criticizes the view that preferences are simply given rather than shaped by society's basic structure. But in one way the Rawlsian approach stops short. Rawls's list of "primary goods," although it includes some capacity-like items, such as liberty and opportunity, also includes thing-like items, particularly income and wealth, and it measures who is least well off simply in terms of the amount of these thing-like resources an individual can command. But people have varying needs for resources: a pregnant woman, for example, needs more calories than a nonpregnant woman, a child more protein than an adult. They also have different abilities to convert resources into functioning. A person in a wheelchair will need more resources to become mobile than a person with unimpaired limbs; a woman in a society that has defined employment outside the home as off limits to women needs more resources to become a productive worker than one who does not face such struggles. In short, the Rawlsian approach does not probe deeply enough to show us how resources do or do not go to work in making people able to function. Again, at least some of our questions about the relationship between tradition and quality of life cannot be productively addressed.

Workers on such issues have therefore increasingly converged on an approach that is now widely known as "the capabilities approach." This approach to quality-of-life measurement and the goals of public policy[26] holds that we should focus on the question: What are the people of the group or country in question actually able to do and to be? Unlike a focus on opulence (say, GNP per capita), this approach asks about the distribution of resources and opportunities. In principle, it asks how each and every individual is doing with respect to all the functions deemed important. Unlike Becker's approach, the capability approach considers people one by one, not as parts of an organic unit; it is very interested in seeing how a supposed organic unit such as the family has constructed unequal capabilities for various types of functioning. Unlike a standard utilitarian approach, the capability approach maintains that preferences are not always reliable indicators of life quality, as they may be deformed in various ways by oppression and deprivation. Unlike the type of liberal approach that focuses only on the distribution of resources, the capability approach maintains that resources have no value in themselves, apart from their role in promoting human functioning. It therefore directs the planner to inquire into the varying needs individuals have for resources and their varying abilities to convert resources into functioning. In this way, it strongly invites a scrutiny of tradition as one of the primary sources of such unequal abilities.[27]

But the capabilities approach raises the question of cultural universalism, or, as it is often pejoratively called, "essentialism." Once we begin asking how people are actually functioning, we cannot avoid focusing on some components of lives and not others, some abilities to act and not others, seeing some capabilities and functions as more central, more at the core of human life, than others. We cannot avoid having an account, even if a partial and highly general account, of what functions of the human being are most worth the care and attention of public planning the world over. Such an account is bound to be controversial.

II. Anti-Universalist Conversations

The primary opponents of such an account of capability and functioning will be "antiessentialists" of various types, thinkers who urge us to begin not with sameness but with difference—both between women and men and across groups of women—and to seek norms defined relatively to a local context and locally held beliefs. This opposition takes many forms, and I shall be responding to several distinct objections. But I can begin to motivate the enterprise by telling several true stories of conversations that have taken place at the World Institute for Development Economics Research (WIDER), in which the anti-universalist position seemed to have alarming implications for women's lives.[28]

At a conference on "Value and Technology," an American economist who has long been a leftwing critic of neoclassical economics delivers a paper urging the preservation of traditional ways of life in a rural area of Orissa, India, now under threat of contamination from Western development projects. As evidence of the excellence of this rural way of life, he points to the fact that whereas we Westerners experience a sharp split between the values that prevail in the workplace and the values that prevail in the home, here, by contrast, exists what the economist calls "the embedded way of life," the same values obtaining in both places. His example: Just as in the home a menstruating woman is thought to pollute the kitchen and therefore may not enter it, so too in the workplace a menstruating woman is taken to pollute the loom and may not enter the room where looms are kept. Some feminists object that this example is repellant rather than admirable; for surely such practices both degrade the women in question and inhibit their freedom. The first economist's collaborator, an elegant French anthropologist (who would, I suspect, object violently to a purity check at the seminar room door), replies: Don't we realize that there is, in these matters, no privileged place to stand? This, after all, has been shown by both Derrida and Foucault. Doesn't he know that he is neglecting the otherness of Indian ideas by bringing his Western essentialist values into the picture?[29]

The same French anthropologist now delivers her paper. She expresses regret that the introduction of smallpox vaccination to India by the British eradicated the cult of Sittala Devi, the goddess to whom one used to pray to avert smallpox. Here, she says, is another example of Western neglect of difference. Someone (it might have been me) objects that it is surely better to be healthy rather than ill, to live rather than to die. The answer comes back; Western essentialist medicine conceives of things in terms of binary oppositions: life is opposed to death, health to disease.[30] But if we cast away this binary way of thinking, we will begin to comprehend the otherness of Indian traditions.

At this point Eric Hobsbawm, who has been listening to the proceedings in increasingly uneasy silence, rises to deliver a blistering indictment of the traditionalism and relativism that prevail in this group. He lists historical examples of ways in which appeals to tradition have been politically engineered to support oppression and violence.[31] His final example is that of National Socialism in Germany. In the confusion that ensues, most of the relativist social scientists—above all those from far away, who do not know who Hobsbawm is—demand that Hobsbawm be asked to leave the room. The radical American economist, disconcerted by this apparent tension between his relativism and his affiliation with the left, convinces them, with difficulty, to let Hobsbawm remain.

We shift now to another conference two years later, a philosophical conference on the quality of life.[32] Members of the quality-of-life project are speaking of choice as a basic good, and of the importance of expanding women's sphere of choices. We are challenged by the radical economist of my first story, who insists that contemporary anthropology has shown that non-Western people are not especially attached to freedom of choice. His example: A book on Japan has shown that Japanese males, when they get home from work, do not wish to choose what to eat for dinner, what to wear, and so on. They wish all these choices to be taken out of their hands by their wives. A heated exchange follows about what this example really shows. I leave it to your imaginations to reconstruct it. In the end, the confidence of the radical economist is unshaken: We are victims of bad universalist thinking, who fail to respect "difference."[33]

The phenomenon is an odd one. For we see here highly intelligent people, people deeply committed to the good of women and men in developing countries, people who think of themselves as progressive and feminist and antiracist, people who correctly argue that the concept of development is an evaluative concept requiring normative argument[34]—effectively eschewing normative argument and taking up positions that converge, as Hobsbawm correctly saw, with the positions of reaction, oppression, and sexism. Under the banner of their fashionable opposition to universalism march ancient religious taboos, the luxury of the pampered husband, educational deprivation, unequal health care, and premature death.

Nor do these anti-universalists appear to have a very sophisticated conception of their own core notions, such as "culture," "custom," and "tradition." It verges on the absurd to treat India as a single culture, and a single visit to a single Orissan village as sufficient to reveal its traditions. India, like all extant societies, is a complex mixture of elements[35]: Hindu, Muslim, Parsi, Christian, Jewish, atheist; urban, suburban, rural; rich, poor, and middle class; high caste, low caste, and aspiring middle caste; female and male; rationalist and mystical. It is renowned for mystical religion but also for achievements in mathematics and for the invention of chess. It contains intense, often violent sectarianism, but it also contains Rabindranath Tagore's cosmopolitan humanism and Mahatma Gandhi's reinterpretation of Hinduism as a religion of universal nonviolence. Its traditions contain views of female whorishness and childishness that derive from the Laws of Manu[36]; but it also contains the sexual agency of Draupadi in the *Mahabharata,* who solved the problem of choice among Pandava husbands by taking all five, and the enlightened sensualism and female agency of the *Kama Sutra,* a sacred text that foreign readers wrongly interpret as pornographic. It contains women like Metha Bai, who are confined to the home; it also contains women like Amita Sen (mother of Amartya Sen), who fifty years ago was among the first middle-class Bengali women to dance in public, in Rabindranath Tagore's musical extravaganzas in Santiniketan. It contains artists who disdain the foreign, preferring, with the Marglins, the "embedded" way of life, and it also contains Satyajit Ray, that great Bengali artist and lover of local traditions, who could also write, "I never ceased to regret that while I had stood in the scorching summer sun in the wilds of Santiniketan sketching *simul* and *palash* in full bloom, *Citizen Kane* had come and gone, playing for just three days in the newest and biggest cinema in Calcutta."[37]

What, then, is "the culture" of a woman like Metha Bai? Is it bound to be that determined by the most prevalent customs in Rajasthan, the region of her marital home? Or, might she be permitted to consider with what traditions or groups she wishes to align herself, perhaps forming a community of solidarity with other widows and women, in pursuit of a better quality of life? What is "the culture" of Chinese working women who have recently been victims of the government's "women go home" policy, which appeals to Confucian traditions about woman's "nature"?[38] Must it be the one advocated by Confucius, or may they be permitted to form new alliances—with one another, and with other defenders of women's human rights? What is "the culture" of General Motors employee Mary Carr? Must it be the one that says women should be demure and polite, even in the face of gross insults, and that an "unladylike" woman deserves the harassment she gets? Or might she be allowed to consider what norms are appropriate to the situation of a woman working in a heavy metal shop, and to act accordingly? Real cultures contain plurality and conflict, tradition, and subversion. They borrow good things from wherever they find them, none too worried about purity. We would never tolerate a claim that women in our own society must embrace traditions that arose thousands of years ago—indeed, we are proud that we have no such traditions. Isn't it condescending, then, to treat Indian and Chinese women as bound by the past in ways that we are not?

Indeed, as Hobsbawm suggested, the vision of "culture" propounded by the Marglins, by stressing uniformity and homogeneity, may lie closer to artificial constructions by reactionary political forces than to any organic historical entity. Even to the extent to which it is historical, one might ask, exactly how does that contribute to make it worth preserving? Cultures are not museum pieces, to be preserved intact at all costs. There would appear, indeed, to be something condescending in preserving for contemplation a way of life that causes real pain to real people.

Let me now, nonetheless, describe the most cogent objections that might be raised by a relativist against a normative universalist project.

III. The Attack on Universalism

Many attacks on universalism suppose that any universalist project must rely on truths eternally fixed in the nature of things, outside human action and human history. Because some people believe in such truths and some do not, the objector holds that a normative view so grounded is bound to be biased in favor of some religious/metaphysical conceptions and against others.[39]

But universalism does not require such metaphysical support.[40] For universal ideas of the human do arise within history and from human experience, and they can ground themselves in experience. Indeed, those who take all human norms to be the result of human interpretation can hardly deny that universal conceptions of the human are prominent and pervasive among such interpretations, hardly to be relegated to the dustbin of metaphysical history along with recondite theoretical entities such as phlogiston. As Aristotle so simply puts it, "One may observe in one's travels to distant countries the feelings of recognition and affiliation that link every human being to every other human being."[41] Kwame Anthony Appiah makes the same point, telling the story of his bicultural childhood. A child who visits one set of grandparents in Ghana and another in rural England, who has a Lebanese uncle and who later, as an adult, has nieces and nephews from more than seven different nations, finds, he argues, not unbridgeable alien "otherness," but a great deal of human commonality, and comes to see the world as a "network of points of affinity."[42] But such a metaphysically agnostic, experiential and historical universalism is still vulnerable to some, if not all, of the objections standardly brought against universalism.

Neglect of Historical and Cultural Differences

The opponent charges that any attempt to pick out some elements of human life as more fundamental than others, even without appeal to a transhistorical reality, is bound to be insufficiently respectful of actual historical and cultural differences. People, it is claimed, understand human life and humanness in widely different ways, and any attempt to produce a list of the most fundamental properties and functions of human beings is bound to enshrine certain understandings of the human and to demote others. Usually, the objector continues, this takes the form of enshrining the understanding of a dominant group at the expense of minority understandings. This type of objection, frequently made by feminists, can claim support from many historical examples in which the human has indeed been defined by focusing on actual characteristics of males.

It is far from clear what this objection shows. In particular it is far from clear that it supports the idea that we ought to base our ethical norms, instead, on the current preferences and the self-conceptions of people who are living what the objector herself claims to be lives of deprivation and oppression. But it does show at least that the project of choosing one picture of the human over another is fraught with difficulty, political as well as philosophical.

Neglect of Autonomy

A different objection is presented by liberal opponents of universalism. The objection is that by determining in advance what elements of human life have most importance, the universalist project fails to respect the right of people to choose a plan of life according to their own lights, determining what is central and what is not.[43] This way of proceeding is "imperialistic." Such evaluative choices must be left to each citizen. For this reason, politics must refuse itself a determinate theory of the human being and the human good.

Prejudicial Application

If we operate with a determinate conception of the human being that is meant to have some normative moral and political force, we must also, in applying it, ask which beings we take to fall under the concept. And here the objector notes that, all too easily—even if the conception itself is equitably and comprehensively designed—the powerless can be excluded. Aristotle himself, it is pointed out, held that women and slaves were not full-fledged human beings, and because his politics were based on his view of human functioning, the failure of these beings (in his view) to exhibit the desired mode of functioning contributed to their political exclusion and oppression.

It is, once again, hard to know what this objection is supposed to show. In particular, it is hard to know how, if at all, it is supposed to show that we would be better off without such determinate universal concepts. For it could be plausibly argued that it would have been even easier to exclude women and slaves on a whim if one did not have such a concept to combat.[44] On the other hand, it does show that we need to think not only about getting the concept right but also about getting the right beings admitted under the concept.

Each of these objections has some merit. Many universal conceptions of the human being have been insular in an arrogant way and neglectful of differences among cultures and ways of life. Some have been neglectful of choice and autonomy. And many have been prejudicially applied. But none of this shows that all such conceptions must fail in one or more of these ways. At this point, however, we need to examine a real proposal, both to display its merits and to argue that it can in fact answer there charges.

IV. A Conception of the Human Being: The Central Human Capabilities

The list of basic capabilities is generated by asking a question that from the start is evaluative: What activities[45] characteristically performed by human beings are so central that they seem definitive of a life that is truly human? In other words, what are the functions without which (meaning, without the availability of which) we would regard a life as not, or not fully, human?[46] We can get at this question better if we approach it via two somewhat more concrete questions that we often really ask ourselves. First is a question about personal continuity. We ask ourselves which changes or transitions are compatible with the continued existence of that being as a member of the human kind and which are not. Some functions can fail to be present without threatening our sense that we still have a human being on our hands; the absence of others seems to signal the end of a human life. This question is asked regularly, when we attempt to make medical definitions of death in a situation in which some of the functions of life persist, or to decide, for others or (thinking ahead) for ourselves, whether a certain level of illness or impairment means the end of the life of the being in question.[47]

The other question is a question about kind inclusion. We recognize other humans as human across many differences of time and place, of custom and appearance. We often tell ourselves stories, on the other hand, about anthropomorphic creatures who do not get classified as human, on account of some feature of their form of life and functioning. On what do we base these inclusions and exclusions? In short, what do we believe must be there, if we are going to acknowledge that a given life is human?[48] The answer to these questions points us to a subset of common or characteristic human functions, informing us that these are likely to have a special importance for everything else we choose and do.

Note that the procedure through which this account of the human is derived is neither ahistorical nor a priori. It is the attempt to summarize empirical findings of a broad and ongoing cross-cultural inquiry. As such, it is both open-ended and humble; it can always be contested and remade. Nor does it claim to read facts of "human nature" from biological observation; it takes biology into account as a relatively constant element in human experience.[49] It is because the account is evaluative from the start that it is called a conception of the good.

It should also be stressed that, like John Rawls's account of primary goods in *A Theory of Justice*,[50] this list of good functions, which is in some ways more comprehensive than his own list, is proposed as the object of a specifically political consensus.[51] The political is not understood exactly as Rawls understands it because the nation state is not assumed to be the basic unit, and the account is meant to have broad applicability to cross-cultural deliberations. This means, given the current state of world politics, that many of the obligations to promote the adequate distribution of these goods must rest with individuals rather than with any political institution, and in that way its role becomes difficult to distinguish from the role of other norms and goals of the individual. Nonetheless, the point of the list is the same as that of Rawlsian primary goods: to put forward something that people from many different traditions, with many different fuller conceptions of the good, can agree on, as the necessary basis for pursuing their good life. That is why the list is deliberately rather general.[52] Each of its components can be more concretely specified in accordance with one's origins, religious beliefs, or tastes. In that sense, the consensus that it hopes to evoke has many of the features of the "overlapping consensus" described by Rawls.[53]

Having isolated some functions that seem central in defining the very presence of a human life, we do not rest content with mere bare humanness. We want to specify a life in which fully human functioning, or a kind of basic human flourishing, will be available. For we do not want politics to take mere survival as its goal; we want to describe a life in which the dignity of the human being is not violated by hunger or fear or the absence of opportunity. (The idea is very much Marx's idea, when he used an Aristotelian notion of functioning to describe the difference between a merely animal use of one's faculties and a "truly human use."[54]) The following list of central human functional capabilities is an attempt to specify this basic notion of the good: All citizens should have these capabilities, whatever else they have and pursue.[55] I introduce this as a list of capabilities rather than of actual functionings, because I shall argue that capability, not actual functioning, should be the goal of public policy.

Central Human Functional Capabilities

1. *Life.* Being able to live to the end of a human life of normal length[56]; not dying prematurely or before one's life is so reduced as to be not worth living
2. *Bodily health and integrity.* Being able to have good health, including reproductive health; being adequately nourished[57]; being able to have adequate shelter[58]
3. *Bodily integrity.* Being able to move freely from place to place; being able to be secure against violent assault, including sexual assault, marital rape, and domestic violence; having opportunities for sexual satisfaction and for choice in matters of reproduction
4. *Senses, imagination, thought.* Being able to use the senses; being able to imagine, to think, and to reason—and to do these things in a "truly human" way, a way informed and cultivated by an adequate education, including, but by no means limited to, literacy and basic mathematical and scientific training; being able to use imagination and thought in connection with experiencing and producing expressive works and events of one's own choice (religious, literary, musical, etc.); being able to use one's mind in ways protected by guarantees of freedom of expression with respect to both political and artistic speech and freedom of religious exercise; being able to have pleasurable experiences and to avoid nonbeneficial pain
5. *Emotions.* Being able to have attachments to things and persons outside ourselves; being able to love those who love and care for us; being able to grieve at their absence; in general, being able to love, to grieve, to experience longing, gratitude, and justified anger; not having one's emotional developing blighted by fear or anxiety. (Supporting this capability means supporting forms of human association that can be shown to be crucial in their development.[59])
6. *Practical reason.* Being able to form a conception of the good and to engage in critical reflection about the planning of one's own life. (This entails protection for the liberty of conscience.)
7. *Affiliation.* (a) Being able to live for and in relation to others, to recognize and show concern for other human beings, to engage in various forms of social interaction; being able to imagine the situation of another and to have compassion for that situation; having the capability for both justice and friendship. (Protecting this capability means, once again, protecting institutions that constitute such forms of affiliation, and also

protecting the freedoms of assembly and political speech.) (b) Having the social bases of self-respect and nonhumiliation; being able to be treated as a dignified being whose worth is equal to that of others. (This entails provisions of nondiscrimination.)

8. *Other species.* Being able to live with concern for and in relation to animals, plants, and the world of nature[60]

9. *Play.* Being able to laugh, to play, to enjoy recreational activities

10. *Control over one's environment.* (a) *Political:* being able to participate effectively in political choices that govern one's life; having the rights of political participation, free speech, and freedom of association (b) *Material:* being able to hold property (both land and movable goods); having the right to seek employment on an equal basis with others; having the freedom from unwarranted search and seizure.[61] In work, being able to work as a human being, exercising practical reason and entering into meaningful relationships of mutual recognition with other workers.

The "capabilities approach," as I conceive it,[62] claims that a life that lacks any one of these capabilities, no matter what else it has, will fall short of being a good human life. Thus it would be reasonable to take these things as a focus for concern, in assessing the quality of life in a country and asking about the role of public policy in meeting human needs. The list is certainly general—and this is deliberate, to leave room for plural specification and also for further negotiation. But like (and as a reasonable basis for) a set of constitutional guarantees, it offers real guidance to policymakers, and far more accurate guidance than that offered by the focus on utility, or even on resources.[63]

The list is, emphatically, a list of separate components. We cannot satisfy the need for one of them by giving a larger amount of another one. All are of central importance and all are distinct in quality. This limits the trade-offs that it will be reasonable to make and thus limits the applicability of quantitative cost-benefit analysis. At the same time, the items on the list are related to one another in many complex ways. Employment rights, for example, support health, and also freedom from domestic violence, by giving women a better bargaining position in the family. The liberties of speech and association turn up at several distinct points on the list, showing their fundamental role with respect to several distinct areas of human functioning.

V. Capability as Goal

The basic claim I wish to make—concurring with Amartya Sen—is that the central goal of public planning should be the *capabilities* of citizens to perform various important functions. The question that should be asked when assessing quality of life in a country—and of course this is a central part of assessing the quality of its political arrangements—is, How well have the people of the country been enabled to perform the central human functions? And, have they been put in a position of mere human subsistence with respect to the functions, or have they been enabled to live well? Politics, we argue (here concurring with Rawls), should focus on getting as many people as possible into a state of capability to function, with respect to the interlocking set of capabilities enumerated by that list.[64] Naturally, the determination of whether certain individuals and groups are across the threshold is only as precise a matter as the determination of the threshold. I have left things deliberately somewhat open-ended at this point, in keeping with the procedures of the *Human Development Report*, believing that the best way to work toward a more precise determination, at present, is to focus on comparative information and to allow citizens to judge for themselves whether their policymakers have done as well as they should have. Again, we will have to answer various questions about the costs we are willing to pay to get all citizens above the threshold, as opposed to leaving a small number below and allowing the rest a considerably above-threshold life quality. It seems likely, at any rate, that moving all citizens above a basic threshold of capability should be taken as a central social goal. When citizens are across the threshold, societies are to a great extent free to choose the other goals they wish to pursue. Some inequalities, however, will themselves count as capability failures. For example, inequalities based on hierarchies of gender or race will themselves be inadmissible on the grounds that they undermine self-respect and emotional development.

The basic intuition from which the capability approach starts, in the political arena, is that human capabilities exert a moral claim that they should be developed. Human beings are creatures such that, provided with the right educational and material support, they can become fully capable of the major human functions. That is, they are creatures with certain lower-level capabilities (which I call "basic capabilities"[65]) to perform the functions in question. When these capabilities are deprived of the nourishment that would transform them into the high-level capabilities that figure on my list, they are fruitless, cut off, in some way but a shadow of themselves. They are like actors who never get to go on the stage, or a person who sleeps all through life, or a musical score that is never performed. Their very being makes forward reference to functioning. Thus, if functioning never arrives on the scene they are hardly even what they are. This may sound like a metaphysical idea, and in a sense it is (in that it is an idea discussed in Aristotle's *Metaphysics*). But that does not mean it is not a basic and pervasive empirical idea, an idea that underwrites many of our daily practices and judgments in many times and places. Just as we hold that a child who dies before getting to maturity has died especially tragically—for her activities of growth and preparation for adult activity now have lost their point—so too with capability and functioning more generally: We believe that certain basic and central human endowments have a claim to be assisted in developing, and exert that claim on others, and especially, as Aristotle saw, on government. Without some such notion of the basic worth of human capacities, we have a hard time arguing for women's equality and for basic human rights. Think, for example, of the remark of Catharine MacKinnon that I quoted as my epigraph. If women were really just trees or turtles or filing cabinets, the fact that their current status in many parts of the world is not a fully human one would not be, as it is, a problem of justice. In thinking of political planning we begin, then, from a notion of the basic capabilities and their worth, thinking of them as claims to a chance for functioning, which give rise to correlated political duties.

I have spoken both of functioning and of capability. How are they related? Getting clear about this is crucial in defining the relation of the capabilities approach to liberalism. For if we were to take functioning itself as the goal of public policy, the liberal would rightly judge that we were precluding many choices that citizens may make in accordance with their own conceptions of the good. A deeply religious person may prefer not to be well nourished but to engage in strenuous fasting. Whether for religious or for other reasons, a person may prefer a celibate life to one containing sexual expression. A person may prefer to work with an intense dedication that precludes recreation and play. Am I saying that these are not fully human or flourishing lives? Does the approach instruct governments to nudge or push people into functioning of the requisite sort, no matter what they prefer?

Here we must answer: No, capability, not functioning, is the political goal. This is so because of the very great importance the approach attaches to practical reason, as a good that both suffuses all the other functions, making them human rather than animal,[66] and figures, itself, as a central function on the list. It is perfectly true that functionings, not simply capabilities, are what render a life fully human: If there were no functioning of any kind in a life, we could hardly applaud it, no matter what opportunities it contained. Nonetheless, for political purposes it is appropriate for us to shoot for capabilities, and those alone. Citizens must be left free to determine their course after that. The person with plenty of food may always choose to fast, but there is a great difference between fasting and starving, and it is this difference we wish to capture. Again, the person who has normal opportunities for sexual satisfaction can always choose a life of celibacy, and we say nothing against this. What we do speak against, for example, is the practice of female genital mutilation, which deprives individuals of the opportunity to choose sexual functioning (and indeed, the opportunity to choose celibacy as well).[67] A person who has opportunities for play can always choose a workaholic life; again, there is a great difference between that chosen life and a life constrained by insufficient maximum-hour protections and/or the "double day" that makes women in many parts of the world unable to play.

The issue will be clearer if we recall that there are three different types of capabilities that figure in the analysis.[68] First, there are *basic capabilities:* the innate equipment of individuals that is the necessary basis for develop-

ing the more advanced capability. Most infants have from birth the basic capability for practical reason and imagination, though they cannot exercise
such functions without a lot more development and education. Second,
there are *internal capabilities:* states of the person herself that are, as far as the
person herself is concerned, sufficient conditions for the exercise of the requisite functions. A woman who has not suffered genital mutilation has the
internal capability for sexual pleasure; most adult human beings everywhere have the internal capability to use speech and thought in accordance
with their own conscience. Finally, there are *combined capabilities,* which we
define as internal capabilities *combined with* suitable external conditions for
the exercise of the function. A woman who is not mutilated but is secluded
and forbidden to leave the house has internal but not combined capabilities
for sexual expression (and work and political participation). Citizens of
repressive nondemocratic regimes have the internal but not the combined
capability to exercise thought and speech in accordance with their conscience. The aim of public policy is the production of *combined capabilities.*
This means promoting the states of the person by providing the necessary
education and care; it also means preparing the environment so that it is favorable for the exercise of practical reason and the other major functions.[69]

This clarifies the position. The approach does not say that public policy
should rest content with *internal capabilities* but remain indifferent to the
struggles of individuals who have to try to exercise these in a hostile environment. In that sense, it is highly attentive to the goal of functioning, and
instructs governments to keep it always in view. On the other hand, we are
not pushing individuals into the function: Once the stage is fully set, the
choice is up to them.

The approach is therefore very close to Rawls's approach using the notion of primary goods. We can see the list of capabilities as like a long list of
opportunities for life functioning, such that it is always rational to want
them whatever else one wants. If one ends up having a plan of life that does
not make use of all of them, one has hardly been harmed by having the
chance to choose a life that does. (Indeed, in the cases of fasting and celibacy
it is the very availability of the alternative course that gives the choice its
moral value.) The primary difference between this capabilities list and
Rawls's list of primary goods is its length and definiteness, and in particular
its determination to place on the list the social basis of several goods that
Rawls has called "natural goods," such as "health and vigor, intelligence
and imagination."[70] Since Rawls has been willing to put the social basis of
self-respect on his list, it is not at all clear why he has not made the same
move with imagination and health.[71] Rawls's evident concern is that no society can guarantee health to its individuals—in that sense, saying that our
goal is full combined capability may appear unreasonably idealistic. Some
of the capabilities (e.g., some of the political liberties) can be fully guaranteed by society, but many others involve an element of chance and cannot be
so guaranteed. We respond to this by saying that the list is an enumeration

of political *goals* that should be useful as a benchmark for aspiration and comparison. Even though individuals with adequate health support often fall ill, it still makes sense to compare societies by asking about actual health capabilities, because we assume that the comparison will reflect the different inputs of human planning and can be adjusted to take account of more and less favorable natural situations.

Earlier versions of the list appeared to diverge from the approach of Rawlsian liberalism by not giving as central a place as Rawls does to the traditional political rights and liberties—although the need to incorporate them was stressed from the start.[72] This version of the list corrects that defect of emphasis. These political liberties have a central importance in making well-being human. A society that aims at well-being while overriding these has delivered to its members a merely animal level of satisfaction.[73] As Amartya Sen has recently written, "Political rights are important not only for the fulfillment of needs, they are crucial also for the formulation of needs. And this idea relates, in the end, to the respect that we owe each other as fellow human beings."[74] This idea has recently been echoed by Rawls: Primary goods specify what citizens' needs are from the point of view of political justice.[75]

The capability view justifies its elaborate list by pointing out that choice is not pure spontaneity, flourishing independently of material and social conditions. If one cares about people's powers to choose a conception of the good, then one must care about the rest of the form of life that supports those powers, including its material conditions. Thus the approach claims that its more comprehensive concern with flourishing is perfectly consistent with the impetus behind the Rawlsian project, which has always insisted that we are not to rest content with merely formal equal liberty and opportunity but must pursue their fully equal worth by ensuring that unfavorable economic and social circumstances do not prevent people from availing themselves of liberties and opportunities that are formally open to them.

The guiding thought behind this Aristotelian enterprise is, at its heart, a profoundly liberal idea,[76] and one that lies at the heart of Rawls's project as well: the idea of the citizen as a free and dignified human being, a maker of choices, Politics has an urgent role to play here, getting citizens the tools they need, both to choose at all and to have a realistic option of exercising the most valuable functions. The choice of whether and how to use the tools, however, is left up to them, in the conviction that this is an essential aspect of respect for their freedom. They are seen not as passive recipients of social planning but as dignified beings who shape their own lives.[77]

Let us now return to the Marglins and to Metha Bai. What would this universalist approach have to say about these concrete cases? Notice how close the Marglin approach is, in its renunciation of critical normative argument, to the prevailing economic approaches of which it presents itself as a radical critique. A preference-based approach that gives priority to the preferences of dominant males in a traditional culture is likely to be especially subversive of the quality of life of women, who have been on the whole badly treated by prevailing traditional norms. And one can see this clearly in the Marglins's own examples. For menstruation taboos, even if endorsed by habit and custom, impose severe restrictions on women's power to form a plan of life and to execute the plan they have chosen.[78] They are members of the same family of traditional attitudes that make it difficult for women like Metha Bai to sustain the basic functions of life. Vulnerability to small-pox, even if someone other than an anthropologist should actually defend it as a good thing, is even more evidently a threat to human functioning. And the Japanese husband who allegedly renounces freedom of choice actually shows considerable attachment to it, in the ways that matter, by asking the woman to look after the boring details of life. What should concern us is whether the woman has a similar degree of freedom to plan her life and to execute her plan.

As for Metha Bai, the absence of freedom to choose employment outside the home is linked to other capability failures, in the areas of health, nutrition, mobility, education, and political voice. Unlike the type of liberal view that focuses on resources alone, my view enables us to focus directly on the obstacles to self-realization imposed by traditional norms and values and thus to justify special political action to remedy the unequal situation. No male of Metha Bai's caste would have to overcome threats of physical violence in order to go out of the house to work for life-sustaining food.

The capabilities approach insists that a woman's affiliation with a certain group or culture should not be taken as normative for her unless, on due consideration, with all the capabilities at her disposal, she makes that norm her own. We should take care to extend to each individual full capabilities to pursue the items on the list—and then see whether they want to avail themselves of those opportunities. Usually they do, even when tradition says they should not. Martha Chen's work with widows like Metha Bai reveals that they are already deeply critical of the cultural norms that determine their life quality. One week at a widows' conference in Bangalore was sufficient to cause these formerly secluded widows to put on forbidden colors and to apply for loans; one elderly woman, "widowed" at the age of seven, danced for the first time in her life, whirling wildly in the center of the floor.[79] In other cases, especially when a woman must negotiate a relationship with a surviving husband, it takes longer for her real affiliations and preferences to emerge. Chen's related study of a rural literacy project in Bangladesh[80] shows that it took a good deal of time for women previously illiterate to figure out, in consultation with development workers, that literacy might offer something to their own concrete lives. Nonetheless, what we do not see in any of these cases is the fantasy that the Marglins describe, a cultural monolith univocally repudiating the outsider and clinging to an "embedded way of life." Why should women cling to a tradition, indeed, when it is usually not their voice that speaks or their interests that are served?

VI. Answering the Objections:
Human Functioning and Pluralism

We still need to show that this approach has answers to the legitimate questions that confronted it. Concerning *neglect of historical and cultural difference,* we can begin by insisting that this normative conception of human capability is designed to make room for a reasonable pluralism in specification. The capabilities approach urges us to see common needs, problems, and capacities, but it also reminds us that each person and group faces these problems in a highly concrete context. The list claims to have identified in a very general way some components that are fundamental to any human life. But it makes room for differences of context in several ways. First, it is open ended and nonexhaustive. It does not say that these are the only important things, or that there is anything unimportant (far less, bad) about things not on the list. It just says that this is a group of especially important functions on which we can agree to focus for political purposes.

Further, the list allows in its very design for the possibility of multiple specifications of each of the components. Good public reasoning about the list will retain a rich sensitivity to the concrete context, to the characters of the agents and their social situation. Sometimes what is a good way of promoting education in one part of the world will be completely ineffectual in another. Forms of affiliation that flourish in one community may prove impossible to sustain in another. Arriving at the best specification will most reasonably be done by a public dialogue with those who are most deeply immersed in those conditions. We should use the list to criticize injustice, but we should not say anything at all without rich and full information.

We see this, for example, in Martha Chen's account of the Bangladeshi literacy project.[81] An initial approach that simply offered the women adult literacy materials met with no response. It was only after a period of "participatory dialogue," during which the local women told their stories and the development workers gave them rich narrative information about the lives of women elsewhere, that a picture of literacy for these women in these circumstances began to emerge and to make sense. Given the opportunity, they made for themselves a concrete local specification of this vague end. And it was clearly no external imposition: The women's narratives express a joy in self-command and agency that seems to come from something very deep in themselves. Rohima, of the West Shanbandha women's group, comments:

> Even my mother said yesterday: "You did not use to visit others' homes, did not speak to others. How have you learnt to speak so many things?" I said: "Ma, how I have learnt I cannot say. Whenever I am alone I sit with the books." Mother asked: "What do you see in the books?" I said: "Ma, what valuable things there are in the books you will not understand because you cannot read and write." If somebody behaves badly with me, I go home and sit with the books. When I sit with the books my mind becomes better.[82]

The books had to have some relation to the women's concrete situation, but it was equally important that the development workers did not back off when they saw that the women's local traditions contained no history of female literacy.

We can say the same of the related value of autonomy. It would have been very wrong to assume, with the Marglins, that these women did not want separateness and choice, that they really wanted to submerge their own aims in those of husband and family. This, again, emerges retrospectively, in their moving accounts of their newfound feeling of selfhood and mental awareness. "My mind was rusty," says one young wife, "and now it shines." On the other hand, it also would have done no good to go into that village and deliver a lecture on Kant—or on human capabilities! The universal value of practical reason and choice would have meant little in the abstract. To make sense, it had to become concretely situated in the stories they told about themselves and their lives.

If we turn to the difficult story of Metha Bai, something similar emerges. Metha Bai's is the story of age-old traditions regarding widowhood in India.[83] Any approach to her situation would have to be based on an understanding of these traditions and their special connection with issues of caste in an upwardly mobile Hindu family. Talk of "the right to work" would have been no use without a concrete local understanding. On the other hand, if the workers in the widows project had simply backed off, saying that the local values did not include a value of right to work for widows, they would have missed the depth at which Metha Bai herself longed for choice and autonomy, both as means to survival for herself and her children and as means to selfhood. These are typical examples of the fruitful ways in which an abstract value can be instantiated in a concrete situation, through rich local knowledge.

One further observation is in order. This objector is frequently worried about the way in which universalist projects may erode the values that hold communities together. We have already seen that traditional community values are not always so good for women. We can now add that universalist values build new types of community. All the women studied by Chen stressed the solidarity promoted by the literacy project, the comfort and pleasure they had in consulting with a group of women (some local, some from the development project) rather than each being isolated in the home. Mallika, a young widow in Dapunia, vigorously expresses this idea:

> The group helped us and taught us many things. I have learned how to live unitedly. Before if any rich person abused or criticized, we could not reply. But now if anybody says anything bad, we, the 17 members of the group, go together and ask that person why he or she passed this comment. This is another kind of help we have gotten. Before we did not know how to get together and help each other. . . . Each one was busy with their own

worries and sorrows, always thinking about food for their children and themselves. Now we, the 17 members of the group, have become very close to one another. [84]

This story is no isolated phenomenon. In women's groups I have visited in both India and China, the first benefit that is typically mentioned is that of affiliation and friendship with other women in pursuit of common goals. This shows us something highly pertinent to the Marglins's nostalgic tale of embeddedness. We do not have to choose between "the embedded life" of community and a deracinated type of individualism. Universal values build their own communities, communities of resourcefulness, friendship, and agency, embedded in the local scene but linked in complex ways to groups of women in other parts of the world. For these women the new community was a lot better than the one they had inhabited before.

The liberal charges the capability approach with *neglect of autonomy,* arguing that any such determinate conception removes from the citizens the chance to make their own choices about the good life. We have already said a good deal about this issue, but let us summarize, stressing three points. First, the list is a list of capabilities, not a list of actual functions, precisely because the conception is designed to leave room for choice. Government is not directed to push citizens into acting in certain valued ways; instead, it is directed to make sure that all human beings have the necessary resources and conditions for acting in those ways. By making opportunities available, government enhances, and does not remove, choice.[85] It will not always be easy to say at what point someone is really capable of making a choice, especially when there are traditional obstacles to functioning. Sometimes our best strategy may well be to look at actual functioning and infer negative capability (tentatively) from its absence.[86] But the conceptual distinction remains critical. Even in the rare case in which the approach will favor compulsory measures—particularly in primary and secondary education—it does so because of the huge role education plays in opening other choices in life.

Second, this respect for choice is built deeply into the list itself, in the role it gives to practical reasoning, to the political liberties, and also to employment, seen as a source of opportunity and empowerment. One of the most central capabilities promoted by the conception will be the capability of choosing itself.[87]

The examples we have considered show the truth of these claims. In the literacy project, a concern for autonomy was fundamental in the method of participatory dialogue itself, which constructed a situation free from intimidation and hierarchy in which the women's own concerns could gradually emerge and develop on the basis of the information they received. Their ex post facto satisfaction with their new situation, in which life choices were greatly enhanced, indicates, I believe, that the focus on a general capability goal was not a violation of their autonomy. (Rohima comments: "It is good now. . . . As my knowledge and understanding are good now, I will be able to do many things gradually."[88]) Indeed, we can see in the project as a whole the construction of full autonomy out of a more inchoate sense of the self. Metha Bai already had a robust sense of her own interests and how they diverged from the expectations of those around her. But the widows project, which extended her thoughts by providing information and advice, was crucial to the further development of her own conception of life.

Finally, the capability view insists that choice is not pure spontaneity, flourishing independently of material and social conditions. If one cares about autonomy, then one must care about the rest of the form of life that supports it and the material conditions that enable one to live that form of life. Thus, the approach claims that its own comprehensive concern with flourishing is a better way of promoting choice than is the liberal's narrower concern with spontaneity alone, which sometimes tolerates situations in which individuals are cut off from the fully human use of their faculties.

We now face the objection about *prejudicial application.* Catharine MacKinnon once claimed that "being a woman is not yet a way of being a human being."[89] As this remark suggests, most traditional ways of categorizing and valuing women have not accorded them full membership in the human species, as that species is generally defined. If this is so, one might well ask, of what use is it to identify a set of central human capabilities? For the basic (lower-level) capacity to develop these can always be denied to women, even by those who grant their centrality—for example, by denying women "rational nature," or by asserting that they are connected to dangerous or unclean animality. Does this problem show that the human function idea is either hopelessly in league with patriarchy or, at best, impotent as a tool for justice?

I believe that it does not. For if we examine the history of these denials we see, I believe, the great power of the conception of the human as a source of moral claims. Acknowledging the other person as a member of the very same kind would have generated a sense of affiliation and a set of moral and educational duties. That is why, to those bent on shoring up their own power, the stratagem of splitting the other off from one's own species seems so urgent and so seductive. But to deny humanness to beings with whom one lives in conversation and interaction is a fragile sort of self-deceptive stratagem, vulnerable to sustained and consistent reflection, and also to experiences that cut through self-deceptive rationalization. Any moral conception can be withheld, out of ambition or hatred or shame. But the conception of the human being, spelled out, as here, in a roughly determinate way, seems much harder to withhold than others that have been made the basis for ethics, such as "rational being" or "person."

VII. Women and Men: Two Norms or One?

But should there be a single norm of human functioning for men and women? One might grant that human capabilities cross cultures while still maintaining that in each culture a division of labor should be arranged along gender lines.

One such position, which I shall call Position A, assigns to both males and females the same general normative list of functions but suggests that males and females should exercise these functions in different spheres of life: men in the public sphere, for example, and women in the home. The second, which I shall call Position B, insists that the list of functions, even at a high level of generality, should be different: for men, citizenship and rational autonomy; for women, family love and care.

Position A is compatible with a serious interest in equality and in gender justice. For what it says, after all, is that males and females have the same basic needs for capability development and should get what they need. It is determined to ensure that both get to the higher (developed) level of capability with respect to all the central functions. It simply holds that this can (and perhaps should) be done in separate spheres. Is this any more problematic than to say that human functioning in India can, and even should, take a different concrete form from functioning in England? Or that some people can realize musical capacities by singing; others by playing the violin?

The trouble comes when we notice that Position A usually ends up endorsing a division of duties that is associated with traditional forms of hierarchy. Even Mill, who made so many fine arguments against women's subordination, did not sufficiently ask how the very perpetuation of separate spheres of responsibility might reinforce subordination. It is hard to find plausible reasons for perpetuating functional distinctions that coincide with traditional hierarchy. Even in the fourth century B.C.E., Plato was able to see that women's role in childbearing does not require, or even suggest, that women be confined to the home.[90] Advances in the control of reproduction are making this less and less plausible. The disability imposed by childbearing on a member of the labor force is to a large extent socially constructed, above all by the absence of support for child care, from the public sphere, from employers, and from male partners.

Sometimes clinging to traditional divisions is a prudent way of promoting social change. Neither Chen nor her colleagues proposed to jettison all gender divisions within the Bangladeshi villages. Instead, they found "female jobs" for the women that were somewhat more dignified and important than the old jobs, jobs that looked continuous with traditional female work but were outside the home and brought in wages. The "revolution" in women's quality of life never would have taken place but for the caution of the women, who at each stage gave the men of the village reason to believe that the transformations were not overwhelmingly threatening and were good for the well-being of the entire group. But such pragmatic decisions in the face of recalcitrant realities do not tell us how things ought to be. And it is likely that women's subordination will not be adequately addressed as long as women are confined to a sphere traditionally devalued, linked with a low "perceived well-being contribution."[91] The *Human Development Report's* Gender Empowerment Measure rightly focuses, therefore, on the ability of women to win entry into the traditional male spheres of politics and administration.

I turn, then, to Position B, which has been influentially defended by many philosophers, including Rousseau and some of his followers in today's world.[92] Insofar as B relies on the claim that there are two different sets of basic innate capacities, we should insist, with John Stuart Mill, that this claim has not been borne out by any responsible scientific evidence. Experiments that allegedly show strong gender divisions in basic (untrained) abilities have been shown to contain major scientific flaws; these flaws removed, the case for such differences is altogether inconclusive.[93] Experiments that cross-label babies as to sex have established that children are differentially handled, played with, and talked to straight from birth, in accordance with the handler's beliefs about the child's biological sex. It is therefore impossible at present to separate "nature" from "culture."[94] There may be innate differences between the sexes, but so far we are not in a position to know them—any more than we were when Mill first made that argument in 1869.[95]

Second, we should note that even what is claimed in this body of scientific material without substantiation usually does not amount to a difference in what I have been calling the central basic capabilities. What is alleged is usually a differential statistical distribution of some specific capacity for a high level of excellence, not for crossing a basic threshold, and excellence in some very narrowly defined function (say, geometrical ability), rather than in one of our large-scale capabilities such as the capability to perform practical reasoning. Thus, even if the claim were true it would not be a claim about capabilities in our capacious sense; nor, because it is a statistical claim, would it have any implications for the ways in which individuals should be treated. The political consequences of such alleged sex differences in our scheme of things, even had they been established, would be nil.

But we can also criticize Position B in a different way, arguing that the differentiated conceptions of male and female functioning characteristically put forward by B are internally inadequate and fail to give us viable norms of human flourishing.[96]

What do we usually find, in the versions of B that our philosophical tradition bequeaths to us? (Rousseau's view is an instructive example.) We have, on the one hand, males who are "autonomous," capable of practical reasoning, independent and self-sufficient, allegedly good at political deliberation. These males are brought up not to develop strong emotions of love and feelings of deep need that are associated with the awareness of one's own lack of self-sufficiency. For this reason they are not well equipped to care for the needs of their family members or, perhaps, even to notice those needs. On the other hand, we have females such as Rousseau's Sophie,[97] brought up to lack autonomy and self-respect, ill equipped to rely on her own practical reasoning, dependent on males, focused on pleasing others, and good at caring for others. Is either of these viable as a complete life for a human being?

It would seem not. The internal tensions in Rousseau's account are a good place to begin.[98] Rousseau places tremendous emphasis on compassion as a basic social motivation. He understands compassion to require fellow feeling and a keen responsiveness to the sufferings of others. And yet, in preparing Emile for autonomous citizenship, he ultimately gives emotional development short shrift, allocating caring and responsiveness to the female sphere alone. It appears likely that Emile will be not only an incomplete person but also a defective citizen, even by the standards of citizenship recognized by Rousseau himself.

With Sophie, things again go badly. Taught to care for others but not taught that her life is her own to plan, she lives under the sway of external influences and lacks self-government. As Rousseau himself shows in his fascinating narrative of the end of her life,[99] Sophie comes to a bad end through her lack of judgment. Moreover, in the process she proves to be a bad partner and deficient in love. For love, as we come to see, requires judgment and constancy. Thus each of them fails to live a complete human life, and each fails, too, to exemplify fully and well the very functions for which they were being trained, because those functions require support from other functions for which they were not trained. The text leads its thoughtful reader to the conclusion that the capabilities that have traditionally marked the separate male and female spheres are not separable from one another without a grave functional loss. Society cannot strive for completeness by simply adding one sphere to the other. It must strive to develop in each and every person the full range of the human capabilities.

This more inclusive notion of human functioning admits tragic conflict. For it insists on the separate value and the irreplaceable importance of a rich plurality of functions. And the world does not always guarantee that individuals will not be faced with painful choices among these functions, in which, in order to pursue one of them well they must neglect others (and thus, in many cases, subvert the one as well). But this shows once again, I believe, the tremendous importance of keeping some such list of the central functions before us as we assess the quality of life in the countries of the world and strive to raise it. For many such tragedies—like many cases of simple capability failure—result from unjust and unreflective social arrangements. One can try to construct a society in which the tragic choices that faced Emile and Sophie would not be necessary, in which both males and females could learn both to love and to reason.

In April 1994, Metha Bai went to Bangalore for the widows' conference. She met widows from all over India, and they spent a week discussing their common problems. During that week, Metha Bai began to smile a lot. She bought beads in the forbidden color of blue, and she seemed pleased with the way she looked. With advice from a local NGO involved in the conference, she applied for and obtained a loan that enabled her to pay off the mortgage on the small property she still owns. Although her economic situation is not secure and she still does not hold a job outside the home, she has managed to stave off hunger. Like many women all over the world, she is fighting for her life, with resilience and fortitude.

Women belong to cultures. But they do not choose to be born into any particular culture, and they do not really choose to endorse its norms as good for themselves, unless they do so in possession of further options and opportunities—including the opportunity to form communities of affiliation and empowerment with other women. The contingencies of where one is born, whose power one is afraid of, and what habits shape one's daily thought are chance events that should not be permitted to play the role they now play in pervasively shaping women's life chances. Beneath all these chance events are human powers, powers of choice and intelligent self-formation. Women in much of the world lack support for the most central human functions, and this denial of support is frequently caused by their being women. But women, unlike rocks and plants and even horses, have the potential to become capable of these human functions, given sufficient nutrition, education, and other support. That is why their unequal failure in capability is a problem of justice. It is up to all human beings to solve this problem. I claim that a conception of human functioning gives us valuable assistance as we undertake this task. ∎

NOTES

I have discussed the capabilities approach in several other papers, to which I shall refer: "Nature, Function, and Capability: Aristotle on Political Distribution," *Oxford Studies in Ancient Philosophy* Supplementary Volume 1 (1988), 145–84, hereafter NFC; "Aristotelian Social Democracy," in *Liberalism and the Good*, ed. R. B. Douglass *et al.* (New York: Routledge, 1990), 203–52, hereafter ASD; "Non-Relative Virtues: An Aristotelian Approach," in *The Quality of Life*, ed. M. Nussbaum and A. Sen (Oxford: Clarendon Press, 1993), hereafter NRV; "Aristotle on Human Nature and the Foundations of Ethics," in *World, Mind and Ethics: Essays on the Ethical Philosophy of Bernard Williams*, ed. J. E. J. Altham and Ross Harrison (Cambridge: Cambridge University Press, 1995), 86–131, hereafter HN; "Human Functioning and Social Justice: In Defense of Aristotelian Essentialism," *Political Theory 20* (1992), 202–46, hereafter HF; "Human Capabilities, Female Human Beings," in *Women, Culture, and Development*, ed. M. Nussbaum and J. Glover (Oxford: Clarendon Press, 1995), 61–104, hereafter HC; "The Good as Discipline, the Good as Freedom," in *The Ethics of Consumption and Global Stewardship*, ed. D. Crocker and T. Linden (Lanham, MD; Rowman and Littlefield, 1998), 312–41, hereafter GDGF; "Capabilities and Human Rights," *Fordham Law Review 66* (1997), 273–300, hereafter CHR.

1. For this case and others like it, see Martha Chen, "A Matter of Survival: Women's Rights to Employment in India and Bangladesh," in *Women, Culture, and Development* (hereafter WCD), ed. M. Nussbaum and J. Glover (Oxford: Clarendon Press, 1995), 37–57. See also M. Chen, *Perpetual Mourning: Widowhood in Rural India.* Delhi: Oxford University Press, 2000.

2. *Bradwell v. Illinois,* 83 U.S. (16 Wall.) 130 (1873).

3. *Carr v. Allison Gas Turbine Division, General Motors Corp.,* 32 F.3d 1007 (1994). Mary Carr won her case on appeal.

4. Martha Chen, *A Quiet Revolution: Women in Transition in Rural Bangladesh* (Cambridge, MA: Schenkman, 1983), 176.

5. *Human Development Report* (New York: United Nations Development Program, 1996) (hereafter *Report*); see also the 1995 *Report,* which focuses on gender. The countries in which women do best in life quality, according to the Gender Development Index (GDI), a measure using the same variables as the HDI (Human Development Index) but adjusted according to disparities between the sexes (see *Report,* 107, for the technical formulation) are, in order, Sweden, Canada, Norway, the United States, Finland, Iceland, Denmark, France, Australia, New Zealand, the Netherlands, Japan, Austria, the United Kingdom, and Belgium.

6. If we subtract the GDI rank from the HDI rank, we get –10 for Spain, –9 for Japan, 8 for Sweden, 10 for Denmark, and 4 for New Zealand.

7. These variables include percentage shares of administrative and managerial positions, percentage shares of professional and technical jobs, and percentage shares of parliamentary seats.

8. The ranking at the top: Norway, Sweden, Denmark, Finland, New Zealand, Canada, Germany, the Netherlands, the United States, Austria, Barbados, and Switzerland. Spain ranks 25; Japan, 37; France, 40; and Greece, 60.

9. These data are from the 1993 report; later reports disaggregate employment data into jobs of various specific kinds and no longer count unpaid agricultural labor as employment.

10. Again, these are 1993 data; the 1996 report gives the absolute percentages, which are, for these examples, Sierra Leone, 16.7%; Afghanistan, 13.5%; Sudan, 32%; Nepal, 13%. Nations in which the female literacy rate is strikingly out of step with the general level of economic development include Saudi Arabia, 47.6%; Algeria, 45.8%; Egypt, 37.0%; Iraq, 42.3%; Pakistan, 23.0%; and India, 36.0%. Striking progress in female literacy, on the other hand, if one can rely on the figures, has been made in Cuba, 94.6%; Sri Lanka, 86.2%; Philippines, 93.9%; and most of the former constituent states of the Soviet Union, in the 90s; Vietnam, 89.5%; and China, 70.9%. On the disparity of achievement between China and India, see Jean Drèze and Amartya Sen, *India: Economic Development and Social Opportunity* (Oxford: Clarendon Press, 1996).

11. Numbers of female students in tertiary education per 100,000 people: Hong Kong, 1,022; Barbados, 1,885; Republic of Korea, 2,866; Philippines, 3,140; Egypt, 499; China, 132; Iran, 764; Laos, 60; Pakistan, 149; Ethiopia, 24; and Rwanda, 19.

12. Countries where women hold a high percentage of parliamentary seats: Norway, 39.4%; Sweden, 40.4%; and Denmark, 33.0%. Bangladesh at 10.6% is ahead of the United States at 10.4%, and India at 8.0% is ahead of Japan at 6.7%.

13. The statistics in this paragraph are taken from Jean Drèze and Amartya Sen, *Hunger and Public Action* (Oxford: Clarendon Press, 1989).

14. This is very likely due to the central role women play in productive economic activity. For a classic study of this issue, see Esther Boserup, *Women's Role in Economic Development* (New York: St. Martin's Press, 1970), 2nd ed. (Aldershot: Gower Publishing, 1986). For a set of valuable responses to Boserup's work, see *Persistent Inequalities,* ed. Irene Tinker (New York: Oxford University Press, 1990).

15. See Drèze and Sen, 52.

16. See Drèze and Sen, *India.*

17. See Sen, "Gender and Cooperative Conflicts," in Tinker, 123–49.

18. See Drèze and Sen *India,* for graphic evidence of the relative independence of educational and health attainment from economic growth, in comparative regional studies.

19. Gary Becker, *A Treatise on the Family* (Cambridge, MA: Harvard University Press, 1981; 2nd ed. 1991).

20. See Sen, "Gender and Cooperative Conflicts"; Partha Dasgupta, *An Inquiry Into Well-Being and Destitution* (Oxford: Clarendon Press, 1993), chap. 11; on food allocation, see Lincoln C. Chen, E. Huq, and S. D'Souza, "Sex Bias in the Family Allocation of Food and Health Care in Rural Bangladesh," *Population and Development Review* 7 (1981), 55–70. Bargaining models of the family are now proliferating; for two valuable recent examples, see Shelly Lundberg and Robert A. Pollak, "Bargaining and Distribution in Marriage," *Journal of Economic Perspectives* 10 (1996), 139–58, and S. Lundberg, R. Pollak, and T. J. Wales, "Do Husbands and Wives Pool Their Resources? Evidence from the U. K. Child Benefit," *Journal of Human Resources* (forthcoming).

21. See, now, Gary Becker, "The Economic Way of Looking at Behavior," the Nobel Address 1992, in *The Essence of Becker,* ed. Ramón Febrero and Pedro S. Schwartz (Stanford, CA: Hoover Institution Press, 1995), 647, on the role of childhood experiences in shaping preferences.

22. Sen, "Gender and Cooperative Conflicts," argues that Becker's account is much stronger as an account of actual preferences in the household than as an account of the real interests (life and death, good and bad health, good and bad nutrition) that underlie the preferences. (He provides evidence that people's perception of their health and nutritional status may be severely distorted by informational deficiencies.)

23. Becker now admits deficiencies in the model: "Many economists, including me, have excessively relied on altruism to tie together the interests of family members." Motives of "obligation, anger, and other attitudes usually neglected by theories of rational behavior" should be added to the models. Becker, "The Economic Way of Looking at Behavior," 648. Elsewhere, Becker mentions guilt, affection, and fear—his example being a woman's habitual fear of physical abuse from men. Ibid., 647. It is unclear whether he still supports an organic one-actor model, with a more complicated motivational structure, or a "bargaining model," of the sort increasingly used by family economists. See Becker, *A Treatise on the Family.*

24. See Sen, "Gender and Cooperative Conflicts"; Jon Elster, *Sour Grapes* (Cambridge: Cambridge University Press, 1993).

25. See John Rawls, *A Theory of Justice* (hereafter TJ) (Cambridge, MA: Harvard University Press, 1970); *Political Liberalism* (hereafter PL) (New York: Columbia University Press, 1993, paper ed. 1996).

26. The "capabilities approach" was pioneered within economics by Amartya Sen and has been developed by both Sen and me in complementary but not identical ways. For an overview, see David Crocker, "Functioning and Capability: the Foundations of Sen's and Nussbaum's Development Ethic," in WCD, 152–98.

27. See Amartya Sen, "Equality of What?," in *Choice, Welfare, and Measurement* (Oxford: Basil Blackwell, 1982), 353–72; and Nussbaum, ASD.

28. Much of the material described in these examples is now published in *Dominating Knowledge: Development, Culture, and Resistance*, ed. Frédérique Apffel Marglin and Stephen A. Marglin (Oxford: Clarendon Press, 1990). The issue of "embeddedness" and menstruation taboos is discussed in S. A. Marglin, "Losing Touch: The Cultural Conditions of Worker Accommodation and Resistance," 217–82, and related issues are discussed in S. A. Marglin, "Toward the Decolonization of the Mind," 1–28. On Sittala Devi, see F. A. Marglin, "Smallpox in Two Systems of Knowledge," 102–44; and for related arguments see Ashis Nandy and Shiv Visvanathan, "Modern Medicine and Its Non-Modern Critics," 144–84. I have in some cases combined two conversations into one; otherwise things happened as I describe them.

29. For Sen's own account of the plurality and internal diversity of Indian values, one that strongly emphasizes the presence of a rationalist and critical strand in Indian traditions, see M. Nussbaum and A. Sen, "Internal Criticism and Indian Relativist Traditions, in *Relativism: Interpretation and Confrontation*, ed. M. Krausz (Notre Dame: Notre Dame University Press, 1989), 299–325 (an essay originally presented at the same WIDER conference and refused publication by the Marglins in its proceedings); and A. Sen, "India and the West," *The New Republic* June 7, 1993. See also Bimal K. Matilal, *Perception* (Oxford: Clarendon Press, 1995) (a fundamental study of Indian traditions regarding knowledge and logic); and B. K. Matilal, "Ethical Relativism and the Confrontation of Cultures," in Krausz, ed., *Relativism*, 339–62.

30. S. A. Marglin, "Toward the Decolonization," 22–3, suggests that binary thinking is peculiarly Western. But such oppositions are pervasive in Indian, Chinese, and African traditions (see HC). To deny them to a culture is condescending: for how can one utter a definite idea without bounding off one thing against another?

31. See Eric Hobsbawm and Terence Ranger, eds., *The Invention of Tradition* (Cambridge: Cambridge University Press, 1983). In his *New Republic* piece, Sen makes a similar argument about contemporary India: The Western construction of India as mystical and "other" serves the purposes of the fundamentalist Bharatiya Janata Party (BJP), who are busy refashioning history to serve the ends of their own political power. An eloquent critique of the whole notion of the "other" and of the associated "nativism," where Africa is concerned, can be found in Kwame Anthony Appiah, *In My Father's House: Africa in the Philosophy of Cultures* (New York: Oxford University Press, 1991).

32. The proceedings of this conference are now published as M. Nussbaum and A. Sen, eds., *The Quality of Life* (Oxford: Clarendon Press, 1993).

33. Marglin has since published this point in "Toward the Decolonization." His reference is to Takeo Doi, *The Anatomy of Dependence* (Tokyo: Kodansha, 1971).

34. See S. A. Marglin, "Toward the Decolonization."

35. See Nussbaum and Sen, "Internal Criticism," and A. Sen, "Human Rights and Asian Values," *The New Republic*, July 10/17, 1997, 33–40.

36. See Roop Rekha Verma, "Femininity, Equality, and Personhood," in WCD.

37. Satyajit Ray, "Introduction," *Our Films, Their Films* (Bombay: Orient Longman, 1976, reprinted New York: Hyperion, 1994), 5.

38. Personal communication, scholars in women's studies at the Chinese Academy of Social Sciences, June 1995.

39. Note that this objection itself seems to rely on some universal values such as fairness and freedom from bias.

40. See HF for a longer version of this discussion.

41. Aristotle, *Nicomachean Ethics* VIII.I. I discuss this passage in HN and NRV.

42. "If my sisters and I were 'children of two worlds,' no one bothered to tell us this; we lived in one world, in two 'extended' families divided by several thousand miles and an allegedly insuperable cultural distance that never, so far as I can recall, puzzled or perplexed us much." Appiah, vii–viii. Appiah's argument does not neglect distinctive features of concrete histories; indeed, one of its purposes is to demonstrate how varied, when concretely seen, histories really are. But his argument, like mine, seeks a subtle balance between perception of the particular and recognition of the common.

43. This point is made by the Marglins, as well as by liberal thinkers, but can they consistently make it while holding that freedom of choice is just a parochial Western value? It would appear not; on the other hand, F. A. Marglin (here differing, I believe, from S. A. Marglin) also held in oral remarks delivered at the 1986 conference that logical consistency is simply a parochial Western value.

44. See Noam Chomsky, in *Cartesian Linguistics* (New York: Harper and Row, 1966). Chomsky argues that Cartesian rationalism, with its insistence on innate essences, was politically more progressive, more hostile to slavery and imperialism, than empiricism, with its insistence that people were just what experience had made of them.

45. The use of this term does not imply that the functions all involve doing something especially "active." See here A. Sen, "Capability and Well-Being," in *The Quality of Life*, ed. M. Nussbaum and A. Sen (Oxford: Clarendon Press, 1993), 30–53. In Aristotelian terms, and in mine, being healthy, reflecting, and being pleased are all "activities."

46. For further discussion of this point, and for examples, see HN.

47. Could one cease to be one's individual self without ceasing to be human? Perhaps, in cases of profound personality or memory change, but I shall leave such cases to one side here. This is ruled out, I think, in Aristotle's conception but is possible in some other metaphysical conceptions.

48. See HN for a more extended account of this procedure and how it justifies.

49. Nor does it deny that experience of the body is shaped by culture. See NRV.

50. Rawls, TJ, 90–95, 396–7.

51. This was implicit in ASD but has become more prominent in recent essays. See A. Sen, "Freedoms and Needs," *New Republic,* January 10/17, 1994, 31–38; Nussbaum GDGF.

52. In ASD I call it "the thick vague theory of the good."

53. Rawls, PL. Note that the consensus is defined in terms of a normative notion of reasonableness. Thus, the failure of some real individuals to agree will not be fatal to the view.

54. On this relationship, see HN.

55. The current version of this list reflects changes suggested to me by discussions during my visits to women's development projects in India. These include a new emphasis on bodily integrity, on employment, on property rights, and on dignity and nonhumiliation.

56. Although "normal length" is clearly relative to current human possibilities and may need, for practical purposes, to be to some extent relativized to local conditions, it seems important to think of it—at least at a given time in history—in universal and comparative terms, as the *Human Development Report* does, to give rise to complaint in a country that has done well with some indicators of life quality but badly on life expectancy. And although some degree of relativity may be put down to the differential

genetic possibilities of different groups (the "missing women" statistics, for example, allow that on the average women live somewhat longer than men), it is also important not to conclude prematurely that inequalities between groups—for example, the growing inequalities in life expectancy between blacks and whites in the United States—are simply genetic variation, not connected with social injustice.

57. The precise specification of these health rights is not easy, but the work currently being done on them in drafting new constitutions in South Africa and Eastern Europe gives reasons for hope that the combination of a general specification of such a right with a tradition of judicial interpretation will yield something practicable. It should be noticed that I speak of health, not just health care; and health itself interacts in complex ways with housing, with education, with dignity. Both health and nutrition are controversial as to whether the relevant level should be specified universally, or relatively to the local community and its traditions. For example, is low height associated with nutritional practices to be thought of as "stunting" or as felicitous adaptation to circumstances of scarcity? For an excellent summary of this debate, see S. R. Osmani, ed., *Nutrition and Poverty* (Oxford: Clarendon Press, WIDER series, 1990), especially the following papers on: the relativist side, T. N. Srinivasan, "Undernutrition: Concepts, Measurements, and Policy Implications," 97–120; on the universalist side, C. Gopalan, "Undernutrition: Measurement and Implications," 17–48; for a compelling adjudication of the debate, coming out on the universalist side, see Osmani, "On Some Controversies in the Measurement of Undernutrition," 121–61.

58. There is a growing literature on the importance of shelter for health; for example, that the provision of adequate housing is the single largest determinant of health status for HIV-infected persons. Housing rights are increasingly coming to be constitutionalized, at least in a negative form—giving squatters grounds for appeal, for example, against a landlord who would bulldoze their shanties. On this as a constitutional right, see proposed Articles 11, 12, and 17 of the South African Constitution, in a draft put forward by the African National Congress (ANC) committee adviser Albie Sachs, where this is given as an example of a justiciable housing right.

59. Some form of intimate family love is central to child development, but this need not be the traditional Western nuclear family. In the development of citizens it is crucial that the family be an institution characterized by justice as well as love. See Susan Moller Okin, *Justice, Gender, and the Family* (New York: Basic Books, 1989).

60. In terms of cross-cultural discussion, this item has proven the most controversial and elusive on the list. It also properly raises the question whether the list ought to be anthropocentric at all, or whether we should seek to promote appropriate capabilities for all living things. I leave further argument on these questions for another occasion.

61. ASD argues that property rights are distinct from, for example, speech rights, in the sense that property is a tool of human functioning and not an end in itself. See also Nussbaum, CHR.

62. Sen has not endorsed any such specific list of the capabilities.

63. See Sen, "Gender Inequality and Theories of Justice," in WCD, 259–73; Becker, "The Economic Way of Looking at Behavior."

64. With Sen, I hold that the capability set should be treated as an interlocking whole. For my comments on his arguments, see NFC.

65. See ibid., with reference to Aristotle.

66. See HN. This is the core of Marx's reading of Aristotle.

67. See chapter 4 in *Sex and Social Justice*. New York: Oxford University Press, 1999.

68. See NFC, referring to Aristotle's similar distinctions.

69. This distinction is related to Rawls's distinction between social and natural primary goods. Whereas he holds that only the social primary goods should be on the list, and not the natural (such as health, imagination), we say that *the social basis of* the natural primary goods should most emphatically be on the list.

70. TJ, 62.

71. Rawls comments that "although their possession is influenced by the basic structure, they are not so directly under its control." TJ, 62. This is of course true if we are thinking of health, but if we think of the social basis of health, it is not true. It seems to me that the case for putting these items on the political list is just as strong as the case for the social basis of self-respect. In "The Priority of Right and Ideas of the Good," *Philosophy and Public Affairs* 17 (1988), 251–76, Rawls suggests putting health on the list.

72. See ASD and GDGF.

73. See HN. For the relation of capabilities to human rights, see CHR.

74. Sen, "Freedoms and Needs," 38.

75. PL 187–8.

76. Though in one form Aristotle had it too. See also GDGF; and CHR.

77. Compare Sen, "Freedoms and Needs," 38: "The importance of political rights for the understanding of economic needs turns ultimately on seeing human beings as people with rights to exercise, not as parts of a 'stock' or a 'population' that passively exists and must be looked after. What matters, finally, is how we see each other."

78. Chapter 3 (in *Sex and Social Justice*) argues that religious norms should not be imposed without choice on individuals who may not have opted for that religious tradition. In that sense, any religiously based employment restriction is questionable.

79. Chen, *The Lives of Widows in Rural India*. Girls in some regions of India are betrothed at a very young age and at that point become members of their husband's family, although the marriage will not be consummated until puberty. Such a girl is treated as widowed even if the male dies before consummation.

80. Chen, *A Quiet Revolution*.

81. Ibid.

82. Ibid., 202. Married at age seven, abandoned by her husband many years later, Rohima lives with her brother. Four of her children have died; one son and one daughter survive. Her son gives her some financial support.

83. See the account of these in Chen, *The Lives of Widows*.

84. Chen, *A Quiet Revolution*, 216.

85. Sen has stressed this throughout his writing on the topic. For an overview, see "Capability and Well-Being." And for some complications, see GDGF.

86. This is the strategy used by Robert Erikson's Swedish team when studying inequalities in political participation. See Robert Erikson, "Descriptions of Inequality," in Nussbaum and Sen, eds., *The Quality of Life*.

87. Rawls proceeds in a similar way, insisting that satisfactions that are not the outgrowth of one's very own choices have no moral worth. He conceives of the "two moral powers" (analogous to our practical reasoning) and of sociability (corresponding to our affiliation) as built into the definition of the parties in the original position, and thus as necessary constraints on any outcome they will select. See ASD.

88. Chen, *A Quiet Revolution*, 199.

89. The remark was cited by Richard Rorty in "Feminism and Pragmatism," *Michigan Quarterly Review* 30 (1989), 263; it has since been confirmed and repeated by MacKinnon herself.

90. Plato, *Republic*, Book V. Although Plato's proposal is theoretical and utopian, it is closely based on observation of the functioning of women in Sparta. See S. Halliwell, *Plato: Republic V* (Warminster: Aris & Phillips, 1994).

91. See Sen, "Gender and Cooperative Conflicts."

92. On Rousseau, see Susan Moller Okin, *Women in Western Political Thought* (Princeton: Princeton University Press, 1979), and Jane Roland Martin, *Reclaiming a Conversation* (New Haven: Yale University Press, 1985). On some related recent arguments, for example, those of Allan Bloom, see Okin, *Justice*, chap. 1.

93. See the convincing summary in Anne Fausto-Sterling, *Myths of Gender*, 2nd ed. (New York: Basic Books, 1992).

94. Ibid.

95. John Stuart Mill, *The Subjection of Women* (1869), ed. Susan Moller Okin (Indianapolis, IN: Hackett, 1988).

96. Here I am in agreement with the general line of argument in Okin, *Women*, and Martin, *Reclaiming*, and with the related arguments in Nancy Chodorow, *The Reproduction of Mothering* (Berkeley: University of California Press, 1978).

97. Jean-Jacques Rousseau, *Emile: or On Education*, trans. Allan Bloom (New York: Basic Books, 1979), Book V.

98. See Okin, *Women*; and Martin, *Reclaiming*.

99. See the discussion in Okin, *Women*.

■ *QUESTIONS FOR MAKING CONNECTIONS WITHIN THE READING* ■

1. Martha Nussbaum takes issue with the ideas of "tradition," "custom," and "culture." To what, specifically, does she object about these ideas? Does she want simply to define the terms themselves in a rather different way, or does she actually believe that there really are no such things as traditions, customs, and cultures?

2. In Nussbaum's discussion of several recent academic conferences, she goes out of her way to emphasize that her opponents are "leftists" or "leftwing." What does the term *left* mean in the context of her argument? Is Nussbaum philosophically unsympathetic to the goals of the left? Would you describe her as a rightist—that is, a political or cultural conservative?

3. Why would anyone object to universalism? Some readers may find Nussbaum's argument so compelling that the position of her opponents might sound unreasonable, even absurd. What arguments might be offered in defense of "otherness"? When considered sympathetically, are the arguments for "otherness" as flat-footed as Nussbaum implies? Can we safely

infer from the success of our society's values that they will offer the same good service in all other places at all other times? Does Nussbaum say that they will?

■ *QUESTIONS FOR WRITING* ■

1. Nussbaum often uses the pronoun *we*, as she does in this passage:

   > We recognize other humans as human across many differences of time and place, of custom and appearance. We often tell ourselves stories, on the other hand, about anthropomorphic creatures who do not get classified as human, on account of some feature of their form of life and functioning. On what do we base these inclusions and exclusions? In short, what do we believe must be there, if we are going to acknowledge that a given life is human?

   Who is Nussbaum's "we," here and throughout the selection? Nussbaum's opponents would allege that her "we" is a false universal: it ostensibly represents everyone but actually represents only educated, white, and relatively wealthy people living in the West. Does this argument seem fair to you? Does such a criticism make it impossible to offer general insights of any kind about human experience?

2. What does Nussbaum mean when she says that her list of "Central Human Functional Capabilities" is "proposed as the object of a specifically political consensus"? Why a *political* consensus? What difference does it make if we understand our obligations to others as political in nature rather than as, say, the product of divine revelation or pure reason? Does Nussbaum imply that the list can grow or shrink over time? If the items on the list can change, in what sense does it remain "universal"?

■ *QUESTIONS FOR MAKING CONNECTIONS BETWEEN READINGS* ■

1. What might Nussbaum learn from reading Deborah Tannen? One question that might arise for Nussbaum is whether our own institutions—especially the educational system—discourage in unacknowledged ways the growth of the "central capabilities." Drawing from your own experience as well as from Tannen's observations, would you conclude that the "argument culture" poses a significant barrier to the achievement of a good life? As you explore this question, consider as well the character of Nussbaum's reasoning. Does she participate in the argument culture? If Nussbaum does, would you say that she undermines her own credibility? Or could it be that the argument culture is less damaging than Tannen assumes?

2. Once humans have been cloned, will it make sense to talk about "central human functional capabilities"? Once humans begin to receive transplants from genetically engineered, cloned animals, will the very meaning of what it means to be human be fundamentally altered? Drawing on Ian Wilmut's discussion of the cloning process, consider the value and applicability of Nussbaum's ideas once cloning becomes a viable option for manufacturing animal donors and for creating human clones. Does the notion of "central human functional capabilities" require that cloning research be curtailed or encouraged?

For additional suggestions about making connections between readings, visit the Link-O-Mat and More Sample Assignments at <www.newhum.com>.

HENRY PETROSKI

HENRY PETROSKI is the Aleksandar S. Vesic Professor of Civil Engineering and a professor of history at Duke University. A recent review declared Petroski "the Stephen Jay Gould of civil engineering" for his ability to make the ideas and concerns of the engineering profession accessible to the lay public. This interest in improving communication between the engineering community and those who live in the world that engineers have helped design is present in all eight books by Petroski. Indeed, Petroski was compelled to write his first book, *To Engineer Is Human: The Role of Failure in Successful Design* (1982), because he wanted to better answer the questions that those outside the engineering profession posed to him whenever a bridge or building collapsed: Why do structures fail, and why can't engineers prevent these catastrophes from happening?

In the selections included here, "Being Human" and "Lessons from Play; Lessons from Life," Petroski explores the role that structural failure inevitably plays in the design process—an exploration that Petroski has pursued throughout his career. Whether writing about a seemingly mundane object like the pencil, as he did in *The Pencil: A History of Design and Circumstance* (1992), or about grander engineering achievements involving concrete and steel, as he did in *Engineers of Dreams: Great Bridge Builders and the Spanning of America* (1996), Petroski's overarching concern is both to demystify and to rehumanize the process of designing, testing, and improving the structures that have made modernity possible. For Petroski, bridges and skyscrapers are such structures, but so too are pencils, books, and educational toys: all have been designed to improve the functioning of civil society and the quality of life of its members. While technological advances will change how engineers go about their work in the future,

Petroski, Henry. "Being Human" and "Lessons from Play; Lessons from Life." *To Engineer Is Human.* New York: Vintage, 1982. 1–10, 21–34.

Biographical information from Henry Petroski's home page <http://www-cee.egr.duke. edu/people/faculty/petroski.shtml> and Henry Petroski, interview by Sloan Career Cornerstone <http://www.careercornerstone.org/video/asce/dslpetroski.html>; quotations from Eric Schatzberg review of Invention by Design: How Engineers Get from Thought to Thing by Henry Petroski, Technology and Culture 40 (1999): 152–154 <http://muse.jhu.edu/ demo/tech/40.1br_petroski.html> and Henry Petroski, interview by Sloan Career Cornerstone <http://www.careercornerstone.org/video/asce/dslpetroski.html>.

what won't change, Petroski believes, "is the method that engineering students learn, the method of how to approach problems and how to solve problems." It is through mastering this method, Petroski insists, that engineers—and those who live in the world engineers have designed—realize their human potential.

To learn more about Henry Petroski and the design process, visit the Link-O-Mat at <www.newhum.com>.

■ ■

Selections from
To Engineer Is Human

Being Human

Shortly after the Kansas City Hyatt Regency Hotel skywalks collapsed in 1981, one of my neighbors asked me how such a thing could happen. He wondered, did engineers not even know enough to build so simple a structure as an elevated walkway? He also recited to me the Tacoma Narrows Bridge collapse, the American Airlines DC-10 crash in Chicago, and other famous failures, throwing in a few things he had heard about hypothetical nuclear power plant accidents that were sure to exceed Three Mile Island in radiation release, as if to present an open-and-shut case that engineers did not quite have the world of their making under control.

I told my neighbor that predicting the strength and behavior of engineering structures is not always so simple and well-defined an undertaking as it might at first seem, but I do not think that I changed his mind about anything with my abstract generalizations and vague apologies. As I left him tending his vegetable garden and continued my walk toward home, I admitted to myself that I had not answered his question because I had not conveyed to him what engineering is. Without doing that I could not hope to explain what could go wrong with the products of engineering. In the years since the Hyatt Regency disaster I have thought a great deal about how I might explain the next technological embarrassment to an inquiring layman, and I have looked for examples not in the esoteric but in the commonplace. But I have also learned that collections of examples, no matter how vivid, no more make an explanation than do piles of beams and girders make a bridge.

Engineering has as its principal object not the given world but the world that engineers themselves create. And that world does not have the constancy of a honeycomb's design, changeless through countless generations of honeybees, for human structures involve constant and rapid evolution. It is not simply that we like change for the sake of change, though some may say that is reason enough. It is that human tastes, resources, and ambitions do not stay constant. We humans like our structures to be as fashionable as our art; we like extravagance when we are well off, and we grudgingly economize when times are not so good. And we like bigger, taller, longer things in ways that honeybees do not or cannot. All of these extra-engineering considerations make the task of the engineer perhaps more exciting and certainly less routine than that of an insect. But this constant change also introduces many more aspects to the design and analysis of engineering structures than there are in the structures of unimproved nature, and constant change means that there are many more ways in which something can go wrong.

Engineering is a human endeavor and thus it is subject to error. Some engineering errors are merely annoying, as when a new concrete building develops cracks that blemish it as it settles; some errors seem humanly unforgivable, as when a bridge collapses and causes the death of those who had taken its soundness for granted. Each age has had its share of technological annoyances and structural disasters, and one would think engineers might have learned by now from their mistakes how to avoid them. But recent years have seen some of the most costly structural accidents in terms of human life, misery, and anxiety, so that the record presents a confusing image of technological advancement that may cause some to ask, "Where is our progress?"

Any popular list of technological horror stories usually comprises the latest examples of accidents, failures, and flawed products. This catalog changes constantly as new disasters displace the old, but almost any list is representative of how varied the list itself can be. In 1979, when accidents seemed to be occurring left and right, anyone could rattle off a number of technological embarrassments that were fresh in everyone's mind, and there was no need to refer to old examples like the Tacoma Narrows Bridge to make the point. It seemed technology was running amok, and editorial pages across the country were anticipating the damage that might occur as the orbiting eighty-five-ton Skylab made its unplanned reentry. Many of the same newspapers also carried the cartoonist Tony Auth's solution to the problem. His cartoon shows the falling Skylab striking a flying DC-10, itself loaded with Ford Pintos fitted with Firestone 500 tires, with the entire wreckage falling on Three Mile Island, where the fire would be extinguished with asbestos hair dryers.

While such a variety may be unique to our times, the failure of the products of engineering is not. Almost four thousand years ago a number of

Babylonian legal decisions were collected in what has come to be known as the Code of Hammurabi, after the sixth ruler of the First Dynasty of Babylon. There among nearly three hundred ancient cuneiform inscriptions governing matters like the status of women and drinking-house regulations are several that relate directly to the construction of dwellings and the responsibility for their safety:

> If a builder build a house for a man and do not make its construction firm, and the house which he has built collapse and cause the death of the owner of the house, that builder shall be put to death.
>
> If it cause the death of the son of the owner of the house, they shall put to death a son of that builder.
>
> If it cause the death of a slave of the owner of the house, he shall give to the owner of the house a slave of equal value.
>
> If it destroy property, he shall restore whatever it destroyed, and because he did not make the house which he built firm and it collapsed, he shall rebuild the house which collapsed from his own property.
>
> If a builder build a house for a man and do not make its construction meet the requirements and a wall fall in, that builder shall strengthen the wall at his own expense.

This is a far cry from what happened in the wake of the collapse of the Hyatt Regency walkways, subsequently found to be far weaker than the Kansas City Building Code required. Amid a tangle of expert opinions, $3 billion in lawsuits were filed in the months after the collapse of the skywalks. Persons in the hotel the night of the accident were later offered $1,000 to sign on the dotted line, waiving all subsequent claims against the builder, the hotel, or anyone else they might have sued. And today opinions as to guilt or innocence in the Hyatt accident remain far from unanimous. After twenty months of investigation, the U.S. attorney and the Jackson County, Missouri, prosecutor jointly announced that they had found no evidence that a crime had been committed in connection with the accident. The attorney general of Missouri saw it differently, however, and he charged the engineers with "gross negligence." The engineers involved stand to lose their professional licenses but not their lives, but the verdict is still not in as I write three years after the accident.

The Kansas City tragedy was front-page news because it represented the largest loss of life from a building collapse in the history of the United States. The fact that it was news attests to the fact that countless buildings and structures, many with designs no less unique or daring than that of the hotel, are unremarkably safe. Estimates of the probability that a particular reinforced concrete or steel building in a technologically advanced country like the United States or England will fail in a given year range from one in a million to one in a hundred trillion, and the probability of death from a structural failure is approximately one in ten million per year. This is equivalent to a total of about twenty-five deaths per year in the United States, so that 114 persons killed in one accident in Kansas City was indeed news.

Automobile accidents claim on the order of fifty thousand American lives per year, but so many of these fatalities occur one or two at a time that they fail to create a sensational impact on the public. It seems to be only over holiday weekends, when the cumulative number of individual auto deaths reaches into the hundreds, that we acknowledge the severity of this chronic risk in our society. Otherwise, if an auto accident makes the front page or the evening news it is generally because an unusually large number of people or a person of note is involved. While there may be an exception if the dog is famous, the old saying that "dog bites man" is not news but that "man bites dog" is, applies.

We are both fascinated by and uncomfortable with the unfamiliar. When it was a relatively new technology, many people eschewed air travel for fear of a crash. Even now, when aviation relies on a well-established technology, many adults who do not think twice about the risks of driving an automobile are apprehensive about flying. They tell each other old jokes about white-knuckle air travelers, but younger generations who have come to use the airplane as naturally as their parents used the railroad and the automobile do not get the joke. Theirs is the rational attitude, for air travel *is* safe, the 1979 DC-10 crash in Chicago notwithstanding. Two years after that accident, the Federal Aviation Administration was able to announce that in the period covering 1980 and 1981, domestic airlines operated without a single fatal accident involving a large passenger jet. During the period of record, over half a billion passengers flew on ten million flights. Experience has proven that the risks of technology are very controllable.

However, as wars make clear, government administrations value their fiscal and political health as well as the lives of their citizens, and sometimes these objectives can be in conflict. The risks that engineered structures pose to human life and environments pose to society often conflict with the risks to the economy that striving for absolute and perfect safety would bring. We all know and daily make the trade-offs between our own lives and our pocketbooks, such as when we drive economy-sized automobiles that are incontrovertibly less safe than heavier-built ones. The introduction of seat belts, impact-absorbing bumpers, and emission-control devices have contributed to reducing risks, but gains like these have been achieved at a price to the consumer. Further improvements will take more time to perfect and will add still more to the price of a car, as the development of the air bag system has demonstrated. Thus there is a constant tension between manufacturers and consumer advocates to produce safe cars at reasonable prices.

So it is with engineering and public safety. All bridges and buildings could be built ten times as strong as they presently are, but at a tremendous increase in cost, whether financed by taxes or private investment. And, it would be argued, why ten times stronger? Since so few bridges and buildings

collapse now, surely ten times stronger would be structural overkill. Such ul-
traconservatism would strain our economy and make our built environment
so bulky and massive that architecture and style as we know them would
have to undergo radical change. No, it would be argued, ten times is too much
stronger. How about five? But five might also arguably be considered too
strong, and a haggling over numbers representing no change from the present
specifications and those representing five- or a thousand-percent improvement in strength might go on for as long as Zeno imagined it would take him
to get from here to there. But less-developed countries may not have the luxury to argue about risk or debate paradoxes, and thus their buildings and boil-
ers can be expected to collapse and explode with what appears to us to be uncommon frequency.

Callous though it may seem, the effects of structural reliability can be
measured not only in terms of cost in human lives but also in material terms.
This was done in a recent study conducted by the National Bureau of Standards with the assistance of Battelle Columbus Laboratories. The study
found that fracture, which included such diverse phenomena as the breaking of eyeglasses, the cracking of highway pavement, the collapse of
bridges, and the breakdown of machinery, costs well over $100 billion annu-
ally, not only for actual but also for anticipated replacement of broken parts
and for structural insurance against parts breaking in the first place. Primarily associated with the transportation and construction industries, many of
these expenses arise through the prevention of fracture by overdesign (making things heavier than otherwise necessary) and maintenance (watching for
cracks to develop), and through the capital equipment investment costs involved in keeping spare parts on hand in anticipation of failures. The 1983
report further concludes that the costs associated with fracture could be
reduced by one half by our better utilizing available technology and by
improved techniques of fracture control expected from future research and
development.

Recent studies of the condition of our infrastructure—the water supply
and sewer systems, and the networks of highways and bridges that we by
and large take for granted—conclude that it has been so sorely neglected in
many areas of the country that it would take billions upon billions of dollars
to put things back in shape. (Some estimates put the total bill as high as $3
trillion.) This condition resulted in part from maintenance being put off to
save money during years when energy and personnel costs were taking
ever-larger slices of municipal budget pies. Some water pipes in large cities
like New York are one hundred or more years old, and they were neither designed nor expected to last forever. Ideally, such pipes should be replaced on
an ongoing basis to keep the whole water supply system in a reasonably
sound condition, so that sudden water main breaks occur very infrequently.
Such breaks can have staggering consequences, as when a main installed in
1915 broke in 1983 in midtown Manhattan and flooded an underground

power station, causing a fire. The failure of six transformers interrupted electrical service for several days. These happened to be the same days of the year that ten thousand buyers from across the country visited New York's garment district to purchase the next season's lines. The area covered by the blackout just happened to be the blocks containing the showrooms of the clothing industry, so that there was mayhem where there would ordinarily have been only madness. Financial losses due to disrupted business were put in the millions.

In order to understand how engineers endeavor to insure against such structural, mechanical, and systems failures, and thereby also to understand how mistakes can be made and accidents with far-reaching consequences can occur, it is necessary to understand, at least partly, the nature of engineering design. It is the process of design, in which diverse parts of the "given-world" of the scientist and the "made-world" of the engineer are reformed and assembled into something the likes of which Nature had not dreamed, that divorces engineering from science and marries it to art. While the practice of engineering may involve as much technical experience as the poet brings to the blank page, the painter to the empty canvas, or the composer to the silent keyboard, the understanding and appreciation of the process and products of engineering are no less accessible than a poem, a painting, or a piece of music. Indeed, just as we all have experienced the rudiments of artistic creativity in the childhood masterpieces our parents were so proud of, so we have all experienced the essence of structural engineering in our learning to balance first our bodies and later our blocks in ever more ambitious positions. We have learned to endure the most boring of cocktail parties without the social accident of either our bodies or our glasses succumbing to the force of gravity, having long ago learned to crawl, sit up, and toddle among our tottering towers of blocks. If we could remember those early efforts of ours to raise ourselves up among the towers of legs of our parents and their friends, then we can begin to appreciate the task and the achievements of engineers, whether they be called builders in Babylon or scientists in Los Alamos. For all of their efforts are to one end: to make something stand that has not stood before, to reassemble Nature into something new, and above all to obviate failure in the effort.

Because man is fallible, so are his constructions, however. Thus the history of structural engineering, indeed the history of engineering in general, may be told in its failures as well as in its triumphs. Success may be grand, but disappointment can often teach us more. It is for this reason that hardly a history can be written that does not include the classic blunders, which more often than not signal new beginnings and new triumphs. The Code of Hammurabi may have encouraged sound construction of reproducible dwellings, but it could not have encouraged the evolution of the house, not to mention the skyscraper and the bridge, for what builder would have found incentive in the code to build what he believed to be a better but untried house? This is not to say that engineers should be given license to experiment with abandon, but rather to recognize that human nature appears to want to go beyond the past, in building as in art, and that engineering is a human endeavor.

When I was a student of engineering I came to fear the responsibility that I imagined might befall me after graduation. How, I wondered, could I ever be perfectly sure that something I might design would not break or collapse and kill a number of people? I knew my understanding of my textbooks was less than total, my homework was seldom without some sort of error, and my grades were not straight As. This disturbed me for some time, and I wondered why my classmates, both the A and C students, were not immobilized by the same phobia. The topic never came to the surface of our conversations, however, and I avoided confronting the issue by going to graduate school instead of taking an engineering job right away. Since then I have come to realize that my concern was not unique among engineering students, and indeed many if not all students have experienced self-doubts about success and fears of failure. The medical student worries about losing a patient, the lawyer about losing a crucial case. But if we all were to retreat with our phobias from our respective jobs and professions, we could cause exactly what we wish to avoid. It is thus that we practice whatever we do with as much assiduousness as we can command, and we hope for the best. The rarity of structural failures attests to the fact that engineering at least, even at its most daring, is not inclined to take undue risks.

The question, then, should not only be why do structural accidents occur but also why not more of them? Statistics show the headline-grabbing failure to be as rare as its newsworthiness suggests it to be, but to understand why the risk of structural failure is not absolutely zero, we must understand the unique engineering problem of designing what has not existed before. By understanding this we will come to appreciate not only why the probability of failure is so low but also how difficult it might be to make it lower. While it is theoretically possible to make the number representing risk as close to zero as desired, human nature in its collective and individual manifestations seems to work against achieving such a risk-free society.

Lessons from Play; Lessons from Life

When I want to introduce the engineering concept of fatigue to students, I bring a box of paper clips to class. In front of the class I open one of the paper clips flat and then bend it back and forth until it breaks in two. That, I tell the class, is failure by fatigue, and I point out that the number of back and forth cycles it takes to break the paper clip depends not only on how strong the clip is but also on how severely I bend it. When paper clips are used normally, to clip a few sheets of paper together, they can withstand perhaps thousands or millions of the slight openings and closings it takes to put them on and take them off the papers, and thus we seldom experience their breaking. But when paper clips are bent open so wide that they look as if we want them to hold all the pages of a book together, it might take only ten or twenty flexings to bring them to the point of separation.

Having said this, I pass out a half dozen or so clips to each of the students and ask them to bend their clips to breaking by flexing them as far open and as far closed as I did. As the students begin this low-budget experiment, I prepare at the blackboard to record how many back and forth bendings it takes to break each paper clip. As the students call out the numbers, I plot them on a bar graph called a histogram. Invariably the results fall clearly under a bell-shaped normal curve that indicates the statistical distribution of the results, and I elicit from the students the explanations as to why not all the paper clips broke with the same number of bendings. Everyone usually agrees on two main reasons: not all paper clips are equally strong, and not every student bends his clips in exactly the same way. Thus the students recognize at once the phenomenon of fatigue and the fact that failure by fatigue is not a precisely predictable event.

Many of the small annoyances of daily life are due to predictable—but not precisely so—fractures from repeated use. Shoelaces and light bulbs, as well as many other familiar objects, seem to fail us suddenly and when it is least convenient. They break and burn out under conditions that seem no more severe than those they had been subjected to hundreds or thousands of times before. A bulb that has burned continuously for decades may appear in a book of world records, but to an engineer versed in the phenomenon of fatigue, the performance is not remarkable. Only if the bulb had been turned on and off daily all those years would its endurance be extraordinary, for it is the cyclic and not the continuous heating of the filament that is its undoing. Thus, because of the fatiguing effect of being constantly changed, it is the rare scoreboard that does not have at least one bulb blown.

Children's toys are especially prone to fatigue failure, not only because children subject them to seemingly endless hours of use but also because the toys are generally not overdesigned. Building a toy too rugged could make it too heavy for the child to manipulate, not to mention more expensive than its imitators. Thus, the seams of rubber balls crack open after so many bounces, the joints of metal tricycles break after so many trips around the block, and the heads of plastic dolls separate after so many nods of agreement.

Even one of the most innovative electronic toys of recent years has been the victim of mechanical fatigue long before children (and their parents) tire of playing with it. Texas Instruments' Speak & Spell effectively employs one of the first microelectronic voice synthesizers. The bright red plastic toy asks the child in a now-familiar voice to spell a vocabulary of words from the toy's memory. The child pecks out letters on the keyboard, and they appear on a calculator-like display. When the child finishes spelling a word, the

ENTER key is pressed and the computer toy says whether the spelling is correct and prompts the child to try again when a word is misspelled. Speak & Spell is so sophisticated that it will turn itself off if the child does not press a button for five minutes or so, thus conserving its four C-cells.

My son's early model Speak & Spell had given him what seemed to be hundreds of hours of enjoyment when one day the ENTER key broke off at its plastic hinge. But since Stephen could still fit his small finger into the buttonhole to activate the switch, he continued to enjoy the smart, if disfigured, toy. Soon thereafter, however, the E key snapped off, and soon the T and O keys followed suit. Although he continued to use the toy, its keyboard soon became a maze of missing letters and, for those that were saved from the vacuum cleaner, taped-on buttons.

What made these failures so interesting to me was the very strong correlation between the most frequently occurring letters in the English language and the fatigued keys on Stephen's Speak & Spell. It is not surprising that the ENTER key broke first, since it was employed for inputting each word and thus got more use than any one letter. Of the seven most common letters—in decreasing occurrence, E, T, A, O, I, N, S, R—five (E, T, O, S, and R) were among the first keys to break. All other letter keys, save for the two seemingly anomalous failures of P and Y, were intact when I first reported this serendipitous experiment on the fatigue phenomenon in the pages of *Technology Review*.

If one assumes that all Speak & Spell letter keys were made as equally well as manufacturing processes allowed, perhaps about as uniformly as or even more so than paper clips, then those plastic keys that failed must generally have been the ones pressed most frequently. The correlation between letter occurrence in common English words and the failure of the keys substantiates that this did indeed happen, for the anomalous failures seem also to be explainable in terms of abnormally high use. Because my son is right-handed, he might be expected to favor letters on the right-hand side of the keyboard when guessing spellings or just playing at pressing letters. Since none of the initial failed letters occurs in the four left-most columns of Speak & Spell, this proclivity could also explain why the common-letter keys A and N were still intact. The anomalous survival of the I key may be attributed to its statistically abnormal strength or to its underuse by a gregarious child. And the failure of the infrequently occurring P and Y might have been a manifestation of the statistical weakness of the keys or of their overuse by my son. His frequent spelling of his name and of the name of his cat, Pollux, endeared the letter *P* to him, and he had learned early that *Y* is sometimes a vowel. Furthermore, each time the Y key was pressed, Speak & Spell would ask the child's favorite question, "Why?"

Why the fatigue of its plastic buttons should have been the weak link that destroyed the integrity of my son's most modern electronic toy could represent the central question for understanding engineering design. Why did the designers of the toy apparently not anticipate this problem? Why did they not use buttons that would outlast the toy's electronics? Why did they not obviate the problem of fatigue, the problem that has defined the lifetimes of mechanical and structural designs for ages? Such questions are not unlike those that are asked after the collapse of a bridge or the crash of an airplane. But the collapse of a bridge or the crash of an airplane can endanger hundreds of lives, and thus the possibility of the fatigue of any part can be a lesson from which its victims learn nothing. Yet the failure of a child's toy, though it may cause tears, is but a lesson for a child's future of burnt-out light bulbs and broken shoelaces. And years later, when his shoelaces break as he is rushing to dress for an important appointment, he will be no less likely to ask, "Why?"

After I wrote about the found experiment, my son retrieved his Speak & Spell from my desk and resumed playing with the toy—and so continued the experiment. Soon another key failed, the vowel key U in the lower left position near where Stephen held his thumb. Next the A key broke, another vowel and the third most frequently occurring letter of the alphabet. The experiment ended with that failure, however, for Stephen acquired a new model of Speak & Spell with the new keyboard design that my daughter, Karen, had pointed out to me at an electronics store. Instead of having individually hinged plastic buttons, the new model has its keyboard printed on a single piece of rubbery plastic stretched over the switches. The new model Stephen has is called an E. T. Speak & Spell, after the little alien creature in the movie, and I am watching the plastic sheet in the vicinity of those two most frequently occurring letters to see if the fatigue gremlin will strike again.

Not long after I had first written about my son's Speak & Spell I found out from readers that their children too had had to live with disfigured keyboards. It is a tribute to the ingeniousness of the toy—and the attachment that children had developed for it—that they endured the broken keys and adapted in makeshift ways, as they would have to throughout a life of breakdowns and failures in our less than perfect world. Some parents reported that their children apparently discovered that the eraser end of a pencil fit nicely into the holes of the old Speak & Spell and thus could be used to enter the most frequently used letters without the children having to use their fingertips. I have wondered if indeed this trick was actually discovered by the parents who loved to play with the toy, for almost any child's finger should easily fit into the hole left by the broken button, but Mommy or Daddy's certainly would not.

Nevertheless, this resourcefulness suggests that the toy would have been a commercial success even with its faults, but the company still improved the keyboard design to solve the problem of key fatigue. The new buttonless keyboard is easily cleaned and pressed by even the clumsiest of adult fingers. The evolution of the Speak & Spell keyboard is not an atypical example of the way mass-produced items, though not necessarily planned that way, are debugged through use. Although there may have been some disappointment among parents who had paid a considerable amount of money for what was then among the most advanced applications of micro-electronics wizardry, their children, who were closer to the world of learning to walk and talk and who were still humbled by their skinned knees and twisted tongues, took the failure of the keys in stride. Perhaps the manufacturer of the toy, in the excitement of putting the first talking computer on the market, overlooked some of the more mundane aspects of its design, but when the problem of the fractured keys came to its attention, it acted quickly to improve the toy's mechanical shortcomings.

I remember being rather angry when my son's Speak & Spell lost its first key. For all my understanding of the limitations of engineering and for all my attempted explanations to my neighbors of how failures like the Hyatt Regency walkways and the DC-10 could happen without clear culpability, I did not extend my charity to the designers of the toy. But there is a difference in the design and development of things that are produced by the millions and those that are unique, and it is generally the case that the mass-produced mechanical or electronic object undergoes some of its debugging and evolution after it is offered to the consumer. Such actions as producing a new version of a toy or carrying out an automobile recall campaign are not possible for the large civil engineering structure, however, which must be got right from the first stages of construction. So my charity should have extended to the designers of the Speak & Spell, for honest mistakes can be made by mechanical and electrical as well as by civil engineers. Perhaps someone had underestimated the number of Es it would take a child to become bored with the new toy. After all, most toys are put away long before they break. If this toy, which is more sophisticated than any I ever had in my own childhood, could tell me when I misspelled words I never could keep straight, then I would demand from it other superhuman qualities such as indestructibility. Yet we do not expect that of everything.

Although we might all be annoyed when a light bulb or a shoelace breaks, especially if it does so at a very inconvenient time, few if any of us would dream of taking it back to the store claiming it had malfunctioned. We all know the story of Thomas Edison searching for a suitable filament for the light bulb, and we are aware of and grateful for the technological achievement. We know, almost intuitively it seems, that to make a shoelace that would not break would involve compromises that we are not prepared to accept. Such a lace might be undesirably heavy or expensive for the style of shoe we wear, and we are much more willing to have the option of living with the risk of having the lace break at an inopportune time or of having the small mental burden of anticipating when the lace will break so that we might replace it in time. Unless we are uncommonly fastidious, we live dangerously and pay little attention to preventive maintenance of our fraying shoelaces or our aging light bulbs. Though we may still ask "Why?" when they break, we already know and accept the answer.

As the consequences of failure become more severe, however, the forethought we must give to them becomes more a matter of life and death. Automobiles are manufactured by the millions, but it would not do to have them failing with a snap on the highways the way light bulbs and shoelaces do at home. The way an automobile could fail must be anticipated so that, as much as possible, a malfunction does not lead to an otherwise avoidable deadly accident. Since tires are prone to flats, we want our vehicles to be able to be steered safely to the side of the road when one occurs. Such a failure is accepted in the way light bulb and shoelace failures are, and we carry a spare tire to deal with it. Other kinds of malfunctions are less acceptable. We do not want the brakes on all four wheels and the emergency braking system to fail us suddenly and simultaneously. We do not want the steering wheel to come off in our hands as we are negotiating a snaking mountain road. Certain parts of the automobile are given special attention, and in the rare instances when they do fail, leading to disaster, massive lawsuits can result. When they become aware of a potential hazard, automobile manufacturers are compelled to eliminate what might be the causes of even the most remote possibilities of design-related accidents by the massive recall campaigns familiar to us all.

As much as it is human to make mistakes, it is also human to want to avoid them. Murphy's Law, holding that anything that can go wrong will, is not a law of nature but a joke. All the light bulbs that last until we tire of the lamp, all the shoelaces that outlast their shoes, all the automobiles that give trouble-free service until they are traded in have the last laugh on Murphy. Just as he will not outlive his law, so nothing manufactured can be or is expected to last forever. Once we recognize this elementary fact, the possibility of a machine or a building being as near to perfect for its designed lifetime as its creators may strive to be for theirs is not only a realistic goal for engineers but also a reasonable expectation for consumers. It is only when we set ourselves such an unrealistic goal as buying a shoelace that will never break, inventing a perpetual motion machine, or building a vehicle that will never break down that we appear to be fools and not rational beings.

Oliver Wendell Holmes is remembered more widely for his humor and verse than for the study entitled "The Contagiousness of Puerperal Fever" that he carried out as Parkman Professor of Anatomy and Physiology at Harvard Medical School. Yet it may have been his understanding of the seemingly independent working of the various parts of the human body that helped him to translate his physiological experiences into a lesson for structural and mechanical engineers. Although some of us go first in the knees and others in the back, none of us falls apart all at once in all our joints. So Holmes imagined the foolishness of expecting to design a horse-drawn carriage that did not have a weak link.

Although intended as an attack on Calvinism, in which Holmes uses the metaphor of the "one-hoss shay" to show that a system of logic, no matter how perfect it seems, must collapse if its premises are false, the poem also holds up as a good lesson for engineers. Indeed, Micro-Measurements, a Raleigh, North Carolina–based supplier of devices to measure the stresses and strains in engineering machines and structures, thinks "The Deacon's Masterpiece" so apt to its business that it offers copies of the poem suitable for framing. The firm's advertising copy recognizes that although ". . . Holmes knew nothing of . . . modern-day technology when he wrote about a vehicle with no 'weak link' among its components," he did realize the absurdity of attempting to achieve "the perfect engineering feat."

In Holmes' poem, . . . the Deacon decides that he will build an indestructible shay, with every part as strong as the rest, so that it will not break down. However, what the Deacon fails to take into account is that everything has a lifetime, and if indeed a shay could be built with "every part as strong as the rest," then every part would "wear out" at the same time and whoever inherited the shay from the Deacon, who himself would pass away before his creation, would be taken by surprise one day. While "The Deacon's Masterpiece" is interesting in recognizing that breaking down is the wearing out of one part, the weakest link, it is not technologically realistic in suggesting that all parts could have exactly the same lifetime. That premise is contrary to the reality that we can only know that this or that part will last for *approximately* this or that many years, just as we can only state the probability that any one paper clip will break after so many bendings. The exact lifetime of a part, a machine, or a structure is known only after it has broken.

Just as we are expected to know our own limitations, so should we know those of the inanimate world. Even the pyramids in the land of the Sphinx, whose riddle reminds us that we all must crawl before we walk and that we will not walk forever, have been eroded by the sand and the wind. Nothing on this earth is inviolate on the scale of geological time, and nothing we create will last at full strength forever. Steel corrodes and diamonds can be split. Even nuclear waste has a half-life.

Engineering deals with lifetimes, both human and otherwise. If not fatigue or fracture, then corrosion or erosion; if not war or vandalism, then taste or fashion claim not only the body but the very souls of once-new machines. Some lifetimes are set by the intended use of an engineering structure. As such an offshore oil platform may be designed to last for only the twenty or thirty years that it will take to extract the oil from the rock beneath the sea. It is less easy to say when the job of a bridge will be completed, yet engineers will have to have some clear idea of a bridge's lifetime if only to specify when some major parts will have to be inspected, serviced, or replaced. Buildings have uses that are subject to the whims of business fashion, and thus today's modern skyscraper may be unrentable in fifty years.

Monumental architecture such as museums and government buildings, on the other hand, should suggest a permanence that makes engineers think in terms of centuries. A cathedral, a millennium.

The lifetime of a structure is no mere anthropomorphic metaphor, for how long a piece of engineering must last can be one of the most important considerations in its design. We have seen how the constant on and off action of a child's toy or a light bulb can cause irreparable damage, and so it is with large engineering structures. The ceaseless action of the sea on an offshore oil platform subjects its welded joints to the very same back and forth forces that cause a paper clip or a piece of plastic to crack after so many flexures. The bounce of a bridge under traffic and the sway of a skyscraper in the wind can also cause the growth of cracks in or the exhaustion of strength of steel cables and concrete beams, and one of the most important calculations of the modern engineer is the one that predicts how long it will take before cracks or the simple degradation of its materials threaten the structure's life. Sometimes we learn more from experience than calculations, however.

Years after my son had outgrown Speak & Spell, and within months of his disaffection with the video games he once wanted so much, he began to ask for toys that required no batteries. First he wanted a BB gun, which his mother and I were reluctant to give him, and then he wanted a slingshot. This almost biblical weapon seemed somehow a less violent toy and evoked visions of a Norman Rockwell painting, in which a boy-being-a-boy conceals his homemade slingshot from the neighbor looking out a broken window. It is almost as innocent a piece of Americana as the baseball hit too far, and no one would want to ban slingshots or boys.

I was a bit surprised, however, to learn that my son wanted to *buy* a slingshot ready-made, and I was even more surprised to learn that his source would not be the Sears Catalog, which might have fit in with the Norman Rockwell image, but one of the catalogs of several discount stores that seem to have captured the imagination of boys in this age of high-tech toys. What my son had in mind for a slingshot was a mass-produced, metal-framed object that was as far from my idea of a slingshot as an artificial Christmas tree is from a fir.

Stephen was incredulous as I took him into the woods behind our house looking for the proper fork with which to make what I promised him would be a *real* slingshot. We collected a few pieces of trees that had fallen in a recent wind storm, and we took them up to our deck to assemble what I had promised. Unfortunately, I had forgotten how easily pine and dry cottonwood break, and my first attempts to wrap a rubber band around the sloping arms of the benign weapon I was making met with structural failure. We finally were able to find pieces strong enough to withstand the manipulation required for their transformation into slingshots, but their range was severely limited by the fact that they would break if pulled back too far.

My son was clearly disappointed in my inability to make him a sling-shot, and I feared that he had run away disillusioned with me when he dis-appeared for an hour or so after dinner that evening. But he returned with the wyes of tree branches stronger and more supple than any I found behind our house. We were able to wrap our fattest rubber bands around these pieces of wood without breaking them, and they withstood as much pull as we were able or willing to supply. Unfortunately, they still did not do as slingshots, for the rubber bands kept slipping down the inclines of the Y and the bands were difficult to hold without the stones we were using for ammunition slipping through them or going awry. After almost a week of frustration trying to find the right branch-and-rubber band combination that would produce a satisfactory slingshot that would not break down, I all but promised I would buy one if we could not make a top-notch shooter out of the scraps of wood scattered about our basement. Stephen was patient if in-credulous as I sorted through odd pieces of plywood and selected one for him to stand upon while I sawed out of it the shape of the body of a sling-shot. He was less patient when I drilled holes to receive a rubber band, and I acceded to his impatience in not sanding the plywood or rounding the edges before giving the device the test of shooting. I surprised him by producing some large red rubber bands my wife uses for her manuscripts, and he began to think he might have a real slingshot when I threaded the ends of a rubber band through the holes in the plywood Y. With the assembly com-pleted I demonstrated how far a little pebble could be shot, but I had to admit, at least to myself, that it was very difficult to keep the pebble bal-anced on the slender rubber band. My son was politely appreciative of what I had made for him, but he was properly not ecstatic. The pebbles he tried to shoot dropped in weak arcs before his target, and he knew that his slingshot would be no match for the one his friend had bought through the catalog.

In my mind I admitted that the homemade slingshot was not well de-signed, and in a desperate attempt to save face with my son I decided to add a second rubber band and a large pocket to improve not only the range but also the accuracy of the toy. These proved to be tremendous improvements, and with them the slingshot seemed almost unlimited in range and very comfortable to use. Now we had a slingshot of enormous potential, and my son was ready to give it the acid test. We spent an entire weekend practicing our aim at a beer bottle a good thirty yards away. The first hit was an historic event that pinged off the glass and the second a show of power that drilled a hole clear through the green glass and left the bottle standing on only a prayer. As we got better at controlling the pebbles issuing from our home-made slingshot we changed from bottles to cans for our targets and hit them more and more.

With all our shooting, the rubber bands began to break from fatigue. This did not bother my son, and he seemed to accept it as something to be expected in a slingshot, for it was just another toy and not a deacon's masterpiece. As rubber bands broke, we replaced them. What proved to be more annoying was the slipping of the rubber band over the top of the slingshot's arm, for we had provided no means of securing the band from doing so. In time, however, we came to wrap the broken rubber bands around the top of the arms to keep the functioning ones in place. This worked wonderfully, and the satisfaction of using broken parts to produce an improved slingshot was especially appealing to my son. He came to believe that his slingshot could outperform any offered in the catalogs, and the joy of producing it ourselves from scrap wood and rubber bands gave him a special pleasure. And all the breaking pieces of wood, slipping rubber bands, and less-than-perfect functioning gave him a lesson in structural engineering more lasting than any textbook's—or any fanciful poem's. He learned to make things that work by steadily improving upon things that did not work. He learned to learn from mistakes. My son, at eleven, had absorbed one of the principal lessons of engineering, and he had learned also the frustrations and the joys of being an engineer. ■

■ QUESTIONS FOR MAKING CONNECTIONS WITHIN THE READING ■

1. As Henry Petroski defines it, "Engineering has as its principal object not the given world but the world that engineers themselves create." What is the difference between "the given world" and "the world that engineers create"? Which world is safer? More hospitable to live in?

2. *To Engineer Is Human* was originally published in 1982, just after the collapse of the Hyatt Regency in Kansas City. Around that time, Petroski maintains, "anyone could rattle off a number of technological embarrassments that were fresh in everyone's mind" Is the same true today? Twenty years after Petroski wrote that statement, is it still the case that the news that grabs the headlines involves engineering disasters? Make a list of the disasters that have dominated the news in the past decade. What does your list say about the recent history of engineering?

3. What are the lessons that Petroski learns in "Lessons from Play; Lessons from Life"? Are the lessons learned from play and from life one and the same? Would you say these lessons are surprising? Obvious? What is gained by learning them?

■ QUESTIONS FOR WRITING ■

1. "[T]he history of engineering in general, may be told in its failures as well as in its triumphs," Petroski writes. "Success may be grand, but disappointment can often teach us more." Why is it that Petroski wants to place

failure at the center of his discussion about engineering? What is the ideal response that Petroski believes engineers and citizens should have to structural failure? If Petroski's readers came to accept the centrality of failure to the engineering process, what, if anything, would change as a result?

2. Petroski maintains, "The exact lifetime of a part, a machine, or a structure is known only after it has broken." What are the implications that this statement has for public safety? For consumer rights? For one's peace of mind?

▪ QUESTIONS FOR MAKING CONNECTIONS BETWEEN READINGS ▪

1. Petroski writes about the inevitability of structural failure with an air of calm that some readers are likely to find unsettling. His assessment of structural reliability in terms of potential loss of life and potential loss of capital is also likely to seem, as Petroski himself puts it, "callous." In this regard, Petroski and Annie Dillard achieve the same level of remove from the emotions that are most frequently evoked by tragedies that take a large toll in human lives. While Petroski and Dillard stand at a distance from such events, do they share the same world view? That is, do the engineer and the poet/naturalist see eye to eye about humanity's place in the "grand scheme of things"? Are they both teaching the same lessons about life and play?

2. In "What Does the Dreaded 'E' Word *Mean*, Anyway?", Stephen Jay Gould distinguishes the biologist's understanding of evolution from the astronomer's understanding. Petroski is describing a different kind of knowledge worker altogether—the engineer—and how the very thoughts of such knowledge workers evolve. Do the ideas of engineers evolve like life forms or like stars? Or do they evolve in some third way that Gould does not discuss? Is their any evolutionary significance to the ways new thoughts emerge?

For additional suggestions about making connections between readings, visit the Link-O-Mat and More Sample Assignments at <www.newhum.com>.

MICHAEL POLLAN

IN HIS RECENT BOOK, *The Botany of Desire: A Plant's-Eye View of the World* (2001), the environmental journalist Michael Pollan has written the "biographies" of four everyday plants—apples, tulips, cannabis, and the potato—that he feels embody the way humans fulfill their desires through nature. The idea of assuming a plant's point of view first came to Pollan when he was working in his garden and realized that he and the bees swarming around him were doing essentially the same thing: they were both at work manipulating the environment to better serve the needs of the plants in his garden. And, in a paradigm shift, Pollan found himself wondering about the degree to which the plants themselves determined his actions by influencing his decisions over what seeds to put down, what to pull out, what to water, and what to cut back.

Pollan explains his shift in perspective as follows: "Think of all the trees that have been cut down to make room for the grasses. It makes just as much sense to a Darwinian to say that agriculture was something that the grasses came up with to get us to cut down the trees." With this insight into the ways that humans and certain plants have coevolved, Pollan realized that one could read in domesticated plants a record of human desire: in the effort to refine the apple, Pollan discerns a partial history of human longings for sweetness; in the tulip, the search for beauty; in cannabis, the call of intoxification; and in the lowly potato, the subject of "Playing God in the Garden," the yearning for control. "Seeing these plants . . . as willing partners in an intimate and reciprocal relationship with us means looking at ourselves a little differently," Pollan believes. We must see ourselves, he goes on to say, "as the objects of other species' designs and desires, as one of the newer bees in Darwin's garden—ingenious, sometimes reckless, and remarkably unself-conscious."

Michael Pollan graduated from Bennington College and received his master's degree in English from Columbia University. The author of *Second Nature:*

Pollan, Michael. "Playing God in the Garden." *The New York Times Magazine.* 25 October 1998, 6–44.

Quotations from Michael Pollan, "Books: In Person," interview by Maria Hong, *The Austin Chronicle* 25 May 2001 and Michael Pollan, introduction to *The Botany of Desire* (New York: Random House, 2000).

A Gardener's Education (1991) and *A Place of My Own: The Education of an Amateur Builder* (1997), Pollan has published widely on gardening, environmentalism, and architecture and is currently an editor-at-large for *Harper's Magazine* and a contributing editor at *The New York Times Magazine*.

To learn more about Michael Pollan and the biotechnology industry, visit the Link-O-Mat at <www.newhum.com>.

■ ■

Playing God in the Garden

Planting

Today I planted something new in my vegetable garden—something very new, as a matter of fact. It's a potato called the New Leaf Superior, which has been genetically engineered—by Monsanto, the chemical giant recently turned "life sciences" giant—to produce its own insecticide. This it can do in every cell of every leaf, stem, flower, root and (here's the creepy part) spud. The scourge of potatoes has always been the Colorado potato beetle, a handsome and voracious insect that can pick a plant clean of its leaves virtually overnight. Any Colorado potato beetle that takes so much as a nibble of my New Leafs will supposedly keel over and die, its digestive tract pulped, in effect, by the bacterial toxin manufactured in the leaves of these otherwise ordinary Superiors. (Superiors are the thin-skinned white spuds sold fresh in the supermarket.) You're probably wondering if I plan to eat these potatoes, or serve them to my family. That's still up in the air; it's only the first week of May, and harvest is a few months off.

Certainly my New Leafs are aptly named. They're part of a new class of crop plants that is rapidly changing the American food chain. This year, the fourth year that genetically altered seed has been on the market, some 45 million acres of American farmland have been planted with biotech crops, most of it corn, soybeans, cotton and potatoes that have been engineered to either produce their own pesticides or withstand herbicides. Though Americans have already begun to eat genetically engineered potatoes, corn and soybeans, industry research confirms what my own informal surveys suggest: hardly any of us knows it. The reason is not hard to find. The biotech industry, with the concurrence of the Food and Drug Administration, has decided we don't need to know it, so biotech foods carry no identifying labels. In a dazzling feat of positioning, the industry has succeeded in depicting these plants simultaneously as the linchpins of a biological revolution—part of a "new agricultural paradigm" that will make farming more sustainable, feed the world and improve health and nutrition—and, oddly enough, as the same old stuff, at least so far as those of us at the eating end of the food chain should be concerned.

This convenient version of reality has been roundly rejected by both consumers and farmers across the Atlantic. Last summer, biotech food emerged as the most explosive environmental issue in Europe. Protesters have destroyed dozens of field trials of the very same "frankenplants" (as they are sometimes called) that we Americans are already serving for dinner, and throughout Europe the public has demanded that biotech food be labeled in the market.

By growing my own transgenic crop—and talking with scientists and farmers involved with biotech—I hoped to discover which of us was crazy. Are the Europeans overreacting, or is it possible that we've been underreacting to genetically engineered food?

After digging two shallow trenches in my garden and lining them with compost, I untied the purple mesh bag of seed potatoes that Monsanto had sent and opened up the Grower Guide tied around its neck. (Potatoes, you may recall from kindergarten experiments, are grown not from seed but from the eyes of other potatoes.) The guide put me in mind not so much of planting potatoes as booting up a new software release. By "opening and using this product," the card stated, I was now "licensed" to grow these potatoes, but only for a single generation; the crop I would water and tend and harvest was mine, yet also not mine. That is, the potatoes I will harvest come August are mine to eat or sell, but their genes remain the intellectual property of Monsanto, protected under numerous United States patents, including Nos. 5,196,525, 5,164,316, 5,322,938 and 5,352,605. Were I to save even one of them to plant next year—something I've routinely done with potatoes in the past—I would be breaking Federal law. The small print in the Grower Guide also brought the news that my potato plants were themselves a pesticide, registered with the Environmental Protection Agency.

If proof were needed that the intricate industrial food chain that begins with seeds and ends on our dinner plates is in the throes of profound change, the small print that accompanied my New Leaf will do. That food chain has been unrivaled for its productivity—on average, a single American farmer today grows enough food each year to feed 100 people. But this accomplishment has come at a price. The modern industrial farmer cannot achieve such yields without enormous amounts of chemical fertilizer, pesticide, machinery and fuel, a set of capital-intensive inputs, as they're called, that saddle the farmer with debt, threaten his health, erode his soil and destroy its fertility, pollute the ground water and compromise the safety of the food we eat.

We've heard all this before, of course, but usually from environmentalists and organic farmers; what is new is to hear the same critique from conventional farmers, government officials and even many agribusiness corporations, all of whom now acknowledge that our food chain stands in need of reform. Sounding more like Wendell Berry than the agribusiness giant it is, Monsanto declared in its most recent annual report that "current agricultural technology is not sustainable."

What is supposed to rescue the American food chain is biotechnology—the replacement of expensive and toxic chemical inputs with expensive but apparently benign genetic information: crops that, like my New Leafs, can protect themselves from insects and disease without being sprayed with pesticides. With the advent of biotechnology, agriculture is entering the information age, and more than any other company, Monsanto is positioning itself to become its Microsoft, supplying the proprietary "operating systems"—the metaphor is theirs—to run this new generation of plants.

There is, of course, a second food chain in America: organic agriculture. And while it is still only a fraction of the size of the conventional food chain, it has been growing in leaps and bounds—in large part because of concerns over the safety of conventional agriculture. Organic farmers have been among biotechnology's fiercest critics, regarding crops like my New Leafs as inimical to their principles and, potentially, a threat to their survival. That's because Bt, the bacterial toxin produced in my New Leafs (and in many other biotech plants) happens to be the same insecticide organic growers have relied on for decades. Instead of being flattered by the imitation, however, organic farmers are up in arms: the widespread use of Bt in biotech crops is likely to lead to insect resistance, thus robbing organic growers of one of their most critical tools; that is, Monsanto's version of sustainable agriculture may threaten precisely those farmers who pioneered sustainable farming.

Sprouting

After several days of drenching rain, the sun appeared on May 15, and so did my New Leafs. A dozen deep-green shoots pushed up out of the soil and commenced to grow—faster and more robustly than any of the other potatoes in my garden. Apart from their vigor, though, my New Leafs looked perfectly normal. And yet as I watched them multiply their lustrous dark-green leaves those first few days, eagerly awaiting the arrival of the first doomed beetle, I couldn't help thinking of them as existentially different from the rest of my plants.

All domesticated plants are in some sense artificial—living archives of both cultural and natural information that we in some sense "design." A given type of potato reflects the values we've bred into it—one that has been selected to yield long, handsome french fries or unblemished round potato chips is the expression of a national food chain that likes its potatoes highly processed. At the same time, some of the more delicate European fingerlings I'm growing alongside my New Leafs imply an economy of small market growers and a taste for eating potatoes fresh. Yet all these qualities already existed in the potato, somewhere within the range of genetic possibilities presented by *Solanum tuberosum*. Since distant species in nature cannot be crossed, the breeder's art has always run up against a natural limit of what a potato is willing, or able, to do. Nature, in effect, has exercised a kind of veto on what culture can do with a potato.

My New Leafs are different. Although Monsanto likes to depict biotechnology as just another in an ancient line of human modifications of nature going back to fermentation, in fact genetic engineering overthrows the old rules governing the relationship of nature and culture in a plant. For the first time, breeders can bring qualities from anywhere in nature into the genome of a plant—from flounders (frost tolerance), from viruses (disease resistance) and, in the case of my potatoes, from *Bacillus thuringiensis*, the soil bacterium that produces the organic insecticide known as Bt. The introduction into a plant of genes transported not only across species but whole phyla means that the wall of that plant's essential identity—its irreducible wildness, you might say—has been breached.

But what is perhaps most astonishing about the New Leafs coming up in my garden is the human intelligence that the inclusion of the Bt gene represents. In the past, that intelligence resided outside the plant, in the mind of the organic farmers who deployed Bt (in the form of a spray) to manipulate the ecological relationship of certain insects and a certain bacterium as a way to foil those insects. The irony about the New Leafs is that the cultural information they encode happens to be knowledge that resides in the heads of the very sort of people—that is, organic growers—who most distrust high technology.

One way to look at biotechnology is that it allows a larger portion of human intelligence to be incorporated into the plant itself. In this sense, my New Leafs are just plain smarter than the rest of my potatoes. The others will depend on my knowledge and experience when the Colorado potato beetles strike; the New Leafs, knowing what I know about bugs and Bt, will take care of themselves. So while my biotech plants might seem like alien beings, that's not quite right. They're more like us than like other plants because there's more of us in them.

Growing

To find out how my potatoes got that way, I traveled to suburban St. Louis in early June. My New Leafs are clones of clones of plants that were first engineered seven years ago in Monsanto's $150 million research facility, a long, low-slung brick building on the banks of the Missouri that would look like any other corporate complex were it not for the 26 greenhouses that crown its roof like shimmering crenellations of glass.

Dave Stark, a molecular biologist and co-director of Naturemark, Monsanto's potato subsidiary, escorted me through the clean rooms where potatoes are genetically engineered. Technicians sat at lab benches before petri dishes in which fingernail-size sections of potato stem had been placed in a nutrient mixture. To this the technicians added a solution of agrobacterium, a disease bacterium whose *modus operandi* is to break into a plant cell's nucleus and insert some of its own DNA. Essentially, scientists smuggle the Bt gene into the agrobacterium's payload, and then the bacterium splices it into the potato's DNA. The technicians also add a "marker" gene, a kind of universal product code that allows Monsanto to identify its plants after they leave the lab.

A few days later, once the slips of potato stem have put down roots, they're moved to the potato greenhouse up on the roof. Here, Glenda De-Brecht, a horticulturist, invited me to don latex gloves and help her transplant pinky-size plantlets from their petri dish to small pots. The whole operation is performed thousands of times, largely because there is so much uncertainty about the outcome. There's no way of telling where in the genome the new DNA will land, and if it winds up in the wrong place, the new gene won't be expressed (or it will be poorly expressed) or the plant may be a freak. I was struck by how the technology could at once be astoundingly sophisticated and yet also a shot in the genetic dark.

"There's still a lot we don't understand about gene expression," Stark acknowledged. A great many factors influence whether, or to what extent, a new gene will do what it's supposed to, including the environment. In one early German experiment, scientists succeeded in splicing the gene for redness into petunias. All went as planned until the weather turned hot and an entire field of red petunias suddenly and inexplicably lost their pigment. The process didn't seem nearly as simple as Monsanto's cherished software metaphor would suggest.

When I got home from St. Louis, I phoned Richard Lewontin, the Harvard geneticist, to ask him what he thought of the software metaphor. "From an intellectual-property standpoint, it's exactly right," he said. "But it's a bad one in terms of biology. It implies you feed a program into a machine and get predictable results. But the genome is very noisy. If my computer made as many mistakes as an organism does"—in interpreting its DNA, he meant—"I'd throw it out."

I asked him for a better metaphor. "An ecosystem," he offered. "You can always intervene and change something in it, but there's no way of knowing what all the downstream effects will be or how it might affect the environment. We have such a miserably poor understanding of how the organism develops from its DNA that I would be surprised if we don't get one rude shock after another."

Flowering

My own crop was thriving when I got home from St. Louis; the New Leafs were as big as bushes, crowned with slender flower stalks. Potato flowers are actually quite pretty, at least by vegetable standards—five-petaled pink stars with yellow centers that give off a faint rose perfume. One sultry afternoon I watched the bumblebees making their lazy rounds of my potato blossoms, thoughtlessly powdering their thighs with yellow pollen grains before lumbering off to appointments with other blossoms, others species.

Uncertainty is the theme that unifies much of the criticism leveled against biotech agriculture by scientists and environmentalists. By planting millions of acres of genetically altered plants, we have introduced something novel into the environment and the food chain, the consequences of which are not—and at this point, cannot be—completely understood. One of the uncertainties has to do with those grains of pollen bumblebees are carting off from my potatoes. That pollen contains Bt genes that may wind up in some other, related plant, possibly conferring a new evolutionary advantage on that species. "Gene flow," the scientific term for this phenomenon, occurs only between closely related species, and since the potato evolved in South America, the chances are slim that my Bt potato genes will escape into the wilds of Connecticut. (It's interesting to note that while biotechnology depends for its power on the ability to move genes freely among species and even phyla, its environmental safety depends on the very opposite phenomenon: on the integrity of species in nature and their rejection of foreign genetic material.)

Yet what happens if and when Peruvian farmers plant Bt potatoes? Or when I plant a biotech crop that does have local relatives? A study reported in *Nature* [in September 1998] found that plant traits introduced by genetic engineering were more likely to escape into the wild than the same traits introduced conventionally.

Andrew Kimbrell, director of the Center for Technology Assessment in Washington, told me he believes such escapes are inevitable. "Biological pollution will be the environmental nightmare of the 21st century," he said when I reached him by phone. "This is not like chemical pollution—an oil spill—that eventually disperses. Biological pollution is an entirely different model, more like a disease. Is Monsanto going to be held legally responsible when one of its transgenes creates a superweed or resistant insect?"

Kimbrell maintains that because our pollution laws were written before the advent of biotechnology, the new industry is being regulated under an ill-fitting regime designed for the chemical age. Congress has so far passed no environmental law dealing specifically with biotech. Monsanto, for its part, claims that it has thoroughly examined all the potential environmental and health risks of its biotech plants, and points out that three regulatory agencies—the U.S.D.A., the E.P.A. and the F.D.A.—have signed off on its products. Speaking of the New Leaf, Dave Stark told me, "This is the most intensively studied potato in history."

Significant uncertainties remain, however. Take the case of insect resistance to Bt, a potential form of "biological pollution" that could end the effectiveness of one of the safest insecticides we have—and cripple the organic farmers who depend on it. The theory, which is now accepted by most entomologists, is that Bt crops will add so much of the toxin to the environment that insects will develop resistance to it. Until now, resistance hasn't been a worry because the Bt sprays break down quickly in sunlight and organic farmers use them only sparingly. Resistance is essentially a form of co-evolution that seems to occur only when a given pest population is threatened with extinction; under that pressure, natural selection favors whatever chance mutations will allow the species to change and survive.

Working with the E.P.A., Monsanto has developed a "resistance-management plan" to postpone that eventuality. Under the plan, farmers who plant Bt crops must leave a certain portion of their land in non-Bt crops to create "refuges" for the targeted insects. The goal is to prevent the first Bt-resistant Colorado potato beetle from mating with a second resistant bug, unleashing a new race of superbeetles. The theory is that when a Bt-resistant bug does show up, it can be induced to mate with a susceptible bug from the refuge, thus diluting the new gene for resistance.

But a lot has to go right for Mr. Wrong to meet Miss Right. No one is sure how big the refuges need to be, where they should be situated or whether the farmers will cooperate (creating havens for a detested pest is counter-intuitive, after all), not to mention the bugs. In the case of potatoes, the E.P.A. has made the plan voluntary and lets the companies themselves implement it; there are no E.P.A. enforcement mechanisms. Which is why most of the organic farmers I spoke to dismissed the regulatory scheme as window dressing.

Monsanto executives offer two basic responses to criticism of their Bt crops. The first is that their voluntary resistance-management plans will work, though the company's definition of success will come as small consolation to an organic farmer: Monsanto scientists told me that if all goes well, resistance can be postponed for 30 years. (Some scientists believe it will come in three to five years.) The second response is more troubling. In St. Louis, I met with Jerry Hjelle, Monsanto's vice president for regulatory affairs. Hjelle told me that resistance should not unduly concern us since "there are a thousand other Bts out there"—other insecticidal proteins. "We can handle this problem with new products," he said. "The critics don't know what we have in the pipeline."

And then Hjelle uttered two words that I thought had been expunged from the corporate vocabulary a long time ago: "Trust us."

"Trust" is a key to the success of biotechnology in the marketplace, and while I was in St. Louis, I asked Hjelle and several of his colleagues why they thought the Europeans were resisting biotech food. Austria, Luxembourg and Norway, risking trade war with the United States, have refused to accept imports of genetically altered crops. Activists in England have been staging sit-ins and "decontaminations" in biotech test fields. A group of French farmers broke into a warehouse and ruined a shipment of biotech corn seed by urinating on it. The Prince of Wales, who is an ardent organic gardener, waded into the biotech debate last June, vowing in a column in *The Daily Telegraph* that he would never eat, or serve to his guests, the fruits of a technology that "takes mankind into realms that belong to God and to God alone."

Monsanto executives are quick to point out that mad cow disease has made Europeans extremely sensitive about the safety of their food chain and has undermined confidence in their regulators. "They don't have a trusted agency like the F.D.A. looking after the safety of their food supply," said Phil Angell, Monsanto's director of corporate communications. Over the summer, Angell was dispatched repeatedly to Europe to put out the P.R. fires; some at Monsanto worry these could spread to the United States.

I checked with the F.D.A. to find out exactly what had been done to insure the safety of this potato. I was mystified by the fact that the Bt toxin was not being treated as a "food additive" subject to labeling, even though the new protein is expressed in the potato itself. The label on a bag of biotech potatoes in the supermarket will tell a consumer all about the nutrients they contain, even the trace amounts of copper. Yet it is silent not only about the fact that those potatoes are the product of genetic engineering but also about their containing an insecticide.

At the F.D.A., I was referred to James Maryanski, who oversees biotech food at the agency. I began by asking him why the F.D.A. didn't consider Bt a food additive. Under F.D.A. law, any novel substance added to a food must—unless it is "generally regarded as safe" ("GRAS," in F.D.A. parlance)—be thoroughly tested and if it changes the product in any way, must be labeled.

"That's easy," Maryanski said. "Bt is a pesticide, so it's exempt" from F.D.A. regulation. That is, even though a Bt potato is plainly a food, for the purposes of Federal regulation it is not a food but a pesticide and therefore falls under the jurisdiction of the E.P.A.

Yet even in the case of those biotech crops over which the F.D.A. does have jurisdiction, I learned that F.D.A. regulation of biotech food has been largely voluntary since 1992, when Vice President Dan Quayle issued regulatory guidelines for the industry as part of the Bush Administration's campaign for "regulatory relief." Under the guidelines, new proteins engineered into foods are regarded as additives (unless they're pesticides), but as Maryanski explained, "the determination whether a new protein is GRAS can be made by the company." Companies with a new biotech food decide for themselves whether they need to consult with the F.D.A. by following a series of "decision trees" that pose yes or no questions like this one: "Does . . . the introduced protein raise any safety concern?"

Since my Bt potatoes were being regulated as a pesticide by the E.P.A. rather than as a food by the F.D.A., I wondered if the safety standards are the same. "Not exactly," Maryanski explained. The F.D.A. requires "a reasonable certainty of no harm" in a food additive, a standard most pesticides could not meet. After all, "pesticides are toxic to something," Maryanski pointed out, so the E.P.A. instead establishes human "tolerances" for each chemical and then subjects it to a risk-benefit analysis.

When I called the E.P.A. and asked if the agency had tested my Bt potatoes for safety as a human food, the answer was . . . not exactly. It seems the E.P.A. works from the assumption that if the original potato is safe and the Bt protein added to it is safe, then the whole New Leaf package is presumed to be safe. Some geneticists believe this reasoning is flawed, contending that the process of genetic engineering itself may cause subtle, as yet unrecognized changes in a food.

The original Superior potato is safe, obviously enough, so that left the Bt toxin, which was fed to mice, and they "did fine, had no side effects," I was told. I always feel better knowing that my food has been poison-tested by mice, though in this case there was a small catch: the mice weren't actually eating the potatoes, not even an extract from the potatoes, but rather straight Bt produced in a bacterial culture.

So are my New Leafs safe to eat? Probably, assuming that a New Leaf is nothing more than the sum of a safe potato and a safe pesticide, and further assuming that the E.P.A.'s idea of a safe pesticide is tantamount to a safe food. Yet I still had a question. Let us assume that my potatoes are a pesticide—a very safe pesticide. Every pesticide in my garden shed—including the Bt sprays—carries a lengthy warning label. The label on my bottle of Bt says, among other things, that I should avoid inhaling the spray or getting it in an open wound. So if my New Leaf potatoes contain an E.P.A.-registered pesticide, why don't they carry some such label?

Maryanski had the answer. At least for the purposes of labeling, my New Leafs have morphed yet again, back into a food: the Food, Drug and Cosmetic Act gives the F.D.A. sole jurisdiction over the labeling of plant foods, and the F.D.A. has ruled that biotech foods need be labeled only if they contain known allergens or have otherwise been "materially" changed.

But isn't turning a potato into a pesticide a material change?

It doesn't matter. The Food, Drug and Cosmetic Act specifically bars the F.D.A. from including any information about pesticides on its food labels.

I thought about Maryanski's candid and wondrous explanations the next time I met Phil Angell, who again cited the critical role of the F.D.A. in assuring Americans that biotech food is safe. But this time he went even further. "Monsanto should not have to vouchsafe the safety of biotech food," he said. "Our interest is in selling as much of it as possible. Assuring its safety is the F.D.A.'s job."

Meeting the Beetles

My Colorado potato beetle vigil came to an end the first week of July, shortly before I went to Idaho to visit potato growers. I spied a single mature beetle sitting on a New Leaf leaf; when I reached to pick it up, the beetle fell drunkenly to the ground. It had been sickened by the plant and would soon be dead. My New Leafs were working.

From where a typical American potato grower stands, the New Leaf looks very much like a godsend. That's because where the typical potato grower stands is in the middle of a bright green field that has been doused with so much pesticide that the leaves of his plants wear a dull white chemical bloom that troubles him as much as it does the rest of us. Out there, at least, the calculation is not complex: a product that promises to eliminate the need for even a single spraying of pesticide is, very simply, an economic and environmental boon.

No one can make a better case for a biotech crop than a potato farmer, which is why Monsanto was eager to introduce me to several large growers. Like many farmers today, the ones I met feel trapped by the chemical inputs required to extract the high yields they must achieve in order to pay for the chemical inputs they need. The economics are daunting: a potato farmer in south-central Idaho will spend roughly $1,965 an acre (mainly on chemicals, electricity, water and seed) to grow a crop that, in a good year, will earn him maybe $1,980. That's how much a french-fry processor will pay for the 20 tons of potatoes a single Idaho acre can yield. (The real money in agriculture—90 percent of the value added to the food we eat—is in selling inputs to farmers and then processing their crops.)

Danny Forsyth laid out the dismal economics of potato farming for me one sweltering morning at the coffee shop in downtown Jerome, Idaho. Forsyth, 60, is a slight blue-eyed man with a small gray ponytail; he farms 3,000 acres of potatoes, corn and wheat, and he spoke about agricultural chemicals like a man desperate to kick a bad habit. "None of us would use them if we had any choice," he said glumly.

I asked him to walk me through a season's regimen. It typically begins early in the spring with a soil fumigant; to control nematodes, many potato farmers douse their fields with a chemical toxic enough to kill every trace of microbial life in the soil. Then, at planting, a systemic insecticide (like Thimet) is applied to the soil; this will be absorbed by the young seedlings and, for several weeks, will kill any insect that eats their leaves. After planting, Forsyth puts down an herbicide—Sencor or Eptam—to "clean" his field of all weeds. When the potato seedlings are six inches tall, an herbicide may be sprayed a second time to control weeds.

Idaho farmers like Forsyth farm in vast circles defined by the rotation of a pivot irrigation system, typically 135 acres to a circle; I'd seen them from 30,000 feet flying in, a grid of verdant green coins pressed into a desert of scrubby brown. Pesticides and fertilizers are simply added to the irrigation system, which on Forsyth's farm draws most of its water from the nearby Snake River. Along with their water, Forsyth's potatoes may receive 10 applications of chemical fertilizer during the growing season. Just before the rows close—when the leaves of one row of plants meet those of the next—he begins spraying Bravo, a fungicide, to control late blight, one of the biggest threats to the potato crop. (Late blight, which caused the Irish potato famine, is an airborne fungus that turns stored potatoes into rotting mush.) Blight is such a serious problem that the E.P.A. currently allows farmers to spray powerful fungicides that haven't passed the usual approval process. Forsyth's potatoes will receive eight applications of fungicide.

Twice each summer, Forsyth hires a crop duster to spray for aphids. Aphids are harmless in themselves, but they transmit the leafroll virus, which in Russet Burbank potatoes causes net necrosis, a brown spotting that will cause a processor to reject a whole crop. It happened to Forsyth last year. "I lost 80,000 bags"—they're a hundred pounds each—"to net necrosis," he said. "Instead of getting $4.95 a bag, I had to take $2 a bag from the dehydrator, and I was lucky to get that." Net necrosis is a purely cosmetic defect; yet because big buyers like McDonald's believe (with good reason) that we don't like to see brown spots in our fries, farmers like Danny Forsyth must spray their fields with some of the most toxic chemicals in use, including an organophosphate called Monitor.

"Monitor is a deadly chemical," Forsyth said. "I won't go into a field for four or five days after it's been sprayed—even to fix a broken pivot." That is, he would sooner lose a whole circle to drought than expose himself or an employee to Monitor, which has been found to cause neurological damage.

It's not hard to see why a farmer like Forsyth, struggling against tight margins and heartsick over chemicals, would leap at a New Leaf—or, in his case, a New Leaf Plus, which is protected from leafroll virus as well as beetles. "The New Leaf means I can skip a couple of sprayings, including the Monitor," he said. "I save money, and I sleep better. It also happens to be a nice-looking spud." The New Leafs don't come cheaply, however. They cost between $20 and $30 extra per acre in "technology fees" to Monsanto.

Forsyth and I discussed organic agriculture, about which he had the usual things to say ("That's all fine on a small scale, but they don't have to feed the world"), as well as a few things I'd never heard from a conventional farmer: "I like to eat organic food, and in fact I raise a lot of it at the house. The vegetables we buy at the market we just wash and wash and wash. I'm not sure I should be saying this, but I always plant a small area of potatoes without any chemicals. By the end of the season, my field potatoes are fine to eat, but any potatoes I pulled today are probably still full of systemics. I don't eat them."

Forsyth's words came back to me a few hours later, during lunch at the home of another potato farmer. Steve Young is a progressive and prosperous potato farmer—he calls himself an agribusinessman. In addition to his 10,000 acres—the picture window in his family room gazes out on 85 circles, all computer-controlled—Young owns a share in a successful fertilizer distributorship. His wife prepared a lavish feast for us, and after Dave, their 18-year-old, said grace, adding a special prayer for me (the Youngs are devout Mormons), she passed around a big bowl of homemade potato salad. As I helped myself, my Monsanto escort asked what was in the salad, flashing me a smile that suggested she might already know. "It's a combination of New Leafs and some of our regular Russets," our hostess said proudly. "Dug this very morning."

After talking to farmers like Steve Young and Danny Forsyth, and walking fields made virtually sterile by a drenching season-long rain of chemicals, you could understand how Monsanto's New Leaf potato does indeed look like an environmental boon. Set against current practices, growing New Leafs represents a more sustainable way of potato farming. This advance must be weighed, of course, against everything we don't yet know about New Leafs—and a few things we do: like the problem of Bt resistance I had heard so much about back East. While I was in Idaho and Washington State, I asked potato farmers to show me their refuges. This proved to be a joke.

"I guess that's a refuge over there," one Washington farmer told me, pointing to a cornfield.

Monsanto's grower contract never mentions the word "refuge" and only requires that farmers grow no more than 80 percent of their fields in New Leaf. Basically, any field not planted in New Leaf is considered a refuge, even if that field has been sprayed to kill every bug in it. Farmers call such acreage a clean field; calling it a refuge is a stretch at best.

It probably shouldn't come as a big surprise that conventional farmers would have trouble embracing the notion of an insect refuge. To insist on real and substantial refuges is to ask them to start thinking of their fields in an entirely new way, less as a factory than as an ecosystem. In the factory, Bt is another in a long line of "silver bullets" that work for a while and then get replaced; in the ecosystem, all bugs are not necessarily bad, and the relationships between various species can be manipulated to achieve desired ends—like the long-term sustainability of Bt.

This is, of course, precisely the approach organic farmers have always taken to their fields, and after my lunch with the Youngs that afternoon, I paid a brief visit to an organic potato grower. Mike Heath is a rugged, laconic man in his mid-50's; like most of the organic farmers I've met, he looks as though he spends a lot more time out of doors than a conventional farmer, and he probably does: chemicals are, among other things, labor-saving devices. While we drove around his 500 acres in a battered old pickup, I asked him about biotechnology. He voiced many reservations—it was synthetic, there were too many unknowns—but his main objection to planting a biotech potato was simply that "it's not what my customers want."

That point was driven home last December when the Department of Agriculture proposed a new "organic standards" rule that, among other things, would have allowed biotech crops to carry an organic label. After receiving a flood of outraged cards and letters, the agency backed off. (As did Monsanto, which asked the U.S.D.A. to shelve the issue for three years.) Heath suggested that biotech may actually help organic farmers by driving worried consumers to the organic label.

I asked Heath about the New Leaf. He had no doubt resistance would come—"the bugs are always going to be smarter than we are"—and said it was unjust that Monsanto was profiting from the ruin of Bt, something he regarded as a "public good."

None of this particularly surprised me; what did was that Heath himself resorted to Bt sprays only once or twice in the last 10 years. I had assumed that organic farmers used Bt or other approved pesticides in much the same way conventional farmers use theirs, but as Heath showed me around his farm, I began to understand that organic farming was a lot more complicated than substituting good inputs for bad. Instead of buying many inputs at all, Heath relied on long and complex crop rotations to prevent a buildup of crop-specific pests—he has found, for example, that planting wheat after spuds "confuses" the potato beetles.

He also plants strips of flowering crops on the margins of his potato fields—peas or alfalfa, usually—to attract the beneficial insects that eat beetle larvae and aphids. If there aren't enough beneficials to do the job, he'll introduce ladybugs. Heath also grows eight varieties of potatoes, on the theory that biodiversity in a field, as in the wild, is the best defense against any imbalances in the system. A bad year with one variety will probably be offset by a good year with the others.

"I can eat any potato in this field right now," he said, digging Yukon Golds for me to take home. "Most farmers can't eat their spuds out of the field. But you don't want to start talking about safe food in Idaho."

Heath's were the antithesis of "clean" fields, and, frankly, their weedy margins and overall patchiness made them much less pretty to look at. Yet it was the very complexity of these fields—the sheer diversity of species, both in space and time—that made them productive year after year without many inputs. The system provided for most of its needs.

All told, Heath's annual inputs consisted of natural fertilizers (compost and fish powder), ladybugs and a copper spray (for blight)—a few hundred dollars an acre. Of course, before you can compare Heath's operation with a conventional farm, you've got to add in the extra labor (lots of smaller crops means more work; organic fields must also be cultivated for weeds) and time—the typical organic rotation calls for potatoes every fifth year, in contrast to every third on a conventional farm. I asked Heath about his yields. To my astonishment, he was digging between 300 and 400 bags per acre— just as many as Danny Forsyth and only slightly fewer than Steve Young. Heath was also getting almost twice the price for his spuds: $8 a bag from an organic processor who was shipping frozen french fries to Japan.

On the drive back to Boise, I thought about why Heath's farm remained the exception, both in Idaho and elsewhere. Here was a genuinely new par adigm that seemed to work. But while it's true that organic agriculture is gaining ground (I met a big grower in Washington who had just added several organic circles), few of the mainstream farmers I met considered organic a "realistic" alternative. For one thing, it's expensive to convert: organic certifiers require a field to go without chemicals for three years before it can be called organic. For another, the U.S.D.A., which sets the course of American agriculture, has long been hostile to organic methods.

But I suspect the real reasons run deeper, and have more to do with the fact that in a dozen ways a farm like Heath's simply doesn't conform to the requirements of a corporate food chain. Heath's type of agriculture doesn't leave much room for the Monsantos of this world: organic farmers buy remarkably little—some seed, a few tons of compost, maybe a few gallons of ladybugs. That's because the organic farmer's focus is on a process, rather than on products. Nor is that process readily systematized, reduced to, say, a prescribed regime of sprayings like the one Forsyth outlined for me—regimes that are often designed by companies selling chemicals.

Most of the intelligence and local knowledge needed to run Mike Heath's farm resides in the head of Mike Heath. Growing potatoes conventionally requires intelligence, too, but a large portion of it resides in laboratories in distant places like St. Louis, where it is employed in developing sophisticated chemical inputs. That sort of centralization of agriculture is unlikely to be reversed, if only because there's so much money in it; besides, it's much easier for the farmer to buy prepackaged solutions from big companies. "Whose Head Is the Farmer Using? Whose Head Is Using the Farmer?" goes the title of a Wendell Berry essay.

Organic farmers like Heath have also rejected what is perhaps the cornerstone of industrial agriculture: the economies of scale that only a monoculture can achieve. Monoculture—growing vast fields of the same crop year after year—is probably the single most powerful simplification of modern agriculture. But monoculture is poorly fitted to the way nature seems to work. Very simply, a field of identical plants will be exquisitely vulnerable to insects, weeds and disease. Monoculture is at the root of virtually every problem that bedevils the modern farmer, and that virtually every input has been designed to solve.

To put the matter baldly, a farmer like Heath is working very hard to adjust his fields and his crops to the nature of nature, while farmers like Forsyth are working equally hard to adjust nature in their fields to the requirement of monoculture and, beyond that, to the needs of the industrial food chain. I remember asking Heath what he did about net necrosis, the bane of Forsyth's existence. "That's only really a problem with Russet Burbanks," he said. "So I plant other kinds." Forsyth can't do that. He's part of a food chain—at the far end of which stands a long, perfectly golden McDonald's fry—that demands he grow Russet Burbanks and little else.

This is where biotechnology comes in, to the rescue of Forsyth's Russet Burbanks and, if Monsanto is right, to the whole food chain of which they form a part. Monoculture is in trouble—the pesticides that make it possible are rapidly being lost, either to resistance or to heightened concerns about their danger. Biotechnology is the new silver bullet that will save monoculture. But a new silver bullet is not a new paradigm—rather, it's something that will allow the old paradigm to survive. That paradigm will always construe the problem in Forsyth's fields as a Colorado potato beetle problem, rather than as a problem of potato monoculture.

Like the silver bullets that preceded them—the modern hybrids, the pesticides and the chemical fertilizers—the new biotech crops will probably, as advertised, increase yields. But equally important, they will also speed the process by which agriculture is being concentrated in a shrinking number of corporate hands. If that process has advanced more slowly in farming than in other sectors of the economy, it is only because nature herself—her complexity, diversity and sheer intractibility in the face of our best efforts at control—has acted as a check on it. But biotechnology promises to remedy this "problem," too.

Consider, for example, the seed, perhaps the ultimate "means of production" in any agriculture. It is only in the last few decades that farmers have begun buying their seed from big companies, and even today many farmers still save some seed every fall to replant in the spring. Brown-bagging, as it is called, allows farmers to select strains particularly well adapted to their needs; since these seeds are often traded, the practice advances the state of the genetic art—indeed, has given us most of our crop plants. Seeds by their very nature don't lend themselves to commodification: they produce more of themselves ad infinitum (with the exception of certain modern hybrids), and for that reason the genetics of most major crop plants have traditionally been regarded as a common heritage. In the case of the potato, the genetics of most important varieties—the Burbanks, the Superiors, the Atlantics— have always been in the public domain. Before Monsanto released the New Leaf, there had never been a multinational seed corporation in the potato-seed business—there was no money in it.

Biotechnology changes all that. By adding a new gene or two to a Russet Burbank or Superior, Monsanto can now patent the improved variety. Legally, it has been possible to patent a plant for many years, but biologically, these patents have been almost impossible to enforce. Biotechnology partly solves that problem. A Monsanto agent can perform a simple test in my garden and prove that my plants are the company's intellectual property. The contract farmers sign with Monsanto allows company representatives to perform such tests in their fields at will. According to *Progressive Farmer*, a trade journal, Monsanto is using informants and hiring Pinkertons to enforce its patent rights; it has already brought legal action against hundreds of farmers for patent infringement.

Soon the company may not have to go to the trouble. It is expected to acquire the patent to a powerful new biotechnology called the Terminator, which will, in effect, allow the company to enforce its patents biologically.

Developed by the U.S.D.A. in partnership with Delta and Pine Land, a seed company in the process of being purchased by Monsanto, the Terminator is a complex of genes that, theoretically, can be spliced into any crop plant, where it will cause every seed produced by that plant to be sterile. Once the Terminator becomes the industry standard, control over the genetics of crop plants will complete its move from the farmer's field to the seed company— to which the farmer will have no choice but to return year after year. The Terminator will allow companies like Monsanto to privatize one of the last great commons in nature—the genetics of the crop plants that civilization has developed over the past 10,000 years.

At lunch on his farm in Idaho, I had asked Steve Young what he thought about all this, especially about the contract Monsanto made him sign. I wondered how the American farmer, the putative heir to a long tradition of agrarian independence, was adjusting to the idea of field men snooping around his farm, and patented seed he couldn't replant. Young said he had made his peace with corporate agriculture, and with biotechnology in particular: "It's here to stay. It's necessary if we're going to feed the world, and it's going to take us forward."

Then I asked him if he saw any downside to biotechnology, and he paused for what seemed a very long time. What he then said silenced the table. "There is a cost," he said. "It gives corporate America one more noose around my neck."

Harvest

A few weeks after I returned home from Idaho, I dug my New Leafs, harvesting a gorgeous-looking pile of white spuds, including some real lunkers. The plants had performed brilliantly, though so had all my other potatoes. The beetle problem never got serious, probably because the diversity of species in my (otherwise organic) garden had attracted enough beneficial insects to keep the beetles in check. By the time I harvested my crop, the question of eating the New Leafs was moot. Whatever I thought about the soundness of the process that had declared these potatoes safe didn't matter. Not just because I'd already had a few bites of New Leaf potato salad at the Youngs but also because Monsanto and the F.D.A. and the E.P.A. had long ago taken the decision of whether or not to eat a biotech potato out of my—out of all of our—hands. Chances are, I've eaten New Leafs already, at McDonald's or in a bag of Frito-Lay chips, though without a label there can be no way of knowing for sure.

So if I've probably eaten New Leafs already, why was it that I kept putting off eating mine? Maybe because it was August, and there were so many more-interesting fresh potatoes around—fingerlings with dense, luscious flesh, Yukon Golds that tasted as though they had been pre-buttered—that the idea of cooking with a bland commercial variety like the Superior seemed beside the point.

There was this, too: I had called Margaret Mellon at the Union of Concerned Scientists to ask her advice. Mellon is a molecular biologist and lawyer and a leading critic of biotech agriculture. She couldn't offer any hard scientific evidence that my New Leafs were unsafe, though she emphasized how little we know about the effects of Bt in the human diet. "That research simply hasn't been done," she said.

I pressed. Is there any reason I shouldn't eat these spuds?

"Let me turn that around. Why would you want to?"

It was a good question. So for a while I kept my New Leafs in a bag on the porch. Then I took the bag with me on vacation, thinking maybe I'd sample them there, but the bag came home untouched.

The bag sat on my porch till the other day, when I was invited to an end-of-summer potluck supper at the town beach. Perfect. I signed up to make a potato salad. I brought the bag into the kitchen and set a pot of water on the stove. But before it boiled I was stricken by this thought: I'd have to tell people at the picnic what they were eating. I'm sure (well, almost sure) the potatoes are safe, but if the idea of eating biotech food without knowing it bothered me, how could I possibly ask my neighbors to? So I'd tell them about the New Leafs—and then, no doubt, lug home a big bowl of untouched potato salad. For surely there would be other potato salads at the potluck and who, given the choice, was ever going to opt for the bowl with the biotech spuds?

So there they sit, a bag of biotech spuds on my porch. I'm sure they're absolutely fine. I pass the bag every day, thinking I really should try one, but I'm beginning to think that what I like best about these particular biotech potatoes—what makes them different—is that I have this choice. And until I know more, I choose not.   ■

■*QUESTIONS FOR MAKING CONNECTIONS WITHIN THE READING* ■

1. Michael Pollan asserts at the opening of his essay that "the intricate industrial food chain that begins with seeds and ends on our dinner plates is in the throes of profound change." How is the food chain being changed by biotechnology? Why does Pollan believe this change to be "profound" rather than, say, "incremental," or just a part of the natural flow of progress?

2. Pollan discusses three governmental regulatory agencies: the USDA, the FDA and the EPA. What do these agencies do? Why haven't any of these agencies been able to control the growth of the biogenetic engineering industry?

3. At the end of "Playing God in the Garden," Pollan decides not to eat the New Leaf Superiors that he has grown in his own garden. Why doesn't he? Is there an answer to the question that is posed to Pollan at the end of

his essay: That is, is there a reason why someone would want to eat bio-genetically engineered food?

1. "Biological pollution will be the environmental nightmare of the 21st century." This is one of the darker pronouncements in Pollan's essay. What is biological pollution, and how does it differ from other forms of pollution? If it is safe to assume that there is no turning back and biogenetically engineered foods are with us to stay, what can be done to control the spread of biological pollution? Who is best equipped to address this problem: the individual, the local community, state or federal government, farmers, or food corporations?

2. Why does Pollan title his essay "Playing God in the Garden"? Does this signal Pollan's disapproval or his admiration of Monsanto's biotechnological research? Does research of this kind violate something sacred? Is it "unnatural" for humans to try to control their environment in this way? On the basis of what principle or principles can questions of this kind be answered?

1. With Peter Drucker's "The Age of Social Transformation" and Michael Pollan's "Playing God in the Garden," we have a description of how dramatically farming has changed over the past century. Does Pollan's essay support Drucker's contention that the age of social transformation has created the need for a social sector? Given the power that agribusiness has over the food supply, is it possible to create a social sector that "can again give individuals . . . a sphere in which they can make a difference in society and re-create community"?

2. In "What Does the Dreaded 'E' Word *Mean,* Anyway?" Stephen Jay Gould provides an extended discussion of what the word *evolution* means in the life sciences. Does genetic engineering, as Pollan describes it, disrupt the evolutionary process Gould describes? Does it participate in that evolutionary process? Does Gould's argument suggest that we should be concerned about genetic engineering or that there is nothing to worry about? That is, does the definition of evolution used in the life sciences put to rest the concerns Pollan has raised about genetic engineering or does it heighten those concerns?

For additional suggestions about making connections between readings, visit the Link-O-Mat and More Sample Assignments at <www.newhum.com>.

Eric Schlosser

In his award-winning article, "In the Strawberry Fields," the investigative journalist Eric Schlosser focuses attention on workers' rights by recounting the tale of how strawberries make their way from the fields to the supermarket, exposing in the process the industry's reliance on illegal immigrants. In *Fast Food Nation: The Dark Side of the All-American Meal* (2001), Schlosser pursues a similar approach by telling the story of how the Big Mac and other fast-food products find their way into the hands of consumers around the world. Who makes this food? Under what conditions? What societal, environmental, and economic changes have been produced by the shift in American eating habits? What are the long-term consequences of the "Americanization" of eating habits around the globe? These are the questions that animate *Fast Food Nation,* Schlosser's book-length study of the fast-food industry.

In criticizing the place that fast food has come to occupy in the American diet, Schlosser aims to go beyond complaining about the architectural tackiness of fast-food restaurants and the blandness of the food—arguments most readers would find unsurprising and could, at any rate, generate on their own. Schlosser's concerns, rather, are with how the fast-food industry treats its workers, what's in the food that those workers sell, and the dramatic changes America's new eating habits have produced in the agricultural industry. In raising these issues, Schlosser means to promote an alternative future, one where people are fed by a "sustainable and largely deindustrialized agriculture, regional production and fast-food restaurants that are locally owned and somehow connected in a real way to the places where they operate." In "Global Realization," Schlosser details ongoing efforts to make certain that food looks and tastes the same the world over and the counter-efforts of those who would resist such attempts to globalize American standards of consumption. Acknowledging that

Schlosser, Eric. "Global Realization." *Fast Food Nation.* Boston: Houghton Mifflin, 2001. 225–252.

Biographical information from Eric Schlosser, interview by Bill Goldstein <http://www.nytimes.com/books/01/01/21/specials/schlosser.html>; Quotations from Eric Schlosser, interview by Patricia Chui, The Nation, <http://www.thenation.com/special/schlosser.mhtml> and Eric Schlosser, interview by Julia Livshin, The Atlantic, 14 December 2000. <http://www.theatlantic.com/unbound/interviews/ba2000-12-14.html>.

"it's very hard to get readers to care about these subjects," Schlosser neverthe-less believes that it is his responsibility to try "to give a voice to people outside of the mainstream."

To learn more about Eric Schlosser and the fast food industry, visit the Link-O-Mat at <www.newhum.com>.

Global Realization

Whenever I told someone in Berlin that I was planning to visit Plauen, I got the same reaction. It didn't matter whom I told—someone old or young, hip or square, gay, straight, raised in West Germany, raised in the East—there'd always be a laugh, followed by a look of slight amazement. "Plauen?" they'd say. "Why would you ever want to go to Plauen?" The way the name was spoken, the long, drawn-out emphasis on the second syllable, implied that the whole idea was vaguely ridiculous. Located halfway between Mu-nich and Berlin, in a part of Saxony known as the Vogtland, Plauen is a small provincial city surrounded by forests and rolling hills. To Berliners, whose city is the present capital of Germany and perhaps the future capital of Europe, Plauen is a sleepy backwater that sat for decades on the wrong side of the Berlin Wall. Berliners regard the place in much the same way that New Yorkers view Muncie, Indiana. But I found Plauen fascinating. The countryside around it is lush and green. Some of the old buildings have real charm. The people are open, friendly, unpretentious—and yet somehow cursed.

For decades Plauen has been on the margins of history, far removed from the centers of power; nevertheless, events there have oddly fore-shadowed the rise and fall of great social movements. One after another, the leading ideologies of modern Europe—industrialism, fascism, communism, consumerism—have passed through Plauen and left their mark. None has completely triumphed or been completely erased. Bits and pieces of these worldviews still coexist uneasily, cropping up in unexpected places, from the graffiti on the wall of an apartment building to the tone of an offhand re-mark. There is nothing settled yet, nothing that can be assumed. All sorts of things, good and bad, are still possible. In the heart of the Vogtland, without much notice from the rest of the world, the little city of Plauen has been al-ternately punished, rewarded, devastated, and transformed by the great unifying systems of the twentieth century, by each new effort to govern all of mankind with a single set of rules. Plauen has been a battlefield for these competing ideologies, with their proudly displayed and archetypal symbols: the smokestack, the swastika, the hammer and sickle, the golden arches.

For centuries, Plauen was a small market town where Vogtland farmers came to buy and sell goods. And then, at the end of the nineteenth century, a local weaving tradition gave birth to a vibrant textile industry. Between 1890 and 1914, the city's population roughly tripled, reaching 118,000 on the eve of World War I. Its new textile mills specialized in lace and in embroidered fabrics, exporting most of their output to the United States. The doilies on dinner tables throughout the American Midwest came from Plauen, as well as the intricate lacework that set the tone of many upper-middle-class Victorian homes. Black-and-white postcards from Plauen before the Great War show lovely Art Nouveau and Neo-Romantic buildings that evoke the streets of Paris, elegant cafés and parks, electric streetcars, zeppelins in the air.

Life in Plauen became less idyllic after Germany's defeat. When the Victorian world and its values collapsed, so did the market for lace. Many of Plauen's textile mills closed, and thousands of people were thrown out of work. The social unrest that later engulfed the rest of Germany came early to Plauen. In the 1920s Plauen had the most millionaires per capita in Germany—and the most suicides. It also had the highest unemployment rate. Amid the misery, extremism thrived. Plauen was the first city outside of Bavaria to organize its own chapter of the Nazi party. In May of 1923, the Hitler Youth movement was launched in Plauen, and the following year, the little city became the Nazi headquarters for Saxony. Long before the Nazi reign of terror began elsewhere, union leaders and leftists were murdered in Plauen. Hitler visited the city on several occasions, receiving an enthusiastic welcome. Hermann Göring and Joseph Goebbels visited too, and Plauen became a sentimental favorite of the Nazi leadership. On the night of November 9, 1938, *Kristallnacht*, a crowd eagerly destroyed Plauen's only synagogue, a strikingly modern building designed by Bauhaus architect Fritz Landauer. Not long afterward, Plauen officially became *Jüden-frei* (Jew-free).

For most of World War II, Plauen remained strangely quiet and peaceful, an oasis of ordinary life. It provided safe haven to thousands of German refugees fleeing bombed-out cities. All sorts of rumors tried to explain why Plauen was being spared, while other towns in Saxony were being destroyed. On September 19, 1944, American bombers appeared over the city for the first time. Instead of rushing into shelters, people stood in the streets, amazed, watching bombs fall on the railway station and on a factory that built tanks for the German army. A few months later, Plauen appeared alongside Dresden on an Allied bombing list.

Plauen was largely deserted on April 10, 1945, when hundreds of British Lancaster bombers appeared over the city. Its inhabitants no longer felt mysteriously protected; they knew that Dresden had recently been fire-bombed into oblivion. During a single raid the Royal Air Force dropped 2,000 tons of high explosives on Plauen. Four days later, the U.S. Army occupied what was left of the town. The birthplace of the Hitler Youth, the most Nazified city in Saxony, gained another distinction only weeks before the war ended. More bombs were dropped on Plauen, per square mile, than on any other city in eastern Germany—roughly three times as many as were dropped on Dresden. Although the carnage was far worse in Dresden, a larger proportion of Plauen's buildings were destroyed. At the end of the war, about 75 percent of Plauen lay in ruins.

When the Allies divided their spheres of influence in Germany, Plauen's misfortune continued. The U.S Army pulled out of the city, and the Soviet army rolled in. Plauen became part of the communist German Democratic Republic (GDR), but just barely. The new border with West Germany was only nine miles away. Plauen languished under Communist rule. It lost one-third of its prewar population. Sitting in a remote corner of the GDR, it received little attention or investment from the Communist party leadership in East Berlin. Much of Plauen was never rebuilt; parking lots and empty lots occupied land where ornate buildings had once stood. One of the few successful factories, a synthetic wool plant, blanketed Plauen in some of East Germany's worst air pollution. According to historian John Connelly, the polluted air helped give the city an "unusually low quality of life, even for GDR standards."

On October 7, 1989, the first mass demonstration against East Germany's Communist rulers took place in Plauen. Small, scattered protests also occurred that day in Magdeberg, East Berlin, and other cities. The size of Plauen's demonstration set it apart. More than one-quarter of the city's population suddenly took to the streets. The level of unrest greatly surprised local government officials. The Stasi (East Germany's secret police) had expected about four hundred people to appear in the town center that day, the fortieth anniversary of the GDR's founding. Instead, about twenty thousand people began to gather, despite dark skies and a steady drizzle. The demonstration had no leadership, no organizers, no formal plan of action. It grew spontaneously, spreading through word of mouth.

The protesters in other East German cities were mainly college students and members of the intelligentsia; in Plauen they were factory workers and ordinary citizens. Some of the demonstration's most fervent supporters were long-haired, working-class fans of American heavy metal music, known in Plauen as *die Heavies,* who rode their motorcycles through town distributing antigovernment pamphlets. As the crowd grew, people began to chant Mikhail Gorbachev's nickname—"Gorby! Gorby!"—cheering the Soviet leader's policies of *glasnost* and *perestroika,* demanding similar reforms in East Germany, defiantly yelling "Stasi go home!" One large banner bore the words of the German poet Friedrich von Schiller. "We want freedom," it said, "like the freedom enjoyed by our forefathers."

Police officers and Stasi agents tried to break up the demonstration, arresting dozens of people, firing water cannons at the crowd, flying helicopters low over the rooftops of Plauen. But the protesters refused to disperse. They marched to the town hall and called for the mayor to come outside and address their demands. Thomas Küttler, the superintendent of Plauen's Lutheran church, volunteered to act as a mediator. Inside the town hall, he found Plauen's high-ranking officials cowering in fear. None would emerge to face the crowd. The equation of power had fundamentally changed that day. A mighty totalitarian system of rule, erected over the course of four decades, propped up by tanks and guns and thousands of Stasi informers, was crumbling before his eyes, as its rulers nervously chain-smoked in the safety of their offices. The mayor finally agreed to address the crowd, but a Stasi official prevented him from leaving the building. And so Küttler stood on the steps of the town hall with a megaphone, urging the soldiers not to fire their weapons and telling the demonstrators that their point had been made, now it was time to go home. As bells atop the Lutheran church rang, the crowd began to disperse.

A month later, the Berlin Wall fell. And a few months after that extraordinary event, marking the end of the Cold War, the McDonald's Corporation announced plans to open its first restaurant in East Germany. The news provoked a last gasp of collectivism from Ernst Doerfler, a prominent member of the doomed East German parliament, who called for an official ban on "McDonald's and similar abnormal garbage-makers." McDonald's, however, would not be deterred; Burger King had already opened a mobile hamburger cart in Dresden. During the summer of 1990, construction quickly began on the first McDonald's in East Germany. It would occupy an abandoned lot in the center of Plauen, a block away from the steps of the town hall. The McDonald's would be the first new building erected in Plauen since the coming of a new Germany.

Uncle McDonald

As the fast food industry has grown more competitive in the United States, the major chains have looked to overseas markets for their future growth. The McDonald's Corporation recently used a new phrase to describe its hopes for foreign conquest: "global realization." A decade ago, McDonald's had about three thousand restaurants outside the United States; today it has about fifteen thousand restaurants in more than 117 foreign countries. It currently opens about five new restaurants every day, and at least four of them are overseas. Within the next decade, Jack Greenberg, the company's chief executive, hopes to double the number of McDonald's. The chain earns the majority of its profits outside the United States, as does KFC. McDonald's now ranks as the most widely recognized brand in the world, more familiar than Coca-Cola. The values, tastes, and industrial practices of the American fast food industry are being exported to every corner of the globe, helping to create a homogenized international culture that sociologist Benjamin R. Barber has labeled "McWorld."

The fast food chains have become totems of Western economic development. They are often the first multinationals to arrive when a country has opened its markets, serving as the avant-garde of American franchising. Fifteen years ago, when McDonald's opened its first restaurant in Turkey, no other foreign franchisor did business there. Turkey now has hundreds of franchise outlets, including 7-Eleven, Nutra Slim, Re/Max Real Estate, Mail Boxes Etc., and Ziebart Tidy Car. Support for the growth of franchising has even become part of American foreign policy. The U.S. State Department now publishes detailed studies of overseas franchise opportunities and runs a Gold Key Program at many of its embassies to help American franchisors find overseas partners.

The anthropologist Yunxiang Yan has noted that in the eyes of Beijing consumers, McDonald's represents "Americana and the promise of modernization." Thousands of people waited patiently for hours to eat at the city's first McDonald's in 1992. Two years later, when a McDonald's opened in Kuwait, the line of cars waiting at the drive-through window extended for seven miles. Around the same time, a Kentucky Fried Chicken restaurant in Saudi Arabia's holy city of Mecca set new sales records for the chain, earning $200,000 in a single week during Ramadan, the Muslim holy month. In Brazil, McDonald's has become the nation's largest private employer. The fast food chains are now imperial fiefdoms, sending their emissaries far and wide. Classes at McDonald's Hamburger University in Oak Park, Illinois, are taught in twenty different languages. Few places on earth seem too distant or too remote for the golden arches. In 1986, the Tahiti Tourism Promotion Board ran an ad campaign featuring pristine beaches and the slogan "Sorry, No McDonald's." A decade later, one opened in Papeete, the Tahitian capital, bringing hamburgers and fries to a spot thousands of miles, across the Pacific, from the nearest cattle ranches or potato fields.

As the fast food chains have moved overseas, they have been accompanied by their major suppliers. In order to diminish fears of American imperialism, the chains try to purchase as much food as possible in the countries where they operate. Instead of importing food, they import entire systems of agricultural production. Seven years before McDonald's opened its first restaurant in India, the company began to establish a supply network there, teaching Indian farmers how to grow iceburg lettuce with seeds specially developed for the nation's climate. "A McDonald's restaurant is just the window of a much larger system comprising an extensive food-chain, running right up to the farms," one of the company's Indian partners told a foreign journalist.

In 1987, ConAgra took over the Elders Company in Australia, the largest beef company in the country that exports more beef than any other in the world. Over the past decade, Cargill and IBP have gained control of the beef industry in Canada. Cargill has established large-scale poultry operations in China and Thailand. Tyson Foods is planning to build chicken-processing plants in China, Indonesia, and the Philippines. ConAgra's Lamb Weston division now manufactures frozen french fries in Holland, India, and Turkey. McCain, the world's biggest french fry producer, operates fifty processing plants scattered across four continents. In order to supply McDonald's, J. R. Simplot began to grow Russet Burbank potatoes in China, opening that nation's first french fry factory in 1993. A few years ago Simplot bought eleven processing plants in Australia, aiming to increase sales in the East Asian market. He also purchased a 3-million-acre ranch in Australia, where he hopes to run cattle, raise vegetables, and grow potatoes. "It's a great little country," Simplot says, "and there's nobody in it."

As in the United States, the fast food companies have targeted their foreign advertising and promotion at a group of consumers with the fewest attachments to tradition: young children. "Kids are the same regarding the issues that affect the all-important stages of their development," a top executive at the Gepetto Group told the audience at a recent KidPower conference, "and they apply to any kid in Berlin, Beijing, or Brooklyn." The KidPower conference, attended by marketing executives from Burger King and Nickelodeon, among others, was held at the Disneyland outside of Paris. In Australia, where the number of fast food restaurants roughly tripled during the 1990s, a survey found that half of the nation's nine- and ten-year-olds thought that Ronald McDonald knew what kids should eat. At a primary school in Beijing, Yunxiang Yan found that all of the children recognized an image of Ronald McDonald. The children told Yan they liked "Uncle McDonald" because he was "funny, gentle, kind, and . . . he understood children's hearts." Coca-Cola is now the favorite drink among Chinese children, and McDonald's serves their favorite food. Simply eating at a McDonald's in Beijing seems to elevate a person's social status. The idea that you are what you eat has been enthusiastically promoted for years by Den Fujita, the eccentric billionaire who brought McDonald's to Japan three decades ago. "If we eat McDonald's hamburgers and potatoes for a thousand years," Fujita once promised his countrymen, "we will become taller, our skin will become white, and our hair will be blonde."

The impact of fast food is readily apparent in Germany, which has become one of McDonald's most profitable overseas markets. Germany is not only the largest country in Europe, but also the most Americanized. Although the four Allied powers occupied it after World War II, the Americans exerted the greatest lasting influence, perhaps because their nationalism was so inclusive, and their nation so distant. Children in West German schools were required to study English, facilitating the spread of American pop culture. Young people who sought to distance themselves from the wartime behavior of their parents found escape in American movies, music, and novels. "For a child growing up in the turmoil of [postwar] Berlin . . . the

Americans were angels," Christa Maerker, a Berlin filmmaker, wrote in an essay on postwar Germany's infatuation with the United States. "Anything from them was bigger and more wonderful than anything that preceded it."

The United States and Germany fought against each other twice in the twentieth century, but the enmity between them has often seemed less visceral than other national rivalries. The recent takeover of prominent American corporations—such as Chrysler, Random House, and RCA Records—by German companies provoked none of the public anger that was unleashed when Japanese firms bought much less significant American assets in the 1980s. Despite America's long-standing "special relationship" with Great Britain, the underlying cultural ties between the United States and Germany, though less obvious, are equally strong. Americans with German ancestors far outnumber those with English ancestors. Moreover, during the past century both American culture and German culture have shown an unusually strong passion for science, technology, engineering, empiricism, social order, and efficiency. The electronic paper-towel dispenser that I saw in a Munich men's room is the spiritual kin of the gas-powered ketchup dispensers at the McDonald's in Colorado Springs.

The traditional German restaurant—serving schnitzel, bratwurst, knackwurst, sauerbraten, and large quantities of beer—is rapidly disappearing in Germany. Such establishments now account for less than one-third of the German foodservice market. Their high labor costs have for the most part been responsible for their demise, along with the declining popularity of schnitzel. McDonald's Deutschland, Inc., is by far the biggest restaurant company in Germany today, more than twice as large as the nearest competitor. It opened the first German McDonald's in 1971; at the beginning of the 1990s it had four hundred restaurants, and now it has more than a thousand. The company's main dish happens to be named after Hamburg, a German city where ground-beef steaks were popular in the early nineteenth century. The hamburger was born when Americans added the bun. McDonald's Deutschland uses German potatoes for its fries and Bavarian dairy cows for its burgers. It sends Ronald McDonald into hospitals and schools. It puts new McDonald's restaurants in gas stations, railway stations, and airports. It battles labor unions and—according to Siegfried Pater, author of *Zum Beispiel McDonald's*—has repeatedly fired union sympathizers. The success of McDonald's, Pizza Hut, and T.G.I. Fridays in Germany has helped spark a franchising boom. Since 1992, the number of franchised outlets there has doubled, and about five thousand more are being added every year. In August of 1999, McDonald's Deutschland announced that it would be putting restaurants in Germany's new Wal-Mart stores. "The partnership scheme will undoubtedly be a success," a German financial analyst told London's *Evening Standard*. "The kiddie factor alone—children urging their parents to shop at Wal-Mart because they have a McDonald's inside the store—could generate an upsurge in customers.

The golden arches have become so commonplace in Germany that they seem almost invisible. You don't notice them unless you're looking for them, or feeling hungry. One German McDonald's, however, stands out from the rest. It sits on a nondescript street in a new shopping complex not far from Dachau, the first concentration camp opened by the Nazis. The stores were built on fields where Dachau's inmates once did forced labor. Although the architecture of the shopping complex looks German and futuristic, the haphazard placement of the buildings on the land seems distinctively American. They would not seem out of place near an off-ramp of I-25 in Colorado. Across the street from the McDonald's there's a discount supermarket. An auto parts store stands a few hundred yards from the other buildings, separated by fields that have not yet vanished beneath concrete. In 1997, protests were staged against the opening of a McDonald's so close to a concentration camp where gypsies, Jews, homosexuals, and political opponents of the Nazis were imprisoned, where Luftwaffe scientists performed medical experiments on inmates and roughly 30,000 people died. The McDonald's Corporation denied that it was trying to profit from the Holocaust and said the restaurant was at least a mile from the camp. After the curator of the Dachau Museum complained that McDonald's was distributing thousands of leaflets among tourists in the camp's parking lot, the company halted the practice. "Welcome to Dachau," said the leaflets, "and welcome to McDonald's."

The McDonald's at Dachau is one-third of a mile from the entrance to the concentration camp. The day I went there, the restaurant was staging a "Western Big Mac" promotion. It was decorated in a Wild West theme, with paper place mats featuring a wanted poster of "Butch Essidie." The restaurant was full of mothers and small children. Teenagers dressed in Nikes, Levis, and Tommy Hilfiger T-shirts sat in groups and smoked cigarettes. Turkish immigrants worked in the kitchen, seventies disco music played, and the red paper cups on everyone's tray said "Always Coca-Cola." This McDonald's was in Dachau, but it could have been anywhere—anywhere in the United States, anywhere in the world. Millions of other people at that very moment were standing at the same counter, ordering the same food from the same menu, food that tasted everywhere the same.

At the Circus

The most surreal experience that I had during three years of research into fast food took place not at the top-secret air force base that got its Domino's pizzas delivered, not at the flavor factory off the New Jersey Turnpike, not at the Dachau McDonald's. It occurred on March 1, 1999, at the Mirage Hotel in Las Vegas. Like an epiphany, it revealed the strange power of fast food in the new world order. The Mirage—with its five-story volcano, its shark tank, dolphin tank, indoor rain forest, Lagoon Saloon, DKNY boutique, and Secret Garden of Siegfried & Roy—is a fine place for the surreal. Even its name suggests the triumph of illusion over reality, a promise that you won't believe your eyes. On that day in March, as usual, Las Vegas was full of spectacles and name acts. George Carlin was at Bally's, and David Cassidy was at the MGM Grand, starring in *EFX*, a show billed as a high-tech journey through space and time. *The History of Sex* was at the Golden Nugget, *The Number One Fool Contest* was at the Comedy Stop, Joacquin Ayala (Mexico's most famous magician) was at Harrah's, the Radio City Rockettes were at the Flamingo Hilton, "the Dream King" (Elvis impersonator Trent Carlini) was at the Boardwalk. And Mikhail Gorbachev (former president of the Supreme Soviet of the USSR, winner of the Orders of Lenin, the Red Banner of Labor, and the Nobel Peace Prize) was at the Grand Ballroom of the Mirage, giving the keynote speech before a fast food convention.

The convention and its setting were an ideal match. In many ways Las Vegas is the fulfillment of social and economic trends now sweeping from the American West to the farthest reaches of the globe. Las Vegas is the fastest-growing major city in the United States—an entirely man-made creation, a city that lives for the present, that has little connection to its surrounding landscape, that cares little about its own past. Nothing in Las Vegas is built to last, hotels are routinely demolished as soon as they seem out of fashion, and the city limits seem as arbitrary as its location, with plastic bags and garbage littering the open land where the lawns end, the desert not far from the Strip.

Las Vegas began as an overnight camp for travelers going to California on the Old Spanish Trail. It later became a ranching town, notable in the early 1940s mainly for its rodeo, its Wild West tourist attractions, and a nightclub called the Apache Bar. The population was about 8,000. The subsequent growth of Las Vegas was made possible by the federal government, which spent billions of dollars to erect the Hoover Dam and build military bases near the city. The dam supplied water and electricity, while the bases provided the early casinos with customers. When authorities in southern California cracked down on illegal gambling after World War II, the gamblers headed for Nevada. As in Colorado Springs, the real boom in Las Vegas began toward the end of the 1970s. Over the past twenty years the population of Las Vegas has nearly tripled.

Today there are few remaining traces of the city's cowboy past. Indeed, the global equation has been reversed. While the rest of the world builds Wal-Marts, Arby's, Taco Bells, and other outposts of Americana, Las Vegas has spent the past decade re-creating the rest of the world. The fast food joints along the Strip seem insignificant compared to the new monuments towering over them: recreations of the Eiffel Tower, the Statue of Liberty, and the Sphinx, enormous buildings that evoke Venice, Paris, New York, Tuscany, medieval England, ancient Egypt and Rome, the Middle East, the

South Seas. Las Vegas is now so contrived and artificial that it has become something authentic, a place unlike any other. The same forces that are ho-mogenizing other cities have made Las Vegas even more unique.

At the heart of Las Vegas is technology: machinery that cools the air, erupts the volcano, and powers the shimmering lights. Most important of all is the machinery that makes money for the casinos. While Las Vegas por-trays itself as a free-wheeling, entrepreneurial town where anyone can come and strike it rich, life there is more tightly regulated, controlled, and moni-tored by hidden cameras than just about anywhere else in the United States. The city's principal industry is legally protected against the workings of the free market, and operates according to strict rules laid down by the state. The Nevada Gaming Control Board determines not only who can own a casino, but who can enter one. In a town built on gambling, where fortunes were once earned with a roll of the dice, it is remarkable how little is now left to chance. Until the late 1960s, about three-quarters of a typical casino's profits came from table games, from poker, blackjack, baccarat, roulette. During the last twenty-five years table games, which are supervised by deal-ers and offer gamblers the best odds, have been displaced by slot machines. Today about two-thirds of a typical casino's profits now come from slots and video poker—machines that are precisely calibrated to take your money. They guarantee the casino a profit rate of as much as 20 percent—four times what a roulette wheel will bring.

The latest slot machines are electronically connected to a central com-puter, allowing the casino to track the size of every bet and its outcome. The music, flashing lights, and sound effects emitted by these slots help disguise the fact that a small processor inside them is deciding with mathematical certainty how long you will play before you lose. It is the ultimate consumer technology, designed to manufacture not a tangible product, but something much more elusive: a brief sense of hope. That is what Las Vegas really sells, the most brilliant illusion of all, a loss that feels like winning.

Mikhail Gorbachev was in town to speak at the Twenty-sixth Annual Chain Operators Exchange, a convention sponsored by the International Foodservice Manufacturers Association. Executives from the major fast food companies had gathered to discuss, among other things, the latest labor-saving machinery and the prospects of someday employing a workforce that needed "zero training." Representatives from the industry's leading suppli-ers—ConAgra, Monfort, Simplot, and others—had come to sell their latest products. The Grand Ballroom at the Mirage was filled with hundreds of middle-aged white men in expensive business suits. They sat at long tables beneath crystal chandeliers, drinking coffee, greeting old friends, waiting for the morning program to begin. A few of them were obviously struggling to recover from whatever they'd done in Las Vegas the night before.

On the surface, Mikhail Gorbachev seemed an odd choice to address a group so resolutely opposed to labor unions, minimum wages, and workplace safety rules. "Those who hope we shall move away from the socialist path will be greatly disappointed," Gorbachev had written in *Perestroika* (1987), at the height of his power. He had never sought the dissolution of the Soviet Union and never renounced his fundamental commitment to Marxism-Leninism. He still believed in the class struggle and "scientific socialism." But the fall of the Berlin Wall had thrown Gorbachev out of power and left him in a precarious financial condition. He was beloved abroad, yet despised in his own land. During Russia's 1996 presidential election he received just 1 percent of the vote. The following year he expressed great praise for America's leading fast food chain. "And the merry clowns, the Big Mac signs, the colourful, unique decorations and ideal cleanliness," Gorbachev wrote in the foreword of *To Russia with Fries*, a memoir by a McDonald's executive, "all of this complements the hamburgers whose great popularity is well deserved."

In December of 1997, Gorbachev appeared in a Pizza Hut commercial, following in the footsteps of Cindy Crawford and Ivana Trump. A group of patrons at a Moscow Pizza Hut thanked him in the ad for bringing the fast food chain to Russia and then shouted "Hail to Gorbachev!" In response Gorbachev saluted them by raising a slice of pizza. He reportedly earned $160,000 for his appearance in the sixty-second spot, money earmarked for his nonprofit foundation. A year later Pizza Hut announced that it was pulling out of Russia as the country's economy collapsed, and Gorbachev told a German reporter that "all my money is gone." For his hour-long speech at the Mirage, Gorbachev was promised a fee of $150,000 and the use of a private jet.

The Twenty-sixth Annual Chain Operators Exchange officially opened with a video presentation of the national anthem. As the song boomed from speakers throughout the Grand Ballroom, two huge screens above the stage displayed a series of patriotic images: the Statue of Liberty, the Lincoln Memorial, amber waves of grain. In one of the morning's first speeches, an executive hailed the restaurant industry's record profits the previous year, adding without irony, "As if things weren't good enough, consumers also dropped all pretense of wanting healthy food." An ongoing industry survey had found that public concerns about salt, fat, and food additives were at their lowest level since 1982, when the survey began—one more bit of news to justify the industry's "current state of bliss." Another executive, a self-described "sensory evaluation specialist," emphasized the importance of pleasant smells. He noted that Las Vegas resorts were now experimenting with "signature scents" in their casinos, hoping the subtle aromas would subconsciously make people gamble more money.

Robert Nugent, the head of Jack in the Box and honorary chairman of the Twenty-sixth Annual Chain Operator's Exchange, broke the cheery mood with an ominous, unsettling speech. He essentially accused critics of the fast food industry of being un-American. "A growing number of groups who represent narrow social and political interests," Nugent warned, "have set their sights on our industry in an effort to legislate behavioral change." Enjoying a great meal at a restaurant was "the very essence of freedom," he declared, a ritual now being threatened by groups with an agenda that was "anti-meat, anti-alcohol, anti-caffeine, anti-fat, anti-chemical additives, anti-horseradish, anti-non-dairy creamer." The media played a central role in helping these "activist fearmongers," but the National Restaurant Association had recently launched a counterattack, working closely with journalists to dispel myths and gain better publicity. Nugent called upon the fast food executives to respond even more forcefully to their critics, people who today posed "a real danger to our industry—and more broadly to our way of life."

Not long afterward Mikhail Gorbachev appeared onstage and received a standing ovation. Here was the man who'd ended the Cold War, who'd brought political freedom to hundreds of millions, who'd opened vast new markets. At the age of sixty-nine Gorbachev looked remarkably unchanged from his appearance during the Reagan years. His hair was white, but he seemed vigorous and strong, still capable of running a mighty empire. He spoke quickly in Russian and then waited patiently for the translator to catch up. His delivery was full of energy and passion. "I like America," Gorbachev said with a broad smile. "And I like American people." He wanted to give the audience a sense of what was happening in Russia today. Few people in the United States seemed to care much about events in Russia, a dangerous state of affairs. He asked the crowd to learn about his country, to form partnerships and make investments there. "You must have a lot of money," Gorbachev said. "Send it to Russia."

A few minutes into Gorbachev's speech, the audience began to lose interest. He had badly misjudged the crowd. His speech might have been a success at the Council on Foreign Relations or at the United Nations General Assembly, but at the Grand Ballroom of the Mirage it was a bomb. As Gorbachev explained why the United States must strongly support the policies of Yevgeny Primakov (the Russian prime minister who was fired not long afterward) row after row of eyes began to glaze. He earnestly asked why there was "some kind of a dislike of Primakov that is widespread in this country," unaware that few Americans knew who Yevgeny Primakov was and even fewer cared about him, one way or the other. I counted at least half a dozen people seated near me in the Grand Ballroom who fell asleep during Gorbachev's speech. The executive right beside me suddenly awoke in the middle of a long anecdote about how the Mongol invasion had affected the Russian character in the Middle Ages. The executive seemed startled and unaware of his surroundings, then glanced at the podium for a moment, felt reassured, and drifted back to sleep, his chin resting flat on his chest.

Gorbachev sounded like a politician from a distant era, from a time before sound bites. He was serious, long-winded, and sometimes difficult to follow. His mere presence at the Mirage was far more important to this crowd than anything he said. The meaning hit me as I looked around at all the fast food executives, the sea of pinstriped suits and silk ties. In ancient Rome, the leaders of conquered nations were put on display at the Circus. The symbolism was unmistakable; the submission to Rome, complete. Gorbachev's appearance at the Mirage seemed an Americanized version of that custom, a public opportunity for the victors to gloat—though it would have been even more fitting if the fast food convention had been down the road at Caesar's Palace.

As a Soviet leader, Mikhail Gorbachev never learned when to leave the stage, a flaw that led to his humiliating defeat in the election of 1996. He made the same mistake in Las Vegas; people got up and left the Grand Ballroom while he was still speaking. "Margaret Thatcher was a lot better," I heard one executive say to another as they headed for the door. Thatcher had addressed the previous year's Chain Operators Exchange.

The day after Gorbachev's speech at the Mirage, Bob Dylan performed at the grand opening of the new Mandalay Bay casino. And billboards along the interstate announced that Peter Lowe's Success 1999 was coming to Las Vegas, with special appearances by Elizabeth Dole and General Colin Powell.

An Empire of Fat

For most of the twentieth century, the Soviet Union stood as the greatest obstacle to the worldwide spread of American values and the American way of life. The collapse of Soviet Communism has led to an unprecedented "Americanization" of the world, expressed in the growing popularity of movies, CDs, music videos, television shows, and clothing from the United States. Unlike those commodities, fast food is the one form of American culture that foreign consumers literally consume. By eating like Americans, people all over the world are beginning to look more like Americans, at least in one respect. The United States now has the highest obesity rate of any industrialized nation in the world. More than half of all American adults and about one-quarter of all American children are now obese or overweight. Those proportions have soared during the last few decades, along with the consumption of fast food. The rate of obesity among American adults is twice as high today as it was in the early 1960s. The rate of obesity among American children is twice as high as it was in the late 1970s. According to James O. Hill, a prominent nutritionist at the University of Colorado, "We've got the fattest, least fit generation of kids ever."

The medical literature classifies a person as obese if he or she has a Body Mass Index (BMI) of 30 or higher—a measurement that takes into account both weight and height. For example, a woman who is five-foot-five and weighs 132 pounds has a BMI of 22, which is considered normal. If she gains eighteen pounds, her BMI rises to 25, and she's considered overweight. If she gains fifty pounds, her BMI reaches 30, and she's considered obese. Today about 44 million American adults are obese. An additional 6 million are "super-obese"; they weigh about a hundred pounds more than they should. No other nation in history has gotten so fat so fast.

A recent study by half a dozen researchers at the Centers for Disease Control and Prevention found that the rate of American obesity was increasing in every state and among both sexes, regardless of age, race, or educational level. In 1991, only four states had obesity rates of 15 percent or higher; today at least thirty-seven states do. "Rarely do chronic conditions such as obesity," the CDC scientists observed, "spread with the speed and dispersion characteristic of a communicable disease epidemic." Although the current rise in obesity has a number of complex causes, genetics is not one of them. The American gene pool has not changed radically in the past few decades. What has changed is the nation's way of eating and living. In simple terms: when people eat more and move less, they get fat. In the United States, people have become increasingly sedentary—driving to work instead of walking, performing little manual labor, driving to do errands, watching television, playing video games, and using a computer instead of exercising. Budget cuts have eliminated physical education programs at many schools. And the growth of the fast food industry has made an abundance of high-fat, inexpensive meals widely available.

As people eat more meals outside the home, they consume more calories, less fiber, and more fat. Commodity prices have fallen so low that the fast food industry has greatly increased its portion sizes, without reducing profits, in order to attract customers. The size of a burger has become one of its main selling points. Wendy's offers the Triple Decker; Burger King, the Great American; and Hardee's sells a hamburger called the Monster. The Little Caesars slogan "Big! Big!" now applies not just to the industry's portions, but to its customers. Over the past forty years in the United States, per capita consumption of carbonated soft drinks has more than quadrupled. During the late 1950s the typical soft drink order at a fast food restaurant contained about eight ounces of soda; today a "Child" order of Coke at McDonald's is twelve ounces. A "Large" Coke is thirty-two ounces—and about 310 calories. In 1972, McDonald's added Large French Fries to its menu; twenty years later, the chain added Super Size Fries, a serving three times larger than what McDonald's offered a generation ago. Super Size Fries have 540 calories and 25 grams of fat. At Carl's Jr. restaurants, an order of CrissCut Fries and a Double Western Bacon Cheeseburger boasts 73 grams of fat—more fat than ten of the chain's milk shakes.

A number of attempts to introduce healthy dishes (such as the McLean Deluxe, a hamburger partly composed of seaweed) have proven unsuccessful. A taste for fat developed in childhood is difficult to lose as an adult. At the moment, the fast food industry is heavily promoting menu items that contain bacon. "Consumers savor the flavor while operators embrace [the] profit margin," *Advertising Age* noted. A decade ago, restaurants sold about 20 percent of the bacon consumed in the United States; now they sell about 70 percent. "Make It Bacon" is one of the new slogans at McDonald's. With the exception of Subway (which promotes healthier food), the major chains have apparently decided that it's much easier and much more profitable to increase the size and the fat content of their portions than to battle eating habits largely formed by years of their own mass marketing.

The cost of America's obesity epidemic extends far beyond emotional pain and low self-esteem. Obesity is now second only to smoking as a cause of mortality in the United States. The CDC estimates that about 280,000 Americans die every year as a direct result of being overweight. The annual health care costs in the United States stemming from obesity now approach $240 billion; on top of that Americans spend more than $33 billion on various weight-loss schemes and diet products. Obesity has been linked to heart disease, colon cancer, stomach cancer, breast cancer, diabetes, arthritis, high blood pressure, infertility, and strokes. A 1999 study by the American Cancer Society found that overweight people had a much higher rate of premature death. Severely overweight people were four times more likely to die young than people of normal weight. Moderately overweight people were twice as likely to die young. "The message is we're too fat and it's killing us," said one of the study's principal authors. Young people who are obese face not only long-term, but also immediate threats to their health. Severely obese American children, aged six to ten, are now dying from heart attacks caused by their weight.

The obesity epidemic that began in the United States during the late 1970s is now spreading to the rest of the world, with fast food as one of its vectors. Between 1984 and 1993, the number of fast food restaurants in Great Britain roughly doubled—and so did the obesity rate among adults. The British now eat more fast food than any other nationality in Western Europe. They also have the highest obesity rate. Obesity is much less of a problem in Italy and Spain, where spending on fast food is relatively low. The relationship between a nation's fast food consumption and its rate of obesity has not been definitively established through any long-term, epidemiological study. The growing popularity of fast food is just one of many cultural changes that have been brought about by globalization. Nevertheless, it seems wherever America's fast food chains go, waistlines start expanding.

In China, the proportion of overweight teenagers has roughly tripled in the past decade. In Japan, eating hamburgers and french fries has not made people any blonder, though it has made them fatter. Overweight people were once a rarity in Japan. The nation's traditional diet of rice, fish, vegetables, and soy products has been deemed one of the healthiest in the world. And yet the Japanese are rapidly abandoning that diet. Consumption of red meat has been rising in Japan since the American occupation after World War II. The arrival of McDonald's in 1971 accelerated the shift in Japanese eating habits. During the 1980s, the sale of fast food in Japan more than doubled; the rate of obesity among children soon doubled, too. Today about one-third of all Japanese men in their thirties—members of the nation's first generation raised on Happy Meals and "Bi-gu Ma-kus"—are overweight. Heart disease, diabetes, colon cancer, and breast cancer, the principal "diseases of affluence" have been linked to diets low in fiber and high in animal fats. Long common in the United States, these diseases are likely to become widespread in Japan as its fast food generation ages. More than a decade ago a study of middle-aged Japanese men who had settled in the United States found that their switch to a Western diet doubled their risk of heart disease and tripled their risk of stroke. For the men in the study, embracing an American way of life meant increasing the likelihood of a premature death.

Obesity is extremely difficult to cure. During thousands of years marked by food scarcity, human beings developed efficient physiological mechanisms to store energy as fat. Until recently, societies rarely enjoyed an overabundance of cheap food. As a result, our bodies are far more efficient at gaining weight than at losing it. Health officials have concluded that prevention, not treatment, offers the best hope of halting the worldwide obesity epidemic. European consumer groups are pushing for a complete ban on all television advertising directed at children. In 1992 Sweden banned all TV advertising directed at children under the age of twelve. Ads have been banned from children's television programming in Norway, Belgium, Ireland, and Holland. The eating habits of American kids are widely considered a good example of what other countries must avoid. American children now get about one-quarter of their total vegetable servings in the form of potato chips or french fries. A survey of children's advertising in the European Union (EU) found that 95 percent of the food ads there encouraged kids to eat foods high in sugar, salt, and fat. The company running the most ads aimed at children was McDonald's.

McLibel

"Resist America beginning with Cola," said a banner at Beijing University in May of 1999. "Attack McDonald's, Storm KFC." The U.S. Air Force had just bombed the Chinese Embassy in Belgrade, Yugoslavia, and anti-American demonstrations were erupting throughout China. At least a dozen McDonald's and four Kentucky Fried Chicken restaurants were damaged by Chinese protesters. For some reason, no Pizza Huts were harmed. "Maybe they think it's Italian," said a Pizza Hut spokesman in Shanghai.

A generation ago American embassies and oil companies were the most likely targets of overseas demonstrations against "U.S. imperialism." Today fast food restaurants have assumed that symbolic role, with McDonald's a particular favorite. In 1995, a crowd of four hundred Danish anarchists looted a McDonald's in downtown Copenhagen, made a bonfire of its furniture in the street, and burned the restaurant to the ground. In 1996, Indian farmers ransacked a Kentucky Fried Chicken restaurant in Bangalore, convinced that the chain threatened their traditional agricultural practices. In 1997, a McDonald's in the Colombian city of Cali was destroyed by a bomb. In 1998, bombs destroyed a McDonald's in St. Petersburg, Russia, two McDonald's in suburban Athens, a McDonald's in the heart of Rio de Janeiro, and a Planet Hollywood in Cape Town, South Africa. In 1999, Belgian vegetarians set fire to a McDonald's in Antwerp, and a year later, May Day protesters tore the sign off a McDonald's in London's Trafalgar Square, destroyed the restaurant, and handed out free hamburgers to the crowd. Fearing more violence, McDonald's temporarily closed all fifty of its London restaurants.

In France, a French sheep farmer and political activist named Jose Bove led a group that demolished a McDonald's under construction in his hometown of Millau. Bove's defiant attitude, brief imprisonment, and impassioned speeches against "lousy food" have made him a hero in France, praised by socialists and conservatives, invited to meetings with the president and the prime minister. He has written a French bestseller entitled *The World Is Not for Sale—And Nor Am I!* In a society where food is a source of tremendous national pride, the McDonald's Corporation has become an easy target, for reasons that are not entirely symbolic. McDonald's is now the largest purchaser of agricultural commodities in France. Bove's message—that Frenchmen should not become "servile slaves at the service of agribusiness"—has struck a chord. During July of 2000 an estimated thirty thousand demonstrators gathered in Millau when Jose Bove went on trial, some carrying signs that said "Non à McMerde."

The overseas critics of fast food are far more diverse than America's old Soviet bloc adversaries. Farmers, leftists, anarchists, nationalists, environmentalists, consumer advocates, educators, health officials, labor unions, and defenders of animal rights have found common ground in a campaign against the perceived Americanization of the world. Fast food has become a target because it is so ubiquitous and because it threatens a fundamental aspect of national identity: how, where, and what people choose to eat.

The longest-running and most systematic assault on fast food overseas has been waged by a pair of British activists affiliated with London Greenpeace. The loosely organized group was formed in 1971 to oppose French nuclear weapon tests in the South Seas. It later staged demonstrations in support of animal rights and British trade unions. It protested against nuclear power and the Falklands War. The group's membership was a small, eclectic mix of pacifists, anarchists, vegetarians, and libertarians brought together by a commitment to nonviolent political action. They ran the organization without any formal leadership, even refusing to join the International Greenpeace movement.

A typical meeting of London Greenpeace attracted anywhere from three people to three dozen. In 1986 the group decided to target McDonald's, later explaining that the company "epitomises everything we despise: a junk culture, the deadly banality of capitalism." Members of London Greenpeace began to distribute a six-page leaflet called "What's Wrong with McDonald's? Everything they don't want you to know." It accused the fast food chain of promoting Third World poverty, selling unhealthy food, exploiting workers and children, torturing animals, and destroying the Amazon rain forest, among other things. Some of the text was factual and straightforward; some of it was pure agitprop. Along the top of the leaflet ran a series of golden arches punctuated by slogans like "McDollars, McGreedy, McCancer, McMurder, McProfits, McGarbage." London Greenpeace distributed the leaflets for four years without attracting much attention. And then in September of 1990 McDonald's sued five members of the group for libel, claiming that every statement in the leaflet was false.

The libel laws in Great Britain are far more unfavorable to a defendant than those in the United States. Under American law, an accuser must prove that the allegations at the heart of a libel case are not only false and defamatory, but also have been recklessly, negligently, or deliberately spread. Under British law, the burden of proof is on the defendant. Allegations that may harm someone's reputation are presumed to be false. Moreover, the defendant in a British court has to use primary sources, such as firsthand witnesses and official documents, to prove the accuracy of a published statement. Secondary sources, including peer-reviewed articles in scientific journals, are deemed inadmissible as evidence. And the defendant's intentions are irrelevant—a British libel case can be lost because of a truly innocent mistake.

The McDonald's Corporation had for years taken advantage of British libel laws to silence its critics. During the 1980s alone, McDonald's threatened to sue at least fifty British publications and organizations, including Channel 4, the Sunday *Times*, the *Guardian*, the *Sun*, student publications, a vegetarian society, and a Scottish youth theater group. The tactic worked, prompting retractions and apologies. The cost of losing a libel case, in both legal fees and damages, could be huge.

The London Greenpeace activists being sued by McDonald's had not written the leaflet in question; they had merely handed it to people. Nevertheless, their behavior could be ruled libelous. Fearing the potential monetary costs, three of the activists reluctantly appeared in court and apologized to McDonald's. The other two decided to fight.

Helen Steel was a twenty-five-year-old gardener, minibus driver, and bartender who'd been drawn to London Greenpeace by her devotion to vegetarianism and animal rights. Dave Morris was a thirty-six-year-old single father, a former postal worker interested in labor issues and the power of multinational corporations. The two friends seemed to stand little chance in court against the world's largest fast food chain. Steel had left school at seventeen, Morris at eighteen; and neither could afford a lawyer. McDonald's, on the other hand, could afford armies of attorneys and had annual revenues at the time of about $18 billion. Morris and Steel were denied legal aid and forced to defend themselves in front of a judge, instead of a jury. But with some help from the secretary of the Haldane Society of Socialist Lawyers, the pair turned the "McLibel case" into the longest trial in British history and a public relations disaster for McDonald's.

The McDonald's Corporation had never expected the case to reach the courtroom. The burden on the defendants was enormous: Morris and Steel had to assemble witnesses and official documents to support the broad assertions in the leaflet. The pair proved to be indefatigable researchers, aided by the McLibel Support Campaign, an international network of activists. By the end of the trial, the court record included 40,000 pages of documents and witness statements, as well as 18,000 pages of transcripts.

McDonald's had made a huge tactical error by asserting that everything in the leaflet was libelous—not only the more extreme claims ("McDonald's and Burger King are . . . using lethal poisons to destroy vast areas of Central American rainforest"), but also the more innocuous ones ("a diet high in fat, sugar, animal products, and salt . . . is linked with cancers of the breast and bowel, and heart disease"). The blunder allowed Steel and Morris to turn the tables, putting McDonald's on trial and forcing a public examination of the chain's labor, marketing, environmental, nutrition, food safety, and animal welfare policies. Some of the chain's top executives were forced to appear on the stand and endure days of cross-examination by the pair of self-taught attorneys. The British media seized upon the David-and-Goliath aspects of the story and made the trial front-page news.

After years of legal wrangling, the McLibel trial formally began in March of 1994. It ended more than three years later, when Justice Rodger Bell submitted an 800-page judgement. Morris and Steel were found to have libeled McDonald's. The judge ruled that the two had failed to prove many of their allegations—but had indeed proved some. According to Justice Bell's decision, McDonald's did "exploit" children through its advertising, endanger the health of its regular customers, pay workers unreasonably low wages, oppose union activities worldwide, and bear responsibility for the cruelty inflicted upon animals by many of its suppliers. Morris and Steel were fined £60,000. The two promptly announced they would appeal the decision. "McDonald's don't deserve a penny," Helen Steel said, "and in any event we haven't got any money."

Evidence submitted during the McLibel trial disclosed much about the inner workings of the McDonald's Corporation. Many of its labor, food safety, and advertising practices had already been publicly criticized in the United States for years. Testimony in the London courtroom, however, provided new revelations about the company's attitude toward civil liberties and freedom of speech. Morris and Steel were stunned to discover that McDonald's had infiltrated London Greenpeace with informers, who regularly attended the group's meetings and spied on its members.

The spying had begun in 1989 and did not end until 1991, nearly a year after the libel suit had been filed. McDonald's had used subterfuge not only to find out who'd distributed the leaflets, but also to learn how Morris and Steel planned to defend themselves in court. The company had employed at least seven different undercover agents. During some London Greenpeace meetings, about half the people in attendance were corporate spies. One spy broke into the London Greenpeace office, took photographs, and stole documents. Another had a six-month affair with a member of London Greenpeace while informing on his activities. McDonald's spies inadvertently spied on each other, unaware that the company was using at least two different detective agencies. They participated in demonstrations against McDonald's and gave out anti-McDonald's leaflets.

During the trial, Sidney Nicholson—the McDonald's vice president who'd supervised the undercover operation, a former police officer in South Africa and former superintendent in London's Metropolitan Police—admitted in court that McDonald's had used its law enforcement connections to obtain information on Steel and Morris from Scotland Yard. Indeed, officers belonging to Special Branch, an elite British unit that tracks "subversives" and organized crime figures, had helped McDonald's spy on Steel and Morris for years. One of the company's undercover agents later had a change of heart and testified on behalf of the McLibel defendants. "At no time did I believe they were dangerous people," said Fran Tiller, following her conversion to vegetarianism. "I think they genuinely believed in the issues they were supporting."

For Dave Morris, perhaps the most disturbing moment of the trial was hearing how McDonald's had obtained his home address. One of its spies admitted in court that a gift of baby clothes had been a ruse to find out where Morris lived. Morris had unwittingly accepted the gift, believing it to be an act of friendship—and was disgusted to learn that his infant son had for months worn outfits supplied by McDonald's as part of its surveillance.

I visited Dave Morris one night in February of 1999, as he prepared for an appearance the next day before the Court of Appeal. Morris lives in a small flat above a carpet shop in North London. The apartment lacks central heating, the ceilings are sagging, and the place is crammed with books, boxes, files, transcripts, leaflets, and posters announcing various demonstrations. The place feels like everything McDonald's is not—lively, unruly, deeply idiosyncratic, and organized according to a highly complex scheme that only one human being could possibly understand. Morris spent about an hour with me, as his son finished homework upstairs. He spoke intensely about McDonald's, but stressed that its arrogant behavior was just one manifestation of a much larger problem now confronting the world: the rise of powerful multinationals that shift capital across borders with few qualms, that feel no allegiance to any nation, no loyalty to any group of farmers, workers, or consumers.

The British journalist John Vidal, in his book on the McLibel trial, noted some of the similarities between Dave Morris and Ray Kroc. As Morris offered an impassioned critique of globalization, the comparison made sense—both men true believers, charismatic, driven by ideas outside the mainstream, albeit championing opposite viewpoints. During the McLibel trial, Paul Preston, the president of McDonald's UK, had said, "Fitting into a finely working machine, that's what McDonald's is about." And here was Morris, in the living room of his North London flat, warmed by a gas heater in the fireplace, surrounded by stacks of papers and files, caring nothing for money, determined somehow to smash that machine.

On March 31, 1999, the three Court of Appeal justices overruled parts of the original McLibel verdict, supporting the leaflet's assertions that eating McDonald's food can cause heart disease and that workers are treated badly. The court reduced the damages owed by Steel and Morris to about £40,000. The McDonald's Corporation had previously announced that it had no intention of collecting the money and would no longer try to stop London Greenpeace from distributing the leaflet (which by then had been translated into twenty-seven languages). McDonald's was tired of the bad publicity and wanted this case to go away. But Morris and Steel were not yet through with McDonald's. They appealed the Court of Appeal decision to the British House of Lords and sued the police for spying on them. Scotland Yard settled the case out of court, apologizing to the pair and paying them £10,000 in damages. When the House of Lords refused to hear their case, Morris and Steel filed an appeal with the European Court of Human Rights, challenging the validity not only of the verdict, but also of the British libel laws. As of this writing, the McLibel case is entering its eleventh year. After intimidating British critics for years, the McDonald's Corporation picked on the wrong two people.

Back at the Ranch

When the first McDonald's opened in East Germany, in December of 1990, the company was unsure how American food would be received there. On opening day the McDonald's in Plauen served potato dumplings, a Vogtland favorite, along with hamburgers and fries. Today hundreds of McDonald's restaurants dot the landscape of eastern Germany. In town after town, statues of Lenin have come down and statues of Ronald McDonald have gone up. One of the largest is in Bitterfeld, where a three-story-high, illuminated Ronald can be seen from the autobahn for miles.

During my first visit to Plauen, in October of 1998, McDonald's was the only business open in the central market square. It was Reunification Day, a national holiday, and everything else was closed, the small shops selling used clothing and furniture, the pseudo-Irish pub on one corner, the pizzeria on another. McDonald's was packed, overflowing not just with children and their parents, but with teenagers, seniors, young couples, a cross-section of the town. The restaurant was brightly lit and spotlessly clean. Cheerful middle-aged women took orders behind the counter, worked in the kitchen, delivered food to tables, scrubbed the windows. Most of them had worked at this McDonald's for years. Some had been there since the day it opened. Across the street stood an abandoned building once occupied by a branch of the East German army; a few blocks away the houses were dilapidated and covered in graffiti, looking as though the Wall had never fallen. That day McDonald's was the nicest, cleanest, brightest place in all of Plauen. Children played with the Hot Wheels and Barbies that came with their Happy Meals, and smiling workers poured free refills of coffee. Outside the window, three bright red flags bearing the golden arches fluttered in the wind.

Life after Communism has not been easy in Plauen. At first there was an outpouring of great optimism and excitement. As in other East German towns, people quickly used their new liberty to travel overseas for the first time. They borrowed money to buy new cars. According to Thomas Küttler, the hero of Plauen's 1989 uprising, thoughts about Friedrich von Schiller and the freedom of their forefathers soon gave way to a hunger for Western consumer goods. Küttler is disappointed by how fast the idealism of 1989 vanished, but feels little nostalgia for the old East Germany. Under Communist rule in Plauen, a person could be arrested for watching television broadcasts from the West or for listening to American rock 'n' roll. Today in Plauen you can get dozens of channels on cable and even more via satellite. MTV is popular there, and most of the songs on the radio are in English. Becoming part of the larger world, however, has had its costs. Plauen's economy has suffered as one after another, old and inefficient manufacturing plants closed, throwing people out of work. Since the fall of the Berlin Wall, Plauen has lost about 10 percent of its population, as people move away in search of a better life. The town seems unable to break free from its past. Every year a few unexploded bombs from World War II are still discovered and defused.

At the moment, Plauen's unemployment rate is about 20 percent—twice the rate in Germany as a whole. You see men in their forties, a lost generation, too young to retire but too old to fit into the new scheme, staggering drunk in the middle of the day. The factory workers who bravely defied and brought down the old regime are the group who've fared worst, the group with the wrong skills and the least hope. Others have done quite well.

Manfred Voigt, the McDonald's franchisee in Plauen, is now a successful businessman who, with his wife, Brigitte, vacations in Florida every year. In an interview with the *Wall Street Journal*, Manfred Voigt attributed his recent success to forces beyond his control. "It was dumb luck," Voigt explained; "fate." He and his wife had no money and could not understand why McDonald's had chosen them to own its first restaurant in East Germany, why the company had trained and financed them. One explanation, never really explored in the *Wall Street Journal* profile, might be that the Voigts were one of the most powerful couples in Plauen under the old regime. They headed the local branch of Konsum, the state-controlled foodservice monopoly. Today the Voigts are one of Plauen's wealthiest couples; they own two other McDonald's in nearby towns. Throughout the former Eastern bloc, members of the old Communist elite have had the easiest time adjusting to Western consumerism. They had the right connections and many of the right skills. They now own some of the most lucrative franchises.

The high unemployment rate in Plauen has created social and political instability. What seems lacking is a stable middle ground. Roughly a third of the young people in eastern Germany now express support for various nationalist and neo-Nazi groups. Right-wing extremists have declared large parts of the east to be "foreigner-free" zones, where immigrants are not welcome. The roads leading into Plauen are decorated with signs posted by the Deutschland Volks Union, a right-wing party. "Germany for the Germans," the signs say. "Jobs for Germans, Not Foreigners." Neo-Nazi skinheads have thus far not caused much trouble in Plauen, though a black person today needs real courage to walk the city's streets at night. The opposition to American fast food voiced by many environmentalists and left-wing groups does not seem to be shared by German groups on the far right. When I asked an employee at the McDonald's in Plauen if the restaurant had ever been the target of neo-Nazis, she laughed and said there'd never been any threats of that kind. People in the area did not consider McDonald's to be "foreign."

Around the time that Plauen got its McDonald's in 1990, a new nightclub opened in a red brick building on the edge of town. "The Ranch" has an American flag and a Confederate flag hanging out front. Inside there's a long bar, and the walls are decorated with old-fashioned farm implements, saddles, bridles, and wagon wheels. Frieder Stephan, the owner of The Ranch, was inspired by photographs of the American West, but gathered all the items on the walls from nearby farms. The place looks like a bar in Cripple Creek, circa 1895. Before the fall of the Berlin Wall, Frieder Stephan was a disc jockey on an East German tourist ferry. He secretly listened to Creedance Clearwater, the Stones, and the Lovin' Spoonful. Now forty-nine years old, he is the leading impresario in Plauen's thriving country-western scene, booking local bands (like the Midnight Ramblers and C.C. Raider) at his club. The city's country-western fans call themselves "Vogtland Cowboys," put on their western boots and ten-gallon hats at night, and hit the town, drinking at The Ranch or joining the Square Dance Club at a bar called the White Magpie. The Square Dance Club is sponsored by Thommy's Western Store on Friedrich Engels Avenue. Plauen now has a number of small westernwear shops like Thommy's that sell imported cowboy boots, cowboy posters, fancy belt buckles, work shirts with snaps, and Wrangler jeans. While teenagers in Colorado Springs today could not care less about cowboys, kids in Plauen are sporting bolo ties and cowboy hats.

Every Wednesday night, a few hundred people gather at The Ranch for line dancing. Members of Plauen's American Car Club pull up in their big Ford and Chevy trucks. Others come from miles away, dressed in their western best, ready to dance. Most of them are working class, and many are unemployed. Their ages range from seven years old to seventy. If somebody doesn't know how to line-dance, a young woman named Petra gives lessons. People wear their souvenir T-shirts from Utah. They smoke Marlboros and drink beer. They listen to Willie Nelson, Garth Brooks, Johnny Cash—and they dance, kicking up their boots, twirling their partners, waving their cowboy hats in the air. And for a few hours the spirit of the American West fills this funky bar deep in the heart of Saxony, in a town that has seen too much history, and the old dream lives on, the dream of freedom without limits, self-reliance, and a wide-open frontier.   ■

NOTES:

Few West Germans are familiar with the unusual history of Plauen, though it is abundantly detailed in a number of locally published books. *Plauen: auf historischen Postkarten* (Plauen, Germany: Plauen Verlag, 1991), by Frank Weiss, uses old postcards to illustrate the history of the city during its most prosperous era. *Plauen: 1933–1945* (Plauen: Vogtländischer Heimatverlag Neupert, 1995) is an oversized book, full of photographs, that traces the effects of the Great Depression and the rise of the Nazi Party. The Allied bombing of the city is vividly documented through before-and-after photographs in *Plauen 1944/1945: Eine Stadt wird zerstört* (Plauen: Vogtländischer Heimatverlag Neupert, 1995), by Rudolf Laser, Joachim Mensdorf, and Johannes Richter. For life near the East German border, I relied on Ingolf Hermann's *Die Deutsch-Deutsch Grenze* (Plauen: Vogtländischer Heimatverlag Neupert, 1998). Plauen's 1989 uprising is chronicled in Rolf Schwanitz's *Zivilcourage: Die friedliche Revolution in Plauen anhand von Stasi-Akten* (Plauen, Vogtländischer Heimatverlag Neupert, 1998). *Plauen: Ein Rundgang Durch die Stadt* (Plauen: Milizke Verlag, 1992) gives a sense of the city after the Wall came down.

John Connelly, an assistant professor of history at the University of California, Berkeley, is one of the few American academics who has both visited and written about postwar Plauen. Professor Connelly shared his recollection of the city with me and sent me the fine article he wrote about its rebellion: "Moment of Revolution: Plauen (Vogtland), October 7, 1989." *German Politics & Society,* Summer 1990. Thomas Küttler, the hero of that uprising, told me how it unfolded and shared his thoughts about its legacy. I am grateful to Cordula Franz for help in arranging interviews in Plauen and to Sybille Unterdoifel for introducing me to The Ranch. Frieder Stephan, the owner of The Ranch, helped me fathom the local youth culture and explained his musical journey from rock to disco to country and western. Christian Pöllmann, who helps run a theater company in Plauen, as well as the German Social Union Party, gave me a strong sense of life under Communism and of the hunger for all things American. The photographer Franziska Heinze and journalist Markus Schneider helped me gather information about their home town. Siegfried Pater—filmmaker, environmentalist, and author of *Zum Beispiel McDonald's* (Göttingen:

Lamuv Verlag, 1994)—described some of McDonald's misbehavior in Germany. Barbara Distil, the curator of the Dachau Museum, spoke to me about the controversy surrounding the local McDonald's. For the history of the camp, I relied on a book that she edited with Ruth Jakusch: *Concentration Camp Dachau 1933–1945* (Brussels: Comité International de Dachau, 1978).

   The Illustrated History of Las Vegas (Edison, N.J.: Chartwell Books, 1997), by Bill Yenne, conveys how the city has been radically transformed in recent years. *The Players: The Men Who Made Las Vegas* (Reno: University of Nevada Press, 1997), edited by Jack Sheehan, provides a good deal of insight into the unique culture that emerged there. Timothy O'Brien's *Bad Bet: The Inside Story of the Glamour, Glitz, and Danger of America's Gambling Industry* (New York: Times Business, 1998) explains precisely how the casinos make their money.

   Much of my information on obesity comes from articles in *Science,* the *Journal of the American Medical Association,* and the *New England Journal of Medicine.* The nutritionist Jane Kirby placed many of the claims and counterclaims about diet into a calm and reasonable perspective for me. Greg Critser's "Let Them Eat Fat: The Heavy Truths about American Obesity," *Harper's,* March 2000, is a provocative essay on fast food and the poor.

   My account of the McLibel trial is based on interviews with the two principals, Helen Steel and Dave Morris, and on the transcripts of the trial (which were available, along with other interesting material, at the anti-McDonald's Web site <www.mcspotlight.org>). Fanny Armstrong—the director of an excellent documentary, *McLibel: Two Worlds Collide*—was extremely helpful. John Vidal's book, *McLibel,* tells the whole, extraordinary story of the trial. The essays collected in *Golden Arches East: McDonald's in East Asia* (Stanford, Calif.: Stanford University Press, 1997), edited by James L. Watson, reveal some of the unpredictable ways in which fast food is now being embraced by other cultures.

▪ QUESTIONS FOR MAKING CONNECTIONS WITHIN THE READING ▪

1. Eric Schlosser begins "Global Realization" with a visit to Plauen, which he writes, "has been alternately punished, rewarded, devastated, and transformed by the great unifying systems of the twentieth century. . . . Plauen has been a battlefield for these competing ideologies, with their proudly displayed and archetypal symbols: the smokestack, the swastika, the hammer and sickle, the golden arches." What are the "competing ideologies" to which Schlosser refers? What do the "archetypal symbols" he mentions represent?

2. Toward the middle of "Global Realization," Schlosser describes an experience he had during a trip to Las Vegas that "revealed the strange power of fast food in the new world order." What is the "new world order," and what role does the fast food industry have to play in it?

3. Schlosser's essay ends with a description of a bar in Plauen called "The Ranch," where he says "the old dream lives on, the dream of freedom without limits, self-reliance, and a wide-open frontier." Is the "old dream" preferable to the "illusion" that Las Vegas sells? If globalization is "the new dream," what are the goals of this dream? How does the new dream differ from the old dream?

■ *QUESTIONS FOR WRITING* ■

1. Schlosser argues that fast food "threatens a fundamental aspect of national identity: how, where, and what people choose to eat." Why are foreign nations threatened by the spread of fast food? Will nations continue to exist if the project of globalization is realized?

2. Schlosser insists that Las Vegas sells "the most brilliant illusion of all, a loss that feels like winning." McDonald's, presumably, is selling a similar illusion. What is lost when the fast food industry succeeds? Is there anything that the consumer can do to combat this "loss that feels like winning"?

■ *QUESTIONS FOR MAKING CONNECTIONS BETWEEN READINGS* ■

1. Schlosser writes, "In many ways Las Vegas is the fulfillment of social and economic trends now sweeping from the American West to the farthest reaches of the globe." Is Las Vegas the logical end point of the "Age of Social Transformation" that Peter Drucker describes? Is globalization the inevitable byproduct of the knowledge society?

2. Is globalization an attempt to flatten human experience and make it more manageable, or is it the realization of an aesthetic ideal, a way of "making special" as Dissanayake defines the term in "The Core of Art"? That is, can successful business practices constitute an aesthetics, or are they necessarily either a violation of or wholly outside the realm of the aesthetic?

For additional suggestions about making connections between readings, visit the Link-O-Mat and More Sample Assignments at <www.newhum.com>.

JAMES C. SCOTT

HOW DO OPPRESSED peoples survive under repressive regimes? What makes revolution possible? At a time when governments have become so powerful and so effective at controlling the behavior of the governed, is resistance a meaningful act? These are some of the questions that James C. Scott, Director of the Program in Agrarian Studies at Yale University and Eugene Meyer Professor of Political Science and Anthropology, has spent his professional life trying to answer. By working across the disciplines of political science, anthropology, ecology, and cultural studies, Scott is expressing his conviction that "the only way to loosen the nearly hegemonic grip of the separate disciplines on how questions are framed and answered is to concentrate on themes of signal importance to several disciplines."

The author of *The Moral Economy of the Peasant: Rebellion and Subsistence in Southeast Asia* (1976), *Weapons of the Weak: Everyday Forms of Peasant Resistance* (1985), and *Domination and the Arts of Resistance: Hidden Transcripts* (1990), Scott has described his most recent book, *Seeing Like a State: How Certain Schemes to Improve the Human Condition Have Failed* (1997), as the result of an "intellectual detour that became so gripping" it forced him to abandon "his original itinerary altogether." Having set out to understand why the state has always cracked down so forcefully on nomadic peoples, Scott ended up seeing state efforts to foster sedentary lifestyles as part of a larger project of making society "legible." With this insight, *Seeing Like a State* evolved into an exploration of the ways that state planners have tended to take "exceptionally complex, illegible, and local social practices . . . and created a standard grid whereby [these practices] could be centrally recorded and monitored."

"Behind the Official Story," the opening chapter of *Domination and the Arts of Resistance*, records Scott's abiding interest in the unruliness of the masses and

Scott, James C. "Behind the Official Story." *Domination and the Arts of Resistance: Hidden Transcripts.* New Haven: Yale University Press, 1990. 1–44.

From the Yale Bioethics Web site <http://www.yale.edu/isps/bioethics/people/scott.html#>; Biographical information and quotations from the Yale Agrarian Studies Web site <http://www.yale.edu/agrarianstudies/real/ashome.html>; and James Scott, introduction to *Seeing Like a State: How Certain Schemes to Improve the Human Condition Have Failed* (New Haven: Yale University Press, 1998). 2.

his commitment to providing alternate understandings of the words and actions of the disempowered. Is it possible to know the story "behind" the official story? Or is this story, which Scott terms "the hidden transcript," forever out of reach of those who are in power? By exposing these questions in these terms, Scott bids his readers to consider the possibility that reading itself might be a form of resistance.

To learn more about James Scott and popular resistance movements, visit the Link-O-Mat at <www.newhum.com>

Behind the Official Story

I tremble to speak the words of freedom before the tyrant.
—CORYPHAEUS, in Euripides, *The Bacchae*

The Labourer and Artisan, notwithstanding they are Servants to their Masters, are quit by doing what they are bid. But the Tyrant sees those that are about him, begging and suing for his Favour; and they must not only do what he commands, but they must think as he would have them [think] and most often, to satisfy him, even anticipate his thoughts. It is not sufficient to obey him, they must also please him, they must harass, torment, nay kill themselves in his Service; and . . . they must leave their own Taste for his, Force their Inclination, and throw off their natural Dispositions. They must carefully observe his Words, his Voice, his Eyes, and even his Nod. They must have neither Eyes, Feet, nor Hands, but what must be ALL upon the watch, to spy out his Will, and discover his Thoughts. Is this to live happily? Does it indeed deserve the Name of Life?
—ESTIENNE DE LA BOETIE, *A Discourse on Voluntary Servitude*

And the intensest hatred is that rooted in fear, which compels to silence and drives vehemence into constructive vindictiveness, an imaginary annihilation of the detested object, something like the hidden rites of vengeance with which the persecuted have a dark vent for their rage.
—GEORGE ELIOT, *Daniel Deronda*

If the expression "Speak truth to power" still has a utopian ring to it, even in modern democracies, this is surely because it is so rarely practiced. The dissembling of the weak in the face of power is hardly an occasion for surprise. It is ubiquitous. So ubiquitous, in fact, that it makes an appearance in many situations in which the sort of power being exercised stretches the ordinary meaning of *power* almost beyond recognition. Much of what passes as normal social intercourse requires that we routinely exchange pleasantries and smile at others about whom we may harbor an estimate not in keeping with our public performance. Here we may perhaps say that the power of social forms embodying etiquette and politeness requires us often to sacrifice candor for smooth relations with our acquaintances. Our circumspect behavior may also have a strategic dimension: this person to whom we misrepresent ourselves may be able to harm or help us in some way. George Eliot may not have exaggerated in claiming that "there is no action possible without a little acting."

The acting that comes of civility will be of less interest to us in what follows than the acting that has been imposed throughout history on the vast majority of people. I mean the public performance required of those subject to elaborate and systematic forms of social subordination: the worker to the boss, the tenant or sharecropper to the landlord, the serf to the lord, the slave to the master, the untouchable to the Brahmin, a member of a subject race to one of the dominant race. With rare, but significant, exceptions the public performance of the subordinate will, out of prudence, fear, and the desire to curry favor, be shaped to appeal to the expectations of the powerful. I shall use the term *public transcript* as a shorthand way of describing the open interaction between subordinates and those who dominate.[1] The public transcript, where it is not positively misleading, is unlikely to tell the whole story about power relations. It is frequently in the interest of both parties to tacitly conspire in misrepresentation. The oral history of a French tenant farmer, Old Tiennon, covering much of the nineteenth century is filled with accounts of a prudent and misleading deference: "When he [the landlord who had dismissed his father] crossed from Le Craux, going to Meillers, he would stop and speak to me and I forced myself to appear amiable, in spite of the contempt I felt for him."[2]

Old Tiennon prides himself on having learned, unlike his tactless and unlucky father, "the art of dissimulation so necessary in life."[3] The slave narratives that have come to us from the U.S. South also refer again and again to the need to deceive:

> I had endeavored so to conduct myself as not to become obnoxious to the white inhabitants, knowing as I did their power, and their hostility to the colored people. . . . First, I had made no display of the little property or money I possessed, but in every way I wore as much as possible the aspect of slavery. Second, I had never appeared to be even so intelligent as I really was. This all colored at the south, free and slaves, find it particularly necessary for their own comfort and safety to observe.[4]

As one of the key survival skills of subordinate groups has been impression management in power-laden situations, the performance aspect of their conduct has not escaped the more observant members of the dominant group. Noting that her slaves fell uncharacteristically silent whenever the latest news from the front in the Civil War became a topic of white conversation, Mary Chesnut took their silence as one that hid something: "They go about in their black masks, not a ripple of emotion showing; and yet on all other subjects except the war they are the most excitable of all races. Now Dick might be a very respectable Egyptian Sphynx, so inscrutably silent he is."[5]

Here I will venture a crude and global generalization I will later want to qualify severely: the greater the disparity in power between dominant and subordinate and the more arbitrarily it is exercised, the more the public transcript of subordinates will take on a stereotyped, ritualistic cast. In other words, the more menacing the power, the thicker the mask. We might imagine, in this context, situations ranging all the way from a dialogue among friends of equal status and power on the one hand to the concentration camp on the other, in which the public transcript of the victim bears the mark of mortal fear. Between these extremes are the vast majority of the historical cases of systematic subordination that will concern us.

Cursory though this opening discussion of the public transcript has been, it alerts us to several issues in power relations, each of which hinges on the fact that the public transcript is not the whole story. First, the public transcript is an indifferent guide to the opinion of subordinates. Old Tiennon's tactical smile and greeting mask an attitude of anger and revenge. At the very least, an assessment of power relations read directly off the public transcript between the powerful and the weak may portray a deference and consent that are possibly only a tactic. Second, to the degree that the dominant suspect that the public transcript may be "only" a performance, they will discount its authenticity. It is but a short step from such skepticism to the view, common among many dominant groups, that those beneath them are deceitful, shamming, and lying by nature. Finally, the questionable meaning of the public transcript suggests the key roles played by disguise and surveillance in power relations. Subordinates offer a performance of deference and consent while attempting to discern, to read, the real intentions and mood of the potentially threatening powerholder. As the favorite proverb of Jamaican slaves captures it, "Play fool, to catch wise."[6] The power figure, in turn, produces a performance of mastery and command while attempting to peer behind the mask of subordinates to read their real intentions. The dialectic of disguise and surveillance that pervades relations between the weak and the strong will help us, I think, to understand the cultural patterns of domination and subordination.

The theatrical imperatives that normally prevail in situations of domination produce a public transcript in close conformity with how the dominant group would wish to have things appear. The dominant never control the stage absolutely, but their wishes normally prevail. In the short run, it is in the interest of the subordinate to produce a more or less credible performance, speaking the lines and making the gestures he knows are expected of him. The result is that the public transcript is—barring a crisis—systematically skewed in the direction of the libretto, the discourse, represented by the dominant. In ideological terms the public transcript will typically, by its accommodationist tone, provide convincing evidence for the hegemony of dominant values, for the hegemony of dominant discourse. It is in precisely this public domain where the effects of power relations are most manifest, and any analysis based exclusively on the public transcript is likely to conclude that subordinate groups endorse the terms of their subordination and are willing, even enthusiastic, partners in that subordination.

A skeptic might well ask at this point how we can presume to know, on the basis of the public transcript alone, whether this performance is genuine or not. What warrant have we to call it a performance at all, thereby impugning its authenticity? The answer is, surely, that we cannot know how contrived or imposed the performance is unless we can speak, as it were, to the performer offstage, out of this particular power-laden context, or unless the performer suddenly declares openly, on stage, that the performances we have previously observed were just a pose.[7] Without a privileged peek backstage or a rupture in the performance we have no way of calling into question the status of what might be a convincing but feigned performance.

If subordinate discourse in the presence of the dominant is a public transcript, I shall use the term *hidden transcript* to characterize discourse that takes place "offstage," beyond direct observation by powerholders. The hidden transcript is thus derivative in the sense that it consists of those offstage speeches, gestures, and practices that confirm, contradict, or inflect what appears in the public transcript.[8] We do not wish to prejudge, by definition, the relation between what is said in the face of power and what is said behind its back. Power relations are not, alas, so straightforward that we can call what is said in power-laden contexts false and what is said offstage true. Nor can we simplistically describe the former as a realm of necessity and the latter as a realm of freedom. What is certainly the case, however, is that the hidden transcript is produced for a different audience and under different constraints of power than the public transcript. By assessing the discrepancy *between* the hidden transcript and the public transcript we may begin to judge the impact of domination on public discourse.

The abstract and general tone of the discussion thus far is best relieved by concrete illustrations of the possibly dramatic disparity between the public and the hidden transcripts. The first is drawn from slavery in the antebellum U.S. South. Mary Livermore, a white governess from New England, recounted the reaction of Aggy, a normally taciturn and deferential black cook, to the beating the master had given her daughter. The daughter had been accused, apparently unjustly, of some minor theft and then beaten while Aggy looked on, powerless to intervene. After the master had finally left the kitchen, Aggy turned to Mary, whom she considered her friend and said,

Thar's a day a-comin'! Thar's a day a-comin'! . . . I hear the rumblin ob de chariots! I see de flashin ob de guns! White folks blood is a runnin on the ground like a ribber, an de dead's heaped up dat high! . . . Oh Lor! Hasten de day when de blows, an de bruises, and de aches an de pains, shall come to de white folks, an de buzzards shall eat dem as dey's dead in de streets. Oh Lor! roll on de chariots, an gib the black people rest and peace. Oh Lor! Gib me de pleasure ob livin' till dat day, when I shall see white folks shot down like de wolves when dey come hungry out o'de woods.[9]

One can imagine what might have happened to Aggy if she had delivered this speech directly to the master. Apparently her trust in Mary Livermore's friendship and sympathy was such that a statement of her rage could be ventured with comparative safety. Alternatively, perhaps she could no longer choke back her anger. Aggy's hidden transcript is at complete odds with her public transcript of quiet obedience. What is particularly striking is that this is anything but an inchoate scream of rage; it is a finely drawn and highly visual image of an apocalypse, a day of revenge and triumph, a world turned upside down using the cultural raw materials of the white man's religion. Can we conceive of such an elaborate vision rising sponta-neously to her lips without the beliefs and practice of slave Christianity having prepared the way carefully? In this respect our glimpse of Aggy's hidden transcript, if pursued further, would lead us directly to the offstage culture of the slave quarters and slave religion. Whatever such an investiga-tion would tell us, this glimpse itself is sufficient to make any naive interpre-tation of Aggy's previous and subsequent public acts of deference impossi-ble both for us, and most decidedly for Aggy's master, should he have been eavesdropping behind the kitchen door.

The hidden transcript Aggy revealed in the comparative safety of friendship is occasionally openly declared in the face of power. When, sud-denly, subservience evaporates and is replaced by open defiance we en-counter one of those rare and dangerous moments in power relations. Mrs. Poyser, a character in George Eliot's *Adam Bede* who finally spoke her mind, provides an illustration of the hidden transcript storming the stage. As tenants of the elderly Squire Donnithorne, Mrs. Poyser and her husband had always resented his rare visits, when he would impose some new, oner-ous obligation on them and treat them with disdain. He had "a mode of looking at her which, Mrs. Poyser observed, 'allays aggravated her; it was as if you was an insect, and he was going to dab his fingernail on you.' How-ever, she said, 'your servant, sir' and curtsied with an air of perfect defer-ence as she advanced towards him: she was not the woman to misbehave to-ward her betters, and fly in the face of the catechism, without severe provocation."[10]

This time the squire came to propose an exchange of pasture and grain land between Mr. Poyser and a new tenant that would almost certainly be to the Poysers' disadvantage. When assent was slow in coming, the squire held out the prospect of a longer term farm lease and ended with the observation—a thinly veiled threat of eviction—that the other tenant was well-off and would be happy to lease the Poysers' farm in addition to his own. Mrs. Poyser, "exasperated" at the squire's determination to ignore her earlier objections "as if she had left the room" and at the final threat, exploded. She "burst in with the desperate determination to have her say out this once, though it were to rain notices to quit, and the only shelter were the workhouse."[11] Beginning with a comparison between the condition of the house—frogs on the steps of the flooded basement, rats and mice coming in through the rotten floorboards to eat the cheeses and menace the children—and the struggle to pay the high rent, Mrs. Poyser let fly her personal accusations as she realized that the squire was fleeing out the door toward his pony and safety:

> You may run away from my words, sir, and you may go spinning underhand ways o' doing us a mischief, for you've got old Harry to your friend, though nobody else is, but I tell you for once as we're not dumb creatures to be abused and made money on by them as ha' got the lash i' their hands, for want o' knowing how t' undo the tackle. An if I'm th' only one as speaks my mind, there's plenty o' the same way o' thinking i' this parish and the next to 't, for your name's no better than a brimstone match in everybody's nose.[12]

Such were Eliot's powers of observation and insight into her rural society that many of the key issues of domination and resistance can be teased from her story of Mrs. Poyser's encounter with the squire. At the height of her peroration, for example, Mrs. Poyser insists that they will not be treated as animals despite his power over them. This, together with her remark about the squire looking on her as an insect and her declaration that he has no friends and is hated by the whole parish, focuses on the issue of self-esteem. While the confrontation may originate in the exploitation of an onerous tenancy, the discourse is one of dignity and reputation. The practices of domination and exploitation typically generate the insults and slights to human dignity that in turn foster a hidden transcript of indignation. Perhaps one vital distinction to draw between forms of domination lies in the kinds of indignities the exercise of power routinely produces.

Notice also how Mrs. Poyser presumes to speak not just for herself but for the whole parish. She represents what she says as the first public declaration of what everyone has been saying behind the squire's back. Judging from how rapidly the story traveled and the unalloyed joy with which it was received and retold, the rest of the community also felt Mrs. Poyser had spoken for them as well. "It was known throughout the two parishes," Eliot writes, "that the Squire's plan had been frustrated because the Poysers had refused to be 'put upon,' and Mrs. Poyser's outbreak was discussed in all the farmhouses with a zest that was only heightened by frequent repetition."[13] The vicarious pleasure of the neighbors had nothing to do with the actual sentiments expressed by Mrs. Poyser—hadn't everyone been saying the same thing about the squire among themselves for years? The content, though Mrs. Poyser may have put it with considerable folk elegance, was stale; it was saying it openly (with witnesses) to the squire's face that was remarkable and that made Mrs. Poyser into something of a local hero. The first open statement of a hidden transcript, a declaration that breaches the etiquette of power relations, that breaks an apparently calm surface of silence and consent, carries the force of a symbolic declaration of war. Mrs. Poyser had spoken (a social) truth to power.

Delivered in a moment of anger, Mrs. Poyser's speech was, one might say, spontaneous—but the spontaneity lay in the timing and vehemence of the delivery, not in the content. The content had, in fact, been rehearsed again and again, as we are told: "and though Mrs. Poyser had during the last twelve-month recited many imaginary speeches, meaning even more than met the ear, which she was quite determined to make to him the next time he appeared within the gates of the Hall Farm, the speeches had always remained imaginary."[14] Who among us has not had a similar experience? Who, having been insulted or suffered an indignity—especially in public—at the hand of someone in power or authority over us, has not rehearsed an imaginary speech he wishes he had given or intends to give at the next opportunity?[15] Such speeches may often remain a personal hidden transcript that may never find expression, even among close friends and peers. But in this case we are dealing with a shared situation of subordination. The tenants of Squire Donnithorne and, in fact, much of the nongentry in two parishes had ample personal reasons to take pleasure in his being publicly humbled and to share vicariously in Mrs. Poyser's courage. Their common class position and their social links thus provided a powerful resolving lens bringing their collective hidden transcript into focus. One might say, without much exaggeration, that they had together, in the course of their social interchange, written Mrs. Poyser's speech for her. Not word for word, of course, but in the sense that Mrs. Poyser's "say" would be her own reworking of the stories, the ridicule, and the complaints that those beneath the Squire all shared. And to "write" that speech for her, the squire's subjects had to have some secure social space, however sequestered, where they could exchange and elaborate their criticism. Her speech was her personal rendition of the hidden transcript of a subordinate group, and, as in the case of Aggy, that speech directs our attention back to the offstage culture of the class within which it originated.

An individual who is affronted may develop a personal fantasy of revenge and confrontation, but when the insult is but a variant of affronts suffered systematically by a whole race, class, or strata, then the fantasy can become a collective cultural product. Whatever form it assumes—offstage parody, dreams of violent revenge, millennial visions of a world turned upside down—this collective hidden transcript is essential to any dynamic view of power relations.

Mrs. Poyser's explosion was potentially very costly, and it was her daring—some would have said foolhardiness—that won her such notoriety. The word *explosion* is used deliberately here because that is how Mrs. Poyser experienced it:

> "Thee'st done it now," said Mr. Poyser, a little alarmed and uneasy, but not without some triumphant amusement at his wife's outbreak. "Yis, I know I've done it," said Mrs. Poyser, "but I've had my say out, and I shall be the'easier for 't all my life. There's no pleasure in living, if you're to be corked up for iver, and only dribble your mind out by the sly, like a leaky barrel. I shan't repent saying what I think, if I live to be as old as the Squire."[16]

The hydraulic metaphor George Eliot puts in Mrs. Poyser's mouth is the most common way in which the sense of pressure behind the hidden transcript is expressed. Mrs. Poyser suggests that her habits of prudence and deception can no longer contain the anger she has rehearsed for the last year. That the anger will find a passage out is not in doubt; the choice is rather between a safer but less psychologically satisfying process of "dribbl[ing] your mind out by the sly" and the dangerous but gratifying full blast that Mrs. Poyser has ventured. George Eliot has, in effect, taken one position here on the consequences for consciousness of domination. Her claim is that the necessity of "acting a mask" in the presence of power produces, almost by the strain engendered by its inauthenticity, a countervailing pressure that cannot be contained indefinitely. As an epistemological matter, we have no warrant for elevating the truth status of Mrs. Poyser's outburst over that of her prior deference. Both are arguably part of Mrs. Poyser's self. Notice, however, that as Eliot constructs it, Mrs. Poyser feels she has finally spoken her mind. Inasmuch as she and others in comparable situations feel they have finally spoken truthfully to those in power, the concept truth may have a sociological reality in the thought and practice of people whose actions interest us. It may have a phenomenological force in the real world despite its untenable epistemological status.

An alternative claim, nearly a logical mirror image of the first, is that those obliged by domination to act a mask will eventually find that their faces have grown to fit that mask. The practice of subordination in this case produces, in time, its own legitimacy, rather like Pascal's injunction to those who were without religious faith but who desired it to get down on their knees five times a day to pray, and the acting would eventually engender its own justification in faith. In the analysis that follows I hope to clarify this debate considerably, inasmuch as it bears so heavily on the issues of domination, resistance, ideology, and hegemony that are at the center of my concern.

If the weak have obvious and compelling reasons to seek refuge behind a mask when in the presence of power, the powerful have their own compelling reasons for adopting a mask in the presence of subordinates. Thus, for the powerful as well there is typically a disparity between the public transcript deployed in the open exercise of power and the hidden transcript expressed safely only offstage. The offstage transcript of elites is, like its counterpart among subordinates, derivative: it consists in those gestures and words that inflect, contradict, or confirm what appears in the public transcript.

Nowhere has the "act of power" been more successfully examined than in George Orwell's essay "Shooting an Elephant," from his days as a subinspector of police in the 1920s in colonial Burma. Orwell had been summoned to deal with an elephant in heat that had broken its tether and was ravaging the bazaar. When Orwell, elephant gun in hand, finally locates the elephant, which has indeed killed a man, it is peacefully grazing in the paddy fields, no longer a threat to anyone. The logical thing would be to observe the elephant for a while to ensure that its heat had passed. What frustrates logic for Orwell is that there are now more than two thousand colonial subjects who have followed and are watching him:

> And suddenly I realized that I should have to shoot the elephant after all. The people expected it of me and I had got to do it; I could feel their two thousand wills pressing me forward, irresistibly. And it was at this moment, as I stood there with the rifle in my hands, that I first grasped the hollowness, the futility of the white man's dominion in the East. Here was I, the white man with his gun, standing in front of the unarmed native crowd—seemingly the leading actor of the piece; but in reality I was only an absurd puppet pushed to and fro by the will of those yellow faces behind. I perceived in this moment that when the white man turns tyrant it is his own freedom that he destroys. He becomes a sort of hollow posing dummy, the conventionalized figure of a sahib. For it is the condition of his rule that he shall spend his life in trying to impress the "natives," and so in every crisis he has to do what the "natives" expect of him. He wears a mask and his face grows to fit it. . . . A sahib has got to act like a sahib; he has got to appear resolute, to know his own mind and do definite things. To come all that way, rifle in hand, with two thousand people marching at my heels, and then to trail feebly away, having done nothing—no, that was impossible. The crowd would laugh at me. And my whole life, every white man's life in the East, was one long struggle not to be laughed at.[17]

Orwell's use of the theatrical metaphor is pervasive: he speaks of himself as "leading actor of the piece," of hollow dummys, puppets, masks, appearances, and an audience poised to jeer if he doesn't follow the established script. As he experiences it, Orwell is no more free to be himself, to break convention, than a slave would be in the presence of a tyrannical master. If subordination requires a credible performance of humility and deference, so domination seems to require a credible performance of haughtiness and mastery. There are, however, two differences. If a slave transgresses the script he risks a beating, while Orwell risks only ridicule. Another important distinction is that the necessary posing of the dominant derives not from weaknesses but from the ideas behind their rule, the kinds of claims they make to legitimacy. A divine king must act like a god, a warrior king like a brave general; an elected head of a republic must appear to respect the citizenry and their opinions; a judge must seem to venerate the law. Actions by elites that *publicly* contradict the basis of a claim to power are threatening. The cynicism of the taped Oval Office conversations in the Nixon White House was a devastating blow to the public transcript claim to legality and high-mindedness. Similarly, the poorly concealed existence of special shops and hospitals for the party elites in the socialist bloc profoundly undercut the ruling party's public claim to rule on behalf of the working class.[18]

One might usefully compare forms of domination in terms of the kinds of display and public theater they seem to require. Another, perhaps even more revealing way of addressing the same question would be to ask what activities are most sedulously hidden from public view by different forms of domination. Each form of rule will have not only its characteristic stage setting but also its characteristic dirty linen.[19]

Those forms of domination based on a premise or claim to inherent superiority by ruling elites would seem to depend heavily on lavish display, sumptuary laws, regalia, and public acts of deference or tribute by subordinates. The desire to inculcate habits of obedience and hierarchy, as in military organizations, can produce similar patterns. In extreme cases display and performance dominate, as in the case of the Chinese emperor Long Qing, whose public appearances were so minutely choreographed that he became virtually a living icon deployed in rituals that risked nothing to improvisation. Offstage, in the Forbidden City, he might carouse as he wished with princes and aristocrats.[20] This may be something of a limiting case, but the attempt by dominant elites to sequester an offstage social site where they are no longer on display and can let their hair down is ubiquitous, as is the attempt to ritualize contact with subordinates so that the masks remain firmly in place and the risk that something untoward might happen is minimized. Milovan Djilas's early critique of Yugoslavia's new party elite contrasted a meaningful but secret backstage with the empty ritual of public bodies: "At intimate suppers, on hunts, in conversations between two or three men, matters of state of the most vital importance are decided. Meetings of party forums, conferences of the government and assemblies, serve no purpose but to make declarations and put in an appearance."[21] Strictly speaking, of course, the public ritual Djilas denigrates does indeed serve a purpose inasmuch as the theater of unanimity, loyalty, and resolve is intended to impress an audience. Public ritual of this kind is both real and meaningful; Djilas's complaint is rather that it is also a performance designed to conceal an offstage arena of politics that would contradict it. Dominant groups often have much to conceal, and typically they also have the wherewithal to conceal what they wish. The British colonial officials with whom Orwell served in Moulmein had the inevitable club to repair to in the evenings. There, except for the invisible Burmese staff, they were among their own, as they might have put it, and no longer strutting before the audience of colonial subjects. Activities, gestures, remarks, and dress that were unseemly to the public role of sahib were safe in this retreat.[22] The seclusion available to elites not only affords them a place to relax from the formal requirements of their role but also minimizes the chance that familiarity will breed contempt or, at least, diminish the impression their ritually managed appearances create. Balzac captures the fear of overexposure, as it now might be termed, among the Parisian magistrates of the mid-nineteenth century,

> Ah what an unfortunate man your true magistrate is! You know, they ought to live outside the community, as pontiffs once did. The world should only see them when they emerged from their cells at fixed times, solemn, ancient, venerable, pronouncing judgment like the high priests of antiquity, combining in themselves the judicial and the sacerdotal powers! We should only be visible on the bench. . . . Nowadays we may be seen amusing ourselves or in difficulties like anybody else. . . . We may be seen in drawing rooms, at home, creatures of passion, and instead of being terrible we are grotesque.[23]

Perhaps the danger that unregulated contact with the public may profane the sacred aura of judges helps explain why, even in secular republics, they retain more of the trappings of traditional authority than any other branch of government.

Now that the basic idea of public and hidden transcripts has been introduced, I will venture a few observations by way of orienting the subsequent discussion. For the study of power relations, this perspective alerts us to the fact that virtually all ordinarily observed relations between dominant and subordinate represent the encounter of the *public* transcript of the dominant with the *public* transcript of the subordinate. It is to observe Squire Donnithorne imposing on Mr. and Mrs. Poyser on all those occasions on which, prior to the explosion, she managed to keep up the pretense of being deferential and agreeable. Social science is, in general then, focused resolutely on the official or formal relations between the powerful and weak. This is the case even for much of the study of conflict, as we shall see, when that conflict has become highly institutionalized. I do not mean to imply that the study of this domain of power relations is necessarily false or trivial, only that it hardly exhausts what we might wish to know about power.

Eventually we will want to know how the *hidden* transcripts of various actors are formed, the conditions under which they do or do not find public expression, and what relation they bear to the public transcript.[24] Three characteristics of the hidden transcript, however, merit clarification beforehand. First, the hidden transcript is specific to a given social site and to a particular set of actors. Aggy's oath was almost certainly rehearsed in various forms among the slaves in their quarters or at the clandestine religious services that we know were common. Orwell's peers, like most dominant groups, would risk less from a public indiscretion, but they would have the safety of the Moulmein Club in which to vent their spleen. Each hidden transcript, then, is actually elaborated among a restricted "public" that excludes—that is hidden from—certain specified others. A second and vital aspect of the hidden transcript that has not been sufficiently emphasized is that it does not contain only speech acts but a whole range of practices. Thus, for many peasants, activities such as poaching, pilfering, clandestine tax evasion, and intentionally shabby work for landlords are part and parcel of the hidden transcript. For dominant elites, hidden-transcript practices might include clandestine luxury and privilege, surreptitious use of hired thugs, bribery, and tampering with land titles. These practices, in each case, contravene the public transcript of the party in question and are, if at all possible, kept offstage and unavowed.

Finally, it is clear that the frontier between the public and the hidden transcripts is a zone of constant struggle between dominant and subordinate—not a solid wall. The capacity of dominant groups to prevail—though never totally—in defining and constituting what counts as the public transcript and what as offstage is, as we shall see, no small measure of their power. The unremitting struggle over such boundaries is perhaps the most vital arena for ordinary conflict, for everyday forms of class struggle. Orwell noticed how the Burmese managed to insinuate almost routinely a contempt for the British, while being careful never to venture a more dangerous open defiance:

> Anti-European feeling was very bitter. No one had the guts to raise a riot, but if a European woman went through the bazaars alone somebody would probably spit betel juice over her dress. . . . When a nimble Burman tripped me up on the football field and the referee (another Burman) looked the other way, the crowd yelled with hideous laughter. . . . In the end the sneering yellow faces of the young men that met me everywhere, the insults hooted after me when I was at a safe distance, got badly on my nerves. The young Buddhist priests were the worst of all.[25]

Tactical prudence ensures that subordinate groups rarely blurt out their hidden transcript directly. But, taking advantage of the anonymity of a crowd or of an ambiguous accident, they manage in a thousand artful ways to imply that they are grudging conscripts to the performance.

The analysis of the hidden transcripts of the powerful and of the subordinate offers us, I believe, one path to a social science that uncovers contradictions and possibilities, that looks well beneath the placid surface that the public accommodation to the existing distribution of power, wealth, and status often presents. Behind the "anti-European" acts Orwell noted was undoubtedly a far more elaborate hidden transcript, an entire discourse, linked to Burman culture, religion, and the experience of colonial rule. This discourse was not available—except through spies—to the British. It could be recovered only offstage in the native quarter in Moulmein and only by someone intimately familiar with Burman culture. Nor, of course, did the Burmans know—except through the tales that servants might tell—what lay behind the more or less official behavior of the British toward them. That hidden transcript could be recovered only in the clubs, homes, and small gatherings of the colonists. The analyst in any situation like this has a strategic advantage over even the most sensitive participants precisely because the hidden transcripts of dominant and subordinate are, in most circumstances, *never in direct contact.* Each participant will be familiar with the public transcript and the hidden transcript of his or her circle, but not with the hidden transcript of the other. For this reason, political analysis can be advanced by research that can compare the hidden transcript of subordinate groups with the hidden transcript of the powerful and both hidden transcripts with the public transcript they share. This last facet of the comparison will reveal the effect of domination on political communication.

Just a few years after Orwell's stint in Moulmein a huge anticolonial rebellion took the English by surprise. It was led by a Buddhist monk claiming the throne and promising a utopia that consisted largely of getting rid of the British and taxes. The rebellion was crushed with a good deal of gratuitous brutality and the surviving "conspirators" sent to the gallows. A portion, at least, of the hidden transcript of the Burmans had suddenly, as it were, leapt onto the stage to declare itself openly. Millennial dreams of revenge and visions of just kingship, of Buddhist saviors, of a racial settling of scores of which the British had little inkling were being acted on. In the brutality of the repression that followed one could detect an acting out of the admission that Orwell struggled against and that undoubtedly found open expression in the white's only club that "the greatest joy in the world would be to drive a bayonet into a Buddhist priest's guts." Many, perhaps most, hidden transcripts remain just that: hidden from public view and never "enacted." And we are not able to tell easily under what precise circumstances the hidden transcript will storm the stage. But if we wish to move beyond apparent consent and to grasp potential acts, intentions as yet blocked, and possible futures that a shift in the balance of power or a crisis might bring to view, we have little choice but to explore the realm of the hidden transcript.   ■

NOTES

1. *Public* here refers to action that is openly avowed to the other party in the power relationship, and transcript is used almost in its juridical sense (*procès verbal*) of a complete record of what was said. This complete record, however, would also include nonspeech acts such as gestures and expressions.

2. Emile Gauillaumin, *The Life of a Simple Man*, ed. Eugen Weber, rev. trans. Margaret Crosland, 83. See also 38, 62, 64, 102, 140, and 153 for other instances.

3. Ibid., 82.

4. Lunsford Lane, *The Narrative of Lunsford Lane, Formerly of Raleigh, North Carolina* (Boston, 1848), quoted in Gilbert Osofsky, ed., *Puttin' on Ole Massa: The Slave Narratives of Henry Bibb, William Wells, and Solomon Northrup*, 9.

5. *A Diary from Dixie*, quoted in Orlando Patterson, *Slavery and Social Death: A Comparative Study*, 208.

6. Ibid., 338.

7. I bracket, for the moment, the possibility that the offstage retraction or the public rupture may itself be a ruse designed to mislead. It should be clear, however, that there is no satisfactory way to establish definitively some bedrock reality or truth behind any particular set of social acts. I also overlook the possibility that the performer may be able to insinuate an insincerity into the performance itself, thereby undercutting its authenticity for part or all of his audience.

8. This is not to assert that subordinates have nothing more to talk about among themselves than their relationship to the dominant. Rather it is merely to confine the term to that segment of interaction among subordinates that bears on relations with the powerful.

9. *My Story of the War*, quoted in Albert J. Raboteau, *Slave Religion: The "Invisible Institution" of the Antebellum South*, 313.

10. *Adam Bede*, 388–89.

11. Ibid., 393.

12. Ibid., 394.

13. Ibid., 398.

14. Ibid., 388.

15. We are, I think, apt to have the same fantasy when we are bested in argument among equals or insulted by a peer. The difference is simply that asymmetrical power relations do not interfere with the declaration of the hidden transcript in this case.

16. Ibid., 395. For readers unfamiliar with *Adam Bede* who would like to know how things turned out, the squire died providentially some months later, lifting the threat.

17. *Inside the Whale and Other Essays*, 95–96.

18. Similar inequalities are not nearly so symbolically charged in Western capitalist democracies, which publicly are committed to defend property rights and make no claims to be run for the particular benefit of the working class.

19. We all recognize homely versions of this truth. It is, parents sense, unseemly to argue publicly in front of their children, especially over their discipline and conduct. To do so is to undercut the implicit claim that parents know best and are agreed about what is proper. It is also to offer their children a political opportunity to exploit the revealed difference of opinion. Generally, parents prefer to keep the bickering offstage and to present a more or less united front before the children.

20. Ray Huang, 1571: A Year of No Significance.

21. *The New Class*, 82.
22. I suspect that it is for essentially the same reason that the subordinate staff in virtually any hierarchical organization tend to work in open view while the elite work behind closed doors, often with anterooms containing private secretaries.
23. *A Harlot High and Low [Splendeurs et misères des courtisanes]*, trans. Reyner Happenstall, 505. The twentieth-century literary figure who made the masks of domination and subordination the center of much of his work was Jean Genet. See, in particular, his plays *The Blacks* and *The Screens*.
24. I overlook, deliberately for the moment, the fact that there are for any actor several public and hidden transcripts, depending upon the audience being addressed.
25. *Inside the Whale*, 91. A shouted insult seems hardly a hidden transcript. What is crucial here is the "safe distance" that makes the insulter anonymous: the message is public but the messenger is hidden.

▪ QUESTIONS FOR MAKING CONNECTIONS WITHIN THE READING ▪

1. At the opening of his essay, James Scott offers a "crude and global generalization" that he acknowledges needs further qualification: "the greater the disparity in power between dominant and subordinate and the more arbitrarily it is exercised, the more the public transcript of subordinates will take on a stereotyped, ritualistic cast." Create a chart that maps out this relationship, using one of the examples that Scott has provided: the master and the slave, the tenant and the landlord, the colonizer and the colonized. How might the behavior of the parties involved change as the disparity in power grows? How would the behavior change as the arbitrariness of the exercise of power increased?

2. Scott provides an approach to reading and understanding the elaborate performance that occurs whenever the powerful and the disempowered engage with one another. In putting on this performance, which Scott terms "the public transcript," "[i]t is frequently in the interest of both parties," Scott maintains, "to tacitly conspire in misrepresentation." What is it, exactly, that gets misrepresented by the public transcript? How does one distinguish between acts of misrepresentation that warrant study and those that are simply acts of civility?

3. Toward the end of his essay, Scott asserts that "virtually all ordinarily observed relations between dominant and subordinate represent the encounter of the *public* transcript of the dominant with the *public* transcript of the subordinate." Provide an example from your own experience that illustrates Scott's assertion. What would it take to gain access to the "private transcripts" of those involved in your example? Does your example confirm Scott's assertion that the analyst of such situations "has a strategic advantage over even the most sensitive participants"?

■ *QUESTIONS FOR WRITING* ■

1. One might argue that in a democracy there is no distinction between the public and the hidden transcript: indeed, in the United States, the freedom of the press guarantees that readers are provided with an unending diet of revelations about the private lives of politicians and ordinary people alike. Would you say that freedom of the press and the advent of modern media serve to eliminate the distinction between the public and the private transcripts that Scott has described? In the United States, has the private transcript been made public and thereby emptied of all its power?

2. Scott is interested in promoting the development of a social science that "uncovers contradictions and possibilities, that looks well beneath the placid surface that the public accommodation to the existing distribution of power, wealth, and status often presents." What is to be gained by developing such a social science? Would it help to promote better forms of government? More effective forms of resistance?

■ *QUESTIONS FOR MAKING CONNECTIONS BETWEEN READINGS* ■

1. One of the most frequent complaints that students make about school is that they are "required to say what the teacher wants to hear." With Scott's essay in mind, we might say that this is a complaint about being trained to perform and reproduce "the public transcript." In Peter Ho Davies' short story, "What You Know," however, we get a glimpse of a teacher's complaint about his students. Has Davies given his readers access to a "personal hidden transcript," or is his story about a "collective hidden transcript"? Has Davies, in other words, used his story to articulate a point of personal dissatisfaction, or is the story a vehicle for making a broader critique of social relations?

2. Susan Faludi's "The Naked Citadel" provides an opportunity to explore the explanatory power and the limits of Scott's approach to studying resistance. How does one determine who is dominant and who is subordinate at The Citadel? Which transcripts has Faludi gained access to in her research? Scott argues that, "by assessing the discrepancy *between* the hidden transcript and the public transcript we may begin to judge the impact of domination on public discourse." What does "The Naked Citadel" reveal about "the impact of domination on public discourse"?

For additional suggestions about making connections between readings, visit the Link-O-Mat and More Sample Assignments at <www.newhum.com>.

MITCHELL STEPHENS

WILL READING BE an important activity in the twenty-first century? Will writing? Have technological advances made previous uses of literacy and older value systems obsolete? These are the questions that Mitchell Stephens tackles in his most recent work, *the rise of the image the fall of the word (1998)*. While most reviewers of contemporary culture decry the decline in the reading and writing abilities of the masses and bemoan the influence of television in the average citizen's life, Stephens argues that the potential for human communication is being revolutionized by the expansion of the visual media. Stephens places particular emphasis on the power of what he calls "the new video"—computer-edited visual essays that are distributed via the Internet—which he believes have the potential "to help resolve [our] crisis of the spirit. Not by taking us back to neighborhoods filled with good conversation, bustling libraries and old-fashioned sincerity. That world is disappearing; it will not return. But by providing the tools—intellectual and artistic tools—needed to construct new, more resilient understandings." In "Thinking 'Above the Stream,'" Stephens bids his readers to consider the new literacies that will be necessary for confronting and making sense of the challenges of contemporary life.

Mitchell Stephens is a professor of journalism and mass communication at New York University and the author of the widely used television and radio journalism textbooks, *Broadcast News* (1980) and *A History of News* (1988), which has been translated into four languages and was a *New York Times* "Notable Book of the Year." Stephens's articles on contemporary thought and the media appear regularly in the *New York Times*, the *Washington Post*, the *Los Angeles Times*, and the *Columbia Journalism Review;* Stephens has also recorded commentaries for *On the Media* for National Public Radio and worked for NBC News.

Stephens, Mitchell. "Thinking 'Above the Stream': New Philosophies." *the rise of the image the fall of the word.* New York: Oxford University Press, 1998. 204–230.

Biographical information from NPR's On The Media Web site <http://www.wnyc.org/new/talk/onthemedia/lehrer030799.html>; quotation from Mitchell Stephens' preface to *the rise of the image the fall of the word* (New York: Oxford University Press, 1998).

To learn more about Mitchell Stephens and the new video, visit the Link-O-Mat at <www.newhum.com>.

■ ■

Thinking "Above The Stream": New Philosophies

Why do you want to pull me in every direction, ye unread?

Heraclitus

In *The Tempest,* the "savage" Caliban has this advice for his drunken coconspirators in the attempt to take control of the island from Prospero: "Remember, first to possess his books; for without them he's but a sot, as I am."[1] All stages of this clumsy revolt fail, of course. But we now live in an age when it appears as if we are surrendering possession of our books. They are disappearing from our homes. Their place in front of our eyes is being usurped by the moving image.

Shakespeare's last play can be read as a disquisition on the power not of the Book of Motion, the magic of our time, but of the book, the magic of his. "My library was dukedom large enough," declares Prospero when recounting his exile. The "art" he finds in one of the books he was able to take with him to the island enables Prospero to conjure up the tempest itself; that's how he "put the wild waters in this roar." "I love my books," he says.[2]

We—maybe not you (If you've read this far, you might consider phoning Michael Kinsley), maybe not I, but we as a society—are losing the love of books, and therefore we risk losing a formidable source of magic, of power. It's not over yet, of course. Indeed, periods of transition from one form of communication to another, like ours, sometimes prove fertile even for old forms. Socrates, for example, perfected a method of developing ideas in spoken words in an Athens energized by written words. Shakespeare wrote for the stage in an England that, as this play indicates, was beginning to sense the power of works written for the printed page.[3] It is conceivable that someone in our time could channel the energy unleashed by the moving image into another transcendent novel. Perhaps James Joyce did. Perhaps some future author will. Still, it would likely be a last hurrah.

America is "on the eve of . . . becoming a literature-free zone," Philip Roth has lamented.[4] He was exaggerating. "To speak today of a famous novelist is like speaking of a famous cabinet maker or speedboat designer," the well-known novelist Gore Vidal has declared. "Adjective is inappropriate to noun. How can a novelist be famous, no matter how well known he may be personally to the press, when the novel itself is of no consequence to the civilized, much less the generality?"[5] Vidal too was exaggerating. Still, the truth is that literature in America and elsewhere continues to lose consequence, and it continues to lose the segment of the generality that controls the future: the young.

Our descendants undoubtedly will still learn to read and write, but they undoubtedly will read and write less often and, therefore, less well. (The tumble in verbal skills as measured by the SATs has abated for the moment. But since these are skills tested exclusively through reading, it would be surprising if they did not begin to decline once again with continued improvement in the selection of moving images available to distract children from reading.) And the language our descendants write and speak will increasingly be a less precise, less subtle language—one designed for use with images.

The end of the printed word—offscreen—won't come tomorrow; it may not come within the next century. Perhaps there won't be a clear, clean end, just continued slippage. Perhaps books, like legitimate theater today, will maintain a small, elite audience. Besides, the schools can always be counted upon to preserve a fading form of communication; look how long they insisted upon rhetoric, recitation, memorization and even the Socratic method. I'm not suggesting that those who work for publishers or newspapers seek new work. My wife edits magazines. I write books. But I would not advise our children to enter these fields.[6] All of them already read less than their father does and did, anyway.[7]

USA Today—that extremely rare phenomenon, a successful new newspaper—recently published an examination of twenty-four hours of American popular culture. In it television was mentioned twenty-three times, film and popular music six times each, radio three times and fiction once (*The Bridges of Madison County*).[8,9] No one who has wandered beyond the graduate schools or Manhattan's Upper West Side should find these numbers surprising.

Every few months or so someone tries to explain in print why the novel, say, is not quite as feeble as measures like this indicate; why, as a *New York Times* editorial in 1994 put it, "Rumors about the death of the book are greatly exaggerated."[10] Usually there is talk of imagination and individualism, of souls and slowness. But I hear mostly nostalgia. I hear, too, echoes of a similar sanguineness expressed by Trithemius of Sponheim, the abbot, bibliographer and fancier of handwritten manuscripts, in 1492: "Yes, many books are now available in print," he wrote early in the previous communications revolution, "but no matter how many books will be printed, there will always be some left unprinted and worth copying."[11] I sense, in other words, that wishes are commandeering thinking.

We wish, of course, because we fear: Without our books, won't we be nothing but "sots"—drunk on images, fooled by appearances, bereft of our intellectual powers? I take this fear very seriously. I have tried not to underplay the disruptions and losses already experienced and likely to be experienced in this transitional period. Yet the message [. . .] is that in the long term the moving image is likely to make our thoughts not more feeble but more robust, that it is likely to lead us to stronger understandings.

Perhaps this book lover's most treasonable thought about print's fall is that it is time. Humankind has a talent for coming up with the new technologies it requires at about the time, give or take a couple of centuries, it requires them—or at least it looks that way in retrospect.[12] I suspect that, in retrospect, we will conclude that sometime in the twentieth century the print method of analyzing the world began to exhaust itself, that its magic began to run out.

"We are threatened by a new and peculiarly American menace," Daniel Boorstin wrote in his prophetic book *The Image,* published in 1962. "It is not the menace of class war, of ideology, of poverty, of disease, of illiteracy, of demagoguery, or of tyranny, though these now plague most of the world. It is the menace of unreality."[13]

This threat has only grown worse in the intervening third of a century, and it has spread to much of the rest of the world. Something, we seem to sense, has been leaking out of our lives: values, perhaps, or meaning, or a kind of surety. Many of us, if I can presume to speak for many of us, upon occasion feel weightless, directionless, uncertain; reality seems to lack realness. [14] That's why we produce so many tributes—in advertising, song, even politics—to "real clothes," "real love," "real experiences," "real events," "real people," "real issues" and, more generally, "making it real."

The villain for Boorstin and the multitudes of professional and amateur cultural observers who have followed is clear: the image. "In our world we sleep and eat the image and pray to it and wear it too," Don DeLillo wrote in *Mao II.*[15] Images are winning—materialistic, entertainment-besotting, civic-life-depleting images; vain, phony, surface-loving, fantasy-promoting, reality-murdering images. I've quibbled with one or two of the particulars in this long indictment; nevertheless Boorstin et al. have a point: Television *has* played a major role in creating what Bill McKibben called "the current emptiness."[16] But so have printed words.

Print's linear, one-word-follows-another, one-thing-at-a-time logic is perhaps its greatest strength. Expanding on the work begun by writing in the time of the pre-Socratic philosopher Heraclitus, print has pulled us in an exceedingly profitable direction. We owe it much: Modern science, modern medicine, modern democracy, our reformations and enlightenments—all were advanced by the printed word. But with the alchemists debunked, the leeches removed and the kings decapitated, it sometimes seems as if print has been reduced to chasing its own long, straight tail.

Print eventually turned the same unyielding logic that had helped over-turn superstitions, monarchies and social hierarchies upon words and logic themselves. Some of the writers who trekked most intrepidly up lines of type—Kafka, Beckett, Camus—found the meanings getting thinner as they ascended. "Nothing, nothing mattered" is the wisdom impending execution brings to Albert Camus's protagonist in *The Stranger*. Philosophers and liter-ary theorists undertook similar journeys. Indeed, close readers, many of them French, discovered that when carefully examined, metaphors conflict, arguments undercut themselves, precepts seem suspended in air. Such print-guided excursions into the absurd or the postmodern, such exercises in existentialism, poststructuralism or deconstruction, left language, mean-ing and reason looking like more "false fronts."[17] No solid ground upon which to construct a secure sense of the real here.

"You taught me language," Caliban fumes at Prospero's daughter, "and my profit on't is, I know how to curse."[18] We have been taught print. We might say, were we to succumb to a similar bitterness, that our "profit on't" is that we now know how to deconstruct.

It is time to repeat a caveat [. . .] I don't mean to discount the contribu-tions made to the uneasinesses of our time by shifts in politics, economics, religion or others of the many social and cultural forces that are not the sub-ject [here]. Still, I believe it is fair to conclude that printed words, like im-ages, have played *a* major role in leading us to this crisis. And I believe it is important to note that printed words may not have the range to help lead us out.

Lines of type seem to have bent themselves into logical circles: trying to find the matter in the fact that nothing matters. In the twentieth century the limits of writing may have been written. "Philosophy is a battle against the bewitchment of our intelligence by means of language," proposed Ludwig Wittgenstein, writing in 1945.[19] That is not a battle easily won by means of language. Perhaps print has taken us as far as it can.

As a writer I feel as if I can describe anything, so I will attempt to describe this: It is a short 1996 public-service film edited by Hank Corwin and di-rected by Samuel Bayer for Boston's Jimmy Fund charity, and in there some-where is a boy whose hair is growing back after treatment for cancer. The film, shot in black and white, is occupied mostly with jaggedly cut images of a number of strange-looking barbers. We see them discussing their work, wielding their combs and brushes, snipping their scissors, smiling some-times almost "demonically" (Corwin's word).[20] I should also mention the odd angles and glaring lighting. In a spot ostensibly about the joy of return-ing to the world, Corwin and Bayer have confronted, through these echoes of childhood (and maybe biblical or historical) barber nightmares, some of the terrors of that world.

It is odd. It is disturbing. Within the limits of the form, a public-service announcement, it looks to me to be art. And whether or not I've had any success describing this film in print, it is difficult to imagine *experiencing* what this film communicates through print.

Print took the world apart and reassembled it in straight, regularly shaped, black-and-white lines. The problem is that not everything can be made to fit.

"What reading does, ultimately," concludes the essayist Sven Birkerts, one of its champions, "is keep alive the dangerous and exhilarating idea that a life is not a sequence of lived moments, but a destiny, that, God or no God, life has a unitary pattern inscribed within it."[21] I would not go that far. Twentieth-century print has certainly not been limited to proselytizing for destiny and unitary patterns. Indeed, I am sympathetic with Milan Kundera's statement that "the novelist teaches the reader to comprehend the world as a question."[22] However, I believe print tends to raise its questions in a way that allows for a limited set of possible answers: a cause-and-effect destiny, for example, an underlying pattern, or its absurd absence ("Nothing, nothing mattered"). Even to think of life as "a sequence of lived moments"—the prosaic view Birkerts sees reading as moving us beyond—is to surrender to prose, to the biases of the sequential line of type.

We have learned from print to squeeze even death into the sequences. Here is Flaubert:

> A spasm flung her down on the mattress. Everyone drew close. She had ceased to exist.[23]

Here is the *New York Times:*

> CHARLESTOWN STATE PRISON, Mass., Tuesday, Aug. 23—Nicola Sacco and Bartolomeo Vanzetti died in the electric chair early this morning, carrying out the sentence imposed on them for the South Braintree murders of April 15, 1920.
>
> Sacco marched to the death chair at 12:11 and was pronounced lifeless at 12:19.
>
> Vanzetti entered the execution room at 12:20 and was declared dead at 12:26.
>
> To the last they protested their innocence, and the efforts of many who believed them guiltless proved futile, although they fought a legal and extra legal battle unprecedented in the history of American jurisprudence.

Events—even events at their most terrible, sensational, unfathomable, tempestuous—tend to display a certain calm, ordered clarity when portrayed in print. (I know it is possible to think of exceptions; perhaps it is time to notice the rule.) Louis Stark, who wrote this story on the execution of Sacco and Vanzetti for the *New York Times* in 1927, later recalled the scene at the prison that night to be one of "the utmost confusion." That confusion does not come through in the procession of isolated facts that form his story.[24]

Shakespeare shows us how the magic contained in books can make and unmake a tempest. A ship is wrecked. "We split, we split, we split!" cries one of those on board.[25] Feelings of recrimination, romance and reconciliation are set loose. A plot is moved forward. Otherwise all the storm's effects, once they have served their narrative purposes, are simply undone: ship restored, victims reunited, their clothes unsullied.

This is a formidable magic. But let's take a closer look at the tempest it has produced. The tempest divides, for a time, daughter from father, prince from king. It erases, in time, confusion between the legitimate and the illegitimate. It splits. It reconciles. It does not muddle, overwhelm or, in the end, even destroy.

Prospero—who deserves the byline on this tempest—ultimately rejects the book he has used to create it. We are presumably to see in this an artist renouncing his art in favor of life. We might also see a conjurer frustrated with the limitations of the book's magic, as conjurers before him must have grown frustrated with the limitations of the spoken word. "Deeper than ever did plummet sound," Prospero vows, "I'll drown my book."[26] It has, after all, been a rather anemic storm.

It would be hypocritical for me to insist too strenuously on the limitations of words while enlisting the services of ninety-some-odd thousand of them. When challenged, print has demonstrated a remarkable ability to expand. That is why I write. As I set sentences after images and ask them to tiptoe into the future, I worry a great deal about my abilities, not much about theirs. However, my ideas—historically based, ultimately rather dualistic—probably don't represent that great a test for this medium.[27] Others have posed sterner tests.

In the twentieth century, some of the best of them that write this writing, to paraphrase Shakespeare once again, have struggled to do our tempests more justice.[28] They have strained to escape the thinness of the line, the flatness of the page.[29] These writers have been trying to say in print what print is not comfortable saying: that the world can't always be split into categories, that our thoughts are often scattered, that contradictions aren't always clarified, that our experiences are determined in part by contingency, that reality sometimes reduces itself to indeterminate clouds, that life resists encapsulation in narratives or processions of facts, that our existences, our cultures, are full of confusions. However, enabling readers to *experience* this has required surrendering some of the strategies that have traditionally made print effective. Avant-garde writers in this century have engaged in sometimes reader-unfriendly subtractions of clarity, message, coherence or entertainment value. (In the *New York Times Magazine,* the impeccably cultured James Atlas recently went so far as to admit that much of the "great literature" of the twentieth century "bores" him.)[30]

Hank Corwin and Samuel Bayer were working in the new video, a much less mature form; they were making a public-service announcement only a couple of minutes long; yet Corwin and Bayer were able to present one or two similarly challenging notions with much less sacrifice, much less strain. The avant-garde energies released by photography and film are finally beginning to settle where they belong: in the successor to photography and film, in the new video.

Corwin and Bayer's messages and the messages of these adventurous novelists and theorists seem dangerous; they have helped raise the specter of unreality. But would they scare us so if our culture did not remain, for the most part, trapped in print's narrow logic? Scattered thoughts, unclarified contradictions, contingency and indeterminacy are direct threats to *print's* reality. The new video, however, is much more comfortable with them. Mark Pellington had no difficulty presenting a few entirely different perspectives on beauty simultaneously in a music video. Corwin and Bayer were willing to intermingle joy and nightmare in a disjointed, stream-of-consciousness montage. They pull us, to use Heraclitus's words, in more than one direction at once.[31,32] In the new video the confusions, the tempests, fit.

In its early centuries print helped spread an older set of frightening messages: that the earth might not be at the center of the universe, that kings might not rule by divine right. It was print itself that eventually helped supply the wisdom the populace needed to survive those shocks. Now, in the midst of a new communications revolution, we face a new set of shocks attributable in part to the exhaustion of print and the arrival of video. Video may be able to help us survive them. It may help reassure us that scattered thoughts, unclarified contradictions, contingency and indeterminacy are not necessarily threats to our reality.

Boorstin insisted that we are foolish to think moving images will ever succeed in giving us "the nub of the matter."[33] Perhaps moving images won't. Perhaps moving images can't. But they may give us other perspectives on reality—less constricted perspectives.

One way of viewing Corwin and Bayer's little film is that it presents barbers and their implements as they might appear to that young cancer patient. We don't see what is going on in that child's head, but this mix of uplifting and nightmarish views gives us an idea of how the world outside might look from in there. This from-the-inside-*out* perspective is more or less the one to which most of us head-bearing creatures are accustomed. It is not, however, the angle of vision that has become characteristic of print.

Print, as I have noted, wants to look from the outside in. Its narrow searchlight is well suited to the dark recesses it finds there. Print must strain mightily to present the visible with anything near the richness or completeness we can get from our own eyes, but in presenting the invisible—in the "attempt to interpret . . . state of mind and inner life," to borrow a phrase from Fyodor Dostoevsky—the printed word has no competition. The novel, back as far as *Don Quixote*, justified its existence by introducing us to the world with*in*. Here, from *Crime and Punishment,* is one of the countless scenes Dostoevsky observed there:

> The hopeless misery and anxiety of all that time, especially of the last hours, had weighed so heavily upon him that he positively clutched at the chance of this new unmixed, complete sensation. It came over him like a fit; it was like a single spark kindled in his soul and spreading fire through him. Everything in him softened at once.[34]

"Novelists," Jonathan Franzen wrote recently in a meditation on the continued relevance of his craft, "are preserving . . . a habit of looking past surfaces into interiors."[35] Humans searching for understanding did not always turn this way. First, we can suppose, they had looked with the aid of spoken language mostly out, toward the edges of their worlds, for signs of the useful or the dangerous. The *Iliad,* the *Odyssey* and the Bible do communicate the urgings of "the heart inside," but often their search for understanding causes eyes to turn *up*—to Olympus, to the heavens.[36] However, the four centuries that are now ending have been dominated by this compulsion to stare not *out* or *up* but *in*.

It is here, under our skins, that our psyches, subconsciouses, "true selves" and souls were found. Descartes, Rousseau, Flaubert, Dostoevsky, Freud, Woolf, Proust—these were explorers of the inner world, of our hidden thoughts, inner selves, hidden natures, inner states and hidden feelings.[37] With their help, we clutched at sensations and kindled sparks in our souls. With their help, we constructed mythologies of the psyche, complete with warring powers and walled-off territories. With their help, we developed a whole profession devoted to guiding people, pilgrims in search of *in*sight, around these hidden inner lands. (Kundera satirized our obsession by having a pretentious professor assert, "Homer's odyssey has been taken inside. It has been interiorized. The islands, the seas, the sirens seducing us, Ithaca summoning us—nowadays they are only the voices of our interior being.")[38]

Although it is about hopes and fears, Corwin and Bayer's film is not a psychological study. Few examples of the new video are. They frequently take their shape, as this film seems to, from the flow of impressions through a single consciousness. However, what we see is not some imagining of the nature of that consciousness but those particular, telling impressions. Such videos show us psyches in action; they do not attempt to conjure up psyches themselves.

There is a reason for this: Video is a bright floodlight. It has its way with the visible and with perspectives on the visible, but has little facility for presenting the buried, the invisible. Our churning ids, deepest selves or immortal souls are even more difficult to capture in a photographic image than hearts, hopes, virtue, integrity or character. Video, consequently, tends not to look in that direction. [39,40]

To those of us still conditioned to the idea that truth is to be found only through such inner vision, video's perspective seems more than just superficial; it seems a blindness, a stupidity. This is one of the largest of the mistakes that has been made about the rise of the image.

For when we speak of our inner natures, it must be remembered, we are speaking metaphorically. Exactly where our own unvoiced thoughts might be located on some topology of consciousness is unclear. But certainly whatever we know of the "inner lives" of others we know not from X rays of their hearts or examinations of their entrails but from surface manifestations. Surgeons have happened upon no Oedipal yearnings, kernels of identity, souls or spirits beneath our skins. After centuries of print's fascinating imaginings, this is easy to forget.

That this metaphor has been hugely productive no one can deny, but it has its limitations. And those limitations have, over time, formed ruts and barriers.

By the middle years of this century we had explored our insides to the point of self-obsession, to the point of solipsism. We had looked into this metaphorical inner world so long and so intently that we sometimes seemed oblivious to what was taking place in that other, more tangible world. We learned, "against the stomach of [our] sense," to borrow another wording from *The Tempest,* to place more stock in the unseen than the seen.[41] We cupped our ears not to the importunings of our fellows but to inner voices. We judged our mental health not by our social circumstances but by unconscious urges. We began to imagine ourselves not so much as actors in the world but as stages for private dramas, as atomistic units—as if we were not so hopelessly dependent on a borrowed language, on borrowed perspectives, so thoroughly covered by the fingerprints of others, that it is almost absurd to speak of us having independent beings.[42] The more we looked inward, into individuals, the less we saw of the connections between individuals.[43]

Why do we assume there is more truth inside us than out? Why is there not as much to be learned by picking apart, rethinking, reimaging our surfaces—from a *superficial* analysis—as there is from an analysis of those mythical insides? Perhaps we have gained what we can gain from this metaphor. Perhaps it is time for it to be dropped, time for our gaze—with all the powers of the new video—to return to what can actually be seen.

"If serious reading dwindles to near nothingness," DeLillo has suggested, "it will probably mean that the thing we're talking about when we use the word 'identity' has reached an end."[44] He may be right. Perhaps we will have to learn to talk of new things.[45]

"The world is all outside," developments in nineteenth-century molecular theory inspired Emerson to conclude; "it has no inside."[46] It could be said, similarly, that human beings are all outside. Our natures—like the atoms of a molecule—are not inside us; they make up us. Oscar Wilde was always sensitive to this point. "It is only shallow people who do not judge by appearances," he remarked in a letter. "The mystery of the world is the visible, not the invisible."[47] Now, for the first time in human history, we have a means of communication, an art form, strong enough to grapple with the all-encompassing outside, with the visible.

In 1993 Mark Pellington took a camera along on a visit to his parents' home, edited in some old 8mm movie footage and other images of memorable family moments, and produced a thirty-minute film. His motivations, sadly, had little to do with those behind the typical home video. The director's father, Bill Pellington, once a star linebacker for the Baltimore Colts, was suffering from Alzheimer's disease. Pellington's film, *Father's Daze*, was broadcast on PBS and screened at a number of film festivals. Nevertheless, this film might be taken as a model of the future home video and of the future world as seen through the new video.

Father's Daze is resolutely, unflaggingly nonnarrative. Words on screen at the beginning inform us of the situation of Pellington's father. But no story of decline is told. No chronology is presented. Various scenes from the father's past—a celebration at the stadium of his career, an afternoon at the beach with his young family, his wedding—are mixed in with various glimpses of him today: an uncomprehending interaction with his son, being fed by a nurse, shuffling in front of the house. Micki Pellington—Bill's wife, Mark's mother—voices her frustration and sadness. Leafless trees are shown against a gray sky. Steep highs and deep lows, to revisit one of McKibben's critiques, are indeed presented. Feeling and emotion flow freely, but they are not channeled into stories. No one explains how long this has been going on. No one remembers him when. No one uses the word *tragedy*.

Moments are pulled out of time in Pellington's film as they are in photographs: the imposing bulk of the aged father immobile on the edge of his bed, the vitality of the young father swinging his son high over the sand. Sometimes all we see is a pajama-covered hip; sometimes the film speeds up to show repetitive routine; sometimes images and sounds are repeated. The film places these moments before us—ungraceful, neither virtuous nor unvirtuous, unburdened by explanatory system.

The subtractions caused by the abandonment of traditional kinds of meaning are as evident in Pellington's film as they are in empty-headed thrillers like *Mission: Impossible.* However, here we can also begin to glimpse—at a very early stage—some of the kinds of meaning this new form might add.

Pellington is forcing us, in part, to examine social behaviors and interactions: son tries to convince father to sit down, football star is interviewed on television, wife places food in husband's mouth. I don't know if Pellington believes there to be a swirling mass of psychological motivations buried beneath these behaviors and interactions, but I know his film doesn't think there is. The new video has neither the talent nor the inclination for such psychological excavations.

What we see here is how his father's situation appeared to Pellington, but the filmmaker did that not by looking from the world into himself but by looking from himself at the world. Eisenstein was probably right: *"The true material of the sound-film is . . . the monologue."*[48] Pellington didn't share the thoughts that might have made this more clearly an "inner monologue" (though he might have). Still, his film can be understood as a representation of the stream of memories and impressions in his head. He presented no models or metaphors for the stream itself; he made no attempt to describe it or his own psychology. All he showed us is the world as seen by his mind's eye. We are not, therefore, on print's centuries-long quest for the essence of a person. Rather, we are on a quest (new and not so new) for an understanding of the perspectives of people: how and what they see.

We are on a quest too—here in the world of the visible—for an understanding of the performances of people, for glimpses of the dexterity and comfort with which they play their roles as, in this case, father, wife, son, athlete, caregiver, patient, filmmaker. The new video observes a ballet of behaviors. It sees not consciences and unconsciousnesses squaring off in private chambers within, but connections and the absence of connections overlapping in society without.

The new video also has the power to see the shadows cast on individuals by larger forces: politics, economics, illness, forms of communication, language. Pellington allowed us to listen in on some phrases: "Let go of his fingers," his mother tells his father. But the director was eavesdropping not so much because, as Renoir maintained, the voice is "the best means of conveying the personality of a human being"; instead Pellington seemed interested in letting us hear what language can and cannot say.[49]

In his film Pellington unabashedly relied on surface images: father and son dive into the ocean together, father sits dumbly in a chair, father makes a dramatic tackle. Again, I don't know whether Pellington thinks there is a hidden, more real world behind these images, but I know that the new video is unable to think that way. It is forced to confront the images—including images of filial love, poignant infirmity, football glory. It can't leave surfaces behind in search of *deeper* truths. Instead, it finds many of its truths through the deft juxtaposition of carefully selected aspects of surfaces: The chair moment was pulled out of time, objectified and held up against the ocean moment and the football moment. All these moments were shaken and transformed in the process. Truths arise that are no less subtle and meaningful for not being "deep." Maybe the new video will help us understand more fully the consequences of the fact that even cores themselves turn out, when exposed, to have surfaces.[50]

In looking *at,* rather than *out* or *up* or *in,* Pellington's film is not simply staring. He is not often asking us to lose ourselves in the intricacies of a scene, as a painting, photo or piece of cinema vérité might. This is instead a jumpy, fragmented, rapidly moving, directed, *analytic* kind of examination.

Pellington mixed an array of isolated glimpses from past and present, from here and there—instants, facets, slants: a cloudy eye, a father swinging his son in the air, large, folded, purposeless hands. Deep contemplation of a single scene is not often possible in the new video, but a guided dissection of the visible world becomes possible. (Jeff Scher's *Milk of Amnesia* also points to this possibility.)

"Behavior items shown in a movie can be analyzed much more precisely and from more points of view than those presented on paintings or on the stage," Walter Benjamin noted.[51] The new video is even more precise and capable of deploying even more points of view. It has the potential to take the surfaces of behaviors, of scenes, and make of them the stuff of a new art. It opens the possibility that we may learn to analyze such surfaces as thoroughly as adept print diagnosticians have analyzed our insides. These surfaces—rippled by the winds of fashion, conformism, rebellion, pretense, longing—are, I contend, the next frontier. There are unexplored territories here, discoveries to be made.

The events Pellington showed us repeatedly fail to arrange themselves in an easily comprehensible order. Again, I don't know if he himself thinks that larger patterns were discernible behind the unhappy present moments and happy past moments that intermingle in his film. I don't know if he believes his father has a core identity or shoulders a destiny. But I do know that his film neither tells such stories nor concerns itself with the absence of such stories. The new video is after different kinds of meanings. As we begin to edit our own home videos, as we are presented with more examples of the new video, we might expect the world to fill with these different kinds of meanings.

One of the key words in the scene from Plato's *Phaedrus* in which the Egyptian god Thoth tries to make the case for writing can be translated in another way. The word is *pharmakon*—usually represented here by "recipe": Thoth's "invention is a recipe for both memory and wisdom." But *pharmakon,* as Jacques Derrida has pointed out, is also the Greek word for "drug," and this translation opens up an interesting new reading.[52]

All technologies can be looked upon as drugs. They have disturbing side effects: The automobile, for example, has puffed poisons into our air, evacuated our downtowns and enfeebled our legs. (Emerson noted a similar effect in 1839: "The civilized man has built a coach, but has lost the use of his feet.")[53,54] And technologies have medicinal powers: The automobile (like the coach) has relieved much physical isolation.

Such drugs are ingested with excitement and anxiety. We spend a great deal of time obsessing about how the warning label should have read. In writing about television, I have acknowledged that it can addict and debilitate, but my main goal has been to raise the possibility that the moving image—particularly in its most concentrated form, the new video—can alleviate, if not cure, certain turn-of-the-millennium maladies.

This particular psychoactive medicine works in two ways. The first is a product primarily of the fourth kind of motion—hopping from scene to scene—which the new video has helped introduce into the world. This new motion enables us to head in a marvelously therapeutic direction: *back,* not in time but in mental space, back to where we can gain perspective.

A 1995 commercial for IBM's Aptiva computers turned out to be a demonstration (probably unintentional) of the new video's proficiency in taking us there. We see, as the ad begins, a computer screen with a small video playing in one corner. The video shows a Native American standing upon a spectacular Southwestern rock formation (of the sort normally reserved in advertisements for something with four-wheel drive). Suddenly the entire screen fills with that video. The commercial, by Ogilvy and Mather, has thus made its main point (which has nothing to do, of course, with Native Americans or precipitous rocks): Aptiva computers offer full-screen video. Now the commercial begins to make my point.

The camera—again suddenly—pulls back, and we learn, to our surprise, that the video we have been watching is only the content of the screen of a computer onstage with a jazz band. Silly us! But then, while we're still coming to grips with our shortsightedness, the camera lurches back once again, and this shot of the jazz band is revealed to be on another computer monitor floating in space next to an astronaut. More shocks follow: Another jump back and we see that our astronaut and his weightless computer are in a video playing on a monitor held by a cross-legged mime. This time the camera, disdaining cuts, retreats in one (relatively) lengthy tracking shot: Said mime is sitting in an exotic glass bubble; then the camera reveals that this bubble is one of many in a surreal carny scene populated by musicians on stilts; then we see the Native American and the astronaut together in another bubble; then a cameraman and director appear in front of the scene. Yet another sudden and surprising break awaits us. The whole carny scene, it turns out, is on a computer screen in a boy's room, complete with fish tank. Thirty seconds have almost passed; an announcer intones the name of the product; the commercial is clearly ending. Is this as far back as we'll go? Maybe not. Just then, in the corner of the screen, a large fish begins to float by, and it appears as if, were there time, our perspective would shift once again.

In the end this commercial, whose purpose is probably just to give a vaguely avant-garde feel to the product being sold, doesn't have all that much on its mind. I don't pretend it extends the breadth of human knowledge; however, the vertiginous cutting of which it makes such a show just might. Words too can "yank" us—to use George Kennan's word—from a particular situation back into a larger context, but words can't do it again and again with such ease, rapidity and verisimilitude. The new video, thanks to its ability to make objects out of scenes, has the power to shift our focus—artistic and intellectual—from changes in particular scenes or situations to changes in the contexts of scenes, and changes in the contexts of contexts. Is this, as Kennan charged, "a massive abuse of the capacity for concentrated thought"? I think not. It is instead a demand for a new kind of concentration. But it is true that such shifts aren't healthy for matters we once concentrated upon, matters such as simple beliefs or basic values. These shifts have philosophic consequences.

Back is, of course, the direction of irony: A dog is attempting some odd feat. Cut back. The grin on the face of the talk-show host reminds us that it is only a "stupid pet trick," to be enjoyed for its absurdity as much as its accomplishment. Back, in this sense, is located "above the stream"—a vantage point from which our flounderings, foolishnesses, inconsistencies and hypocrisies become apparent, the object of talk-show chuckles.

Ironies obviously predate moving images by many millennia. Authors have certainly proven themselves capable of standing back from their modest proposals as they are making them. It is possible to write a line and then, in the next line, comment upon, even contradict what has been written. It is even possible to lift above lines as they are written through sarcasm or satire (as might be accomplished by italicizing the word *possible* in this sentence).

But video appears to have made a special contribution to irony. Even without fast cutting and the rapid shifts back it facilitates, even in the first era of video, these electronically distributed moving images have encouraged a detached, lighthearted point of view—a David Letterman point of view. A world parades before us on television—small, slight, without consequence for our lives or purchase on our emotions. Relieved of responsibility for caring a whole lot about that world, we settle into the role of detached observers. We examine, in our usual half-alert fashion, whatever is on-screen. Is it pretentious? Is it hypocritical? Is it wearing some silly Spanish-cowgirl outfit? We're the experts. We hold the "zapper." Inevitably we smirk.

"Television was practically *made* for irony," the young novelist David Foster Wallace has concluded.[55] Pretty soon we lost whatever ability we may have had to watch the McGuire Sisters without seeing them as camp. Pretty soon that which was on-screen began to defend itself against our smirks by smirking along with us, by including ironic comments on its own conventions: Talk-show hosts seemed to wink at the audience as they held up a sponsor's product; commercials mocked commercials; sportscasters camped their way through the prohibition against rebroadcast of their events. Actions, gestures, behaviors were increasingly presented as if in quotations marks.

And that was *before* the new video, which dramatically accelerates the ironic distancing. Each element in these rapid flows of images and words is in a position to smirk at the one that proceeded it. The new video is continually stepping back from what it has just shown. My favorite example is the last of a series of slogans flashed on the screen in a 1993 Planet Reebok commercial: "No Slogans." The new video lifts us higher and higher "above the stream."

I am aware that, at century's end, many have come to conclude that this is not a good thing. All this smirking has come to seem unattractive. Our indifference about that which is on television seems to have metastasized into an indifference about much of life. "The 'girl-who's-dancing-with-you-but-would-obviously-rather-be-dancing-with-somebody-else' expression," Wallace reported, "has become my generation's version of cool."[56] From these cold altitudes that old, lazy stream has come to look rather warm and comfortable; our position up on the bluffs has come to seem rather sad. We yearn, even the undeniably with-it Wallace yearns, for an escape from this incessant irony, for reimmersion in a world of caring, commitment and concern. We yearn for sincerity.

Fortunately, our position above the stream does not prevent us from sometimes taking a dip. Eventually, whatever out expression, we find ourselves dancing with someone we deeply desire. Caring, commitment and concern continue to retain a place in the lives of most of us. Still, enlarging that place—restoring what has been eroded by irony—seems a swell idea, the obvious solution to our irony problem. But how exactly might that be accomplished? Are we capable, as Wallace imagined, of shrinking "away from ironic watching," of returning to "single-entendre principles"? Are we capable once again of rhyming *June* and *moon*, of selfless devotion to a political party, of saying "I truly love you" without stepping back and noting that we have arrived at a moment when we are saying "I truly love you"?

This solution to the drawbacks of irony seems similar to the monarchist's solution to the drawbacks of democracy: If only we could believe once again in divine right. If only we could believe once again in simple virtue or in the unclouded wisdom of giving to each according to need or in endless, unquestioned love. If only we could, without giggling, stick a carnation in our lapel, don a red beret or dress up like Spanish cowgirls. I don't think we can—most of us. I don't think we can even say "without the express consent of the National Football League" anymore without the hint of a smile. I think those forms of sincerity are gone—gone, for most of us, like omens and kings.

However, there is another possible response to the pull of irony. We might, instead, go with it; we might choose to see what tricks this great, ghostly genie might perform for us.

The new video cuts with such ease to ironic distances that it has no difficulty stacking them on top of each other. It gives us an opportunity to be not only ironic about irony (which Wallace is) or ironic about irony about irony (my goal?) but to jitterbug among these various ironies. We have a chance to do this repeatedly and engagingly. We have a chance to become adept at juxtaposing and negotiating the various levels of irony. We have a chance to become reconciled to their existence, to grow comfortable with them, to understand them. The new video, to pick up Wallace's wording, was *made* for mastering irony. Perhaps we will learn better how to replace some of our smirks with knowing but affectionate smiles. Perhaps we will learn better how to increase the space for caring, commitment and concern between the quotation marks. Or perhaps we will learn something else entirely.

Two paths, it might be said, lead away from the joke-fest with David Letterman in which we now seem to find ourselves: One would return to old certainties, to a bygone seriousness. It calls to us; I know that. However, I think this other path—while certainly unfamiliar, even frightening—is more promising.

Irony travels with an even less reputable companion, of course: cynicism. There's no doubt that the new video's propensity for stepping back also encourages a kind of cynicism. The president delivers a speech. Cut to the handlers behind him, feeding lines and dispensing spin. Silly us! It is as foolish to accept that speech as a sincere expression of the president's own thoughts as it is to believe that Aptiva commercial will stick with the Native American. We are being taught by the moving image in general, and by this new kind of motion in particular, that there is always a broader perspective to be had. We are learning to view art, politics and life as scenes from which it is always possible to move back.

This seems, initially, rather dispiriting. Hence the disturbing nihilism that seems as common in the young as acne. Hence all the critical, cynical earfuls we've been getting from our pundits lately about how critical and cynical we've all become. But perhaps we might be a little cynical about this cynicism about cynicism. Yes, there are higher states, but does the path to them pass through gullibility? Might not a clear view of the imperfections of the world and of ourselves be a prerequisite to changing or accepting them? Might these additional steps back be useful in finally getting a handle on spins and those who dispense them?

Back is the direction of self-consciousness, too: A comment is made at a party. Cut. Cut. Cut. We see three other people making the same comment. A simple unselfconscious self-consciousness can paralyze. But there is a freedom in a self-consciousness that is aware of itself and of its own limits, that can accept the extent to which party chatter is predictable. A Nike commercial from 1993 starring Michael Jordan and Bugs Bunny steps back for an instant to place a sign reading, "Product Shot," next to a picture of the sneakers it is hawking. In that too there is a freedom, though I realize applying this word to a Nike commercial is at the very least problematic.

The rise of moving images has certainly been associated with the rise of a commercial, product-oriented culture, with the rise, for instance, of corporations like Nike. There's no getting around the extent to which television and the techniques I celebrate in particular have been put to the task of selling.[57] And we have bought a lot—too much, many would say—of what they have sold: The Nike logo is now proudly displayed on our hats, our socks, our shorts and our shirts, as well as on sneakers probably made in whatever country currently has the lowest-paid workers. Some might tattoo that logo on their foreheads if they thought it would increase the chance of their being perceived to be like Michael Jordan.

The new video, with its heavy debt to television commercials, can hardly separate itself from this commercial culture. But I note that as we become more ironic, cynical and self-aware, as we become alert to how and why product shots are inserted, we become somewhat more difficult to sell to, harder marks. Irony, cynicism and self-consciousness may have helped undercut the alternatives to acquisitiveness—thrift, selflessness, spiritual values; but they may also begin to call into question our compulsion to acquire. It is hard to see uses of the new video beyond Nike commercials because there have been, to date, so few of them and so many Nike commercials. However, the new video—with its irony, cynicism and self-consciousness—may ultimately be more at home presenting, as Mark Pellington did in a video for Information Society's song "Peace and Love, Inc.," a sneaker displaying the logo "ENVY."

I won't underestimate the resourcefulness of advertisers armed with these techniques in anticipating and responding to our changing attitudes, in following us back. But I do suspect we may visit places they may not want us to reach. A Sprite commercial from 1996 that makes use of the slogan "Image Is Nothing/Thirst Is Everything" is a good example of the chase on which advertisers now find themselves. Sprite is clearly after what philosopher Jacques Derrida has called "the image of the nonimage."[58] But this is a tougher image to sell than older, pre-selfconscious images of virility, beauty, athleticism, femininity, suavity. It is too wispy, too amorphous, too negative, and it gives away too much of the image/product-shot/slogan game. These ads are making us into experts.

A series of Miller Lite commercials in 1997, the source of considerable controversy within the advertising industry, illustrates part of the problem: in a burst of ironic pseudo-self-consciousness, the commercials, produced by Fallon McElligott, credit themselves to a young "creative superstar" named Dick, and then proceed to present such unattractive images as a bunch of aged, bedraggled singing cowboys walking off into a men's room.[59] Perhaps a rare satiric sensibility is on display here; perhaps not. Still, it must have been easier to sell beer when audiences were content with chummy old football stars on-screen and advertisers could stay hidden away in their plush offices.

Following us further in this backward spiral away from obvious enticements—to the image of the non-nonimage, for example, the "shot of product shot" shot, the "no slogan about no slogans" slogan—may create even more problems. This is a chase advertisers—early experts in the new video—may prove good at (though not as good as some twenty-seven-year-old singer-songwriters), and no doubt it will get some of their creative juices flowing. However, we shouldn't therefore conclude that this is a chase advertisers want to be on. It will force them to surrender more and more of their tools for selling, and it will increasingly enable us to watch ourselves being sold to. The freedom of that Nike commercial's self-consciousness may ultimately be our freedom.

And as the scenes shift and recede, we can be taken back further still: We might, for instance, be given an opportunity to watch ourselves watching ourselves watching. The new video allows us, in Roland Barthes's phrase, to "take off the brake" on this kind of reflective awareness.[60] Is there not a chance that a new wisdom might manifest itself amongst all these mirrors?

For back is, most crucially, the direction of perspective. "There is only a perspective seeing, only a perspective 'knowing,'" maintained Friedrich Nietzsche (producing, not for the first time, an archetypal twentieth-century thought in the nineteenth century). He then concluded: "The more eyes, different eyes, we can use to observe, the more complete our vision will be."[61] The new video, thanks to its ability to dance from perspective to perspective, gives us more eyes.

Were I to produce a video version of this [chapter] it would necessarily rest on my ideas a bit less firmly. It would want to include other perspectives: questioning voices (asking whether changes in communications really are that important), cynical voices (pouncing on the inanity of some current exercises in fast cutting), ironic and self-conscious voices (proclaiming, perhaps in words printed on-screen, that all this irony and self-consciousness is *well* beyond the capabilities of mere print).

I have tried to hone the words [here] into an argument. That argument would wend its way through the video version too—well served by pictures, film clips, video clips, words on-screen, graphics and narration. But there would be many more opportunities to step back from it. Moving images are not easily honed; they tend to swell and engulf.

A more substantial example, if only hypothetical, would seem to be in order. The following brief script—really a mind experiment—was conceived some years ago.[62]

The subject of this hypothetical script was a very serious one: At the time the Serbs were brutalizing sections of Bosnia. Say we edited together a second or two from a shot of a Serb-run prison camp with a shot of a Nazi concentration camp and a shot of the Clinton White House, whose responses to the Serbian outrages struck many at the time as insufficient. A simple (then rather familiar) point would have been made. A different point, reflecting another school of thought at the time, might have been made by editing together quick shots of similarly armed and aggressive-looking Croats, Bosnian Muslims and Serbs, with the words *Croats, Muslims and Serbs* on-screen below their pictures. But what point would be made were these two little montages edited together, with some music and a couple of phrases from statements by politicians tacked on? That would be a fair amount of complexity for perhaps twenty seconds.

Then we might have edited in some similarly contradictory sequences from Somalia and Azerbaijan—two other places where outrages were then being committed against innocents. And that half minute on the world's moral tangles could have been used as an element in a larger juxtaposition on the difficulties of action, mixing in sections on, for example, inner-city poverty. That could then have been a piece in a production evaluating possible strategies for living a life: moral action, hedonistic pursuits, material acquisitions, etc. Finally, the issue of whether such life strategies have any meaning might have been raised through further juxtapositions involving representative instants selected from a wide variety of lives.

Back and back and back. The "stream" is still there—in front of us in photographic moving images—but we are also making ourselves at home above the "stream." The new video allows our thoughts to explore places that before they had only visited.

The second strength of the new video as a philosophical pharmaceutical is a product of its speed and our growing ability to grasp things that move at such speeds. So much is happening in such short segments of time that those segments seem to expand before a fast and alert consciousness. Half a minute, when filled with a few dozen images, gains depth and breadth. New artistic and philosophical spaces are opened up in time. Words, of course, create some substantial spaces of their own. They can grow scenes in our thoughts, but the new video, because it tends to swarm rather than queue up, can fill our thoughts with flurries of such scenes.

According to the laws that govern the world of the moving image, I'm asserting, speed generates space. It gives the new video an unprecedented capaciousness. Some of those who work in this form have indeed felt themselves to be exploring new realms: "I'm playing this four-dimensional chess in my head," Hank Corwin reported.[63]

There is room in the dimensions opened by these flocks of pictures, graphics and words for numerous, overlapping trains of thought; for digressions, exceptions and contradictions; for indeterminacy and even confusion; for ideas too oddly shaped or freighted with paradox to settle comfortably between the covers of a book. Multiple levels of understanding can exist simultaneously here.[64,65] The new video, because it moves so quickly among these levels, has room for thoughts that protrude onto more than one, such as the views of normal life expressed in Corwin and Bayer's public-service announcement.

Consider, for a larger example, a particular philosophic dance, stomped out in one version or another by a number of twentieth-century philosophers.[66] It involves rejecting the possibility of various forms of beliefs/ truths/meanings while at the same time rejecting the possibility of making it through the day without various forms of beliefs/truths/meanings. (Other variants of this dance have appeared in this chapter: climbing up above the stream, then taking a dip in the stream, for example.) The leaps and turns this dance demands have made for some strained sentences and convoluted paragraphs. (Not here, of course; in other books.) These are moves that don't *print* well. However, it is possible to imagine such a dance captured in a video of no great length or loftiness, in which scenes from a life of engagement might simply be mated with a narration summing up a seminar's worth of philosophic doubts.

This is the sort of double-jointed dance the new video enjoys and is capable of helping its audiences enjoy. Indeed, when transferred to the screen, our grand philosophic enigma might appear perhaps not so confounding after all; it might appear rather obvious, as the beginning and not the end of the discussion. The new video, in the hands of an inventive editor, seems able to manage more complex steps. It seems able to help *us* manage more complex steps. And we have an obligation to wonder whether our puzzlement about such existential questions may someday appear as quaint as that of those preliterate Soviet peasants when Alexander Luria confronted them with the syllogism about white bears.

Italo Calvino's name belongs on a list I have alluded to but not presented: that of twentieth-century authors whose words seem to strain against the narrowness and regularity of print's long word queue. Calvino's name also belongs on a second list, one I have not before discussed but have kept in my head: that of subjects mentioned [elsewhere] to which a lingering fidelity to aged rules of composition compels me to return. The words of this Italian novelist, who died in 1985 at the age of sixty-one, introduced the book's introduction; now we are within hailing distance of the conclusion of its conclusion.

Calvino's novel *If on a Winter's Night a Traveler . . .* , first published in 1979, experiments with a number of the ways of thought that will, I argue, be facilitated by the new video. It refuses, to begin with, to restrict itself to a simple narrative. Calvino certainly did not forgo narrative entirely, as Mark Pellington did in *Father's Daze.* But his stories in this book come and go—a superabundance of them. Just when readers have lost themselves in one, it disappears. A character in the novel talks of "producing too many stories at once because what I want is for you to feel, around the story, a saturation of other stories that I could tell and maybe will tell." Calvino's narratives are not as condensed as they are in some videos; most are a dozen or so pages long. Nevertheless, we begin to feel that saturation.

This novel is also compulsively self-conscious. The reader is even made a character in it; "You are about to begin reading. Best to close the door; the TV is always on in the next room." And the pleasures and frustrations of reading this procession of incomplete tales are formed into a story of their own. We are asked to climb to some airy vantage points here: asked to examine the nature of narrative and the process of reading.

My kind of stuff, right? It's true; I much admire Calvino's novel. However, I must admit I had a difficult time pulling myself through it. The problem was that each time one of the stories in the book ended, I had to force myself, with phone calls to make and a book of my own to write, to pick the novel up once again and begin a new one.

I don't think this would happen in "the next room," the room where the videos are playing. For video not only can execute with more speed and dexterity the sorts of jumps and twists in which Calvino delighted, it can make them considerably more entertaining.

Our Platos and King Thamuses have managed, typically, to portray video's remarkable ability to captivate as a failing, a cheap trick. (The novel, of course, was subject to similar criticism.) Recall Susan Sontag's distress at the thought that fast-cut images might be "attention grabbing." Yet it is precisely this facility for grabbing attention, for entertaining, that makes it possible to surrender many of the devices, the crutches, of traditional storytelling. With video we might head out in Calvino-like directions, in Joyce-like directions and still remain confident that audiences—maybe not huge audiences, but certainly audiences as large as those interested in authors such as Calvino—will be able to follow, that they won't (like James Atlas) grow bored.

And video might give us the reserves of entertainment value needed to venture beyond Calvino, beyond Joyce: We might be able to disdain narrative entirely or overwhelm with dozens of almost simultaneous narratives; we might layer on multiple levels of selfconsciousness; we might hop and skip stream-of-consciousness-like not only through this world but through various possible worlds. This new medium should allow our scouts, our explorers, once they get their hands on it, to take many new risks. Let me propose a rule: The more entertaining the medium, the more artistically and intellectually adventurous it has the potential to become.

As our transition from print to moving images proceeds, most of us spend more and more of our time in Calvino's "next room." It is my purpose to suggest that we may find there a better form for saying the sorts of things Calvino was straining to say. It is my purpose to raise the possibility that the video you are about to begin watching—perhaps next year, perhaps in the next decade, perhaps decades from now—may make possible some grand adventures.

A frequently asked question: Can we entrust video with the education of our young? I've tried to suggest how ideas might find their way into this medium as it matures. But can ideas formulated under the influence of such a *pharmakon*, such a drug, be trusted? Can such a melange of juxtapositions, ironic perspectives, oddly shaped notions and philosophic high stepping "mold a brain," as the author and "techno-skeptic" David Shenk has put it, "into a disciplined thinking organ"?[67]

The answer, I believe, is yes, though I add my usual qualification: in time. New ways of thinking generally seem unruly at first; their initial *raison d'être*, after all, is often to loosen the grip of the old rules. However, these new cognitive tools are not trotted out in high-school or college classes with any great haste. First they must be corralled and saddled—categorized, interpreted, tested, made accessible. In the process various kinds of intellectual discipline—some familiar, some not—are located in them. New orthodoxies form.

We will have to learn how to undertake this process in video, just as our ancestors (worrying all the while about the education of their young)[68] had to learn how to undertake it in writing and then again in print. We will have to develop kinds of digitally accessed video textbooks and journals. We might even expect, as the decades pass, the accumulation of a "canon" of *old* new videos. In time some sufficiently sturdy molds should be at the disposal of young brains.

A question of my own: Don't we have a responsibility to these same young to find fresh approaches to the conundrums that seem to have left a residue of nihilism in much of their music and in many of their minds? Two other related (and similarly rhetorical) questions present themselves: Can we continue to submit our responses to Nirvana songs and Nike commercials only in print? As equipment for shooting and editing plummets in price, are we to continue to leave video, with all its power, to rock stars and advertising agencies?

When the strains inherent in a revolution like this become evident, retreat seems an increasingly attractive alternative: Publish some more celebrations of reading. Grumble about "the menace of unreality." Suggest to some green-haired, body-pierced, fast-eyed, image-bedazzled young persons that all their answers await them in books. I don't think this is, in the end, an acceptable alternative. I think we must push on. I think we must learn some new steps.

New philosophies made possible by moving images might begin to fill the current emptiness. A medicine of such power might begin to cure our children's reality sickness and our own. Put some ideas on video and call me in a millennium.

All this will not happen, if it happens, without pain. "Poison" is another meaning that lurks in the Greek word *pharmakon.* Indeed, it may come closest to what Plato was getting at when he applied the term to the invention of writing.[69] New intellectual tools do not merely polish old ways of thinking or fill gaps in them; they tear some of them down.

The mind-set that preceded the arrival of writing was poisoned. The mind-set that preceded our communications revolution is being poisoned. "I can no longer think what I want to think," lamented the French novelist Georges Duhamel in 1930. "My thoughts have been replaced by moving images."[70]

This new form of communication, wherever it is leading us, is probably not going to restore our old ways of looking at the world. Fondly remembered certitudes about reality are unlikely to return. Truths revealed on brightly lit surfaces are unlikely to resemble truths uncovered in dark spaces within. The place beyond irony and cynicism, if there is such a place, is unlikely to look like sincerity. We are going to have to deal with new, unfamiliar and often discomfiting notions. Many of us will find that we "can no longer think what [we] want to think." Indeed, many of us already have.

What might be our reward for going through this transition? The arts may regain their steam. Political thought may awake from its slumber. But life won't seem significantly easier or become significantly fairer. We likely will find our way around our current philosophic crisis, but new crises inevitably will arise. I doubt the effort will make us much happier. I foresee no "brave new world"—no Huxleyan nightmare of cheerfully drugged video watchers, but no utopia similar to that one of the characters in *The Tempest* proclaims when Shakespeare introduces this phrase, either.[71]

Nevertheless, I can't look at the history of human communication without concluding—unfashionable as such a conclusion may currently be in the historical community—that a kind of progress has been made. Yes, we've lost some wisdom along the way, but I believe we've gained more. And I can't look at the magical devices we are coming up with for capturing, editing and making available moving images without concluding that they will help us make additional progress.

I know this is hard to accept. Believe me, on an evening when each of my children lies prone before a different TV carrying a different vapid program, it is hard to write. The fall of the printed word—the loss of our beloved books—is a large loss. Nevertheless, the rise of the moving image, as we perfect new, nonvapid uses of video, should prove an even larger gain.

All our enlightenments are not behind us. We are beginning again, and in this new beginning is the moving image. ∎

NOTES

1. *The Tempest,* act 3, scene 2, 93–95. Shakespeare, William. *The Complete Works.* New York, 1980.

2. *The Tempest,* act 1, scene 2, 1–2; 109–10; 166.

3. Harold Innis makes a similar point; Innis 148. Innis, Harold A. *Empire and Communications.* Toronto, 1980.

4. In a blurb for Alfred Kazin's *A Lifetime Burning in Every Moment.*

5. Vidal 3. Vidal, Gore. *Screening History.* Cambridge, Mass., 1992.

6. The *New York Times* recently ran an article noting difficulties in finding "extra content for multichannel broadcasting" under a lengthy feature on the problems "midlist" authors are having getting their books published. The career advice lurking there for creative types went unremarked upon.

7. Doren Carvajal, "Middling (and Unloved) in Publishing Land," and Joel Brinkley, "A Gulf Develops Among Broadcasters on Programming Pledge," *New York Times,* August 18, 1997.

8. Andy Seiler, "How Bad Is the Message: Audience's Options Run the Gamut," *USA Today,* June 6, 1995. Jonathan Franzen, "Perchance to Dream," *Harper's Magazine,* April 1996.

9. Jonathan Franzen did the counting.

10. "Don't Believe the Cyberhype," *New York Times,* August 21, 1994.

11. Trithemius 65. Trithemius, Johannes. *In Praise of Scribes.* Edited by Klaus Arnold. Lawrence, Kan., 1974.

12. See Raymond Williams, *Television,* 13; on print, Febvre and Martin 28. Williams, Raymond. *Televison: Technology and Cultural Form.* Hanover, N.H., 1992. Febvre, Lucien, and Henri-Jean Martin. *The Coming of the Book: The Impact of Printing, 1450–1800.* Translated by David Gerard. London, 1976.

13. Boorstin 240. Boorstin, Daniel J. *The Image.* New York, 1962.

14. The *Utne Reader* went so far as to wonder in its July–August 1997 issue: "Is Real Life Possible Anymore?"

15. DeLillo 37. DeLillo, Don. *Mao II.* New York, 1992.

16. "The current emptiness is not television's fault," he said, surprisingly, "but television has made it visible"; McKibben 134. McKibben, Bill. *The Age of Missing Information.* New York, 1993.

17. For my take on these subjects, see my articles: "The Theologian of Talk: Jurgen Habermas," *Los Angeles Times Magazine,* October 23, 1994; "Jacques Derrida," *New York Times Magazine,* January 23, 1994; "The Professor of Disenchantment (Stephen Greenblatt and the New Historicism)," *West, San Jose Mercury,* March 1, 1992; "Deconstruction and the Get-Real Press," *Columbia Journalism Review,* September/October 1991; "Deconstructing Jacques Derrida," *Los Angeles Times Magazine,* July 21, 1991; "Deconstruction Crew," *Tikkun,* September–October 1990.

18. *The Tempest,* act 1, scene 2, 364–65.

19. Wittgenstein 47. Wittgenstein, Ludwig. *Philosophical Investigations.* Translated by G.E.M. Anscombe. New York, 1968.

20. Interview with Hank Corwin, New York, April 5, 1996.

21. Birkerts 85. Birkerts, Sven. *The Gutenberg Elegies.* New York, 1995.

22. Cited, Cervantes xvi. Cervantes, Miguel de. *Don Quixote.* Translated by Charles Jarvis. Edited with an introduction by E.C. Riley. Oxford, 1992.

23. Flaubert, *Madame Bovary,* 370. Flaubert, Gustave. *Madame Bovary.* Translated by Francis Steegmuller. New York, 1957.

24. Stephens, *A History of News,* 246–48. Stephens, Mitchell. *A History of News.* Fort Worth, Tex., 1997.

25. *The Tempest,* act 1, scene 1, 61.

26. *The Tempest,* act 5, scene 1, 56–57.

27. Some of the philosophic noodlings here may be exceptions.

28. *The Tempest,* act 1, scene 2, 434.

29. Poetry—an oral form, never entirely comfortable in print—has long been engaged in that effort.

30. James Atlas, "Literature Bores Me," *New York Times Magazine,* March 16, 1997.

31. Raymond Williams: "The flow of hurried items establishes a sense of the world: of surprising and miscellaneous events coming in, tumbling over each other, from all sides." And he was just talking about early 1970s newscasts.

32. Williams, *Television,* 110.

33. Boorstin 148.

34. Dostoevsky 452–53, 464. Dostoevsky, Fyodor. *Crime and Punishment.* Translated by Constance Garnett. New York, 1987.

35. Jonathan Franzen, "Perchance to Dream," *Harper's Magazine,* April 1996.

36. Homer 231. Homer. *The Iliad.* Translated by Robert Fagles. New York, 1991.

37. See Watt 18, 205–6. Watt, Ian. *The Rise of the Novel.* Berkeley, 1967.

38. Kundera 125. Kundera, Milan. *The Book of Laughter and Forgetting.* Translated by Aaron Asher. New York, 1996.

39. Bertolt Brecht, writing about film, put it bluntly (too bluntly): "Character is never used as a source of motivation; the inner life of the persons never supplies the principal cause of the plot and seldom is its main result." Brecht, Bertolt. *Brecht on Theatre: The Development of an Aesthetic.* Translated by John Willet. New York, 1994.

40. Brecht, *Brecht on Theatre,* 48; cited, Benjamin, *Illuminations,* 246n (I rely on the translation in Benjamin). Benjamin, Walter. *Illuminations.* Edited by Hannah Arendt. Translated by Harry Zohn. New York, 1988.

41. *The Tempest,* act 2, scene 1, 109.

42. Joseph Brodsky described the book as encouraging a "flight in the direction of . . . autonomy, in the direction of privacy."

43. Joseph Brodsky, "The Nobel Lecture: Uncommon Visage," *New Republic,* January 4 and 11, 1988. For a different interpretation of the same symptoms, see Sass. Sass, Louis A. "The Epic of Disbelief: the Postmodernist Turn in Contemporary Psychoanalysis," in *Psychology in a Postmodern Landscape.* Edited by S. Kvale. London, 1992.

44. In a letter to Jonathan Franzen; cited, Jonathan Franzen, "Perchance to Dream," *Harper's Magazine,* April 1996.

45. For alternative theories of identity, see Gergen; also Mitchell Stephens, "To Thine Own Selves Be True (Postmodern Psychology)," *Los Angeles Times Magazine,* August 23, 1992. Gergen, Kenneth J. *The Saturated Self: Dilemmas of Identity in Contemporary Life.* New York, 1991.

46. Cited, Robert D. Richardson Jr. 382. Richardson, Robert D., Jr. *Emerson: The Mind on Fire.* Berkeley, 1995.

47. Cited, Sontag, *Against Interpretation,* 3. Sontag, Susan. *Against Interpretation and Other Essays.* New York, 1990.

48. Sergei Eisenstein, *Film Form,* 103–6. Eisenstein, Sergei. *Film Form.* Translated and edited by Jay Leyda. San Diego, 1977.

49. A similar preoccupation with the strengths and limitations of language has evidenced itself in more traditional television, particularly in such situation comedies as *Friends* and *Seinfeld.*

50. One of the final sentences in Susan Sontag's book *On Photography* is, "Images are more real than anyone could have supposed." Sontag, Susan. *On Photography.* New York, 1990.

51. Benjamin, *Illuminations,* 235–36.

52. See Derrida 70–77. Derrida, Jacques. *Dissemination.* Translated by Barbara Johnson. Chicago, 1981.

53. Emerson 165. Emerson, Ralph Waldo. *Selections from Ralph Waldo Emerson.* Edited by Stephen E. Whicher. Boston, 1960.

54. This entire passage in "Self-Reliance" discusses the debilitations of technologies, from watches to notebooks.

55. David Foster Wallace 35. Wallace, David Foster. *A Supposedly Fun Thing I'll Never Do Again.* Boston, 1997.

56. David Foster Wallace 64.

57. Newspapers and magazines sell too, but the spiels somehow haven't seemed as loud or unavoidable in print.

58. Cited, Mitchell Stephens, "Jacques Derrida," *New York Times Magazine,* January 23, 1994.

59. See Stuart Elliott, "Advertising: A Big Brouhaha Erupts When *Advertising Age* Takes a Few Shots at a Miller Lite Campaign," *New York Times,* February 24, 1997.

60. Barthes, *Roland Barthes,* 66. Barthes, Roland. *Roland Barthes.* Translated by Richard Howard. New York, 1988.

61. Nietzsche, *Genealogy of Morals,* III, 12. Nietzsche, Friedrich. *Genealogy of Morals.* New York, 1968.

62. Speaking of ironies: I am aware that the better the job I do of describing here, the worse it is for my case. However, I ask the skeptical reader to focus on the extent to which the sentences that follow outline rather than present.

63. Interview with Hank Corwin, New York, April 5, 1996.

64. T.W. Adorno, writing in 1954, also spoke of televison being "multilayered," but he saw those layers as mostly hidden. Now they are often overt, sometimes even celebrated.

65. Adorno 478–82. Adorno, T.W. "Television and the Patterns of Mass Culture," in *Mass Culture.* Edited by Bernard Rosenberg and David Maning White. London, 1994.

66. "Continental" philosophers, for the most part; analytic philosophers tend not to be as light on their feet.

67. See Shenk. Shenk, David, *Data Smog.* San Francisco, 1997.

68. In 1756, when print was the upstart, Thomas Sheridan traced an increase in "Immorality, Ignorance and false Taste" to a decline in the study of "the Art of Speaking" in the schools.

69. See Derrida 70–77.

70. Duhamel 52; I have used the translation in Benjamin, *Illuminations,* 238. Duhamel, Georges. *Scènes de la vie future.* Paris, 1930.

71. *The Tempest,* act 5, scene 1, 184.

■ *QUESTIONS FOR MAKING CONNECTIONS WITHIN THE READING* ■

1. How, in Mitchell Stephens's opinion, does the new video enlarge the range of questions we can ask? What sorts of questions might the new video be incapable of asking? What questions are best suited to the medium of print, and what questions does print tend to ignore? Are print and the image destined to be rivals, or might it turn out that each can supplement the other? Can you think of anything both media—the moving image as well as print—leave out?

2. Stephens quotes the philosopher Ludwig Wittgenstein as saying, "Philosophy is a battle against the bewitchment of our intelligence by means of language." How can language "bewitch" us? Is it possible to think without words? Can the new media help us to avoid getting bewitched? If our words can bewitch us, what about images? In the age of the moving image, do we need a new kind of philosophy that battles against its spell? What might that new philosophy look like?

3. What does Stephens mean in this passage: "[W]hen we speak of our inner natures, it must be remembered, we are speaking metaphorically. Exactly where our own unvoiced thoughts might be located in some topology of consciousness is unclear." What does he mean when he says that the distinction between our inner and outer natures is metaphorical? Does experience have an "inside" or an "outside," or do we attach these terms to our experience after the moment has passed? If our thoughts do not come from inside us, where might they come from?

▪ QUESTIONS FOR WRITING ▪

1. Do you feel that Stephens offers an accurate account of the way you approach the new media and the contemporary world in general? Or does Stephens give both videos and books too much importance? For most readers of times past, after all, even the greatest novels, poems, and plays were fundamentally entertainment, a point easily lost on those who study them professionally. Do you really view the new media as opening doors into uncharted reality, or is most of what you see just mind candy?

2. Do images have meanings in the same way as poems or stories? Is there any single, correct way to appreciate a video or understand a television program? To determine the meaning of a video or television episode, might it be more appropriate simply to ask viewers what they got out of it?

▪ QUESTIONS FOR MAKING CONNECTIONS BETWEEN READINGS ▪

1. Would Jan Willis agree with Stephens's celebration of the new culture of images? Would she agree, in particular, with his claim that although the "fall of the printed word . . . is a large loss," the "rise of the moving image, as we perfect new, nonvapid uses of video, should prove an even larger gain"? Is Stephens's notion of liberation from the power of print comparable in some respects to Willis's attempt to recognize that the "mind is like the sky"? What is the relationship between spiritual and philosophical liberation?

2. In a note, Stephens praises "Continental" European philosophers for their willingness to accept that "multiple levels of understanding can exist at the same time." By contrast, he contends that "analytic philosophers tend not to be as light on their feet." Would you say that Nussbaum's treatment of "multiple levels of understanding" is more, or less, sophisticated than that of Stephens? Does she see, in other words, problems and solutions that Stephens overlooks, or is it the other way around? Once we have recognized the coexistence of "multiple levels of understanding," what are we supposed to do?

For additional suggestions about making connections between readings, visit the Link-O-Mat and More Sample Assignments at <www.newhum.com>.

ALEXANDER STILLE

HOW WILL THE environmental problems of the twenty-first century be solved? And who will do this work? Will it be scientists? Members of the business community? Religious leaders? In "The Ganges' Next Life," Alexander Stille ['Shtē-la] shows how these questions are being answered by those who are working to clean up the Ganges River, the center of India's spiritual and commercial life. By focusing on the collaboration between Veer Bhadra Mishra, a Hindu religious leader and environmental engineer, and William Oswald, an American scientist specializing in renewable energy sources, to design a sustainable system for purifying the water that flows through the Ganges, Stille documents just how fluid the relationships between science and religion, environmentalism and capitalism, tradition and modernity can be. In so doing, Stille bids his readers to consider the essential role that cross-cultural collaboration has to play in making change possible.

Stille, who writes for the *New York Times* and the *New Yorker,* specializes in Italian political culture and has covered subjects as diverse as Primo Levi's suicide, the resurgence of interest in the 1960s media theorist Marshall McLuhan, and recent efforts by sociologists to quantify happiness. He is the author of two books: *Benevolence and Betrayal: Five Italian Jewish Families under Fascism* (1993), a documentary that captures the life of Italy's Jews during the Holocaust, and *Excellent Cadavers: The Mafia and the Death of the First Italian Republic* (1995), a study of two prosecutors who sought to put an end to the Mafia's control of Sicily in the mid-1980s. *Excellent Cadavers,* which has been praised as "totally absorbing and distinctly chilling. . . . An altogether outstanding work of contemporary history," was made into a feature-length film by HBO in 1999.

To learn more about Alexander Stille and the effort to clean up the Ganges, visit the Link-O-Mat at <www.newhum.com>.

Stille, Alexander. "The Ganges' Next Life." *New Yorker.* January 19, 1998. 58–67.

Quotation from "Barry Unsworth's Favorite Books," <http://www.randomhouse.com/nanatalese/exclusive/unsworthfavs.html>.

The Ganges' Next Life

Shortly after dawn, Veer Bhadra Mishra, a silver-haired Brahman in a traditional Indian dhoti, or loincloth, walks slowly and stiffly down a long, steep stairway from his temple in the city of Varanasi to the banks of the Ganges, as he has done almost every day of his fifty-eight years. All around him, along a seven-kilometre stretch of the river dominated by majestic, crumbling temples, palaces, and ashrams, the pageant of Indian life passes by. Tens of thousands of bathers, at eighty different ghats, or landing areas, plunge into India's holiest body of water. White-bearded ascetics raise their emaciated arms to salute the sun god; housewives in bright-colored saris toss garlands of marigolds to Mother Ganges, the river goddess; adolescent boys in G-strings do pushups, flex their muscles, and wash their bodies; naked children splash in the water; and families carry their dead to the "burning ghats" to cremate them and scatter their ashes on the river.

The tug of these traditions, some of which go back three thousand years, to the founding of Varanasi (also known as Banaras), the holiest city in India, pulls Mishra to the river, despite having suffered a broken thigh, which makes walking painful. But on this particular day, in early March, he remains on the bank, because of a nagging cold and also because of the poor quality of the water: it is filled with raw sewage, human and industrial waste, the charred remains of bodies, and animal carcasses. Normally, Mishra tries to perform five full immersions—five is an auspicious number, he explains. But even when he is feeling well he holds his nose as he puts his head in, and he no longer drinks the river water.

"There is a struggle and turmoil inside my heart," Mishra says. "I want to take a holy dip. I need it to live. The day does not begin for me without the holy dip. But, at the same time, I know what is B.O.D."—biochemical oxygen demand—"and I know what is fecal coliform." He is referring to some of the scientific indices of water pollution.

For Mishra, this struggle of the heart is particularly acute because he has a complex double identity: he is the mahant—the head—of Sankat Mochan Temple, one of the principal temples of Varanasi, and he is also a professor of hydraulic engineering at Banaras Hindu University.

As a devout Hindu, Mishra views the Ganges as a goddess, a river that, because of its divine origin, is pure and purifies all those faithful who immerse themselves in her. Just as Muslims vow to visit Mecca, it is the dream of all good Hindus to visit Varanasi and bathe in the Ganges at least once in their lives. It is said that one drop of Ganges water carried by a breeze that lands on your cheek hundreds of miles away is enough to cleanse a lifetime of sins. All Hindus seek to have their ashes scattered along the Ganges at their deaths, and it is considered particularly lucky to die in Varanasi, because from there your soul will travel straight to Heaven.

But, as a scientist, Mishra cannot forget what he knows about the condition of the river water. Up in the temple complex behind him stands a state-of-the-art laboratory where bacteria cultures are being grown in special incubators in order to measure the level of pathogens at various points along the river. In some places at Varanasi, the fecal-coliform count has been known to reach a hundred and seventy million bacteria per hundred millilitres of water—a terrifying three hundred and forty thousand times the acceptable level of five hundred per hundred millilitres.

Some five hundred million people—one out of every twelve people in the world—now live in the basin of the Ganges and its tributaries. A hundred and fourteen cities dump their raw sewage directly into the river, which starts at Nepal, in the Himalayas, flows fifteen hundred miles through India and Bangladesh, and empties into the Bay of Bengal at Calcutta. Not surprisingly, waterborne illnesses—hepatitis, amebic dysentery, typhoid, and cholera—are common killers, helping to account for the deaths of more than two million Indian children each year.

What is particularly disturbing about these numbers is that they come at the end of a ten-year government cleanup project called the Ganga Action Plan—a project that most people, even in government, concede has failed. Now the government is preparing for the second phase of the Ganga Action Plan, and Mishra is trying to keep the government from repeating its mistakes: he is pushing a new plan to save the river.

The battle to clean the Ganges is about much more than the environmental future of a river. Just as the river is a symbol of India, its cleanup is a test of India's condition fifty years after independence, and its outcome may answer some of the fundamental questions about the country's future. Will India (and other parts of the Third World) master its problems, or will it descend into a nightmarish Malthusian struggle over diminishing natural resources? Will India find creative ways to preserve its rich cultural traditions, or will it become homogenized into the new global economy? Will its ancient rituals, such as bathing in the Ganges, survive beyond the next century?

Varanasi is one of the oldest continuously occupied cities in the world, contemporary with the dynasties of ancient Egypt or Mesopotamia. But while no one sacrifices to the Egyptian sun god Ra or to Baal anymore, some sixty thousand devotees take the holy dip each day in Varanasi, lighting fires along the shores of the Ganges to Lord Shiva, the god who is believed to have caught the river in the tangled locks of his hair as it descended to earth from Heaven.

"Please consider them an endangered species, these people who still have this faith, this living relationship with the river," Mishra says with passion. "If birds can be saved, if plants can be saved, let this species of people be saved by granting them holy water."

Mishra, as the mahant of Sankat Mochan Temple, is himself the living link to one of Varanasi's most cherished legacies. He is spiritual heir to a greatly revered Hindu saint, Tulsi Das, who in the sixteenth century wrote a famous Hindi version of the Ramayana, one of the most important texts of Hinduism, originally written in Sanskrit. Mahantji, as Mishra is almost universally known in Varanasi (Indians add the suffix "ji" to a name to denote affection and respect), lives, with his family, in the house that Tulsi Das built, overlooking the Ganges and above the landing Tulsi Ghat. The house contains an original manuscript of Tulsi Das's Ramayana and a pair of the saint's wooden sandals. Mishra's position as mahant, which has been passed from father to son in his family for many generations, accords him a semidivine status among the disciples of Tulsi Das. As Mishra is speaking about things like biomass and biogas, a steady stream of worshippers stop by to touch his feet—a traditional sign of respect in India.

Mishra wears his status lightly. He is a person of exquisite courtesy and genuine warmth, without a hint of arrogance or self-regard. He has a handsome tan face, dark-brown eyes, an elegant head of white hair with a shock of black in the center, and a gray mustache. If his lower body is slow and awkward, from his broken thigh, his face is highly mobile and expressive, as if to underscore the Hindu belief that the body is but an imperfect vessel for the noble spirit. He smiles easily and laughs a lot, frequently at himself. He jokes about his "throne room"—the name his Western friends have teasingly given a room where he receives guests. It is in fact a modestly decorated room on the ground floor of his house, in which a large wooden platform covered with mattresses provides the mahant a place to sit cross-legged or lean back on a cushion. He dresses almost invariably in nothing but a light-blue dhoti—a single swath of cotton that wraps around his waist and covers his shoulders like a toga—and generally goes barefoot. The one exception is when he lectures at the university: then he puts on a pair of loafers and a brown Western-style suit, in which he looks somewhat ill at ease.

In 1982, after years of speaking out about the deteriorating condition of the river, Mishra founded, with two other engineers from Banaras Hindu University, the Sankat Mochan Foundation, a private secular organization dedicated to cleaning the Ganges. This has taken Mishra far from the traditional, religious role of mahant and brought him into contact with politicians in New Delhi, American State Department officials, and environmentalists and scientists around the world. Overcoming a certain amount of criticism and ridicule among some Hindus in Varanasi, he has travelled to places like Sydney, New York, and San Francisco in order to attend water-resource conferences and explore alternative waste technologies. Like India itself on the eve of the millennium, Mishra is trying to incorporate what is best from the West in order to preserve the Hindu traditions that he loves.

In his attempt to clean the Ganges, the mahant finds himself teamed with a seeming unlikely partner—William Oswald, an emeritus professor of engineering at Berkeley, who is a gray-haired seventy-eight-year-old with elephantlike ears, two hearing aids, an impish smile, and an earthy sense of humor. On being told that the Hindus believed that they would go straight to Heaven if they died in Varanasi, Oswald replied, "They'll get there a lot faster if they go in that water."

Mishra and Oswald were brought together by Friends of the Ganges, a San Francisco–based group of environmentalists who have been working closely with the Sankat Mochan Foundation to help find a solution to Varanasi's water-pollution problems.

Oswald is the pioneer of a kind of "back to the future" approach to modern urban waste, called Advanced Integrated Wastewater Pond Systems, in which sewage is treated in a carefully engineered series of natural algae ponds. Waste decomposes naturally in water through a combination of microbial fermentation and photosynthesis. It works like this: In a pond, bacteria grow on sewage and, in the process, decompose it into its elements—carbon, nitrogen, hydrogen, oxygen, etc. Algae in the pond assimilate these nutrients and, as their green biomass grows, produce oxygen through photosynthesis. Algae are the most efficient producers of oxygen on the planet: they supply more than one and a half times their weight in oxygen, and are the largest single source of atmospheric oxygen in the air we breathe. The oxygen that algae produce sustains the aquatic life of a pond or a river; fish both feed on algae and breathe the oxygen that algae produce; bacteria also use the oxygen to keep the process of decomposition going in a self-sustaining cycle of creation and decay.

Oswald is to algae what Michael Jordan is to basketball. When he and I first met, in Delhi, he excused himself in advance for not remembering my name: "For every new person's name I learn, I forget the name of an alga." Back in the late sixties, at the request of the United States Air Force's space program, Oswald invented something called the Algatron—a system for growing algae in space to provide oxygen for astronauts. Although it has been tried out only on mice in a California laboratory, Oswald proved, in principle, that you could create a self-sustaining ecosystem in a weightless environment. In his view, algae are among the great unacknowledged heroes of the planet. Algae and bacteria have a symbiotic relationship that performs miracles in converting toxic or disease-carrying waste into oxygen, new plant life, and valuable protein for other forms of life to feed on.

Oswald's system is not a utopian environmentalist's fantasy. Before the age of mechanical treatment plants, ponds were one of the primary means of taking care of sewage. They are cheaper than mechanical treatment plants and clean wastewater more thoroughly, but they generally require more land. As a result, most major United States cities have switched to mechanized plants in recent decades, relegating pond systems to smaller cities and towns—some seventy-five hundred of them throughout the United States.

Oswald has devoted his life to devising pond systems that improve on nature's by handling waste in an accelerated fashion while using less space. He has created a system that moves water, by means of gravity and paddle wheels, through a linked sequence of ponds, each with its own special environment, meant to encourage a particular kind of waste treatment. The first group of ponds are dug very deep, in order to create a dark, sunless environment without oxygen, where anaerobic bacteria decompose the heavier solid wastes. The second group are shallow, so that all the water is exposed to sunlight in order to encourage algae to grow through photosynthesis and kill off harmful bacteria. The third ponds are deep, still ponds, in which the algae settle and can be easily "harvested," to be fed to pigs or chickens, or else left in the water for fish farming. In the final phase, the water passes into large, reservoirlike ponds from which it will be reused in irrigation.

This technology appears ideally suited to India, one of whose most abundant resources is sunlight. And it seems fitting that the scientific key to the modern problems of Varanasi, one of India's most ancient cities, could be one of the most ancient and also one of the simplest life-forms: algae.

In 1994, Mishra travelled to Northern California and visited three pond systems built by Oswald. Last summer, Earl Kessler, a member of the State Department's Agency for International Development, or AID, sent a delegation as well. Kessler was sufficiently impressed to commission both Oswald and Mishra's Sankat Mochan Foundation to prepare a feasbility study for a waste-pond system at Varanasi. Last spring, Oswald and his partner, Bailey Green, an acquaintance of mine, were scheduled to fly to India in order to complete the study and try to win Indian government support for the plan, and I decided to accompany them.

When we arrived, Mishra and two of his close colleagues at the foundation presented the American engineers with a surveyor's map they had prepared of the area where the ponds would be constructed, with carefully traced markings for ground elevation and soil composition. Oswald and Green have proposed a system of thirty-two ponds in a dried-up river channel near the island of Dhab, downstream from Varanasi. They spread the map on a table in a guesthouse overlooking a grassy lawn where a colored tent and a marigold-festooned stage were decked out for the foundation's annual festival of *dhrupad*—the most ancient form of Indian classical music—which was to begin later that evening.

As they pored over the map, Oswald worried about possible hitches in the successful completion of the pond project, which, if it should be carried out, would be the largest of his career. "Are you sure that a dike that is seventy-five metres above sea level will be high enough for the monsoon?" he asked. During the last thirty years, Oswald had seen many ambitious pond projects in the Third World evaporate for a host of technical, political, and financial reasons.

But, after fifteen years of work, the mahant was anxious that the project's momentum not be slowed by nettlesome details. "We will show that Dr. Oswald's pond system can work even in India," he said grandly.

"I don't want to be a hero," responded Oswald the pragmatist. "I just want to be right."

The musicians outside began to tune up their instruments, and the conversation about the soil composition of the proposed pond site continued to the drone of sitars. The musicians played until six-thirty in the morning, and as we lay under our mosquito nets later that night ancient ragas ran through our waking and sleeping thoughts.

The following afternoon, we set off by boat down the Ganges to examine the site where the ponds would be constructed. There were about twenty of us on a long, flat, beat-up wooden boat with a put-put motor and a canvas sheet stretched over us for protection against the midday sun. Besides us visitors and the mahant, the passengers were mostly volunteers from the Varanasi area, devotees of the temple who also donated their time to the Clean the Ganges campaign. (The foundation can afford only two full-time staff members. Its laboratory was provided through the efforts of the Swedish chapter of Friends of the Ganges, and one of Mishra's household servants doubles as a laboratory assistant.)

Because Tulsi Ghat is at the far south end of Varanasi, the trip took us in slow motion past the entire city. The ghats rise up dramatically out of the water, at the top of tall stairways, and so serve as a kind of two-way theatre: people on the ghats observe the activity on the river below, while those passing by in boats observe the doings of people up above.

Although Varanasi is the chief center of Hindu learning and culture, almost every religious practice and every region of India are represented along the river. There is a ghat for the Dandi Panth ascetics and a ghat leading to a temple surrounded by erotic Nepalese sculptures. There are pagodalike ghats reminiscent of southern India, and fortresslike ghats, which recall the Mogul conquerors of the north. Some ghats are old and are built of sombre, earth-colored stone; others are made of modern concrete and are painted white, yellow, pink, red, or green.

Along with all the different religious practices, all the different forms of pollution along the Ganges were similarly evident. There were ghats where herds of water buffalo cooled off in the water. At others, washerwomen rinsed out their laundry on the shore while a rainbow of colored saris lay drying on the steps. Hinduism contains many rituals of purification and hygiene, including a prohibition against using soap in the Ganges, which is widely ignored.

After a few minutes, we slowly passed the first of the burning ghats. At all hours of the day and night, the funeral pyres burn on the shore, with family members circling the fire and saying prayers. When the firewood has been consumed, the remains of the dead are consigned to the river to begin their journey from this world to the next, but in some cases the bodies may not have been fully consumed. On the average, about forty thousand traditional funerals are performed on the banks of the Ganges at Varanasi each year. In addition, about three thousand other dead bodies—those of people too poor to afford a funeral—and about nine thousand dead cattle are tossed into the river annually. As part of the government's Ganga Action Plan, close to twenty-nine thousand turtles were released at Varanasi a few years ago, in the hope that they would consume any decomposing body parts. But the turtle farm is now empty, and there are no turtles in the river. Many people suspect that they were poached for food.

The government cleanup, however, did include the building of an electric crematorium at one of the two main burning ghats, in order to cut back on the traditional funerals. The program seems to be working, for the lines in front of the brick crematorium are much longer than the ones in front of the firewood sellers. This, in Mishra's view, is an instance of India's adaptability: "The reasons are economic," he explained. "A traditional funeral today will cost between fifteen hundred and two thousand rupees, and the charge for the electric crematorium is seventy rupees."

The traditional forms of Indian life visible along the shores of the Ganges—the funeral pyres, the water buffalo, the washerwomen—are not the principal source of pollution at Varanasi. Looking closely, even along the bathing ghats you can see large sewage pipes draining directly into the river. The city's trunk sewer, which was built by the British in 1917, is strained beyond capacity. As recently as fifty years ago, the population of Varanasi was just over a quarter million; now it is a million four hundred thousand, and growing.

Upon leaving Varanasi, we reached the point where the Varuna River meets the Ganges, and there the surface of the water was bubbling like soup on a low flame—raw sewage turning into methane gas. Just a mile or so up the Varuna is a huge new pumping station, which is supposed to transport Varanasi's sewage to a large treatment plant a few miles downstream. Able to handle but a fraction of the city's two hundred million litres of sewage per day, the plant pumps the sewage of Varanasi up several hundred yards, only to dump the bulk of it into the Varuna, where it then travels back to the Ganges.

A few miles farther downstream, there was a sudden explosion of algae blooms, in such unnatural quantities that for several hundred yards the Ganges took on the unhealthy appearance of a swamp. It is here that the Indian government has placed its treatment plant, but the plant only performs what in the waste business is called "primary treatment"—the equivalent of going through just the first of Oswald's four ponds. Because the plant's "cleaned" effluent is still full of sewage and harmful bacteria, it, together with the hot Indian sun, stimulates the growth of far more algae than the natural resources of the river can absorb. As they decompose they consume, rather than create, oxygen, putting a strain on the marine life of the river. This condition shows up when the oxygen level of the water is tested in a laboratory: biological oxygen demand, or B.O.D., is one of the principal measures of water pollution. Where pollution places a high demand on oxygen, less is available for fish and other organisms.

The central government, in New Delhi, has recently spent about a hundred and fifty million dollars building Western-style high-technology wastewater plants along the Ganges, like the one we just passed, which are particularly ill-suited to Indian conditions. The treatment facilities run on electricity, and when the power goes out—as happens several times a day in many Indian cities—they stop operating. Similarly, the plants become overwhelmed during the monsoon season and simply shut down. Even when they are working, the facilities are so expensive and so difficult to operate that many of the cities say they cannot afford to maintain them.

In Varanasi, sewage is backing up into people's toilets or forming fetid puddles in their yards and in the streets. Local residents became so enraged about a year ago that they forced a city water engineer to stand for several hours in a pool of sewage in order to better acquaint him with the problem.

After decades of supporting this type of expensive, high-technology project, the United States State Department is now a proponent of "sustainable technology"—projects like Oswald's ponds, which cost less, use little electricity, and can be maintained with relatively little training by local people. (The pond system designed for Varanasi is estimated to cost between ten and sixteen million dollars, as opposed to twenty-five million for the city's mechanized treatment plant, which handles only a quarter to a third as much waste.)

In 1985, the government in New Delhi also adopted Western waste-treatment technology without considering the radically different ways that people use the rivers in India. It is still common in Europe for sewage-treatment plants to discharge partly cleaned effluent into rivers, but the inhabitants of London and Paris would not dream of bathing in or drinking out of the Thames or the Seine. "They have made such blunders," the mahant said. "It is like a theme park of failed technology."

Although our trip downriver to the island of Dhab was only about ten miles long, it took us nearly five hours, because the boat kept running aground. With each successive stop, more members of our party were out in the river pushing the boat and fewer of us were in it. The small Western contingent was calculating the probability of catching some dread tropical disease if it was forced to take an unanticipated holy dip to reach shore.

The Ganges is generally a mile wide throughout its course, but it becomes shallow in the dry months leading up to the summer monsoon. The problem has grown worse in recent years as more and more river water has been diverted for irrigation. Throughout our journey, we saw large pipes sucking water out of the Ganges toward distant fields. While India has twenty percent of the world's people, it has only four percent of the world's fresh water. With its population approaching a billion, the country is scheduled to overtake China as the world's most populous nation, and its future growth could mean mass starvation. Some three hundred million Indians are already classified as "Food Insecure"—a bad monsoon away from starvation.

Under these circumstances, wars over water—a prospect that haunts the twenty-first century—have already become a reality in India. India and Bangladesh have come close to breaking off diplomatic relations over the use of Ganges water. And in 1994 the Indian state of Haryana simply diverted a sizable portion of New Delhi's water supply, claiming it needed the water for irrigation. The struggle for water can only get worse as India's growing urban population demands Western standards of plumbing. The seventeen five-star hotels of New Delhi consume eight hundred thousand litres of water daily—enough to fulfill the requirements of a million three hundred thousand slum dwellers, who have no plumbing whatever. And as the number of flush toilets increases so will the amount of sewage.

As I was contemplating the prospect of ecological Armageddon during our on-again, off-again voyage in the shallow waters of the Ganges, we heard the distant sound of a brass band. A large crowd was massed on the banks of the island of Dhab, and, even though it was nearly sunset and they had been waiting all afternoon, they greeted the arrival of the Sankat Mochan Foundation and its Western guests with triumphal music and wild jubilation.

Dhab is one of the pockets of rural India that have been largely left out of the past fifty years of development: it has no electricity and no year-round bridge to the mainland. About ten miles long, Dhab, with a population of forty thousand, has a curious geographical configuration: it is an island during the rainy season and a tenuous part of the mainland the rest of the year. As the course of the Ganges gradually shifted over centuries toward the southeast, it exposed a former channel to the north of the island, which can be crossed during the drier months of the year but still floods during the summer. This wide former river channel is sandy and infertile, and has no proper road. It is here that the Sankat Mochan Foundation would like to put its system of wastewater ponds. The plan also involves building three main roads across the dikes of the ponds to connect Dhab to the mainland—roads that cable could be laid in, providing the electric spark that would connect the people of Dhab to the rest of the world.

Amid cries of "Hail to the gods!" we climbed up the banks of a shore thick with eagerly waiting crowds, who were waving painted banners and were ready to hand us armfuls of carefully stitched flower wreaths. So we proceeded slowly, in cars sent ahead by the foundation, stopping at every village cluster for a new celebration. Again and again, there were bands and painted banners, and entire canopies of marigolds. At each stop, mothers sent their children forward to touch our feet, lay on wreaths, and say prayers.

It was dark before we reached our final stop and the main ceremony, in which we were invited to eat a sticky orange sweet and drink some lemon tea. The mahant and the elected chiefs of the villages read a declaration. The people of Dhab stated their support for the Oswald pond project. The declaration ended with the fervent hope that this good deed would bring them *mukti* and *bhukti*—liberation in the next life and happiness in this one.

The wild sense of expectation and hope on the island—the sense that the pond project would instantly transform people's lives for the better—was both moving and sobering. While there is a legitimate worry about the levelling effect of every remote outpost's plugging into the world grid, Dhab's desire to be part of the wider world is palpable and overpowering. On a clear night, villagers on certain parts of the island can see the lights of a distant railroad yard. They stand and watch this bright symbol of the world they yearn to be a part of—a world of lights, power tools, modern appliances, and, of course, television.

"Our moral responsibility is now very great," the mahant said as we set off for Varanasi amid final cheers.

The next ten days back at Tulsi Ghat were filled with activity on various fronts. The foundation members were trying to set up a series of high-level seminars in which to present the American engineers and their plan to local officials, including the mayor of Varanasi; to technocrats at the Water Commission in Lucknow, the capital of the state of Uttar Pradesh, the region in which Varanasi lies; and to national ministers, politicians, and environmental activists at a major conference in New Delhi. Oswald and Green were working day and night with their pencils and calculators, as they drew up a new set of site-specific engineering plans and came up with precise figures on the money and the land that would be needed to build the pond system. Staff members and volunteers of the foundation were trying to track down things like the cost of moving a ton of earth in Varanasi.

Also during those ten days a stream of special visitors passed through the mahant's "throne room": engineers, village chiefs, politicians, local bureaucrats, university professors—anyone thought to have access to some important decision-making body. In between meetings, the mahant was on his cordless phone, lining up support and making sure that people who had promised to attend a particular meeting would actually show up.

The day after we returned from the island, Mishra received a phone call from a member of the Indian parliament representing Varanasi, who was eager to hear about the trip. The people of Dhab had evidently become so disappointed with the traditional politicians that they would no longer receive them. It seemed that the mahant had inadvertently uncovered a small political gold mine—a unified group of approximately twenty-five thousand highly motivated voters. As a result, the mahant found himself in the role of power broker—a role in which he felt some discomfort. "We are not political people, and it is still not clear to me what we should do with this consensus," he explained to me, as we sat in the throne room overlooking the Ganges.

And yet perhaps the only way to realize the pond project is through judiciously applied political pressure. "We have to have a more effective way to influence the politicians and harness the support we have built," Mishra said. So far, the political work appears to be paying off. The foundation has succeeded in winning the support of both the central government in New Delhi and the municipal government of Varanasi. The final obstacle to building the ponds remains the state government of Uttar Pradesh.

In the midst of all this engineering, organizing, and politicking, life at Tulsi Ghat continued as if it were a medieval village within the city. Devotees trooped through at all hours to worship at one of several pagodalike shrines in the courtyard. Sanskrit students passed through on their way to a school that the temple runs. Behind Mishra's house is an arena with a round corrugated-tin roof, in which each morning young men practiced a traditional form of Hindu wrestling. Sacred cows also wandered through, while goats walked into the shrines to eat the flowers that worshippers had left for the gods.

While this ritual-filled life moved at the stately pace of the Ganges, the activity of the Sankat Mochan Foundation marched to the high-pitched squeal of the fax machine. Mishra himself shuttled between these two worlds, finding time, despite long meetings and conferences, to keep up his religious duties, from his holy dip at dawn to the closing ceremonies at the temple, which sometimes did not end until midnight. Somewhere in between, he and I managed to have a series of conversations about his own double role as holy man and environmental activist, and about his own curious blend of science and Hinduism. "Even in my wildest dreams, I would not have thought that something like this would happen in my life," the mahant said, with a burst of laughter. Nothing in Mishra's early life prepared him for a life of science and political activism. "My father and my grandfather had the traditional education, which means Sanskrit and wrestling and music," he said. "There was no reason to deviate." In 1952, Mishra's father died, and Mishra, only fourteen, had the role of mahant thrust upon him. His destiny seemed even more fixed. "From that time onward, there would be a distance between me and the other people," he said, rather ruefully. "Because of traditional respect, even old people would come and touch my feet to pay respect, so there was no intimate interaction. My life was very protected."

When Mishra reached the age of seventeen, however, he made a radical and unprecedented move: he enrolled at Banaras Hindu University: "I don't know why this happened," he said, his voice rising with genuine perplexity. "In my family, I am the first person to go to the university." When he got there, his path became even more unusual: he started taking science courses. "Why I studied physics, chemistry, and mathematics, I don't know. Why I became a civil engineer with a specialty in hydraulics, I don't know. I can now see this as a scheme of the god."

Although there are no other known cases of someone's combining the vocation of mahant and that of civil engineer, it seems typical of India's uncanny ability to preserve its culture while surviving countless foreign occupations and absorbing new influences, from the Persians and the Islamic Mogul conquerors to the departure of the British, in 1947. The Indian writer Gita Mehta, in her latest book "Snakes and Ladders," tells a story that sums up this quality of Indian culture very well:

> There were two men who were considered the holiest in India, one called the Diamond-Hard Ascetic and the other called the Field of Experience. The Diamond-Hard Ascetic challenged his rival to a duel to prove that he was the holiest of all. I have become so hard through countless austerities, he said, that you can strike me with a sword of steel. And indeed the sword bounced off him. When he took the sword to the Field of Experience, it simply went through him, at which point the Ascetic conceded that the other man was holier.

The Field of Experience is India: seeming to offer no resistance, it is nevertheless impregnable. Other traditional societies—like China, Burma, and nations governed under strict Islamic law—preserve themselves by steeling themselves against the outside world, but they may become much more vulnerable as they begin to open up. India is a wide-open society, through which numerous armies have marched, and yet it remains remarkably itself.

India's economy, which has been frequently written off, came to life as a result of a policy of liberalization started in 1991. Growing at the rate of six percent a year ever since, India has been enjoying a boom similar to China's, but it has done so while remaining the world's largest democracy. Though its problems, in their scale, are almost unimaginable, so are its assets. It has more poor people than any other country in the world, but it also has a huge well-educated middle class. More than a hundred million Indians speak English, the lingua franca of the computer world, which is more than the number of speakers of English in Great Britain, Australia, and New Zealand combined. It is not an accident that software developers have turned to India for highly skilled software engineers. Half a world away, computer companies in Silicon Valley send their work problems to technicians in Bangalore, and those technicians work on them all day while the people in California sleep. Bill Gates arrived in Delhi while I was there, and his arrival was accorded the pomp of Queen Victoria's Diamond Jubilee during the days of Raj.

"These things—satellite television, this Internet surfing—are with us whether we like it or not," Mishra says. "They are means. They can be used in a beautiful way. It is as if you were riding a lion—you should be strong enough to tame the lion, or it will eat you." In keeping with that spirit, the Sankat Mochan Foundation is believed to be the first group in Varanasi to sign up for an E-mail and Internet connection.

This extremely open attitude toward the outside, however, has—so far, at least—in no way lessened the country's intense religiosity. To a remarkable degree, Indians have adapted new technology to their own traditional purposes. When Indian television broadcast a movie version of the Ramayana, many Indian families moved their sets up onto their household altars and worshipped before them. Some observers might be scandalized by this, but these people were not worshipping the television; they were worshipping their gods. In Varanasi, on the night celebrating the wedding anniversary of the gods Shiva and Parvati, I saw numerous shrines to Shiva elaborately decorated with flashing electric lights, pulsing to the beat of Indi-pop disco music. To Western eyes, these shrines, built around an ancient phallic symbol and decked out like entrances to Las Vegas night clubs, seemed sacrilegious and surreal, but ordinary Indians were clustered around them in devout worship, just as they would have been a generation or a millennium ago.

"I think in India this lion will be tamed!" Mishra said, with a delighted laugh, when I mentioned the disco shrine.

The mahant is also convinced that science and religion have to mesh if the Ganges is to be saved. The Western approach, based on fear of a possible ecological disaster, will not work, he said. "If you go to people who have a living relationship with Ganga and you say, 'Ganga is polluted, the water is dirty,' they will say, 'Stop saying that. Ganga is not polluted. You are abusing the river.' But if you say 'Ganga is our mother. Come and see what is being thrown on the body of your mother—sewage and filth. Should we tolerate sewage being smeared on the body of our mother?' you will get a very different reaction, and you can harness that energy."

One attraction of the Oswald pond system is that it seems to combine modern science with traditional Hindu ideas, relying mainly on the self-cleansing properties of nature. Indeed, there is a curious parallel between Oswald's descriptions of the self-sustaining ecology of a pond system and certain traditional Hindu beliefs about the fundamental nature of the universe. "All living organisms fit into one of three categories," Oswald explained to me. "Either they are producers, like algae and other plants that create oxygen, or they are consumers, like cows, which eat plants, or human beings, who eat plants and cows, or they are decomposers, like fungi, which dispose of things when they're dead." Hinduism, in its mythopoetic description of the universe, may have intuited something similar. Mishra told me, "There are three gods: Brahma, the creator, Vishnu, the sustainer, and Shiva, the god who provides us happiness in this world, which is decaying every day."

When I pointed out the analogy to Mishra, he seemed fascinated. "What did Professor Oswald say when you mentioned this?" he asked. I told him that Oswald had replied, with humor, "I'll leave that to your literary imagination. If I go back to California talking about Lord Shiva, they'll put me in a straitjacket."

Mishra, however, sees no necessary contradiction between the mythological and the scientific. Indeed, the practice of harnessing the metaphors of Hindu mythology to create a new environmental ethos is common in India. Even secular magazines, like *India Today,* invoke Lord Krishna's love of the forest in writing about the need for protection against the denuding of the Indian landscape. "With the Clean the Ganges campaign," Mishra says, "a meaning has been given to my religious background and to my scientific background. If both these backgrounds were not there, probably I would not have done this." He concludes by saying, "Life is like a stream. One bank is the Vedas"—the earliest Hindu Sanskrit texts—"and the other bank is the contemporary world, which includes science and technology. If both banks are not firm, the water will scatter. If both banks are firm, the river will run its course." ∎

▪ QUESTIONS FOR MAKING CONNECTIONS WITHIN THE READING ▪

1. Why does Mishra value the Ganges? Why does Oswald? Why does Stille?

2. Describing governmental efforts to clean up the Ganges, Mishra says, "They have made such blunders. It is like an theme park of failed technology." Chart out all the efforts Stille describes that have been made to clean up the Ganges. Why does Mishra see these as examples of "failed technology" rather than, say, a "failed politics" or even a "failed world view?"

3. At one point while he is moving down the Ganges River, Stille finds himself "contemplating the prospect of ecological Armageddon." What is "ecological Armageddon" exactly? Why might the failure to clean up the Ganges matter to anyone who doesn't live on its banks?

▪ QUESTIONS FOR WRITING ▪

1. Stille is intrigued by Mishra's "complex double identity" and spends much of the essay trying to make sense of how Mishra can be both a devout Hindu and a scientist at the same time. Stille seems surprised that

Mishra can maintain such an identity. What is a "complex double identity," exactly? Why is Mishra able to maintain his? Does everyone have one? Or only a few people? What other types of identity are there?

2. In his discussion of efforts to clean up the Ganges, Stille declares that "wars over water—a prospect that haunts the twenty-first century—have already become a reality in India." Is it possible that there could be struggles—if not wars—over water in the United States this century? To respond to this question, you might begin by finding out where the water you drink at your school and at your home comes from. Where does this water go? How is it cleaned?

■ *QUESTIONS FOR MAKING CONNECTIONS BETWEEN READINGS* ■

1. In Michael Pollan's essay, "Playing God in the Garden," we learn about the efforts multinational agricultural corporations are making to genetically modify the food chain, a project that they justify, in part, in the name of better feeding the world's inhabitants. In "The Ganges' Next Life," we learn how religious practice, the population explosion, and governmental incompetence have combined to contaminate the Ganges River. Should science be working to provide the means for the human population to continue to increase? Is feeding the world objectively good? Does it matter if this project is motivated by reason, spirituality, or hopes for financial gain?

2. According to Henry Petroski, "It is the process of design, in which diverse parts of the 'given-world' of the scientist and the 'made-world' of the engineer are reformed and assembled into something the likes of which Nature had not dreamed, that divorces engineering from science and marries it to art." Does engineering, as Petroski defines it, become an art when Veer Bhadra Mishra practices it? Is it an art when William Oswald practices it? Do spiritual beliefs or political concerns, including concerns about the environment, have any place in the practice of science?

For additional suggestions about making connections between readings, visit the Link-O-Mat and More Sample Assignments at <www.newhum.com>.

DEBORAH TANNEN

DEBORAH TANNEN BECAME interested in cross-cultural communication after she graduated from college in 1966 and taught English in Greece for two years. After earning a master's degree in English from Wayne State University and teaching writing in the United States for a few years, Tannen decided to pursue a doctorate in linguistics at Berkeley. It was just Tannen's luck that the first linguistics institute she attended focused on language in a social context. "Had I gone another summer," Tannen has said, "it's quite likely I would have concluded linguistics was not for me."

Tannen is currently University Professor on the faculty of the linguistics department at Georgetown University. Tannen, who has published sixteen books and more than eighty-five articles and is the recipient of four honorary doctorates, is best known as the author of *You Just Don't Understand: Women and Men in Conversation* (1991), which is credited with bringing gender differences in communication style to the forefront of public awareness. This book was on the *New York Times Bestsellers* list for nearly four years, including eight months as number one, and has been translated into twenty-five languages.

"The Roots of Debate in Education and the Hope of Dialogue" is drawn from one of Tannen's most recent books, *The Argument Culture* (1998), which examines the social, political, and emotional consequences of treating discussions as battles to be won or lost. Tannen's goal in this work is to get her readers to notice "the power of words to frame how you think about things, how you feel about things, how you perceive the world. The tendency in our culture to use war metaphors so pervasively, and to frame everything as a metaphorical battle, influences how we approach each other in our everyday lives."

To learn more about Deborah Tannen and styles of argumentation, visit the Link-O-Mat at <www.newhum.com>.

Tannen, Deborah. "The Roots of Debate in Education and the Hope of Dialogue." *The Argument Culture: Moving from Debate to Dialogue.* New York: Random House, 1998. 256–290.

Biographical information from Deborah Tannen's home page "<http://www.georgetown.edu/tannen/> on the Georgetown University Web site; quotation Deborah Tannen, interview by Michael Toms <http://www.newdimensions.org/article/tannen.html>. "Agreeing to Disagree: The Culture of Argument in America." *New Dimensions World Broadcasting Network.*

The Roots of Debate in Education and the Hope of Dialogue

The teacher sits at the head of the classroom, feeling pleased with herself and her class. The students are engaged in a heated debate. The very noise level reassures the teacher that the students are participating, taking responsibility for their own learning. Education is going on. The class is a success.

But look again, cautions Patricia Rosof, a high school history teacher who admits to having experienced that wave of satisfaction with herself and the job she is doing. On closer inspection, you notice that only a few students are participating in the debate; the majority of the class is sitting silently, maybe attentive but perhaps either indifferent or actively turned off. And the students who are arguing are not addressing the subtleties, nuances, or complexities of the points they are making or disputing. They do not have that luxury because they want to win the argument—so they must go for the most gross and dramatic statements they can muster. They will not concede an opponent's point, even if they can see its validity, because that would weaken their position. Anyone tempted to synthesize the varying views would not dare to do so because it would look like a "cop-out," an inability to take a stand.

One reason so many teachers use the debate format to promote student involvement is that it is relatively easy to set up and the rewards are quick and obvious: the decibel level of noise, the excitement of those who are taking part. Showing students how to integrate ideas and explore subtleties and complexities is much harder. And the rewards are quieter—but more lasting.

Our schools and universities, our ways of doing science and approaching knowledge, are deeply agonistic. We all pass through our country's educational system, and it is there that the seeds of our adversarial culture are planted. Seeing how these seeds develop, and where they came from, is a key to understanding the argument culture and a necessary foundation for determining what changes we would like to make.

Roots of the Adversarial Approach to Knowledge

The argument culture, with its tendency to approach issues as a polarized debate, and the culture of critique, with its inclination to regard criticism and attack as the best if not the only type of rigorous thinking, are deeply rooted in Western tradition, going back to the ancient Greeks.[1] This point is made by Walter Ong, a Jesuit professor at Saint Louis University, in his book

Fighting for Life. Ong credits the ancient Greeks[2] with a fascination with adversativeness in language and thought. He also connects the adversarial tradition of educational institutions to their all-male character. To attend the earliest universities, in the Middle Ages, young men were torn from their families and deposited in cloistered environments where corporal, even brutal, punishment was rampant. Their suffering drove them to bond with each other in opposition to their keepers—the teachers who were their symbolic enemies. Similar in many ways to puberty rites in traditional cultures, this secret society to which young men were confined also had a private language, Latin, in which students read about military exploits. Knowledge was gleaned through public oral disputation and tested by combative oral performance, which carried with it the risk of public humiliation. Students at these institutions were trained not to discover the truth but to argue either side of an argument—in other words, to debate. Ong points out that the Latin term for school, *ludus,* also referred to play or games, but it derived from the military sense of the word—training exercises for war.

If debate seems self-evidently the appropriate or even the only path to insight and knowledge, says Ong, consider the Chinese approach. Disputation was rejected in ancient China as "incompatible with the decorum and harmony cultivated by the true sage."[3] During the Classical periods in both China and India, according to Robert T. Oliver, the preferred mode of rhetoric was exposition rather than argument. The aim was to "enlighten an inquirer," not to "overwhelm an opponent." And the preferred style reflected "the earnestness of investigation" rather than "the fervor of conviction." In contrast to Aristotle's trust of logic and mistrust of emotion, in ancient Asia intuitive insight was considered the superior means of perceiving truth. Asian rhetoric was devoted not to devising logical arguments but to explicating widely accepted propositions. Furthermore, the search for abstract truth that we assume is the goal of philosophy, while taken for granted in the West, was not found in the East, where philosophy was concerned with observation and experience.

If Aristotelian philosophy, with its emphasis on formal logic, was based on the assumption that truth is gained by opposition, Chinese philosophy offers an alternative view. With its emphasis on harmony, says anthropologist Linda Young, Chinese philosophy sees a diverse universe in precarious balance that is maintained by talk. This translates into methods of investigation that focus more on integrating ideas and exploring relations among them than on opposing ideas and fighting over them.

Onward, Christian Soldiers

The military-like culture of early universities is also described by historian David Noble, who describes how young men attending medieval universities were like marauding soldiers: The students—all seminarians—roamed the streets bearing arms, assaulting women, and generally creating mayhem. Noble traces the history of Western science and of universities to joint origins in the Christian Church. The scientific revolution, he shows, was created by religious devotees setting up monastery-like institutions devoted to learning. Early universities were seminaries, and early scientists were either clergy or devoutly religious individuals who led monklike lives. (Until as recently as 1888, fellows at Oxford were expected to be unmarried.)

That Western science is rooted in the Christian Church helps explain why our approach to knowledge tends to be conceived as a metaphorical battle: The Christian Church, Noble shows, has origins and early forms rooted in the military. Many early monks[4] had actually been soldiers before becoming monks. Not only were obedience and strict military-like discipline required, but monks saw themselves as serving "in God's knighthood," warriors in a battle against evil. In later centuries, the Crusades brought actual warrior-monks.

The history of science in the Church holds the key to understanding our tradition of regarding the search for truth as an enterprise of oral disputation in which positions are propounded, defended, and attacked without regard to the debater's personal conviction. It is a notion of truth as objective, best captured by formal logic, that Ong traces to Aristotle. Aristotle regarded logic as the only trustworthy means for human judgment; emotions get in the way: "The man who is to judge would not have his judgment warped by speakers arousing him to anger, jealousy, or compassion. One might as well make a carpenter's tool crooked before using it as a measure."[5]

This assumption explains why Plato wanted to ban poets from education in his ideal community. As a lover of poetry, I can still recall my surprise and distress on reading this in *The Republic* when I was in high school. Not until much later did I understand what it was all about.[6] Poets in ancient Greece were wandering bards who traveled from place to place performing oral poetry that persuaded audiences by moving them emotionally. They were like what we think of as demagogues: people with a dangerous power to persuade others by getting them all worked up. Ong likens this to our discomfort with advertising in schools, which we see as places where children should learn to think logically, not be influenced by "teachers" with ulterior motives who use unfair persuasive tactics.

Sharing Time: Early Training in School

A commitment to formal logic as the truest form of intellectual pursuit remains with us today. Our glorification of opposition as the path to truth is related to the development of formal logic, which encourages thinkers to regard truth seeking as a step-by-step alternation of claims and counterclaims.[7] Truth, in this schema, is an abstract notion that tends to be taken out of context. This formal approach to learning is taught in our schools, often indirectly.

Educational researcher James Wertsch shows that schools place great emphasis on formal representation of knowledge. The common elementary school practice of "sharing time" (or, as it used to be called, "show-and-tell") is a prime arena for such training. Wertsch gives the example of a kindergarten pupil named Danny who took a piece of lava to class.[8] Danny told his classmates, "My mom went to the volcano and got it." When the teacher asked what he wanted to tell about it, he said, "I've always been taking care of it." This placed the rock at the center of his feelings and his family: the rock's connection to his mother, who gave it to him, and the attention and care he has lavished on it. The teacher reframed the children's interest in the rock as informational: "Is it rough or smooth?" "Is it heavy or light?" She also suggested they look up "volcano" and "lava" in the dictionary. This is not to imply that the teacher harmed the child; she built on his personal attachment to the rock to teach him a new way of thinking about it. But the example shows the focus of education on formal rather than relational knowledge—information about the rock that has meaning out of context, rather than information tied to the context: Who got the rock for him? How did she get it? What is his relation to it?

Here's another example of how a teacher uses sharing time to train children to speak and think formally. Sarah Michaels spent time watching and tape-recording in a first-grade classroom. During sharing time, a little girl named Mindy held up two candles and told her classmates, "When I was in day camp we made these candles. And I tried it with different colors with both of them but one just came out, this one just came out blue and I don't know what this color is." The teacher responded, "That's neat-o. Tell the kids how you do it from the very start. Pretend we don't know a thing about candles. OK, what did you do first? What did you use?" She continued to prompt: "What makes it have a shape?" and "Who knows what the string is for?" By encouraging Mindy to give information in a sequential manner, even if it might not seem the most important to her and if the children might already know some of it, the teacher was training her to talk in a focused, explicit way.

The tendency to value formal, objective knowledge over relational, intuitive knowledge grows out of our notion of education as training for debate. It is a legacy of the agonistic heritage. There are many other traces as well. Many Ph.D. programs still require public "defenses" of dissertations or dissertation proposals, and oral performance of knowledge in comprehensive exams. Throughout our educational system, the most pervasive inheritance is the conviction that issues have two sides, that knowledge is best gained through debate, that ideas should be presented orally to an audience that does its best to poke holes and find weaknesses, and that to get recognition, one has to "stake out a position" in opposition to another.

Integrating Women in the Classroom Army

If Ong is right, the adversarial character of our educational institutions is inseparable from their all-male heritage. I wondered whether teaching techniques still tend to be adversarial today and whether, if they are, this may hold a clue to a dilemma that has received much recent attention: that girls often receive less attention and speak up less in class.[9] One term I taught a large lecture class of 140 students and decided to take advantage of this army (as it were) of researchers to answer these questions. Becoming observers in their own classrooms, my students found plenty of support for Ong's ideas.

I asked the students to note how relatively adversarial the teaching methods were in their other classes and how the students responded. Gabrielle DeRouen-Hawkins's description of a theology class was typical:

> The class is in the format of lecture with class discussion and participation. There are thirteen boys and eleven girls in the class. In a fifty-minute class:
> Number of times a male student spoke: 8
> Number of times a female student spoke: 3
> . . . In our readings, theologians present their theories surrounding G-D, life, spirituality and sacredness. As the professor (a male) outlined the main ideas about the readings, he posed questions like "And what is the fault with /Smith's/ basis that the sacred is individualistic?" The only hands that went up were male. Not one female <u>dared</u> challenge or refute an author's writings. The only questions that the females asked (and all female comments were questions) involved a problem they had with the content of the reading. The males, on the other hand, openly questioned, criticized, and refuted the readings on five separate occasions. The three other times that males spoke involved them saying something like: "/Smith/ is very vague in her theory of XX. Can you explain it further?" They were openly argumentative.[10]

This description raises a number of fascinating issues. First, it gives concrete evidence that at least college classrooms proceed on the assumption that the educational process should be adversarial: The teacher invited students to criticize the reading. (Theology, a required course at Georgetown, was a subject where my students most often found adversarial methods—interestingly, given the background I laid out earlier.) Again, there is nothing inherently wrong with using such methods. Clearly, they are very effective in many ways. However, among the potential liabilities is the risk that women students may be less likely to take part in classroom discussions that are framed as arguments between opposing sides—that is, debate—or as attacks on the authors—that is, critique. (The vast majority of students' observations revealed that men tended to speak more than women in their classes—which is not to say that individual women did not speak more than individual men.)

Gabrielle commented that since class participation counted for 10 percent of students' grades, it might not be fair to women students that the agonistic style is more congenial to men. Not only might women's grades suffer because they speak up less, but they might be evaluated as less intelligent or prepared because when they did speak, they asked questions rather than challenging the readings.

I was intrigued by the student's comment "/Smith/ is very vague in her theory of XX. Can you explain it further?" It could have been phrased "I didn't understand the author's theory. Can you explain it to me?" By beginning "The author is vague in her theory," the questioner blamed the author for *his* failure to understand. A student who asks a question in class risks appearing ignorant. Prefacing the question this way was an excellent way to minimize that risk.

In her description of this class, Gabrielle wrote that not a single woman "<u>dared</u> challenge or refute" an author. She herself underlined the word "dared." But in reading this I wondered whether "dared" was necessarily the right word. It implies that the women in the class wished to challenge the author but did not have the courage. It is possible that not a single woman *cared* to challenge the author. Criticizing or challenging might not be something that appealed to them or seemed worth their efforts. Going back to the childhoods of boys and girls, it seems possible that the boys had had more experiences, from the time they were small, that encouraged them to challenge and argue with authority figures than the girls had.

This is not to say that classrooms are more congenial to boys than girls in every way. Especially in the lowest grades, the requirement that children sit quietly in their seats seems clearly to be easier for girls to fulfill than boys, since many girls frequently sit fairly quietly for long periods of time when they play, while most boys' idea of play involves at least running around, if not also jumping and roughhousing. And researchers have pointed out that some of the extra attention boys receive is aimed at controlling such physical exuberance. The adversarial aspect of educational traditions is just one small piece of the pie, but it seems to reflect boys' experiences and predilections more than girls'.

A colleague commented that he had always taken for granted that the best way to deal with students' comments is to challenge them; he took it to be self-evident that this technique sharpens their minds and helps them develop debating skills. But he noticed that women were relatively silent in his classes. He decided to try beginning discussion with relatively open questions and letting comments go unchallenged. He found, to his amazement and satisfaction, that more women began to speak up in class.

Clearly, women can learn to perform in adversarial ways. Anyone who doubts this need only attend an academic conference in the field of women's studies or feminist studies—or read Duke University professor Jane Tompkins's essay showing how a conference in these fields can be like a Western shoot-out. My point is rather about the roots of the tradition and the tendency of the style to appeal initially to more men than women in the Western cultural context. Ong and Noble show that the adversarial culture of Western science and its exclusion of women were part and parcel of the same historical roots—not that individual women may not learn to practice and enjoy agonistic debate or that individual men may not recoil from it. There are many people, women as well as men, who assume a discussion must be contentious to be interesting. Author Mary Catherine Bateson recalls that when her mother, the anthropologist Margaret Mead, said, "I had an argument with" someone, it was a positive comment. "An argument," to her, meant a spirited intellectual interchange, not a rancorous conflict. The same assumption emerged in an obituary for Diana Trilling, called "one of the very last of the great midcentury New York intellectuals."[11] She and her friends had tried to live what they called "a life of significant contention"—the contention apparently enhancing rather than undercutting the significance.

Learning by Fighting

Although there are patterns that tend to typify women and men in a given culture, there is an even greater range among members of widely divergent cultural backgrounds. In addition to observing adversarial encounters in their current classrooms, many students recalled having spent a junior year in Germany or France and commented that American classrooms seemed very placid compared to what they had experienced abroad. One student, Zach Tyler, described his impressions this way:

> I have very vivid memories of my junior year of high school, which I spent in Germany as an exchange student. The classroom was very debate-oriented and agonistic. One particular instance I remember well was in physics class, when a very confrontational friend of mine had a heated debate with the teacher about solving a problem. My friend ran to the board and scribbled out how he would have solved the problem, completely different from the teacher's, which also gave my friend the right answer and made the teacher wrong.

> STUDENT: "You see! This is how it should be, and you are wrong!"
> TEACHER: "No! No! No! You are absolutely wrong in every respect! Just look at how you did this!" (He goes over my friend's solution and shows that it does not work.) "Your solution has no base, as I just showed you!"
> STUDENT: "You can't prove that. Mine works just as well!"
> TEACHER: "My God, if the world were full of technical idiots like yourself! Look again!" (And he clearly shows how my friend's approach was wrong, after which my friend shut up.)

In Zach's opinion, the teacher encouraged this type of argument. The student learned he was wrong, but he got practice in arguing his point of view.

This incident occurred in high school. But European classrooms can be adversarial even at the elementary school level, according to another student, Megan Smyth, who reported on a videotape she saw in her French class:

> Today in French class we watched an excerpt of a classroom scene of fifth-graders. One at a time, each student was asked to stand up and recite a poem that they were supposed to have memorized. The teacher screamed at the students if they forgot a line or if they didn't speak with enough emotion. They were reprimanded and asked to repeat the task until they did it perfectly and passed the "oral test."

There is probably little question about how Americans would view this way of teaching, but the students put it into words:

> After watching this scene, my French teacher asked the class what our opinion was. The various responses included: French schools are very strict, the professor was "mean" and didn't have respect for the students, and there's too much emphasis on memorization, which is pointless.

If teaching methods can be more openly adversarial in European than American elementary and high schools, academic debate can be more openly adversarial there as well. For example, Alice Kaplan, a professor of French at Duke University, describes a colloquium on the French writer Céline that she attended in Paris:

> After the first speech, people started yelling at each other. "Are you suggesting that Céline was fascist!" "You call that evidence!" "I will not accept ignorance in the place of argument!" I was scared.[12]

These examples dramatize that many individuals can thrive in an adversarial atmosphere. And those who learn to participate effectively in any verbal game eventually enjoy it, if nothing else than for the pleasure of exercising that learned skill. It is important to keep these examples in mind in order to avoid the impression that adversarial tactics are always destructive. Clearly, such tactics sometimes admirably serve the purpose of intellectual inquiry. In addition to individual predilection, cultural learning plays a role in whether or not someone enjoys the game played this way.

Graduate School as Boot Camp

Although the invective Kaplan heard at a scholarly meeting in Paris is more extreme than what is typical at American conferences, the assumption that challenge and attack are the best modes of scholarly inquiry is pervasive in American scholarly communities as well. Graduate education is a training ground not only for teaching but also for scientific research. Many graduate programs are geared to training young scholars in rigorous thinking, defined as the ability to launch and field verbal attacks.

Communications researchers Karen Tracy and Sheryl Baratz tapped into some of the ethics that lead to this atmosphere in a study of weekly symposia attended by faculty and graduate students at a major research university. When they asked participants about the purpose of the symposia, they were told it was to "trade ideas" and "learn things." But it didn't take too much discussion to uncover the participants' deeper concern: to be seen as intellectually competent. And here's the rub: To be seen as competent, a student had to ask "tough and challenging questions."

One faculty member commented, when asked about who participated actively in a symposium,

> Among the graduate students, the people I think about are Jess, Tim, uh let's see, Felicia will ask a question but it'll be a nice little supportive question.[13]

"A nice little supportive question" diminished the value of Felicia's participation and her intelligence—the sort of judgment a student would wish to avoid. Just as with White House correspondents, there is value placed on asking "tough questions." Those who want to impress their peers and superiors (as most, if not all, do) are motivated to ask the sorts of questions that gain approval.

Valuing attack as a sign of respect is part of the argument culture of academia—our conception of intellectual interchange as a metaphorical battle. As one colleague put it, "In order to play with the big boys, you have to be willing to get into the ring and wrestle with them." Yet many graduate students (and quite a few established scholars) remain ambivalent about this ethic, especially when they are on the receiving rather than the distribution end. Sociolinguist Winnie Or tape-recorded a symposium at which a graduate student presented her fledgling research to other students and graduate faculty. The student later told Or that she left the symposium feeling that a truck had rolled over her. She did not say she regretted having taken part; she felt she had received valuable feedback. But she also mentioned that she had not looked at her research project once since the symposium several weeks before. This is telling. Shouldn't an opportunity to discuss your research with peers and experts fire you up and send you back to the isolation of research renewed and reinspired? Isn't something awry if it leaves you not wanting to face your research project at all?

This young scholar persevered, but others drop out of graduate school, in some cases because they are turned off by the atmosphere of critique. One woman who wrote to me said she had been encouraged to enroll in graduate school by her college professors, but she lasted only one year in a major midwest university's doctoral program in art history. This is how she described her experience and her decision not to continue:

> Grad school was the nightmare I never knew existed. . . . Into the den of wolves I go, like a lamb to slaughter. . . . When, at the end of my first year (masters) I was offered a job as a curator for a private collection, I jumped at the chance. I wasn't cut out for academia—better try the "real world."

Reading this I thought, is it that she was not cut out for academia, or is it that academia as it was practiced in that university is not cut out for people like her. It is cut out for those who enjoy, or can tolerate, a contentious environment.

(These examples remind us again of the gender dynamic. The graduate student who left academia for museum work was a woman. The student who asked a "nice little supportive question" instead of a "tough, challenging one" was a woman. More than one commentator has wondered aloud if part of the reason women drop out of science courses and degree programs is their discomfort with the agonistic culture of Western science. And Lani Guinier has recently shown that discomfort with the agonistic procedures of law school is partly responsible for women's lower grade point averages in law school, since the women arrive at law school with records as strong as the men's.)

The Culture of Critique: Attack in the Academy

The standard way of writing an academic paper is to position your work in opposition to someone else's, which you prove wrong. This creates a need to make others wrong, which is quite a different matter from reading something with an open mind and discovering that you disagree with it. Students are taught that they must disprove others' arguments in order to be original, make a contribution, and demonstrate their intellectual ability. When there is a need to make others wrong, the temptation is great to oversimplify at best, and at worst to distort or even misrepresent others' positions, the better to refute them—to search for the most foolish statement in a generally reasonable treatise, seize upon the weakest examples, ignore facts that support your opponent's views, and focus only on those that support yours. Straw men spring up like scarecrows in a cornfield.

Sometimes it seems as if there is a maxim driving academic discourse that counsels, "If you can't find something bad to say, don't say anything." As a result, any work that gets a lot of attention is immediately opposed. There is an advantage to this approach: Weaknesses are exposed, and that is surely good. But another result is that it is difficult for those outside the field (or even inside) to know what is "true." Like two expert witnesses hired by opposing attorneys, academics can seem to be canceling each other out. In the words of policy analysts David Greenberg and Philip Robins:

> The process of scientific inquiry almost ensures that competing sets of results will be obtained. . . . Once the first set of findings are published, other researchers eager to make a name for themselves must come up with different approaches and results to get their studies published.[14]

How are outsiders (or insiders, for that matter) to know which "side" to believe? As a result, it is extremely difficult for research to influence public policy.

A leading researcher in psychology commented that he knew of two young colleagues who had achieved tenure by writing articles attacking him. One of them told him, in confidence, that he actually agreed with him, but of course he could not get tenure by writing articles simply supporting someone else's work; he had to stake out a position in opposition. Attacking an established scholar has particular appeal because it demonstrates originality and independence of thought without requiring true innovation. After all, the domain of inquiry and the terms of debate have already been established. The critic has only to say, like the child who wants to pick a fight, "Is not!" Younger or less prominent scholars can achieve a level of attention otherwise denied or eluding them by stepping into the ring with someone who has already attracted the spotlight.

The young psychologist who confessed his motives to the established one was unusual, I suspect, only in his self-awareness and willingness to articulate it. More commonly, younger scholars, or less prominent ones, convince themselves that they are fighting for truth, that they are among the few who see that the emperor has no clothes. In the essay mentioned earlier, Jane Tompkins describes how a young scholar-critic can work herself into a passionate conviction that she is morally obligated to attack, because she is fighting on the side of good against the side of evil. Like the reluctant hero in the film *High Noon*, she feels she has no choice but to strap on her holster and shoot. Tompkins recalls that her own career was launched by an essay that

> began with a frontal assault on another woman scholar. When I wrote it I felt the way the hero does in a Western. Not only had this critic argued *a, b,* and *c,* she had held *x, y,* and *z!* It was a clear case of outrageous provocation.[15]

Because her attack was aimed at someone with an established career ("She was famous and I was not. She was teaching at a prestigious university and I was not. She had published a major book and I had not."), it was a "David and Goliath situation" that made her feel she was "justified in hitting her with everything I had." (This is analogous to what William Safire describes as his philosophy in the sphere of political journalism: "Kick 'em when they're up.")[16]

The claim of objectivity is belied by Tompkins's account of the spirit in which attack is often launched: the many motivations, other than the search for truth, that drive a critic to pick a fight with another scholar. Objectivity would entail a disinterested evaluation of all claims. But there is nothing disinterested about it when scholars set out with the need to make others wrong and transform them not only into opponents but into villains.

In academia, as in other walks of life, anonymity breeds contempt. Some of the nastiest rhetoric shows up in "blind" reviews—of articles submitted to journals or book proposals submitted to publishers. "Peer review" is the cornerstone of academic life. When someone submits an article to a journal, a book to a publisher, or a proposal to a funding institution, the work is sent to established scholars for evaluation. To enable reviewers to be honest, they remain anonymous. But anonymous reviewers often take a tone of derision such as people tend to use only when talking about someone who is not there—after all, the evaluation is not addressed to the author. But authors typically receive copies of the evaluations, especially if their work is rejected. This can be particularly destructive to young scholars just starting out. For example, one sociolinguist wrote her dissertation in a firmly established tradition: She tape-recorded conversations at the company where she worked part-time. Experts in our field believe it is best to examine conversations in which the researcher is a natural participant, because when strangers appear asking to tape-record, people get nervous and may change their behavior. The publisher sent the manuscript to a reviewer who was used to different research methods. In rejecting the proposal, she referred to the young scholar "using the audiotaped detritus from an old job." Ouch. What could justify the sneering term "detritus"? What is added by appending "old" to "job," other than hurting the author? Like Heathcliff, the target hears only the negative and—like Heathcliff—may respond by fleeing the field altogether.

One reason the argument culture is so widespread is that arguing is so easy to do. Lynne Hewitt, Judith Duchan, and Erwin Segal came up with a fascinating finding: Speakers with language disabilities who had trouble taking part in other types of verbal interaction were able to participate in arguments. Observing adults with mental retardation who lived in a group home, the researchers found that the residents often engaged in verbal conflicts as a means of prolonging interaction. It was a form of sociability. Most surprising, this was equally true of two residents who had severe language and comprehension disorders yet were able to take part in the verbal disputes, because arguments have a predictable structure.

Academics, too, know that it is easy to ask challenging questions without listening, reading, or thinking very carefully. Critics can always complain about research methods, sample size, and what has been left out. To study anything, a researcher must isolate a piece of the subject and narrow the scope of vision in order to focus. An entire tree cannot be placed under a microscope; a tiny bit has to be separated to be examined closely. This gives critics the handle of a weapon with which to strike an easy blow: They can point out all the bits that were not studied. Like family members or partners in a close relationship, anyone looking for things to pick on will have no trouble finding them.

All of this is not to imply that scholars should not criticize each other or disagree. In the words of poet William Blake, "Without contraries is no progression."[17] The point is to distinguish constructive ways of doing so from nonconstructive ones. Criticizing a colleague on empirical grounds is the beginning of a discussion; if researchers come up with different findings, they can engage in a dialogue: What is it about their methods, data, or means of analysis that explains the different results? In some cases, those who set out to disprove another's claims end up proving them instead—something that is highly unlikely to happen in fields that deal in argumentation alone.

A stunning example in which opponents attempting to disprove a heretical claim ended up proving it involves the cause and treatment of ulcers. It is now widely known and accepted that ulcers are caused by bacteria in the stomach and can be cured by massive doses of antibiotics. For years, however, the cure and treatment of ulcers remained elusive, as all the experts agreed that ulcers were the classic psychogenic illness caused by stress. The stomach, experts further agreed, was a sterile environment: No bacteria could live there. So pathologists did not look for bacteria in the stomachs of ailing or deceased patients, and those who came across them simply ignored them, in effect not seeing what was before their eyes because they did not believe it could be there. When Dr. Barry Marshall, an Australian resident in internal medicine, presented evidence that ulcers are caused by bacteria, no one believed him. His findings were ultimately confirmed by researchers intent on proving him wrong.[18]

The case of ulcers shows that setting out to prove others wrong can be constructive—when it is driven by genuine differences and when it motivates others to undertake new research. But if seeking to prove others wrong becomes a habit, an end in itself, the sole line of inquiry, the results can be far less rewarding.

Believing as Thinking

"The doubting game" is the name English professor Peter Elbow gives to what educators are trained to do. In playing the doubting game, you approach others' work by looking for what's wrong, much as the press corps follows the president hoping to catch him stumble or an attorney pores over an opposing witness's deposition looking for inconsistencies that can be challenged on the stand. It is an attorney's job to discredit opposing witnesses, but is it a scholar's job to approach colleagues like an opposing attorney?

Elbow recommends learning to approach new ideas, and ideas different from your own, in a different spirit—what he calls a "believing game." This does not mean accepting everything anyone says or writes in an unthinking way. That would be just as superficial as rejecting everything without thinking deeply about it. The believing game is still a game. It simply asks you to give it a whirl: Read *as if* you believed, and see where it takes you. Then you can go back and ask whether you want to accept or reject elements in the argument or the whole argument or idea. Elbow is not recommending that we stop doubting altogether. He is telling us to stop doubting exclusively. We need a systematic and respected way to detect and expose strengths, just as we have a systematic and respected way of detecting faults.

Americans need little encouragement to play the doubting game because we regard it as synonymous with intellectual inquiry, a sign of intelligence. In Elbow's words, "We tend to assume that the ability to criticize a claim we disagree with counts as more serious intellectual work than the ability to enter into it and temporarily assent."[19] It is the believing game that needs to be encouraged and recognized as an equally serious intellectual pursuit.

Although criticizing is surely part of critical thinking, it is not synonymous with it. Again, limiting critical response to critique means not doing the other kinds of critical thinking that could be helpful: looking for new insights, new perspectives, new ways of thinking, new knowledge. Critiquing relieves you of the responsibility of doing integrative thinking. It also has the advantage of making the critics feel smart, smarter than the ill-fated author whose work is being picked apart like carrion. But it has the disadvantage of making them less likely to learn from the author's work.

The Socratic Method—Or Is It?

Another scholar who questions the usefulness of opposition as the sole path to truth is philosopher Janice Moulton. Philosophy, she shows, equates logical reasoning with the Adversary Paradigm, a matter of making claims and then trying to find, and argue against, counterexamples to that claim. The result is a debate between adversaries trying to defend their ideas against counterexamples and to come up with counterexamples that refute the opponent's ideas. In this paradigm, the best way to evaluate someone's work is to "subject it to the strongest or most extreme opposition."[20]

But if you parry individual points—a negative and defensive enterprise—you never step back and actively imagine a world in which a different system of ideas could be true—a positive act. And you never ask how larger systems of thought relate to each other. According to Moulton, our devotion to the Adversary Paradigm has led us to misinterpret the type of argumentation that

Socrates favored: We think of the Socratic method as systematically leading an opponent into admitting error. This is primarily a way of showing up an adversary as wrong. Moulton shows that the original Socratic method—the *elenchus*—was designed to convince others, to shake them out of their habitual mode of thought and lead them to new insight. Our version of the Socratic method—an adversarial public debate—is unlikely to result in opponents changing their minds. Someone who loses a debate usually attributes that loss to poor performance or to an adversary's unfair tactics.

Knowledge as Warring Camps

Anne Carolyn Klein, an American woman who spent many years studying Tibetan Buddhism, joined a university program devoted to women's studies in religion. It was her first encounter with contemporary feminist theory, which she quickly learned was divided into two warring camps. In one camp are those who focus on the ways that women are different from men. Among these, some emphasize that women's ways are equally valid and should be respected, while others believe that women's ways are superior and should be more widely adopted. Both these views—called "difference feminism"—contrast with those in the other camp, who claim that women are no different from men by nature, so any noticeable differences result from how society treats women. Those who take this view are called "social constructionists."[21]

Klein saw that separating feminist theory into these two camps reflects the Western tendency to rigid dichotomies. Recalling how Buddhist philosophy tries to integrate disparate forces, she shows that there is much to be gained from both feminist views—and, in any case, both perspectives tend to coexist within individuals. For example, even though the constructionist view of gender has won ascendancy in academic theory (that's why we have the epithet "essentialist" to describe those who hold the view that is in disfavor but no commonly used epithet to sneer at the constructionist view), "feminists still struggle to recognize and name the commonalities among women that justify concern for women's lives around the world and produce political and social alliances." Klein asks, "Why protest current conditions unless the category 'women' is in some way a meaningful one?"[22] She shows, too, that the very inclination to polarize varied views of women and feminism into two opposing camps is in itself essentialist because it reduces complex and varied perspectives to simplified, monolithic representations. This also makes it easy to dismiss—and fight about—others' work rather than think about it.

Reflecting this warring-camps view, journalist Cynthia Gorney asked Gloria Steinem, "Where do you stand in the current debate that the feminist world has divided into 'equity' feminism versus 'difference' feminism—

about whether women are to be treated like men or as different from men?" This question bears all the earmarks of the adversarial framework: the term "debate" and the separation of a complex domain of inquiry into two opposed sides. Steinem responded:

> [*Sighs.*] Of course, you understand that I've turned up in every category. So it makes it harder for me to take the divisions with great seriousness, since I don't feel attached to any of them—and also since I don't hear about the division from women who are not academics or in the media. The idea that there are two "camps" has not been my experience. The mark to me of a constructive argument is one that looks at a specific problem and says, "What shall we do about this?" And a nonconstructive one is one that tries to label people. "Difference" feminist, "gender" feminist—it has no meaning in specific situations.[23]

In this short comment, Steinem puts her finger on several aspects of the argument culture. First, she identifies academics and journalists as two groups that have a habit of—and a stake in—manufacturing polarization and the appearance of conflict. Second, she points out that this view of the world does not describe reality as most people live it. Third, she shows that polarizing issues into "a debate" often goes along with "labeling" the two sides: Lumping others together and sticking a label on them makes it easy to ignore the nuances and subtleties of their opinions and beliefs. Individuals are reduced to an oversimplification of their ideas, transformed into the enemy, and demonized.

False dichotomies are often at the heart of discord.

Question the Basic Assumption

My aim is not to put a stop to the adversarial paradigm, the doubting game, debate—but to diversify: Like a well-balanced stock portfolio, we need more than one path to the goal we seek. What makes it hard to question whether debate is truly the only or even the most fruitful approach to learning is that we're dealing with assumptions that we and everyone around us take to be self-evident. A prominent dean at a major research university commented to me, "The Chinese cannot make great scientists because they will not debate publicly." Many people would find this remark offensive. They would object because it generalizes about all Chinese scientists, especially since it makes a negative evaluation. But I would also question the assumption that makes the generalization a criticism: the conviction that the only way to test and develop ideas is to debate them publicly. It may well be true that most Chinese scientists are reluctant to engage in public, rancorous debate. I see nothing insulting about such a claim; it derives from the Chinese cultural norms that many Chinese and Western observers have documented. But we also know that many Chinese have indeed been great scientists.[24] The falsity of the dean's statement should lead us to question whether debate is the only path to insight.

Consensus Through Dissension?

The culture of critique driving our search for knowledge in the scientific world of research is akin to what I have described in the domains of politics, journalism, and law. In those three institutions, an increasingly war-like atmosphere has led many people already in those professions to leave, and many who would have considered entering these professions in the past are now choosing other paths. Those who remain are finding it less fun; they don't look forward to getting up and going to work in the same way that they and others used to. And in all these areas, raised voices and tempers are creating a din that is drowning out the perhaps more numerous voices of dialogue and reason. In law, critics of the principle of zealous advocacy object on the grounds of what it does to the souls of those who practice within the system, requiring them to put aside their consciences and natural inclinations toward human compassion— just what some among the press say about what aggression journalism is doing to journalists.

Forces affecting these institutions are intertwined with each other and with others I have not mentioned. For example, the rise of malpractice litigation, while prodding doctors to be more careful and providing deserved recompense to victims, has also made the doctor-patient relationship potentially more adversarial. At the same time, physicians are finding themselves in increasingly adversarial relationships with HMOs and insurance companies—as are the patients themselves, who now need the kind of advice that was offered under the headline "When Your HMO Says No: How to Fight for the Treatment You Need—and Win."[25]

People in business, too, report an increasingly adversarial atmosphere. There are, of course, the hostile takeovers that have become common, along with lawsuits between companies and former employees. But there is also more opposition in the day-to-day doing of business. A man who works at a large computer company in Silicon Valley told me that he sees this daily. Disagreement and verbal attack are encouraged at meetings, under the guise of challenging assumptions and fostering creativity. But in reality, he observes, what is fostered is dissension. In the end, the company's ability to do business can be threatened. He has seen at least one company virtually paralyzed by trying to seek consensus after assiduously stirring up dissension.

Who Will Be Left to Lead?

If this seems to describe an isolated phenomenon in a particular industry, take note: A comparable situation exists in our political life. The culture of critique is threatening our system of governance. Norman Ornstein, a political analyst at the American Enterprise Institute, articulates how.[26]

Ornstein offers some astonishing statistics: Between 1975 and 1989, the number of federal officials indicted on charges of public corruption went up by a staggering 1,211 percent. During the same period, the number of non-federal officials indicted doubled. What are we to make of this? he asks. Does it mean that officials during that decade were far more corrupt than before? Not likely. Every systematic study, as well as all anecdotal evidence, suggests just the opposite: Public officials are far less corrupt now; fewer take bribes, get drunk in the middle of their duties, engage in immoral conduct, and so on.

What we have is the culture of critique. The press is poised to pounce on allegations of scandal, giving them primacy over every other kind of news. And the standards by which scandals are judged have declined. Allegations make the news, no matter where they come from, often without proof or even verification. (Remember the ruckus that accompanied reports that planes were forced to circle and travelers were delayed while President Clinton got a haircut on Air Force One in the Los Angeles airport?[27] And that George Bush did not know what a supermarket scanner was? Both turned out to be false.) Political opponents seize on these allegations and use them to punish or bring down opponents. The sad result is that laws designed to improve ethics have not improved ethics at all. Instead, they have made government almost impossible. Allegations trigger long investigations that themselves damage reputations and suggest to the public that terrible things are going on even when they aren't.

Prosecutors, too, are part of the web, Ornstein continues. In the past, an ambitious prosecutor might set out to snare a criminal on the FBI's ten most wanted list. Now the temptation is to go after a senator or cabinet member—or a vice president. That's where attention is paid; that's where the rewards lie.

The threat is not only to those at the highest levels of government but to public servants at every level. I spoke to someone prominent in the arts who was invited to join a federal commission. But first there was a questionnaire to fill out—pages and pages of details requested about the prospective nominee's personal, professional, and financial life. Special request was made for anything that might be embarrassing if it became public. The person in question simply declined the invitation.

The artist I spoke to typified a situation Ornstein described: It is becoming almost impossible to get qualified people to serve in public positions, from the highest executive nominations to part-time or even honorary appointments. Leaving private life for public service has always required personal sacrifice: Your family life is disrupted; you take a pay cut. But now those contemplating such a move must be willing to make an even greater sacrifice: putting their personal reputation at risk. Instead of enhancing reputations, going into public services now threatens them, whether or not the officials have done anything to be ashamed of.

Disruption of family life is intensified, too, by the inordinate delay, Ornstein explained. While a nominee waits to be confirmed, life goes on hold: A spouse's job is in limbo; children await a change in schools; houses must—but can't—be found or rented or bought or sold. What is causing the delays to become so much more protracted than they were before? Every step in the process: Presidents (and their staffs) must take much more time in choosing potential nominees, to make absolutely sure there is nothing in their lives or backgrounds that could embarrass not just the nominee but the president. Once people are selected, the FBI takes weeks or months longer than it used to for background checks, because it too wants to make sure it is not embarrassed later. Finally, the nomination goes to the Senate, where political opponents of the president or the nominee try to go for the jugular on ethics charges.

The result of all these forces is a much smaller pool of qualified people willing to consider public service, long periods when important posts are left vacant, a climate of suspicion that reinforces public doubts about the ethics of people in government, and real disruption in the running of our country.

We have become obsessed with the appearance of impropriety, as Peter Morgan and Glenn Reynolds show in a book with that title. Meanwhile, real impropriety goes unnoticed. We have to ask, as Ornstein does, whether the price we're paying to have pristine individuals fill every public post is worth what we're getting—and he (like Morgan and Reynolds) doubts that what we're getting is less impropriety.

The Cost in Human Spirit

Whatever the causes of the argument culture—and the many causes I have mentioned are surely not the only ones—the most grievous cost is the price paid in human spirit: Contentious public discourse becomes a model for behavior and sets the tone for how individuals experience their relationships to other people and to the society we live in.

Recall the way young boys on Tory Island learned to emulate their elders:

> All around milled little boys imitating their elders, cursing, fluffing, swaggering, threatening. It was particularly fascinating to see how the children learned the whole sequence of behavior. Anything that the men did, they would imitate, shouting the same things, strutting and swaggering.[28]

Tory Island may be an especially ritualized example, but it is not a totally aberrant one. When young men come together in groups, they often engage in symbolic ritual displays of aggression that involve posturing and mock battles. Without pressing the parallel in too literal a way, I couldn't help thinking that this sounds a bit like what journalists and lawyers have observed about their own tribes: that the display of aggression for the benefit of peers is often more important than concrete results.

Consider again law professor Charles Yablon's observation that young litigators learn to value an aggressive stance by listening to their elders' war stories about "the smashing victories they obtained during pretrial discovery in cases which ultimately were settled." Litigators

> derive job satisfaction by recasting minor discovery disputes as titanic struggles. Younger lawyers, convinced that their future careers may hinge on how tough they *seem* while conducting discovery, may conclude that it is more important to look and sound ferocious than act cooperatively, even if all that huffing and puffing does not help (and sometimes harms) their cases.[29]

Against this background, recall too the observations made by journalists that their colleagues feel pressured to ask tough questions to get peer approval. Kenneth Walsh, for example, commented that "it helps your stature in journalism" if you ask challenging questions because that way "you show you're tough and you're independent." Just as litigators trade war stories about how tough they appeared (whether or not that appearance helped their client), Walsh points out that a journalist who dares to challenge the president takes on a heroic aura among his peers. He recalled a specific incident to illustrate this point:

> Remember Brit Hume asking the question . . . about the zigzag decision-making process of President Clinton? And of course President Clinton cut off the questions after that one question because he felt it was not appropriate. That's what we all remember about the Ruth Bader Ginsburg period, is that Brit asked that question.[30]

Let's look at the actual exchange that earned Brit Hume the admiration of his peers. President Clinton called the press conference to announce his nomination of Judge Ruth Bader Ginsburg to the Supreme Court. After the president introduced her, Judge Ginsburg spoke movingly about her life, ending with tributes to her family: her children, granddaughter, husband, and, finally, her mother, "the bravest and strongest person I have known, who was taken from me much too soon." Following these remarks, which moved listeners to tears, journalists were invited to ask questions. The first (and, as it turned out, also the last) asked by correspondent Hume was this:

The withdrawal of the Guinier nomination, sir, and your apparent focus on Judge Breyer and your turn, late, it seems, to Judge Ginsburg, may have created an impression, perhaps unfair, of a certain zigzag quality in the decision-making process here. I wonder, sir, if you could kind of walk us through it and perhaps disabuse us of any notion we might have along those lines. Thank you.

This question reminded everyone—at the very moment of Judge Ginsburg's triumph and honor—that she was not the president's first choice. It broke the spell of her moving remarks by shifting attention from the ceremonial occasion to the political maneuvers that had led up to the nomination—in particular, implying criticism of the president not from the perspective of substance (whether Judge Ginsburg would make a good Supreme Court Justice) but strategy (the decision-making process by which she was chosen). Remarking, "How you could ask a question like that after the statement she just made is beyond me," the president closed the event.

The answer to how Brit Hume could have asked a question like that lies in Walsh's observation that journalists value a display of toughness. In this view, to worry about Judge Ginsburg's feelings—or those of the viewing audience—would be like an attorney worrying about the feelings of a witness about to be cross-examined. But public ceremonies play a role in the emotional lives not only of participants but also of observers, an enormous group in the era of television. Viewers who were moved by Judge Ginsburg's personal statement shared in the ceremony and felt connected to the judge and, by implication, to our judicial system. Such feelings of connection to public figures whose actions affect our lives is a crucial element in individuals' sense of community and their feeling of well-being. Breaking that spell was harmful to this sense of connection, contributing a little bit to what is often called cynicism but which really goes much deeper than that: alienation from the public figures who deeply affect our lives and consequently from the society in which we live.

In this sense, the valuing of the appearance of toughness is related to another theme running through all the domains I discussed: the breakdown in human connections and the rise of anonymity. Lieutenant Colonel Grossman points out that this, too, was one of many ways that the experience of serving in Vietnam was different for American soldiers than was the experience of serving in previous wars. Remember my Uncle Norman, who at the age of eighty-seven was still attending annual reunions of the "boys" he had served with in World War II? This was possible because, as Grossman describes, soldiers in that war trained together, then went to war and served together. Those who were not killed or wounded stayed with the group until they all went home together at the end of the war. No wonder the bonds they forged could last a lifetime. Vietnam, in contrast, was a "lonely war" of individuals assigned to constantly shifting units for year-long tours of duty (thirteen months for Marines). Grossman's description is graphic and sad:

In Vietnam most soldiers arrived on the battlefield alone, afraid, and without friends. A soldier joined a unit where he was an FNG, a "f——ing new guy," whose inexperience and incompetence represented a threat to the continued survival of those in the unit. In a few months, for a brief period, he became an old hand who was bonded to a few friends and able to function well in combat. But then, all too soon, his friends left him via death, injury, or the end of their tours . . . . All but the best of units became just a collection of men experiencing endless leavings and arrivals, and that sacred process of bonding, which makes it possible for men to do what they must do in combat, became a tattered and torn remnant of the support structure experienced by veterans of past American wars.[31]

Though this pattern is most painful in this context, it parallels what we have seen in all the other domains of public dialogue. Recall attorney Susan Popik's observation "You don't come up against the same people all the time. That encouraged you to get along with them because you knew that in six months, you would be across the table from them again."[32] Recall journalists' lamenting that the present White House press corps is a large group, often unknown to aides and leaders, kept at a distance from the leaders they are assigned to cover: confined in a small room, in the back of the president's plane, behind ropes at public events. Contrast this with the recollections of those old enough to remember a small White House press corps that had free run of official buildings and lots of private off-the-record meetings with public officials, including the president and first lady, so that they actually got to know them—as people. And recall departing Senator Heflin's regret about the decline of opportunities for legislators of opposing parties to socialize, which led to friendships developed "across party and ideological lines" that "led to more openness and willingness to discuss issues on a cordial basis" and to finding "common ground." We could add the demise of the family doctor who came to your home, replaced by an overworked internist or family practitioner—if not an anonymous emergency room—and, if you're unlucky enough to need them but lucky enough to get to see them, a cadre of specialists who may not talk to each other or even much to you, or surgeons who may spend hours saving your life or limb but hardly ever see or speak to you afterward.

In all these domains, wonderful progress has been accompanied by more and more anonymity and disconnection, which are damaging to the human spirit and fertile ground for animosity.

Getting Beyond Dualism

At the heart of the argument culture is our habit of seeing issues and ideas as absolute and irreconcilable principles continually at war. To move beyond this static and limiting view, we can remember the Chinese approach to yin and yang. They are two principles, yes, but they are conceived not as irreconcilable polar opposites but as elements that coexist and should be brought into balance as much as possible. As sociolinguist Suzanne Wong Scollon notes, "Yin is always present in and changing into yang and vice versa."[33] How can we translate this abstract idea into daily practice?

To overcome our bias toward dualism, we can make special efforts not to think in twos. Mary Catherine Bateson, an author and anthropologist who teaches at George Mason University, makes a point of having her class compare *three* cultures, not two.[34] If students compare two cultures, she finds, they are inclined to polarize them, to think of the two as opposite to each other. But if they compare three cultures, they are more likely to think about each on its own terms.

As a goal, we could all try to catch ourselves when we talk about "both sides" of an issue—and talk instead about "all sides." And people in any field can try to resist the temptation to pick on details when they see a chance to score a point. If the detail really does not speak to the main issue, bite your tongue. Draw back and consider the whole picture. After asking, "Where is this wrong?" make an effort to ask "What is right about this?"—not necessarily *instead*, but *in addition*.

In the public arena, producers can try to avoid, whenever possible, structuring public discussions as debates. This means avoiding the format of having two guests discuss an issue, pro and con. In some cases three guests—or one—will be more enlightening than two.

An example of the advantage of adding a third guest was an episode of *The Diane Rehm Show* on National Public Radio following the withdrawal of Anthony Lake from nomination as director of central intelligence. White House Communications Director Ann Lewis claimed that the process of confirming presidential appointments has become more partisan and personal.[35] Tony Blankley, former communications director for Newt Gingrich, claimed that the process has always been rancorous. Fortunately for the audience, there was a third guest: historian Michael Beschloss, who provided historical perspective. He explained that during the immediately preceding period of 1940 to 1990, confirmation hearings were indeed more benign than they have been since, but in the 1920s and the latter half of the nineteenth century, he said, they were also "pretty bloody." In this way, a third guest, especially a guest who is not committed to one side, can dispel the audience's frustration when two guests make opposite claims.

Japanese television talk shows provide a window on other possibilities. Sociolinguist Atsuko Honda compared three different current affairs talk shows televised in Japan. Each one presents striking contrasts to what Americans take for granted in that genre. (The very fact that Honda chose to compare three—not two—is instructive.) The Japanese shows were structured in ways that made them less likely to be adversarial. Within each structure, participants vigorously opposed each other's ideas, yet they did so without excessively polarizing the issues.

Consider the formats of the three shows: *Nichiyoo Tooron (Sunday Discussion)* featured a moderator and four guests who discussed the recession for an hour. Only the moderator was a professional news commentator; two guests were associated with research institutes. The two other shows Honda examined concerned Japanese involvement in a peacekeeping mission in Cambodia. *Sunday Project* featured three guests: one magazine editor and two political scientists; the third show was a three-and-a-half-hour discussion involving fourteen panelists sitting around an oval table with a participating studio audience composed of fifty Japanese and Cambodian students. Viewers were also invited to participate by calling or faxing. Among the panelists were a history professor, a military analyst, a movie director, a scholar, a newscaster, and a legislator.

It is standard for American shows to provide balance by featuring two experts who represent contrasting political views: two senators or political consultants (one Republican, one Democrat), two journalist commentators (one on the left, one on the right), or two experts (one pro and one con). These Japanese shows had more than two guests, and the guests were identified by their expertise rather than their political perspectives. Another popular Japanese show that is often compared to ABC's *Nightline* or PBS's *Jim Lehrer News Hour* is called *Close-up Gendai*.[36] Providing thirty minutes of nightly news analysis, the Japanese show uses a format similar to these American TV shows. But it typically features a single guest. Japanese shows, in other words, have a wide range of formats featuring one guest or three or more—anything but two, the number most likely to polarize.

The political talk shows that Honda analyzed included many disagreements and conflicts. But whereas moderators of American and British talk shows often provoke and stoke conflict to make their shows more interesting, the Japanese moderators—and also the other guests—expended effort to modulate conflicts and defuse the spirit of opposition, but not the substance of disagreement. One last example, taken from Honda's study, illustrates how this worked.

In the long discussion among fourteen panelists, a dispute arose between two: Shikata, a former executive of the Japanese Self-Defense Forces, supported sending these forces to Cambodia. He was opposed by Irokawa, a historian who believed that the involvement of these forces violated the Japanese constitution. This exchange comes across as quite rancorous:

> SHIKATA: Why is it OK to send troops to the protecting side but not OK to the protected side?
> IROKAWA: Because we have the Japanese Constitution.
> SHIKATA: Why is it so, if we have the Constitution?

IROKAWA: Well, we have to abide by the Constitution. If you don't want to follow the Constitution, you should get rid of your Japanese nationality and go somewhere else.

These are pretty strong words. And they were accompanied by strong gestures: According to Honda, as Shikata posed his question, he was beating the table with his palms; as Irokawa responded, he was jabbing the air toward Shikata with a pen.

Yet the confrontation did not take on a rancorous tone. The television cameras offered close-ups of both men's faces—smiling. In Japanese and other Asian cultures, smiling has different connotations than it does for Americans and Europeans: It tends to express not amusement but embarrassment. And while Shikata and Irokawa smiled, other panelists rushed to add their voices—and everyone burst out laughing. The laughter served to defuse the confrontation. So did the loud cacophony of voices that erupted as several panelists tried to speak at once. When individual voices finally were distinguished, they did not take one side or the other but tried to mediate the conflict by supporting and criticizing both sides equally. For example, Ohshima, a movie director, said:

OHSHIMA: I think that both parties overestimate or underestimate the realities for the sake of making a point.

Atsuko Honda found this to be typical of the televised discussions she analyzed: When a conspicuous conflict arose between two parties, other participants frequently moved in with attempts to mediate. In this way, they supported the Japanese ideal of avoiding winners and losers and helped everyone preserve some measure of "face." This mediation did not prevent varying views from being expressed; it resulted in different kinds of views being expressed. If two sides set the terms of debate and subsequent comments support one side or the other, the range of insights offered is circumscribed by the original two sides. If the goal instead is to mediate and defuse polarization, then other panelists are more likely to express a range of perspectives that shed nuanced light on the original two sides or suggest other ways of approaching the issue entirely.

Moving from Debate to Dialogue

Many of the issues I have discussed are also of concern to Amitai Etzioni and other communitarians. In *The New Golden Rule*, Etzioni proposes rules of engagement to make dialogue more constructive between people with differing views. His rules of engagement are designed to reflect—and reinforce—the tenet that people whose ideas conflict are still members of the same community.[37] Among these rules are:

- Don't demonize those with whom you disagree.
- Don't affront their deepest moral commitments.
- Talk less of rights, which are nonnegotiable, and more of needs, wants, and interests.
- Leave some issues out.
- Engage in a dialogue of convictions: Don't be so reasonable and concilia-tory that you lose touch with a core of belief you feel passionately about.

As I stressed [. . .] earlier [. . .], producers putting together television or radio shows and journalists covering stories might consider—in at least some cases—preferring rather than rejecting potential commentators who say they cannot take one side or the other unequivocally. Information shows might do better with only one guest who is given a chance to explore an idea in depth rather than two who will prevent each other from developing either perspec-tive. A producer who feels that two guests with radically opposed views seem truly the most appropriate might begin by asking whether the issue is being framed in the most constructive way. If it is, a third or fourth partici-pant could be invited as well, to temper the "two sides" perspective.

Perhaps it is time to reexamine the assumption that audiences always prefer a fight. In reviewing a book about the history of *National Geographic*, Marina Warner scoffs at the magazine's policy of avoiding attack. She quotes the editor who wrote in 1915, "Only what is of a kindly nature is printed about any country or people, everything unpleasant or unduly criti-cal being avoided."[38] Warner describes this editorial approach condescend-ingly as a "happy-talk, feel-good philosophy" and concludes that "its deep wish not to offend has often made it dull." But the facts belie this judgment. *National Geographic* is one of the most successful magazines of all time—as reported in the same review, its circulation "stands at over 10 million, and the readership, according to surveys, is four times that number."

Perhaps, too, it is time to question our glorification of debate as the best, if not the only, means of inquiry. The debate format leads us to regard those doing different kinds of research as belonging to warring camps. There is something very appealing about conceptualizing differing approaches in this way, because the dichotomies appeal to our sense of how knowledge should be organized.

Well, what's wrong with that?

What's wrong is that it obscures aspects of disparate work that overlap and can enlighten each other.

What's wrong is that it obscures the complexity of research. Fitting ideas into a particular camp requires you to oversimplify them. Again, disinfor-mation and distortion can result. Less knowledge is gained, not more. And time spent attacking an opponent or defending against attacks is not spent doing something else—like original research.

What's wrong is that it implies that only one framework can apply, when in most cases many can. As a colleague put it, "Most theories are wrong not in what they assert but in what they deny."[39] Clinging to the elephant's leg, they loudly proclaim that the person describing the elephant's tail is wrong. This is not going to help them—or their readers—understand an elephant. Again, there are parallels in personal relationships. I recall a man who had just returned from a weekend human development seminar. Full of enthusiasm, he explained the main lesson he had learned: "I don't have to make others wrong to prove that I'm right." He experienced this revelation as a liberation; it relieved him of the burden of trying to prove others wrong.

If you limit your view of a problem to choosing between two sides, you inevitably reject much that is true, and you narrow your field of vision to the limits of those two sides, making it unlikely you'll pull back, widen your field of vision, and discover the paradigm shift that will permit truly new understanding.

In moving away from a narrow view of debate, we need not give up conflict and criticism altogether. Quite the contrary, we can develop more varied—and more constructive—ways of expressing opposition and negotiating disagreement.

We need to use our imaginations and ingenuity to find different ways to seek truth and gain knowledge, and add them to our arsenal—or, should I say, to the ingredients for our stew. It will take creativity to find ways to blunt the most dangerous blades of the argument culture. It's a challenge we must undertake, because our public and private lives are at stake.   ∎

NOTES

1. This does not mean it goes back in an unbroken chain. David Noble, in *A World Without Women,* claims that Aristotle was all but lost to the West during the early Christian era and was rediscovered in the medieval era, when universities were first established. This is significant for his observation that many early Christian monasteries welcomed both women and men who could equally aspire to an androgynous ideal, in contrast to the Middle Ages, when the female was stigmatized, unmarried women were consigned to convents, priests were required to be celibate, and women were excluded from spiritual authority.

2. There is a fascinating parallel in the evolution of the early Christian Church and the Southern Baptist Church: Noble shows that the early Christian Church regarded women as equally beloved of Jesus and equally capable of devoting their lives to religious study, so women comprised a majority of early converts to Christianity, some of them leaving their husbands—or bringing their husbands along—to join monastic communities. It was later, leading up to the medieval period, that the clerical movement gained ascendancy in part by systematically separating women, confining them in either marriage or convents, stigmatizing them, and barring them from positions of

power within the church. Christine Leigh Heyrman, in *Southern Cross: The Beginnings of the Bible Belt*, shows that a similar trajectory characterized the Southern Baptist movement. At first, young Baptist and Methodist preachers (in the 1740s to 1830s) preached that both women and blacks were equally God's children, deserving of spiritual authority—with the result that the majority of converts were women and slaves. To counteract this distressing demography, the message was changed: Antislavery rhetoric faded, and women's roles were narrowed to domesticity and subservience. With these shifts, the evangelical movement swept the South. At the same time, Heyrman shows, military imagery took over: The ideal man of God was transformed from a "willing martyr" to a "formidable fighter" led by "warrior preachers."

3. Ong, *Fighting for Life*, p. 122. Ong's source, on which I also rely, is Oliver, *Communication and Culture in Ancient India and China*. My own quotations from Oliver are from pp. 259.

4. Pachomius, for example, "the father of communal monasticism . . . and organizer of the first monastic community, had been a soldier under Constantine" and modeled his community on the military, emphasizing order, efficiency, and military obedience. Cassian, a fourth-century proselytizer, "'likened the monk's discipline to that of the soldier,' and Chrysostom, another great champion of the movement, 'sternly reminded the monks that Christ had armed them to be soldiers in a noble fight'" (Noble, *A World Without Women*, p. 54).

5. Aristotle, quoted in Oliver, *Communication and Culture in Ancient India and China*, p. 259.

6. I came to understand the different meaning of "poet" in Classical Greece from reading Ong and also *Preface to Plato* by Eric Havelock. These insights informed many articles I wrote about oral and literate tradition in Western culture, including "Oral and Literate Strategies in Spoken and Written Narratives" and "The Oral/Literate Continuum in Discourse."

7. Moulton, "A Paradigm of Philosophy"; Ong, *Fighting for Life*.

8. The example of Danny and the lava: Wertsch, *Voices of the Mind*, pp. 113–14.

9. See David and Myra Sadker, *Failing at Fairness*.

10. Although my colleagues and I make efforts to refer to our students—all over the age of eighteen—as "women" and "men" and some students in my classes do the same, the majority refer to each other and themselves as "girls" and "boys" or "girls" and "guys."

11. Jonathan Alter, "The End of the Journey," *Newsweek*, Nov. 4, 1996, p. 61. Trilling died at the age of ninety-one.

12. Kaplan, *French Lessons*, p. 119.

13. Tracy and Baratz, "Intellectual Discussion in the Academy as Situated Discourse," p. 309.

14. Greenberg and Robins, "The Changing Role of Social Experiments in Policy Analysis," p. 350.

15. These and other quotes from Tompkins appear in her essay "Fighting Words," pp. 588–89.

16. Safire is quoted in Howard Kurtz, "Safire Made No Secret of Dislike for Inman," *The Washington Post*, Jan. 19, 1994, p. A6.

17. I've borrowed the William Blake quote from Peter Elbow, who used it to open his book *Embracing Contraries*.

18. Terence Monmaney, "Marshall's Hunch," *The New Yorker*, Sept. 20, 1993, pp. 64–72.

19. Elbow, *Embracing Contraries*, p. 258.

20. Moulton, "A Paradigm of Philosophy," p. 153.

21. Social constructionists often deride the ideas of those who focus on differences as "essentialist"—a bit of academic name-calling: it is used only as a way of criticizing someone else's work: "Smith's claims are repugnant because they are essentialist." I have never heard anyone claim, "I am an essentialist," though I have frequently heard elaborate self-defenses: "I am not an essentialist!" Capturing the tendency to use this term as an epithet, *Lingua Franca,* a magazine for academics, describes "essentialist" as "that generic gender studies *j'accuse!*" See Emily Nussbaum, "Inside Publishing," *Lingua Franca,* Dec.–Jan. 1977, pp. 22–24; the quote is from p. 24.

22. Klein, *Meeting the Great Bliss Queen,* pp. 8–9.

23. Cynthia Gorney, "Gloria," *Mother Jones,* Nov.–Dec. 1995, pp. 22–27; the quote is from p. 22.

24. See, for example, Needham, *Science and Civilization in China.*

25. Ellyn E. Spragins, *Newsweek,* July 28, 1997, p. 73.

26. This section is based on an interview with Ornstein. See also Ornstein's article, "Less Seems More."

27. The story behind the haircut story is told by Gina Lubrano, "Now for the Real Haircut Story . . . ," *The San Diego Union-Tribune,* July 12, 1993, p. B7. That the supermarket scanner story was not true was mentioned by George Stephanopoulos at a panel held at Brown University, as reported by Elliot Krieger, "Providence Journal/Brown University Public Affairs Conference," *The Providence Journal-Bulletin,* Mar. 5, 1995, p. 12A.

28. Fox, "The Inherent Rules of Violence," p. 141.

29. Yablon, "Stupid Lawyer Tricks," p. 1639.

30. Kenneth Walsh made this comment on *The Diane Rehm Show,* May 28, 1996.

31. Grossman, *On Killing,* p. 270.

32. Susan Popik made this comment on the *U.S. Business Litigation* panel.

33. Suzanne Wong Scollon: Personal communication.

34. Mary Catherine Bateson: Personal communication.

35. At the time of this show, Ms. Lewis was deputy communications director.

36. Yoshiko Nakano helped me with observations of *Close-up Gendai.*

37. Etzioni, *The New Golden Rule,* pp. 104–106. He attributes the rule "Talk less of rights . . . and more of needs, wants, and interests" to Mary Ann Glendon.

38. Marina Warner, "High-Minded Pursuit of the Exotic," review of *Reading National Geographic* by Catherine A. Lutz and Jane L. Collins in *The New York Times Book Review,* Sept. 19, 1993, p. 13.

39. I got this from A. L. Becker, who got it from Kenneth Pike, who got it from . . .

REFERENCES

Elbow, Peter. *Embracing Contraries: Explorations in Learning and Teaching* (New York and Oxford: Oxford University Press, 1986).

Etzioni, Amitai. *The New Golden Rule: Community and Morality in a Democratic Society* (New York: Basic, 1996).

Fox, Robin. "The Inherent Rules of Violence." In *Social Rules and Social Behaviour,* Peter Collet, ed. (Totowa, N.J.: Rowman and Littlefield, 1976), pp. 132–49.

Greenberg, David H., and Philip K. Robins. "The Changing Role of Social Experiments in Policy Analysis." *Journal of Policy Analysis and Management* 5:2 (1986), pp. 340–62.

Grossman, Dave. *On Killing: The Psychological Cost of Learning to Kill in War and Society* (Boston: Little, Brown, 1995).

Havelock, Eric A. *Preface to Plato* (Cambridge, Mass.: Belknap Press, Harvard University Press, 1963).

Heyrman, Christine Leigh. *Southern Cross: The Beginnings of the Bible Belt* (New York: Knopf, 1997).

Kaplan, Alice. *French Lessons: a Memoir* (Chicago: University of Chicago Press, 1993).

Klein, Anne Carolyn. *Meeting the Great Bliss Queen: Buddhists, Feminists, and the Art of the Self* (Boston: Beacon Press, 1995).

Kurtz, Howard. *Hot Air: All Talk, All the Time* (New York: Times Books, 1996).

Moulton, Janice. "A Paradigm of Philosophy: The Adversary Method." In *Discovering Reality,* Sandra Harding and Merrill B. Hintikka, eds. (Dordrecht, Holland: Reidel, 1983), pp. 149–64.

Needham, Joseph. *Science and Civilization in China* (Cambridge, England: Cambridge University Press, 1956).

Noble, David. *A World Without Women: The Christian Culture of Western Science* (New York and Oxford: Oxford University Press, 1992).

Oliver, Robert T. *Communication and Culture in Ancient India and China* (Syracuse, N.Y.: Syracuse University Press, 1971).

Ong, Walter J. *Fighting for Life: Contest, Sexuality, and Consciousness* (Ithaca, N.Y.: Cornell University Press, 1981).

Ornstein, Norman J. "Less Seems More: What to Do About Contemporary Political Corruption." *The Responsible Community* 4:1 (Winter 1993–94), pp. 7–22.

Tompkins, Jane. "Fighting Words: Unlearning to Write the Critical Essay." *Georgia Review* 42 (1988), pp. 585–90.

Tracy, Karen, and Sheryl Baratz. "Intellectual Discussion in the Academy as Situated Discourse." *Communication Monographs* 60 (1993), pp. 300–20.

Wertsch, James V. *Voices of the Mind: A Sociocultural Approach to Mediated Action* (Cambridge, Mass.: Harvard University Press, 1991).

Yablon, Charles. "Stupid Lawyer Tricks: An Essay on Discovery Abuse." *Columbia Law Review* 96 (1996), p. 1618–44.

▪ *QUESTIONS FOR MAKING CONNECTIONS WITHIN THE READING* ▪

1. In the course of her argument Deborah Tannen refers to "our adversarial culture," "the culture of critique," and to maleness, logic, formalism, and polarization. She refers as well to the customs and discourses of Western religion and science, and to contemporary educational practices. Define these terms and explain how they fit together. What is the relation between logic and aggression, religion and science, and ancient Greece and the education offered by our universities?

2. In what ways has the "boot camp" model shaped your own educational experience? In an actual boot camp, is it the drill sergeant alone who cre-

ates the tension, or does everyone collaborate in creating and sustaining an atmosphere of rivalry and violence? How about in the case of schooling: In what ways do the students themselves actively collaborate in making the classroom into a "camp"? In what ways does the system—the culture and the institutions of schooling—reinforce these behaviors?

3. In the section entitled "Getting Beyond Dualism," Tannen describes the dynamics of three Japanese television programs, which she offers as examples of a less agonistic style of public discussion. What features distinguish these programs from comparable discussions in the U.S. media and in places like the classroom? Does disagreement have a different significance in the context of Japanese culture? When people disagree in Western settings, what might be at stake? What values and outcomes matter the most? In the Japanese context, what values and outcomes are most significant? How might an American misunderstand the Japanese programs?

▪ QUESTIONS FOR WRITING ▪

1. University professors routinely study communities and institutions outside the university, and they are often quite critical of what they discover there, but the university itself is seldom the object of comparable scrutiny. In what ways—if any—does the culture of critique stifle inquiry and thwart constructive change within the university itself? If Tannen is correct in her estimations, then would it be fair to say that the advancement of knowledge is only one of the university's many goals and perhaps not even the most important one? What might the other goals be?

2. The university in the United States is a unique institution in many ways. For one thing, all faculty above the level of assistant professor have lifetime employment and cannot be dismissed except for gross dereliction of duty. Most public universities receive automatic funding from state coffers. Many private universities have enormous endowments, sometimes in the billions of dollars. And most professors are shielded from any assessment of their effectiveness as teachers, except through course evaluations. In what ways does the university's unique situation contribute to the persistence of the culture of critique? What about the media?

▪ QUESTIONS FOR MAKING CONNECTIONS BETWEEN READINGS ▪

1. Was the attack on the World Trade Center and the Pentagon an act of war or a crime? What difference does it make what words one chooses in describing this—or any other—act of violence? Drawing on the work of Tannen and Mary Kaldor, discuss the relationship between the terms we use

to describe acts of violence and the ways we elect to respond to acts of violence. Would changing the words we use and the ways we use them create new options for responding to violence, or are such concerns a luxury during times of great danger?

2. How does Malcolm Gladwell's discussion of the dynamics of social change confirm, contradict, or complicate Tannen's argument? Does Gladwell's account suggest that social change is decided by the strongest argument? Does debate even play a significant role? If public debate and rational deliberation have a marginal influence, why does the university place so high a premium on them? Have professors depicted the social world in ways that are flattering to themselves? In what ways is this depiction both accurate *and* inaccurate?

For additional suggestions about making connections between readings, visit the Link-O-Mat and More Sample Assignments at <www.newhum.com>.

FRANS DE WAAL

FRANS DE WAAL [de Vaal] began his work on the link between human and primate behavioral patterns in 1975 with a six-year project studying the world's largest captive colony of chimpanzees at the Arnhem Zoo in the Netherlands. De Waal discussed the initial results of his research into how primates resolve conflict in *Chimpanzee Politics* (1982) and has since published a series of books that seek to further establish the continuum of conciliatory and aggressive behavioral patterns that link humans and primates: *Peacemaking Among Primates* (1989), *Good Natured: The Origins of Right and Wrong in Humans and Other Animals* (1996), and *Bonobo: The Forgotten Ape* (1997).

Originally trained as a zoologist and ethologist in the Netherlands, de Waal is currently the C. H. Candler Professor of Primate Behavior at Emory University and director of the Living Links Center at the Yerkes Regional Primate Research Center in Atlanta, Georgia. The goal of the Living Links Center is to study the four extant breeds of great apes—the bonobos, chimpanzees, gorillas, and orangutans—that connect humans to our primate relatives. By exploring these links, de Waal and his colleagues hope "to reconstruct human evolution, pinpoint the differences and similarities between humans and apes, and educate the public about apes and promote their well-being and conservation." By insisting primates have a "culture" that they learn through observation, de Waal sees himself as challenging both the humanities and the social sciences, which have assumed a sharp distinction between humans and animals, and the sciences, which have depicted humans as "taking over the world by means of aggression." In "Survival of the Kindest" and "Down with Dualism," two chapters drawn from de Waal's most recent book, *The Ape and the Sushi Master: Cultural Reflections by a Primatologist* (2001), de Waal offers an alternate understanding of the relationship between primates and humans. As de Waal explained in a re-

de Waal, Frans. "Survival of the Kindest" and "Down with Dualism." *The Ape and the Sushi Master: Cultural Reflections by a Primatologist.* New York: Basic Books, 2001. 315–335, 337–357.

Biographical information drawn from the Living Links Center's Web site <http://www.emory.edu/LIVING_LINKS/>; quotations from Frans de Waal, interview by Ira Flatow, "Science Friday," National Public Radio, 1 June, 2001 <http://search.npr.org/cf/cmn/cmnpd01fm.cfm?PrgDate=06/01/2001&PrgID=5>.

cent interview, it is by studying the compassionate and altruistic behavior of the bonobo and the other great apes that we can gain access "to a side of ourselves that the textbooks have put under the table."

To learn more about Frans de Waal and the study of primates, visit the Link-O-Mat at <www.newhum.com>.

■ ■

Selections from
The Ape and the Sushi Master

Survival of the Kindest

Of Selfish Genes and Unselfish Dogs

"How selfish soever man may be supposed, there are evidently some principles in his nature, which interest him in the fortune of others, and render their happiness necessary to him, though he derives nothing from it, except the pleasure of seeing it."

Adam Smith, 1759

"Altruism may arise in the chimpanzee, in some modest degree, where there has been no training in generosity. On any reasonable view, this requires reinterpretation of the traditional hedonistic, law-of-effect view of human nature and human motivation."

Donald Hebb, 1971

The most absurd animal exhibit I have ever seen was at a small zoo in Lop Buri, Thailand. Two medium-sized dogs shared a cage with three full-grown tigers. While the tigers cooled their bodies in dirty water, the dogs moved around, hopping unconcernedly over the huge striped heads that rested on the concrete rim of the pool. The dogs were walking snacks, but the tigers evidently failed to perceive them as such.

I learned that one of the dogs had raised the tiger cubs along with her own puppy, and that the whole family had happily stayed together. The mother was said to be top dog over everyone else.

The tigers were no pushovers, though. They silently stalked the three-year old son of my hosts when he strolled by the cage, their yellow eyes glued to the boy, ready to pounce if some miracle removed the bars holding them back. In the forest, a member of the same species once roared at the boy's father, a tall German primatologist, making his blood curdle, and permanently changing his perspective on the risk factors of his job.

A couple of meters from this exhibit stood a statue depicting combat between a tiger and an eagle, both of them larger than life. The eagle seemed to be trying to scratch out the tiger's eyes with its talons, an implausible encounter because the two animals normally don't get in each other's way. But it was a dramatic rendition of the ubiquitous struggle for existence, the cutthroat competition between organisms over limited resources, or, as Tennyson immortalized it, "nature, red in tooth and claw."

Both the statue and the cage with tigers and dogs presented artificial situations, but with conflicting messages. While the animals demonstrated how well teeth and claws can be held under control, the statue arrogantly declared: "Who cares what you actually see in nature? This is how it works!" Unintentionally, the zoo thus offered grounds for reflection on observed versus theorized nature.

The incredible sacrifice of the mother dog in rearing three tigers falls under the biological definition of altruism—that is, she incurred a serious cost for the benefit of others. She didn't do it for herself, her family, or even her species, so why did she do it? What energy she must have put into raising three giant animals so totally unlike herself! The difference in size was every big as large as that between, say, a tiny hedge sparrow and the enormous cuckoo nestling she is raising. But the hedge sparrow had been tricked by an egg similar to her own, whereas it is hard to imagine that a dog is unable to tell a tiger cub from a puppy by sight, let alone smell.

Biologists often explain altruism by so-called kin selection. Kindness towards one's kin is viewed as a genetic investment, a way of spreading genes similar to one's own. Assisting kin thus comes close to helping oneself. Sacrifices on behalf of kin are pervasive, from honey bees that die for their colony by stinging intruders to birds—such as scrub jays—that help their parents raise a nest full of young. Humans show the same bias toward kin, giving rise to expressions such as "Blood is thicker than water." No wonder awards for heroism are rarely bestowed on those who have saved members of their own family.

The bitch of our story qualifies as a heroine, though, since she gave tender loving care and nourishing milk to individuals that could not possibly be her relatives. Kin selection, therefore, cannot explain her behavior. The alternative hypothesis is the "You scratch my back, I'll scratch yours" argument, where the help is directed to someone willing to repay the service. In my own work, I have tested this idea by recording grooming sessions among chimpanzees at the Yerkes Primate Center's Field Station, near Atlanta, after which I watched food sharing among the same apes. I found that if chimpanzee A had groomed B in the morning, A's chances of getting food from B in the afternoon were greatly improved. All parties stand to gain in such an economy of exchange.

Could this account for the dog's behavior? It might be argued that the cats repaid her by not devouring her, but such altruism-by-omission is a bit of a stretch. It certainly doesn't explain the mother's generosity. Had she simply rejected the cubs, she would not have had to contend with them as dangerous adults to begin with. Clearly, she got little or nothing out of the whole deal.

Does this mean that the evolutionary paradigm is fundamentally flawed? The answer depends on how broad or narrow a vision of evolution one embraces. The above theories explain cooperation reasonably well, but they do not apply—and do not need to apply—to each and every single instance. The beauty of unnatural arrangements, such as placing tiger cubs on a dog's nipples, is that they expose the disjunction between motive and function. The original *function* of maternal care is obviously to raise one's own offspring, but the *motivation* to provide such care reaches beyond that function. The motivation has become strong and flexible enough to reach out to other young, even those of other species, regardless of what is in it for the mother. Motives often acquire lives of their own. As a result, they do not always neatly fit biology's dominant metaphors, which emphasize ruthless competition.

The Spider and the Fly

Anyone who has seen the film *Il Postino* (The Postman) realizes the extraordinary lure of the metaphor. The apprentice poet of the movie learns to offer a fresh look at the world through carefully selected analogies. Shy at first, he soon relishes the poet's proverbial "license" to transform reality, which helps him greatly in wooing the opposite sex.

People are animists by nature, always interpreting reality in their own image. It starts early when children freely ascribe inner lives to clouds, trees, dolls, and other objects. This tendency is commercially exploited with pet rocks, chia pets, and Tamagotchi, which show remarkably little resemblance to the usual recipients of human love.[1] The phenomenon is not even limited to our species; chimpanzees, too, care for imaginary young. Richard Wrangham observed a six-year-old juvenile, Kakama, carry and cradle a small wooden log as if it were a newborn. Kakama did so for hours on end, one time even building a nest in a tree and putting the log into it on its own. Kakama's mother was pregnant at the time. The field-worker notes: "My intuition suggested a possibility that I was reluctant, as a professional skeptical scientist, to accept on the basis of a single observation: that I had just watched a young male chimpanzee invent and then play with a doll in possible anticipation of his mother giving birth."[2]

Scientists are not immune to the urge to project needs and desires onto inanimate objects. Unfortunately for us, however, we lack the license of the poet and the innocence of the child. Metaphors are used in science to great effect and advantage, but also at great peril. Taken literally, they often obscure the truth. This lot befell the well-known "struggle for existence" view of the natural world. It kept generations of biologists from recognizing the shared interests among individuals and species even though Charles Darwin—always wiser than his followers—had warned in *The Origin of Species*: "I use the term Struggle for Existence in a large and metaphorical sense including dependence of one being on another."[3]

In chemistry and physics, metaphors are common, as when we say that elements are "attracted" to each other (not to mention that they "like" each other), or when we use concepts such as "force" and "resistance." Anthropomorphic interpretations are attempts to make sense of the world around us. In modern biology, this has led to the characterization of genes as "selfish" and of organisms as "adapting" to their environment. Genes are said to be our rulers, and to strive for their own replication. But really, all that is going on is that genes, a mere batch of DNA molecules, replicate at different rates depending on the success of the traits that they produce. Rather than doing the selecting themselves, genes are *being* selected. Adaptation, too, is a blind and passive process resulting from the elimination of less successful forms. All of this is known to every biologist, but we are unable to resist infusing evolution with direction and intent.

It is only a small step from calling genes selfish to slapping the same label onto the carriers of those genes: plants, animals, and people. Thus, according to George Williams, one of the world's leading evolutionary biologists, "natural selection maximizes short-sighted selfishness."[4] He thus extends the utilitarian language of his discipline to the domain of motivation. This is a slippery extrapolation, because the selfishness of genes is entirely metaphorical—genes have no self, hence cannot possibly be selfish—whereas animals and people do qualify for the literal application.

Thus, the concept of "selfishness" has been plucked from the English language, robbed of its vernacular meaning, and applied outside of the psychological domain where it used to belong. It is now often used as if it were a synonym for "self-serving," which of course it is not. Selfishness implies the *intention* to serve oneself, hence knowledge of what one stands to gain. Without such knowledge, selfishness is a much more problematic concept than many evolutionary thinkers realize. A vine may serve its own interests by overgrowing and suffocating a tree, but since plants lack intentions and knowledge they cannot possibly be selfish except in a rather meaningless sense.

The question then becomes whether animals and people possess the knowledge to act selfishly. In nature, the future is mostly hidden behind a veil of ignorance. The spider builds her web in order to catch flies and the squirrel hides nuts to get through the winter, but it is unlikely that spiders and squirrels do so knowingly. This would require previous experience, whereas even the youngest, most naïve spiders and squirrels weave webs and store nuts. They have no clue how useful their actions will turn out to be. Both species would have become extinct long ago if it were otherwise. And these are only the simplest examples I can think of. Many behavioral functions are much harder to recognize. The stallion fights at great risk against other stallions so as to claim a harem of mares and sire offspring with them, but it would be ridiculous to suggest that the stallion himself knows how a victory might affect his reproductive chances. For this, he would need to know the relation between sex and procreation, an understanding yet to be demonstrated in any nonhuman animal.

Even human behavior doesn't necessarily depend on awareness of its results. The healthy appetites of children and pregnant women, for instance, serve their need for growth. It would be a mistake, however, to assume that these individuals eat out of a desire to grow: hunger does the trick. Motivations follow their own rules, fulfill their own goals, and require their own set of explanations.

Instead of the piecemeal evolution of individual acts—such as bite, scratch, flee, lick, or nurse—natural selection has produced entire psychologies that orchestrate a species' whole repertoire of behavior. Animals weigh choices, absorb information, learn which behavior yields rewards, and solve problems intelligently, and they do all of this within a framework of natural tendencies that have proven their value over the ages. Genes are definitely part of the equation, but to say that animals are nothing but machines controlled by genes is like saying that a Rembrandt is nothing but fabric and paint, or that a brain is a mere collection of neurons. While not incorrect, such statements miss by a mile the higher levels of organization.

Returning to our mother dog, it is easy to recognize in her behavior a complex psychology shaped by a long history of reliance of maternal care. The tendency to feed and clean dependent young is well established for excellent reasons. At the same time, the entrenched nature of the tendency makes it vulnerable to exploitation, as when people gave the dog tiger cubs to raise. Not that this matters much to the mother. From an evolutionary perspective, care for non-offspring may be maladaptive, but from a psychological perspective, it remains entirely authentic and fitting behavior for the species. Another dog, at Beijing Zoo, recently acted as wet nurse for three snow-leopard cubs whose mother had abandoned them.[5]

And so, the dog at the Thai zoo really hadn't done anything unusual, nothing that a good canine wouldn't or shouldn't do. Her behavior did provide a stark reminder, though, of how narrow a portrayal of nature the nearby statue offered. The statue was intended to show selection at work, but could not begin to convey the variety of outcomes evolution has produced. Paradoxically, harsh selection processes have led to some amazingly cooperative species with character traits such as loyalty, trust, sympathy, and generosity.

The Midwife Bat

Before we now conclude that animals and people can be truly unselfish, we need to subject the terms "altruism" and "kindness" to the same scrutiny as was just applied to "selfishness." Here, too, we risk confusion: functional altruism—in which one individual gains from another's actions—does not necessarily rest on intended kindness, in which someone else's well-being is the goal.

When a blue jay gives alarm shrieks for a red-tailed hawk gliding around the corner, does he do so in order to warn others? All potential prey of the hawk take immediate action, and thus profit from the jay's alert, whereas the jay takes enormous risks, telling the hawk, in effect: "Here I am!" On the surface, this seems an act of unmitigated altruism. The critical question remains, however, whether the jay cared about the others: did he even realize the wider impact of his calls?

There exist many examples of altruism in which awareness of what the behavior means to others is questionable. This is especially true for social insects, which sacrifice themselves on a massive scale for their colony and queen. Many other animals help each other find food and water, avoid predation, raise offspring, and so on. Only a few of the largest-brained animals, however, seem to operate with a solid understanding of how their behavior affects others. When these animals go out of their way to help others without any clear benefits for themselves, it is possible that the other's welfare is their goal. I am thinking, for example, of how Binti Jua, the lowland gorilla at Chicago's Brookfield Zoo, scooped up and gently transported an unconscious boy who had fallen into her enclosure. Binti followed a chain of action no one had taught her, resulting in the boy's rescue.[6]

In another incident, a British tourist was protected by dolphins in the Gulf of Akaba off the Red Sea. While cavorting with dolphins, the man was attacked by sharks. When his companions on the vessel heard his screams, they thought at first it was a joke, until they saw blood stain the water. Three dolphins surrounded the injured victim, leaping up and smacking the water with their tails and flippers, and successfully kept the sharks at bay.[7]

In my work on the evolution of morality, I have found many instances of animals caring for one another and responding to others' distress. For example, chimpanzees will approach a victim of attack, put an arm around her and gently pat her back, or groom her. These reassuring encounters, termed *consolations*, are so predictable that my students and I have recorded hundreds of instances.[8] In monkeys, on the other hand, consolation has never been demonstrated. On the contrary, monkeys often avoid victims of aggression. Our closest relatives, the anthropoid apes, thus seem more empathic than monkeys. Apes may be able to perceive the world from someone else's perspective, and hence understand what is wrong with the other, or what the other needs.

Nadie Ladygina-Kohts noticed similar empathic tendencies in her young chimpanzee, Yoni, whom she raised in Moscow at the beginning of the twentieth century. Kohts, who analyzed Yoni's behavior in the minutest detail, discovered that the only way to get him off the roof of her house (much more effectively than by holding out a reward) was to appeal to his feelings of concern for her:

> If I pretend to be crying, close my eyes and weep, Yoni immediately stops his plays or any other activities, quickly runs over to me, all excited and shagged, from the most remote places in the house, such as the roof or the ceiling of his cage, from where I could not drive him down despite my persistent calls and entreaties. He hastily runs around me, as if looking for the offender; looking at my face, he tenderly takes my chin in his palm, lightly touches my face with his finger, as though trying to understand what is happening, and turns around, clenching his toes into firm fists.[9]

In previous books, such as *Good Natured* (1996), I have amassed other examples in support of this empathic capacity in the chimpanzee and its closest relative, the bonobo. For instance, an adult daughter brought fruit down from a tree to her aging mother, who was too old to climb. In another instance, juveniles interrupted their rambunctious play each time they got close to a terminally sick companion. There is also the report of an old male leading a blind female around by the hand, and of an ape who released a damaged bird by climbing to the highest point of a tree, spreading the bird's wings, and sending it off through the air. This individual seemed to have an idea of what kind of assistance might be best for an injured bird. There exist ample stories of this sort about apes that suggest a capacity to assist others insightfully.

But even though apes may be special in this regard, we cannot exclude similar capacities in other animals. A well-documented instance of possible altruism concerns a very different species: Rodrigues fruit bats in a breeding colony in Florida, studied by Thomas Kunz, a biologist at Boston University.[10] By chance, Kunz witnessed an exceptionally difficult birthing process in which a mother bat failed to adopt the required feet-down position. Instead, she continued to hang upside-down. Taking on a midwife role, another female spent no less than two and a half hours assisting the inexperienced mother. She licked and groomed her behind, and wrapped her wings around her, perhaps so as to prevent the emerging pup from falling. She also repeatedly fanned the exhausted mother with her wings. But what amazed the biologist most was that the helper seemed to be *instructing* the mother: the mother adopted the correct feet-down position only after the helper had done so right in front of her. On four separate occasions the helper adopted the correct position in full view of the mother—a position normally used only for urination or defecation, which the helper didn't engage in—and each time the mother followed the helper's example.

It looked very much as if the midwife bat was aware of the difficulties the mother's unorthodox position was causing, and that she tutored the mother to do the right things. If she indeed monitored the effects of her actions and deliberately strove for a successful delivery, the helper's behavior was not just functionally but also intentionally altruistic. When the pup was finally born, it climbed onto its mother's back assisted by head-nuzzling from the helper female.

We easily recognize such helping tendencies, because they are prominent in our own species. This is abundantly clear when people crawl into smoking ruins to save others, such as during earthquakes and fires. Given our talent for risk assessment, there can be nothing inadvertent about such behavior. When Lenny Skutnik dove into the icy Potomac River in Washington, D.C., to rescue a plane-crash victim, or when European civilians sheltered Jewish families during World War II, incredible risks were taken on behalf of complete strangers. Even if reward comes afterward in the form of a medal or a moment on the evening news, this is of course never the motive. No sane person would willingly risk his life for a piece of metal or five minutes of televised glory. The decision to help is instantaneous and impulsive, without much time to think. When fugitives knock on the door, one determines there and then whether to take them in.

But even if many heroic acts escape traditional biological explanations in terms of "short-sighted selfishness," this doesn't make the underlying tendencies counterrevolutionary. More than likely, the helping responses of dolphins, gorillas, or people toward strangers in need evolved in the context of a close-knit group life in which most of the time such actions benefited relatives and companions able to repay the favor. The impulse to help was therefore never totally without survival value to the one showing the impulse. But, as so often, the impulse became dissociated from the consequences that shaped its evolution, which permitted it to be expressed even when payoffs were unlikely. The impulse thus was emancipated to the point where it became genuinely unselfish.

Depressed Rescue Dogs

The animal literature is filled with examples of normal behavior under unusual circumstances. Followed by a single file of goslings, Konrad Lorenz demonstrated the tendency of these birds to imprint on the first moving object they lay their eyes on. He thus permanently confused their sense of species-belonging. Niko Tinbergen saw stickleback fish in a row of tanks in front of his laboratory window, in Leiden, make furious territorial displays at the mail delivery van in the street below. At the time, Dutch mail vans were bright red, the same color as the male stickleback's underbelly during the breeding season, and the fish mistook the van for an intruder of their own species.

Artificial situations sometimes help us see more clearly how behavior is regulated. When goslings do the normal thing, following their mom around all day, one might think that they share our exalted view of motherhood. We are quickly disabused of this notion, however, when they follow a bearded zoologist with equal devotion. And when sticklebacks defend their territory, we might think that they want to keep competitors out, whereas in reality they are only reacting to a species-typical red flag. What animals really are after is not always evident, and tinkering with conditions is a way to find out.

For altruistic behavior, an informative context is that of rescue dogs. Trainers tap into the inborn tendency of these cooperative hunters to come to each other's aid. Time and again, dogs demonstrate this ability spontaneously towards their human "pack members." An example is the occasion on which a rottweiler and golden retriever crawled side by side on their bellies toward their master, who had broken through the ice on a frozen lake. The heavy man managed to grab their collars, one in each hand, upon which both dogs inched backward, pulling him out.[11]

Rescue dogs are trained to perform such responses on command, often in repulsive situations, such as fires, that they would normally avoid unless the entrapped individuals are familiar. Training is accomplished with the usual carrot-and-stick method. One might think, therefore, that the dogs perform like Skinnerian rats, doing what has been reinforced in the past, partly out of instinct, partly out of a desire for tidbits. If they save human lives, one could argue, they do so for purely selfish reasons.

The image of the rescue dog as a well-behaved robot is hard to maintain, however, in the face of their attitude under trying circumstances with few survivors, such as in the aftermath of the bombing of the Murrah Federal Building in Oklahoma City. When rescue dogs encounter too many dead people, they lose interest in their job regardless of how much praise and goodies they get.

This was discovered by Caroline Hebard, the U.S. pioneer of canine search and rescue, during the Mexico City earthquake of 1985. Hebard recounts how her German shepherd, Aly, reacted to finding corpse after corpse and few survivors. Aly would be all excited and joyful if he detected human life in the rubble, but became depressed by all the death. In Hebard's words, Aly regarded humans as his friends, and he could not stand to be surrounded by so many dead friends: "Aly fervently wanted his stick reward, and equally wanted to please Caroline, but as long as he was uncertain about whether he had found someone alive, he would not even reward himself. Here in this gray area, rules of logic no longer applied."[12]

The logic referred to is that a reward is just a reward: there is no reason for a trained dog to care about the victim's condition. Yet, all dogs on the team became depressed. They required longer and longer resting periods, and their eagerness for the job dropped off dramatically. After a couple of days, Aly clearly had had enough. His big brown eyes were mournful, and he hid behind the bed when Hebard wanted to take him out again. He also refused to eat. All other dogs on the team had lost their appetites as well.

The solution to this motivational problem says a lot about what the dogs wanted. A Mexican veterinarian was invited to act as stand-in survivor. The rescuers hid the volunteer somewhere in a wreckage and let the dogs find him. One after another the dogs were sent in, picked up the man's scent, and happily alerted, thus "saving" his life. Refreshed by this exercise, the dogs were ready to work again."[13]

What this means is that trained dogs rescue people only partly for approval and food rewards. Instead of performing a cheap circus trick, they are emotionally invested. They relish the opportunity to find and save a live person. Doing so also constitutes some sort of reward, but one more in line with what Adam Smith, the Scottish philosopher and father of economics, thought to underlie human sympathy: all that we derive from sympathy, he said, is the pleasure of seeing someone else's fortune. Perhaps this doesn't seem like much, but it means a lot to many people, and apparently also to some big-hearted canines.

Under certain conditions and for certain species, therefore, we can drop the customary quotation marks around "altruism." At least in some cases, we seem to be dealing with the genuine article: a good deed done *and* intended.

Apples and Oranges

It is not hard to see why biologists call the problems they deal with multi-layered. At the evolutionary level a behavior may be self-serving; at the psychological level it may be kind and unselfish; and at yet another level it may be best understood by the effects of hormones on certain brain areas. Similarly, from the performer's perspective a behavior may be a mere reflex or fully deliberate, yet this matters little to the recipient, who mainly cares about whether the behavior helps or harms him.

When we freely jump from one level or perspective to another we run the risk of forgetting to keep our language straight. For example, nature documentaries now customarily discuss animal behavior in the shorthand of evolutionary biology ("The croaking frog advertises his genetic superiority to potential mates"), making us forget that animals know nothing about the genetic story. Even worse is that scientists who operate on one level sometimes can't stand another level's idiom, and vice versa. This explains why some flinch at the same behavior being called selfish. In fact, both may be right within their respective frameworks.

If one biologist's apples are another's oranges, this obviously creates a communication problem. We usually resolve the difficulty by asking whether someone is talking at the "proximate" (direct causation) or "ultimate" (adaptive value) level, but this distinction has never caught on outside of biology. The tension between the two is forever there, however. The mother dog who raises tiger cubs is at once extraordinarily generous and doing what her genes, based on millions of years of self-service, nudge her to do. By following her natural impulses, she illustrates the contradictions that lend so much richness to evolutionary accounts that we will never be done mining their meaning.

Down with Dualism!

Two Millennia of Debate About Human Goodness

"We approve and we disapprove because we cannot do otherwise. Can we help feeling pain when the fire burns us? Can we help sympathizing with our friends? Are these phenomena less necessary or less powerful in their consequences, because they fall within the subject sphere of experience?"

Edward Westermarck, 1912

Edward Westermarck's writings, including those about his journeys to Morocco, kept me busy as I leaned back in a cushy seat on a jet from Tokyo to Helsinki. More comfortable than a camel, I bet! I was on my way to an international conference in honor of the Swedish-Finn, who lived from 1862 until 1939, and who was the first to bring Darwinism to the social sciences.

His books are a curious blend of dry theorizing, detailed anthropology, and secondhand animal stories. He gives the example of a vengeful camel that had been excessively beaten on multiple occasions by a fourteen-year-old "lad" for loitering or turning the wrong way. The camel passively took the punishment, but a few days later, finding itself unladen and alone on the road with the same conductor, "seized the unlucky boy's head in its monstrous and mouth, and lifting him up in the air flung him down again on the earth with the upper part of the skull completely torn off, and his brains scattered on the ground."[1]

I don't know much about camels, but stories of delayed revenge abound in the zoo world, especially about apes and elephants. We now have systematic data on how chimpanzees punish negative actions with other negative actions—a pattern called a "revenge system"—and how if a macaque is attacked by a dominant member of its troop it will turn around to redirect aggression against a vulnerable, younger relative of its attacker.[2] Such behavior falls under what Westermarck called the "retributive emotions," but for him "retributive" went beyond its usual connotation of getting even. It included positive tendencies, such as gratitude and the repayment of services. Depicting the retributive emotions as the cornerstone of human morality, Westermarck weighed in on the question of its origin while antedating modern discussions of evolutionary ethics, which often take the related concept of reciprocal altruism as their starting point.[3]

That Westermarck goes unmentioned in the latest books on evolutionary ethics, or serves only as a historic footnote, is not because he paid attention to the wrong phenomena or held untenable views about ethics, but because his writing conveyed a belief in human goodness. He felt that morality comes naturally to people. Contemporary biologists have managed to banish this view to the scientific fringes under the influence of the two Terrible Toms—Thomas Hobbes and Thomas Henry Huxley—who both preached that the original state of humankind, and of nature in general, is one in which selfish goals are pursued without regard for others. Compromise, symbiosis, and mutualism were not terms the Toms considered particularly useful, even though these outcomes are not hard to come by in both nature and human society.

Are we naturally good? And if not, whence does human goodness come? Is it one of our many marvelous inventions, like the wheel and toilet training, or could it be a mere illusion? Perhaps we are naturally bad, and just pretend to be good?

Every possible answer to these questions has been seriously advocated by one school of thought or another. I myself have struggled with the question of human nature, contrasting the views of present-day biologists—from whom an admission of human virtue is about as hard to extract as a rotten tooth—with the belief of many philosophers and scientists, including Charles Darwin, that our species moderates its selfishness with a healthy dose of fellow-feeling and kindness. Anyone who explores this debate will notice how old it is—including, as it does, explicit Chinese sources, such as Mencius, from before the Western calendar—so that we can justifiably speak of a perennial controversy.

Westermarck Beats Freud

In a stately building on a wintry, dark Helsinki day, not far from his childhood home, we discussed Westermarck's brave Darwinism, which was initially applauded but soon opposed by contemporary big shots such as Sigmund Freud and Claude Lévi-Strauss. Their resistance was so effective that the Finn has been largely forgotten.

His most controversial position concerned incest. Both Freud and many anthropologists were convinced that there would be rampant sex within the human family if it were not for the incest taboo. Freud believed that the earliest sexual excitations and fantasies of children are invariably directed at close family members, while Lévi-Strauss declared the incest taboo the ultimate cultural blow against nature—it was what permitted humanity to make the passage from nature to culture.

These were high-flown notions, which carried the stunning implication that our species was somehow predestined to free itself of its biological shackles. Westermarck didn't share the belief that our ancestors started out with rampant, promiscuous sex over which they gained control only with great difficulty. He instead saw the nuclear family as humanity's age-old reproductive unit, and proposed that early association within this unit (such as normally found between parent and offspring and among siblings) kills sexual desire. Hence, the desire isn't there to begin with. On the contrary, individuals who grow up together from an early age develop an actual sexual *aversion* for each other. Westermarck proposed this as an evolved mechanism with an obvious adaptive value: it prevents the deleterious effects of inbreeding.

In the largest-scale study on this issue to date, Arthur Wolf, an anthropologist at Stanford University, spent a lifetime examining the marital histories of 14,402 Taiwanese women in a "natural experiment" dependent on a peculiar Chinese marriage custom. Families used to adopt and raise little girls as future daughters-in-law. This meant that they grew up since early childhood with the family's son, their intended husband. Wolf compared the resulting marriages with those arranged between men and women who did not meet until their wedding day. Fortunately for science, official household registers were kept during the Japanese occupation of Taiwan. These registers provide detailed information on divorce rates and number of children, which Wolf took as measures of, respectively, marital happiness and sexual activity. His data supported the Westermarck effect: association in the first years of life appears to compromise marital compatibility.[4]

These findings are especially damaging to Freud, because if Westermarck is right then Oedipal theory is wrong. Freud's thinking was premised on a supposed sexual attraction between members of the same family that needs to be suppressed and sublimated. His theory would predict that unrelated boys and girls who have grown up together will marry in absolute bliss, as there is no taboo standing in the way of their primal sexual desires. In reality, however, the signs are that such marriages often end in misery. Co-reared boys and girls resist being wed, arguing that they are too much like brother and sister. The father of the bride sometimes needs to stand with a stick by the door during the wedding night to prevent the two from escaping the situation. In these marriages, sexual indifference seems to be the rule, and adultery a common outlet. As Wolf exclaimed at the conference, Westermarck may have been less flamboyant, less self-assured, and less famous than any of his mighty opponents; the fundamental difference was that he was the only one who was right!

A second victim is Lévi-Strauss, who built his position entirely on the assumption that animals lead disorderly lives in which they do whatever they please, including committing incest. We now believe, however, that monkeys and apes are subject to exactly the same inhibitory mechanism as proposed by Westermarck. Many primates prevent inbreeding through migration of one sex or the other. The migratory sex meets new, unrelated mates, while the resident sex gains genetic diversity by breeding with immigrants. In addition, close kin who stay together avoid sexual intercourse.

This was first observed in the 1950s by Kisaburo Tokuda in a group of Japanese macaques at the Kyoto Zoo. A young adult male who had risen to the top rank made full use of his sexual privileges, mating frequently with all of the females except for one: his mother.[5] This was not an isolated case; mother-son matings are strongly suppressed in all primates. Even in the sexy bonobos, this is the one partner combination in which intercourse is rare or absent. Observation of thousands of matings in a host of primates, both captive and wild, has demonstrated the suppression of incest.

The Westermarck effect serves as a showcase for Darwinian approaches to human behavior because it so clearly rests on a *combination* of nature and nurture: it has a developmental side (learned sexual aversion), an innate side (the way early familiarity affects sexual preference), a cultural side (some cultures raise unrelated children together and others raise siblings of the opposite sex apart, but most have family arrangements that automatically lead to sexual aversion among relatives), a likely evolutionary reason (suppression of inbreeding), and direct parallels with animal behavior. On top of this comes the cultural *taboo*, which is unique for our species. An unresolved issue is whether the taboo merely serves to formalize and reinforce the Westermarck effect or adds a substantially new dimension.

That Westermarck's integrated view was underappreciated at the time is understandable, as it flew in the face of the Western dualistic tradition. What is less understandable is why these dualisms remain popular today. Westermarck was more Darwinian than some contemporary evolutionary biologists, who are best described as Huxleyan.

Bulldog Bites Master

In 1893, before a large audience in Oxford, Huxley publicly tried to reconcile his dim view of the nasty natural world with the kindness occasionally encountered in human society. Huxley realized that the laws of the physical world are unalterable. He felt, however, that their impact on human existence could be softened and modified if people kept nature under control. Comparing us with the gardener who has a hard time keeping weeds out of his garden, he proposed ethics as humanity's cultural victory over the evolutionary process.[6]

This was an astounding position for two reasons. First, it deliberately curbed the explanatory power of evolution. Since many people consider morality the essence of our species, Huxley was in effect saying that what makes us human is too big for the evolutionary framework. This was a puzzling retreat by someone who had gained a reputation as "Darwin's Bulldog" owing to his fierce advocacy of evolutionary theory. The solution that Huxley proposed was quintessentially Hobbesian in that it stated that people are fit for society only by education, not nature.

Second, Huxley offered no hint whatsoever where humanity could possibly have unearthed the will and strength to go against its own nature. If we are indeed born competitors who don't care one bit about the feelings of others, how in the world did we decide to transform ourselves into model citizens? Can people for generations maintain behavior that is out of character, like a bunch of piranhas who decide to become vegetarians? How deep does such a change go? Are we the proverbial wolves in sheep's clothing: nice on the outside, nasty on the inside? What a contorted scheme!

It was the only time Huxley visibly broke with Darwin. As aptly summarized by Huxley's biographer, Adrian Desmond: "[He] was forcing his ethical Ark against the Darwinian current which had brought him so far.[7] Two decades earlier, in *The Descent of Man*, Darwin had stated the continuity between human nature and morality in no uncertain terms. The reason for Huxley's departure has been sought in his suffering at the cruel hand of nature, which had just taken his beloved daughter's life, and in his need to make the ruthlessness of the Darwinian cosmos palatable to the general public. He could do so, he felt, only by dislodging human ethics, declaring it a cultural innovation.

This dualistic outlook was to get an enormous respectability boost from Freud's writings, which throve on contrasts between the conscious and subconscious, the ego and superego, Eros and Death, and so on. As with Huxley's gardener and garden, Freud was not just dividing the world in symmetrical halves: he saw struggle everywhere! He explained the incest taboo and other moral restrictions as the result of a violent break with the freewheeling sexual life of the primal horde, culminating in the collective slaughter of an overbearing father by his sons. And he let civilization arise out of a renunciation of instinct, the gaining of control over the forces of nature, and the building of a cultural superego. Not only did he keep animals at a distance, his view also excluded women. It was the men who reached the highest peaks of civilization, carrying out tortuous sublimations "of which women are little capable."[8]

Humanity's heroic combat against forces that try to drag us down remains a dominant theme within biology today. Because of its continuity with the doctrine of original sin, I have characterized this viewpoint as "Calvinist sociobiology."[9] Let me offer a few illustrative quotations from today's two most outspoken Huxleyans.

Declaring ethics a radical break with biology, and feeling that Huxley had not gone far enough, George Williams has written extensively about the wretchedness of Mother Nature. His stance culminates in the claim that human morality is an inexplicable accident of the evolutionary process: "I account for morality as an *accidental* capability produced, in its boundless *stupidity*, by a biological process that is normally opposed to the expression of such a capability" (my italics). In a similar vein, Richard Dawkins has declared us "nicer than is good for our selfish genes," and warns that "we are never allowed to forget the narrow tightrope on which we balance above the Darwinian abyss." In a recent interview, Dawkins explicitly endorsed Huxley: "What I am saying, along with many other people, among them T. H. Huxley, is that in our political and social life we are entitled to throw out Darwinism, to say we don't want to live in a Darwinian world."[10]

Poor Darwin must be turning in his grave, because the world implied here is totally unlike what he himself envisioned. Again, what is lacking is an indication of how we can possibly negate our genes, which the same authors at other times don't hesitate to depict as all-powerful. Thus, first we are told that our genes know what is best for us, that they control our lives, programming every little wheel in the human survival machine. But then the same authors let us know that we have the option to rebel, that we are free to act differently. The obvious implication is that the first position should be taken with a grain of salt.

Like Huxley, these authors want to have it both ways: human behavior is an evolutionary product except when it is hard to explain. And like Hobbes and Freud, they think in dichotomies: we are part nature, part culture, rather than a well-integrated whole. Their position has been echoed by popularizers such as Robert Wright and Matt Ridley, who say that virtue is absent from people's hearts and souls, and that our species is potentially but not naturally moral.[11] But what about the many people who occasionally experience in themselves and others a degree of sympathy, goodness, and generosity? Wright's answer is that the "moral animal" is a fraud: "[T]he pretense of selflessness is about as much part of human nature as is its frequent absence. We dress ourselves up in tony moral language, denying base motives and stressing our at least minimal consideration for the greater good; and we fiercely and self-righteously decry selfishness in others."[12]

To explain how we manage to live with ourselves despite this travesty, theorists have called upon self-deception and denial. If people think they are at times unselfish, so the argument goes, they must be hiding the selfish motives from themselves. In other words, all of us have two agendas: one hidden in the recesses of our minds, and one that we sell to ourselves and others. Or, as philosopher Michael Ghiselin concludes, "Scratch an 'altruist,' and watch a 'hypocrite' bleed." In the ultimate twist of irony, anyone who doesn't believe that we are fooling ourselves, who feels that we may be genuinely kind, is called a wishful thinker and thus stands accused of fooling himself![13]

This entire double-agenda idea is another obvious Freudian scheme. And like a UFO sighting, it is unverifiable: hidden motives are indistinguishable from absent ones. The quasi-scientific concept of the subconscious conveniently leaves the fundamental selfishness of the human species intact despite daily experiences to the contrary.[14] I blame much of this intellectual twisting and turning on the unfortunate legacy of Huxley, about whom evolutionary biologist Ernst Mayr didn't mince any words: "Huxley, who believed in final causes, rejected natural selection and did not represent genuine Darwinian thought in any way. . . . It is unfortunate, considering how confused Huxley was, that his essay [on evolutionary ethics] is often referred to even today as if it were authoritative."[15]

Moral Emotions

Westermarck is part of a long lineage, going back to Aristotle and Thomas Aquinas, which firmly anchors morality in the natural inclinations and desires of our species. Compared to Huxley's, his is a view uncompounded by any need for invisible agendas and discrepancies between how we are and how we wish to be: morality has been there from the start. It is part and parcel of human nature.

Emotions occupy a central role in that, as Aristotle said, "Thought by itself moves nothing." Modern cognitive psychologists and neuroscientists confirm that emotions, rather than being the antithesis of rationality, greatly aid thinking. They speak of emotional intelligence. People can reason and deliberate as much as they want, but if there are no emotions attached to the various options in front of them, they will never reach a decision or conviction.[16] This is critical for moral choice, because if anything, morality involves strong convictions. These don't—or rather can't—come about through a cool Kantian rationality; they require caring about others and powerful gut feelings about right and wrong.

Westermarck discusses, one by one, a whole range of what philosophers before him used to call the "moral sentiments." He classifies the retributive emotions into those derived from resentment and anger, which seek revenge and punishment, and those that are more positive and prosocial. Whereas in his time there were few good animal examples of the moral emotions—hence his occasional reliance on Moroccan camel stories—we know now that there are many parallels in primate behavior. Thus, he discusses "forgiveness," and how the turning of the other cheek is a universally appreciated gesture: we now know from our studies that chimpanzees kiss and embrace and that monkeys groom each other after fights.[17] Westermarck sees protection of others against offenders resulting from "sympathetic resentment"; again, this is a common pattern in monkeys and apes, and in many other animals, who stick up for their friends, defending them against attackers. Similarly, the retributive kindly emotions ("desire to give pleasure in return for pleasure") have an obvious parallel in what biologists now label reciprocal altruism, such as providing assistance to those who assist in return.[18]

When I watch primates, measuring how they share food in return for grooming, comfort victims of aggression, or wait for the right opportunity to get even with a rival, I see very much the same emotional impulses that Westermarck analyzed. A group of chimpanzees, for example, may whip up an outraged chorus of barks when the dominant male overdoes his punishment of an underling, and in the wild they form cooperative hunting parties that share the spoils of their efforts. Although I shy away from calling chimpanzees "moral beings," their psychology contains many of the ingredients that, if also present in the progenitor of humans and apes, must have allowed our ancestors to develop a moral sense. Instead of seeing morality as a radically new invention, I tend to view it as a natural outgrowth of ancient social tendencies.

Westermarck was far from naïve about how morality is maintained; he knew it required both approval and negative sanctions. For example, reflecting on an issue that today we might relate to developments taking place in South Africa's Truth and Reconciliation Commission, he explains how forgiveness prohibits revenge but not punishment. Punishment is a necessary component of justice, whereas revenge—if let loose—only destroys. Like Adam Smith before him, Westermarck recognized the moderating role of sympathy: "The more the moral consciousness is influenced by sympathy, the more severely it condemns any retributive infliction of pain which it regards as undeserved."[19]

The most insightful part of his writing is perhaps where Westermarck tries to come to grips with what defines a moral emotion as moral. Here he shows that there is much more to these emotions that raw gut feeling. In analyzing these feelings he introduces the notion of "disinterestedness." Emotions, such as gratitude and resentment, directly concern one's own interests—how one has been treated or how one wishes to be treated—and hence are too egocentric to be moral. Moral emotions, in contrast, are disconnected from one's immediate situation: they deal with good and bad at a more abstract, disinterested level. It is only when we make general judgments of how *anyone* ought to be treated that we can begin to speak of moral approval and disapproval. This is an area in which humans go radically farther than other primates.[20]

Westermarck was ahead of his time, and he went well beyond Darwin's thinking on these matters. In spirit, however, the two were on the same line. Darwin believed that there was plenty of room within his theory to accommodate the origins of morality, and he attached great importance to the capacity for sympathy. He by no means excluded animals from this view: "Many animals certainly sympathize with each other's distress or danger."[21] He has been proven right; laboratory experiments on monkeys and even rats have shown powerful vicarious distress responses. The sight of a conspecific in pain or trouble often calls forth a reaction to ameliorate the situation. These reactions undoubtedly derived from parental care, in which vulnerable individuals are tended with great care, but in many animals they stretch well beyond this situation, including relations among unrelated adults.[22]

Darwin did not see any conflict between the harshness of the evolutionary process and the gentleness of some of its products. As discussed in the previous chapter with regard to the distinction between motive and function, all one needs to do is make a distinction between how evolution operates and the actual psychologies it has produced. Darwin knew this better than anyone, expressing his views most clearly when he emphasized continuity with animals even in the moral domain. In *The Descent of Man*, he takes exactly the opposite position of those who, like Huxley, view morality as a violation of evolutionary principles: "Any animal whatever, endowed with well-marked social instincts, the parental and filial affections being here included, would inevitably acquire a moral sense or conscience, as soon as its intellectual powers had become as well developed, or nearly as well developed, as in man."[23]

The *Ke* Willow

There is never much new under the sun. Westermarck's emphasis on the retributive emotions, whether friendly or vengeful, reminds one of Confucius' reply to the question whether there is any single word that may serve as prescription for all of one's life. Confucius proposed "reciprocity" as such a word. Reciprocity is also, of course, the crux of the Golden Rule ("Do unto others as you would have them do unto you"), which remains unsurpassed as a summary of human morality.

A follower of the Chinese sage, Mencius, wrote extensively about human goodness during his life, from 372 to 289 B.C.[24] Mencius lost his father when he was only three, and his mother made sure he received the best possible education. The mother is at least as well known as her son, and still serves as a maternal model to the Chinese for her absolute devotion.

Called the "second sage" because of his great influence, Mencius had a revolutionary bent in that he stressed the obligation of rulers to provide for the common people. Recorded on bamboo clappers and handed down to his descendants and their students, his writings show that the debate about whether we are naturally moral, or not, is ancient indeed. In one exchange, Mencius reacts against Kaou Tsze's views, which are strikingly similar to Huxley's gardener and garden metaphor: "Man's nature is like the *ke* willow, and righteousness is like a cup or a bowl. The fashioning of benevolence and righteousness out of man's nature is like the making of cups and bowls from the *ke* willow."[25]

Mencius replied:

> Can you, leaving untouched the nature of the willow, make with it cups and bowls? You must do violence and injury to the willow, before you can make cups and bowls with it. If you must do violence and injury to the willow, before you can make cups and bowls with it, *on your principles* you must in

the same way do violence and injury to humanity in order to fashion from it benevolence and righteousness! Your words alas! would certainly lead all men on to reckon benevolence and righteousness to be calamities.

Evidently, the origins of human kindness and ethics were a point of debate in the China of two millennia ago. Mencius believed that humans tend toward the good as naturally as water flows downhill. This is also evident from the following remark, in which he seeks to exclude the possibility of a double agenda on the grounds that the moral emotions, such as sympathy, leave little room for this:

> When I say that all men have a mind which cannot bear to see the suffering of others, my meaning may be illustrated thus: even nowadays, if men suddenly see a child about to fall into a well, they will without exception experience a feeling of alarm and distress. They will feel so, not as a ground on which they may gain the favor of the child's parents, nor as a ground on which they may seek the praise of their neighbors and friends, nor from a dislike to the reputation of having been unmoved by such a thing. From this case we may perceive that the feeling of commiseration is essential to man.

Mencius' example is strikingly similar to both the one by Westermarck ("Can we help sympathize with our friends?") and Smith's famous definition of sympathy ("How selfish soever man may be supposed to be . . ."). The central idea underlying all three statements is that distress at the sight of another's pain is an impulse over which we exert no control: it grabs us instantaneously, like a reflex, leaving us without the time to weigh the pros and cons. Remarkably, all of the alternative motives that Mencius considers occur in the modern literature, usually under the heading of reputation building. The big difference is, of course, that Mencius rejects these explanations as too contrived given the immediacy and force of the sympathetic response. Manipulation of public opinion is entirely possible at other times, he says, but not at the moment a child falls into a well.

I couldn't agree more. Evolution has produced species that follow genuinely cooperative impulses. I don't know whether people are, deep down, good or evil, but I do know that to believe that each and every move is selfishly calculated overestimates human mental powers, let alone those of other animals.[26]

Interesting additional evidence comes from child research. Freud, B. F. Skinner, and Jean Piaget all believed that the child learns its first moral distinctions through fear of punishment and a desire for praise. Like Huxleyan biologists who see morality as culturally imposed upon a nasty human nature, they conceived morality as coming from the outside, imposed by adults upon a passive, naturally selfish child. Children were thought to adopt parental values to construct a superego, the moral agency of the self.

Left to their own devices, like the children in William Golding's *Lord of the Flies*, they would never arrive at anything even close to morality.

Already at an early age, however, children know the difference between moral principles ("Do not steal") and cultural conventions ("No pajamas at school"). They apparently appreciate that the breaking of certain rules distresses and harms others, whereas the breaking of other rules merely violates expectations about what is appropriate. Their attitudes don't seem to be based purely on reward and punishment. Whereas pediatric handbooks still depict young children as self-centered monsters, we know now that by one year of age they spontaneously comfort people in distress, and that soon thereafter they begin to develop a moral perspective through interactions with other members of their species.[27]

Rather than being nicer than is good for our genes, we may be just nice enough. Thus, the child is not going against its own nature by developing a caring, moral attitude, and civil society is not like an out-of-control garden subdued by a sweating gardener. We are merely following evolved tendencies.

How refreshingly simple!   ■

NOTES FOR "SURVIVAL OF THE KINDEST"

1. In the 1975 Christmas season, millions of Americans spent five dollars each to purchase ordinary rocks as pets. The rocks were sold in boxes with air holes and came with a manual explaining how to train the rock to roll over, to play dead, and to protect its owner. Tamagotchi is a popular Japanese electronic gadget that mimics a chick. It eats, sleeps, defecates, gets cranky, and beeps for attention. If the owner does not take care of it, Tamagotchi dies.

2. Wrangham and Peterson (1996). Playing with "dolls" is not unusual in nonhuman primates. I have seen young chimpanzees in captivity act the same as Kakama with a piece of cloth or a broom. A wild mountain gorilla was seen to pull up a mass of soft moss, which she carried and held like an infant under her chest, cuddling and "nursing" it (Byrne, 1995).

3. Darwin (1859).

4. Quoted from an interview by Roes (1998).

5. Also, let us not forget that many people volunteer to adopt children—some even kidnap newborns from the maternity ward—following urges that evidently transcend genetic self-interest.

6. See Chapter 1 ("The Whole Animal").

7. Reported in *The Jerusalem Post*, July 26, 1996.

8. De Waal and Aureli (1996).

9. Ladygina-Kohts (in press).

10. Kunz and Allgaier (1994).

11. Jewell (1997).

12. Whittemore and Hebard (1995).

13. Whittemore and Hebard (1995).

NOTES FOR "DOWN WITH DUALISM"

1. Westermarck (1912).

2. de Waal and Luttrell (1988) and Aureli et al. (1992).

3. For recent debate about evolutionary ethics, see the *Journal of Consciousness Studies*, vol. 7 (1–2), edited by L. D. Katz (2000).

4. Wolf (1995). Others before him studied marriages in Israeli kibbutzim and found that children do not have sexual intercourse, let alone marry unrelated children of the opposite sex with whom they have grown up in the same peer group (reviewed by Wolf, 1995).

5. Tokuda (1961–62).

6. Huxley (1894).

7. Desmond (1994).

8. Freud (1913, 1930).

9. de Waal (1996a). See also Flack and de Waal (2000).

10. Williams quoted in Roes (1998), Dawkins in *Times Literary Supplement* (November 29, 1996), and Dawkins in another interview by Roes (1997). The profound irony, of course, is that contrary to Dawkins's warning against a Darwinian world, such a world is eminently more livable than a Huxleyan one, which is devoid of natural moral tendencies. Dawkins seems almost a reincarnation of Huxley in terms of both combativeness (e.g., Dawkins, 1998) and his departure from Darwinism. Such notions as that we are survival machines, that we are born selfish and need to be taught kindness, and especially that morality and biology are miles apart were alien to Darwin yet typical of Huxley. Darwin never looked at any life form as a machine. He had a Lorenz-like rapport with animals and didn't shy away from attributing intentions and emotions to them. Crist (1999) discusses at length Darwin's anthropomorphism, which has irritated some scholars, but confirms that those with an integrated view of nature don't necessarily have a problem with it (see also Chapter 1, "The Whole Animal"). Given their differences of opinion, Darwin couldn't resist referring, in his final letter to Huxley, to the latter's depiction of all living things (including humans) as machines: "I wish to God there were more automata in the world like you." (Cited in Crist, 1999).

11. In view of their cynical positions, the titles of the books by Wright (*The Moral Animal*) and Ridley (*The Origins of Virtue*) don't exactly cover their message (Wright, 1994; Ridley, 1996).

12. Wright (1994).

13. Sober and Wilson (1998) write about this accusation: "We feel we should address a criticism that is often leveled at advocates of altruism in psychology and group selection in biology. It is frequently said that people endorse such hypotheses because they *want* the world to be a friendly and hospitable place. The defenders of egoism and individualism who advance this criticism thereby pay themselves a compliment; they pat themselves on the back for staring reality squarely in the face. Egoists and individualists are objective, they suggest, whereas proponents of altruism and group selection are trapped by a comforting illusion."

14. Ideas about the subconscious and its evolutionary *raison d'être* have been around since Badcock (1986) and Alexander (1987). The first explicitly sought to provide Freudian-Darwinian solutions to the "problem" of altruism.

15. Mayr (1997).

16. Damasio (1994).

17. Aureli and de Waal (2000).

18. Westermarck lists moral approval as a kind of retributive kindly emotion, hence as a component of reciprocal altruism. These views antedate discussions about "indirect reciprocity" and reputation building in the modern literature on evolutionary ethics (e.g., Alexander, 1987).

19. Smith (1759).

20. These reflections by Westermarck parallel Smith's (1759) idea of an "impartial spectator."

21. Darwin (1871).

22. Reviewed by Preston and de Waal (in press).

23. Darwin (1871).

24. This makes Mencius a contemporary of Aristotle—born 384 B.C. in Greece—the first and foremost Western philosopher to root morality in human biology (Arnhart, 1998).

25. All quotations are from Mencius (372–289 B.C.), *The Works of Mencius.*

26. See Chapter 10 ("Survival of the Kindest"), which also contains the full quotation from Smith.

27. Killen and de Waal (2000).

REFERENCES

Alexander, R. A. (1987). *The Biology of Moral Systems.* New York: Aldine de Gruyter.

Arnhart, L. (1998). *Darwinian Natural Right: The Biological Ethics of Human Nature.* Albany, N.Y.: SUNY Press.

Aureli, F., Cozzolino, R., Cordischi, C., and Scucchi, S. (1992). Kin-oriented redirection among Japanese macaques: An expression of a revenge system? *Animal Behaviour* 44: 283–291.

Aureli, F., and de Waal, F. B. M. (2000). *Natural Conflict Resolution.* Berkeley: University of California Press.

Badcock, C. R. (1986). *The Problem of Altruism: Freudian-Darwinian Solutions.* Oxford, England: Blackwell.

Crist, E. (1999). *Images of Animals: Anthropomorphism and Animal Mind.* Philadelphia: Temple University Press.

Damasio, A. R. (1994). *Descartes' Error: Emotion, Reason, and the Human Brain.* New York: Putnam.

Darwin, C. (1964 [1859]). *On the Origin of Species.* Cambridge, Mass.: Harvard University Press.

Darwin, C. (1981 [1871]). *The Descent of Man, and Selection in Relation to Sex.* Princeton, N.J.: Princeton University Press.

Dawkins, R. (1998). *Unweaving the Rainbow: Science, Delusion and the Appetite for Wonder.* New York: Houghton Mifflin.

Desmond, A. (1994). *Huxley: From Devil's Disciple to Evolution's High Priest.* New York: Perseus.

Flack, J. C., and de Waal, F. B. M. (2000). "Any animal whatever": Darwinian building blocks of morality in monkeys and apes. *Journal of Consciousness Studies* 7 (1–2): 1–29.

Freud, S. (1989 [1913]). *Totem and Taboo.* New York: Norton.

Freud, S. (1989 [1930]). *Civilization and Its Discontents.* New York: Norton.

Huxley, T. H. (1989 [1894]). *Evolution and Ethics*. Princeton, N.J.: Princeton University Press.

Jewell, D. (July 14, 1997). Brave hearts. *People*.

Killen, M., and de Waal, F. B. M. (2000). The evolution and development of morality. In F. Aureli and F. B. M. de Waal (eds.), *Natural Conflict Resolution*, pp. 352–372. Berkeley: University of California Press.

Kunz, T. H., and Allgaier, A. L. (1994). Allomaternal care: Helper-assisted birth in the Rodrigues fruit bat, *Pteropus rodricensis. J. Zool., London* 232: 691–700.

Ladygina-Kohts, N. N. (in press). *Infant Chimpanzee and Human Child* (F. B. M. de Waal, ed.). New York: Oxford University Press.

Mayr, E. (1997). *This is Biology: The Science of the Living World*. Cambridge, Mass.: Belknap.

Mencius (372–289 B.C.). *The Works of Mencius*. English transl. Gu Lu. Shanghai: Shangwu Publishing House.

Preston, S. D., and de Waal, F. B. M. (in press). The communication of emotions and the possibility of empathy in animals. In *Altruistic Love: Science, Philosophy, and Religion in Dialogue*. Oxford, England: Oxford University Press.

Ridley, M. (1996). *The Origins of Virtue*. London: Viking.

Roes, F. (1998). A conversation with George C. Williams. *Natural History* 5: 10–15.

Smith, A. (1937 [1759]). *A Theory of Moral Sentiments*. New York: Modern Library.

Sober, E., and David Wilson, D. S. (1998). *Unto Others: The Evolution and Psychology of Unselfish Behavior*. Cambridge, Mass.: Harvard University Press.

Tokuda, K. (1961–62). A study of sexual behavior in the Japanese monkey. *Primates* 3(2): 1–40.

de Waal, F. B. M. (1996a). *Good Natured*. Cambridge, Mass.: Harvard University Press.

de Waal, F. B. M., and Aureli, F. (1996). Consolation, reconciliation, and a possible cognitive difference between macaque and chimpanzee. In A. E. Russon, K. A. Bard, and S. T. Parker (eds.), *Reaching into Thought: The Minds of the Great Apes*, pp. 80–110. Cambridge, England: Cambridge University Press.

de Waal, F. B. M., and Luttrell, L. M. (1988). Mechanisms of social reciprocity in three primate species: symmetrical relationship characteristics or cognition? *Ethology and Sociobiology* 9: 101–118.

Westermarck, E. (1912). *The Origin and Development of the Moral Ideas*, vol. 1. London: Macmillan.

Whittemore, H., and Hebard, C. (1995). *So That Others May Live*. New York: Bantam.

Wolf, A. P. (1995). *Sexual Attraction and Childhood Association: A Chinese Brief for Edward Westermarck*. Stanford, Calif.: Stanford University Press.

Wrangham, R. W., and Peterson, D. (1996). *Demonic Males: Apes and the Evolution of Human Aggression*. Boston: Houghton Mifflin.

Wright, R. (1994). *The Moral Animal; The New Science of Evolutionary Psychology*. New York: Pantheon.

■ *QUESTIONS FOR MAKING CONNECTIONS WITHIN THE READING* ■

1. In "Survival of the Kindest," Frans de Waal distinguishes between "functional altruism" and "intended kindness." In "Down with Dualism," he

looks at the difference between "emotions" and "moral emotions." Using examples from your own experience, define these key terms. What relationships do you see between these terms? Is altruism, for example, "an emotion"?

2. Why does de Waal find the animal exhibit in Lop Buri to be "absurd"? What kind of animal exhibit would best represent his understanding of the essential characteristics that have governed evolution in the animal kingdom?

3. What evidence does de Waal present to support his belief that nature is governed by "survival of the kindest"? How does his evidence differ from the evidence offered by those who believe that nature is governed by "survival of the fittest?"

■ *QUESTIONS FOR WRITING* ■

1. de Waal concludes "Survival of the Kindest" with a description of the animal kingdom that is bound to shock some readers: he describes dogs who became "depressed" when exposed to a great deal of death; he discusses a strategy meant to help the dogs recover their "emotional investment" in helping others; finally, he concludes with the assertion that there are species of animals who intend to do good deeds. What would change if de Waal were right? That is, what would the consequences be if de Waal's account of the evolutionary value of kindness replaced the dominant account of evolution as the arena of "survival of the fittest"? Is de Waal's revision of the evolution narrative simply an academic matter, or does it have social, cultural, and spiritual ramifications?

2. As de Waal sees it, Westermarck's ideas were ignored because they "flew in the face of the Western dualistic tradition." What is this tradition and why would one want to work in some other tradition? What is de Waal's relationship to this tradition? If those who live in the West can't escape or avoid this tradition, what other relationships might they have to it?

■ *QUESTIONS FOR MAKING CONNECTIONS BETWEEN READINGS* ■

1. "Down with Dualism" concludes with de Waal's assertion "that distress at the sight of another's pain is an impulse over which we exert no control." In "The Wreck of Time," Annie Dillard reflects on major events in the last millennium, including great tragedies that involved the deaths of untold numbers of innocent victims. Do the stories that Dillard has to tell support de Waal's argument about nature or Huxley's? If "moral emotions" are part of the genetic makeup of humans, then how can we account for the

disasters that Dillard describes? And how do we account for the fact that some, perhaps including Dillard, feel so little distress at learning about the pain others have experienced?

2. In making his argument for an alternate explanation of the evolutionary process, de Waal relies on the work of Edward Westermarck, who believed that "human goodness" was part of our genetic makeup. If de Waal and Westermarck are correct, how does one account for the changes in human society that Peter Drucker describes in "The Age of Social Transformation"? That is, what are we to make of the fact that the "knowledge society" has evolved apparently, according to Drucker, at the expense of the social sector?

For additional suggestions about making connections between readings, visit the Link-O-Mat and More Sample Assignments at <www.newhum.com>.

JAN WILLIS

WHILE COMPLETING HER Bachelor's Degree in Philosophy at Cornell University in the 1960s, Jan Willis found herself pulled in two directions: on the one hand, having lived in fear of the Ku Klux Klan where she grew up in Alabama, she was drawn to the revolutionary politics of the Black Panthers; on the other hand, after traveling to Nepal in her junior year, she was taken with the possibility of learning more about Tibetan Buddhism. Now that value systems travel around the globe as easily as passengers do, how does one decide which values to embrace? And now that tradition has become dynamic and everchanging, how does one decide which tradition to claim as one's own? How does one decide between becoming a Black Panther or a Buddhist? These are the questions that have animated Willis's life, and they are the questions that are at the heart of her most recent book, *Dreaming Me: An African American Woman's Spiritual Journey* (2001).

Having resolved in the end to follow the contemplative path, Willis returned to a monastery in Nepal, where she found herself the only woman among sixty monks being trained in Tibetan Buddhism. And now, some thirty years later, after completing her doctorate at Columbia University in Indic and Buddhist Studies, Willis is a professor of religion and the Walter A. Crowell Professor of the Social Sciences at Wesleyan University. As a scholar and as a practitioner, Willis has committed herself to making the value of Buddhism more evident to people of all races. As the passages from *Dreaming Me* included here demonstrate, Willis believes that this spiritual practice has much to offer those who seek peace in troubled times, particularly African Americans trying to find relief from the despair and rage that are the legacy of slavery in the United States. Willis remains attracted to the contemplative life because, as she puts it, "Buddhism is a come-and-see model. Meditation is the path. You don't have to accept dogma. You have to spend time on the cushion."

Willis, Jan. "Decision Time: A 'Piece' or Peace?," "This, Too, Is Buddha's Mind," and "My Great Seal Retreat." *Dreaming Me: An African American Woman's Spiritual Journey.* New York: Riverhead Books, 2001. 124–129, 155–158, 211–226.

Biographical information from Nadya Labi, "Of Color and The Cushion," *Time.Com Spiritual Innovators Series* <http://www.time.com/time/innovators/spirituality/profile_willis.html> and Jan Willis's home page at Wesleyan University; quotation from Nadya Labi, "Of Color and The Cushion," *Time.Com Spiritual Innovators Series.*

To learn more about Jan Willis, the Black Panthers, and Buddhism, visit the Link-O-Mat at <www.newhum.com>.

＿＿

Selections from
Dreaming Me

Decision Time: A "Piece" or Peace?

I had already made up my mind to return to Nepal after leaving Cornell when I picked up a copy of *Time* magazine and read the story about Fred Hampton's tragic death. As they slept in an apartment at 2337 W. Monroe Street in Chicago, he and another of his comrades had been shot to death. The pictures of the room showed blood-splattered walls and bodies lying in disarray. I had personally met Fred Hampton earlier that same year when he had given a talk at the University of Wisconsin. Now, that young warrior was dead. The photos churned my stomach. Against guns, we had no chance.

During the summer and early fall of 1969, I had had to make the most important decision of my life: whether to join the Black Panther party or return to the Tibetan Buddhist monastery in Nepal. After the experience at Cornell, I was convinced that as a thinking black person in this country, I was left no choice but to join the party; to lay my life on the line for my beliefs and for my people's freedom. Making the choice troubled my every waking moment and invaded my nights.

After graduation I had agreed to a job as a teaching assistant for a philosophy course at Cornell. It was a way to earn income and a place to live after school. I took an apartment just at the edge of Cornell's Collegetown. As summer's end approached, I met one of my former professors to say good-bye. He asked about my future plans, and I told him they weren't decided but that I was considering the two alternatives of Panther party or Nepal. In a matter of days, he had arranged a luncheon for me with my thesis advisor, himself, and the dean of the college. At that meeting, the three men made me a unique offer: if I chose to, I would be admitted to graduate studies in philosophy at Cornell *and* I'd be granted my first year there, *in absentia*. In short, I could return to the monastery in Nepal at Cornell's expense, with a University Traveling Fellowship.

Before that, however, when I'd participated in the Straight takeover, one of the men brought in from outside had given me the name of a key contact with the Panther party in Oakland, California. If I was serious about my commitment to revolution, he'd said, I had better have a meeting with this man. I felt that I had to follow through and check out this path, this choice, as well.

At summer's end I hitchhiked across the country with Rand and Rob. On the way, we stopped off to visit other hippie and politico friends. One of our stops was at the University of Wisconsin in Madison. There we were told to check out the campus lecture one evening that was being given by Fred Hampton, the head of the Chicago Black Panthers. Flanked on either side by my friends, I marched into the lecture hall proudly sporting my tall Afro. The three of us were strangers there, and we could tell that among some of the students, there was speculation going on about our identity. At such moments, I felt proud that I might actually be thought already to be a Black Panther. Several students moved over and offered us seats up front.

On the stage, two young Panthers stood at attention, clothed all in black, wearing leather jackets and berets. Fred Hampton was introduced. I was surprised that he was so young; I think only nineteen at the time. He was tall and eloquent, delivering a flawlessly rousing speech. He mentioned that as a child he had stuttered very badly but that watching and listening to Panther party members had inspired him to work on improving his speech so that, now, he could speak like the best of them. It was a moving revelation. The Chicago chapter of the Black Panther party provided free school meals and health facilities for inner-city blacks and other poor. For me, Hampton represented the promise of a better future—through pride and confident action.

After the speech I was invited to join with Hampton and members of the all-black radical student alliance for a reception. When I was introduced to Hampton as being from Cornell, Fred said to me, "Hello, sister. You guys saw some action at Cornell. Yeah . . . I guess you know how to use your piece. Glad to meet you." His handshake was warm and firm, his smile infectious. At that moment, I felt genuinely close to him. I knew, however, that I had *just* learned how to use a "piece" very recently when Mack had taught me how to shoot a rifle just after the Straight stand-off. I also knew that I did not look forward *ever* to having to demonstrate that particular ability. In fact, I now recognized that I was scared to death of guns, preferring peace much more than a piece.

Shortly after Rand, Rob, and I arrived in California, we had another fortunate meeting. We were looking for a friend of theirs who lived somewhere on Mt. Tamalpais. As we climbed the mountain roads on foot, a rain began to fall, gently at first and then more freely. At one house, we saw a petite young woman, red-haired and freckle-faced, doing something or other on a raised deck. We asked if she knew the person, and rather surprisingly, she said she didn't know anyone at all in the area or anything about the place itself. Noting the weather, she told us that if we didn't find him, we should feel free to return and come in from the rain. We had no luck locating the friend, so shortly afterward, we took her up on her offer.

She met us at the door with a large plate of sliced oranges and several marijuana cigarettes rolled in brown wrappers. We settled in to a pleasant and, as always, political conversation. Her own story left me spellbound. She'd been offered this house as a refuge and respite before she had to begin serving a three-and-a-half-year prison sentence in Washington State for encouraging draft resisters. The house, she said, belonged to an artist famous for his anti-American political posters. We knew his name and one of his posters in particular: a graphic portrayal of several police officers gang-raping the Statue of Liberty.

It turned out that this diminutive woman also personally knew the Black Panther party contact person I was supposed to meet in Oakland. She said there had been recent rumblings about his abusive tactics with female Panther party members. Just as had been the case at Cornell, black women were to keep in the background; they were to be the black man's natural complement, but they were not to take any leadership positions. Yet at Cornell, in spite of being a black female, I had tasted power. The leadership had consisted of eight seniors, seven men and myself. There I had been in charge of women's safety. Though I admired the Panthers' cause, I did not want to have to be a doormat in the background. In a certain sense the power dynamics that operated in society separating blacks and whites were being duplicated here all over again between black men and women. All this information added to my confusion about the decision I faced.

Every place we went in California, we saw newspaper photos of Huey Newton and other Black Panthers brandishing shotguns on the steps of the Sacramento State Capitol. Everywhere I looked, this brazenly militant movement seemed my only alternative. The images and rhetoric of the Black Panthers pervaded all conversations. Many a morning I woke up in a cold sweat.

Unrelenting questions pummeled my mind: Was I ready to be shot and killed by Alameda County police? Was I ready to serve a prison term like the one that freckled-faced girl at Mt. Tamalpais was awaiting? Would any of my activities really help to turn things around in this country? No matter, wasn't it time to stand up? Wasn't it time to stop pleading for justice and to take up a gun and demand it? A piece or peace? The questions literally shook my mind. I walked around with a constant fever and a buzzing in my head. The closer we got to Oakland, the more the questions tormented me.

My choices could not have been farther apart, and no assurances of success were offered by either. I had always been a good girl, eager to please. I had always shunned the limelight, knowing since early childhood that conspicuousness brings with it danger. It was not in my nature to desire to fight back; the day the Klan showed up, I had wanted to talk. I sought the more peaceful path. Though I thought it seemed awfully cowardly on my part, I could not see myself standing defiantly on the statehouse steps brandishing a shotgun. I talk to myself a lot. The real truth was that I was scared, scared down to my bones.

Right then in California there was a fractional war within the Panther party. Though the Northern wing, headed by Huey Newton and Bobby Seal, got all the notoriety, a Southern branch out of L.A. was busy trying to disseminate information in written form. Huey had dubbed them the "Paper Panthers." I didn't know how to contact the folk in the South. If I had, perhaps I might have decided differently. But it seemed to me that my only choice was between this Northern faction of the Panthers and Nepal.

I was, and am, a Pisces, always deliberating between choices. I knew that either of these choices would freak out my family. I did not want to worry them, but I had to do something. Amid the revolutionary timbre of the times, I was tossed and pushed along, it seemed inevitably, toward guns and violence. But then, just before taking that fateful step, I bolted. My whole being—mind, body, and soul—bolted. And even though doing so made me feel like a coward and chicken-shit deserter, I had to turn away from it.

True, I had learned to shoot a piece. I had even helped deliver guns to the Straight when I had to. But I had also marched, nonviolently amid violence, in Birmingham with King. And I had wanted to talk with those Klan folk who'd burned a cross in front of our house. "To thine own self be true," the saying goes, and my sister, San, had always said, "Trust your *first mind*." I decided not to meet with the Panthers.

I didn't know where the path of Buddhism would ultimately take me, but it seemed to offer at least the possibility of peaceful transformation. I told myself that it offered the best opportunity for clarity—about personal as well as political strategies. Now that I had made that westward journey, turning eastward seemed the best and most viable alternative. I took a deep breath. I felt calmer than I had in months. I picked up the phone to call that professor at Cornell. I would go back to Nepal.

Only a few months passed before I saw the article about Hampton's death. My heart was saddened to think of him, cut down in his shining prime. But I had made the right decision.

This, Too, Is Buddha's Mind

Randy and Robbie, with Zina's help, had managed to secure lodging with a Nepalese family—the Bahadurs—right on the other side of the hill where Lama's fledgling Kopan monastery was housed. I was living in Bodhanath, in the Gelukpa Monastery there. Though my own situation was an exceptionally generous arrangement, made possible by Lobsang Chonjor and the other monks at the monastery, I had to admit that I was pretty envious of Rand and Rob's arrangement so near to our main teacher. I had to walk over an hour up the rugged sandy road to Kopan to spend time with Lama Yeshe, whereas for them only a quick jaunt separated them from Lama Yeshe's establishment.

The Behadur family had welcomed Rand and Rob with open arms in spite of the fact that, being Hindus themselves, they were pretty suspicious of the Buddhists living on top of the hill. In fact, once the deal to house Rand and Rob was reached, the Bahadurs had actually divided their own tiny mud-brick house into two equal parts. With lightning speed, they installed new walls on both stories and reshuffled all eleven members of their family—Laxman and his brother, their parents, wives, and five children—into one side, giving the other side over to Rand and Rob. Randy's outgoingness aided in the Bahadurs' ready acceptance of them. The extra rupees, curiosity, and sincere openness of the Bahadurs to this new friendship helped as well. Rob, too, was happy to be at long last living in Nepal.

But the trek from Bodhanath up to Kopan often took its toll on me. So sometimes, after a long and usually very fruitful day of teachings and meals with Lama Yeshe, I'd spend the night at Rand and Rob's place. This required an adjustment from my more private space at Bodhanath. Life at the Bahadurs' was fully communal. Everything happened in the tiny mud-caked courtyard out in front of their house. The family's big water buffalo lived in its own hut just at the corner of the yard, and Laxman's two sons brought in freshly cut grass to feed it. The brother's wives were usually carrying cut grass, or spreading corn to dry, or pounding the family's wash on the rocks nearby. The three of us sat on the one-step porch watching these various activities and trying to speak Nepali. Often Laxman brought puffed rice or popped corn to us, and with all the family peering and laughing, we sat together. Several times during those early months, the family tried to get me to eat and drink the flimsy yogurt substance known as *bigotie* they'd painstakingly produced. "Just try a little," they'd urge. Rand and Rob had no problem with the thin sour stuff, but I didn't like yogurt of the more substantial variety even in the States, and I found this form even more repugnant. I was uneasy in the public environment.

One morning after spending the night there, I woke up a little late. Rand and Rob had already gone downstairs, probably, I thought, to do their morning bathroom ritual out in the field behind the Bahadurs' house. I was determined to do the new sitting meditation Lama Yeshe had recently given us. Rolling out of my sleeping bag onto the smooth mud-caked floor, I quickly reshuffled the bag to form a cushion and began my meditation. Only a minute or two went by before great plumes of heavy smoke began filling up the whole of the second floor. Feeling that I was about to suffocate to death, I ran down and out of the house into the tiny courtyard out front, coughing and gagging. I stumbled right past Randy, who was fanning the hearth in an attempt to start a fire for breakfast. I was furious. From the courtyard, I shouted back inside to her, "What the hell are you doing? Didn't you know I was trying to meditate?" With a nervous chuckle, Rand began to make some reply. I didn't hear her because I was racing up the slick footpath away from the two of them, away from the Bahadurs, who'd come running out at all the commotion, and away from my remarkably insensitive and inconsiderate so-called friends.

At the crest, just where the footpath broke out onto the sunny side of the hill, stood Lama Yeshe. With my head down and in my fury, I almost knocked him over. "Good morning!" he said cheerfully. "How is your meditation going?" This was Lama's typical greeting to each of us. Usually whenever he asked it, always gently smiling, we melted into smiles ourselves.

But this time, nothing doing. "I cannot work with these people, Lama! I will not work with them! Randy just built a fire under my meditation. She knew I was meditating. I don't want to be friends with them anymore!"

With a broad smile, he asked, "But aren't the three of you going into town later today?" The question stopped me. Hadn't he heard what I was just saying? I asked him, "Lama, you are very kind and compassionate, but didn't you just hear me? I don't think the three of us can be friends anymore."

"You *are* friends," he said, "and friends for life. More important, you three are *Chos-ru*, Dharma sisters and brothers. You will feel differently later." My body bristled. Then, stepping forward and looking deep into my eyes, he whispered, "Sometimes, when anger rises up so forcefully, it's good to say to yourself, 'Buddha's mind is angry today.'" Because of the way he told me this, as though it were a secret teaching just between the two of us, I listened. The suggestion that *my* mind, even filled with anger, was also the Buddha's mind brought a big smile to my face. My body began to release its tension. Then, almost abruptly, Lama turned away and continued his morning stroll down the sunny side of the footpath. Over his shoulder, he said softly, "Don't forget your town trip." I was never able to look at myself the same way again. And of course, I went to town with my two best friends.

I had come to Lama Yeshe loaded down with guilt, shame, anger, and a feeling of utter helplessness. I couldn't think or see past the rage I felt from the untold indignities I'd experienced in life prior to meeting him. Such anger had crippled me in countless ways and had almost sent me down the path of violence. Yet wounds like mine had a flip side too, a false and prideful view of entitlement: Look at all that I've endured. I'm great. In time, Lama Yeshe would find a way to pull the rug out from under this pride.

My Great Seal Retreat

He did not mean the sea mammal of that name. Lama Yeshe was offering me the chance to try out the advanced system of tantric meditation perfected by Tibetan yogic masters who had quickly attained enlightenment by using it. It was the early summer of 1981. I had been living in Nepal for a year and a half. I had gone there on a National Endowment for the Humanities fellowship to work primarily on collecting the oral histories of certain living Tibetans. But first Lama Yeshe had asked me to translate the lives of some of the early Gelukpa saints who had gained full enlightenment very quickly. These particular practitioners had followed the meditative instructions developed by Tsongkhapa, the founder of the Gelukpa school. His system was known either as the Ganden Oral Tradition or the Gelukpa Mahamudra, though the great yogi Milarepa had first brought prominence to the method.

Mahamudra means "Great Seal" or "Great Gesture," referring both to the subtle shift, or gesture, of the mind, which ushers in enlightenment, and to the badge or "seal" of this attainment. For more than a year I had worked on the translations Lama wanted, which became the basis of my book *Enlightened Beings*. Now, I planned to get on with my oral history work.

Though the translation work had been challenging, as well as inspiring, it had never crossed my mind to try out the grueling methods of the Great Seal tradition. For example, one of its practitioners, a sage named Jampel Gyatso, had chosen to sustain himself while he meditated for almost three years by eating only tiny pills fashioned from crushed juniper berries mixed with mud. Another, Gyelwa Ensapa, had continued his strenuous practices even while his body was being ravished by smallpox. Even though by 1981 I had been doing some meditations for about twelve years, the commitment required to tackle Great Seal practices seemed to me almost superhuman.

Lama Yeshe was preparing to leave Nepal for a tour abroad that would begin in Australia and keep him away from Nepal for the remainder of my stay there. One day he asked me, in quite a serious tone, "Don't you want to know what the system these people practiced was like? I mean, don't you want to *try it yourself?*"

One part of me was flattered. The other part of me was scared. Immediately I thought, "Right. Does he really think that *I* would actually sample anything so lofty as the practices that had ensured these men enlightenment?" I had meditated a bit during the years I'd known Lama—had even had some pretty good results—but this was serious stuff and a big commitment. I didn't think I was ready or brave enough to undertake it. My response to Lama Yeshe's offer came out of my mouth with far too little reflection. It was a cowardly and knee-jerk response. I said, "No. Thank you, Lama, but *no way!*" He looked a bit stunned.

"Why, daughter, wouldn't you want to try something so wonderful?" I said, with emphasis, "Thank you, Lama. I am happy you'd consider introducing me to such mysteries, but I don't think I'm ready." Probably sensing my fear, his response then was compassionate and gentle: "Well, think about it, dear. Think about it." When he turned toward other activities, I left the monastery and literally ran down the hill away from Kopan.

All the way home, his offer stayed with me. I had been translating the lives of these saints for a year. I had studied other *nam-thar*, or "liberation life stories," for many years before. These were exceptional practitioners. Devout from the beginning, committed to the Dharma until the end. I didn't think I could practice like they had. I didn't have the will, the determination. I was chicken, right down to my toes.

Moreover, those Great Seal practitioners had felt the great Mahayana wish to liberate all beings from suffering from the time they had issued from their mothers' wombs. I wasn't sure I wanted to save all sentient beings. I surprised myself with that thought. In a flood of emotions, all the hesitations and doubts I had previously only thought about regarding Buddhist renunciation, about giving up everything in order to help others, came rising up. One thing seemed certain: I did not possess it. Could it actually be that I liked suffering too much? And then, I didn't know what to expect from the practice. I was afraid I might end up in some strange place, like Castaneda's Itxalan, catatonic and alone. I was afraid that I might actually *succeed*, and thereby *lose* myself. These fears surfaced all together and at once. I was a wreck by the time I reached home.

I tried, with no success, to have a restful afternoon. In spite of my fears, there was something so tantalizing about Lama Yeshe's offer. I knew it would be stupid to let it slip away. "Be brave," a stray thought encouraged me. "Be a Buddhist, girl! Here's a chance to really practice. Put your actions where all your study and thinking has been. Answer Lama with your heart."

Almost without full awareness, I called Lakshman, my young, ever-smiling yardman, and gave him a scribbled note to carry back up to Lama Yeshe. The note said simply, "I would be happy to try the practice. Thank you so much. Your Daughter."

Lakshman had recently purchased a new bicycle with the ample rupees I was paying him and he liked nothing better than a mission such as this. I had asked him to please hurry back, but several hours passed before his return. When he did enter the front gate, ringing the bell loudly, I raced out to the porch to meet him. I could see that he was grinning from ear to ear. In fact, his face was luminous, as though Lama Yeshe had performed some special magic just for him. Which, of course, he had.

"Ma'am *sahib!* Ma'am *sahib!*" Lakshman blurted out through gleaming white teeth. "Your Lama has sent you a special present!" From his *jola* bag Lakshman pulled out an object wrapped in layers of rice paper. Cook Kanchi joined us in the living room as Lakshman excitedly narrated the details of his splendid adventure. After reading my note, Lama Yeshe had been very pleased. He had ordered a very fine meal for Lakshman, with tea and dessert. Lakshman had eaten on the top patio of the monastery while Lama Yeshe rushed back and forth preparing the statue that was contained in the rice paper.

"That statue, ma'am *sahib*, is very precious. Your guru, Lama Yeshe, told me so. And he has *filled* it, ma'am *sahib*, with many precious things!"

In their presence, I carefully unwrapped the gift Lama had sent me. It was Nepalese terra-cotta Buddha about eight inches in height. My first impression was that the little image was rather gaudy, painted in thick and overly bright colors. I had seen lots of statues much more subtly executed. Perhaps, I thought, Lama Yeshe's student Lama Zopa had painted this one himself. I was not taken by the statue's attractiveness. It was clear, however, as Lakshman had reported, that the statue had been very recently sealed up at the bottom; rice paper was freshly glued around its lotus base. The idea of Lama Yeshe's having stuffed the statue with many precious things made me smile. I knew that lamas did this when their statues were ritually consecrated, stuffing every available nook and cranny with everything from soil from sacred Buddhist sites to hairs from famed teachers to gemstones and minutely written mantras. Lama Yeshe had consecrated this Buddha image just for me and my practice. It was a gift from him. And it seemed to carry along with it his joy that I was willing to undertake the practice. I touched it to my head in reverence and I treasured it.

The next day I walked up to the monastery at Kopan to meet with Lama and discuss the details of my upcoming retreat. He met me with a broad smile and said, "I am happy, dear, that you will do this practice. And I am sure—one-hundred-percent sure—that you will be able to taste the great Mahamudra bliss. Don't worry, dear. You will."

I apologized for having at first turned down his offer, to which he responded, "All right, dear. Now you will do it. That is very good." He then reminded me that I was extremely fortunate at this time to possess all the external necessities for doing such a retreat, namely, a nice, sturdy, and quiet house; a cook to prepare my meals; a yardman to handle any needed shopping; and a fireplace in which to conduct nightly fire-offerings. The external conditions, in fact, could not have been better. The retreat would last six weeks. It would be a *silent* retreat. I could walk inside my house's compound but could not go farther than the yard. I could not read or enjoy any form of entertainment. Nor could I receive visitors. I balked a bit at the silence part but, upon reflection, thought that it might be a relief. So far so good. I was still willing to give it a try.

Next, Lama told me that we would discuss the specific details of the practice at a later time but that for the time being there were certain requisites that I needed to begin assembling. First, I would need to have another statue made, one of Dorje Sampa, whose Sanskrit name is Vajrasattva. The Buddhist deity used primarily for purification, his meditative practice is a necessary requisite to all advanced tantric meditation. I had been doing a practice that focused on this deity since 1969. The statue required now would need to be a special one, one that I had myself commissioned, made to certain specified standards. *And* it would need to be specially consecrated by a group of monks. Lama suggested that I request someone at Samteling Monastery, my earliest monastic home, to handle the consecration for me. I should also begin collecting the necessary grains and various other offering materials to be used in the fire rituals I would have to perform each evening during the retreat.

The preparations for my retreat took a full two weeks. As it turned out, I was fortunate to get everything done by then because Lama Yeshe was leaving on his trip just a day or two later. I had Lakshman shop for most of the grains I needed. He had to purchase big bags of rice and black sesame seeds, enough to last for six weeks. Some of the offering materials, like *kusha* grass, I had to shop for myself.

To have a statue made just for me required several trips out to Patan, the little town that had once served as a capital of Nepal. Many artisan families lived in Patan, descendants of people who had been supplying monasteries in Tibet with their statuaries for centuries. Visiting a number of stores that sold such statues, I finally found my way to a respected and trustworthy clan of artisans. Before a deal was actually struck, I was guided through numerous back alleys and up and around several darkened stairways. Finally, I stood in a room, lit only by the light from a tiny window. The chief bronze-caster offered me a wooden stool and then reached under a low thatched Nepali bed. Pulling out a tray, there suddenly appeared twenty or so bronze molds of statues, lying on their backs. They were each about ten inches tall, half-bodied and still rough, but somehow wondrously lifelike.

The bronzecaster asked me to choose the statue I liked most. Surveying them, one in particular caught my eye. Even in this early stage of production, its limbs were graceful and its face sublime. Watching me, the bronze-caster gently lifted out that particular form and, holding it up, said to me, "This is your Dorje Sampa." I smiled.

I saw my Dorje Sampa statue twice more in differing stages of completion. I decided at the next meeting that the statue should have its exposed limbs gilded and, on the subsequent viewing, that its face should be delicately painted with gold. When, after ten days, the statue was finally presented to me, it was magnificent. In fact, it was the most beautiful Dorje Sampa I had ever seen.

Still, I had to have the statue filled and consecrated. Lama Yeshe's suggestion proved right about who would be best to handle this part. I took the statue to my friend Lama Thubten Palden, a respected monk at Samteling who was also the monastery's ritual specialist. Lama Palden listened attentively as I explained that I needed the statue in order to do a six-week Mahamudra retreat under Lama Yeshe's guidance. Moreover, he seemed unruffled when I added that I needed the consecration done in just a few days. I learned later that Lama Palden had begun work on the statue as soon as I left him. He himself had made trips around Kathmandu Valley gathering various materials with which to fill the image. He had traveled up to Swayambhunath to get certain substances from teachers living there: dust from Bodhgaya, diamond chips and rubies from other lamas, hairs from revered lamas of the past. Back at Samteling, he had filled the statue with these items, dressed it, and then recruited three other lamas to help him perform the consecration rituals. The four monks conducted special ceremonies that lasted two complete days and nights. When next I saw my statue, it was as if it had become alive. It was draped in a tiny brocade robe and wore a necklace of coral and turquoise, and it evinced a living spiritual presence. As the traditional Buddhist saying goes, "Its eyes had been opened." I thanked the lamas and Lama Palden and made them a small offering. The preparations for my Great Seal retreat were done.

During that week, Lama Yeshe had sent me a note asking me to come to Kopan to receive final instructions for the retreat. When I arrived, I found the *gompa* in a buzz. Lama was leaving the next day. He motioned me over to his own small room.

A huge suitcase was flopped open on his bed. Various articles were scattered all over the tiny room. Lama searched through his stack of *pejas*, Tibetan woodblock-printed texts, wrapped in various colors, until he found the one he wanted. He turned to me, licking his fingers and flipping through the long pages, as he said, "As you know, dear, you are about to undertake the great Mahamudra retreat, the retreat taken by so many precious Gelukpa saints, and that brought them to the experience of actually *tasting* the Dharma's power and richness. This great meditation involves both deity-yoga and voidness-yoga, both generation-stage and completion-stage practice. Its central deity during the deity-yoga stage is Dorje Sampa."

Suddenly he paused, as if having an afterthought, and asked me, "How many Dorje Sampa mantras have you already completed, dear?"

"Well, now. Let's see. . . . I did the practice for two hours each night while I lived in Ithaca," I said as I began trying frantically to tally the specific number of sessions I'd completed, then counting 100 mantras for each session and multiplying. Fortunately, at that point a nun came in holding up for Lama's inspection a sleeveless yellow shirt worn by Geluk monks under their robes.

"This one, Lama?" she asked. Lama Yeshe gave his quick assent, "Yes, all right, dear. That one will be okay." The interruption gave me a chance to complete my tally.

"I'd say roughly thirty-five thousand Dorje Sampa mantras, Lama."

He looked at me with a startled expression on his face. *"That's all?"* he asked in disbelief.

"Well, yes. I think so. Maybe a few more, but not many more than that." No need to lie to your guru at this point, I thought. He began flipping through the *peja* again, perhaps, I thought, to find a watered-down version of the practice, one more suitable for a lazy practitioner like me.

Another nun entered the room carrying a monk's shawl. "This *dzen*, Lama?"

"No, dear, I have enough *dzens* already. Thank you."

I was thinking, "What a way to get such a powerful initiation!" Yet amid all the busyness of Lama Yeshe's packing and all the things he'd no doubt have to attend to later in the evening, he kept instructing me. Things began to calm down. Lama Yeshe was now reading aloud from instructions on the retreat. He began to speak slowly, intently, and directly.

"This retreat requires some strict, that is, some rigid meditation, and some relaxation meditation. It is important that you do the relaxation part fully as well." I took out the small notebook I'd brought up and began to scribble notes.

"You are to practice in six sessions for a total of eight hours each day," he said, "and to perform a two-hour fire-offering *puja* every evening. The schedule should be like this: Wake at five-thirty A.M. Take tea. Begin your first session at six, six to seven. From seven to seven-thirty, attend to your altar. From seven-thirty to eight-thirty, second session. Break nine to ten, third session. Ten A.M.—one P.M., break and lunch. One to two, fourth session. Two to four, break. Four to five, fifth session. Five to six, break. Six to eight, Fire-*puja*. Eight to nine-thirty, dinner. Nine-thirty to ten-thirty, sixth session. Then, sleep!"

I asked Lama questions about the overall practice, and he cleared them up quickly and easily. He checked that I knew how to correctly perform the fire-*puja*. I did. He stressed to me again that *relaxation* was very important to the success of this retreat. No visitors. No talking. No reading, even. It was to be a completely silent, completely relaxed retreat experience.

Satisfied that I'd grasped the details of the retreat, Lama Yeshe closed the *peja* hurriedly rewrapped it, and sat it back upon his stack. Looking kindly at me and almost shyly, he then said, "Now, I have to do this little thing, and tell you this." He made a quick gesture of pointing up to the sky, while he leaned forward and said to me, "Mind is like the sky."

I felt something quite simple and quite extraordinary at the same time; something akin to grace. A vast, blissful calmness. A stillness that was, in its immensity, all of a piece and all peace-filled. I had glimpsed such peacefulness only once in my life, as I emerged from the baptismal waters outside our little church in Docena. Then, the touch of hands reaching down for me had kept my mind from completely spacing out. Lama Yeshe never actually touched me, but, I am absolutely convinced, his blessings allowed me to touch, and to taste the richness of, that vast infinity of peace. Years later, I would read Buddhist texts that described that special moment of instruction as the "deep pointing out."

"Okay, dear," Lama was saying. "That's all. Have a good retreat. Lama will be praying for you."

I don't know how long I sat there. When I came back to myself, a nun was walking out of the room carrying some other item of clothing. I thanked Lama Yeshe. He told me again that he would pray for me and that I should remember to relax!

Of course, relaxation was the farthest thing from my mind. I was, after all, a Pisces, determined to *do* anything that I could. Now, with the jewel of a practice, I wanted nothing more than to throw myself completely and wholeheartedly into it. Lama Yeshe flew out of Kathmandu the next day.

At my cozy house in Maharaj-ganj, everything for my Great Seal retreat was in order. Kanchi understood that I could speak to her only sparingly, to give assent or not to meals. She agreed to keep Lakshman busy, making sure that fire-*puja* materials were sufficient and that a fire was prepared at the appropriate time each evening. Under ideal conditions, my retreat began.

Each evening, my retreat practice required that I perform a two-hour fire-offering. To my amazement, Lakshman proved totally inadequate as a fire-maker. Perhaps it was the modern fireplace. The first couple of days I demonstrated for him, in silence. Still, it took him a few days to catch on. The practice itself was simple but powerful: I sat on a raised seat before the fire. Within the flames of the fire, I envisioned a squatting, dwarflike deity called Dorje Khandro, with an upturned face and gaping mouth. I made mental offerings to this deity, who is viewed as the great destroyer of negativities.

Next, I thought about all the suffering beings throughout the realms of existence. Thereafter, I visualized taking into myself all those beings' various sufferings in the form of smoky streams that I inhaled, letting them come to rest at my heart-center. After some minutes of such inhalations, I breathed out several times into the mixture of grains and butter that had been prepared beforehand. It was this mixture that I then offered, in ladle-fuls, to the gaping mouth of Dorje Khandro, visualized inside the fire. The crackling sounds of the mixture's being consumed by the fire brought the day of meditation to its completion and assured me that countless negativities and situations—whether of harmful emotions or physical ailments, mine as well as those of all other sentient beings—were being purified. It was a very satisfying way to end each day.

Keeping silent has an uncanny way of sharpening one's other senses. During the early days of my meditations, especially during break times, I found my sense of vision in particular to be greatly enhanced. I began to take special notice of the birds that came each day to rest on the wall of my house's compound. Indeed, the wall seemed to be a favorite spot of these tiny blackbirds with bright yellow beaks. One particular morning, early on in my retreat, I noticed that each bird, though of the same species, had its own distinctive face, body, and idiosyncrasies. I noticed. I took notice. I was astounded: each was different. I began to take special delight in watching the birds, *seeing* whole families, *seeing* individuals and mates, *seeing* what they talked about. Lama Yeshe had continually reminded me to relax. I found that relaxing with the birds was a joy beyond measure. Wasn't this the same bliss the Christian mystics had spoken of? For the first time, I felt I had some understanding of the great joy and peace that St. Francis enjoyed with God's creatures. This kind of peacefulness was not limited to Buddhism.

Then one day during one of my breaks, after I'd been practicing hard for about two weeks, quite unexpectedly a most tantalizingly blissful awareness occurred. I was sitting on my bed, looking out of the window. Thinking about nothing in particular, I noticed that I could see myself standing on the roof of a house some distance away. I had the strange sensation that I was not only standing there but that I could also look back toward the house I was actually in and see myself sitting there. My mind and body felt completely free and unhindered. My normal seeing orientation just suddenly, and subtly, shifted. It was no longer anchored to my physical eyes. I could see myself anywhere I chose, and I could see anywhere. It felt as though my mind suddenly became immeasurably vast. It encompassed everything, the very universe, itself. There was no longer any separation between me and everything else in the universe. The duality of "subject" and "object" simply dropped away and disappeared. The birds and I were of one essence. I was completely convinced that I had tasted that ineffable knowledge about which only the saints can speak. I felt happy, light, ecstatic, completely blissful.

My meditation sessions thereafter became seamless with the rest of the day. There was no distinction between my meditation periods and my non-meditation periods. My awareness was consistently lucid, vast, and fully attuned to life. Nothing was a distraction any longer because everything was part and parcel of the great encompassment I had directly experienced. This new way of seeing, and the state of utter bliss it engendered, lasted for several days. Kanchi must have thought I was nuts. I moved around, silently, with a permanent grin on my face.

Then the bottom dropped out. It was not that the luminous state of mind departed. Rather, it was that my physical body began to fail me. I began to notice a sort of dizziness. Later this state turned to one of slight nausea. My head started to droop and fall forward. I could not look down or to the side without almost falling over. Things began to spin. Because this was a tantric retreat, it followed the guidelines of earlier Indian practices wherein tantric practitioners, in reversal of traditional religious norms, imbibed forbidden substances: alcohol, meat, fish, and some others. Consequently, for the practice, I was required to sip of tablespoon of *rakshi*, Nepali liquor, at the beginning of each session. Always watchful, Kanchi began to worry. She suggested that perhaps the *rakshi* that I was taking was bad. *"Rakshi karaab, ma'am sahib!"* She strongly encouraged me to discontinue taking it. But I was as stubborn as ever. Taking a sip of *rakshi* was part of the requirements of this retreat, and even though I suspected she might be right, I didn't want to leave off following any of the directions I had been given. Why it didn't occur to me to have Lakshman search out another brand of *rakshi* I don't know. The sickness got progressively worse.

I began to do my meditations propped against the wall. During break times, I literally had to hold my head up with my hands. Kanchi was beside herself with worry. "Please, ma'am *sahib*. Stop this meditating. Your Lama would not want you to suffer so!" But I tried to keep at it.

Sometime, after I'd been suffering like this for a few days, two Tibetans came to the door. I was on break and had decided to sit in a chair downstairs in my living room. Visitors were off-limits, but no one had told these Tibetans that. I recognized one of the men. I had met him in California some years before. He had come to Nepal to visit friends while on his way to Tibet. Not knowing about my retreat but knowing where I lived, he and the other monk had decided to visit me. Kanchi gladly let them in; she wanted me to get help.

I, too, decided that, given my physical condition, I needed to talk to someone, and these teachers were certainly capable of offering me advice. After listening to me and seeing the shape I was in, the two monks counseled with each other. Then one gently spoke: "It seems that you are experiencing what we call *"tsok-loong,"* a type of inner-wind disorder. Because of your strenuous efforts with this Mahamudra practice, your winds have become crossed and entangled. It is a condition that often happens when performing such retreats. Even in Tibet, monks used to make several attempts at this practice before succeeding with it. Also, it can be life-threatening. We suggest that you consult with your guru right away and that, for the time being, you take things very slowly."

I felt like crying. I did cry. Lama Yeshe was far away. I didn't know if I could reach him. But I thought until I could reach him, and until he advised me, I shouldn't break off doing the meditations. Lama had said over and over again that I should relax. I blamed myself. Because of my ambition, my overzealousness, I was suffering. I told myself to just try and take things easier.

Wisely, and weakly, I did manage to scribble a note to Lama Yeshe and asked Lakshman to send it as a telegram to the center in Australia where I hoped Lama would be. I described my symptoms and told him what the two lamas had said. I ended the message with the straightforward, and urgent, question: "What should I do?"

A couple of days after the lamas left, I could not get out of bed. Everything was spinning all the time. I could no longer walk on my own. Even Lakshman had become concerned. When Kanchi arrived, I called her upstairs. "Have Lakshman go for the American doctor, Kanchi. Ask him to come right away." I could see the relief in Kanchi's face as she ran from the room screaming, "Lakshman! Ho, Lakshman!"

Hours went by. Miserable, I lay helpless on my bed. I heard the ring of Lakshman's bicycle bell. Then Kanchi's angry rejoinders. Lakshman had not found the doctor in. He had waited, but he'd never returned. But Lakshman had not left a note or message for the doctor. Kanchi was furious. When she came up to report Lakshman's incompetence, I found myself trying to soothe her: "Tomorrow," I told her, "I'll send Lakshman with a note and forbid him to return without the doctor. If he's not at his office, Lakshman should go to his house." The American doctor lived somewhere in Maharajganj; it could not be too far from my house. I made it through one more night.

The next day around noon, Chad, the doctor taking care of American AID people and other American officials in Nepal, came to my house. When he observed my condition and listened to my symptoms, he made two recommendations. The first was to stop doing the retreat. I told him I didn't think so. The second was to begin taking that most dreadful stuff, Flagil, for amoebic dysentery.

"But I don't have dysentery!" I whined. "I just can't hold my head up."

"Nevertheless," he said, it was still indicated.

I took the Flagil, and for the next day and a half literally crawled into my bathroom and threw up globs of red stuff that looked like stewed tomatoes. The dizziness and weakness continued.

I stopped trying to sit. Chad began dropping by in the evenings on his way home. In spite of the Flagil misprescription, we became friends. He didn't have a clue about what was happening to me, but I enjoyed his company.

I was a little more than halfway through my Great Seal retreat. I had had incredible experiences and had gained actual insights in a really short time. Perhaps if my desire for success had not been so all-consuming, I might have done better.

One day, feeling slightly better when I woke up, I determined to move from my bedroom into the adjoining room where I'd set up my altar and where I meditated. I would stay here permanently. I would meditate when I could. A part of me resigned myself to the idea that I might very well die here, as well. This Joy of the Dharma, I mused, was anything but joyous now. A little while later, Kanchi came running upstairs with a telegram. It was from Lama Yeshe. Trembling and weak, I took out the typed note from its envelope. Its message read: "Health most important. Stop retreat!"

Seeing those words, I finally really broke down. Perhaps the retreat had been too much of a strain. At any rate, my sickness certainly pushed it over the edge. Stopping the sessions altogether, slowly, slowly I regained some steadiness. I still could not walk well on my own. And I found Chad's advice not to move very fast—"No bicycles or taxi rides!"—to be, in fact, very helpful.

Years after my Great Seal retreat, I discovered that I am allergic to the sulfates in liquor. Taking a tablespoon of *rakshi* six times a day had been slowly but surely poisoning me. Yet I believe the diagnosis offered by my two Tibetan visitors was more on the mark. Tibetan Buddhist medical theory says that the root of all sickness, whether of body or mind, is holding too rigidly to the self. The mental poisons that arise from this grasping are the harmful emotions of ignorance, hatred, and desire. The physical ones are closely related and are, therefore, also classified into three main divisions: a disharmony of bile is said to be caused by hatred; of phlegm, by ignorance; and a disharmony of wind energy is caused by desire. During that retreat, desire was clearly my problem. Though Lama Yeshe had constantly encouraged me to take it easy, I had gone after the goal of the practice with greediness and with a vengeance. Telling myself it was a tantric and, therefore, speedy practice, I went for overnight results. It was like getting my Buddhist name—stubbornly, on one knee—all over again. How many times had I heard Lama say, "Be gentle with yourself, with your mind and your body. If you are gentle with yourself, then you can be truly gentle with others"? How many times, as we meditated together, had he counseled, "Let go, dear.

Just let go"? The point was to let the drives and the worries go, to let the ambitions go.

Tantric Buddhism offers methods for transformation, but change doesn't happen overnight. It is a gradual process. When I look back at myself, at the timid and insecure self that first arrived before Lama Yeshe, I can clearly see how I have changed, how I have become less fearful and more confident and capable. These changes occurred in small increments and over some time. The point is to allow them to happen, without grasping and attachment; to have faith that positive change will come and, in the meantime, to try to be gentle with yourself. It was like this for all the Buddhas throughout the ages. They were each, at the beginning of their journeys, beings just like us: tossed and pummeled by ordinary fears, worries, and insecurities. And yet, with steady and patient practice, they each became Awakened Ones. They have given us a model of moderation to follow. If we practice as they did, who knows? We might just become the next Buddhas.   ■

■ *QUESTIONS FOR MAKING CONNECTIONS WITHIN THE READING* ■

1. What might be the link, if there is one, between the consecration of statues and the practice of meditation that Willis describes in her essay? Are the two statues—one of the Buddha, the other of a deity known as Vajrasattva—primarily objects of devotion, or do they serve some other purpose? Is it important that Willis obtained the statues through her own efforts? Why must they conform to certain standards of representation?

2. What can be learned from Willis's account about the social organization of Tibetan Buddhist meditation practice? How does the social organization of this practice differ from the organization of religions with which you are perhaps more familiar? Can you think of other institutions in the West, possibly secular ones, that operate along similar lines?

3. What might Lama Yeshe have meant when he told Jan, "Mind is like the sky"? Does Willis herself give us any hints about what this skylike mind actually feels like when it is experienced?

■ *QUESTIONS FOR WRITING* ■

1. Willis tells us that at the height of her meditation retreat she felt her awareness "was consistently lucid, vast, and fully attuned to life. Nothing was a distraction any longer because everything was part and parcel of the great encompassment I had directly experienced." At the same time, however, Willis also recalls that "it didn't occur to me to have Lakshman search out another brand of *rakshi*." Is it possible that Willis's feel-

ings of lucidity were actually a distortion of consciousness rather than a liberation from illusion? Why was she unable to recognize the causes of her own illness if she had, indeed, caught a glimpse of enlightenment? Shouldn't enlightenment make a person all-knowing, or is knowing just one form of awareness?

2. At the end of the chapter "Decision Time," which recounts the circumstances behind her choice to leave the Black Panthers and return to Nepal, Willis decisively announces, "I had made the right decision." At several later points in her narrative, however, she bears witness to an inner uneasiness. For example, she writes, "I had come to Lama Yeshe loaded down with guilt, shame, anger, and a feeling of utter helplessness." And later she recalls, "Because of my ambition, my overzealousness, I was suffering." Is there any connection between her initial decision and these expressions of self-doubt and self-deprecation? If they might have another source, what could it be?

■ *QUESTIONS FOR MAKING CONNECTIONS BETWEEN READINGS* ■

1. After rereading Ellen Dissanayake's essay, "The Core of Art," consider whether there may be a link between the modern banishment of art as a mode of experience and the disappearance of activities like meditation. Why and how did art cease to be something that anybody could do? Who benefited and who lost out from this change? By extension, who stands to benefit if people never learn how to control their own minds?

2. In "The Ecology of Magic," David Abram argues with great conviction that the deep sense of connection with the world achieved by Balians and shamans cannot be achieved "without long and sustained exposure to wild nature, its patterns and its vicissitudes." Western healers who try to assume the mantle of the shaman "without [an] intimate knowledge of the wider natural community cannot . . . do anything more than trade certain symptoms for others." Judging from your reading of Willis and Abram, is the experience of the Balian or the shaman the same as the experience of the Tibetan meditator? Does an "intimate knowledge" of the "wider" world always assume the same form? Would Abram say that Tibetan meditation brings people closer to nature? Would Willis accept Abram's experience as a form of enlightenment?

For additional suggestions about making connections between readings, visit the Link-O-Mat and More Sample Assignments at <www.newhum.com>.

Ian Wilmut

Although his is not yet a household name, Ian Wilmut has played a central role in developing cloning, the reproductive technology now dominating the headlines. Wilmut's success in this area has unleashed worldwide concern about the dangers and the promise of dramatically increasing the role scientists and genetic engineers play in the reproductive process. Should humans be cloned? Should research into the cloning process be allowed to continue? Although Wilmut makes clear his opposition to human cloning in the essay included here, he also acknowledges that he cannot control how the technology will be used.

Wilmut had his first success with reproductive technology in 1973, when he created Frostie, the first calf ever produced from a frozen embryo. In 1974, he joined the Animal Research Breeding Station in Scotland, which is now known as the Roslin Institute, and has conducted research there ever since. While working on a project involving the insertion of genes into sheep embryos in the mid-1980s, Wilmut began experimenting with the process of cloning, and in 1990 he hired cell cycle biologist Keith Campbell to assist him in his research. Their work produced its first success with the 1995 birth of Megan and Morag, two Welsh mountain sheep cloned from differentiated embryo cells. On July 5, 1996, Wilmut and Campbell used a new technique of starving embryo cells before transferring their nuclei to fertilized egg cells to produce the first clone from adult cells, a Finn Dorset lamb named Dolly. In 1997, Wilmut and Campbell succeeded in creating Polly, a sheep cloned from fetal skin cells that had been genetically altered to contain a human gene. And by 2000, there was already news that groups of scientists were competing to be the first to successfully clone a human.

Wilmut's hope is that the cloning process will not be used to reproduce humans but to create two different kinds of animals: those that can manufacture donor organs for humans in need of transplants and those that can mimic

Wilmut, Ian. "Cloning People." *The Second Creation: Dolly and the Age of Biological Control.* New York: Farrar, Straus and Giroux, 2000. 267–298.

Biographical information drawn from Ann On-line <http://www.annonline.com/interviews/970701/biography.html>; ThinkQuest <http://library.thinkquest.org/24355/data/details/profiles/wilmut.html> and Ian Wilmut "Cloning for Medicine," *Scientific American,* December 1998 <http://www.sciam.com/1998/1298issue/1298wilmut.html>.

human genetic defects for testing purposes. "Cloning People" introduces non-scientists to the moral and ethical issues involved in pursuing such research and offers an argument for allowing research of this kind to go forward.

To learn more about Ian Wilmut and the cloning process, visit the Link-O-Mat at <www.newhum.com>.

Cloning People

We believe that the science and technology that will emerge from our method of cloning, and from the genetic manipulations thus made possible, should benefit humankind and the other creatures, for whom human beings have become responsible in countless ways. It has been obvious to everyone from the outset that if sheep can be cloned, so, in principle, can human beings. Both Keith and I see human cloning as a rather ugly diversion, superfluous as a medical procedure and repugnant in general. But although we have patented certain aspects of the cloning technique, that does not give us a legal right to tell the rest of the world how the technology should be used. Human cloning is now in the spectrum of future possibilities, and we, more than anyone else, helped put it there. We wish this were not the case, but there it is and will remain for as long as civilization lasts.

What should we do? What should our responsibility be? As scientists, closer to the action than most, we take it to be our duty to make the facts as we see them as clear as possible—because although the facts must not be allowed to determine the ethics ("is" is not "ought"), they clearly do bear on the moral arguments in many ways. But simply as members of a democratic society, we share every citizen's right to express a personal opinion. We do not suggest that our feelings should carry any more weight than anyone else's. But it's clear that people at large do attach weight to our opinions, and for this reason alone we should say what we think.

This [essay], then, has three functions. We want to look at the factual issues that relate to cloning and its associated technologies. Then we will survey the kinds of ethical arguments that are being made with respect to human cloning—although many of them apply just as strongly to other areas of biotechnology—and try to show how the facts of the case bear on such arguments. Finally, we want to offer our personal opinions on human cloning, not because we assume any particular moral authority but in the spirit of throwing pebbles into the pool of discussion. Discussions on human cloning and the technologies that might spring from it will last for the rest of time. People the world over still ponder moral issues that were current at the time of Christ, and indeed long before. In 2,000 years' time, or 5,000, or 10,000, our descendants will no doubt still be turning over the ethical implications of human cloning even if, by then, it has long since become routine (although we suspect that it may not).

We might reasonably begin by asking whether cloning really is as outlandish as many commentators suggest. Present-day reproductive technologies are already fantastical, to borrow Hans Spemann's excellent term once more. Does cloning really represent a new age, or is it just one more technique among many?

Just Another Reproductive Technology?

Reproduction does not come easily to human beings. About one in every eight young couples of reproductive age are estimated to suffer some kind of shortfall in fertility: shortage of sperm, or sperm that lacks motility; lack of eggs; blocked fallopian tubes; lack of womb; incompatibility between sperm and reproductive tract; poor communication between egg and sperm; and so on. Techniques to enhance childbirth are at least as old as civilization—probably much older—but, apart from various drugs, tinctures, and quack remedies, the first recorded technology specifically to enhance fertility is only about 200 years old. An Italian priest, Lazzaro Spallanzani, impregnated bitches by artificial insemination in 1782. In the following decade the great Scottish physician John Hunter used a syringe to impregnate a woman with sperm from her husband, who had a deformed penis. AI [Artificial insemination] was recorded from time to time throughout the nineteenth century, and in 1884 William Pencoast at Jefferson Medical School in Philadelphia inseminated a married woman with sperm from an anonymous donor described as "the handsomest student in the class."

Although AI is technically simple, it was difficult to organize in the early days because the sperm had to be fresh, ejaculation had to be timed to the woman's ovulation, and this could be embarrassing and inconvenient for both parties. Cryopreservation, freezing and thawing cells without killing them, was developed in 1953 and made all the difference; in particular, it became easy to preserve the donor's anonymity (although nowadays children born by AI have sometimes claimed the right to trace their fathers). As a medical practice, AI for human beings really took off in the 1970s, and by 1978 single and gay women in the United States could legally obtain AI by anonymous donor. Many must have conceived by AI without the mediation of physicians. In *Remaking Eden*, Lee Silver estimates that a million people worldwide may now have been conceived by AI.

The next significant technique, in vitro fertilization, or IVF, was a huge leap forward from AI but was a logical extension of it. The first baby to be conceived by IVF—inevitably called a test-tube baby—was Louise Joy Brown, who weighed in at 5 pounds 12 ounces at the Oldham and General District Hospital in the north of England on July 25, 1978. Patrick Steptoe was the obstetrician, but the driving force behind the whole exercise was Robert Edwards, a Cambridge physiologist who had worked on IVF, primarily in mice, through the 1960s and began his partnership with Dr. Steptoe in 1968. It took them ten years to transfer the technique to humans, which may seem a long time. But the first attempt in humans could not simply be speculative: it had to be a serious clinical endeavor with a high expectation of success. If doctors really press ahead with cloning, then they should surely proceed in the same cautious spirit as Edwards and Steptoe. The bullishness that some enthusiasts display is surely irresponsible.

Many different conditions can be helped by IVF. A woman with damaged fallopian tubes might still provide an egg that could be fertilized in vitro, and the embryo could then be reimplanted in her womb. If a woman is unable to produce her own eggs, then her partner's sperm might fertilize a donor's egg in vitro, and again, the embryo could be implanted in the woman. If a woman does produce eggs but her womb is damaged, then the couple might produce an embryo in vitro to be brought to term in a surrogate mother. By 1994, thirty-eight countries were running IVF programs with more than 100 births each, including Britain, where it all began, the U.S., Australia, France, Belgium, Holland, Malaysia, Pakistan, Thailand, Egypt, Venezuela, and Turkey. Worldwide in 1995 there were an estimated 150,000 IVF babies, and Lee Silver estimates that by 2005 half a million babies might be born by IVF in the U.S. alone, with many millions more throughout the world. In short, IVF is becoming commonplace. We are already at the point where everyone knows someone who has had a child by IVF, or knows someone who knows someone.

Cryopreservation now assists reproduction in many ways. Cells of all kinds are generally preserved in liquid nitrogen at –196 degrees C. The trick is to take them down to this temperature, where flesh becomes hard as stone, and bring them back again to normality without turning the water into crystals of ice that slice the fabric of the cell to pieces. The first cells were frozen and recovered successfully in the 1940s; bull semen followed in 1950, with enormous consequences for the world's cattle industry; and human sperm joined the ranks in 1953. The first embryos, of mice, were successfully frozen and thawed in 1971, and the technique was soon applied to the embryos of rabbits, sheep, goats, and cattle. In the late 1970s when I was at Cambridge, I made Frostie, the first calf to be produced from an embryo that had been frozen, thawed, and nurtured in the womb of a surrogate mother. The first human child to be born from a frozen embryo was Zoe Leyland in Melbourne, Australia, on March 28, 1984. Since then, the cryopreservation of human embryos has become routine.

Artificial insemination, in vitro fertilization, and cryopreservation may now be seen as standard reproductive technologies. The first may be done with kitchen equipment, but the second two are definitely high tech, although they can now be carried out by technicians with the aid of standard kits, albeit directed by clinicians. To this basic repertoire, however, is now appended a steadily growing catalogue of refinements, usually known by acronyms. ICSI, intracytoplasmic sperm injection, was developed in 1992 and is now widespread in U.S. clinics. Up to 80 percent of eggs that are fertilized by ICSI develop normally into two-celled embryos that, once formed, develop to term as frequently as those produced by traditional IVF. ROSNI is round spermatic nucleus injection. In some men, the sperm fail to mature properly; they get to the spermatid stage, when they are haploid and more or less devoid of cytoplasm, but fail to develop tails, remain immobile, and cannot penetrate the egg. So they are injected into the egg in tailless form, while they are still "round."

The refinements grow ever more extraordinary. Ralph Brinster of the University of Pennsylvania Medical School has now taken early male germ cells that are still diploid—spermatogonia—and introduced them into the testes of other males whose own germ cells have been stripped out (which can be achieved with the aid of drugs).

The spermatogonia then mature and undergo meiosis in the "foster testes" and are ejaculated as mature sperm. Remarkably, spermatogonia can be successfully transferred between species: mouse into rat, for example. Exactly what species combinations are possible has not yet been established—particular genetic barriers between species will probably count for as much as overall genetic distance—but it might in principle be possible to mature human spermatogonia in the testes of a pig.

Techniques involving donation of eggs are far newer than those of AI partly because oocytes are so much harder to collect, and partly because there was no point in collecting them until IVF came on line after 1978. The first successful pregnancy initiated in humans with a donated egg was reported in November 1983 from Monash University in Melbourne, Australia. Egg donation is not pleasant—the donor must undergo both a course of hormones that can have uncomfortable side effects and minor surgery—but women volunteer nonetheless, either in a spirit of altruism, to help relatives or friends, or in return for money. Perhaps, though, the traumas of egg donation are numbered, because scientists in Britain and in Sweden are developing techniques to take immature eggs from the ovary by needle biopsy and mature them in vitro. This would provide a virtually inexhaustible supply of eggs. Eggs are difficult to freeze and thaw successfully, but this too can now be done, and in 1998, Britain allowed embryos to be created from frozen eggs.

Many women are able to donate their own eggs but need to borrow the womb of another. Surrogacy is an ancient practice: the Old Testament tells us that Rachel, Sarah, and Leah, all of whom were "barren," persuaded their husbands to impregnate their handmaidens and then claimed the babies at birth. Such ad hoc arrangements must have been common in the past. As a formal clinical treatment, perhaps abetted by AI or embryo transfer, surrogacy has been available since the 1970s. The surrogate mothers may be friends or relatives acting altruistically, or they may be employed through agencies.

The three most significant technologies listed above—AI, IVF, and cryopreservation—all caused tremendous controversy, which still comes to the surface. Perhaps that is right: human reproduction is a serious business, and whatever we take seriously should be argued through at length. Artificial insemination provoked tremendous opprobrium even when it was first developed for cattle in the 1930s, by Sir John Hammond at Cambridge. Bishops objected to its unnaturalness, while others felt that animals should not be deprived of their sexual rights. In human beings, AI was used increasingly in the early decades of this century—but far less than it might have been, largely because husbands objected to their wives' insemination. Many men (and women) are still not comfortable with the procedure. In the U.S., Canada, and Britain, AI was held to be adulterous and the children it produced were officially illegitimate, a foolish piece of lawmaking that persisted until the 1960s.

In vitro fertilization provoked at least as much opprobrium in the late 1970s and 1980s as cloning does now—perhaps more, because people in those days were less attuned to high-tech fertility treatments. The inevitable wastage of conceptuses was one of many objections, seen by many Catholics as a form of abortion and thus quite unacceptable.

Cryopreservation raises practical problems. IVF follows superovulation, so it is generally possible to make many more embryos at any one time than can immediately be implanted. Those that are not needed immediately can be frozen and perhaps used for later pregnancies, saving the trauma and expense of later superovulations. But current British law says that frozen embryos should not be stored for more than five years without the express request of the genetic parents, and in the early 1990s the problem of disposal again prompted waves of revulsion and protest. Some saw it as a kind of mass abortion.

Maternal surrogacy remains highly controversial. Surrogate mothers have sometimes changed their minds and wanted to keep the babies they have carried. Critics have suggested, too, that surrogacy is immoral, carrying overtones of prostitution, adultery, and/or incest, or that it is "dehumanizing." Herbert Krimmel, a professor of law, has said that "surrogate mother arrangements . . . encourage and tempt the adopting parents to view children as items of manufacture." "Commodify" has become a common verb in this kind of context. But some ethicists argue that women have a right to be surrogates if they choose, with Lori Andrews of the Chicago-Kent College of Law maintaining that a woman's individual rights should override state interventions—which, of course, is a common theme in U.S. politics.

What can we learn from all these apparent precedents? First, it is clear that people (including theologians, lawyers, and politicians) tend to object as a matter of course to any new, exotic technology that affects the human body. Novelty in general and invasive medical procedures in particular are innately suspect. As time passes, however, the fuss dies down and eventually, at least sometimes, the technology that once seemed outlandish, or even diabolical, is widely accepted as normal practice. AI and IVF are key examples. With all such procedures, however, a hard core of objectors remains. We may be reasonably sure that in 100 years, or 500, some people will still be objecting to IVF for one reason or another.

If we acknowledge, as the present authors do, that at least some of these reproductive technologies are acceptable, then we may regard the initial distaste simply as a passing phase, which most people will soon get over. Of course people are suspicious at first, and quite rightly, but once they grow used to the new technology, and see what benefits it can bring, their misgivings fall away.

But that is not the end of the matter. It does not follow that just because we grow used to some phenomenon or other that phenomenon is good. We grow used to bad things as well as to good. You don't have to be in Bombay for very long before you begin to ignore the beggars: the underlying reality remains horrifying; it's just that the visitor becomes hardened. The public seems largely to have grown used to IVF and accepts it as standard medical procedure, but perhaps people are wrong to be so complaisant. Perhaps they have simply grown accustomed to something that is bad. But to us, now that the dust has settled, IVF does not *feel* like an evil procedure. In the hands of good clinicians and responsible patients, it really does seem to emerge as a benign and worthwhile technology.

Does the same kind of principle apply to cloning? Is the present aversion felt by many people—including us—simply a fear of novelty? Or is there really a qualitative difference between the technology of cloning and the reproductive technologies that are already commonplace and seem on the whole to be acceptable even when they seem exotic?

Of course there is a qualitative difference, which has nothing to do with the nature of the technique. All the current technologies are designed to abet sexual reproduction: the creation of a new embryo by the fusion of egg and sperm. This is the normal method of reproduction among human beings, and among all mammals. Furthermore, the sexual fusion of egg and sperm produces a new individual who is genetically unique. Biologically, this fusion is first and foremost an exercise in genetic recombination. Sex ensures that no two human beings—indeed, no two creatures of any kind—are ever exactly alike. Genetically identical human beings are produced only occasionally, by the division of an embryo in the womb, at various stages of early development. Among people, as among all mammals and most vertebrates, genetic uniqueness is the rule.

But cloning is not intended to abet normal sexual reproduction. It is exclusively an exercise in replication. To be sure, the creation of a clone like Dolly involves many components of sexual reproduction. Once the embryo is made, it has to be inserted into the womb of a surrogate mother to be brought to term. But the essential part of the creation process—the fusion of eggs and sperm—is missing. Fertilization is replaced by another process, that of nuclear transfer. Thus cloning provides a *substitute* for normal sexual reproduction. It is a qualitatively new addition to the canon of mammalian capabilities. Crucially, it does not produce a genetically unique individual. It produces a new individual who is genetically identical to some preexisting individual.

Cloning is different conceptually from all previous technologies. In truth, it is also more complex technically than most existing reproductive techniques because it combines elements from several different standard technologies, but technical complexity is not the prime issue. What really matters is the intention, which is to bypass normal sexual reproduction, and the result, the creation of a new individual that is not genetically unique.

This last issue—the sacrifice of uniqueness—is the one that has bothered critics most. We should ask what it really entails. To begin with, are cloned individuals really identical to one another, or are they merely similar? And how similar are they?

Are Clones Identical?

Sometimes in the womb an embryo splits and each half develops into a new individual. Then we have identical twins.

Analyzed molecule by molecule, identical twins produced in this natural way really do seem to be as identical as it is possible to be. Each set of genes, in each new individual, is a facsimile of the other's genes, and although the cytoplasm is not duplicated precisely, the two sets of cytoplasm are *qualitatively* the same.

Sometimes the similarities between twins who are created in this way are startling; there are classic cases of twins separated at birth who, when compared many years later, are found to be wearing identical clothes, have the same hobbies, are married to remarkably similar partners, and so on. There are identical twins brought up together whose thinking is so alike they can finish each other's sentences. Many twins, however, are irritated by these "classic" examples, which they regard merely as clichés. They prefer to emphasize their differences; the contrasts, given the underlying genetic resemblance, can be striking, too. There are various reasons why this should be so.

First, genes are not as constant as we imagine. They mutate. Everyone's body probably contains hundreds of mutated genes. A conscientious analyst who trawled all the body cells (and gametes) of two identical human twins would undoubtedly find increasing genetic differences as they grew older, caused by these constant mutations. This may be a small point in practice, since most genetic mutations have little or no discernible effect on the phenotype, but it is a point nonetheless. Nature might intend to produce perfect genetic replication each time a cell divides, but absolute perfection is a tall order.

More important is the point emphasized [elsewhere], that genes operate in constant dialogue with their surroundings. The DNA is surrounded by the environment of the nucleus, which in turn is surrounded by the cytoplasm of the cell, which is in touch with the rest of the cells of the organism, which is assailed by the outside world—first the womb, and then the great outdoors. The surroundings affect gene expression. For simple reasons of physics, no two entities can be in exactly the same place at the same time. Identical twins may share a womb, but they do not share the same part of the womb, and there is evidence in many contexts and various species that the difference in location can affect development. The twin babies may share a crib, but one will be on one side, and one on the other, and their view and experience of the world will be ever-so-slightly different.

Ever so slightly, perhaps, but enough to make a difference to gene expression. Indeed, Davor Solter [. . .] has suggested in *Nature* that although two cloned creatures may have identical genomes, they may nonetheless *express* different genes, and if they express different genes, they are *functionally* different genetically. Furthermore, the genetic differences are liable to increase as the cloned individuals develop because a gene that comes on line at one point in time (or fails to come on line) will affect the expression of others that are due to come on line later.

For two reasons—recurrent mutation and variable expression—even *identical twins*, formed by splitting an embryo, may be genetically different, physically and perhaps functionally. The differences are liable to be slight, but they can be obvious nonetheless.

Then there is the point that Jaques encapsulates so neatly in Shakespeare's *As You Like It*: As people grow older (Jaques specifically spoke of men, but the principle applies to women just as well), they change, radically—from mewling infant, in Jaques's jaundiced view, to foul-mouthed soldier and then to enfeebled "pantaloon." How does this happen? A geneticist would say because each of us, as time passes, runs through our genetic program. In infancy, the genes appropriate to babyhood are expressed, producing simple, touching souls with big domed heads and tiny hands. In manhood, the appropriate genes generate testosterone by the dram so that the beard flourishes, the voice booms, and the temper grows worse. In old age, the genomic program is increasingly in disarray until, as Jaques dyspeptically put the matter, we are left sans teeth, sans everything.

Consider, then, a child who has been cloned from his father or from her mother. Clone parent and clone child are at different points of their genetic program. Leaving aside differences in mutation and expression, they are operating different permutations of their genes, taken from different points on the program. Functionally, at any one point in time, they will be very different people, just as adults reading this [. . .] are different in appearance and attitudes from the children they once were, while children can expect to become different as they grow older. On the other hand, the influence of the genes is pervasive. The cloned child would be working through the same genetic program that its clone parent was still embarked on and could expect, to some extent, to reenact and re-create the person the parent had been. Clone parent and clone child alike would be constantly confronted by the immediate differences between them, yet also by the overall similarity.

But of course—and biologists are at least as aware of this as anybody—genes do not *determine* in tight detail how a creature turns out. In general, the genome merely sets broad limits on the possibilities. A person may decide to be a slob, or have little opportunity to be anything else, and become fat and short-winded; or he or she may decide to train, and might perhaps have been raised in the shadow of a gymnasium, and become an Olympic athlete. Same person, same genes, but completely different outcome. Nutrition in infancy influences height (and hence weight) at maturity. The nutrition of the mother influences the birth weight of the infant, which in turn influences that child's final height and weight. Hence children who are well nourished are taller than their parents who were less well fed, and this effect continues through several generations. In Britain, today's fifteen-year-olds typically tower over their parents. Modern pinups, the supermodels, are commonly around six feet tall, while the Victorian factory girls who posed for pocket money rarely reached five feet.

The effect of environment on personality and on educational achievement is clearly stupendous. This issue has become politically charged but the generalization is undeniable. Children who are given well-directed musical education at a young age, for example, may become virtuosi, while those who do not handle a musical instrument until they are in their teens are most unlikely ever to achieve more than competence. Children of diplomats or immigrants commonly grow up to be bilingual, or even polylingual, while those plucked from their homelands and brought up on plantations among people from many lands who share no common language may not progress beyond their own reinvented pidgin. Genes, in short, merely propose possibilities. It is the environment that shapes the final outcome.

We can see the physical realities of this principle in the brain. Thoughts and memories seem to be contained within and framed by the brain cells, neurons, of which there are billions. What matters most is not the number or the distribution of the cells, but the connections between them: the synapses. Two individuals may possess similar neurons, but the neurons in the two individuals become wired up to each other in different ways, and so form different neural "circuits." Thus two brains with similar cells are nonetheless qualitatively different. If there are billions of different brain cells, then there is an infinity of possible ways in which the circuits could form. Do the genes determine the circuitry in fine detail? Well, if we have only 80,000 genes, and billions upon billions of possible arrangements of synapses, how could it be so? It seems rather that the genes lay down the broad structure, but the structure then works itself out in ways that are beyond their fine control. The final distribution of the synapses depends, again, on environmental influences, in the womb and out of it. There is no reason to assume that the elusive quality of "free will" would be less apparent in a person produced by nuclear cloning than in the rest of us. Once the brain is formed, it does its own thing.

Genes lay down the ground rules, but in the end our upbringing and experience make us what we are. Pygmies could never star at basketball, Masai warriors could never be jockeys, and very few of us could ever emulate Mozart, no matter how many hours we practiced. Our genes provide the clay or the marble from which we are made, and this influences the kind of people we can become. But our own experiences, and our perception of those experiences, impose the sculpting. Here is another crucial set of reasons that two individuals will be different even if, like "identical" twins, they arise from two apparently identical cells of the same embryo.

But with clones like Dolly, or Megan and Morag, there is yet another layer of difference. For such clones do not arise in the manner of identical twins. They are not made by splitting an embryo. They are made by introducing a nucleus into the cytoplasm of an egg *which usually is taken from another individual*. Dolly has the same genes as the old Finn-Dorset ewe who provided the mammary gland cells in the original culture, but her cytoplasm came from a Scottish Blackface ewe. The cytoplasm, as we have seen [. . .], profoundly affects the expression of the genes. The cytoplasm even contains genes of its own, within the mitochondria. So Dolly and her clone mother are not like identical twins. Dolly is merely a "DNA clone" or a "genetic clone" or a "genomic clone" of her clone mother. We have already listed a series of reasons that true identical twins, produced in the womb by the schism of an embryo, nonetheless grow into different people. How much greater will the difference be if the clones are merely genomic clones, who begin with different cytoplasm?

Since these are early days, and there are so far very few genomic clones in the world, we cannot yet answer this question. Already there are signs, however, that genomic clones may vary significantly. We have mentioned Cedric, Cyril, Cecil, and Tuppence, the four young rams we cloned from cultured embryo cells at the same time as Dolly. They are genomic clones, and yet they are very different in size and personality, with Tuppence the shrinking violet among the four. People who are now hoping to replicate their beloved cats and dogs by genomic cloning will be disappointed, at least sometimes. The personality of the newfound pet may differ profoundly from that of the original; even the coat color may be different because the expression of the genes that "determine" color is very sensitive to early stimuli in the womb.

Cloning of course can and generally does produce sets of individuals who can be almost indistinguishable, and since we are accustomed to seeing human beings (and most other animals) in ones, the similarities can sometimes seem almost uncanny. Yet cloned creatures may also be noticeably different, sometimes remarkably so; genomic clones differ more, one from another, than conventional identical twins. So those who contemplate human cloning face a paradox. Sometimes the differences between two cloned individuals might be upsetting; at other times, it is the similarity that could give cause for disquiet. We are opposed to human cloning in either case, but for the sake of completeness, we should look at the various contexts in which such cloning might be carried out and see where the two different kinds of objection might apply.

Why Clone People?

In January 1998, Dr. Richard Seed—who was educated at Harvard as a physicist (not a physician!)—launched a campaign to clone a human being. He lacked funds, a suitable laboratory, and appropriate expertise. Although Seed's grand plan was bruited on many a front page, Alexander Morgan Capron, a professor of law and medicine at the University of Southern California and a member of the National Bioethics Advisory Commission, remarked somewhat archly that "it belongs in the entertainment section."[1] At the time of writing, however—well into 1999—Seed was still promising to clone a human being by the end of the twentieth century. At one point he intended to begin by cloning himself, but later, lest he be accused of egoism, he decided to clone his wife instead.

Unfortunately, Seed is not alone in his enthusiasm. Though most commentators have been repelled by the notion of human cloning, a significant few have welcomed it—and basically for four kinds of reasons. Some would simply like to copy themselves. Others would like to re-create departed loved ones. Some suggest that we should clone outstanding individuals—Mozart, Einstein, Gandhi, Michael Jordan, and Marilyn Monroe have been among the nominees. And, most commonly, some suggest that cloning be regarded as another of the many technologies that already help infertile couples (or individuals, or conceivably consortia) produce their own genetic offspring. Of course, none of these proposals is technically feasible at present, and it may never be possible to make another Mozart, even if his body still exists, since his DNA has probably long since decayed. But a great deal will eventually be possible, and we should examine these different motivations.

Why, first of all, should people want to clone themselves? Not everyone has given reasons, but Richard Dawkins, expressing such a desire in his essay

"What's Wrong with Cloning?" says unequivocally, "My feeling is founded on pure curiosity."[2] Others, no doubt, are motivated by a desire to increase their own influence. It has often been suggested that dictators might want to clone themselves, as Ira Levin anticipated in *The Boys from Brazil*. Actually, we know of no living despot who has expressed a desire to be cloned, and perhaps dictators prefer to be as unique as possible (for there are degrees of uniqueness, despite what the grammarians say). Perhaps some people who want to be cloned are simply vain. Others clearly feel that by duplicating themselves they will achieve a kind of immortality, though this, as we shall see, is one of the many misconceptions surrounding cloning.

Is curiosity, vanity, the wish for personal power, or an undoubtedly misguided desire for immortality really a good enough reason for bringing a child into the world? I have two daughters and an adopted son, while Keith has two daughters, and we both feel that to bring a new human being into the world is a sacred thing—the most serious thing that most of us do in the course of our lives. The birth of a child affects its parents, its family, society as a whole, and of course, above all, the child. Is any motive apart from an unassuageable desire to be a parent, with all that that connotes, truly acceptable? In truth, even without reproductive high technology, children have often been brought into this world for dubious reasons: to prop up failing marriages, to give status in societies where motherhood is a woman's only route to status, to be sold into slavery, and so on. But that is not the point. We should not add insouciantly to the catalogue of unacceptability.

I have been the main spokesman for the cloning work at Roslin, and I have often been asked—although I dread the question—whether it is possible to re-create some dead loved one. I was first asked this over the telephone within days of announcing Dolly's birth, by distraught parents from another country. Over the telephone, or in a lecture hall, it is not possible to say much more than "No, at this time it is not possible." The more expanded answer, however, is that there are two caveats, which, as already have been outlined, are opposite in nature.

First, for all the reasons described above, the child (or cat or dog) that was cloned by the kind of technique that produced Dolly would not simply be a facsimile of the original. We might rejoice in the difference, that the new person or animal was a new individual, after all, despite the manner of his or her creation. On the other hand, people who *wanted* a precise facsimile would surely be disappointed. The new baby would not simply follow in its brother's or sister's footsteps. The anxious parents would surely be puzzled and perhaps upset by the difference. Cloned cats or dogs might look completely different from their clone siblings or clone parents; notably, they might have significantly different markings. A puppy cloned from a black-and-white dog would itself be black-and-white, but the patch over the eye that made the original so lovable might be lacking. Those who are planning to offer a service in cloning pets (and there are some already) had better be careful about lawsuits. You might well find a closer match to your much-loved original at the pet shop. Dolly's clone mother is not around for comparison, but Cedric, Cyril, Cecil, and Tuppence already show how different genomic clones may be.

Parents or pet owners seeking a facsimile of lost loved ones could well be disappointed, and this brings me to what I think is perhaps the most important of all the objections to human cloning, and the one I have stressed in many a lecture and article. For what we should surely consider above all—even above the interests of the parents—is the welfare, including the psychological welfare, of the unborn child. Parents may already require too much of their children, at least in expecting them to conform to their own ideals. How much worse would it be if the child had been brought into this world as a replica of some other individual! How would the parents avoid making comparisons with the dead brother or sister? How would this affect the growing child?

Or suppose that the child was made in the image of one of the parents. As I have said to many an audience on both sides of the Atlantic, suppose my wife and I had decided to clone me, and the Wilmut clone was now a teenage boy. My wife and I met while we were both still at school—not the same, but neighboring schools—so this hypothetical lad would now be as old as I was when we met. How would Vivienne regard this near-facsimile of the boy she once fell in love with? How would he think of his own future as he regarded me—now aging, bearded, and balding but nonetheless demonstrating the prospect of life to come? Perhaps he would look up to me as I looked up to my own father, and perhaps he would welcome the transition. But perhaps not. There is clearly a risk. I fear that a child brought into a family as a clone could severely compromise family life—and that the child himself or herself would suffer the most. It surely is not proper to bring a child into the world in the expectation of such confusion and possible unhappiness.

What of the second commonly proposed motive for human cloning—to replicate special individuals? Mozart, Einstein, and Gandhi have commonly been suggested as candidates. The decision in this case would presumably be made not by an individual wanting to regain a loved one but by society, although the child would have to be brought up in a loving family.

Then again, for all the reasons already outlined, a genomic clone might not share the talents, and certainly not the inclinations, of his or her clone parent. A cloned Einstein would almost certainly be highly gifted, but he would not necessarily be a great physicist. To what extent, too, would it be possible or desirable to simulate the upbringing of the original, which obviously had such an influence? Newton, one of the supreme talents of all time, had an extraordinary and unhappy childhood. He was abandoned by his mother at the age of three, although she continued to live in the next village with a new husband. Did the loneliness imposed by this gratuitous separation contribute to the intensity and obsessiveness that later made him so remarkable? It is certainly possible. Should a Newton clone be subjected to similar cruelty? Surely not. Would a Newton clone brought up with siblings and taken out on picnics like any other child become so dedicated? Perhaps. Perhaps not.

There is of course another side to this particular coin: the hypothetical cloning of crazed dictators, effected at their own command or through the offices of their followers. In the days and weeks that followed Dolly's birth, many a commentator raised this possibility as one of several "worst-case scenarios," hence the battalion of Hitlers on the cover of *Der Spiegel*. But a cloned dictator would not replicate the original any more than a cloned genius would. It has often been suggested that Hitler might have become a perfectly innocuous landscape painter if only the Vienna Academy of Fine Arts had accepted him as a student before World War I, and we might reasonably hope that the Hitler clone would be luckier in his choice of university.

A genetic nuclear clone of Hitler would not necessarily strive to create a Fourth Reich. This would be most unlikely. If he inherited his clone father's oratorical powers, he might as soon be a schoolteacher—or a priest, which was one of Hitler's own boyhood ambitions. If he was as fond of dogs, he might become a vet. Of course, the clone's genetic inheritance would set limits on his achievements. Richer postwar nutrition would most likely ensure that a Hitler clone would be taller than the original, but still, he would never shine at basketball, or trouble the Olympic scorers in the high jump. Unless he grew a poky mustache and smeared his hair across his forehead few would spot the resemblance to his infamous father. The Führer's cloned offspring would surely disappoint their clone pater no end.

The cartoonists' vision of an instant battalion of Hitlers is further nonsense. Clones like Dolly may be produced from adult cells, but they begin their lives as one-celled embryos and then develop at the same rate as others of their kind. Adolf Hitler was forty-four years old when he became dictator of Germany and fifty at the outbreak of World War II. It would take just as long to produce the doppelgänger as it did to shape the original, and by that time the political moment that brought the first Hitler to power would be well and truly past, as indeed is the case.

It is always worth raising worst-case scenarios when contemplating the future. We should examine every idea we can think of. But it must be a mistake to take worst-case scenarios at their face value, or to base general policy on them. As lawyers say, "Hard cases make bad law." We have made clear by now that we are not apologists for human cloning. We do believe that all possible caveats—all that anyone can think of—should be laid out for discussion. It is the case, though, that some of the bogeys, when confronted head on, prove to be insubstantial.

Finally, however, there is one worst-case possibility that might have some substance. In the film *Blade Runner*, the cloned eponymous hero was shown becoming steadily more flawed as the generations passed, just as successive photocopies lose quality. Taken literally, this is nonsense—clones are not photocopies—yet the general notion does give cause for concern. Sexual reproduction ensures that new individuals are made from the fusion of gametes. Gametes are produced by meiosis, [. . .]. In meiosis, it seems likely that any damaging mutations that arise during the life of the individual are shuffled off; indeed, this might be the chief selective pressure that drove meiosis—and hence sex—to evolve in the first place. But clones are not produced by fusion of gametes. There is no meiosis in the prefatory phase to purge damaging mutations. Any mutations that are present in the particular cell nucleus from which the clone is made will be present in all the cells of the new individual. Cloning so far has proved difficult: most of the reconstructed embryos die. Mutation within those cells *could* be a cause. This has yet to be investigated. The survivors could just be the lucky ones—but they might still carry mutations of a sublethal nature. But if the cloned individual was cloned again, and then again and again, the results could well prove increasingly disorderly.

In practice, this scenario is surely unlikely. We reproduce our own cloned animals by normal sexual means, and we may presume that cloned human beings (if ever there are any) would also reproduce by sex. It is hard to imagine circumstances in which a cloned individual would then be cloned again. If this did happen, we could envisage an accumulation of flaws, as in *Blade Runner*.

But we are now well into the realms of fancy and should return to the final, most important, down-to-earth reason human cloning has been seriously considered. It could in principle be employed as an aid to fertility. Here again there are two clear-cut possibilities. The first is to help heterosexual couples in which both partners are infertile and who cannot be helped by any other means; the second is to extend the traditional concept of "family," and of "parent." Again, we do not advocate human cloning in this context or any other, but the arguments should be explored.

Cloning to Overcome Infertility

The techniques outlined at the start of this chapter are intended to help couples who are unable to reproduce sexually because of some specific shortfall: lack of sperm, a defective womb, or any other reason. In some cases, however, reproduction by sex is out of the question: when one person alone seeks to reproduce, without a sexual partner; or when two partners either fail to produce gametes at all or produce incompatible gametes—as is the case with homosexual partners. In mammals, new embryos cannot be created by placing two sperm nuclei or two egg nuclei in a single egg because of the phenomenon of genomic imprinting: nuclei of both sexes are needed. But male homosexual couples might conceivably be cloned with the aid of egg donors and surrogate mothers, while female couples could be far more independent; indeed, cloning could help realize the dream of some extreme feminists, of reproduction without males. One member of a lesbian couple might provide a nucleus from a body cell, and the other could provide the cytoplasm; next time around they could reverse the procedure. Of course, by such means, a lesbian couple could produce only daughters. A woman could clone herself precisely if one of her own nuclei was introduced into one of her own enucleated oocytes. Many combinations can be imagined.

It is certainly not up to us to comment on where the limits of parenthood ought to lie. Clearly, however, society has become more liberal. In the decade up to the mid-1990s, fifteen U.S. states allowed adoption by gay couples, and what any one state allows, the other states are obliged to recognize—though not, of course, to emulate. Lee Silver estimates that up to 6 million children in the United States may now be living in families of same-sex couples, either male or female. Mere liberality, however, is not enough if homosexual couples are to produce their own genetic offspring. Various third parties—clinicians, technicians, and sometimes donor mothers (to provide egg cytoplasm) and surrogate mothers—must lend their active assistance. In this context John Robertson, an American lawyer and moralist, has coined the expression collaborative reproduction, although we could say that this is a matter of degree since human birth in general is collaborative, as it is usual and desirable at least to involve a midwife.

Even so, is cloning justified? We believe it is not. Keith, in particular, stresses that he can envisage no circumstances that could not be aided simply by adapting present techniques. Male homosexuals *could*, for example, borrow or buy the services of egg donors and surrogate mothers, to produce a genetic facsimile of at least one of them. Lesbian couples already have recourse to anonymous sperm donors. Heterosexual couples who are doubly infertile could buy or borrow the services of egg donors and sperm donors to produce a child by IVF and, if necessary, raise the child within the womb of a surrogate mother. There is no circumstance in which a couple would absolutely *need* to produce a child by nonsexual means. Of course, a child produced with the help of an egg donor or sperm donor is genetically related to only one of the prospective parents (unless the donor is related to the other parent). But, Keith asks, why is genetic relationship considered to be such a big deal? What truly matters is that a child, however produced, should be brought up within a loving home. If this is taken to be the criterion of acceptability, then there can be no circumstances in which cloning is the only option.

Keith also suggests that doctors in the future might view cloning, in the manner that produced Dolly, as a crude, late-twentieth-century intermediate technology. As we have seen, it is already becoming possible to direct the differentiation of cells in culture—to induce stem cells to develop into particular tissues. Within a few decades, such techniques will be standard. If this is the case, then it surely will be possible one day to induce cultured cells to develop into eggs or sperm. When this technology comes on board, it will be possible to produce embryos by IVF, from gametes made from body cells. These embryos could then be taken to term by surrogate mothers. This technology will not be cloning, although it will partake of the methods now being developed through cloning research.

Whatever way you turn the arguments, we can see no unequivocal reason to adopt human cloning, and we can foresee many shortcomings. It is the case, though, that cloning qua cloning is not the only issue. As we have stressed [elsewhere], we have developed cloning technology primarily as a means by which to realize the potential of genetic engineering.

People Engineered

Cloning and genetic engineering are conceptually linked because they are technically linked. The transgenesis of zygotes is a hit-and-miss affair, offering only limited possibilities. But when cells are cultured by the million, and laid out in a dish for months at a stretch, genetic engineers can work their full repertoire. Then the cells that are satisfactorily transformed can be made into new individuals by the same method that enabled us to create Dolly. Genetic engineering is a quite different concept, but cloning is involved in it. Genetic engineering also seems to raise much bigger issues, for cloning merely duplicates what exists already—though only up to a point—while genetic engineering can, in principle, change the nature of living creatures, which means it might change the nature of humanity, the meaning of *Homo sapiens*. All this is feasible—but how could it come about? By what route, and with what motivation? When?

Genetic engineering might be applied to human beings in two quite different contexts. In the first, damaged tissues might be removed, manipulated, and then returned to the body. Alternatively, and this is the approach that I am already involved in with Roslin Bio-Med, each person might be provided with his or her own personal store of cultured fetal cells that could, when required, be cultured and differentiated in vitro to replace or supplement damaged tissue of whatever kind is required. Such approaches are already being worked on for a diversity of disorders, from cystic fibrosis to Parkinson's disease. This is high-tech, twenty-first-century medical biology, but it does not seem to raise outstanding ethical issues. The physical changes made by such means are not passed on to the next generation. The only serious caveat seems to be that in some circumstances transformed cells intended for one person might escape into another—which at least is theoretically possible if such cells were delivered to the lung by aerosol, for example. But this is a technical issue, and surely resoluble.

The second possibility does raise ethical issues: adding, subtracting, or altering genes in the germ line, so that future generations are affected. If an animal (including a human animal) is genetically transformed as a zygote, or by the method that made Dolly, then the transformations should finish up in the eggs or sperm and be passed into the dynasty. Whatever the nature of the gene—even if it is the most innocuous conceivable, even if it has no discernible effect at all—this is a serious thing to do.

Thomas Paine suggested at the end of the eighteenth century that no one generation has a right to impose its will on the next, though in practice this is unavoidable, and at least in some instances future generations can reverse the decisions of their predecessors. But to add genes to future generations—that changes the nature of future people. It is difficult to imagine a greater imposition. We might indeed simply leave the matter there and declare that germ-line transformation of human beings is, in principle, forever beyond the pale.

But every possibility should be thought through, and some serious physicians are already envisaging cases where, they suggest, germ-line transformation would be justified. So we should look further.

To begin with, we can draw the traditional distinction that runs through all medicine: on the one hand, the correction of obvious disorder; on the other, the enhancement of what already works reasonably well. In this way physicians distinguish between medicines and tonics. The distinction is not always easy in practice, but in principle it seems clear enough. Also, as we discussed in the context of Tracy, we should distinguish between characters that can be modified cleanly and discretely by adding, knocking out, or altering a single gene, and those that are polygenic, where each gene is merely a player in a larger consortium. Bear in mind, too, that most genes are pleiotropic, often having many effects besides the one the engineers might intend.

An obvious goal is to correct the many different single-gene disorders—at least 3,000 are known in human beings—that are caused by single mutated alleles. Robert Winston has suggested Duchenne muscular dystrophy as a prime target. It is a sad and crippling disease: those who inherit the causative gene in a double dose become increasingly disabled and die young.

There is an alternative approach. Most of the deleterious alleles that cause single-gene disorders in human beings are recessive. They have no obvious effect unless inherited in a double dose, from both parents. Individuals who carry only one copy of the "bad gene" are carriers and have a fifty-fifty chance of passing the gene on to any one of their offspring, but they are not themselves affected. The simplest Mendelian rule shows that if two carriers of Duchenne muscular dystrophy (or cystic fibrosis or sickle-cell anemia or other disorders) have children, then two out of every four are liable to be carriers themselves (having inherited the bad gene from one parent but not the other); one out of four will inherit a double dose of the bad gene, and so will manifest the disorder; and one out of every four will inherit a normal allele from each parent, and so be free of the disorder altogether—neither affected nor even a carrier. These figures are averages: Lucky parents who were both carriers might have half a dozen children totally free of the disease, or they might have one affected child after the other.

More and more of the mutant alleles that cause such disorders can now be diagnosed within very young embryos simply by taking a single cell and examining its DNA by techniques that are becoming ever more simple and surefire. So in families in which there is a history of disorder and therefore some reason to look for trouble, it should soon be relatively simple to produce a batch of embryos by superovulation and IVF and to pick out the ones—one in four—that are free of the bad gene altogether. One of these can be implanted in the mother.

In practice, I see nothing wrong ethically with the idea of correcting single-gene defects. But I am very concerned about any other kind of intervention, for anything else would simply be an experiment. How could we possibly foretell the outcome? Thus, if we practiced germ-line intervention *except* to correct very special defects that are well understood, we would not only be imposing our will on future generations, we would also be taking a chance—and potentially a very serious one—with their welfare. The chanciness alone seems to me to put such intervention beyond the scope of consideration. This brings us to an issue that must run through all debate and prophecy, whether about cloning qua cloning, or cloning as a means to genetic engineering. The universal issue is that of risk.

Risk

Risk is a tricky concept. It clearly has ethical implications: Likelihood of success or of hideous failure must influence consideration of right and wrong. It is also one of those ethical regions to which science must contribute, for risk should be quantified, and science alone can provide the necessary data and mathematics. But it is hard to get a feel for risk. We may estimate by the best possible means that such-and-such a procedure has a one in 100 chance of causing a particular disaster and feel that such a risk is worthwhile, only to find that the first three attempts are disasters. If the estimate was right, then the chance of three failures in a row is one in a million; but one in a million odds sometimes come up. Risk means that the outcome of any one endeavor is uncertain, and of course, except in well-defined circumstances where we can enjoy the thrill, we greatly prefer certainty.

There are risks that can be quantified, because we have a great many examples from the past by which to make judgments, or some theory to tell us what ought to happen; risks that cannot be quantified, because we simply don't have enough data to make a judgment, and risks that are yet unknown (a risk of risk). We must balance small risks of terrible disasters (in this context, the risk of a child being seriously deformed, for example) against large risks of mere inconveniences. Always we must exercise judgment. There are no absolute criteria of acceptability.

We do know, though, that risk cannot be avoided altogether, even at the best of times. All action is potentially risky, yet we have to act to survive: Miss Havisham's life of irreducible inactivity in *Great Expectations* probably did not extend her life (house mites must have played havoc, if nothing else) and certainly was not life-enhancing. Babies conceived in the best circumstances sometimes die or are deformed, and this unpleasant fact at least provides us with a yardstick. The risk of death or deformity in a cloned baby born to a surrogate mother can be measured against the risk of such disasters in more natural circumstances. In addition, we must balance the risk of action against the known disadvantage of inaction. Desperate couples faced with infertility have already shown that they are prepared to run considerable risk. People who know they carry harmful genes often risk having children. Perception of acceptability varies with circumstances, as it must.

How can such discussion throw light on the risk of cloning a human being by the method that produced Dolly? Work on sheep and mice already suggests that the chances are low of producing an embryo that is able to go to term from a given cell: Dolly was the only success out of 277 reconstructed embryos. Such statistics, however, do not tell us all we need to know. Perhaps we were unlucky; perhaps if we had made ten more embryos, we would have had ten more Dollys. Perhaps we were lucky; perhaps another 10,000 embryos would have yielded no more Dollys at all. Much more experience with more animals will give a clearer idea of the odds and also improve the rate of success—for practice always reduces imperfection, although, unfortunately, the reasons for the improvement are not always clear. All the results so far at Roslin suggest that by present techniques, fetuses produced by nuclear transfer are ten times more likely to die in utero than fetuses produced by normal sexual means, while cloned offspring are three times more likely to die soon after birth. Deformities also occur. These setbacks are very distressing for people who work with animals—and surely mean that any immediate extension into human medicine is unthinkable.

In addition, with Dolly, there is a list of unresolved issues that cannot at present be quantified—and if they could, what should we make of them? Dolly's genes came from a six-year-old animal, and although Dolly after two years looks like an eminently normal two-year-old, we have yet to see how her life will pan out. The telomeres on her chromosomes are reduced in length. The shortening of the telomeres does not *cause* aging, it merely reflects aging, but when the telomeres have disappeared altogether, the cell dies. There is no reason to suppose that Dolly's telomeres have shortened enough, or will do so, to affect her life span, but we cannot foresee how a longer-lived animal like a human being would be affected. Neither does Dolly seem to have suffered side effects from genomic imprinting—but her embryo siblings, who did not make it to term, may have. Certainly the potential issue of genomic imprinting is not resolved, and it is difficult to see how it can be until the phenomenon itself is better understood. Then there is the matter of large-fetus syndrome. This is clearly a hazard in cattle and is certainly a potential hazard in sheep, even though, because of the cross-breeding that has gone on, it is impossible at present to assess the extent of the problem in sheep. Yet these are only the potential hazards that we know about, or at least have some intimation of. Others will surely crop up that cannot at present be anticipated.

How can all the potential hazards be identified and quantified so that we could know in advance what the risks would be, if anyone ever attempted to clone a human? They can't, is the answer. Dolly and her daughter Bonnie must live their allotted spans, and perhaps their early promise of total normality will be confirmed. The Hawaiian cloned mice have already bred through several generations and will generate far more data far more quickly. Other species surely will be cloned before humans are—they certainly should be—such as dogs and, of course, monkeys, which are primates like us. But still, until we try we cannot know whether the lessons learned from all those other species are strictly applicable to us. As Keith has often observed, there are huge similarities in the biology of different creatures, stretching from humans to yeasts and well beyond. But there are many differences of detail, too, as he also stresses, and details can make all the difference. At present there is no obvious reason to suppose that human cloning will raise problems that could not be foreseen in sheep or mice or monkeys. Besides, human reproductive biology has been well studied, and already remarkable manipulations are possible. So human cloning might prove to be reasonably straightforward, once biologists have gained experience in a range of other species. But nobody will know until they try.

Whenever we speak of risk, too, we must ask, "Risk to whom?" and "Risk of what?" Our first thoughts turn to the physical well-being of the baby: Will it live? Will it be normal? But others are physically involved too, notably the surrogate mother, and, so many would insist, the reconstructed embryos that are not implanted or are implanted but fail. Many people will be involved psychologically, including the baby who becomes the child, the social parents who bring it up, its surrogate mother, and so on.

What is the risk of cloning people? At present the question is unanswerable, even if we confine discussion to the physical well-being of the newly cloned individual. There are too many unknowns. How long would it take to reduce the unknowns to the point at which the transition to humans seems acceptable? There is a "How long is a piece of string?" quality to this question. The transition will always be a risk. The procedure is bound to carry some hazard, which seems likely to be higher than that of normal conception and childbirth, and the data from animals, however exhaustive, cannot in the end tell us all we would like to know. If, however, we were to insist that a range of species should be examined, that cloned animals and their offspring should be allowed to live their complete lives, and that the hazards we can anticipate already (like those that might ensue from genomic imprinting) should be understood more thoroughly, then surely we should be thinking in terms of decades.

But some people are impatient. Some are already offering cloning, or proposing to do so. Richard Seed is not the only one. I told a government committee that "significant progress" toward human cloning could be made within three years—and this was reported as if I had said that it will, in fact, be technically possible. Actually it might be technically possible in that time, but only in the sense that if someone who is prepared to take risks and is competent attempts it; then if they are lucky, they might get away with it. But "getting away with it" is not what is normally meant by offering a clinical service. In the end, the date of the first human cloning will be determined by the amount of risk that potential parents, and those who attend to them, are prepared to take. Perhaps clinicians should warn their patients not to take the risks—just as we now advise sixteen-year-olds that they ought to wear crash helmets, even when they would rather not.

Advice is not always taken, and clinicians do not always behave like this, so is human cloning, in the end, inevitable? The market forces are certainly strong, but nothing is inevitable. At present, human cloning is illegal in Britain and much of the United States, but mere illegality is not quite the issue. All that is required in the initial stages, to produce a clone like Dolly, is a flask of cultured body cells. This could be prepared in any competent laboratory. A technician merely has to take a tissue biopsy and from that create a culture. Once the culture is growing in a stable fashion, it can be frozen and transported anywhere in the world. The only laws that would seem to apply so far are those that restrict transportation of biological materials; if they do apply, it surely would not be difficult to get around them. The cultured cells could then be sent to a country where cloning (or genetic manipulation) is not illegal. This could be anywhere: anywhere, preferably, where local women are willing to act as surrogate mothers. In any case, a person who wanted to be cloned could simply travel to the appropriate laboratory, like any tourist. In short, a practice that is illegal in one country can become a minor industry in another.

Would people go to such lengths? The answer seems obvious. Many people are not against human cloning and have little regard for the laws that now restrict it. In all walks of life, laws that are not respected are routinely flouted. Many physicians would be perfectly willing to offer such a service. Many doctors certainly feel that they should make ethical choices, but others argue that it is not up to them to decide what is right or wrong; their duty is merely to meet their patients' requests. Many would argue that it is morally wrong to withhold their services from people they could help, especially if they see nothing wrong with the procedure in the first place. Would patients be willing to take the risks and pay the price? Undoubtedly. There is no stronger human instinct than to reproduce. People in America routinely pay $50,000 for a course of IVF, with no guarantee of success. In the present culture of the U.S. the marketplace leads, and there is surely a huge potential market for cloning: eager, affluent buyers; willing and capable suppliers.

There is a broader point, perhaps best illustrated by reference to the United States. In the Western world we generally subscribe to the notion of democracy and also tend to support the idea of free enterprise. The philosophy of democracy differs enormously in different parts of the world. In Britain, for example, it tends to mean "majority rule," although Britons pay increasing attention to the demands of various minorities. But some, at least, of the founders of the United States saw majority rule in an unsavory light. Much more important, they felt, was personal freedom, the right of an individual to do what he or she wants. Personal liberty remains the guiding light of the U.S. (manifested most grotesquely in the perceived "right" to carry firearms). Thus it is that people in the U.S. who themselves object to the idea of human cloning are quite likely to defend the rights of people who welcome it. It is always difficult to maintain unpopular laws in democracies. In societies in which personal liberty is perceived effectively to be sacrosanct, it is surely almost impossible.

On the face of things, then, it may seem that human cloning (and perhaps, from this, germ-line engineering) is very likely to happen: perhaps in the first half of the twenty-first century, if not in the first decade. But it is not inevitable, and it may never have anything like the impact that IVF has had.

First, various societies in recent years have shown that they *can* resist new technologies of many kinds, whatever the market forces. Various European countries have now rejected nuclear power. The forces massed behind the nuclear industry are prodigious, but the Swedish, among others, have said they simply do not want it. In Britain, popular feeling has effectively condemned the high-rise, which as recently as the 1970s was seen as the only efficient form of mass housing and had huge financial backing. Spectacularly, as the new millennium dawns, there is widespread rejection on both sides of the Atlantic of genetically modified—GM—crops. Worldwide, we may perceive a trend toward libertarianism. But countries do become more restrictive, as well as less so. The U.S. and Europe now have laws to protect wildlife and to restrict the sales of many different items, including drugs, which 100 years ago would have been seen simply as an affront to freedom. Similarly, we need not assume that future societies will inevitably become more relaxed about human cloning than we are now; even if they did, their successors may later decide that enough is enough, and set themselves against it. There are precedents. There is no inevitable "slippery slope."

Then again, the extent to which people do *not* adopt novel technologies is striking. AI has been available for 200 years. It is far more common now than in the past, yet it remains very much a minority pursuit. Some extreme feminists have envisaged "families" of women, living like prides of lionesses, employing men (or AI) simply for their genes and raising the children in day-care centers. Why should a woman tie herself to some fickle and self-indulgent couch potato when such freedom could so easily be achieved? Why indeed? Well, social conservatism is obviously one answer. But another, perhaps, is that women prefer to live in a family with a single mate, however imperfect he may be. Human beings are not quite so flexible as it has become fashionable to argue. Some ways of life come easier to us than others. By the same token, human beings are sexual beings. Other routes do not come naturally to us. Of course, as moral philosophers remind us, what is "natural" is not necessarily right, and what is "unnatural" is not necessarily wrong. It is true, however, that what comes naturally to us also tends to come easily. When it comes to the point, many people surely will find themselves averse to cloning, and perhaps that aversion will prove to be deep-seated. Perhaps, however great the market forces or the desire to reproduce, that aversion will prevail. This cannot be predicted. Clearly, though, there is reason to doubt whether human cloning will ever become fully respectable, let alone fashionable, and it surely will never be the norm. It may seem crude, but it is accurate to suggest that reproduction by cloning goes against our nature.

Overall, as with all powerful technologies, there are contradictions. On the one hand, cloning has immense potential for good, especially in combination with the other great modern biotechnologies, genetic engineering and genomics. But such power can be abused, and the most obvious possible abuse—at least, we believe it to be so—would be human cloning. The pressures for human cloning are powerful, but although it seems likely that somebody, at some time, will attempt it, we need not assume that it will ever become a common or significant feature of human life. Society does not have to adopt technologies with which it feels uncomfortable, and people have already shown that they are perfectly able to resist what they do not like.   ∎

NOTES

1. *Nature,* January 15, 1998, page 218.
2. *Clones and Clones,* edited by Martha C. Nussbaum and Cass R. Sunstein, W. W. Norton, New York, 1998, page 55.

■ *QUESTIONS FOR MAKING CONNECTIONS WITHIN THE READING* ■

1. When confronted with new problems such as those raised by the possibility of human cloning, people sometimes try to address them by appealing to moral absolutes or to abstract philosophical principles. Approached in this way, cloning might be viewed as either right or wrong, ethical or unethical, humane or dehumanizing. How does Wilmut approach the issue? What do you see as the advantages and disadvantages of his approach?

2. Much of Wilmut's thinking depends on a crucial distinction between cloning and all other existing reproductive technologies. Do you find this distinction compelling, or do you feel that it amounts to a distinction without difference? Does it really matter, in other words, whether science duplicates biological reproduction or invents a new way of reproducing human life?

3. Search the Web for sites that deal with human cloning. After conducting an informal review of your findings, describe the broad contours of the current debate. What positions would you say occupy the extremes? What positions lie close to the middle of the road? Does there seem to be a consensus on some aspects of the issue? Where would you place Wilmut? Is his position well-represented by sources on the Internet, or would you describe it as relatively marginal?

▪ QUESTIONS FOR WRITING ▪

1. Wilmut recognizes the influence of financial forces on the development of cloning technology, but he tends to overlook the personal and emotional dimensions of this innovation. In what ways are all reproductive technologies shaped by our needs, dreams, and anxieties—our ideas about personal fulfillment and a life well-lived? In what ways, conversely, has technology shaped those ideas? Feel free to consider technologies other than those directly tied to reproduction. Cars, television and movies, medical innovations, and the Internet might all be considered as shaped by, while also shaping, human desires.

2. Less than two years after Wilmut published this essay, there was news that teams of scientists in Europe and in the United States were competing to be the first to successfully clone a human. What do you think the appropriate response to these developments is? Should governments intervene to stop this research? Should average citizens have a say in whether work of this kind should go forward? Discuss Wilmut's argument against human cloning and the possible impact the development of this reproductive technology may have on human behavior.

▪ QUESTIONS FOR MAKING CONNECTIONS BETWEEN READINGS ▪

1. In "Does God Have a Future?", Karen Armstrong traces recent changes in our society's thinking about God. How are these changes likely to affect our responses to the issue of human cloning? Would the disappearance of a personal God lead to a diminished respect for human life, or might it have the opposite effect?

2. What lessons might Wilmut learn from Michael Pollan's essay? Are the forces shaping reproductive technology fundamentally different from those shaping agriculture? Given what we learn from Wilmut about uses of procedures like artificial insemination, is there really any chance that McBabies—a commercialization of human life—will become commonplace in our near future? If people want french fries without blemishes, would they be likely to make similar choices in the preselection of their offspring?

For additional suggestions about making connections between readings, visit the Link-O-Mat and More Sample Assignments at <www.newhum.com>.

ACKNOWLEDGMENTS

p. 1   From THE SPELL OF THE SENSUOUS by David Abram. Copyright © 1996 by David Abram. Used by permission of Pantheon Books, a division of Random House, Inc.

p. 25   From WRITING WOMEN'S WORLDS: Bedouin Stories by Lila Abu-Lughod. Copyright © 1992 The Regents of the University of California. Used by permission.

p. 54   From SCIENCE ON TRIAL: The Clash of Medical Evidence and the Law in the Breast Implant Case by Marcia Angell, M.D. Copyright © 1996 by Marcia Angell, M.D. Used by permission of W.W. Norton & Company, Inc.

p. 71   From A HISTORY OF GOD by Karen Armstrong. Copyright © 1993 by Karen Armstrong. Used by permission of Alfred A. Knopf, a division of Random House, Inc.

p. 94   From A PLACE FOR US by Benjamin R. Barber. Copyright © 1999 by Benjamin R. Barber. Reprinted by permission of Hill and Wang, a division of Farrar, Straus and Giroux, LLC.

p. 115   Reprinted with the permission of The Free Press, a division of Simon & Schuster, Inc., from HUNGRY GHOSTS: Mao's Secret Famine by Jasper Becker. Copyright © 1996 by Jasper Becker.

p. 145   Reprinted from Jonathan Boyarin, "Waiting for a Jew: Marginal Redemption at the Eighth Street Shul," in BETWEEN TWO WORLDS: Ethnographic Essays on American Jewry, edited by Jack Kugelmass. Chapter copyright © 1988 by Jonathan Boyarin. Copyright © 1988 by Cornell University. Used by permission of the publisher, Cornell University Press.

p. 168   "What You Know" by Peter Ho Davies, originally published in Harper's, January 2001. Reprinted by permission of the author.

p. 182   "The Wreck of Time" by Annie Dillard, Harper's, January 1998. Copyright © 1998 Annie Dillard. Reprinted by permission of the author.

p. 192   "The Core of Art: Making Special" from HOMO AESTHETICUS by Ellen Dissanayake. Copyright © 1995 Ellen Dissanayake. Reprinted by permission of the University of Washington Press.

p. 221   "The Age of Social Transformation" reprinted by permission of the author. First published in The Atlantic Monthly, November 1994. Copyright © 1994 Peter F. Drucker.

p. 249   "The Naked Citadel" by Susan Faludi. Originally appeared in The New Yorker, September 5, 1994. Used by permission of the Sandra Dijkstra Agency.

p. 285   From THE TIPPING POINT by Malcolm Gladwell. Copyright © 2000, 2002 by Malcolm Gladwell. By permission of Little, Brown and Company (Inc.).

p. 597 "The Ganges' Next Life" by Alexander Stille, first appeared in *The New Yorker,* January 19, 1998. Copyright © 1998 by Alexander Stille. Used by permission of the Wylie Agency.

p. 613 From THE ARGUMENT CULTURE by Deborah Tannen. Copyright © 1997 by Deborah Tannen. Used by permission of Pantheon Books, a division of Random House, Inc.

p. 646 From THE APE AND THE SUSHI MASTER by Frans de Waal. Copyright © 2001 by Frans de Waal. Reprinted by permission of Basic Books, a member of Perseus Books, LLC.

p. 673 "Decision Time: A 'Piece' or Peace?," "This, Too, is Buddha's Mind," "My Great Seal Retreat," from DREAMING ME by Jan Willis. Copyright © 2001 by Jan Willis. Used by permission of Riverhead Books, a division of Penguin Putnam, Inc.

p. 692 "Cloning People" from THE SECOND COMING by Ian Wilmut, Keith Campbell, and Colin Tudge. Copyright © 2000 by Ian Wilmut, Keith Campbell, and Colin Tudge. Reprinted by permission of Farrar, Straus and Giroux, LLC.

AUTHOR AND TITLE INDEX